Oil, Gas & Government

Oil, Gas & Government

The U.S. Experience

Volume I

Robert L. Bradley Jr.

CATO INSTITUTE

ROWMAN & LITTLEFIELD PUBLISHERS, INC.

ROWMAN & LITTLEFIELD PUBLISHERS, INC.

Published in the United States of America
by Rowman & Littlefield Publishers, Inc.
4720 Boston Way, Lanham, Maryland 20706

3 Henrietta Street
London WC2E 8LU, England

British Cataloging in Publication Information Available

Library of Congress Cataloging-in-Publication Data

Bradley, Robert L.
Oil, gas, and government : the U.S. experience / Robert L. Bradley, Jr.
p. cm.
Includes bibliographical references and index.
1. Petroleum industry and trade—Government policy—United States—History. 2. Gas
industry—Government policy—United States—History. 3. Petroleum law and
legislation—United States—History. 4. Gas—Law and legislation—United States—
History. 5. Natural gas pipelines—Law and legislation—United States—History. 6.
Public utilities—Law and legislation—United States—History. 7. Antitrust law—
United States—History. 8. Trade regulation—United States—History. I. Title.
HD9566.B62   1995   95-21325   338.2'728'0973—dc20   CIP

ISBN 0–8476–8110-6 (set: alk. paper)

Printed in the United States of America

⊖™ The paper used in this publication meets the minimum requirements of
American National Standard for Information Sciences—Permanence of
Paper for Printed Library Materials, ANSI Z39.48–1984.

Contents

Volume I

Acknowledgments

This book is a revised version of my dissertation for the degree of doctor of philosophy in social sciences with specialization in political economy, received from International College in 1985. I am particularly indebted to my dissertation committee that supported the methodological approach and the scope of the book: Professors Dominick T. Armentano, Donald C. Lavoie, and the late Murray N. Rothbard.

A book of this magnitude reflects not only the perseverance of the author but the contributions of many individuals. My first debt is to the Cato Institute, which underwrote a project that was far longer and more costly than originally planned. I thank Edward Crane, president, and David Boaz, executive vice president, in particular. A second driving force behind this book was my father, Robert L. Bradley, whose unflinching support and encouragement were instrumental throughout. I dedicate the book to him. For the emotional support necessary to spend years researching and writing the manuscript, I thank my wife, Nancy. I do not know if I could have persevered without her. The legacy of my late grandparents, Genevra and Palmer Bradley, was also crucial to the book from conception to completion.

Important early encouragement and support were received from Jerry Finger, the late Bud Hadsell, Gerald Marshall, the late L. F. McCollum, and A. K. McLanahan.

With great respect I acknowledge many intellectual debts. My deepest debt is to Murray Rothbard, whose interdisciplinary worldview, encouragement, and review of the manuscript as head of my dissertation committee helped to shape the effort. My academic interest in the social sciences owes much to over a decade of seminars sponsored by the Institute for Humane Studies. Executive Enterprises kindly accommodated repeated requests to participate in important energy conferences on regulatory developments. The

American Petroleum Institute and many other industry trade associations generously provided me with publications. Last, several seminars in applied market-process (Austrian school) economics at New York University and George Mason University provided useful forums for airing the ideas in several chapters of the book.

Helpful comments on the manuscript came from a variety of individuals, particularly Dom Armentano, an antitrust specialist who focused on energy regulation in the eventful 1970s. His presence on my dissertation committee gave me a wealth of expertise to fall back on. Fellow committee member Don Lavoie, whose prolific work on the theoretical problems of government intervention and the methodology of economics speaks for itself, also provided much needed input. Tyler Cowen read many chapters and gave several of them needed criticism. I also wish to thank the following individuals, many of them recognized industry experts, for evaluating the parts of the manuscript that dealt with their areas of specialization: Clyde Ball, William Block, Leonard Coburn, Carroll Gilliam, Richard Gonzalez, T. Crawford Honeycutt, William Huie, Israel Kirzner, Charles Koch, John McGuire, Stephen McDonald, Robert Plett, Robert Perdue, William Johnson, Henry Steele, Arlon Tussing, William Vail, R. Graham Whaling, George Wolbert, and M. K. Woodward. This list does not include countless individuals in government and industry whom I bothered with a "quick question or two." Each of them shared a desire to help set the record straight, and I hope the expenditure of their time is justified by the end product.

Helpful research assistance was provided by Allen Brain, Matt Hoffman, Richard Kest, Jerry Mildner, Robb Rauth, and Murfee Worsham. Mike Hamilton did yeoman work reading the entire manuscript and researching incomplete citations. Copyeditor JoAnne Platt and Cato editor Elizabeth W. Kaplan and senior editor Sheldon Richman patiently improved the manuscript. I thank all these individuals for their contributions. Needless to say, any errors of fact or analysis are my responsibility alone.

List of Acronyms and Abbreviations

AAA	American Automobile Association
AFL	American Federation of Labor
AICPA	American Institute of Certified Public Accountants
ANS	Alaskan North Slope
API	American Petroleum Institute
APRA	American Petroleum Refiners Association
ASF	allocable supply fraction
BAT	best available technology
Bcf	billion cubic feet
bl	barrel
BLM	Bureau of Land Management
BPCL	base-period control level
CBT	Chicago Board of Trade
CDS	construction differential subsidy
CFTC	Commodity Futures Trading Commission
CLC	Cost of Living Council
CO	carbon monoxide
CPA	certified public accountant
DOE	U.S. Department of Energy
ECPA	Energy Conservation and Production Act of 1976
EPA	Environmental Protection Agency
EPAA	Emergency Petroleum Allocation Act of 1973
EPCA	Energy Policy and Conservation Act of 1975
ERA	Economic Regulatory Administration
ERDA	Energy Research and Development Administration
ESA	Economic Stabilization Agency

FASB   Financial Accounting Standards Board
FBI   Federal Bureau of Investigation
FEA   Federal Energy Administration
FEO   Federal Energy Office
FERC   Federal Energy Regulatory Commission
FOCB   Federal Oil Conservation Board
FPC   Federal Power Commission
FTB   Federal Tender Board
FTC   Federal Trade Commission

GAAP   generally accepted accounting principles
GAO   General Accounting Office
GATT   General Agreement of Tariffs and Trade
GOR   gas-oil ratio

HC   hydrocarbon
HEW   U.S. Department of Health, Education, and Welfare
HHI   Herfindahl-Hirschman index

I.T.   Income Tax Division Ruling
ICC   Interstate Commerce Commission
IDC   intangible drilling costs
IEA   International Energy Agency
IOCC   Interstate Oil Compact Commission
IPAA   Independent Petroleum Association of America
IRAA   Independent Refiners Association of America
ISP   Industrial Sales Program

LDC   local distribution company
LNG   liquefied natural gas
LOOP   Louisiana Offshore Oil Port
LPG   liquefied petroleum gas
Mcf   thousand cubic feet
MDF   market-demand factor
MDP   market-demand proration
MER   maximum efficient rate
MMBtu   million British thermal units
MMcf   million cubic feet
MMS   Minerals Management Service
MMT   methycyclopentadienyl manganese
MOIP   Mandatory Oil Import Program
MPAB   Military Petroleum Advisory Board

xiv

mpg	miles per gallon
mph	miles per hour
NGA	Natural Gas Act of 1938
NGPA	Natural Gas Policy Act of 1978
NIRA	National Industrial Recovery Act of 1933
NO$_x$	nitrogen oxide
NPA	National Production Authority
NPC	National Petroleum Council
NPN	National Petroleum News
NPR	naval petroleum reserve
NPRA	National Petroleum Refiners Association
NRA	National Recovery Administration
NYMEX	New York Mercantile Exchange
OCC	Oklahoma Corporation Commission
OCS	outer continental shelf
ODA	operating differential subsidy
ODM	Office of Defense Mobilization
ODT	Office of Defense Transportation
OES	Office of Economic Stabilization
OGJ	Oil & Gas Journal
OHA	Office of Hearings and Appeals
OIA	Oil Import Administration
OOG	Office of Oil and Gas
OPA	Office of Price Administration and Civilian Supply
OPC	Office of Petroleum Coordinator
OPEC	Organization of Oil Exporting Countries
OPS	Office of Price Stabilization
OSAC	Oil States Advisory Committee
OSHA	Occupational Safety and Health Administration
OW	Oil Weekly
PAB	Petroleum Administrative Board
PAC	Petroleum Advisory Committee
PAD	Petroleum Administration for Defense
PAW	Petroleum Administration for War
PCC	Planning and Coordination Committee
PIWC	Petroleum Industry War Council
PMPA	Petroleum Marketers Practices Act of 1978
ppm	parts per million
PWSC	Petroleum War Service Committee

resid   residual fuel oil
RFC   Reconstruction Finance Corporation
RRA   reserve-recognition accounting

SBA   Small Business Administration
SEC   Securities and Exchange Commission
SFC   Synthetic Fuels Corporation
SMP   Special Marketing Program
SPR   Strategic Petroleum Reserve
SR-1   Special Rule no. 1

TAPS   Trans-Alaska Pipeline System
TBA   tires, batteries, and accessories
Tcf   trillion cubic feet
TET   Texas Eastern Transmission
TGT   Tennessee Gas Transmission
TLP   term-limit pricing
TRC   Texas Railroad Commission

WPT   Windfall Profit Tax

Introduction

This book is intended to provide interested laypersons, industry members, social scientists, and policymakers a detailed history and analysis of government intervention in the U.S. oil and gas market. Although there have been numerous books published in this field, particularly after energy matters took center stage in the 1970s, no single work has attempted to trace the history of oil and gas regulation, taxation, and subsidization from the last century to the present era from an economic and political perspective.

This void exists despite many eminent works in the oil and gas literature. John Ise's *The United States Oil Policy* (1926), the treatise of its day, had admirable scope but was flawed in interpretation. Gerald Nash's *United States Oil Policy, 1890–1964* is a succinct historical overview but is short on economic analysis and conclusions. Robert Engler's *The Politics of Oil* (1961) and *The Brotherhood of Oil* (1977) present a wealth of factual information about industry-government relations, but both books lack a sound theoretical framework for interpretation and policy recommendation. Harold Williamson and Arnold Daum's *The American Petroleum Industry* (2 vols., 1959, 1965), which remains the lone major business history of the domestic U.S. oil industry, is less thorough on the regulatory side and has become dated. Legal edifices such as the revised editions of W. W. Thorton's *The Law Relating to Oil and Gas* do not cover political themes and interpretive economics. Edward Chester's *United States Oil Policy and Diplomacy* (1983) and M. A. Adelman's *The World Petroleum Market* (1972) concentrate on the international oil market, the former from the political side and the latter from the business-history side, and only briefly examine domestic regulation. The more recent best-selling tome by Daniel Yergin, *The Prize* (1992), provides a highly readable account of the development of the international petroleum industry but understates important developments on the domestic U.S. regulatory front. Many other industry classics and government documents have examined particular

1

themes, periods, companies, and episodes, but although they achieve their stated purposes, none presents the big picture of government intervention in the world's primary energy market. That is the goal of the present work.

This book is divided into three sections: theory, history, and policy. Chapter 1, on theory, which contrasts the market process with government intervention, precedes the historical section by design. All historical investigation is influenced by the author's conception of cause and effect. Which facts are important, the relationships between facts, and the evidential conclusions reached all presuppose a theoretical framework. While the theoretical section does not attempt to fully develop a theory of the market process and government intervention, which is the domain of a treatise on political economy, the concepts introduced are revisited many times in historical contexts to illuminate the theory and give the reader ample opportunity to test their applicability and validity.

The third and final section on public policy is built on theory and history. Concepts of socially beneficial and socially detrimental public policies are theory laden and draw upon the historical experience of market processes and government intervention. The basis for chapter 31, in short, is found in chapters 1 through 30.

The heart of the book is the four-part historical review of government intervention in oil and gas. Chapters 2 through 28 are organized vertically by industry phase, beginning at the wellhead (Part I) and continuing downstream through transportation (Part II), refining (Part III), and retailing (Part IV). Unlike oil, natural gas is divided into only wellhead (chapter 8) and pipeline (chapter 15) regulation. Municipal regulation of distribution is integrated into chapter 15 because it is complementary to natural-gas pipeline regulation. This integration is also necessitated by a relative dearth of research, city by city and state by state, on the rise of public-utility regulation of the manufactured- and natural-gas business.

Part I, Intervention in Exploration and Production, contains nine chapters. The wellhead is the center of the oil industry, and it is no coincidence that more intervention has taken place here than in any other industry sector.

Chapter 2, Early Years and Legal Development, sketches the birth of the oil industry and the formation of property rights in oil and gas extraction. The chapter develops an alternative legal framework

2

for first title to oil and gas production based on the homestead principle. This reformulated private-property assignment, which gives first title to contiguous reservoirs to the first finder, with certain stipulations, overcomes the multiple-ownership problem common under the rule of capture.

Chapters 3 and 4, on state petroleum conservation regulation, trace controversies over oil and gas extraction under the rule of capture as well as ensuing regulation. Although many writers have interpreted petroleum extraction practices as a case study of market failure—and consequently have been sympathetic to oil-state regulation of output—the present analysis paints a far different picture. A variety of government activities, from taxation to first-purchaser regulation to the "solution" of conservation law itself, created greater obstacles to cooperative solutions to overdrilling and overproduction than did incentives under the rule of capture. These chapters also show that imperfect knowledge of hydrocarbon reservoirs and extraction created an *inherent* problem for which the market cannot be blamed and which government intervention could not solve. The revisionist interpretation in chapters 3 and 4, and the alternate private-property legal framework introduced in chapter 2, constitute a challenge to the widely held view that government intervention is necessary to rationalize petroleum extraction within a private-property framework.

Chapter 5 examines wartime regulation of oil and gas production. While government planning has been sanctified as necessary in emergency situations such as wartime, the actual results of intervention are shown to be unnecessary and counterproductive. After the historical records of World War I, World War II, and the Korean conflict are examined, and the contingency planning efforts of the 1950s and 1960s are reviewed, the chapter concludes with a theoretical discussion of the inherent problems of substituting central planning for market entrepreneurship. This theoretical detour becomes particularly relevant in chapter 6, Petroleum Leasing and Environmental Policy on Government Land, which examines the major example of U.S. government resource ownership of oil and gas.

Chapter 7 is dedicated to taxation issues surrounding oil and gas extraction. Excise taxation, including the Crude Oil Windfall Profit Tax, is studied along with controversial oil-related deductions from the corporate tax—the depletion allowance, intangible drilling costs, and the foreign tax credit. State and Indian-tribe taxation, involving primarily wellhead production, is also reviewed.

Chapter 8 traces the history of wellhead natural-gas price regulation, which began with judicial interpretations of the Natural Gas Act of 1938 and continued under the Natural Gas Policy Act of 1978. The tumultuous experience with price ceilings, featuring the interplay between administrative regulation and the political process, has been one of the most academically scrutinized episodes in the U.S. energy experience. Chapter 9, on regulation and decontrol of crude-oil prices, studies maximum price ceilings on oil production that began with President Nixon's price-control program in 1971 and continued until 1981 under the Emergency Petroleum Allocation Act of 1973. The lessons of oil-price controls were not dissimilar from those of wellhead controls on the natural-gas side—a demonstration of the workings of economic law.

Chapter 10 concludes Part I by examining residual state and federal intervention in wellhead oil and gas production—labor-market regulation, government loans, securities regulation, accounting regulation, and subsidization of synthetic fuels. Despite the variety of interventions, their common ability to cause harm by departing from the discipline of the market is revealed.

Part II, comprising chapters 11 through 17, details intervention in oil and gas transportation and allocation. The opening chapter describes the dawn of the petroleum transportation phase in the 1860s and related rail, pipeline, and waterway regulation until the turn of the century. Chapter 12, one of the more significant chapters in the book, covers various episodes of petroleum allocation regulation, beginning with World War I planning and continuing with the East Texas "hot-oil war," World War II planning, Korean-conflict planning, and energy-crisis regulation in the 1970s. Of particular importance is the detailed study of the oil-reselling industry that blossomed under the regulatory incentives of the Emergency Petroleum Allocation Act of 1973. This episode unlocks the mystery of why U.S. consumers paid world prices for petroleum products despite tip-to-tail oil-price regulation designed to ensure that they would not.

Chapter 13 summarizes the long history of petroleum protectionism from the Civil War to the present; that history includes tariffs enacted in the Revenue Act of 1932 and quotas established in the

Mandatory Oil Import Program of 1959. Traditional arguments for and against oil tariffs and quotas are reviewed. The chapter is followed by an appendix on oil-export regulation.

Chapter 14 reviews oil-pipeline regulation on the state level after the turn of the century and federal regulation that began for interstate carriers with a 1906 amendment to the Interstate Commerce Act. The chapter concludes by critically reviewing ongoing arguments for applying traditional public-utility regulation to federally regulated carriers.

Chapter 15 covers both natural-gas pipeline and gas-distribution regulation. The criticism of public-utility regulation of gas pipelines is a variation on the discussion in chapter 14. Two appendices follow chapter 15. The first surveys the transportation and spot-gas revolution that began in the 1970s to alleviate curtailments and came into full bloom with the natural-gas surplus of the 1980s. The second examines the regulation of natural-gas imports, which became a controversial high-priced supply source during gas shortages caused by domestic price controls.

Chapter 16, beginning where chapter 11 leaves off, reviews railway, motor-carrier, and waterway regulation after the turn of the century. Chapter 17 examines some remaining miscellaneous interventions in transportation and allocation: intervention in storage (including the Strategic Petroleum Reserve) and regulation of the petroleum futures market.

Part III on refinery intervention is composed of four chapters. Chapter 18 revisits the Standard Oil Trust controversy that revolved around John D. Rockefeller's consolidation of the refining (and pipeline) phase and examines the state antitrust suits and the famous federal suit that led to the dissolution of the trust in 1911. Chapter 19 focuses on refinery regulation that occurred between World War I and the Korean conflict. Intervention from 1953 to the present, prominently including the Mandatory Oil Import Program from 1959 to 1973 and the buy-sell and entitlements programs under the Emergency Petroleum Allocation Act of 1973, is the subject of chapter 20. Chapter 21 concludes Part III by studying refinery-related land and air pollution. A free-market approach to dealing with pollution externalities is presented as an alternative to the "command-and-control" approach of regulation.

Part IV consists of seven chapters on petroleum-product and service-station regulation. The length and detail of the chapters are inspired by the fact that, unlike the other areas of the industry, relatively little has been written on gasoline marketing from both a business-history and a regulatory viewpoint. Thus, not only are the effects of regulation scrutinized, but the rivalry of free-market competition and the results of spontaneous order also are revealed.

Chapter 22 revisits Standard Oil to examine some of the trust's marketing controversies as well as other related intervention of the period. Chapter 23 studies the first period of gasoline regulation that began prior to World War I and continued through the New Deal in a "quest for stability." The beginning of gasoline taxation is also described. Chapter 24 chronicles wartime planning for gasoline and fuel oil, including the nation's only major experiment to date with coupon rationing, during World War II. The chapter summarizes wartime controversies, including the aborted planning effort during the Korean conflict. Chapter 25 describes the market rivalry and respondent regulation that flowered in the 1950s and 1960s. Many earlier interventions intensified in this period, as did motor-fuel taxation and public-road building.

Applications of antitrust law to gasoline marketing are the subject of chapter 26. The origin of federal antitrust statutes and price-fixing, discrimination, exclusive-dealing, and merger policies are examined. The chapter ends with an appendix that discusses a question debated in academic circles for several decades: has there been too much or too little competition in gasoline retailing?

Chapter 27 reexamines the 1970s' energy crises from the whole-sale-retail side. It surveys the price and allocation regulation of petroleum products with particular attention to the economic distortions that caused the two major periods of gasoline shortages. Chapter 28 traces the continuance, in the 1972–84 period, of gasoline regulation and taxation that were independent of, but influenced by, price and allocation controls.

Chapters 29 and 30, which draw economic and political conclusions, respectively, tie together major themes that were previously addressed in individual chapters. The chapter on economics finds that interventions not only distorted market processes responsible for consumer welfare but led to complementary regulation, taxation, or subsidization, thus creating an *interventionist dynamic*. The chapter on politics concludes that, except in rare instances, government intervention was conceived and implemented with active industry support.

Chapter 31 promulgates a market-driven oil and gas policy for the local, state, and federal levels. It argues that a comprehensive free market is in the self-interest of a wide cross-section of the industry and consumers.

Brief mention should be made of major government interventions and free-market reforms that have taken place since 1984. With regard to petroleum, the interventionist dynamic of the 1970s was replaced by a deregulation dynamic in the 1980s—greatly facilitated by falling oil prices. In addition to petroleum price and allocation deregulation described in this book, the Synthetic Fuels Corporation and the Windfall Profit Tax were repealed effective December 19, 1985, and August 23, 1988, respectively.[1] At the same time, "soft" regulation spurred by environmental concerns began to accelerate. In comparison with the major interventions of decades past, current U.S. oil policy can be described as market oriented.[2]

On the natural-gas side, a new regulatory era has commenced. While the Powerplant and Industrial Fuel Use Act of 1978 was significantly weakened and incremental pricing was repealed in May 1987, and wellhead regulation was repealed effective January 1, 1993,[3] mandatory contract carriage has been implemented for interstate pipelines under the Natural Gas Act. A broader analysis of these particular interventions reveals familiar economic and political themes.[4]

***

Two distinguishing characteristics of the book should be acknowledged at the outset. One is the methodology of the social sciences and

[1]Public Law 99-190, 100 Stat. 1185 at 1249 (1985); and Public Law 100-418, 102 Stat. 1107 at 1322 (1988).

[2]For discussions of post-1984 petroleum regulation, see Robert L. Bradley, Jr., *The Mirage of Oil Regulation* (Lanham, Md.: University Press of America, 1989); idem, "Energy Policy: A Few Bright Spots," in *Assessing the Reagan Years*, ed. David Boaz (Washington, D.C.: Cato Institute, 1988), pp. 305–19; and idem, "What Now for U.S. Energy Policy? A Free-Market Perspective," Cato Institute Policy Analysis no. 145, January 29, 1991.

[3]Public Law 100-42, 101 Stat. 319 (1987); and Public Law 101-60, 103 Stat. 157 (1989).

[4]For discussions of post-1984 natural-gas regulation, see Robert L. Bradley, Jr., *Reconsidering the Natural Gas Act* (Atlanta: Southern Regulatory Policy Institute, 1991); and idem, "The Distortions and Dynamics of Gas Regulation," in *New Horizons in Natural Gas Deregulation*, ed. Jerry Ellig and Joseph Kalt (New York: Praeger, 1995), chap. 1.

applied economics in particular; the other is the book's consistently negative spotlight on government intervention in the oil and gas market.

The applied economist is part historian and part economist. He or she must not only sift through the statistical information on a situation (the "outside" of an event) but thoroughly understand the anecdotal or "inside" of an event. The motivations of the economic actors are crucial. As R. G. Collingwood states: "[The historian's] work may begin by discovering the outside of an event, but it can never end there; he must always remember that the event was an action, and that his main task is to think himself into this action, to discern the thought of its agent."[5] That point is emphasized because applied economists tend to neglect—and even sacrifice—the "inside" of events in order to model, measure, and statistically test the "outside" of events to falsify hypotheses and make forecasts. Although a technical approach to economic history has its place, it also has inherent limitations that make it less useful for understanding than a broader anecdotal approach. There are several reasons for this. First, by the time applied economists start their work, it is too late to compile many relevant and informative statistics. Second, statistics have a range of error that often precludes a "tight" interpretation. In other words, it is much safer to use statistics to generally support a logically defensible hypothesis than to rigorously defend a speculative judgment. Third, assuming for the sake of argument the completeness and accuracy of the relevant statistics, specifying an econometric model is problematic, because reality is always more complex than the model's finite number of independent variables. The real world is not a laboratory in which the social scientist can "prove" that a particular cause created a measurable result. Therefore, the resulting statistical relationships must remain imprecise and tentative. It is not a mystery that applied economics has never found a constant in purposeful human action and that forecasting remains an art, not a science.

The "first cut" and core of applied economics, for these reasons, is "inside," not "outside," analysis. Understanding the situation from general motivations and facts, interpreted with sound economic theory, takes precedence over more empirical methods that

<hr>

[5]R. G. Collingwood, *The Idea of History* (Oxford: Clarendon Press, 1946), p. 213.

ape the laboratory sciences. To rely primarily on quantitative cost-benefit analysis is to demand perfection at the expense of the achievable. Such analysis is only a tool, a secondary and tentative tool, compared to the realism and understanding provided by the "inside" method. The focus of this book, consequently, is more qualitative than quantitative.

Turning from methodology to public policy, this book will be recognized by both friend and foe as highly critical of government intervention in the oil and gas market. Given the unsatisfactory outcomes of federal energy regulation in the 1970s, a free-market outlook should be anything but controversial. In fact, the burden of proof has been thrust on the shoulders of those who espouse government intervention in energy markets. What will be controversial to some is the book's consistently negative descriptions of government intervention, regardless of decade, industry phase, or geographical setting.

This consistency reflects several economic principles. The *knowledge problem* (defined in chapter 1) inherent in government intervention applies to a wide variety of situations. The *political problem* of government intervention (also defined in chapter 1) typically assures that results deviate from intentions and goals. The alternative, relying on the market, recognizes the *self-ordering* nature of the market process and the positive role of *entrepreneurship* that, while imperfect and occasionally resulting in what critics have called "market failure," is, as a rule, superior to government planning. Thus, it should not be surprising that the many government-versus-market case studies lead to similar conclusions and underline the superiority of well-defined private-property rights and voluntary exchange to government subsidy, taxation, and regulation.

SECTION 1

THEORY

1. Economic Alternatives and Applications

The United States oil and gas market offers historians, applied economists, and other social scientists a rich history of industry performance and public policy. Dating the petroleum industry from the first commercial oil well, the industry turned 125 years old in 1984. The manufactured- and natural-gas industry is nearly a half century older. Market processes and government intervention have coexisted in different degrees and contexts from the beginning.

As an introduction to the rest of the book, chapter 1 contrasts the major forms of economic organization and applies them to the domestic oil and gas industry. It begins by identifying the attributes of a free-market economy as seen by modern economics. The next section applies spontaneous-order theory to understand the industry's development and growth. The key insight is that private property and voluntary exchange have achieved a coordinated and complex industry without government planning.

The alternatives to the free market are *government ownership* of industry resources or *planning and regulation* of privately held resources. The balance of the chapter examines socialism and nationalization, macroeconomic planning, and microeconomic intervention. While comprehensive government planning of the domestic industry has been limited to "emergency" episodes, selected intervention has a long and varied history on all levels of government. Government ownership of oil and gas resources, on the other hand, has been the exception to the rule of private ownership.

The Market as Spontaneous Order

The free market is self-regulated, not government regulated. Freely negotiated contracts and business norms shape the relationships that determine the macroeconomic structure of the economy and the industries and firms that constitute it. Government involvement is limited to enforcing contractual obligations and keeping the peace.

13

The belief that self-regarding behavior in a free market unintentionally promotes the general well-being is as old as economics itself. In the late eighteenth century, economist and social philosopher Adam Smith wrote of an "invisible hand" that led an individual's self-interest to unintentionally achieve social good.

> As every individual, therefore, endeavours as much as he can both to employ his capital in the support of domestic industry, and so to direct that industry that its produce may be of the greatest value; every individual necessarily labours to render the annual revenue of the society as great as he can. He generally, indeed, neither intends to promote the public interest, nor knows how much he is promoting it. . . . He intends only his own gain, and he is . . . led by an invisible hand to promote an end which was no part of his intention. Nor is it always the worse for the society that it was no part of it. By pursuing his own interest he frequently promotes that of the society more effectually than when he really intends to promote it.[1]

Far from being an atomistic and selfish profit maximizer, Smith's "economic man" is part of a rich, diverse, and complex social order that is itself unintended, according to F. A. Hayek, a theorist in the classical or market-liberal tradition. Hayek recognized the existence and beneficial nature of what is called "the results of human action but not of human design."[2] Hayek expounded the thesis that much of social life—law, language, morals, customs, rules, and market exchange itself—was not the purposeful invention of a genius or political ruler possessing a grand design, but an unintended by-product of numerous individuals' engaging in self-interested behavior. As one interpreter summarized:

> We have not designed our social institutions but rather it is they that have structured us as we are. We are studying the *unintended* consequences of our actions when we study the truly social.[3]

Examples of beneficial, unintended order abound. Self-regarding individuals endeavoring to communicate created the societal good

---

[1]Adam Smith, *An Inquiry into the Nature and Causes of the Wealth of Nations*, ed. Edwin Cannan (1776; New York: G. P. Putnam's Sons, 1904), vol. 1, p. 421.

[2]Hayek attributes this phrase to the eighteenth-century British philosopher, Adam Ferguson. F. A. Hayek, "The Results of Human Action but Not of Human Design," *Studies in Philosophy, Politics, and Economics* (New York: Simon and Schuster, 1969), p. 96.

[3]Walter Weimer, "For and against Method," *Pre/Text* 1 (1980): 168.

of language without a blueprint. Money was not invented by an economic architect but arose spontaneously as exchange value gradually replaced the direct-use value of certain durable goods. The unintended social consequence was the facilitation of exchange. Neither was financial accounting invented; it emerged from a long process of trial and error by merchants eager to judge the performance and state of their enterprises. The American oil and gas industry, as discussed below, has achieved its present shape much less by government design than as the result of millions of incremental entrepreneurial innovations within a private-property environment. These invisible-hand occurrences are "the task of social theory to explain."[4]

The argument that the free market results in a productive economic order rests on the fact that the market effectively processes "dispersed bits of incomplete and frequently contradictory knowledge which all the separate individuals possess."[5] The market grapples with that "division of knowledge" through the price system, which can be viewed as a "mechanism for communicating information" about supply and demand.[6] Prices are economically meaningful because they reflect the knowledge of the market—consumers' buying or not buying and entrepreneurs' entering and leaving the market. The economy of information in prices minimizes the problem created by the division of knowledge and, in fact, serves as a proxy for the nonrealizable "knowledge in whole form" that otherwise would be needed for modern economic organization. In Hayek's words, "The whole acts as one market, not because any of its members survey the whole field, but because their limited individual fields of vision sufficiently overlap [through relative prices] so that through many intermediaries the relevant information is communicated to all."[7]

Such knowledge is unavailable in the absence of freely determined prices. Volumes of economic data on supply and demand could be

[4]F. A. Hayek, "The Results of Human Action," p. 97. For a history of the spontaneous-order thesis and its applications to economics, see Norman Barry, "The Tradition of Spontaneous Order," *Literature of Liberty* (Summer 1982): 7–58.

[5]F. A. Hayek, "The Use of Knowledge in Society," *Individualism and Economic Order* (Chicago: Henry Regnery, 1948), p. 77.

[6]Ibid., p. 86.

[7]Ibid.

compiled to address the relative scarcities of goods and services. But continually changing objective data and the economic actors' subjective interpretation of them make this approach a burdensome and inaccurate proxy for information spontaneously derived from the demonstrated choices of market participants.

Nonreproducible (depletable) resources are not an exception to the "invisible hand" of the price system but rather an application of it. As existing supply is depleted, its increased scarcity raises the price. Higher prices, in turn, incite profit-seeking entrepreneurs to locate new sources of supply, develop substitutes, and discover new technologies to meet consumer demand. On the demand side, higher prices help to direct supply to its most urgent uses. Some consumers are "priced out of the market" and reduce their use of the resource. This process of *conservation* tends to prevent wasteful uses of scarce resources and encourage the substitution of less scarce alternatives. Shortages (surpluses), during which consumers (producers) cannot buy (sell) goods and services at any price, are prevented.

The price system is also known as the profit-and-loss system. Entrepreneurs drive the economy by discovering new input-output combinations that reallocate resources in response to consumer demand. The alertness of entrepreneurs to profit opportunities and their resourcefulness in implementing their visions are key to the market order. Entrepreneurs promote short-run efficiency and long-term growth by their arbitrage, speculative, and innovative activities.[8] The legal freedom of anyone to pursue entrepreneurial ideas in a free market, moreover, promotes its uniquely competitive aspects.

The market is not a flawless system of economic organization. Entrepreneurial and consumer error misallocates resources compared to what an economy predicated on perfect knowledge would produce. That can be called "market failure." But the attraction of the market is relative, not absolute. Economists who attack the notions of the invisible hand and spontaneous order because they do not meet a standard of perfect knowledge are not dealing with the real world. The fact that the invisible hand "trembles or fails" in comparison with ideal resource allocation does not condemn the theory of market

---

[8]See Israel Kirzner, *Discovery and the Capitalist Process* (Chicago: University of Chicago Press, 1985), pp. 84–85.

order.[9] The economic problem is how to allocate resources in a world of imperfect knowledge and true uncertainty. The important insight of the invisible-hand theory is that, unlike the case with nonmarket (governmental) alternatives, beneficial processes exist in unregulated markets to *minimize* economic error.[10]

Price information is not the only conduit between individual knowledge and economic and social coordination. Nonprice decisions and institutions are also integral aspects of the market's undesigned order. Well-defined property laws impart important information about "the rules of the game." Commonly accepted customs and modes of behavior promote predictability and stability in interpersonal dealings. Institutions, from business firms to families, promote coordination outside financial transactions.[11] This "nonprice planning" is privately conceived and effectuated; it is distinguishable from government planning that relies on edicts.

Tacit knowledge is essential to both social cooperation and the market order. Individuals skillfully perform many tasks with little knowledge they can articulate. Examples include playing a sport without knowing the physical laws involved or communicating without knowing the formal rules of language. Without inarticulate knowledge (more commonly called intuition), everyday tasks crucial to social success would become problematic. All these things promote coordination or order, defined as "a state of affairs in which a multiplicity of elements of various kinds are so related to each other that we may learn from . . . part of the whole to form correct expectations concerning the rest, or at least expectations which have a good chance of proving correct."[12]

---

[9]Frank Hahn, "Reflections on the Invisible Hand," *Lloyds Bank Review*, April 1982, pp. 1, 5. Hahn's "pure theory" is characterized by perfect knowledge and perfect competition creating the normative benchmark of perfect markets where all supplies and demands mesh, allocation is optimal (Pareto efficient), production and prices are at marginal cost for all firms, and futures markets exist for all goods at all time intervals.

[10]Hahn does stop short of the non sequitur that failures of the "invisible hand" require government intervention. Ibid., p. 9.

[11]See R. H. Coase, "The Nature of the Firm," *Economica* (November 1937): 386–405.

[12]F. A. Hayek, *Law, Legislation, and Liberty*, 3 vols., (Chicago: University of Chicago Press, 1973), vol. 1, p. 36.

Market theory explains how an economy can "run itself" without central direction from governmental czars. In the oil and gas industry, the stages of production are numerous, highly specialized, and remote from the consumption level. The major phases are exploration and production, transportation (by truck, pipeline, barge, tanker, and rail), refining, and marketing. Behind the scenes are numerous secondary production processes whose output is critically responsible for the output of the primary phases. The specialized phases are all interdependent and necessary; without one of them, the integrated structure breaks down for consumers. Amid such complexity, coordination rather than bottlenecks tends to prevail in market settings because adverse situations offer incentives—profit opportunities—for their prevention and removal. The result is unintended order since no individual entrepreneur or government agency masterminds that overall result.

The Petroleum Market as Spontaneous Order

The theory of spontaneous order can be used to understand the development of the U.S. petroleum industry.[13] As one economist has observed, the formative years of the industry represented "a virtual textbook example of a laissez-faire market economy."[14] The free-market era in petroleum, which saw isolated intervention but was free of price and allocation regulation and other major intrusions, can be dated from the beginning of the industry to 1911, when the Standard Oil Trust was dissolved. The great maturation and growth of the industry during the laissez-faire era and after—market forces continued to dominate after 1911—can be comprehended and appreciated in light of the economic environment surrounding its development.

Between the 1859 discovery of the Drake well and 1865, more than 900 oil companies, representing aggregate capital of $580 million, sprang into operation in the complementary phases of production, transportation, refining, and retailing.[15] Virtually all this growth

---

[13]While the natural-gas industry has experienced significant growth, government intervention has been more pronounced to dilute the application of spontaneous-order theory.

[14]D. T. Armentano, "The Energy Crisis: Historical Roots and Political Consequences," *Libertarian Review*, July–August 1979, p. 25.

[15]Andrew Cone and Walter Johns, *Petrolia* (1870; Westport, Conn.: Hyperion Press, 1976), p. 587. In 1993 dollars, this investment would be over $8 billion. See Appendix A for conversions from nominal to inflation-adjusted dollars.

was privately financed and directed without government planning. Coordination crises between industry sectors were the exception rather than the rule. Crude-oil producers secured transportation and refining; transportation and refining attracted crude oil. Refined products found transportation and marketing outlets; transportation and marketing outlets secured refined products. There were many temporary problems and challenges along the way, as documented in industry histories of the period, but profitable solutions were found. Under market incentives, necessity was indeed the mother of invention. Ida Tarbell attributed this success to "free opportunity," an explanation akin to Smith's invisible hand and Hayek's spontaneous order. In her words:

> It is certain . . . the development [of the petroleum industry] could never have gone on at anything like the speed that it did except under the American system of free opportunity. Men did not wait to ask if they might go into the Oil Region: they went. They did not ask how to put down a well: they quickly took the processes which other men had developed for other purposes and adopted them to their purpose. . . . Taken as a whole, a truer exhibit of what must be expected of men working without other regulation than that they voluntarily give themselves is not to be found in our industrial history.[16]

In 1861, oil from Pennsylvania exceeded domestic refining demand and began to be exported to other countries. The United States would be a net exporter of crude for the rest of the century. The Petroleum Board, one of the earliest organized stock exchanges, opened in New York City in 1864 to facilitate capital procurement for the budding industry. These early years also witnessed innumerable mechanical innovations that lowered business costs and reduced oil waste.[17] Less satisfactory was the evolution of first-title, lease, and tort law at the wellhead, as seen in the next chapter.[18]

With the development of the industry, the United States became the world leader in petroleum production and consumption. Until

---

[16]Ida Tarbell, Introduction to Paul Giddens, *The Birth of the Oil Industry* (New York: Macmillan and Co., 1938), p. xxxix.

[17]See, generally, Harold Williamson and Arnold Daum, *The Age of Illumination, 1859 to 1899*, vol. 1 of *The American Petroleum Industry* (Evanston, Ill.: Northwestern University Press, 1959).

[18]See chapter 2, pp. 59–69.

the turn of the century, between 80 and 90 percent of world production originated from the United States to satisfy demand domestically, in Europe, and elsewhere.[19] The Standard Oil Trust was the first to supply the masses. "[Standard] gradually extended its services," John D. Rockefeller later recalled, "first to the large cities, and then to towns, and now to the smallest places, going to the homes of its customers, delivering the oil to suit the convenience of the actual users."[20] This also was true in international markets, to which Standard became the world's leading exporter of kerosene in the 1870s and 1880s.

Crude output in the United States, which began modestly at several thousand barrels in 1859, rose to 2 million barrels in 1861, 5 million barrels in 1871, 10 million barrels in 1874, and over 60 million barrels by 1900. By 1911, yearly crude production surged to 220 million barrels. The production of refined products, chiefly kerosene, increased more than proportionately as a result of improvements in storage, transportation, and distillation technology. Crude prices per barrel fell from the $3 to $9 range in the 1860s to under $1 during most of the 1890–1915 period.[21] The race for production under the rule-of-capture legal framework (described in chapter 2), growing demand, and a multi-billion-dollar petroleum infrastructure, led by Standard Oil's investments in the pipeline and refining sectors, underlay this growth.

While the largest industry in the world took shape and matured in the United States, other petroleum-endowed areas remained in ignorance of their hydrocarbon wealth because of a lack of private-property rights and market incentives. Potential changed into actual only when major U.S. companies internationalized the petroleum industry with their exports of capital, equipment, technological expertise, and profit-and-loss entrepreneurship. U.S. oilmen introduced many countries to their subsurface oil wealth beginning with Brazil (1887) and Mexico (1900) and continuing with Venezuela

[19]J. Stanley Clark, *The Oil Century* (Norman: University of Oklahoma Press, 1958), p. 27.

[20]John D. Rockefeller, *Random Reminiscences of Men and Events* (New York: Doubleday, Page and Company, 1909), p. 57.

[21]U.S. Department of Commerce, Bureau of the Census, *Historical Statistics of the United States: Colonial Times to 1970* (Washington, D.C.: Government Printing Office, 1975), pp. 593–94.

(1913), Canada (1914), Bolivia (1926), Iraq (1927), Hungary (1937), Saudi Arabia and Kuwait (1939), Chile (1945), and Libya (1956).[22] This has continued to recent times. The development of the North Sea fields in the 1960s and 1970s led Edward Chester to state, "The economic efficiency and long-standing technological superiority of the great American petroleum firms, so frequently displayed elsewhere, at this time manifested itself in the backyards of Great Britain and Western Europe."[23]

Investments by U.S. firms in foreign petroleum markets have been substantial. From $1.1 billion in 1929, constituting the lion's share of world petroleum investment, the total grew to $3.4 billion (68 percent of the total) in 1948, $5 billion (66 percent) in 1953, and a high of $6.4 billion (56 percent) in 1957. In the next decade, nationalization, import restrictions, and regulatory uncertainty dropped U.S. oil and gas investment overseas to under 50 percent of the world total for the first time. The growth in U.S. investment in international oil and gas projects resumed in the 1970s, increasing from $10.6 billion in 1973 to $22 billion in 1976, $32 billion in 1979, and a peak of $63 billion in the early 1980s.[24] U.S. market share, however, remained below 50 percent because of nationalization and regulatory disincentives.

In addition to pioneering the development of the world petroleum market, the U.S. oil industry intensely developed its own reserves, which for most of the twentieth century constituted over 50 percent of world supply.[25] U.S. refining projects also dotted the international map, as did pipeline and marketing facilities. In some destitute areas of the world, entire infrastructures—from housing to schools and

[22]Eugene Holman, "American Oil Companies in Foreign Petroleum Operations," in *Our Oil Resources*, ed. Leonard Fanning (New York: McGraw-Hill, 1945), pp. 38–50.

[23]Edward Chester, *United States Oil Policy and Diplomacy* (Westport, Conn.: Greenwood Press, 1983), p. 101.

[24]Leonard Fanning, *Foreign Oil and the Free World* (New York: McGraw-Hill, 1954), p. 347; and American Petroleum Institute, *Basic Petroleum Data Book*, 1983 ed. (Washington, D.C.: API, 1983), sec. V, table 8, and 1986 ed., sec. V, table 6.

[25]U.S. output fell below 50 percent of world production for the first time in the early 1950s. The decline accelerated, and U.S. output dropped below 20 percent in the mid-1970s. The decline reflected the rapid development of foreign reserves, mainly by U.S. firms. American Petroleum Institute, *Basic Petroleum Data Book*, 1986 ed., sec. IV, table 1. Secondary factors in the transformation were domestic proration and, later, domestic price controls and taxation.

hospitals—were built by profit-seeking American firms to supplement their higher cost domestic properties with high-volume foreign output. Foreign production reflected government permission—approval by the State Department to do business abroad and concessions by host governments to explore, drill, and build—rather than government subsidies.[26]

Symbolic of the preeminent position of the United States in the world petroleum market is the fact that of the seven major world oil firms, the so-called seven sisters, five were U.S. companies—Jersey Standard (Exxon), New York Standard (Mobil), California Standard (Chevron), Texaco, and Gulf. The two foreign firms, providing stout competition for the other five, were Royal Dutch Shell and British Petroleum.[27]

Where the U.S. oil industry has not been directly involved in world production, refining, and marketing, it has been indirectly involved through applications of American technology. Geology and geophysics, applying advanced science to locate hydrocarbon deposits, were developed in the United States. Rotary drilling, offshore production, long-distance oil and gas pipelines, major refinery techniques, and innumerable smaller innovations were also U.S. contributions to "technology—the great multiplier."[28] Standardization of equipment specifications and advances in oil and gas accounting were achieved through cooperative efforts within the American Petroleum Institute beginning in the 1920s.[29] Another example of cooperative success was the formation of the Natural Gasoline Association in 1921 to formulate distillation and blending standards to improve the quality of motor gasoline and increase consumer acceptance.

The march of innovation within the market's spontaneous order has continued to the present. New market institutions created to manage instability include the reestablishment of petroleum futures

[26]Eugene Holman, "American Oil Companies," pp. 52–81.

[27]Gulf would later merge with Chevron to create six sisters in place of seven.

[28]See O. D. Donnell and A. Jacobsen, "Technology—The Great Multiplier," in *Our Oil Resources*, pp. 71–111.

[29]American Petroleum Institute, *History of Petroleum Engineering* (Washington, D.C.: API, 1961), pp. 1193–1210. Also see Isaac Marcosson, "Oil and Conservancy," *Saturday Evening Post*, February 18, 1928, p. 141.

markets, discussed in chapter 17, and natural-gas spot markets, discussed in appendix 15.1.[30] Another development, the rise of international spot markets in petroleum, occurred in conjunction with the erosion of the Organization of Petroleum Exporting Countries (OPEC) cartel in the post-1980 decontrol era. The spot market, which by 1984 accounted for nearly half of all international crude movements compared with under 5 percent a decade before, "just happened" according to one participant. "There was no grand design. . . . [I]t was a response to a hunger for a hedging mechanism, given the uncertainties of the time."[31] In a related development, spontaneous order has shaped international oil contracts regarding the laws of nonperformance. Sophisticated legal instruments, devised by multinational oil firms, have facilitated oil trading and fostered growth and efficiency in the world oil market.[32]

A résumé of the American petroleum industry in the present century must highlight the growth of supply and demand. From under half a billion barrels in 1920, crude production increased to around 1 billion barrels in the 1927–35 period, 2 billion barrels in 1948, and 3 billion barrels in 1966. Pervasive regulation in the next decade arrested this growth. Crude-oil prices declined in real terms in the 1900–73 period despite state and federal regulation intended to promote the opposite. After 1973, prices reached record levels but declined greatly after 1981 as market forces reasserted control. Reflecting crude-oil costs, the price of petroleum products fell as well.[33]

With economic growth and the mass application of new energy-intensive technologies, annual per capita U.S. petroleum consumption escalated from 4.3 barrels in 1920 to over 30 barrels by 1980. In 1984, the United States accounted for over one-fourth of world consumption.[34] Far from being a black mark, this level of consumption was indicative of a high—and growing—standard of living for Americans in the technological age.

[30]See chapter 17, pp. 1052–55, and appendix 15.1, pp. 944–60.

[31]*Houston Chronicle*, December 3, 1984, sec. 2–2.

[32]Leon Trakman, "Nonperformance in Oil Contacts," *Oil and Gas Tax Quarterly*, June 1981, pp. 716–50.

[33]See appendix A, pp. 1911–18, for nominal and real prices of crude oil, fuel oil, and motor gasoline.

[34]DeGolyer and MacNaughton, *Twentieth Century Petroleum Statistics* (Dallas, Tex.: DeGolyer and MacNaughton, 1980), pp. 20, 100; and American Petroleum Institute, *Basic Petroleum Data Book*, 1986 ed., sec. IV, table 1.

Not only economic growth but the absence of shortages and other performance crises during the industry's free-market periods suggests that a spontaneous order was at work. Age-old predictions of oil shortages—either because demand was rapidly increasing or future supply was uncertain—have been repeatedly belied by new discoveries, technological advances, and conservation.[35] Oil (and natural-gas) shortages, on the other hand, were closely associated with pervasive price and allocation regulation that demonstrated the opposite of spontaneous order—imposed disorder.

A subtle part of the industry's success story has been the compilation and dissemination of industry data in publications such as the *American Gas Light Journal/Pipeline & Gas Journal* (1859), *Oil & Gas Journal* (1902), *National Petroleum News* (1909), *Oil Weekly* (1916), *Platt's Oilgram* (1923), and *Oil Daily* (1951). Distilled supply, demand, and price statistics improved economic calculation, and how-to technical articles shared the wealth. The international basing point for world pricing for most of this century, the Texas-Louisiana Gulf Coast, confirmed the United States as the world petroleum center and the U.S. trade press as its informational nexus. Warren Platt, founder and editor of the *National Petroleum News* and *Oilgram*, paid modest tribute to his forty-five years of industry reporting: "The quick and accurate gathering and distribution of plain unvarnished industry facts, we believe, has been of some aid in helping the industry to develop the degree of vigorous and constructive competition that it has."[36]

An overlooked characteristic of the U.S. petroleum industry in its first 125 years has been the social mobility of industry figures and philanthropic applications of business and personal income. History is replete with examples of industry executives from humble origins who worked their way up the business ladder.[37] With governmental considerations largely absent, merit as revealed by the marketplace dominated hiring and promotion decisions. Many of these successful individuals had strong charitable instincts because of their modest

[35]For an examination of these forecasts and why they proved wrong, see Leonard Fanning, "A Case History of Oil-Shortage Scares," in *Our Oil Resources*, pp. 306–405.

[36]Warren Platt, "To My Friends of the Oil Industry," *National Petroleum News*, January 6, 1954, p. 33. Cited hereafter as *NPN*.

[37]For some examples of the career histories of early industry executives, see *NPN*, February 5, 1936, pp. 478–82.

backgrounds and accumulations of wealth far in excess of their consumption habits. Major industry figures in the present century, from John D. Rockefeller to J. Howard Pew to Hugh Roy Cullen, donated hundreds of millions of dollars of personal wealth to philanthropic causes.[38] Such indirect social benefits joined the more direct benefits of reliable oil supplies at affordable prices.

These varied contributions of the industry have not been the result of a unique inbred genius possessed by the American people or of a monopoly of resources within the United States. They are the result of an economic system characterized by

1. private ownership of the means of production, including, for the most part, mineral rights;
2. the incentive of profit and the disincentive of loss to find new and better ways to serve consumers;
3. market pricing to economically guide production and consumption; and
4. the ability of the industry to finance growth from retained earnings and expanding private capital markets.

The general result of market reliance has been a reliable synchronization of the complex phases of the petroleum industry, as well as mass energy production for mass energy consumption. The U.S. oil and gas market is a case study of the practical operation of the Smith-Hayek spontaneous-order theory, although property-rights misapplications and government intervention have challenged this coordination and growth, as future chapters will detail.

Economic Constructivism

Various social scientists have rejected the spontaneous-order paradigm and advocated an array of "corrective" interventions. Even some market-oriented scholars have stopped short of anchoring their analyses in the Smith-Hayek worldview. They have embraced the competing *constructivist* worldview, advocating government intervention to achieve utilitarian goals. That view has been dominant for much of the present century.

---

[38]Reflecting on his own experience, Rockefeller wrote, "If [the rich] get pleasure from the possession of money, it comes from their ability to do things which give satisfaction to someone besides themselves." *Random Reminiscences of Men and Events*, p. 140.

Constructivism is the belief that "since man has created the institutions of society and civilization, he must be able to alter them at will to satisfy his wishes and desires."[39] It also entails the belief that "reason is capable of directly manipulating all the details of a complex society," a belief from which "all modern socialism, planning, and totalitarianism derive."[40]

A corollary to constructivism is scientism, the idea that knowledge in the social sciences can be quantitatively derived by the same methods employed by the physical sciences.[41] Under the "unified-science" approach, the social scientist can statistically model economic data to develop predictive theories about human action. In constructivist hands, predictive theories justify substituting economic planning for the free-market economy. As one proponent put it, "Mathematical programming assisted by electronic computers . . . [by solving] large numbers of equations and inequalities . . . becomes the fundamental instrument of long-term planning." In contrast, "The market process . . . appears old fashioned . . . a computing device of the preelectronic age."[42]

The theory that society should control its own destiny and avoid a "naive" dependence on spontaneous forces draws inspiration from the impressive record of the physical sciences in controlling inanimate matter. It is also driven by the alluring quest to impose stability, security, and equality on human affairs. Both rationales have inspired the theory and application of economic intervention. Arising from a dissatisfaction with market outcomes, economic constructivism ranges from full-scale government ownership of economic assets to broad economic planning to selected regulation of privately held resources.

Central Planning

Socialism and Nationalization. Socialism—state ownership of the means of production—represents a radical denial of the spontaneous

---

[39]F. A. Hayek, "The Errors of Constructivism," *New Studies in Philosophy, Politics, Economics and the History of Ideas* (Chicago: University of Chicago Press, 1978), p. 3.

[40]F. A. Hayek, "Kinds of Rationalism," *Studies in Philosophy, Politics, and Economics,* pp. 85, 88.

[41]It should be emphasized that while constructivism implies a belief in scientism, the reverse need not be true.

[42]Oskar Lange, "The Computer and the Market," in *Comparative Economic Systems,* ed. Morris Bornstein (Homewood, Ill.: R. D. Irwin, 1974), pp. 137, 139.

order; the "invisible hand" of market processes is replaced with the visible hand of government in the conduct of economic affairs.[43] Although socialist theory has only a small voice in economic theory and policy debates today, socialism has been widely implemented in various forms in the oil-producing regions of the world.

Resource allocation under socialism is very different from allocation in the free market, because bureaucratic management produces different results than does profit-and-loss entrepreneurship. The government assumes the position of a monopoly firm, immune from interfirm rivalry and potential entry. Pricing based on cost or bureaucratic rules fails to duplicate scarcity pricing of the market. Political control cannot replicate impersonal market forces. Socialism, in short, cannot be expected to provide the right incentives for production, avoid politicization, and utilize the decentralized knowledge of its economic participants to approach sound resource allocation. Any application of socialism to the energy market faces those problems.

In the United States, proposals for full socialization of the energy market have been rare and lacking in scholarly justification or detail. Socialists have advocated economy-wide nationalization of industry—and thus implicitly of oil and gas—but no attempt has been made to explain how efficiency and economic order could be successfully achieved in practice.[44]

Market socialism, a compromise version of full, or Marxian, socialism, formulated by Oskar Lange and Abba Lerner, attempts to set efficiency rules to mimic a competitive market. This purely theoretical construct has not been proposed for the U.S. oil and gas market. Neither has the Lerner-Lange proposal been seriously considered for implementation in either socialist or nonsocialist countries.[45]

The U.S. petroleum market has been subject to occasional calls for *nationalization,* a forced transfer of private resources to government

---

[43]Gerald Sirklin, *The Visible Hand: The Fundamentals of Economic Planning* (New York: McGraw-Hill, 1968), p. viii.

[44]For instance, see Michael Harrington, *Socialism* (1970; New York: Saturday Review Press, 1972), pp. 371–72; and idem, "The Oil Crisis—Socialist Answers," *Dissent* (Spring 1974): 139–42.

[45]Market socialism as a program for the entire economy is described in Oskar Lange and Fred Taylor, *On the Economic Theory of Socialism* (1938; New York: McGraw-Hill, 1964), pp. 65–98.

ownership and operation. Sentiment for this variant of socialism has surfaced several times during oil shortages and once during overproduction and falling prices, as will be discussed below. United industry opposition prevented nationalization.[46]

During and immediately after World War I, a tight crude-oil market caused by wartime price controls led to concern over the government's ability to satisfy its petroleum needs. Fuel czar Harry Garfield openly considered nationalization of oil based on the precedents of the coal-mining, railroad, telephone, and telegraph industries.[47] A Federal Trade Commission report in 1918 warned of nationalization if the problem was not corrected. In the same year, at their inaugural meeting, the Oil, Chemical, and Atomic Workers International Union called for oil nationalization. Two years later, Secretary of the Navy Josephus Daniels advocated the same policy to assure the U.S. Navy of a steady supply of fuel oil at acceptable prices.[48] Those warnings failed to materialize, although in another context the Mineral Leasing Act of 1920 nationalized subsoil rights by reserving minerals to the state in contrast to the prior policy of awarding patents to discoverer-claimants.[49]

When unprecedented oil production depressed prices, exacerbating industry problems during the Great Depression, the unwelcome specter of nationalization again arose. The industry backed the less severe remedy of increased regulation and successfully implemented state and federal policies to that end.

The energy shortages of the 1970s again found the oil industry on the defensive. The AFL-CIO Executive Council in August 1979 unanimously asked Congress to consider nationalization if "the oil monopoly fails to adequately serve the public interest."[50] Although

---

[46]On the local level, the Osage Indian tribe nationalized individual allotments of mineral rights for tribal income equality. John Ise, *The United States Oil Policy* (New Haven, Conn.: Yale University Press, 1926), p. 391.

[47]*Oil & Gas Journal*, May 30, 1919, p. 2. On the sectoral level, an Oklahoma senator unsuccessfully introduced a bill in Congress in 1914 to nationalize long-distance oil pipelines and associated facilities.

[48]George Nash, *United States Oil Policy* (Westport, Conn.: Greenwood Press, 1968), pp. 35, 45.

[49]See chapter 6, pp. 266–72.

[50]Lester Sobel, ed., *Energy Crisis*, 4 vols. (New York: Facts on File, 1980), vol. 4, p. 89.

nationalization was never formalized in a bill, congressional sentiment for nationalization intensified. But as it had forty years earlier,
Congress intensified regulation instead.

Another advocate of energy nationalization was Barry Commoner,
author of several books and articles on energy and a presidential
candidate in 1980. Although admittedly not an expert in economics,
he staunchly recommended nationalization as a cure for an energy
crisis created by "produc[ing] for profit rather than social value."[51]
Commoner, however, was oblivious to the free-market arguments
about social knowledge and economic calculation, issues crucial to
any case for national energy planning.

Commoner's pronouncements on energy were paralleled by the
normative program of Robert Engler, a political scientist whose
books on oil and natural-gas regulation detailed the political influence of the industry over government policy. Engler's exposés, along
with his distrust of profit seeking, led him to advocate "public
ownership and democratic planning of all domestic energy
resources."[52]

Although Engler's historical study of the politicization of oil is
valuable, his case for nationalization is a non sequitur. His facts can
support the opposite policy position of deregulating oil, and he
does not attempt to refute the economic case against socialism. Like
Commoner, Engler defaults on the crucial question of how a nationalized energy sector could obtain the intricate knowledge of a decentralized market to effectively serve consumers.

In each of the above cases, the rationale for nationalization arose
from the crisis situation itself, not from a demonstration that government ownership could efficiently plan the energy sector. The implicit
assumption—that a market-created lack of coordination requires
imposed order—will be questioned throughout this book.

---

[51]Barry Commoner, "Energy, Environment, and Economics," in *Energy: The Policy
Issues,* ed. Gary Eppen (Chicago: University of Chicago Press, 1975), p. 40. Also see
idem, *The Poverty of Power: Energy and the Economic Crisis* (New York: Alfred A. Knopf,
1976), p. 258; and idem, *The Politics of Energy* (New York: Alfred A. Knopf, 1979), p. 82.

[52]Robert Engler, *The Brotherhood of Oil* (Chicago: University of Chicago Press, 1978),
pp. 213–14. Also see his prior work, *The Politics of Oil* (New York: Macmillan,
1961), chap. 16.

The Federal Corporation. A second planning mechanism is government enterprise within an essentially private economy.[53] This piecemeal form of socialism has economic advantages over comprehensive socialism because the surrounding market allows the government enterprise to compare its costs and revenues. This mechanism may be inefficient, but it does not suffer from calculational chaos. The weakness of bureaucratic enterprise is that it is internally sheltered from market discipline. The enterprise cannot "test" itself to know which cost and revenue changes best serve the consumer. Without profit and loss, government firms lack the necessary economic clues to know how best to differentiate products, arrange inputs, and choose a proper scale of operation. Bureaucracy is also protected from the marketplace because its capitalization is obtained through government edict, not the competitive loan market. Thus, the important market process of channeling scarce investment funds into the most skilled hands is circumvented.

A popular form of bureaucratic enterprise is euphemistically referred to as the federal corporation.[54] This entity is designed to increase rivalry in a market by being an additional competitor (a "yardstick enterprise") or to monopolistically perform a function considered uneconomical by profit-and-loss firms or unimportant by nonprofit private institutions. A sophisticated federal corporation may emulate its free-market counterparts by preparing business-type budgets, having commercial audits and accounting opinions, retaining a board of directors, and having contractual autonomy. But it remains fundamentally different from a private-sector concern nonetheless.[55] A federal corporation may be allowed to seek profits ("surpluses"), although this has not been the norm.

[53]Free-market and government institutions should be carefully distinguished. This has not been done in the energy literature by Robert Engler and Anthony Sampson who have characterized major oil companies as "private governments." See Engler, *The Brotherhood of Oil*, p. 94; and Sampson, *The Seven Sisters* (1975; New York: Bantam Books, 1980), p. 9. The close interplay between private companies and the political process can be appreciated without blurring this distinction.

[54]The term "corporation" is a misnomer when used to describe a government agency since there is no private ownership or trading of stock. Similarly, it is misleading to use the phrase "government on a business basis" to describe the operation of a bureaucracy.

[55]A discussion of federal corporate charters and enabling legislation, such as the Government Corporation Control Act of 1945 (Public Law 248, 59 Stat. 597) and the Budget and Accounting Procedures Act of 1950 (Public Law 81-784, 64 Stat. 832), is contained in Sidney Goldberg and Harold Seidman, *The Government Corporation:*

In both discussion and practice, the federal corporation has been a small part of the oil and gas market. In 1943, the Federal Petroleum Reserves Corporation was established to develop oil and gas abroad, although it never became operational. Other wartime corporations, the Defense Supplies Corporation and the Defense Plants Corporation, affected petroleum investments and sales. In 1980, the U.S. Synthetic Fuels Corporation was founded to subsidize the private development of alternative fuels. It was instructed by Congress to "function much like a private corporate entity such as a bank or other financial institution."[56] On the local level in the early years of the industry, city and county governments occasionally set up agencies to explore for, produce, and transport oil and gas to meet local needs. Those nonprofit bureaucracies were created to supplement market activity.[57]

Public and congressional agitation for a federal energy firm surfaced on several other occasions. In the 1909–17 period, U.S. naval officials advocated federal production, transportation, and refining of crude oil to assure the navy of ample supplies at attractive prices. The navy began drilling in the newly established Naval Petroleum Reserves. In 1920, worries about a shortage of domestic supply prompted congressional debate on whether to set up a United States Oil Corporation to conduct exploratory activity abroad. In 1971, proposals were aired for a Coal Gasification Development Corporation, a government-industry partnership but a federal entity nevertheless. And during the energy crisis of 1973–74, when more than 800 energy bills were introduced in over 30 subcommittees, citizen groups lobbied Congress for a federal agency to compete against private oil firms. Sen. Adlai Stevenson III's (D-Ill.) Consumer Energy Act of 1974 proposed to create a Federal Oil and Gas Corporation to explore for oil and gas on federal and private lands.[58] A year

---

Elements of a Model Charter (Chicago: Public Administration Service, 1953). For a chronological summary of federal laws cited in this book, see Appendix B.

[56]Conference Report, H. R. Rep. no. 96-1104, 96th Cong., 2d sess. (1980), p. 203. See chapter 10, pp. 578–83.

[57]Other examples in the energy field are the federal power marketing agencies, such as the Tennessee Valley Authority (founded 1933) and the Bonneville Power Agency (founded 1937), and hundreds of municipal power agencies.

[58]The bill's stated purpose was to "secure adequate and reliable supplies of natural gas and oil at the lowest reasonable cost to the consumer." For the text of the bill and a critical analysis of it, see American Enterprise Institute, *Federal Oil and Gas Corporation Proposals* (Washington, D.C.: AEI, May 21, 1974).

later, Sen. Henry Jackson (D-Wash.) proposed a National Energy Production Board to develop oil resources on the federal domain.[59] Also in 1975, Sen. Frank Church (D-Idaho) introduced a bill to create a federal corporation to directly buy petroleum imports from oil-exporting countries. The oil monopsony plan, supported by economist M. A. Adelman as an alternative to higher oil-import fees, was also defeated.[60]

The perceived need to increase competition in free-market settings is predicated on two questionable assumptions. The first is that the market lacks rivalry and the government can measure competition to determine the optimal amount of rivalry to introduce. The second assumption is that government must perform the tasks that the private economy will not perform. Both assumptions are questionable. Competition in a free market—which prominently includes *potential* competition—is inherent in all entrepreneurial activity where legal barriers to entry do not exist. Government cannot "know" how to supplement market rivalry—nor does it need to do so. The assumption that government should do what private business will not risk is suspect, given the meaning of profit and loss. The market produces goods and services that can command a revenue high enough to cover expenses and earn a return. When government produces what the market will not support, it destroys economic value by preventing resources from being employed in more urgent (profitable) areas. Further, the belief that government is more far-sighted and knowledgeable than the market overlooks the informational content of market prices, which assimilate the knowledge of all market participants rather than only the relatively limited knowledge of government planners.

A federal corporation remains a government bureaucracy. Even if it is allowed to seek profits, it still suffers from nonmarket capitalization and the likely prospect of losses. There is little reason to conclude that the government can discover profit opportunities better than market entrepreneurs in fields to which private entry is not

---

[59]*Oil & Gas Journal*, February 24, 1975, p. 36. Another Senate bill in 1975 proposed to establish an Energy Production Board, modeled after World War II's War Production Board, to add 2 million barrels per day to domestic production. *Oil & Gas Journal*, February 10, 1975, p. 33.

[60]*Oil & Gas Journal*, February 3, 1975, pp. 60–61. Also see Robert Pindyck, "Should the Federal Government Enter the Oil Business?" *Challenge*, May–June 1976, pp. 48–51.

restricted. Another problem has been emphasized by the public-choice school of economics. Incentives to managers under political rule are often perverse in contrast to market incentives that unintentionally promote the general welfare. Lower prices, increased sales, and improved service—paramount in a free market—may be precluded by the pursuit of political objectives. This is the *political problem* of government intervention in the market economy.

The Poverty of Planning. Constructivism suffers from a poverty of knowledge. Economic planning requires substituting the knowledge of a few, expressed through legal edicts that alter market outcomes, for the knowledge of the many, which is impersonally transmitted through the freely functioning price system. Seen another way, constructivism replaces individual and business planning with government central planning and loses a very effective director of economic activity—the "man on the spot."[61]

This impoverishment of results can occur despite good intentions. Many intellectuals and politicians have trumpeted the need and ability to substitute planning for what is seen as the autonomous, cold forces of the market. In fact, their efforts have created unintended detrimental social consequences in the oil and gas market.

Going from theory to the world energy market, there is a close correspondence between the wealth of an economy and its utilization of knowledge. That knowledge includes the ability of consumers to choose the best purchases, the ability of financiers to choose the best investments, and the ability of entrepreneurs to discover and produce what the market demands at least cost. In contrast to the U.S. oil and gas market, where a wealth of knowledge has spawned general economic wealth, many other regions of the world—some enjoying comparable or greater endowments of hydrocarbons[62]— have depended on the knowledge of a political elite and, consequently, have largely failed to benefit their general populations.

---

[61]F. A. Hayek calls this the "very important but unorganized knowledge ... of people, of local conditions, and of special circumstances." Hayek, "The Use of Knowledge in Society," *Individualism and Economic Order*, p. 80.

[62]Of the world's proven reserves in 1984, the United States held only 4 percent of crude oil and 7.7 percent of natural gas. American Petroleum Institute, *Basic Petroleum Data Book*, 1986 ed., sec. II, table 3; and DeGolyer and MacNaughton, *Twentieth Century Petroleum Statistics*, 1980 ed., pp. 1, 14.

The absence of private-property rights and arbitrary regulatory and tax impositions in many petroleum-endowed countries have led to delayed development, underdevelopment, nondevelopment, and negative growth. In 1927, the *Oil & Gas Journal* reported "a progressively increasing world tendency to control and regulate the petroleum industry by legislative action."[63] In this period and after, U.S. companies working under foreign concessions were subject to arbitrary requirements and contracts. Favoritism to host countries regarding employment, directorships, investment, and stock ownership was often required. Public-works construction was sometimes required. Mandatory worker benefits were imposed. Inventory levels were prescribed. Taxes and royalties were unilaterally increased. Price controls were implemented along with foreign exchange controls. The rules of the game could change at any time.[64]

Nationalization has taken a heavy toll. Russia's thriving petroleum industry, which rivaled that of the United States at the turn of the century, was devastated by nationalization and Marxist reform. A writer in *Nation's Business* noticed, "As to the effect of government control on potential supply, the record shows 20 years of experience with government control in Russia, which in 1900 produced the same amount of oil as the United States, in 1916 produced one-fifth as much, and in 1929 less than a tenth as much."[65]

Closer to home, the promising growth of Mexico's oil industry in the first decades of this century was hampered by high production and export taxes and was severely arrested by nationalization in 1938. Over the next decade, not one new field was discovered, and new development wells failed to keep pace with retirements. In 1947, twenty wells were drilled in Mexico compared to 9,000 in neighboring Texas.[66] In the 1950s, U.S. know-how and capital came

[63]*Oil & Gas Journal,* January 29, 1927, pp. 108, 184.

[64]For a discussion of petroleum constructivism outside the United States, see Henri Madelin, *Oil and Politics* (New York: Praeger, 1966), part III. A summary of regulation per country as of 1922 is contained in Boverton Redwood, *Petroleum: A Treatise* (London: Charles Griffin & Co., 1922), pp. 979–1154. Lease and tax regulations of selected countries are presented in Ernest Lilley, *The Oil Industry* (New York: D. Van Nostrand, 1925), chap. V. Also see D. M. Phelps, "Petroleum Regulation in Temperate South America," *American Economic Review* (March 1939): 48–59.

[65]Thomas Read, "Should Bureaucracy Rule Petroleum?" *Nation's Business,* August 1941, p. 25.

[66]Edward Chester, *United States Oil Policy and Diplomacy,* pp. 133–34.

to the rescue, but large-scale corruption and inefficiency prevented the great potential wealth of the Mexican petroleum industry from helping to eradicate the country's chronic poverty problem. In the late 1970s, prolific discoveries reconfirmed Mexico as an oil power. But what was hailed as a new era of abundance crashed from new heights of corruption and inefficiency, high debt, declining world prices, inflation and peso devaluations, and petrodollars misspent on prestige and industrial projects. Excruciating poverty remains.

In Canada, the Petroleum Administration Act of 1975 and the National Energy Program of 1980 comprehensively intervened in oil and gas activity.[67] Oil prices and allocation were regulated, energy sectors were subsidized, industry revenues were redistributed, nationalistic ownership requirements were set ("Canadianization" policy), new energy taxes were levied, oil imports were licensed, and oil exports were restricted. These responses to the energy crisis, which created problems similar to those in the United States (as a result of many similar regulations), began to be dismantled in 1984 amid their widely recognized distortions and falling oil prices.

In other countries, nationalization has reduced or reversed oil-sector growth. Examples of nationalization include Argentina (1937), Bolivia (1937, 1969), Romania (1921, 1944), Hungary (1948), Iran (1951), Cuba (1960), Iraq (1961, 1972), Brazil (1964), Algeria (1967–70), Peru (1968, 1975), Libya (1973–74), and Venezuela (1976).[68] The largest nationalization in history was the ownership transfer of the Arabian American Oil Company (Aramco) from Texaco, Chevron, Exxon, and Mobil to the Saudi government after the 1973 embargo. Operational control had been assumed in 1972–73, a condition that facilitated the price increases that followed.[69]

State petroleum monopolies, some in conjunction with national-ization, were established in Argentina (1922), Spain (1927), Manchu-kuo (1934), Bolivia (1936), Mexico (1938), Colombia (1948), Iran

---

[67]See, generally, G. Bruce Doern and Glen Toner, *The Politics of Energy* (New York: Methuen, 1985).

[68]Edward Chester, *United States Oil Policy and Diplomacy*, pp. 157, 166, 169, 181, 200, 205, 231; Leonard Fanning, *Foreign Oil and the Free World* (New York: McGraw-Hill, 1954), pp. 242–48, 314–15; and Eugene Holman, "American Oil Companies in Foreign Petroleum Operations," in *Our Oil Resources*, pp. 38–44.

[69]See Walter Mead, "An Economic Analysis of Crude Oil Price Behavior in the 1970s," *Journal of Energy and Development* (Spring 1979): 212–28.

(1951), Brazil (1953), Venezuela and Kuwait (1960), Saudi Arabia (1962), Algeria (1963), Iraq (1964), Indonesia (1968), Libya (1970), Canada and Britain (1975), and other countries.[70] With oil wealth concentrated in the public sector, these countries engineered industrial modernization programs that have turned out far different from entrepreneurial investments in a free market. In fact, looking at relative performance, the ironic conclusion is that private-sector firms have been more public, benefiting wide sections of the population, while public-sector firms have really been private—primarily benefiting the politically favored and corrupt few.

The poverty of constructivism is not entirely foreign to the U.S. experience. There have been clearly identifiable periods of malcoordination and underachievement as a result of pronounced government intervention. Large amounts of human capital and financial resources have been wasted under regulations that had the negative effect of hampering the market's ability to produce unintended beneficial order. But because the market has continued to play an important role, oil and gas crises have been the exception rather than the rule as coming chapters will illustrate.

Intervention

Short of government ownership, economic constructivism can prescribe selected intervention to tax, regulate, and subsidize individual firms or sectors in the industry. All-encompassing interventionism can take the form of de facto socialism, since government makes business decisions as if it owned the resources. This was virtually the case in the U.S. petroleum market during World War I, World War II, and, to a lesser extent, during the Korean conflict when government orchestration of private oil and gas activity replaced market competition. Outside of these years, oil and gas intervention has been piecemeal and fragmented rather than coordinated according to a central plan, which led some critics to conclude that the United States does not have a national energy policy.

Government intervention can be subdivided into two general categories. One variant attempts to broadly control ("fine-tune") the aggregates of an economic system or a sector thereof. The other variant intervenes in market decisions on a particularized basis

---

[70]Edward Chester, *United States Oil Policy and Diplomacy*, p. 315.

according to individual situations. The former may be labeled *macroeconomic interventionism*, the latter *microeconomic interventionism*.

Macroeconomic Planning. Macroeconomic planning is linked to the ideas presented in John Maynard Keynes's *General Theory of Employment, Interest and Money*.[71] The book sounded an optimistic note during the Great Depression: government manipulation of macroeconomic variables could promote noninflationary full employment. Keynes's theory represented a "middle way" between full planning and the unfettered market. The "Keynesian Revolution" not only denied the unintended beneficence of the market economy but put forward a scientistic-constructivist theory of imposing macroeconomic order on the economy.

In energy economics, the shortages of the 1970s invited macroeconomists to analyze the effects of oil shocks and government policies designed to deal with them. This was an implicit, not explicit, application. As Paul Samuelson, a leading contemporary Keynesian economist, observed:

> There is nothing in Keynes' *General Theory* that tells you how to handle an oil crisis. There are multipliers and accelerators there, but they apply to models too gross to apply to oil shortages.[72]

Although a Keynesian program specifically for petroleum-market disequilibrium has not gained currency, there are several post-Keynesian legacies in energy scholarship. One is the use of econometrics to derive causal relationships for policy fine-tuning.[73] Energy economists have quantified relationships between such energy aggregates as consumption, supply, demand, price levels, elasticities

---

[71]John Maynard Keynes, *General Theory of Employment, Interest and Money* (1936; New York: Harcourt Brace and World, 1964).

[72]Paul Samuelson, "Discussion," *Technology Review*, March–April 1974, p. 51.

[73]The econometric revolution was the doing of later Keynesians rather than Keynes himself. While Keynes invited statistical inquiry in a descriptive sense (*General Theory*, pp. 9–10, 127), he forwardly criticized inferential statistics and econometrics. See Keynes's book review of J. Tinbergen, *On Method and Its Application to Investment Activity*, in *Economic Journal* (September 1939): 558–68; and "Reply to Tinbergen," *Economic Journal* (March 1940): 154–56. Despite Keynes's own reservations, econometrics closely complemented his "new economics" as later Keynesians would demonstrate.

of supply and demand, and refinery utilization to compare them to economy-wide aggregates such as output, employment, and prices.[74] As an illustration of historical relationships and as a forecasting tool, energy econometrics can be a benign academic exercise. But in the public policy arena, where quantitative relationships are assumed to be invariant, the temptation becomes great to employ energy econometrics to plan private activities. That is exactly what happened in the 1970s when government energy planners welcomed a "scientific" basis for their work, much as the New Deal of the 1930s found a "scientific" basis in Keynesian economics. As W. T. Ziemba and others stated:

> In the wake of the 1973–74 energy crisis . . . the field of energy policy modeling became one of the fastest growing in the industrialized world. . . . The suddenly felt need for sound government action to alleviate the economic shock caused by these dislocations has led to increased use of quantitative modeling techniques by various government agencies [since] it was apparent that many economic, operations research, and scientific studies could aid in the solution and understanding of this crisis.[75]

F. A. Hayek pointed out that error in social science theory and policy is most commonly "based on the presumption of knowledge which in fact we do not possess."[76] The bane of econometric research,

[74]For an explicit Keynesian Y = C + I + G adaptation to energy econometrics, see Alan Manne, "ETA-MACRO: A Model of Energy-Economy Interactions," in *Advances in the Economics of Energy and Resources,* ed. R. S. Pindyck (Greenwich, Conn.: JAI Press, 1979), vol. 2, pp. 205–33.

[75]W. T. Ziemba, S. L. Schwartz, and E. Koenigsberg, *Energy Policy Modeling: United States and Canadian Experiences,* 2 vols. (Boston: Martinus Nijhoff, 1980), vol. 1, p. xviii. Milton Searl similarly remarked on the progress of energy econometrics by 1973: "Energy modeling in some areas of application is now capable of making useful contributions to planning and policy formation." *Energy Modeling,* ed. Milton Searl (Washington, D.C.: Resources for the Future, 1973), p. 13. For a list of over 170 econometric and predictive studies conducted by the U.S. Department of Energy as part of its regulatory program as of 1980, see *1980 EIA Publications Directory: A User's Guide* (Washington, D.C.: U.S. Department of Energy, 1981), chap. 2. Other empirical energy studies are listed in R. W. Rycroft et al., *Energy Policy Making: A Bibliography* (Norman: University of Oklahoma Press, 1977), pp. 19–23. The first government-sponsored econometric energy study was prepared in 1939 for the National Resources Committee. Econometrics' first major application in regulatory policy was in the debate over regulation of natural gas at the wellhead. See chapter 8, pp. 398.

[76]F. A. Hayek, "The Errors of Constructivism," p. 20.

in so far as it tries to translate quantitative "laws" into social policy, is the simple fact that there are no constants in purposeful human action. Unlike the physical sciences, human action cannot be studied in a laboratory where constants and variables can be arranged to derive cause and effect.[77] Unless other factors are held constant, high correlations can reflect a noncausal relationship, and low correlations can hide a strong causal relationship. Intuition must decide, which places the debate on a qualitative plane. While this has led some economists and many philosophers to question the fertility of econometrics for hypothesis falsification, this is not the major point here. The danger of energy econometrics is that alleged statistical relationships can become the basis of interventionist public policy, as was the case during the energy crisis. In the same period, Nobel prize–winning economists Wassily Leontief and Gunnar Myrdal advocated broad national planning for major industrial sectors, including energy, on the basis of historical input/output ratios.[78]

In 1977, national planning was proposed for the petroleum industry by the president of Atlantic Richfield (ARCO), Thornton Bradshaw. He complained that the petroleum market never had been able to avoid the swings of shortages and surpluses and recommended government planning of output and price for certain energy resources to achieve stabilization.[79] A fellow energy executive replied that the ills Bradshaw identified were the result not of the market but of government interference with the market.[80]

[77]For a soft critique of energy scientism from a mainstream perspective, see Robert Stobaugh and Daniel Yergin, "Limits to Models," *Energy Future* (New York: Ballantine Books, 1979), pp. 305–37. For brief looks at the unsatisfactory record of energy forecasting in the 1970s and early 1980s, see *Wall Street Journal,* May 5, 1982, pp. 1, 17, and March 16, 1984, p. 26.

[78]For an illuminating discussion of the academic and political drive for national planning, along with a critique of the input/output econometric program, see F. A. Hayek, "The New Confusion about Planning," pp. 232–46.

[79]Thornton Bradshaw, "My Case for National Planning," *Fortune,* February 1977, pp. 103–4. Bradshaw's thesis is similar to that of economist Paul Frankel, who argued that instability inheres in the market because of inelastic demand coupled with incentives to rapidly produce under the rule of capture. Frankel, *Essentials of Petroleum* (London: Chapman and Hall, 1946).

[80]Charles Koch, "Energy: The Case for a Free Market," *Libertarian Review,* August 1977, pp. 34–37.

In addition to scientism, a second Keynesian legacy in the modern energy debate was provided by Paul Davidson in his "post-Keynesian" perspective on the cause and cure of U.S. energy market instability.[81] Resurrecting Keynes's view of the destabilizing effects of market expectations, Davidson questioned the reliability of energy prices and profits for guiding production. Although he stopped short of advocating government management of energy aggregates, he did prescribe a "regulated wellhead price [to] . . . squelch producer speculation in all energy sources."[82]

The Keynes-Davidson view of market expectations fails to acknowledge the tendency of expectations, when they prove correct (profitable), to smooth out price fluctuations by encouraging purchases when the price is low, driving the price up, and encouraging sales when the price is high, driving the price down. This reduces price uncertainty (fluctuations) and works to stabilize the market. Although the Keynes-Davidson view contains a germ of truth, namely that incorrect expectations destabilize prices and generate speculative losses, the view neglects how profits encourage good speculation and losses discourage bad speculation. The market contains error and waste, but it is equally true that, unlike nonmarket alternatives, the market contains incentives to minimize error. Davidson's call for wellhead price controls would introduce as many problems as it attempts to solve, as is seen in chapters 8 and 9.

A third Keynesian legacy has been the propensity of government to neglect—or at least assume the constancy of—the supply side of the energy equation. Wellhead price controls on crude oil and natural gas are excellent examples. Instead of market-oriented supply reform, the government has introduced conservation ("demand-management") programs—a regulatory "solution" to a problem caused by regulation.[83] President Carter's approach to energy problems from 1977 through 1980 was heavily conservation oriented.

[81]Paul Davidson, "The Economics of Natural Resources," *Challenge*, March–April, 1979, pp. 40–46.

[82]Ibid., p. 45.

[83]For a summary of the demand-management energy programs as of 1980, see John Carlin, David Hatcher, and Mark Rodekohr, "A Qualitative Assessment of the Impact of Energy Demand-Management Programs," U.S. Department of Energy, March 1980, pp. 22–62.

An economic literature using Keynesian precepts has proliferated to measure the negative aggregate effects on the economy of higher oil prices resulting from a hypothetical cutoff. The "macroanalysis of an oil disruption,"[84] positing a government role in import policy to alleviate "market failure," is critically reviewed in chapter 13.[85]

Microeconomic Policies. Government ownership and macroeconomic planning have been the exception, not the rule, in the U.S. oil and gas market. The "rule" has been specific regulation, taxes, and subsidies. Some microeconomic interventions have been intended to correct "market failures" and implement "user fees" for government services. But many interventions have been purely political—the result of industry pressures to improve particular competitive positions. The common categories and applications of microeconomic intervention are examined below as a prelude to their more systematic description and evaluation in the chapters to follow.

The government can regulate the transactions of buyers and sellers by setting a maximum or a minimum price. Maximum price decrees on petroleum occurred during World War I, World War II, the Korean conflict, and from 1971 to 1981 under Nixon's price control program and the Emergency Petroleum Allocation Act of 1973. In each case, maximum selling prices or cost-plus price ceilings prevented downstream industry parties from capturing the economic rent denied to upstream parties.

Wellhead natural gas dedicated in interstate commerce had been regulated in various forms since 1940, and regulation became comprehensive in 1954. Intrastate price maximums were introduced in 1978. Public-utility regulation has set maximum prices at the gas-distribution level since the 1880s and at the interstate-transmission level since 1938.

Price minimums have been implemented briefly by several states to reduce the physical waste of natural gas, as detailed in chapter 3.[86] With petroleum, price floors have been rare, since market-demand proration by state governments and federal import restrictions have

---

[84]George Horwich, "Government Contingency Planning for Petroleum-Supply Interruptions: A Macroperspective," in *Policies for Coping with Oil-Supply Disruptions,* ed. George Horwich and Edward Mitchell (Washington, D.C.: American Enterprise Institute, 1982), pp. 33–65.

[85]See chapter 13, pp. 757–62. Also see chapter 17, pp. 1043–47.

[86]See chapter 4, pp. 195–97.

41

achieved a similar result. Federal price floors were seriously considered as part of the Code of Fair Competition for the Petroleum Industry under the National Industrial Recovery Act of 1933. The Department of the Interior abandoned the idea because of its complexity and relied on wellhead production (output) control instead.

The experience with oil and gas price controls vividly illustrates how unregulated exchange coordinates activities and how nonmarket pricing creates economic distortion and social discord. Although interference with rising oil prices is always for the sake of a noble cause—fighting inflation or the "OPEC monopoly," correcting "macroeconomic dislocation," or opposing "monopoly profits"— price controls create severe unintended consequences. Shortages, black markets, superfluous entrepreneurship, arbitrary wealth redistribution, and resource misallocation have resulted from legal edicts establishing a price lower than market levels.[87] Price minimums, on the other hand, have created economically immobile surpluses.[88]

These negative results have occurred despite the best efforts of energy scientism to discover the "optimum" price. With no more than ambiguous historical data and subjective calculations of the alterations needed to reflect changed conditions, there is no reliable anchor for computing the "right" price. There are only constantly changing market prices, discoverable by the free interplay of buyers and sellers, and nonmarket prices, derived from the whim or sophisticated econometrics of government authorities.

In addition to direct price regulation, the government may take an indirect approach by influencing the underlying conditions that determine price and output. In these situations, price and output do not reflect only consumer preference; they reflect governmental influences as well.

The government has manipulated supply and demand in the petroleum market in numerous and varied instances with wellhead and end-use conservation regulations, import and export restrictions, nonneutral tax provisions, public-land leasing policies, subsidies, safety and environmental standards, licensing and permit regulation, and product-quality regulations. Sometimes, these interventions have been ambitiously packaged as part of an integrated energy

[87]See, specifically, chapter 8, pp. 457–64; chapter 9, pp. 528–32; chapter 12, pp. 680–81, 687–710; and chapter 27, pp. 1630–49, 1662–83.

[88]See chapter 4, pp. 195–97.

strategy. President Nixon created such a peacetime policy in a June 1971 Presidential Message, "A Program to Insure an Adequate Supply of Clean Energy in the Future." President Ford proudly referred to the Energy Policy and Conservation Act of 1975, a 98-page warehouse of intervention, as "the first elements of a comprehensive national energy policy."[89] President Carter's National Energy Plan of 1977 and Second National Energy Plan of 1979 proposed to manipulate virtually all energy policy variables in excruciating detail. Although these interventions are too numerous and varied to be critically examined outside their historical context, several common aspects may be pointed out.

Manipulation of supply and demand produces more subtle distortions than those produced by price controls. Each intervention increases costs and reduces supply, leading to higher prices. The consumer, however, is often not able to separate the interventionist component of price (the "price premium" attributable to regulation and taxation) from the underlying scarcity price—hence the subtlety. Consequently, there can be a call for further intervention to offset the effects (higher prices, lower output) of prior intervention. Indeed, in responding to political incentives, officeholders have often misidentified causal relations in order to deflect blame from existing policies and allow greater scope for future policy activism.

Through the antitrust laws, enforced by the Federal Trade Commission and the Justice Department, government can reshape business competition from its natural market structure. Officials, drawing on the perfect-competition model to demonstrate the welfare losses of deviations from marginal-cost pricing, may decide that the undesigned market structure is noncompetitive; they may intervene to "create" competition, believing that output will increase and prices will fall.

Antitrust prosecution (or its threat) has increased the number of nonaffiliated firms and reduced each firm's market share or "economic power." In the U.S. oil and gas market, the antitrust movement

---

[89]Congressional Quarterly, Inc., *Energy Policy*, March 1981, p. 150. Senator Henry Jackson (D-Wash.) stated: "The nation desperately needs a coordinated, reasoned national energy program that will accelerate development of our domestic energy supplies, end wasteful consumption, and redress arbitrary and unfair fuel pricing policies. The 93rd Congress recognized this need and began development of a national energy policy." Jackson, "Rational Development of Outer Continental Shelf Oil and Gas," *Oregon Law Review* 54 (1975): 567.

has prevented and destroyed large, integrated businesses; preserved small, nonintegrated business concerns; and penalized certain price behavior as "noncompetitive."

The most dramatic antitrust breakup in U.S. history occurred in 1911 when the Standard Oil Trust was found in violation of the Sherman Antitrust Act and divided into more than thirty separate companies. In addition, numerous companies in all petroleum phases have been investigated and prosecuted on the state and federal levels under antitrust law. The two most active periods were after the New Deal (1935–41) and during the energy crisis (1973–80).[90] Although divestiture has been rare, business cooperation and mergers have been discouraged. Ironically, authorities have also encouraged cartelization and monopolization during significant periods in the industry's history.[91]

A voluminous academic literature has attempted to assess the competitiveness of the U.S. petroleum industry. Interventionists have concluded that vigorous antitrust scrutiny and even horizontal and vertical divestiture are necessary to achieve competitive pricing.[92] Other economists have concluded that the existing structure of the industry is competitive.[93]

Two assumptions in this technical debate deserve scrutiny. First, the theoretical benchmark of perfect competition has been uncritically adopted by energy economists on each side of the question, resulting in a neglect of the role of intertemporal competition and entrepreneurship (pure profits and losses) in efficiently allocating resources. Second, both sides of the debate have tried to measure

[90]See chapter 14, pp. 785–87, 792–94, 799–801, 808–10, 816–18; chapter 18, pp. 1074–89; chapter 22, pp. 1297–1305; and chapter 26 for discussions of competition and antitrust theory and cases in the oil industry. Major congressional studies of energy-market competitiveness include those undertaken in 1922 (LaFollette Committee), 1926 (Federal Trade Commission investigation), 1936 (Madison investigation), 1939 (Temporary National Economic Committee hearings), and 1972 (Multinational Subcommittee hearings).

[91]For a summary of these episodes, see chapter 29, pp. 1799–1800.

[92]Economist John Blair has advocated strict antitrust rules and enforcement rather than regulation for industry reform. See Blair, *The Control of Oil* (New York: Pantheon Books, 1976), chap. 16. Also see Stanley Ruttenberg, *The American Oil Industry: A Failure of Anti-trust Policy* (New York: Marine Engineers Association, 1973).

[93]See Jesse Markham, Anthony Hourihan, and Francis Sterling, *Horizontal Divestiture and the Petroleum Industry* (Cambridge, Mass.: Ballinger, 1977); and Edward Mitchell, ed., *Vertical Integration in the Oil Industry* (Washington, D.C.: American Enterprise Institute, 1976).

competition from profit levels, market share, price behavior, joint venture propensities, capital expenditures, financial interlocks, and so on. Rivalry, however, is not an objectively measurable process from which the presence (or "degree") of competition can be established. Not only are the "facts" inexact and open to opposing interpretations, but economic theory provides no quantitative definition of what is and is not competitive.[94] Entrepreneurial competition in a free market, for example, prominently includes the possibility of new entry. Yet it is impossible for outsiders to know or measure the strength of potential rivalry.

The evaluation of competition and efficiency requires a qualitative rather than a quantitative standard. A market is not competitive because its firms are configured a particular way but because entry is free of legal restrictions and competitive business practices have minimum constraints. The market-process view of competition and efficiency, in contrast to the structuralist view, is presented in Chapter 26 on antitrust regulation.[95]

"Market failure" is a revered justification for government interference in the energy markets (as elsewhere). James Griffin and Henry Steele have written:

> Market failures provide a guideline for government intervention in energy markets. To the extent that observed phenomena fit into one of these [failure] classifications, there is an economic justification for government intervention in the market.[96]

Market failures fall into three main areas: externalities, public goods, and natural monopoly.

The *externality* argument holds that individuals or firms may not be influenced by all the pertinent costs and benefits of an activity. When there is a difference between private costs and social costs or private benefits and social benefits, output or demand is nonoptimal.

[94]On the difficulty of objectively interpreting profit levels, a popular barometer of competition to many energy economists, see Shyam Sunder, *Oil Industry Profits* (Washington, D.C.: American Enterprise Institute, 1977), pp. 9–50. Sunder's attempt to break out of subjectivity by quantifying risk is beset with the same difficulty as the initial interpretation of profits, however.

[95]See chapter 26, pp. 1542–51, 1567–69, 1585–93, 1601–3.

[96]James Griffin and Henry Steele, *Energy Economics and Policy* (New York: Academic Press, 1980), p. 43. The caveat is added that a quantitative cost-benefit analysis must justify the intervention (p. 44), a procedure which is critically examined below.

Under those conditions, the price system, which normally dissemi-
nates valuable information, imparts misinformation and misallocates resources.

Some oft-cited externalities in the petroleum industry are oil production under the rule of capture and oil imports. In both cases,
social costs are said to exceed private costs. In the case of oil production, short-term gains are won by overdrilling and reducing the
recoverable output of petroleum reservoirs; in the pollution case,
air and water resources are damaged by profit-maximizing practices.

Oil imports and private inventory have attracted criticism as nonoptimal. The price (private cost) of imports, critics charge, does not
account for the social cost of imports—the macroeconomic losses
from supply disruptions, given import dependence. Private inventory in preparation for import disruptions, relatedly, is suboptimal
from society's viewpoint. In these examples, the "invisible hand"
seems to work in reverse—what is profit maximizing for individual
firms is bad for society.

The outstanding characteristic of externalities is that they tend to
occur in pronounced fashion when private-property rights are either
nonexistent, poorly formulated, or invaded.[97] With the example of
oil production, the allocation of property rights, not the free market
per se, is at issue. Introducing, redefining, or extending property
rights can internalize externalities and allow the market to bring
individual costs and benefits more nearly into line with their general
effects, as will be shown in chapters 2 and 3.[98]

The alleged externalities of underpriced, overpurchased imports
and understocked private inventory may be more imagined than
real. Market expectations include the risk of supply interruptions,
and the market's expectation in the 1980s was that debilitating cutoffs
would not recur. In retrospect, the market was right and the critics
wrong. The government's major response, the Strategic Petroleum
Reserve, has carried a high price tag, whatever its contribution to
reducing the alleged externality.[99] There is not only "market failure"
but "government failure."

[97]"In order for a society to use its resources efficiently, property rights must be well
defined, enforced, and transferable." Terry Anderson and Peter Hill, "Establishing
Property Rights in Energy: Efficient vs. Inefficient Processes," *Cato Journal* 1, no. 1
(Spring 1981): 87–105.

[98]See chapter 2, pp. 70–74, and chapter 3, p. 107–31, respectively.

[99]See chapter 13, pp. 760–62, and chapter 17, pp. 1036–48, respectively.

To take issue with these examples is not to suggest that the market is omniscient and that every price signal is correct. It does suggest that the market, as collectively expressed, is resourceful about perceiving and exploiting profit opportunities to improve suboptimal resource allocations. Nevertheless, externalities and market failure occur, although not as severely as in economic systems where private-property rights are poorly defined, invaded, or absent. To make their case, the advocates of government intervention must unambiguously show not only that error exists but that the correction is known and obtainable at less cost than the cost of the alleged market imperfection. Quantitative cost-benefit analysis, however, introduces more ambiguity to the debate than science can allow.

The attempt to measure social costs and benefits presumes that a unit of measurement exists for calculating the "goods" and "bads" of economic life. But subjective value is incapable of being added or subtracted, because no unit of comparison exists. There is nothing in the social sciences that corresponds to the time, distance, and weight measurements of the physical sciences. The economist's value proxy, the monetary unit, is not an "equilibrium" fixture; it constantly fluctuates because of changes in demand and supply.[100]

Subjective economic perception undermines the rationale behind intervention to mitigate externalities. There is no scientific basis upon which the government can determine what the "social" benefits and costs are, much less equate the two.[101] Instead, the case for eradicating particularly acute externalities can go little further than to provide a clear, all-encompassing system of property rights so that the cost-benefit analysis can be internalized within the market by the involved parties. The myriad less prominent externalities that remain are a fact of life; correction by intervention—regulation, subsidy, or taxation—politicizes the issue and introduces costs that could well be greater than the externality itself.

---

[100]Even in the hypothetical world of general equilibrium, monetary outlays do not measure costs and benefits because forgone opportunity remains in the mind of the beholder. See James Seldon, "The Relevance of Subjective Costs: Comment," *Southern Economic Journal* (May 1982): 216–21.

[101]For a more detailed criticism of quantitative cost-benefit analysis, see James Buchanan, *Cost and Choice* (Chicago: Markham, 1969), pp. 70–83; and Mario Rizzo, ed., *Time, Uncertainty, and Disequilibrium* (Lexington, Mass.: Lexington Books, 1979), pp. 71–95, 117–22.

The public-goods argument for government intervention involves an externality: the market is believed to inadequately produce goods of which the net social benefits exceed the net private benefits. In some cases, the market may be entirely unable to produce what the public collectively wants because a normal sales market cannot exist. Such cases occur when one person's consumption does not prevent or reduce another's consumption and the exclusion of nonpayers is not possible. The resulting "free rider" problem, the argument concludes, can only be overcome if the government (taxpayer) provides the "public good" and requires everyone to pay. The classic example is national defense.

The public-goods argument as applied to oil and gas is limited. Exclusion of users is always theoretically possible; the question is, at what cost? The matter thus reduces to a technological argument over whether the means exist to collect revenue for the "public" good in a private setting, and, indeed, whether or not the good should be produced. In a different institutional context, many public goods can be redefined as private goods with rivalrous consumption.[102]

Energy economists John Holloman and Michel Grenon have identified certain large-scale energy research and development projects as public goods deserving government subsidy. They assert that large amounts of capital, which the market cannot afford, are needed, yet the resulting supply enhancement benefits everyone.[103] However, market "underinvestment" is evidence not of capital-market failure but of a calculated entrepreneurial decision in a surplus energy market. If an investment opportunity is sufficiently attractive and a firm does not have enough resources, interfirm capital pooling can be undertaken. The example of the multi-billion-dollar trans-Alaskan pipeline, financed entirely by private companies through pooled capital despite their tax obligations and heavy regulatory impediments, is proof that even megaprojects can attract the necessary private capital.

Heavy capital requirements for certain projects indicate the need to lessen the tax burden. Lower taxation expands the capital market

---

[102]See Tyler Cowen, "On the Definition of Public Goods and Their Institutional Context," *Review of Social Economy*, April 1985, pp. 53–63.

[103]John Holloman and Michel Grenon, *Energy Research and Development* (Cambridge, Mass.: Ballinger, 1975), p. 17.

generally and affords more firms the means to internally finance large projects. A multi-trillion-dollar world capital market exists to be tapped by entrepreneurs as long as a competitive profit is envisioned; that huge pool can be enhanced by tax reduction and antitrust reform.

The "general benefits" argument can be used against government expenditure per se. Government expenditures as a rule have been a welfare loss for taxpayers, while private research and development projects are replete with positive results. The government's inability to determine "optimal" research and development outside of market preferences makes overinvestment by bureaucrats as likely as under-investment by entrepreneurs. The record of the multi-billion-dollar federal energy research effort by the Department of Energy and the Synthetic Fuels Corporation is an excellent example of the perils of government investment.[104]

Natural monopoly occurs when it is feasible for only one firm to produce a good or service in a certain geographical area. In more technical terms, it occurs when economies of scale throughout the entire relevant range of production (demand) are such that only one firm can efficiently serve the entire market. Although practically every petroleum-related firm enjoys a monopoly in its own small area, natural monopolies over larger geographical areas are said to exist with gas-distribution companies and major oil and gas pipelines.

Critics of the market charge that unregulated natural monopolists will overcharge and underproduce. To create competitive prices while preventing "monopoly profits," public-utility regulation is imposed. Public-utility regulation sets maximum prices based on prudent costs and a "normal" return on invested capital; entry, exit, and other service modifications are also regulated to conform to the "public convenience and necessity."

Public-utility regulation of the entire oil and gas industry has been supported as an alternative to nationalization. In 1931, a period of wellhead overproduction, falling prices, and sagging industry morale, public-utility regulation was advocated by Sen. William Borah (R-Id.) with support from Bainbridge Colby, Woodrow Wilson's secretary of state. In 1935, sentiment for declaring the entire

---

[104]See chapter 10, pp. 575–85.

petroleum industry a public utility was formalized in the Thomas Bill, supported by Interior secretary Harold Ickes, among others. It was opposed by President Roosevelt and the industry, and state wellhead regulation with federal embellishment prevailed. Interstate oil pipelines, natural-gas transmission and distribution, and, for a period, natural-gas production have been regulated as public utilities by either state or federal agencies.[105]

The traditional case for public-utility regulation has come under increasing attack by some economists who have looked more closely at the costs and undesired consequences of actual regulation.[106] Other economists have found flaws in the theoretical underpinnings of natural monopoly. Within the neoclassical orthodoxy, Harold Demsetz questioned whether the existence of natural-monopoly characteristics automatically means that firms reduce output below and set prices above competitive levels.[107] Demsetz argued that in the absence of prohibitive contracting costs, firms competing to serve the whole market in the initial bidding period would bid down monopoly gains. The same would be true for subsequent bidding when the initial contract came up for renewal. "Natural monopoly theory," Demsetz concluded, "provides no logical basis for monopoly prices."[108]

Although fellow economists have criticized certain areas of his theory, Demsetz's general argument has set the tone for a debate that was once closed. When the shortcomings of the regulatory alternative are understood from a market-process and public-choice perspective, the argument for natural-monopoly regulation is weakened.[109]

---

[105]Another example from the energy field is electric power, which has been regulated as a public utility for nearly a century. Although the specific regulatory history of the power industry will not be dealt with in this book, the general arguments made against price and profit regulation of oil and gas firms also apply to the generation, transmission, and distribution of electricity.

[106]For one early example, see George Stigler and Claire Friedland, "What Can Regulators Regulate? The Case of Electricity," *Journal of Law and Economics* (October 1962): 1–13.

[107]Harold Demsetz, "Why Regulate Utilities?" *Journal of Law and Economics* (April 1968): 55–65.

[108]Ibid., p. 59.

[109]Public-choice theory is described in chapter 30, pp. 1816–18.

In an equilibrium world where entrepreneurship becomes obsolete, the welfare norms of marginal-cost pricing and production at minimum average cost hold. But in real-world disequilibrium, where consumer welfare is better served by shaking up the status quo, the welfare rules change. In natural-monopoly situations, pure profits and losses (i.e., prices unequal to marginal costs) are necessary not only to incite entrepreneurial activity but also to impart knowledge to the market in order to propel the entrepreneurial process further. Traditional public-utility regulation has discouraged risky entrepreneurial strategies and encouraged firms to loosely manage operating costs and "pad the rate base" to maximize returns. Certification has delayed projects that consumers would have paid "monopoly rents" for much sooner. The command-and-control effort has imposed deadweight losses. Those combined costs, particularly forgone entrepreneurship, powerfully counteract the "gains" from public-utility regulation.[110] As Stephen Breyer concluded:

> In trying to overcome [market failures] the regulatory process introduces so many distortions of its own. . . . Thus, only serious market failure will, even arguably, warrant the adoption of cost-of-service ratemaking as a cure.[111]

Conclusion

The U.S. petroleum industry has "delivered the goods" for well over a century. Growth statistics tell part of this story; supply coordination, except during price-regulated periods, tells another important part. The disappointing experience of other countries that have relied on a political allocation of resources—Russia and Mexico, for example—highlights the success of the capitalistic U.S. oil and gas industry.

But beneath the free-market success story lie many controversies. Was there a dark side to the rise and domination of the Standard Oil Trust in the 1870–1911 period? Was the rule of capture an insurmountable obstacle to rational drilling and production strategies that required state conservation regulation? Was oil-pipeline regulation

[110]See chapter 14, pp. 834–47, on oil pipelines and chapter 15, pp. 922–39, on natural-gas pipelines.

[111]Stephen Breyer, *Regulation and Its Reform* (Cambridge, Mass.: Harvard University Press, 1982), p. 59.

appropriate to protect wellhead interests from economic exploitation? Was emergency regulation necessary to meet unprecedented military and civilian demand during the world wars? Was a government response needed during the heyday of OPEC's market power? Did the plethora of special-interest regulations affecting gasoline service stations intentionally or unintentionally achieve a greater good?

Similar questions can be asked on the manufactured- and natural-gas side. Was unregulated distribution in the nineteenth century chaotic and in need of public-utility regulation to rationalize the industry? Was downstream gas regulation—first with interstate transmission and then with production—imperative to make upstream regulation effective?

If regulation did not work, was it a failure only of administration and not of theory? Could it benefit from experience and work the next time? These important questions are live issues for the applied economist, economic historian, policymaker, industry participant, and interested public. The remaining chapters address these questions and many more to increase understanding of the consequences of past government intervention in the U.S. oil and gas market, the policy prospects for future government intervention in oil and gas, and the rationale for a market-based energy policy.

SECTION 2

HISTORY

PART I

INTERVENTION IN EXPLORATION AND PRODUCTION

2. Early Years and Legal Development

In the decades preceding the birth of the American nation, records kept by Indians, missionaries, and explorers first told of surface crude-oil deposits in areas that later became Pennsylvania and New York.[1] Early use of seepage crude was for medicinal applications for persons and animals.

One particularly noticeable oil spring was in an area early settlers called Oil Creek (Pennsylvania). Located on a tributary of the Allegheny River, this spring became the source of a crude-oil retail trade by the late 1700s. The oil supply, gathered by bucket in the high-water season and by blanket-dipping in the dry season, fetched around one dollar a gallon at Pittsburgh in 1843, substantially cheaper than several decades earlier when incremental barrels had been imported from Britain.

Early exploration and production were also conducted with picks and shovels. In California in the 1850s and 1860s, Colonel A. C. Ferris offered a steady $20 per barrel for oil provided by oil diggers from a variety of locations.

Throughout the first half of the 1800s, drilling was taking place—but not for oil and gas. The precious preservative salt was the primary target, although oil was produced as a less desired by-product. Abundant whale oil, which only later would become scarce because of overkilling of the animals, reduced the incentive to drill for petroleum. As demand for petroleum as an illuminant increased, however, some entrepreneurs, most notably Samuel Kier, transformed their salt-well operations into crude-oil sources. The era of modern petroleum was foreshadowed.

The Titusville Beginning and After

The birth of the modern petroleum industry is dated by many as the August 27, 1859, drilling discovery of oil by Colonel E. L. Drake

---

[1]This discussion is adopted from Harold Williamson and Arnold Daum, *The Age of Illumination, 1859 to 1899*, vol. 1 of *The American Petroleum Industry* (Evanston, Ill.: Northwestern University Press, 1959), chap. 1.

and the Seneca Oil Company in Titusville, Pennsylvania. The 69.5-foot strike was the culmination of eight long years of creative effort, setbacks, and coincidence, in which people from all walks of business life had participated—entrepreneurs, venture capitalists, land-owners, lawyers, stockbrokers, engineers, bankers, and chemical consultants. Many professional and technological procedures were inaugurated that would thereafter be employed in the continuing search for and production of petroleum.

When oil-lamp producers and middlemen converged at the well site to buy Seneca's crude at $20 per barrel, the third era of energy—after wood and coal—came of age. As William Berger and Kenneth Anderson explained, "At last the combination had come together: the need for oil, an established market and price, and a method of obtaining oil in quantity."[2]

News of the Titusville hit spread quickly, and within days would-be producers, land speculators, crude purchasers, and hangers-on came in search of opportunity. New wells were put into place as fast as money, materials, and charters could be secured.[3] With crude supply, the complementary phases of refining, transportation, and retailing took shape. Those activities, in some respects comparable to the California gold rush, were not without risks. The oil community would discover that the price of crude oil was volatile and could fall drastically.

Within a year of Drake's discovery, the price of a barrel of crude oil fell from $20 to around $2 as dozens of new producing wells entered the market. In the next decade, prices fluctuated between $0.10 and $9 per barrel; annual swings averaged several hundred percent.[4] Despite price fluctuations, production increased significantly except during the Civil War. Price declines caused by the discovery of gushers closed marginal wells, but new wells were hastily developed. Explained Melvin de Chazeau and Alfred Kahn, "Entry was too easy, producers too numerous, conflicts of interest between them too great, the lure of a lucky strike too irresistible for the affected parties to organize themselves and effect necessary

[2]William Berger and Kenneth Anderson, *Modern Petroleum* (Tulsa: PennWell, 1978), p. 6.

[3]State business charters, the earliest government intervention in petroleum production, were not restrictively employed to slow industry development.

[4]*Oil & Gas Journal–Oil City Derrick*, August 27, 1934, p. 47.

control over supplies."[5] Rising demand from an industrializing economy countered increased production, but supply-side developments
ensured a buyer's market.[6]

Outside Pennsylvania, commercial wells were first drilled in Ohio,
West Virginia, Tennessee, and Kentucky in 1860; New York in 1864;
California in 1875; Wyoming in 1883; Colorado and Texas in 1887;
Missouri and Illinois in 1889; Kansas in 1892; and Oklahoma in
1897.[7] In those areas, the pattern of production followed that of
Pennsylvania. Oil finds led to the development of numerous neighboring wells producing full-out, which resulted in rapid depletion
of the oil table. Decades later this would be scrutinized as drilling and
subsurface waste; the then-recognized problems were aboveground
waste and safety hazards. As a consequence, many oil states passed
legislation to combat these problems.

Before examining legislation of the so-called conservation movement, the subject of chapters 3 and 4, an examination of oil and gas
property law is necessary. Many scholars have identified the legal
framework surrounding oil reservoirs as a contributing factor to the
wellhead instability that characterized the petroleum industry both
in the early years and later.

Oil and Gas Property Law

Concurrent with the birth of petroleum drilling came the need to
establish property rights to oil and gas deposits. This was a novel
and perplexing task for three reasons: (1) oil and gas reservoirs
transcended fixed surface property boundaries; (2) the magnitude
of hydrocarbon deposits is not approximately determinable for purposes of apportioning ownership according to surface property titles;
and (3) the pool could be drained from any one person's surface
property above it.

The U.S. Development

Private Oil Lease Contracts. The U.S. system of private property
rights borrowed heavily from the established tradition of English

---

[5]Melvin de Chazeau and Alfred Kahn, *Integration and Competition in the Petroleum Industry* (New Haven, Conn.: Yale University Press, 1959), p. 76.

[6]Production rose from 82,000 barrels in 1859 to 500,000 barrels in 1860, 2,113,000 barrels in 1861, 3,056,000 barrels in 1862, and 5,795,000 barrels in 1871. Rolland Maybee, *Railroad Competition and the Oil Trade* (Philadelphia: Porcupine Press, 1974), p. 244.

[7]Max Ball, Douglas Ball, and Daniel Turner, *This Fascinating Oil Business* (Indianapolis: Bobbs-Merrill, 1940, 1979), p. 361.

common law. Until the question of mineral pools arose, the question of subsurface rights had been relatively clear: the owner of the surface had title to the subsurface too.[8] Early thinking about oil and gas deposits was that as long as a person owned the land, he could drill vertically and take possession of the fruits of his labor or empower another to do so by a lease or royalty agreement. The first executed oil production contract, dated July 4, 1853, read:

> Agreed . . . with J. D. Angier of Cherrytree Township, in the County of Venango, Pa., that he shall repair up and keep in order the old oil spring on land in said . . . or dig and make new springs, and the expenses to be deducted out of the proceeds of the oil, and the balance, if any, to be equally divided . . . for the full term of five years from this date. If profitable.[9]

The two-party arrangement was an example of pioneering entrepreneurship and a building block of spontaneous order. Victor Kulp described the evolution of what was early called the oil and gas lease:

> Except for western lands, which were part of the public domain, the lands from which the oil and gas were to come were in private ownership, and it was assumed that the right to produce oil and gas was part of the fee simple title. But the owners of land were not in a position to drill for oil and gas, because of lack either of funds or of knowledge where they might be found. In spite of the hazards incurred, the promise of rich rewards created a spirit of adventure in others, who, however, did not want to buy the land. So landowner and operator got together on a special contract, wherein the operator agreed to bear the expense of the undertaking and, if successful, to pay the landowner a share of the production.[10]

The Rule of Capture. Simple extensions of private-property contracts sufficed until the fugacious character of oil and gas created a

---

[8]The most common alternative to this legal assignment, sovereign (state) ownership, is criticized in the appendix to this chapter.

[9]W. W. Thornton, *The Law Relating to Oil and Gas* (Cincinnati: W. H. Anderson Co., 1912), pp. 28–29. The first common-law legal decision regarding oil production, concerning oil found in a salt well, was in 1854 (*Hail v. Reed*, 54 Ky. 383). See A. W. Walker, Jr., "Property Rights in Oil and Gas and Their Effect upon Police Regulation of Production," *Texas Law Review* (April 1938): 370.

[10]Victor Kulp, *Oil and Gas Rights* (Boston: Little, Brown, 1954), p. 507. Oil minerals were clearly recognized as land by the courts. For some early cases, see George Bryan, *The Law of Petroleum and Natural Gas* (Philadelphia: George T. Bisel, 1898), pp. 20–36.

property-rights problem. When multiple wells demonstrated that oil deposits could be punctured and drained at different points by different property owners, the courts had to consider competing claims to title. To tackle this question, precedents were sought.

Unable to find direct precedents, the courts worked from analogies of fact with near-precedents of English experience. One case was *Acton* v. *Blundell* in 1843 wherein a water-well owner brought a damage suit against the owner of a nearby coal mine.[11] Although the water well was damaged by pollution from the coal operation, the court decided against the plaintiff—hence against the extrapolation of surface rights to subsurface property—to rule in effect that a person had the right to drill on his land even if a neighbor's underground minerals were adversely affected. In *Brown* v. *Vandergrift*, an 1875 Pennsylvania case, the *Acton* decision was cited to rule against the claim that one owner's well draining another owner's well, being part of the same pool, constituted a theft of oil.[12]

Another influence of English law on U.S. courts in this period concerned the legality of decoying wild game. The law held that luring an animal to one's own property from another's property was legal and that, if captured, the game constituted rightfully acquired property. In an 1889 case, the Pennsylvania Supreme Court likened petroleum pools to wild animals, making well bores, in effect, hydrocarbon decoys.[13] Hence the *rule of capture* emerged as a major tenet of oil and gas property law, modifying the ownership-in-place legal title to hard minerals to encompass the unique case of migrant minerals.

From the fixed-mineral, subterranean-water, and wild-game cases, the legal conclusion was reached that the surface owner had the right to drill and capture oil and gas from the reservoir as long as

[11]12 M. and W. 324 (1843). For extending cases, see Robert Hardwicke, "The Rule of Capture and Its Implication as Applied to Oil and Gas," *Texas Law Review* (June 1935): 409.

[12]80 Pa. 142 (1875).

[13]"Water and oil, and still more strongly gas, may be classed by themselves, if the analogy be not too fanciful, as minerals *ferae nature*. In common with animals, and unlike other minerals, they have the power and the tendency to escape without the volition of the owner." *Westmoreland* v. *DeWitt*, 130 Pa. 235 (1889). This analogy is borrowed from James Griffin and Henry Steele, *Energy Economics and Policy* (New York: Academic Press, 1980), p. 236.

surface nuisances were not committed.[14] The economic effect, as later detailed and qualified, was to promote dense drilling and rapid production instead of production from fewer wells over a longer period.

What common reservoir owners could do in the face of a fellow driller's draining the pool soon became clear. Without legal recourse, they could, in the language of a 1907 court decision,

> only go and do likewise. . . . The oil is wild and will run away if it finds an opening and it is the driller's business to keep it at home. This may not be the best rule; but neither the legislature nor our highest court has given us any better.[15]

With the nonliability of drainage established, the race to take physical possession of oil was on.

Implied Covenants. The substance of the rule of capture was significantly strengthened by judicial interpretation of oil and gas lease law.[16] In several important cases, precedents were established as the court liberally interpreted lease agreements in favor of the lessor since, in the court's eyes, the interest of the landowners as well as the public was better served by drilling than by delay.[17] Implied covenants, distinguishable from contractual covenants, meant that

[14]In Robert Hardwicke's words: "Disregarding refinements and apart from implications or incidental corollaries, and reduced to its fundamentals, the Rule of Capture may be stated as follows: The owner of a tract of land acquires title to the oil or gas which he produces from wells drilled therein, though it may be proved that part of such oil or gas migrated from adjoining lands." Hardwicke, "The Rule of Capture and Its Implication as Applied to Oil and Gas," p. 393.

[15]*Barnard* v. *Monongahela Gas Company*, 216 Pa. 362 (1907). The self-help remedy was aptly stated in a 1931 decision: "The common sense of the common law has recognized that it is wiser to leave the individual to protect himself, if harm results to him from the exercise of another's right to use his property in a reasonable way, than to subject that other to the annoyance, and the public to the burden, of actions at law." *Michalson* v. *Nutting*, 275 Mass. 232 (1931). Quoted in A. W. Walker, Jr., "Property Rights in Oil and Gas," p. 374.

[16]Harold Williamson and Arnold Daum, in *The Age of Illumination*, p. 760, described the court's interpretation of lease provisions as "the practical working of the [capture] rule" since the great majority of land was leased rather than owned by oil operators.

[17]Walter Summers, "The Modern Theory and Practical Application of Statutes for the Conservation of Oil and Gas," in American Bar Association, *Legal History of Conservation of Oil and Gas* (Baltimore: Lord Baltimore Press, 1939), pp. 4–5; and Maurice Merrill, "The Evolution of Oil and Gas Law," *Mississippi Law Journal* (March 1941): 286–87.

once a neighboring well began production, the lessee had to act "prudently" by quickly sinking a well to protect the lessor from drainage, even if not specified in the lease agreement.[18] In legal terminology, the obligation became known as the *offset drilling rule*. Once begun, "continuous and diligent" operation was required thereafter to avoid abandonment at law and forfeiture. The pro-lessor doctrine, in addition to addressing drainage, required lessors to drill additional wells to develop a commercial find, market output on the most favorable terms, and properly maintain the lease.[19]

An explicit area of biased court interpretation concerned delay rentals, which came into regular use after 1874. Despite lessors' agreeing in the contract to accept payment for delayed drilling, decisions by lessors to refuse payment and claim forfeiture were upheld in court.[20]

These extracontractual covenants reinforced the capture rule to promote rapid production from many wells. Given the legal frame-work, the state of knowledge, and the economics of the situation, production could not have proceeded otherwise.

Correlative Rights. Just as a case can be made for the rule of cap-ture's being a convenient derivation to allow the industry to continue its rapid development, the next stage in oil and gas property law can be viewed as a similarly pragmatic attempt to correct the excesses of the capture rule and its corollary, the offset drilling rule. In *Ohio Oil Company* v. *State of Indiana* (1890), a landmark case involving a state statute prohibiting natural-gas wastage, U.S. Supreme Court Justice White introduced the concept of correlative rights as a subsur-face adjunct to the surface law of riparian rights.[21] By this precedent,

---

[18]The obligation of the lessee to develop the property "reasonably" grew out of earlier stone-quarry and iron-mine court cases. The first affirmation of the implied covenant in petroleum to drill quickly to avoid drainage was in an 1875 Pennsylvania court case followed by similar decisions in Ohio and West Virginia (1897), California, Indiana, and Texas (1903), and other states thereafter. See Maurice Merrill, *The Laws Relating to Covenants Implied in Oil and Gas Leases* (St. Louis: Thomas Law Book Co., 1926), chap. 1.

[19]Jacqueline Lang Weaver, *Unitization of Oil and Gas Fields in Texas* (Washington, D.C.: Resources for the Future, 1986), p. 220.

[20]Harold Williamson and Arnold Daum, *The Age of Illumination*, pp. 760–61.

[21]Correlative rights were also known as the "American rule," the "reasonable use rule," and the "beneficial use rule." They were derived from the *sic utere tuo ut alienum non laedas* maxim (so use your own that you do not injure that of another) versus the *cujus est solum ejus est usque ad coelum* (do as you please) tenet.

the rule of capture was significantly modified. Now one could capture oil only as long as one's actions did not lead to the "annihilation of rights of the remainder" to their "just distribution" of the pool.[22] Resurrected was the property-in-place view, which assigned title, if only in abstract, to oil and gas prior to possession. Co-owners now had a reasonable opportunity to capture instead of an absolute right to capture.

This decision brought the age of interventionism to petroleum production. Deeply embedded in correlative rights was the illegality of committing waste since it had an unfavorable impact on fellow well owners.[23] By 1900, several states had passed public-interest conservation laws prohibiting natural-gas wastage, and this ruling put these aims, however valid in themselves, safely within the protection of correlative rights. The common law, in short, had been interpreted to require government regulation of oil and gas production.[24]

A Critique of U.S. Property Law

The Rule of Capture. Given that property rights to the subsurface automatically accrue to the surface owner, the evolution of American oil and gas law seems to have been a reasoned, if imperfect, attempt to grapple with the legal labyrinths involved. However, this legal framework created operational problems. Some of these shortcomings are detailed below as a preliminary to a reconsideration of oil and gas property law.

The subsumption of subsurface rights under surface rights established *luck* as a major element for landowners compared with the

[22]*Ohio Oil Company* v. *Indiana*, 177 U.S. 190 at 210 (1900). Correlative rights were reaffirmed in the 1932 *Danciger Oil* case (49 S.W.2d 837 [Tex. Civ. App. 1932]): "No particular lease or well can ... be taken as a unit, but must be considered in its relation to adjacent leases or wells, with a view to conserving the whole, and is subject to regulation accordingly."

[23]"[L]egislative power ... can be manifested for the purpose of protecting all the collective owners, by securing a just distribution, and to reach the like-end [of protecting correlative rights] by preventing waste." 177 U.S. 190 at 210. Erich Zimmermann, in *Conservation in the Production of Petroleum* (New Haven, Conn.: Yale University Press, 1957), p. 113, has called correlative rights and waste prevention "twin objectives," although the tension between the two will be seen in chapters 3 and 4.

[24]For early court decisions upholding state petroleum regulation as a valid exercise of state "police power," see Robert Hardwicke, "The Rule of Capture and Its Implication as Applied to Oil and Gas," pp. 410–11.

effort and risk of drillers. The good fortune of the landowner whose property simply overlies oil and gas deposits is perhaps the most dramatic example of overnight rags to riches in the American experience. Consider the following report in the January 1919 *Oil & Gas Journal.*

> Some of the West Texas farmers who deserted their homes last summer in pitiful white lines of old prairie wagons are now going back in automobiles. Driven out by . . . drought, they are going back as oil men. . . . Stretches of land . . . from which the disheartened farmers departed . . . are within the new oil district. Some of the farmers who struggled, almost penniless . . . can qualify as oil magnates.[25]

The blind luck of early landowners was diminished by the development of a secondhand market in mineral rights, where wily oilmen and speculators bought mineral rights from surface owners on the gamble of discovery. This market "correction," as it were, transferred resource rights from passive landowners to alert entrepreneurs. But revenue from mineral rights received by the surface owner was an extramarket gain, unearned in the first-title sense by the creative effort of discovery. It can be asked whether an alternative legal theory exists to better reward the efforts of the discoverer of a mineral asset than the accidental owner of the surface area above it.[26]

---

[25]*Oil & Gas Journal*, January 31, 1919, p. 48. Cited hereafter as *OGJ*. Indians on oil-laden reservations were another example of sudden fortune: "A few short years ago the docile Navajo Indians grubbed about in their 25,000 sq.-mi. desert reservation at the four corners where Utah, Arizona, Colorado, and New Mexico meet. Disease-ridden, undernourished, ignorant, they lived in ramshackle hogans and crumbling shacks. . . . Then, in 1956, big-time oil drillers on Navajo land hit the jackpot, and the dollars began gushing in. By last week, their numbers [had] grown to 85,000 . . . their treasury to $60 million, their ancient weapons supplanted by grosses of ballpoint pens, lawyers, bookkeepers, geologists, oil consultants—even a press agent." *Time*, November 10, 1958, p. 31.

[26]This analysis should not be construed as being against a positive reversal of fortunes per se. It is a philosophic/economic analysis of just ownership and proper incentives or rewards associated with an asset that, it will be argued, is not owned until discovery. Far from being obtuse and inconsequential, arguments for regulation and taxation of oil production have stemmed from arguments of "unjust" ownership based on such luck. John Ise, for example, argues for stiff taxation of oil royalties because "incomes accruing from the accidental ownership of oil lands certainly stand in a different position from incomes earned by productive service." Ise, *The United States Oil Policy* (New Haven, Conn.: Yale University Press, 1926), p. 521.

Another inadequacy of the rule-of-capture framework was sanctification of a *law of piracy*, whereby the first finder of a reservoir had his prize diluted by the very act of discovery.[27] Predation commonly occurred when a deposit extended beyond the finder's property or lease area. In such situations, neighboring property owners or lessees would either drill into the reservoir to share in the finder's discovery or extract higher rent from the finder to lease the entire surface area above the deposit. The protection of block leasing was an expensive and risky alternative, particularly in the early days of the industry, compared with "checkerboarding," where mineral-right holdings were scattered to "pirate" as many potential reservoirs as possible. The result was that wildcat drilling was penalized, and developmental drilling was subsidized, by a "free-rider" effect. In other words, new fields were discouraged, while existing fields were overdeveloped. These deterrents provide another reason to seek an alternative legal framework to better define the finder's rights in relation to the followers'.

While drainage was accepted as a fact of life under the capture rule, another practice was less accepted but beyond the arm of the law as originally interpreted. A common-pool producer with relatively poor production could and would threaten fellow owners with reservoir damage unless they purchased his well or agreed to share their higher output with him.[28] Simply removing his well casing would allow salt water to penetrate the oil-bearing sand and flood and ruin neighboring oil production. (Casing inadequacies, encouraged by the rush of speculative drilling by some underfinanced, unsophisticated operators, inadvertently caused the same result.) One Titusville farm lost sixty producing wells from "promiscuous and sometimes vindictive withdrawals of tubing."[29] This problem generated sentiment for a legislative solution that led to the first set of conservation regulations for casing and plugging wells.[30] Short of correlative rights and formal regulation, another allocation of private-property rights was called for.

---

[27]The capture rule in this regard has been called "the law of the jungle" and "the law of piracy." Robert Hardwicke, "The Rule of Capture and Its Implications as Applied to Oil and Gas," p. 392.

[28]Harold Williamson and Arnold Daum, *The Age of Illumination*, p. 161.

[29]Ibid., p. 162.

[30]See chapter 4, pp. 134–36.

On the economic plane, the capture rule played a role, although overestimated as shown in the next two chapters, in the annual sound resource allocation normally associated with market processes. Lamented economists James Griffin and Henry Steele, "Although the rule of capture may have been a godsend to judges burdened with a heavy case load, it was anathema to the goal of economic efficiency."[31]

The capture-rule incentive to produce at an almost panic rate, fortified by implicit covenants, created economic distortion because oil and gas in the ground had the legal status of a wild animal, owned by no one. To gain ownership, physical possession was required. Overdrilling and overproduction were the result. Too many wells were sunk in the same area. The large number of pool perforations, many poorly located, and subsequent all-out production reduced reservoir recoverability from certain rate-sensitive reservoirs.[32] Once brought to the surface, oil was handled wastefully; storage facilities were often inadequate because major oil finds were not geographically predictable and exploitation was immediate and rapid. In all, oil production had little time structure; proven reservoirs were not managed to yield an optimal future income stream, or, in financial jargon, the capital values of oil wells were not maximized. Much of the problem, as argued in the next chapter, was inherent because, in its infant state, reservoir engineering had not produced the knowledge required to "optimally" deplete reservoirs, and drillers and their lenders could not afford delayed production in many cases. Hence, to a large extent, a conservation problem did not exist given the realities of early-year production. But undoubtedly the rule of capture contributed to existing problems by skewing time preference toward the present in the race for possession and raising transaction costs by increasing the number of pool owners required to orchestrate their actions to allow greater intertemporal production.[33] In

[31]James Griffin and Henry Steele, *Energy Economics and Policy*, p. 237. For a neoclassical interpretation of the "common-pool problem" under the capture rule, see Alan Friedman, "The Economics of the Common Pool: Property Rights in Exhaustible Resources," *U.C.L.A. Law Review* 18 (1971): 855–87.

[32]For a discussion of geologic waste, see the appendix to chapter 4, pp. 218–21.

[33]The capture rule prompted this second tendency by encouraging lease speculation where profit-maximizing brokers would divide and subdivide lease tracts to sell to drillers, even to 1/32 of an acre, to multiply the number of pool owners needing to cooperate to effectuate slower production. One example of extreme small-tract leasing occurred in the Signal Hill field in California where a well was drilled on a plot

contrast to operator-lessors, furthermore, less sophisticated lessors have been less amenable to the cooperative development that is commonly necessary to most efficiently develop a commonly owned reservoir.[34]

The instability that characterized oil and gas production in the early years and beyond can be understood. With little reservation demand with underground inventory, the market process of speculation to stabilize swings in supply and price was stymied. Instead, cycles of scarcity and abundance characterized production.

Another deficiency in the capture rule has concerned lease properties with more than one vertical reservoir.[35] As long as production is diligently pursued from one formation, the traditional capture-rule lease is powerless to compel development of other formations. Neighboring drillers are unable to break the inaction because of the trespass prohibition on slant drilling. The leaseholder thus exercises a vertical monopoly over the underdeveloped reservoirs until current production ceases to place the lease in jeopardy. Innovative lease agreements can deal (and have dealt) with the relative development of multiple formations, but in many agreements, no provision exists to prevent potential problems of monopolization. Another property-rights assignment is necessary to avoid the problem of "banked" reservoirs altogether.

Severed ownership of mineral rights and surface rights under the rule of capture has introduced another problem. Because the mineral-rights owner has the right to use the surface area for drilling, the surface owner must be on standby indefinitely to acquiesce to exploration and production activity. The surface owner is entitled to "fair market" compensation for use of his property, but the royalty owner holds the perpetual right to drill. This not only creates uncertainty for landowners without subsurface rights, it obstructs potential surface development where mineral-rights ownership is sufficiently fragmented that purchase by the surface owner is discouraged or prevented. This problem commonly occurs, for example,

---

measuring 24 by 30 feet. The "world's smallest oil lease" measured 0.0165 acre. *OGJ*, June 25, 1936, p. 31.

[34]Jacqueline Lang Weaver, *Unitization of Oil and Gas Fields in Texas*, pp. 221, 230.

[35]A controversy in this regard arose from the Hugoton field in Kansas where landowners complained that deeper pockets of oil and gas were being purposefully neglected for economic reasons, given that shallower production protected the lease. *Wall Street Journal*, May 4, 1983, p. 29.

with real estate development where the project cannot proceed until all drilling rights are retired. Even where minerals are unlikely, exploration rights can be a nuisance to surface owners and developers. This conflict also suggests a need for an alternative theory of property rights.

Implied Covenants. Implied covenants have reinforced the proclivity of the capture rule to promote autonomous decisionmaking about commonly owned reservoirs.[36] The requirement to rapidly drill offset wells and continually produce from them makes cooperative development of a reservoir more problematic than if self-help were the only recourse for neighboring mineral-rights owners. (This is truest with primary production and less so with secondary operations where cooperative decisions are typically required to introduce artificial lift.) With or without reform of the rule of capture, implicit covenants are open to censure from a private-property, economic-efficiency perspective.

Correlative Rights. The advent of correlative rights marked an attempt to address some problems of the law of capture, but it created its own problems as well. Within the broad authority of a welfare statute, various subterfuges could now be carried out under the banner of waste prevention. Vested interests could restrict ("prorate") supply to stabilize price—ostensibly to protect common-law rights or, in political language, to achieve "conservation." The impracticability of apportioned ownership made the correlative concept a mental construct only; the fallacy of in-place ownership was demonstrated by the fact that it was illegal for co-owners to "waste" their "shares." Correlative rights, consequently, did little more than open the door for politically defined conservation legislation, discussed in the next two chapters, that would usurp market solutions and create difficulties of a different kind.

A Homestead Theory of Oil and Gas Law

In chapter 1, the importance of a proper delineation of property rights to the effective operation of the market economy was stressed. Given the intertemporal production problem, first-finder disincentives, potential monopolization of virgin reservoirs, and surface-owner uncertainty under the rule of capture, and vague apportionability and politicization problems under the doctrine of correlative

---

[36]Jacqueline Lang Weaver, *Unitization of Oil and Gas Fields in Texas*, p. 220.

rights, the sacrosanct first-title cornerstone of U.S. mineral-rights law—the assumption that subsurface and surface rights are inseparable—can be questioned. A new legal theory for the allocation of first title to oil and gas reservoirs that offers a private-property solution to some of the aforementioned problems will then be presented.[37]

A Reconsideration of Anglo-Saxon Property Law. U.S. property law, under the dominance of the English law of the commons, uncritically adopted the notion that possession of the surface also entailed ownership of the sky above it and the ground below it. Writing in the mid-eighteenth century, English jurist Sir William Blackstone described his country's formulation of the law as follows:

> Land hath also, in its legal signification, an indefinite extent, upwards as well as downwards. . . . [U]pwards, therefore, no man may erect a building, or the like to overhang another's land; and downwards, whatever is in a direct line, between the surface of any land and the center of the earth. . . . So the word land includes not only the surface of the earth but everything under it or over it. . . . [Therefore], if a man grants all his lands, he grants thereby all his mines of metal and other fossils. . . . This is incorporated in the fundamental law of the land.[38]

Little did early American jurists realize that their acceptance of this conception of mineral-right ownership would lead to a bevy of problems in the unique case of oil and gas.

The common-law logic of assigning initial surface ownership to the first user of property has an inherent logic.[39] For it is the homesteader who transforms a state of nature into a state of human usefulness. Natural-rights philosopher John Locke derives homestead ownership from self-ownership.

> [E]very man has a property in his own person. Nobody has any right to this but himself. . . . The labor of his body and the work of his hands, we may say, are properly his. . . . As much land as a man tills, plants, improves, cultivates and can use the product of, so much

---

[37]For a similar application to airspace, see chapter 21, pp. 1268–74.

[38]William Blackstone, *Commentaries on the Laws of England* (Philadelphia: J. B. Lippincott, 1908), pp. 404–5.

[39]In Blackstone's words, "Occupancy is the thing by which the title was in fact originally gained." Ibid., pp. 396–97.

is his property. He by his labour does, as it were, enclose it from the common.[40]

Then by trade or gift, the first owner can renounce title to another party, fully in keeping with the established tradition of private-property rights.[41]

Under the homestead assignment of first title, the extension of the unit of ownership from the surface area to the center of the earth and to the sky above is not inferable. In the case of first title, it is the surface land that has been transformed, not the minerals below or the airspace above. Certainly the landowner has the further right to homestead these additional areas, acquire them from the title-holder, and have recourse if other parties damage his surface property, but it does not logically follow that the surface homesteader should claim an a priori monopoly to exclude mineral owners beneath him. A tenable theory of first-title rights should have consistent application whether on, above, or below the surface area.

Subsurface Homestead Rights. With an extension of the homestead principle to subsurface areas, a number of significant changes in U.S. property law would take place. First and most obvious, mineral rights would not automatically accompany surface rights. Minerals would be unowned until homesteaded by the act of discovery and the intent to possess. In the case of oil and gas, initial ownership would occur when the oil or gas entered the well bore and was formally claimed by the driller. The reservoir would then turn into owned inventory from its prior "state of nature." The homesteader (discoverer) could be the property owner directly overhead, another landowner, or a lessee of either.[42] This variety of potential first finders

---

[40]John Locke, *An Essay Concerning the True Original Extent and End of the Civil Government,* in *Social Contract,* ed. Ernest Barker (London: Oxford University Press, 1947), pp. 17, 20. For a modern restatement of the homestead argument, see Murray Rothbard, *For a New Liberty* (New York: Collier Books, 1978), pp. 31–37.

[41]For a modern restatement of Lockean natural rights, see Robert Nozick, *Anarchy, State, and Utopia* (Oxford: Blackwell, 1974).

[42]When the surface is also unowned, as is that of an offshore tract, the driller would homestead the water area by establishing drilling operations and then homestead the discovered minerals. If the water area were previously homesteaded (for aquaculture or shipping purposes, for example), then a surface lease would be required.

resulted from the fact that slant (horizontal) drilling would be permissible as long as subsurface or surface property previously homesteaded (or rightfully acquired through gift or trade) was not violated. If it should be violated, tort liability with legal redress would be incurred.

The oil and gas lease under homestead rights would be the right to conduct drilling operations on a person's surface property. It would not be, as under the capture rule, the right to any mineral found under a particular surface area. Since surface-land rental is much less valuable than rights to the mineral, and since many reservoir target areas could be reached by slant drilling, the economic rent of a homestead lease would be far below the value of a capture-rule lease. The difference would accrue to the driller-finder.

The homestead lease would not be subject to implicit covenants; neutral judicial interpretation and the primacy of explicit covenants over implicit covenants would prevail. Under a homestead theory of subsurface rights, the first finder of a mineral area would have claim to the entire recognized deposit, this being the relevant technological unit. In the case of oil and gas, the geologic unit is the entire reservoir, however shaped, as long as it is contiguous. Separate and distinct reservoirs in the same general area, whether vertical or horizontal, would require separate and distinct discovery and claim. The owner of alien wells draining an already-claimed reservoir would be liable if the homesteader could reasonably prove invasion (whether by well distance, well depth, crude type, geological formation, reservoir pressure, or other means).[43] Last, the pool owner would be able to use his discovery as he chose. He might leave his pool untapped, deplete its contents, or upon removal use the space

---

[43]In certain rare cases, such as the East Texas field or the Prudhoe Bay field, the relevant technological unit could be less than the entire reservoir. Definition of property in these cases would be difficult, and courts of law would have to define invasion, for example, as a certain quantitative change in bottom hole pressure resulting from a neighboring well. If the reservoir were larger than an operator realized and another driller claimed a discovery later found to be a part of it (as occurred in East Texas, which had at least three "discoverers"), the pool would be apportioned to each homesteader using equidistant principles in the absence of compelling reasons for an unequal division. If reasonable uncertainty about the boundaries of unusually large reservoirs existed, new wells would delineate ownership. The first homesteader, appropriately, would have the advantage of beating the competition with frontier wells to mark the field.

for storage. The reservoir space, in addition to the virgin contents of the reservoir, is newfound property.

The operation of a homestead property-rights system could be facilitated by pragmatic rules established by either law or judicial opinion. When a new oil or gas field was discovered, the surrounding acreage could be declared off-limits to other producers until the discoverer had a reasonable opportunity to drill frontier wells to delineate the field. An exception would be made if another operator had begun to drill before the nearby discovery was made. If the discoverer chose not to drill development wells, then other operators could drill and become part owners of the same contiguous reservoir upon discovery. A more likely scenario, however, would be for the discoverer to contract with another producer to help develop the field.

Advantages of Subsurface Homestead Law. The application of home-steading to underground resources is not entirely foreign to the Anglo-Saxon common-law tradition. In both substance and intention, it is similar. In substance, it is an extension of the surface law of first title to below the surface; in intention, it affords protection to the property rights of the surface owner against invasion from above or below.

The law of homestead has the dual attractiveness of remaining firmly within the private-property ethic and mitigating the deficiencies associated with the capture rule–correlative rights system. Problems of sheer luck, piracy, and overdrilling and overproduction waste would be averted by sole reservoir ownership.[44] Political control of production, necessitated by the "fair-share" apportionment "correction" of the capture rule, would also be avoided. The first finder would have incentive to quickly locate reserves and would receive a full reward for developing them. Production instabilities would be arrested because extraction would be governed by cost and price considerations instead of drainage conditions. The homestead

---

[44]Sole ownership is natural not only in the philosophical sense but the economic sense as well. As Wallace Lovejoy and Paul Homan conclude, "It is universally recognized today in expert quarters that the efficient way to develop a reservoir in the usual case is to treat it as a single producing unit." Lovejoy and Homan, *Economic Aspects of Oil Conservation Regulation* (Baltimore: Johns Hopkins University Press, 1967), p. 63.

principle is thus well supported by moral and economic considerations. This alternate private-property, free-market legal framework will have important implications in the next chapter, where the "market failure" of conservation under the rule of capture is reinterpreted, and in chapter 31, which suggests first title for offshore oil and gas in accordance with homestead principles.[45]

---

[45]See chapter 31, pp. 1899–1900.

Appendix to Chapter 2:
Private versus Sovereign Mineral Rights

Some critics of U.S. oil and gas law have condemned private ownership and development to suggest, implicitly or explicitly, sovereign ownership under Roman law or civil law. George Stocking characterized capture-rule production as "uncontrolled private ownership and operation of a community resource which does not lend itself to the methods of competition."[1] Also writing in the 1920s, John Ise stated that

> the great need [is] . . . to slow down the present production in the interests of the future. In this connection, we cannot but regret that more of the oil is not federally owned or controlled, so that it could be conserved without danger of interstate difficulties.[2]

Arguments for natural-resource socialism based on the U.S. experience encounter many difficulties. First, the private-property alternative of homestead rights, which addresses the problem of competitive drilling, is neglected. Second, historical conservation problems under the rule of capture have predominantly resulted from government intervention, not the free market, as detailed in chapters 3 and 4. Third, political control in theory and practice is little solution. Sovereign ownership, as discussed in chapter 6, inherently suffers from the problem of economic calculation—not having the knowledge generated from a competitive process to make rational decisions. Another theoretical problem occurs on the political side. Even if economic calculation could be practiced, there is no guarantee, or even likelihood, that political rule would choose to be efficient. "Profit maximization" in the public sector can be very different

---

[1] George Stocking, *The Oil Industry and the Competitive System* (New York: Augustus M. Kelley, 1925, 1973), p. 264.

[2] John Ise, *The United States Oil Policy* (New Haven, Conn.: Yale University Press, 1926), p. 520.

from profit maximization in the private sector that is responsible for economic efficiency. Historically, the record of government as steward of the public domain has been very unsatisfactory in the United States and even worse abroad. If there has not been overproduction, there has been underproduction; if there has not been resistance to reform, there has been misplaced trust.[3]

From a philosophical perspective, a priori government ownership of property is an arbitrary act of power. Nothing is discovered or produced, just claimed by virtue of a monopoly of force over a geographical area. The "common good" of common ownership is not a persuasive justification. The record demonstrates the opposite. Despite its shortcomings, U.S. oil and gas property law has spawned greater public wealth from private land ownership than other countries, even those with greater endowments of oil and gas, have created from public ownership.

---

[3]Problems of foreign development in the absence of private property are surveyed in chapter 1, pp. 33–36. Development problems on government land are examined in chapter 6, pp. 304–18.

3. The Rise of Wellhead Conservation Regulation

The oil-state wellhead conservation movement is chiefly associated with the tumultuous era between 1915 and 1935; although broadly defined, that movement stretches from the water-pollution legislation of the late nineteenth century to the mandatory unitization statutes of recent decades.[1] Defined as "an exercise of state police power to conserve natural resources, protect individual property interests, and make safety regulations,"[2] the conservation movement has spawned state and federal regulation of crude-oil production under the broad legal authority to prevent waste and protect the correlative rights of reservoir co-owners.

The problems of overproduction and waste have not only generated spirited debate within the industry, they have also attracted considerable scholarly attention from economists and historians. From the economic point of view, important questions are, what constitutes waste, did it actually occur, and if so, why did it occur? If waste was present, did it result from ignorance, perverse market incentives, or government interference with the market? From the historical viewpoint, the key question is, what was the reason for the change from voluntary arrangements to government intervention? Who was responsible, why did the parties agitate for the transformation, and how did they succeed?

This chapter attempts to answer those questions. After the mainstream view is presented, a historical review of the development of conservation legislation at the state and federal levels is undertaken.

---

[1]Chapter 4 will examine each major area of conservation; this chapter focuses on the historical sequence of events that led to wellhead production control in the major oil states.

[2]*Petroleum Hearings before the Temporary National Economic Committee* (New York: American Petroleum Institute, 1942), p. 66. Cited hereafter as *TNEC Petroleum Hearings.*

Then a revisionist interpretation of the alleged necessity of mandatory conservation to rectify drilling and production incentives under the rule of capture is outlined.

Part of the revisionist argument presented herein concerns the state of scientific knowledge of the oil community in the important 1915–35 era. The appendix to chapter 4 describes geologic waste to aid understanding of the nature of reservoir damage from rapid extraction rates and overdrilling, the two central aspects of petroleum conservation and waste.

The Mainstream Interpretation Examined

Market Conservation and Petroleum:
Zimmermann's Challenge

Reflecting the sentiment of the majority of his peers, petroleum conservation writer Erich Zimmermann has staunchly maintained the necessity of government intervention in oil and gas production to achieve what laissez faire could not—the prevention of flagrant waste of a vital, nonrenewable resource.

> If there are those who believe that mere passive reliance on market forces can solve the grave problems of the industry, the burden of proof is on them. They have to make peace with a historical record of events and a set of established facts that in this writer's opinion admit but one answer: free automatic forces cannot even halfway solve the problems, and resort to police power is inevitable if they are to be solved satisfactorily.[3]

Accepting the burden of proof, this chapter attempts to demonstrate that it was not the free market per se that made restrained drilling and a rational time structure of reservoir production difficult but facts inherent in the situation and a series of government interventions that discouraged entrepreneurial reform. Hence the swings of instability, associated exclusively with free-market competition

---

[3]Erich Zimmermann, *Conservation in the Production of Petroleum* (New Haven, Conn.: Yale University Press, 1957), p. 110. Later he adds, "The old theory of economics, sometimes called harmonics, according to which spontaneous free market forces are the sole guides to the social weal, has long fallen into disrepute" (p. 126).

based on the rule of capture, are explained by other sources.[4] Further, it will be shown that waste, seen in static, technological terms rather than in dynamic, economic terms by Zimmermann and others, is, in part, a misidentified problem.

From Market to Mandatory Conservation: The Nash Thesis

As renowned as Zimmermann's economic interpretation of the necessity of conservation legislation is the "consensus" thesis of historian Gerald Nash regarding the drive to substitute government petroleum conservation for market conservation. In fact, Nash's thesis can be considered the historical ancillary to Zimmermann's theoretical foundation. Given Zimmermann's argument, it naturally follows that a pluralist-oriented government, as the caretaker of the common wealth, would weigh the evidence and lead the drive to preserve the country's irreplaceable resources through appropriate conservation law. This essentially is the viewpoint of Nash—that national and state leaders, as impartial arbiters between self-interested oil company executives and society, saw the need for conservation legislation and responded accordingly. Those leaders formed a natural consensus, as it were, without the impurities of politics and favoritism. As Nash summarizes:

> The Chief Executives [of government] . . . cannot be properly characterized as having been for or against business; rather, they were responding to particular problems emanating from structural changes in the American economy. . . . Cooperation in public policy arose out of far-reaching technological and economic changes that frequently overrode political considerations.[5]

The Nashian view is shared by David Leven, particularly in regard to the petroleum conservation movement: "Despite the opposition of many operators in many flush producing fields, public-spirited

---

[4]In addition to Zimmermann, petroleum economist P. H. Frankel concludes, "The basic feature of the petroleum industry *is that it is not self-adjusting.* . . . Hectic prosperity is followed all too swiftly by complete collapse." Frankel, *Essentials of Petroleum* (New York: Augustus M. Kelley, 1969), p. 67. Industry executive Thornton Bradshaw made a case for national planning on the basis of a similar observation. "The free-market mechanism never has worked for oil because there has always been too much oil or too little." Bradshaw, "My Case for National Planning," *Fortune,* February 1977, p. 103.

[5]Gerald Nash, *United States Oil Policy: 1890–1964* (Westport, Conn.: Greenwood Press, 1968), pp. vii–viii.

and far-sighted men in and out of the industry have waged a hard and victorious fight to compel the industry to recommend the adoption of state conservation laws."[6]

As the developments of the conservation movement are sketched in this chapter, this thesis on the political transformation of oil and gas production will be challenged. What will be found instead is that organized interests within the oil industry enlisted state and federal support for their desired ends. The lofty-sounding goal of conservation was a subterfuge—albeit persuasive—for achieving the less noble end of limiting production to maintain prices and maximize revenues.

This counterthesis explains the anomaly of both industry factions' and federal authorities' advocating and securing legislation that blatantly contradicted petroleum conservation, whether conservation is defined as nonuse or as the absence of physical and economic waste. Such legislation demonstrated a lack of consensus between conservation and stabilization, the common good and the private good.[7] A consensus did not exist among oil company executives. State and federal "conservation" policies were the political result of clashes between integrated and nonintegrated producers, as well as between marginal-well and flush-well owners, each interested in his relative economic position rather than in the "common good."

Rise of Conservation Legislation

Three Aims of Early Legislation: 1878–1914

The opening decades of petroleum drilling were marked by capacity production and haphazard storage. Water pollution was a visible consequence. Belowground waste from inefficient use of reservoir energy was less detected; only later would a debate emerge within the scientific community and producing industry about whether

---

[6]David Leven, *Done in Oil* (New York: Ranger Press, 1941), p. 189.

[7]This revisionist view, in sharp contrast to Nash, was first developed by Norman Nordhauser, "Origins of Federal Oil Regulation in the 1920's," *Business History Review* (Spring 1973): 53–71; and idem, *The Quest for Stability* (New York: Garland Publishing, 1979), especially pp. iv–vii, 163–65. The present analysis will extend Nordhauser's thesis by emphasizing economic considerations.

unrestrained production lowered recoverability against economic self-interest.[8]

Prevention of External Damage. The drive for oil conservation legislation began in 1867 when a state representative from the oil-rich Pennsylvania county of Venago introduced a measure to regulate the casing and plugging of wells. Although the measure was unsuccessful, Pennsylvania passed a plugging law eleven years later, reflecting producer sentiment against subsurface, freshwater contamination and oil-sand flooding that often resulted from interstrata contact through open drill holes.[9] Similar legislation followed, often with the addition of casing requirements, in New York (1879), Ohio (1883), Kansas (1891), Kentucky and Utah (1892), Indiana (1893), Tennessee (1895), West Virginia (1897), Texas (1899), California (1903), Illinois (1905), Oklahoma (1909), Louisiana (1910), Alabama (1911), and New Mexico (1912).[10] Many of these states would revise their anti-pollution statutes on the basis of their experience with the law and the advance of technology.

This legislation—and the sentiment behind it—reflected a failure to properly identify subsurface damage as invasion subject to

[8]A 1913 article by L. G. Huntley was a significant beginning of an explanation of reservoir mechanics that other members of the scientific community would later advance. Huntley, "Possible Cause of the Decline of Oil Wells, and Suggested Methods of Prolonging Yield," Technical paper 51, *Petroleum Technology* (September 1913). The majority of oil company executives, as scientists, however, did not understand (and practice) the business implications of reservoir maintenance until over a decade later. Noticed W. P. Z. German, "Apparently no one [in 1915], not even technologists with the Bureau of Mines, had an understanding of the presence of gas energy in oil pools and its use-value in the increased recovery of oil." German, "Legal History of Conservation of Oil and Gas in Oklahoma," in American Bar Association, *Legal History of Oil and Gas* (Baltimore: Lord Baltimore Press, 1939), p. 135. Cited hereafter as *Legal History,* 1939. The debate over recoverability and extraction rates, far from black and white, is examined in the appendix to chapter 4.

[9]Harold Williamson and Arnold Daum, *The Age of Illumination, 1859 to 1899,* vol. 1 of *The American Petroleum Industry* (Evanston, Ill.: Northwestern University Press, 1959), p. 163.

[10]Dates of various state laws taken from numerous sources are presented in Appendix C. Subsequent dates in this chapter and chapter 4 will not be footnoted. The best single source for the year of enactment of major state conservation laws is the revised editions of W. W. Thornton, *The Law Relating to Oil and Gas* (Cincinnati: W. H. Anderson, 1904; revised 1912, 1918, 1925, 1933, 1935, 1939, 1944, 1948, 1953, 1956, 1960, 1962, 1977). Also see Northcutt Ely, *The Oil and Gas Conservation Statutes* (Washington, D.C.: Government Printing Office, 1933).

redress. In fact, some common-pool operators, as discussed in chapter 2, used the threat of deliberate damage to blackmail neighboring well operators. The deficiencies of the regulatory approach, compared with a nonregulatory, tort approach, are presented in chapter 4.[11]

Aboveground Waste Prevention: Natural Gas. A second aim of early conservation legislation was to ban the wastage of casinghead gas—natural gas obtained as a by-product of crude oil—as well as the open-air flow (venting) of gas wells after the initial discovery period, flambeau-light burning, natural-gas flaring, and carbon-black manufacture with natural gas. Typically, the laws allowed gas illumination only during darkness. Crude-oil waste was also referred to in the language of many state statutes, but only as an aside.

Natural gas, although useful in consumer hands, was of negligible value unless found near transportation facilities or consumer markets in this period. Long-distance natural-gas pipelines were still decades away, so gas was often used for "inferior" purposes, such as illuminating the well site or manufacturing carbon black, a material used in rubber, paint, and ink manufacture. Alternatively, the gas was often simply discharged into the air.

The first gas-conservation law was enacted in Indiana in 1891; it prohibited open-air flambeau lights as "wasteful and extravagant." Two years later, a revised statute banned "the flow of gas or oil . . . into the open air . . . for a longer period of two days next after gas or oil shall have been struck in such well." This statute was invoked against a violator, tested in court, and upheld in *Ohio Oil Company v. State of Indiana*.[12] The prevention of waste to further the common good of gas consumers and promote industrial growth was affirmed.

Following Indiana's lead with similar natural-gas laws were Ohio (1889); West Virginia (1891); Texas (1899); Kansas (1901); Tennessee (1905); Louisiana (1906); and Alabama, California, and North Dakota (1911). These laws were passed to outlaw inferior uses of a scarce natural resource, not to enhance oil recoverability; general awareness of the latter conservation end did not exist. In later years, other states passed similar legislation restricting the consumption of natural gas in inferior uses, as discussed in chapter 4.[13]

[11]See chapter 4, pp. 136–38.
[12]177 U.S. 190 (1899).
[13]See chapter 4, pp. 192–93.

Maintenance of Reserves. Maintenance of oil reserves had a different meaning in the pre-1915 era than it had several decades later. Originally it meant keeping reserves in the ground for future depletion; it later meant achieving maximum recovery through efficient production practices. The earlier "nonuse" of public-land oil deposits constituted a third area of early petroleum conservation law.

Early petroleum leasing on federal lands was fraught with difficulties. Misguided federal lease provisions powerfully supplemented the rule of capture to encourage frenzied production, waste, and rapid reservoir depletion. These problems led the General Land Office to withdraw substantial acreage in 1900 and 1901, only to return most of it within the decade. In 1909, responding to fears of future shortage raised by the director of the U.S. Geological Survey, George Otis Smith, Interior Secretary Richard Ballinger, and U.S. Navy officials, President William Howard Taft withdrew approximately 3 million acres of public land in Wyoming and California for later government usage. Several dozen more limited withdrawals followed and, as had the original one, created adversity for oil operators in various stages of development at the time of the lease cancellations. These withdrawals also discouraged production that would contribute to supply problems in subsequent years.[14]

Despite the withdrawals, naval officials remained unsure about adequate supply at stable prices. Two proposals were advocated. One would have established a federal corporation for production and refining and earmarked its output for exclusive military use. The second proposal, first recommended in 1900 by the U.S. Geological Survey, would have established naval reserves in areas likely to have oil deposits for future defense needs.

After active discussion in government, the latter course was chosen. In 1912, President Taft reserved 39,000 acres in Elk Hills, California (Reserve no. 1) and 30,000 acres in Buena Vista Hills, California (Reserve no. 2) for the exclusive use of the navy. In 1915, a third area was added, 9,400 acres near Salt Creek, Wyoming (Reserve

---

[14]Early federal-land policy is described in chapter 6. Withdrawals were also encouraged by a Bureau of Mines consulting engineer who reported to the Senate in 1916 that the nation's supply would be exhausted within ten years, leaving the United States "with a national crisis of the first magnitude." Quoted in August Giebelhaus, *Business and Government in the Oil Industry: A Case Study of Sun Oil* (Greenwich, Conn.: Jai Press, 1980), p. 113.

no. 3, also known as the Teapot Dome reserve). A fourth naval reserve covering 35,000 square miles was added in southern Alaska in 1923 by President Warren Harding.[15]

Since rudimentary geological principles provided only very limited information about remaining deposits, the best indicator of future supply was past experience, which did not offer shortage precedents. What past experience offered was price volatility, reflecting different supply-demand configurations. Assuming this fact was comprehended, it can be surmised that price, not supply, worried the General Board of the U.S. Navy and other agitators for postponed use. That explained the alternative proposal of federal oil development, which was not a conservation measure at all. The concern was simply for dollars and cents—a fact verified by U.S. Navy secretary Josephus Daniels, who stated in his annual address, "The only possible relief from . . . a staggering item in the expense account of the Navy in the future is in the control of oil wells and the refining of its own oil."[16] Whether by means of a reserves policy or of a federal corporation, what navy planners really sought was an affordable means for realizing foreign policy ambitions, not preserving oil supply for its own sake.

Proponents of postponed use who were not affiliated with the navy, George Otis Smith being foremost, were very presumptuous in advocating radical policies such as government ownership. No one knew the extent of remaining deposits; all that was known was that petroleum had been found, was being found, and that vast areas remained to be explored. Less excusable was the failure to understand the economic function of price to provide incentive for locating new supplies and rationing demand for existing supplies. In retrospect, not only did the free market prove governmental concerns wholly wrong, a tradition of erroneous government forecasts of petroleum supply and demand was born. The mistakes of the first generation of petroleum pessimists would be repeated in later decades.

Prevention of General Waste: 1915–26

The second era of conservation legislation focused on Oklahoma and Texas. Along with the development of the Texas Gulf Coast oil

---

[15]The subsequent operation of the naval reserves is described in chapter 6, pp. 278–81.

[16]Quoted in Gerald Nash, *United States Oil Policy*, p. 18.

region, launched by the discovery of the prolific Spindletop field in 1901, several large producing areas were uncovered in Oklahoma, making this state an oil power. In 1905, the Glenn Pool field was discovered, followed by the Cushing field in 1912 and the Healdton field in 1913. Rapid production, in ignorance of reservoir mechanics, created aboveground waste as the flow of oil exceeded storage and transportation capabilities.[17] Flush production also depressed prices to well under a dollar per barrel in the 1904–15 period.[18] For political relief, demoralized industry leaders turned to the state legislature, also interested in higher prices for reasons of self-interest. The result was the Oklahoma Oil Conservation Act of 1915, recognized by Gerald Nash as "a remarkable statute . . . which provided for closer state control over the oil business than for any other industry in the United States."[19]

The distinguishing feature of the 1915 act was that it plainly established *stabilization* as its primary focus, not *conservation*. The legislation was conceived and spearheaded not by the scientific community or far-sighted legislators but by influential local independent oil producers, organized as the Independent Producers League, with a vested interest in higher prices. Leonard Logan explained:

> At that time the industry leaned little on science. The early operators were not concerned with conservation. [T]heir efforts [were] to curb production and that was profits.[20]

The 1915 statute broadly defined waste as "economic waste, underground waste, surface waste, and waste incident to the production of crude oil or petroleum in excess of oil transportation or marketing facilities or reasonable market demands."[21] Although at first glance the statute might seem to be genuinely conservation

---

[17]See Erich Zimmermann, *Conservation in the Production of Petroleum*, pp. 135–37.

[18]Harold Williamson et al., *The Age of Energy, 1899 to 1959*, vol. 2 of *The American Petroleum Industry* (Evanston, Ill.: Northwestern University Press, 1963), p. 39.

[19]Gerald Nash, *United States Oil Policy*, p. 16.

[20]Leonard Logan, *Stabilization of the Petroleum Industry* (Norman: University of Oklahoma Press, 1930), pp. 127–28.

[21]Quoted in W. P. Z. German, "Legal History of Conservation of Oil and Gas in Oklahoma," pp. 126–27. Also in the act was proration language to protect correlative rights.

oriented, *economic waste* meant low-priced crude encouraging "inferior" uses, while *underground waste* meant water pollution and oil contamination occurring as a result of improper casing and plugging. *Geologic waste* from rapid withdrawals was not part of the legislative intention.[22]

This landmark statute followed earlier attempts in Oklahoma to stabilize production. In 1909, Oklahoma passed a law requiring crude-oil purchasers (pipelines) to deal equitably with all producers. In 1914, the Oklahoma Corporation Commission (OCC), founded in 1907, unsuccessfully set minimum prices and storage regulations in an attempt to keep more oil in the ground in the Cushing and Healdton fields.[23] Such measures were inadequate to stem the oil flow and were superseded by the 1915 act.

Oklahoma's efforts were followed in Texas by a 1919 conservation law prohibiting underground and surface—but not economic— waste. The Texas Railroad Commission (TRC), founded in 1891, was responsible for enforcement.[24] Also included in the Texas law was a well-spacing rule, the first of its kind. In 1923, Arkansas, a second-tier producing state behind California, Oklahoma, and Texas, passed legislation similar to Oklahoma's 1915 statute, including a prohibition on underground waste.

Conservation law underwent a highly significant transformation in 1915–26. The TRC and the OCC gained jurisdiction over oil and

[22]Regarding Arkansas's 1923 conservation act, which copied Oklahoma's 1915 law, W. H. Rector contends, "By [underground waste], the lawmakers obviously meant physical waste committed . . . [by] improper withdrawal . . . as to prematurely exhaust reservoir energy." Rector, "Legal History of Conservation of Oil and Gas in Arkansas," in *Legal History,* 1939, p. 21. That presumption is highly debatable. It will be contended that the oil community and state legislatures learned of geologic waste well after 1925. Underground waste probably referred to water invasion from improperly cased or plugged wells. Textbook treatments of waste in the 1920s typically made no mention of geologic waste from gas dissipation or water coning. For example, in his chapter "Waste of Oil and Gas," James Westcott identifies waste as resulting from "the sudden blowing in of wells or their unexpected drilling in where operators had failed to provide tankage for the proper storage of the crude or pipe line connections had not been made." Westcott, *Oil: Its Conservation and Waste* (New York: Beacon, 1928), p. 202. Waste, in other words, was synonymous with aboveground waste.

[23]M. P. Z. German, "Legal History of Conservation of Oil and Gas in Oklahoma," pp. 124–25. State pipeline regulation, a direct consequence of wellhead overproduction, is examined in chapters 11 and 14.

[24]For a summary of state agencies regulating wellhead oil and gas activity, see appendix D, pp. 1936–39.

gas production comprising 40 percent of national output. The interest of stabilization was securely in place within the broad language of conservation law. The next stage of legislation, one of more pronounced state control, was set to begin.

Rise of Mandatory Proration: 1927–33

Mandatory proration, a sophisticated form of state regulation restricting open-flow production to a predetermined "market demand," began almost simultaneously in the sister oil states of Oklahoma and Texas in 1927. Other important oil states followed later—except California and Illinois, which practiced either voluntary production cutbacks or none at all.[25]

The Texas-Oklahoma oil community, and hence locally elected officials,[26] was divided over the importance of limiting the natural flow of production in the pre-1926 period. Numerous wells and full production, many believed, constituted efficient practice. This conclusion was expressly stated in the final report by the American Petroleum Institute's (API's) Committee of Eleven, which investigated industry production practices in 1925.[27] Consequently, the majority of oil company executives were against regulatory programs to curtail production, such as Henry L. Doherty's plan for mandatory unitization, first presented before the API in 1923. A special resolution of the API denounced Doherty's proposal as "not resulting in the production of more oil and gas than is produced by present methods," while having the unfavorable potential of "eliminating the small producer."[28]

---

[25]For the interesting case of California, see J. Howard Marshall, "Legal History of Conservation of Oil and Gas in California," in *Legal History*, 1939, pp. 28–36; see also Myron Watkins, *Oil: Stabilization or Conservation?* (New York: Harper & Brothers, 1937), pp. 230–46. Illinois, like California, operated solely on rule-of-capture competition until 1942 when wartime planning prorated crude output.

[26]The influence of dominant oil interests on local politics is a major theme of the conservation movement. Virtually every major regulation passed and enforced in the period had organized industry support behind it.

[27]"The cheapest oil produced is that obtained by flowing, hence every effort is made to keep wells flowing naturally. . . . Present production methods are as efficient as is warranted by the value of the product handled. The waste in the industry is virtually negligible and the oil left in the ground becomes a reserve for the future." API, Committee of Eleven, *American Petroleum: Supply and Demand* (New York: McGraw-Hill, 1925), p. 55.

[28]API Special Resolution, December 1924. Quoted in Leonard Logan, *Stabilization of the Petroleum Industry*, pp. 144–45.

Beginning in late 1926, the rapid development of the large Seminole field in Oklahoma made the pendulum swing the other way. Voluntary proration was first tried with little success. Local producers appealed to the OCC for compulsory action. Output of one-half million barrels per day was driving prices down, which threatened many firms. A commission hearing found waste, and a mandatory proration order was issued pursuant to the 1915 act on August 9, 1927. This action represented the first major attempt by a state or federal agency to restrict oil production outside of public-land withdrawals.[29]

Development of the Seminole field signaled a major change in the outlook of oil companies in just a short period. As Norman Nordhauser noted:

> Those optimistic API members who had, a few months earlier, testified that there was neither waste nor shortage of American oil, now cried that there was an urgent need to check overproduction and to prevent prodigal practices. Only the rapid change in price and production of the industry wrought by the wealth of oil at Seminole could explain this turnabout.[30]

With this turnaround came the beginning of another bellwether transformation: the serendipitous discovery by the oil community that stabilization of production, by restricting the open flow of producing wells, preserved reservoir energy that could increase future crude-oil recoverability. Petroleum legal scholar Robert Hardwicke described the nature of this second development.

> A great movement often originates largely through accident. It is evident that the enforcement of conservation statutes was originally urged by most oil men, and attempted by most public officials, as a smoke screen for achieving stabilization, but with the result that the industry finally awoke to the realization that the conservation policies were, for themselves alone, highly desired ends.[31]

[29]In Oklahoma, isolated proration orders were issued in 1915, 1921, and 1923 for smaller fields, but the 1927 order began "the period of continuous proration." W. P. Z. German, "Legal History of Conservation of Oil and Gas in Oklahoma," pp. 149–51.

[30]Norman Nordhauser, *The Quest for Stability,* pp. 27–28. Elsewhere Nordhauser refers to the Seminole experience as "the great reversal." Nordhauser, "Origins of Federal Oil Regulation," p. 68. The first *Oil & Gas Journal* editorial espousing wellhead proration appeared on April 28, 1927. Cited hereafter as *OGJ.*

[31]Robert Hardwicke, "Legal History of Proration of Oil Production in Texas," *Proceedings, Texas Bar Association* (October 1937): 99.

Now the previously vague terms "underground waste" and "economic waste" could have meaning, the former being the dissipation of crude-recovering reservoir energy and the latter unnecessary drilling costs. But it took more than Seminole to change the face of conservation. It took other major fields to continue to make the stabilization of price—and therefore of production—the utmost priority.

Oklahoma

The Seminole proration edict, the beginning of modern petroleum regulation on the state level, was reinforced by a statewide order in Oklahoma in September 1928. Another first in U.S. oil regulation, the order was necessary to prevent other oil regions within Oklahoma from stepping up production to replace Seminole's curtailment. The Seminole order prorated production between wells; the statewide mandate allocated production by field with a further division of output between wells in a field.

The Seminole region was joined by another significant oil-producing area in 1929—the Oklahoma City field. Rapid production occurred when there were only limited transportation facilities, and downward pressures on price prompted voluntary, and then mandatory, production restraints.[32] In 1930, the OCC consolidated control by replacing industry-appointed "umpires" with their own enforcement personnel.[33]

Allowables assigned to the Oklahoma City region were far below capacity, and complaints of discrimination were heard from the field. From this particular proration program, originally endorsed by a wide cross section of producers, came two factions that marked a polarization in the debate over production restrictions. Anti-prorationists consisted of oil operators desiring full-scale production, even at lower prices. Their number included favorably situated operators with relatively high output and integrated well owners who enjoyed a direct link to the market. Pro-prorationists were producers with

[32]The first order for the field, discovered in December 1928, was issued on July 22, 1929. From 1929 until shutdown of the field, the allowable per well ranged from a low of 2.75 percent to a high of 40 percent of potential production. W. P. Z. German, "Legal History of Conservation of Oil and Gas in Oklahoma," pp. 158, 184.

[33]Ibid., p. 164. Robert Hardwicke called the 1930 action the OCC's "first detailed . . . and . . . vigorous effort." Hardwicke, "Legal History of Conservation of Oil in Texas," in *Legal History*, 1939, p. 222.

marginal wells or without distribution outlets, as well as major companies interested in price stabilization for their nationwide production. Consumers were not organized to lobby for lower prices through nonregulation. The overriding factor was pecuniary, evidenced by the fact that operators reversed their stands when it became profitable to do so.[34] There was little philosophizing about preserving supply for generations yet unborn or the more immediate "common good." The nonneutral effects of production regulation would continue to create dissension in the industry.

Factionalism culminated in several legal challenges to the OCC's 1930 proration edict. The plaintiffs were local, integrated companies desiring to produce in excess of allowables rather than purchase more expensive crude from their competitors to feed their refineries. In *Julian Oil and Royalties Company* v. *Carpshaw* in 1930, the Oklahoma Supreme Court denied Julian Oil's Fourteenth Amendment due process argument and upheld both the constitutionality of the 1915 conservation statute and the OCC's enforcement jurisdiction.[35] In *Champlin Refining Company* v. *Oklahoma Corporation Commission* a year later, however, a federal district court granted an injunction against OCC proration in favor of Champlin, an integrated producer seeking to produce more than its allowables.[36] This decision, setting the stage for a breakdown of the production-control system, prompted Oklahoma governor William "Alfalfa Bill" Murray to take the drastic step of declaring martial law and shutting down the Oklahoma City and Seminole fields until "we get dollar oil."[37] The date was August 4, 1931—one day after *Champlin*.

Several months later, the National Guard, under the command of the governor's nephew, Cicero Murray, reopened the field to production under a strict allowable. Conditions worsened, and martial law was declared again in June 1932. This time it was more severe. All private associations were abolished, pertinent records

---

[34]Quipped one observer, "It would seem that virtue is comparable with capital investment." *OGJ*, September 13, 1934, p. 13.

[35]145 Okla. 237 (1930).

[36]W. P. Z. German, "Legal History of Conservation of Oil and Gas in Oklahoma," p. 180.

[37]Ruth Knowles, *The Greatest Gamblers* (New York: McGraw-Hill, 1959), p. 265. One of the first fields shut down under Murray's order belonged to Champlin Oil. Norman Nordhauser, *The Quest for Stability*, p. 86.

were seized, and physical violence lead to the use of tear gas by the militia.

The field remained unstable despite troop presence, and on March 4, 1933, a ten-day shutdown was imposed on all wells of the Oklahoma City field except those taking in 10 percent or more water. The *Champlin* case, meanwhile, had been appealed to the U.S. Supreme Court, which on May 16, 1932, reversed the federal district court decision by upholding state proration as a means of preventing waste, whether economic or physical, surface or subsurface.[38]

With this definitive victory and the troops entrenched in the oil fields, Oklahoma, on April 10, 1933, passed a conservation law to strengthen the 1915 act, especially to detect and prosecute producers of "hot" oil—oil produced in excess of allowables. Power was transferred from the governor to the Oklahoma Conservation Commission. Six years after the first proration order, political control over Oklahoma crude production was complete.

Texas

The course of events in Texas remarkably paralleled the Oklahoma experience. Under authority of the 1919 statute, the TRC issued its first proration order in late 1927 after voluntary efforts in the large Yates field, led by Humble Oil, fell short. A year later, the productive Hendricks field was given a similar edict. As had been the case in Oklahoma, statewide proration was required to prevent the transfer of production from regulated areas to unregulated areas. After hearings to determine "market demand," in August 1930 the TRC issued its first comprehensive order based on the Texas Conservation Act of 1929, which prohibited physical (but not economic) waste.[39]

As had been the case in Oklahoma, the statewide order created dissent among those producing advantageously in the absence of regulation. In 1930, an injunction suit was filed against the TRC by Danciger Oil and Refining Company protesting its allowable in the Panhandle field. Danciger argued that the proration order was based

---

[38]*Champlin Refining Co.* v. *Oklahoma Corporation Commission,* 286 U.S. 210 (1932). Prior to oil proration, Humble Oil executives pushed for a gas conservation law, which indirectly achieved the same end for most wells. Henrietta Larson and Kenneth Porter, *History of Humble Oil & Refining Company* (New York: Harper and Brothers, 1959), p. 307.

[39]Robert Hardwicke, "Legal History of Conservation of Oil in Texas," p. 222.

on economic waste, not physical waste, and constituted an attempt to fix prices in violation of the 1929 statute. The Texas Supreme Court disagreed in a February 1931 decision, declaring that prevention of physical waste was intended and that price consequences were incidental.[40]

The next chapter in the rise of proration regulation in Texas also resembled the Oklahoma experience. As the Oklahoma City field threatened to annul the fragile Seminole proration plan, full-scale development of the enormous East Texas field, a four-county field of relatively shallow oil pockets, threatened the same thing for the Yates and Hendricks fields, if not also for the state and entire midcontinent region.[41] After seven months of unregulated flush production, the TRC issued a proration order in April 1931 that was twice revised before it became effective on May 1. Injunction actions were immediately filed by many operators—as many as 2,000 by one account—to continue unconstrained production while their suits were pending.[42] In *Alfred MacMillan et al. v. Railroad Commission of Texas et al.*, in May 1931, the plaintiffs, a group of East Texas oil operators, argued for relief from proration on the Fourteenth Amendment grounds used by Danciger Oil. In July, the federal district court unexpectedly sided with MacMillan, declaring that the TRC had illegally prohibited economic waste, violating the 1929 statute.[43]

[40]*Danciger Oil and Refining Company* v. *Railroad Commission of Texas,* 495 W.2d 837 (Civil Appeals: Austin, March 23, 1932).

[41]Discovered in late 1930, the 211-square-mile East Texas field was producing over 350,000 barrels per day by June 1932. On the eve of the August 17, 1931, shutdown, despite proration orders, output approached 1 million barrels per day, which accounted for over 30 percent of national output. Norman Nordhauser, *The Quest for Stability,* pp. 80–83.

[42]Yandell Boatner, "Legal History of Conservation of Oil and Gas in Louisiana," in *Legal History,* 1939, p. 68. Not unlike operators in the Oklahoma City field, many independents and small refiners in East Texas favored unregulated production, while the majors desired proration. See Gerald Forbes, *Flush Production* (Norman: University of Oklahoma Press, 1942), p. 89; and Norman Nordhauser, *The Quest for Stability,* pp. 70–71. Also see chapter 12, pp. 637–54.

[43]Appealing the case with Robert Hardwicke as legal counsel were Sun, Texas, Shell, and Humble. Clearly, the major companies favored proration. Henrietta Larson and Kenneth Porter, *History of Humble Oil & Refining Company,* p. 458. Key legal experts associated with early proration were Hardwicke, John Kilgore, Lewis Foster (Sun Oil), W. O. Crane (Texas), W. P. Z. German (Skelly), James Vessey (Carter Oil), and the brothers Hines and Rex Baker (Humble).

With the reversal of *Danciger*, the Texas legislature hastily passed the Anti-Market Demand Act of 1931. At the same time, the East Texas field, producing three times the legal amount, saw prices fall to $0.10 per barrel with attendant demoralization.[44] This state of affairs, along with the Oklahoma precedent a few weeks before, influenced Texas governor Ross Sterling to employ 1,200 Texas National Guardsmen on August 17 to stop all production in the East Texas field under a declaration of martial law.

The shutdown of the East Texas field was closely associated with the majors' viewpoint, particularly that of Humble Oil, the largest landholder in the field with 13 percent. Sun Oil's J. Edgar Pew was another instrumental figure on the day of reckoning with flush output.[45] Governor Ross Sterling, formerly president of Humble Oil & Refining and still a financial beneficiary of the company, placed General Jacob F. Walters, chief counsel of Texaco, in charge.[46] The shutdown was successful, and the heavily policed field was subsequently ordered to produce at a fraction of capacity on a barrels-per-well allowable.[47] "Sterling's summary action," remarked Carl Rister, "literally lifted crude oil prices at the point of a bayonet."[48]

With the Supreme Court victory in March 1932 in *Champlin*, the Texas legislature took the offensive and passed the Market Demand Act of 1932, a law that reversed the act of a year earlier by expressly allowing the legislative prevention of economic waste along with physical waste and proration based on "market demand." The

---

[44]In some cases, spot sales were as low as $0.02 per barrel. Prior to the field's development, the average price was over $1.00 per barrel in most Texas fields. Ibid., p. 453.

[45]August Giebelhaus, *Business and Government in the Oil Business*, pp. 202–5. In the proration debate of the early 1930s, Gulf Oil and Sinclair Oil broke ranks with the other majors because of their philosophical concerns with government intervention in the oil business. Some independents, on the other hand, favored proration. Jacqueline Lang Weaver, *Unitization of Oil and Gas Fields in Texas* (Washington, D.C.: Resources for the Future, 1986), p. 385.

[46]Sterling in 1931 received a $225,000 advance royalty payment from Humble. Ibid., p. 44.

[47]The detrimental effects of flat per well allowables will be examined when market-demand proration is criticized in chapter 4, pp. 175–79.

[48]Carl Rister, *Oil: Titan of the Southwest* (Norman: University of Oklahoma Press, 1949), p. 321. Prices rose from $0.24 per barrel at the time of the shutdown to $0.67 per barrel at the end of the shutdown period.

improved political climate for proration reflected independent-producer support that had been won five months earlier with oil tariffs
on imported crude oil and petroleum products. Another sign of the
times was a new head at the TRC, E. O. Thompson, who took an
activist stance favoring proration.

Even with legislation in place and an increased commitment at
the TRC, the East Texas field would not be easily tamed to a predetermined price-quantity configuration. A second shutdown in December 1932 was only a sign of continuing troubles. Unlike the major
Oklahoma fields, East Texas was one of a kind; it would be three
long years before production control was achieved.[49]

Other States

In the development of state proration law, there is a rough (positive) correspondence between the quantity of production and legislation. Along with Texas and Oklahoma, Kansas, accounting for over 4
percent of U.S. production, adopted a market-demand conservation
law. The Proration Act of 1931 was based on the 1915 Oklahoma
statute.[50] Louisiana did not have any major fields to spur proration
sentiment and, instead, relied on neighboring-state regulation for
price stabilization until 1935. New Mexico, Arkansas, and Mississippi also followed Louisiana, passing effective legislation only after
internal production increased.[51]

California, a significant producing state along with Texas and
Oklahoma, bucked the mandatory proration trend, reflecting the
sentiment of independent producers. Voluntary proration was practiced through the Central Committee of California Oil Producers
and the Executive Committee for Equitable Curtailment of the Oil
Industry. In 1931, a production-control act, the Sharkey bill, was
overwhelmingly defeated by referendum after it had been passed
by the legislature. Sheltered somewhat geographically from midcontinent production, enjoying high demand, and helped by other state
restrictions, California producers, many of whom were integrated
into refining, preferred the higher quantity, lower price combination
to the opposite. To them, as well as the public they convinced at

---

[49]The East Texas hot-oil war is described in chapter 12, pp. 637–54.

[50]Innis D. Harris, "Legal History of Conservation of Oil and Gas in Kansas," in
Legal History, 1939, p. 45.

[51]See chapter 4, pp. 162–63.

the voting booth, free-market production was the best policy—a far cry from their brethren to the east.[52]

Coordination of Control: The Federal Effort from 1917 to 1935

Birth of Cooperation

Federal involvement with the conservation movement, outside of land policy, began in World War I. In January 1917, the United States Fuel Administration, a wartime planning agency, established the Oil Division with fourteen subsidiaries, including the Bureau of Conservation.[53] This relatively inactive bureau supplemented state conservation efforts dealing with well practices and the prevention of natural-gas wastage. Of greater importance was a fundamental transformation that took place within the industry as a result of war planning. With interfirm *competition* replaced to a large extent by government-directed *cooperation*, oil companies found a pleasant refuge from the rigors of the marketplace. W. C. Teagle, president of Jersey Standard, described the change.

> The war was still young when we found ourselves in company, strange at first and then congenial and helpful. Industries apparently hopelessly and permanently divided by the bitterness begotten by years of relentless competition closed ranks at the call of government.[54]

The industry during this brief period changed from laissez faire to the government's actively determining the success of individual firms. The *political means* of favorable government intervention was born on a national scale to join the *economic means* of consumer service in a free market, never to be forgotten by oil companies in the heat of competition.

Wartime regulation began to ease after hostilities ceased in November 1918, suggesting a return to the prewar rivalry between firms. But much of the industry, especially the major oil companies, which occupied a preeminent position in the coordination effort,

[52]J. Howard Marshall, "Legal History of Oil and Gas in California," p. 28. Michigan, for reasons similar to California's, defeated wellhead proration laws in 1935 and 1937.

[53]For greater detail on World War I planning of petroleum production, see chapter 5, pp. 223–33.

[54]Quoted in William Kemnitzer, *Rebirth of Monopoly* (New York: Harper Brothers, 1938), p. 22.

wished to continue the government-engineered cartelization in some form. The *Oil & Gas Journal* reported "a growing sentiment among oil men of the various divisions of the industry favoring a permanent organization, similar to that which now regulates the oil business."[55] A leading light was the former World War I oil czar Mark Requa, whose worldview revolved around the beneficence of cooperation.

> Cooperation has been the dominant note that has made victory possible. Cooperating under General Foch, the United States won; the cooperative effort of the Allied Navies kept the seas free for commerce; and behind the lines at home the splendid cooperation of industry, of labor and of capital supplied the armies and the navies with all that made the victory possible. It has taken a world war to bring the lesson home to us. The case has been proved; the demonstration made; it remains for us to make use of knowledge so dearly bought.[56]

With the demise of petroleum planning in sight, the industry advisory group, the Petroleum War Service Committee (PWSC), voted on March 24, 1919, to disband and create the API to, in the words of its charter, "afford a means of cooperation with the government in all matters of national concern."[57] The PWSC's membership was carried forward with the addition of Requa, who was soon at work with the Sinclair Oil Company.

From the Federal Oil Conservation Board to the Oil States Advisory Committee

Several years after the API was established as a clearinghouse of industry opinion, a debate over federal intervention in conservation matters was launched against a background of increasing crude supplies and weakening prices. Henry Doherty, a prominent oil executive and API director, used the institute as a forum in 1923 to

[55]*OGJ*, November 22, 1918, p. 36.

[56]*National Petroleum News*, December 11, 1918, p. 17. Cited hereafter as *NPN*. Requa was described by Gerald Nash as "a passionate advocate of cooperation among businessmen . . . and the government." Nash, *United States Oil Policy*, p. 30.

[57]Leonard Fanning, *The Story of the American Petroleum Institute* (New York: World Petroleum Policies, 1959), p. 30. In an address that would lead to the founding of the API, Requa advised, "I see no other way for the petroleum industry to cooperate among its own members and the government as it will have to cooperate unless it takes some form to perpetuate the [National Petroleum War Service Committee]." Quoted in Gerald Nash, *United States Oil Policy*, p. 40.

press his case for mandatory unitization of oil reservoirs to replace rule-of-capture competition to achieve conservation.[58] Doherty, head of Cities Service, was once a laissez-faire advocate. But capture-rule competition had caused major financial losses from his California investments in the Huntington Beach, Signal Hill, and Santa Fe Springs fields beginning in the late 1920s.[59]

Encountering more hostility than support from his fellow API members (except for Requa, who, as before, favored federal direction), the determined and energetic Doherty went to President Calvin Coolidge, a personal friend, to present his case orally as well as in writing. Impressed, Coolidge sent letters to the secretaries of war, navy, interior, and commerce announcing their role in the creation of the Federal Oil Conservation Board (FOCB) to "study the Government's responsibilities [and] . . . enlist the full cooperation of representatives of the oil industry [to] . . . safeguard the national security through conservation of our oil."[60] A further factor in Coolidge's quick action was the Teapot Dome scandal, which was unfolding in congressional hearings at virtually the same time as Doherty's lobbying campaign. A new agency dedicated to conservation and preservation, in the president's mind, could rewin the public trust in natural-resource matters and differentiate the Coolidge administration from, in Herbert Hoover's words, the "Fall-Doheny-Sinclair scandals of the Harding Administration."[61]

In a series of reports issued from 1926 to 1932, the FOCB, under the chairmanship of Interior Secretary Hubert Work, reached conclusions similar to Doherty's but urged interstate cooperation rather

---

[58]For discussion of Doherty's significant role during the post–World War I period in the drive for federal intervention in petroleum, see Norman Nordhauser, *The Quest for Stability*, pp. 9–18. Doherty's recommended plan is presented in his article, "Suggestions for Conservation of Petroleum by Control of Production," in American Institute of Mining and Metallurgical Engineering, *Production of Petroleum in 1924* (New York: AIMME, 1925), pp. 11–12.

[59]August Giebelhaus, *Business and Government in the Oil Industry*, p. 125. To his credit, Doherty studied reservoir mechanics as the basis for advancing the virtues of a singular production plan per reservoir to efficiently use reservoir energy.

[60]Calvin Coolidge, letter of December 19, 1924. Reprinted in Samuel Pettengill, *Hot Oil: The Problem of Petroleum* (New York: Economic Forum, 1936), pp. 209–11.

[61]August Giebelhaus, *Business and Government in the Oil Business*, pp. 126–27. The Teapot Dome scandal is examined in chapter 6.

than federal control. A role for the national government, neverthe-less, was secured to provide economywide statistics to assist state conservation efforts. This task was begun by the FOCB's Voluntary Committee on Petroleum Economics in 1930.[62] The board sent questionnaires to oil companies in 1925 requesting information and opinions on production practices—the first peacetime reporting requirement imposed by the federal government outside of public-land activity. Responses, however, were slow in coming and uninformative.

At the time of the disbandment of the FOCB in 1932, efforts to form an interstate conservation group were already under way. The industry was anti-federal but not anti-government. In early 1931, Oklahoma governor Murray called a meeting of representatives from the midcontinent oil states to deal with the destabilizing East Texas situation. From their participation came the formation of the Oil States Advisory Committee (OSAC), also known as the Governor's Committee. It was held that for proration to work within states, a common plan for the states was necessary to prevent a redistribution of production from states that practiced proration to those that did not. But while the groundwork was being laid to establish an inter-state allowable plan within a federal estimate of national demand, the legal and physical situation in the East Texas and Oklahoma City fields prompted more immediate action by the respective governors: declarations of emergency and shutdowns of the fields.

Within a year of the closings, an attempt was made by the OSAC to create an interstate compact and a federal interstate oil board to oversee its operation with the Thomas-McKeon bill. However, distrust of federal regulation, particularly the possibility of public-utility status for oil and gas producers, caused dissension within the OSAC, which led to the bill's demise.[63]

[62]*TNEC Petroleum Hearings,* pp. 546–47. National crude-oil and gasoline demand estimates were published at three-month and six-month intervals. From 1930 until 1932, the FOCB, with the cooperation of the Bureau of Mines, issued national demand estimates. This task was assumed by the bureau after the FOCB was dismantled in 1932. From August 1933 until May 1935, the bureau supplied the forecasts to the National Industrial Recovery Act's (NIRA's) Petroleum Administrative Board. After the NIRA codes were invalidated, the bureau continued to publish monthly figures for state usage until November 1973.

[63]For a history of OSAC activities from its February 28, 1931, founding until its replacement by the Interstate Oil Compact Commission on September 12, 1935, see the reprinted documents contained in Interstate Oil Compact Commission, *The Compact's Formative Years* (Oklahoma City: IOCC, 1968).

The New Deal

The drive to coordinate conservation efforts to this point had come from the states. The federal effort under Herbert Hoover, who took a "states' rights" position, was tantamount to inaction. But with the defeat of Hoover in November 1932 and the new presidency of Franklin D. Roosevelt in March 1933, a New Deal for oil would emerge.

Recognizing the increased likelihood of government action at the national level, industry officials and the API actively entered federal politics. In March 1933, the Committee of Fifteen was formed by Harold Ickes, the newly appointed secretary of the interior, to hammer out an industry-supported oil and gas conservation program. Large-scale production cutbacks, which were desirable from the majors' viewpoint, were recommended. As a consequence, a counter-group, the Independent Petroleum Association Opposed to Monopoly, was formed to represent East Texas and California producers enjoying flush production and small refineries desiring cheap feedstock. Their program mentioned nothing about production cutbacks and recommended stricter import restrictions and antitrust action against the majors.

The majors were the stronger of the two groups, and the committee's "big oil" program emerged in Congress as the Marland-Capper bill, giving broad authority to Washington to control both production and price. This bill, however, was in competition with Senator Robert Wagner's (D-N.Y.) popular National Industrial Recovery Act (NIRA), a national public-works program promising federal support for all industries to recover from the depression. The Marland-Capper bill, consequently, became amendment 9(c) to the NIRA. In the amending process, Senator Tom Connally (D-Tex.) added an important provision granting enforcement power to the Interior Department to combat the transportation of hot oil, a measure designed to plug the main leak in the proration dike. The NIRA, including the so-called Connally amendment, became law on June 16, 1933.[64]

The following month, President Roosevelt invoked section 9(c) of the NIRA by executive order and gave Interior Secretary Ickes jurisdiction to combat the hot-oil problem. Establishing the Division

---

[64]Public Law 67, 48 Stat. 195 (1933).

of Investigation, Ickes sent federal agents straight to the source of the problem, East Texas, and achieved immediate results by curtailing hot-oil production, refining, and distribution by approximately one-third. This successful beginning, however, would soon entail problems requiring new federal strategies.

With the federal government attuned to East Texas, the API convened a meeting in Chicago to compose an industry code under the NIRA in the summer of 1933. While many industry parties favored restricted production to increase revenue, price fixing to achieve the same result was hotly debated. The "Chicago Code" revolved around price legislation and other less crucial issues. Against price floors were majors whose marketing operations helped them to weather wellhead storms. They questioned whether price fixing could work if overproduction continued and were also concerned that favorable price regulation could turn into unfavorable price regulation.[65] Nonintegrated refiners also opposed higher prices supported by price minimums. Favoring price-setting, on the other hand, were independents, led by Wirt Franklin and the two-year-old Independent Petroleum Association of America (IPAA).[66] Warren Platt, editor of the *National Petroleum News* and closely aligned with downstream independents, argued that price fixing was a false substitute for restricted production and warned of socialized production in all but name should licensing and other measures follow.[67]

In addition to industry factionalism, a bureaucratic rivalry developed between Interior Secretary Harold Ickes, who favored price fixing, and National Recovery Administrator Hugh Johnson, who did not. The stalemate was broken by FDR who, on August 19, 1933, compromised by allowing discretionary price fixing on a ninety-day basis. Ickes was also appointed code administrator with autonomy from Johnson and the other NIRA codes. An industry advisory board, the Planning and Coordination Committee (PCC), chaired by Wirt Franklin, was also created to assist Ickes.[68]

---

[65]See Donald Brand, "Corporatism, the NRA, and the Oil Industry," *Political Science Quarterly* (Spring 1983): 113–14.

[66]August Giebelhaus, *Business and Government in the Oil Business*, pp. 207–12. The formation and early history of the IPAA concerned proration versus import restrictions. See chapter 13.

[67]*NPN*, July 11, 1934, p. 16.

[68]For an organizational chart of the PCC, see appendix E, p. 1941.

On September 2, 1933, the Code of Fair Competition for the Petroleum Industry (Oil Code) became effective. The tone of the new code was stated by Petroleum Administrator Harold Ickes. "Our task," Ickes told the PCC, "is to stabilize the oil industry upon a profitable basis."[69]

Article I, setting price floors, was not activated. Article II set wage and hour regulations for drilling and production firms.[70] Article III, Production, limited withdrawals from storage to 100,000 barrels per day and gave discretionary authority to the PCC to impose other restrictions. Output was regulated to demand, which was to be determined "at intervals" by authorities and allocated by state.

Price fixing was detailed in case of activation: average retail gasoline prices were to be multiplied by 18.5 to set a wellhead price per barrel, below which "it shall be an unfair practice . . . to buy, sell, receive in exchange, or otherwise acquire."[71] Coordinator Ickes established the Petroleum Administration Board (PAB) to administer the code, which "in functions and in structure . . . greatly resembled the old Oil Division of the United States Fuel Administration in World War I."[72] The PCC established a network of local-level committees staffed by oil executives to apportion quotas to each producing state (fourteen states did not have proration authority) and deal with code violations.

Improved price conditions delayed Ickes's expected price order until mid-October when he announced that effective December 1, the published price floors would be activated.[73] Major companies immediately protested, and independent producers began to have second thoughts. With a promise by majors to dedicate $10 million to a gasoline purchase pool to stabilize prices, Ickes changed his mind.[74]

[69]Quoted in 310 U.S. 150 at 172 (1939). The natural-gas industry, represented solely by the American Gas Association, debated a code confined to labor provisions but never adopted one.

[70]On July 9, 1934, the derrick and rig industries received additional code coverage defining unfair trade practices. *NPN*, July 11, 1934, p. 16.

[71]National Recovery Administration, *Code of Fair Competition for the Petroleum Industry* (Washington, D.C.: Government Printing Office, 1933), p. 9.

[72]Gerald Nash, *United States Oil Policy*, p. 140. Applauding events in the background was former Oil Division head Mark Requa.

[73]Nationwide crude price floors are reprinted in *OGJ*, October 19, 1933, p. 8.

[74]*OGJ*, September 7, 1933, p. 8; October 19, 1933, p. 8; and November 23, 1933, p. 9. The gasoline purchase plan is discussed in chapter 23, pp. 1351–52.

Although price-fixing remained in the code, it would never see the light of day. Ickes instructed his assistant solicitor and right-hand man, J. Howard Marshall, to prepare an order fixing minimum prices for every grade of crude oil and petroleum product for all points in the United States. With the help of fellow assistant solicitor Norman Myers and economist J. Elmer Thomas, Marshall spent weeks on the project before telling Ickes that "we didn't know enough to devise a national price-fixing order—and no one else did either!"[75] Ickes reluctantly agreed. Volumetric regulation was the key.

The PAB reflected the wishes of the majority of the industry it was intended to serve. Federal *coordination* was provided in place of federal *control*. Production-quota decisions were left to state con-servation agencies; the main function of the PAB in the production phase was assisting the Bureau of Mines' Petroleum Economics Division with its monthly oil-demand forecast.[76]

In September 1933, the PAB issued its first national demand fore-cast ("recommendation") to apportion supply among producing states. By the end of the month, the recommendations resulted in a 10 percent drop in national production and a 40 percent drop in East Texas.[77] Crude prices increased from $0.64 to $1.00 per barrel in September alone and remained relatively high for the rest of the Oil Code period. This reversed the profit picture for many oil interests that initially had been politically active in establishing the regulations.[78]

By no means did the code produce its full intended effect. PAB quota recommendations increasingly became the starting point from which state conservation agencies increased allowables according

[75]J. Howard Marshall, *Done in Oil* (College Station: Texas A&M University Press, 1994), p. 28.

[76]Beginning in August 1933, the Petroleum Economics Division also issued statistics on interstate vs. intrastate petroleum movements, pipeline vs. truck transport, and inventory levels, all of which were valuable for hot-oil enforcement, especially in East Texas. *TNEC Petroleum Hearings*, p. 547.

[77]Norman Nordhauser, *The Quest for Stability*, p. 134.

[78]Ibid., p. 135. A notable example given by Nordhauser (pp. 135–36) concerned the Wirt Franklin Corporation. Franklin, head of the PCC and founder of the protectionist-minded Independent Producers Association of America, saw his company rebound from a loss before depletion and depreciation of $234,000 for the six months ending in June 1933 to a net profit of $268,000 in the same period a year later.

to local industry desires. Under pressure from local constituents, the TRC in late 1933 began to exceed recommended quotas by over 10 percent.[79] Oklahoma and California also consistently produced in excess of allocations as table 3.1 indicates.

In addition to state allowable assignments in excess of federal recommendations, excess oil came from other sources. Wildcat production was not recorded in the states' figures of oil output. Exports went unreported or were grossly underestimated.[80] Above all, hot oil was the main problem as overproducing well operators found ingenious ways to escape detection. To avoid a total breakdown of proration, federal authorities redoubled their enforcement efforts in East Texas in 1934. After several years of practical difficulties and legal setbacks, described in chapter 12, control of the great field was finally achieved for good in 1936.

The courts ended the several-year experiment with economic petroleum planning and then invalidated the NIRA itself. On January 7, 1935, the Supreme Court invalidated section 9(c) of the Oil Code on a technicality; the section had been inadvertently deleted in a formally adopted prior draft.[81] With hot-oil transportation no longer prohibited, the end of proration seemed near. A legislative substitute was quickly provided by Texas senator Tom Connally, however, that took effect on February 22.[82] A potentially ruinous "regulatory gap" was closed.

On May 27, 1935, the Supreme Court declared the entire NIRA unconstitutional.[83] With the book closed, a total of 627 administrative orders had been given under the Oil Code, several hundred of which certified allowables and approved allocations among the states.[84]

Interstate Coordination:
The Interstate Oil Compact Commission

Substitute legislation was sought to replace the defunct Oil Code. As it had under World War I planning, the industry had tried regulation, liked it, and sought a facsimile. Waiting in the wings was a plan

[79]Ibid., pp. 141–42.

[80]Myron Watkins, *Oil: Stabilization or Conservation?* pp. 104–5.

[81]*Panama Refining Company* v. *Ryan,* 293 U.S. 388 (1935).

[82]Public Law 14, 49 Stat. 30 (1935).

[83]*Schechter Poultry Corp.* v. *United States,* 295 U.S. 495 (1935).

[84]"The Government in the Exercise of the Power over Foreign Commerce," in American Bar Association, *Conservation of Oil and Gas, A Legal History, 1948,* ed. Blakely M. Murphy (Chicago: ABA, 1949), p. 645.

Table 3.1
RECOMMENDED AND ACTUAL OUTPUT: SEPTEMBER 1933–MAY 1935
(thousands of barrels per day)

Month	United States		Texas		Oklahoma		California	
	PAB	Actual	PAB	Actual	PAB	Actual	PAB	Actual
1933								
Sept.	2,414	2,611	975	1,123	540	554	480	486
Oct.	2,339	2,454	965	1,060	495	499	455	470
Nov.	2,338	2,332	965	939	495	498	455	461
Dec.	2,210	2,328	888	952	457	491	450	471
1934								
Jan.	2,183	2,321	884	957	446	491	438	457
Feb.	2,183	2,338	884	987	446	482	438	450
Mar.	2,283	2,437	948	1,022	456	498	454	475
Apr.	2,366	2,526	981	1,064	476	523	463	482
May	2,366	2,576	981	1,079	476	531	463	462
June	2,528	2,668	1,032	1,108	512	551	550	516
July	2,530	2,631	1,042	1,106	490	504	509	518
Aug.	2,449	2,550	1,001	1,072	480	484	490	493
Sept.	2,342	2,527	968	1,113	461	462	457	468
Oct.	2,326	2,477	956	1,044	457	470	452	466

Nov.	2,340	2,415	957	986	459	468	462	478
Dec.	2,384	2,420	973	982	470	474	465	479
1935							
Jan.	2,460	2,539	1,007	1,031	489	491	474	500
Feb.	2,526	2,599	1,032	1,077	497	490	489	499
Mar.	2,520	2,629	1,020	1,082	491	505	493	498
Apr.	2,527	2,614	1,021	1,056	493	522	493	473
May	2,561	2,660	1,040	1,067	500	523	494	495

SOURCE: Myron Watkins, *Oil: Stabilization or Conservation?* p. 91.

first devised by Humble Oil's Hines Baker in 1929 (and embodied in the Oil States Advisory Committee) to coordinate state regulatory activities and yet steer clear of federal regulation. On February 16, 1935, the Interstate Compact to Conserve Oil and Gas created the Interstate Oil Compact Commission with four states as members and recommendations from four other states. It was ratified upon the additional memberships of New Mexico and Kansas and received congressional consent on August 27, 1935.[85] Article III of the compact recommended that "within a reasonable time" states ban production practices causing aboveground waste, belowground waste, and fire hazards.[86]

The Interstate Compact defeated a rival measure, the Thomas-Disney bill, which would have relinquished state authority to control production and, indirectly, price to the Department of the Interior. Its defeat reaffirmed the regulatory limits the industry preferred and successfully implemented in this period—federal direction and enforcement but not federal control.[87]

With a single federal law prohibiting the movement of illegally produced oil in interstate commerce, a combined state-federal enforcement effort, a tariff on crude oil and petroleum products, and a multistate coordinating agency, effective wellhead production regulation was set to begin. Until radically changed market conditions made output ceilings superfluous in the early 1970s, this system of control would endure.

[85]The original states providing ratification in 1935 were New Mexico, Oklahoma, Kansas, Colorado, Texas, and Illinois. States joining later were Louisiana (1940); Pennsylvania, New York, and Arkansas (1941); Kentucky (1942); Ohio and Michigan (1943); Montana, Florida, Alabama, and West Virginia (1945); Georgia (Associate, 1946); Tennessee and Indiana (1947); Mississippi (1948); North Dakota and Nebraska (1953); Oregon (Associate, 1954); South Dakota, Nevada, Arizona, and Wyoming (1955); Utah and Alaska (1957); Washington (1958); Maryland (1959); and Idaho (Associate, 1960).

[86]The text of this law is reprinted in Samuel B. Pettengill, *Hot Oil*, pp. 284–87. To Leonard Fanning, Congress's consent to the Interstate Oil Compact Commission "put a federal seal on conservation procedures." Fanning, *The Story of the American Petroleum Institute*, p. 155.

[87]Part of the sentiment against Thomas-Disney came from the Cole committee, which undertook one of the most exhaustive congressional investigations of the oil industry ever. The majority of the committee recommended state rather than federal regulation. See Gerald Nash, *United States Oil Policy*, p. 145.

The Need for Mandatory Petroleum Conservation: A Reconsideration

After the preceding summary of the major events leading to the substitution of mandatory conservation for voluntary production practices, what was earlier designated as "Zimmermann's challenge" can now be reconsidered. Zimmermann forthrightly denounced the ability of market forces to prevent waste in petroleum production and placed the burden of proof on critics of wellhead regulation.

Zimmermann's interpretation has been held by practically every important writer on the subject.[88] Even the few critics of conservation law, recognizing the entire legislative effort as an attempt by politically powerful oil interests to achieve higher prices and profitability, fail to address the important issue of whether some type of regulation was necessary to correct the "market failure" under capture-rule competition.[89]

The revisionist perspective presented herein begins with a definition of economic conservation. Upon this foundation, the historical events that led to government control of production are reinterpreted to find that government intervention played a prominent role in the creation of preventable conservation problems. The rule of capture, consequently, is found to be a contributing—but not a primary— factor in the industry's commonly cited problems.

Economic Conservation and Petroleum

In chapter 1, economic conservation was linked with the preservation of the capital value of a privately held asset. In petroleum production, the asset is the oil or gas reservoir, making conservation the extent to which the resource is being managed to maximize discounted future profits.

---

[88]Well-known writers include Gerald Nash, *United States Oil Policy*, pp. 8–9 and passim; Stephen McDonald, *Petroleum Conservation in the United States* (Baltimore: Johns Hopkins University Press, 1971), pp. 30–34; and Wallace Lovejoy and Paul Homan, *Economic Aspects of Oil Conservation Regulation* (Baltimore: Johns Hopkins University Press, 1967), p. v.

[89]Norman Nordhauser is an outstanding example. See also the books of Myron Watkins and W. J. Kemnitzer. An exception is D. T. Armentano, who questions the case for mandatory conservation since government intervention was in part responsible for the problem. Armentano, "Petroleum, Profits, and Prices," *Reason*, June 1974, p. 1.

The starting point for understanding free-market petroleum conservation is the distinction between *physical conservation* and *economic conservation*. From the purely physical viewpoint, all waste—the avoidable loss of any quantity of oil or gas—should be prevented. Production under this standard should proceed at a rate no greater than the maximum efficient rate, a petroleum-engineering term denoting the rate of extraction that recovers the most oil from a deposit, regardless of other considerations.

From the economic viewpoint, purely physical output is tempered by such other factors as cost minimization and the preference for present output over future output. The present-oriented nature of production stems from the economic law of time preference and from omnipresent uncertainty.[90] These economic influences require *present-oriented* production that, in the unique case of petroleum, may require physical waste. The amount of waste depends on the situation, but it might be considerable since

1. the life of a well can be long even with rapid production, making the discount placed on future production great;
2. unique uncertainty characterizes petroleum production given the technological and political influences that bear upon the industry;
3. financial indebtedness requires a minimum cash flow; and
4. expectations about continued plentiful crude and low prices often prevail.

The legitimacy of "quick payouts" for the producer, and the value of immediate consumption to the consumer, even at the cost of lost production or higher cost recovery, must be respected.[91]

---

[90]Time preference means, other things being equal, that individuals prefer to satisfy wants sooner than later. Uncertainty means that the individual would rather have a sure thing today than a not-so-sure thing tomorrow, all other things the same. For a detailed explanation of time preference and uncertainty as the factors making up the interest rate used to discount future satisfactions, see Frank Fetter, *Capital, Interest, and Rent: Essays in the Theory of Distribution* (Kansas City, Mo.: Sheed, Andrews and McMeel, 1977), pp. 172–316; and Ludwig von Mises, *Human Action* (Chicago: Contemporary Books, 1966), pp. 483–89, 524–37.

[91]Erich Zimmermann fails to recognize economic factors requiring present-oriented production when he asserts that "all waste is economic waste." Zimmermann, *Conservation in the Production of Petroleum*, p. 310.

Petroleum conservation (or more precisely, economic conservation) must be intrinsically linked to the *technological knowledge available to the relevant decisionmaker at any given point in time.* This precludes false retrospective judgments made by imposing the illegitimate standard of superior (or perfect) knowledge. For example, nineteenth-century horse-and-buggy transportation cannot be called wasteful because mechanized transportation is known and used today. By today's standards, yesterday's travel options were not efficient, but it cannot be said that a problem of transportation inefficiency existed. Analogously, petroleum production must be judged in light of the relevant technological development at a point in time, not evaluated by superimposing a superior standard.

The Problem of Petroleum Conservation Historically Contemplated

For many decades after its Titusville beginning, the petroleum industry suffered from problems associated with a young developing industry. *The problems, however, were not of conservation.*[92] Belowground geologic waste from rapid production was not a conservation problem because the knowledge did not exist to alert producers to the fact that they were damaging oil recoverability and, to an extent, their own future profits by dissipating gas energy.[93] *Surface waste* was not so much a problem of economic conservation as it was a by-product of three factors: low petroleum prices due to abundant supply that outdistanced a demand limited to kerosene lighting, an infant distribution phase trying to keep pace with the quickly developing production phase, and financing constraints that made delayed production difficult. Regarding the last factor, the unbankability of the reservoir as collateral, coupled with price instability,

---

[92]In one sense, a conservation problem arguably existed when producers used such public property as creeks and rivers to dump unwanted crude, creating pollution and fire-hazard externalities. If, alternatively, these water areas had been privately owned, this practice could have been priced or subject to pecuniary restitution, making possible alternative (i.e., higher) uses of crude oil. The difference between the (practiced) lower and (unpracticed) higher uses of crude oil would be economic waste and a problem of conservation. This also applies to oil-well gushers that damaged neighboring farmland and structures with impunity, given that successful prosecution under tort law would have discouraged these occurrences.

[93]"In the 'old days,' 'reservoir energy' was sometimes referred to as 'rock pressure,' and it was thought that the quicker the rock pressure was utilized, the greater the recovery of oil would be. This reasoning was based upon the fact that quite often

made petroleum production a noncompetitive risk to the external capital market in many cases.

Aboveground waste also resulted from a lack of understanding of belowground waste; slower production would have lessened the strain on surface activities to reduce leakage, evaporation, and contamination. *Capital waste* from overdrilling was not yet recognized as the problem it would later come to be. The widely believed Cutler theory preached that more wells recovered more oil.[94] The rule of capture *did* contribute to dense drilling and rapid production as drillers vied for the same underlying oil, but it was powerfully supplemented by a problem of technical misinformation. "Overproduction" and "waste," in other words, may well have been common complaints without drainage competition. Thus exclusive emphasis on the rule of capture must be relaxed vis-à-vis the embryonic state of the industry to explain some of the practices that created instability and a "conservation problem."

With time, progress in science, technology, and capital markets transformed the industry by eliminating or reducing many of the aforementioned problems. The invention and commercial adaptation of the gasoline-powered internal-combustion engine created a demand for crude oil as *energy*, in addition to its use as an illuminant.

---

when a gas well came in, it was found that if the gas was blown off, the oil would follow. So it was reasoned that if they flowed the gas quickly, they would get an oil well." Leslie Moses, "The Constitutional, Legislative and Judicial Growth of Oil and Gas Conservation Statutes," *Mississippi Law Journal* (March 1941): 372. In matter-of-fact textbook language, John Diehl instructed the reader in 1927: "Whenever any 'wild-catting' takes place it is with the hope that an oil field will be discovered. If gas be found, it is temporarily wasted under the assumption that eventually oil will be produced." Diehl, *Natural Gas Handbook* (Erie, Pa.: Metric Metal Works of the American Meter Co., 1927), p. 16. This is not to suggest that all thinking on the subject was fallacious. Particularly among technical academics, in contrast to many oil producers, there was understanding of underground waste. The following quotation dates from 1916. "Town-lot development . . . means uneconomical production throughout—drilling more wells than are necessary, pumping too fast, wasting gas pressure (and the gas itself), in flooding wells, and pumping one well against another, thereby creating underground conditions favorable for the encroachment of water." Raymond Bacon and William Hamor, *The American Petroleum Industry*, 2 vols. (New York: McGraw-Hill, 1916), vol. 1, pp. 398–99.

[94]This theory, formulated in 1924 and widely believed until the 1940s, suggested that absolute recovery was inversely related to the distance between wells. See chapter 4, pp. 146–47.

In the 1920s, natural gas began to assume greater importance as new pipeline technology eased the problem of distance. Another significant breakthrough for wellhead production was the belated recognition of a non-barrel-for-barrel tradeoff between current and future production in certain reservoirs.[95] Slower depletion and better utilization of gas-cap reservoirs, it was advanced, enhanced future recoverability compared with open-flow production by preserving reservoir pressure.

For an industry accustomed to wells' producing at their maximum rate, the new theory of reservoir mechanics had important ramifications. Self-interest now required in some cases that production philosophies be radically altered to preserve future profits. This meant substituting a common plan of reservoir development for autonomous capture-rule competition. It required, in Leslie Moses's view, "an educational campaign," although this was "not the quickest remedy for waste."[96] This also constituted the problem, or, more accurately, the challenge, of petroleum conservation.

The conservation problem is the difference between what producers *could do* to maximize future discounted profits, given their means-ends framework, and what they *actually practiced*. There was not a major gap between the two until advances in reservoir engineering became generally known. In what year did this new knowledge become widely enough disseminated to inspire common application? Robert Hardwicke listed a series of technological papers commencing in 1913 that presented the new theory of reservoir energy and its role in recoverability.[97] But it was not until Doherty's effort in 1923 and 1924 to convince the industry of the need for unitization that the radical new ideas were widely introduced to producers.[98]

[95]See the appendix to chapter 4, pp. 218–21, for a discussion of rate-sensitive and rate-insensitive reservoirs.

[96]Leslie Moses, "The Constitutional, Legislative, and Judicial Growth of Oil and Gas Conservation Statutes," p. 359.

[97]Robert Hardwicke, *Antitrust Laws et al. v. Unit Operation of Oil or Gas Pools* (New York: American Institute of Mining and Metallurgical Engineers, 1948), pp. 4–8. Erich Zimmermann uncovered two earlier articles from 1865 and 1880 identifying the importance of gas pressure to recoverability. Zimmermann, *Conservation in the Production of Petroleum*, p. 121. Both discoveries, however, were forgotten until L. G. Huntley's rediscovery in 1913.

[98]"While engineers urged its use prior to 1924, it was in that year that the question was brought forcibly to the attention of the oil industry, the government, and the public by Henry L. Doherty." Raymond Myers, *The Law of Pooling and Unitization*, 2 vols. (New York: Banks and Co., 1967), vol. 1, p. 20.

Doherty's crusade, unfortunately, had a counterproductive side. Not only did he advocate federal intervention to compel unitization, he turned to top federal officials when the industry gave him a cold shoulder. Production reform thus took on *political* meaning instead of *scientific* meaning for oil producers wary of federal involvement. This hardened old ways and delayed reform. The blunt denial of production inefficiency by the Committee of Eleven in its famous 1925 report for the API was intended, in part, to avoid the political consequences of a different conclusion.[99]

Despite the staggered start, unitization entered into an "organized study period" from 1925 to 1930.[100] The American Bar Association's Committee on Conservation of Mineral Resources debated the legality of cooperative reform in light of antitrust law. The American Institute of Mining and Metallurgical Engineers' Committee on Unit Operations addressed unitization issues and published their findings. The API's Gas Conservation Committee publicized new theories of reservoir mechanics beginning in 1927. In 1929, they published H. C. Miller's definitive *Function of Natural Gas in the Production of Oil* and formally endorsed unit operations. API's Production Division held a symposium, "A New Conception of Oil Proration," at its 1931 annual meeting. Research on production methods to prevent waste was also carried out by the API with industry contributions, such as Humble Oil's $500,000 grant in 1926. The Mid-Continent Oil and Gas Association published *The Handbook of Unitization of Oil Pools* to educate oil producers about the "three cardinal virtues" of unitization—economy, greater recovery, and stability of output.[101]

[99]See Leonard Logan, *Stabilization of the Petroleum Industry*, pp. 144–45; and API Special Resolution, December 1924. That resolution did not represent all views within the API. Earl Oliver rebutted that "the report does not reflect the attitude of the industry" but certain influential members who feared Doherty's plan of federal intervention. Waste, the counterstudy concluded, was the "inevitable" result of "competitive drainage conditions" where there existed a "failure to utilize the natural forces of gas and encroaching water in the expulsion of product." Oliver, "The So-Called A.P.I. Report: An Analysis," October 16, 1925, unpublished; copy in the American Petroleum Institute library.

[100]Rex Baker and Robert Hardwicke, "History of Conservation Law," in *History of Petroleum Engineering* (New York: API, 1961), p. 1126. In *Antitrust Laws et al. v. Unit Operation of Oil or Gas Pools*, p. 35, Hardwicke uses the slightly different dates of 1927–31.

[101]Mid-Continent Oil and Gas Association, *The Handbook of Unitization of Oil Pools* (Tulsa: Mid-Continent Oil and Gas Association, 1930), p. 9.

An appendix to that book listed approximately eighty articles discussing unitization in theory and practice that were published between 1927 and 1930 in industry trade magazines. Scholarly books outside the industry orbit were also published on the subject.[102] Finally, the federal government, through the Bureau of Mines and the FOCB, studied singular-plan pool production.

By the early 1930s, "the new conception" of production, as Humble Oil executive John Suman described it, faded into the background of active discussion and application.[103] In the majority of fields, voluntary production agreements, facing competitive vulnerability as free-market cartels, broke down. Formal unit agreements were no longer sought or failed to pass. Instead of unitization, the new concept was proration; instead of conservation, the industry goal was stabilization.[104] The 1925–30 "organized study period" turned into the "state regulation period."[105]

The East Texas field was also responsible for the new emphasis on mandatory allowables instead of on cooperative production. Although casinghead gas waste was not an issue with the water-driven field, there was simply too much oil for industry profitability given previous expectations and investments. In 1926–27, proration was in its infancy; by 1931–32, it came of age in Oklahoma and Texas and would expand to other oil states by the middle of the decade. Unitization as the answer to industry problems was an idea whose time had come and gone.

The Paradox of Petroleum Waste

The fact that voluntary methods were not generally successful before mandatory conservation became widespread suggests that a conservation problem, that is an *economic error* and not a *technical*

---

[102]See, for example, Leonard Logan, *Stabilization of the Petroleum Industry;* and Myron Watkins, *Oil: Stabilization or Conservation?*

[103]Robert Hardwicke, *Antitrust Laws et al. v. Unit Operation of Oil or Gas Pools,* pp. 89–90. A 1931 API symposium was called "The New Conception of Oil Production."

[104]A sign of the times was the American Institute of Mining and Metallurgical Engineers' renaming its Committee on Unit Operation the Stabilization Committee in 1932. Ibid., pp. 84–85.

[105]Robert Hardwicke, *Antitrust Laws et al. v. Unit Operation of Oil or Gas Pools,* p. 33.

error, existed during part or all of the 1927–35 period, perhaps from 1930 on.[106]

The existence of economic error seems to present a paradox between "is" and "ought," between practice and theory. As Wallace Lovejoy and Paul Homan stated:

> Looking backward at the history of conservation regulation, the most astonishing fact to an outside observer is that the interests desiring to make money out of producing oil have supported policies that required them to incur much greater costs than were necessary and that greatly curtailed the amount of oil they could ultimately recover from their properties. This does not look at all like the behavior of "economic men" who are supposed to be eager to maximize their profits.[107]

The paradox can be appreciated when seen another way. Of all privately held mineral assets, petroleum was the only one experiencing an obvious conservation problem. The U.S. experience did offer isolated examples of nonmineral resource exhaustion—of certain forests, grasslands, and fisheries—but these overdepletions were associated with publicly owned resources subject to the "tragedy of the commons."[108]

---

[106]On these two categories of error, see Israel M. Kirzner, *Perception, Opportunity, and Profit: Studies in the Theory of Entrepreneurship* (Chicago: University of Chicago Press, 1979), chapter entitled "Economics and Error," pp. 130–36. The precise date when the industry "knew" better than to engage in open-flow drainage competition cannot be known with certainty. Rex Baker and Robert Hardwicke stated, "The technical men, by 1930, were largely in agreement that, as to most pools, such operation caused underground waste, even if every barrel of the oil and every cubic foot of gas that was produced should be promptly used for current consumption." Baker and Hardwicke, "History of Conservation Law," p. 1135. Additional time should be added to allow for the knowledge transfer from the technical to the entrepreneurial side of the business.

[107]Wallace Lovejoy and Paul Homan, *Economic Aspects of Oil Conservation Regulation*, pp. 261–62. Ludwell Denny also refers to this as "the paradox of the American Capitalist system deliberately destroying profits." Denny, *We Fight for Oil* (Westport, Conn.: Hyperion Press, 1928, 1976), p. 249.

[108]This term reflects the fact that nonowned resources are overused since no one has the financial incentive to preserve the asset's capital value. See Garrett Hardin, "The Tragedy of the Commons," reprinted in *Pollution, Resources, and the Environment*, ed. Alain Enthoven and Myrick Freeman (New York: W. W. Norton, 1973), pp. 1–13.

Government Intervention and Petroleum Waste: The Neglected Link

Government Intervention and Multiple Ownership.[109] Students of petroleum conservation have agreed on the central role that uncoordinated multiple ownership of individual petroleum deposits played in overproduction, overdrilling, and the wastes therein. This problem has been equated with the rule-of-capture legal framework and unregulated competition based upon it. The consensus, therefore, has been that private property and the free market formed the root of the problem.

While the formulation of the problem can be agreed upon, the conclusion that the free market was responsible does not follow. The first reason is that the free market and the rule of capture are not synonymous. The market could have been assigned a *homestead* allocation of first-title oil and gas rights, more in keeping with a Lockean private-property system, and avoided the problem of multiple ownership altogether.[110] The transition to new production practices would have been far more easily achieved, and the free market would have avoided a major part of the problem. Second, the powerful incentive of profit maximization is still present to modify behavior within the capture-rule framework. The "common-pool" problem under the capture rule was *not* the same as the "tragedy of the commons" experienced with publicly owned resources. Resource abuse (versus calculated depletion) under the former is not commonly profit maximizing as is the latter. To establish this point, it can be shown how market forces, propelled by the desire for profit and the avoidance of loss, *could have worked* to replace the monetarily destructive environment of capture-rule competition, yet were thwarted by a series of government interventions.

The rule of capture was destructive to producers since it bred resource inefficiency and encouraged overdrilling, overproduction, and price instability; hence it sowed the seeds of its own demise.

---

[109]This section overlaps in places with the next section, "Government Intervention and Consolidation." This reflects the similarity of formal consolidation where reservoir co-owners purchase properties in the same reservoir to reduce the number of firms involved and informal consolidation where through unit agreements singular operation is contractually achieved although ownership remains diffuse.

[110]See chapter 2, pp. 69–74. Although the capture-rule legal framework cannot be categorized as an intervention in the free market, it can be recognized as a misapplication of private-property rights.

Further misapplications of property rights and a variety of government interventions, however, kept market forces from annulling ruinous drainage competition.

Government Intervention and Consolidation. The modification of the capture rule by implicit covenants, correlative rights, and, ultimately, regulation was intended to mitigate the problems of piracy and waste. Instead, *it detracted from the market alternative of consolidating ownership to achieve singular plans of reservoir development to achieve true conservation.* The effect of such law was to establish a mandatory program, consisting of compulsory shutdowns, well-spacing rules, mandatory proration, and, later, compulsory unitization, which replaced incentive for voluntary consolidation and autonomous cooperation.

Beginning with mandatory proration in the Seminole field in 1927, the drive toward free-market solutions was replaced by political "solutions." In the Oklahoma City and East Texas fields in 1931, the problem reached its peak. Tremendous production depressed prices precipitously, and "chaos" loomed by all accounts. What would this have meant? A prominent API executive warned at the time, "East Texas will bankrupt 95 percent of the independent operators of the United States and shake the majority of the major companies if allowed to produce at its present rate."[111] Unfortunately, the threat—or occurrence—of bankruptcy was exactly what was needed to eradicate the numbers problem that prevented efficient, intertemporal production. Marginal wells needed to be plugged and resources transferred to more productive wells; "mom-and-pop" producers needed to be replaced with strongly capitalized firms; and large sections of producing areas needed single-company management to operate fewer wells at disciplined production rates.

---

[111]Quoted in Norman Nordhauser, *The Quest for Stability,* p. 85. One of the conclusions reached in petroleum-industry hearings before the Temporary National Economic Committee in the late 1930s was that "had the industry continued to suffer from the violent overproduction and severely depressed prices of the early 1930s, most small enterprises would have been forced out of business and only the strong well-financed companies would remain." *TNEC Petroleum Hearings,* p. 77. In early 1934, an estimated 250,000 stripper wells produced a barrel per day. *OGJ,* April 19, 1934, p. 24. Lloyd Unsell, executive vice president of the IPAA, similarly interpreted the "chaos" to have potentially resulted in "only five or six major companies controlling production instead of thousands of little people looking for oil in little places." Personal interview with the author, July 23, 1981.

It was recognized in the industry, as one executive testified before the Federal Trade Commission, that "the only way to cut down the production of crude is to cut the price" and that "low prices were especially hard on small producers who were often near bankruptcy because of costly competitive drilling."[112] In fact, serious consideration was given to abandoning proration entirely to allow this painful solution. In early 1933, the *Oil & Gas Journal* reported "a well-defined and growing feeling among many conservative oil men that the petroleum industry might more quickly get back to a solid foundation if the policy of proration was abandoned and the different fields permitted to produce without legal or regulatory restrictions."[113] Six weeks later, the same influential trade journal editorialized, "It would now be better to open up all the fields, go through the comparatively brief period of 15-cent oil, and then start the recovery with politicians eliminated from the picture."[114]

In Oklahoma, the free-market solution almost prevailed. The OCC voted to continue proration by a single deciding vote cast after long hesitation by a commissioner previously against proration.[115] It was the narrowest of victories, the most consequential of decisions. Shutdowns and a program designed to make the marginal well profitable—at the expense of more efficient wells—usurped powerful market forces that promised a healthy consolidation of offset wells, the retirement of marginal properties, and disciplined future production.

Instead of continued consolidation, which was evident before proration, the proration period saw the transfer of market share from large firms to small firms. In 1920, the twenty-four largest producing companies accounted for 52 percent of the market, a percentage that grew to 64 percent in 1926 and 70 percent a year later. In 1938, in

---

[112]Henry Seager and Charles Gulick, *Trust and Corporation Problems* (New York: Harper and Brothers, 1929), p. 139; and Henrietta Larson and Kenneth Porter, *History of Humble Oil & Refining Company*, p. 18.

[113]*OGJ*, February 2, 1933, p. 7. Also see "Is Proration Doomed?" *OGJ*, January 5, 1933, p. 18; and *Business Week*, January 25, 1933, p. 10.

[114]*OGJ*, March 16, 1933, p. 7.

[115]*NPN*, March 1, 1933, p. 23. Had Commissioner E. R. Hughes voted differently, Governor Murray could still have declared martial law. But with the legality of proration in grave doubt, a return to unregulated conditions, which might have impelled Texas and other oil states to follow suit, could have occurred. A different vote by Hughes is one of the great "what ifs" in the history of U.S. oil regulation.

contrast, this figure fell below 58 percent.[116] In East Texas in 1935, more than 1,000 firms, over 800 of which operated 9 or fewer wells, made concerted reform impossible for field leaders, such as Humble Oil (1,800 wells), Gulf (1,000 wells), and 7 other majors with over 500 wells each.[117]

A related disincentive to ownership consolidation was a well-sale tax, which stood at 16 percent from 1922 to 1936 and 30 percent thereafter.[118] Because of the considerable difference between the cost and the sales price of commercial wells, entrepreneurs could justify independence as a "political" alternative in the face of low prices and other difficulties.

Another example of government intervention that discouraged consolidation was state and federal laws that regulated purchases by oil and gas pipeline companies from independent producers.[119] "Discrimination," whether favoritism toward an affiliate, reduced terms, or absolute refusals to purchase, was sorely needed to discourage poorly located or low-producing wells and to encourage plugging, integration, or consolidation once they were in operation. Beginning in the 1880s, Standard Oil successfully used purchaser leverage to reduce crude production to marketable amounts; in 1927 and 1928, Humble Oil did the same to encourage conservation in the big Yates field.[120] Despite the different eras, both times the strategy was effective against overproduction. But future use of that strategy would be precluded by common-purchaser and common-carrier oil pipeline laws that in the crucial 1930s forced transporters

---

[116]*TNEC Petroleum Hearings*, p. 277. Small firms increased in number during the proration era. An estimated 4,000 oil companies in 1932 grew to 13,000 by 1953. Simon Whitney, *Antitrust Policies* (New York: Twentieth Century Fund, 1958), pp. 168–69.

[117]*Oil Weekly*, April 22, 1935, p. 14. In 1931, an influential independent tried to organize his fellow independents in the East Texas field into a large corporation to enter into a unitization agreement with the majors. See Jacqueline Lang Weaver, *Unitization of Oil and Gas Fields in Texas*, p. 390n. 59.

[118]See chapter 7, pp. 349–50.

[119]See chapters 11, pp. 612–18, and 14, pp. 776–85.

[120]For an agreement between Standard Oil and producers, see Ida Tarbell, *History of the Standard Oil Company*, 2 vols. (New York: McClure, Phillips, 1904), vol. 1, pp. 379–80. On Humble Oil's discipline of producers, see Henrietta Larson, Evelyn Knowlton, and Charles Popple, *New Horizons* (New York: Harper & Row, 1971), pp. 88–89, 317.

to buy oil ratably from all producers and accept shipments ratably from all shippers.[121]

The importance of consolidation for production efficiency, and the superior position of large firms in this regard, was clearly noted in 1926 by John Ise.

> Over-production was generally worse in those fields where many small companies were operating. The oil-producing industry has in most fields been burdened with a multitude of small companies, often controlled by men utterly unfamiliar with the business. . . . Generally, the larger companies were more conservative in their operations at times when oil was too cheap [unlike] . . . the town-lot promoters [who] have often forced the orgies of rapid production.[122]

A telling statistic of the forgone alternative was the number of abandoned and shut-in wells (table 3.2) that peaked after the solidification of state control in 1930—particularly with the 1931 shutdowns—and fell with mandatory conservation.

It was precisely the inexperienced "town-lot" operators and owners of marginal wells who needed to be pressured by market forces into more disciplined production or replaced by stronger companies possessing the expertise and financial strength to block lease and practice efficient production, even if it meant slowing output.[123] But

[121]In Texas, however, the 1930 Common Purchaser Act had more bark than bite. Jacqueline Lang Weaver, *Unitization of Oil and Gas Fields in Texas*, p. 41.

[122]John Ise, *The United States Oil Policy* (New Haven, Conn.: Yale University Press, 1926), pp. 125–26. Also see "Small Operators Do Most of Drilling," *OGJ*, December 24, 1931, p. 14; and the empirical findings of Gary Libecap and Steven Wiggins, "Contractual Responses to the Common Pool: Prorationing of Crude Oil Production," *American Economic Review* (March 1984): 87–98.

In chap. 19, Ise provides examples of efficient production in areas of concentrated ownership in California and in sections of the Texas Gulf Coast. Ise also mentions the important role of landowners in forcing "orgies of production." The implicit "quick-drill" covenant was at fault in this regard. Assuming *express* quick-drill covenants were desired by present-oriented landowners, properly scaled companies could have provided present money to modify the lease agreement to legally practice slower, longer production. This, for example, was sometimes done by Humble Oil. Henrietta Larson and Kenneth Porter, *History of Humble Oil & Refining Company*, p. 323. Also see Jacqueline Lang Weaver, *Unitization of Oil and Gas Fields in Texas*, p. 53.

[123]Block leasing was an important free-market strategy as larger companies knew. "The large company, while seldom reselling to any great extent, always desires a solid block covering any structure that its geologists have outlined both because of the greater return if the well proves successful and the security given against competitive drilling. Where the definite structure has been outlined, the lease man must get leases on the area contained or none at all." Ernest Lilley, *The Oil Industry* (New York: Van

Table 3.2
WELL INACTIVATIONS: 1926–35

Year	Abandoned/Shut-In U.S. Oil Wells
1926	6,126
1927	9,682
1928	7,848
1929	14,962
1930	8,823
1931	22,231
1932	4,880
1933	2,720
1934	6,899
1935	7,498

SOURCE: DeGolyer and MacNaughton, *Twentieth Century Petroleum Statistics,* 1980 ed. (Dallas: DeGolyer and MacNaughton, 1981), p. 39.

government interference prevented the corrective signals of profit and loss from effecting the urgently needed transformation.

Integration. Consolidation of wellhead operations with complementary downstream (pipeline, refinery, and marketing) operations was also discouraged by government intervention—with negative implications for conservation. The Standard Oil breakup in 1911 and the Texas anti-integration incorporation law from 1897 to 1917 were prominent examples. Another example was the aforementioned pipeline regulation, which diluted the value of integration.

Integration favored disciplined production for several reasons. First, downstream profitability required that crude output be limited to marketable amounts. Second, pipeline investments required longevity of connected wells that, in turn, required husbanding reservoir energy in selected cases. Legislative favoritism toward nonintegrated producers at the expense of integrated producers, consequently, hurt the cause of conservation and stability.[124]

___

Nostrand, 1925), p. 68. Humble Oil was active in block leasing in Texas and Louisiana. Henrietta Larson et al., *New Horizons,* p. 79.

[124]Referring to Texas's law against petroleum firms' participating in more than one phase, Henrietta Larson and Kenneth Porter raise an interesting point: "Whether a more tolerant attitude toward the experienced companies would have enabled them to operate as a stabilizing and progressive influence it is impossible to say, although the rapid and more orderly development of the oil industry in certain other states

Government Intervention and Cooperation. Short of concentrated ownership, what was needed to mitigate overdrilling and overproduction was reservoir operation *as if* reservoirs were singularly owned. This meant cooperative development. Many writers have automatically assumed that the free market and "individual freedom of action deeply imbedded in the American tradition" prevented individuals from submitting their will to the common will.[125] Although to an extent this may have been true, the fact remains that it was in their self-interest to submit to one plan to decrease drilling costs and increase discounted revenue and capital values. Why, then, was voluntary unitization the exception rather than the rule? Again, government intervention, neglected by writers such as Lovejoy, Homan, and Zimmermann, played a prominent role.

Antitrust Obstacles. State and federal antitrust laws discouraged community action in reservoir development. The offset-drilling requirement invited agreements among neighbors to share oil and gas revenue without drilling offset wells, but antitrust law foreclosed such "restrictive" agreements.[126] Voluntary pooling and unitization were likewise hindered. As early as 1891, eighteen states, including Kansas, Oklahoma, and Texas, had antitrust laws.[127]

---

indicates that such might have been the effect." Larson and Porter, *History of Humble Oil & Refining Company,* p. 21.

[125]Wallace Lovejoy and Paul Homan, *Economic Aspects of Oil Conservation Regulation,* p. 262. This popular explanation blames overproduction and waste on psychological considerations, such as pride of ownership and control and mistrust. But surely the quest for profits would encourage cooperation, buyouts, and sellouts to overcome these surface obstacles. But to the extent other ends were valued more than monetary gain, the economist must view the prevention of such ends as a form of waste and inefficiency since the individual was unable to realize his plans.

Failure to unitize also has been blamed on greed. Posits R. B. Sherman, "Simple greed is sufficient explanation why few examples of unitized operations exist." Sherman, *The Petroleum Industry: An Economic Survey* (Norman: University of Oklahoma Press, 1940), p. 263. Yet greed should encourage lower costs—reduced drilling—and higher capital values—the optimal depletion that unitization could achieve. If, on the other hand, rapid production from many wells was profit maximizing, physical waste was not economic waste.

[126]Offset drilling is defined in chapter 2, pp. 62–63. For a dramatic example of the effect of the offset rule on well location in the Cushing field, see Simon Simon, *Economic Legislation of Taxation* (New York: Arno Press, 1979), p. 6.

[127]See chapter 4, pp. 206–7.

In Texas, as in Kansas, antitrust had long been used in the oil industry, specifically against Standard Oil and its affiliates as discussed in chapters 18 and 22. Other integrated firms were put on notice by Standard's harsh treatment. A 1907 revision prohibited agreements limiting or reducing production of the parties as a felony, subject to stiff fines and expulsion from the state. As Jacqueline Lang Weaver noted, "The Texas antitrust laws originating in 1889 were antithetical to the very concept of unitization."[128] With *political* enforcement, restrictive voluntary agreements represented significant risks for major companies.[129]

The Sherman Act, passed in 1890, made national in scope that "every contract, combination in the form of a trust or otherwise . . . in restraint of trade . . . is hereby declared to be illegal."[130] This cast a legal shadow on cooperative action designed to curtail current oil production since a per se "restraint of trade" would have been committed with a product actively engaged in interstate markets. Writing in the mid-1920s, John Ise noticed the negative effect of antitrust laws on production efficiency.

> To some extent, state and national governments have contributed to the overproduction by refusing to sanction agreements among operators to limit production. The theory of our law has been that such agreements are in restraint of trade, and therefore contrary to the antitrust laws; and, not a few times, state and federal officials have taken alarm at the laudable efforts of oil producers to limit production by agreement.[131]

In 1927, when Seminole's output became an overproduction "problem," law professor Vernon Gibbs forcefully wrote in the *Oil & Gas Journal:*

---

[128]Jacqueline Lang Weaver, *Unitization of Oil and Gas Fields in Texas,* p. 303.

[129]In 1935, Texas Railroad Commission chairman Ernest Thompson expressed his state's anti-monopoly sentiment: "Texas has always disliked monopolies. . . . In any number of ways, its legislation has reflected that attitude." Thompson, "The Purpose and Operation of Laws Prorating Production of Oil among Fields, Pools, and Wells to Balance Output with Demand," *16 Annual Proceedings* (New York: American Petroleum Institute, 1935), p. 21.

[130]The origins of the Sherman Act are discussed in chapter 26, pp. 1526–31.

[131]John Ise, *The United States Oil Policy,* p. 125. Moreover, as Ise points out, the legality of the very act of collecting production statistics from which a concerted plan could be formulated was in doubt.

Conservation and unlimited competition in oil production are diametrically opposed. There will be overcompetition and overproduction until nature's supply is prematurely exhausted unless there is relaxation of the Sherman law's mandate forcing unlimited competition applying to oil production. Conservation depends upon cooperation, cooperation depends upon Congress. An unsound economic condition can be remedied only by the removal of the cause.[132]

The oil community repeatedly tried without success to remove the antitrust deterrent.[133] In 1926, a Committee of Nine, appointed by the FOCB and the American Bar Association, recommended:

> (1) Federal legislation which shall (a) unequivocally declare that agreements for the cooperative development and operation of single pools are not in violation of the Federal antitrust laws, and (b) permit, under suitable safeguards, the making, in times of overproduction, of agreements between oil producers for the curtailment of production. . . .
> (2) Similar legislation by the various oil-producing states.[134]

The fact that the application of antitrust law to the oil industry was a legal gray area did not necessarily mitigate the law's discouraging effect on cooperation. As Will Farish, president of Jersey Standard and a member of the Committee of Nine, expressed it:

> It is all very well to say that [antitrust revision] amounts to asking the authorities to lower an unloaded gun. [But] the world is full of people whom the pulling of a trigger on an unloaded gun pointed straight at them could discomfort.[135]

---

[132]"Oil Industry Must Have Moratorium," *OGJ*, December 1, 1927, p. 143. Norman Nordhauser noted, "The word 'conservation,' as used by industry leaders, became synonymous with the call for a suspension of the antitrust laws, which prevented oil companies from making local, as well as national, arrangements for production control." Nordhauser, *The Quest for Stability*, p. 33.

[133]For a history of these efforts, see Gerald Nash, *United States Oil Policy*, pp. 91–95, 99, 102, 129, 147; and Robert Hardwicke, *Antitrust Laws et al. v. Unit Operation of Oil or Gas Pools*, pp. 53, 91, 95, 100, 154. Also see *NPN*, October 7, 1931, pp. 11–12. For a popularized version of the tension between antitrust law and production reform, complete with dramatic cartoons, see Isaac Marcosson,, "What Price the Sherman Law?" *Saturday Evening Post*, February 1931.

[134]Reprinted in Samuel Pettengill, *Hot Oil*, p. 218.

[135]Quoted in Norman Nordhauser, *The Quest for Stability*, p. 31.

Humble Oil, the most prominent producer in Texas, as did the other major oil companies, had reason to be gun-shy. When Humble Oil asked for an opinion sanctioning the voluntary Yates field agreement, the state attorney general refused and promised only to give notice before prosecution.[136] The year was 1927, a crucial time in the saga of regulation versus cooperation to restrain production. It would not be until 1976, with immunity from antitrust law, that Yates was unitized.

An attempt by Humble to pass a voluntary unitization law in Texas failed in 1929. Going the other way, Texas's 1932 Market-Demand Prorationing Act emphatically upheld the state's antitrust law.[137] Output reductions from unitized operations were "condemned as a monopolistic scheme of the major oil companies" by the Texas legislature and other state politicians.[138] Even Texas's 1949 Voluntary Unitization Act created as much alarm as relief. "Ironically," summarized Jacqueline Lang Weaver, "the 1949 Act which was to encourage unitization leaves Texas operators with the worst of both worlds: a statute which offers limited antitrust immunity only to certain types of cooperative agreements and which thereby increases the antitrust risks of entering into other types of voluntary agreements."[139]

Oklahoma, the other major oil state of the day, was also inhospitable to self-help. For example, in 1933, a senator from Oklahoma introduced a resolution that the Federal Trade Commission investigate the majors to see if predatory pricing was present in light of Gulf's stated policy of acquiring properties from companies in distress.[140]

The antitrust disincentive lingered in the 1940s and the decades beyond. "At the time that economics, technology, and the [Texas] Railroad Commission's orders were pushing producers into the types of operations requiring unitization," stated Weaver, "the threat of antitrust liability for entering into cooperative agreements seemed

[136]Henrietta Larson and Kenneth Porter, *History of Humble Oil & Refining Company,* p. 317.
[137]See Jacqueline Lang Weaver, *Unitization of Oil and Gas Fields in Texas,* p. 62.
[138]Ibid., p. 303.
[139]Ibid., p. 97. Also see chapter 4, pp. 205–11.
[140]*OGJ,* January 26, 1933, p. 12.

to increase."[141] Until a 1983 revision, Texas's antitrust law "essentially condemned voluntary unitization agreements as per se violations of the antitrust laws."[142] And even the 1983 revision left the prosecution door ajar, where it remains today.[143]

The result of the antitrust obstacle was to substitute mandatory "conservation" for "failed" voluntary conservation. As D. T. Armentano concluded, "With voluntary cooperation illegal, the door was opened to State and then Federal 'conservation' regulation."[144]

Tax Incentives. The perception that joint operating agreements would *subject earnings to a double tax,* unlike nonincorporated business income, which was taxable only as individual income, constituted a major government-created disincentive for voluntary associations seeking to counter inefficient production practices. Stated Raymond Myers:

> One of the early objections to unitization was the fear that under a joint operating agreement the operators would form themselves into an association taxable as a corporation under Federal Income Tax Law. . . . Not only would the unit be taxed as a corporation on all taxable income produced by the unit, but all payments made to interest holders would be considered dividends and taxable again as income to the recipients.[145]

An association did not have to be formally incorporated to be taxable as a corporation. Since before 1918, the Internal Revenue Service had included "associations, joint stock companies, and insurance companies" under the term corporation, and joint production ventures were clearly associations.[146] Only later would the "limited liability" attribute differentiate partnership associations from corporate associations for tax purposes.[147] The choice, as perceived by

---

[141]Jacqueline Lang Weaver, *Unitization of Oil and Gas Fields in Texas,* p. 79.

[142]Ibid., p. 131.

[143]Ibid., p. 304.

[144]D. T. Armentano, "Petroleum, Profits, and Prices," p. 11.

[145]Raymond Myers, *The Law of Pooling and Unitization,* vol. 1, pp. 21, 337. Myers refers to joint operating agreements in light of federal tax policy as the "new entity problem."

[146]Ibid., p. 338.

[147]In a 1935 decision, the Supreme Court listed five characteristics of associations taxable as corporations: (1) continuing existence, (2) centralized management, (3) transferable interests, (4) property titleholder, and (5) limited liability. *Morissey* v. *Commissioner,* 296 U.S. 344 (1935). See Raymond Myers, *The Law of Pooling and Unitization,* vol. 1, pp. 341–42.

many, was to operate individually and have income taxed only as personal income or to operate collectively and be subject to both a business tax and a personal tax on income from oil and gas production. Only in the late 1940s would cooperative unit agreements finally be declared noncorporations for tax purposes.[148] Although this was probably less of a deterrent to voluntary pooling and unitization than was the specter of antitrust prosecution, it made concerted production decidedly less attractive given the double-digit amount of the corporate tax after 1914.

A second tax issue that contributed to drilling inefficiencies involved the depletion allowance as interpreted between 1918 and 1926. The Bureau of Internal Revenue defined discovery value as the quantity of oil contained in a 160-acre area. This led to several perversities. By drilling three other wells at the far boundaries of the 160-acre square, an operator could claim four discovery values from the same area. Other operators, moreover, could drill offset wells at each of the four locations and also receive tax benefits from the same reservoir.[149]

Federal-Land Restrictions. Another hindrance to efficient production practices involved cooperative development on federal lands. Until 1930, unit operations were prohibited altogether. Thereafter, they were subject to approval by the secretary of the interior, but approval proved difficult.[150] Not only did submitted plans encounter bureaucratic delays of several months to several years, they were rejected if operators failed to grant the Department of the Interior the power to dictate the rate and quantity of production. By 1935,

---

[148]Income Tax Division Ruling (I.T. hereafter) 3930 (1948), reaffirmed a year later by I.T. 3948, ruled that joint operating agreements in oil and gas production were not for "joint profit" since "profits arise not from mere extraction or from processing of mineral, but from the sale thereof." Raymond Myers, *The Law of Pooling and Unitization,* vol. 1, pp. 343–44. Also see Robert Shepherd, "Some Problems of Administering Oil and Gas Properties Having Large Number of Owners," *12 Oil and Gas Institute* (New York: Matthew Bender, 1961), pp. 243–47. The importance of the rulings was reflected in a 1956 Arizona law stating, "Any unit agreement approved by the commission shall contain language suggested by the Internal Revenue Service under I.T. 3930 and I.T. 3948 so that owners in the unitized area will not be held taxable as a corporation." Arizona Revised Statutes, Title 27.

[149]Simon Simon, *Economic Legislation of Taxation,* pp. 144–52. Discovery depletion is described in chapter 7, pp. 336–37.

[150]See the discussion in chapter 6, pp. 269–70.

only 6 of 500 submitted unitization plans had been approved, leaving drainage competition and waste as the only alternative for public-land operators.[151]

Conservation Law Disincentives. State regulatory policies discouraged community development by unintentionally creating an "either-or" between voluntary and mandatory wellhead production reform. In Texas and other market-demand proration states, allowable assignments designed to allow poorer wells to produce profitably replaced natural incentives for forming unit operations to reduce drilling costs and, with rate-sensitive reservoirs, increase recoverability. Robert Hardwicke, a leading proponent of state conservation law predicated on correlative rights, admitted that "frequently those who refuse to enter into a unit-operation program do so because of an advantage obtained as a result of a regulation by an administrative agency, such as that which fixes allowables for wells or properties which are relatively greater than those given to comparable wells or properties of others."[152]

Well-spacing exceptions, which were the rule rather than the exception in Texas,[153] gave the recalcitrant small producer a license to drain his more widely spaced neighbors. Once the wells were sunk, the incentive to unitize diminished. "The opportunities for profitable obstructionism," concluded Jacqueline Lang Weaver, "were enhanced by the regulatory system that gave independent producers and small tract owners a disproportionate share of the oil and gas in Texas reservoirs."[154]

Not only did legislative and administrative regulation discourage self-help. In Texas, the judiciary was hostile to the implied right of oil operators to pool.[155] The result of the aforementioned disincentives to cooperative development was noted by Herman Kaveler.

---

[151]William Holloway, "Unit Operations of Public Lands," 3 *Oil and Gas Institute* (New York: Matthew Bender, 1952), p. 239.

[152]Robert Hardwicke, *Antitrust Laws et al. v. Unit Operation of Oil or Gas Pools*, p. 155. This was particularly true in Texas where small-tract drilling offered substantial advantage over well spacing based on the reservoir as a unit.

[153]See chapter 4, pp. 143–44.

[154]Jacqueline Lang Weaver, *Unitization of Oil and Gas Fields in Texas*, p. 109. Weaver calls this a "vested . . . regulatory inheritance" (p. 108).

[155]Ibid., p. 206.

[By 1933] the subject of unit-operation passed out of the light of live interest. The reason was that "proration" under state conservation laws was working well, and the days of crisis had passed.[156]

Government Intervention and General Instability

The most unstable period in petroleum production occurred in conjunction with the most unstable period in American business history—the Great Depression. Although this point has been glossed over by petroleum conservation writers as coincidental or a foregone conclusion, it is important to fully appreciate the role of government in the problems of petroleum production.

The Boom: 1921–29. The maladjustment between consumer demand and producer output did not begin with the stock market crash in October 1929. It began with the business boom that resulted from easy-money policies during the early and mid-1920s. The stated goal of the Federal Reserve Act of 1913 was to "furnish an elastic currency," and authorities used their power liberally.[157] New money, entering the economy exclusively as bank business credit, artificially lowered interest rates, which led to investments and speculation that were unsound compared with the investment discipline exerted by nonexpansive monetary policy and market interest rates. Malinvestments centered around durable-good manufacturing; speculation centered around stocks, bonds, land, and *oil mineral leasing*. It is true that advances in geology and geophysics in the 1920s were the primary reason for prolific finds in Oklahoma and Texas, but the "easy-money" investment atmosphere certainly encouraged subsequent lease speculation and small-lot drilling. Statistics are unavailable to quantitatively express how much extra bank credit and venture capital was involved in exploration and production as a result of monetary inflation, but an understanding of causal relations suggests that the artificial boom of the general economy contributed to the oil production boom of 1926–29.[158]

---

[156]Herman Kaveler, "Unitization," in *History of Petroleum Engineering*, p. 1179.

[157]Public Law 43, 38 Stat. 251 (1913). See Lionel Robbins, *The Great Depression* (1934; reprint, Salem, N.H.: Ayer, 1976), pp. 10, 44–49. Also see Murray Rothbard, *America's Great Depression* (Los Angeles: Nash Publishing, 1963), chap. 4.

[158]The fact that lease speculation and high drilling activity continued into the depression seems to suggest that fundamental economics and not inflationary credit drew resources into oil exploration and production. But import restrictions and market-demand proration subsidized oil producers to allow them to continue their predepression activities. Reinflation was also at work. Chase Bank vice-president and petroleum lender Joseph Pogue complained in 1938 that "cheap and redundant

The Depression Years: 1929–38. The painful aftermath of the October 23–29 stock market crash of 1929, consisting of credit contractions and plummeting consumer demand, caught many major oil companies with high inventories and expanded operations.[159] Accompanying falling demand and full inventories was the development of the huge East Texas field. With a new federal gasoline tax and rising state gasoline taxes further reducing demand, and with pessimistic expectations for the future, conditions were ripe for rapid development from low-cost wells, depressed prices, and the "waste" that low prices made possible.[160] While bountiful production was a blessing from nature to the consumer, and certainly for the East Texas community,[161] a conservation problem was created, in part, by governmental measures that depressed demand from its free-market level. With higher demand from a stable, growing economy, better business conditions would have existed for a transition to single-plan reservoir development.[162]

Summary. The legal framework of the rule of capture, coupled with a faulty conception of reservoir mechanics and the infant state of the petroleum market, created a barrier against what later became recognized as efficient production. As technical progress brought forth a new age in petroleum supply and demand, a series of federal and state interventions prevented the industry from making needed adjustments away from drainage competition and marginal-well development toward single-plan pool production and fewer, better situated wells. The free market, guided by market entrepreneurs practicing economic calculation, was set to make the transition to formal cooperation but was prevented from doing so by misguided government intervention and special-interest politics.

---

credit" was "overcapitalizing the production department." *TNEC Petroleum Hearings,* p. 228.

[159]William Kemnitzer, *Rebirth of Monopoly,* p. 122.

[160]See chapter 23, pp. 1370–74, for state and federal gasoline tax rates.

[161]East Texas was pulled out of the depression by oil. See, for example, *NPN,* July 8, 1931, pp. 24–25. The prosperity of East Texas was also felt in the emerging capital of the oil industry, Houston.

[162]For an analysis of federal policies prolonging the depression, see Murray Rothbard, *America's Great Depression,* pp. 167–95; and idem, "Herbert Hoover and the Myth of Laissez-Faire," in *New History of Leviathan,* ed. Ronald Radish and Murray Rothbard (New York: E. P. Dutton, 1972), pp. 111–45.

Undoubtedly, there would have been many more cooperative agreements and greater scientific interest in the new theories of reservoir development without the disincentives of antitrust law, corporate taxation, state conservation law, first-purchaser regulation, federal-land policy, and general economic growth. Most certainly there would have been a "cleaning out" of inefficient, underscaled producers by stronger companies able to practice controlled production had not shutdowns and allowable programs replaced market incentives in the crucial "overproduction" period. This is not to suggest that unit operations and consolidation would have entirely replaced drainage competition from offset wells and open-flow production. As powerful as the quest for profits is, not all opportunities for efficient production would have been noticed, and still fewer opportunities would have been seized, for several reasons.[163]

One is *prohibitive transaction costs*—the difficulty of obtaining total (or nearly total)[164] agreement for certain reservoirs with diffuse ownership, particularly where relative shares are plagued by estimation problems. The second reason is *entrepreneurial error*—the failure of less talented businesspeople to recognize profit opportunities. The result of forgone profits or losses, however, works to discourage these situations—to fight "market failure"—while profits and improvements in knowledge and experience encourage individual and general gains. The unregulated market, as explained in the opening chapter, is not perfect but an institution promoting the systematic discovery and correction of error. In this light, it must be compared with real-world alternatives, namely government intervention, not a hypothetical standard of perfection.

---

[163]Lost oil associated with underground waste, it should be mentioned, is not necessarily gone forever. Advanced secondary and tertiary recovery techniques have dislodged oil once deemed unrecoverable. In the future, more oil lost from earlier inefficient production practices can be expected to become extractable. See E. B. Miller, "Old Fields Never Die," in Institute on Exploration and Economics of the Petroleum Industry, *Economics of the Petroleum Industry* (Houston: Gulf Publishing, 1965), vol. 3, pp. 139–50.

[164]It has been argued that the benefits of unit operations over drainage competition can accrue even without 100 percent agreement. But certainly a large portion of the reservoir would need to be under singular control to profitably absorb the drainage of recalcitrant operators. See the discussion in Allen King, "Pooling and Unitization of Oil and Gas Leases," *Michigan Law Review* (January 1948): 327–28.

Zimmermann's challenge has been met. The effective working of a free market in petroleum production, even based upon the rule of capture, can be recognized, and a successful conclusion to the industry's previous problems can be imagined had not government intervention been in place. Chapter 4 turns to the wasteful consequences created by the "solution" of state conservation law.

4. Modern State Conservation Regulation Reconsidered

The legal authority of state regulation was articulated by Supreme Court Justice Brown in 1894: "To justify the State in . . . interposing its authority in behalf of the public, it must appear, first, that the interests of the public . . . require such interference; and second, that the means are reasonably necessary for the accomplishment of the purpose, and not unduly oppressive upon individuals."[1] Upon this authority, forty states, thirty-two of which have produced oil, have passed petroleum statutes regulating the production phase.[2] Of the states with conservation regulation, only Missouri, Virginia, Iowa, and Maine are not members of the Interstate Oil Compact Commission (IOCC).[3]

Federal regulation and administration would coordinate state control in the post-1936 era as they had during the East Texas hot-oil war of the 1931–35 period. Subagencies within the Department of the Interior led the way. The Bureau of Mines assisted state agencies with market-demand estimates. The Federal Tender Board, which played a primary role in the hot-oil war, came under the Petroleum Conservation Division in 1937.[4] Within the Interior Department, the Federal Petroleum Board was created in 1942, the same year the Connally Hot-Oil Act was extended indefinitely by Congress. With the termination of the Petroleum Administration for War in May 1946, and a desire among officials to consolidate the petroleum

---

[1]*Lauton v. Steele*, 152 U.S. 133 at 137 (1894). The Supreme Court would later find that state rather than federal courts had jurisdiction over fact issues concerning petroleum conservation law. This internalized most challenges to such regulation to contribute to the politicization of conservation law.

[2]For a state-by-state summary of historical regulation and an updated summary of present regulation, see appendices C and F, pp. 1934–35, 1948–49.

[3]Of these four states, Missouri and Virginia have produced oil; Iowa and Maine have not.

[4]See chapter 12, pp. 650–51.

activities of over thirty agencies, the Oil and Gas Division was created within the Interior Department as the focal point of federal
petroleum activities. On the industry side, the National Petroleum
Council was formed in the same year to assist the Oil and Gas
Division, which in 1958 merged with the Geological Survey.

Other federal measures vitally assisted the effort to limit production. Congress sanctioned the IOCC, which meant that Texas, Oklahoma, New Mexico, Kansas, and other oil states could openly discuss
and informally coordinate their market-demand programs. Oil
imports were limited from 1959 through the early 1970s under the
Mandatory Oil Import Program. Without import regulation, domestic cartelization would have been difficult if not impossible.[5]

State petroleum conservation law has had three main aims: abatement of surface nuisances, prevention of natural-resource waste, and
protection of correlative rights. Regulatory activity, correspondingly,
has centered around preventing external damage, restricting production, and mandating cooperative production. In addition, two auxiliary rules evolved: the right of the marginal-well owner to produce
profitably and the right of the owner of each well to receive equal
treatment from economic and political interests.[6] These state oil regulations represent, in Erich Zimmermann's estimation, "one of the
most remarkable systems of economic control ever attempted in
this country."[7]

The Prevention of External Damage

History

Protecting freshwater from oil and saltwater was the original end
of production regulation. Beginning in the late nineteenth century,
"surface nuisance" laws, which required casing wells in progress
and plugging abandoned wells, were passed in a number of states.[8]

---

[5]See chapter 13, pp. 726–27, 734–35, 764.

[6]Limits to state intervention have resulted from court challenges based on deprivation of property without "due process," denial of equal protection under the law,
impairment of contractual obligations, and interference with interstate commerce.
See Leslie Moses, "The Constitutional, Legislative, and Judicial Growth of Oil and
Gas Conservation Statutes," *Mississippi Law Journal* (March 1941): 363–64.

[7]Erich Zimmermann, *Conservation in the Production of Petroleum* (New Haven, Conn.:
Yale University Press, 1957), p. 139.

[8]See chapter 3, pp. 81–82.

Regulations combatting well-site pollution have remained unchanged in intent and become more rigorous and specific in application. In the post-1948 period, over twenty states upgraded their regulations in response to the growing number of abandoned polluting wells, operating wells taking on saltwater, and heightened demand for freshwater as a result of industrialization.[9] Revised statutes commonly provide for plugging oil wells, limiting saltwater disposal, prohibiting certain practices that contribute to water pollution, and extending the authority of state conservation commissions over resources such as coal and water.[10]

Regulations that affect saltwater disposal are among the most important revisions in modern well-site pollution law. Earthen pits, once the most common disposal method, have been legislatively discouraged in favor of reinjection into underground reservoirs. Texas, for example, prohibited the use of earthen pits in 1969.[11] Some states have virtually outlawed saltwater disposal in streams and rivers and granted tax incentives to develop underground saltwater disposal systems.[12]

Abatement of surface nuisances encompasses not only oil or saltwater invasion of freshwater but well-site accidents due to fires, blowouts, well shootings, cave-ins, and land subsidence. To prevent fires, states often require waste oil and other flammable materials to be placed away from well tanks and separators. In Texas, for example, blowout prevention rules dictate mud circulation, mud-fluid density, bradenhead pressure, check-valve maintenance, and on-location blowout equipment.[13] To prevent cave-ins, states with underground coal mines near petroleum deposits have prescribed

---

[9]Stephen McDonald, *Petroleum Conservation in the United States* (Baltimore: Johns Hopkins University Press, 1971), pp. 146–47.

[10]Ibid., p. 143.

[11]Saltwater leakage not only contaminates freshwater but surrounding soil, vegetation, and wildlife. See Ira Butler, "The Oil and Gas Industry and Water Conservation," *16 Oil and Gas Institute* (New York: Matthew Bender, 1965), pp. 301–42. Also see Jacqueline Lang Weaver, *Unitization of Oil and Gas Fields in Texas* (Washington, D.C.: Resources for the Future, 1986), pp. 170–72.

[12]Stephen McDonald, *Petroleum Conservation in the United States*, pp. 145–47.

[13]See Texas Railroad Commission, "Rules Having Statewide General Application to Oil, Gas and Geothermal Resource Operations within the State of Texas," Austin, 1981, pp. 59–66.

rules to prevent drill bits from piercing coal deposits.[14] Well shooting—lowering explosive materials into the well to dislodge oil pockets—has been regulated as a dangerous activity.[15] The California
Subsidence Act, passed in 1958, mandated cooperative development
to maintain bottom hole pressure to prevent land from sinking into
water areas.

The model statute of the IOCC recommends that its member
states require

> the drilling, casing, operating and plugging of wells in such manner
> as to prevent (a) the escape of oil and gas out of the reservoir into
> another formation, (b) the detrimental intrusion of water into an Oil
> or Gas Reservoir that is avoidable by efficient operations, (c) the
> pollution of fresh water supplies by Oil, Gas, or salt water, and (d)
> blowouts, cave-ins, seepages, and fires.[16]

As of 1984, all thirty-six member states (and two nonmember states,
Missouri and Virginia) required drilling permits, and thirty-one
members (and Missouri and Virginia) required compliance bonds
to ensure proper well casing and plugging.[17]

Evaluation

The alternative to surface-nuisance regulation is a private-property approach that recognizes pollutive damage as invasive of
another person's property and therefore subject to restitution. The
nonregulatory tort approach was formulated in *Fletcher* v. *Rylands*,
an 1866 English case:

> The person whose grass or corn is eaten down by the escaping cattle
> of his neighbour, or whose mine is flooded by the water from his
> neighbour's reservoir, or whose cellar is invaded by the filth of his
> neighbour's privy, or whose habitation is made unhealthy by the
> fumes and noisome vapours of his neighbour's alkali works, is dam-
> nified without any fault of his own; and it seems but reasonable

[14]Such states include Colorado and California (1915), Pennsylvania (1921), Illinois
(1925), West Virginia (1929), Ohio (1931), and Kentucky (1932).

[15]Louisiana (1924), Texas (1925), Indiana (1927), and Mississippi (1932), among
other states, have established procedures and conditions for well shooting.

[16]Interstate Oil Compact Commission, *A Form for an Oil and Gas Conservation Statute*
(Oklahoma City: IOCC, 1981) pp. 7–8.

[17]Interstate Oil Compact Commission, *Summary of State Statutes and Regulations for
Oil and Gas Production* (Oklahoma City: IOCC, 1979). States not requiring bonding
are Arkansas, Kansas, Louisiana (in certain cases), Mississippi, and Pennsylvania.

and just that the neighbour, who has brought something on his own property which was not naturally there, harmless to others so long as it is confined to his own property, but which he knows to be mischievous if it gets on his neighbour's, should be obliged to make good the damage which ensues if he does not succeed in confining it to his own property. But for his act in bringing it there no mischief could have accrued, and it seems but just that he should at his peril keep it there so that no mischief may accrue, or answer for the natural and anticipated consequences. And upon authority, this we think is established to be the law whether the things so brought be beasts, or water, or filth, or stenches.[18]

While some states accepted strict liability, other states tended toward a pragmatic standard that forgave invasion if a higher societal good resulted. Important in this regard was a 1886 Pennsylvania case, *Pennsylvania Coal Co. v. Sanderson*, wherein water pollution caused by a coal mine was legally forgiven to promote industry growth, given that no ready alternative existed for disposing of the pollutive matter.[19] With tort liability weakened, the door was opened to the regulatory approach to combatting nuisances.

The regulatory approach to surface and subsurface nuisances has several distinct drawbacks compared with a market-oriented tort approach:

1. A politicized environment in which firms lobby for stringent regulations to achieve competitive advantages; strong firms, for example, may desire or at least accept costly regulations to penalize competitors less able to absorb additional costs;
2. Potentially low standards created by industry pressures;
3. A potentially higher incidence of damage since the regulations represent a minimum standard past which actual damage is legally forgiven;
4. Monolithic rules that are inflexible in particular situations; and
5. The cost of creating and administering the regulations.

In addition, once the regulation is in place, firms that comply are at a disadvantage compared with grandfathered firms, noncomplying

---

[18]L.R.1 Ex 265 at 280 (1866).

[19]113 Pa. 126 (1886). See the discussion in John Knodell, "Liability for Pollution of Surface and Underground Waters," *12 Oil and Gas Institute* (New York: Matthew Bender, 1967), pp. 37–39.

firms, or new entrants should the regulation be revoked. Consequently, within the regulated industry, inertia develops to make the regulation both comprehensive and perpetual.[20] Alternatively, the private-property approach bypasses political issues and before-the-fact generalized standards to focus on the act of wrongdoing itself. Retributive penalties fit the tort, while discouraging its occurrence prospectively.[21] Contractual norms may also stipulate predrilling bonds or insurance protection in case an accident occurs.

The Restriction and Control of Production

Shutdowns

The most severe production restriction a state conservation agency can impose is a well, pool, or field shutdown. This is legally possible when state authorities determine that waste is occurring where ordinary regulation failed to control practices considered wasteful. "Oil holidays" have afforded regulators time to bring the insurgent activities under control, while addressing the "waste" problem in the interim.

History. The most dramatic and far-reaching shutdowns occurred in 1931 when the East Texas and Oklahoma City fields were closed by martial law and declared "military zones" by the respective state governors. On July 28, 1931, Oklahoma governor William Murray dramatically announced that if crude did not reach $1 per barrel within several days, he would close the field.[22] This came to pass and set an example Texas governor Ross Sterling soon followed.[23] The Oklahoma City closing lasted from August 4 until October 10; the East Texas shutdown lasted from August 17 until September 2.[24] Both fields reopened under strict production allowables and military

---

[20]For a more recent example, see "EPA's Drive to Loosen Some Rules Angers Firms That Have Complied," *Wall Street Journal,* September 23, 1982, p. 33.

[21]For further consideration of the tort versus regulatory approach, see chapter 21, pp. 1268–74.

[22]*National Petroleum News,* July 29, 1931, p. 23. Cited hereafter as *NPN.*

[23]See chapter 3, pp. 93–94.

[24]Texas's martial-law shutdown was successfully challenged in *Constantin* v. *Smith,* 57 F.2d 227 (E.D. Tex.), aff'd sub nom. *Sterling* v. *Constantin,* 287 U.S. 378 (1932). In the same year, the Ritz-Canton pool in Kansas was shut down by orders given on August 22 and 26. This closing did not require military intervention. The East Texas and Oklahoma City fields would again be closed by military command.

presence, yet considerable hot-oil production, particularly in East Texas, continued through 1935.[25] The next major shutdown occurred in Kansas on August 15, 1939, when the State Corporation Commission closed 19,268 wells for fifteen days to decrease crude output by a targeted 2,460,000 barrels to meet "demand."[26] Almost to the day, fifteen-day shutdowns were ordered in New Mexico and Texas to stabilize prices.[27] Louisiana, Oklahoma, and Arkansas followed suit in a concerted interstate effort to cut output and raise price.[28] Illinois bucked the trend and allowed liberal production, while unregulated California watched from afar. Unlike earlier experiences, police units were not necessary and few injunctions were filed.[29]

Subsequent large-scale shutdowns were in response to natural-gas venting in Texas. On March 17, 1947, the Texas Railroad Commission (TRC) issued a "flare gas order" for the Seeligson field. This order shut down all 615 oil wells until "all the casinghead gas produced incident to such production is made available and is used for one or more of the lawful uses as set out for sweet gas."[30] Legal uses were confined to lighting, fuel, "efficient" chemical manufacturing, and reservoir reinjection. With natural gas in demand, the TRC challenged majors and independents alike by requiring that the gas either be reinjected into the reservoir or channeled into pipelines.

[25]See chapter 12, pp. 637–51.

[26]"Whereas it appears that the immediate production of crude oil tends to create waste because of unstable conditions in the petroleum industry, an emergency is hereby declared" (Emergency Order no. 196, 1939). Quoted in Rosser Malone, "New Mexico, 1938–1948," in American Bar Association, *Conservation of Oil and Gas: A Legal History, 1948,* ed. Blakely M. Murphy (Chicago: ABA, 1949), p. 327. Cited hereafter as *Legal History,* 1949.

[27]A year before, Texas had ordered a six-week sabbatical shutdown of its 79,000 oil wells to stabilize price. *Business Week,* February 5, 1938, p. 22.

[28]Henrietta Larson and Kenneth Porter, *History of Humble Oil & Refining Company* (New York: Harper and Brothers, 1959), p. 532. All told, an estimated two-thirds of U.S. production was idled. *Business Week,* August 26, 1939, p. 18.

[29]In Kansas, the producers "did it apparently willingly, without scratching or biting and without a single attempt at subterfuge. It has been done without policing the oil field. The cooperation has been 100% from every single interest in the industry." Jay Kyle, "Kansas, 1937–1948," in *Legal History,* 1949, p. 165.

[30]Robert Sullivan, "Texas," in American Bar Association, *Conservation of Oil and Gas: A Legal History, 1958,* ed. Robert Sullivan (Chicago: ABA, 1960), p. 231. Cited hereafter as *Legal History,* 1960.

In the *Shell Oil* case the same year, the commission's order was upheld.[31] In 1948, the TRC closed down sixteen fields from December 1948 until April 1949 until gas flaring was eliminated. The order was sustained in the *Flour Bluff* case in 1949.[32]

Another shutdown to prevent casinghead gas wastage occurred in April 1953 when the TRC shut down an estimated 2,400 wells in the Sprayberry field. In the *Rowan* case, the Texas Supreme Court invalidated the entire order on grounds that the commission shut down legal wells along with illegal ones.[33] In response, the commission achieved the same result by issuing a lowered oil allowable on July 1, 1953, that reduced gas output to levels easily absorbed into legal uses.

As it was with crude oil, the power to prevent natural-gas wastage was firmly established. The shutdown, in real or potential form, was the ultimate enforcer.

Evaluation. For advocates of private property, free markets, and the simple right to produce, the shutdown is the most objectional weapon in the arsenal of state conservation law. It denies—however temporarily—oil and gas producers the right to a livelihood. And to the extent a true conservation problem exists, the shutdown annuls market processes that shift resources from wasteful to efficient producers.

The martial-law shutdowns in Oklahoma and Texas in the dark days of 1931 are particularly open to censure, not only from an economic perspective but from moral and legal viewpoints as well. Andrew Bruce, former chief justice of the North Dakota Supreme Court, wrote shortly after the martial-law declarations:

> We cannot allow our executives themselves to make the law and to enforce it by means of their control over state militias. No matter how good the motives may have been or difficult the situation . . . the militia has been called out to enforce a gubernatorial fiat and not to enforce any court mandate. . . . America is not yet ready for Oliver Cromwells or for Mussolinis.
>
> The danger in the Texas and Oklahoma experiments lies in the fact that they may elsewhere be repeated with disastrous consequences and not only in regard to oil but other personal and property

[31]*Railroad Commission* v. *Shell Oil Co.*, 206 S.W.2d 235 (1947).

[32]*Railroad Commission* v. *Flour Bluff Oil Co.*, 219 S.W.2d 506 (Tex. Civ. App. 1949).

[33]*Railroad Commission* v. *Rowan Oil Co.*, 195 Tex. 439, 259 S.W.2d 173 (1953).

rights. . . . There is such a thing as playing with fire, even in the most foolish of all games—the game of politics.[34]

Given the dangerous precedent of Governors Murray and Sterling, what were their motives? Was it a case of "the ends justify the means"? Murray's explicitly stated reason was price—to shut down the Oklahoma City field until the price of oil reached $1 per barrel. This is what most of the industry desired, and it meant more tax revenue for Oklahoma, which was $3 million in debt.[35] Governor Sterling of Texas, in his martial-law proclamation, declared that "a state of insurrection against the conservation laws existed" and that mass violence loomed because depressed prices threatened many small producers.[36] But why did not authorities allow market forces to correct the chaotic situation and increase police protection to ensure that property rights were respected in the event of violence fueled by widespread business failures and ownership rearrangements? Sterling, like Murray, wanted not only to stabilize price but to preserve the status quo of predominantly independent control of the field.[37] The shutdowns may have been politically expedient, but they prevented a free-market resolution of the problem and set the stage for the inferior "solution" of state conservation regulation.

Well-Spacing Restrictions

History. Well-spacing regulation began in 1905 when Kansas forbade wells within 100 feet of railroad rights-of-way. In 1919, under pressure from major companies, the TRC enacted Rule 37 forbidding wells within 300 feet of each other and 150 feet from property lines

---

[34]Andrew Bruce, "The Oil Situation and the Military," *American Bar Association Journal* (June 1931): 643–44.

[35]Governor Murray's ambition to be the Democratic nominee in the 1932 presidential election was also prominent in this decision. The *National Petroleum News* reported several weeks before the shutdown, "He was eager to go ahead [with the shutdown], for he is a 'publicity hound' and such an order would give him front page notice all over the nation." *NPN*, July 29, 1931, p. 24. Murray also threatened to build state refineries because of a dearth of $1 per barrel oil bids. *NPN*, September 9, 1931, p. 27, and August 12, 1931, p. 29.

[36]Norman Nordhauser, *The Quest for Stability* (New York, Garland Publishing, 1979), p. 84.

[37]Andrew Bruce, "The Oil Situation and the Military," p. 643.

unless "showing good cause, and provided no injustice be done."[38] While other spacing laws such as those of Arkansas (1923), Montana (1927), Michigan (1929), and California (1931) were passed to reduce fire hazards and pollution, other spacing minimums, beginning with a 10-acre rule in Texas (1931) and Oklahoma (1935), were primarily intended to arrest reservoir waste from offset well drainage and prevent unnecessary drilling. Laws with similar intent were passed in New Mexico (1935) and Louisiana (1936).

In the 1930s, 10-acre rules were often widened to 20 acres to discourage drainage competition. During World War II, well-spacing minimums were widened to 40 acres to conserve materials.[39] After the war, Wyoming (1951), Alaska (1955), and some states introduced well spacing, while other states, such as Texas in 1962, revised their laws toward the 40-acre standard. Correlative rights and waste prevention, two major tenets of modern conservation law, replaced the original aim of well-spacing law of preventing external damage.

Proponents of conservation law have identified well spacing as "among the most needed and effective means to prevent all forms of waste and to protect correlative rights."[40] As of 1984, twenty-nine states had well-spacing regulations, twenty-five of which are of a predetermined distance—commonly 40 acres per oil well and 640 acres per gas well. Four states had no predetermined acreage minimums but established spacing by hearing.[41] While most of these states employ spacing restrictions in conjunction with other regulations, nine states, including Alaska and California, rely solely on spacing law to regulate production. On the other hand, nine states

[38]Robert Hardwicke, "Oil Well Spacing Regulations and Protection of Property Rights in Texas," *Texas Law Review* (December 1952): 105. The "no injustice" clause was strengthened in 1921 to allow spacing exceptions to prevent waste and protect correlative rights. In *Oxford Oil Co.* v. *Atlantic Oil Co.*, 277 U.S. 585 (1928), the U.S. Supreme Court rejected the Fourteenth Amendment "due process" argument to uphold Texas's spacing rule.

[39]See chapter 5, pp. 239–40.

[40]Interstate Oil Conservation Commission, *A Study of Conservation of Oil and Gas in the United States* (Oklahoma City: IOCC, 1964), p. 180.

[41]See appendix F, pp. 1948–49. The most lenient spacing rule is in California where one well every acre is allowed; the most strict is in West Virginia where both oil and gas wells are allowed one per 640 acres. In many of the states with fixed distances, "field rules" are made for new discoveries that allow exceptions.

have no spacing regulations and rely instead on incentives provided by allowables regulation to achieve a similar end.[42]

The Texas Experience. State spacing minimums historically have been weakened by commission leniency and court decisions. In Texas, political pressure from small-tract drillers influenced the TRC to place correlative rights above conservation per se. The result was the "profligate grant of Rule 37 exception wells during the era from the 1930s to the 1960s."[43]

Small-tract drilling in Texas was allowed by the following rules.

1. The "separate tract" (or "fair share") rule, which allowed well-spacing exceptions, even if wasteful, to prevent drainage by other wells. One well was allowed for every separately owned tract, no matter how small.[44]

2. The "equidistant offset" rule, which granted the operator an exception to drill a well as close to his property line as a neighbor's well to prevent drainage.[45] This rule penalized large lease-holders and benefited small landowners since the latter generally had more neighboring offset wells than the former.

3. The "eight-times-area" rule, which allowed operators of any tract to obtain additional well permits if other wells located within an area eight times as large as his tract were more closely spaced than his to expose him to drainage. Not only did this favor leaseholders who had more well-intensive neighbors over those who did not, it incited a prolonged adjustment process whereby each permit changed the well-density average to create further exceptions to begin the process anew.[46]

---

[42]Of the nine states, only Colorado and Arkansas have significant production.

[43]Jacqueline Lang Weaver, *Unitization of Oil and Gas Fields in Texas* (Washington, D.C.: Resources for the Future, 1986), p. 294.

[44]*Daily v. Railroad Commission,* 133 S.W.2d 219 (Tex. Civ. App. 1939); *Magnolia Petroleum Co.* v. *Railroad Commission,* 120 S.W.2d 553 (Tex. Civ. App. 1938); and *Railroad Commission* v. *Humble Oil and Ref. Co.,* 193 S.W.2d 824 (Tex. Civ. App. 1946). The last case, known as the *Hawkins* case, reaffirmed the right of small tracts to produce while adding another important right discussed below.

[45]David Prindle, *Petroleum Politics and the Texas Railroad Commission* (Austin: University of Texas Press, 1981), p. 51.

[46]The Texas Railroad Commission arbitrarily arrived at this rule for the East Texas field. Howard Williams, "Conservation of Oil and Gas," *Harvard Law Review* (May 1952): 1165.

4. The "discretion" rule, which allowed the TRC to grant exceptions on the broad basis of preventing waste or protecting correlative rights, or both. In the pre-1934 period, exceptions were routinely granted when personally appealed for. After this time, power struggles and block voting among the three commissioners influenced the majority decision in an arbitrary, yet lenient, manner.[47]

As can be imagined, small-tract drilling loopholes were exploited. An eyewitness to the early development of the East Texas oil field in the 1930s observed, "Many lease owners, in order to increase the number of wells on their leases, formed dummy corporations to whom they sold off a portion of the acreage to enable the new corporation to apply for permits to drill wells that, under the spacing rule, would not have been permissible."[48] In response, the Texas Supreme Court in 1937 established the "Century Doctrine" to disallow exceptions for tracts subdivided and sold after oil was discovered. An exception could be granted only if the *reconstituted* area was greater than the spacing-law minimum.[49] But opportunistic behavior would continue. In 1959, for example, a Rule 37 exception was granted an operator to drill a $75,000 well on a 0.625-acre tract estimated to contain, if strictly proportioned, only $250 in oil reserves.[50]

Throughout its history, Rule 37 has been the most litigated of all state conservation regulations. Between 1931 and 1950 in East Texas alone, over 13,000 wells were drilled in exception to the spacing minimum.[51] More recently, approximately 85 percent of all spacing exceptions (or an average of 2,657 exceptions a year) have been granted by the TRC as seen in table 4.1.

It has been estimated that over 70 percent of all oil and gas wells in Texas violate the spacing rules of 40 acres for oil and 640 acres for gas.[52]

[47]David Prindle, *Petroleum Politics and the Texas Railroad Commission,* pp. 47–49.

[48]Harry Harter, *East Texas Oil Parade* (San Antonio: Naylor, 1934), p. 152.

[49]*Railroad Commission* v. *Magnolia Petroleum Co.,* 105 S.W.2d 787 (Tex. Civ. App. 1937).

[50]*Foster* v. *Railroad Commission,* 326 S.W.2d 533 (Tex. Civ. App. 1959). Many examples exist of huge differentials between in-place reserves of small-tract drillers and potential revenue from an allowable assignment to the wells.

[51]Stuart Buckley, ed., *Petroleum Conservation* (Dallas: E. J. Storm, 1951), p. 263.

[52]Michel Halbouty, "Conservation and the Public Interest," in *Ahead of His Time: Michael T. Halbouty Speaks to the People,* ed. James Clark (Houston: Gulf Publishing, 1971). Halbouty states, "Today the United States has about 10% of the world's oil

Table 4.1
FILED AND GRANTED WELL-SPACING EXCEPTIONS

Year	Exceptions Requested	Exceptions Granted	Percentage
1976	2,250	2,197	98
1977	2,765	2,493	90
1978	2,319	2,042	88
1979	2,809	2,392	85
1980	3,769	3,031	80
1981	3,791	2,725	72
1982	3,522	2,564	73
1983	3,530	2,881	82
1984	3,775	3,592	95
Total	28,530	23,917	84

SOURCE: Texas Railroad Commission Hearing Files. Personal communication with the commission.

Evaluation. The problematical nature of well spacing results from the tension between waste prevention and correlative rights. To prevent waste, from the conservationist point of view, small-tract operators must be prevented from overdrilling and overproducing. Yet to uphold correlative rights, the same operators must be permitted to recover their "fair share" of commonly owned reservoirs. What should the authorities do—address alleged wastage by not allowing drilling in areas smaller than the spacing minimum or give small-tract operators their economic freedom to drill as they please?[53] The TRC, which, as seen above, historically regulating one-third to two-fifths of national output, has adopted small-tract drilling during most of its history. This raises the important question of whether spacing regulation, even from the conservationist viewpoint, justifies its large administrative costs.

State spacing minimums substitute monolithic rules for scientific considerations and hard-and-fast obstacles. Optimal well location

---

and about 90% of its oil wells" (p. 243). This statistic reflects not only the far larger size of foreign oil and gas pools but also the effects of drainage competition and incentives created by conservation law in the United States.

[53]A third alternative for addressing this dilemma—mandatory cooperation to form pro rata units—will be discussed later in this section.

depends on reservoir characteristics that dictate pressure per location; surface choices are moderated by legal restrictions and existing structures. In hearings, exceptions are made for these facts, but far from legitimating spacing regulation, the exceptions reveal the artificiality of set rules. From a free-market perspective, these exceptions reduce the distortions caused by artificially rigid spacing rules. Yet since the spacing minimums still constrain many competitors, a nonmarket advantage for the politically astute distorts competition.

The alleged need for statutory spacing minimums fails to acknowledge two important factors: artificial drilling incentives created by government intervention and the state of knowledge about drilling choices.

Historically, taxation and regulation have promoted overdrilling. Discovery depletion under the depletion allowance handsomely rewarded offset wells until 1926.[54] Per well allowables meant that more wells qualified for more production.[55] Offset drilling, coupled with legal uncertainty over pooling and unit agreements, precluded innovative lease terms whereby reservoir co-owners could share production proceeds without drilling their own wells. Offset to arrest drainage production was virtually required.

Purely scientific considerations also encouraged close spacing. The closer the well to an existing well, the less the risk of a dry hole, which was an important consideration to financially constrained operators and investors. Although development wells can be widely spaced with greater assurance today, reservoir boundaries for most of drilling history had to be determined by cautiously drilling incrementally spaced frontier wells. Reinforcing this proclivity was the Cutler theory, first presented in 1924, which was interpreted to mean that recoverability was negatively correlated with the distance between wells.[56] This erroneous theory held sway over the oil industry—even over scientists through the 1930s and 1940s—to the detriment of exploration and production budgets. In 1939, the eminent petroleum geologist Everette DeGolyer testified:

[54]See chapter 7, pp. 336–37.

[55]Per well allowables are discussed in this chapter, pp. 175–79.

[56]On the basis of experiments, W. W. Cutler of the U.S. Bureau of Mines concluded that "doubling the distance between wells doubles the ultimate production per well and halves the ultimate recovery per acre." Quoted in Rupert Craze, "Development Plan for Oil Reservoirs," in Thomas Frick, ed., *Petroleum Production Handbook*, 2 vols. (Dallas: Society of Petroleum Engineers, 1962), vol. 2, pp. 33–35. For a history of the Cutler theory, erroneous interpretations of it, and later refutations of it, see Rupert

We do not know too much about well spacing. Unfortunately, the individual oil pool, once exhausted under a certain well pattern, cannot be restored and again produced under a different well pattern for comparative purposes.[57]

Imperfect knowledge, not drainage instincts, created what was later recognized as drilling waste. Moreover, the other side of the coin is that spacing that is too wide or misplaced can cause physical and economic waste just as its opposite can.[58]

Under free-market conditions where consolidation and cooperation are viable alternatives, the decision of when and where to drill is a fundamental entrepreneurial decision. Potential problems, such as drainage competition from offset wells and reservoir energy dissipation from poorly located wells, create incentives for avoidance because costs are unnecessarily increased and the capital value of the reservoir is decreased. The belief that legal spacing minimums are required to prevent waste falsely denies that operators wish to minimize costs, wish to maximize (discounted) revenues, and are able to creatively achieve those goals in an environment unhampered by government intervention.

Crude-Oil Production Ceilings

The heart of state petroleum regulation has been the control of wellhead production. Production limitations have been achieved by

---

Craze and James Glanville, *Well Spacing* (Houston: Humble Oil & Refining Co., 1955). In 1951, Stuart Buckley, in *Petroleum Conservation,* commented, "Much confusion still exists, not only in the minds of laymen, but even in the technical literature, regarding the effects of well density on ultimate oil recovery" (p. 164).

[57]*Petroleum Hearings before the Temporary National Economic Committee* (New York: American Petroleum Institute, 1942), p. 297. Cited hereafter as *TNEC Petroleum Hearings.* The role of scientific imperfection, or at least ambiguity, in drilling waste was also acknowledged by industry economist Richard Gonzalez. "Lack of understanding of the behavior of oil and gas in reservoirs, and a widespread belief that the area that could be drained by a well was quite limited, caused the drilling of many more wells than necessary for efficient recovery." Gonzalez, "Oil and Gas," in *Economics of the Mineral Industries* (New York: American Institute of Mining and Metallurgical Engineers, 1976), p. 489. Wallace Lovejoy and Paul Homan stated, "As late as the early 1940's many in the industry still held the opinion that more wells got out more oil." Lovejoy and Homan, *Economic Aspects of Oil Conservation Regulation* (Baltimore: Johns Hopkins University Press, 1967), pp. 50–51. Also see Henrietta Larson and Kenneth Porter, *History of Humble Oil & Refining Company,* p. 253.

[58]Jacqueline Lang Weaver, *Unitization of Oil and Gas Fields in Texas,* p. 478n. 84.

assigning a "maximum efficient rate" of production, dictating a maximum gas-oil ratio, and, most controversially, setting output to "market demand." Each of these three control programs is historically reviewed and critically evaluated.

Depth-Acreage Allowables. With the birth of mandatory proration in the late 1920s, the question of apportionment arose. The simplest solution was to assign output per well, but given the incentive for overdrilling, regulators resorted to other means. Acreage distance between wells and bottom hole pressure came into use in Texas in 1928 and in other states soon thereafter.[59]

During World War II, the maximum efficient rate (MER) criteria, explained below, joined the depth-acreage allowables: after the war, the two began a coexistence that has continued to this day. While MER assignments were given to larger fields, allowables from a standard formula or published chart were assigned to smaller fields for which elaborate data for tailor-made assignments were not available. Table 4.2 presents depth-acreage (yardstick) charts for Texas, Louisiana, Oklahoma, New Mexico, and Kansas. These amounts place an upper ceiling on production to which a market-demand percentage, discussed below, is applied.

Maximum-allowable schedules have been imbued with political elements throughout their history. The Texas "1947 Yardstick," the first state allowables schedule, showed a notable bias toward closely spaced wells (10 and 20 acres) as opposed to more widely spaced wells (40 acres). This stimulated overdrilling. This bias cannot be explained by technological necessity or economic desirability.[60]

The schedules are highly influenced by firm profitability in light of drilling costs. Although the reservoirs may be technically similar,

---

[59]Bottom hole pressure, also called well potential, was measured as production under open flow. On April 24, 1928, Winkler County, Texas, production was set at 150,000 barrels per day with allowables per well assigned at 50 percent to acreage and 50 percent to potential. The Yates field in Texas in May 1928 was prorated at 25 percent to acreage and 75 percent to potential. Henrietta Larson and Kenneth Porter, *History of Humble Oil & Refining Company,* p. 319.

[60]This was largely removed in Texas's 1965 yardstick. In Louisiana, similarly, the 1953 yardstick was modified in 1960 and 1967 to reduce incentives for close well spacing.

Table 4.2
MER Allowable Chart
(barrels per day)

Depth (ft.)	Texas[a]	Louisiana[b]	Oklahoma[c]	New Mexico[d]	Kansas[e]
			10 Acres		
0– 2,000	21	104	60	80	25
2,000– 3,000	22	124	60	80	25
3,000– 4,000	23	148	66	80	25
4,000– 5,000	24	174	76	80	34
5,000– 6,000	26	207	88	107	46
6,000– 7,000	28	242	106	142	54
7,000– 8,000	31	278	126	187	60
8,000– 8,500	34	322	142	230	60
8,500– 9,000	36	322	152	230	60
9,000– 9,500	40	385	164	275	60
9,500–10,000	43	385	178	275	60
10,000–10,500	48	454	200	320	60
10,500–11,000	–	454	226	320	60
11,000–11,500	–	550	260	365	60
11,500–12,000	–	550	298	365	60
12,000–12,500	–	670	346	410	60
12,500–13,000	–	670	396	410	60

(Continued on next page)

Table 4.2—Continued
MER Allowable Chart
(barrels per day)

Depth (ft.)	Texas[a]	Louisiana[b]	Oklahoma[c]	New Mexico[d]	Kansas[e]
13,000–13,500	–	816	446	455	60
13,500–14,000	–	816	496	455	60
14,000–14,500	–	988	546	500	60
14,500–15,000	–	988	586	500	60
15,000–16,000	–	1,190	–	545	60
16,000–17,000	–	1,411	–	590	60
17,000–18,000	–	1,674	–	635	60
			20 Acres		
0– 2,000	39	104	90	80	PH
2,000– 3,000	41	124	90	80	PH
3,000– 4,000	4	148	94	80	PH
4,000– 5,000	48	174	102	80	PH
5,000– 6,000	52	207	114	107	PH
6,000– 7,000	57	242	132	142	PH
7,000– 8,000	62	278	152	187	PH
8,000– 8,500	68	322	172	230	PH
8,500– 9,000	74	322	188	230	PH
9,000– 9,500	81	385	202	275	PH
9,500–10,000	88	385	222	275	PH

10,000–10,500	96	454	250	320	PH
10,500–11,000	106	454	282	320	PH
11,000–11,500	119	550	324	365	PH
11,500–12,000	131	550	372	365	PH
12,000–12,500	144	670	432	410	PH
12,500–13,000	156	670	496	410	PH
13,000–13,500	169	816	556	455	PH
13,500–14,000	181	816	620	455	PH
14,000–14,500	200	988	681	500	PH
14,500–15,000	–	988	732	500	PH
15,000–16,000	–	1,190	–	545	PH
16,000–17,000	–	1,141	–	590	PH
17,000–18,000	–	1,674	–	635	PH

40 Acres

0– 2,000	74	104	114	80	PH
2,000– 3,000	78	124	114	80	PH
3,000– 4,000	84	148	118	80	PH
4,000– 5,000	93	174	126	80	PH
5,000– 6,000	102	207	142	107	PH
6,000– 7,000	111	242	166	142	PH
7,000– 8,000	121	278	192	187	PH
8,000– 8,500	133	322	216	230	PH
8,500– 9,000	142	322	234	230	PH
9,000– 9,500	157	385	254	275	PH

(Continued on next page)

151

Table 4.2—Continued
MER Allowable Chart
(barrels per day)

Depth (ft.)	Texas[a]	Louisiana[b]	Oklahoma[c]	New Mexico[d]	Kansas[e]
9,500–10,000	172	385	278	275	PH
10,000–10,500	192	454	312	320	PH
10,500–11,000	212	454	352	320	PH
11,000–11,500	237	550	404	365	PH
11,500–12,000	262	550	466	365	PH
12,000–12,500	287	670	540	410	PH
12,500–13,000	312	670	618	410	PH
13,000–13,500	337	816	700	455	PH
13,500–14,000	362	816	776	455	PH
14,000–14,500	400	988	851	500	PH
14,500–15,000	–	988	914	500	PH
15,000–16,000	–	1,190	–	545	PH
16,000–17,000	–	1,411	–	590	PH
17,000–18,000	–	1,674	–	635	PH
			80 Acres		
0– 2,000	129	104	–	160	PH
2,000– 3,000	135	124	–	160	PH
3,000– 4,000	144	148	–	160	PH
4,000– 5,000	158	174	158	160	PH

			160 Acres		
5,000– 6,000	171	207	176	187	PH
6,000– 7,000	184	242	208	222	PH
7,000– 8,000	198	278	240	267	PH
8,000– 8,500	215	322	270	310	PH
8,500– 9,000	229	322	294	310	PH
9,000– 9,500	250	385	318	355	PH
9,500–10,000	272	385	346	355	PH
10,000–10,500	300	454	390	400	PH
10,500–11,000	329	454	440	400	PH
11,000–11,500	365	550	508	445	PH
11,500–12,000	401	550	584	445	PH
12,000–12,500	436	670	676	490	PH
12,500–13,000	471	670	776	490	PH
13,000–13,500	506	816	872	535	PH
13,500–14,000	543	816	970	535	PH
14,000–14,500	600	988	1,068	580	PH
14,500–15,000	–	988	1,147	625	PH
15,000–16,000	–	1,190	–	625	PH
16,000–17,000	–	1,411	–	670	PH
17,000–18,000	–	1,674	–	715	PH
0– 2,000	238	104	–	–	PH
2,000– 3,000	249	124	–	–	PH

(Continued on next page)

Table 4.2—Continued
MER ALLOWABLE CHART
(barrels per day)

Depth (ft.)	Texas[a]	Louisiana[b]	Oklahoma[c]	New Mexico[d]	Kansas[e]
3,000– 4,000	265	148	–	–	PH
4,000– 5,000	288	174	–	–	PH
5,000– 6,000	310	207	–	347	PH
6,000– 7,000	331	242	–	382	PH
7,000– 8,000	353	278	–	427	PH
8,000– 8,500	380	322	–	470	PH
8,500– 9,000	402	322	–	470	PH
9,000– 9,500	435	385	–	515	PH
9,500–10,000	471	385	–	515	PH
10,000–10,500	515	454	702	560	PH
10,500–11,000	562	454	792	560	PH
11,000–11,500	621	550	890	605	PH
11,500–12,000	679	550	1,052	605	PH
12,000–12,500	735	670	1,218	650	PH
12,500–13,000	789	670	1,398	650	PH
13,000–13,500	843	816	1,568	695	PH
13,500–14,000	905	816	1,746	695	PH
14,000–14,500	1,000	988	1,924	740	PH
14,500–15,000	–	988	2,065	785	PH

154

15,000–16,000	—	1,190	—	—	875	PH
16,000–17,000	—	1,411	—	—	830	PH
17,000–18,000	—	1,674	—	—	875	PH

SOURCE: Various state conservation agencies.

[a]Texas 1965 postdiscovery allowable schedule as of 1981.

[b]Louisiana allowable schedule as of 1981. Note that all well distances have the same allowable conforming to their spacing rule.

[c]Oklahoma postdiscovery allowable schedule as of 1978. Each figure has been averaged for depths under 3,000 feet.

[d]New Mexico postdiscovery allowable schedule as of 1978. Note that 40-acre well allowables apply to all wells spaced under that acreage.

[e]For spacing greater than 10 acres, the Kansas allowable is determined per hearing (PH). Allowables are averaged for depths under 4,000 feet.

higher allowables are given for deeper pools to allow deep production. This creates waste by encouraging high-cost production.[61]

Another political element found in many state schedules is bonus
("discovery") allowables awarded to wells drilled in new fields.
Although a new reservoir may be comparable to a reservoir underlying an existing well, the allowable for the former can be as much
as 100 percent higher than that for the latter.[62] This causes several
major distortions. Since discovery allowables are generally awarded
to the first wells sunk in the new area (such as the first eleven in
Texas) and for a specified period of time (twenty-four months in
Texas), rapid drilling and maximum withdrawals are encouraged.
Cooperative arrangements such as pooling and unitization lose their
free-market luster. Furthermore, wildcat drilling is artificially stimulated at the expense of development wells in proven areas.[63]

Maximum Efficient Rate. Regulatory control of production can be
achieved by limiting the rate of an oil well's flow to a predetermined
MER. An engineering-geological determination, the MER allowable
restricts open-flow production to a level perceived to maximize
future reservoir recoverability by natural means.[64]

MER regulation began with World War II petroleum planning.[65]
Studies before this time established a correlation between reservoir

[61]"Compensation [for deeper drilling] is waste. For under competition, the higher
costs of deeper wells would shut them out of the market, except as offset by cost-
reducing factors such as greater productivity." M. A. Adelman, *The World Petroleum
Market* (Baltimore: Johns Hopkins University Press, 1972), p. 148.

[62]The first state to grant bonus allowables was New Mexico on June 1, 1944. The
Texas bonus for new reservoir production begins at depths of 4,000 feet and reaches
135 percent of regular allowables at 14,000 feet. In Oklahoma, discovery allowables
increase with depth in amounts commonly over 100 percent of regular "allocated"
well output. In Kansas, the discovery allowable is fixed at 150 percent of regulated
allowables. In New Mexico, discovery allowables are greater by either 5 or 10 barrels
per day per 1,000 feet of depth. Louisiana, on the other hand, does not award bonus
allowables for discoveries.

[63]W. P. Z. German, "State Regulation of Oil and Gas Production," *Lectures on Texas
Oil and Gas Law* 59, no. 8 (December 1959): 1468–1510.

[64]For discussion of the MER concept, see Stuart Buckley, ed., *Petroleum Conservation*, pp. 151–63.

[65]For a discussion of early theoretical attempts to formulate a workable MER concept, see Edgar Kraus, "'MER'—A History," in *Drilling and Production Practices* (Washington, D.C.: American Petroleum Institute, 1947), pp. 108–9. J. Howard Marshall II
credits Robert Allen, assistant oil umpire of the Central Committee of California Oil
Producers, with coining the term *maximum efficient rate* in the late 1930s. Conversation
with Marshall, April 13, 1991.

energy and recoverability, but what range of production could achieve the highest output was highly unsettled. Despite this uncertainty, the Petroleum Administration for War (PAW) and the Production Committee for District V employed MER estimates in early 1942 to determine reservoir production ceilings in California, the key oil state for the Pacific war theater, that did not have market-demand proration.[66] Soon thereafter, the PAW and the Production Committee for Section III (the Ivy Committee) estimated MERs for Texas for allowables regulation by the TRC.[67] A nationwide MER survey for pools and individual wells was first undertaken in early 1943 by special industry subcommittees assigned by the PAW. From this point until the end of the war, quarterly revisions were made to compare MER benchmarks to actual production.

Since World War II, ten states have established upper limits on daily well production based on MER estimates, the most recent major producing state being Louisiana in 1969. While most states establish MERs by individual hearings, Texas, Oklahoma, Louisiana, Kansas, and New Mexico, as seen in table 4.2, publish MERs in surrogate form as "depth-acreage" charts for their older wells to follow, reserving MER hearings for new fields. MER ceilings would now establish an upper production limit for non-market-demand states and provide the base figure for market-demand percentages in market-demand states.

In 1973, the MER assumed new importance when nominations by crude purchasers set state market-demand factors at 100 percent. For the first time in decades, only MER assignments, and yardstick allowables for wells without MER assignments, stood between regulated and free-market production. The Energy Policy and Conservation Act, passed December 20, 1975, confirmed the newfound importance of MER by defining the term, ordering its determination for all fields on public and private land, and giving standby authority

---

[66]The engineering subcommittee defined MER as "the highest daily rate of production that can be sustained by a field or pool for a period of six months without jeopardizing maximum practical ultimate recovery from the reservoir." Edgar Kraus, "'MER'—A History," p. 109.

[67]The federal government has also relied on MER regulation to address physical wastage of oil and gas on onshore and offshore federal lands. See Stephen McDonald, *The Leasing of Federal Lands for Fossil Fuels Production* (Baltimore: Johns Hopkins University Press, 1979), pp. 127–29.

to the president to order production at such levels.[68] This authority would not be used; MER production was already in wide use, and forced production outside of regular practice would have created unnecessary difficulties.

Evaluation. To the extent that MER regulation is a lenient, nonrestrictive determination and authorities rely instead on market-demand factors to control output, it is a superfluous regulation. But to the extent that it has restricted output from unregulated levels, particularly in the post-1972 period when market-demand considerations have ceased to restrict production with minor exceptions, it has sacrificed consumer welfare to the earlier criticized goal of physical conservation.[69] Economic conservation, reflecting present-oriented human action, is a higher goal than the MER physical-waste prevention ideal. Don Knowlton, a PAW engineer involved with early MER work, pointed this out in 1947:

> We would do well to consider MER as a temporary expedient employed during the war period and to refocus our attention on the truer objective of maximum economic recovery. . . . Economic carries the more accurate connotation . . . to the extent it results in economic benefit to all parties in interest.[70]

The problem with the MER as a regulatory concept and goal runs much deeper than its neglect of economic value. There is serious question about whether many reservoirs have a single, definable MER, and, even if they have, whether reservoir changes over time make statutory assignments obsolete. These points require elaboration.

Assigned MER figures are necessarily imprecise. As Dan Bruce states, "Two geologists separately viewing the same basic data would almost certainly arrive at different answers."[71] In fact, many reservoirs, as discussed in the appendix to this chapter, have no

---

[68]Public Law 94-163, 89 Stat. 871 (1975). MER is defined as "the maximum rate of production of crude oil or natural gas, or both, which may be sustained without loss of ultimate recovery of crude oil or natural gas, or both, under sound engineering and economic principles" (p. 880).

[69]See chapter 3, pp. 107–9.

[70]Don Knowlton, "Discussion," in *Drilling and Production Practices*, p. 111.

[71]Dan Bruce, "'Maximum Efficient Rate'—Its Use and Misuse in Production Regulation," *Natural Resources Lawyer* 9 (1976): 445.

MER; they are rate insensitive. While some large reservoirs of years past were rate sensitive (but not East Texas whose recoverable output was independent of the extraction rate), the majority of modern finds have little or no tradeoff between extraction rates and absolute recovery. This leaves economic considerations paramount in the absence of regulatory assignment. Many reservoir engineers would not disagree with economist Paul MacAvoy's characterization of MER as "a religious term."[72] Therefore, a range of MER determinations that can be politically decided to favor some firms and penalize others is always available. Consumer or producer pressure can result in "high" or "low" MER assignments. Without binding determinations, on the other hand, entrepreneurial calculations would narrow engineering estimates to the "right" production level.

A second problem with the MER benchmark for regulators was stated by Dan Bruce: "MER is not only an imprecise concept, but a dynamic one."[73] Far from being set in concrete, MER rates change with reservoir performance due to changes in the reservoir itself as it is depleted and as new technological information is collected. As is characteristic of regulation in general, MER determinations are rigid and do not change with new conditions. Rather than continually hold hearings to revise the assignment, regulators allow past determinations to hold sway until a particularly obvious need for revision prompts a rehearing. In the interim, either the regulation becomes superfluous or it increasingly restricts production to the detriment of consumers.

Engineering data are only one factor the profit-maximizing operator calculates in making decisions about present versus future production. Also of importance are investor expectations, lease provisions, present versus anticipated costs, and present versus anticipated revenues. Because MER regulation ignores these elements in favor of engineering criteria, economic inefficiency results.

Gas-Oil Ratio. A sister regulation to MER allowables is the gas-oil ratio (GOR), which, by limiting the amount of gas producible per barrel of oil, restricts the amount of oil a well is allowed to produce. Like MER regulation, the GOR is intended to enhance

---

[72]Paul MacAvoy, Comment in *Challenge,* March–April 1974, p. 50.

[73]Dan Bruce, " 'Maximum Efficient Rate'—Its Use and Misuse in Production Regulation," p. 447.

crude recoverability by preserving the reservoir's natural energy.[74] Thus, in theory at least, expensive secondary recovery methods using artificial lift can be deferred until a later date by prohibiting open-flow production that prematurely exhausts reservoir energy.

The first GOR statute was passed in California in 1929 to combat open-air discharges of natural gas.[75] It was upheld by the Supreme Court in the *Bandini* case, but enforcement proved difficult.[76] In 1933, the Oklahoma Corporation Commission, under authority to prevent crude-oil and natural-gas waste, issued two "emergency orders" requiring a ratio of 5,000 cubic feet of gas per barrel of oil for the Holdenville field and a ratio of 10,000 cubic feet per barrel in the Oklahoma City Wilcox zone.[77] Other states to pass GORs in the early years were Texas, Kansas, and New Mexico (1935); Louisiana (1936); Arkansas (1937); and Mississippi (1938). In the next several decades, approximately fifteen other states adopted similar conservation laws.[78] The current standard regulation is a maximum ratio of 2,000 cubic feet of gas for every barrel of oil produced.

Under the GOR statutes, three alternatives are possible for wells producing excess gas. First, the operator may reinject ("cycle")

---

[74]Explains Stephen McDonald, "Gas-oil regulations . . . reduce the drop in reservoir pressure accompanying a given amount of oil production; . . . limit channeling of gas through the oil zone; and . . . help create or maintain a gas cap which may contribute to the efficiency of recovery of both oil and gas." McDonald, *Petroleum Conservation in the United States*, p. 46.

[75]Three years earlier, Louisiana passed a statute regulating casinghead gas that was similar to a gas-oil ratio. It prohibited the release of gas that, if priced at $0.03 per Mcf, would have a greater market value than the oil produced. Yandell Boatner, "Legal History of Conservation of Oil and Gas in Louisiana," in American Bar Association, *Legal History of Conservation of Oil and Gas* (Baltimore: Lord Baltimore Press, 1939), p. 67. Cited hereafter as *Legal History, 1939*. In 1927, a GOR was introduced in the Oklahoma legislature to restrict fields in the state (Seminole in particular) to 500 cubic feet of gas per barrel of oil. August Giebelhaus, *Business and Government in the Oil Industry: Case Study of Sun Oil* (Greenwich, Conn.: Jai Press, 1980) pp. 134–35; and Norman Nordhauser, *The Quest for Stability*, p. 29.

[76]*Bandini Petroleum Co. v. Superior Court*, 284 U.S. 8 (1931). See Northcutt Ely, "The Conservation of Oil," *Harvard Law Review* (May 1938): 1238–39.

[77]W. P. Z. German, "Legal History of Conservation of Gas and Oil in Oklahoma" in *Legal History, 1939*, pp. 197–98; and T. Murray Robinson, "Oklahoma, 1938–1948," in *Legal History, 1949*, pp. 377–78.

[78]See appendix C for historical dates and appendix F (updated to 1990) for a summary of states with GOR laws.

casinghead gas into the reservoir to lower the ratio to the legal limit.[79] Second, the operator might reduce production rates if this measure decreases the ratio. Finally, authorities might allow production above the legal limit by penalizing the well with a reduced crude-oil allowable.

Evaluation. To the extent that entrepreneurial decisions are modified by GOR statutes, economic waste is substituted for the physical waste prevented by regulation. If reinjection was not originally practiced, the entrepreneur most likely calculated that the costs of reinjection, or revenue from sales of marketable gas, did not justify the (discounted) value of increased future production or future production at lower cost. Changing this decision by regulation creates economic waste by increasing present costs or forgoing present revenue. If the operator reduces crude output to lower the ratio to the legal level (or to avoid a reduced allowable), the economic waste is the forgone present supply the consumer loses minus the (discounted) satisfactions the consumer gains from greater or cheaper future output. The difference can be assumed to be positive since the entrepreneur, estimating the present price (value) of output against the discounted price (value) of future output, originally chose not to delay production or to recover oil at a lower cost at a later date.[80]

The belief that mandatory GORs are necessary to prevent waste denies the propensity of entrepreneurs, within a free-market setting, to make correct decisions regarding consumer preference, and in the process to reduce physical waste in so far as it represents economic waste. This mistaken notion rests in part on a faulty comprehension of the role of profit and loss in minimizing error behind true waste; it also stems from the historical misconception that free-market incentives in oil and gas production led to withdrawals neglectful of the role of casinghead gas in crude-oil recoverability.

---

[79]The first cycling operation was in the Cayuga field (Texas) in 1938, three years after cooperative cycling was legalized in the state's antitrust law, subject to permission from the state attorney general. Four years later, cycling plants in Texas increased to twenty-nine in response to regulatory pressure to reinject gas. David Prindle, *Petroleum Politics and the Texas Railroad Commission*, pp. 60–61. In Louisiana (1940), Oklahoma (1945), Alabama (1945), Florida (1945), and Georgia (1945), gas cycling was simultaneously legalized and made compulsory. H. P. Pressler, "Legal Problems Involved in Cycling Gas in Gas Fields," *Texas Law Review* (December 1945): 19–33.

[80]These scenarios assume the entrepreneur makes correct decisions, given the role of profits in encouraging correct economic behavior and losses (or forgone profits) in discouraging incorrect decisionmaking.

GOR statutes have another serious problem. Like MER regulations, they lose whatever questionable validity they have with reservoirs that are rate insensitive. As explained in the appendix to this chapter, this is true of the majority of wells.

Market-Demand Proration. Of all state oil regulations, market-demand proration (MDP) is the most complex, controversial, and consequential. Eugene Rostow has called it "the keystone to the entire [conservation] plan."[81] Given its importance in comparison with other more technically oriented regulations affecting production, an in-depth review of its determination, legislative and administrative history, historical consequences, and theoretical justification is merited.

The crucial distinction between normal manifestations of market demand and the "market demand" of state proration programs is that while the former unfolds at the moment of purchase against existing prices, the latter is predetermined at estimated prices. States estimate market demand by conducting hearings where crude purchasers give sworn estimates ("nominations") of the supply they intend to purchase in the next selling period. The demand of each buyer is based on the going or expected posted price for crude in areas where it will be purchased. The total estimate, the "market demand," is then compared with supply—the sum of MER assignments and depth-acreage allowables—to arrive at a market-demand factor (MDF). If demand is greater than supply, the MDF is set at 100 percent of the MER-yardstick allowable; if demand is less than supply, the factor is set at less than 100 percent of the MER-yardstick allowable as a legal ceiling on production. For example, if demand is 1.5 million barrels per day and nonexempt capacity is 2 million barrels per day, then an MDF of 75 percent would be assigned to each (nonexempt) well under either its MER assignment or the yardstick ceiling.[82]

Authority to prevent crude-oil waste by limiting production to a predetermined market demand began with the Oklahoma Conservation Act of February 11, 1915. Although not invoked until years

---

[81]Eugene Rostow, *A National Policy for the Oil Industry* (New Haven, Conn.: Yale University Press, 1948), p. 29.

[82]The Texas Railroad Commission's procedure is described in E. O. Thompson, "The Texas Market Demand Statute on Oil and Gas and Its Application," *Texas Law Review* (December 1960): 145–46. The important role of exempt wells is explained in this chapter, pp. 179–81.

later, the act defined waste as crude oil produced "in excess of transportation or marketing facilities or reasonable market demands." After high production and instability set in during the late 1920s, other states joined Oklahoma with market-demand statutes—Kansas (1931), Texas (1932),[83] Louisiana and New Mexico (1935), Mississippi (1936), Arkansas (1937), and Michigan (1939). New Mexico defined "reasonable" market demand as "demand for such crude petroleum oil for reasonable current consumption and use within or outside the state, together with the demand for such amounts as are reasonably necessary for building up or maintaining reasonable storage reserves."[84] This language has come to define "market demand" outside the hearings process.

Interstate coordination of MDP, with federal assistance, began in 1930 and reached a high point in the 1933–35 New Deal period. During World War II, MDP yielded to full production, only to reemerge after wartime petroleum demand subsided in 1945. From the postwar period until crude-price controls in 1971, MDP would prove to be very restrictive, as can be seen by examining the MDFs, expressed as a percentage of MER-yardstick production, for Texas, Louisiana, Oklahoma, and New Mexico in table 4.3.

Caution is necessary when comparing MDF percentages state by state. Because market-demand states have varying allowables for depth and well distance, percentages can be *different* and be equally restrictive, or they can be the *same* and be unequally restrictive. For example, Oklahoma has a more liberal allowable schedule than Texas but has had lower MDF percentages, bringing the two states' output ceilings closer together. The allowable schedule can also have figures above a well's production capacity, which would effectively increase the MDF percentage in relation to well capacity. The *effective* MDF, the percentage of a well's capacity that can be legally produced, would be the well's allowable divided by the well's capacity multiplied by the MDF. For example, if a well's capacity is 16 barrels per

---

[83]Texas, under the broad authority to prevent physical waste, began market-demand proration several years before it was specifically permitted to do so. Texas's first statewide proration order was issued on August 18, 1930; the Texas Market Demand Act was passed on November 12, 1932. The 1932 act was the work of major companies led by Will Farish of Humble and J. Edgar Pew of Sun. Henrietta Larson and Kenneth Porter, *History of Humble Oil & Refining Company*, p. 471.

[84]J. A. O'Connor, "The Role of Market Demand in the Domestic Oil Industry," *Arkansas Law Review* (Fall 1958): 349–50.

Table 4.3
PERCENTAGE OF MARKET DEMAND

Year	Texas[a]	Louisiana[b]	Oklahoma[c]	New Mexico[d]
1947	89	–	–	–
1948	100	–	–	63
1949	65	–	–	61
1950	63	–	–	69
1951	76	–	–	74
1952	71	–	–	68
1953	65	93	–	63
1954	53	70	–	57
1955	53	49	30	57
1956	52	44	27	56
1957	47	43	26	56
1958	33	33	23	49
1959	34	34	21	50
1960	28	34	18	49
1961	28	32	16	49
1962	27	32	17	50
1963	28	32	16	54
1964	28	32	14	54
1965	29	33	14	56
1966	34	35	19	65
1967	41	38	23	74
1968	45	42	37	64
1969	52	44	49	68
1970	72	56	59	85
1971	73	73	77	80
1972	94	100	100	87
1973–84	100	100	100	100

SOURCE: Various state conservation agencies.

[a] The market-demand factor is expressed as a percentage of yardstick-MER production based on the 1947–65 depth-acreage yardsticks or individually computed reservoir MERs. From 1938 until 1946, the MDF was expressed as a percentage of open-flow production. (Note that the 1947–62 "number of producing days" has been converted to a percentage figure to correspond to the percentage format begun in 1963.)

[b] The market-demand factor is basd on statewide allowable tables or MER allocation. Prior to 1953, MDP and MER allowables were combined into a single barrel-per-day figure to preclude a precise estimate of proration.

[c] Before 1955, the MDF was built into the allowable figures to preclude a precise estimate of proration.

[d] The normal unit allowable (NUA) is a percentage of the state's depth-acreage allowable. In September 1972, the MDF replaced the NUA and was set at 100 percent.

day, and its allowable is 20 barrels per day, then an MDF of 50 percent equates to an effective rate of 62.5 percent of capacity output; if capacity were 20 barrels per day with an allowable of 16 barrels per day, a 50 percent MDF would be equal to 40 percent of potential. With such adjustments, a convergence between state allowables, a necessity for political support, is evident.

In the 1960s, Texas and Louisiana published yardsticks for offshore allowables to determine maximum daily production. To these ceilings, both states applied market-demand percentages. Dissatisfaction expressed by President Nixon led to a December 5, 1970, order to allow full-MER production.[85] This was replaced, effective May 1, 1974, by an order that allowed production at full MER levels as defined by federal statute.[86] By this time, the question was moot; both states were allowing 100 percent of MER-yardstick production.

Because of federal price controls and reduced imports as a result of the Arab embargo, demand increased relative to supply to end the overproduction era. "Market demand" was determined to be within each state's MER-yardstick allowables in the 1972–73 period. All states set their MDF at 100 percent, with slight exceptions, from this period through 1984.[87]

The prospects for returning to a market-demand limitation appear small given the changed economic and political climate in the last decade. Despite the oil "glut" since mid-1981 that has lowered prices from an early-1981 high of nearly $40 per barrel to under $30 per barrel, there have been no serious proposals or attempts to return to the pre-1973 restrictive assignments on the oil side. Unlike before, strong consumer and political interests are well positioned to demand full production.

Four major economic distortions have resulted from substituting proration "demand" for the true demand of an unhampered market:

[85]35 *Fed. Reg.* 18559 (December 5, 1970).

[86]Geological Survey, OCS Order 11 (1974).

[87]In Texas, the market-demand factor was set between 98 and 99 percent from December 1976 until February 1977 to protest federal oil policies, especially crude oil price controls. The East Texas field has been given a separate MDF of 86 percent since 1974 because of "reservoir problems." *Oil & Gas Journal*, April 3, 1974, p. 40. Cited hereafter as *OGJ*. The East Texas allowable reflects political constraints, namely less favorably situated independents that fear water encroachment from full production.

the misdirection of market share between production areas, the construction of unnecessary wells, the stabilization of price, and the subsidization of marginal wells. Separately and together, they constitute a major area of economic waste caused by the substitution of mandatory conservation for market conservation.

Distortion of Market Share. Although there was never a rigid quota system among Texas, Oklahoma, Kansas, New Mexico, and Louisiana in the early years of proration, these states informally adhered to the National Industrial Recovery Act's Oil Code and to the Bureau of Mines' forecasts of relative shares of national demand. From 1930 until 1940, and particularly from 1933 until 1935, market-demand states represented an effective cartel. The result, noted legal historian Innis Harris, was to "freeze the channels of trade as they were established at the time stabilization [proration] was commenced." He explained, "As long as a purchaser can supply his markets through existing channels and as long as stabilization of markets and prices removes any incentive to move out into new flush production areas, then markets remain as they are."[88]

MDP prevented price competition from new production areas able to offer lower prices. True market demand was unable to follow supply, a distortion that was magnified with oil and gas, which are found in certain areas rather than being widely distributed. This favored Texas and Oklahoma, which made their major finds by the early 1930s, and penalized Kansas, which between 1933 and 1937 increased its proven reserves tenfold, yet could only incrementally increase its market share as seen in table 4.4.[89]

---

[88]Innis D. Harris, "Legal History of Conservation of Oil and Gas in Kansas," in *Legal History,* 1939, p. 50.

[89]Ibid., p. 51. In 1933, Kansas's allowable represented 50 percent of output capacity; in 1938, the allowable was only 5 percent of open flow. Oklahoma wells, meanwhile, were producing at 85 percent of capacity. This situation prompted Kansas governor Alfred Landon to call a conference to urge oil purchasers to increase their demand for Kansas oil compared to that of other states. Unable to persuade them because of the expense of greater distances to market, Landon threatened to seek federal control of proration "to preserve the interests of the Kansas oil producers." See Jay Kyle, "Kansas, 1937–1948," pp. 155–56. Statistics detailing proven reserves for the major producing states, if at all determinable during these years, are unavailable. Written accounts identify Kansas as experiencing the largest increase and Oklahoma the largest decrease in proven reserves in the 1930–37 period.

Table 4.4
NATIONAL MARKET SHARE: TEXAS, KANSAS, AND OKLAHOMA
(percentage)

Year	Texas	Kansas	Oklahoma
1930	32.3	4.6	24.1
1931	39.1	4.4	21.2
1932	39.8	4.4	19.5
1933	44.5	4.6	20.0
1934	42.0	5.2	19.8
1935	39.4	5.5	18.6
1936	38.9	5.3	18.8
1937	39.9	5.5	17.9
1938	39.2	5.0	14.4
1939	38.2	4.8	12.7

SOURCE: DeGoyler and MacNaughton, *Twentieth Century Petroleum Statistics*, 1981 ed. (Dallas: DeGoyler and MacNaughton), tables 2, 20, 21, 23.

Another distortion of MDP has been a redistribution of production from market-demand states to states not practicing proration.[90] While market-demand states extended proration from particular fields to the entire state to prevent a shift of production to unregulated areas, these states were powerless to prevent unregulated states from capturing a larger market share.[91] The IOCC did not have regulatory power to force participation, and formal federal cartelization, being a step away from public-utility regulation of prices and profits, was not desired by the industry. Consequently, while Texas, Oklahoma, Kansas, and Louisiana imposed production ceilings on their operators, unregulated states such as California and Illinois benefited. Between 1936 and 1940, Illinois's share of national production increased from 0.4 percent to 10.9 percent. California was able to retain its large market share despite the rise of the midcontinent

[90]Erich Zimmermann referred to this in 1957 as the "unsolved problem" of state proration. Zimmermann, *Conservation in the Production of Petroleum*, p. 211.

[91]Influence, however, could and would be used. An example was the Rodessa field, discovered in 1935 in northwest Louisiana, that stretched into Texas and Arkansas. Rather than let this field produce at capacity from the Louisiana side and drain regulated Texas operators, Louisiana used the occasion to pass a market-demand law as requested by the Texas Railroad Commission. Yandell Boatner, "Legal History of Conservation of Oil and Gas in Louisiana," p. 68. Arkansas followed two years later with proration.

producing area in the post-1927 period.[92] TRC chairman E. O. Thompson, seeing Texas as a victim, went so far as to suggest abandoning market-demand proration.[93] Clearly, producer interests rather than an a priori commitment to conservation weighed heavily on the influential commissioner.

Changes in market shares have also occurred between regulated states. In theory, if one market-demand state decides to allow greater demand by allowing lower prices, it stands to gain over a state administering proration more strictly. A report from the Antitrust Division of the Department of Justice warned in 1963, "Even moderate liberalization of controls in one area might swamp stabilization efforts in others."[94] Quarreling over this issue developed when Louisiana increased its market share at the expense of Texas in the late 1950s and 1960s.[95] While Louisiana doubled its market share in this period, Texas's share decreased over 10 percent.[96]

A third redistribution of market share as a result of MDP has occurred within regulated states. Not only are flush fields restrained relatively more than less productive fields by the MDF, which applies equally to both, inequality occurs because some fields are regulated by allowable schedules and other fields are regulated by MER assignment. MER restrictions further distort production between fields and within the state.

[92]DeGoyler and MacNaughton, *Twentieth Century Petroleum Statistics*, 1981 ed. (Dallas: DeGoyler and MacNaughton), pp. 20–21, 23. Northcutt Ely noted in 1938 that "there has been agitation for a production law in California, where production at times has failed to recede in phase with the reductions in the Compact states." Ely, "The Conservation of Oil," p. 1240.

[93]*NPN*, November 15, 1939, pp. 17, 29.

[94]M. A. Adelman, *The World Petroleum Market*, p. 149.

[95]"The more severely a State restrains output, the more it raises unit costs of operation within its borders. Hence, Louisiana's increased market share is, in part, because Louisiana is more permissive and lower-cost. Resentment is voiced in Texas, and indeed a recent report to the governor (Sixth World Petroleum Congress Committee, *Report to Hon. John B. Connally*) cannot mention its neighbor without snarling." M. A. Adelman, "Efficiency of Resource Use in Petroleum," *Southern Economic Journal* (October 1964): 107. Also see Wallace Lovejoy and Paul Homan, *Economic Aspects of Oil Conservation Regulation*, pp. 219–26.

[96]DeGoyler and MacNaughton, *Twentieth Century Petroleum Statistics*, 1979 ed. (Dallas: DeGoyler and MacNaughton), p. 21.

Table 4.5
CRUDE IMPORTS AND TOTAL U.S. DEMAND: 1947–71

Year	Imports/Demand	Year	Imports/Demand
1947	8.0%	1960	18.5%
1948	8.9	1961	19.2
1949	11.1	1962	20.0
1950	13.0	1963	19.8
1951	11.9	1964	20.5
1952	13.1	1965	21.4
1953	13.6	1966	21.3
1954	13.5	1967	20.2
1955	14.7	1968	21.2
1956	16.3	1969	22.4
1957	17.8	1970	23.3
1958	18.6	1971	25.8
1959	18.7		

SOURCE: American Petroleum Institute, *Basic Petroleum Data Book* (Washington, D.C.: API, 1981), vol. 1, no. 2, sec. 9, table 1.

To the extent that market-demand proration has increased industry costs, it has artificially reduced the competitiveness of the domestic industry against lower cost foreign sources. The consequence is a redistribution of market share away from domestic sources toward foreign production. This led directly to oil import restrictions beginning in 1932 and again beginning in 1959 to shield domestic producers, especially in the heavily regulated midcontinent area. Despite protectionism, high-cost American oil from proration contributed to a steady rise in the percentage of total U.S. demand supplied by imports from 1947 until 1971 (table 4.5).

Distortion of Market Price. Early motives for proration centered on a perceived need within Texas and Oklahoma to stabilize (i.e., support at existing or recent levels) price to prevent the "chaos" of financial ruin of owners of small wells. Scientific conservation was secondary. John McLean and Robert Haigh identified 1932 as particularly important.

> Because of the strong economic forces tending toward lower oil prices in 1932, the proration machinery of the important oil states in that year, as never before, became dedicated to the ulterior purpose of price maintenance rather than . . . the avoidance of physical waste.

169

The result was that during 1932 posted crude oil prices at practically all times of the year were kept at a level which made it impossible for the purchaser of crude oil at such posted prices to refine it and to secure a revenue from the finished product equal to the cost.[97]

From that time until the price escalation of the 1970s, stabilization of price was a major result of market-demand proration.[98]

Proration officials, particularly in Texas, have vigorously denied that price was an important variable in the market-demand estimation process. Ernest Thompson, the leading voice at the TRC from 1933 until 1965, declared that "in Texas we do not permit price to even be discussed at our hearings."[99] This opinion is still voiced at the TRC.[100]

Several points can be made about this denial of price fixing. First, price *was* of great concern to Thompson, a man described as "the father of petroleum conservation."[101] Protecting marginal wells was a high priority as he admitted in 1939 testimony before Congress: "[Price is important] to the extent that it seems to be proper not to let the little stripper wells be squeezed out of the picture."[102] In the same year, Thompson wrote to the governor after a large price reduction by producers: "This act is wholly unwarranted. . . . I am advocating to my colleagues on the Railroad Commission that we

---

[97]John McLean and Robert Haigh, *The Growth of Integrated Oil Companies* (Norwood, Mass.: Plimpton Press, 1954), p. 241.

[98]Hines Baker has linked MDP to the "stabilization of price rather than the fixing of price." Baker, "Achievements and Unsolved Problems in Oil and Gas Conservation," Company pamphlet, Humble Oil & Refining Company, 1949, p. 17. But to prevent prices from reaching their natural level *is* to fix price, albeit more subtly than by setting a direct price floor.

[99]Quoted in Robert Engler, *The Politics of Oil* (New York: Macmillan, 1961), p. 146. In 1932, Thompson testified, "I tell you that it has never mattered to me about the price." Kenneth Davis and York Wilbern, "Administrative Control of Oil Production in Texas," *Texas Law Review* (February 1944): 155.

[100]Conversation with George Singletary, senior staff engineer and former administrator, TRC, May 20, 1981.

[101]James Clark, *Three Stars for the Colonel* (New York: Random House, 1954). Cover quotation.

[102]Quoted in Kenneth Davis and York Wilbern, "Administrative Control of Oil Production in Texas," p. 155.

shut down all Texas oil fields for thirty days."[103] Elsewhere Thompson wrote:

> Texas wants a good price for crude petroleum. . . . I am convinced
> that the people of Texas do not want us so to administer the oil law
> in a manner that would lower the price of crude oil.[104]

Price *was* important—if it dropped to threaten the status quo of production. The fact that prices are not mentioned in nomination hearings is not an escape from price fixing. The nature of market-demand proration does not require the express treatment of price. If price is unmentioned—and especially if no *schedule of prices is allowed from which crude purchasers can alter existing demand*—the only price left is the *historical* price. This is precisely where stabilization comes into play. Since demand is based on prices of the last period, past prices form the basis for future prices, and therefore, period-to-period changes have a tendency to be cushioned. The overwhelming success of this inertia is evident in table 4.6 where changes in MDF for four major oil states are compared with changes in price.

Table 4.6 shows that MDFs, not price, were the equilibrating factors between supply and demand before MDP reached 100 percent from 1973 forward.[105] The MDF fluctuated between 27 percent and 100 percent in Texas between 1948 and 1968, while prices varied only from $2.58 to $3.06 per barrel. From 1953 to 1968, Louisiana saw prices in the $2.81–$3.14 range, while the MDF changed from 32 percent to 93 percent. In Oklahoma, prices moved between $2.92 and $3.40 between 1955 and 1971, while the MDF fluctuated between 17 percent and 77 percent. New Mexico witnessed MDFs of between

---

[103]Ibid. The record of the TRC under Thompson led Will Farish, proration advocate and Jersey Standard president, to testify: "I say unhesitatingly that price has influenced these proration authorities. There isn't any argument about that. The record is so clear that it would be stupid to say it hadn't." *TNEC Petroleum Hearings,* p. 75.

[104]E. O. Thompson, "The Purpose and Operation of Laws Prorating Production of Oil among Fields, Pools, and Wells to Balance Output with Demand," *16 Annual Proceedings* (New York: American Petroleum Institute, 1935), p. 21.

[105]Melvin de Chazeau and Alfred Kahn, focusing on the 1934–51 period, concluded that MDP resulted in "much fewer and less extreme price changes . . . [and] with one minor exception, the only way it ever moved was up." De Chazeau and Kahn, *Integration and Competition in the Petroleum Industry* (New Haven, Conn.: Yale University Press, 1959), pp. 146, 163.

Table 4.6
PRICE AND PRORATION FACTORS: 1947–72

	Texas		Louisiana		Oklahoma		New Mexico	
Year	MDF (%)	Price ($/bl)	MDF (%)	Price ($/bl)	MDF (%)	Price ($/bl)	MDF (%)	Price ($/bl)
1947	89	1.95	–	2.01	–	1.92	–	1.77
1948	100	2.61	–	2.68	–	2.58	63	2.45
1949	65	2.59	–	2.66	–	2.56	61	2.44
1950	63	2.59	–	2.65	–	2.57	69	2.43
1951	76	2.58	–	2.65	–	2.57	74	2.45
1952	71	2.58	–	2.64	–	2.56	68	2.47
1953	65	2.73	93	2.81	–	2.70	63	2.63
1954	53	2.84	70	2.93	–	2.79	57	2.75
1955	53	2.84	49	2.93	30	2.78	57	2.74
1956	52	2.83	44	2.93	27	2.78	56	2.75
1957	47	3.11	43	3.32	26	3.03	56	2.99
1958	33	3.06	33	3.26	23	2.96	49	2.98
1959	34	2.98	34	3.16	21	2.92	50	2.85
1960	28	2.96	34	3.14	18	2.92	49	2.85
1961	28	2.97	32	3.15	16	2.91	49	2.86
1962	27	2.99	32	3.15	17	2.92	50	2.88
1963	28	2.97	32	3.12	16	2.91	54	2.88
1964	28	2.96	32	3.11	14	2.90	54	2.87
1965	29	2.96	33	3.10	14	2.89	56	2.81

Year							
1966	34	2.97	35	3.11	19	2.91	65	2.84
1967	41	3.01	38	3.12	23	2.93	74	2.92
1968	45	3.04	42	3.14	37	2.99	64	2.95
1969	52	3.21	44	3.30	49	3.12	68	3.13
1970	72	3.28	56	3.38	59	3.19	85	3.20
1971	73	3.48	73	3.59	77	3.40	80	3.40
1972	94	3.48	100	3.59	100	3.41	87	3.41

SOURCES: American Petroleum Institute, *Basic Petroleum Data Book*, sec. 6, table 8; and various state conservation agencies.

49 percent and 74 percent in the 1948–68 period, while prices were steady in the $2.43–$2.95 range. Inflation flattened prices even further. The historical record reinforces the theoretical conclusion that MDP cushioned price fluctuations and prevented crude prices from falling when increased production from new discoveries and imports outdistanced increases in demand.

Several counterarguments have been raised against the charge that MDP inflated the price of oil and was economically inefficient. Fuel oil steadily outcompeted coal in industrial and utility markets in the 1950s and 1960s, suggesting that oil was priced at competitive levels.[106] The acknowledged pricing superiority of fuel oil, however, does not refute the contention that oil prices were artificially maintained; it only affirms the favorable energy economics and convenience of fuel oil over coal in many applications and that regulatory policies dared not restrict oil output to the point where market share would go to substitutes. The fact remains that consumers paid higher prices for oil as a result of regulation, and coal gained market share at the margin, although the price of oil remained below that of coal. It should be added that to the extent higher oil prices have caused prices of substitutes such as coal to rise, energy consumers in general have been injured.[107]

Another argument is that since the price of oil declined when adjusted for inflation, its price was not really increased by the MDP.[108] To the extent real prices did not fall more, however, proration negatively affected consumers. In fact, prices of natural resources can be expected to fall to the extent that technological advances allow additions to supply to outpace consumption.[109] Regulation simply prevented the price of crude oil from falling more than it did.

A third counterargument is that because oil prices were increased in the short run by proration, greater reserves resulted that lowered

[106]Draft comments from Richard Gonzalez, April 20, 1982.

[107]The price of interstate natural gas, on the other hand, has been controlled by government partially since 1940 and comprehensively since 1954. In some cases, oil prices were pressured downward by price-regulated gas, and in other cases, where gas was simply not available, oil prices were pressured upward.

[108]Stanley Learned, "Petroleum Conservation—The Myths and Realities," in *Exploration and Economics of the Petroleum Industry* (New York: Matthew Bender, 1968), pp. 186–87.

[109]See Julian Simon, *The Ultimate Resource* (Oxford: Martin Robertson, 1981), chap. 3.

prices for consumers in the longer run. But the market recognized higher prices as a mirage since only a fraction of a well's output could command them. Shut-in deliverability received nothing. On a total-revenue basis, the effect on reserves was ambiguous. Foreign reserves not subject to allowables, on the other hand, were stimulated by state regulation (at least prior to import restrictions), but domestic reserve additions were not. Nonprorated output at lower prices could have stimulated domestic production as much as the higher price-restrained output combination that historically existed.

Nonmarket prices engender economic distortion. Oil prices from proration were no exception. Consumer welfare is lowered because above-market wellhead prices translate into higher prices for derived retail products. Overconservation, it can be concluded, has taken place at the expense of the buyer. Oil producers, to the extent that revenue is increased from the higher price-lower output combination rather than the lower price-higher output mix, gain at the expense of consumers. MDP, therefore, is anti-consumer and pro-producer, particularly for producers with exempt (stripper) wells. Another consequence of nonmarket pricing is that misinformation is imparted to the market. Consumers believe that oil is scarcer than it really is and unnecessarily conserve. Producers think consumers value their product more than they really do, yet if they respond with new discoveries, they create a "surplus" that must be prorated by lowering the MDF. This consequence, complicated by other attributes of MDP, points toward another result of the historical practice of proration—overdrilling.

Overdrilling and Overcapacity. When mandatory proration began in the late 1920s and early 1930s, conservation authorities treated each well identically by assigning "demand" to each well on a flat per well basis determined by each well's potential. This created incentive to drill as many wells as could profitably operate at the existing and anticipated allowable rate.[110] So while authorities attempted to reduce production by limiting flush well output, more wells producing less oil substituted for fewer wells producing more oil. The net effect still reduced oil production because new well

---

[110]Spacing regulations in Texas proved to be no hindrance because routine exceptions were made to uphold correlative rights over waste prevention. Oklahoma, on the other hand, did not pass well-spacing regulation until 1935.

construction was constrained by cost, but the consequence was a significant misallocation of resources toward superfluous wells.

Several examples of proration-related overdrilling may be given. In the Oklahoma City field in 1929–30, spacing shrank from 40 acres per well to 10 acres and finally to 50-foot-by-140-foot plots as more and more wells were sunk in response to allowables based on potential output per well.[111] As many as 400 out of 700 wells in this field were unnecessary, representing an estimated expense of $31 million in 1934 dollars.[112] In Kansas, allowables based on the individual well created the same wasteful incentive until acreage allowables began in mid-1937.[113]

The most dramatic case of overdrilling spawned by proration occurred in the relatively shallow East Texas field between 1931 and 1938. As table 4.7 indicates, a vicious circle of allowables assignments, then new-well construction, then reduced allowables for the greater number of wells, then new-well construction, and so forth was experienced.

By 1935, over 19,000 wells, the great majority of which were Rule 37 exceptions, littered the East Texas landscape at a cost of approximately $25,000 per well. Commissioner Thompson acknowledged the cycle:

> The stricter you prorate the lower the allowance you set—the more wells are drilled; then you must still further reduce the allowable. It is a merry-go-round, with the railroad commission getting a lot of the abuse.[114]

By 1939, another 5,000 wells were drilled to give the entire field a density of one well per 4 acres, a far cry from the spacing "rule" of one oil well per 20 acres.[115]

---

[111]W. P. Z. German, "Legal History of Conservation of Oil and Gas in Oklahoma," pp. 158–61.

[112]Northcutt Ely, "The Conservation of Oil," p. 1233.

[113]Innis D. Harris, "Legal History of Conservation of Oil and Gas in Kansas," p. 47.

[114]E. O. Thompson, "The Purpose and Operation of Laws," p. 20.

[115]One East Texas acre contained twenty-seven wells with each well producing at 0.2 percent of capacity. David Prindle, *Petroleum Politics and the Texas Railroad Commission*, p. 50.

Table 4.7
East Texas Allowables Program: 1931–38

Date	Allowable (well/day)[a]	Wells	Production Well (bl/day)[b]	Price ($/bl)	Total Production (bl/day)
1931					
May	—	703	417	0.67	293,452
June	—	1,057	450	0.15	475,081
August[c]	—	1,644	234	0.25	385,227
September[d]	225 bl	2,188	157	0.68	344,368
November	125 bl	3,291	128	0.83	422,527
1932					
January	100 bl	3,934	99	0.83	389,762
March	75 bl	4,659	82	0.83	383,868
May	61 bl	5,919	70	0.75	414,216
July	50 bl	7,246	57	0.75	410,748
September	46 bl	8,195	57	0.75	468,385
November	40 bl	9,057	51	0.75	457,095
1933					
January	28 bl	9,612	37	0.50	351,012
March	1/3 W, 2/3 O	9,898	57	0.25	550,900
May	15% hr-pt	10,123	96	0.25	969,466
July	10% hr-pt	10,335	64	0.50	656,827
September	7.5% hr-pt	10,830	50	0.90	545,344
November	5.75% hr-pt	11,550	38	1.00	441,453

(Continued on next page)

Table 4.7—Continued
EAST TEXAS ALLOWABLES PROGRAM: 1931–38

Date	Allowable (well/day)[a]	Wells	Production Well (bl/day)[b]	Price ($/bl)	Total Production (bl/day)
1934					
January	5% hr-pt	12,191	37	1.00	447,504
April	5% hr-pt	13,038	40	1.00	526,241
July	4.5% hr-pt	14,069	39	1.00	540,921
November	3.6% hr-pt	15,233	30	1.00	454,127
1935					
February	3.6% hr-pt	16,138	30	1.00	490,968
April	3.45% hr-pt	17,002	28	1.00	473,053
July	3.3% hr-pt	18,275	27	1.00	494,953
October	2.8% hr-pt	19,048	24	1.00	464,494
1936					
March	2.85% hr-pt	20,137	23	1.15	462,824
July	2.32% hr-pt	21,087	21	1.15	437,617
1937					
January	2.32% hr-pt	22,104	21	1.15	454,911
July	2.32% hr-pt	23,201	21	1.35	476,953
November	2.32% hr-pt	24,066	19	1.35	456,499
1938					
May	2.32% hr-pt	25,161	15	1.35	379,543

SOURCE: East Texas Engineering Association, *The East Texas Oil Field: 1930–1950* (Kilgore, Tex.: ETEA, 1953), pp. 143–51.
[a]B is barrels; W is per well; hr-pt is hourly potential; O is other: average sand thickness and bottom hole pressure.
[b]The difference between these figures and the allowable figures represents the amount of hot oil produced per well.
[c]Preshutdown

After the war when MER-yardstick allowables became distinct from MDP and spacing exceptions were routinely allowed, the problem of overdrilling would shift from the latter to the former. But in the 1931–39 market-demand period, overdrilling threatened the very heart of proration. Robert Hardwicke warned in 1938, "The reckless investment in unnecessary wells throughout the United States has reached the point where it may cause a breakdown in the entire conservation program."[116]

Subsidization of Marginal Wells. A final distortion of MDP, working in concert with well-spacing exceptions, has been the express intent of creating and maintaining the conditions necessary for submarginal wells to produce profitably. This effort has been twofold: to exempt low-producing wells and some high-cost secondary-recovery wells from the MDF, and to restrict supramarginal production to maintain prices to allow less productive wells to profitably produce.

On April 16, 1931, the Texas legislature unanimously passed the Marginal Well Statute to exempt from MDP wells producing 10 barrels or less at 2,000 feet, 20 barrels or less from 2,000 to 3,500 feet, and 40 barrels or less from 3,500 feet or more. A special minimum of 40 barrels per day was established for the East Texas field. An amendment two years later changed the categories to 20 barrels from 2,000 to 4,000 feet, 25 barrels from 4,000 to 6,000 feet, 30 barrels from 6,000 to 8,000 feet, and 35 barrels from wells deeper than 8,000 feet.[117] Oklahoma passed a similar exemption for wells producing under 25 barrels per day in 1933.[118] Other states granting legislative favor to marginal wells were Kansas (1933), New Mexico (1935), and Louisiana (1936). In the 1946 *Hawkins* case, the Texas Supreme Court opined that not only could every tract owner drill at least one well on his property but that "his allowable cannot be cut down to

---

[116]Robert Hardwicke, "Legal History of Conservation of Oil in Texas," in *Legal History*, 1939, p. 257. Hardwicke, perhaps the country's foremost market-demand proration advocate in the 1930–60 period, goes on to admit, "It is clear that conservation orders with respect to spacing and distribution of spacing and distribution of allowables have been large factors [in overdrilling]."

[117]Ibid., pp. 258–59. For the exempt-well schedule as of 1984, see appendix G, pp. 1957–58.

[118]Beginning with the first proration order in the Oklahoma City field in 1930, marginal wells were given special treatment in the state. W. P. Z. German, "Legal History of Conservation of Oil and Gas in Oklahoma," p. 164.

the point where his well would no longer produce, nor below the point where it could not be drilled and operated at a reasonable profit."[119] Although this ruling would later be abandoned, the TRC's support of prices by lowering the MDF would achieve a similar result. This reflected the political strength of the so-called little guys, numerous independents operating small-tract wells in Texas and other oil states.

The economic consequence of market-demand exemptions and price support has not been only to preserve the active status of low-yield wells. It has also encouraged some well owners to reduce output to obtain marginal-well status. Robert Hardwicke and M. K. Woodward identified commonly employed methods to lower output to achieve exempt-well classification:

1. For pumping wells,
   a. Use small tubing;
   b. Use small pumps and short strokes;
   c. Reduce pumping speed;
   d. Use choke in the bottom of the well's tubing;
   e. Place the pump at a high level in the tubing's oil column; and
   f. Neglect to clean the well or well tubing.
2. For gas-lift wells,
   a. Restrict valve openings;
   b. Set the valves high; and
   c. Reduce the gas supply.[120]

The result was to institutionalize inefficiency by making it profitable for producers to decrease output. This increased excess capacity and left less supply for consumption. And increasing the number of marginal wells (and certain secondary projects falling into the same category), and decreasing the number of nonmarginal wells to increase the exempt-to-nonexempt oil ratio, subjected high-yield wells to greater allowable reductions. The gain of high-cost, low-yield wells, in other words, was at the expense of low-cost, high-yield wells.[121]

[119]*Railroad Commission* v. *Humble Oil and Refining*, 193 S.W.2d 824, at 832 (Tex. Civ. App. 1946).

[120]Robert Hardwicke and M. K. Woodward, "Fair Share and the Small Tract in Texas," *Texas Law Review* (November 1962): 90–91.

[121]M. A. Adelman, "Efficiency of Resource Use in Crude Petroleum," p. 104. Adelman identified the marginal well as a "liability parading as an asset."

The Case for Market-Demand Proration Reconsidered

Table 4.8 reveals how marginal wells were preserved during the proration era. In the absence of regulation, free-market processes would have retired and consolidated many of the wells.[122] Robert Hardwicke, a leading legal authority, advocate, and writer on petroleum conservation law for over four decades, has penned the most elaborate defense of MDP.[123] In a 1949 article, "Market Demand as a Factor in the Conservation of Oil," he defends proration as an integral part of the conservation effort to prevent waste and protect correlative rights.[124] Given the overriding historical importance of MDP compared with other conservation regulations, his argument, complemented by the arguments of others, deserves extended critical analysis.

Six major claims have been advanced for the social beneficence of wellhead proration based on market demand:

1. It prevents physical waste;
2. It prevents economic waste;
3. It preserves competition and innovation;
4. It protects correlative rights;
5. It can be scientifically determined; and
6. It is in the interest of national security.

These points led former Texas railroad commissioner W. J. Murray to contend that market-demand proration "is as essential to sound

---

[122]Information before 1947 is unavailable, but estimates of the number of stripper wells in the early 1930s are near 300,000. In the East Texas field alone, wells producing under 20 barrels per day averaged around 1,500 between 1940 and 1947. See East Texas Engineering Association, *The East Texas Oil Field; 1930–1950* (Kilgore, Tex.: ETEA, 1953), pp. 124–26.

[123]During Hardwicke's career as a regulatory lawyer, he was associated with such major companies as Humble Oil and Magnolia Petroleum, which supported proration but not favoritism to marginal wells.

[124]Robert Hardwicke, "Market Demand as a Factor in the Conservation of Oil," 1 *Oil and Gas Institute* (New York: Matthew Bender, 1949), pp. 149–82. Also see "Limitation of Oil Production to Market Demand," *OGJ*, October 6, 1932, pp. 54–55; "Some Legal and Economic Aspects of Conservation Regulation," in *Essays on Petroleum Conservation Regulation*, ed. Wallace Lovejoy and I. James Pikl, Jr. (Dallas: Southern Methodist University Press, 1960), pp. 93–94, 101–7; "Oil Conservation: Statutes, Administration, and Court Review," *Mississippi Law Review* (March 1941): 386–90; and Hardwicke and Rex Baker, "History of Conservation Law," in *History of Petroleum Engineering* (American Petroleum Institute, 1961), pp. 1116–67.

Table 4.8
U.S. STRIPPER PRODUCTION: 1947–71

Year	Wells in Operation[a]	Average Production[b]	Percentage of Total Production
1947	294,672	2.6	15.1
1948	310,892	3.1	17.5
1949	313,970	3.1	19.0
1950	321,287	3.2	19.0
1951	320,689	2.9	15.2
1952	332,058	3.1	16.3
1953	332,552	3.2	16.3
1954	340,276	3.5	18.7
1955	357,931	3.5	18.7
1956	370,489	3.6	18.6
1957	372,519	3.5	18.1
1958	373,870	3.8	20.9
1959	392,535	3.7	20.7
1960	403,323	3.9	22.4
1961	406,102	4.0	22.6
1962	406,051	3.9	21.7
1963	401,031	3.8	20.2
1964	394,107	3.7	19.9
1965	398,299	4.0	20.7
1966	380,549	3.5	16.0
1967	376,851	3.6	15.5
1968	367,205	3.6	14.6
1969	358,650	3.5	13.5
1970	359,130	3.4	12.5
1971	353,696	3.3	12.3

SOURCE: American Petroleum Institute, *Basic Petroleum Data Book*, 1981 ed., sec. 4, table 4.
[a] At year-end.
[b] Barrels per day.

conservation as is MER proration," although admittedly it is "less understood."[125]

[125]W. J. Murray, "Market Demand Proration," in *Essays on Petroleum Conservation Regulation*, p. 69.

Physical Waste. Without MDP, it is argued, physical waste would occur because less supply would be produced, and even less oil would be preserved for market. Less oil would be extracted because low prices would close poorly situated and low-producing wells, make certain enhanced recovery operations uneconomic, and cause uneven reservoir withdrawals (due to purchaser discrimination) leading to reservoir damage.[126] Less would be consumed, the argument continues, because certain forms of waste would result from aboveground storage of surplus oil.

It is true that if conservation agencies did not stabilize price when production increased relative to demand, a number of marginal wells—many created and preserved by regulation—would face shut-ins or outright abandonment. Yet this is not a compelling argument for MDP; it is a reason for abolishing subsidization to permit resources to shift to more urgent uses, namely, the exploration for and development of larger, better located reserves. Today's stripper wells more often than not were yesterday's big producers, and it is entirely logical for one to recognize that at some point an economic limit is reached and retirement must occur. These reserves can be considered "lost" until changes in price and technology make them economical to extract again. But it is misleading to infer, as Hardwicke does, that total output and proven reserves decrease as active marginal wells do. The opposite is more the case, as Jacqueline Lang Weaver concludes:

> Producers who were lucky enough to discover good-sized pools found their wells prorated to about one-third of their capacity. This reduced the incentive to explore for new discoveries, and from 1956 to 1966, little change occurred in the level of proved reserves of crude oil in the United States.[127]

By abolishing market-demand subsidies, a market process is unleashed whereby new discoveries increase the supramarginal-to-marginal proven reserve ratio, and high-yield well production is relatively increased over marginal-well output. Both changes reflect the elimination of the MDF, which at once discourages exploration

---

[126]Robert Hardwicke, "Market Demand as a Factor in the Conservation of Oil," pp. 169–72. Also see Hines Baker, "Achievement and Unsolved Problems in Oil and Gas Conservation," pp. 15–16.

[127]Jacqueline Lang Weaver, *Unitization of Oil and Gas Fields in Texas*, p. 99.

for rich fields and limits flush well output. Lost output from aged, depleted reserves is replaced by fresh supply.

A related argument is that without MDP, purchaser discrimination would cause physical waste by inciting drainage competition and the dissipation of reservoir energy. This, too, is not persuasive. Assuming that a shut-in or a cooperative selling arrangement could not address the situation, an excellent entrepreneurial opportunity would exist for a buyout, either by an outside company or by a fellow well owner, to preserve the reservoir's capital value. Beyond these self-help and potentially profitable alternatives, recalcitrant operators—and other pool owners who continued to produce with them—would have to suffer the consequences of inefficient behavior as all businesspeople do in a market economy.

The second half of the physical-waste argument asserts that without proration, aboveground waste would occur since excess supply would be held in storage subject to "weathering, leakage, evapora-tion, fire loss, and general deterioration."[128] But why would oil pro-duced in the absence of a restrictive MDF automatically be unmarket-able inventory, incapable of being moved by price reductions? Hard-wicke, ignoring the elementary function of price, asserts, "Unquestionably, when production is greatly in excess of demand, the excess must go into surface storage for an indefinite time."[129] So immersed is Hardwicke in the market-demand straitjacket that the mobility of prices and physical resources—so characteristic of the market economy—is overlooked. Such mobility would prevent sup-ply from being "greatly" in excess of demand and would undercut an "indefinite" storage of crude oil. If prices and therefore demand were fixed by law in the absence of proration, economic theory does point to overproduction and surface waste incidental to it. Yet the disequilibrating factor is not overproduction per se but demand and price manipulation by MDP. Absent intervention, equality between supply and demand can be expected.

The physical-waste-prevention argument tacitly assumes that pro-duction without a market-demand limitation would proceed at open-flow levels. This is not necessarily true. Production depends

<hr>

[128]W. J. Murray, "Market Demand Proration," p. 72.
[129]Robert Hardwicke, "Market Demand as a Factor in the Conservation of Oil," p. 104.

not only on present costs and revenues but also on anticipated costs and revenues. If future revenues are anticipated to be sufficiently high, production will be reserved until the future. Inventory in this case would have a tendency to be held in the reservoir rather than in expensive, wasteful aboveground storage.

Economic Waste. Without MDP, Hardwicke contends, economic waste would occur because all physical waste "results in a loss, without use, of a valuable commodity."[130] Even without physical waste, economic waste would result because low prices from unregulated production make possible "inferior" uses of the product.[131]

To the extent economic waste and physical waste are equated, earlier arguments against the latter overlap to make a case that economic waste as a result of unregulated production is illusory. Moreover, recalling the economic distortions of MDP—the misallocation of market shares, overdrilling, and the penalization of high-yield wells to subsidize marginal wells—proration, not its opposite, can be allied with economic waste. Regarding the argument that "low" prices encourage "inferior" uses of oil, the free-market price—resulting from mutual valuations of demanders and suppliers—must be recognized as the "right" price rather than prices constructed from regulation.[132] An MDP price that is above market levels creates waste rather than prevents waste by precluding certain consumptions that would have been allowed. Economic waste can be associated with MDP, not its absence.

Competition and Innovation. The belief that small independent producers perform a competitive service for the industry and the public at large and therefore should be protected by MDP, implicit in the writings of Hardwicke and others, is prominently argued in the concluding chapter of David Prindle's study of the petroleum policies of the TRC. After detailing the political nature of commission decisions and the wasteful consequences thereof, he justifies their actions as promoting competition and innovation. He concludes:

[130]Ibid.

[131]Although Hardwicke does not use the latter argument, it has been cited by proponents of market demand.

[132]See the discussion on market versus nonmarket pricing in this chapter, pp. 169–75.

By restraining production, supporting prices, and rationing participation in the market, the Commission ensured that the relatively
independent companies would not be exterminated by competition
from the major integrated companies. . . . By protecting the smaller
companies of the industry from the rigors of the free market, the
Commission performed a valuable service to the industry as a whole
[because] . . . the independents are the source of a significant proportion of the creative risk taking in the industry.

Of course, protecting all those relatively inefficient producers in
order to encourage those who might be creative involved a considerable amount of short-run waste. . . . But that is a small cost to pay
for keeping the entrepreneurial spark alive.[133]

Prindle's argument is as follows. Independent producers, because
they are vulnerable in an industry dominated by larger firms, should
be protected by government favor. No matter how high their costs or
limited their production, they should be shielded from the corrective
forces of the free market. Why? Because some small firms might
become innovative in the long run; because economic theory (viz.,
that of Joseph Schumpeter) teaches that the free market will "destroy
itself with its own success" by replacing the would-be innovative
firm with the bureaucratic big firm.[134]

This rationalization of the wastes of state petroleum conservation
law is a blend of three deceptive doctrines: infant-industry protectionism, pure and perfect competition, and the entrepreneurial stagnation thesis.

Protectionism is a doctrine that claims that a noncompetitive firm
helped by government to survive can become competitive and self-
supporting in the long run. Prindle argues that some inefficient
producers will blossom into industry leaders with the crutch of the
MDF. But how long will such a firm need to be propped up? Proration was used for decades in Texas and in other states to help many
of the same wells and companies. How much short-run inefficiency,
at the expense of consumers and efficient producers, should be
tolerated for the sake of late bloomers? Further, are there not certain
independents sufficiently efficient to successfully compete in both
the short and long run without proration? Restated, is there not a
happy medium in many cases between marginal-well owners and

---

[133]David Prindle, *Petroleum Politics and the Texas Railroad Commission*, pp. 191–92.
[134]Ibid., p. 190.

major integrated companies? Surely the fallacy of "one big firm" wielding "economic power" to take over competitors one by one, prevent new entry, and forever enjoy "monopoly profits" does not lurk behind Prindle's petroleum production protectionism.[135]

Another misconception of Prindle's is that a larger number of smaller companies are inherently more competitive and "Pareto optimal" than a smaller number of larger firms. But larger, properly scaled firms are able to do what a "perfect competitor" cannot do— innovate and minimize costs. By reaching optimum size of plant where increasing returns to scale are exhausted, the firm is best able to compete with pricing. This is the "welfare ideal" of the unhampered market—the ability of firms to innovate toward a point of cost minimization.

In petroleum production, optimum size requires larger operations than in a mom-and-pop firm. The majority of ongoing firms must pool the risks of drilling, block-lease to avoid or minimize drainage competition, and have the financial strength to practice delayed production when necessary to serve the market.[136] The latter two attributes require capital from either cash flow or borrowing based on producing-property income. Historically, small companies with only proven reserves have had difficulty obtaining credit because scientific shortcomings in reservoir estimation prevent loan collateralization. Larger integrated firms with cash flow and fixed assets, on the other hand, escape this limitation.

The nature of petroleum production makes the "perfect competitor" of neoclassical theory an inefficient participant in the market. In most cases, only large properly scaled firms able to actively conduct drilling programs and properly manage their reservoirs can satisfy the "rigors of the market." It is a tribute to the market that producers are disciplined to constantly adjust their actions to use a minimum of resources to satisfy consumer preferences.

---

[135]The fallacy of predatory pricing will be examined when the Standard Oil Trust is studied in chapters 18 and 22.

[136]Economists have long recognized important advantages of medium- to large-scale oil production. For nineteen reasons given in 1922 for the "overwhelming advantage of large units of capital and management," see Roswell Johnson, L. G. Huntley, and R. E. Somers, *The Business of Oil Production* (New York: John Wiley and Sons, 1922), pp. 63–64. Financial strength is needed for independents to practice block-leasing before drilling or make adjacent land purchases after oil is located.

Drawing upon economist Joseph Schumpeter's theory of capitalistic evolution, Prindle cements his argument by postulating that the short-run success of the competitive process sours into entrepreneurial stagnation as obese, clumsy firms emerge from the fray. In Schumpeter's words:

> Since capitalist enterprise, by its very achievements, tends to automatize progress, we conclude that it tends to make itself superfluous—to break to pieces under the pressure of its own success. The perfectly bureaucratized giant industrial unit not only ousts the small or medium-sized firm . . . but in the end it also ousts the entrepreneur.[137]

Schumpeter's theory, adopted by Prindle, fails to recognize innovation as an ongoing process fueled by constant changes in consumer preferences, entrepreneurial ideas, and technological possibilities. In the imaginary world of equilibrium where perfect knowledge reigns, entrepreneurship and innovation would indeed become obsolete. But in the real world of disequilibrium, the barometers of change, profit and loss, are always at work, signaling the presence of entrepreneurial activity. The transfer of resources from inefficient to efficient producers, in petroleum production as elsewhere, takes place continually. It does not halt mysteriously after the initial resource transfer from small, weak firms to large, strong firms.[138]

The view that MDP can increase competition and innovation suffers from a "pretense of knowledge" that the right mix of firms and their relative market shares can be determined outside freely expressed consumer preferences. Major companies and independents of varying sizes each have unique capabilities for locating and extracting oil and gas deposits.[139] Only the market can decide to what extent they can parlay their talents to compete successfully.

[137]Joseph Schumpeter, *Capitalism, Socialism, and Democracy* (New York: Harper & Brothers, 1950), p. 134. Elsewhere he adds: "[Capitalism] proceeds by competitively destroying old businesses. . . . There always corresponds to it a process of decline, of loss of caste, of elimination." Schumpeter, *The Theory of Economic Development* (Cambridge, Mass.: Harvard University Press, 1936), p. 156.

[138]For a defense of entrepreneurial activity as equilibrating, and a critique of Schumpeter's description of profit seeking as disequilibrating, see Israel Kirzner, "Entrepreneurship and the Market Approach to Development," in *Toward Liberty*, 2 vols. (Menlo Park, Calif.: Institute for Humane Studies, 1971), vol. 2, pp. 174–208.

[139]In farm-out arrangements, acreage-rich majors use the exploratory talents of independents by assigning leases to them in return for a percentage of oil and gas discovered. Acreage-rich independents benefit from cash-rich and technically skilled major companies through farm-outs, land sales, and mergers. For a discussion of the complementary relationship between major and independent producers, see James

Correlative Rights. The fallacy of equating the absence of MDP with large unsold and wasting inventory leads Hardwicke to argue that correlative rights would be violated where, if supply exceeded demand, purchasers discriminated against certain common-pool owners to injure their right to produce a "fair share" of the reservoir.[140] As explained previously, price reductions offer well owners a chance to move inventory, and cooperative arrangements or mergers are available to avoid the problem entirely. Producers in a free market have the opportunity to adjust their actions in the face of discrimination or other threatening forms of business behavior; they should not, under the banner of correlative rights, be guaranteed impunity in the face of wasteful, autonomous behavior within a common supply source as the law has allowed them to do. Correlative rights based on the equal opportunity to obtain "fair shares" do not depend on proration.

Scientific Determination. Defenders of MDP have emphasized the precision of crude-oil-demand forecasts to defend its practicality as a regulatory program. While early proration was admittedly haphazard and crudely intended to fix prices, Hardwicke contends that the "development of a scientific method of determining reasonable market demand removed [the price-fixing] objection."[141] Prior to the "scientific methods," state regulators and purchasing companies used market demand exclusively to determine well allowables. In 1933, the U.S. Bureau of Mines developed a technical forecast to determine national and state demand by extrapolating seasonal trends, motor vehicle demand, fuel-oil use, imports, inventory changes, and other factors. As a result of these estimates and regular nomination hearings, the argument continues, not only did price considerations become obsolete, but industry stabilization was achieved and "the oil industry [became] bankable, particularly as the independent was concerned."[142]

Critics of the entire market-demand exercise have understood the subtle implications of the absence of price in its determination. But

---

McKie, "Market Structure and Uncertainty in Oil and Gas Exploration," *Quarterly Journal of Economics:* (November 1960): 543–71.

[140]Robert Hardwicke, "Market Demand as a Factor in the Conservation of Oil," p. 163.

[141]Ibid., p. 162.

[142]W. J. Murray, "Market Demand Proration," p. 73.

market-demand proponents see banishment of explicit price discussions as a rescue from the price-fixing charge.[143] It is not. By failing to recognize that changes in price affect supply and demand, as well as inhibit demand revisions up until the moment of purchase, authorities introduce rigidities based on historical magnitudes that are not present in a true market.

When the federal government prepares its monthly forecast of national demand, and crude purchasers submit binding estimates at state hearings, there is no schedule of demands corresponding to different prices. There is only one demand based on an unmentioned but assumed-to-be-constant (or nearly constant) price. This stabilizes the crude-oil market, enhances the marginal well as a bankable asset, and makes the forecast self-fulfilling, but does not make a case for MDP. Stability is not to be valued if the "instability" of declining prices is forgone. The free market is an institution satisfying consumers, not guaranteeing producers a certain price. Access to credit markets by marginal-well operators is not to be valued if these loans are at the expense of high-yield wells penalized by a low MDF. And the accuracy of a particular supply-demand configuration is not to be applauded if it was accomplished by precluding the market's spontaneous, albeit unpredictable, outcomes.

MDP is not a program of science but of price manipulation to achieve political ends. As William Kemnitzer argued:

> Any statistician can study, compute, and chart trends of supply and demand at *fixed* prices, perchance with great accuracy. But he cannot predict price in a competitive market. And if he cannot predict prices, then he cannot predict either supply and demand. If, therefore, any statistician, economist, or other "authority" attempts to predict or to forecast supply and demand and such forecasts are enforced, those persons become parties, albeit perhaps unwittingly, to restraint of trade, price fixing, and attendant monopolistic practices.[144]

National Security. Proponents of MDP have argued that the creation of excess capacity by limiting wells to a fraction of capacity

---

[143]Robert Hardwicke in his 1949 article, "Market Demand as a Factor in the Conservation of Oil," went so far as to say that "the price of oil does not control the size of demand" (p. 179). By 1960, having witnessed years of low market-demand factors to stabilize price, he admitted that price and demand were linked. See Hardwicke, "Some Legal and Economic Aspects of Conservation Regulation," p. 106.

[144]William Kemnitzer, *Rebirth of Monopoly* (New York: Harper Brothers, 1938), p. 102.

serves as a reserve in case a large production increase is necessary to meet an emergency. Hardwicke and Murray credit victory in World War II to excess well capacity created by prewar proration.[145] Consequently, support for MDP is urged for "patriotic reasons."[146]

The rationale of national security and national defense has used to justify a host of interventions in the petroleum market that could not be supported by economic considerations alone.[147] Yet on national defense grounds, the argument is suspect. Efficiency is needed as much—if not more—in wartime as in peacetime.

Wartime petroleum requirements include judicious employment of scarce drilling equipment; full production from productive, low-cost fields; and continual development of new reserves. As previously explained, MDP interferes with these ends by encouraging overdrilling and marginal wells. Patriotism, therefore, dictates that MDP not weaken a country's peacetime production structure by subsidizing poor wells at the expense of productive fields in case full-scale production is suddenly needed. This is particularly true should the conflict become protracted, necessitating the continual replacement of supply sources.

Conclusion. Market-demand proration can be effectively rebutted by its own criteria. What is good for the marginal-well owner cannot be shown to be good for the flush-well owner, the industry, the consumer, or the economy in general. MDP is fundamentally a political program, rationalizing the short-run profitability needs of vested interests. It is a total government-planning effort at odds with market ordering and economic efficiency.

Natural-Gas Regulation

Natural gas production has been regulated at the state level by

1. setting maximum gas-oil ratios,
2. prohibiting certain end-uses of production,
3. setting a percent-of-open-flow limit on production,
4. restricting output to "market demand," and
5. setting a minimum price in certain fields.

---

[145]Robert Hardwicke, "Market Demand as a Factor in the Conservation of Oil," p. 180; and W. J. Murray, "Market Demand Proration," p. 73.

[146]Ibid., p. 74.

[147]See chapter 13, pp. 757–61.

The first limitation, previously studied, concerns gas production from oil wells (casinghead or associated gas); the other four regulations deal primarily with gas from gas wells (nonassociated gas).[148]

End-Use Restrictions. Banning open-air discharges of natural gas was one of the three original aims of conservation law and the first regulation to directly prevent the perceived waste of a natural resource.[149] From the beginning, laws against venting casinghead and nonassociated gas have been hotly debated, especially in Texas where historically over one-third of U.S. gas production has centered.

An 1899 Texas natural-gas statute required that nonassociated gas be used for light, fuel, or power purposes within ten days after a well's discovery. Venting was prohibited past this time.[150] Resistance to this law developed, and on April 25, 1933, the Texas legislature rescinded a ban on "stripping," whereby gasoline condensate is extracted before the gas is released into the open air, so long as the discharges did not exceed 25 percent of well capacity or "reasonable market demand."[151] This victory by gas producers was challenged by pipeline companies that waged an intense educational campaign to outlaw venting as "waste" to indirectly force producers to sell supply to them as an inexpensive alternative to expensive reinjection.[152] The pipelines' effort resulted in a comprehensive gas statute

[148]See this chapter, pp. 159–62. Oil wells are defined in most states as producing more than 1 barrel of crude oil per 100,000 cubic feet (100 Mcf) of natural gas; gas wells are defined as producing less than 1 barrel per 100,000 cubic feet. Oklahoma delineates between the two at 10,000 cubic feet per barrel.

[149]See chapter 3, p. 82.

[150]Maurice Cheek, "Legal History of Conservation of Gas in Texas," in *Legal History,* 1939, p. 269.

[151]Texas Railroad Commission, *A Chronological Listing of Important Historical Events, Legislative Acts, Judicial Decisions, Orders, and Other Relevant Data, Regarding the Railroad Commission of Texas* (Austin: TRC, October 1, 1980), p. 9. The flaring issue concerned the 125-mile, 1.5-million-acre Panhandle field, called the "East Texas" of gas fields. David Prindle, *Petroleum Politics and the Texas Railroad Commission,* p. 61.

[152]"Conservation associations were organized by the pipeline companies which throughout 1934 carried on a ceaseless campaign by newspaper advertisements, billboards, radio talks, distribution of literature, legislative tours, and the like, all to the end that the law be repealed." Maurice Cheek, "Legal History of Conservation of Gas in Texas," pp. 279–80. Whether coincidental or not, the commission issued the Agua Dulce no-flare order in the same year as the pipelines' effort that forced producers in this condensate field to either market, recycle, or shut in their gas. Jacqueline Lang Weaver, *Unitization of Oil and Gas Fields in Texas,* pp. 139–40.

in 1935, the Gas Conservation Act, which outlawed venting nonassociated gas before or after stripping and prohibited the use of low-sulfur ("sweet") gas in the manufacture of carbon black.[153] Voluntary unitization and MDP for gas fields were also authorized. With this law, and laws in other major gas-producing states modeled after it, gas cycling became an important oil-patch industry. In Texas, for example, over twenty-nine such plants were operating by 1942 compared to only one experimental plant less than a decade before.[154]

With the issue of nonassociated gas settled, the next political tussle in Texas concerned venting casinghead gas. The 1935 gas-to-oil ratio law proved unenforceable, and flaring gas above and even below this ratio was perceived as a major conservation problem. After completing a study in 1945 documenting that over one-half of all gas produced in the state was flared, Texas Railroad Commissioner W. J. Murray issued shutdown orders ("flare orders") for the Seeligson field in 1947 and sixteen smaller fields between December 1948 and April 1949. By 1949, casinghead gas, along with nonassociated gas, was restricted to pipeline use or reinjection. The Texas gas war was a victory for self-described conservationists and burgeoning natural-gas transmission companies. It was also a victory for the state treasury, which had many more transactions to tax.[155]

Percent-of-Open-Flow Ceilings. Before and during market-demand gas proration, examined below, several states passed regulations to limit gas-well output to a percentage of open flow. The Oklahoma Conservation Act of 1915, considered the first comprehensive gas statute passed by any state, gave the corporation commission the authority to limit nonassociated gas withdrawals to a percentage of

---

[153]Oklahoma (1905), Wyoming (1919), Texas and Montana (1921), and Louisiana (1922), along with Arkansas, Kansas, Michigan, and several other states, restricted or prohibited the use of natural gas in the manufacture of carbon black, an ingredient used by the rubber and ink industries. See Leslie Moses, "Statutory Regulations in the Carbon Black Industry," *Tulane Law Review* (October 1945): 83–97. Restrictions on natural-gas consumption by carbon-black manufacture were upheld as a lawful end of state regulation in *Henderson* v. *Thompson et al.,* 300 U.S. 258 (1937). Natural-gas-exhaustion scares were behind early carbon-black regulation. See, for example, *OGJ,* January 10, 1918, p. 32.

[154]Jacqueline Lang Weaver, *Unitization of Oil and Gas Fields in Texas,* p. 140.

[155]For detailed discussions of this episode, see Maurice Cheek, "Legal History of Conservation of Gas in Texas," pp. 274–86; and David Prindle, *Petroleum Politics and the Texas Railroad Commission,* pp. 61–67.

well capacity.[156] A 25 percent maximum would be adopted. In 1924, six years after passing a gas statute with market-demand language, Louisiana issued a maximum production schedule tying a well's percentage of open flow to its proximity to other wells.[157] Other early statutes specifying output percentage limits were passed in Michigan (1929), Mississippi (1932), Kansas (1935), and South Dakota (1939). The TRC, under its general authority to prevent waste, set maximum percentages in the prolific Panhandle field beginning in 1932. Today, approximately twelve states, including the major gas-producing states of Louisiana, Texas, Oklahoma, New Mexico, and Kansas, either have percentages in force or have the authority to implement them.

Market-Demand Proration. Prorating natural-gas production to a predetermined market demand is distinguishable from crude-oil proration in several important respects. The rationale rests on correlative right protection for producers against purchaser discrimination rather than waste per se,[158] because recoverability from gas reservoirs is not damaged by high withdrawal rates as it is from some oil reservoirs.

Because natural gas is not as flexibly transported and stored as crude oil, market demand is established for individual gas fields, rather than for the entire state, at periodic hearings. Output restrictions reflect demand conditions in specific areas, unlike crude-oil proration, which also reflects national demand and imports.[159]

[156]In 1913, Oklahoma began ratable gas production, set at 25 percent of capacity, that became embodied in the 1915 statute. W. P. Z. German, "Legal History of Conservation of Oil and Gas in Oklahoma," pp. 133–34.

[157]The Louisiana gas-well schedule was as follows:

Acreage between Wells	Open-Flow Maximum (%)
160	24
80	21
40	18
20	15
10	12
5	9
Below 5	7

Yandell Boatner, "Legal History of Conservation of Oil and Gas in Louisiana," p. 66.

[158]Stephen McDonald, *Petroleum Conservation in the United States*, p. 49.

[159]A hot-gas statute was considered in 1935 by the Texas legislature to accompany hot-oil legislation but was not enacted. "Federal Price Control of Natural Gas Sold

The first mention of market demand in conjunction with a natural-gas statute was in a 1918 Louisiana law that limited gas production to 25 percent of capacity if greater output was in excess of "market demand." In 1935, Texas passed the aforementioned Gas Conservation Act (also called the Gas Waste Act), which limited gas-well output to "reasonable" market demand determined by hearing. "The impetus of the 1935 Act," stated Jacqueline Weaver, "was to protect the correlative rights of nonintegrated producers by instituting an equitable system of prorationing and end-use controls that either would encourage or force the pipeline-owners and producers to cooperate with the independents."[160] Other states to pass natural-gas proration laws were Arkansas and Mississippi (1933), Kansas (1935), Michigan and Oklahoma (1937), Alabama (1945), and New Mexico (1949). As of 1984 (and 1990), approximately nineteen states had authority to restrict gas reservoir output to market demand.[161]

In the early 1980s, when an excess deliverability problem became apparent with natural gas, proration assumed new importance. In April 1983, the Oklahoma Corporation Commission sharply cut gas allowables statewide in response to a request by Oklahoma Natural Gas, an intrastate pipeline company.[162] In Texas, industry interest surfaced to reform the state's market-demand law. The IOCC called a meeting to discuss allowables and ratable takes. A national market-demand proposal, unveiled by Pennzoil chairman J. Hugh Liedtke, was similar to state regulation.[163] Because of the inherent conflicts between producers and pipelines, wide industry support necessary to adopt the proposal has been absent.

Price Floors. Statutory price floors have been used in the effort to limit nonassociated gas production.[164] In 1920, the Oklahoma Corporation Commission issued an order fixing the price of natural gas

to Interstate Pipelines," *Yale Law Review* (1950): 1479. The FTC later sought to extend the Connally Act to natural gas without avail. *Business Week,* January 2, 1937, p. 31.

[160]Jacqueline Lang Weaver, *Unitization of Oil and Gas Fields in Texas,* p. 71.

[161]See appendix F, pp. 1948–49. Texas in 1977 changed from submitted producers' forecasts to purchaser nominations, similar to crude-oil market-demand hearings. *OGJ,* February 28, 1977, p. 59. This methodology was made permanent in 1979.

[162]*OGJ,* April 11, 1983, p. 58. Also see *OGJ,* May 9, 1983, p. 66, and May 16, 1983, p. 45.

[163]*OGJ,* January 3, 1983, p. 44.

[164]On one occasion, a price minimum was used to prevent oil waste. On September 22, 1914, the Oklahoma Corporation Commission issued an order setting a price floor

in the Cushing field at $0.09 per Mcf. The order rested on a 1913 statute subjecting first purchasers of gas to price regulation if, after notice and hearing, "said owners and the party taking such . . . cannot agree."[165] Foreshadowing the reasoning behind the 1954 *Phillips* decision, which placed wellhead gas sales in interstate commerce under federal price regulation, the Oklahoma Corporation Commission argued that because the gas pipeline company was under public-utility regulation at retail, the gas-well owner, by dealing with him, "becomes one of the essential parts of that utility and is subject to the same rules and regulations by the Commission as the pipe lines of said utility are subject to."[166] The order was not contested.

Decades later, the Oklahoma commission again set minimum gas prices. A pricing dispute between two pipeline companies led to a pricing order in 1946 of $0.07 per Mcf to prevent economic and physical waste.[167] Upheld by the Oklahoma Supreme Court in the 1950 *Cities Service* case, the price floor was raised to $0.09 per Mcf in 1952. The order remained in effect until the U.S. Supreme Court voided the price law on April 11, 1955, as conflicting with the 1938 Natural Gas Act.[168]

The Louisiana legislature set a price floor for natural gas in 1946 and 1948. Similar talk was heard in the Texas legislature in 1950. Kansas set an $0.08 per Mcf minimum for the Hugoton gas field in 1948. The Kansas Corporation Commission order followed a strong lobbying effort by royalty owners and producers anxious to link waste to prevailing prices. Sustained by the Kansas Supreme Court in the 1950 *Nebraska Natural Gas* case, the price was increased to

---

of $0.65 per barrel on October 1, 1914, for the Cushing and Healdton pools. On November 25, 1914, the minimum was lowered to $0.50 per barrel. With the 1915 conservation law, the pricing law became a dead letter until it was formally abolished in 1933. W. P. Z. German, "Legal History of Conservation of Oil and Gas in Oklahoma," pp. 126–27. In 1973, the Kansas Corporation Commission received the authority to set field gas prices to prevent waste.

[165]Ibid., p. 148.

[166]Ibid.

[167]Order 19514, December 9, 1946. In the commission's words, "The taking of gas at the prevailing prices resulted in both economic and physical waste of gas, loss to producer and royalty owners, loss to the state in gross production taxes, inequitable taking of gas from the common source of supply and discrimination against various producers in the field."

[168]*Natural Gas Pipeline Co. of America* v. *Panama Corporation*, 349 U.S. 44 (1955).

$0.11 per Mcf in 1953, whereupon a purchasing company filed suit. The order was again upheld by the state supreme court. The price remained in effect until May 12, 1958, when the U.S. Supreme Court invalidated state authority to regulate wellhead gas prices as being in conflict with the Federal Power Commission's authority to do likewise.[169]

A final attempt to fix wellhead prices for natural gas would be made at the state level despite two Supreme Court decisions declaring such action unconstitutional. On October 5, 1972, the Oklahoma Corporation Commission set a floor price of $0.20 per Mcf for intrastate and interstate gas. With certain exceptions, wells that sold gas under this price were to be shut in. The commission argued that such action was not price fixing but "prohibit[ing] the production of gas under circumstances which we find will produce waste." The order was stayed and then dismissed in U.S. district court as restraining interstate commerce.[170]

Natural Gas Conservation Law: A Summary Critique. The major economic objection to state regulation of natural-gas production—whether by prorating demand, restricting end-use, setting price minimums, or capping output—is that the authorities are artificially imputing a higher value to the resource than its particular economic circumstances allow it to have. Natural gas has commercial value, but only if its value, measured by consumer expenditure, is greater than the resources expended to bring it to market, measured by cost. This has often not been the case. One reason has been the large expense of constructing pipelines directly to each field and to wells within a field, which is unlike the situation with crude oil that can be conveniently trucked or barged to pipeline connection points and easily stored aboveground. Plentiful supply provided by favorably located wells has kept gas prices low and "crowded out" poorly located competitors. The conflict between conservation and profitability (a barometer of economic value) has been recognized by the courts, which have blessed the former at the expense of the latter.[171]

---

[169]*Cities Service Gas Co.* v. *Corporation Commission,* 355 U.S. 391 (1958). For a discussion of the case, see Robert Sullivan, "Kansas," in *Legal History,* 1960, pp. 93–95.

[170]*OGJ,* October 16, 1972, p. 98, and July 2, 1973, p. 33.

[171]For several examples, see Jacqueline Lang Weaver, *Unitization of Oil and Gas Fields in Texas,* pp. 298–300.

Price regulation of natural gas dedicated to interstate markets unintentionally added to the conservation problem. Some oil operators were discouraged from selling residue gas to interstate pipeline companies for fear that the Federal Power Commission, under authority of the Natural Gas Act of 1938, could apply public-utility regulation to them—for reasons similar to those given by the Oklahoma Corporation Commission in 1920.[172] Moreover, interstate pipeline companies were wary of paying increased wellhead prices because rate-increase filings could be challenged by the commission in prolonged, costly hearings.[173] The alternative of cycling gas back into the reservoir was little known prior to the 1930s and required unitization after that time to be in anyone's self-interest. But government-created disincentives to unit operations, not the least of which were antitrust law and the allowables preference given to small tracts, hindered cooperation that would have facilitated cycling efforts to increase future profits for the reservoir as a whole.[174] The Cotton Valley suit brought by the Justice Department in 1947 against a unitized gas-condensate field in Louisiana, just six months after U.S. Attorney General Tom Clark had commended the IOCC for "great advances" in cooperative reservoir development, reminded the producer community of the latent power of antitrust law.[175]

Early natural-gas "waste" was a fact of life. If nearby carbon-black plants were not present to demand gas as a substitute for coal, the alternative was stripping out the liquids for motor gasoline and flaring the residue. For decades, venting was also encouraged by the erroneous belief that oil followed gas in the well bore. When

[172]Howard Williams, "Conservation of Oil and Gas," pp. 1177–78. Also see chapter 8, p. 458.

[173]William Holloway, "State Regulation of Minimum Field Gas Prices," *Oklahoma Law Review* (February 1951): 75.

[174]Hines Baker wrote in 1949, the year Texas legalized secondary recovery agreements, that "the lack of a statute in Texas specifically authorizing voluntary unitization of oil pools has greatly hindered the development of gas-return projects." Baker, "Achievements and Unsolved Problems," p. 25.

[175]See Burns Errebo, "Unit Operation at Cotton Valley: An Alleged Violation of the Sherman Act," *Tulane Law Review* (October 1949): 80–81. Although the government complaint was directed at marketing and not production itself, the IOCC complained of the "difficulty . . . in determining the dividing line" between the two. The case would be dismissed, but that "close call" increased the uncertainty of the legal status of wellhead cooperation. Ibid., p. 81.

more became known about the role of gas in the recovery of crude oil, and particularly when pipeline technology allowed linkage between major supply areas in the Southwest and major consuming areas in the Northeast, the market came of age. What had been a waste by-product turned into a coveted product to the extent that marketability problems and counterproductive regulation could be overcome.[176]

Occasional use of price minimums by major producing states was a particularly self-defeating measure. Mandating prices above free-market levels merely create surpluses that breed marketing difficulties, the very problem gas-conservation law attempts to lessen. Although some producers who enjoyed sales at the higher prices gained from the intervention, other producers with unmarketable supply had an increased propensity to perform wasteful activities with their surplus. This cost was in addition to what the consumer lost to higher prices and less supply.

Limiting gas output to "market demand" is susceptible to the same criticisms that were earlier leveled against crude-oil proration. Although natural-gas proration is less restrictive than oil proration, the freedom of buyers to alter purchases until the point of sale and to tailor demand to an array of prices is inhibited. Proration can also be "gamed," which means that the forecasts favor some producers over other producers—often small-tract operators over their larger brethren.[177]

Natural-gas conservation law, outwardly promoted as being in the common interest because it supposedly preserves a depletable natural resource, has been the province of special-interest battles. While producers and royalty owners have historically lobbied for price floors and otherwise nonrestricted production, pipeline companies have fought for unregulated pricing and prohibitions on flaring and stripping to decrease price and increase commercial supply. In addition, in Texas as elsewhere, the drive to tighten gas-well

---

[176]The economics of natural-gas conservation was stated by James Westcott in 1930: "A by-product natural resource may be wasted when it has a low value, but when the dollars and cents become important and mount to fair figures, means are devised for its conservation." Westcott, *Oil: Its Conservation and Waste* (New York: Beacon, 1928), p. 209.

[177]Jacqueline Lang Weaver, *Unitization of Oil and Gas Fields in Texas*, pp. 276–77, 498–99.

allowables relative to crude oil was supported and led by the Independent Refining Association of America, which correctly saw natural gas as a competitor to fuel oil.[178] Coal interests have long advocated federal and state policies that would raise the price and decrease the supply of natural gas.[179] The consumer's interest, and the scientific cause of conservation, have been incidental in these political spats.

Compulsory Pooling and Unitization

Forced cooperative development of commonly owned oil and gas reservoirs has been described by petroleum geologist and conservation writer Michel Halbouty as "total conservation" in contrast to the "partial conservation" of well spacing, proration, and the like.[180] Mandatory cooperation is the "correction" of piecemeal conservation regulation that has discouraged, and, in fact, precluded, the operation of the reservoir as a single unit.

Mandatory Cooperation: Some Legal Precedents

Mandatory cooperation in the United States predated compulsory pooling and unitization in oil and gas by a half-century. In two 1885 decisions, the U.S. Supreme Court upheld state laws forcing communal action on water projects on the grounds that the general welfare of the owners was served.[181] A number of subsequent cases concerning partition fences, grazing districts, water-improvement districts, and cotenancy likewise have been decided on the principle that "the otherwise absolute right of each owner must yield or be modified by the correlative rights of others for what is determined to be the common good."[182]

---

[178]The Independent Refiners Association of America estimated that in 1950 in Texas alone gas production was displacing 1.4 million barrels of crude oil daily. *OGJ*, April 13, 1950, p. 57. Also see *OGJ*, March 23, 1950, p. 156.

[179]See, for example, *NPN*, August 18, 1954, p. 57. Also see chapter 30, pp. 1853–55.

[180]Michel Halbouty, "Conservation—Total or Partial?" in *Ahead of His Time*, pp. 196–210.

[181]"The Legislature [may] establish regulations by which adjoining lands, held by various owners in severalty, and in the improvement of which all have a common interest, but which, by reason of the peculiar natural condition of the whole tract, cannot be improved by any of them without the concurrence of all, may be reclaimed and made useful to all at their joint expense." *Wurts v. Hoagland*, 114 U.S. 606 (1885).

[182]R. M. Williams, "Compulsory Pooling and Unitization," *15 Oil and Gas Institute* (New York: Matthew Bender, 1964), p. 232.

Mandatory Pooling

Mandatory petroleum pooling, the forced integration of tracts to form an acceptable spacing unit under state law, first became a legal controversy in 1927 when Oxford, Kansas, passed an ordinance to limit drilling to one well per city block. The producers involved were required to combine royalty interests with all other city owners on a block on a square-foot basis. This led to the landmark *Marrs v. City of Oxford* case in which a circuit judge upheld the ordinance, which paved the way for other, similar city and state statutes. He reasoned:

> It is sufficient to say that the police power is not limited to the protection of the health, peace and morals of the community. It has been said to extend to acts that increase the industries of the state, develop its resources and . . . promote the public convenience and the general prosperity.[183]

Three years later, Oklahoma City passed a similar ordinance to restrict dense city drilling. In *Grant v. Oklahoma City* a year later, the order was upheld by the circuit court of appeals on the basis of the *Marrs* decision.[184]

Mandatory pooling on the state level began in 1935 when Oklahoma and New Mexico passed such laws in conjunction with well-spacing requirements. Indeed, unless a state, such as Texas, grants spacing exceptions to allow drilling on every small tract, pooling law is required to allow small-tract owners to share in production.[185] The New Mexico statute stated that if co-owners within a spacing unit could not agree on a plan, pooling might "be required" to "afford to the owner of each tract in the pool the opportunity to

---

[183]Quoted in W. P. Z. German, "Compulsory Unit Operation of Oil Pools," *American Bar Association Journal* (June 1931): 399.

[184]See Allen King, "Pooling and Unitization of Oil and Gas Leases," *Michigan Law Review* (January 1948): 323. In 1935, an ordinance by the city of South Houston creating 16-acre drilling districts with one well per district was sustained by a federal court in Texas. Northcutt Ely, "Conservation of Oil," p. 1236.

[185]This is an example of a further intervention attempting to correct the distortive effects of a prior intervention, a major theme of government involvement presented in chapter 29.

recover or receive his just and equitable share of the oil and gas."[186] Oklahoma's statute was virtually identical except for requiring an 80 percent acreage agreement for units greater than 10 acres and limiting compulsory units to 40 acres or less.[187] In 1936, Louisiana passed a similar regulation that was litigated and upheld by the Supreme Courts of Louisiana and the United States. In *Hunter Co. v. McHugh*, the U.S. Supreme Court held that "a state has constitutional power to regulate production of oil and gas so as to prevent waste and to secure equitable apportionment among landholders . . . fairly distributing among them the costs of production and of the apportionment."[188]

Upon this legal basis, approximately thirty-seven states have passed mandatory pooling statutes. Texas, which joined the list with the Mineral Interest Pooling Act of 1965, had allowed spacing exceptions for small-tract drilling for decades. The new law reflected two Texas Supreme Court decisions, inspired by the economic plight of large-tract drillers, that invalidated the one-third well, two-thirds acreage formula that favored small-tract production. The *Normanna* (1961) and *Halbouty* (1962) decisions had created "compulsory pooling by judicial decree" by inciting small-tract operators to join together to qualify for higher allowables. The 1965 law applied to reservoirs found or first produced after March 8, 1961, the day of the *Normanna* decision.

Texas's pooling law was not entirely a repudiation of the correlative rights of small-tract owners. Its provisions reflected the views of independent producers such as Michel Halbouty, himself a victim of small-tract drilling, who undertook a six-month crusade to change industry and public opinion. The law excluded new discoveries, required that voluntary pooling be tried first, and set a maximum acreage to stop short of forced unitization.[189]

---

[186]"Law Providing for the Conservation of Oil and Gas in New Mexico," Reprinted in *Legal History*, 1939, p. 294.

[187]W. P. Z. German, "Conservation of Oil and Gas in Oklahoma," pp. 209–10.

[188]320 U.S. 222 at 227 (1943).

[189]See Jacqueline Lang Weaver, *Unitization of Oil and Gas Fields in Texas*, pp. 124–31; David Prindle, *Petroleum Politics and the Texas Railroad Commission*, pp. 78–80; and James Keahey, "The Texas Mineral Interest Pooling Act: End of an Era," *Natural Resources Lawyer* (April 1971): 359–67.

Mandatory Unitization

Whereas pooling refers to the integration of tracts to achieve a particular spacing unit, *unitization* or *unit operations* refers to a consolidation of interests in the entire reservoir.[190] In 1929, the first unitization plan, voluntarily agreed upon, was spearheaded by the Pure Oil Company for the 5,450-acre Van field in Texas.[191] Such agreements, however, proved to be the exception rather than the rule before the 1940s for the aforementioned reasons.

Mandatory unitization began in 1940 with a Louisiana law that required cooperative development of secondary recovery operations. The act stated, "In order to prevent waste and to avoid the drilling of unnecessary wells, the commissioner shall . . . require the re-cycling of gas in any pool or portion . . . and promulgate rules to unitize separate ownership and to regulate production of the gas and reintroduction of the gas into productive formations."[192] This statute was used several months later to force unitization of the Cotton Valley field, which was sustained by the Louisiana Supreme Court.[193]

In 1945, the Oklahoma legislature, after unsuccessful attempts in 1941 and 1943, followed Louisiana's lead with a statute mandating poolwide operation when "reasonably necessary" to "substantially increase" secondary recovery.[194] Unlike the Louisiana statute, it applied to both oil and gas fields. Industry interests, led by the Mid-Continent Oil and Gas Association, were instrumental in the law's passage in 1945 and in avoiding its repeal in 1947, 1949, and 1951. The law stipulated that 50 percent of the involved owners could petition for a hearing, after which consent of 85 percent of the owners

---

[190]Henry Doherty originally used the term "plan of unit operation." Herman Kaveler, "Unitization," in *History of Petroleum Engineering* (New York: American Petroleum Institute, 1961), p. 1175.

[191]J. Howard Marshall and Norman Meyers, "Legal Planning of Petroleum Production," *Yale Law Journal* (November 1931): 60. Early unit and cooperative development is described in Vance Rowe, "Production Engineering, Unitization Proves Itself," *NPN*, July 30, 1934, pp. 19–22.

[192]Quoted in R. M. Williams, "Compulsory Pooling and Unitization," p. 253.

[193]*Crichton* v. *Lee*, 25 So.2d 229 (1946).

[194]Noticed R. M. Williams, "The Oklahoma act was patterned to a large extent after the laws in numerous states creating drainage, irrigation, flood control, grazing, and similar statutory districts." Williams, "Compulsory Pooling and Unitization," pp. 254–55.

was required to invoke the Plan of Unitization. After several court battles, the statute was declared constitutional by the U.S. Supreme Court in 1952.[195]

Mandatory-unitization law has been applied to two other areas besides secondary recovery—well spacing with primary production and public-land development. Oklahoma, in the same 1945 act, became the first state to require unitization for primary production. Since that time, approximately twenty states have claimed the authority to force unit operations of natural lift production, subject to a typical proviso that 75 percent or more of the owners of the involved acreage agree. Public-land unitization statutes were passed more slowly, with the majority becoming law in the 1950s and 1960s. While most states with secondary unitization statutes have the authority to compel primary unitization, a number of states that can compel unitization of primary operations do not have the authority to compel unitization of secondary operations. Among the major oil states, Texas is in a class by itself; unitization is done voluntarily or not at all with both primary and secondary operations.[196] Jacqueline Weaver explained why:

> Texas entered the 1930s without compulsory pooling or unitization because such laws were anathema to the independent producers who had discovered and secured an advantageous position in the East Texas field, and to legislators who feared—with some justification—that such acts would allow the major oil companies to monopolize the oil fields. Henceforth, without compulsory pooling or unitization, small-tract owners and producers in other fields could be protected against confiscation only by being granted Rule 37 exception permits and per-well allowables. Once this regulatory inheritance became vested, no compulsory pooling or unitization bill would be supported by the independent producers and, without this support, no such bill could pass.[197]

Only in 1965 did Texas pass mandatory pooling, which, as discussed, covered an acreage unit rather than a field.

---

[195]*Palmer Oil Corp.* v. *Amerada Petroleum Corp,* 343 U.S. 390 (1952).

[196]Unsuccessful attempts to pass a unitization law in Texas occurred in 1933, 1947, and 1968. See *OGJ,* April 19, 1947, p. 64; and Wallace Lovejoy, "Oil Conservation, Producing Capacity, and National Security," *Natural Resources Journal* (January 1970): 63.

[197]Jaqueline Lang Weaver, *Unitization of Oil and Gas Fields in Texas,* p. 108.

Mandatory Cooperation as a Market Alternative

Compulsory pooling and unitization have been strongly supported by economists as the least costly and most effective of all conservation regulations designed to prevent waste.[198] Indeed, by making the reservoir rather than the well the competitive unit, the wastes of overdrilling, shutdowns, and market-demand proration are avoided. But this view severely underestimated the crippling effect of government intervention on "self-help" market associations and the commonplace implementation of voluntary unit agreements once the industry fully understood the implications of reservoir mechanics in the post-World War II period.[199] One telling intervention may be highlighted here: the almost immediate transformation, as seen in table 4.9, from the time when voluntary cooperation was prohibited by state and federal antitrust laws to the time when cooperation became mandatory. Because of this—not to mention other disincentives created by state and federal policies—volunteerism was given a suspect opportunity to address the inefficiency of multiple recovery plans working within a common reservoir in the crucial 1926-40 period.

To what extent greater market cooperation would have occurred in the absence of government-created disincentives cannot be known. Some time undoubtedly would have been needed to educate producers about the implications of the new theories of reservoir mechanics. But with the cost savings of fewer wells and the enhancement of capital value as a result of greater recoverability from rate-sensitive reservoirs, a powerful incentive existed to prorate expenses and revenues within a plan of pooling or plan of unitization, even if some sacrifice or uncertainty existed.[200]

---

[198]For instance, see Melvin de Chazeau and Alfred Kahn, *Integration and Competition in the Petroleum Industry*, chap. 10; and Stephen McDonald, *Petroleum Conservation in the United States*, chap. 11.

[199]See chapter 3, pp. 112–31.

[200]"Companies and individuals with large experience in unitization feel that it is a matter of give and take, and that where a particular formula may be slightly to their disadvantage, the rewards of unitization are so great that the sacrifice is worth taking." Raymond Myers, *The Law of Pooling and Unitization*, 2 vols. (New York: Banks and Co., 1967), vol. 1, p. 109. With cost and revenue escalations in the 1960s and particularly the 1970s, the incentive to unitize reached new highs. Wallace Lovejoy remarked in 1970, "Economic pressures have forced more and more voluntary unitization everywhere." Lovejoy "Oil Conservation, Producing Capacity, and National Security," p. 63.

Table 4.9
Prohibition and Compulsion in Cooperative Petroleum Production

Jurisdiction	Antitrust Law Passed	Antitrust Law Relaxed (oil & gas)	Antitrust Law Relaxed[a] (state land)	Mandatory Pooling	Mandatory Unitization	
					Primary Production	Secondary Production
State						
Alabama	1896	1945	1945	1945	1945	1957
Alaska	1955	1955	1955	1955	1955	1955
Arkansas	1897	1939	1943	1941	1951	1957
California	1907	1929	1941	1947	1971	1971
Colorado	1937	1951	1947	1951	X	1965
Florida	1915	1945	1945	1945	1945	1945
Illinois	1965	1941	1941	1951	X	X
Indiana	1897	1947	1947	1947	X	X
Kansas	1889	1939	1939	X	1967	1967
Kentucky	1890	1944	1944	1960	X	X
Louisiana	1890	1936	1936	1936	1960	1940
Michigan	1889	1937	1937	1939	X	X
Mississippi	1890	1932	1932	1938	X	1972
New Mexico	1891	1929	1941	1935	X	1975
New York	1889	1963	1963	1963	X	X
N. Carolina	1889	1945	1945	1945	X	X

N. Dakota	1890	1953	1941	1953	X	X
Ohio	1892	1967	1965	1967	1967	1967
Oklahoma	1890	1945	1945	1935	1945	1945
Pennsylvania	X	X	–	1963	X	X
Tennessee	1889	1943	1943	1943	1974	1974
Texas	1889	1935	1945	1965	X	X
		1949[b]	1949[c]			
Utah	1898	1955	1945	1955	X	X
Wyomong	1911	1945	1945	1951	X	1951
Federal						
Public domain	1890	1930	–	1935	1935	1935
Acquired lands	1890	1947	–	1947	1947	1947
Indian lands	1890	1938	–	1938	1938	1938
Naval reserves	1890	1935	–	1938	1938	1938

SOURCE: Various state conservation commissions.

NOTE: X = no law exists.

[a] Subject to permission from state conservation agencies.

[b] Antitrust law was relaxed for oil in 1935 and for gas in 1949.

[c] Antitrust law was relaxed for oil in 1945 and for gas in 1949.

One state, Texas, offers a glimpse into the natural incentives to voluntarily unitize.[201] Voluntary unitization occurs despite the state's multidecade "anti-unitization policy."[202] Agreements in this state were voluntary since the threat of compulsion was not present to prod operators into such agreements. Over 1,000 unitization agreements were made in this state in the "legal" 1949–78 period by hundreds of different applicants despite incentives for small-tract drilling that remained until the 1960s. Earlier examples of unitization, such as the Van field in 1929 between four majors and Humble Oil's wholly owned Sugarland and Olney fields in 1930, add to this total (table 4.10).[203] On the natural-gas side, approximately forty units were sanctioned by the attorney general under the 1935 Gas Conservation Act.[204] In the 1970s, however, pervasive government intervention in oil production continued a time-honored tradition of discouraging unit agreements, however unintentionally (table 4.10)[205] Another sixteen unitization agreements were approved by 1982.[206]

Although not a precise case study, the Texas experience dispels the simple notion that diffuse ownership creates ipso facto market failure. In the most detailed examination of the Texas experience,

---

[201]California offers another case study of voluntary unitization. Between 1929, the year when unit operations were legalized, and 1971, when secondary operations could be ordered (and 1973 when primary operating units could be ordered), over 100 primary and secondary units were formed. Letter to author from James Campion, Division of Oil and Gas, California Department of Conservation, November 24, 1982. As far back as 1948, it was observed that poolwide agreements in California "ha[ve] overcome the practical difficulties of unitization to some extent." William Holloway, "California, 1931–1948," in Legal History, 1949, pp. 49–50. In Wyoming, prior to 1951 when pooling and unitization became mandatory, an estimated forty poolwide cooperative plans were made, although many were on federal land where coercion was potentially present. Conversation with Chuck Farmer, Wyoming Oil and Gas Conservation Commission, November 17, 1981. In other states, voluntary agreements have been more common than forced agreements. "The great majority of unit operations in this country have been voluntary." Interstate Oil Compact Commission, A Study of Conservation of Oil and Gas, p. 61. But this fact is open to multiple interpretations because the threat of force has been present.

[202]Jacqueline Lang Weaver, Unitization of Oil and Gas Fields in Texas, p. 68.

[203]Ibid., pp. 53–54.

[204]Ibid., p. 78.

[205]See chapter 9, pp. 515–17.

[206]Jacqueline Lang Weaver, Unitization of Oil and Gas Fields in Texas, p. 317.

Table 4.10
APPROVED OIL AND GAS UNIT OPERATIONS IN TEXAS: 1949–78

Year	Number	Year	Number	Year	Number
1949	1	1959	44	1969	49
1950	11	1960	64	1970	38
1951	19	1961	57	1971	20
1952	14	1962	65	1972	23
1953	14	1963	56	1973	22
1954	13	1964	75	1974	26
1955	19	1965	74	1975	12
1956	23	1966	59	1976	12
1957	22	1967	70	1977	13
1958	22	1968	59	1978	15

SOURCE: Texas Railroad Commission hearing files.

Jacqueline Weaver has questioned the assumption of prohibitive transaction costs.

> Most often, the large operators make every effort to negotiate fairly with all interested owners and the result is usually a compromise formula that all owners can accept. The large operators generally bargain fairly in order to avoid . . . administrative hassles and legal entanglements.[207]

The holdout problem, she adds, is surmountable.

> If a large number of owners refuse to join a proposed unit, the unitization allocation formula will often be renegotiated to attract the holdouts. If only a few owners refuse to join, restrictions of the unit's activities will be privately negotiated with the nonconsenters who then become silent. Because unitization can increase oil and gas production so much, the unit can pay these economic rents to the nonconsenters and still make a profit. Of course, if enough owners in the field refuse to unitize, their considerable power . . . may defeat the unit's formation.[208]

[207]Ibid., p. 189.

[208]Ibid., p. 248. She adds: "Those who sign the agreements generally receive fair treatment. The lack of compulsory process allows owners of tracts with structural or regulatory advantage to capture the economic rents of their favorable position. . . . Negotiated formulas which perpetuate vested rights to some degree are inevitable" (p. 192).

The TRC has encouraged unitization by regulatory means. Field orders prohibiting gas wastage, for example, "reduc[ed] the differential between a producer's vested interest in the regulatory status quo and his expected interest under a unitization agreement."[209] The commission has reduced allowables for holdouts when a plan of unitization has been in progress and has indirectly forced unitization (since 1964) by invoking forced pooling to eliminate holdouts. Nonetheless, this is not sufficient to explain the volume of voluntary agreements over a thirty-year period.

Disincentives to formal unitization would have remained without government intervention. Informational problems, particularly early in a field's life, can prevent "fair and reasonable participation formulas."[210] Obtaining the prerequisite geologic and engineering data, not to mention the legal process itself, is costly.[211] Some operators have been hesitant to enter into agreements when they have felt the lead company, often the company owning the largest land share, would incur greater operating expenses than if it operated independently. Thus, in some cases the quest for cost minimization has prevented formal unitization, leaving operators to run wells separately or form subgroups to do so.[212]

Economics aside, an evaluation of compulsory cooperation should consider the impropriety of denying property rights to a minority in order to side with the majority's preference. There is also the potential situation where holdouts are assigned unfair shares in the pooling or unitization plan—a "tyranny of the majority." The major problem of voluntary unitization, imperfect knowledge about the reservoir and relative shares of surface owners above it, is not eliminated by forced cooperation but is placed on the shoulders of holdouts.[213] "Reluctance to pool or unitize . . . due to the fear of making

---

[209]Ibid., p. 166.

[210]Ibid., p. 83.

[211]Ibid., p. 111. For one example that took two years and $2 million (in 1960 dollars), see ibid., p. 379n. 39.

[212]W. J. Murray, "Engineering Aspects of Unit Operations," 3 *Oil and Gas Institute* (New York: Matthew Bender, 1952), p. 3.

[213]Economist Henry Steele refers to the mandatory solution as making "an imperfect situation still more imperfect." Steele, "Public Policy Problems of the Domestic Crude Oil Industry: Comment," *American Economic Review* (March 1964): 119.

a bad bargain"[214] is mental unrest made permanent by forced participation.

Mandatory Conservation as a Political Program: A Concluding View

State conservation law has not been a common-good program— contradicting the Nashian "consensus" interpretation of the transformation from unregulated to regulated production. Economic perversities occurred every step of the way. Market rigidities were introduced, supply was withheld from consumers, overdrilling raised industry costs, imports were artificially encouraged, producers acted inefficiently by "playing the regulations," and special interests skewed the regulations toward their own ends.

Special-Interest Battles

An initially flawed program, based on the presumption that a legislative solution was needed to correct free-market competition predicated on the rule of capture, was predictably politicized. Michel Halbouty, an industry advocate for conservation law based on unit production, has lamented that conservation as it has historically been practiced, particularly in Texas, has been "political conservation" or "conservation as practiced when political expedience rather than sound engineering and geological considerations guide the decisions of a regulatory or legislative body."[215] Six layers of special-interest battles can be identified.

First, there was an intraindustry clash, centered in Texas, over the implementation and control of mandatory proration that would affect all oil-producing regions in the country. Although injunctions against proration orders were effectively used by the relatively unorganized anti-prorationists—the flush-well independents, small integrated companies, and small refineries located in the East Texas field—their opponents were too strong to defeat in the political arena. The great majority of independents outside East Texas, including North Texas and Southwest Texas, favored state production

---

[214]Ralph Shank, "Pooling Problems," *Texas Law Review* (May 1950): 686.
[215]Michel Halbouty, "Conservation—Total or Partial?" p. 199.

limitations.[216] Humble Oil & Refining, the largest landholder in East Texas, openly worked for mandatory proration, as did other majors active in the field.[217] A number of East Texas independent producers favored the lower output, higher price combination, as did state authorities desiring higher severance tax revenue. The preservation of stripper wells was crucial to both.[218] Many citizens in East Texas, concerned about pollution and the safety hazards of unrestrained production, also worked for state regulation.[219] These groups prevailed.

Outside East Texas, proration in the major oil states was generally advocated by major oil companies and opposed by independents. Price stability was the primary aim of the majors, and prorated domestic output could be replaced by imports from South America and elsewhere. Independents, without foreign production, looked first to restrict imports. In fact, both domestic production and imported crude would be restricted by 1932 by a political compromise. According to William Kemnitzer, the majors bought support for proration by accepting tariffs advocated by the Independent Petroleum Association of America and erasing a $40,000 debt of the association.[220]

[216]Lobby groups favoring East Texas proration, if not proration throughout the Southwest, were the North Texas Oil and Gas Association, Central Proration Committee, Southern Oklahoma Stripper Well Association, Northwest Oklahoma Stripper Well Association, Kansas Stripper Well Association, and Pennsylvania Grade Crude Oil Association.

[217]For an account of Humble Oil's involvement with wellhead proration before and during the East Texas oil boom, as well as the division within the industry over the proration question, see Henrietta Larson and Kenneth Porter, *History of Humble Oil & Refining Company*, pp. 316–26, 447–87.

[218]A major factor influencing independent operators in and outside East Texas to support proration was concern for their low-output wells. As Charles Roeser, president of the Texas Oil and Gas Association, stated: "Conservation is important to the 30,000 stripper wells in Texas, which should be preserved. It is possible to preserve them only by conservation." *OGJ*, November 12, 1931, p. 136. The Texas Oil and Gas Association, led by such members as H. L. Hunt, a major East Texas landowner, gave early support to Sterling's martial-law declaration and remained on the side of mandatory proration.

[219]Sentiment of the local townsfolk against unregulated production was expressed by J. Lewis Thompson, president of the East Texas Home and Landowners Association, in "East Texas and East Texans," *12 Annual Proceedings* (New York: American Petroleum Institute, 1931), pp. 9–12.

[220]William Kemnitzer, *Rebirth of Monopoly*, pp. 134–35.

Once the machinery of proration was in place, the independents succeeded in tailoring the program for the "little guy" at the expense of the major companies. By 1935, all five major Southwest producing states had special legislation for marginal wells that predominately belonged to shoestring operators. Spacing rules were routinely violated by small-tract operators who captured production predominantly from under land belonging to acreage-rich majors. Ironically, independents took control of the majors' program to neutralize, if not reverse, its intended benefit.

Second, there was the "little guy-big guy" controversy, centered in Texas, over small-tract drilling. As detailed by political scientist David Prindle, this has been the single most debated, litigated, and time-consuming aspect of this state's regulatory effort.[221] Other major oil states, such as Louisiana, Oklahoma, New Mexico, and, later, Alaska, have relied on compulsory cooperation; California and some other states have avoided the problem altogether by not having strict spacing rules. Behind the scenes has been a muted effort by drilling firms and well supply and service companies, interested in a liberal exceptions policy, to create more demand for their goods and services.[222]

Third, there was a clash between those producers who spearheaded regulations that decreased supply and raised price and consumers who desired the opposite. Production ceilings, justified as being in the long-run interest of consumers, reflected the political strength of certain organized industry segments and the lack of consumer organization. A participant in the conservation debate in the 1930s, Rep. Samuel Pettengill (D-Ind.), titled a chapter of his book about the hot-oil war, "The Forgotten Man—The Consumer."[223] Northcutt Ely made the same point when he described conservation

[221]David Prindle, *Petroleum Politics and the Texas Railroad Commission,* pp. 44–55, 73–81. Two of the seven major policy episodes in the fifty-year history of the Texas Railroad Commission's effort with petroleum regulation concerned well-spacing exceptions.

[222]The role of drilling, well service, and well supply trade groups, such as the International Association of Oil Well Drilling Contractors, the American Association of Oil Well Drilling Contractors, and the Petroleum Equipment Supply Association, in obtaining favorable spacing policies was passive. Spacing exceptions were as much a judicial as an administrative outcome, and these associations left well enough alone, unlike their producer counterparts.

[223]Samuel Pettengill, *Hot Oil: The Problem of Petroleum,* pp. 29–43.

law as "producers' legislation" passed over the "indifference of the consuming public."[224]

The power of consumers to change anti-consumer conservation law at the voting booth was limited by two key factors. First, the oil industry and its infrastructure were so important in major oil states that pro-producer policies overwhelmed support for lower prices. Commissioner Thompson, for example, estimated that 2 million of 7 million Texans benefited directly from higher oil prices.[225] Millions more benefited indirectly. The second factor was that voters from states without significant production were powerless to change oil-state policies.

Fourth was the interest in higher prices of net oil-exporting states prevailed over that of net oil-importing states. By preventing price declines, major producing states in the Gulf Coast and midcontinent areas increased oil revenues at the expense of consuming areas, such as the Northeast. Further, shielding marginal wells from market forces raised industry costs to benefit the home-state industry at the expense of out-of-state consumers.[226]

A prominent example occurred in 1962 when a cost-cutting proposal offered by two major operators to close seven-eighths of the wells in the East Texas field was vetoed by the TRC. Although production would not have been changed, concern centered around job losses in an area dependent on oil-related employment.[227] Above-market costs represented more jobs and demand for drilling, well service, and well supply companies centered in oil states. Again, a nonmarket interregional wealth transfer occurred between "have" and "have not" oil states.

---

[224]Northcutt Ely, "The Conservation of Oil," p. 1241.

[225]NPN, September 15, 1948, p. 42. In California, voters who rejected market-demand proration did so in part because of active opposition within the industry. A unified industry in favor of the law would have revealed that voters were less sophisticated.

[226]Texas was particularly at fault by allowing high-cost small-tract drilling, which fostered an overbuilt drilling service and supply industry. See the discussions in M. A. Adelman, "Efficiency of Resource Use in Crude Petroleum," pp. 106–7; and David Prindle, *Petroleum Politics and the Texas Railroad Commission,* pp. 125–27.

[227]Wallace Lovejoy and Paul Homan, *Economic Aspects of Oil Conservation Regulation,* p. 121. In 1970, Lovejoy calculated the overall investment in unused capacity to be over $9 million with yearly maintenance of over $1 billion. Lovejoy, "Oil Conservation, Producing Capacity, and National Security," pp. 92, 95.

Fifth, corruption, conflict of interest, and inefficiency on the part of oil conservation agencies tainted their desire and ability to protect basic property rights.[228] In the case of the TRC, this went further than scattered controversies; it resulted in the greatest oil robbery in U.S. history.

The East Texas slant-well scandal began in the 1940s and intensified in the following decade when oil from the great field began to migrate eastward because of a water drive propelled by depletion.[229] Operators, mostly independents in the western half of the field, used existing technology to aim their well bores eastward to capture the retreating oil, located mainly under major-company property. Slant wells became common knowledge, but the TRC, given its limited budget in light of its broad regulatory functions and an unwritten rule to favor independents over majors, was not alert to the ongoing violations.[230] The commission did issue several new rules to stem the illegal activity, but it was not until the early 1960s that the controversy came to a head. In April 1961, a Shell Oil well encountered a slant well, and a group of victimized major companies, led by Humble Oil, launched a private investigation. Soon thereafter, Commissioner W. J. Murray instructed the commission to do the same. To head off both groups, the East Texas Producers Group, which included many guilty independents, was created.[231]

The inquiry continued, and it was discovered that, with the help of the private companies running fraudulent directional surveys and corrupt TRC field personnel falsifying inspection reports, hundreds of wells had pirated millions of barrels of oil through slant-well drilling.[232] Three hundred eighty wells were closed and $1 million in penalties was assessed, but the damage had been done by a

---

[228]This also has interfered with the ability of conservation agencies to enforce the regulations themselves. For example, see "Conservation Is a Mockery in Oklahoma," *OGJ*, March 2, 1950, p. 28. Agency corruption hit its peak in the Oklahoma and East Texas hot-oil war. See chapter 12, pp. 652–54.

[229]This discussion is adopted from David Prindle, *Petroleum Politics and the Texas Railroad Commission*, pp. 81–94.

[230]Their effort was also discouraged by the political clout of independents who were almost entirely the guilty parties.

[231]Among other things, the East Texas Producers Group demanded that the U.S. attorney general press antitrust charges against the major companies.

[232]Estimates of the value of illegally obtained oil ranged from $40 million to $1 billion. David Prindle, *Petroleum Politics and the Texas Railroad Commission*, p. 84.

corrupt political climate that favored independents and a conservation agency so encumbered by regulatory activity that it neglected its most basic duty—the protection of property rights.

A second property rights problem has been more recent. Thefts of oil and oil-related equipment amounted to an estimated $18 million a day in the early 1980s and involved as much as 3 to 6 percent of all oil and oil products produced in the United States. Such thefts translated into an estimated $100 million per year that consumers paid in higher prices.[233] In response, industry trade groups and oil field supply companies organized the Petroleum Industry Security Council to curtail the theft epidemic. This private-sector initiative again reflects the failure of authorities to perform their most basic duty.

State oil regulation, like all regulation, faces an inherent administrative problem. If the administrator is from the oil industry, he is prone to conflicts of interest, such as occurred in the incident that led to the resignation of W. J. Murray from the TRC in 1963.[234] On the other hand, an outsider suffers from ignorance of the industry his decisions are affecting. An example was Olin Culberson of the TRC, who candidly admitted: "I am a cowpuncher and don't know much about [oil and gas]. If voters had put me on meat packing, maybe I would know a little bit more about it."[235] The problem of "who regulates" has caused innumerable errors in state oil and gas regulation as has other government interference with the petroleum industry.

Sixth, producers of competing fuels lobbied to persuade authorities to reduce oil and gas output to achieve greater relative market shares. In 1950, as previously mentioned, the Independent Refiners Association of America lobbied the TRC to impose a strict market-demand proration on natural gas and natural-gas liquids. From the beginning of the conservation debate, the National Coal Association has actively urged federal officials to reduce oil output sold at

---

[233]*Wall Street Journal*, December 24, 1980, p. 7; *OGJ*, February 8, 1982, p. 79.

[234]See David Prindle, *Petroleum Politics and the Texas Railroad Commission*, pp. 92–94.

[235]Federal Power Commission, "Natural Gas Investigation," Docket G-580, pp. 3518, 3526.

"demoralizing" prices and restrict gas usage for "unworthy" purposes.[236]

Summary

The primary result of production restrictions to achieve "conservation" has been to create waste of the oil and gas resource itself, as well as to misuse resources both within the industry and by other industrial sectors. This waste represents a large margin of error, much of which might have been avoided had the free-market alternative been allowed to work against the problems confronting the industry in the 1920s and later. There can be no laboratory experiment—much less an agreed-upon quantitative measure of waste—to compare precisely how the market alternative would have fared against the regulatory alternative, but three things are known. First, conservation regulation historically has been wasteful and abused by political interests. Second, self-interest and market processes work to combat economic waste. And third, despite all obstacles, voluntary unitization agreements have been made over a five- to six-decade period. These conclusions suggest that mandatory conservation law to restrict production was the wrong road to take.

---

[236]Comments of John Battle, executive secretary of the National Coal Association, before the Senate Committee on Mines and Mining (1933). Quoted in Samuel Pettengill, *Hot Oil—The Problem of Petroleum*, p. 102.

Appendix to Chapter 4: Geologic Waste

In chapters 3 and 4, reference is made to oil wastage from rapid extraction under drainage competition. Underground or geologic waste is contrasted with drilling waste—overdrilling—and surface waste—evaporation and contamination. This appendix describes geologic waste to provide a better understanding of oil conservation and the regulatory issues surrounding it.

Efficient oil production requires efficient utilization of reservoir energy to maximize recovery by natural means. Oil left behind by primary (natural) recovery requires more expensive secondary and tertiary techniques to extract, and some oil is nonrecoverable with existing technology. Oil is driven to the surface by gas pressure, water pressure, the force of gravity, or a combination of the three. These energy agents are activated when penetration of a hydrocarbon reservoir creates a point of least pressure.

Gas-driven reservoirs are either solution-gas driven, where the gas is dissolved in oil, or gas-cap driven, where in addition to dissolved gas there is a gas phase over the oil liquid phase. Both provide drive to propel oil to the surface: the gas cap by exerting downward pressure on oil and expanding when a penetrating drill bit creates a low-pressure point; and dissolved gas by expanding, which physically moves oil toward the pressure drop at the wellbore. In water-driven reservoirs, the aquifer (water-bearing rocks) exerts pressure from beneath or from the edge of the oil zone and, when there is a drop in pressure, moves in to push oil to the wellbore. In classic reservoirs, both a gas cap and an aquifer provide energy for primary recovery.[1]

Inefficient use of reservoir energy, resulting in a loss of oil that could have been recovered by natural means, occurs most frequently under the following scenarios. In gas-cap reservoirs, the driving

[1] Primary or natural recovery can be contrasted with secondary and tertiary recovery where the oil is propelled to the surface by artificial means.

energy can be dissipated by depleting the gas-cap displacing agent. This was a common practice during the prescientific recoverability era when gas was blown off in hopes that oil would follow.[2] A second waste of cap-gas reservoirs, less detectable, is an oil extraction rate so rapid that gas is drawn down to cone the extraction area so gas is produced instead of oil. Gas coning can reduce the percentage of total oil in the reservoir that is recovered by primary means from the normally expected 20 to 25 percent to less than 10 percent.

In a dissolved-gas reservoir, waste occurs when extraction is at such a high rate that a reservoir pressure drop breaks gas out of solution near the wellbore. Separated, or free, gas does not act as an efficient energy agent but is immobilized in countless pore spaces in the oil sands, which inhibits oil movement or permeability around the wellbores. Reduced permeability can mean that less than 5 percent of the reservoir is recovered by primary means as opposed to 10 to 15 percent.

Water-drive-reservoir waste occurs when a sufficiently high extraction rate causes water coning, which is analogous to gas coning. Water is drawn to the low-pressure point, which obstructs oil from reaching the wellbore. The result is a high water-to-oil ratio and separated pockets of nonrecovered oil.

Lawyers and economists who have analyzed historical production problems with petroleum have cavalierly assumed that open-flow production created geologic waste. An influential book written by geologists and reservoir engineers in 1951, *Petroleum Conservation,* gives credence to their presumption. In the chapter on "Efficient Operation of Petroleum Reservoirs," it is concluded that "ultimate oil recovery from most pools is directly dependent on the rate of production."[3] For each reservoir, there is a "maximum rate of production that will permit reasonable fulfillment of the basic requirement for efficient recovery."[4] Production, it is added, must be "sufficiently low."[5] An essay written in the late 1950s by reservoir engineer Rupert Craze, "Development Plan for Oil Reservoirs," made the same points.

[2]See chapter 3, p. 109n. 93.
[3]Stuart Buckley, ed., *Petroleum Conservation* (Dallas: E. J. Storm, 1951), p. 151.
[4]Ibid.
[5]Ibid.

Experience has proved that one of the most essential factors in meeting the requirements for efficient oil recovery is control (and by control is meant restriction) of the rate of oil production. Control of excessive production of oil and gas is also necessary to prevent premature dissipation of these displacing agents. The ultimate oil recovery from most pools is directly dependent on the rate of production. For each reservoir . . . there is a maximum efficient rate of production, or MER.[6]

Each author uses the adjective "most" to describe rate-sensitive reservoirs, which raises a red flag that some reservoirs are rate insensitive and, contrary to Craze's final point, have no MER of production. Yet virtually all lawyers and economists erroneously equate full production with reservoir damage.

A revisionist interpretation of reservoir mechanics is in order. Modern thinking on the subject has tended to conclude that many, if not most, reservoirs are rate insensitive. In other words, a significant proportion of oil reservoirs has no MER or at least a very wide MER range. B. C. Craft and M. F. Hawkins concluded in 1959:

> Recovery from true solution gas-drive reservoirs by primary depletion is essentially independent of both individual well rates and total or reservoir production rates. . . . The recovery from very permeable, uniform reservoirs under very active water drives may also be essentially independent of the rates at which they are produced.[7]

Reservoir engineers today concur that most modern reservoirs do not have damagingly high production rates, which removes geologic waste as a rationale for government intervention. The next question is, to what extent did major reservoirs of the past (e.g., East Texas, Oklahoma City, Seminole, Signal Hill) have a well-defined MER that was acutely violated to significantly reduce oil recoverability? (Small reservoirs of the past were probably rate insensitive.) To the extent that recoverability was not significantly impaired by past unregulated production rates, historical conservation waste collapses into

---

[6]Rupert Craze, "Development Plan for Oil Reservoirs," in *Petroleum Production Handbook*, ed. Thomas Frick and R. William Taylor, 2 vols. (Dallas: Society of Petroleum Engineers, 1962), vol. 2, pp. 33-28 to 33-29.

[7]B. C. Craft and M. F. Hawkins, *Applied Petroleum Reservoir Engineering* (Englewood Cliffs, N.J.: Prentice-Hall, 1959), p. 197.

drilling waste and surface waste (and intertemporal production problems from a nontechnical viewpoint), which constitute a different and much smaller problem than hitherto believed.

5. Wartime Planning of Exploration and Production

Government direction of economic activities, rare in U.S. history, has typically accompanied situations perceived as abnormal and of special urgency. In petroleum, government planning has occurred on five occasions, thrice during wartime and twice during peacetime.

In this chapter, the experiences with planning of the heavily regulated exploration and production phase during World War I, World War II, and the Korean conflict are studied for historical content and economic consequence.[1] Standby oil and gas planning, which followed the Korean conflict, is also examined. The chapter concludes with a theoretical discussion of the relative merits of government-directed interfirm cooperation and consumer-directed interfirm rivalry during emergency periods. Other planning experiences—the "hot-oil" crisis and New Deal regulation of the 1930s and price and allocation regulation in the 1970s—are treated in separate chapters.[2]

Wartime Planning

World War I

During America's period of neutrality in World War I (August 1914–April 1917), preparations for economic planning were made for petroleum as well as for other industries. The importance of fuel oil for ships, aircraft, and land vehicles attracted this early interest. In August 1915, President Woodrow Wilson created the Council

[1]Wartime planning for phases other than exploration and production is examined for transportation in chapter 12, pp. 630–36; for refining in chapter 19, pp. 1109–14, 1134–47, 1151–57; and for retailing in chapter 23, pp. 1313–19, and chapter 24, pp. 1396–1430.

[2]New Deal planning is studied in chapter 3, pp. 99–103; chapter 12, p. 637–51; chapter 19, pp. 1119–31; and chapter 23, pp. 1344–63. Energy-crisis planning in the 1970s is examined in chapter 9, pp. 486–532; chapter 12, pp. 667–81; chapter 20, pp. 1185–1234; and chapter 27, pp. 1624–91.

of National Defense with the secretaries of war, navy, agriculture, commerce, interior, and labor as appointees.[3] In April 1916, the Petroleum Advisory Committee (PAC) was formed within the Defense Council. Composed of prominent industry leaders, with Alfred Bedford, president of Jersey Standard, as chairman, the PAC had no regulatory functions.

"Although sincere patriotism was involved," George Gibb and Evelyn Knowlton remarked, "the Cooperative Committee on Petroleum of the Council of National Defense grew out of some shrewd and long-range thinking in the industry."[4] Foremost in this strategic outlook was favorably shaping government involvement with their industry. Oil producers were aware of the regulatory precedents set by such agencies as the Interstate Commerce Commission, the Department of Agriculture, the Federal Reserve Bank, and the Federal Trade Commission. Oil producers were also familiar with the Oklahoma Oil Conservation Act, which gave unprecedented powers of intervention to a state government. If there was to be federal oil regulation, the industry would not wait to hear about it; they planned to have a major say in its formulation.[5]

After the United States entered the war on April 6, 1917, President Wilson replaced the PAC with the producer-dominated National Petroleum War Service Committee. The new agency was placed within the War Industries Board, which had replaced the Defense Council on July 28, 1917.

The War Industries Board would become "the most powerful of all the wartime government agencies."[6] With Bedford continuing as chairman, the War Service Committee offered the government a united industry front to facilitate wartime planning.[7]

[3]Public Law 191, 39 Stat. 493 (1916); and Public Law 85, 39 Stat. 166 (1916). See James Weinstein, *The Corporate Ideal in the Liberal State: 1900–1918* (Boston: Beacon Press, 1968), pp. 217–18.

[4]George Gibb and Evelyn Knowlton, *The Resurgent Years, 1911–1927* (New York: Harper & Brothers, 1956), p. 238.

[5]Pre–World War I regulation in a context of industry advocacy is documented in Gabriel Kolko, *The Triumph of Conservatism* (New York: Free Press, 1963); and James Weinstein, *The Corporate Ideal in the Liberal State*.

[6]George Gibb and Evelyn Knowlton, *The Resurgent Years*, pp. 221–22.

[7]Along with Bedford, the other thirteen members were W. C. Teagle, president, Jersey Standard; E. C. Lufkin, president, Texaco; G. S. Davison, president, Gulf; E. L. Doheny, Pan American; H. F. Sinclair, president, Sinclair; J. W. Van Dyke, president, Atlantic; W. S. Farish, president, Gulf Coast Oil Producers Association, and vice president, Humble; E. W. Clark, Refiners of California and vice president, Union;

On August 10, 1917, Congress passed the Food and Fuel Control Act (Lever Act), which gave the president broad powers to direct the petroleum industry by wartime planning. The stated purpose of the act was to "provide for the national security and defense by encouraging the production, conserving the supply, and controlling the distribution of food products and fuel" and to "prevent, locally or generally, scarcity, monopolization, hoarding, injurious speculation, manipulations, and private controls, affecting such supply, distribution, and movement; and to establish and maintain governmental control of such necessities during the war."[8]

The act defined fuel as fuel oil and coal. Gasoline and kerosene, two major petroleum staples, were not mentioned; neither was natural gas, which was only indirectly involved in the war effort. Agriculture was the major focus of the statute, and, reflecting oil-industry sentiment, there was reservation about the inclusion of oil at all.[9]

Under Lever Act authority, President Wilson on August 23 created the U.S. Fuel Administration, with Harry Garfield as fuel administrator, to regulate the pricing and distribution of coal. On January 11, 1918, the Oil Division was created within the Fuel Administration by executive order to extend price and allocation regulation to petroleum. The Oil Division was headed by Mark Requa, a California oil producer and mining engineer.[10] Within its fourteen subdivisions, the Oil Division would regulate the petroleum industry more closely

---

J. S. Cosden, Western Petroleum Refiners Association, and president, Cosden & Co.; Frank Haskell, president, Mid-Continent Oil and Gas Association, and vice president, Tidal Oil Co.; Samuel Messer, president, National Petroleum Association, and treasurer, Emlenton Refining; J. H. Markham, producer; and V. H. Manning, director, Bureau of Mines.

[8]Public Law 41, 40 Stat. 276 (1917).

[9]*Oil & Gas Journal*, February 14, 1918, p. 34. Cited hereafter as *OGJ*.

[10]Mark Requa, a leading voice in the Independent Oil Producers Agency and a tireless advocate of oil-production tax benefits, was perceived as an ally by most of the industry. Prominent oil producer E. L. Doheny commented, "I can safely say that the appointment [of Requa] will meet with the approval of every oil producer in the country." *OGJ*, January 17, 1918, p. 36. Two characteristics of Requa's were evident on the eve of his tenure as fuel czar: as a Herbert Hoover protege, he was a cooperativist; regarding oil supply, he was a pessimist. In 1916, he warned the Bureau of Mines that only five or ten years worth of oil was left in the ground. August Giebelhaus, *Business and Government in the Oil Industry: A Case Study of Sun Oil* (Greenwich, Conn.: Jai Press, 1980), pp. 113–14.

than ever before, especially the exploration and production phase.[11] It had taken nearly sixty years, but systematic federal regulation of oil had arrived.

The Lever Act did not grant Garfield or Requa authority to set crude-oil, natural-gas, or petroleum-product prices. Supply was the primary concern despite the "Cushing Depression," which had given the industry a taste of the "overproduction" and the low prices a big Southwest field could bring. In his first week, Requa ordered a supply survey, and in February 1918, regional committees were appointed to find ways to increase production.[12]

Requa originally thought that pricing was "an economic question, the solution of which should rest with the industry itself."[13] This would change. Already a precedent had been established by the Federal Trade Commission, which embarked on a fact-finding study to estimate production cost to determine the "fair" price the government should pay for fuel oil purchased by the navy.[14] With oil prices beginning to rise as a result of wartime demand, monetary inflation, and coal shortages, Requa reversed his laissez-faire position in May 1918 and appealed to the industry to treat current quotations as price maximums.[15] Since he could not order price controls, cooperation was necessary.

The industry responded favorably. Independent refiners welcomed relief from paying premiums above the posted price of crude, premiums that integrated refiners did not have to pay their production affiliates. The *Oil & Gas Journal* editorialized that price maximums "should have the effect of bringing about a stronger spirit of confidence among certain refiners."[16] Criticism was muted by

[11]Within the Oil Division, the Bureaus of Production, Oil Well Supplies, and Conservation regulated the exploration and production phase. For an organizational chart of the Oil Division, see appendix E, pp. 1942–43. Coal was more heavily regulated than oil, reflecting its preeminence as a fuel source.

[12]*OGJ*, January 17, 1918, p. 36; and Gerald Nash, *United States Oil Policy: 1890–1964* (Westport, Conn.: Greenwood Press, 1968), p. 32.

[13]*OGJ*, March 31, 1918, p. 32.

[14]*OGJ*, August 30, 1917, p. 32, and October 18, 1917, p. 30.

[15]*OGJ*, May 15, 1918, p. 36, and May 30, 1918, p. 34. Also see Joseph Pogue, *Prices of Petroleum and Its Products* (Washington, D.C.: Government Printing Office, 1919), p. 28.

[16]*OGJ*, May 23, 1918, p. 36. On refiner support of price regulation, see *OGJ*, July 12, 1918, p. 40, and August 2, 1918, p. 46.

patriotism on the maiden voyage of federal intervention throughout the industry.

In July 1918, Requa formalized "voluntary" crude-oil price ceilings—the first such regulation in the history of the U.S. petroleum industry.[17] In a July 12 address, the Oil Division head stated:

> The law of supply and demand has broken down in the face of a demand far exceeding the available supply. . . . I do not believe there would be any stimulation of moment to production of petroleum by an increase in the price of crude oil.[18]

Through jawboning, public appeals, and the threat of mandatory price controls, Requa's Oil Division and Bedford's War Service Committee worked out a "voluntary" plan to freeze posted crude prices and limit premium payments in excess of such prices.[19] Effective for all contracts entered into after May 17, 1918, until at least November 1, 1918, the plan, finalized on August 9, 1918, with the unanimous recommendation of the War Service Committee, "suggested" the following price behavior.

- Appalachian division: (1) That the large purchasing companies continue to purchase crude oil at their posted market price, and that all other purchasers who now pay a premium for crude oil be hereafter permitted to pay a premium not to exceed 10 cents per barrel above the posted prices for the various grades of crude oil. (2) That all producers are requested to make monthly sales of their crude oil.
- Mid-continent division: (1) That the large purchasing companies continue to purchase crude oil at their posted price in the Mid-continent field, and that all other purchasers who now pay a premium for crude oil are permitted hereafter to pay up to a maximum premium above posted market prices as follows:
  For Cushing crude, a maximum premium of 75 cents per barrel.
  For Yale and Inay, a maximum premium of 50 cents per barrel.
  For Garber crude, a maximum premium of $1.50 per barrel.

[17]*Oil Weekly*, July 13, 1918, p. 8. Cited hereafter as *OW*.

[18]Quoted in Joseph Pogue, *Prices of Petroleum and Its Products*, p. 28.

[19]Gerald Nash, *United States Oil Policy*, pp. 33–34. Bedford misleadingly called the price stabilization plan "wholly a voluntary action of the industry." With a mandatory program touted as the alternative, Requa's "suggestions" were equivalent to regulation.

For Billings crude, a maximum premium of 75 cents per barrel.

For Kay County crude, a maximum premium of 75 cents per barrel.

For Healdon crude, a maximum premium of 30 cents per barrel.

For all other crudes for the whole Mid-continent division, including Kansas, Oklahoma, and northern Texas, a maximum premium not to exceed 25 cents per barrel with the strict understanding that in no district in which premiums are being paid of less than 25 cents per barrel, will the United States Fuel Administration permit the paying of a higher premium than is now in effect.

- Gulf coast and northern Louisiana division: (1) That the large purchasing companies in the Gulf coast territory be requested to establish a posted price for crude oil effective as of August 1, 1918, of $1.80 per barrel, and continue to pay said price until November 1918; and a maximum premium established above the posted price of 10 cents per barrel, with strict understanding that in no district in which premiums are being paid of less than 10 cents per barrel will the United States Fuel Administrator permit the paying of a higher premium than is now in effect. (2) That the large purchasing companies establish a differential of 25 cents per barrel below the posted price of Gulf coast oil for northern Louisiana heavy oil below 32d. gravity, and that a premium of 10 cents per barrel be permitted, on this grade of oil; that on light crude oil a premium of 25 cents per barrel be permitted, with the strict understanding that in no case where premiums of less than 10 cents and 25 cents per barrel, respectively, have been paid, will the fuel administrator permit the paying of higher premiums than are now in effect.[20]

Besides wellhead prices, government involvement in wartime exploration and production included regulation of entry by new firms, mandatory conservation, exemptions from military service for drilling personnel, "voluntary" price controls on and rationing of drilling equipment, and special tax breaks.

The Capital Issues Committee restricted new entry into the production phase on the rationale that "the emergencies of war [are]

---

[20]Reprinted in Paul Garrett, *Government Control over Prices* (Washington, D.C.: Government Printing Office, 1920), pp. 663–64.

above the calls of speculative business enterprise."[21] Labor shortages, which idled numerous drilling rigs in West Texas and elsewhere, inspired legislation to allow servicemen to return to civilian life under certain conditions to work in industries vital to the war effort, including oil.[22] The Advisory Committee on Oil Well Supplies, in conjunction with the Petroleum War Service Committee, regulated the price and manufacture of oil field equipment to "promote efficiency" and regulated distribution to "prevent speculation" and ensure "equitable procurement" between firms.[23] The War Revenue Act of 1918 liberalized the depletion allowance to permit deductions based on the market value of production rather than the cost of discovery. This deduction, however, was offset by stiff war taxes.[24] In its final major regulation, the Fuel Administration, citing waste of 800 billion cubic feet of gas a year, issued an order making such "inefficient" end-uses as burning gas in flambeau lights illegal.[25]

On October 29, 1918, price controls were extended by the War Services Committee to February 1, 1919.[26] With the armistice on November 11, 1918, planning partners Requa and Bedford emphasized the continuation of regulation until official word that the war had ended. For the interim, the *National Petroleum News* warned readers that the government still had "the authority to make a man discontinue his business."[27] The peace did end ambitious plans for more regulation, such as limiting gasoline and kerosene to one grade and setting profit-based price ceilings.

An explanation of why wartime authority lingered was given by the same trade journal.

> That the President is fond of power no one can gainsay. . . . Legislation means power for the executive. It means new duties and new duties mean more men to command and larger fields to cover. Another incontrovertible fact is that Congress has as members in

[21]*OGJ*, October 25, 1918, p. 2.

[22]Public Law 105, 40 Stat. 450 (1918).

[23]*OGJ*, March 14, 1918, p. See also Gerald White, *Formative Years in the Far West* (New York: Appleton-Century-Crofts, 1962), p. 543.

[24]See chapter 7, pp. 336–37.

[25]*OGJ*, January 10, 1919, p. 38.

[26]Announcement of the extension by A. C. Bedford, reprinted in *OW*, November 9, 1918, p. 33.

[27]*National Petroleum News*, November 13, 1918, p. 1. Cited hereafter as *NPN*.

both House and Senate, a large number of men with a decided leaning toward making the world perfect by legislation.[28]

Effective December 16, 1918, prices were deregulated by Requa after seven months of official "suggestion" and several previous months of less formal "suggestion."[29] Refiners were now free to bid any premium they desired to secure crude, and producers were allowed to receive it. All other petroleum-related regulations, including the natural-gas conservation order, were terminated. On June 30, the position of fuel administrator and the Oil Division were terminated.[30] A novel business-government relationship ended that would be remembered in future wartime situations.

The commonly perceived success of World War I petroleum planning, exemplified by Lord Curzon's oft-quoted statement, "The Allies floated to victory on a sea of oil," does not prove the efficacy of wartime petroleum planning.[31] If the goal of petroleum planning was to increase supply and coordinate the industry along common lines, government policies were counterproductive both before and during the war. The 1911 breakup of Standard Oil into over thirty separately managed firms had a deleterious effect on market coordination and cooperation.[32] More small firms, instead of fewer large firms, complicated the planning effort. Federal and state antitrust laws had the same effect. Public-land policies, detailed in the next

---

[28]Ibid., p. 13.

[29]OGJ, December 20, 1918, p. 42. The order said: "The Fuel Administration today announced that, in line with the general policy of the government of lifting all restrictions as rapidly as conditions would warrant, it has asked the oil industry to suspend its voluntary plan to stabilize prices ... and at the same time has taken similar action as to any voluntary understandings or agreements with respect to prices of crude oil or its refined products. This suspension will be permanent unless events prove the necessity of again exercising control." Reprinted in NPN, December 18, 1918, p. 1.

[30]OGJ, May 23, 1919, p. 2; and Northcutt Ely, "The Government in the Exercise of the War Power," in Conservation of Oil and Gas: A Legal History, 1948, ed. Blakely Murphy (Chicago: American Bar Association, 1949), p. 665.

[31]The legitimacy of U.S. participation in the war is beyond the scope of this book. The German threat, however, was stressed, even exaggerated, in industry publications to rally industry support for petroleum regulation. For example, see "Fuel Oil Control Necessary," OGJ, March 28, 1918, p. 2; and "For Perpetuating Democracy," OGJ, April 18, 1918, p. 2.

[32]See chapter 18, pp. 1088–89.

chapter, prevented production on vast oil-laden lands during the war period.[33] Commenting on the ill-timed dead period, William Holloway remarked:

> [The] withdrawals removed from the field of exploration millions of acres of the public land and contributed in no small degree to the petroleum shortage during and following World War I. . . . During these years and until 1921 exploration of the public domain remained at a standstill.[34]

The case for price controls and other regulation was questionable. The problems could be addressed by free-market policies. Drilling and production on private land certainly did not merit government intervention. The industry had recovered from a depressed price of $0.64 per barrel in 1915, and prices averaging around $1.56 per barrel two years later inspired record drilling and production. Aggregate crude output exceeded 300 million barrels in 1916 and rose 11.5 percent in 1917. This set the stage for more output and lower prices, with growing demand during the neutrality and war periods. Because of regulation, those things did not happen until after the war.[35]

Requa, with the ready support of Bedford and the War Service Committee, instituted price ceilings because of rising prices and concern over "demand far exceeding the available supply." With such economic misunderstanding, it is not surprising that he spearheaded counterproductive regulation. Free price movements *prevent* demand and supply from losing balance—that is the purpose of a price system, although it was not "invented" to do so. Higher prices also provide incentive for increasing supply for the future and for husbanding supply in the present. Encouraging consumption and waste by keeping prices low—and then regulating consumption to eliminate marginal uses—was an inferior strategy.

[33]See chapter 6, p. 266.

[34]William Holloway, "Unit Operation of Public Lands," 3 *Oil and Gas Institute* (New York: Matthew Bender, 1952), p. 231. Also see Federal Trade Commission, *Report of the Pacific Coast Petroleum Industry* (Washington, D.C.: Government Printing Office, 1921), pp. 84–88. During the war the Pacific Coast industry attempted to resolve public-land issues and begin exploration and production but to no avail. Gerald White, *Formative Years in the Far West*, p. 548.

[35]This analysis is from Simon Simon, *Economic Legislation of Taxation* (New York: Arno Press, 1979), pp. 26–34.

Table 5.1
CRUDE-OIL SUMMARY: 1915–20

Year	Wells Drilled	Production (000 bl)	Consumption (000 bl)	Inventory (000 bl)	Year-End Price ($/bl)
1915	14,185	281,104	290,772	194,185	0.64
1916	24,728	300,767	324,420	179,372	1.10
1917	23,503	335,316	378,312	159,452	1.56
1918	25,687	355,928	412,273	128,586	1.98
1919	29,173	378,367	420,462	136,213	2.01
1920	33,911	442,929	530,532	146,028	3.07

SOURCE: Department of the Interior, Bureau of Mines.

Monetary inflation, not free-market conditions, was chiefly responsible for the price rise. From 1 percent inflation in 1915, prices rose by 7.6 percent in 1916 and over 17 percent in 1917 and again in 1918—all from "an immense expansion of bank credit . . . from the beginning of 1915 to April 1917." That expansion consisted of gold inflows and reductions in reserve requirements.[36]

For these reasons, price interference was a wrong and unstudied course of action. Price controls merely chased causes rather than addressed effects. Production was discouraged. Production increased less than demand, with inventory drawdowns bridging the gap as shown in table 5.1.

A 37 percent increase in inventory during 1915, due partly to unprecedented flush production in Oklahoma and partly to expectations of higher prices during the European conflict, rescued the industry from the relatively short period of price controls. This inventory buildup, ironically, was decried as "hoarding" and "profiteering" by government planners. A longer war would have revealed the distortions of price regulation more vividly—as World War II petroleum planning would. As it was, a drilling boom and

[36]Bureau of Labor Statistics, Consumer Price Index. Benjamin Anderson, *Economics and the Public Welfare* (Indianapolis: Liberty Press, 1949, 1979), p. 56. An estimated 5 percent of total government expenditure in the March 1917–November 1918 period, or $1.5 billion, was inflation financed. As opposed to 70 percent borrowing and 25 percent taxation, this revenue source represented "an implicit tax on money balances levied through the rise in prices." Milton Friedman and Anna Schwartz, *A Monetary History of the United States* (Princeton, N.J.: Princeton University Press, 1963), p. 221.

falling prices after the war—from a high of $3.00 per barrel in 1920 to under $2.00 per barrel for the rest of the decade—indirectly proved the point.

A number of government-related reasons explained why the wartime petroleum boom that should have happened did not. Shortages of drilling equipment due to price restraints and rationing inefficiencies discouraged new wells, particularly wildcats.[37] Only inventory depletion and equipment recycling by the industry kept things from becoming worse. Transportation problems, discussed in chapter 13, hampered drilling by delaying delivery of well supplies and pipeline construction.[38] Labor problems closed rigs and forced legislative reform. Rising drilling costs due to inflation created profitability problems given fixed selling prices. High wartime tax rates enacted in the Revenue Act of 1917 siphoned retained earnings from new drilling projects and discouraged risk taking.[39] General fear of regulation—in particular more restrictive price ceilings and the unknown longevity of petroleum planning—discouraged greater efforts at the wellhead. High profits were continually derogated by government officials as "unfair," and even as the "unconscionable" result of "inordinate greed."[40] The beneficial role of profits aside, federal policy restricting entry of new firms contributed to the very problem that planners tried to legislate and jawbone away. In July 1918, a study by the Federal Trade Commission reported that oil-industry profits were 40 percent higher than prewar levels.[41] Assuming the accuracy of the study—which is contradicted by effective price ceilings placed on most firms—a contributing factor was the cartelization afforded to established firms by war planning.[42]

---

[37]See Simon Simon, *Economic Legislation of Taxation*, pp. 36–38.

[38]Ibid.

[39]Ibid., p. 43. Also see *OGJ*, May 16, 1918, p. 40.

[40]*OGJ*, May 30, 1918, p. 34, and July 5, 1918, p. 49. Within the industry, "profiteering" and "hoarding" were pejorative terms. For example, see the advertisement in *OGJ*, May 9, 1918, p. 13.

[41]Ibid.

[42]War cartelization also tended to favor large, established firms over smaller, younger firms. Not only were priority requests for equipment more readily granted, large prewar inventories served the former to advantage. For example, see *OW*, October 5, 1918, p. 38.

World War II

Although World War II planning was described by Deputy Petroleum Administrator Ralph K. Davies as "an unprecedented program
of Government-industry cooperation," it was more accurately a reen-
actment, albeit on a larger scale, of the seventeen-month planning
experience of World War I.[43] It did not initiate, but only furthered,
the relationship between the oil industry and the federal government
that began in 1917 and reappeared in the New Deal.

In preparation for war, President Roosevelt on May 27, 1941,
declared an "unlimited national emergency." The next day, he created the Office of Petroleum Coordinator for National Defense (OPC)
to coordinate the energy programs of approximately thirty agencies.[44] The OPC was charged with gathering information on petroleum supply and demand, recommending price policy to the Office
of Price Administration and Civilian Supply (created April 11, 1941),
and recommending materials policy to the Office of Production Management (created January 7, 1941). A week later, Interior Secretary
Harold Ickes was appointed coordinator—a surprising choice given
his refusal to testify on behalf of the industry at the Madison trial.[45]
Ickes lessened the controversy by appointing Ralph Davies, vice
president of California Standard, as deputy coordinator. The machinery of wartime planning was taking shape along familiar lines.

In the summer of 1941, Ickes began laying the groundwork for
government petroleum planning. With cooperation a major theme,
outstanding antitrust actions against the industry were settled.[46]
Understanding was reached, by letters of June 3 and June 18 from
the attorney general, that cooperative industry actions sanctioned
by Ickes would not be prosecuted.[47] In July, five district OPC offices
were established across the country to correspond to geographical
oil divisions. Jawboning and suasion of producers began.[48] Illinois

[43]Ralph Davies in the foreword to John Frey and H. Chandler Ide, *A History of the
Petroleum Administration for War* (Washington, D.C.: Government Printing Office,
1946), p. xvii.

[44]6 *Fed. Reg.* 2760 (June 7, 1941); and *OGJ*, June 5, 1941, pp. 27–28.

[45]See chapter 19, p. 1129.

[46]See chapter 19, pp. 1134–35; and chapter 26, pp. 1533, 1540.

[47]Antitrust immunity became law a year later in the Small Business Mobilization
Act, Public Law 603, 56 Stat. 351 at 357 (1942).

[48]Jawboning was particularly evident on the retail-consumer level. See chapter 24,
pp. 1397–1400.

and California, two states without mandatory proration laws, were the targets of Ickes's regulatory blackmail, which was predicated on his erroneous understanding of the rise of regulation. Ickes stated:

> The way for you to avoid an oil "czar" is to eliminate such wasteful practices . . . . People endured patiently for a long time the unlimited taking of game. Remember, too, it was the transgressions of the railroads that resulted in the creation of the Interstate Commerce Commission. It was disregard by business of the rights of the individual that brought about the anti-trust laws. Public power is well on its way because of the oppressive practices of the private utilities. The securities-exchange act sprang from the loins of Wall Street itself.[49]

In fact, the demand for regulation came from within the oil industry as well as from from outside.[50] Ickes's inverted view of history, coupled with a vacuum of economic understanding, resulted in a false confidence that would inspire activist regulation during World War II—as had been the case during the New Deal.

On November 28, 1941, the Petroleum Industry Council for National Defense, consisting of sixty-six members from oil companies and trade associations, was established.[51] Closely resembling the War Service Committee of World War I and the Planning and Coordination Committee of the New Deal, this committee, later renamed the Petroleum Industry War Council (PIWC), was the industry's voice in regulatory policy. The first meeting was held the day after Pearl Harbor; monthly meetings were held thereafter.

After war was declared immediately following the December 7, 1941, attack on Pearl Harbor, the OPC was renamed the Office of Petroleum Coordinator for War. On December 2, 1942, that office was reorganized by executive order with regulatory power as the

---

[49]Harold Ickes, "National Defense and the Oil Industry," *23 Annual Proceedings* (New York: American Petroleum Institute, 1941), p. 23. Illinois would succumb to pressure and pass a proration law in 1941.

[50]On railroads, see chapter 11, pp. 619–23; on antitrust, see chapter 26, pp. 1551–55; on public utilities, see chapter 15, pp. 851–58; and generally, see chapter 30, pp. 1823–51.

[51]Previously, the Advisory Commission to the Council of National Defense, a general business group formed in mid-1940, had existed.

Petroleum Administration for War (PAW). The PAW would conduct petroleum planning until the end of the war.[52]

Price Regulation. Significant regulation of the exploration and production phase commenced in mid-1941, when the Office of Price Administration and Civilian Supply (OPA) began a "voluntary" price-control program for crude oil. Price interference began on June 7 when California producers were ordered to roll back recent price increases to May 23 levels. A hearing was held, and after uncontested evidence was presented by oil firms to cost-justify the increases, government representatives, led by Price Division director John Kenneth Galbraith, refused to rescind the order.[53] Although eventually those prices were allowed to rise, other requests for increases, submitted in accordance with mandatory prenotification instituted June 26, 1941, were denied. An August 22 order by the OPA disallowed a $0.23 to $0.25 per barrel increase of Pennsylvania-grade crude. Two reasons were given: it was "inflationary," and it tended "to weaken the defense effort by causing economic dislocations and price spiraling and profiteering."[54] The same reasons were given for denying crude increases in the Gulf Coast, Midcontinent, and Midwest divisions, although higher prices were eventually allowed in Pennsylvania and North Texas.[55]

In January 1942, official price ceilings were established in the Emergency Price Control Act, which set individual prices for each field at their October 1, 1941, levels.[56] This froze relative price imbalances along with prices themselves, since the unique circumstances determining prices on this day for each field and well had become obsolete with time. Changed underlying conditions of supply and

[52]For an uncritical summary of PAW activities, see John Frey and H. Chandler Ide, *History of the Petroleum Administration for War*, and *Petroleum Industry Committees in World War II: District V*, ed. Charles Scott (San Francisco: Petroleum Industry Committee, 1947). For an organization chart of the PAW and constituent planning groups, see appendix E, pp. 1942–43.

[53]Complained one industry participant, "It was apparent that [Galbraith] had made his decision before the meeting was held, which was a cruel act as the oil men came to the meeting expecting a square deal." *OGJ*, June 12, 1941, p. 20.

[54]*OGJ*, August 28, 1941, p. 30.

[55]*NPN*, November 5, 1941, p. 11; *OGJ*, November 13, 1941, p. 12; and *NPN*, December 17, 1941, p. 24, and April 1, 1942, p. 19.

[56]Public Law 421, 56 Stat. 23 (1942). The October data resulted from a production cost study by the U.S. Tariff Commission, which concluded that prices on this day

demand, coupled with rising production costs, caused in large part by monetary inflation, led certain high-cost fields to face curtailments if not shutdowns.[57] To avoid supply disruption, the OPA began to grant price exceptions for certain areas, which created new price distortions.[58] Between 1943 and 1945, more than 100 exceptions were granted, with the amount of the price increases determined by crude grade.[59] Overall price increases, twice requested by the PAW in May and August 1943, were denied by the OPA in conformity with President Roosevelt's "hold the line" price directive.[60]

In May 1942, an autonomous division within the OPC was established to regulate natural gas.[61] On October 1, 1942, natural-gas prices at the wellhead came under price regulation and remained regulated until the end of the war.[62] As they did with gasoline, wellhead ceilings on natural gas created shortages. An abnormally cold winter in early 1944 increased demand, and regulated rates at the distribution level could not clear the market. Severe curtailments were experienced in Michigan and particularly Ohio. Natural-gas curtailments were blamed for the loss of an estimated 300,000 tons of steel for the war program.[63]

---

were equitable. John Frey and H. Chandler Ide, *History of the Petroleum Administration for War*, p. 185. On April 28, 1942, the OPA released the General Maximum Price Regulation to freeze prices at March 1942 highs. See Victor Abramson, "Price Freezing under the Office of Price Administration," *American Economic Review* (December 1942): 760–74.

[57]Monetary inflation during World War II is discussed in this chapter, pp. 243, 246n. 103.

[58]See, for example, *NPN*, April 14, 1943, p. 18. Ray Dudley of the *Oil Weekly* noticed the inherent problem of date price fixing: "If prices are frozen at the level of any certain date, such freezing might easily find important commodities in the process of a change in price vital to their existence. On the other hand, if adjustments are attempted after freezing, each adjustment on one commodity will affect the well being of another." *OW*, July 7, 1941, p. 9.

[59]John Frey and H. Chandler Ide, *History of the Petroleum Administration for War*, p. 185. Twenty-seven price increases were granted in 1943, fifty-nine were allowed in 1944, and thirty-nine were allowed in the first nine months of 1945. Most of the exemptions were in California and Wyoming.

[60]Executive Order 9328, 8 *Fed. Reg.* 4681 (April 10, 1943); *OGJ*, May 13, 1943, p. 36; and John Frey and H. Chandler Ide, *History of the Petroleum Administration for War*, p. 186.

[61]*OGJ*, May 7, 1942, p. 25.

[62]*OGJ*, January 28, 1943, p. 106.

[63]John Frey and H. Chandler Ide, *History of the Petroleum Administration for War*, pp. 231–32.

Table 5.2
STRIPPER-WELL SUBSIDIES

Subsidy ($/bl)	Well Output (bl/day)
0.35	1–4
0.25	5–6
0.20	7–8
0.35	9 or more[a]
0.75	Penn grade only

SOURCE: John Frey and H. Chandler Ide, *A History of the Petroleum Administration for War*, p. 186 n. 22.
[a]For certain high-cost fields.

Stripper-Well Subsidies. Price regulation had an adverse effect on marginal wells and new drilling because of rising costs due to less regulated inputs. Recommendation 47, effective April 21, 1942, prohibited "premature" abandonment of wells—but did nothing to change the economics of price regulation, which created the problem initially.[64]

During 1943, a noticeable decline in drilling activity was in progress, and "political" alternatives to the free-market solution of deregulated prices came forth. Russell Brown of the Independent Petroleum Association of America proposed that federal funds help underwrite wildcat wells. In return, the U.S. Treasury would receive a one-fourth override on any oil and gas discovered.[65] While this proposal floundered, government authorities decided on another. On July 5, 1944, Jesse Jones of the Reconstruction Finance Corporation (RFC) announced that, beginning August 1, subsidies of up to $50 million would be available from the Office of Economic Stabilization (OES) for stripper wells and certain other high-cost fields.[66] The schedule of payments, paid by the RFC to the first purchaser of crude oil, who in turn paid the producer the amount of the subsidy over the price ceiling, is given in table 5.2.

Oil producers favored price increases much more than stripper subsidies, but they readily cashed their checks. One prominent critic

[64]*OGJ*, January 28, 1943, p. 106.
[65]*NPN*, May 4, 1943, p. 3.
[66]*OGJ*, May 13, 1943, p. 36.

was J. C. Harter, president of the Mid-Continent Oil and Gas Association, who stated, "The plan [will] not attract exploration by experienced oil men but [will] encourage promoters [to] drill for the so-called subsidy instead of for oil."[67] It also encouraged "bracket-gaming," whereby production was artificially altered to maximize subsidy income and preserve output for the future when prices would be decontrolled.

Disputes over eligibility for the subsidies predictably arose, and the OES took the path of least resistance by leniently defining eligible properties.[68] From August 1 until the program's completion on November 30, 1945, the OES paid $65 million to 308 operators for 177 million barrels of stripper crude. The average subsidy was $0.367 per barrel.[69]

Synthetic-Fuel Subsidies. In 1944, the Synthetic Liquid Fuels Act allocated $30 million to the Bureau of Mines to construct and operate demonstration plants for turning coal, shale, or other products into crude oil.[70] Output was to be sold to the armed services at cost with the residual sold at whatever the market would bear.

As is explained in more detail in chapter 10, this subsidy and greater postwar grants, totaling nearly $107 million, produced minimal quantities of crude oil at two facilities.[71] The hoped-for commercialization of new technologies never occurred. While the taxpayer contribution was far from negligible, the contribution of synthetic crude to the war effort was indeed negligible.

Regulation of Materials. In addition to price regulation and output subsidization, other intervention affected exploration and production. On July 7, 1941, the oil and gas industry became one of twenty-four industries that began a rationing (priority allocation) program for materials and equipment to prevent stockpiling and "hoarding."[72] On December 23, 1941, the Office of Production Management

[67]*NPN*, July 12, 1944, p. 3.

[68]Northcutt Ely, "The Government in the Exercise of the War Power," p. 676.

[69]John Frey and H. Chandler Ide, *A History of the Petroleum Administration for War*, p. 186. Also see *OGJ*, September 9, 1944, p. 52.

[70]Public Law 290, 58 Stat. 190 (1944).

[71]See chapter 10, pp. 569–75.

[72]E. Stettinius, priorities director of the Office of Production Management, warned of court action and equipment withholding to enforce the "voluntary" program. *OGJ*, July 10, 1941, p. 20.

issued Conservation Order M-68 that required minimum spacing of one oil well per 40 acres for new wells to limit demand for scarce drilling supplies.[73] Recognized as "the first step toward forced unitization of all oil and gas fields," the regulation was relaxed in February 1942 for physical obstacles and irregular tracts and removed entirely in March 1943 for wildcat wells. Exceptions were made in October 1942 for particular fields in California and elsewhere.[74]

Conservation Order 68 also promulgated a spacing rule for natural gas that limited wells to one per 640 acres. Exceptions and amendments were made in a February 13, 1942, order to allow 160-acre spacing for deep wells and 60-acre spacing for shallow wells in the Appalachian gas fields.[75]

Conservation Regulation. National demand estimates by the Bureau of Mines, previously used for state proration assignments, were used for the same purpose by the Office of Price Stabilization beginning in January 1942. The "recommendations," later changed to "certificates of necessity" by the PAW, were enforced by the National Conference of Petroleum Regulatory Authorities (founded January 17, 1942), which was staffed by state conservation agency personnel.[76] In Texas, Oklahoma, Louisiana, New Mexico, Kansas, Arkansas, and several other oil states, previous regulatory customs carried forward. In Illinois, Ickes's threat of federal regulation led to passage of the Oil and Gas Conservation Act, a market-demand proration law, in 1941. California remained a holdout; market-demand proration would come from above.

World War II brought about a radical change in production policy. Instead of restricting output to support prices, wells were ordered to produce at, or above, calculated maximum efficient rates (MERs) to meet civilian and military demand stimulated by artificially low

---

[73]John Frey and H. Chandler Ide, *History of the Petroleum Administration for War*, p. 179.

[74]*NPN*, February 25, 1942, p. 14; and *OGJ*, January 28, 1943, p. 106, and April 1, 1943, p. 12.

[75]Northcutt Ely, "The Government in the Exercise of the War Power," p. 677. Also see P. Thomas Curtin, *Men, Oil, and War* (Chicago: Petroleum Industry Committee, 1946), pp. 69–70.

[76]In California, a crucial state for the war effort, market-demand proration was entirely new, and a special committee had to be formed to implement it.

prices.[77] Yet even with maximum and above-maximum production, state conservation efforts were alive and well under the aegis of federal planning. As legal scholar Northcutt Ely summarized:

> The broad PAW policy toward conservation was based on encouraging state agencies to improve existing laws, and to induce states without conservation laws to adopt them. . . . Principles and practices long sought by advocates of conservation were put into widespread use and received thorough testing under the emergencies of war. . . . [T]he cause of conservation received a tremendous boost.[78]

These "boosts" included well-spacing minimums for oil and gas, MER calculations for each field,[79] and, directly or indirectly, forced unitization and secondary-recovery plans.[80] The act of June 11, 1942, provided immunity from antitrust law for cooperative agreements.[81] These initiatives would later become integral parts of state conservation regulation. Another advance for peacetime conservation regulation made during the war was the Connally Hot-Oil Act, which was made permanent on June 22, 1942.[82]

As was the case for peacetime conservation regulation, wartime conservation regulation had unintended detrimental consequences. National production quotas were an example. Early in the war, production quotas were so low in some areas that refinery inventories became depleted and producers experienced hardship.[83] Mississippi took matters into its own hands by producing at a rate 40

---

[77]Production was above the MER total in the last half of 1944 and all of 1945. John Frey and H. Chandler Ide, *A History of the Petroleum Administration for War*, pp. 176, 444.

[78]Northcutt Ely, "The Government in the Exercise of the War Power," p. 673. Also see John Frey and H. Chandler Ide, *A History of the Petroleum Administration for War*, pp. 188–89.

[79]See this chapter, pp. 239–40, on MER regulation that began in early 1942 in District V.

[80]Robert Hardwicke, *Antitrust Laws et al. v. Unit Operation of Oil and Gas Pools* (New York: American Institute of Mining and Metallurgical Engineers, 1948), pp. 105–6. Between June 1942 and June 1944, almost 100 secondary projects were undertaken. Northcutt Ely, "The Government in the Exercise of the War Power," pp. 676–77.

[81]Public Law 239, 61 Stat. 449 (1942). The so-called O'Mahoney Act would be repealed on July 25, 1947.

[82]Public Law 624, 56 Stat. 381 (1942). Hot-oil violations in East Texas occurred during the war. See *NPN*, October 18, 1944, p. 40.

[83]*OGJ*, May 7, 1942, p. 33.

percent above OPC recommendations.[84] Later in the war, at the same time adverse government policies curtailed additions to proven reserves, OPC production assignments were so high that operators feared reservoir damage in the East Texas field.[85] Questions were also raised about the disproportionate burden placed by the OPA on major fields to meet increased demand relative to that placed on the more numerous, smaller reservoirs.[86]

Other Regulation. In addition to subsidizing stripper-well output and allowing MER or above-MER production, government policies attempted to increase supply by lowering royalty payments on federal land and creating the Foreign Operations Committee to secure foreign supplies. Although largely advisory, that committee worked to gain concessions for American companies drilling abroad. In 1943, concern on the part of U.S. officials about domestic supplies led to the secret formation of the Petroleum Reserves Corporation with a charter to explore for and produce petroleum abroad. Strong industry protest prevented the federal corporation from becoming operational.[87] On October 1, 1943, in response to skilled-labor shortages experienced by the industry, draft exemptions were awarded to men in certain drilling occupations such as oil-well perforators, foremen, cementers, and drillers. Seismologists and geologists were also given preferential treatment.[88]

Decontrol. Wartime petroleum planning would not terminate until after the surrender of Nazi Germany on May 7, 1945, and Japan on August 14, 1945. On September 1, 1945, all regulations governing well spacing and well construction and servicing were dropped.[89] Price decontrol was another matter. Chester Bowles of the OPA

---

[84]With the number of production days per month fixed, increased quotas had to be met by increasing withdrawal rates on those days rather than producing for more days at lower rates. *OGJ*, May 21, 1942, p. 20.

[85]*OGJ*, August 26, 1943, p. 44.

[86]*OGJ*, July 29, 1943, p. 94.

[87]Northcutt Ely, "The Government in the Exercise of the War Power," pp. 679–80. The industry planning group, the Petroleum Industry War Council, denounced the proposed activity as "a program of imperialism." PIWC Release, "United States Foreign Policy and Petroleum Reserves Corporation," February 28, 1944, p. 9.

[88]*OGJ*, August 19, 1943, p. 32.

[89]*NPN*, August 22, 1945, p. p. 7; and *OGJ*, September 1, 1945, p. 38.

adamantly favored continuing controls through 1946, citing high industry profits and inflation as reasons.[90]

The Texas Railroad Commission returned to the fore by holding its first proration hearing since before the war to set September 1945 allowables. The agency first ordered wells to return to an MER basis from wartime production levels. It then declared twenty days' production for the month, a 67 percent market-demand factor, ushering in a twenty-five-year era of restrictive proration.[91]

On the pricing front, the OPA granted a token $0.10 per barrel increase for crude oil effective April 1, 1946. Consideration of price deregulation in mid-1946 was ended because of a coal strike.[92] On May 8, 1946, the PAW was dissolved by executive order, which left a stubborn OPA between the industry and state regulation.[93] In late July, oil prices and oil-equipment prices were finally deregulated. Prices increased, primarily to pass through the cost inflation incurred since 1941.[94]

Evaluation. Like petroleum planning during World War I, the experience of World War II has received high marks from historians.[95] John Frey and H. Chandler Ide gave the planning effort a nearly perfect score, noting that the OPC and the PAW "supplied the essential civilian requirements for petroleum products while meeting every demand for the armed forces *in full and on time.*"[96] This judgment is highly misleading, however. Many existing wells were left idle because of planning errors, and many potential wells,

---

[90]*NPN*, March 7, 1945, p. 8.

[91]*NPN*, September 5, 1945, p. 26.

[92]*NPN*, March 13, 1946, p. 3, and May 15, 1946, p. 3.

[93]John Frey and H. Chandler Ide, *History of the Petroleum Administration for War*, p. 38.

[94]*NPN*, July 31, 1946, p. 11. Standby regulation expired August 20, 1946, when the Decontrol Board failed to reimpose price ceilings.

[95]One exception to this view was David Novick et al. who saw the planning errors of World War I reappear in World War II. "Probably the most important lesson to be learned from the record of the administration of industrial mobilization from 1940 through 1945 is that experience neither compels learning nor guarantees that subsequent administrators in a comparable national emergency will not repeat the documented errors. The management control problems of World War I reappeared in World War II." David Novick, Melvin Anshen, and W. C. Truppener, *Wartime Production Controls* (New York: Columbia University Press, 1949), p. 370.

[96]John Frey and H. Chandler Ide, *A History of the Petroleum Administration for War*, p. 2.

in both existing fields and wildcat domain, were not drilled because of disincentives. Supply was not always adequate, as evidenced by pervasive gasoline rationing and shortages, nor was it secured at least cost.[97]

As had been the case in America's first wartime planning experience, misconceived and conflicting policies curtailed petroleum activities. A dispute between the navy, the Justice Department, and the PAW prevented increased output and new drilling in the oil-laden Elk Hills naval reserve at a time when California was short of crude.[98] Maximum-price policies of the OPA severely discouraged development wells and wildcat drilling, which worked against the pro-production policies of the PAW and OES.[99] This was particularly wasteful because, while price controls reduced supply from flush sources, marginal wells were subsidized to take up the slack. The Canol project was another cost perversity. Canol, a taxpayer-financed drilling project in northwestern Canada, had average costs of over $40 per barrel for the several hundred thousand barrels produced, refined, and transported for army use in 1944 and 1945.[100] Synthetic-fuels subsidies, which began in 1944, were far beyond uneconomical on a cost-per-barrel basis. Thanks to output lost as a result of price regulation and incremental barrels from stripper wells, the Canol project, and synthetic crude oil, government planners succeeded in substituting the most expensive for the least expensive crude sources to fuel America's war machine.

The Office of Production Management's allocation of drilling equipment on the basis of well spacing uneconomically favored risky wildcat wells over development wells in proven areas. Ray Dudley, publisher of the *Oil Weekly*, expressed industry opinion when he warned that "OPM may be cutting the cloth entirely too

---

[97]World War II rationing is discussed in chapter 24, pp. 1402–28.

[98]See *Business Week*, December 18, 1943, pp. 34, 37; and *NPN*, January 5, 1944, p. 5, and July 5, 1944, p. 36.

[99]The effect of price controls in Texas was not unlike that in other producing states. "Drilling was deeper, labor was more expensive, supplies and equipment were almost twice their prewar prices, but still the price of crude oil was pegged.... Only 307 wildcats were drilled in Texas in the first five months of 1943, and of those, all except twenty-three were dry." James Clark, *Three Stars for the Colonel* (New York: Random House, 1954), pp. 186–87.

[100]*NPN*, July 14, 1944, p. 26, and March 7, 1945, p. 11.

Table 5.3
WORLD WAR II OIL-PRODUCTION SUMMARY

Year	Output (bl)	Reserve Additions (bl)	Well Completions	Commercial Finds
1938	1,213,186	3,054,064	26,712	19,106
1939	1,264,256	2,399,122	25,987	17,734
1940	1,351,847	1,893,350	28,124	19,843
1941	1,404,182	1,968,963	29,070	19,590
1942	1,385,479	1,878,976	18,151	10,977
1943	1,503,427	1,484,786	17,884	9,887
1944	1,678,421	2,067,500	23,106	13,502
1945	1,736,717	2,100,299	24,677	13,944
1946	1,726,348	2,658,062	26,991	16,087
1947	1,850,445	2,464,570	30,842	17,613
1948	2,022,448	3,795,207	37,508	22,197

SOURCE: DeGolyer and MacNaughton, *Twentieth Century Petroleum Statistics,* 1981 ed., pp. 18, 33, 39.

small for the garment required." He recommended that scarce supplies be allocated to development areas, even when closely spaced, to maximize production.[101]

A comparison of prewar and postwar drilling and production statistics with those of the war period strongly suggests that not all was well under federal petroleum regulation. A 22 percent increase in oil production during wartime was not satisfactory, given the replacement of proration with maximum output and given unprecedented demand. As table 5.3 shows, yearly well completions decreased after 1941, and the number of discoveries dropped precipitously, in part as a result of the artificial incentives for wildcat drilling. Particularly telling was the large drop in yearly additions to wartime proven reserves compared with those reserves before and after the war.

It is true that scarce drilling supplies and labor problems reduced the means for increasing oil production, but supply shortages, skilled and unskilled labor shortages, and squandered incentives were directly attributable to price and allocation controls.[102] If petroleum

[101]Ray Dudley, "Cutting the Cloth Too Small?" *OW,* January 26, 1942, p. 37.
[102]Material and labor shortages closed or threatened many drilling operations. See, for example, *OGJ,* January 28, 1943, p. 106; and *NPN,* May 10, 1944, p. 34.

had been truly vital to the war effort, higher prices would have been readily paid in the absence of regulation, and higher costs, much of which was attributable to monetary inflation,[103] could have been absorbed to increase oil supplies for the home front and for war export. More oil at higher prices was not inflationary—relative price changes do not increase general prices[104]—but deflationary—increasing goods and services for dollars to buy.

As they had been during World War I, complaints of "profiteering" and "hoarding" were used to justify government allocation of drilling equipment.[105] Yet both practices are beneficial market processes that help, not hurt, consumers. Exploiting profit opportunities improves resource allocation. Hoarding vital equipment, like speculating with oil inventory, has a beneficial role in the economic system. If supplies are stockpiled when they are available, production need not be interrupted when supplies become scarce. Forced reallocation from inventory-rich firms to inventory-poor firms, on the other hand, penalizes foresight (and rewards its opposite) and overemphasizes present productive capacity in relation to the future ability of the production structure to satisfy war needs.

Instead of depending on self-interest within the discipline of the market, petroleum planners attempted to mastermind inventory positions of all exploration and production firms to balance equipment demand with inventories. In late 1942, the OPC tallied ten thousand inventory sheets to try to accomplish this Herculean task.[106] However superficially plausible this may have seemed, firms themselves or independent brokers could have been relied upon to reduce whatever economic error accounted for disparate inventory positions. As explained earlier, the market, because of its superior use of the knowledge revealed by profit and loss, can discover and remove economic error far better than can government centralization. The government's inventory procedure, on the other hand, in

---

[103]Between 1939 and 1948, the money stock rose over 11 percent per year. The doubled money supply went mainly toward war finance and debt retirement thereof. See Milton Friedman and Anna Schwartz, *A Monetary History of the United States*, p. 570.

[104]See the argument in chapter 9, pp. 510–12.

[105]*OGJ*, July 10, 1941, p. 20, and September 24, 1942, p. 61.

[106]*OGJ*, November 19, 1942, p. 16.

addition to the administrative burden it imposes on both firms and regulators, is static and prone to self-interested misreporting.[107]

Economic calculation that is crucial to efficiency is dependent not only on scarcity prices but on the reasonable accuracy of financial accounting information, which translates scarcity values into income-statement and balance-sheet information. Wartime practices, however, distorted business accounting.

A major debate developed in the accounting profession over the "tentativeness . . . of financial statements in wartime."[108] Revenue timing under government cost-plus contracts was ambiguous.[109] Depreciation and amortization schedules of war-related assets with little or no peacetime conversion value were very imprecise.[110] Particular policies during World War II increased the tentativeness of financial information. Profit and loss statements became tentative because of retroactive income adjustments on government contracts, deemed by authorities to have resulted in "excessive" or "unreasonable" profits.[111] Postwar tax refunds had the same effect.[112]

Accountants also called attention to the economic distortion created by government planning of private-sector activity. Price control, reported E. L. Kohler and W. W. Cooper, "caused real hardship on some business concerns and has presented bonanzas to others."[113] Disincentives to minimize costs, inherent in cost-plus war contracts, were worsened because of (1) a refund policy if high profits were made and (2) high taxes, which represented a large pass-through

---

[107]Henry Dawes, president of the Pure Oil Company, estimated that from 8 to 10 percent of his company's net profit went to prepare the "mass of uncoordinated, immaterial and irrelevant data" required by governmental and quasi-governmental (industry advisory) groups. *OGJ*, March 4, 1943, p. 37.

[108]George Farrand, "Wartime Problems of Financial Statements," *Journal of Accountancy* (January 1943): 36. Also see C. Oliver Wellington, "Financial Statements in Wartime," *Journal of Accountancy* (July 1943): 54–65.

[109]George Farrand, "Wartime Problems of Financial Statements," p. 37.

[110]Ibid., p. 38.

[111]Two laws in 1942 brought about contract adjustments: Public Law 507, 56 Stat. 176 (1942); and Public Law 528, 56 Stat. 226 (1942).

[112]George Farrand, "Wartime Problems of Financial Statements," pp. 38–39.

[113]E. L. Kohler and W. W. Cooper, "Costs, Prices and Profits: Accounting in the War Program," *Accounting Review* (July 1945): 268.

item.[114] Urgent contracts that the government excused from a bid process, moreover, represented open season on cost.[115] Finally, excessive accounting and legal demands created a competitive imbalance that favored large over small firms and thus lessened competition and reduced variety in the production structure.[116]

The fact that essential war needs received enough petroleum supply was more a testimonial to the wealth of the country and strength of the industry to absorb inefficiency than to the genius of government planning of petroleum production. The $18.6 million administrative cost on the government side[117] (a figure that would have been much higher except for voluntary industry aid) was no bargain. That cost was in addition to the costs of the aforementioned regulatory distortions and of the forgone opportunity for profit-seeking entrepreneurship. Only in a free market could the industry have met war and civilian demands in a least-cost manner.

The Korean Conflict

Prewar Bureaucracy. During 1946, the petroleum regulations and the planning apparatus of World War II were dismantled. What remained were certain petroleum-related assets built or acquired by the government for the war effort and a legacy of cooperation, similar to that at the end of World War I, that would ensure the return of planning under similar conditions. In early 1946, President Truman remarked, "I have been impressed with the great contribution of Government-industry cooperation in the success of the war petroleum program, and feel that the values of such close and harmonious relations between government and industry should be continued."[118] To this end, the Oil and Gas Division was created in the Department of the Interior on May 6 to administer the Connally Act and serve as the locus of federal petroleum regulation.[119] A month later,

---

[114]Ibid. Said Kohler and Cooper: "It leaves the contractor no incentive other than patriotism, pride, and maintenance of industrial efficiency to reduce costs. In fact, the economic incentive is in the opposite direction" (p. 279).

[115]Ibid., p. 285.

[116]Ibid., p. 282. Price controls also forced small companies with less staying power to sell out to large firms. *NPN*, November 10, 1943, p. 36.

[117]John Frey and H. Chandler Ide, *A History of the Petroleum Administration for War*, p. 34.

[118]Ibid., p. 55.

[119]Northcutt Ely, "The Government in the Exercise of the War Power," p. 697.

the National Petroleum Council (NPC) was founded as an industry-government liaison—a peacetime version of the PIWC. On March 29, 1947, an unpublicized organization was created to undertake a three-year study of petroleum supply needs should a global conflict occur. The Military Petroleum Advisory Board (MPAB) was composed of twenty industry volunteers, most of whom were veterans of the PAW.[120]

In the National Security Act of 1947, a semblance of petroleum planning reemerged with the creation of the National Security Resources Board. The purpose of this agency was to develop "programs for the effective use in time of war . . . for military and civilian needs."[121] Finally, in late 1950 the Office of Assistant Secretary for Mineral Resources was formed within the Interior Department to oversee the Bureau of Mines, the Geological Survey, and the Oil and Gas Division.

War Planning. On June 25, 1950, communist North Korea invaded U.S. ally South Korea, and a "limited police action" was declared by the United States under the aegis of the United Nations (founded in 1945). On September 8, the Defense Production Act was passed, which gave the president wide regulatory authority to set priorities and allocate supply, regulate prices and wages, control credit, requisition assets, settle labor disputes, and expand industrial capacity to increase supply.[122] On October 3, President Truman by executive order created the Petroleum Administration for Defense (PAD), which immediately assumed some functions of the Oil and Gas Division.[123] Headed by Oscar Chapman, former assistant interior secretary, the PAD, modeled after the PAW of World War II, was

[120]The Military Petroleum Advisory Board is described in Bruce Brown, *Oil Men in Washington* (El Dorado, Ark.: Evanil Press, 1965), pp. 1–7.

[121]Public Law 253, 61 Stat. 495 (1947). Also see *NPN*, April 14, 1948, pp. 40–41. Craufurd Goodwin characterized the National Security Resources Board as "a creature of the early cold war." Goodwin, "The Truman Administration," in *Energy Policy in Perspective*, ed. Craufurd Goodwin (Washington, D.C.: Brookings Institution, 1981), p. 17.

[122]Public Law 774, 64 Stat. 798 (1950).

[123]Executive Order 10161, 15 *Fed. Reg.* 6105 (October 3, 1950). For an organizational chart of the PAD, see appendix E, p. 1945.

empowered to allocate petroleum products, coordinate transportation, and prepare forecasts of petroleum supply and demand for the war effort.[124]

As they had been in earlier war efforts, industry groups were formed to advise the PAD on planning. Joining the MPAB were the Military Fuels General Advisory Committee and, reflecting the increasing stature of natural gas, the Gas Industry Advisory Council. The reestablishment of close industry-government relations only four years after the World War II partnership had ended was noticed by Craufurd Goodwin. "Once again, the bywords were 'teamwork' and 'cooperation' rather than 'conflict of interest' or 'restraint of trade.'"[125]

Price Regulation. Price regulation began in December 1950 when the Office of Price Stabilization, headed by Mike DiSalle, sent telegrams to forty East and Midwest oil companies urging them to hold prices at December 8 levels and to give the Economic Stabilization Agency (ESA) seven days' notice of price increases.[126] (The OPA reported to the ESA, which, in turn, reported to the Office of Defense Mobilization.) The author of the order was Orville Judd, a former OPA official and head of the ESA's Fuels Division. In conjunction with the "voluntary" request, certain crude-oil producers in the western United States were asked to roll back their recent $0.25 per barrel increase. While the California rollback was in dispute, Michigan refiners agreed to rescind a $0.12 per barrel increase posted December 16–22.[127]

---

[124]Craufurd Goodwin, "The Truman Administration," pp. 40–41, 46. While the PAW had a maximum employment of over 1,400 in July 1943, the PAD reached a high of only 350 in June 1952. Roger Wallstadt, *Oil Industry Participation in Emergency Planning* (Washington, D.C.: American Petroleum Institute, 1981), pp. 6, 8.

[125]Craufurd Goodwin, "The Truman Administration," p. 47.

[126]*NPN*, December 27, 1950, p. 11. For some initial industry response, see ibid., pp. 30–31. *Business Week* (December 23, 1950, p. 73) correctly envisioned the price control scenario in a sub-headline: "At first, piecemeal regulation will plug leaks in the dike of voluntary freeze. Overall enforcement will come as fast as machinery can be set up. Immediate effects: price increases, uptrading." "Uptrading" is when a firm discontinues less profitable lines to concentrate on more profitable lines to weather increased costs during the control period.

[127]*NPN*, January 3, 1951, pp. 27, 30. Clarified price rules were issued at this time. See *NPN*, December 27, 1950, p. 28, and January 3, 1951, p. 28. Several weeks later, the California rollback request was withdrawn. *NPN*, January 17, 1951, p. 22.

Temporary ceiling prices for crude became effective January 25, 1951, freezing prices at their highest level during the preceding January 19–25 period for the next six months.[128] Anticipating circumvention of the regulation, the Economic Stabilization Administration directive added:

> Any practice which results in obtaining indirectly a higher price than is permitted by this regulation is a violation of this regulation. Such practices include, but are not limited to, devices making use of commissions, services, cross sales, transportation arrangements, premiums, discounts, special privileges, tie-in arrangements and trade understandings.[129]

The formal regulatory order, described by the *National Petroleum News* as a "sneak attack from the clear blue," brought skeletons out of the closet. World War II price controls were described by the same journal as "political" and responsible for "cut[ting] down severely the country's war supplies."[130] Patriotism, at least in the oil patch, was strained from the start of the Korean "police action."

Effective May 12, permanent controls set maximum crude prices at "the ceiling price at a receiving tank [on] . . . January 25, 1951."[131] In August, the Independent Petroleum Association of America began to lobby for cost-based price increases.[132] The Office of Price Stabilization, ambivalent about the request, conferred with the PAD about a stripper subsidy plan in October.[133] On October 3, the first crude-price liberalization allowed prices that had been out of line on January 25 to be raised to the highest frozen price for similar crude in the area.[134] An amendment to the Defense Production Act in late 1951 allowed cost increases between the base period and July 26, 1951, to be passed through, although it was uncertain whether oil, like manufactured items, was eligible.[135]

[128]*NPN*, January 31, 1951, p. 13; and *OGJ*, February 1, 1951, p. 32. A recognized irony of the price freeze was that it immediately followed a forced rollback of automobile prices, which increased petroleum demand to pressure crude prices upward.

[129]*NPN*, January 31, 1951, p. 14.

[130]*NPN*, May 16, 1951, p. 33.

[131]*OGJ*, May 10, 1951, p. 81.

[132]*OGJ*, August 9, 1951, p. 62.

[133]*NPN*, October 31, 1951, p. 19.

[134]Pricing Order 23, October 3, 1951.

[135]Public Law 96, 65 Stat. 43. (1951). Also see *NPN*, December 13, 1951, p. 64.

Requests for increased prices in 1952 fell on deaf ears. The OPA's "inflation fighters" were not to be distracted from their top priority of price stability. On the drilling front, incentives to drill marginal fields were explicitly denied by the same agency to conserve scarce oil-field supplies.[136]

On February 12, 1953, five months before the July 27 armistice, crude prices were decontrolled pursuant to President Eisenhower's directive to remove wartime regulation. Crude prices rose on the West Coast and in Pennsylvania because of abnormally low ceiling prices. Prices were little changed elsewhere.[137] Pending price applications, numbering between 600 and 700, were closed with letters announcing decontrol. There was informed speculation that without maximum-price psychology, prices would drop, but state proration officials stepped in to prevent that by limiting production.[138]

Material Allocation. In the fall of 1950, steel used in oil exploration and production, such as drill pipe, tubing, and casing, began to be crowded out by military hardware manufacture. Price-system restrictions interfered with a natural resolution of competing demands, and in January 1951, the PAD met with the National Production Administration to secure priority for oil-industry steel requirements. The PAD also requested control of 5 percent of oil tubular inventory per warehouse in District V (Washington, Oregon, Nevada, California, and Arizona) for emergency allocation, particularly to small producers who were inventory poor.[139] A lack of regulation, not the results of prior regulation, was perceived as creating the developing shortage.[140]

Formal allocation directives would come.[141] After the 5 percent request was granted, the National Production Administration in

---

[136]*NPN*, May 21, 1952, p. Also see *NPN*, April 21, 1952, p. 98.

[137]*NPN*, February 18, 1953, p. 53.

[138]Ibid., pp. 33–34. For proration factors, see chapter 4, p. 164.

[139]Bruce Brown, *Oil Men in Washington*, pp. 92–94.

[140]Said Brown, "We were plagued by the shortage of materials and the absence of any real system for carrying out our principal function which was to get the materials that were actually needed for an industry operation, so that the operation could proceed." Ibid., p. 132.

[141]Government loans were already made to tubular-goods companies to increase production. See, for example, the discussion of the $73-million loan to Lone Star Steel in *NPN*, January 17, 1951, p. 18.

late February gave its first equipment-priority assignment to the industry. This was superseded on March 12, 1951, by the Controlled Materials Plan, which began oil tubular allocation on an "emergency" basis on April 1 and on a "normal" basis on July 1, according to a priority system based on past demand.[142] The PAD also joined the material-allocation effort, advising state conservation agencies to widen spacing rules and encourage secondary unitization, more economical pipe size, and dual completions.[143]

By mid-1951, controversy developed over steel allocations between domestic drilling and foreign drilling. This was a tiff between independents and majors. Russell Brown of the Independent Petroleum Association of America complained that, according to National Production Council estimates, the foreign side received 30 percent more than required while the domestic side received 10 percent below requirements.[144] The independents' view was stated by PAD deputy administrator Bruce Brown:

> There was a world-wide shortage of oil country tubular goods. The domestic producers were distressed about the shortage and suspicious of the allocation system. To them every shipment of oil country tubular goods abroad made it harder to get the material together to complete a well at home.[145]

The exasperation of one independent with the NPC's allocation requests was quoted verbatim by Brown:

> You so-in-so's can use these forms for toilet paper. It would not do a damn bit of good for me to waste my time filling out such tripe. Your entire organization is a waste of Public Money, a delusion and a snare as far as the "little man" in the Oil Business is concerned. . . . However, that does not alter the fact that I have to go out on the Black Market and buy twenty-five thousand dollars worth of casing on a "wildcat" well because of you—AND—there was plenty and is plenty of casing available. Boy, if I told you what I thought of you, I'd probably go to jail—so I'll just THINK IT.[146]

---

[142]*OGJ*, March 1, 1951, p. 21, March 15, 1951, p. 41, and March 22, 1951, p. 61.

[143]Bruce Brown, *Oil Men in Washington*, p. 99.

[144]*NPN*, June 6, 1951, p. 29.

[145]Bruce Brown, *Oil Men in Washington*, p. 165.

[146]Ibid., p. 216. For prosecution of black-market ("grey-market") activity in oil tubular goods, see *OGJ*, November 24, 1952, p. 82.

Although admitting that foreign drilling was more economical than domestic drilling because of larger reservoirs abroad, Brown emphasized a PAD goal of "sustaining smaller operators such as independent producers."[147] The favoritism dispute led to hearings by the House Small Business Committee chaired by Wright Patman (D-Tex.). The PAD was found neither negligent nor discriminatory.[148]

After almost a year and a half of forced redistribution of company inventories and priority allocation, regulation was relaxed when war demands slackened in the spring of 1952.[149] As late as November 1952, however, California producers complained to the PAD about inadequate materials.[150]

Other. Natural gas, an increasingly important fuel, was regulated under price controls and drilling equipment allocation. A separate bureaucracy for methane matters, proposed by the American Gas Association's National Defense Committee, was turned down by Secretary of the Interior Oscar Chapman in early 1951. The Federal Power Commission continued to exert regulatory jurisdiction over rates and service issues of interstate gas pipelines and, increasingly, production dedicated to the interstate market.[151]

Early in the Korean crisis, producers lobbied the PAD to finance wildcat drilling in return for a royalty override and to otherwise loan money for drilling to increase crude supply. These requests were denied.[152] One debacle, however, similar to the Canol project during World War II, occurred. In quest of a cheap source of fuel oil, the navy financed a multimillion-dollar exploratory program in the Alaskan naval reserve. Although oil was found, poor transportation facilities and climate difficulties—reasons the industry had left

---

[147]Bruce Brown, *Oil Men in Washington,* p. 144. Brown said elsewhere, "By regulating distribution of the pipe needed to drill oil and gas wells, PAD is restoring freedom of action to smaller operators, reducing excess inventories, and breaking up a black market" (p. 145).

[148]Ibid., pp. 222–25.

[149]Ibid., pp. 226.

[150]*OGJ,* December 1, 1952, p. 59; and Bruce Brown, *Oil Men in Washington,* pp. 226–27.

[151]See chapter 8, pp. 367–70.

[152]Bruce Brown, *Oil Men in Washington,* p. 46.

the areas untapped—led to the program's termination a year ahead of schedule with little to show for its effort.[153]

Evaluation. On April 23, 1954, the PAD was abolished.[154] While planning during the Korean conflict had not approached the magnitude and thus the distortion of World War II petroleum planning, it was nonetheless counterproductive and unnecessary. Simple reliance on the price system would have sufficed to coordinate military and civilian access to supply. Whether the "police action" constituted a crisis was highly debatable, and in any case petroleum supply was never seriously in doubt. Crude-oil "overproduction" was evident at the height of hostilities, judging from market-demand proration factors below 80 percent in Texas and New Mexico and prorated output in other producing states except California.[155] Open lobbying by the Independent Petroleum Association of America and the Texas Independent Producers and Royalty Owners for restrictions on crude imports was another sign that the problem was quite different from the one supposedly addressed by emergency planning. Whatever the emergency, an opposite free-market strategy of reduced monetary growth,[156] reduced taxes, relaxed state conservation law, and resolution of the state-federal "tidelands controversy" over offshore mineral ownership[157] should have been employed. The price system and entrepreneurship would have done the rest.

Standby Planning, 1954–65

After the demise of the PAD in April 1954, emergency planning was relocated in the Interior Department's Office of Defense Mobilization, which included the Oil and Gas Division and several advisory groups: the reactivated MPAB, the Military Fuels General Advisory

---

[153]*OGJ*, August 9, 1951, p. 58. An editorial had the last word on the navy's effort: "The greatest conclusion from the Alaskan failure is that it shows up the fallacy of the 'naval reserve' type of thinking. . . [that] because the Navy uses oil it should also have to own oil fields. It would be just sensible to say that the Navy should mine its own iron ore, or grow its own beans" (p. 53).

[154]Department of the Interior order 2755, 19 *Fed. Reg.* 2503 (April 30, 1954).

[155]See chapter 4, p. 164.

[156]The money supply rose at an annual rate of 3.5 to 5 percent in the war period. See Milton Friedman and Anna Schwartz, *A Monetary History of the United States*, pp. 610–14.

[157]See chapter 6, pp. 282–83.

Committee, the Foreign Oil Supply Committee, and the NPC. Almost immediately, the Committee on Oil and Gas Emergency Defense Organization of the NPC recommended war emergency committees for each PAD district with separate subcommittees for oil and gas.[158] Later, the presidential-level Office of Emergency Planning and the army's Office of Civil Defense assumed the role previously held by the Office of Defense Mobilization. A director of the Office of Emergency Planning described the agency's function as "postattack management . . . to minimize the chaos and confusion that could smother our society economically, politically, and socially."[159] In addition, the Comprehensive Program for the Survival of Government and Management of Resources was implemented with planning directors and boards in each state.

In 1958, the Office of Emergency Planning and the Office of Civil Defense merged to form the Office of Civil and Defense Mobilization, only to return to their original separate states in 1961. Peacetime preparedness was again reshaped on August 28, 1963, with the establishment of the Emergency Petroleum and Gas Administration, staffed by "executive reservists"—leading industry figures who consented to plan petroleum matters in the event of an emergency.[160] The Emergency Petroleum and Gas Administration, in conjunction with the NPC, published a series of pamphlets describing the need for emergency mobilization, government planning, and civilian protection should an emergency arise.

> In peacetime, and to a large extent in war, Americans rightfully rely on the marketplace to work out the intricate matching-up of supply and demand. The business community recognizes, however, that some direction from the government is necessary in time of war. A balance has to be struck between civilian and military needs. There has to be some government coordination in securing scarce materials and manpower to accomplish wartime goals.[161]

[158]*NPN*, July 28, 1954, p. 16.

[159]Edward McDermott, "Address," *44 Annual Proceedings* (New York: American Petroleum Institute, 1964), p. 33.

[160]National Petroleum Council, *Civil Defense and Emergency Planning for the Petroleum and Gas Industries*, 2 vols. (Washington, D.C.: National Petroleum Council, 1964), vol. 1, p. 11. For an organizational chart of the Emergency Petroleum and Gas Administration, see appendix E, pp. 1946–47.

[161]National Petroleum Council, *What Is the Emergency Petroleum and Gas Administration?* (Washington, D.C.: National Petroleum Council, 1966), p. 5.

Elsewhere, Emergency Petroleum and Gas Administration planning was justified on the grounds that "no company should stand to gain a more favorable position in the industry or profit inequitably from a national disaster."[162]

Beginning in the late 1960s, emergency planning for petroleum would enter a new era. In 1966, the *National Petroleum News* speculated on whether growing involvement in Vietnam would trigger a return to Korean conflict controls. In fact, little thought was given to special wartime regulation. Emergency planning within the Office of Contingency Planning, meanwhile, was dormant.

After the 1973 Arab embargo, "emergency" assumed new meaning—higher prices and shortages—in place of the traditional sense of a physically demanding war effort or the aftermath of a disaster. "Economic warfare" by oil-exporting countries using the "oil weapon" was the new basis for regulatory control, and it inspired such government agencies as the Contingency Planning Office, the Emergency Response Planning Office, and the Office of Policy, Planning, and Analysis. Programs such as the Strategic Petroleum Reserve, the Synthetic Fuels Corporation, and the International Energy Agency arose several years later as buffers to anticipated oil-supply cutoffs. Traditional wartime planning—even contingency wartime planning—was a fading memory in the 1980s.

Cooperation versus Competition in Emergency Situations: A Theoretical View

In the first two chapters, a theoretical case was developed to demonstrate the superiority of market entrepreneurship to interventionism and socialism. Consumers, it was concluded, are best served when entrepreneurs are not subsidized or penalized by government involvement. The consumer, conceived abstractly, could be a private individual or even a government agency. Furthermore, the conditions surrounding production and consumption were not defined; it could have been during wartime, the aftermath of a calamity, or a period of relative tranquillity. In this section, the analysis will be tailored to emergency-type situations with particular reference to

---

[162]National Petroleum Council, *Petroleum and Gas in a National Emergency* (Washington, D.C.: National Petroleum Council, 1964), p. 9. "National disaster" meant a nuclear attack rather than a conventional war.

petroleum to present an economic case for market reliance under abnormal circumstances as well as under normal conditions.

It has been almost a foregone conclusion that centralized planning is necessary for wartime and emergency mobilization to replace market competition with cooperation and replace interfirm rivalry with pooling of managerial talent, physical facilities, and stocks on hand. It is true, as planning proponents point out, that rivalry entails experimentation and error (waste) by some firms and that, in unique circumstances such as war and disaster aftermaths, the complexity of end-uses is simplified by government coordination. But this assumes far too much to establish even a conditional case for economic constructivism. Competitive experimentation through market entrepreneurship performs a vital role in wartime as in peacetime for "the discovery of such facts as, without resort to it, would not be known to anyone, or at least would not be utilized."[163] Government-engineered cooperation, on the other hand, discards the trial-and-error process in favor of the status quo, which becomes less innovative and more inefficient as conditions change.[164]

For example, if plan x represents cooperative pooling to achieve a particular end (such as a transatlantic shipment of petroleum product), in a competitive market there are also plans $x+1$, $x-1$, $x+2$, $x-2$, and so on, distinguished by price, location, and means of service. In the latter rivalrous situation, it may be that several alternatives are inferior to the best alternative and that waste is created in the process of revealing what indeed is the best process. Even so, the best alternative is discoverable, from which the consumer benefits and to which rivals beneficially adjust, and constant pressure is placed on entrepreneurs to employ new ways to minimize cost and improve the quality of goods and services. Dependence on the status quo, on the contrary, makes the elementary constructivist error that all relevant facts are known or can be discovered outside the market process and that this information can be used by planners and government-appointed industry councils. If the constructivist assumptions were true, the issue of centralization and interfirm pooling

---

[163]F. A. Hayek, "Competition as a Discovery Procedure," *New Studies in Philosophy, Politics, Economics, and the History of Ideas* (Chicago: University of Chicago Press, 1978), p. 177.

[164]This suggests that World War II petroleum planning created more inefficiencies than the other two wartime planning experiences.

versus decentralization and interfirm rivalry would become moot. Since it is not, a case is made for allowing unhampered market processes to provide economic calculation to rationally decide which goods and services should be produced and which firms should enter, exit, contract, or expand in "emergency" situations.

Economic calculation in the market instructs firms on the relative merits of cooperative versus autonomous strategies. Where the government is a major demander in the market, contracts can be expected to be larger and more uniform than under conditions of predominantly private-sector demand. This suggests that cooperative strategies and scale economies will have a greater role than they would otherwise. Thus, under imperfect calculational conditions where the government crowds out private-sector activity, there is a role for cooperation, whether informal agreements or joint ventures, without government planning. This assumes that antitrust law is suspended and that such cooperation passes the market test of profitability.

Planning has not emerged from market failure. It has arisen because government interventions, such as monetary creation, subsidies, antitrust law, and price regulation, damaged the ability of the price system and entrepreneurship to effectively perform.[165] This was the case in all three wartime experiences.

The government alternative raises questions about the mentality of the planners themselves. Either a regulator is from the industry and is thus often favorably inclined toward particular firms (such as, for example, the firm he was with most recently or the firm with which he expects to be), or he is from outside the petroleum sector and lacks basic knowledge of the industry. Either way, there exists a propensity for decisionmaking that is different from the market's tendency to favor the least cost, highest quality alternatives.

Historically, wartime regulators have come overwhelmingly from the petroleum industry, and whatever their patriotism, the pressure to at least preserve, if not to enhance, the position of firms with which their loyalties lie in relation to other firms, both existing enterprises and would-be entrants, must be recognized.

---

[165]For some historical examples of the negative effect of regulation in emergency situations in the United States, see Jack Hirshleifer, *Disaster and Recovery* (Santa Monica, Calif.: Rand Corporation, 1963), pp. 113–24.

The decision not to implement petroleum planning in the Vietnam War, although the matter was scarcely considered, was the correct one. The decisions to regulate prices and allocate materials during World War I, World War II, and the Korean conflict were mistakes. Assuming good intentions, intellectual error was involved.

There were various reasons that an inferior economic means of planning was chosen over the more prosperous means of market entrepreneurship. Government planners were attracted to the power to command. Officials were also attracted to fuel-cost savings for the war effort that ceiling prices and requisitioned supply could provide—at least for the short term.[166] The industry, in turn, was attracted to a safe harbor of cooperation over the competitive gales of the market. But the importance of preexisting intervention "necessitating" greater government involvement cannot be overstated. Currency expansion and antitrust, as mentioned, created the problems that planning sought to correct by regulating pricing and encouraging cooperation. Allocation regulation, in turn, sought to cure the problems created by price regulation. Succeeding chapters examining downstream government intervention in the war episodes will bring to light other examples of regulation's begetting other regulation, a major theme of peacetime intervention as well.

---

[166]On requisition controversies, see chapter 23, pp. 1320–21.

6. Petroleum Leasing and Environmental Policy on Government Land

The previous chapters of Section II have concentrated on state and federal regulation of drilling and production on private land. This chapter focuses on the long and controversial history of petroleum exploration and production on government and Indian land. After the federal and respective state laws are summarized, environmental law, affecting primarily offshore drilling, is examined.

In the historical review of governmental lease policies to follow, many instances of malincentives and inefficient outcomes are uncovered. The final section presents a theoretical justification of why these problems are inherent, not the unique result of managerial errors. Specifically, centralized leasing suffers from calculational problems not present in a competitive market, and political choices are unstable. Policy reform to balance the ends of production and environmentalism in an efficient, nonconfrontational manner is postponed until chapter 31.

Leasing Policy on Federal and Indian Land: A History

The Constitution of the United States gives Congress jurisdiction over federally owned land. It states, "The Congress shall have power to dispose of and make all needed rules and regulations respecting the territory or other property belonging to the United States; and nothing in this Constitution shall be so construed as to prejudice any claims of the United States or any particular state."[1] Separate laws have been promulgated to govern petroleum leasing on federal land: the public domain, acquired land, the naval reserves, multiple mineral development land, military land, and submerged land. The

---

[1] Article IV, section 3, clause 2. The Supreme Court acknowledged in *Light* v. *United States,* 220 U.S. 523 at 537 (1911): "'All the public lands of the nation are held in trust for the people of the whole country.' And it is not for the courts to say how that trust shall be administered. That is for Congress to determine."

leasing of Indian land is overseen by the Department of the Interior's Bureau of Indian Affairs, although authority has increasingly been transferred to the tribes.

Public Domain

Early Years. Prior to 1866, mineral development on federal lands acquired by treaty or cession, the public domain, did not exist. It was illegal. "The Government," Edward Weeks explained, "had the undoubted *legal* right to treat every miner upon the public domain as a naked trespasser."[2] An early example of no-use policy occurred in 1865 when a report of likely oil deposits on the public domain in California led the U.S. land commissioner to immediately order the land reserved from entry or prospecting.[3]

In a policy reversal, the act of July 26, 1866, declared the public domain "free and open to exploration and occupation by all citizens of the United States" if, pursuant to the act of July 4, 1866, the land had not been previously reserved.[4] The act specified that "veins or lodes" of hard minerals were subject to claim, but petroleum was not mentioned.

The General Mining Laws Act of 1870, known as the Placer Act, qualified the "open season" with certain conditions on prospecting.[5] Placer claims applied to "all forms of deposits, excepting veins of quartz, or other rock in place." Whether petroleum qualified was ambiguous. The law was concerned with hard minerals—and uplifting the people who mined them. The bill's House sponsor stated, "The effect . . . will be that our mining population will be attached to the soil, that they will be changed from the nomadic, wandering character which they now have to settle communities."[6]

Revisions in 1872 to the Placer Act still did not settle the petroleum question.[7] That question remained largely academic; oil exploration

[2]Edward Weeks, *Commentary on the Mining Legislation of Congress* (San Francisco: Summer Whitney, 1880), p. 2.

[3]Federal Trade Commission, *Report on the Pacific Coast Petroleum Industry*, 3 vols. (Washington, D.C.: Government Printing Office, 1920), vol. 1, p. 72. Cited hereafter as *Report.*

[4]14 Stat. 251 (1866); and 14 Stat. 86 (1866).

[5]16 Stat. 217 (1870).

[6]*Oil & Gas Journal*, April 11, 1919, p. 50. Cited hereafter as *OGJ.*

[7]17 Stat. 92 (1872).

was in its infancy, and private lands offered plenty of wildcat territory in the several oil-producing states.

In the mid-1870s, with commercial oil wells becoming common and oil established as a valuable consumer good, the status of public-domain oil rights became more urgent. In early 1875, Land Commissioner Samuel Burdett opined that oil located in the public domain might be patentable. In 1880, the first oil claim was entered. In 1882, Commissioner Thomas McFarland reiterated the possibility of oil as a Placer Act mineral.[8] The suspense heightened the next year when Interior Secretary Henry Teller overruled the land commissioner by stating that the legality of petroleum findings on the public domain was "an undetermined question."[9] Petroleum claims were being entered in growing numbers.

The uneasy truce between explorers and land officials was shattered in 1896 when Secretary of the Interior Hoke Smith stated that petroleum was not a mineral under the law. Congressional agitation for amendatory law followed, led by congressmen from California and Wyoming where drilling on the public domain was concentrated. The result was the act of February 11, 1897, entitled "An Act to Authorize the Entry and Patenting of Lands Containing Petroleum and Other Mineral Oil under the Placer Mining Laws of the United States."[10] Public lands containing petroleum were now unambiguously "free and open to occupation, exploration, and purchase by citizens of the United States." The problem of mining a fugacious mineral under a law designed for hard minerals, however, remained.

The new law gave prospectors license to explore for petroleum and, if a discovery was made, claim ownership. But this was not a homestead private-property-right situation like the one discussed in chapter 3.[11] A previous claim for another mineral voided the oilman's discovery rights.[12] Government ownership and jurisdiction

[8]John Ise, *The United States Oil Policy* (New Haven, Conn.: Yale University Press, 1926), p. 296.

[9]Ibid.

[10]29 Stat. 526 (1897).

[11]See chapter 3, pp. 69–74.

[12]Stated John Ise: "The operators under the Placer Law were always subject to the danger that, after they had expended thousands of dollars in drilling, someone else might make discovery first and so take the claim. . . . In many cases, oil prospectors found the their land taken from them by claimants who asserted discovery of asphaltum, or gypsum, or some other mineral mentioned in the Placer Law." Ise, *The United States Oil Policy*, p. 297.

made all discovery work and discoveries uncertain. Because of limited acreage, oil finds incited piracy through drainage. Ownership was not of the entire contiguous deposit. Limited-term patents assured open-flow, maximum production, as did the legal requirement to drill "diligently." Complicating matters were the claims of script holders—military veterans, land-grant railroads, and speculators (particularly lawyers in the know)—who had public-domain land rights pursuant to an 1897 federal law.[13] Even if the rights of these public-domain titleholders did not supersede mineral ownership claims, the titleholders could complicate matters by exercising their legal right to trade grants located within forest reserves for "vacant and unoccupied" public domain.

The "clandestine atmosphere" of drilling on federal land produced fraud, subterfuge, protracted litigation, and outright violence.[14] A common practice was for individuals or associations to enlist friends and relatives as "dummy entrymen" to lay claim to thousands of acres to circumvent the acreage maximums. Dummy derricks (locators) and tunnels in the sides of hills satisfied the work-in-progress requirement, and questionable discoveries from oil seeps to "gypsum claims" kept areas reserved until actual drilling could take place.[15] Assessment work, necessary to preserve the driller's placer license, encouraged make-work projects, such as road building, and incited overdrilling.

In the 1880s and 1890s, and even after the 1897 Placer Law revisions, much criticism surrounded petroleum exploration and production on federal land. Drillers encountered many obstacles not present with private-land development. The government required no royalty payments to encourage supply; instead, it encouraged practices that penalized the government (as asset owner) and drillers as oil was wasted, prices were driven downward, superfluous wells

---

[13]30 Stat. 36 (1897).

[14]Paul Gates, *History of Public Land Law Development* (Washington, D.C.: Government Printing Office, 1968), p. 732. Also see Roswell Johnson, L. G. Huntley, and R. E. Somers, *The Business of Oil Production* (New York: John Wiley and Sons, 1922), p. 35.

[15]John Ise, *The United States Oil Policy*, pp. 298, 301–2. Prominent explorationist Thomas O'Donnell testified before Congress that "90 percent of all locators in California on these lands were dummy locators." Federal Trade Commission, *Report*, p. 77.

were drilled, and extraction was reckless. Only lawyers unambiguously benefited.[16] The underlying problem was recognized by the
Oil & Gas Journal.

> The law under which the oil lands of the Public Domain were leased
> . . . forced operators to drill, drill more wells and then drill in between
> in order that he might drain the territory as fast as possible. Unless
> he followed this procedure, the operator was very likely to have his
> production drained from his wells by other leaseholders close by,
> or at the end of his term, find himself suddenly bereft of his wells
> without recourse.[17]

This would lead to an enveloping concern: conservation of a highly
valued, nonreplaceable resource.

The Withdrawal Movement. Problems with drilling and production
on the public domain led to stark and varied measures after the
turn of the century. Between 1900 and 1909, President Theodore
Roosevelt presided over the removal of 225 million acres of land in
a general "conservation movement."[18] Public domain in California
and Wyoming was withdrawn from agricultural entry to protect oil
prospectors and improve incentives for oil conservation. Restorations occurred when lands were found to be non-oil-bearing. In
December 1908, over 6,000 acres were removed from hydrocarbon
development in Louisiana to arrest natural-gas wastage.[19] A year
later, a major withdrawal was made—not to check overproduction
but to preserve supply for later military usage by the U.S. Navy. In
the "aid of proposed legislation," almost 3 million acres of oil-proven
or likely oil lands in California were withdrawn as were 170,000
acres in Wyoming, which "caught a large number of operators in
every conceivable stage of development."[20]

In addition to the withdrawals, a July 1909 decision by the Department of the Interior (the *Yard* case), which challenged placer location
transfers and placed many patents in question, unsettled petroleum
activity in the public domain. Work in progress continued, while

[16]*OGJ*, April 11, 1919, p. 50.

[17]*OGJ*, September 20, 1918, p. 46.

[18]E. Louise Peffer, *The Closing of the Public Domain* (Stanford, Calif.: Stanford University Press, 1951), pp. 107–8.

[19]John Ise, *The United States Oil Policy*, p. 300.

[20]Ibid., p. 313.

public-domain drillers sought legislative relief. In response, Congress passed the Pickett Act of 1910 to protect those "in diligent prosecution of work leading to the discovery of oil or gas."[21] The Assignment Act of 1911 was also enacted to uphold claims from *Yard* if otherwise "valid and regular."[22]

Between 1910 and 1916, another thirty-five withdrawals aggregating 3.5 million acres were made. Net of restorations, total oil-land removals were over 5.5 million acres, not including the Alaska Territory. Significantly affected states were Utah (1,952,326 acres), California (1,507,547 acres), Wyoming (668,094 acres), Montana (641,622 acres), Louisiana (414,720 acres), Arizona (230,400 acres), Colorado (87,474 acres), and North Dakota (84,894 acres).[23] All of these withdrawals were "temporary," however, pursuant to the Pickett Act.

With work in progress protected, and some unsanctioned post-withdrawal exploratory work in progress, $18 million was expended in withdrawn areas by 1916, mostly in California.[24] Complaints of overproduction continued. In the 1914 *United States* v. *Midwest Oil Co.* case, the Supreme Court upheld the government's power to unilaterally withdraw public lands from mineral activity.[25] Prosecution of illegal drilling began in earnest in the second half of 1915.[26] Drilling was stopped, and reduced supply reversed the California picture to bring complaints of oil shortages prior to and during World War I.

Mineral Leasing Act of 1920. Between 1910 and 1920, Congress grappled with public-land problems and debated legislative reform.[27] Industry lobbyists desired open prospecting and clear title in disputed domain. Legislators desired more control over public-domain development and recognized in mineral extraction a revenue

---

[21]36 Stat. 847 (1910). For the politics behind the bill, see John Ise, *The United States Oil Policy*, pp. 314–19.

[22]Public Law 187, 38 Stat. 708 (1911).

[23]John Ise, *The United States Oil Policy*, p. 321.

[24]Federal Trade Commission, *Report*, p. 85.

[25]236 U.S. 459 (1914). "The acquiescence of Congress, as well as the decisions of the courts, all show that the President had the power to make the [withdrawal] order." 236 U.S. at 483.

[26]John Ise, *The United States Oil Policy*, pp. 321–22.

[27]See ibid., chap. 23.

source to supplement income taxation. The result of these preferences was the Mineral Leasing Act of February 25, 1920, drafted by
Secretary of the Navy Josephus Daniels, which made major changes
to the Placer Law.[28] A quasi-homestead system of property rights
was replaced by a leasing system with government as royalty owner
of all minerals, both discovered and to be found. Although scarcely
recognized as doing so, the law nationalized public-domain minerals
by formalizing ownership and control. Industry interests who did
not favor the bill's royalty obligations supported the legislation as
an alternative to federal development. They also welcomed the restoration of withdrawn areas subject to the leasing rules.

Prospecting permits covering 2,560 acres were available for two-
year terms in areas without known petroleum deposits. Exploration
work had to begin within six months, and within one year a well
depth of 500 feet had to be reached. Within two years, a depth of
2,000 feet had to be penetrated unless a discovery was made. Upon
discovery, one-fourth of the permit area, 160 acres, could be leased
for twenty years at a royalty rate of 5 percent of oil or gas sales. On
the remaining permit land, a "B Lease" could be secured at a royalty
rate of between 12.5 and 33.5 percent. This applied to all public
domain except in the Alaska Territory, where more liberal provisions
were designed to encourage development.

In Alaska, a maximum of 640 acres could be leased in areas of
known deposits at competitive royalty rates commencing at 12.5
percent. If production fell below 10 barrels per day per well, a royalty
reduction was possible. Another provision prohibited wells within
200 feet of the boundaries of leased land unless another well was
on private land. In addition, discretionary powers were given to
the Interior Department to curb undesired practices and encourage
conservation.

An anti-monopoly provision limited individuals and corporations
to one lease per field and three fields per state. This limitation and
the strict acreage maximums rested on the view that the greater the
number of distinct competitors, the greater the competition.[29]

---

[28]Public Law 146, 41 Stat. 437 (1920). The formal title was "An Act to Promote the
Mining of Coal, Phosphate, Oil, Oil Shale, Gas, and Sodium on the Public Domain."

[29]Commented John Ise, "The outstanding feature of the new law, and the feature
which contrasts most decisively with the laws of most foreign oil-producing countries,
is the smallness of the leases, suggesting, of course, our reliance upon competition."
Ise, *The United States Oil Policy*, p. 352.

This, like other provisions, would have unintended detrimental consequences.

The centerpiece of the law was the royalty clause, which was based on private-land rates; the end of the law was revenue. Of all rentals, royalties, and bonuses, 52.5 percent was to go to the Reclamation Fund to retire land in its virgin state; 37.5 percent was earmarked for the respective states for public schools and public roads; and the remaining 10 percent was to be distributed, along with filing fees, to the U.S. Treasury. This newfound revenue source would be a contributing factor to the expansion of government on all levels.

Operation and Amendment. In anticipation of the new law, geologists and scouts were in the fields and poised to apply for exploration permits. On February 25, the rush began, and by the end of the year, 5,000 applications had been filed.[30] In 1921, in response to slumping prices, the Interior Department relaxed drilling obligations. To John Ise, this flexibility demonstrated the superiority of public-land operations because "during the time when the government was allowing operators to cease drilling, many private owners were compelling operators on their lands to drill regardless of the market."[31]

By mid-1924, over 32,000 applications had been made under the Mineral Leasing Act. Discoveries, however, were far fewer; the main contribution of the law was "quieting the title to lands which were already proved."[32]

The wasteful conditions of petroleum production on the public domain under the Placer Law would not be alleviated under the Leasing Law. Writing in 1925, George Stocking criticized the latter as wasteful because

> it fails to take complete account of the fundamental nature of petroleum and its occurrence. . . . It fails to recognize the fact that the only logical unit for exploiting an oil pool is the geological unit— the underground pool itself . . . [and not] legal divisions and subdivisions of public land surveys.

[30]Ibid., p. 353.

[31]Ibid., p. 354. This "market failure" had governmental sources. See chapter 3, pp. 115–31.

[32]John Ise, *The United States Oil Policy*, p. 353.

"The law," he continued, "seems to be inadequate to ensure an orderly development of our petroleum resources."[33]

Also of concern was the fixed twenty-year lease, given operator ignorance of reservoir life. Quick-drill covenants promoted fast discovery work and drainage to public-land neighbors. Adjacent private lands also presented the choice between rapid withdrawal and drainage. The specter of arbitrary federal actions that would affect ongoing production work, which had historically been the case, encouraged wasteful, short-sighted strategies. "The characteristic of the present Federal system," concluded Charles Hughes in 1926, "appears to be prompt, continuous and competitive drilling."[34] In response to these problems, Herbert Hoover, in his only major presidential act regarding petroleum conservation, closed the public domain to further leasing on March 12, 1929.[35] At the same time, some 20,000 outstanding permits were reviewed for violations, which resulted in the cancellation of approximately 16,600 permits before April 4, 1932.[36] Falling oil prices and declining revenue also figured in Hoover's decision.

Another significant event would lead to a major revision of the 1920 act. The wasteful development of the Kettleman Hills field in California, 30 percent of which was located on the public domain, prompted the Department of the Interior to close the field, effective July 25, 1929, until a plan for restricted production could be implemented.[37] After two years of inactivity, the first unitization plan for federal land was developed by the operators and approved by federal officials. This experience led to the act of July 3, 1930, which

[33]George Stocking, *The Oil Industry and the Competitive System* (Westport, Conn.: Hyperion Press, 1925, 1976), pp. 278–79.

[34]Quoted in Samuel Pettengill, *Hot Oil: The Problem of Petroleum* (New York: Economic Forum, 1936), p. 187.

[35]Said Hoover, "There will be no leases or disposal of Government oil lands, no matter what category they may lie in . . . except those which may be mandatory by Congress. . . . There will be complete conservation of Government oil in this administration." *Public Papers of the Presidents: Herbert Hoover* (Washington, D.C.: Government Printing Office, 1974), p. 21. See also Northcutt Ely, "The Government in the Capacity of Land Owner," in *Conservation of Oil and Gas: A Legal History, 1948,* ed. Blakely M. Murphy (Chicago: American Bar Association, 1949), p. 602. Cited hereafter as *Legal History, 1949.*

[36]Ibid., pp. 602–3.

[37]See *National Petroleum News,* May 8, 1929, pp. 47–48. Cited hereafter as *NPN.*

temporarily exempted joint-production plans from antitrust law if they were approved by the interior secretary.[38] This law was joined by the act of March 4, 1931, which amended sections 17(b) and 27 of the 1920 act to exempt unitization and other forms of cooperative development on federal lands from acreage limitations.[39] Yet by 1935, only 6 of 500 submitted unitization plans had been approved by the secretary of the interior. Bureaucratic delay and stringent federal requirements interfered significantly with private efforts to avert the wastes of drainage competition.[40]

The act of August 21, 1935, again amended section 17(b) to give the interior secretary authority to require prediscovery unit or cooperative operations as a condition for obtaining lease rights.[41] The same act terminated prospecting permits and replaced them with five-year noncompetitive leases within known geologic structures. Standard twenty-year competitive leases were also replaced by ten-year leases.

Other changes would be made to liberalize the 1920 Mineral Leasing Act, which has governed petroleum development of the public domain to this day. The per state limitation was increased to 7,680 acres in 1926, 15,360 acres (with options on 100,000 acres) in 1946, 46,080 acres (with options on 200,000 acres) in 1954, and 246,080 acres (with options on 200,000 acres) in 1960, except in Alaska where 300,000 acres (with options on 200,000 acres) were allowed.[42] New sections were added in 1933 and 1934 to suspend production and lease payments under certain conditions and to enter water-well leases.[43] A 1954 revision established judicial review of Interior

[38]Public Law 527, 46 Stat. 1007 (1930).

[39]Public Law 853, 46 Stat. 1523 (1931). See Leroy Hines, *Unitization of Federal Lands* (Denver: F. H. Gowen, 1953), p. 20.

[40]In addition to delays of several months to several years before the government ruled on the submitted agreements, unitization plans were rejected if the owners did not consent to Interior Department control of the rate and quantity of production. See William Holloway, "Unit Operation of Public Lands," 3 *Oil and Gas Institute* (New York: Matthew Bender, 1952), pp. 237–41.

[41]Public Law 297.5, 49 Stat. 674 (1935).

[42]Public Law 157, 44 Stat. 373 (1926); Public Law 696, 60 Stat. 950 (1946); Public Law 561, 68 Stat. 648 (1954); and Public Law 86-705, 74 Stat. 781 (1960).

[43]Public Law 330, 47 Stat. 798 (1933); and Public Law 373, 48 Stat. 977 (1934). Other early amendments of lesser importance were Public Law 456, 46 Stat. 822 (1930); Public Law 726, 54 Stat. 742 (1940); Public Law 192, 57 Stat. 593 (1943); Public Law 212, 57 Stat. 608 (1943); Public Law 442, 58 Stat. 755 (1944); Public Law 231, 59 Stat.

Department decisions for lessor-plaintiffs.[44] This was important because, in the 1947–54 period, the burden of proof regarding lease applications went from the Bureau of Land Management to the driller.[45] Amendments in 1960, in addition to revising the acreage limitation, introduced noncompetitive bidding on land not known to be oil laden or unlikely to contain favorable geologic structures. In such cases, the first qualified applicant got the lease, subject to a minimum royalty of 12.5 percent.[46] Changes in 1962 and 1970 concerned royalty nonpayment and lease reinstatement.[47] More recently, the Combined Hydrocarbon Leasing Act of 1981 redefined oil under the 1920 act to include tar sands and other solid-state hydrocarbon deposits to facilitate and encourage production.[48]

Cooperative development, which started very slowly in the early and mid-1930s, picked up late in the decade with Interior's power to require unitization. Statistics for federally owned or operated domain, which includes Outer Continental Shelf (OCS) lands in addition to the public domain, reveal this point. In 1940, over 100 units covering 1.8 million acres had been approved, which grew to 373 units and 5.7 million acres a decade later. In 1960, over a thousand plans had been approved on 21 million acres. In 1970, these figures approximately doubled, and by 1980, cumulative approval stood at 3,581 agreements covering 58 million acres. This accounted for 64 percent of oil and 48 percent of gas produced on federal land, chiefly the public domain.[49]

Until 1975, bonuses and royalties from the public domain were allocated under the original 1920 law. Since 1975, states except Alaska have received 50 percent, the Reclamation Fund 40 percent, and the U.S. Treasury 10 percent. Since becoming a state on January

---

587 (1945); and Public Law 696, 60 Stat. 950 (1946). Also see Lewis Hoffman, *Oil and Gas Leasing on Federal Lands* (Denver: Ray Frey, 1957), pp. 4–7.

[44]Public Law 555, 68 Stat. 583 (1954).

[45]H. Byron Mock, "Human Obstacles to Unitization of the Public Domain," *12 Oil and Gas Institute* (New York: Matthew Bender, 1967), p. 214.

[46]Public Law 86-705, 74 Stat. 781 (1960).

[47]Public Law 87-822, 76 Stat. 943 (1962); and Public Law 91-245, 84 Stat. 206 (1970).

[48]Public Law 97-78, 95 Stat. 1070 (1981).

[49]U.S. Department of the Interior, *Federal and Indian Lands: Oil and Gas Production, Royalty Income, and Related Statistics* (Washington, D.C.: Government Printing Office, June 1981), pp. 63–65.

3, 1959, Alaska has received 90 percent of public-domain oil and gas revenues with the remainder going to the federal treasury.

Acquired Lands

With passage of the Acquired Lands Leasing Act on August 7, 1947, existing laws applicable to the public domain were extended to lands acquired by the federal government from individuals or states.[50] Exempted from this law—and leasing in general—were areas "situated within incorporated cities, towns and villages, national parks or monuments; set apart for military and naval purposes; and tidelands or submerged lands." Pursuant to the act of July 29, 1954, amended regulations were issued for acquired lands to incorporate updated public-domain provisions contained in the amended Mineral Leasing Act of 1920.[51]

As of 1980, acquired lands accounted for 727 active wells on 8.8 million leased acres with annual production of approximately 211 million barrels of oil and 778 billion cubic feet of natural gas. This accounted for 0.7 percent of the oil and 0.04 percent of the natural gas produced in the United States.

Bonus and royalty income from acquired land is distributed differently than that from the public domain, depending on the category of land. If the land is within the national forests, 25 percent goes to the state, 65 percent to the U.S. Treasury, and 10 percent to the Forests, Roads, and Trails Fund. If the leased land is within the national grasslands, 25 percent goes to the county, 65 percent to the U.S. Treasury, and 10 percent to forest maintenance. Revenue from other types of acquired land goes to other funds in addition to state and federal treasuries.

Indian Lands

Laws governing petroleum leasing on Indian lands, administered by the Bureau of Indian Affairs within the Department of the Interior since 1898,[52] have had separate provisions for land purchased by Indian tribes and land allotted to individual tribal members by the

---

[50]Public Law 382, 61 Stat. 913 (1947).
[51]Public Law 555, 68 Stat. 583 (1954).
[52]30 Stat. 495 (1898).

federal government. In addition, special treatment has been given certain tribes situated in particularly rich oil regions.[53]

In 1983, 20 million barrels of oil and 118 billion cubic feet of natural gas were produced from 3,865 producing leases owned by 58 tribes. This accounted for 0.6 percent of the oil and 0.01 percent of the natural gas produced domestically and generated royalties of $141 million held in trust by the U.S. Treasury for all tribes, nations, and allottees except the Osage tribe.[54]

Tribal Leasing. The act of February 28, 1881, began petroleum leasing of lands purchased by tribal members. Certain restrictions applied, such as a maximum ten-year lease period.[55] Later acts in 1926 and 1927 enlarged leasable lands to include Indian school land, agency land, and unallotted lands within Indian areas.[56] The next major change, the act of May 11, 1938 (Tribal Leasing Act), paralleled the 1935 act pertaining to the public domain by giving the interior secretary power to require unit operation before or after issuing leases.[57] This act, as amended, is the central law governing tribal leasing today, although increased tribal autonomy has limited its authority.

Allotted-Land Leasing. The General Allotment Act of 1887 (Dawes Act) assigned individual land tracts to Indians, twenty-five years after which title would be transferred from the government to the individuals.[58] Section 5 of the act, however, disallowed mineral leasing. This was reversed in the act of March 3, 1909, subject to Interior Department approval of the lease plan.[59] The power of the interior secretary was further delineated and minor changes in the lease

[53]This section relies upon discussions in Northcutt Ely, "The Government in the Capacity of Land Owner," in *Legal History,* 1949, pp. 614–22; Northcutt Ely, "The Government in the Capacity of Land Owner," in *Conservation of Oil and Gas: A Legal History, 1958,* ed. Robert E. Sullivan (Chicago: American Bar Association, 1960), pp. 308–9; cited hereafter as *Legal History,* 1960; and Alfred McLane, *Oil and Gas Leasing on Indian Lands* (Denver: Bradford-Robinson, 1955), pp. 55–58.

[54]U.S. Department of the Interior, *Mineral Revenues* (Washington, D.C.: Government Printing Office, 1983), p. 38.

[55]26 Stat. 794 (1891).

[56]Public Law 133, 44 Stat. 300 (1926); and Public Law 702, 44 Stat. 1347 (1927).

[57]Public Law 505, 52 Stat. 347 (1938).

[58]24 Stat. 388 (1887).

[59]Public Law 316, 35 Stat. 781 (1909).

provisions were made in subsequent amendments to the 1909 law.[60] Mandatory unitization of allotted lands, upon request of the interior secretary, was authorized in the Tribal Leasing Act of 1938. The 1909 act, as amended, remains the basic law governing leasing of allotment land today.

Osage Tribe Land Leasing and Five Civilized Tribes. Because of their location in oil-rich midcontinental areas, the Osage tribe and the Five Civilized Tribes—the Cherokees, Choctaws, Chickasaws, Creeks, and Seminoles—have been governed by special legislation.[61] The act of June 28, 1906, established a special trust fund for the Osage tribe's 1.5-million-acre reservation in northern Oklahoma and allowed the tribe to negotiate leases on the western half of the reservation. At the end of twenty-five years—on January 1, 1932— the trust was to be transferred from the Interior Department to the tribe.[62] In 1921, retention of the trust by the government was extended until 1946, and in 1938, it was extended again to 1984.[63] In 1978, a law was passed to hold Osage land minerals in perpetuity.[64] Clearly, the government was reluctant to relinquish control and grant fiscal sovereignty to these tribes.

Unique among tribes are the supervisory powers the Osage tribe holds over petroleum leasing. The Department of the Interior only provides staff services and support work. Because of tribal control and the obvious incentives therein, mismanagement problems that have plagued other tribes subservient to the Bureau of Land Management and the Minerals Management Service (MMS) have been largely avoided.

Petroleum leasing of land held by the Five Civilized Tribes, also located in Oklahoma, began with the act of May 27, 1908, which

---

[60]36 Stat. 855 (1910); 39 Stat. 123 (1916); Public Law 329, 42 Stat. 994 (1922); Public Law 732, 54 Stat. 745 (1940); and Public Law 257, 69 Stat. 540 (1955).

[61]For an early history of petroleum leasing for these tribes, see John Ise, *The United States Oil Policy*, chap. 26; and *OGJ*, December 17, 1936, pp. 15–16.

[62]Public Law 321, 34 Stat. 539 (1906). The first royalty income was received by this tribe in 1901. By 1914, over $14 million was received annually. Yearly income reached $10 million by 1919 and $30 million by 1923 before declining to $5 million by 1936. Income has steadily risen in recent decades, peaking at $50 million in the early 1980s.

[63]Public Law 360, 41 Stat. 1249 (1921); and Public Law 711, 52 Stat. 1034 (1938).

[64]Public Law 95-496, 92 Stat. 1660 (1978).

amended the lease prohibition in the act of March 3, 1893.[65] As with other Indian lands, the power to force unit operations came with the aforementioned Tribal Leasing Act of 1938. Although not of significance for the purposes of this book, many legislative amendments and much litigation have surrounded these petroleum-laden tribal lands.[66]

Management Problems. As a government monopoly, petroleum leasing on Indian land suffered problems similar to those of public-domain leasing. Rigid rules required minimum lease sales in bad times as in good times. The requirement of continuous production forced maximum production even in times of overproduction and market demoralization. Red tape delayed development and timely royalties for Indians. Stiff bonding requirements discouraged bidding.[67] Small-tract sales, such as the 160-acre-per-person maximum on Osage land and 4,800 acres elsewhere, promoted overdrilling and drainage competition. So did quick-drill provisions. Commented a member of the Kansas Geological Survey in 1905:

> With the entire area controlled by one good business head, development would be stopped until the stocks had decreased greatly and the price of oil advanced; but with the Secretary of Interior insisting on the "development clause," no one cares to jeopardize the title of valuable leases by declining to drill. Therefore, the price goes downward and production continues to increase.[68]

Acreage limitations per individual and per company kept "the oil business in the hands of small and inefficient units" that had a propensity to overdrill and overextract.[69] Acreage limitations were intended to reduce speculation and increase competition, but by hampering calculated production and reducing scale economies, they created a far more wasteful state of affairs.

In addition to lease regulations, paternalist politics skewed leasing decisions away from decisions enlightened by economic calculation.

---

[65]Public Law 140, 35 Stat. 312 (1908).

[66]Major court decisions and amending acts are examined in Northcutt Ely, "The Government in the Capacity of Land Owner," in *Legal History*, 1949, pp. 617–22.

[67]Harold Williamson et al., *The Age of Energy, 1899 to 1959*, vol. 2 of *The American Petroleum Industry*, (Evanston, Ill.: Northwestern University Press, 1963), p. 52.

[68]Quoted in John Ise, *The United States Oil Policy*, p. 396.

[69]Ibid.

Revenue maximization, for example, was not good but bad. Interior Secretary Franklin Lane curtailed mineral leasing on Osage land in 1917 because he felt per capita income of $2,000 from oil was enough.[70] By the early 1920s, however, this tribe enjoyed an average yearly per capita oil income of $10,000, and some families received as much as $80,000.

An irony of Indian wealth from oil was the original intention of the federal government to saddle the Indians with marginal land, not to mention to moderate "demoralization" once their lands became valuable. This irony, as well as the demoralization problem of sudden wealth and the conservation problem under federal leasing rules, was noted by John Ise.

> The extraordinary fortunes that have fallen to many of the Indians seem fair and just in one way, at least. The government established the Indian reservations in Oklahoma because the land there was thought to be of little value; and when oil was later discovered there, it almost looked as if there were some sort of justice in the turn of fortune's wheel. In other ways, however, the situation is far from happy. Such wealth as many Indians have . . . is said to be a demoralizing influence. Furthermore, while they are smothering in their wealth now, it is likely that the time will come when oil royalties will cease; and the decline to poverty again will be a more painful change than was the elevation to riches. It is greatly to be regretted that the Indian lands could not have been . . . exploited much more slowly than they have been. Had they been so, we would have had less distress in the oil industry, less waste of oil, less demoralization of the Indians; and we should have more oil left for the future, and a longer future of financial competence for the Indians.[71]

Paternalistic control also meant less revenue for the tribes. Lease-area restrictions reduced the attractiveness of Indiana properties to lessors. The Osage tribe complained to Congress that private royalty owners received two to three times more lease revenue than they did thanks to the absence of acreage restrictions.[72] A March 1922

---

[70]*OGJ*, February 22, 1917, p. 3.

[71]John Ise, *The United States Oil Policy*, p. 399. The "sudden wealth" problem also applies to the rule of capture itself. See chapter 2, pp. 64–65.

[72]*OGJ*, February 1, 1917, p. 26.

ruling by the Interior Department that prohibited Indian-land leasing by foreigners, later reversed, also narrowed competitive bidding.[73]

Indian-land management problems would prove to be persistent and resistant to reform. Decades of royalty undercollection and haphazard lease plans by the Bureau of Indian Affairs were revealed by General Accounting Office investigations beginning in the 1950s.[74] Alarmed at the lack of progress in resolving royalty mismanagement problems, documented periodically by later General Accounting Office reports, Congress passed the Indian Mineral Development Act of 1982, which allowed tribes to negotiate directly with oil companies for the first time. Title II of the Federal Oil and Gas Royalty Management Act instructed the Interior Department to enter into cooperative arrangements with the tribes to increase efficiency.[75] A year later, agreements were made with Indian tribes to "carry out inspection, auditing, investigation or enforcement" of lease agreements.[76] A 1982 Court decision sanctioned tribal taxation, which centered on oil and gas production.[77]

Despite promotion of tribal governance and the corresponding demotion of the Bureau of Indian Affairs, long-standing problems continued through 1984. According to David Lester of the Council of Energy Resource Tribes, royalty collections were from three to four months late, and specific information for monitoring purposes was lacking. Innovations to traditional lease agreements such as joint ventures, equity ownership, and service contracts are slow to gain the approval of the Department of the Interior. Security and monitoring services by the U.S. Geological Survey's Bureau of Land

[73]For an example of a blocked sale of Osage properties by Dutch-Shell, see Ludwell Denny, *We Fight for Oil* (New York: A. A. Knopf, 1928), p. 253.

[74]See this chapter, pp. 308–14. The royalty problem was one reason Indians desired to eliminate, or at least reduce, the guardian-ward relationship between themselves and the Interior Department. In 1975, a victory was won in the Indian Self-Determination and Education Act, which permitted Indians to provide their own social services and education. Public Law 93-638, 88 Stat. 2203 (1975).

[75]Public Law 97-382, 96 Stat. 1938 (1982). Only the Osage tribe has enjoyed relative autonomy in mineral management.

[76]Public Law 97-451, 96 Stat. 2447 at 2457 (1983).

[77]See chapter 7, pp. 362–63.

Management are lacking. Furthermore, noted Lester, "The problem is growing worse."[78]

Multiple Mineral Development

The Mineral Leasing Act of 1920 prevented prospecting for different minerals on the same land by awarding a monopoly lease to the first applicant and a monopoly claim upon the first mineral discovery. "Large areas of public lands," Northcutt Ely observed, "were hence closed to development of minerals other than those authorized under the first valid lease or location."[79] In 1954, this was changed to allow multiple development of the same tract, in this case uranium prospecting on leased federal oil and gas properties.[80] This law was primarily intended to open some 60 million acres of oil-reserved land to uranium prospecting. The August 13, 1954, law also helped petroleum exploration in reverse situations, but not as much as exploration for other minerals.

Naval Petroleum Reserves

With the establishment of four naval reserves in Elk Hills, California (no. 1-1912, 38,969 acres), Buena Vista, California (no. 2-1912, 30,080 acres), Teapot Dome, Wyoming (no. 3-1915, 9,418 acres), and Southern Alaska (no. 4-1923, 35,000 square miles) by the federal government for indefinite naval use, the problem of existing petroleum leases became apparent. Reserve no. 2 in Buena Vista, California, in particular, was heavily leased by private interests.[81] After the titles in this reserve were reviewed to revoke fraudulent claims, titleholders engaged in "diligent" development as of February 25, 1920, were allowed to continue operations subject to permission

[78]Conversation with the author, August 1, 1984.

[79]Northcutt Ely, "The Government in the Capacity of Land Owner," in *Legal History*, 1960, p. 298.

[80]Public Law 585, 68 Stat. 708 (1954). Before the question of multiple minerals arose, agricultural entry on potential mineral lands was authorized in the act of July 17, 1914 (Public Law 128, 38 Stat. 509) and the Stockraising Homestead Act of December 29, 1916 (Public Law 290, 39 Stat. 862).

[81]The Buena Vista field was discovered in June 1909, followed by production and further leasing. At one time, 20,320 acres were privately held and 9,760 acres were publicly held on the reserve. The other three reserves also had private leaseholders and production. Reginald Ragland, *History of the Naval Petroleum Reserves and of the Development of the Present National Policy Respecting Them* (Washington, D.C.: Government Printing Office, 1944), pp. 84–89.

from the Interior Department.[82] These wells, located throughout the reserve areas, created drainage problems for the U.S. Navy's adjoining tracts. When authority over the reserves was transferred from the navy to the Interior Department in the act of June 4, 1920, the problem was addressed by leasing unallotted reserve areas and requiring rapid production.[83] Unlike the Department of the Navy, which advocated and practiced a conservationist policy of nonuse, the Interior Department under Secretary Albert Fall favored development, and by 1923, almost the entire reserve areas except Reserve no. 4 in Alaska were leased for private production.[84] In return for naval reserve leases, royalty payments in oil (in-kind royalties) were required, which the navy could trade for fuel oil, which it could strategically store.

Of all the arrangements made with private companies, the most remembered was between Secretary Fall and the Pan American and Sinclair companies. The highly publicized Teapot Dome scandal, the Watergate of its day, concerned secretive leases awarded to Pan American in Reserves no. 1 and no. 2 and to Sinclair in Reserve no. 3. What made the transactions notorious was not that they were made—Fall for many years had been critical of conservationist policy and had sought expanded leasing—or the terms of the leases but the fact that the principals of the involved firms, E. L. Doheny and Harry Sinclair, gave gifts and loaned $404,000 to Fall, who was experiencing financial difficulties.[85] Although evidence pointed more to a conflict of interest than a bribe, given Fall's predilection for reserve development, the wrath of both Democrats and fellow Republicans descended upon him and pro-development policy in general.[86] President Coolidge, whom critics viewed as having close ties to the affair, sought to make amends by appointing a commission

---

[82]Public Law 146, 41 Stat. 437 (1920). Under the leasing law, a 12.5 percent royalty on previous production was required to continue production on the reserve. For litigation surrounding the rights of existing claimants on the reserves, see Northcutt Ely, "The Government in the Capacity of Land Owner," in *Legal History*, 1949, p. 625.

[83]The Interior Department's commitment to counterdevelopment overrode the alternative of using eminent domain to end drainage from existing wells.

[84]George Stocking, *The Oil Industry and the Competitive System*, p. 286.

[85]John Ise, *The United States Oil Policy*, pp. 360–64.

[86]"Both Democrats and Republicans made him a convenient scapegoat . . . [for] uncovered close relationships between oilmen and important politicians." Gerald Nash, *United States Oil Policy*, p. 80.

in March 1924 to study naval reserve policy. Simultaneously, further leasing in the reserves stopped. But far from replacing exploitation with nonuse, the new policy ensured that drainage, estimated at almost 7 million barrels before the Fall leasing program began, would resume. The question in the three reserves was not whether oil would remain in place but who would gain possession—neighboring private-land operators or sanctioned reserve lessors. When severe drainage occurred in Reserves no. 1 and no. 2 in 1938, the navy belatedly asked Congress to allow an offset program and to engage in lease swaps with private-land owners.[87] Conflict of interest aside, subsequent events would vindicate Fall for his pragmatic strategy of depleting the reserves for naval supplies stored above ground.

In 1935 amendments to the Mineral Leasing Act, the secretary of the navy was authorized to allow cooperative agreements to develop the naval reserves.[88] In the Act of June 30, 1938, as amended by the act of June 17, 1944, unitization was made mandatory. The secretary of the navy had the power to purchase, acquire by trade, or condemn adjoining tracts. Outstanding leases outside an approved unit plan as of July 1936 would expire after an initial twenty-year period. Unit production, furthermore, could be reduced by the interior secretary if deemed necessary for national defense.[89]

In the 1940s and 1950s, production in Reserves no. 1 and no. 2 continued at a steady pace. In 1944, a unit plan was devised with Chevron for Reserve no. 1. In 1958, the navy began a program to drill offset wells on dormant Reserve no. 3 to counter drainage from the east side.[90] The Naval Petroleum Reserve Act of 1976 instituted full maximum-efficient-rate (MER) output for a period of six years, which was later extended to April 5, 1985.[91] In late 1980, Congress instructed the Interior Department to conduct competitive bidding

---

[87]John Ise, *The United States Oil Policy*, p. 372.

[88]Public Law 297.5, 49 Stat. 674 (1935).

[89]Public Law 786, 52 Stat. 1253 (1938); and Public Law 343, 58 Stat. 280 (1944). For certain exceptions and other developments, see Northcutt Ely, "The Government in the Capacity of Land Owner," in *Legal History*, 1949, pp. 627–29.

[90]Northcutt Ely, "The Government in the Capacity of Land Owner," *Legal History*, 1960, p. 308.

[91]Public Law 94-258, 90 Stat. 303 (1976).

for private companies on the 23-million-acre Alaskan reserve beginning August 1982.[92] Prior to this time, navy funds, amounting to
over $50 million by the mid-1950s, had been used exclusively to
explore and develop the field.

In 1984, the Department of Energy began a fourteen-well drilling
program on Reserve no. 3 to avoid natural-gas drainage from a
nearby private field.[93] In 1983, government production from the three
active reserves totaled 45.9 billion barrels of oil and 124 billion cubic
feet of natural gas, which generated $1.5 billion in revenue to offset
expenses of under $200 million. Oil from Reserves no. 1 and no. 3 was
sold entirely to the Defense Fuel Supply Center of the Department of
Defense, which in turn sold the oil to 30 private firms.

Over 95 percent of current oil production in the naval reserves
has come from Elk Hills, the second most active field in the United
States after Prudhoe Bay. Approximately 700 million barrels of oil
have been produced, and estimated future recovery is 811 million
barrels. In contrast, the Buena Vista field, its history punctuated by
drainage and rapid extraction, is in its twilight phase with 636 million
barrels down and an estimated 16 million barrels to go. The Teapot
Dome reserve is estimated to be at the half-way mark of a field
estimated to contain 27 million barrels. Reserve no. 4 in Alaska
awaits development.[94]

Military Land

Federal lands purchased by the defense establishment are designated as military lands. Prior to 1976, these lands were available for
lease only to protect against drainage; since that time, leasing has
been more aggressive (although still slow by private standards),
reflecting national energy policy.

Historical production on military lands through 1983 totaled 29
million barrels of oil and 970 million cubic feet of natural gas. In
1980, 1 million barrels of oil and 1.7 million cubic feet of natural
gas were produced from 268 wells, mostly situated in Louisiana.
Revenues in 1983 totaled $4.6 million. Other states with current

---

[92]Public Law 96-514, 94 Stat. 2957 (1980).

[93]U.S. Department of Energy, *DOE This Month*, December 1984, p. 7.

[94]This discussion is taken from the 1983 Annual Report, Department of Energy, *Naval Petroleum and Oil Shale Reserves* (Washington, D.C.: Government Printing Office, 1984).

military-land production are Alaska, Arkansas, Kentucky, Oklahoma, and Texas.

As is the case with other federal lands, leasing decisions are made within the Interior Department with consent of the Department of Defense.

Submerged Land

Origins of Federal Ownership. The private-property tradition of the United States has never applied to coastal waters and the land beneath them.[95] While it has been a foregone conclusion that state and local governments controlled nontidal navigable waters within their purview, the question of ownership of coastal waters has been less clear. This does not include water areas within federal lands, which are leased pursuant to the amended Mineral Leasing Act of 1920.

Offshore production in shallow depths began off California in 1899 and Texas in 1913, at which time these states claimed ownership and assumed jurisdiction. Texas passed an offshore leasing law in 1913 (revised 1917), followed by Louisiana in 1915 and California in 1921.[96] This assumption of jurisdiction went unchallenged until 1937 when Sen. Gerald Nye of North Dakota, upon the urging of Interior Secretary Harold Ickes, introduced Senate Bill 2164 to declare this territory part of the public domain.

This bill did not pass, but the movement for federal control had begun. The Department of the Navy, interested in national defense priority claims on the offshore deposits, and the Interior Department, interested in conservation practices for offshore production, joined the federal initiative.

---

[95]Under Roman law, the sea was considered community property belonging to the sovereign, a view adopted by English common law in the belief that open water was incapable of being exclusively enjoyed or occupied. This view carried over to American jurists who never considered private ownership in this area. For a history of early law and the "territorial concept of the marginal sea," see Ernest Bartley, *The Tidelands Oil Controversy* (Austin: University of Texas Press, 1953), pp. 7–29.

[96]Ibid., pp. 66–67, 88–89. Previously, the Gulf states claimed seaward boundaries upon statehood. Gordon Ireland, "Marginal Seas around the State," *Louisiana Law Review* (November 1940): 252–93; ibid. (December 1940): 436–78. The state boundaries were extended to 27 miles offshore by Louisiana in 1938 and Texas in 1941. Texas again extended its boundary in 1947 to reach the Outer Continental Shelf.

Following World War II, the debate resumed. On September 28, 1945, President Truman declared federal jurisdiction over all coastal waters.[97] Forty-six of forty-eight states responded by backing a quit-claim measure renouncing federal ownership of submerged lands three miles seaward from state coastlines. Introduced as House Joint Resolution 225, the bill passed Congress, only to be vetoed by President Truman on August 2, 1946, without an override.[98]

During the controversy, the states continued to grant leases and collect royalty income pursuant to existing statutes. In late 1945, the United States filed suit against California in the U.S. Supreme Court. In a disputed decision issued in June 1947, Justice Black opined for the majority that the federal government had "paramount rights in [and] full dominion over the resources" off the coastline.[99] The "paramount rights" doctrine was reaffirmed in two 1950 Supreme Court cases.[100]

Having lost in the legal arena, the states turned to Congress. After several setbacks, they won a compromise in the Submerged Lands Act of 1953, which deeded to the coastal states an area three statute miles off the low-water mark of their Pacific and Atlantic shorelines, and, in the case of the Gulf of Mexico states, ten and one-half miles (three marine leagues) from the low-water mark.[101] In the Outer Continental Shelf Lands Act of August 7, 1953, federal sovereignty, with Interior Department jurisdiction, was assigned to the area beyond the states' limits.[102] Royalty divisions between federal and state governments corresponded to these jurisdictions.[103]

With the jurisdictional matter settled, the curtailed production that occurred between 1948 and 1953 as a result of legal uncertainties would end. Other controversies, however, would arise. Following

[97]Proclamation 2667, 59 Stat. 884 (1945).

[98]Ernest Bartley, *The Tidelands Oil Controversy*, p. 145.

[99]*United States* v. *California*, 332 U.S. 19 at 38–39 (1947).

[100]*United States* v. *Louisiana*, 339 U.S. 699 (1950); and *United States* v. *Texas*, 339 U.S. 707 (1950).

[101]Public Law 31, 67 Stat. 29 (1953).

[102]Public Law 212, 67 Stat. 462 (1953).

[103]Establishment of precise boundaries has spawned much litigation between the federal government and the states. See John Connally, "Government Regulation of Operations on Submerged Lands," *21 Oil and Gas Institute* (New York: Matthew Bender, 1970), pp. 31–36.

oil-product price increases in late 1970, President Richard M. Nixon transferred authority over production rates per well on the OCS from state conservation agencies, which used market-demand factors to limit output, to the Interior Department to allow full MER output. A recent dispute, discussed below, is over sharing royalties from reservoirs on the OCS that also underlie the state side. The states' argument is that vital information for federal production is gleaned from exploration and production on their side.

Lease Activity: 1954–78. Because of wildcat domain and technical limits to deep-water drilling, not to mention Interior Department conservatism and heavily prorated offshore oil, offshore leasing proceeded at a cautious pace in the early years. Between 1954 and 1971, twenty-nine sales leased 7.3 million acres, generating bonus revenue of $4.4 billion.[104]

Environmental restrictions on offshore petroleum activity were of secondary importance until the Union Oil blowout in the Santa Barbara channel in January 1969. That highly publicized event marshaled environmental sentiment, particularly among Californians, into a politically powerful force, as discussed below. Reflecting the new environmentalism, total activity during 1969–71 was less than in the year preceding the accident.

A strong comeback began in 1972–73 as a result of growing oil-supply problems. In response to the embargo, President Nixon announced that 10 million acres of the OCS would be open to bids, matching the total offerings of the previous sixteen years. Frontier areas in both oceans and off Alaska were targeted. After a promising beginning, activity became sluggish despite an era of record prices and record imports. In the "energy vs. environment" debate, the latter prevailed as table 6.1 suggests.

Lease Activity under the OCS Amendments: 1978–84. Under the 1953 Outer Continental Shelf Act, the interior secretary had wide latitude in making leasing decisions—when to lease, where to lease, and on what terms. With the growing political clout of environmentalism and the coastal states, a movement began in Congress in 1974 to amend the law. Another undercurrent of legislative reform was stagnant domestic output in the face of growing petroleum demand,

---

[104]U.S. Department of the Interior, *Mineral Revenues: 1982 Report* (Washington, D.C.: Government Printing Office, 1983), p. 16.

Table 6.1
OUTER CONTINENTAL SHELF ACTIVITY: 1971–78

Year	Leased Acres	Oil Output (bl)	Gas Output (MMcf)	Bonuses Paid ($000)
1971	37,222	418,548,946	2,777,044	96,305
1972	826,195	411,885,893	3,038,555	2,251,348
1973	1,032,570	394,729,999	3,211,588	3,082,463
1974	1,762,158	360,594,065	3,514,724	5,022,861
1975	1,679,877	330,237,452	3,458,693	1,088,134
1976	1,277,937	316,920,109	3,595,924	2,242,898
1977	1,100,734	303,948,240	3,737,747	1,568,565
1978	1,297,274	292,265,042	4,385,061	1,767,042

SOURCE: U.S. Department of the Interior, *Annual Report,* various years.

the difference being rising imports. With the OCS containing the majority of remaining U.S. reserves, federal offshore policy was an important spigot of "national energy policy."

The result of these conflicting pressures was the eclectic Outer Continental Shelf Act Amendments of 1978, which had laudable aims. Listed among their purposes were

> expedited exploration and development . . . to achieve national economic and energy policy goals, assure national security, reduce dependence on foreign sources, and maintain a favorable balance of payments in world trade. . . . Orderly energy resource development with protection of the human, marine, and coastal environments. . . . Ensure the public a fair and equitable return. . . . Preserve and maintain free enterprise competition.[105]

State and local governments were given consideration in the new law with lease sales contiguous to their waters. Two funds were created in case of an oil spill, a fisherman contingency fund and an oil liability fund.

Gasoline shortages in 1979 again focused attention on dormant OCS production. In April 1979, President Jimmy Carter announced an accelerated leasing program. The following month, Interior Secretary Cecil Andrus proposed the first five-year plan under the 1978 act, which became final in June 1980. Twenty-six sales covering 55

[105]Public Law 95-372, 92 Stat. 628 at 631–32 (1978).

million acres were planned through 1985, which brought lawsuits from the Natural Resources Defense Council, Alaska, and California.

The change of administrations six months later would greatly accelerate the planned increase in OCS leasing. In April 1981, Interior Secretary James Watt announced proposed revisions to Andrus's program, and three months later a new five-year plan to lease the entire OCS was unveiled by Watt as "the most important oceanic and energy proposal of the Reagan administration."[106] The new plan drew lawsuits from the same parties that had challenged Andrus, and on October 6, 1981, a federal court sided with the plaintiffs and remanded the lease plan back to Interior for further consideration.[107] Watt resubmitted his proposal with minor changes, and on July 21, 1982, the "billion acre plan" became final.[108]

Between 1983 and 1987, 200 million acres were to be offered each year with emphasis on frontier development. Behind the full-throttle program were the pro-production philosophy of the Reagan administration that would replace foreign tankers with offshore wells, a desire to inventory the OCS in a period of ten to fifteen years, and the desire for increased revenue to balance the budget. This program, eighteen times larger than Andrus's plan and twenty-five times larger than the entire acreage offerings in the history of federal offshore leasing, led to a major suit by the earlier petitioners joined by Florida, Washington, and Oregon. On July 5, 1983, the U.S Court of Appeals for the District of Columbia affirmed the plan as being in compliance with the amended Outer Continental Shelf Act.[109] Another environmentally inspired lawsuit to annul Watt's program was rebuffed by the Supreme Court, which in a five-to-four verdict ruled that Interior did not have to submit to state coastal-zone management plans, which in effect would have given veto power to militant states.[110]

Despite federal court support, the billion-acre program was not to be. Specific lease sales met lawsuits that bought time for opponents.

---

[106]Hearing before the Subcommittee on Energy Conservation and Supply, *Proposed 5-Year Plan for Oil and Gas Development in the Outer Continental Shelf,* 97th Cong., 1st sess. (Washington, D.C.: Government Printing Office, October 6, 1981) p. 1.

[107]*State of California by and through Brown* v. *Watt,* 668 F.2d 1290 (1981).

[108]U.S. Department of the Interior, News Release, July 21, 1982.

[109]*State of California* v. *Watt,* 712 F.2d 584 (1983).

[110]*Secretary of the Interior et al.* v. *California et al.,* 104 S. Ct. 656 (1984).

Table 6.2
OUTER CONTINENTAL SHELF ACTIVITY: 1978–84

Year	Leased Acres	Oil Output (bl)	Gas Output (MMcf)	Bonuses Paid ($000)
1978	1,297,274	292,265,042	4,385,061	1,767,042
1979	1,767,443	285,565,538	4,672,979	5,078,862
1980	1,134,238	277,388,975	4,641,457	4,204,640
1981	2,237,005	289,765,405	4,849,537	6,602,666
1982	1,886,360	321,211,454	4,679,511	3,987,490
1983	6,593,506	340,703,336	3,939,826	5,749,016
1984	7,304,655	339,634,000	4,073,043	3,877,673

SOURCE: U.S. Department of the Interior, *Annual Report,* various years.

Whereas only five of twenty sales were challenged between 1978 and 1982, six of eight sales were challenged within a year of Watt's announcement.[111] Another tactic used by opposing state congressmen was to deny Interior Department funding for lease sales. In 1982, less than a million acres encountered moratoriums; in 1983, that number increased to 36 million acres with even more on hold for 1984.[112] Another blow was the controversy surrounding Secretary Watt, who resigned in November 1983. His replacement, William Clark, was a pragmatist careful to satisfy critics and follow an appeasing course. Thus in 1983, only 120 million acres were offered instead of 200 million; in 1984, only 154 million acres were submitted for bid instead of 200 million more.[113] Watt's program was replaced by Secretary Clark's case-by-case approach, not uninfluenced by election-year politics.

A review of 1978–84 OCS activity reveals the Andrus-Watt acceleration, increased production, and a fiscal boom due to rising oil prices (table 6.2).

With declining prices, a world oil glut, and appeased environmentalists under the Clark regime, the energy vs. environment debate faded. The major ongoing controversy was between the Department

[111]*OGJ,* June 20, 1983, p. 58.

[112]American Petroleum Institute, *Response Letter,* February 29, 1984.

[113]U.S. Department of the Interior, Minerals Management Service, *OCS Lease Offerings Statistics* (Washington, D.C.: Government Printing Office, 1984). Actual leased acreage was 6.6 million acres in 1983 and 7.5 million in 1984.

of the Interior and several major oil states that desired OCS revenue to augment their 50 percent share of onshore federal-land bonuses and royalties. In two suits filed by Louisiana and Texas, all claims were denied except one of Texas's for compensation for the fact that a common reservoir discovered on the state side was responsible for a high OCS bid.[114] More court action, if not amendatory federal legislation, could be necessary to decide how to share OCS revenue between states and the federal government. Sharing the OCS pie would placate state opposition to federal lease sales; one motivation for legal challenges has been that federal sales decrease interest in state leases with negative revenue effects.

In addition to the U.S. Treasury, revenue from OCS leasing goes to the Land and Water Conservation Fund to maintain a $900-million balance and the Historic Presentation Fund in amounts of $150 million per year.

Federal- and Indian-Land Policy Today

Onshore

Oil and gas leasing, administered by the Bureau of Land Management (BLM), is governed by the following rules. If the land is within a known geological structure, competitive bidding by sealed bid or auction is required with a maximum lease area of 640 acres, maximum lease life of five years, and minimum royalty of 12.5 percent, with the highest up-front bonus winning the lease. The limit per state for any individual or association is 246,000 acres except for Alaska where the limit is 300,000 acres in each of two leasing districts. Options are limited to 200,000 acres. Renewal lease royalties range from 12.5 percent if production is below 110 barrels per day to 25 percent if output is above 400 barrels per day.

If the area to be leased is not within a known geological structure, noncompetitive leases are allowed with a 10,240-acre maximum, ten-year lease life, and straight 12.5 percent royalty. Leases are issued to the first qualified applicant who, as in the case of competitive bidding, must be a U.S. citizen, an adult under state law, or an association, partnership, or corporation organized under U.S. law.[115]

---

[114]*Texas* v. *Secretary of Interior*, 580 F. Supp. 1197 (E.D. Tex 1984); and *Louisiana* v. *Watt*, Civil Action no. 79-2965-I (2) (E.D. La. 1984).

[115]See the summary of lease regulations in 48 *Fed. Reg.* 33648 (July 22, 1983).

Offshore

Until recently, two agencies within the Department of the Interior have administered OCS leasing, exploration, and production programs. The BLM sets five-year lease schedules, conducts environmental studies, and invites public and coastal-state comment. Upon approval by the interior secretary and the Council on Environmental Quality, lease sales are conducted. Tracts, with a maximum lease area of 5,760 acres (nine square miles) per company, are awarded to the offerer of the highest sealed bonus bid. The minimum royalty is 12.5 percent, and standard leases run five years or more.[116] Offshore operations are regulated by the U.S. Geological Survey, which formulates and administers operating standards. In 1982, the MMS assumed all offshore leasing functions from the BLM and the survey.

Agencies and subagencies that perform tasks related to offshore leasing are the Department of Defense, the Federal Energy Regulatory Commission, the Environmental Protection Agency, the Federal Aviation Administration, the Department of Commerce, the Fish and Wildlife Service, the Coast Guard, the U.S. Army Corps of Engineers, the Occupational Safety and Health Administration, and the National Oceanic and Atmospheric Administration. In addition, more than thirty coastal-zone commissions participate in federal decisionmaking about activities off their respective coasts.[117]

[116]The original 1953 OCS Act authorized two bidding systems: a variable-bonus, fixed-royalty system and a fixed-bonus, variable-royalty system. In virtually all cases, the bonus bid option was used with the royalty fixed at 16 2/3 percent. In the 1978 amendments to the 1953 law, Congress, sensitive to criticism that only major companies could competitively bid under the traditional "up-front" system, authorized ten bidding alternatives and instructed the interior secretary to use the "nontraditional" nine from 20 percent to 60 percent of the time during an experimental five-year period. The interior secretary (then Cecil Andrus, later James Watt, and then William Clark) was to periodically report to Congress on his bidding choices. The ten options were (1) the traditional bonus bid with a fixed royalty and the nontraditional (2) fixed bonus, variable royalty; (3) variable bonus, (set) sliding royalty scale; (4) variable bonus, fixed profit-sharing; (5) fixed dollar bonus, variable royalty; (6) fixed work commitment, variable royalty; (7) fixed dollar bonus and fixed work commitment, variable royalty; (8) fixed bonus, variable profit-sharing; (9) fixed dollar bonus, fixed work commitment, (set) sliding royalty; and (10) fixed cash bonus, available work commitment, fixed royalty. Of the nine options, Secretaries Andrus and Watt used only variable cash bonus schemes to satisfy the experimentation requirement, as discussed later in this section.

[117]For a summary and comparison of state offshore mining provisions as of the early 1970s, see J. Leslie Goodier, *U.S. Federal and Seacoast State Offshore Mining Laws* (Washington, D.C.: Nautilus, 1972), pp. 5–7. Also see C. Deming Cowles, "Environ-

State Lease Policy: A Historical Survey

State and local governments at present own and manage approximately 136 million acres or 6 percent of the nation's land. An overview of petroleum lease law in major producing states is presented below.

Texas

The Texas constitution of 1866 broke from tradition to allow private ownership of mineral rights.[118] Previously, minerals belonged to the sovereign under the Spanish constitution, which had remained unchanged upon Texas's independence in 1840.

The 1866 privatization succeeded from ignorance; governments as a rule do not surrender valuable claims without strong voter or special-interest motivations. As A. W. Walker explained:

> The amendment was made without any conception of the tremendous mineral wealth that was being released to the state. Oil had not been discovered in Texas at that time, and mining operations were of little importance. . . . It is pertinent to observe that many years later, after the mineral wealth of the state came to be more fully appreciated, the legislative reverted to the civil-law policy by enacting statutes which required public free school and asylum lands to be sold with express mineral reservations in favor of the state.[119]

In 1883, and again in 1907 and 1913, Texas reserved to the state mineral rights on public lands. Private development of state-land minerals was first allowed in the Relinquishment Act of 1919.[120] While previous public-land sales had reserved mineral properties to the state, this act made the lessor the state's agent with an even

---

mental Regulation of Offshore Exploration, Production, and Development," *27 Oil and Gas Institute* (New York: Matathew Bender, 1976), pp. 55–65, 76.

[118]Section 39, article 7 of the 1866 constitution stated, "The state of Texas hereby releases to the owners of the soil all mines and minerals substance, that may be the same, subject to such uniform rate of taxation, as the Legislature may impose." Cited in *Cox v. Robison*, 105 Tex. 426 150 S.W. 1189 (1912). For an early history of Texas land law, see Wallace Hawkins, *El Sal del Rey* (Austin: Texas State Historical Association, 1947).

[119]A. W. Walker, Jr., "Book Review of *El Sal del Ray*," *Texas Law Review* (December 1947): 242.

[120]For a detailed analysis of the 1919 act, see A. W. Walker, Jr., "The Texas Relinquishment Act," *1 Oil and Gas Institute* (New York: Matthew Bender, 1949), pp. 245–312.

split of royalties. This applied to over 40 million acres of public-school and asylum lands that were sold in increments each year. The provisions of the 1919 act remained in effect until the Sales Act of 1931, which reduced the state's royalty to 1/16th on public-school lands to encourage development.

In 1983, lease bonuses and production from 4.9 million acres of state land generated $348 million from production of 72 million barrels of crude oil and 670 million cubic feet of natural gas. Revenue is invested in two funds, the Permanent School Fund and the Permanent University Fund. Moneys invested in the Permanent School Fund (which has a $4-billion balance) provide investment income for the Available School Fund (which has a balance of nearly $2 billion) for the state's public-school system below the college level. Earnings from the Permanent University Fund are placed in the Available University Fund for distribution to the University of Texas colleges (2/3) and the Texas A&M colleges (1/3).

A change in the Texas constitution was made in 1984 to allow the other twenty-six state universities to receive $100 million in Available University Fund proceeds annually. This amendment could attract attention from other quarters, educational as well as noneducational, interested in sharing in this pocket of public-sector wealth.

Alaska

Seventeen years after the United States purchased the Alaskan Territory from Russia, the Alaska Organic Act of 1884 was passed to extend the Placer Mining Law of 1870 to this area.[121] In ensuing decades, laws were passed to facilitate the transfer of federal lands to private ownership—the act of 1890, the Trade and Manufacturing Sites Act of 1891, and the Native Allotment Act of 1906, which allowed limited acreage to be sold to citizens or corporations. Yet upon statehood in 1959, over 99 percent of Alaska's 366 million acres still remained in federal hands with mineral leasing conducted by the BLM under the Leasing Act of 1920, as amended.

Upon becoming the forty-ninth state in 1959, Alaska received ownership of the three-mile tidelands area, covering 35 million to 45 million acres, and a promise of 102.6 million "vacant, unappropriated and unreserved" acres from the federally owned public

---

[121]This discussion is taken from Richard Cooley, *Alaska: Challenge in Conservation* (Madison: University of Wisconsin Press, 1966), pp. 18–31.

Table 6.3
OWNERSHIP OF ONSHORE ALASKAN LAND
(million acres)

Category	1959[a]	1982
Private land	0.7	1.8
State land	–	104.5
Native Corp. land	–	43.7
Federal land		
Naval Reserve no. 4	23.0	22.4
Indian land[b]	4.1	43.7
Military land	2.3	2.5
Public domain	271.2	42.6
Other[c]	64.2	106.5
Total federal	364.8	217.7
Total	365.5	367.7

SOURCES: Alaska Department of Natural Resources; and Richard Cooley, *Alaska*, p. 23.
[a]Year of Statehood.
[b]Land conveyed to Indians and other Alaskan natives pursuant to the Alaska Native Claims Settlement Act.
[c]Includes land under the jurisdiction of the Forest Service, the U.S. Fish and Wildlife Service, and the National Park Service.

domain. Since this time, over 100 million acres have been transferred from federal to state ownership, while private ownership has increased only incrementally as shown in table 6.3.

In 1959, oil and gas leasing on state land began. As of 1983, 3.9 million acres were leased for petroleum activity, which generated production of 587 million barrels of crude oil and 170 million cubic feet of natural gas. Royalties from these lands, along with the state's share of federal royalties, totaled $1.69 billion. Twenty-five percent of these funds are invested in the Alaska Permanent Fund along with oil and gas severance income. Revenue earned by the $6.1-billion corpus as of 1984 is distributed as dividends to state residents each year.

Louisiana

Private ownership of mineral rights in Louisiana began in 1870.[122] Public-land leasing began in the Caddo Levee District with Act 267

[122]This discussion is taken from Harriet Daggett, *Mineral Rights in Louisiana* (Baton Rouge: Louisiana State University Press, 1939), chap. 2; and John Madden, *Federaland State Lands in Louisiana* (Baton Rouge: Claitors, 1973), pp. 411–33.

of 1908 and began statewide with Act 258 of 1912, which gave the governor authority to lease vacant and unappropriated lands.[123] Act 9 of 1928 extended this authority to state-land proprietors other than the governor—school superintendents, municipalities, and police authorities.

Widespread dissatisfaction with these laws, including charges of political favoritism, led to the passage of Act 93 of 1936, which created the State Mineral Board and set acreage maximums, established royalty minimums, and instituted competitive bidding. Four years later, Act 162 consolidated all previous statutes into one comprehensive statute. Retaining the 1936 changes, the 1940 act, as amended, governs state-land leasing in Louisiana today.

In 1983, the state generated revenues of $422 million from 9.5 million barrels of crude oil and 115 million cubic feet of natural gas from 2 million leased acres. The royalty and bonus income is invested in the Royalty Road Fund (10 percent) and the General Fund (90 percent).

California

The California Mineral Reservation Act of 1921 began leasing for "all coal, oil, oil shale, gas . . . and other mineral deposits in lands belonging to the state, or which may become the property of the state."[124] Patterned after the federal Mineral Leasing Act of a year before, the law particularly addressed tideland production, which had become widespread.[125] Although acreage restrictions created drainage competition, the act continued to be in effect without major change until the State Lands Act of 1938. This act restricted leasing in certain areas, increased the royalty scale, and established a State Lands Commission with jurisdiction over the entire state, onshore and offshore. The 1938 act was modified in 1955 and 1957 to increase revenue and encourage leasing, particularly offshore.

In 1983, 161,600 acres of leased state land, all offshore, produced 11.9 million barrels of crude oil and 7.1 million cubic feet of natural gas, generating royalty and bonus income of approximately $69.3

---

[123]The governor's lease authority was extended to navigable water beds in Act 30 of 1915 and Act 9 of 1928.

[124]Cal. Stats. 1921, c. 303, sec. 1, p. 404. See Robert Krueger, "State Tidelands Leasing in California," *UCLA Law Review* 5 (1958): 429.

[125]Tidelands drilling began in California in 1899 and grew to 412 wells by 1906. Ibid.

million. Income is invested in various educational funds that distribute proceeds to public education.

Oklahoma

Before Oklahoma became a state in 1907, the Organic Act of May 2, 1890, extended federal leasing regulations to Indian lands and public-domain lands within the territory. Upon statehood, the Enabling Act of June 16, 1906, transferred federal land to state ownership and allowed mineral leasing under certain regulations beginning January 1, 1915. A complete leasing law, which included oil and gas extraction from "any of the school or other lands owned by the state," followed in 1917.

In 1983, Oklahoma received over $39 million in oil and gas royalties and bonus income from 650,000 acres of leased lands. (Oil and gas production figures for state land were not made available.) The money is invested in a variety of educational funds, ranging from the Common School Fund to the Oklahoma University Fund.

Wyoming

From statehood to the present, the federal government has been the major landholder in Wyoming. The 1870 Placer Mining Law thus governed early public-land leasing. In 1909, all federal land in Wyoming was withdrawn from mineral exploration because of conservation concerns, only to be partially returned within several years. Between 1912 and 1920, much of the same land was again removed from entry until mineral leasing was again allowed in the 1920 Mineral Leasing Act. In this year, state-land leasing joined federal-land development.

In 1983, 3.3 million acres of Wyoming state land generated revenues of approximately $36 million from 6.6 million barrels of crude oil and 23.8 million cubic feet of natural gas. Royalty income is invested, with the proceeds going to the Department of Education Fund (6 percent) and the Permanent Land Fund (94 percent). Both funds invest the royalties, and interest goes to the state school system. Money from the fund can also be borrowed by counties, municipalities, cities, or farmers for uses deemed in the general interest of the state.

Other States

In 1915, the Arizona legislature passed a statute allowing mineral leasing on state lands. In 1927, the legislature specifically identified oil and gas as minerals under the 1915 act. This law was modified by the Oil and Gas Land Act of 1939, which, as amended, serves as the centerpiece of state-land leasing today.

In Michigan, the Public Domain Commission Act of 1909 reserved for the state mineral ownership and a royalty percentage for all sold lands. Upon statehood in 1912, New Mexico received 12.5 million acres of federal land, whereupon private development on a royalty basis was allowed. In 1928, a major state-land lease law was enacted. Kansas began state-land leasing in 1923 and allotted $10,000 for drilling by the State Board of Administration. Mineral (petroleum) leasing on state land was first allowed in Colorado in 1876; New York in 1894; Washington and Minnesota in 1901; Pennsylvania in 1907; Ohio in 1916; Idaho, Utah, South Dakota, and Tennessee in 1919; Nevada in 1921; Florida and Idaho in 1923; Montana in 1927; Arkansas in 1929; Alabama in 1931; Mississippi in 1932; West Virginia in 1937; Illinois in 1941; Nebraska in 1943; South Carolina in 1944; Indiana in 1947; Virginia in 1950; North Carolina in 1957; and Missouri in 1966.

Environmental Law and Government Lease Policy

Environmental regulation was among the earliest legislation passed in the petroleum field. In the late nineteenth and early twentieth centuries, laws administered by state agencies attempted to protect underground freshwater from oil contamination at the drill site and to protect neighboring lakes and creeks from the effects of inadequate oil storage.[126]

While all producing states have specific rules governing well-site pollution control today,[127] a second layer of anti-pollution regulation has been promulgated on the federal level. These regulations have limited exploration and production on federal onshore and offshore lands, while preserving land and water areas in their original state.

[126]In addition to plugging and casing requirements, discussed in chapter 5, laws forbidding oil in rivers or creeks were passed in Pennsylvania (1863), Colorado (1889), Oklahoma (1909), and Kansas (1913).

[127]See Interstate Oil Compact Commission, *Summary of State Statutes and Regulation for Oil and Gas Production* (Oklahoma City: IOCC, 1979). For a history of the Texas Railroad Commission's concern with water pollution, see Ira Butler, "The Oil and Gas Industry and Water Conservation," *16 Oil and Gas Institute* (New York: Matthew Bender, 1965), pp. 321–30. State agencies are immune from federal lawsuits regarding pollution (as in other areas) on the grounds of sovereign immunity.

Onshore

As of 1984, the federal government owned 720 million acres of a total 2.1 billion acres, or 34 percent of the nation's land area. Government ownership is concentrated in Alaska (95 percent) and the thirteen western states (63 percent). Petroleum leases are in force on 167 million acres, or 8 percent of the federal landholdings. The small percentage of federal lands leased for oil and gas exploration and development reflects not only the perceived absence of petroleum deposits in many areas but environmental roadblocks as well. A number of land withdrawals since the 1960s have restricted prospecting, while the burden of proof of possible adverse environmental consequences has fallen on the lessee to discourage petroleum activity.

While most land in early withdrawals was returned to mineral leasing by 1910, and the authority to mandate future withdrawals was weakened by several measures, in the next decades certain areas became reserved for exclusive nonmineral use.[128] On the majority of federal land, mineral leasing was allowed, although beginning in the middle 1960s, oil and gas leasing would become more and more encumbered by environmental legislation.

The Wilderness Act of 1964 started a several-decade movement that restricted or delayed petroleum development on public land.[129] This act established the National Wilderness Preservation System and set aside 9.1 million acres of wilderness, which subsequently has grown to 88.7 million acres.[130] Although the act allowed petroleum leasing and development through 1984, such operations have been effectively excluded, since roads, mechanical devices, or man-made

---

[128]The National Park Service Act (Public Law 190, 39 Stat. 446 [1916]) prescribed that national parks be managed to "leave them unimpaired"; the Migratory Bird Conservation Act (Public Law 770, 45 Stat. 1222 [1929]) set aside lands for bird sanctuaries; and the Taylor Grazing Act (Public Law 482, 48 Stat. 1269 [1934]) set aside lands for exclusive animal use. These restricted areas were small in comparison with later environmental withdrawals.

[129]Public Law 88-577, 78 Stat. 890 (1964).

[130]In 1981, another 40 million acres were under consideration for inclusion in the National Wilderness Preservation System. American Petroleum Institute, "The Wilderness Act," Briefing Paper, June 26, 1981, pp. 1–2.

structures are not permitted in these designated areas.[131] Reinforcing this de facto prohibition was the Clean Air Act, which banned air emissions common to well-site operations in wilderness areas.[132] Together, these acts have greatly reduced oil and gas development on major portions of the federal domain.

The next major legislation that inhibited petroleum leasing was the historic National Environmental Policy Act of 1969, which placed the burden of proof on drillers, via environmental impact statements, to show that "the quality of the human environment" would not be impaired by their activity.[133] Both federal officials and interested citizens and groups could—and would—examine the submitted environmental impact statements, issue court challenges, and delay or stop drilling operations.[134]

A third major legislative deterrent to federal leasing was the 1976 Federal Land Policy and Management Act, which established a comprehensive body of regulations pertaining to 398 million acres under the control of the Interior Department's BLM.[135] Although "multiple use" and "sustained yield" are in the language of the statutes, petroleum leasing has been given low priority by the BLM.[136] Of potentially greater consequence, however, is an ongoing inventory of all federal lands by the BLM and the Forest Service (U.S. Department of Agriculture) to be used in recommending further withdrawals.

In 1981, there were seventy-nine Areas of Critical Environmental Concern covering 620,000 acres, which two years later were increased to over 52 million acres by congressional action. Forgone

---

[131]In the words of the Wilderness Act, "There shall be . . . no temporary road, no use of motor vehicles, motorized equipment or motorboats, no landing of aircraft, no other form of mechanical transport, and no structure or installation within any such area" (p. 894).

[132]Public Law 88-206, 77 Stat. 392 (1963).

[133]Public Law 91-190, 83 Stat. 852 (1969).

[134]Ruth Knowles identified the law as "a powerful weapon which [the environmentalists] would use in every area affecting energy development." Knowles, *America's Oil Famine* (New York: Coward, McCann, and Geoghegan, 1975), p. 36.

[135]Public Law 94-579, 90 Stat. 2743 (1976).

[136]See sec. 102(a)(12). Two previous acts encouraged multiple use of federal land: the Multiple-Use and Sustained Yield Act of 1960 (Public Law 86-517, 74 Stat. 215) and the Classification and Multiple-Use Act of 1964 (Public Law 88-607, 78 Stat. 986). Multiple use in the language of the federal acts refers to a balance between present and future use of the land rather than multiple resource development per se.

output during the moratorium has been estimated by the Interior Department at 318 million barrels in 1984 alone.[137]

Other less important federal laws that have either delayed or restricted the use of onshore federal lands for petroleum operations include the

- Antiquities Act (1906),
- Taylor Grazing Act (1934),
- Arctic National Wildlife Range Act (1960),
- Classification and Multiple Use Act (1964),
- Land and Water Conservation Fund Act (1965),
- National Historic Preservation Act (1966),
- Endangered Species Conservation Act (1966, amended 1973),
- Wild and Scenic Rivers Act (1968),
- National Trails System Act (1968),
- Alaska Native Claims Settlement Act (1971),
- Archaeological and Historic Data Conservation Act (1974),
- Resource Conservation and Recovery Act (1976),
- Federal Land Policy and Management Act (1976),
- Federal Mine Safety and Health Act (1977),
- Surface Mining Control and Reclamation Act (1977), and
- Endangered American Wilderness Act (1978).

Restrictions on oil and gas exploration and production on federal lands were removed by several other laws, such as the Naval Petroleum Reserves Production Act (1976), the Central Idaho Act (1980), the Colorado Wilderness Act (1980), and the Alaska National Interest Lands Conservation Act (1980).

The 1964–80 legislative movement to restrict petroleum development on federal lands has been mitigated in the last few years by Secretary Watt's reversal of the policy of previous administrations and a recognized need to increase domestic production and reduce imports. As of 1984, a record 140 million acres of federal land were under petroleum lease, an acreage that would be even greater except for wilderness areas reserved by Congress in Interior Department appropriations bills beginning with fiscal year 1982. Although no

---

[137]American Petroleum Institute, "Bureau of Land Management Areas of Critical Environmental Concern," Briefing Paper, June 22, 1981, p. 1; and American Petroleum Institute, *Response Letter*, August 1, 1984, pp. 1–2. Also see *OGJ*, May 21, 1984, p. 59.

new anti-leasing bills are on the horizon, dozens of small wilderness bills are emerging that increasingly affect major petroleum states.

Offshore and Inland Waterways

The history of federal efforts to combat water pollution began with discharges from refineries and crude-oil barges and was later expanded to cover oil tankers and offshore drilling. Because these laws prominently overlap with platform exploration and production, water environmentalism is briefly examined in this section.

Early Legislation. The first federal legislation that dealt with water pollution was the act of August 5, 1886, which attempted to regulate inland pollution that commonly resulted from well-site, refinery, and barge discharges.[138] This ineffectual law, covering New York Harbor only, was replaced by the Rivers and Harbors Act of 1889, which stated, "It shall not be lawful to throw, discharge, or deposit . . . any refuse matter of any kind or description whatever, other than that flowing from streets and sewers and passing therefrom in a liquefied state, into any navigable waters of the United States."[139] Whether Congress included oil as refuse under the act was not clear; the law's major intent was to prevent hard objects that would hinder navigation from being discarded into waterways.[140] Later, the 1889 act would turn into the "sleeping beauty of federal water pollution control" when the courts included oil as refuse and assigned liability.[141]

Oil discharges were directly addressed for the first time in the Oil Pollution Act of 1924, which prohibited "discharges of oil by any method . . . into or upon the coastal navigable waters of the United States" with certain exceptions for discharges that were not "deleterious" to users of the water.[142] The law would prove ineffectual because a permit system was never systematized and prosecution was nonexistent.

In 1948, Congress passed the Federal Water Pollution Control Act, which, according to one informed observer, "marked the entry of

---

[138]24 Stat. 310 (1886).

[139]26 Stat. 426 at 453 (1889).

[140]Frank Grad, *Treatise on Environmental Law,* 3 vols. (New York: Matthew Bender, 1980), vol. 1, p. 3-70.

[141]Frank Trelease, *Water Law* (St. Paul, Minn.: West, 1974), pp. 587–88.

[142]Public Law 238, 43 Stat. 604 at 605 (1924).

the United States into active participation in water quality control."[143] The act's intent was to "prepare or adopt comprehensive programs for eliminating or reducing the pollution of interstate waters and tributaries thereof and improving the sanitary conditions of surface and underground waters."[144] Standards and enforcement were left to the states, and problems developed because some states were inactive, some promulgated standards that were vague, and jurisdictional authority was in question.[145] These problems led to greater federal responsibility beginning in the early 1960s.

The International Oil Pollution Convention of 1954. In 1954, an international convention was held in Geneva, Switzerland, to "prevent pollution of the sea by oil discharged from ships."[146] An agreement was ratified to prohibit oil discharges within fifty miles of the nearest land including U.S. coastlines.

The provisions agreed to at the meeting did not become law in the United States until passage of the Oil Pollution Act of 1961, which made foreign vessels subject to U.S. law with full liability for accidents.[147] This act was amended in 1966 to cover smaller oil tankers and again in 1973 to set more stringent discharge limits.[148] Although the importance of the 1961 act would be overshadowed by the plethora of federal legislation following it, the era of federally directed water-pollution control had begun.

Federalization of Water-Pollution Control: 1966–72. In a six-year period beginning with the 1966 Clean Water Restoration Act,[149] the federal government passed anti-pollution laws that had as a by-product restricting or delaying petroleum development offshore and in inland waters. States also began actively regulating water quality,[150] but federal laws, which were uniform and comprehensive in scope, took center stage.

[143]Frank Trelease, *Water Law,* p. 586.

[144]Public Law 845, 62 Stat. 1155 (1948).

[145]See J. Gordon Arbuckle, *Environmental Law Handbook* (Washington, D.C.: Government Institutes, 1978), pp. 95–96.

[146]Frank Grad, *Treatise on Environmental Law,* vol. 3, pp. 13-60 and 13-61.

[147]Public Law 87-167, 75 Stat. 402 (1961).

[148]Public Law 89-551, 80 Stat. 372 (1966). Frank Grad, *A Treatise on Environmental Law,* vol. 3, pp. 13-59 to 13-60. Other amendments in 1969 and 1971 were less significant.

[149]Public Law 89-753, 80 Stat. 1246 (1966).

[150]State laws included the Delaware Waters Protection Law of 1965, Michigan Environmental Protection Act of 1970, Washington Oil Spill Act of 1970, Maine Coastal

The Clean Water Restoration Act broadened the 1924 Oil Pollution Act to include inland waterways in addition to offshore waters. Prosecution, however, was restricted to accidents caused by "gross" or "willful" negligence.[151] To expand liability to all polluters regardless of intent, the 1889 Rivers and Harbors Act was resurrected by a 1966 Supreme Court decision, *Standard Oil Co. v. United States,* that included petroleum as refuse prohibited by the act.[152] After the decision, a 1970 executive order created a new discharge permit system with the U.S. Army Corps of Engineers in charge. Effective enforcement became achievable for the first time.[153]

Permanent legislation followed when Congress overhauled water-pollution law in the Federal Water Pollution Control Act Amendments of 1972.[154] This law stringently mandated that "the discharge of pollutants into the navigable waters be eliminated by 1985" and set an interim goal of ensuring the "protection and propagation of fish, shellfish, and wildlife" by 1983.[155] This act effectively replaced the 1889 law and provided for citizen and state action to aid enforcement. The exacting federal standards, administered by the Environmental Protection Agency (established by the National Environmental Policy Act of 1969), restricted offshore as well as onshore leasing and resulted in widespread prosecution.[156]

Conveyance of Petroleum Act of 1970, Washington Coastal Waters Protection Act of 1971, and Delaware Coastal Zone Act of 1971.

[151]William Ross, *Oil Pollution as an International Problem* (Seattle: University of Washington Press, 1973), p. 83. This liberal qualification meant that accidents the size of the Torrey Canyon spill off the English coast would be exempt from liability in U.S. waters.

[152]*Standard Oil Co. v. United States,* 384 U.S. 224 (1966). Gasoline, and thus oil in general, was defined as refuse under the act.

[153]"By using this authority to require . . . permits . . . the administration was able, for the first time, to pose a credible threat of prosecution. Hundreds of cases were initiated under the Refuse Act." J. Gordon Arbuckle, *Environmental Law Handbook,* p. 96. The Water Quality Improvement Act of 1970, "expressly complement[ing] the provisions of Section 13 of the 1899 act," aided the permit process by coordinating federal and state efforts. Frank Grad, *A Treatise on Environmental Law,* vol. 1, p. 3-79.

[154]Public Law 92-500, 86 Stat. 816 (1972). These amendments to the 1948 law were again amended in 1977 in Public Law 95-217, 91 Stat. 1566, although no major provisions of the statute were affected.

[155]The National Pollutant Discharge Elimination System, which issued permits for the discharge of any pollutant as long as Federal Water Pollution Control Act standards were not violated, was created.

[156]For a discussion of the major court decisions surrounding this far-reaching law, see Frank Grad, *A Treatise on Environmental Law,* vol. 1, pp. 3-109 to 3-120.

Legislative Impediments to Offshore Leasing: 1972–78. The aforementioned legislation directly involved offshore leasing and, in fact, was inspired by the 1969 Santa Barbara accident.[157] But it was not until 1976 that offshore leasing began to be heavily litigated. The litigation centered around Atlantic leasing and was based not only on the 1972 Federal Water Pollution Control Act Amendments but also on other statutes summarized below.[158]

- The Coastal Zone Management Act of 1972: Amended in 1976 and 1980, this act gave coastal states the power to veto federal lease proposals (the doctrine of "federal consistency").[159] Militant states, such as California, Massachusetts, Alaska, and Maine, would succeed in delaying or canceling many offshore lease sales with this law.[160]

- The Marine Protection, Research and Sanctuaries Act of 1972: Title III empowered the interior secretary to designate ocean areas as "sanctuaries for their conservation, recreational, ecological, or aesthetic values."[161] Various groups used this act, administered by the National Oceanic and Atmospheric Administration, in conjunction with the Endangered Species Act and the Coastal Zone Management Act, to hinder offshore drilling.

- The Endangered Species Act of 1969: As amended in 1973, 1978, and 1979, this act required all federal agencies to ensure that

---

[157]The Union Oil offshore well blowout in California's Santa Barbara Channel spilled an estimated 10,000 barrels of crude oil over several hundred square miles of ocean. See Ruth Knowles, *America's Energy Famine* (Norman: University of Oklahoma Press, 1980), pp. 35–36.

[158]Gulf Coast leasing off Texas and Louisiana, which began in the 1950s, was relatively free of litigation, reflecting the amicable relationship between the industry and these oil states.

[159]Public Law 92-583, 86 Stat. 1280 (1972). Subsection 307(c)(1) of the 1972 law stated, "Each federal agency conducting or supporting activities directly affecting the coastal zone shall conduct or support those activities in a manner which is, to the maximum extent possible, consistent with approved state management programs." The amendments were Public Law 94-370, 90 Stat. 1013 (1976), and Public Law 94-464, 94 Stat. 2060 (1980).

[160]For a list of several delayed exploration and production projects, mostly offshore, see "Major Legislative and Regulatory Impediments to Energy Development," American Petroleum Institute, *Response Letter*, October 1, 1979, pp. 5–6.

[161]Public Law 532, 86 Stat. 1052 (1972), as amended in 1980 by Public Law 96-332, 94 Stat. 1057, sec. 302 (a).

their policies, including those on offshore leasing, "do not jeopardize the continued existence of . . . endangered species or threatened species" or critically affect their habitats.[162] Individuals were allowed to petition the National Marine Fisheries Service (U.S. Department of Commerce) and the Fish and Wildlife Service (U.S. Department of the Interior) to delay or cancel lease sales and file suit if necessary.

Transformation of Environmental Water Law: An Overview. Frank Grad, in his three-volume history of environmental law, identified the 1972 Federal Water Pollution Control Act Amendments as the beginning of "expansive regulatory philosophy."[163] The transformation was from moderate environmentalism, accepting an amount of water impurity as optimal, to radical environmentalism, accepting none if scientifically possible. In Grad's words,

> While the pre-1972 law accepts pollution as inevitable and attempts to set regulations so as to reduce it to a relatively harmless limit, the 1972 legislation takes the position that all pollution is unlawful and that some degree of pollution will be permitted for as long as no technology is available to cope with it.[164]

This regulatory stringency, buttressed by other legislation examined above, shifted priority from the previous policy of "multiple use," however imperfect, toward water purity, nonuse, and species preservation. Advocates of multiple use, who emerged as a political counterforce in the early 1980s, have documented the cost of that extremism: limited, costly federal-land production contributing to greater reliance on unstable, expensive foreign crude supplies.[165]

Government Leasing and Environmental Policy: A Critical Appraisal

Chapters 2, 3, and 4 described petroleum leasing on private land—origins, development, regulation, and controversies. It was found that government intervention was no panacea for alleged problems

[162]Public Law 93-205, 87 Stat. 903 (1973). The amendments were Public Law 95-632, 92 Stat. 3751 (1978); and Public Law 96-159, 93 Stat. 1225 (1979).

[163]Frank Grad, *A Treatise on Environmental Law*, vol. 1, p. 3-85.

[164]Ibid., pp. 3-85 to 3-86.

[165]For example, see Ruth Knowles's criticism of environmentalism as a contributing factor to the 1970s "oil famine." Knowles, *America's Oil Famine*, pp. 171–213.

and, in fact, was initially responsible for many problems. In this section, government ownership and leasing of petroleum-bearing land are found to be even more problematic. After some theoretical arguments about why this is necessarily so are presented, the checkered past of public-land leasing is reviewed.

Theoretical Problems

The Dilemma of Public Land and Private Purpose. The dilemma surrounding private use of federal land is how to balance resource development with environmental maintenance. Just as production benefits many consumers and certain producing interests, other ends such as "pristine beauty" and natural habitats, not to mention alternative commercial uses such as tourism and fishing, have value to other citizens and economic interests. To the extent that mineral (petroleum) development is incompatible with these ends (i.e., to the extent that the ends of society clash), how are we to balance the two? Or in Robert Smith's words, "If the land belongs to 'all of the people,' how are 'we' going to decide how to use it?"[166] Under private ownership, anticipated profits from each course of action would guide the entrepreneur's decision and "spontaneously" settle conflicts. With public ownership, however, market pricing and capital values do not exist to use in calculating economic tradeoffs between competing uses and preferences. Consequently, the answer can be only a political one. Pro-development forces gather evidence and formulate arguments to impress upon lawmakers and the voting public the benefits of immediately developing public resources; anti-development interests make a case for accepting the status quo and waiting for better conditions in the future. Both arguments have appeal: the former stresses lower prices for consumers as a result of greater present supply; the latter emphasizes environmental maintenance and the resource needs of future generations. Lobbying and time-consuming, expensive litigation follow. The political exercise explodes the myth of a single-minded society deciding what to do with "its" resources. Some "owners" have their preferences violated, while other "owners" achieve their ends. The decisionmaking process, unlike the market where true owners make sovereign choices,

---

[166]Robert Smith, *Private Ownership vs. Public Waste* (Washington, D.C.: National Libertarian Party, 1980), p. 28.

is a tyranny of the more politically powerful over the less politically powerful.

Complicating the environmental tradeoff is the inherent problem of public resources imbued with negative externalities. Without incentives for individual owners to maximize asset values in a present-value sense, overuse—overconsumption—is promoted. Resources either freely used or leased for a finite period, after all, cannot have a long horizon. This created environmental problems, absent under market conditions, that conservationists recognized and desired to correct through regulation. But far from balancing the bias, environmental restrictions have introduced bias as well.

Environmentalism, not just development, is a special interest that, through legislation, achieves *concentrated benefits* and *dispersed costs* at the expense of the welfare of a more general constituency. The benefits flow to the well-organized environmental lobby; the costs fall upon the relatively unorganized public who are left with fewer choices and less supply. As Lawrence Chickering explained in regard to a particular coastline incident involving offshore oil drilling:

> The "public interest" is represented by an extremely narrow self-interested coalition of high-income environmentalists and local, coastal fishing and recreational groups which include wealthy people with seaside homes and views. . . . Actually, the very narrowness of the environmental coalition explains why it has been so easy to organize and is so powerful politically—while the very breadth of the public interest served by drilling explains the difficulty of organizing an effective political coalition to lobby for it.[167]

Motives for nondevelopment by other parties also have been blatantly self-interested. State governments have opposed federal lease sales to increase the economic rent of state leasing. Leasing in state waters, which are closer to the shore, is certainly less "environmental" than drilling in federal waters, which are further away from recreational and commercial activities.[168]

Sometimes anti-development can be an inconsistent creed. Both the Department of the Interior and the *Wall Street Journal* publicized energy development in the 26,000-acre Rainey Wildlife Refuge in

---

[167]*Newsweek*, June 1, 1981, p. 10. Also see William Tucker, "Environmentalism and the Leisure Class," *Harper's*, December 1977, pp. 49–80.

[168]For the case of Louisiana, see *OGJ*, May 7, 1984, p. 71.

Louisiana by the National Audubon Society, an environmental group that heavily criticized Secretary Watt for despoiling wildlife areas by allowing similar development elsewhere.[169] Environmentalism and consumerism are more often adversaries than allies. Postponed consumption, especially indefinitely postponed consumption, is inferior to more immediate supply and use. Self-styled consumerists toeing the environmental line can sound far less pro-consumer than development advocates. Arguing against accelerated development, Energy Action's Edwin Rothschild, for example, could easily be mistaken for a market-demand proration advocate of decades past: "What's the rush? Oil and natural gas reserves left in the ground do not disappear. . . . They do not lose value. They certainly provide an important cushion for the future."[170]

In contrast, Interior Secretary Watt defended his pro-development program:

> The Reagan administration . . . now intends to advance the consumer. . . . My previous successors frequently played this program to meet short-term budget needs rather than focusing on the consumer, but if you are interested in consumers, you want to deliver energy to them. If you are interested in national security, you want energy, and energy comes about through competition, not through restricting supply as my predecessors did.[171]

The "energy versus environment" conflict over petroleum leasing is complex and not easily divided into a special interest versus the public interest. This results from (1) an inability to weigh preferences of different groups of current users or of present and future users outside the realm of private property and voluntary exchange and (2) the imperfections of political choices.

Economic Calculation and Bureaucracy. Given the dilemma of public-resource decisionmaking in light of heterogeneous and nonquantifiable preferences within society, final choices nonetheless have legal instruction to promote an efficient use of resources. A 1978

---

[169]*Wall Street Journal,* August 4, 1983, p. 18.

[170]*OGJ,* June 20, 1983, p. 60.

[171]*Final 5-Year Plan for Oil and Gas Development in the Outer Continental Shelf,* Hearing before the Subcommittee on Energy Conservation and Supply of the Senate Committee on Energy and Natural Resources, 97th Cong., 1st sess. (Washington, D.C.: Government Printing Office, 1982), pp. 9, 12.

congressional report spelled out eight major considerations in public-land leasing to be observed by the Interior Department: market
return, competitive bidding, hazard prevention, avoidance of speculation, avoidance of delays in exploration and production, increased
production, timely development, and economical administration.[172]
As is the case for all decisionmaking, public or private, the degree
to which this can be achieved depends on whether sound economic
calculation can be performed. This requires scarcity prices generated
from market conditions and entrepreneurs who are able to work
within free-market situations of profit and loss.[173]

Do the necessary conditions exist for the government as lessor to
make such economic calculations? Can it discover competitive lease
terms, which tracts to lease, and when to lease them? Competitive
market conditions exist on the demand side with private firms and
unregulated entry, but is there a true market on the supply side?
With government as sole provider of offshore mineral rights and a
major supplier of onshore rights, the answer must be negative. Only
a quasi, or distorted, market exists because public land was not
competitively acquired, profit and loss are not at work, and all
decisions come from the center, that is, from the Department of the
Interior, as instructed by Congress, or state mineral boards. If the
government monopolized all mineral rights and produced all oil
and gas—if the government "bought" from and "sold" to itself—
economic calculation would be completely lacking. But with a free
market on the demand side and a partially competitive onshore
market on the supply side, the Interior Department and state agencies are able to gain valuable clues about the specifics of their lease
programs. Consequently, their decisions are inefficient compared
with those of a pure market, although not totally so. The practical
result is that it is highly unlikely that the authorities can know when
to conduct sales, where to sell, and on what terms to sell in order
to maximize discounted revenues to achieve the "market" return
and efficiency mandated by Congress. The unsatisfactory record of
government leasing policies over a century of practice lends credence
to these theoretical observations.

---

[172]H.R. Conference Report no. 95-1474, p. 92 (1978).
[173]See chapter 1, pp. 13–18.

Historical Consequences

Onshore at the Federal Level. Early public-land leasing occurred under conditions of underpricing in comparison with the private sector,[174] lease-area restrictions, and stringent expiration clauses, all of which institutionalized rapid, wasteful production by making it the most profitable alternative. The absence of royalties from public land until 1920, unlike the situation on private land, misallocated resources from the latter to the former. Acreage limitations per individual and per firm caused overparticipation by undersized independents whose time horizons were shorter and production practices less efficient than those of larger operators. Problems of drainage from private land adjacent to federal holdings were never properly addressed. Since many of these shortcomings were uncorrectable—partly because of economic-calculation difficulties and partly because of bureaucratic rigidity and political constraints—resort was had to property-right upheavals. Millions of acres in the western United States, the most active area of public-land oil exploration and production, were withdrawn and restored both before and after the 1920 Mineral Leasing Act. Petroleum supply during World War I and the postwar period was adversely affected by the unsettled state of oil leasing on the public domain.

Lease decisions tainted by favoritism and conflicts of interest were made in the 1920s. These problems were compounded by government policy on the state and federal levels that prohibited sorely needed unitization agreements in the 1920s and made such agreements practically unobtainable in the 1930s. Overdrilling and drainage competition thus could not be arrested by innovative private arrangements on federal land. By the 1940s, a raft of conservation regulation, which had the wasteful consequences described in chapters 3 and 4, addressed the overdrilling and overproduction problems of petroleum production on public land. In place of this traditional problem, however, another serious problem was documented—accounting mismanagement.

Before the situation was brought to the attention of the public and Congress, it was known within the industry and within the

---

[174]For concern within the Interior Department over below-market pricing in the early 1900s, see Reginald Ragland, *History of the Naval Petroleum Reserves and of the Development of the Present National Policy Respecting Them,* p. 84.

Interior Department that public-domain and Indian-land record keeping was inadequate. Consequently, systematic royalty under-payments were occurring.[175] Yet it was not until 1959 that suspicions led Congress to assign the General Accounting Office (GAO) to investigate the extent of mismanagement. In its initial report, the GAO found that

> a number of serious deficiencies exist in the [Geological] Survey's royalty accounting activities. The billing and collection of royalties due the Government are delayed at times for prolonged periods. Large unexplained differences exist [in the] . . . royalty receivable records . . . resulting from the manner in which the Survey's responsibilities in this area have been delegated and are being carried out.[176]

One recognized reason for the problem was the fact that scientists and geologists, instead of bookkeepers and accountants, were responsible for devising and maintaining a complex record-keeping system. Recognizing this elementary error, the report advised that the task be transferred from the Geological Survey to the Administration Division of the Department of the Interior. The recommendation, however, was not implemented.

In a follow-up study five years later, the GAO reported a "continuation of certain of the deficiencies . . . in our prior report" but added that "corrective action had been taken or that serious consideration was being given to our recommendations."[177] A third report in 1972

---

[175]Inefficient mineral management within the Interior Department has a long history. One example is so extreme that it is humorous—except to the victimized company. A patent, application for which was submitted in 1909 and processed three years later—itself testament to bureaucratic delay—was finally issued in 1950. Investigation revealed that the thirty-eight-year wait was the fault of an Interior employee who placed the file under a seat cushion for extra chair height. When the employee retired in 1950, the file was discovered and the claim was quickly patented with a form letter stating that no recent objections had been made as justification for issuance. For the story of the "most sat on case" in oil and gas bureaucratic history, see H. Byron Mock, "Human Obstacles to Unitization of the Public Domain," pp. 189–90.

[176]General Accounting Office, "Review of Supervision of Oil and Gas Operations and Production on Government and Indian Lands" (December 1959). Reprinted in General Accounting Office, *Fiscal Accountability of the Nation's Energy Resources* (Washington, D.C.: Government Printing Office, 1982), pp. D-1 to D-2.

[177]General Accounting Office, "Certain Deficiencies in Financial Management of Oil and Gas Activities" (August 1964). Reprinted in GAO, *Fiscal Accountability,* p. D-3.

found that little corrective action had been taken, and it drew attention to "numerous inconsistencies in the manner in which regional oil and gas supervisors have carried out their responsibilities."[178] As before, corrective measures were recommended to the director of the Geological Survey.

A fourth GAO report in 1976 focused on government mismanagement of mineral royalties on Indian lands. The Bureau of Indian Affairs was censored for "hinder[ing] mineral development of tribal lands by failing to conduct inventory studies, devise management plans, and properly monitor lease agreements."[179]

A fifth GAO report in April 1979 was more specific and alarming. Decades of mismanagement without reform had caused "a breakdown in the Survey's financial management system."[180] An estimated $359 million in royalties out of a collected $1.2 billion, a disturbing 34 percent, was past due when received. The "need for major changes" was emphasized, and the interior secretary was addressed outright.[181] Two years later, a sixth GAO report again summarized the problem and pointed out the futility of earlier reports and recommendations:

> Since 1959, GAO has been reporting on the need for major improvements in the Geological Survey's oil and gas royalty accounting system. Possibly hundreds of millions of dollars in royalties due from Federal government and Indian leases are not being collected annually. Although the Geological Survey has readily acknowledged that it is not collecting all royalties due, it has been slow to correct the reported problems.[182]

[178]General Accounting Office, "More Specific Policies and Procedures Needed for Determining Royalties on Oil from Leased Federal Lands" (February 1972). Reprinted in GAO, *Fiscal Accountability*, p. D-4.

[179]General Accounting Office, "Coal, Oil, and Gas: Better Management Can Improve Development and Increase Indian Income and Employment" (March 1976). Reprinted in GAO, *Fiscal Accountability*, p. D-5.

[180]General Accounting Office, "Oil and Gas Royalty Collections—Serious Financial Management Problems Need Congressional Attention" (April 1979). Reprinted in GAO, *Fiscal Accountability*, p. D-6.

[181]Ibid., p. D-7.

[182]General Accounting Office, "Oil and Gas Royalty Collections—Longstanding Problems Costing Millions" (October 1981). Reprinted in GAO, *Fiscal Accountability*, p. D-9.

The 1979 report drew the attention of President Ronald Reagan and Interior Secretary Watt. As part of the president's pledge to cut government waste, Watt appointed a five-member panel in January 1981, the U.S. Commission on Fiscal Accountability of the Nation's Energy Resources, to exhaustively detail the problems and recommend corrective measures.[183] In a several-hundred-page study issued in January 1982, the commission concluded:

> Management of royalties for the Nation's energy resources has been a failure for more than twenty years. Because the Federal government has not adequately managed this multibillion dollar enterprise, the oil and gas industry is not paying all the royalties it rightly owes.
> The government's royalty recordkeeping for Federal and Indian lands is in disarray. . . . [I]ndividual audits . . . suggest that hundreds of millions of dollars due the U.S. Treasury, the States, and Indian tribes are going uncollected every year.
> In addition, oil thefts are occurring on Federal and Indian leases. . . . [I]t is well-documented that security at many Federal and Indian lease sites is lax and is an open invitation to theft.[184]

Sixty separate recommendations were given for revamping internal controls, improving site security, increasing enforcement cooperation with state and Indian officials, raising the royalty rate from 12.5 percent to 16.66 percent, and creating a new office of royalty management.[185] Within several months of the report, a new royalty program was implemented with a new accounting system and greatly enlarged staff. In early 1982, the MMS was created in the Interior Department to handle royalty management and activities on the OCS in place of the BLM and the U.S. Geological Survey. Later that year, onshore

---

[183]Among the members was Michel Halbouty, a well-known geologist and independent producer critical of public-land and Indian-land mismanagement.

[184]General Accounting Office, *Fiscal Accountability*, p. xv. The Interior Department would not disagree with the major finding of the commission: "The same methods which had been utilized when income from the program produced $50 million a year in revenue (60 years ago) were still in place for a $5 billion a year program. Worse still, the royalty management activities of the Department of the Interior continue to trail along in the backwash of the scientifically oriented Geological Survey." U.S. Department of the Interior, *Annual Report: Mineral Accountability in the Department of Interior* (Washington, D.C.: Government Printing Office, 1983), p. v.

[185]General Accounting Office, *Fiscal Accountability*, pp. 237–67.

leasing administration was removed from the MMS and placed in the BLM.[186] The Geological Survey has not become reinvolved.

In response to underpayments estimated at between 7 and 10 percent, amounting to annual revenue of $500 million to $650 million, Congress enacted the Federal Oil and Gas Royalty Management Act on January 12, 1982.[187] The interior secretary was instructed to implement a "comprehensive inspection, collection, and fiscal and production accounting and auditing system to provide the capability to accurately determine oil and gas royalties, interest, fines, penalties, fees, deposits, and other payments owed, and to collect and account for such amounts in a timely manner."[188] Record-keeping requirements were tightened for lessees and operators, and penalties for nonpayment or late payment were prescribed.

Secretary Watt moved to implement many of the commission's sixty recommendations to satisfy the legislative instruction. By early 1983, it was reported that $60 million had been collected under the new policies, lease inspection had doubled, and penalties had been increased.[189]

On September 20, 1983, rule changes were made by the MMS and the BLM pursuant to the Federal Oil and Gas Royalty Management Act.[190] The MMS established two new systems, the Auditing and Financial System and the Production Accounting and Auditing System, within its Royalty Management Program. In addition, reporting requirements were stiffened, audit and inspection powers were increased, payment procedures were streamlined, and civil penalties for nonpayment were increased. More rules are promised as "MMS gains experience with compliance problems."[191] The bureau rules upgraded inspection, expanded record keeping, set specific penalties, and required first-purchaser documentation for trucks traveling from lease areas.

The short-run results of the 1982 reorganization fell short of expectations. The first report of the MMS concluded,

[186]U.S. Department of the Interior, *Annual Report: Mineral Accountability in the Department of Interior*, 1983, pp. v, 36.

[187]Public Law 97-451, 96 Stat. 2447 (1983).

[188]Ibid., pp. 2449–50.

[189]*OGJ*, February 28, 1983, p. 51.

[190]49 *Fed. Reg.* 37336 and 37356 (September 21, 1984).

[191]49 *Fed. Reg.* 37336.

The results of this oversight review indicate that although a great deal of time, effort, and money has gone into system design and development efforts over the last several years, many of the problems . . . not only persist, but have become worse in some areas.[192]

Royalty and general accounting problems represent more bureaucratic mismanagement than does fraud on the part of oil and gas production companies. As firms pay as little tax as legally required, the same firms can be expected to pay as little royalty as need be and no sooner than absolutely required. The government, by failing to inspect leases, alter royalty rates with regulatory changes, adjust royalties to market conditions, and properly bill for royalties due, not only mispriced assets but placed the industry "essentially on an honor system."[193] Some deliberate underpayment undoubtedly occurred, but federal mismanagement legalized the deliberate and encouraged the undeliberate.[194]

Thefts of oil and gas from federal and Indian land in the early 1980s have been estimated at between 3 and 6 percent of daily production.[195] Entrusted with the responsibility of properly administering public and Indian property, the government has failed to do so. Because the companies bear around seven-eighths of the loss and the government and Indians the remainder, it can be concluded that the government as custodian has not only shortchanged the public and the Indians but oil and gas companies even more. These losses are akin to a hidden tax because the government has chosen to let the situation exist rather than tax and spend the money required to correct the problem, albeit inefficiently compared with the private sector.

---

[192]U.S. House of Representatives, Committee on Interior and Insular Affairs, *Federal Minerals Royalty Management* (Washington, D.C.: Government Printing Office, 1985), p. 2.

[193]General Accounting Office, *Fiscal Accountability*, p. 15. For regulatory complications with the royalty system, see pp. 4, 23. In 1982, there were only sixty-three field personnel to monitor 17,522 onshore leases and over 55,000 wells. Offshore, there were seventy-five inspectors to monitor 1,240 leases. Ibid., p. 34.

[194]For selected audits of underpayments (and overpayments), see ibid., appendix E.

[195]Testimony of David Linowes, chairman of the Commission on Fiscal Accountability of the Nation's Energy Resources, *Mineral Royalty Collection, Accounting, and Distribution*, Hearing before the Senate Committee on Energy and Natural Resources, 97th Cong. 1st sess. (Washington, D.C.: Government Printing Office, 1982) p. 4.

The most recent onshore lease controversy is the noncompetitive simultaneous leasing program, known as the lottery, which began in 1959. The Simultaneous Oil and Gas Leasing System allocates government land in wildcat areas where the chance of finding oil is remote to random applicants who have paid a modest filing fee. The lottery has come under considerable criticism for two reasons: many unknowing persons have lost money to middlemen "filing companies" who exaggerate the prospects of winning valuable acreage, and second, knowledgeable persons have heavily filed for acreage inaccurately classified by government geologists. Thus, while thousands of ordinary persons have lost their money, professional players have made fortunes as a result of the Interior Department's miscalculations. In 1983, an estimated 240,000 to 500,000 acres within known geologic structures were placed in the lottery system instead of being offered under competitive procedures.[196] Because of these problems, Secretary Clark suspended the program between October 1983 and August 1984 to correct manpower and procedural problems. Congressional critics will watch for improved performance to decide whether to eliminate noncompetitive leasing altogether.

Leasing and production choices on federal lands are politically shaped. Lease offerings have been decided not only by environmental questions and broad-based "energy policy" but by other criteria as well. In 1978 and 1979, Carter's "voluntary" wage and price guidelines were backed by a threat to deny federal leases (as government contracts) to noncomplying oil firms.[197] Oil was produced from onshore and offshore federal lands under state proration laws until the early 1970s to support stable prices. In the future, as in the past, federal leasing and production policies will be determined politically and only secondarily by market conditions—if indeed market conditions can be known short of a true market (privatization).

Onshore at the State Level. On the state side, inefficiency has been less publicized but real. The reorganization of the petroleum activities of the Texas General Land Office in 1983 by ambitious newcomer Gary Mauro revealed glaring inefficiencies—uncollected royalties,

---

[196]*Wall Street Journal,* March 29, 1984, p. 27, and April 4, 1984, p. 2.

[197]William Lane, *The Mandatory Petroleum Price and Allocation Regulations: A History and Analysis* (Washington, D.C.: American Petroleum Institute, 1981), pp. 57–58.

expired leases, calculation mistakes, unsophisticated lease procedures, and, for many decades, unperformed audits.[198] Correction of some of these problems in the first year alone resulted in $45 million in new revenues. By conjecture, other producing states may well have "patsy" agencies and institutionalized inefficiency that will attract reforms as fiscal pressures mount.[199]

State petroleum leasing has not been immune from politics and arbitrary action. For decades, Louisiana policy favored the politically well-to-do. In the 1920s, political boss Leander Perez of Plaquemines Parish, as principal owner of the Delta Development Company, secured lucrative leases from the local Levee Board; those leases are in litigation. In 1936, just prior to the creation of the State Mineral Board, a huge state lease covering 240,000 acres of onshore and offshore land was awarded by Governor James Noe to William Burton, who in turn assigned rights to Texaco and the Win or Lose Corporation, principally owned by relatives of late governor Huey Long. Because of this connection and the absence of competitive bidding, State Lease 340, the most prolific single state lease ever awarded, was generally believed to have been a political plum. Although occasional litigation has led to newspaper inquiries, the "coincidences" of early state and local lease decisions in Louisiana await rigorous scholarly attention.[200]

State-land politics has spawned regionalism. In 1973, New Mexico passed a law giving the state the right to buy oil and gas from state leases to keep supply within the state.[201] Complained the New Mexico Oil and Gas Association, "Any contract of sale would grant to the purchaser only the most illusory and unpredictable rights, because deliveries would be subject to threat of interruption at any time and for any length of time." In the same year, gas curtailments

---

[198]*Wall Street Journal,* May 9, 1984, p. 29.

[199]In his testimony, David Linowes reported that all states except Louisiana had inspection programs that were worse than the maligned federal program. *Mineral Royalty Collection, Accounting, and Distribution,* p. 53.

[200]Numerous individuals spoken to requested anonymity because of the sensitive nature of the subject. Bribes and secret dealings between the industry and public officials, whether state lease officials or the local sheriff, have been a way of life in Louisiana for over fifty years. See, for example, *Wall Street Journal,* October 22, 1984, pp. 1, 22–23.

[201]*OGJ,* March 26, 1973, p. 39.

led Louisiana to suspend onshore and offshore leasing to prod companies to keep gas produced from state land intrastate.

Offshore. Controversy over the relatively young federal government offshore leasing system has concerned the method of competitive bidding. The original Outer Continental Shelf Act in 1953 authorized cash bonus bidding with a fixed royalty rate. This placed smaller companies at a disadvantage compared with major companies better able to afford the risk of preexploration payments. Influenced by consumer-group lobbying, congressional mistrust of major companies, and token pressure from smaller companies standing to benefit from rule changes, the 1978 OCS amendments offered nine new "experimental" lease systems for the interior secretary to use for between 20 percent and 60 percent of the acreage leased in a five-year period ending in 1983.[202] A loophole existed, however, that the Department of the Interior could exploit. One experimental system retained the cash-bid variable, and both Secretary Andrus and Secretary Watt used this option to satisfy the 20–60 percent requirement. This led to a court challenge by the same groups and individuals who had initially lobbied for the fixed-cash-bid alternatives.[203] In *Watt, Secretary of Interior, et al.* v. *Energy Action Educational Foundation, et al.,* the Supreme Court concluded that Congress did not restrict the interior secretary to any particular mix of the eight experimental bidding systems and that the decision to rely entirely on cash bidding was made in good faith to satisfy the "fair market value" criterion of the law.[204]

Many economists believe that the government would shoulder heavy risk by fixing the cash bonus and allowing bids on royalty rates or profit sharing. Not only would dry holes leave the government without revenue, smaller companies, for a variety of reasons, might be unable to explore and develop resources in a timely manner to provide royalty income. Further, high royalty (profit-sharing) rates would encourage earlier well abandonment than would lower rates

[202]See this chapter, p. 289n. 116.

[203]They included Energy Action Educational Foundation, Citizens/Labor Energy Coalition, Consumer Federation of America, Consumer Energy Council of America, Michigan Citizens Lobby, Arkansas Consumer Research, Inc., and the Texas Consumer Association.

[204]80 U.S 1464 (December 1, 1981).

under a cash-bid system.[205] It is true that a larger number of bids would emerge if producer risk under the royalty-bid system were lessened, but more bids per se do not mean more rental revenue for the government—just as more competitors do not necessarily mean lower product prices or increased efficiency. It could well mean less and has meant less.[206]

The debate over the most fair and financially sound offshore bidding system clearly demonstrates the enigma of public leasing. To some, "fair" means increasing the opportunity for the average company to bid—and use of the fixed-cash system. To others, cash bidding is fair because it ensures the highest return to the public with a minimum of risk. Who is right? In a free market, entrepreneurs would make choices based on perceived profits from each course of action. This would result in a variety of lease arrangements instead of a monolithic system of standard bidding, fixed lease terms, and periodic block sales.[207] Market variety would be economic calculation at work, coordinating levels of price and supply in particular situations. Bureaucratic management, on the other hand, cannot economically calculate market preferences. Under political rule, it must substitute arbitrary homogeneous procedures despite the underlying reality.

Conclusion

Inefficiency and controversy surrounding government petroleum leasing stem from four intrinsic factors:

- different preferences among the "owners" of public land;
- political constraints imposed by Congress, reflecting the imperfections of the political process;

---

[205]On the problems with royalty-based bidding, see Stephen McDonald, *The Leasing of Federal Lands for Fossil Fuels Production,* pp. 95–120. Also see Robert Kalter and Wallace Tyner, "Disposal Policy for Energy Resources in the Public Domain," in *Energy Supply and Government Policy,* ed. Robert Kalter and William Vogely (Ithaca, N.Y.: Cornell University Press, 1976), pp. 51–75; and Walter Mead and Gregory Pickett, "Federal Leasing Policies" in *Free Market Energy,* ed. Fred Singer (New York: Universe Books, 1984), pp. 189–217.

[206]See, for example, *OGJ,* May 2, 1977, pp. 132–33.

[207]Greater variety in a free-market situation would result from the greater number of sellers, different attitudes toward risk (risk takers versus risk averters), and different perceptions of future events.

- the inability to economically calculate, resulting from the government's position as resource owner; and
- bureaucratic mismanagement without the discipline and informational feedback from profit and loss.

Removal of these impeding factors would require that the government transfer ownership and operation of public lands to the private market, a question considered in chapter 31.

7. Taxation of Exploration and Production

Taxation of oil and gas extraction, ranging from Civil War taxes in the 1860s to the Crude Oil Windfall Profit Tax Act of 1980, has a history as long as that of government intervention in petroleum itself. This chapter examines direct federal production taxation, business-income taxation and petroleum-related deductions, and severance and miscellaneous production taxation by states, localities, and Indian tribes.[1]

While mostly descriptive of the features and political motivations of these taxes, this chapter critically evaluates taxation as a resource transfer from the industry to the public sector. This is not only detrimental from the industry's viewpoint; it also occurs at the expense of the consumers' interest in greater supply and lower prices. Various tax deductions, by mitigating this effect, thus are found to be pro-consumer and pro-industry. On a more specific level, the historic calculation of the depletion allowance, long a target of industry critics, is identified as a special tax provision distinct from capital-cost recovery.

Federal Taxation

Although federal taxation of wellhead oil production has been intermittent, it has had important consequences. The original tax in 1865 was soon rescinded because of its detrimental impacts on the developing industry. The 1934 crude license tax served its purpose of identifying and discouraging hot-oil production in East Texas. More recently, the Windfall Profit Tax of 1980, passed as a political compromise on price decontrol, has raised tens of billions of dollars, making it one of the largest excise taxes in U.S. history.

---

[1]Personal income taxation (1862, 1913–present) will not be discussed, although its relationship with petroleum production is direct for noncorporations and indirect for corporations.

Excise Taxation

Revenue Act of 1865. Taxation of petroleum production began when the North passed the Internal Revenue Act of March 3, 1865, which placed a $1.00 per barrel duty on crude-oil inventory and production to help finance the Civil War. Record-keeping requirements were also imposed for enforcement purposes.[2] The stiff levy, constituting over 13 percent of the wellhead crude price, caused well abandonments and slowed drilling to a virtual standstill. Consequently, the tax was repealed a year later in the act of May 9, 1866, as a result of strong industry protest led by the Petroleum Producers Association of Pennsylvania.[3] Also instrumental in repeal were the end of the war and stout representation from Representative (and later president) James Garfield of Ohio, himself a royalty owner.

During its short life, the production tax "put hundreds of marginal producers out of business."[4] An explanation was provided by two contemporaries.

> After repeated experiment it became evident to the General Government that any tax laid upon the crude material could only result in ruin to the business. . . . The fact of the business being free of taxation is the chief inducement for investment in it. The aggregate of [drilling] failures are not deemed to involve so great a loss as a burdensome tax. . . . The producer cannot afford to be thus burdened unless he has a large flowing well, and of this class there are at present none in the Oil Region.[5]

Vigorous production activity soon resumed in Pennsylvania, Ohio, and New York.

After the Civil War, special revenue needs were met by tariff income, liquor and tobacco "vice" taxes, estate taxes, sales of public

[2]13 Stat. 469 (1865). This was the second tax imposed on the petroleum industry; the first was a retail tax on kerosene passed in 1862. See chapter 22, p. 1293.

[3]14 Stat. 355 (1866). Also see John Ise, *The United States Oil Policy* (New Haven, Conn.: Yale University Press, 1926), p. 24; Harry Smith, *The United States Federal Internal Tax History from 1861 to 1871* (New York: Houghton Mifflin, 1914), pp. 234, 237; and Paul Giddens, *The Early Petroleum Industry* (Philadelphia: Porcupine Press, 1974), pp. 155–56.

[4]J. Stanley Clark, *The Oil Century* (Norman: University of Oklahoma Press, 1958), p. 100.

[5]Andrew Cone and Walter Johns, *Petrolia* (New York: D. Appleton and Company, 1870), p. 643.

land, and, later, surcharges on individual and corporate income.[6] Petroleum production would not be subject to direct federal taxation until more than a half century later.

Revenue Act of 1934. On May 10, 1934, a $0.001 (one mill) per barrel federal tax was placed on oil production from wells producing more than 5 barrels per day.[7] Payable by the producer to the first purchaser effective June 10, the modest levy was not so much a New Deal revenue measure as an attempt to identify and curtail hot-oil production in the prolific East Texas field.[8] Nonetheless, this tax and related levies on refineries and natural gasoline production were expected to yield $1.7 million to underwrite enforcement of the National Industrial Recovery Act's Oil Code.

Designed by Petroleum Administrator Harold Ickes, the tax gave authorities entrance and inspection powers that otherwise were legally assailable. The law instructed producers to

> keep such records and make such reports with respect to production and disposition of crude petroleum . . . [and] be open to inspection at all reasonable hours by any duly authorized representative of the [Revenue] Commissioner or any agency of the United States or any State having supervisory or regulatory powers over the production of crude petroleum.[9]

Producers were to keep detailed records for the most recent four years, submit to monthly swearings that all crude was accounted for and stamped tax-paid, and, if required, post bond.[10] Willful violations carried a maximum six-month jail term and $1,000 fine, and interference during inspection had a $500 penalty.

Recognized by the *Oil Weekly* as "the most effective weapon yet devised for stamping out 'hot' oil production and refining," the hot-oil tax was feared by oil producers[11] Said one:

[6]See Sidney Ratner, "Taxation," in *Encyclopedia of American Economic History,* ed. Glenn Porter, 3 vols. (New York: Charles Scribner's Sons, 1980), vol. 1, pp. 455–56.

[7]Public Law 216, 48 Stat. 680 (1934).

[8]The 1931–35 hot-oil war in Texas and Oklahoma is described in chapter 12, pp. 637–54.

[9]Public Law 216, 48 Stat. 766 (1934), sec. 604(e).

[10]By previous regulation, all crude was required to have tender papers documenting authenticity of "allowable" oil, which were now stamped upon tax payment.

[11]*Oil Weekly,* August 13, 1934, p. 7.

> We're not afraid of the Texas Railroad Commission. We're not afraid of the Attorney General's department. What we are afraid of is the Federal Government's Internal Revenue Department when it starts collecting that one mill tax![12]

The Texas Petroleum Council, an industry trade group that was against hot-oil production, journeyed to Washington to lobby for strict enforcement, and on September 11, final regulations were released by the Petroleum Administration Board and the Internal Revenue Bureau. Along with other measures, the tax was instrumental in checking illegal crude output, which would finally be controlled in 1935. The tax was decreased to $0.00025 per barrel in the Revenue Act of 1935 (indicative of its primary nonrevenue function), where it remained into the next decade.[13]

Along with the crude-oil stamp tax, a $0.01 per gallon tax was placed on "gasoline sold by the producer," that is, natural gasoline made from natural gas.[14] A tax on the extraction of natural gas, a policy pushed by the National Coal Association, was not enacted.[15]

Crude Oil Windfall Profit Tax Act of 1980. The prehistory of the Crude Oil Windfall Profit Tax (WPT) relates directly to crude-oil price controls examined in chapter 9. Congressional concern about "energy windfall profits" began shortly after the Arab embargo in late 1973 and continued until the tax was passed as a condition for phased decontrol in 1979.

President Nixon introduced the idea of an excess profits tax to Americans on December 19, 1973.

> Because of the abrupt nature of the present shortage, prices could temporarily exceed the price levels required to increase supply, and oil producers could reap unanticipated "windfall" profits. I want to assure all Americans that there will be no windfall profits at their expense. When the Congress reconvenes in January, I will ask it to enact an Emergency Windfall Profits Tax.[16]

---

[12]*Oil Weekly*, August 7, 1934, p. 9.

[13]Public Law 407, 49 Stat. 1014 (1935).

[14]Public Law 216, 48 Stat. 764 (1934), sec. 603(b).

[15]*Oil & Gas Journal*, January 11, 1934, p. 18. Cited hereafter as *OGJ*.

[16]Office of the President, *Executive Energy Documents* (Washington D.C.: Government Printing Office, 1978), p. 113.

In early 1974, the head of the Federal Energy Office, William Simon, pushed the tax as part of a decontrol package. The proposal, which ranged from 10 to 85 percent of the May 15, 1973, price plus $0.35 per barrel, was lost in the push or continued regulation and would wait for another day.[17]

President Gerald Ford resurrected the "windfall profits" theme in a national address on January 13, 1975.[18] As proposed in the Nixon era, the levy was forwarded to accompany price deregulation. Although the Senate Finance Committee readied a bill, it failed to clear the Senate.

In 1977, President Jimmy Carter first proposed a windfall profits tax. In April 1979, when Carter announced a twenty-eight-month phase-out of crude price controls, he asked Congress to enact a tax to recapture the increased revenues, the "windfall," of decontrol. Given the unpopularity of higher prices that resulted from decontrol, the tainted image of the industry, highly publicized industry profit increases in the first half of 1979, and the wish for "quick-fix" synfuel subsidization—not to mention the government's insatiable appetite for revenue—the tax was enacted as the political "price" for crude-oil decontrol in 1980.[19]

The tax was huge, easily the largest in the history of the oil and gas industry. Revenues of $220 billion were anticipated in the 1980s alone. It was, admitted Carter, "the largest tax ever levied on any industry in the history of the world."[20]

The Windfall Profit Tax Act of 1980 stated, "An excise tax is hereby imposed on the windfall profit from taxable crude oil removed from the premises during each taxable period ... [to] be paid by the producers of the crude oil."[21] Applicable to crude oil removed (sold) after February 29, 1980, the "windfall profit" is the difference between the adjusted base price (considered a "normal" profit price)

---

[17]*OGJ*, January 7, 1974, p. 23.

[18]Office of the President, *Executive Energy Documents*, p. 172.

[19]Public Law 96-223, 94 Stat. 229 (1980). For a discussion of political maneuvering between oil-state and Northeast congressmen and final compromises leading to enactment, see Joseph Yager, "The Energy Battles of 1979," in *Energy Policy in Perspective* (Washington, D.C.: Brookings Institution, 1981), pp. 628–29; and *OGJ*, December 24, 1979, p. 24.

[20]Jimmy Carter, *Keeping Faith* (New York: Bantam Books, 1982), p. 122.

[21]Public Law 96-223, 94 Stat. 230 (1980).

Table 7.1
WINDFALL PROFIT TAX OUTLINE

Tier	Crude Types[a]	Adjusted Base Price ($/bl)	Major Tax (%)	Independent Tax (%)
1	Lower and upper tier under June 1979 producer regulations	$12.81 (approx.) adjusted for inflation, grade, quality, and field	70	50
2	Stripper, Naval Petroleum Reserve	$15.20 adjusted for inflation, grade, quality, and field	60	30
3	Newly discovered, heavy, and incremental tertiary crude	$16.55 adjusted for inflation, grade, quality, and field	30	30

SOURCE: Windfall Profit Tax Act of 1980.
NOTE: Original tax table for oil produced on or after March 1, 1980.
[a]For definitions of these categories, see chapter 9, pp. 497, 500, 504–8.

plus any state severance tax and the actual selling price per barrel. This "windfall" is multiplied by the tax rate to determine the tax amount—not to exceed 90 percent of net income—to be collected and remitted to the U.S. Treasury by the first purchaser of crude oil. The adjusted base price and the tax rate depend on the tier of crude oil and the producing company, as shown in table 7.1.

Taxable crude oil includes all domestically produced crude except exempt Alaskan oil (which accounts for approximately 18 percent of state production and comes from remote areas where such a tax would make production uneconomical), exempt Indian oil, exempt tertiary oil, state or local government oil used for public purposes, and oil owned by charitable medical facilities or educational institutions.[22] The WPT was scheduled to be phased out at 3 percent per month over thirty-three months, beginning either in December 1987

---

[22]For greater detail on exempted oil under the original regulations, see Paul Osterhuis, "The Windfall Profit Tax," *Petroleum Regulation Handbook*, ed. Joseph Bell (New York: Executive Enterprises, 1980), pp. 59–60.

or when $227.3 billion in revenue is received, but no later than December 1990.

With revenue well below the trigger phase-out amount ($66 billion had been collected through fiscal 1984) and little chance of legislative retirement, the tax faced a January 1991–October 1993 phase-out unless extended by legislation. Market conditions, however, could deactivate the tax if oil prices fall below base-price levels, as occurred in several situations in 1983 and 1984. Under such conditions, repeal of the tax ahead of schedule is more probable.

Expenditure of WPT revenues was never statutorily defined, although President Carter concurrently signed the multi-billion-dollar Energy Security Act to subsidize synthetic fuels and related the two measures verbally.[23] A House-Senate conference report suggested that 60 percent of WPT revenues go toward income-tax reductions, 25 percent toward welfare programs, and 15 percent toward energy and transportation programs.[24] These guidelines never assumed importance; the tax soon became an entrenched source of general revenue that first Carter and later Reagan, despite campaign rhetoric, embraced.[25]

Legislative Amendment. President Reagan's Economic Recovery Tax Act of 1981, containing several oil-industry "sweeteners" to help gain passage, lessened the WPT tax bite for individual royalty owners, stripper production, and new discoveries.[26] The tax concessions reflected the political strength of "little oil," independent producers and royalty owners.[27] For qualifying royalty owners, a $1,000 tax credit was allowed for 1980, a $2,500 credit for 1981, a 730 barrel per year exemption for 1982 through 1984, and a 1,095 barrel per year exemption thereafter. Stripper oil (Tier 2) working interests of independent producers were made exempt beginning in 1983, and the Tier 3 tax on newly discovered oil was phased down from 30 percent in 1981 to 15 percent in 1986.[28]

---

[23]See chapter 10, pp. 578–79.

[24]Stephen Chapman, "Government's Windfall from Windfall Profits," *Fortune,* March 24, 1980, p. 60.

[25]On Reagan's campaign promise to abolish the tax, see *Business Week,* October 19, 1981, p. 7.

[26]Public Law 97-34, 95 Stat. 172 (1981).

[27]See Kaye Northcott, "Little Oil," *Texas Monthly,* February 1982, pp. 132–37.

[28]The phase-down schedule was as follows: 1982, 27.5 percent; 1983, 25 percent; 1984, 22.5 percent; 1985, 20 percent; 1986, 15 percent.

The Tax Equity and Fiscal Responsibility Act of 1982, the largest tax increase in U.S. history one year after the largest tax decrease in history, made minor technical amendments concerning Alaskan oil to the WPT.[29] Over six pages of language corrections and minor changes in the WPT were made several months later in the Technical Corrections Act of 1982.[30]

The first major legislative amendments to the WPT were enacted on July 18, 1984, in the Deficit Reduction Act, which scaled back scheduled Tier 3 tax reductions on newly discovered oil from 20 percent in 1985 and 15 percent thereafter to 22.5 percent from 1985 to 1987, 20 percent in 1988, and 15 percent thereafter.[31]

Ambiguities in the law required administrative rulings by the Internal Revenue Service (IRS). "Three years into the WPT program," the *Oil & Gas Journal* reported, "many basic terms are still not defined and regulations are not in place."[32] Definitions were promulgated for property and condensate, and issues concerning the net income limitation, tertiary recovery projects, removal prices, and base prices were clarified.[33]

Judicial Review. Burdened by heavy tax obligations under the WPT, several individuals and over thirty independent-producer trade associations and royalty-owner groups, led by the Independent Petroleum Association of America, filed suit on June 29, 1981, to have the WPT declared unconstitutional and receive refunds of all past payments from the U.S. Treasury. With over $60 billion collected, and monthly intakes of $1.5 billion, much was at stake for plaintiffs and defendant alike.[34]

The plaintiffs argued on Fifth Amendment grounds that the tax was confiscatory and that the Alaska exemption violated the uniformity clause of the Constitution, which requires levies to be equally

[29] Public Law 97-248, 96 Stat. 324 (1982).

[30] Public Law 97-448, 96 Stat. 2365 (1983).

[31] Public Law 96-369, 98 Stat. 494 (1984).

[32] *OGJ*, March 7, 1983, p. 30.

[33] For example, see 47 *Fed. Reg.* 50858 (November 10, 1982) on property, 48 *Fed. Reg.* 35092 (August 3, 1983) on base prices, and Revenue Ruling 83-185, 52 *Int. Rev. Bull.* 10 (1983) on the net income limitation.

[34] Collected amounts were $6.2 billion in 1980, $23.3 billion in 1981, $18.9 billion in 1982, $14.3 billion in 1983, and $10 billion in 1984. Net of lost income-tax revenue, these figures have been estimated at $4 billion in 1980, $14.2 billion in 1981, $8.4 billion in 1982, $7.2 billion in 1983, and 5.0 billion in 1984.

applied "throughout the United States."[35] In U.S. district court, Judge Ewing Kerr on November 4, 1982, rejected the Fifth Amendment argument—the wide latitude of state taxation powers from previous court decisions was not a live issue—but sided with the plaintiffs to rule that "distinctions based on geography are simply not allowed."[36] The next question was whether to invalidate the entire tax act or delete the unconstitutional section. Following time-honored judicial instruction not to "alter legislative intent or usurp legislative authority," the entire law was ruled unconstitutional.[37]

The Reagan administration immediately appealed the decision. Burgeoning spending and record deficits overwhelmed distant campaign promises and anti-tax philosophy. Collections of the tax were allowed to continue pending a Supreme Court decision.

As is the case in virtually all debates over government intervention, it was self-interest rather than philosophy that guided industry positions. While most oil firms were disadvantaged by and therefore were against the levy, Atlantic Richfield was not. ARCO, a major producer in a tax-preferred section of Alaska, sought to preserve its relative competitive advantage and filed with the Supreme Court an elaborate brief supporting the levy. The major defended the WPT as constitutional, on the basis of a narrow interpretation of the uniformity clause as prohibiting "only those taxes that have no basis other than preference for or discrimination against particular states."[38]

The Supreme Court, in oil and gas regulation as elsewhere, has long interpreted the Constitution as sanctifying wide powers of government to regulate and tax.[39] Its decision in this landmark tax case would not be different.

---

[35]Article 1, sec. 8, clause 1.

[36]*Harry Ptasynski, et al., v. United States*, 550 F. Supp. 549 at 553 (1982).

[37]Ibid., p. 555.

[38]*OGJ*, March 14, 1983, p. 27. Given the small earmarked expenditure for synthetic fuels compared to revenues from the WPT, $20 billion versus over $200 billion, not to mention the general-revenue dedication of the tax, organized support did not develop for the tax from industry members anticipating government subsidies.

[39]For a review of other Supreme Court decisions supporting government intervention in the oil and gas field, see chapter 30, pp. 1856–59. For general decisions along the same lines, see Bernard Siegan, *Economic Liberties and the Constitution* (Chicago: University of Chicago Press, 1980).

Justice Lewis Powell, admitting that the "Court has not addressed the [uniformity clause] squarely,"[40] broke new ground to find that geographical differences—the tax was paid on some Alaskan oil while other state oil was exempt—were not constitutionally forbidden, and the WPT was not geographically discriminatory because it exempted high-cost oil. The uniformity clause was finely interpreted to mean that "a tax is uniform when it operates with the same force and effect in every place where the subject of it is found" instead of straight proportionality or equality per state.[41]

Not only was taxation quantitatively limitless, it could be qualitatively tailored by Congress to achieve regulatory and political goals. Concluded Justice Powell for the unanimous court, "Where, as here, Congress has exercised its considered judgement with respect to an enormously complex problem, we are reluctant to disturb its determination."[42]

The Supreme Court decision parlayed constitutional ambiguity into an interpretation favorable to expansive government. The key constitutional word "uniform" could have been easily interpreted to retain its virginal meaning of equality or state-to-state proportionality. The substituted *neutrality* interpretation was not a clean replacement. No tax, as argued below, can have "the same force and effect in every place" because of differing subjective evaluations of individuals.

Theoretical Evaluation. Justification for the WPT, a misnamed graduated excise tax on crude production, rests on the assumption that high prices and profits from decontrol are abnormal and unearned—a "windfall"—because they resulted from "artificial" pricing by the Organization of Petroleum Exporting Countries and a favorable change in government policy (decontrol). Accordingly, authorities were entitled to tax the "windfall" for such "social" purposes as alternative-fuel development.

This argument is flawed. First, the argument, based on *price,* not *profit,* applied to producers who were losing money. Second, there does not exist "normal" or "average" profit from which an "abnormal" or "windfall" profit can be differentiated.[43] In the real world,

---

[40]*United States* v. *Harry Ptasynski et al.,* 103 U.S. 2239 at 2244 (1983).

[41]Ibid., p. 2239.

[42]Ibid., p. 2246.

[43]See chapter 15, pp. 932–33.

all profits and losses refer to particular circumstances of time and place that are incapable of being equated. Crude-oil prices and profits with decontrol were *not* abnormal given the market-clearing actions of OPEC and nine years of U.S. price controls suppressing domestic-producer prices and profits; they were simply belated adjustments to changed world conditions and misguided domestic policies. Third, even if existing wells received a "windfall," undiscovered oil has not and, by the government's logic, should not be taxed. Regarding expenditure, there is no monolithic "social purpose" toward which producers' or royalty owners' "windfalls" can be directed. There are only purposes of individuals, some of which are disappointed by the tax and others of which are advanced by the redistribution of wealth. In no sense can the WPT income transfer increase "social utility" by benefiting all members of society.

A change in government policy benefited producers, but this is no more an argument for taxation than an unfavorable policy change (such as price controls) is for subsidizing producers. Compared with government intervention, which intentionally and unintentionally benefits and penalizes parties in the economic system, the market is relatively neutral because voluntary exchange impersonally decides prices, profits, and the economic rent of resources.

Economic Effects. Before the discernible historical results of the tax are examined, several necessary theoretical effects may be elucidated.[44]

With revenues lowered by the amount of the tax, fewer prospects are profitable and more producing properties reach their economic limit more quickly. Fewer secondary and tertiary projects are initiated. When its production income is lowered, a firm has less capital, as a result of either smaller retained earnings or less ability to attract external capital, with which to drill marginal projects. Other things unchanged, forgone prospects transfer supply to the future, or in the case of prematurely retired wells, supply is lost. The unambiguous result is less near-term supply, which increases price and contracts the entire domestic petroleum industry from well-supply firms to gasoline stations. The door is opened for more imports, greater foreign petroleum investment relative to the U.S. industry, and

---

[44]This analysis is also applicable to the 1865–66 crude-oil tax, which provided a near textbook example of a punitive excise tax because of its severity and short life.

implicit wealth transfers from domestic parties (production companies, royalty owners, oil-field service and supply companies, and consumers) to foreign suppliers. To the extent foreign supply is less secure than domestic deposits, price premiums and higher inventory costs result.[45]

Despite the design of the tax "to impose relatively high tax rates where production cannot be expected to respond very much to further increases in price and relatively low tax rates on oil whose production is likely to be responsive to price," negative output effects occur.[46] The "perfectly designed windfall-profits tax," defined by Kenneth Arrow and Joseph Kalt as one that "leaves the incremental production . . . incentives of the unregulated market unaffected," is recognized by the authors as mythical.[47] To know the price sensitivity of every existing well is inconceivable, as is a tax code with all the tiers—continually updated—to implement it. Equally indeterminable is the price elasticity of new supply, which is the unquantifiable sum of shifting entrepreneurial expectations. The WPT may have identified certain production sources generally susceptible to premature abandonment that would receive a lower tax rate, but the tax structure remains relatively monolithic. Instead of three tiers, there could have been dozens, but never can the "perfect tax" be approximated. The code is also politically imbued. Indian, local-government, education-fund, and charity oil paid no WPT for no reason other than political favor and compromise.

Uneven tax provisions create intraindustry distortions. Production of major companies is relatively more penalized than is independent production because of the tax-rate differential. "Independents," concluded Stephen McDonald, "will probably displace 'majors' in many bare supramarginal oil operations."[48] High-cost crude production is

---

[45]See Stephen McDonald, "The Incidence and Effects of the Crude Oil Windfall Profit Tax," *Natural Resources Journal* (April 1981): 336–38. For further discussion of the economic consequences of the WPT and early quantitative estimates of forgone production and lost reserves, see H. J. Gruy, "Effect of Windfall Profit Tax on Recoverable Reserves," *19 Exploration and Economics of the Petroleum Industry* (New York: Matthew Bender, 1981), pp. 386–400.

[46]H.R. 96-304 at 307 (1979). Quoted in 103 U.S. 2241 (1983).

[47]Kenneth Arrow and Joseph Kalt, *Petroleum Price Regulation: Should We Decontrol?* (Washington, D.C.: American Enterprise Institute, 1979), p. 35.

[48]Stephen McDonald, "The Incidence and Effects of the Crude Oil Windfall Profit Tax," p. 339. To prevent opportunistic transactions of producing properties from majors to independents, oil-well transfers could not lower the tax.

encouraged over low-cost production by tax exemptions and the tax-tier differential, which favor oil properties that are either low yield, high cost, or poorly located. These inequalities create inefficiency within the producing industry and encourage the infamous practice of "playing the regulations" where perverse economic behavior maximizes income.[49]

Historical Effects. The early effects of the huge tax seem to suggest an anomaly. In a dramatic editorial on the day of the bill's enactment, the *Wall Street Journal* predicted that the tax would "run the American crude oil production industry into the ground."[50] Yet during 1980–81, a drilling boom was in evidence, checked more by scarcities of equipment and skilled labor than by lack of incentive. It so happened that the high price-WPT combination of decontrol outdistanced the controlled price, pretax combination, and that a production catch-up period was under way. A drilling exodus from Canada to escape relatively harsh regulation also kept drilling brisk in the lower forty-eight. But when this pocket of incentive became exploited (i.e., when marginal properties became developed), the chilling effects of the WPT became more apparent. This began in mid-1981 when world oil prices, which peaked near $40.00 per barrel, began to fall as a result of increased conservation and a recessionary economy. With a drop in oil prices, drilling budgets pared wildcat wells in favor of development wells. By 1983, the rotary-rig count, which had stood at over 4,000 two years before, was under 2,000. Abandonments increased. The one escape, invalidation of the WPT and a refund of nearly three years' collections, was struck down in mid-1983 by the Supreme Court. In 1984, the slump was arrested, but price erosion set in near year-end. Although the WPT cushions price declines by applying lower tax takes, the tax takes away the upside of higher prices and thus contributes to petroleum-industry problems.

The complexity of the tax, which sought to provide huge revenue and yet retain production incentives, invariably had nonneutral competitive effects. A prominent example is ARCO's interpretation of

---

[49]For some early examples of opportunism regarding the net income limitation and tertiary-recovery provisions of the tax, see John Jennrich, "Lemonade from the 'Windfall Profit' Tax," *OGJ*, August 4, 1980, p. 31.

[50]"The Close-the-Wells Tax," *Wall Street Journal*, January 22, 1980, p. 20.

an ambiguous section of the tax code, whereby the "removal value" of over 200,000 barrels per day of Prudhoe Bay crude oil was reduced to create less WPT liability. This allowed product prices to be discounted below those of the competition.

Beginning in 1982, ARCO imputed a transfer price for crude purchased by its California refineries that was higher than the price of similar crude sold by Sohio and Exxon by the amount of additional transportation expense from California to the Gulf Coast. The greater the transportation cost, the lower the removal value and the lower the tax. By saving an estimated $200 million annually from lower feedstock costs, ARCO significantly increased its share of the gasoline market on the West Coast and in New England, which raised protests of "unfair" competition. Rival independent dealers called for congressional investigation and amendatory action.[51] Several probes followed, and in October 1983, the IRS rejected ARCO's methodology and ordered repayments. As of 1984, the matter remained in dispute.

Business Taxation and Drilling Deductions

The corporate tax is a fixture of modern American capitalism. However, the nonexistence of a business tax accelerated the growth of the petroleum industry through the turn of the century. When the tax was implemented, its stifling effect was mitigated by the enactment of distinctive tax deductions. In recent years, however, the oil-production industry has gone from being one of the least taxed to being one of the most taxed major industries in the United States.

History of the Corporate Business Tax. Federal business taxation began in 1894 when a 2 percent flat tax was levied on corporate income.[52] The tax was found to be a direct tax and was declared unconstitutional by the Supreme Court soon after it went into effect.[53]

---

[51]See chapter 20, pp. 1221–23.

[52]State corporate taxation will not be discussed because firms are allowed to deduct state taxes from federal taxes. Shortcomings with the federal corporate tax also apply to the theory and practice of state and local business taxation. For a history of the origins of state taxation, see National Industrial Conference Board, *State Income Taxes,* 2 vols. (New York: NICB, 1930). As of 1982, forty-five states had a corporate tax. Among those that did not were several major oil states (Texas and Alaska) that had been able to depend on oil revenue instead.

[53]28 Stat. 509 (1894). *Pollock* v. *Farmers' Loan and Trust Co.,* 157 U.S. 249 (1894).

Corporate taxation again appeared in the Revenue Act of 1909 on the rationale that it was not a direct tax on income or capital but a fee for the privilege of conducting business in corporate form.[54] The 1 percent tax on corporate profits over $5,000 was doubled in 1916, grew to 6 percent a year later, and rose to 12 percent in the War Revenue Act of 1918.[55] Also in the 1918 act was an excess-profits tax and a maximum tax rate on the sale of oil and gas properties by corporations.[56] The same act included a tax on undistributed profits, first passed in the Revenue Act of 1917, which for the first time defined partnerships as corporations.[57]

The corporate tax rate rose after World War I and reached new heights during the New Deal and again during World War II. The excess-profits tax rate rose from a maximum of 35 percent in 1934 to a top rate of 95 percent by 1944; the basic corporate tax rate rose from 12.5 percent to 24 percent in the same period.

After the Korean conflict, during which the excess-profits tax continued at lower levels, growing peacetime revenue needs kept the corporate tax rate between 48 to 52 percent until 1976. As of 1984, the rate stood at 46 percent of corporate income, a far cry from the 1909 rate and a clear indication of the growth of government in peacetime as in wartime. The *effective rate,* however, has been much less as the result of various incentives such as the investment tax credit, although political pressures for more revenue may limit deductions in the future to bring the effective rate, estimated at 17 percent for 1983, closer to the nominal rate.[58]

All taxes have the effect of reducing consumption and investment wealth of the private sector, while penalizing the creative effort that in a market economy rewards individuals with personal income and business profits. "Excess" profit taxes magnify the disincentive to

[54]Public Law 5, 36 Stat. 11 (1909).

[55]Public Law 271, 39 Stat. 756 (1916); Public Law 377, 39 Stat. 1000 (1917); and Public Law 254, 40 Stat. 1057 (1918). Taxation of income became constitutional with the Sixteenth Amendment, ratified February 25, 1913. For a history of its ratification, see Arthur Ekirch, Jr., "The Sixteenth Amendment: The Historical Background," *Cato Journal* 1, no. 1 (Spring 1981): 161–82.

[56]The excess-profits rate was from 30 to 80 percent of eligible income. The well-sales tax is examined below.

[57]Public Law 50, 40 Stat. 300 (1917).

[58]Congressional Joint Committee on Taxation, "Study of 1983 Effective Tax Ratios of Selected U.S. Corporations," Committee Print JCS-40-84, November 28, 1984.

successful entrepreneurship.[59] Not only are *noticed* opportunities to improve resource allocation not chosen because of the tax disincentive, resource-improving opportunities themselves are not perceived because of the taxation.[60]

The corporate income tax has an additional distorting effect because it is a *double tax*. There is a tax on corporate earnings, which, when distributed as wages or dividends, are again taxed as income or capital gains. Consequently, less efficient forms of business organization than the corporation are made relatively more attractive. An outstanding example in the oil and gas field has been individual ownership and operation of portions of a commonly held reservoir.[61] A second prominent example in the petroleum industry is the strategy used by some crude-rich corporations to spin off oil and gas properties into royalty trusts and limited partnerships to escape corporate taxation. Distributed as dividends, shareholders' revenue is subject only to personal income taxes. Since 1979, Houston Oil and Minerals (Tenneco), Mesa Petroleum, Louisiana Land and Exploration, Southland Royalty, Sabine, and Transco Exploration have followed this strategy. A determined effort in late 1983 by Mesa Petroleum's T. Boone Pickens to restructure Gulf to separate a portion of its hydrocarbon properties into a royalty trust, following earlier attempts with other merger targets, dramatized the hard choices that result from the corporate tax—forgo separation and pay double taxes or separate and lose the advantages of integration.

In 1984, critics of the industry trend to remove producing properties from the corporate umbrella for tax purposes succeeded in removing the incentive for doing so. Effective March 31, 1985, a "recapture" clause in the Deficit Reduction Tax taxed the appreciation of the royalty trust over cost when transferred from the corporation to stockholders.[62]

Another distortion of corporate taxation involves the retention of income. While the pool of income to be distributed or reinvested is partially siphoned off by the tax, the remaining pool has a tendency

---

[59]Favorable treatment of business losses, conversely, subsidizes entrepreneurial error.

[60]Israel Kirzner, "Taxes and Discovery: An Entrepreneurial Perspective," *Discovery and the Capitalist Process* (Chicago: University of Chicago Press, 1985), pp. 93–118.

[61]See chapter 3, pp. 125–26.

[62]Public Law 96-369, 98 Stat. 494 (1984).

to be overretained because of double taxation. This impairs the mobility of capital to respond to new investment opportunities created by changing consumer preferences.[63]

Petroleum-Related Deductions. The Sixteenth Amendment allowed taxation of income but not capital.[64] This constitutional limitation required that capital involved in creating income, be it a fixed asset or a mineral deposit, be given a replacement allowance in the form of a tax-reducing expense to be matched against the income created by the wasting asset. For fixed assets, a depreciation allowance was created; for mineral deposits, a *depletion allowance* was devised.[65] Explained Supreme Court Justice Brandeis in 1927:

> The depletion charge permitted as a deduction from the gross income in determining taxable income . . . represents the reduction in the mineral contents of the reserve from which the product is taken. The reserves are recognized as wasting assets. The depletion effected by operation is likened to the using up of raw material in making the product of a manufacturing establishment. As the cost of the raw material must be deducted from the gross income before the net income can be determined, so the estimated cost of the part of the reserve used up is allowed.[66]

The substance of the depletion allowance, however, would stray from cost to other determinations that would differentiate it from depreciation and raise controversy.

While the Federal Excise Tax of 1909 introduced the depreciation deduction, the Revenue Act of 1913 began the depletion tax writeoff. The 1913 act set "a reasonable [depletion] allowance . . . not to exceed

---

[63]Murray Rothbard, *Power and Market* (Kansas City, Mo.: Sheed Andrews and McMeel, 1977), p. 102.

[64]"The Congress shall have power to lay and collect taxes on incomes, from whatever source derived." Sixteenth Amendment to the Constitution of the United States (February 25, 1913).

[65]Arthur Dewing defines depletion as "a loss arising directly from the functional consumption of a capital asset through the normal operation of the business." Dewing, *The Financial Policy of Corporations* (New York: Ronald Press, 1953), p. 557.

[66]*United States* v. *Ludey*, 274 U.S. 302 (1927). In 1965, the Supreme Court reaffirmed the depletion rationale: "The allowance for depletion is to compensate the owner of wasting mineral assets for the part exhausted in production so that when the minerals are gone, the owner's capital and his assets remain unimpaired." *Paragon Jewel Coal Co.* v. *CIR*, 380 U.S. 624 at 631 (1965).

. . . 5 percentum of the gross value . . . of the output."[67] The 1913 law was changed in 1916 to a "reasonable" allowance based on either *cost* or *market value* as of March 1, 1913.[68] A year later, a Treasury Department ruling disallowed depletion for the first year of a well's life if production did not decline. As production declined, the ratio of flush production to current production multiplied by cost was allowed as the depletion deduction.[69]

The one-year dead period before the depletion allowance was allowed, coupled with rising business-tax rates, created hardship for many drillers, which was brought to the attention of lawmakers. In the Revenue Act of 1918, the "reduction in flow" methodology was liberalized to allow depletion based on *discovery value* for deposits discovered after March 1, 1913, if the property was not purchased.[70] The new law was intended to encourage exploration for new reserves, a policy priority resulting from the important role petroleum played during World War I. It also resulted from a skilled lobbying effort by independent oil producers, and Oil Division head Mark Requa in particular, who portrayed the existing tax structure as promoting shortages by discouraging wildcatting.[71] The law was drafted by the Treasury Department with much industry input, which, according to critic Senator Robert LaFollette, resulted in "loopholes, side doors, 'pads,' 'cushions,' and various devices giving administrators wide discretion in construction and execution of the

[67]38 Stat. 114 at 167 (1913). For analysis of the congressional debate surrounding the law, see Simon Simon, *Economic Legislation of Taxation* (New York: Arno Press, 1979), pp. 63–67.

[68]Public Law 271, 39 Stat. 759 (1916).

[69]Simon Simon, *Economic Legislation of Taxation*, p. 68. This strict interpretation was mitigated by a provision in the same act that allowed intangible drilling and development costs to be expensed (discussed below).

[70]Public Law 253, 40 Stat. 1067 (1918). "Discovery value" was computed thirty days after the reservoir was found. The advantage of this methodology over market value for the industry was that it was leniently based on high World War I prices and was applicable to new wells in existing fields. See Charles Galvin, "The 'Ought' and 'Is' of Oil-and-Gas Taxation," *Harvard Law Review* (June 1960): 1459.

[71]See Simon Simon, *Economic Legislation of Taxation*, chaps. 5–7. Charles Galvin recognized discovery depletion as "not an accounting device for cost recoupment but an incentive device built into the federal revenue system to permit tax-free receipts in excess of cost as a bonus for discovery." Galvin, "The 'Ought' and 'Is' of Oil-and-Gas Taxation," p. 1459. This demonstrated the *political* nature of the tax provision that at this early date was overtaking the theoretical rationale for the deduction.

law."[72] Estimates under the law were consequently liberal, and an arbitrary definition of 160 acres as the reservoir area allowed opportunistic overdrilling to inflate discovery value above reservoir value.[73]

The next modification in petroleum-depletion tax law began a series of reductions. In 1921, discovery value was limited to 100 percent of a property's yearly profits to prevent diversified corporations from using the depletion allowance to lower taxable income from other sources.[74] In 1924, discovery value was further reduced to 50 percent of income. The cost-depletion option, however, remained unchanged from its 1916 beginning.

In the 1918–25 period, determination of discovery value for thousands of new producing wells became burdensome for tax authorities. Disputes between producers and the U.S. Treasury were commonplace. Overdrilling and drainage were unintentionally promoted at the expense of wildcat wells, which the law was intended to benefit. Simplicity was coveted, and after debate on figures ranging from 20 percent to 40 percent of gross income, the Revenue Act of 1926 adopted an allowance of 27.5 percent to replace discovery value, while retaining both the 50 percent income limitation and the cost-depletion alternative.[75] Studies of the 27.5 percent rule showed a slight tax increase for producers compared with the previous discovery-value procedure because the 50 percent limitation often came into play.[76]

From 1926 until 1969, the depletion allowance remained unchanged except for a limitation on the cost method imposed in 1932.[77] Uncertainty and litigation that previously plagued the allowance ended. Congressional challenges to lower the 27.5 percent

---

[72]Simon Simon, *Economic Legislation of Taxation*, p. 142.

[73]Ibid., p. 126. Also see chapter 3, p. 126.

[74]Cross-deductions were common because a large drop in crude prices in 1920–21 created loss positions that were used to reduce taxable income from other sources. For an example, see Simon Simon, *Economic Legislation of Taxation*, pp. 168–69.

[75]Public Law 20, 44 Stat. 16 (1926). See Simon Simon, *Economic Legislation of Taxation*, chap. 9. Unlike the situation under discovery depletion, purchased properties could enjoy the 27.5 percent allowance.

[76]John Lichtblau and Dillard Spriggs, *The Oil Depletion Issue* (New York: Petroleum Industry Research Foundation, 1959), pp. 41–42.

[77]Public Law 154, 47 Stat. 169 (1932).

depletion rate in 1951, 1954, 1958, and 1959 were defeated by the political strength of the major producing states, particularly Texas. By the 1960s, political winds had begun to change, and late in the decade the first of a series of reductions occurred. The Tax Reform Act of 1969 reduced the oil and gas depletion allowance from 27.5 percent to 22 percent for all producers.[78] The Tax Reduction Act of 1975, supported by ARCO, which openly favored abolition of the depletion allowance, eliminated the deduction for all integrated companies, foreign production, and proven properties exchanged after December 31, 1974 (to prevent transfers of property from integrated to independent companies able to qualify for percentage depletion).[79] Natural gas regulated under long-term contract or produced from certain formations was exempted from the rule.

For firms that still qualified for percentage depletion, limitations were specified in the 1975 act depending on the year, amount of crude produced, and type of production (table 7.2).[80]

A year later, the Tax Reform Act of 1976 weakened the percentage basis for those eligible—independents with domestic production and royalty owners—by limiting the deduction to 65 percent of the taxpayer's taxable income computed on the cost basis.[81] As of 1984, the schedule's percentages were in effect for independents and royalty owners.

In a space of seven years, the percentage depletion allowance was eliminated for roughly 85 percent of the industry and reduced for the rest. This made the cost method, matching adjusted cost to total production to establish a per unit deduction limited to the basis

[78]Public Law 91-172, 83 Stat. 487 (1969).

[79]Public Law 94-12, 89 Stat. 26 (1975). Regarding ARCO's support for repeal of the depletion allowance, see *National Petroleum News*, February 1974, p. 38; and *New York Times*, December 27, 1973, p. 57. Senator William Proxmire (D-Wis.) stated, "The Atlantic Richfield Corp. has asked for exactly this and says that they're going to lead the fight to eliminate the oil depletion allowance." *Business and Society Review* (Spring 1974): 84. Nonintegrated marketers opposed the depletion allowance on competitive grounds. See, for example, *National Petroleum News*, December 1983, p. 12.

[80]Table 7.2 is adopted from Ted Englebrecht and Richard Hutchins, "Percentage Depletion Reductions from Oil and Gas Operations: A Review and Analysis," in *Basic Oil and Gas Taxation*, ed. Lewis Mosberg (Oklahoma City: Institute for Energy Development, 1978), pp. 138–39. Englebrecht and Hutchins identified the 1975 tax act as "effectively end[ing] the history of what was one of the most lucrative of the special industry provisions in the Internal Revenue Code" (p. 134).

[81]Public Law 94-455, 90 Stat. 1520 (1976).

Table 7.2
INDEPENDENT PRODUCER DEPLETION TABLE: 1975–84

| | Percentage Depletion Rate | | Depletable Quantity |
Year	Primary Recovery	Secondary & Tertiary Recovery	without Rate Reduction (bl/day)[a]
1975	22%	22%	2,000
1976	22	22	1,800
1977	22	22	1,600
1978	22	22	1,400
1979	22	22	1,200
1980	22	22	1,000
1981	20	22	1,000
1982	18	22	1,000
1983	16	22	1,000
1984	15	15	1,000

SOURCE: Ted Englebrecht and Richard Hutchins, "Percentage Depletion Reductions from Oil and Gas Operations," pp. 138–39.
[a]For Mcf of natural-gas production, multiply the barrels per day oil figure by 6,000.

amount, mandatory for most and competitive with percentage depletion for the remainder.[82]

While the depletion allowance attempted to avoid a tax on capital, the tax treatment of drilling and development costs liberalized a gray area in accounting theory to provide incentive to an industry deemed important to national welfare. The two tax deductions stem from different reasoning and must be separately evaluated.

A pillar of accounting theory is to match costs as closely as possible with revenues to gain a realistic picture of income over a period.[83] Certain costs are expensed to match current revenues, while other costs are capitalized to match associated multiperiod revenues. In oil

[82]Alexander Bruen and Willard Taylor, *Federal Income Taxation of Oil and Gas Investments* (New York: Warren, Gorham and Lamont, 1980), p. 7-5. For an explanation of the current law of cost depletion, see ibid., pp. 7-12 to 7-20; and Boris Bittker, *Federal Taxation of Income, Estates and Gifts* (Boston: Warren, Gorham, & Lamont, 1983), pp. 24-23 to 24-25.

[83]In accounting theory, this is the *matching principle*. Glenn Welsch, Charles Zlatkovich, and Walter Harrison, *Intermediate Accounting* (Homewood, Ill.: R. D. Irwin, 1979), p. 32.

and gas production, costs associated with dry holes and commercial wells raised the issue of whether their costs should be expensed in the current period or capitalized over several accounting periods. Under capitalization, costs would be amortized over the life of the well if commercial or over the life of the firm's other wells if not commercial. Although the amount of tax to be paid is identical under both approaches, the timing difference creates a tax advantage under the expensing option since less tax is paid on less stated income in the current period.

Special treatment for petroleum drilling and development costs was first clarified in a February 1917 Treasury Department ruling, which allowed expensing (noncapitalization) of "incidental expenses of drilling wells . . . which do not necessarily enter into and form a part of the capital invested or property account."[84] A second ruling a year later added that costs not expensed were recoverable through depreciation and that dry-hole expenditures could be entirely expensed in the current year.[85] In 1943, a general restatement of the law was released that primarily incorporated court decisions and administrative interpretations of the last several decades.[86]

Several early court cases questioned the ruling's favoritism toward expensing over capitalization, but it was not until 1945 that a legal challenge came forth. In *F.H.E. Oil Company* v. *Commissioners*, the Fifth Circuit Court of Appeals declared that incidental (intangible) costs could not be expensed because they made permanent improvements that increased the value of the property.[87] Congress, responding to industry concern, passed a concurrent resolution recognizing

[84]Treasury Decision 2447, 19 *Treasury Decisions under Internal Revenue Law* 31 at 35 (1917).

[85]Treasury Decision 2690, 20 *Treasury Decisions under Internal Revenue Law* 127 (1918). In 1933, this ruling was amended to subject capitalized costs with certain exceptions to cost depletion rather than to depreciation as with intangible expenses. In 1943, the intangible-drilling-cost deduction was first allowed for wells drilled under turnkey contracts or as consideration for a lease. See Stephen McDonald, *Federal Tax Treatment of Income from Oil and Gas* (Washington, D.C.: Brookings Institution, 1963), pp. 14–15; and Charles Galvin, "The 'Ought' and 'Is' of Oil and Gas Taxation," pp. 1466–67.

[86]Treasury Decision 5276, 1943 *Commerce Bulletin* 151.

[87]147 F.2d 1002 (5th Cir. 1945). The court based its decision on sec. 24(a)(2) of the 1939 Internal Revenue Code, which required capitalization of such costs. Frank Burke, "Intangible Drilling and Development Costs," in *Basic Oil and Gas Taxation,* ed. George Hardy (Oklahoma City: Institute for Energy Development, 1981), pp. 152–53.

the validity of current treatment of intangibles, although the resolution was more symbolic than statutory.[88] Implied sanction for expensing intangibles was given in the Revenue Act of 1954, which stated that "regulations shall be prescribed . . . [to] gran[t] the option to deduct as expenses intangible drilling and development costs in the case of oil and gas wells."[89] What had been practiced by the industry for thirty-seven years under administrative rulings officially became law.[90]

Intangible drilling and development costs (IDC), which constitute approximately 70 percent of all well costs, are those onshore and offshore expenses without salvage value such as labor, materials and supplies, payments to drilling contractors, and fuel used to prepare the well site and run production operations. Repairs, redrilling, and enhanced-recovery projects are included as intangibles and eligible for current-year writeoffs. *Tangible* costs, to be capitalized and recovered through cost depletion, are costs deemed to have a salvage value such as fixed assets at the well site, even casing cement.[91] Companies commonly kept two sets of books—one in which intangibles were expensed for tax purposes and one in which intangibles were capitalized for internal accounting purposes.

Until 1976, investors had widely and ingeniously employed the IDC tax option as an income-sheltering device, which provoked congressional criticism and, eventually, action. If expensed in the first year of drilling, intangible costs created large losses that could be used to reduce taxable ordinary income from other sources. Individuals and partnerships magnified this tax-minimization strategy by leveraging with borrowed funds, which allowed tax writeoffs many times greater than one's "true" investment.

The Tax Reform Act of 1976 attempted to end this practice by individuals and partnerships and reduce the corporate deduction. Four major revisions were made:

1. A 15 percent tax on part of the tax reduction from IDC expensing for individuals and partnerships. The tax is levied on the

---

[88]H. Con. Res. 50 (July 21, 1945), 79th Cong., 1st sess.

[89]Public Law 591, 68A Stat. 77 (1954), sec. 263(c).

[90]As before, these costs were limited to 50 percent of yearly taxable income when added to the depletion deductions.

[91]Frank Burke, "Intangible Drilling and Development Costs," pp. 166–70.

"excess" IDC minus the taxpayer's net income, with "excess" defined as the difference between capitalized IDC and expensed IDC.[92]

2. A reduction of the IDC deduction from 70 to 50 percent for personal-service income subject to a maximum rate.[93]

3. For domestic or foreign petroleum-property sales in which IDC is expensed and a gain is made, profit is to be taxed as ordinary income instead of capital gains to "recapture" the tax benefit.

4. A limit to the IDC expensing deduction for capital "at risk," that is, collateralized borrowings.

Reduction of IDC expensing, especially for noncorporations as well as for corporations, joined reductions in the depletion allowance to weaken incentives for oil and gas exploration and production that had historically existed. Although new drilling marginally increased as a result of other factors under the new tax regime, proven reserves declined from 31 million barrels in 1977 to 27.8 million barrels in 1979 because of those changes in combination with other factors. Unlike the situation before the 1975–76 period, the disincentive of price controls was reinforced by the removal of tax incentives associated with IDC expensing and percentage depletion.

The Tax Equity and Fiscal Responsibility Act of 1982 reduced the IDC deduction for integrated companies to 85 percent of the amount otherwise eligible, with the remaining 15 percent to be ratably deducted from income over a three-year period.[94] Only minor changes were made for independents, in keeping with their favorable tax treatment compared to majors.

From 1909 until 1918, U.S. corporations operating abroad were subject to foreign taxes in addition to their domestic obligations. The double-tax disincentive was recognized and largely removed in the Revenue Act of 1918, which allowed a 100 percent credit on domestic taxes for foreign "income, excess profits, or war profits

---

[92]The Tax Reduction and Simplification Act of 1977 (Public Law 95-30, 91 Stat. 126) amended this provision to allow offsets for oil and gas income for 1976 and 1977. The offset was then made permanent in the Energy Tax Act of 1978 (Public Law 95-618, 92 Stat. 3174).

[93]This provision was repealed in the Economic Recovery Tax Act of 1981 (Public Law 97-34, 95 Stat. 172).

[94]Public Law 97-248, 96 Stat. 324 (1982).

tax" on a "per country" basis.[95] In 1921, an "overall" basis limitation was enacted to discourage offsets used to reduce taxes on domestic income.[96] The credit was granted not only to avoid double taxation but also because of federal policy to encourage the development of foreign fields to preserve domestic supply. It was not only tax policy but energy policy in the wake of World War I.

At the close of World War II, the tax credit assumed new importance as U.S. companies became active in the Middle East and involved foreign countries looked toward taxation of earnings in addition to royalty income. Venezuela in 1946 and Saudi Arabia in 1950 introduced 50–50 profit-sharing "partnerships," which soon became standard fare in other major oil-exporting countries.[97] The IRS ruled that the host government's 50 percent share constituted foreign taxation subject to the tax credit.[98] Subsequent rulings upheld profit calculations based on posted prices, which critics charged were set "artificially" low by U.S. multinational companies, at the bequest of foreign governments,[99] to increase profits on outside sales, increase outside refining costs, increase foreign tax liabilities to deduct from U.S. taxes, and reduce price competition for their U.S. crude.[100] In 1958, a final liberalization of the foreign tax credit took place when Congress enacted a carryback-carryover provision to allow excess (unusable) credits to be retroactively or prospectively used.[101]

[95]Public Law 254, 40 Stat. at 1073 (1918).

[96]Public Law 98, 42 Stat. 227 at 258 (1921).

[97]Carl Nordberg and Linda Schwartzstein, "The Foreign Tax Credit for Foreign Oil and Gas Income," *29 Oil and Gas Institute* (New York: Matthew Bender, 1978), p. 482.

[98]Income Tax Division Ruling 4038, 1950–2 C.B. 54 (Venezuela). Revenue Ruling 55-296, 1955-1 C.B. 386 (Saudi Arabia). Carl Nordberg and Linda Schwartzstein, "The Foreign Tax Credit for Foreign Oil and Gas Income," pp. 480, 482.

[99]"Posted prices were originally market prices at which oil companies were willing to sell to third parties. In the early 1960's the setting of these prices was taken over— at first informally and now officially—by the governments of the producing countries and were set above actual market values." Carl Nordberg and Linda Schwartzstein, *The Foreign Tax Credit and The U.S. Oil Industry* (New York: Petroleum Industry Research, 1974), p. 25.

[100]Edith Penrose, "Middle East Oil: The International Distribution of Profits and Income Taxes," *Economica* (August 1960): 208–9.

[101]Public Law 85-866, 72 Stat. 1606 at 1639 (1958).

Integrated U.S. companies could also use high posted prices to derive accounting losses for their U.S. refining and retailing operations to reduce, if not escape, domestic taxation. With high profits centered on foreign production, a combination of 50–50 profit sharing, the foreign tax credit, and the depletion allowance could negate taxable profits to minimize taxes for multinationals.

Much bad press about this alleged strategy was generated in such periodicals as the *New Republic* and the *Nation*. Congressional inquiry and "price audit" investigations by the IRS and Treasury Department began in the middle 1960s. Of particular concern to critics was whether foreign taxes were "in lieu of" royalty income to host governments.[102]

After Congress unsuccessfully tried to limit foreign tax credits in the 1969 and 1974 tax bills, the Tax Reduction Act of 1975 limited creditable foreign taxes to 52.8 percent in 1975, 50.4 percent in 1976, and 50 percent thereafter.[103] The same act replaced the per country limitation with an overall basis to reduce offsets. Another "revenue enhancer" was a recapture clause that limited foreign losses applicable to domestic income.

Creditable taxes were again lowered in the Tax Reform Act of 1976 to 48 percent of total sales ending after 1976.[104] This helped settle the vexing question of whether tax payments to the host government were disguised royalty payments. In the words of a 1977 report by the Task Force on Foreign Source Income:

> The problem dealt with in the case of petroleum companies is different than that which arises in the case of multinationals in general. The question with petroleum companies was whether payments made to foreign governments were in the nature of creditable income taxes or deductible royalty payments. Since it is generally quite difficult to distinguish between royalties and taxes in the case of most

[102]Congressional hearings in 1959 produced evidence that the Arabian American Oil Company (Aramco), consisting of Exxon, Mobil, California Standard, and Texaco, with exclusive concessions to Saudi Arabia petroleum deposits, encouraged higher taxes to renegotiate obsolete lease terms. Evidence was also presented that the U.S. State Department encouraged the Aramco partners and host governments to do the same for foreign policy reasons. See Robert Schmidt, "Operation of the Foreign Tax Credit in the Petroleum Industry: a 'Dry Hole'?" *Virginia Journal of International Law* (Winter 1975): 428–29.

[103]Public Law 94-12, 89 Stat. 26 (1975).

[104]Public Law 94-455, 90 Stat. 1520 (1976).

foreign operations of U.S. petroleum companies, it is felt necessary to provide for a special limitation on these payments.[105]

The foreign tax credit is currently capped at 46 percent of a corporation's yearly foreign earned income with levies greater than this amount usable as credits two years backward and five years forward. In the case of oil and gas, the carryback-carryforward is limited to 2 percent of yearly income.[106] In 1982, the Tax Equity and Fiscal Responsibility Act required firms to consolidate foreign exploration and production income into one sum to compute creditable foreign taxes.[107]

A View of Corporate Taxation and Deductions. Critics of corporate tax deductions associated with oil and gas extraction have emphasized the special treatment of this industry compared with other industries. Free-market advocate Milton Friedman has called the depletion allowance a "special favor" or "subsidy" that "simply gives the oil industries . . . a lower tax rate than other industries."[108] Free-market critic Paul Davidson has belittled the depletion allowance as "primarily an ad valorem subsidy to mineral rights owners who have no alternative use for their resource."[109]

Before the fundamental question of the economic effects of taxation per se is addressed, the theory behind the depletion allowance and the allowance in practice will be evaluated.

The rationale of the depletion allowance is to avoid a tax on capital because reservoir extractions, other things equal, lower an asset's salable or capital value. The tax deduction as practiced, while compensatory, has deviated from this premise. Unlike depreciation, which is calculated on the lower of cost or market principle, depletion is arbitrarily calculated as a percentage of yearly income. Depletion,

---

[105]Cited in Carl Nordberg and Linda Schwartzstein, *The Foreign Tax Credit and the U.S. Oil Industry,* pp. 490–91.

[106]U.S. Department of Energy, *A Taxonomy of Energy Taxes* (Washington, D.C.: DOE, October 1979), p. 23.

[107]Public Law 97-248, 96 Stat. 324 (1982).

[108]Milton Friedman, *An Economist's Protest* (Glen Ridge, N.J.: Thomas Horton and Daughters, 1975), pp. 309–10.

[109]Paul Davidson, "Policy Problems of the Crude Oil Industry," *American Economic Review,* March 1963, p. 106. For a representative critique of depletion from a journalistic perspective, see Harvey O'Connor, "How to Make a Billion," *Nation,* February 26, 1955, pp. 175–76.

on the contrary, should be linked to the cost of the producing well, whether computed using the successful-efforts or the full-cost method, unless market value is below cost.[110] It is true that when market value is above cost, as it is with virtually all commercial wells, a capital tax is incurred. But what is taxed is *capital gains*, which are recognized only when the asset is sold in accordance with lower of cost or market valuation.

A second defect also concerns the historical setting of the depletion allowance. Cost recovery (capital recovery) has been achieved short of the depletion allowance by expensing intangible drilling costs and capitalizing tangible drilling costs. The depletion allowance, consequently, superaccelerates cost recovery and reduces income-tax liabilities after cost (capital) recovery is completed.

Under the 27.5 percent standard, the effective tax rate for oil and gas production firms was estimated to be significantly below the effective rate for downstream companies within the industry and firms in other sectors. Senator Paul Douglas (D-Ill.) in the 1950s documented that oil and gas companies paid little or no taxes because of the depletion allowance, which foreshadowed congressional debates that several decades later would lead to reform.[111]

Favorable tax treatment drew resources into exploration and production at the expense of other employments. As Stephen McDonald explained:

> Differential tax treatment is *unneutral*, having induced a reallocation of resources. . . . Under the assumption that the corporate income tax is not shifted forward in higher prices, percentage depletion and related expensing provisions in mineral production result in significant misallocations of resources, both between minerals production and other activities and among different minerals.[112]

With commercial finds more profitable on an after-tax basis, dry holes were more affordable and frequent, which from the viewpoint

[110]Successful efforts and full-cost accounting alternatives are examined in chapter 10, pp. 561–66.

[111]Robert Engler, *The Politics of Oil* (Chicago: University of Chicago Press, 1961), p. 155. Also see Stephen McDonald, *Federal Tax Treatment of Income from Oil and Gas*, pp. 16–22.

[112]Stephen McDonald, "Taxation System and Market Distortion," in *Energy Supply and Government Policy*, ed. Robert Kalter and William Vogely (Ithaca, N.Y.: Cornell University Press, 1976), pp. 34, 50.

of a nonpreferential (neutral) tax represented overdrilling and resource waste. With more wildcats and development wells, the latter relatively more encouraged by IDC expensing,[113] production was artificially stimulated in relation to the output that a neutral tax would have created. Higher drilling and production, in turn, influenced state conservation laws to restrict the same, an example of cumulative intervention that had as an end result state and federal cartelization of the domestic production industry.[114] Another distortion caused by the nonneutral levy was an apparent advantage for integrated firms who could employ high upstream profits to aggressively compete downstream against nonintegrated firms. Independent marketers became vocal critics of the depletion allowance and successfully worked for its partial repeal in the 1970s for this reason.

Although the depletion allowance is a distinctive tax provision and a distortion of resource allocation and competition from a more neutral tax environment, it confuses the issue to equate the tax break to a government subsidy. Taxation is an intervention, and reducing taxes lessens the intervention. A government subsidy is a self-contained intervention wholly separate from taxation. To reduce one intervention is not to create another intervention.

The foreign tax credit was an understandable attempt to avoid a double corporate tax on firms operating outside the United States. The rationale of the foreign tax credit has been stated by Treasury secretary George Shultz.

> The basic concept of a tax credit system is that the country in which the business activity is carried on has the first right to tax the income from it even though the activity is carried on by a foreigner. The foreigner's home country also taxes the income, but only to the extent the home tax does not duplicate the tax of the country where the income is earned. The duplication is eliminated by a foreign tax credit.[115]

---

[113]Stephen McDonald, *Federal Tax Treatment of Income from Oil and Gas*, p. 83.

[114]See Alfred Kahn, "The Depletion Allowance in the Context of Cartelization," *American Economic Review* (June 1964): 286–314. Also see chapter 29, pp. 1775–76.

[115]George Shultz, Testimony before the House Ways and Means Committee, February 4, 1974. Quoted in Carl Nordberg and Linda Schwartzstein, *The Foreign Tax Credit and the U.S. Oil Industry*, p. 16.

This is not a tax advantage over domestic firms, and it is not preferential as long as the foreign tax is not in lieu of market payments such as land rental or equipment purchases from the host government. When the tax is in lieu of other concessions—if indeed market rents can be known outside of a true market to separate the two—a favorable situation arises since the involved firm either pays less U.S. tax or acquires resources at below-market prices. This furthers a nonneutral situation between and within industries, which is a source of economic inefficiency but not its cause, as explained below.

The historical treatment of intangible drilling and development costs is partly an attempt to adhere to the matching principle, a prerequisite to accurate financial accounting, and partly favorable treatment of the oil and gas production industry. To the extent that special treatment has been received, uneconomic resource allocation has resulted because, other things unchanged, resources leave high-tax areas for low-tax areas.

The conclusion can be reached that the depletion allowance in combination with IDC expensing has promoted nonneutrality. But a more fundamental point can be made. The problems of nonneutrality and economic misallocation are inherent characteristics of taxation. No tax, even if pegged at a fixed rate with uniform deductions, is neutral or "fair," given subjective entrepreneurial perceptions and differing economic circumstances. Taxation, moreover, diverts resources from the private sector to the public sector, which creates economic waste in transfer costs and the final pattern of production. The pattern of production that would have existed without the intervention of taxation is not proportionally diminished relative to before the tax—it is nonneutrality skewed.[116] Uneven tax provisions may aggravate the nonneutral effects of taxation, but the theoretical case must bring the critics of petroleum-tax provisions face to face with the wider question of taxation itself. Taxation is the intrinsic carrier of economic dislocation from which other inefficiencies, such as uneven tax provisions, stem. Taxation as a political act, moreover, is always likely to be tailored to special ends and purposes rather than the "social welfare."

---

[116]See Murray Rothbard, "The Myth of Neutral Taxation," *Cato Journal* 1, no. 2 (Fall 1981): 519–64. For a critique of the "Just Tax," see Rothbard, *Power and Market*, pp. 135–62.

Nonneutrality cuts both ways. If taxation of oil and gas extraction favored the industry in decades past, recent amendments have discriminated against the industry. Since 1980, it can be argued, the WPT has disadvantaged the producing industry as much or more than past tax deductions advantaged the industry. Resources that in a neutral world would go to petroleum production could well have been going to other industries since the mid-1970s and certainly since 1980.[117] A study of 17 large oil companies in the 1980–82 period by the Petroleum Industry Research Foundation found a 26 percent effective income-tax rate compared to a 16 percent rate for 213 major nonoil companies.[118] This discrimination is the other side of the political coin.

A new area of nonneutrality has been created from the differential tax provisions for majors and independents. Because independents have a depletion allowance, albeit reduced, and can fully write off IDC in the year incurred, whereas majors have no depletion allowance and have to capitalize 15 percent of intangibles, a two-tiered exploration and production industry has been fostered. James Wetzler has identified "a division of labor within the oil industry under which the majors specialize in lease acquisitions and geological and geophysical work and the independents specialize in the actual drilling of the wells."[119]

Well Sales and Capital-Gains Taxation

Capital-gains taxation has been particularly important to the petroleum-extraction industry because of the active market for the sale of interests in oil and gas wells and the advantage of using this tax option in conjunction with other petroleum-related tax deductions.[120]

From the beginning of the corporate tax in 1909 until the Revenue Act of 1917, sales of petroleum-related assets, as of other business

---

[117]The reduction in personal-income tax rates in the Economic Recovery Tax Act of 1981, with the upper bracket reduced from 70 percent to 50 percent, has also reduced the attractiveness of petroleum-drilling deductions and consequently petroleum drilling itself.

[118]*OGJ*, April 2, 1984, pp. 64–65. Also see American Petroleum Institute, *Response Letter*, November 15, 1983, and December 18, 1984.

[119]James Wetzler, "Taxation of Energy Producers and Consumers," in *Free Market Energy*, ed. Fred S. Singer (New York: Universe Books, 1984), p. 161.

[120]Stephen McDonald, *Federal Tax Treatment of Income from Oil and Gas*, pp. 92–93.

assets, were taxed at the corporate rate for corporations and the personal-income rate for noncorporations. With a large jump in tax rates in the Revenue Act of 1918, a special ceiling rate of 20 percent was placed on petroleum-well sales.[121] In the Revenue Act of 1921, the maximum rate remained at 20 percent, which was reduced the next year to 16 percent where it remained until 1936.[122]

A capital-gains tax of 12.5 percent was introduced for nonpetroleum assets in the 1921 act. In 1934, the rate was increased to the 30 and 100 percent range before being lowered to 24 percent in 1944.[123] Petroleum-well sales, meanwhile, continued to be preferentially treated thanks to effective political representation, underscoring their importance to the oil lobby. In the Revenue Act of 1936, the maximum profit tax was increased from 20 percent to 30 percent where it has remained.[124]

Well-sale tax ceilings and the capital-gains tax, both passed to offer relief from higher individual and corporate tax rates, stimulated this market compared to the absence of special treatment. Nonetheless, the existence of taxed transactions has distorted (lessened) the transfer of well interests. This point was of great importance for the market drive toward consolidating common pool interests in the late 1920s and early 1930s, a transformation that was hampered by the high taxable differential between the cost and the postdiscovery value of wells.

Taxation of Farm-Out Well Transactions

A common arrangement has been for major companies with substantial acreage to "farm out" a drill site to independents in return for a royalty interest in any oil or gas produced.[125] The "farmee" is obligated to drill the well, while returning the option to purchase the surrounding acreage to the "farmer."

---

[121]The base rate in the 1918 law was well below 20 percent, but the "excess profit" tax ranged from 20 to 80 percent, which, according to the Mid-Continent Oil and Gas Association, "resulted in stopping all sales and exchanges of [oil] properties." Simon Simon, *Economic Legislation of Taxation*, p. 98.

[122]Public Law 98, 42 Stat. 227 (1921); and Public Law 740, 49 Stat. 1648 (1936).

[123]Public Law 216, 48 Stat. 680 (1934); and Public Law 235, 58 Stat. 21 at 53 (1944).

[124]Public Law 740, 49 Stat. 1648 (1936).

[125]This is commonly referred to as the "obligation well farm-out arrangement" and serves to spread concentrations of risk among producers, while allowing acreage-rich companies with limited technical staffs to team with firms with opposite strengths.

In 1951, the IRS adopted the "nonrealization of income" approach to rule that farm-out transactions did not represent taxable income because an interest in uncertain production took place rather than an exchange of goods or services. Taxable income would arise only with production.[126] Relatedly, drilling-company services were interpreted as capital pooled with the farmer company. In 1977, this view was reversed by Revenue Ruling 77-176 to tax the farm-out; the taxable income of the *farmee* being equal to its interest in the "fair market value" of the acreage and the taxable income of the *farmer* being the difference between the acreage's market value and its original purchase price.[127] The consequence of the ruling was to discourage farm-out activity through either the tax obligation or the paperwork and liability associated with forming a partnership.[128] Overshadowed by price controls and the WPT, this tax change was a mitigating factor in the production of marginal properties in the post-1977 period.

State and Local Taxation

State and local governments have exercised taxing authority from the beginning of U.S. history. Although not expressly granted in the Constitution, state and local taxation has received legal sanction as necessary for "the privileges of living in an organized society, established and safeguarded by the devotion of taxes to public purposes."[129] The Constitution does, however, impose constraints on nonfederal taxation. In addition to specific prohibitions on import, export, or tonnage duties, implicit restrictions derive from the Constitution's supremacy, commerce, and due-process clauses.[130] These limits were spelled out in a 1977 U.S. Supreme Court decision, *Complete Auto Transit, Inc.* v. *Brady,* that declared constitutional a state

---

[126]See Patricia Chicoine, "New Tax Treatment of Oil and Gas Farm-Outs: A Threat to Domestic Production," in *Basic Oil and Gas Taxation*, pp. 236–41.

[127]See William Linden and L. Price Manford, "How to Avoid the New Ruling Which May Currently Tax Oil and Gas 'Farmout' Deals," *Basic Oil and Gas Production*, p. 262. This preproduction tax is applicable only to properties farmed out after April 27, 1977.

[128]Independent Petroleum Association of America, *Oil and Gas Facts and Issues* (Washington, D.C.: IPAA, 1981), pp. 2–15.

[129]*Carmichael* v. *Southern Coal and Coke Co.,* 301 U.S. 495 at 522 (1936).

[130]John Due, *Government Finance: Economics of the Public Sector* (Homewood, Ill.: R. D. Irwin, 1968), pp. 98–99.

or local tax that "is applied to an activity with a substantial nexus within the taxing state, is fairly apportioned, does not discriminate against interstate commerce, and is fairly related to services provided by the State."[131] If these criteria are met, said the high court elsewhere, the taxing body is "free to pursue its own fiscal policies, unembarrassed by the Constitution, if by the practical operation of a tax the state has exerted its power in relation to opportunities which it has given, to protection which it has afforded, benefits which it has conferred."[132]

State taxation of petroleum production has taken several forms, the most important of which is the *severance tax*. Severance levies are a direct tax on minerals removed, or severed, from the land within a state's jurisdiction.[133] A separate but identical tax is the *conservation tax*, a "user tax" levied on oil and gas production to finance state petroleum-regulation programs. These twin taxes— along with other similar exploration and production taxes on the state and local levels—constitute the start of a series of levies by all branches of government on the single most taxed item in the United States, petroleum.[134]

State Severance Taxation

Except under the common-law property-right traditions of England and the United States, governments have claimed ownership of mineral resources and the value thereof. The Spanish constitution, for example, reserved all minerals to the sovereign in areas later to become the states of Florida, Texas, New Mexico, Arizona, and Louisiana. These states each broke the Regalian Law tradition to allow mineral-right ownership by private landowners but retained subsoil rights on state-owned lands.[135] As the need to raise revenue grew, the memory and tradition of sovereign rights led to a private-land state royalty—the severance tax.

---

[131]430 U.S. 274 at 279 (1977).

[132]*Wisconsin* v. *J.C. Penney Co.*, 311 U.S. 435 at 444 (1940).

[133]Harley Lutz, *Public Finance* (New York: D. Appleton-Century, 1947), p. 481.

[134]A compilation of oil-industry taxes in 1936 totaled 71 industry-specific taxes and 134 general taxes. *National Petroleum News*, February 5, 1936, p. 96. Today, not only is the number of specific and general taxes higher, but the magnitude of oil and gas taxation is much greater.

[135]Also see chapter 2, pp. 75–76, and chapter 6, pp. 290–91.

The first oil and gas severance tax, a "net proceeds tax" applicable to salable extractions, was passed by Nevada upon statehood in 1864.[136] In Pennsylvania, an attempt was made in 1879 to tax crude output at $0.05 per barrel and enact a stiff drilling tax. Designed to curtail "overproduction," the bill failed despite support from certain producers with high inventories and existing wells who desired to penalize latecomers.[137]

In Texas, the Kennedy Gross Receipts Law of 1907 taxed oil production at 1.5 percent of net sales.[138] In 1908, Oklahoma passed a tax identical to Texas's, which was upheld by the Oklahoma Supreme Court in 1914. Louisiana passed an ineffectual tax near the turn of the century, which was raised to 2 percent and amended to provide for enforcement in 1920.

Other states that passed similar levies on oil and gas production in the period were Kentucky (1917), Montana (1921), Arkansas (1923), West Virginia and New Mexico (1925), and Michigan (1929). Twenty-three states would later follow, the most recent being Alaska (1955), Wyoming (1974), and Idaho (1980).

Indian lands received special treatment under state and local severance taxation. Because of the "guardian-ward" relationship between the federal government and the Indians, Indian lands were originally considered federal instrumentalities immune from nonfederal taxation unless permitted by Congress.[139] Taxation was first allowed by Congress in the act of May 29, 1924, for unallotted Indian lands leased at Interior Department auctions if the tax applied equally throughout the state and was not used as a lien against Indian property.[140] The act of March 3, 1927, extended the privilege

---

[136]The first severance tax applying to fixed minerals was passed by Michigan in 1846.

[137]John Ise, *The United States Oil Production*, p. 15.

[138]The tax withstood a court challenge two years later. Earlier Supreme Court cases had upheld the constitutionality of severance and related state taxes: *Postal Telegraph Cable Co.* v. *Adams*, 155 U.S. 688 (1895); *Western Union Telegraph Co.* v. *Missouri ex rel. Gottlieb*, 190 U.S. 412 (1903); and *Old Dominion Steamship Co.* v. *Virginia*, 198 U.S. 299 (1905). Cited in *Commonwealth Edison Co. et al.* v. *Montana et al.*, 453 U.S. 609 at 624 (1981).

[139]Early court decisions affirming tax immunity were *United States* v. *Richert*, 188 U.S. 432 (1903); *Indian Territory Illuminating Oil Co.* v. *Oklahoma*, 240 U.S. 522 (1915); and *Large Oil Company* v. *Howard*, 248 U.S. 549 (1919). See Alfred McLane, *Oil and Gas Leasing on Indian Lands* (Denver: Bradford-Robinson, 1955), pp. 117–23.

[140]Public Law 158, 43 Stat. 244 (1924). This was upheld in *British–American Oil Producing Company* v. *Board of Equalization of State of Montana*, 299 U.S. 264 (1936).

Table 7.3
STATE PETROLEUM PRODUCTION TAXATION: 1968–84
(thousand dollars)

Year	Tax Total[a]	Year	Tax Total[a]
1968	$ 565,921	1977	$2,012,505
1970	624,240	1978	2,207,195
1971	668,631	1979	2,541,219
1972	685,289	1980	4,131,658
1973	752,675	1981	6,127,874
1974	1,219,261	1982	7,132,376
1975	1,596,684	1983	6,606,884
1976	1,769,210	1984	6,803,677

SOURCE: Independent Petroleum Association of America, *The Oil Producing Industry in Your State*, various issues.
NOTE: Information for 1969 was not compiled.
[a] Includes all state and local production taxes.

of state and local taxation to all allotted and unallotted executive-order Indian lands.[141] Not only could oil and gas production be taxed at the states' regular severance rates, well improvements could be taxed, too.

With federal approval, the courts reversed their earlier position on immunity to rule that severance taxation on Indian lands was constitutional unless explicitly denied by Congress.[142] Congress has not been so inclined.

Twenty-seven states currently have severance taxes on oil and gas production, which peaked at over $7 billion in 1982 before falling in 1983 and 1984 (table 7.3). The tax amount is stated in units (cents per barrel) or ad valorem (percentage of value). The dramatic rise in state-government receipts resulted not only from higher tax rates but from higher wellhead prices beginning in 1973. In 1983, oil-producing states collected the wellhead taxes given in table 7.4.

Texas's oil revenue has obviated the need for a state income tax. Alaska, cashing in relatively late on its wealth of mineral resources, abolished its state income tax in 1980. Several petroleum-rich states,

[141] Public Law 702, 44 Stat. 1347 (1927).

[142] *Helvering* v. *Mountain Producers Corporation*, 303 U.S. 376 (1938); and *Oklahoma Tax Commission* v. *Texas Company*, 335 U.S. 342 (1949).

Table 7.4
Petroleum Production Taxation by State for 1983

State	Year Passed	Current Rates Oil	Current Rates Gas	Revenue (000)	End Use
Texas	O, 1907 G, 1931	4.6%	7.5%	$2,215,647	S, Gen.
Alaska	1955	12.25%	10%	1,393,100	Gen.
Louisiana	O, 1901 G, 1918	12.5%	7¢/Mcf	803,183	Gen.
Oklahoma	1908	7%	7%	709,917	S, R, Gen.
New Mexico	1925	3.75%	$12.60/Mcf	381,537	Gen.
Florida	1945	8%	5%	28,837	Gen., E
Mississippi	1945	6%	6%	96,888	Gen.
Wyoming	1957	6%	6%	270,180	Gen.
N. Dakota	1953	6.5%	5%	160,436	R, S, Gen.
Michigan	1911	6.6%	5%	82,556	Gen.
Alabama	1945	10%	10%	114,302	S, Gen.
W. Virginia	1925	4%	4%	44,125	F, Gen.
Arkansas	1921	5%	3¢/Mcf	21,329	F, Gen.
Montana	1921	5%	2.65%	134,862	S, Gen.
Utah	1955	2%	2%	38,443	S, R, Gen.
Colorado	1953	2–5%	2–5%	20,598	Gen.

(Continued on next page)

355

Table 7.4—Continued
PETROLEUM PRODUCTION TAXATION BY STATE FOR 1983

State	Year Passed	Current Rates Oil	Current Rates Gas	Revenue (000)	End Use
California	1939	1.4¢/bl	1.4¢/Mcf	17,018	R
Nebraska	1955	3%	3%	5,128	Gen.
Indiana	1947	1%	–	1,546	R
Ohio	1971	3¢/bl	–	4,396	E
Kentucky	1917	4.5%	–	13,461	Gen.
S. Dakota	1974	4.5%	4.5%	1,557	Gen.
Kansas	1917	1.25¢/bl	0.33¢/Mcf	243,011	R
Tennessee	1943	1.5%	1.5%	1,201	Gen.
Oregon	1919	6.9%	6%	318	S
Arizona	1967	2.5%	2.5%	3,135	S

SOURCE: Various state commissions.
NOTE: O = oil, G = gas, S = schooling, Gen. = general, R = roads, E = environmental, F = forestry, R = regulation.

the most important of which are California and Kansas, have forgone reliance on severance-tax income in favor of more general revenue sources. They limit production taxation to paying for administration of their conservation laws. For major severance-tax states, such as Texas, Louisiana, and Oklahoma, the revenue bonanza of the 1970s and early 1980s was accompanied by dramatic budget growth that would necessitate unprecedented belt tightening and new taxes in the wake of declining severance-tax income.

Severance taxes have been tailored to meet particular political and economic ends in some states. Tax-rate reductions are offered for low-producing wells in Alabama (40 barrels per day or less), Alaska (the "economic limit" factor),[143] Arkansas (10 barrels per day or less), Colorado (10 barrels per day or less), Florida (100 barrels per day or less), Louisiana (25 barrels per day or less), Michigan ("marginal" properties), and Wyoming (10 barrels per day or less). Florida has a blanket reduction for tertiary production, while Louisiana has a lower tax rate for wells producing 50 percent or more saltwater with crude oil. Montana exempts gas wells over 5,000 feet deep from its severance tax. Alabama has a higher tax rate for oil and gas produced from the rich Smackover field.[144]

Several states offer lower severance-tax rates for new discoveries; thes lower rates are reminiscent of higher maximum-efficient-rate "discovery allowables" that various states offer for new finds, discussed in chapter 4. Reduced tax rates are offered for new fields in Alabama for five years after discovery and in Louisiana for two years after discovery.

As do federal production taxes, severance taxation has the general effect of transferring wealth from producers and royalty owners of oil and gas to recipients of the tax revenue. This redistribution distorts the "reward" (incentive) system between producers and consumers that voluntary transactions make possible. As one attorney summarized in the early years of severance tributes:

> It is a tax on industry, a tax on thrift, a tax on energy, a tax on discovery. It discourages the man who tries to develop a great natural

---

[143]The complicated formula behind Alaska's economic limit factor is presented in U.S. Department of Agriculture, *State Taxation of Mineral Deposits and Production* (Washington, D.C.: USDA, 1979), p. 21.

[144]American Petroleum Institute, "State and Local Oil and Gas Severance and Production Taxes," typescript, November 1, 1981.

resource. The tax gatherer is ever at his elbow, and the minion of the State ever looking over his shoulder to observe every entry on his books.[145]

Another distortion results when the tax differs from state to state and within states. The distribution of drilling activities, decided in a market by purely economic considerations, is distorted by the advantages and disadvantages created by unequal tax rates. Intra-state tax breaks encourage such distortions as lowering output to qualify for the marginal-well tax reduction and taking uneconomic risks, such as neglecting development drilling in favor of wildcat exploration to qualify for the discovery-well tax reduction.

An argument has been made that severance taxation promotes conservation because oil production is discouraged "in the interests of the future."[146] This argument has several flaws. One, postponed use is not necessarily good. Nearer satisfactions are preferred to more distant ones, and future use, by the same argument, could be postponed forever. If mitigating overproduction under the rule of capture is a motivating force of this argument, the reinterpretation of chapters 3 and 4, demonstrating the primary role of government intervention in historic problems, should be emphasized. Further-more, while a severance tax would discourage exploration, produc-tion from proven reserves might be accelerated to achieve the same payout or in anticipation of future tax increases, lessening conserva-tion defined as nonuse.

A major problem surfaced regarding the limit to which a state can tax natural resources without unconstitutionally burdening interstate commerce (i.e., without unduly damaging the economic interests of importers). The case involved a 30 percent net sales tax imposed by Montana on coal exported to utility companies in New York. Under public-utility regulation, the tax was passed as rate increases. In *Commonwealth Edison Co. et al.* v. *Montana et al.*, the U.S. Supreme Court ruled on July 2, 1981, that a tax of any size was "a matter for legislative, not judicial, resolution."[147] By upholding the tax, the Supreme Court invited resource-rich states to legislate high

---

[145]*OGJ*, May 24, 1917, p. 2.

[146]John Ise, *The United States Oil Policy*, p. 520.

[147]453 U.S. 581 at 610 (1981). Prior to the decision, several unsuccessful bills were introduced in Congress to impose limits on state autonomy to tax resource production.

prices for importing-state interests to bear. This is true not only for resources purchased by firms under public-utility regulation but particularly for oil and state severance taxes, which are deductible from the WPT. Such action can only contribute to ill will and regionalism between net importing states and net exporting states that could lead to "corrective" legislation at the federal level to regulate state as well as industry practices.

Other State Taxation

A second state tax on oil and gas production is the *conservation tax,* levied to finance the regulatory efforts of state conservation commissions. This tax is identical to the severance assessment in all but name and, in fact, is often included as part of it.[148]

In 1910, Louisiana enacted a small production tax of 4 mills per barrel on oil and 2 mills per million cubic feet (MMcf) on gas to establish a conservation fund.[149] In 1915, California levied a conservation tax to finance the State Mining Bureau's program to "supervise the drilling, operation, and maintenance and abandonment of petroleum and gas wells."[150] New Mexico in 1935 passed a tax to be deposited in an Oil Conservation Fund for exclusive use by the state Oil Conservation Commission.[151] In the same year, House Bill 188 was passed in Oklahoma to tax oil and gas output, with 87.5 percent of the revenue to go to the Proration Fund for use by the Oklahoma Commission and the remainder to fund the newly created Interstate Oil Compact Fund of Oklahoma.[152] Other states that have passed conservation taxes are Oregon (1923), Arkansas (1927), Kansas and Alabama (1939), Georgia (1945), Montana (1947), Mississippi (1948), Colorado (1951), Utah and Wyoming (1953), Idaho (1963), and Nevada (1971).

---

[148]This is usually the case in regulatory states that have a severance tax but not a conservation tax.

[149]John Ise, *The United States Oil Policy,* p. 517.

[150]Howard Marshall, "Legal History of Conservation of Oil and Gas In California," in American Bar Association, *Legal History of Conservation of Oil and Gas, 1938* (Baltimore: Lord Baltimore Press, 1939), p. 31. Cited hereafter as *Legal History,* 1939.

[151]"Appendix: New Mexico Statute," in ibid., p. 302.

[152]W. P. Z. German, "Legal History of Conservation of Oil and Gas in Oklahoma," in *Legal History,* 1939, p. 209. Since this time, member states have continued to underwrite the budget of the Interstate Oil Compact Commission.

Today, eighteen states have special taxes to finance petroleum-regulation programs. Tax rates vary from percentage of sales to cents per barrel (or cents per Mcf). These taxes represent the cost to the government of having mandatory conservation laws.

In 1983, the budgets of the thirty-eight state conservation agencies totaled over $50 million, led by Texas ($15.2 million), Louisiana ($6.4 million), Oklahoma ($6.1 million), California ($5.7 million), and Kansas ($2.3 million). Of this amount, the Interstate Oil Compact Commission received $350,000 from thirty-six member and associate states for its coordinating activities.

Several other categories of state production taxes exist. Two states, Montana and Wyoming, tax output and place the revenues in trust for use in the future when revenue from depletable sources is expected to decline. In 1949, Kansas levied a pollution tax on oil output for "cleaning out and properly plugging suspect wells where no one can be found who has legal responsibility to do so." In 1977, Arkansas passed a small oil tax to build and maintain the Arkansas Oil Museum. In New Mexico, production-tax revenues have been placed in the Emergency School Fund since 1935 to finance public education. (State-land royalty income, as in other states, has been used for the same purpose.) In California, a special tax on producers operating in subsidence areas such as the Wilmington field has been assessed for environmental reasons.

Several states tax the exploration and production phase without directly taxing quantities removed and sold. Minnesota, a state without production, has a levy on acreage leased for oil and gas prospecting. Indiana and New Mexico have special (higher) property taxes on oil- and gas-drilling equipment. During 1977 and 1978, Alaska taxed proven reserves with the state's regular property tax.[153] A similar tax in Louisiana, proposed by Governor David Treen in 1982 to close a deficit in the state budget, expenditures under which tripled between 1973 and 1981, was defeated.

The foregoing array of production-related taxes reflects the political popularity of raising state revenue in this way rather than depending on more broad-based levies, such as the sales or income tax. One reason is that because oil and gas reservoirs are immobile,

---

[153]American Petroleum Institute, *State and Local Oil and Gas Severance and Production Taxes.*

a state does not worry about relocations. Another reason is that the tax falls on a smaller number of people, persons perceived to be wealthy, lucky, or both. Writing in 1926, John Ise opined:

> Incomes accruing from the accidental ownership of oil lands certainly stand in a different position from incomes earned by productive service. A tax on the millions received thus as windfalls would be no discouragement to enterprise, and no injustice; in fact, it would be nothing less than mere justice.[154]

The stigma of "windfall wealth," it can be conjectured, results in part from the property-right system under which the surface owner automatically and without effort has original claim to any wealth beneath him. It can be questioned whether in a "finders-keepers" world of subsurface homestead law the same opinion would prevail. But psychological and political considerations aside, severance taxes, like other taxes, cause higher prices, less supply, and resource dislocations from what a structure of production based on consumer preferences alone would be.

Local Taxation

Six states allow local taxation of production—California, Kentucky, Maryland (gas only), South Dakota, Tennessee (Scott County only), and Virginia. In Virginia, local taxes take the place of a statewide levy. These "mini-severance" taxes are in addition to ad valorem property taxes, which virtually all localities levy on petroleum equipment as on other property.

In recent years, several coastal cities in Texas have taken advantage of the state's liberal annexation law to extend their city limits into the Gulf of Mexico to impose property taxes on offshore drilling equipment. Beginning in 1978, Port Arthur, Texas, incrementally extended its city limits until the ten-mile legal maximum was reached. Within the annexed property was one large offshore operation that in 1981 alone paid over $750,000 in ad valorem property

---

[154]John Ise, *The United States Oil Policy*, p. 521. A related argument is that natural resources are common to all mankind and that "society generally should benefit from the[ir] exploitation and depletion" through a tax. Eugene Kuntz, *A Treatise on the Law of Oil and Gas* (Cincinnati: W. H. Anderson, 1962), p. 61. Virgin resources, however, are valueless until discovered and harnessed by creative effort. Creation, not the undiscovered resource, benefits society, and with discovery commonality is gone. An extraction tax simply transfers wealth between individuals, depending on political clout. It does not unambiguously benefit the "public."

taxes.[155] Corpus Christi, Texas, annexed Corpus Christi Bay where approximately 200 oil and gas wells bring in annual income of nearly $700,000.[156] Galveston, on the other hand, enjoys less controversial offshore property income, having annexed a three-mile area in the gulf in 1901.

Taxation by Indian Tribes

The Indian Reorganization Act of 1934 authorized tribal constitutions subject to the approval of the secretary of the interior.[157] Whether or not constitutions signified sovereignty became a hotly debated issue when the Jicarilla Apache tribe, located in the mineral-rich San Juan basin in north-central New Mexico, placed an oil- and gas-production tax on their 740,000-acre reservation in 1976.[158] The Oil and Gas Severance Tax Ordinance, the first passed by an Indian nation in over 80 years, taxed natural gas at $0.05 per million British thermal units (MMBtu) and crude oil and condensate at $0.29 per barrel. Given federal regulation of oil and gas prices, that tax amounted to approximately 29 percent of the gas price and 12 percent of the oil wellhead price, which made it among the highest production taxes in the country. It was challenged in federal district court by all nineteen oil companies involved, including Mobil, Gulf, Marathon, and ARCO, who, in the first year alone, paid $4 million in tribal taxes. The plaintiffs argued that the tribe did not possess sovereign power to tax and that such levies, in addition to New Mexico's severance tax, imposed a burden on interstate commerce. The companies further contended that the original lease agreements froze conditions of entry and production that could not be retroactively changed in the lessor's favor. In the *Merrion* case in 1982, the

---

[155]*Wall Street Journal,* January 12, 1982, p. 29. The involved company, Superior Oil, filed suit, and as of 1984 the matter was in litigation with the disputed tax held in escrow.

[156]*Houston Post,* December 13, 1981, p. 78.

[157]Public Law 383, 48 Stat. 984 (1934). The Interior Department interpreted the new law as giving Indians powers "of local self-government . . . similar to those exercised by any state or nation in regulating the use and disposition of private property, save insofar as it is restricted by specific statutes of Congress." 55 *Interior Decisions* 14 at 51 (1934).

[158]The tribe's 1937 constitution was amended in 1968 to "impose taxes and fees on non-members of the tribe doing business on the reservation." Approved a year later by the interior secretary, this amendment set the stage for the 1976 enactment. *Revised Constitution of the Jicarilla Apache Tribe,* Article XI.

U.S. Supreme Court upheld the tribe's sovereign right to tax and denied that double severance taxation unconstitutionally burdened commerce.[159] Only Congress, concluded Justice Marshall for the majority, could explicitly deny tribal authority to tax.

The implication of the Supreme Court decision is that, by granting Indian tribes taxation powers, a new layer of government has been created. On a par with state and local governments, Indian tribes cannot only tax but they can do so almost without limit (subject only to Interior Department approval) per the 1981 *Commonwealth* decision.[160] The Supreme Court argued that the "advantages of a civilized society" apply to tribal governments as they do to the state and federal governments, and outsiders entering into financial contracts with them are retroactively obligated to pay for Indian-government services. But surely the "advantages of civilization" can be maintained by contractual means. If tribal services are provided (such as roads and police services), why was this not calculated into the original lease contract, and if new services are desired, why not allow voluntary means to provide for them? The fact that this was not done implies that "public" services were not at issue; rather, a unilateral increase in royalty rates was desired, an increase the Jicarilla tribe indirectly achieved through the power to tax.[161]

Energy-company activity is explicitly taxed by nine tribal nations, seven of which currently tax oil and gas extraction (table 7.5).

In addition, the Navajo tribe has indirectly taxed wellhead activity through a business activity tax of 5 percent and a possessory interest tax of 3 percent applicable to all commercial activity (Indian and

---

[159]*Merrion et al., DBA Merrion and Bayless et al.* v. *Jicarilla Apache Tribe et al.*, 455 U.S. 130 (January 25, 1982).

[160]The limitations of the Indian tax would follow the constitutional basis established in *Complete Auto Transit.* In the dissenting opinion, Justice Stephens pointed out the discomforting implications of the Supreme Court decision. "If this retroactive imposition of a tax on oil companies is permissible, however, an Indian tribe may with equal legitimacy contract with outsiders for the construction of a school or hospital, or for the rendition of medical or technical services, and then—after the contract is partially performed—change the terms of the bargain by imposing a gross receipts tax on the outsider." 455 U.S. at 190.

[161]Since 1953 when leasing began on the Jicarilla reservation, over 70 percent of the tribe's acreage has been leased. This underscores the retroactive nature of the tax and benefits gained by imposing it in 1976 rather than earlier, which would have resulted in lower lease bids.

Table 7.5
OIL AND GAS SEVERANCE TAXES: INDIAN LANDS

Tribe	Date Passed	State	Rate and Base
Jicarilla Apache	2–77	New Mexico	29¢/bl, 5¢/MMBtu
Blackfeet	2–77	Montana	Max. 10¢/bl, 10¢/Mcf
Blackfeet	10–82	Montana	Max. 2.65% of market value
Shoshone-Arapaho	4–79	Wyoming	4% of wellhead value
Fort Peck Sioux	10–80	Montana	1% of market value
Sac and Fox	4–82	Oklahoma	8% of market value
Southern Ute	4–82	Colorado	5% of wellhead value
Ute Mountain Ute	8–82	Colo.-N.M.	5% of wellhead value
Cheyenne and Arapaho	6–80	Oklahoma	7% of wellhead value

SOURCE: Council of Energy Resource Tribes.

non-Indian) on its Arizona reservation. The 1978 levies applied to oil and gas extractions, and the Kerr-McGee Corporation went to court to protest what was characterized as a unilateral amendment to their lease agreements made in the 1960s.[162] The question of Indian sovereignty would again be tested.

The imposition of new production taxes has economic implications that can work against the sovereign entity imposing them. The precedents of tribal taxation will likely lower future bids to develop mineral resources on Indian land. The economic limits of wells on developed properties subject to the tax will be reached sooner, and future royalty income will be lower. The combination of lower bids and reduced future royalty income will mitigate additional revenue from new mineral-extraction and general business taxes.

[162]The tax included not only "Navajo goods," such as oil and gas "produced, processed, and extracted within the Navajo nation," but "Navajo services" as well including oil and gas transportation. Regulations of the Navajo Tax Commission, December 21, 1984, p. 5. See chapter 15, p. 943.

8. Regulation of Natural-Gas Prices: 1940–84

This chapter examines the history of natural-gas price regulation at the wellhead. The jurisdictional dispute over whether field prices could be regulated along with interstate pipeline tariffs pursuant to the Natural Gas Act of 1938 (NGA)[1] is traced. Early price regulation of pipeline production affiliates—and legislative attempts by independent producers to reword the NGA to unambiguously exempt them from regulation—are described.

Comprehensive price control of wellhead production dedicated to interstate commerce began with a 1954 Supreme Court decision. This sparked a political debate over legislative decontrol. Failing reform, regulation went through three tumultuous phases of cost-based pricing. Widespread shortages, which first occurred in the winter of 1971–72 and peaked in the winter of 1976–77, led to the current phase of statutory assignments under the Natural Gas Policy Act of 1978 (NGPA).[2] Problems under the NGPA, in turn, led to an unsuccessful attempt by the Reagan administration in 1983 to reform regulation further.

The chapter ends with a summary evaluation of regulatory experience with trying to achieve "just and reasonable" producer prices. The failure of wellhead regulation has direct implications for traditional NGA regulation that applies the "just and reasonable" criterion to interstate gas transmission. This subject is taken up in chapter 15 on gas pipeline regulation.

Jurisdictional Interpretation under the Natural Gas Act: 1940–47

Soon after public-utility regulation of interstate gas pipelines, described in chapter 15, began in 1938, a controversy developed over whether the Federal Power Commission (FPC) had jurisdiction

[1]Public Law 688, 52 Stat. 821 (1938).
[2]Public Law 95-621, 92 Stat. 3350 (1975).

over the field price of natural gas. This was understandable. To effectively regulate pipeline tariffs, more than the relatively small component of profit had to be controlled; the pipelines' cost of goods sold, the acquisition cost of natural gas, had to be regulated also. This was particularly important when the post–World War II boom and expansionary monetary policy led wellhead gas prices to new heights, which became a politically sensitive issue for the interventionist-minded FPC and the courts.

The Natural Gas Act of 1938 stated that "the production or gathering of natural gas" was a local activity under state jurisdiction not subject to federal regulation. The act, however, granted the FPC authority to "investigate and determine the cost of the production . . . of natural gas."[3] This contradiction was not fully recognized by producers, who took a neutral, if not a cautiously supportive, stance toward the NGA, or by regulators, who did not relish double duty of regulating producers along with interstate gas pipelines. But as the perimeters of pipeline regulation came to be defined by the agency and the courts, the tension between these two sections of the act came to light.

The first jurisdictional test came on October 31, 1939, when the FPC suspended a scheduled increase in the field price charged Warfield Natural Gas Company, an interstate pipeline, by Columbian Fuel Corporation, an independent producer. Columbia requested dismissal of the order before the full commission, which was granted on grounds of absence of congressional intent to regulate producers, lack of agency resources to expand regulation, and fear of extending authority to other local production activities.[4] The verdict, however, was hedged in language that "set the tone for the 10-year controversy which followed."[5]

> Further experience with the administration of the Natural Gas Act may reveal that the initial sales of large quantities of natural gas which eventually flows in interstate commerce are by producing or gathering companies which, through affiliation, field agreement, or

[3]Public Law 688, 52 Stat. 821 (1938), sec. 1(b) at 821 and sec. 5(b) at 824.

[4]*Columbian Fuel Corporation*, 2 FPC 200 (1940). Discussion of this case is contained in Kenneth Marcus, *The National Government and the Natural Gas Industry* (New York: Arno Press, 1979), pp. 150–54.

[5]"Federal Price Control of Natural Gas Sold to Interstate Pipelines," *Yale Law Journal* (December 1950): 1479.

dominant position in a field, are able to maintain unreasonable price despite the appearance of competition. Under such circumstances the Commission will decide whether it can assume jurisdiction over arbitrary field prices under the present or should report the facts to Congress with the recommendation for such broadening of the act and provision of additional machinery as may appear necessary to close *this gap in effective regulation of the natural gas industry.*[6]

Later the same year, a second FPC decision upheld a field-price order given to a natural-gas producer-transmission company engaged in interstate commerce.[7] Accepted without appeal, the decision brought under federal jurisdiction integrated firms with affiliates that purchased gas prior to interstate movement. Independent producers remained unregulated by virtue of their "arm's-length" transactions. This meant the former's imputed price could be disallowed for pass-through, while the latter's price was automatically an operating expense fully deductible from pipeline revenues prior to calculation of permissible return. For the first time in the history of the natural-gas market, prices were subject to maximum price control, albeit of selected transactions within integrated operations.

A series of cases during and following World War II proved consistent with the *Columbian* and *Billings* decisions, which defined jurisdiction by the arm's-length, continuous-flow criterion.[8] One case, although consistent with the rest, deserves separate analysis because it hinted at regulation of independents, which caused consternation within the industry.

On April 27, 1943, the FPC assumed jurisdiction over gas rates charged to three interstate pipelines by Interstate Natural Gas Company, an interstate pipeline that also gathered and produced gas.[9]

---

[6]*Columbian Fuel Corporation,* 2 FPC 200 at 208 (1940); emphasis added. Commissioner John Scott in his dissenting opinion (at 209–17) also foreshadowed forthcoming debate by favoring regulation of producers on the grounds that Congress intended to close the regulatory gap, and the "sale . . . for resale" clause predominated the later wording in sec. 1(b) to exempt producers and gatherers.

[7]*Billings Gas Company,* 2 FPC 288 (1940).

[8]*Peoples Natural Gas Company* v. *Federal Power Commission,* 127 F.2d 153 (1942); and *Colorado Interstate Gas Company* v. *Federal Power Commission,* 324 U.S. 581 (1945). Eight other cases are listed in Charles Crenshaw, "The Regulation of Natural Gas," *Law and Contemporary Problems* (Summer 1954): 336.

[9]*Interstate Natural Gas Company,* 2 FPC 416 (1943).

Commingling its production with purchases from independent producers, Interstate piped the gas intrastate before it was sold for interstate carriage. The importance of the case was not the decision but its reasoning; the FPC, instead of claiming authority because Interstate was an interstate line selling gas to another interstate pipeline, made the sweeping interpretation that its jurisdiction included the price of all "sales . . . for resale" in interstate commerce. Before the Supreme Court, the commission switched its lower court argument to the firmer ground of *Billings* and other cases, but in upholding FPC jurisdiction, Justice Fred Vinson rekindled uncertainty for independent producers by opining for the court:

> These sales are in interstate commerce. It cannot be doubted that their regulation is predominately a matter of national, as contrasted to local concern. All the gas sold in these transactions is destined for consumption in the States other than Louisiana. Unreasonable charges extracted at this stage of the interstate movement become perpetuated in large part in fixed items of cost which must be covered by rates charged subsequent purchasers of the gas, including the ultimate consumer. It was to avoid such situations that the Natural Gas Act was passed.[10]

Reflecting the interventionist leaning of the so-called New Deal Court, the Supreme Court's reasoning parlayed the act's ambiguity into language suggestive of a wholesale extension of FPC jurisdiction to prices paid to producers—independent and integrated—by interstate pipelines on the controversial grounds of congressional intent and the public interest.

In the same case, appeals court judge Curtis Waller criticized the lower court's reasoning in a dissent that would become a "standard reference" and "rallying point" in the future debate over regulation of the independent sector.[11] "Believing that courts should construe statutes instead of making them," he said, "I am unwilling to participate in writing into the act that which Congress expressly undertook to keep out, even if by so doing a better statute would result."[12]

---

[10]*Interstate Natural Gas Company* v. *FPC*, 331 U.S. 682 at 692–93, rehearing denied, 332 U.S. 785 (1947). For a succinct discussion of the case, see "Federal Price Control of Natural Gas Sold to Interstate Pipelines," p. 1481.

[11]Kenneth Marcus, *The National Government and the Natural Gas Industry*, p. 178.

[12]*Interstate Natural Gas Company* v. *Federal Power Commission*, 156 F.2d 949 at 956 (1946).

Legislative Activity: 1947–50

The drive to amend the NGA in the 1947–50 period produced one of the most intense and illustrative legislative debates and lobbying efforts in U.S. regulatory history, approached only by several later efforts to deregulate wellhead natural-gas prices. It actively involved not only Congress but the FPC and the president, and not only the gas industry but coal interests and consumer representatives. Much was at stake. With an estimated 40 percent of natural-gas production under FPC jurisdiction (that is, affiliated with interstate pipelines and dedicated interstate)[13] and the remaining 60 percent at issue, gas properties priced under original-cost valuation would be able to command only a fraction of their true market value.[14] This represented more than a redistribution of wealth from southwestern producers and royalty owners to northern, eastern, and western consumers; it represented uncertainty over maintaining and attracting reserve dedications to supply a rapidly expanding interstate market.

With FPC regulation, the incentive for pipeline firms with affiliated gas properties went from expanding their reserve base to acquiring market value for their present properties. This meant escaping regulation by selling proven reserves for market value and buying gas as needed at arm's length.[15] Yet independent producers were wary about entering into long-term contracts with interstate carriers, lest a drift in FPC policy, already foreshadowed, should place them under original-cost regulation also. This not only created gas-acquisition problems for existing interstate lines, it threatened new pipeline projects that required long-term throughput agreements to receive FPC certification. Hence, the existence of regulation and the potential for expanded regulation meant that instead of supplying interstate markets where demand was greatest, gas would remain undiscovered or untapped in located reservoirs, be flared, or go toward inferior intrastate uses.

In addition to interstate gas producers, pipelines, and consumers, a fourth group vitally affected by regulation were coal interests—coal producers, coal-carrying railroads, and coal marketers. Natural

[13]"Comments," *University of Chicago Law Review* (Spring 1950): 483.

[14]With lease-acquisition cost reflecting only a *chance* of underlying gas reserves, market value of such property became far greater once gas was located. Original-cost valuation failed to account for the risk of nondiscovery. For further discussion, see this chapter, pp. 392–93, 411–14.

[15]See this chapter, pp. 390–91.

gas was a cleaner, less expensive fuel, which had displaced coal in commercial markets and was in the process of capturing many industrial markets as well. To maintain their dwindling industrial market, coal interests turned to the political process, which offered opportunities to inflate the price of gas, reduce interstate supplies, and restrict pipeline expansion.

Finally, there were governmental parties to the debate. The FPC was interested in maintaining jurisdiction over the industry if not expanding its calling. State authorities were interested in reducing gas "wastage" at the wellhead. Republicans and Democrats, meantime, were attempting to reconcile party philosophies to the wishes of the electorate. Against this backdrop, the stage was set for the major events to follow.

In 1947, four identical bills, authored by the Independent Natural Gas Association and other industry sources, were introduced in Congress to reword section 1(b) of the NGA to unambiguously exempt independent producers from the long arm of the FPC. Amendments were also proposed to replace original-cost valuation of pipeline production with a passthrough cost based on the market price of gas and to deregulate gas at the distribution level. This would leave only wholesale transactions between interstate pipelines and gas distributors under FPC authority.[16]

Hearings followed. Favoring the bill were natural-gas and oil-industry groups and individuals and legislators from gas-producing states; against the bill were state and federal public-utility regulators and representatives from established urban gas markets in the North and the Northeast.[17] Supporting a weakened version of the bill were coal interests, who desired unregulated production to keep gas prices high and continued regulation of gas utilities to check expansion.[18] Regulation of distributors was also supported by fuel-oil and

---

[16]Kenneth Marcus, *The National Government and the Natural Gas Industry*, pp. 191–92.

[17]The consumer groups were the Committee on Electric and Gas Rates, the National Institute of Municipal Law Officers, and the U.S. Conference of Mayors. These groups represented *established* gas markets more than "waiting-list" areas. On this distinction, see this chapter, pp. 374–75.

[18]The coal lobby included the National Coal Association, the Eastern States Retail Solid Fuel Conference, the Railway Labor Executives' Association, the Chesapeake and Ohio Railroad, and the Central Railroad Company of New Jersey. Kenneth Marcus, *The National Government and the Natural Gas Industry*, p. 227.

gas wholesalers, represented by the Eastern Gas and Fuel Associates, who desired to continue to operate in a cost-plus environment.

During House and Senate debate, the FPC attempted to forestall passage of the Rizley-Moore bill. On April 10, 1947, the commission requested that legislative activity be postponed until its investigation of the natural-gas industry (Docket G-580) was complete.[19] Two commission decisions a month later rejected regulation of arm's-length transactions, even where an interstate pipeline, Tennessee Gas Transmission, owned 81 percent of the production company that supplied it.[20] On August 7, Order 139 expressed the agency's interpretation that the NGA precluded regulation of independent producers (Commissioner Claude Draper dissenting). All of these actions had a common purpose as noted by Kenneth Marcus:

> By proposed rules, by early release of staff reports, by actual Commission decisions, by public statements and testimony before the respective congressional committees, the Commission tried to convince the Congress, the natural gas industry, the consumer groups, and the general public that it had no desire or intention to regulate any aspect of the activities of independent producers and gatherers.... These various manifestations of self-abnegation were designed to defeat the various proposals to amend the Natural Gas Act.[21]

In the case of Commissioners Harrington, Wimberly, and Nelson Smith, these actions would prove to be consistent applications of nonregulatory philosophy, not a strategic attempt to get the industry to lower its guard. But of Commissioner Leland Olds, judging from his lifelong beliefs and subsequent decisions, the same cannot be said.[22]

Unconvinced by FPC actions, proponents of the bill did not relax. On July 11, a surprisingly easy victory was won in the House with

---

[19]Gerald Nash, *United States Oil Policy* (Westport, Conn.: Greenwood Press, 1968, 1976), p. 217.

[20]*Fin-Ker Oil and Gas Case*, 6 FPC 92 (May 22, 1947); and *Tennessee Gas Transmission Case*, 6 FPC 98 (May 28, 1947).

[21]Kenneth Marcus, *The National Government and the Natural Gas Industry*, pp. 274–75.

[22]M. Elizabeth Sanders also explained Olds's uncharacteristic support of pro-industry positions as an attempt to quell growing Senate unpopularity. Sanders, *The Regulation of Natural Gas* (Philadelphia: Temple University Press, 1981), p. 84.

373

support from consumer-state Republicans, producer-state Democrats, and northern lawmakers of both parties influenced by supply problems experienced the preceding winter.[23] Senate passage, however, would not be forthcoming. Two attempts to report the bill out of committee failed, reflecting strong Democratic opposition.

With the Rizley-Moore bill dead for the eightieth legislative session, the attention of the gas industry turned to a commission vacancy created May 5, 1947, by the resignation of Richard Sachse. The five-member agency, with a shift in Olds's stance in 1948, was deadlocked between pro-regulation Olds and Draper and anti-regulation Smith and Wimberly, which made the new member pivotal.[24] Despite House rejection, Thomas Buchanan, a proponent of regulation, was given an interim appointment by President Truman, a setback that redoubled industry efforts to amend the NGA.

New bills, which were narrower versions of the ill-fated Rizley-Moore bill of the previous session, were introduced in the House and Senate in 1949. Independent producers were to be exempt from FPC purview as before, but no mention was made of end-use deregulation or market value replacing original-cost valuation for pipeline production affiliates.[25] It was now independent gas producers and integrated gas companies for themselves, a split necessitated by political realities. Along the voting lines of the Rizley-Moore bill, the House approved the Harris bill on August 5 despite an announcement by Truman four days earlier that he would veto the measure.[26] The scene then shifted to the crucial Senate where the issue became intensely political. Whereas a year before the debate over price versus supply had scholarly overtones, the second time around the issue was superficially packaged as producer versus consumer and big versus little. Major consuming areas favored lower fuel bills in the short term and discounted the longer run threat of curtailments, while markets desiring gas service supported the bill to increase

[23]Ibid., p. 83; and Kenneth Marcus, *The National Government and the Natural Gas Industry*, pp. 311–22.

[24]The April 1948 release of Docket no. G-580 ("Natural Gas Investigation") contained two reports: the Olds-Draper report favoring wellhead regulation and the Smith-Wimberly report favoring exemption.

[25]Kenneth Marcus, *The National Government and the Natural Gas Industry*, pp. 393–94.

[26]Ibid., p. 439.

their chances of timely hookups.[27] This support, combined with unanimous backing from producing-state senators, including such influential Democrats as Subcommittee on Interstate and Foreign Commerce chairman Lyndon Johnson (D-Tex.), and fear of federal regulation on the part of neutral ("observant") Republicans, who were well represented in the Senate, led to approval of the Harris-Kerr bill on March 29, 1950.[28] It now remained to be seen whether President Truman would make good on his veto threat of seven months before.

Congressional approval of the Harris-Kerr bill came on top of, and indeed was aided by, the defeat of Leland Olds for a third commission term on October 19, 1949. Olds's demise resulted not only from his anti-industry positions but from a full airing of his earlier socialist leanings at a time when the seeds of McCarthyism had been planted. Subsequent Truman appointees, however, would retain the commission's regulatory favor, which made legislative victory, now in the president's hands, of utmost importance to independent producers and, to a lesser extent, interstate pipelines.

Truman's actions to date put him on the side of an activist FPC, and his decision on the bill would be no different. In the six weeks between congressional approval and his decision, an outpouring of veto support came from gas utility companies in major consuming areas, press editorials in major urban markets, the FPC (by a three-to-two preference), members of Congress, and several major interstate pipelines.[29] With November elections on the horizon and an image of the "little man's friend" to preserve for himself and the Democratic party, Truman returned H.R. 1758 unsigned on April 15, after which no attempt was made to override the veto. Citing a "record of accomplishment under the present law," Truman hesitated to amend the NGA because of an alleged lack of seller competition to "hol[d] prices to reasonable levels" and his "confidence" that FPC pricing decisions would maintain incentives for production and

---

[27]Interestingly, senators from areas desiring gas service who voted for the Rizley-Moore bill voted against the Kerr bill once the gas mains were in service to their areas. M. Elizabeth Sanders, *The Regulation of Natural Gas*, p. 92.

[28]See the discussion of voting patterns in ibid., pp. 88–93, and Kenneth Marcus, *The National Government and the Natural Gas Industry*, pp. 541–56.

[29]Ibid., pp. 576–82.

interstate dedications of natural gas.[30] In language that would continue to mark the issue of natural-gas regulation (and decades later
crude-oil price controls), Truman spoke of "large windfall profits
to gas producers, at the expense of consumers, with no benefit . . .
of added exploration and production."[31] Future events under an
unamended NGA would prove Truman's self-serving anticipa-
tions wrong.

With the veto, an air of activism came over the FPC. The changed
tenor was manifested in Order 154 on July 13, 1950, which rescinded
Order 139 of three years before.[32] The earlier order favoring blanket
exemption for independent producers was replaced by a veiled
threat of regulation in the form of open-ended investigations.[33] Comprehensive regulation of field prices of natural gas sold interstate
was at hand.

The 1954 *Phillips* Decision: Birth of Comprehensive Regulation

The case that decided the jurisdictional question under the NGA,
and ended more than a decade of ambiguity, involved Phillips Petroleum, the nation's largest independent natural-gas producer. Phillips
supplied interstate pipelines equally from its own production and
outside purchases. Although integrated into refining and gas processing, Phillips did not own or operate an interstate natural-gas
pipeline.

The original dispute concerned whether a certificate of convenience and necessity should be given to the Michigan-Wisconsin
Pipe Line Company. Phillips was brought into the case on October 11,
1946, by the Detroit City Council because the firm supplied gas to
the defendant. In early 1947, the FPC ruled that an inquiry was
merited to determine whether Phillips was a natural-gas company
under the NGA. After several lengthy delays, in April and May 1951
hearings were held at which over 10,000 pages of testimony were

[30]*96 Cong. Rec.* 5304 (1950).

[31]Reprinted in Kenneth Marcus, *The National Government and the Natural Gas Industry*,
appendix F, p. 1053.

[32]Joining Olds for the majority were Draper and recent Truman appointee, Mon
Wallgren.

[33]"Where . . . the sales of individual producers or gatherers have a material effect
on interstate commerce and the rates therefore appear excessive, appropriate investigations will be undertaken." Order 154, 15 *Fed. Reg.* 4633 (July 20, 1950).

presented. On July 18, 1951, the commission ruled, Commissioner Buchanan dissenting, that Phillips was not a natural-gas company under the act, since its sales were local in nature and ended before the interstate journey began. Regulation of producer prices, the majority added, could be achieved by approving rates before issuing certificates of convenience and necessity to applicant pipelines.

In a sharp thirty-two-page dissent, Buchanan demonstrated the thin ground the FPC stood on by forgoing jurisdictional expansion. By neglecting the 1943 *Interstate* decision, he charged, the commission "embraced the same abnegation of its authority which pervaded the adoption of Order no. 139."[34] Phillips's sales, he argued, were subsequent to production and gathering and thereby were part of the interstate flow of natural gas.[35]

The decision, combined with Dwight D. Eisenhower's election in 1952, the predominantly Republican eighty-third Congress, and the replacement of Commissioner Buchanan with the more conservative Seaborn Digby on May 15, 1953, painted a bright picture for the industry, the majority of which favored state but not federal regulation. The *Oil & Gas Journal* spoke of a "new era" for the FPC and the gas industry.[36] With confidence that the courts would uphold the conservative FPC, it seemed that, for all practical purposes, the veto of April 15, 1950, had been overturned. The euphoria of the moment, however, was short-lived. Powerful interests within the industry—namely gas distributors and some interstate gas pipelines—favored regulation of independent producers and appealed the case.[37] On May 2, 1953, the Court of Appeals for the District of Columbia reversed the FPC on grounds similar to Buchanan's dissent. The sale of natural gas by Phillips, two of the three judges decided, was an interstate "sale . . . for resale," making Phillips a natural-gas company pursuant to the NGA.[38] The independent producing industry was further stunned on November 30, 1953, when the Supreme Court denied a writ of certiorari. A request for rehearing, strengthened by six states that joined the original

---

[34]*Phillips Petroleum Company*, 10 FPC 246 at 308 (1951).

[35]In Buchanan's words, "Gathering may be an incident of sale, but sale, an incident of gathering, as the majority holds, never."

[36]*Oil & Gas Journal,* May 4, 1953, p. 63. Cited hereafter as *OGJ.*

[37]Gerald Nash, *United States Oil Policy,* p. 233.

[38]*State of Wisconsin* v. *Federal Power Commission*, 205 F.2d 706 (1953).

petitioners, led to a grant of certiorari on January 18, 1954. On June 7 of the same year, the landmark verdict was announced: "The statutory language, the pertinent legislative history, and the past decisions of the Court," Justice Vinson argued for the majority, "give the Commission jurisdiction over the rates of all wholesales of natural gas in interstate commerce, whether by a pipeline company or not and whether occurring before, during, or after transmission by an interstate pipeline company." Congress, Vinson continued, intended to "plug the 'gap' in regulation . . . [for] . . . protection of consumers against exploitation," noting that legislative attempts to amend the NGA to "weaken this protection . . . have repeatedly failed." He concluded, "We refuse to achieve the same result by a strained interpretation of the existing statutory language."[39] Production of interstate gas was now subject to the "just and reasonable" criterion of the NGA.

A reinterpretation of the 1954 decision is needed to better understand the fourteen-year struggle to define jurisdiction under the NGA. The act's original language was contradictory, which left the jurisdictional question open to opposite interpretations. Whether a sale of natural gas to an interstate carrier at the wellhead, terminus of a gathering line, or processing station is part of the production phase and thus *local*, or part of the transmission phase and thus *interstate*, is inherently debatable. If one falls back on congressional intent, it would seem that Congress wrote a law outwardly designed to protect consumers by closing a regulatory loophole but in so doing opened another loophole, one stage back, that not only threatened the practical effectiveness of the law but involved an area explicitly exempted from regulation. How does one square the circle? Without amendatory legislation, the guiding light of a decision must be the interpreter's personal biases. It was not by coincidence or a mere aside that the landmark *Phillips* opinion concluded on a utilitarian note. Further regulation was constitutional not because the NGA unambiguously allowed it but because the Court felt it was needed to achieve the act's purpose of protecting consumers. Ambiguity thus led to a decision based on the tenet that further government intervention was good.

---

[39]*Phillips Petroleum Co.* v. *Wisconsin*, 347 U.S. 672 at 677, 682, 685 (1954).

In the same year as *Phillips*, a small victory for the gas-producer industry was won when the FPC ruled that interstate pipelines could receive a fair field price for their own production instead of a depreciated-cost price.[40] The four-to-one decision was based on the concern that original-cost valuation of pipeline properties vastly understated true worth and was not in the public interest because pipeline production was discouraged, supply availability was threatened, and conservation was lessened.[41] Also, the commission noted, the proposed gas price for Panhandle Eastern would not greatly affect the city-gate price. The decision meant that although the door to comprehensive regulation was opened by the Supreme Court, the FPC would regulate on equal terms all producers selling interstate, independent or not.

Appealed by the city of Detroit, the FPC decision was reversed on December 15, 1955, as in conflict with the "just and reasonable" price criterion of the NGA.[42] The verdict, underscoring the judicial system's bias toward short-run consumer goals at the expense of producer needs, not to mention longer run consumer ends, made another try at amendatory legislation imperative.

Legislative Activity: 1955–56

Soon after *Phillips*, the FPC, upon judicial instruction, ordered gas producers with interstate sales to file schedules and apply for certification. Interpretative relief would not be forthcoming. Reconsideration of the case by the Supreme Court was denied on October 14, 1954, which left only the legislative option. Independent spokesmen, such as Phillips chairman Kenneth Adams, began groundwork

---

[40]Opinion 269, 13 FPC 53 (1954).

[41]Said the commission, "We cannot but be struck by the fact that no new major pipeline which has been certificated since the Commission's pricing practice was first established—including some of the largest systems serving enormous new markets—produces any significant portion of its total supply" (p. 75). Elsewhere the opinion stated, "[Current policy] does not promote that conservation in both the production and the use of natural gas which is in the natural interest" (p. 74). Quoted in Kenneth Marcus, *The National Government and the Natural Gas Industry*, pp. 661–62.

[42]Argued the court, "In view of the primary orientation of the act toward the maintenance of low prices for the consumer, we do not preclude the possibility that a rate increase might be unlawful even though no lower rate could encourage gas production by pipeline companies." *City of Detroit* v. *Federal Power Commission*, 230 F.2d 810 at 818 (1955).

by calling for a united industry effort to amend the NGA.[43] Such unity was sorely lacking. Gas distributors, indeed, were leading advocates of wellhead regulation, and many interstate pipelines preferred a regulated weighted average cost of gas, known as a WACOG, to higher market prices.

Failing to attract broad industry support, gas-producing interests created the General Gas Committee in October 1954 and the Natural Gas and Oil Resources Committee the next month. The latter, headed by Conoco president L. F. McCollum, mounted a nationwide grass-roots educational campaign to sway the public toward deregulation. Congress waited for the opportune moment, which occurred several days after a deregulation recommendation was issued by President Eisenhower's Advisory Committee on Energy Supplies and Resources Policy. On March 2, 1955, Oren Harris (D-Ark.) introduced H.R. 4560; on April 28, William Fulbright (D-Ark.) introduced S. 1853. Neither bill was strictly deregulatory; although pipelines were to receive a fair field price for self-production and independents were exempted from cost-based public-utility control, the FPC was pragmatically allowed to determine the "reasonable market price" pipelines paid for gas and regulate "malignant" escalator clauses.[44]

During House hearings in March and April and Senate hearings in May and June 1955, the positions of proponents and opponents of partial deregulation were reminiscent of those on the Harris-Kerr bill debate five years before. One difference was the increased presence of interstate gas pipelines that were openly courted by wellhead interests. Leading the opposition were 28 gas utility companies and over 250 municipal groups from areas served by natural gas.[45] Both complained about "escalator clauses" in producer contracts that put pipelines and utilities in the position of passing on higher rates, which, allegedly, was becoming harder to do given fuel-oil and coal substitution. For consumers, field-price escalations

---

[43]This discussion is taken from Kenneth Marcus, *The National Government and the Natural Gas Industry*, chap. 9. See also ibid., pp. 668–69.

[44]Most-favored-nation and other "escalation clauses" increased existing contract prices when higher priced contracts were made in the same area. See Rayburn Foster, "Natural-Gas Regulation from the Producers' Standpoint," *Georgetown Law Journal* (June 1956): 668–71.

[45]For a list of these groups and companies, see Kenneth Marcus, *The National Government and the Natural Gas Industry*, pp. 713–18.

meant higher prices; for utilities, they potentially represented a profit squeeze and loss of market share.

Waiting-list areas desiring gas service and growth markets seeking expanded service, in contrast, supported the bill. They preferred certain supply at market prices to uncertain supply at below-market prices.[46] Coal interests opposed NGA reform for the same reason prospective consumers wanted it—expanded gas service to further displace their fuel. Fuel-oil interests were willing to take their chances against unregulated gas, although support for the bill hinged in part on the gas industry's dropping its drive to restrict imports of residual oil.[47] Natural-gas producers and oil producers, the latter of whom produced gas, too, and feared an expansion of regulation to them, were united behind the two similar bills.[48]

On July 28, the House narrowly approved H.R. 6645. Senate approval followed on February 6, 1956, after virtually identical debate except for one development that changed the complexion of the issue completely. Three days before passage, Sen. Francis Case (R-S.D.) emotionally told the chamber that a $2,500 gift with industry origins had been received in connection with his support of S. 1853. To opponents of the bill, particularly members of the press, this was a ringing confirmation of all that was wrong with a society in which monied interests could tempt the democratic process toward their ends. As such sentiment unfolded, the quasi-deregulatory bill, which awaited presidential approval, became more political than ever. In a move interpreted as "an opening move in the President's campaign to win reelection," President Eisenhower vetoed the bill on February 17, 1956, on grounds smacking of politics.[49] Although he was "in accord with the basic objective of H.R. 6645," the veto was necessary because behind the bill were "efforts . . . so arrogant and so much in defiance of acceptable standards of propriety as to risk creating doubt among the American people concerning the integrity of government processes."[50] No attempt was made to override the veto.

[46]M. Elizabeth Sanders, *The Regulation of Natural Gas*, p. 98.

[47]Kenneth Marcus, *The National Government and the Natural Gas Industry*, pp. 762–63; and *National Petroleum News*, January 1955, p. 62. Cited hereafter as *NPN*.

[48]For a list of individuals, firms, and groups testifying in favor of the bill, see Kenneth Marcus, *The National Government and the Natural Gas Industry*, pp. 707–12.

[49]Ibid., p. 900.

[50]Ibid., p. 899. Privately, Eisenhower remarked that he "hated to have any part of the Administration program open to the charge that business could get this bill by throwing sufficient money around" and that he was "sensitive to the tendency of

The Eisenhower veto invites rigorous censure. Regardless of the ethical or legal nature of the Case transaction—gift or bribe, legal or illegal—the merits of the issue, painstakingly presented by both sides, were thrown aside. (In fact, the payment was made *after* Case's position on the bill was known, making the money a political gift rather than a bribe.) That a single isolated act and the several individuals involved—including John Neff, a registered lobbyist of the Superior Oil Company in the employ of Superior president Howard Keck—were showcased to discredit the entire quasi-deregulatory effort can itself be said to reflect "defiance of acceptable standards" and "doubt . . . concerning the integrity of governmental processes."[51] If Keck was "buying" the right for his company to sell natural gas on voluntary terms, Eisenhower was buying a political future for himself and his party by appeasing major urban centers. Who was "pathetic and despicable,"[52] Keck or the man who admitted he was performing an act "contrary not only to the national interest but especially to the interests of consumers"? The malaise was deeper than the $2,500 payment; the problem was that important economic transactions could be taken out of the marketplace and decided by politicians on emotional and self-serving grounds.

Subsequent attempts to soften wellhead regulation of natural gas would fall short of previous unsuccessful attempts. In the next session of Congress, the Harris-O'Hara bill (H.R. 8525), a weakened version of Harris-Fulbright that allowed direct regulation of field

---

labeling Republicans as the party of big business." Quoted in William Barber, "The Eisenhower Energy Policy: Reluctant Intervention," in *Energy Policy in Perspective*, ed. Craufurd Goodwin (Washington, D.C.: Brookings Institution, 1981), p. 264. L. F. McCollum, a leading industry spokesman for the bill, recalled the sudden turn of events and his last-ditch effort to avoid a veto:

> I first heard the news [of the Case incident and Eisenhower's reaction] and promptly took a plane back to Washington. I found President Eisenhower very apologetic in his attitude toward continuing to support the decontrol bill. He felt there were too many—though perhaps unfounded—accusations going around and that the best thing would be to let this bill be defeated and propose another later. I felt keenly that the chances of getting another bill would be absolutely impossible. He didn't agree with this. I was right—the opportunity came and went!

Letter from McCollum to the author, April 29, 1983.

[51] See Henry Hazlitt, "That Gas Bill Veto," *Newsweek*, March 12, 1956, p. 88.

[52] Michael Straight, "Down Payment on a Purchase," *New Republic*, March 12, 1956, p. 10.

prices on an arm's-length, fair-field basis, rather than on a public-utility, cost-of-service basis, never reached a vote. A year later in 1958, Congressman Harris again introduced a similar bill, H.R. 366, which failed to be reported out of committee. By 1960, not even partial deregulation was in the political mainstream. Reform of the NGA had its chance and lost in a most unpredictable way. Even with passage, price control by indirection would nonetheless have remained, the use of which would have depended on the makeup of the FPC. But without reform, forthcoming stringent regulation would have consequences that would make Eisenhower's veto warning right—and his veto action wrong.

Comprehensive Price Regulation under the NGA

With gas politics settled, the task before the FPC was to apply public-utility regulations to thousands of independent producers in Texas, Oklahoma, Louisiana, Kansas, New Mexico, and other gas-exporting states. This unprecedented experience would be more difficult, and its results more controversial, than its judicial and legislative architects had anticipated.

Regulation of Individual Producers: 1954–60 (Phase I)

Quick action to protect consumers against "exploitation" followed the *Phillips* verdict of June 7, 1954, in which independent natural-gas producers and gatherers (as opposed to production affiliates of interstate pipelines already under NGA regulation) were defined as natural-gas companies under the NGA.[53] Without notice or hearing, FPC Order 174 on July 16 brought any firm "engaged in the production or gathering of natural gas and who transports natural gas in interstate commerce or sells natural gas in interstate commerce for resale" under public-utility regulation retroactive to the day of the Supreme Court decision.[54] By October 1, such firms were to file for a certificate of public convenience and necessity, file rate schedules, and comply with reporting requirements and the Uniform System of Accounts.[55] Whereas approximately 157 firms previously reported

[53]347 U.S. 672 at 685 (1954).

[54]19 *Fed. Reg.* 4534 (July 22, 1954).

[55] Order 174-A, issued August 12, extended the filing deadline to December 1. 19 *Fed. Reg.* 5081 (1954).

to the FPC, now more than 4,000 firms were under the commission's jurisdiction.[56]

The task was to regulate each producer on a traditional public-utility cost-of-service basis, despite the fact that important differences abounded between gas producers and franchised utilities. Despite FPC attempts to substitute other criteria for regulation, the courts mandated cost of service as the "anchor . . . by which to hold the terms 'just and reasonable' to some recognizable meaning."[57] After Congress denied a $300,000 supplemental allocation to expand operations, reflecting an undercurrent of anti-regulatory sentiment, the FPC began Phase I of natural-gas regulation, an application of public-utility control neither sought nor relished by the agency.[58]

Certification Issues. Pursuant to Order 174, all natural-gas sales in interstate commerce—at the wellhead, gathering line, or processing plant—required certification from the FPC. Intrastate gas—gas produced, transmitted, and distributed in home states—remained free of federal control. The first demonstration of the agency's newfound authority occurred several weeks after the order when a proposed pipeline was denied certification because several of its field suppliers were not licensed.[59] The FPC, noticed the *Oil & Gas Journal*, "flexed its new muscles."[60] By early 1955, over 5,600 applications for certification had been made, none of which would receive formal commission approval until several years later.[61] During the delay, firms were allowed to operate as before unless submitted rate schedules were found to be excessive.

---

[56]Clark Hawkins, *The Field Price Regulation of Natural Gas* (Tallahassee: Florida State University Press, 1969), p. 37.

[57]*City of Detroit* v. *Federal Power Commission*, 230 F.2d 810 (D.C. Cir. 1955).

[58]In addition to supporting Phillips's position before the Supreme Court in 1953–54, the commission called for legislative relief in each annual report from 1955 through 1960. See *OGJ*, September 7, 1953, p. 67; and William Ross, "The Area Rate Proceedings: An Unsettled Experiment in Public Control of Natural Gas Prices," *Southwestern Law Journal* (June 1964): 166.

[59]Opinion 276, 13 FPC 380 (1954).

[60]*OGJ*, August 9, 1954, p. 70.

[61]Kenneth Marcus, *The National Government and the Natural Gas Industry*, p. 722. For an in-depth discussion of the filing requirements for certification, see Lewis Mosburg, "Regulation of the Independent Producer by the Federal Power Commission," *Oklahoma Law Review* (August 1963): 12–19.

Outside of price, the major controversy surrounding certification concerned abandonment of service. The first major abandonment case concerned the activation of an "escape clause" designed to void long-term contracts should the FPC claim jurisdiction over the sales of an independent producer. The intent was to escape potentially harsh price regulation by rededicating supply to the unregulated intrastate market. Following *Phillips*, the Huber Corporation acted on an escape clause and was immediately enjoined by the commission under authority of section 7(b) of the NGA.[62] The court of appeals sided with the FPC on grounds that the clause frustrated the intent of *Phillips* and was not in the public interest.[63]

Also favoring the historic purchaser was the commission's position against allowing depleted fields to be abandoned, unless sufficiently convinced by the producer that the "public interest" would not be "disserved."[64] When the commission was unconvinced, the buyer could continue to receive gas at a price deemed uneconomical by the seller.

The ability of gas to move to its most highly valued uses was hindered by two more certification and abandonment issues in the 1954–60 era. A contract clause allowing a producer to abandon a buyer if a higher price presented by a third party was not met was stricken by the FPC.[65] In a similar vein, the commission rejected limited certifications timed to expire with long-term contracts to avoid abandonment proceedings. Between 1956 and 1960, Sunray

[62]"No natural gas company shall abandon all or any portion of its facilities subject to the jurisdiction of the Commission, or any service rendered by means of such facilities, without the permission and approval of the Commission." Public Law 688, 52 Stat. 824 (1938).

[63]"We think the sense of the *Phillips* decision is altogether opposed to permitting the Commission's control over sales to be nullified by the independent producer's abandonment of those sales at will. The money losses to distribution lines and to ultimate consumers would be stupendous in actual equipment etc. but a far greater loss would be the deprivation of the vital gas itself to the public." *J. M. Huber Corp.* v. *FPC*, 236 F.2d 500 at 558 (3d Cir. 1956).

[64]Carroll Gilliam, "Wellhead Regulation under the Natural Gas Act and the Natural Gas Policy Act," in American Gas Association, *Regulation of the Gas Industry*, 4 vols. (New York: Matthew Bender, 1982), vol. 1, p. 20-57.

[65]See Willard Satchell, "Independent Producers under the Natural Gas Act," *George Washington Law Review* (March 1958): 384. This ruling expanded previously discussed Order 174-B.

Table 8.1
PRODUCER CERTIFICATION: 1954–60

Year	Requests	Approved	Pending
1955	11,000	10,836	164
1956	4,442	4,332	274
1957	6,947	6,751	470
1958	7,665	7,653	482
1959	8,769	8,583	668
1960	8,805	8,822	651

SOURCE: FPC, *Annual Report*, various years.

Mid-Continent Oil unsuccessfully sought a limited-duration certificate from the FPC. The Supreme Court ruled that the commission could, but did not have to, tailor the certificate to the contract.[66]

The policies of the FPC were identified by Gene Woodfin as part of the FPC's "unremitting zeal" to break contracts in favor of the pipeline purchaser with the intent to pass through lower prices to consumers.[67] Certification was a powerful supplement to rate regulation because out-of-date, below-market contracts were tied to the life of the well.

In the six years under review, almost all producer certificates were routinely granted without hearings. Franchise rights were not at issue, limited agency resources were available to cover thousands of requests, and rival fuels as intervenors focused attention at the gas-transmission and gas-distribution levels. Table 8.1 summarizes certification activity from 1954 to 1960.

Price Issues. Order 174, embodying the NGA mandate of "just and reasonable" prices, froze field prices of natural gas at their June 7, 1954, level. Contractual escalations were subject to a change-in-rate review and approval by the commission. The first pricing action by the FPC occurred less than a month after the freeze order when

---

[66]*Sunray Mid-Continental Oil Co.* v. *FPC*, 364 U.S. 137 (1960). On the day of the decision, the Court also ruled that certificates were unlimited in duration where not specified by the commission. *Sun Oil Co.* v. *FPC*, 364 U.S. 170 (1960).

[67]Gene Woodfin, "Recent Developments in Federal Power Commission Control of Independent Producers," *10 Oil and Gas Institute* (New York: Matthew Bender, 1959), p. 44.

an escalator clause between Phillips Petroleum and Michigan-Wisconsin Pipe Line was invalidated and a $8.3-million refund to the latter was ordered.[68]

Subsequent FPC orders and court decisions set a pattern of allowing the original rate filing (which gave incentive to firms to build into present prices higher future prices) with subsequent rate hikes subject to a five-month suspension and refund liability beyond the suspension period if the effectuated price was not found "just and reasonable."[69] One exception, hailed by gas distributors and consumer-state utility commissions, was made in 1955 when an original contract rate was modified as a precondition for the producer's receiving certification. This prevented the price from triggering escalator clauses of agreements governing neighboring wells and causing a general price increase—and rate-change requests—"until," said the commission, "experience and time have given us the opportunity to develop more comprehensive criteria governing determination of rates of independent producers."[70]

Only once more would a conditional certification be given to modify a wellhead contract. Direct rate regulation came with each producer's request for a price increase. But the fact remained: broad judgments, not fact or formula, could determine the legality of natural-gas prices under the NGA.

The FPC first attempted to devise a ratemaking methodology for field gas on November 17, 1954, when a rulemaking proceeding solicited comments from gas-industry parties to use in deciding whether cost-based or value-based pricing should be used.[71] The complexity of the issue and conflicting recommendations—producers and pipelines favored contract ("fair field") pricing and distributors and consumer interests favored prohibition of escalator clauses—led to termination of the proceedings without resolution on December 1, 1955.[72]

---

[68]Order 174-B, 19 *Fed. Reg.* 8807 (December 23, 1954). *OGJ*, August 9, 1954, p. 70.

[69]See the discussion in Gene Woodfin, "Recent Developments in Federal Power Commission Control of Independent Producers," pp. 26–34.

[70]Cities Service Gas Co., 12 P.U.R. 3d 3 (1955). This opinion was upheld in *Signal Oil and Gas Co.* v. *FPC* 238 F.2d 771 (3d Cir. 1956), which affirmed the FPC's authority to precondition producer certification on price.

[71]19 *Fed. Reg.* 7696 (November 27, 1954).

[72]20 *Fed. Reg.* 8992 (December 7, 1955). For selected testimony, see "Arguments at the FPC Gas Rate Hearings," *Public Utility Fortnightly* (February 17, 1955): 217–22.

When amendatory legislation to weaken the FPC's power over gas producers was killed by Eisenhower's veto in 1956, the commission displayed newfound activism in dealing with thousands of pending rate increases on file. Between this time and 1960, approximately twenty larger cases were picked for rate proceedings pursuant to sections 4(e) and 5(a) of the NGA.[73] The rest of the disputed rates, which after a five-month suspension automatically became effective, would wait because of the workload of the commission.

Although no set formula was used, cost was the constant determinant of whether to allow rate increases pursuant to *City of Detroit* (1956), in which arm's-length transactions had been rejected as prima facie proof of a just and reasonable price.[74] When cost evidence was not presented, rate hikes were denied. Cost data considered inadequate or unrealistic also led to disallowed increases. Decisions concerning cases where cost evidence was considered imperfect but adequate for passing judgment resulted in mixed decisions depending on particular facts. In one case in which cost support was considered impossible to reasonably formulate, an increase was allowed.[75]

Two decisions would shape future price regulation—the 1959 *CATCO* Supreme Court decision and the 1960 *Phillips* FPC opinion. In August 1956, four independent producers, collectively known as CATCO, contracted to sell gas from various offshore Louisiana properties to Tennessee Gas Transmission for carriage to New England markets. The transaction was important—it involved the most gas ever dedicated to one sale, and the sale was made at the highest price ever paid by Tennessee Gas. Taking a hard line, the commission twice denied certification to the transaction. CATCO and Tennessee were finally offered a temporary permit pending a rate proceeding. Because of the risk of a rollback and refund order, the CATCO producers nixed the deal as well as a later conditional permanent certificate and began looking toward intrastate markets. Fearing this loss of supply, the commission granted an unconditional certificate, which brought court action by the New York Public Service Commission. The lower court overturned the FPC opinion,

---

[73]William Ross, "The Area Rate Proceedings: An Unsettled Experiment in Public Control of Natural Gas Prices," p. 170.

[74]*City of Detroit* v. *FPC*, 230 F.2d 810 (D.C. Cir. 1956), cert. den. 352 U.S. 829.

[75]See Gene Woodfin, "Recent Developments in Federal Power Commission Control of Independent Producers," pp. 48–49.

which was upheld by the Supreme Court in 1959. The high court ruled that the intrastate threat was not an important consideration and that the contract price was unacceptable because

> the price certificated will in effect become the floor for future con-tracts in the area. . . . New price plateaus will thus be created as new contracts and unless controlled will result in "exploitation" at the expense of the consumer, who eventually pays for the increases in his monthly bill.[76]

The Court's language gave a subtle twist to "just and reasonable" to require new contracts to be in line with existing contracts in the general area. It foreshadowed across-the-board restrictive regulation that led one natural-gas attorney to characterize the *CATCO* opinion as "the most significant document in natural gas regulation since the 1938 Act."[77]

The second major case in the opening stages of comprehensive price regulation was a rate determination pursuant to the 1954 *Phillips* case. In elaborate proceedings that took 82 hearing days and over 10,000 pages of testimony, four cost-of-service studies to deter-mine the "just and reasonable" rate were presented by the FPC, Phillips, the Wisconsin Public Utility Commission, and a consortium of utility firms.[78] The futility of trying to make the subjective objective and the tremendous burden it placed on the regulatory process amid a growing backlog led a discouraged commission to reject the firm-by-firm cost-of-service approach altogether. Concluded the FPC in an April 6, 1959, opinion:

> Experience . . . in this case, as well as in many other producer rate cases during the last five years, has shown, beyond any doubt, that the traditional original cost, prudent investment rate base method of regulating utilities is not a sensible, or even workable method of fixing the rates of independent producers of natural gas. The fact that, in this case, we can, by making numerous arbitrary allocations and estimates, arrive at a calculated unit cost of gas does not prove to anyone's satisfaction, including ours, that we have thus solved the problem of fixing prices. . . . While the examiners felt that the

---

[76]*Atlantic Refining Company* v. *Public Service Commission*, 360 U.S. 378 at 390 (1959).

[77]Nicholas Johnson, "Producer Rate Regulation in Natural Gas Certification Pro-ceedings: CATCO in Context," *Columbia Law Review* (April 1962): 788.

[78]An examination of the four approaches is contained in Clark Hawkins, *The Field Price Regulation of Natural Gas*, pp. 48–74.

traditional method of rate regulation could ultimately be successfully used to regulate producers' rates, we are convinced that such a method is unworkable, and will produce fallacious results.[79]

This marked the end of Phase I regulation of individual firms and the beginning of Phase II "area price" regulation.

Phase I in Review. The initial phase of producer regulation was an unmitigated failure. Advocates of regulation questioned whether field prices were constrained at all and, if so, at what cost. To them, the commission was a rubber-stamp agency that, in Senator Paul Douglas's words, was "the servant of the industry it was supposed to regulate."[80] Initial rate schedules were almost universally allowed with later increase requests becoming effective because of the physical impossibility of case-by-case review. The most the commission did to lower prices from market (contract) levels was to suspend proposed increases for the maximum five months and order refunds after this time in the select cases where prices were found unreasonable. And even in these cases, the amount of effective price regulation could have been overstated. With initial contracts uncontested by virtue of arm's-length agreements, a recognized strategy was to inflate the base price to cover later disputes.[81] Given the alternative of unregulated intrastate market sales, producers generally had the ability to alter contracts to reflect regulatory risk.[82] Thus, regulation worked against lower prices for consumers. Indeed, it may have had the opposite effect of raising prices.

Circumvention also prevented regulation from holding prices below market levels. At least three escapes were possible. One was to divert supply to the unregulated intrastate market. A second was to withhold undedicated supply from both the intrastate and the interstate market (given the saturation of the former and uncertainty of the latter) in hopes of higher future prices. A third was to replace wellhead sales with producing-property transactions. The sale of

---

[79]Opinion 338, *Phillips Petroleum Co.*, 24 FPC 537 (1960).

[80]Quoted in Kenneth Marcus, *The National Government and the Natural Gas Industry*, p. 734.

[81]Gene Woodfin, "Recent Developments in Federal Power Commission Control of Independent Producers," p. 31. Contract provisions were also made to mitigate the commission's strict abandonment policy, which gave benefits to gas sellers at the expense of the purchaser.

[82]Nonjurisdictional sales were increasing at this early date because of interstate regulation. Ibid., p. 41.

the large Rayne field to Texas Eastern Transmission Company, for example, gave producers a market price for their reserves (as well as a capital gains tax advantage), while giving the pipeline coveted supply and a higher cost basis that was eligible for passthrough.[83]

To critics of regulation, not only was the entire exercise of price regulation ineffectual, it was dearly paid for by all concerned. Regulatory uncertainty reduced capital-market access by the industry and chilled interstate dedications of new gas packages, which meant reduced alternatives and supply for consumers. In early 1955, warnings were heard from banks and insurance companies, traditionally large sources of credit for producers and pipelines, that further commitments could cease because of the unsettled state of regulation.[84] New supply dedications to the interstate market virtually ceased after the 1954 *Phillips* decision and only slowly reappeared.[85] Diversion of gas supplies to intrastate markets prevented supply from going to its most highly valued (interstate) uses and artificially promoted industrial expansion in gas-producing states. Paul Endacott, president of Phillips Petroleum, explained:

> There's little regulation of the producers by the FPC, mostly denial. Today it's worth accepting at least a couple of cents a thousand cubic feet less to sell gas intrastate in preference to . . . interstate. . . . That's little to pay for the assurance that your selling prices will remain firm over the contract period.

Noting the irony of regulation, he continued:

> Each of several chemical plants in Texas keeps off the interstate market enough gas to supply all the householders in a city like Milwaukee. People who've been fighting about "high" gas prices to producers are simply precipitating further relocation of industry. This is absolutely the reverse of their intention.[86]

[83]Richard Smith, "The Unnatural Problems of Natural Gas," *Fortune*, September 1959, p. 125.

[84]*OGJ*, January 24, 1955, p. 64.

[85]"By far the greatest impact of *Phillips* upon the pipelines has been the systematic withholding of uncommitted reserves which would otherwise have been available to support new projects or to augment existing pipeline supplies. . . . Virtually overnight, [Midwestern Gas Transmission Co.'s] gas supply had vanished. . . . It is significant that nearly all major post *Phillips* projects have been based upon foreign gas supplies, three of them Canadian, and the other Mexican." Raymond Shibley and George Mickum, "The Impact of Phillips upon the Interstate Pipelines—The Riddle in the Middle," *Georgetown Law Journal* (June 1956): 633–34.

[86]Quoted in Richard Smith, "The Unnatural Problems of Natural Gas," pp. 124–25.

Costs eligible for passthrough to consumers were increased to comply with regulatory requirements.[87] Consumers as taxpayers paid the mounting expenses of the FPC's undertaking detailed proceedings in the late 1950s. Because these items raised effective gas costs, it can be questioned whether a consumer honeymoon existed during the first era of price control.

The mirage of the "just and reasonable" price was discovered the hard way by the FPC. Traditional cost-based public-utility pricing was particularly ill suited for gas production in which the risk of nondiscovery was not represented in the well's financial history. Furthermore, costs varied from well to well—as the result of different capital costs, lease acquisition costs, and prospecting and drilling costs—which provided a myriad of prices for an identical good that were anything but "just" even if they were "reasonable."

Another serious problem with individualized cost-of-service price determination, emphasized by economists Alfred Kahn and M. A. Adelman, who both entered the debate to give expert testimony, was the presence of *joint costs* since gas was almost always produced with crude oil or gas liquids. The problem, however, was more than a "distinct regulatory problem" because these other extractions were not regulated along with natural gas.[88] By-product costs cannot be allocated precisely (outside of hypothetical situations of perfect information) to find true money cost–based prices for each individual product.[89] Placing all well output under public-utility regulation would address monetary cost-revenue problems as a whole but

---

[87]By 1961, these costs were placed at $100 million. Lloyd Thanhouser, "Paradise Lost for Natural Gas," *Business Lawyer* (April 1961): 638. In the first year of regulation, Phillips Petroleum reported that 250,000 pages were prepared in conjunction with regulatory matters, which occupied twenty-five full-time employees. Harry Fair, "The Natural Gas Dilemma—How, What, and Why?" *35 Proceedings* (New York: American Petroleum Institute, 1955), p. 114.

[88]Stephen Breyer and Paul MacAvoy, *Energy Regulation by the Federal Power Commission* (Washington, D.C.: Brookings Institution, 1974), p. 67.

[89]Alfred Kahn estimated that from "three-fourths to four-fifths of total operating expenses and investment costs cannot be assigned directly to a single product." Kahn, "Economic Issues in Regulating the Field Price of Natural Gas," *American Economic Review* (May 1960): 511. Commented one attorney close to cost-based litigation, "Possible methods of allocating joint costs run into hundreds." Dale Doty, "Current Problems in the Regulation of Independent Producers of Natural Gas by the Federal Power Commission," *Oklahoma Law Review* (November 1959): 466.

would not simplify relative cost-revenue matchups for assigning cost-based prices.

Economists working within the neoclassical "objective-cost" framework have failed to see that the problem of cost-derived, natural-gas pricing is deeper than joint costs. Even for the approximately one-third of gas production that is nonassociated, accurate computation of money costs, risk return included, is not the cost of the well from the economic point of view. Economic cost is the *opportunity cost*, which is unknowable, of any other course of action that was forgone.[90] It is the gas well that would have been drilled or whatever else the entrepreneur had in mind to do with the expended resources. Only at the moment of decision does the relevant decisionmaker know the cost of his choice. It is subjective to him, not objective to others, and makes the cost-derived "just and reasonable" price illusory. Reasonable people can forever disagree on what the cost of a gas well is. What is "just" or "reasonable" to one person may not be to another because of heterogeneous preferences and subjective perceptions. Only if perfect knowledge made cost objective and discernible to all—only if the general-equilibrium world of neoclassical economics existed—would rate proceedings be able to achieve their desired result.

Cost-based pricing distorts incentive by granting higher prices to higher cost producers and assigning lower prices to lower cost producers. The market discipline of cost minimization is partially negated with the consequence that not only do consumers pay more for particular gas packages, but fewer resources are available for alternative uses in the economy.

The Phase I period from June 1954 to September 1960 was an example of what economist Ludwig von Mises called *planned chaos*.[91] Based on the rationale of substituting "competition" for market "monopoly," planned disorder replaced a spontaneous order. The

---

[90] Explains Ludwig von Mises, "Costs are a phenomenon of valuation. Costs are the value attached to the most valuable want-satisfaction which remains unsatisfied because the means required for its satisfaction are employed for that want-satisfaction the cost of which we are dealing with." Von Mises, *Human Action* (Chicago: Henry Regnery, 1966), p. 397. For a historical review and modern restatement of subjective cost theory, see James Buchanan, *Cost and Choice* (Chicago: Markham, 1969).

[91] Ludwig von Mises, *Planned Chaos* (Irvington-on-Hudson, N.Y.: Foundation for Economic Education, 1947, 1972), chap. 1.

chaos, fortunately, was confined for the most part to the FPC rather than the industry because of the former's inefficient, undermanned efforts and the NGA's safeguards against regulatory delay (e.g., rate changes becoming effective after a five-month suspension if still awaiting review). While at the close of 1956, approximately 350 rate-increase filings were pending, by 1960, the number had swelled to over 6,000, several thousand of which had been suspended.[92] The commission estimated that it would take a tripled staff until the year 2043 to complete the 1960 caseload.[93] Producers had to "pancake" filings—apply for new increases while earlier requests for increases were pending. This created prodigious uncertainty for firms and consumers alike as to what the real terms of the transaction were. Crisis was at hand. The Landis Commission, appointed by President John F. Kennedy to evaluate the regulatory agencies, concluded:

> The FPC without question represents the outstanding example in the field of government of the breakdown of the administrative process. . . . The Commission has literally done nothing to reduce the delays which have constantly increased. . . . There is a large measure of agreement on separating from the Commission its entire jurisdiction over natural gas and creating a new commission.[94]

Area Price Regulation: 1960–73 (Phase II)

The second phase of producer price regulation was area regulation, covering the period from 1960 to 1973. Stage I began shortly after the Landis report and was characterized by a "get-tough" commission attitude toward the task at hand. Phase II was a retreat from the activist approach of the Kennedy commissioners in recognition of the realities of the marketplace.

---

[92]Rate-change filings and pending requests are contained in the annual reports of the Federal Power Commission for the respective years.

[93]Opinion 338, *Phillips Petroleum Co.*, 24 FPC 537 at 545–46 (1960).

[94]J. M. Landis, *Report on Regulatory Agencies to the President-Elect* (Washington, D.C.: Government Printing Office, 1960), p. 54. Also see idem, "What's Wrong with the Regulatory Agencies?" *41 Proceedings* (New York: American Petroleum Institute, 1961), pp. 19–22. Landis in a private memorandum to President Kennedy charged that the rate-backlog problem was a purposeful attempt by the commission to "prove that rate regulation of natural gas production was an administrative impossibility." Quoted in William Barber, "Studied Inaction in the Kennedy Years," in *Energy Policy in Perspective*, p. 321.

Stage I: 1960–70. The *Phillips: 2* opinion, released September 30, 1960, not only abandoned individualized ratemaking but suggested a new pricing program. The overhaul, necessitated by an unmanageable and growing backlog of rate cases, was also influenced by the Supreme Court's *CATCO* decision a year before, described as a "guiding flare in a field of otherwise utter darkness," that interpreted NGA regulation of independent producers as setting uniform *initial* prices according to common geographical-geological areas.[95] The FPC's new approach would be

> to establish fair prices for the gas itself and not for each individual producer. . . . It appears that the ultimate solution to producer regulation will be in the determination of fair prices for gas, based on reasonable financial requirements of the industry and not on the particular rate base and expenses of each natural gas company.[96]

The new program coincided with a new set of activist commissioners to implement it. In the wake of the Landis report, President Kennedy's five new appointees shared a "belief in the necessity of vigorous regulation in order to protect the interests of the public."[97] The predictable result of stringent intervention is described below.

Concurrent with Opinion 338, the FPC released a statement of general policy, which set two guideline prices for twenty-three natural-gas regions of the country—one for new contracts ("initial service") and one for existing contracts (table 8.2).[98] "New gas" was set at the highest certified price in an area; "old gas" was set at the average price for all existing contracts in an area.[99] Published prices were considered temporary until formal rate proceedings could determine "just and reasonable" prices. Geographical areas were also subject to revision. In the interim—a period that turned out to be prolonged—unconditional certification required contracts to be priced at or below published levels. If above

[95]Nicholas Johnson, "Producer Rate Regulation in Natural Gas Certification Proceedings: CATCO in Context," p. 773.

[96]Opinion 338, *Phillips Petroleum Co.*, 24 FPC 537 (1960). Area pricing was narrowly upheld by the Supreme Court in *Wisconsin* v. *FPC*, 373 U.S. 294 (1963).

[97]Charles Ross, "Producer Regulation: A Commissioner's Viewpoint," in *Regulation of the Natural Gas Producing Industry*, ed. Keith Brown (Baltimore: Johns Hopkins University Press, 1972), p. 93.

[98]Statement of General Policy no. 61-1, 24 FPC 818 (1960).

[99]Edmund Kitch, "Regulation of the Field Market for Natural Gas by the Federal Power Commission," *Journal of Law and Economics* (October 1968): 264.

Table 8.2
AREA PRICE GUIDELINES

Area	Initial Service (¢/Mcf)	Old Contracts (¢/Mcf)
Texas		
District 1	15.0	14.0
District 2	18.0	14.0
District 3	18.0	14.0
District 4	18.0	14.0
District 5	14.0	14.0
District 6	15.0	14.0
District 7-B	14.0	11.0
District 7-C	16.0	11.0
District 8	16.0	11.0
District 9	14.0	14.0
District 10	17.0	11.0
Louisiana		
Southern	Not set	13.7
Northern	16.6	13.7
Oklahoma		
Panhandle	17.0	11.0
Cartier-Knox	16.8	11.0
Other	15.0	11.0
New Mexico		
Permian Basin	16.0	11.0
San Juan Basin	12.7	12.7
Mississippi	Not set	13.7
Kansas	16.0	11.0
Colorado	14.6	12.7
Wyoming	15.0	12.7
West Virginia	26.8	23.9

SOURCE: FPC, various orders.

published levels, rates were automatically suspended and a temporary certificate was issued. Even at the guideline level, a formal hearing ensued if a formal protest was made against the applicant.

This could reduce prices *below* the guidelines.[100] Thus began a decade of rigorous price regulation.

On December 23, 1960, the FPC announced its first area rate proceeding to "develo[p] facts relevant and appropriate to the determination of a just and reasonable area producer rate, or rates" for southeastern New Mexico and western Texas (Districts 7-C and 8, the Permian Basin).[101] All pending rate requests, numbering in the hundreds, were suspended and consolidated for singular determination. On April 5, 1961, the commission announced that 336 respondents and 47 intervenors could present evidence. Although cost data were required, cost-of-service determinations, for either a firm or a group of firms, were not.[102]

With mandatory data obtained from all producers with jurisdictional sales over 10 million cubic feet (MMcf) in 1960, composite evidence was introduced in hearings, which began on October 11, 1961. Five aggregate cost studies were presented and discussed for the bulk of the 250 hearing days, which concluded on October 4, 1963.[103] Unregulated pricing was dismissed because "pipelines [in the Permian Basin] are far from being in a bargaining position [to] validate the theory that a market price will necessarily be a just and reasonable price."[104] A decision was reached by the commission on August 5, 1965, which from the "basic ingredient" of composite cost set a two-level price—a $0.145 per thousand cubic feet (Mcf) "old" gas price and a $0.165 per Mcf "new" gas price.[105] These maximums were below the temporary 1960 guidelines despite general inflation that did not spare gas-drilling costs and burner-tip prices.[106]

---

[100]The power of intervenors (mainly distributors and state public-utility agencies) manifested itself in "their own lower guidelines . . . which if exceeded would . . . forc[e] . . . a full evidentiary hearing on the application." John Carver, "The Future of Area Rate Gas Pricing," *16 Oil and Gas Institute* (New York: Matthew Bender, 1971), p. 403.

[101]Area Rate Proceeding, 24 FPC 1121 (1960).

[102]Clark Hawkins, *The Field Price Regulation of Natural Gas*, pp. 80–81.

[103]For a discussion of the cost studies, see ibid., chap. 5.

[104]Opinion 468, 34 FPC 159 at 182 (1965).

[105]Ibid. at 190; and Opinion 468-A, 34 FPC 1068 (1965).

[106]The rollback was approximately 3.2 percent for new gas and even more for old gas. Robert Helms, *Natural Gas Regulation* (Washington D.C.: American Enterprise Institute, 1974), p. 23.

Two-tiered "vintaging" defined *old gas* as all casinghead gas and gas-well gas flowing into interstate commerce prior to January 1, 1961. *New gas* was defined as all nonassociated gas entering interstate commerce after January 1, 1961. A moratorium on price-increase requests until January 1, 1968, was also established.

Near the end of the proceedings, the FPC's Office of Economics introduced findings from an elaborate econometric model, the Permian model, that estimated supply-and-demand responses to hypothetical gas prices. A surprising conclusion, the "result of comprehensive analysis," was that

> an increase in wellhead prices of new contracts has not resulted in additional new gas reserves (except, perhaps, temporarily). If the past is any guide to the future, price increases will lessen exploration, and hence result in the long run, in less gross additions of new reserves.[107]

With a counterintuitive conclusion and incomprehensible derivation, the model was largely ignored by the hearing examiner and the commission. Respondent witnesses demonstrated numerous errors in data selection, technique, and interpretation.[108] What the model did prove was that correlation does not equal causation, a fundamental problem of econometrics. In any case, scientism—predictive econometrics with a policy orientation—made its entrance in the constructivist effort to set "just and reasonable" prices. The first of seven rate hearings in the 1960s and early 1970s, the *Permian* decision was firmly upheld by the Supreme Court on May 1, 1968: area (group) pricing and vintaging—as well as a two-and-one-half-year price freeze—were affirmed as consonant with "just and reasonable" under the NGA.[109] Summarized Carroll Gilliam:

---

[107]Quoted in Harold Wein, *Natural Gas Supply and Demand* (Washington D.C.: FPC, 1963), p. 10.

[108]See Joe Steele, *The Use of Econometric Models by Federal Regulatory Agencies* (Lexington, Ky.: Heath Lexington Books, 1971), pp. 33–38.

[109]*Permian Basin Area Rate Cases*, 390 U.S. 747 (1968). The Supreme Court's sturdy support of in-line pricing, beginning with *CATCO* (1959), continued in *FPC v. Hunt*, 376 U.S. 515 (1964) and *United Gas Improvement Co. v. Callery Properties, Inc.*, 382 U.S. 223 (1965) before the *Permian* opinion. In the *Hunt* case, the court reasoned that "a triggering of price rises often results from the out-of-line initial pricing of certified gas. These effects become irreversible and splash over into intrastate sales, thus generating reciprocal pressures that directly affect jurisdictional rates [of which] . . . the possibility of refund does not afford sufficient protection" (p. 524).

[T]he Court bestowed its blessing not only upon continuation of the area method in general, but also upon each of the specific underlying, contested Commission decisions of major or minor substance in this particular case. Throughout, the Court did point out that novelty of issues and uncertainties in the pilot case warranted relaxation of what otherwise are fundamental, continuing requirements in administrative law . . . except for clear abuse of power.[110]

Permian was a landmark case. It cleared the way for similar FPC decisions and sanctified a multitiered pricing scheme that would continue henceforth in natural-gas price regulation.

The second major rate case, announced May 10, 1961, concerned southern Louisiana where sizable offshore gas deposits had been located by the CATCO producers.[111] Hearings began in the spring of 1964 with cost information similar to that given in the recently completed *Permian* testimony. A decision was reached by the commission on September 26, 1968, based on 1963 costs that extended the price tiers from two to three: (1) $0.185 per Mcf for pre-1961 interstate gas properties and all casinghead gas, (2) $0.195 per Mcf for 1961–68 gas-well gas, and (3) $0.20 per Mcf for post-1968 gas.[112] Market pricing was rejected for reasons similar to those given in *Permian*—imbalanced bargaining in the producers' favor, which "often tends to make price a second level consideration to the purchaser."[113] Price-increase requests were disallowed until January 1, 1984, but on rehearing, increases were allowed for new gas and offshore gas.[114]

In 1970, the Fifth Circuit Court of Appeals affirmed the *Southern Louisiana* opinion but not without expressing reservations about the "experimental nature" of the pricing orders and the overattention to composite cost rather than market conditions. The court invited the FPC to revise its decision as needed, retrospectively as well as

---

[110]Carroll Gilliam, "The Permian Basin Area Rate Cases: New Landfalls in Rate Regulation," *Natural Resources Lawyer* (July 1969): 197.

[111]Area Rate Proceeding, 25 FPC 942 (1961).

[112]Opinion 546, 40 FPC 530 (1968).

[113]Ibid., p. 554.

[114]Opinion 546-A, 41 FPC 301 (1969). Late in the same year, recognized supply disincentives initiated a new hearing for southern Louisiana (onshore and offshore) with uniform (higher) prices.

prospectively.[115] By this time, unmistakable signs of supply problems were present that even a highly sympathetic court could not ignore. Other rate hearings under way in the 1960s would not be resolved until the early 1970s. By this time, necessitated by the stark reality of shortage, a change in the commission's pricing philosophy had occurred. In retrospect, Stage I of area rate regulation constituted the high years of gas-price constructivism when the FPC demonstrated "more dedication to its view of statutory mandates than . . . wit, wisdom, or apparent concern over the impact of its actions and inactions on the economic well-being of the natural gas industry."[116]

In addition to *Permian, Southern Louisiana,* and several other hearings in which rate increases for existing contracts were disallowed and "guideline" contracts were certified instead, a stringent in-line philosophy prevailed over the dictates of changing market conditions. The courts went as far as to interpret the *CATCO* "hold-the-line" verdict retroactively. In four lower court decisions in late 1960 and early 1961, past unconditional certifications were labeled "suspect" if contract prices were above "in-line" levels.[117] The commission could then roll back prices to "true" in-line levels to prevent the "out-of-line" contracts from forming higher in-line levels. This magnified the effect of regulation since not only could prices be held to in-line levels, but the level itself could be redefined even if past administrative orders were annulled.[118] This was regulation with a vengeance that led one observer to comment, "The absence of rational regulation may be obscured by 'getting tough.' "[119]

A sampling of conditional certificates that rolled back initial prices from their contract level is presented in table 8.3.

[115]*Southern Lousiana Area Rate Cases*, 428 F.2d 407 (5th Cir. 1970).

[116]Carroll Gilliam, "Wellhead Regulation under the Natural Gas Act and the Natural Gas Policy Act," p. 20-67.

[117]See Lewis Mosburg, "Regulation of the Independent Producer by the Federal Power Commission," p. 21. Prominent decisions were Order 232, 25 FPC 39 (1960); Order 232-A, 25 FPC 609 (1961); and Order 242, 27 FPC 339 (1962). In 1966, another price-limiting order was issued (Order 329, 36 FPC 925).

[118]For a ringing censure of the Suspect Order Rule on judicial grounds, see Joseph Morris, "Recent Independent Producer Certificate Cases: The 'Suspect Order' Rule," *George Washington Law Review* (March 1964): 489–503.

[119]Cecil Munn, "The Lesson of the Independent Gas Producer Regulatory Experiment," *Administrative Law Review* (Fall 1961): 57.

Table 8.3
IN-LINE PRICING DECISIONS

Date	Area	Contract ($/Mcf)	Allowed ($/Mcf)
10-31-61	Southern Louisiana	$0.215	$0.2125
8-30-62	Texas–District 4	0.180	0.160
3-27-63	Texas–District 3	0.200	0.160
7-17-63	Southern Louisiana	0.21–0.248	0.200
10-26-64	Mississippi	0.215	0.205
11-17-64	Oklahoma-Other	0.20495	0.179

SOURCE: Various FPC decisions.

The commission stated in its 1965 *Annual Report* that these roll-backs "characterize[d] a new era in pipeline company regulation . . . to hold the line on producer rates."[120] Between 1961 and 1965, almost $1 billion in producer refunds had been ordered as a result of the almost carefree "consumerist pricing" of the period.[121] Consumers who were directly involved could claim short-run gains from lower rates; producers were discouraged from creating new reserves and making interstate dedications. The stage was set for the backlash to follow.

New measures to circumvent the NGA came with effective regulation in the post-1960 period.[122] Dedicating gas to the unregulated intrastate market rather than the regulated interstate market was the most obvious and widely used alternative; home-state diversion would be the bane of federal regulation until 1978 when regulation was extended to intrastate gas.[123]

[120]Federal Power Commission, *Annual Report* (Washington, D.C.: Government Printing Office, 1965), p. 137.

[121]Testimony of FPC chairman Joseph Swidler in 1971. Quoted in M. Elizabeth Sanders, *The Regulation of Natural Gas*, p. 113.

[122]William Coleman and Robert Maris usefully define such circumvention as when "existing and traditional institutions in the industry are manipulated or altered in some way so that a member of a regulated class, or one of its 'transactions,' assumes a form which does not appear to fall within the strict language of Section 1 of the Natural Gas Act." Coleman and Maris, "Federal Power Commission Proceedings Involving Jurisdictional Issues: Of Loopholes, Gaps and End Runs," *Natural Resources Lawyer* (October 1968): 44.

[123]See *OGJ*, September 27, 1971, p. 63. Another problem of interstate dedications that encouraged intrastate contracts was regulatory lag with interstate supply certification that delayed commencement of actual deliveries and consequent revenue.

One response was to leave reserves undeveloped for a more favorable future.[124] Diversionary action was taken by Consolidated Edison, a major New York gas-distribution company, which contracted with a group of Texas producers to bypass a "sale for resale" that would have occurred if the producers had contracted with a pipeline to resell to the utility. Con Ed then contracted with Transcontinental Pipe Line to carry the gas to New York State. Although the FPC could not regulate the producer-distributor contract, it squelched the deal—and other similar pending contracts—by refusing to certify Transco because Con Ed's demand for gas reserves ostensibly increased its price by increasing the number of bidders.[125] The Supreme Court upheld the opinion, while recognizing that the commission had acted pragmatically in skirting the jurisdictional issue to preserve the effectiveness of regulation.[126]

As a result of the *CATCO* verdict, a group of producers in the Rayne field in southern Louisiana withdrew their certification applications, voided their sales contracts, and arranged to sell their reserves to Texas Eastern for renumeration similar to the present value of the original sales contract. The pipeline then could pass on the purchase price as a cost of service. Upon review, the FPC asserted nonjurisdiction and certified Texas Eastern. On appeal by affected gas-distribution interests, the lower court ruled that the commission did not have jurisdiction but had authority to judge Texas Eastern's cost of service reasonable.[127] On remand, the FPC reversed its earlier opinion to claim jurisdiction and find the certification imprudent because

> [a]ny other result would exalt form over substance, would give greater weight to the technicalities of contract draftsmanship than to the achievement of the purposes of the Natural Gas Act ... to the detriment of the ultimate consumer.[128]

[124]Suspicions existed, for example, that Humble was sitting on the Katy and Pledger gas fields in Texas waiting for higher interstate prices. *Fortune*, January 1966, p. 133.

[125]Opinion 315-A, 21 FPC 138 (1959).

[126]*FPC* v. *Transcontinental Gas Pipe Line Corp.*, 365 U.S. 1 (1961).

[127]*Public Service Commission* v. *FPC*, 287 F.2d 143 (D.C. Cir. 1960).

[128]Opinion 378, 29 FPC 249 at 256 (1963). Commented Commissioner Charles Ross, "The most blatant ... attempts by the industry to circumvent regulation ... were the attempts to dispose of holdings by 'sales in place'—the Bastian Bay, Ship Shoal, and Rayne Field cases." Ross, "Producer Regulation: A Commissioner's Viewpoint," p. 94.

Once again, a jurisdictional question was pragmatically decided by sympathetic courts to preserve comprehensive—hence effective—regulation.

Another attempt to circumvent the NGA occurred where producer contracts required the interstate pipeline purchaser to either sell gas intrastate, sell gas directly to consumers, or consume the gas. Thus, the field sale would be either intrastate or not for resale to avoid federal involvement. In the *Lo-Vaca* opinion, the FPC claimed jurisdiction over such transactions because nonregulated gas was commingled with regulated gas.[129] The lower court reversed.[130] Before the Supreme Court in 1965, the commission's opinion was resurrected on grounds of commingling and the inability to sort out nonjurisdictional gas and also, more accurately, because a contrary finding would work against the purpose of the NGA.[131] Again, the Supreme Court became the bodyguard of the FPC's broad construction of authority to make prices "just and reasonable."

Although not strictly matters of jurisdiction, several common practices of producers in the 1960s were designed to improve the terms of trade to partially circumvent price maximums. Producers were prepaid under "take-or-pay" covenants that guaranteed minimum payments regardless of the quantity of gas taken. The FPC allowed these "sweeteners." Purchasers also "tied in" purchases of gas liquids with natural gas, so the former's unregulated high price would cover the latter's regulated price. Flagrant use of these circumventions attracted FPC action, but to various extents they were successfully employed to mitigate area price control.[132]

Stage 2: 1970–73. The regulatory process is driven not only by exogenous factors but by its own shortcomings.[133] Wellhead-price regulation under the NGA is a case in point. Worsening supply problems led to revamped regulation in the 1970–73 period.

[129]Opinion 348, 26 FPC 606 (1961).

[130]*Lo-Vaca Gathering Co.* v. *FPC,* 323 F.2d 190 (5th Cir. 1963).

[131]*California* v. *Lo-Vaca Gathering Co.,* 379 U.S. 366 (1965). Also, *FPC* v. *Amerada Petroleum Corp.,* 379 U.S. 687 (1965). The commingling doctrine was subsequently qualified. See Carroll Gilliam, *Regulation of the Natural Gas Industry,* vol. 1, pp. 20-23 to 20-24.

[132]Edmund Kitch, "Regulation of the Field Market for Natural Gas by the Federal Power Commission," pp. 275–76.

[133]For a discussion of interventionist dynamics, see chapter 29, pp. 1769–72.

The cumulative effect of below-market pricing since at least 1960—and general uncertainty since the 1954 *Phillips* decision—led to long-predicted consequences by decade's end. A warning signal of gas-market disequilibrium was an American Gas Association study released in early 1969 that reported that for the first time in recorded history, additions to proven reserves had fallen short of the previous year's production (equaling consumption).[134] With demand increasing and interstate supply declining as a result of artificially low prices, a concerned FPC warned that "only a few years remain before demand will outrun supply."[135] In 1970, three major interstate pipelines notified customers that they would be unable to acquire enough gas to comply with their contracts.[136] Within several years, curtailment spread to fourteen other interstate carriers, affecting as much as one-third of contracted deliveries for some. This interrupted many business and recreational arrangements and forced substitutions of less economical, more polluting fuels.[137] Curtailments of nearly 1 billion cubic feet (Bcf) per day in 1971 were followed the next year by lost sales of 2.5 Bcf per day, before returning to 1971 levels in 1973.[138]

For the FPC, shortages meant a retreat from "just and reasonable" prices toward supply enhancement for interstate markets. (Intrastate supply was generally ample and growing thanks to its unregulated status.)[139] This meant succumbing to the inevitable—higher prices to approach market-clearing and incentive levels. Robert Helms noticed the irony: "It seems that the purpose of regulation has

---

[134]Robert Helms, *Natural Gas Regulation*, p. 25.

[135]Richard Merriman and Peyton Bowman, "The 1970s—A Period of Momentous Change," in *Regulation of the Gas Industry* (New York: Matthew Bender, 1982), vol. 1, p. 5-7.

[136]See chapter 15, pp. 906–8, 920. In early 1968, a subzero cold spell created gas shortages in Maine and New Hampshire that closed factories and businesses in many communities and required heat shelters to be set up by the Red Cross and the Salvation Army. *NPN*, February 1968, p. 71.

[137]Patricia Starratt, *The Natural Gas Shortage and the Congress* (Washington, D.C.: American Enterprise Institute, 1974), pp. 3–4.

[138]*OGJ*, March 19, 1973, p. 29. A summary of utility curtailments is contained in *NPN*, July 1972, pp. 62–63.

[139]Texas, however, began to experience problems when intrastate gas was coaxed to interstate markets by FPC emergency programs described in this chapter, pp. 441–42. See *Business Week*, December 16, 1972, p. 28.

changed from protecting consumers from higher prices to protecting consumers from natural gas shortages by allowing higher prices."[140] Higher price assignments, along with other "quick-fix" adjustments, constituted the second stage of area price regulation, itself the second phase of price regulation of independent gas producers.

In the early 1970s, several unfinished area rate proceedings from the 1960s were brought to a close and several previously concluded proceedings were reopened when moratoriums on new filings expired. On November 17, 1963, an area rate hearing was announced for the Hugoton-Anadarko region, which covered the entire state of Kansas, the Oklahoma Panhandle, the Oklahoma-Anadarko area, and Texas District 10.[141] Price maximums based on a cost methodology similar to that of *Permian* and *Southern Louisiana* were announced on September 18, 1970, with a moratorium on rate increases until July 1, 1977.[142] Old gas under contracts made prior to November 1, 1969, ranged from $0.125 per Mcf in Kansas to $0.19 per Mcf in Oklahoma; new gas contracted for after November 1 ranged from $0.19 per Mcf in Kansas to $0.205 per Mcf in Oklahoma. The old gas–new gas price differential remained the same, except all rates were scheduled to increase by $0.01 per Mcf on July 1, 1972. This last concession was a hint of complicating modifications to come, necessitated by shortage conditions.

Also on November 17, 1963, an area proceeding was announced for the Texas Gulf Coast area, composed of Texas Railroad Commission Districts 1 (sixteen southeastern counties only), 2, 3, and 4. On May 16, 1971, the FPC announced a complicated pricing structure, based on historical and predicted cost, and a moratorium on nonprescribed rate increases until January 1, 1976.[143] Old gas, under contracts from before October 1, 1968, was priced at $0.19 per Mcf until October 1, 1973, when a $0.01 per Mcf increase would take effect. New gas, under post–October 1, 1968, contracts, was priced at $0.24 per Mcf until October 1, 1973, when a $0.25 per Mcf rate would take effect. As a reaction to growing intrastate sales at a time when

[140]Robert Helms, *Natural Gas Regulation*, p. 27.

[141]30 FPC 1354 (1963).

[142]Opinion 586, 44 FPC 761 (1970).

[143]Opinion 595, 45 FPC 674 (1971). Said the commission, "Slavish adherence to a test period can be self-defeating. . . . Predictive elements are included . . . to reflect the various dynamics which illuminate the future" (p. 690).

interstate supply was below demand, special incentives were offered to producers to increase interstate sales. Price ceilings could be increased by $0.05 per Mcf if 4 trillion cubic feet of new reserves were contracted interstate, another $0.05 per Mcf for 6 trillion cubic feet, and another $0.01 for 10 trillion cubic feet. Refund credit was also offered for new interstate dedications.

On February 28, 1967, a proceeding was initiated for the Other Southwest Area, comprising the states of Mississippi and Arkansas, northern Louisiana, southern and eastern Oklahoma, and Texas Districts 5, 6, and 9.[144] On October 29, 1971, a rate-schedule decision was reached, based on cost from test year 1962, by the FPC with a rate-hike moratorium until July 1, 1976. For old gas contracted for prior to October 1, 1968, rates varied from $0.1825 per Mcf (southern Arkansas) to $0.206 per Mcf (northern Louisiana) with a $0.01 per Mcf escalation on October 1, 1973; gas contracted for after this time ranged from $0.225 per Mcf (southern Arkansas) to $0.26 per Mcf (offshore Mississippi) with a $0.01 per Mcf hike scheduled on October 1, 1973.[145] On January 17, 1972, another FPC opinion gave price incentives to new reserves dedicated interstate; below-market interstate rates were sending new reserves intrastate, a condition that regulators intended to reverse.[146]

On October 16, 1969, an area rate proceeding began for the Appalachian–Illinois Basin gas fields. Instead of holding prolonged adjudicatory hearings, the FPC finalized rate opinions by the rulemaking method whereby the commission solicited comments on rate schedule notices.[147] This expedited evaluation of cost evidence from test year 1962, and on October 2, 1970, an order was issued that set area prices of from $0.16 per Mcf to $0.32 per Mcf.[148] Deteriorating supply conditions led pipeline purchasers to petition for higher rates, which

---

[144]37 FPC 400 (1967).

[145]Opinion 607, 46 FPC 900 (1971).

[146]Opinion 607-A, 47 FPC 99 (1972).

[147]For a discussion of the methodology used to set area prices, see William Diener, "Producer Rate Regulation—Rulemaking at the Federal Power Commission," *Natural Resources Lawyer* (Summer 1972): 378–88.

[148]Order 411, 44 FPC 1112 (1970), as amended by Order 411-A, 44 FPC 1334 (1970) and Order 411-B, 44 FPC 1487 (1970).

were denied by the commission on December 12, 1972.[149] In its decision, however, the FPC admitted that area ratemaking was in need of replacement by *uniform nationwide pricing*, and vintaging would be phased out by making gas from expired ("rollover") contracts eligible for new-gas rates.

On June 17, 1970, it was announced that area rates would be established for Arizona, New Mexico, Colorado, Wyoming, Nebraska, Montana, North Dakota, South Dakota, and Colorado.[150] In a rulemaking, the FPC set "interim" rates on July 15, 1971, based on 1962 test-year costs for contracts made after June 17, 1970, at prices ranging from $0.225 per Mcf to $0.24 per Mcf.[151] Upon judicial approval of area pricing by rulemaking procedures, an opinion dated April 11, 1973, increased new rates for pre–October 1, 1968, gas and pre–December 31, 1972, gas from $0.15 per Mcf to $0.24 per Mcf.[152]

The moratorium on rate increase requests expired January 1, 1968, for the Permian Basin area. On June 17, 1970, a second area rate proceeding was begun to establish new maximum rates (new rates had last been set on August 5, 1965).[153] On August 7, 1973, new area rates were announced. The rate for pre–October 1, 1968, gas was set at $0.23 per Mcf from October 1, 1968, until September 30, 1974, and $0.24 per Mcf thereafter; the rate for post–October 1, 1968, gas was set at $0.35 per Mcf prior to October 1, 1975, and $0.36 per Mcf thereafter.[154]

Although rate-increase requests were not allowed until January 1, 1974, a second rate proceeding for Southern Louisiana was initiated in 1967.[155] The involved gas had been badly underpriced by the last hearing, and declining interstate sales and shortage conditions prompted the unscheduled rehearing. On July 16, 1971, new rates were implemented to replace the existing $0.17 to $0.20 per Mcf rates with new rates ranging from $0.21375 to $0.26 per Mcf. As further impetus, prices for gas contracted prior to October 1, 1968,

---

[149]Opinion 639, 48 FPC 1299 (1972). This opinion was upheld in *Shell Oil Co.* v. *FPC*, 491 F.2d 82 (5th Cir. 1974).

[150]35 *Fed. Reg.* 10152 (June 20, 1970).

[151]Order 435, 46 FPC 68 (1971).

[152]Ibid.

[153]43 FPC 899 (1970).

[154]Opinion 662, 50 FPC 390 (1973).

[155]Opinion 546, 40 *Fed. Reg.* 530 at 544 (1967).

could be increased, and "workoffs" of refund liabilities could be reduced in return for new reserves contracted interstate.[156] With these opinions, some 85 percent of interstate supply was price controlled under maximum area rates. The balance, representing dispersed fields outside the reach of area proceedings, were regulated by guidelines published in 1960 or individualized assignments made thereafter.

The 1970–73 period witnessed a number of modifications to area pricing to cope with interstate gas shortages. Curtailments, despite growing admittance of high-priced natural-gas imports and the embarrassing existence of an abundantly supplied intrastate market, made the problem and the solution obvious. Scientistic cost-derived area prices had to be relaxed to provide incentives for exploration and production, to redirect available supply interstate, and to ration demand to supply. Rather than abandon area pricing, however, authorities sought to fine-tune the program to take into account the heterogeneity that the area-pricing methodology had to neglect.

In 1970, the year curtailments were announced by several major pipelines, three measures were undertaken by the FPC to alleviate the crisis. Sixty-day "emergency sales" could be made by producers to interstate carriers without notification or approval of the FPC.[157] By 1972, fourteen pipelines were purchasing emergency gas under the program.[158] Such rates were reviewable by the FPC only as a pipeline cost of service; if a passthrough was not allowed, the pipeline would bear the consequences. After sixty days, the producer was eligible for a limited-term certificate at a rate above the area ceiling with prearranged abandonment. Contracts were generally for three years or less.[159] The commission was serious about promoting limited certificates; quick action was taken on applications, and rates as high as $0.45 per Mcf were awarded.[160]

---

[156]Opinion 598, 46 FPC 86 (1971).

[157]Order 402, 43 FPC 707 (1970); and Order 418, 44 FPC 1574 (1970).

[158]Gordon Gooch, "Current Developments in FPC and Natural Gas Matters," 23 *Oil and Gas Institute* (New York: Matthew Bender, 1972), p. 104.

[159]Order 431, 45 FPC 570 (1970). On September 4, 1973, the emergency-sale period was extended to 180 days (Order 491, 50 FPC 742 [1973]) before being returned to sixty days (Order 491D, 51 FPC 947 [1974]).

[160]Carroll Gilliam, "Recent Developments in Regulation of Natural Gas Sales," *Rocky Mountain Law Review* (1974): 184.

A second 1970 measure was FPC approval of purchaser prepayments to producers, which could be recorded as capital assets in the pipelines' rate bases.[161] On November 10, 1971, rate-base treatment was narrowed to apply to contracts made prior to December 31, 1972.[162] Order 465 on December 29, 1972, extended the cutoff date one year, and Order 499 on December 28, 1973, extended it for another two years.[163] Prepayments were used as exploratory capital, and gas discoveries were to be dedicated to the prepaying pipeline to retire the obligation. Between 1970 and the program's termination at the close of 1975, advance payments of over $3 billion were committed (with nearly $2 billion advanced) to producers, mitigating the lack of internally generated funds due to price ceilings.[164]

A third stopgap measure in troubled 1970 was to allow producers to earmark gas produced and sold from federal waters (technically in interstate commerce) for self-use (the Chandeleur Doctrine).[165] After a stormy five-year existence, the "reserved-gas" program was restricted on March 7, 1977, to "high-priority" end uses and was completely terminated a year later, without noticeably increasing interstate over intrastate dedications.[166]

On March 18, 1971, the commission deregulated small producers with annual output under 10 Mcf to encourage new production.[167] In December of the following year, the D.C. Circuit Court of Appeals ruled that unregulated prices were not prima facie just and reasonable, which was upheld by the Supreme Court.[168] With market pricing again not sanctified as just and reasonable, the commission's

---

[161]Order 410, 44 FPC 1142 (1970).

[162]Order 441, 46 FPC 1178 (1971).

[163]48 FPC 1550 (1972); and 50 FPC 2111 (1973).

[164]Exploration activity in this program centered in offshore Texas and Louisiana, which, as of September 1975, accounted for $1.4 billion in advances and $2.7 billion in commitments. One of the most active interstates in the program was Transco with $147 million in advances and $1.1 billion in commitments. *OGJ*, September 29, 1975, pp. 45–49. In June 1975, advance payment regulations were tightened. See *OGJ*, June 30, 1975, p. 47.

[165]Opinion 560, 40 FPC 20 (1970).

[166]Opinion 789, 57 FPC 1306 (1977); and Opinion 10, 2 FERC 61,549 (March 20, 1978).

[167]Order 428, 45 FPC 454 (1971); and Order 428-B, 46 FPC 47 (1971).

[168]*FPC v. Texaco, Inc.*, 417 U.S. 380 (1974).

agenda was confined to loosening rather than freeing natural-gas prices.[169]

Relaxed price regulation was sidetracked in February and March of 1972 when the Cost of Living Council's Price Commission, as part of the economywide wage and price control program implemented in August 1971 by President Nixon, exercised authority over the FPC's public-utility pricing functions.[170] After hearings, autonomous control over pricing of interstate production and transportation was returned to the FPC.

The next major modification to increasingly unsatisfactory area pricing occurred August 3, 1972, when the FPC announced that, with sufficient supporting evidence, certain long-term contracts could receive above-maximum rates as a "one-shot" deal.[171] Approved supra-area prices and fixed escalations could not be increased again during the lives of contracts with interstate carriers made after April 6, 1972. This special treatment was an inducement for new interstate commitments of gas, but many members of Congress and the judiciary thought this strayed beyond the FPC's administrative discretion. This uncertainty, coupled with reopened hearings on national rate determination, lessened incentive for optional rate proceedings by the mid-1970s.[172]

Another important amendment to area pricing in the hectic four years under review was announced on April 12, 1973.[173] Producers could petition for relief from designated ceiling prices if cost evidence or reservoir performance information, or both, sufficiently proved that higher prices were needed to maintain output or to undertake well-workover projects. The intention was to prevent premature abandonment or forgone enhancement of supply. A related commission order provided relief if lack of incentive promoted gas flaring or venting.[174] Such relief would be successfully used and later incorporated into the Natural Gas Policy Act of 1978.

[169]See the discussion in Rush Moody, "1974—The Gathering Storm," 26 *Oil and Gas Institute* (New York: Matthew Bender, 1975), pp. 8–11.

[170]*OGJ*, February 21, 1972, p. 26. As of December 31, 1971, there were 1,820 pending suspensions involving $75.3 million in increases.

[171]Order 455, 48 FPC 218 (1972); and Order 455-A, 48 FPC 477 (1972).

[172]See Carroll Gilliam, "Wellhead Regulation under the Natural Gas Act and the Natural Gas Policy Act," p. 20-97.

[173]Order 481, 49 FPC 992 (1973).

[174]Order 482, 49 FPC 996 (1973).

Fine-tuning area pricing prevented a bad situation from becoming worse. The regulatory clamp was not removed but relaxed. The basic problems of area pricing—as a regulatory program interfering with market prices—ensured that modification alone would not be enough to arrest continuing distortions of the gas market.

Area Pricing Critically Reviewed. Elizabeth Sanders has identified the move from individual-firm pricing to area pricing as "the transformation of federal involvement . . . from conventional utility regulation to redistributive policy."[175] Prior to area price regulation, the hallmarks of producer controls were uncertainty and large administrative and compliance costs; now "pro-consumer" below-market pricing was the norm with detrimental consequences to follow. What began as a crisis in bureaucratic administration (1954–60) turned into a performance crisis within the gas industry by 1970. The compounded errors of the area approach were at fault.

Group Price Determination. The area or group approach to price control sacrificed heterogeneous reality for administrative simplicity. The exercise was characterized by arbitrary distinctions and illegitimate extrapolations from aggregates to their individual parts. Defining separate areas at the beginning of the program was described by Commissioner Arthur Kline as "one of the biggest problems confronting the Commission in its attempts to hold the line on initial prices."[176] Indeed, neighboring reservoirs could be different as distant reservoirs could be similar; high-cost and low-cost gas properties were lumped together for geographical, not geologic or economic, reasons. The locational hodgepodge of fields and basins led the commission to hedge by stating that "the areas . . . will be adjusted from time to time as such facts as may become before us compel such adjustments."[177]

Cost estimates as a base for area prices were ambiguous and illegitimate. Databases compiled from firms' answers to questionnaires are hardly the informational foundation for "scientific" pric-

---

[175]M. Elizabeth Sanders, *The Regulation of Natural Gas*, p. 113. Paul MacAvoy similarly described price regulation as a "'welfare' policy in the sense of redistributing income." MacAvoy, "The Regulation-Induced Shortage of Natural Gas," in *Regulation of the Natural Gas Producing Industry*, p. 169.

[176]24 FPC 106 at 108 (1960).

[177]Statement of General Policy no. 61-1, 24 FPC 818 at 819–20 (1960).

ing.[178] The inherent subjectivity of cost assignment was never acknowledged by regulators. Such subjectivity allowed room for "fudging" costs toward desired prices. It is natural to believe that firms with individual data and the FPC with composite data produced results biased toward preconceived ends.[179] Indeed, differing studied opinions of what the "cost" of produced gas is, the FPC's loose talk of "objective cost" notwithstanding,[180] guaranteed controversy and political resolution.

The choice of the test year, crucial for cost-based price determination, varied from proceeding to proceeding and from case to case, making legal prices uneven and discriminatory on a current basis. The later the test year, the higher the cost and derived ceiling prices, yet "selecting appropriate [test] years is certainly as difficult, and significant, as selecting areas."[181]

As were determinations of area and cost, determination of allowed rates of return was fraught with difficulty.[182] Producers understandably were allowed greater margins than were franchised pipelines because of drilling risk, but the size of the differential was an open question. In the *Permian* proceeding, a 12 percent return (compared to gas pipeline assignments of from 6 to 6.5 percent) was decided upon by calculating the average profit from production in the area.[183]

The fundamental flaw of profit averaging is that returns are *individual phenomena*. Profits and losses are inextricably tied to the individual project and the entrepreneur's ability to minimize costs and successfully locate commercial finds. Averaging treats the talent

[178]In October 1963, the FPC sent a 400-page questionnaire to the 114 largest producers in the country, which required an estimated 2 million staff-hours and $10 million to complete. John Bitner, "Federal Regulation of the Natural Gas Producer—A Reappraisal after 10 Years," 44 *Proceedings* (New York: American Petroleum Institute, 1964), p. 28.

[179]See the discussion of Edmund Kitch on the cost methodology used in the *Permian* and *Southern Louisiana* proceedings. Kitch, "The *Permian Basin Area Rate Cases* and the Regulatory Determination of Price," *University of Pennsylvania Law Review* (December 1967): 208–9, 213–15.

[180]"Basic to [the area approach] is . . . objective cost standards." 34 FPC 159 (1965).

[181]Nicholas Johnson, "Producer Rate Regulation in Natural Gas Certification Proceedings: CATCO in Context," p. 803.

[182]For a more detailed critique of statutory margins used in public-utility regulation, see chapter 15, pp. 927–33.

[183]As Edmund Kitch noticed, this allowance was really higher because negative margins from nonproductive wells were excluded. Kitch, "The *Permian Basin Area Rate Cases* and the Regulatory Determination of Price," p. 202.

for locating and extracting gas as nonspecific and shared by all. Consequently, a predetermined cost-plus allowance cannot provide the same incentive under regulated conditions that it provides under free-market conditions.

Because of the subjectivity of the area-pricing methodology—the area chosen, the determination of cost, the test year of cost, and computed margin—not only absolute prices but relative prices in the various production regions are likely to be different from market prices. Falsified relative prices mislead producers' decisions about where to dedicate resources; they also misalign consumption because misallocated production is captive to its contract. Area pricing creates economic inefficiency not only because of below-market pricing in absolute terms but also because of falsified relative prices in different areas.

Cost-derived price ceilings, which are problematic when set on an individual basis, are error compounded when established for an area. What is true for the whole may not be true for its individual components upon which supply depends.[184] A more subtle flaw has been noticed by Stephen Breyer and Paul MacAvoy.[185] Regulators set prices above costs to provide incentive for production, and they later judge their success by whether prices remain above average costs. However, cost-based prices perpetuate themselves and mislead regulators because once a regulated price is in place, only low-cost projects can be profitably undertaken. This reduces average costs over time, which in turn reduces prices based on them. And to the extent that drilling costs escalate and profitable gas deposits become harder to find, *marginal costs* tend to rise above historic average costs to further dampen incentives to replace extractions

---

[184]"Group regulation . . . is highly protracted. . . . The presence of large numbers of parties operating under related circumstances tends to swallow up legitimate distinctions. There is a dangerous tendency toward generalization which may be true of only a part of those being regulated." Or due to inadequate considerations of legitimate details, the generalization may not be "representative of the regulated class as a whole." Lewis Mosburg, "The Permian Decision—A Study in Group Regulation," *Oklahoma Law Review* (May 1966): 139. Also see Justice Douglas's dissenting argument that the area approach was inconsistent with the "just and reasonable" criterion because individualized cost, risk, or profit was not known. 392 U.S. 829–30 (1968).

[185]Stephen Breyer and Paul MacAvoy, *Energy Regulation by the Federal Power Commission*, p. 70.

with new reserves. A raft of high-cost projects are legislated into nonexistence, while authorities falsely think proper production inducements are in place.[186] In other words, the informational content provided by area pricing cannot guide authorities to enlightened regulation—quite the opposite. Once begun, the program works in the dark to discover the "right" price to spur production at the lowest cost to consumers.

Related to the preclusion of high-cost drilling was the competitive hardship placed on smaller firms. The narrowed range of profitable opportunities put firms with less capital to pool for drilling ventures in a riskier position than larger firms. While a series of noncommercial finds could be absorbed by the latter, it could devastate the former. Restated, optimum size of drilling operations was artificially increased by price regulation. A second anti-competitive result of legislatively pricing older gas below newer gas, discussed later in this chapter, was that established pipelines enjoyed lower gas acquisition costs than did later entrants.[187]

An oft-cited rationalization by the FPC, the simplicity of the area approach compared with its predecessor, deserves comment.[188] Economy in regulation does not mean economy *resulting* from regulation. Simplification, while a blessing for the commission, falsified heterogeneous reality with numerous subtle distortions. In this regard, unmanageable regulation in the 1954–60 period, while worse for regulators, was *better* for the gas market. Inefficient regulation, which allowed market forces more leeway, outperformed efficient regulation.

Multitiered Pricing. The most distinctive characteristic of area pricing, outside the group approach itself, was the implementation of a dual gas price, one for older committed gas and one for newer gas. The brainchild of Alfred Kahn, a technical economist representing the utility interests in several important area proceedings, the

---

[186]Rush Moody censured average-cost pricing as having "the inevitable effect of sealing off from exploration and development all but the most profitable drilling opportunities. . . . Thus, an FPC rate is, in practical effect, a ceiling on what gas wells are drilled—but it is not a ceiling on profits." Moody, "1974—The Gathering Storm," pp. 44–45.

[187]See this chapter, pp. 440–41.

[188]"The area approach offers a regulatory method which is best adapted to the discharge of our responsibilities." 34 FPC 180 (1965).

lower old-gas price reflected its lower elasticity of supply while the higher price for new gas reflected its greater supply responsiveness to price.

Although the multitiered-price approach was a novel application of technical economics to oil and gas production, serious theoretical and practical difficulties prevented its success.[189] First, qualitative acknowledgment of two different supply elasticities does not mean that quantitative estimates can pinpoint the price at which a certain supply will be forthcoming. Empirical evidence, if one has faith in the ceteris paribus assumption, can at best reveal how sensitive supply has been to price *historically*. What price elasticity is *today* or will be *tomorrow* is unknowable, especially in an open-ended situation such as that under area planning. Moreover, Kahn's program achieved its measure of success by tricking the market. Producers originally make investments based on certain prices and do not expect the "rules of the game" to change, which belittles the producers' sunk investment by lowering legal prices to cover only out-of-pocket expenses. Such trickery can only fool the market so long; once implemented, the new-gas incentive is dulled because producers know that once investments are committed, a lower Kahnian "old-new-gas" price could result. Thus, the very implementation of a price differential narrows the elasticity gap that serves as the rationale of the pricing scheme.

The presence of two prices, not attributable to transportation costs, for a homogeneous good distorts the market by imparting misinformation to producers and consumers. Consumers of old gas are "told" that supply is plentiful and they can conserve less than consumers of new gas. Producers of old gas are "told" to explore less than new-gas producers because they can make less profit and have less capital to draw on. Yet some old-gas consumers may be better able than new-gas users to conserve, and some old-gas producers may be better explorationists than their new-gas counterparts. This is a waste that dual pricing superimposes on a market already distorted by effective price control.

One contribution that dual pricing can make is to bring prices closer to market levels than they would be under homogeneous

---

[189]The origin of supply-elastic price regulation can be traced to late World War II when subsidies were granted to stripper wells to alleviate hardship and possible abandonment as a result of ceiling prices. See chapter 5, pp. 238–39.

pricing. This is not an attribute of the price tiers per se, however, but of a relaxation of regulation.

Prices derived solely from elasticity (supply) considerations do not necessarily clear the market because the demand side of the equation is neglected. The death knell of area pricing and multitiered pricing was rung when prices failed to restrain demand, supply effects aside, and gas-market disequilibrium continued to reign. In retrospect, Kahn regretted that he had "bequeathed to the nation an impractical system."[190]

Realities of Area Pricing. The result of area pricing, as of all effective efforts to fix prices below market levels, was shortage. Elaborate cost testimony, competitive studies, group averaging, and dual pricing were no escape. A below-market price, however sophisticated its derivation, remains a below-market price. Late in the area program when (1) expensive imports from Canada, Algeria (in liquefied form), and to a lesser extent Mexico were allowed to supplement inadequate domestic interstate gas and (2) higher prices for interstate gas had to be awarded to compete with the intrastate market, the wolf was at the door. As Commissioner Carl Bagge commented in early 1971, "Regulation cannot now escape the fact that it is in the process of being deluged by the very market forces for which it was intended as a substitute."[191] Previous hearings were reopened and record price increases were sanctioned in later area proceedings because of market realities. Area pricing had only postponed the will of the market. Bagge had the last word:

> The Supreme Court held that price regulation must substitute for the lack of competition in field sales of natural gas. But neither that decision nor price regulation nullified the long-term forces of the market. The impact of the market may have been delayed by regulation but it is the market that is controlling in the end.[192]

Failures of interstate-production regulation inspired another commissioner, Rush Moody, to lead a one-man crusade for price deregulation by legislative amendment of the NGA.[193] In 1972, the National

---

[190]Thomas McCraw, *Prophets of Regulation* (Cambridge, Mass.: Harvard University Press, 1984), p. 235.

[191]Carl Bagge, "Gas Producer Price Legislation: An Alternative to Whistling in the Dark," *Natural Resources Lawyer* (January 1971): 93.

[192]Ibid., pp. 93–94.

[193]*OGJ*, July 17, 1972, p. 56. Also see Moody's dissent in Opinion 622, 47 FPC 1624 at 1653–56 (1972).

Industrial Pollution Control Council lobbied Nixon to raise prices significantly to arrest shortages and encourage substitution to fuel oil. Even gas distributors questioned the efficacy of "just and reasonable" price assignments. The Associated Gas Distributors in September 1972 asked the FPC to review and increase pre-1961 contract gas prices under area ceilings.[194] President Nixon's Oil Policy Committee and the Office of Emergency Preparedness favored relaxed regulation to increase competition against oil imports that were beginning to cause concern.[195] At the same time, advocates of regulation were not ready to concede. There was talk of expanding regulation intrastate through legislative amendment to reduce competition in the interstate market. The FPC, in addition to Congress, was also ready for another phase of administrative regulation.

National Rate Proceedings: 1974–78 (Phase III)

Stage I: 1974–76. On July 21, 1970, the FPC began a nationwide investigation "to determine the terms and conditions which will result in an adequate supply of natural gas at the lowest rate consistent with [incentives] to provide service with its attendant risks." This led to the third phase of gas-producer regulation on June 21, 1974, when the FPC announced a national $0.42 per Mcf rate for contracts made on or after January 1, 1973, for reserves that were new or freed from expired contracts.[196] Pricing "rollover" contract gas at the new rate would eventually cause vintaging to be replaced by uniform pricing, as had been intended in earlier orders.[197] Based on average-cost estimates from a 1972 base year and a 15 percent return, the higher rate reflected increased drilling costs attributable to general inflation and shortages caused by inadequate past pricing.[198]

For producers with limited-term certificates and producers with sixty-day emergency sale contracts who received as much as $0.55

[194]*OGJ*, September 4, 1972, p. 54.

[195]*OGJ*, September 25, 1972, p. 70.

[196]Opinion 699, 51 FPC 2212 (1974). The new rate applied to all jurisdictional sales onshore and offshore except in Alaska.

[197]See Kenneth Heady, "Gas Producer Regulation in a New Environment," *24 Oil and Gas Institute* (New York: Matthew Bender, 1973), pp. 22–23; and Rush Moody, "1974—The Gathering Storm," pp. 12–14.

[198]Stated the commission: "The continuing and deepening natural gas shortage . . . requires that this Commission take all prudent steps to insure . . . adequate . . . supplies to fulfill reasonable demand while protecting the 'consumers against exploitation at the hands of natural-gas companies.' . . . Thus the Commission faces a formidable task: establishing rates high enough to provide the economic incentive for . . . finding

per Mcf, the universal pricing order was a setback.[199] Sharp criticism of the cost methodology and the computation of national rates, led by Commissioner Moody, prompted the commission to issue a new opinion on December 4 to raise the national rate to $0.50 per Mcf for contracts allowed $0.42 per Mcf six months before.[200] Fixed escalations of $0.01 per Mcf were allowed each January 1 thereafter, along with a biennial rate review for changes as needed. The $0.08 per Mcf increase reflected several changes that increased cost determination, the most prominent being inclusion of expenses associated with unsuccessful drilling.

The Fifth Circuit Court of Appeals on October 14, 1975, upheld the 699 opinions in all major areas—national ratemaking, renewal contract repricing over vintaging, and the cost methodology of rate determination. Nonetheless, the court let it be known that the area rate–national rate experiment had not been successful and that changes—the foremost of which was better predictions of the effects of assigned rates—were needed or the court would lose its fatherly patience. In the words of the court:

> The national rate structure under review . . . demonstrates that the Commission does not believe that any of the total [area] rate structures . . . had the desired effect of providing developmental incentive while preventing exploitation. . . . [T]he effort to protect consumer interests as to price is at odds with the long-range consumer interest in maintaining an adequate supply of natural gas for the interstate market. Finding and maintaining this point of delicate balance is a difficult task. . . . We must express our regret . . . that the FPC continues to issue orders which would be inadequate but for our "kid glove" treatment. . . . For over fourteen years the Commission has been experimenting in area rate regulation and yet it still "supports" many of the essential elements of its new national rate order with little more than *ipse dixit*. . . . As experiment lapses into experience, the courts may well expect the Commission to justify its policies with reasoned projections.[201]

---

enormous reserves . . . but not so high that the natural gas consumer is exploited during a time of shortage." 51 FPC 2212 at 2217–18.

[199]*OGJ*, July 1, 1974, p. 16.

[200]Opinion 699-H, 52 FPC 1064 (1974). The new ceiling may have been influenced by Senate bill 2506, which set maximum prices between $0.40 and $0.60 per Mcf. The Consumer Energy Act would not be reported out of committee.

[201]*Shell Oil Company* v. *FPC*, 520 F.2d 1061 at 1072 (5th Cir. 1975).

On December 1, 1975, rates for gas contracts in force prior to January 1, 1973 (excluding contracts that would expire after that date, which could obtain the new gas price) were revised upward to $0.235 per Mcf with an escalation to $0.295 per Mcf on June 30, 1976, to account for the end of percentage depletion.[202] As with post–January 1, 1973, gas, cost studies using base year 1972 and a 15 percent return were used to arrive at the ceiling rate.[203]

A more drastic, and counterproductive, measure taken by the FPC to alleviate the shortfall in supply in the national rate years was to compel interstate service from properties historically committed intrastate.[204] This gave authorities the upper hand in curtailment matters and reallocation of dedicated reserves, contracts notwithstanding. For producers, compulsory perpetual dedication increased an already uncertain interstate situation; new reserves now had extra reason to stay in home-state markets.

Stage II: 1976–78. Although the series of rate increases that began in 1970 set new highs, the effort was clearly piecemeal and catch-up, not an attempt to approach market-clearing levels. Shortages, despite price increases and historically high interstate prices, confirmed that. The first serious, if still inadequate, attempt to jump prices toward market levels, in response to deteriorating interstate supply and record oil prices caused by the first major price hike by the Organization of Oil Exporting Countries (OPEC), occurred in the second national rate proceeding, which began in late 1974. On July 27 and November 5, 1976, two opinions were released by a Republican-oriented commission that set rates at unprecedented levels. For contracts made on or after January 1, 1975, price ceilings were set at $1.42 per Mcf with quarterly escalations of $0.01 per Mcf beginning October 1, 1976. For contracts made between January 1,

---

[202]Opinion 749, 54 FPC 3090 (1975). Also see Opinion 749-C, 56 FPC 303 (1976).

[203]The 749 opinions were upheld in *Tenneco Oil Co.* v. *FPC*, 571 F.2d 834 (5th Cir. 1978), dismissed 439 U.S. 801 (1978).

[204]Order 539 (54 FPC 1576 [1975]) gave the FPC "full authority to enforce the rendition of natural gas to meet certified . . . services . . . quantities, volumes, or sales, earlier espoused in the *Bass* (1972) and *Southland* (1975) cases." See Rush Moody, "Uncertainty in Natural Gas Regulation and Legislation—A Dilemma for the Gas Producer and His Attorney," 22 *Rocky Mountain Institute* (New York: Matthew Bender, 1976), pp. 718–22; and idem, "The FERC Inheritance—Unresolved Problems in Producer Regulation," 29 *Oil and Gas Institute* (New York: Matthew Bender, 1978), p. 420.

1973, and January 1, 1975, a rate of $0.93 per Mcf was permitted with yearly escalations of $0.01 per Mcf. For gas under expired contracts, previously given the maximum ceiling rate, new contracts could be made for $0.52 per Mcf with yearly escalations of $0.01 per Mcf.[205] These increases were magnified by an August 28, 1975, provision that allowed output from producers with annual output under 10 Bcf a ceiling price of 130 percent of the otherwise maximum rate.[206] Certain restrictions were included to limit opportunistic ownership rearrangements, a provision that carried over to the next phase of producer regulation beginning in 1978.

Drastic, but long-overdue, price increases provided in Opinion 700 were based on "many factors" besides the *Permian 1* cost methodology, including "the price of competitive fuels, the impact upon supply and demand, inflationary pressures, the nation's natural gas shortage and conservation factors."[207] Historic cost was abandoned as a primary consideration: pragmatism that led to its previous use now dictated its quiet burial and replacement by trended (predicted future) cost and the aforementioned factors. The "scientific" approach to price setting was not so successful after all compared with unheralded spontaneous pricing of the market.

The new rates, representing over $1 billion in increased yearly income for producers, prompted quick action for judicial reversal on all sides. Consumer interests sought a rollback, while producer interests sought still higher rates. With legislative action in process to amend the NGA to establish a new pricing approach, the District of Columbia Circuit Court of Appeals affirmed the 770 opinions, as it had the 699 and 749 opinions, regarding procedure, facts, and conclusions.[208] The court expressed faith in the agency's "devotion to the public interest" at a time when "the nation is engaged in a searching review of its entire energy policy and a possible restructuring of agency powers."[209] Higher prices, although short of unregulated levels, were necessarily the order of the day.

---

[205]Opinion 770, 56 FPC 509 (1976); and Opinion 770-A, 56 FPC 2698 (1976). The commission described such pricing as "monitored decontrol." FPC, *Annual Report* (Washington, D.C.: Government Printing Office, 1975), p. 36.

[206]Opinion 742, 54 FPC 853 (1975).

[207]Opinion 770, 56 FPC at 516 (1976).

[208]*American Public Gas Association* v. *FPC*, 567 F.2d 1016 (D.C. Cir. 1977).

[209]Ibid., p. 1064.

Summary. The experiment with national rate pricing, the third phase of gas-producer regulation, yielded unsatisfactory results, which led to its demise. Flaws of the area approach were exacerbated by national averaging. Arbitrary cost determinations lumped together high-cost and low-cost reservoirs to arrive at a cost-based nationwide price.[210] A uniform return, neglecting relative entrepreneurial abilities, was adopted. The demand-side implications of regulation were ignored. Multitiered pricing was abandoned only to be reinstated, but either way, since they produced nonmarket prices, both approaches produced economic distortion. The end result was no different than before—below-market pricing that failed to elicit supply and ration demand to end shortages. Shortages experienced in the early 1970s were lessened by warmer winters and the 1974–75 recession, but the cold winter of 1976–77 revealed a supply crisis to crush any hopes of national ratemaking, despite liberalized pricing. Frustrated Commissioner Rush Moody, his reasoned pleas for deregulation and higher administrative pricing ignored, resigned with the statement, "I can no longer participate in a regulatory system which is inflicting grave damage to our national economic structure."[211] Radical price increases in Stage II only admitted the inability of maximum price controls to restrain prices and yet avoid economic distortion.

The administrative simplicity of aggregate price setting would be again outweighed by the result. When increasing simplicity failed to "cure" the problem, a return to complexity to fine-tune the problem would be tried.

The Natural Gas Policy Act of 1978 (Phase IV)

Toward Legislative Reform

With the advent of curtailments in the early 1970s, consumer unrest joined long-standing producer dissatisfaction to make the status quo vulnerable to legislative reform. The choice was to *deregulate* to ration demand, spur production, and reallocate intrastate

---

[210]For a wholesale critique of the *Permian 1* cost-estimation methodology used in Opinion 699 to arrive at $0.42 per Mcf, verified by subsequent revisions to cost justify price hikes, see the dissent of Commissioner Moody, 51 FPC 2307-40 (1974). Also see his dissent to the revision to $0.50 per Mcf in Opinion 699-H, 52 FPC 1604 (1974).

[211]*OGJ*, March 17, 1975, p. 83. In Opinion 699, Moody advocated a national rate based on cost estimated as high as $0.71 per Mcf. *OGJ*, July 1, 1974, p. 16.

supply interstate or to *expand regulation* by regulating intrastate and forcing conversions from natural gas to other fuels.

In the 1960s, the distortive effects of regulation had not yet arrived to inspire reform. Pro-regulation interests, such as the AFL/CIO, the United States Conference of Mayors, the American Municipal Association, and the National Committee for Fair Gas Prices, would not be budged without a crisis of supply. But in the 1970s, the scene changed.

In 1971, thirty-one northern Democrats from areas affected by curtailments introduced H.R. 2513 to deregulate small-producer contracts, forbid administrative rollbacks of contract prices, and set gas prices on the basis of "other economic factors besides cost."[212] Two similar bills were introduced in the Senate. Despite support from the American Gas Association, a trade group of interstate gas pipelines and gas distributors that had traditionally favored regulation, the bill did not reach a vote because of consumer-state opposition and a belief that the FPC could achieve the same ends administratively. A Senate try at partial deregulation during the following session of Congress (the ninety-third) narrowly failed by a 45 to 43 vote. An amendment to S. 2776 by Senator James Buckley (R-N.Y.) would have deregulated new gas contracts.[213]

Heightened debate between pro-regulation and anti-regulation forces occurred in the ninety-fifth Congress. Shortages had grown more severe, and the worst yet was feared for the next winter (1975–76). S. 2310 was introduced as an "emergency gas bill" that allowed high-priority users to purchase gas at up to three times its legal price. It was then amended to deregulate onshore gas contracts made after January 1, 1975, while phasing out price controls on offshore gas over six years—measures strongly supported by President Ford. On October 22, 1975, the Senate passed S. 2310 with the

---

[212]M. Elizabeth Sanders, *The Regulation of Natural Gas*, p. 129.

[213]*OGJ*, December 24, 1973, p. 24. The reemergence of gas decontrol (if only partial) as a live political issue was explained by the *OGJ* of October 8, 1973: "When the results of regulation were only a theory, Congress twice passed decontrol bills, only to have them vetoed. . . . Now that the shortage is here, and the problem is far better understood by the public, the issue is much more controversial in Congress. And it is the President who is leading the campaign for decontrol, with strong support from disillusioned producer regulators on the Federal Power Commission" (p. 33).

Pearson-Bentsen amendment somewhat weakened. In the House, H.R. 9764, which began as a companion measure to S. 2310, was amended into an opposite measure to expand regulation intrastate for large producers, set a national price from cost-of-service data, and require power plants to convert from gas to coal. Backed by a coalition from consumer states and coal states, the bill narrowly passed the House on February 5, 1976. Compromise with the Senate bill would be virtually impossible; any amendatory bill would have to find new political drive.

After his election in November 1976, President Carter reversed his campaign pledge to deregulate natural gas and embarked on a far-ranging constructivist program to fine-tune a legislative solution to the "energy crisis."[214] Dependence on market forces to balance supply and demand in the short run and set longer run configurations of supply, cost, and price was ruled out. At the center of Carter's National Energy Plan was natural gas that, in the winter of 1976–77 ran unprecedentedly short in the West, Midwest, and Northeast. Those shortages were responsible for thousands of business closings, millions of disrupted jobs, and several deaths in homes short of gas heat.[215] By early 1977, proposals were being made to extend regulation within states to close the intrastate-interstate gap and to price gas by cost-of-extraction and vintaging criteria—seventeen categories in all. The major premise of the pricing scheme was that sensitivity of supply to price was small, or in the words of the National Energy Plan, "market incentives cannot improve on nature."[216] Therefore, higher prices due to decontrol would result in a wealth transfer without corresponding benefits. Coupled with mandatory fuel-saving measures, the Carter plan became recognized by friend and foe as a *conservation*, not a *production*, policy.

---

[214]Carter's change of heart was political. Stated M. Elizabeth Sanders in *The Regulation of Natural Gas:* "By aligning administrative policy with the urban consumer interests, a Democratic President cast his lot with traditional, reliable partisans whose electoral votes could give the incumbent President a second term" (p. 165).

[215]William Simon, *A Time for Truth* (New York: McGraw-Hill, 1978), p. 81. Emergency sixty-day sales outside of FPC authorization transferred 400 MMcf per day from surplus to shortage areas to prevent even worse hardship. *OGJ*, February 14, 1977, pp. 43–48.

[216]Executive Office of the President, Energy Policy and Planning Office, *The National Energy Plan* (Washington D.C.: Government Printing Office, 1977), p. 11.

On April 20, 1977, a comprehensive energy plan—some "one hundred interdependent proposals consisting of pricing policies and the creation of regulatory mechanisms and administrative actions"—was presented to a joint session of Congress by the president.[217] Behind the recommendations were "energy czar" James Schlesinger and a staff of fifteen energy planners.[218] The thorniest area of the entire energy plan was natural gas, as the 1976 congressional stalemate had suggested. It would take a nearly unprecedented executive lobbying effort to turn a compromise version of Carter's proposals into what on November 9, 1978, became Phase IV of the regulation of natural-gas producers.

The House of Representatives, under the guidance of Speaker Thomas O'Neill passed H.R. 8444 on August 5, 1977, Title I of which contained the administration's complex natural-gas proposals. In the Senate the going would be tougher. S. 2104 was reported out of committee without recommendation, and, surviving a filibuster, a phased deregulation plan was substituted for the administration bill. Compromise legislation was then forged by the House-Senate conference committee on July 31, 1978. Between this time and passage three months later, White House lobbyists went into high gear. Government projects were dangled before members of Congress who could trade support for the bill for jobs in their home areas. Lame-duck members were offered government jobs upon expiration of their terms in return for support. Leaders in major nonoil industries favoring deregulation were summoned to White House conferences and told to support the bill or potentially suffer at the hands of government policy in their areas. With such strong-arm tactics, enough support was garnered to override the adamant opposition of independent producers (except deep-gas drillers represented by the Independent Gas Producers Committee who were not regulated under the bill) who abhorred extension of regulation intrastate, and labor unions and certain consumer groups who rebelled at the compromise pricing provisions.[219] Interstate pipelines supported the

---

[217]James Cochrane, "Carter Energy Policy and the Ninety-Fifth Congress," in *Energy Policy in Perspective*, p. 564.

[218]Commented Cochrane, "Schlesinger's views on national economic policy were closer to French indicative planning than to the invisible hand of Adam Smith, Alfred Marshall, or Milton Friedman." Ibid., p. 553.

[219]M. Elizabeth Sanders, *The Regulation of Natural Gas*, pp. 187–88. Sanders called the Carter blitzkrieg "one of history's most impressive lobbying efforts" (p. 187). Underscoring the media (and intellectual) bias toward regulation, the 1956 Keck affair

compromise bill on pragmatic grounds as did some intrastate carriers.[220] For example, Houston Natural Gas, a major Texas utility with a vast intrastate pipeline network, favored the bill on grounds that a lower cost of service due to regulation of intrastate producers would increase its market share.[221] Other major industry groups, such as the American Petroleum Institute and the Natural Gas Supply Committee, viewed the bill neutrally with its intricate mix of improvements to and retrogradations from the status quo.[222]

The Senate approved the compromise gas act on September 27, 1978, followed by House approval October 15. The following month, President Carter signed the NGPA into law.[223]

Provisions of the NGPA

The Natural Gas Policy Act of 1978 substituted a new regulatory program for the Natural Gas Act's tenuous section 1(b) authority. The new law expanded regulation intrastate and shifted wellhead pricing powers from the discretion of the Federal Energy Regulatory Commission (prior to November 1, 1977, the FPC) to Congress. All cost bases for determining ceiling prices were replaced by statutory formulas. The last vestiges of public-utility regulation, certificates of public convenience and necessity, were dropped for gas contracts. Nonprice deregulation provided in section 601, which in one fell swoop did away with entry, rate, and abandonment requirements, was called the "single most important section in the NGPA" by principal draftsman

---

(a political donation by an appreciative oilman) was turned into a national scandal while Carter's pork-barrel politics—legitimized bribery—was viewed as pragmatic "ends justify the means" politics.

[220]Ibid., pp. 186–87. As early as 1975, one chairman of a major interstate pipeline, Transco's Jack Bowen, advocated intrastate federal regulation as a second-best alternative to higher interstate pricing to compete with the intrastate market. *OGJ*, April 21, 1975, p. 42. With a $0.51 per Mcf ceiling price compared to $2.00 per Mcf intrastate, 97 percent of new onshore gas offered in 1973 went intrastate. *Business Week*, May 19, 1975, p. 91.

[221]M. Elizabeth Sanders, *The Regulation of Natural Gas*, p. 236.

[222]John Jimison, "Natural Gas Policy," in *Energy Initiatives of the 95th Congress* (Washington, D.C.: Government Printing Office, 1979), p. 53.

[223]Public Law 95-621, 92 Stat. 3350 (1978). Carter's version of NGPA lobbying, absent description of hardball tactics, is contained in his autobiography, *Keeping Faith* (New York: Bantam Books, 1982), pp. 102–7.

William Demarest.[224] Price deregulation, in contrast, was incremental and partial. Effective December 1, 1978, the NGPA contained Congress's outline that the Federal Energy Regulatory Commission (FERC) and the judiciary had to hammer into defined law.

Title I: Pricing. Maximum-price regulation revolved around the concept of first sale, which encompassed transactions between the producer, gatherer, processor, broker (reseller), and intrastate pipeline. Sales from intrastate pipelines to interstate pipelines and distribution companies were not covered by NGPA regulation but by NGA regulation instead. Broad price-ceiling coverage of field gas sales was designed to prevent opportunistic resales to bring prices to market-clearing levels. The implications of the ongoing oil-resale boom were understood by the drafters of the gas bill.[225]

Eight gas categories were established for first-sale pricing purposes with subsections pertaining to well location, vintage of production, and the nature of the contract. The assigned price ceilings, noticed Carroll Gilliam, "consisted of a combination of broadly applicable rates and vestigial remnants of each of the Commission's approaches ... between 1954 and 1978."[226] *New gas* ("102 gas"), defined as onshore output from wells drilled 1,000 feet below or 2.5 miles from existing ("marker") wells after April 20, 1977, along with Outer Continental Shelf wells drilled after July 26, 1976, was allowed a price of $1.75 per million British thermal units (MMBtu) for April 1977 plus a monthly inflation and growth factor (3.5 percent to April 1981 and 4 percent thereafter). Gas from the Prudhoe Bay (Alaska) unit was excluded.[227] *New onshore gas* ("103 gas"), defined as output

[224]Comments before the Executive Enterprise Conference, "FERC Natural Gas Regulation," Houston, Texas, October 10, 1984. At the time of the bill, Demarest was counsel to the Subcommittee on Energy and Power of the House Committee on Interstate and Foreign Commerce.

[225]Ibid. Fixed long-term contracts also precluded resale of natural gas.

[226]Carroll Gilliam, "Wellhead Regulation under the Natural Gas Act and the Natural Gas Policy Act," p. 20-104.

[227]NGPA, sec. 102. One million British thermal units (MMBtu's) is virtually equivalent to one thousand cubic feet (Mcf) of gas. The Btu standard was already fairly common in private contracts, but as a statutory term it would bring unforeseen problems. Specifically, it was not defined whether Btu was calculated on the basis of actual delivery conditions or under water-saturated conditions. The latter understated Btu content compared to the former by approximately 1.7 percent, and pipelines went to court contending that NGPA ceiling prices were overstated by the difference. On August 9, 1983, the U.S. court of appeals overruled FERC Order 93 (15 FERC 49247) and Order 93-A (15 FERC 61169) to side with the "wet rule" over the "dry

from post–February 19, 1977, gas wells within 1,000 feet vertically and 2.5 miles horizontally of existing wells if properly spaced under state law, was priced at $1.75 per MMBtu for April 1977, adjusted monthly for inflation. After 1984, gas from wells less than 5,000 feet deep drilled after April 20, 1977, would revert to this category except for Prudhoe Bay gas, which was to be priced midway between the 103 gas price, inflation adjusted, and the current 102 price. Contracts for *dedicated interstate gas* ("104 gas") from pre–November 10, 1978, could be priced at the higher of the FPC-approved contract price as of April 20, 1977, inflation adjusted, or the November 9, 1978, price. An extension of the NGA just and reasonable price, this price could be increased further at FERC discretion. *Dedicated intrastate gas* ("105 gas") from pre–November 10, 1978, contracts could be priced at the higher of the new-gas price or the inflation-adjusted contract price.[228]

In lieu of contract escalation clauses, if the December 3, 1984, price for such gas was over $1.00 per MMBtu, then the ceiling would be the higher of the new-gas or the inflation-adjusted contract price. Three price determinations were made for *rollover-contract gas* ("106 gas"), defined as gas from contracts made before the NGPA that subsequently expired. For the interstate ("106a") variety, a ceiling of $0.54 per MMBtu, inflation adjusted, was designated unless a higher FERC discretionary price was allowed; for intrastate ("106b") gas, the higher of the expired contract price, inflation adjusted, or $1.00 per MMBtu, inflation adjusted from May 1977, was legal.

For Indian-land gas, the new-gas price was allowed. A sixth category, *high-cost gas* ("107 gas"), was also permitted to receive the new-gas price. Such gas included production from below 15,000 feet from post–February 19, 1977, wells, from geopressured brine, from Devonian shale, and from coal seams where the gas was occluded. For projects the FERC felt were sufficiently high cost or risky, such as enhanced production and tight sand production, the FERC was to set incentive (not cost) prices. *Stripper-well gas* ("108 gas"), defined

---

rule." *Interstate Natural Gas Association* v. *Federal Energy Regulatory Commission*, 716 F.2d 1 (D.C. Cir. 1983). Refunds of over $1 billion, representing the first-sale overcharge from December 1, 1978, forward, were scheduled for repayment by November 5, 1984, for producers with 1983 sales of 10 Bcf or more and by May 3, 1985, for the remainder.

[228]The roundabout NGPA method was to take the lower of the contract or *new-gas* price and then, if the contract price was higher, pick the higher of the *new-gas* or adjusted contract price.

as gas from wells with output under 60 Mcf per day at maximum-efficient-rate levels for ninety straight days (or greater than 60 Mcf per day from qualifying enhanced-recovery projects), was priced at $2.09 per MMBtu for May 1978 with monthly inflation adjustments and growth adjustments (3.5 percent before April 20, 1981, and 4 percent thereafter).

The last category, *other gas* ("109 gas"), was priced at $1.45 per MMBtu for April 1977 with inflation adjustments every month thereafter. Included in this category were Prudhoe Bay gas and other differentiable gas, to be determined, worthy of separate pricing in the commission's estimation.[229]

If gas qualified under more than one of the above categories, the highest price was allowed—the "producer always wins" rule.[230] Commingled gas from different categories was priced on a weighted-average basis. Higher NGPA prices could not trigger indefinite escalator clauses; also voided were regulatory escape clauses designed to void contracts in the event of expanded federal jurisdiction. Last, NGPA regulation applied to most but not all natural gas. Synthetic gas remained regulated under the "just and reasonable" price authority of the NGA as did natural gas dedicated to interstate commerce prior to November 9, 1978, except for new gas, high-cost gas, and new onshore gas. NGA price ceilings are given in table 8.4.

Reflecting the Senate's position, the compromise bill scheduled some categories of gas for decontrol. High-cost gas was to be deregulated first, the sooner of November 9, 1979, or when the incremental pricing rule was promulgated. This occurred on November 1, 1979. Four categories were decontrolled, entirely or in part, on January 1, 1985: new gas, new onshore production-well gas from post–April 20, 1977, gas from wells over 5,000 feet deep, and interstate-dedicated gas priced over $1.00 per MMBtu on December 31, 1984. Scheduled for decontrol on July 1, 1987, was post–April 20, 1977, gas from wells within 5,000 feet of the surface (shallow 103 gas). This would

---

[229]For twelve subcategories of other gas as of 1980, see Michael Silva and Phyllis Rainey, "Learning to Live with the NGPA—The Cents and Nonsense," 26 *Rocky Mountain Institute* (New York: Matthew Bender, 1980), pp. 720–21.

[230]See NGPA, sec. 101(b)(5). When overpricing and surplus deliverability became a problem several years later, commission opinions began to tend the other way to reduce first-sale prices.

Table 8.4
NGA Prices under the Natural Gas Policy Act

Type of Gas	Price Ceiling
Small producer	130 percent of assigned rate
Rollover contract	$0.52 per Mcf plus $0.01 per year escalation
Pre–January 1, 1973, flowing gas	$0.93 per Mcf or area rate, whichever is greater
January 1, 1973–January 1, 1975, wells	$0.93 per Mcf plus $0.01 per year escalation
Post–January 1, 1975, wells	$1.42 per Mcf plus $0.01 per year escalation

Source: NGPA, Title I, "Wellhead Pricing," Subtitle A1, "Wellhead Price Controls."

leave under perpetual price ceilings, by way of contrast, stripper-well gas, other gas, rollover-contract gas, intrastate-dedicated gas, interstate-dedicated gas under $1.00 per MMBtu on December 31, 1984, new onshore production-well gas from less than 5,000 feet, and gas from wells drilled between February 20 and April 19, 1977.

Reimposition of price controls on deregulated gas except high-cost gas was allowed if done by Congress or the president between July 1, 1985, and June 30, 1987, for a maximum period of eighteen months. If deregulated again within this period, a second reimposition was not allowed.

Title II: Incremental Pricing. Title II of the NGPA dealt with the question of which interstate consumers would bear the burden of the higher wellhead price categories contained in the act. Because of the relative political strength of utility companies, residential consumers were protected and the higher price (cost) increments were directed at industrial users—steam and electric boiler fuel customers—which came under federal regulation for the first time.[231] Between the favored and the penalized were commercial users. One

[231]To be passed through were higher prices for new gas, rollover-contract gas, new onshore production-well gas, imported gas (natural and liquefied), stripper-well gas, higher cost gas, and Prudhoe Bay gas along with any price increase resulting from state severance taxes, emergency gas sales, and special interstate pipeline surcharges.

429

constraint, intended to prevent fuel substitution, was that higher gas costs could not exceed the cost of an alternative fuel (no. 2 fuel oil). Exempted from incremental pricing were industrial users of less than 300 Mcf per day, agricultural users, schools, hospitals, and other public institutions. [232]

Other Sections. Title III set forth the authority of the president to declare a gas emergency, make emergency gas purchases, and make emergency gas allocations. Mandatory carriage of interstate pipeline gas by an intrastate line and vice versa could be ordered by the FERC.[233] The commission was allowed to set a minimum duration for onshore producer contracts at the lower of fifteen years or the commercial life of the reservoir. For offshore producers, this contract minimum was mandatory. Title IV dealt with curtailment policies largely borrowed from earlier FPC opinions. Title V dealt with FERC administration and enforcement and judicial review of the NGPA. Title VI, finally, set forth the interrelationship between the NGPA, the NGA, and state energy law.

Modifications to the NGPA: 1978–84

The broad features of the NGPA provided by Congress would become specific with FERC pronouncements and interpretations from the Department of Energy's Office of General Counsel. On December 1, 1978, the effective date of the NGPA, 364 pages of interim regulations were released.[234] This began "a seemingly endless stream of interim rules, revised rules, changes on rehearing, 'final' rules, and modification of those 'final' rules on rehearing."[235]

Prices set under the interim regulations, along with later adjustments and modifications, are given in table 8.5.

Administrative rulings shaped and modified the act. Several early orders reduced notice and filing responsibilities for monthly rate changes for small producers and interstate dedications.[236] Interpretative orders further defining major gas categories were issued in 1979

---

[232]Phase I of the program covering only large industrial users was not extended to all users as originally planned. See 49 *Fed. Reg.* 12207 (March 29, 1984).

[233]See chapter 15, pp. 946–47.

[234]43 *Fed. Reg.* 56448 (December 1, 1978).

[235]Carroll Gilliam, "Wellhead Regulation under the Natural Gas Act and the Natural Gas Policy Act," p. 20-106.

[236]Order 15, 43 *Fed. Reg.* 55756 (November 17, 1978); and Order 25, 44 *Fed. Reg.* 19387 (April 3, 1979).

Table 8.5
NGPA Price Ceilings: 1978–84

NGPA Gas Category (section of act)	Price ($/MMBtu) as of							
	12-78	1-79	1-80	1-81	1-82	1-83	1-84
New gas (102)	2.08	2.10	2.36	2.67	3.00	3.30	3.59
New onshore gas (103)	1.97	1.98	2.16	2.36	2.57	2.72	2.85
Interstate-dedicated gas (104)							
Minimum rate	0.20	0.20	0.22	0.24	0.27	0.28	0.29
Replacement contract							
Small producer	0.78	0.78	0.85	0.93	1.01	1.07	1.12
Large producer	0.59	0.60	0.65	0.71	0.77	0.82	0.86
Flowing							
Small producer	0.39	0.40	0.43	0.47	0.51	0.54	0.57
Large producer	0.33	0.33	0.36	0.40	0.43	0.46	0.48
Permian Basin[a]							
Small producer	0.46	0.47	0.50	0.55	0.60	0.64	0.67
Large producer	0.41	0.41	0.44	0.49	0.53	0.56	0.59
Rocky Mountain[a]							
Small producer	0.46	0.47	0.50	0.55	0.60	0.64	0.67
Large producer	0.39	0.40	0.43	0.47	0.51	0.54	0.56
Appalachian Basin[a]							
Post-10-7-69	0.37	0.37	0.40	0.44	0.48	0.51	0.54
Other	0.34	0.35	0.38	0.42	0.45	0.48	0.50

(Continued on next page)

Table 8.5—Continued
NGPA Price Ceilings: 1978–84

NGPA Gas Category (section of act)	Price ($/MMBtu) as of							
	12-78	1-79	1-80	1-81	1-82	1-83	1-84
Post-1974[b]	1.63	1.64	1.79	1.96	2.13	2.25	2.36
1973–74 decade[b]							
Small producer	1.38	1.39	1.51	1.66	1.80	1.91	2.00
Large producer	1.06	1.06	1.16	1.27	1.38	1.46	1.53
Intrastate, contract (105)	Per contract							
Interstate, rollover contract gas (106)							
Small producer	0.70	0.72	0.73	0.74	0.79	0.84	0.88
Large producer	0.60	0.61	0.66	0.72	0.79	0.84	0.88
High-cost gas (107)	2.08	2.10	4.73	5.14	—[c]	—[c]	
Stripper-well gas (108)	2.22	2.24	2.86	3.22	3.54	3.84	
Other gas (109)	1.63	1.64	1.96	2.13	2.25	2.36	

SOURCE: *Foster Natural Gas Report*, various issues.

[a]Certain types.

[b]This category also reflects NGA pricing.

[c]Various.

and 1980.[237] Effective September 3, 1980, pipeline production became eligible for NGPA maximum prices in place of NGA assignments.[238] Several subsequent rulings relaxed pricing constraints to the chagrin of some who charged that "backdoor" or "administrative" decontrol was taking place in violation of congressional intent and administrative authority under the NGPA.[239] Order 23, issued March 13, 1979, allowed NGA area prices to escalate to NGPA ceiling prices.[240] On August 15, 1980, gas produced from tight sands was given a price ceiling of 200 percent of the 103 price.[241] Over the next eighteen months, approximately seventy geological formations would be designated for incentive pricing.[242]

Two proposed rulemakings to extend incentive pricing were considered but not adopted: deep-water gas, gas from reservoirs 300 feet below the mean water drilling surface, was to receive 200 percent of the 103 gas price, and "near-deep gas," gas found between 10,000 and 14,999 feet below the drilling surface, was to receive 150 percent of the 103 gas price. The urgency of increasing prices toward market or incentive levels was dissipated when a stark reality hit the gas market. Falling fuel-oil prices, coupled with rising prices for incentive-priced and decontrolled NGPA gas categories, prevented use of the latter from increasing in industrial and power-plant markets

---

[237]Section 102 gas: Order 42-A, 44 *Fed. Reg.* 69642 (December 4, 1979); section 103 gas: Order 43-A, 44 *Fed. Reg.* 67108 (November 23, 1979); section 104 gas: Order 64-A, 45 *Fed. Reg.* 16171 (March 13, 1980); section 105 gas: Order 68, 45 *Fed. Reg.* 5678 (January 24, 1980); section 107 gas: Order 78, 45 *Fed. Reg.* 28092 (April 28, 1980); section 108 gas: Order 43, 44 *Fed. Reg.* 49651 (August 24, 1979); section 109 gas: Order 72, 45 *Fed. Reg.* 18915 (March 24, 1980).

[238]45 *Fed. Reg.* 53091 (August 11, 1980). Also see 49 *Fed. Reg.* 33849 (August 27, 1984).

[239]See, for instance, the testimony of Edwin Rothschild, *Natural Gas Policy and Regulatory Issues*, Hearings before the Senate Committee on Energy and Natural Resources, 97th Cong., 2d sess. (Washington, D.C.: Government Printing Office, 1980), pp. 698–99. Cited hereafter as *Natural Gas Policy*.

[240]This was upheld in *Pennzoil Co.* v. *FERC*, 645 F.2d 360 (5th Cir. 1981) cert. denied, 454 U.S. 1142 (1982).

[241]Order 99, 45 *Fed. Reg.* 56034 (August 22, 1980). This was upheld in *Pennzoil Co.* v. *FERC*, 671 F.2d 119 (5th Cir. 1982).

[242]See *Natural Gas Policy*, p. 29. Quipped Arie Verrips, "It appears the entire state of Ohio may soon qualify for the 107(c)(5) incentive price." Testimony of Verrips, *Implementation of Title I of the Natural Gas Policy Act of 1978*, Hearings before the Senate Committee on Energy and Natural Resources, 97th Cong,. 2d sess., 1982 (Washington, D.C.: Government Printing Office, 1982), p. 324. Cited hereafter as *Implementation*.

short of fuel switching. Despite regulation of gas prices from well-head to burner tip, consumer resistance in the alternate-fuel market effectively capped the price of natural gas. Higher regulated gas prices would lose market share and thus would be self-defeating.

On January 1, 1985, three categories of regulated gas became deregulated to leave 40 percent of natural gas under control—primarily 104 gas dedicated interstate prior to the NGPA. Although technically unregulated, price and other contract provisions for freed gas came under indirect government control as a pipeline cost of service. Interstate lines came under FERC review under the NGA and section 601(c)(2) of the NGPA, the latter of which barred gas cost recovery if "excessive" due to "fraud, abuse, or similar grounds."[243] In the 1984 *Columbia* opinion, the FERC gave substance to this section by questioning the pipeline's choice of a substitute fuel on which to base pricing.[244] Another policy declaration limited take-or-pay commitments to 75 percent for new contracts.[245] Pipelines' collection of the variable-cost portion of minimum-bill contracts for gas not taken by distributors was prohibited, with upstream ramifications.[246]

In the 1981–82 debate over the NGPA, much concern was raised about the January 1, 1985, date of partial deregulation. Critics predicted that escalator clauses (favored nation, deregulation, indefinite, and area) would be triggered to create spiraling price increases that would injure consumers. What was not realized then is realized now: the market, not only regulators, sets prices. No price can be greater than the market price without self-defeating consequences. Gas prices cannot and did not increase on the deregulation date because of the fuel-switching capabilities of a major segment of the market. In fact, some NGPA-regulated ceiling prices—contractually unassailable—turned from price ceilings to price floors. A producer strategy thus became to strictly interpret contracts so as to remain regulated.[247]

---

[243]Public Law 95-621, 92 Stat. 3411.
[244]47 *Fed. Reg.* 6253 (February 11, 1982).
[245]47 *Fed. Reg.* 57268 (December 23, 1982).
[246]Order 380, 27 FERC 61594 (1984).
[247]See, for example, *OGJ*, October 29, 1984, pp. 44–46.

NGPA Distortions and Policy Discontent
The first six years under the NGPA, the fourth stage of natural-gas price regulation, were stormy. Senator Bennett Johnson (D-La.) characterized the act as

> very much like the Treaty of Versailles after the First World War. It was a lot better than a continuation of the war, but we redrew the map in such a way that it guaranteed a new conflict. And indeed, we are in a new conflict.[248]

Few proponents or opponents hailed the early returns. The patchwork bill, in fact, gave the gas market the worst of both worlds—high prices for consumers and ambivalent incentives for producers. Production efficiency, in any case, was not advanced. This was documented at extensive hearings before a Senate subcommittee investigating the pricing features of the NGPA in late 1981.

Before considering prices and production during the first six years of the act, a review of the policy positions of hearing participants is instructive. The biggest supporters of the NGPA were the same groups that had actively secured its passage in 1978—interstate gas carriers and gas distributors.[249] Artificially low acquisition costs under old-gas contracts protected the competitive edge over competing fuels, and availability of supply was improved by intrastate regulation and expedited transportation in section 311. Also supporting the status quo was a group of fifteen gas producers, represented by GHK Companies, who were heavily committed to decontrolled deep gas and incentive-priced tight gas.[250] A middle position was taken by the Consumer Energy Council of America, a self-styled consumer group, which found more fault with FERC administration than with the act itself.[251] Taking an adversarial position in favor of

[248]*Natural Gas Legislation: Part 1*, Hearings before the Senate Committee on Energy and Natural Resources, 98th Cong., 1st sess., 1983 (Washington D.C.: Government Printing Office, 1983), p. 67. Cited hereafter as *Natural Gas Legislation: 1*.

[249]See the testimony of the Interstate Natural Gas Association of America in *Implementation*, pp. 326–45; the Associated Gas Distributors, pp. 357–75; and the American Gas Association, pp. 286–97.

[250]Ibid., pp. 502–22. This group was soon organized as the Independent Gas Producers Committee. Deep drilling would be concentrated in the Oklahoma Anadarko Basin, the Louisiana Tuscaloosa Trend, and the Rocky Mountain Overthrust Belt.

[251]Ibid., pp. 129–50. In testimony four months later, another consumer group, the Citizen Labor Energy Coalition, expressed dissatisfaction with both the NGPA, which it lobbied against originally, and its implementation. *Natural Gas Policy*, pp. 698–712.

immediate deregulation or greater deregulation were general producers,[252] fuel-oil interests,[253] industrial users,[254] and producer-state interests.[255] The diversity of dissatisfaction with the NGPA was noteworthy: producers were unhappy with incentives, consumerists were against rising prices, fuel-oil interests complained of "legalized predatory pricing,"[256] industrial users worried about inadequate and uncertain feedstock, intrastate pipelines complained about shortages, and environmentalists expressed concern over substitution to polluting fuels.[257] How the NGPA led to these positions brings us to the economic effects of the law itself.

Production Disincentives. The NGPA, with seven major pricing categories and over twenty pricing subcategories, was a complicated transition for producers and regulators. Rush Moody and Allan Garten speculated that the act was "the most complicated and ambiguous statute ever enacted."[258] Involved firms experienced as much as a 10 percent increase in administrative costs.[259] Early processing of thousands of category determinations by state agencies verged on chaos.[260] In the first two years of the program, over 10,000 determinations were challenged by outside parties without resolution, which

[252]See the testimony in *Implementation* of the Independent Producers Association of America (pp. 526–34) and of the Natural Gas Supply Association (pp. 580–93).

[253]Testimony of National Oil Jobbers Council. Ibid., pp. 797–99. Several months later, a similar trade group, the Northeast Coalition for Energy Equity, would boomerang the "consumerist" logic to argue, "Working people in the Northeast . . . [pay] doubly for gas price controls: They pay a higher price for oil to heat their homes and they receive lower wages so their employers may remain competitive." *Natural Gas Policy*, p. 599.

[254]See the testimony in *Implementation* of the National Association of Manufacturers (pp. 272–79), the Process Gas Consumers Group (pp. 182–207), the Petrochemical Energy Group (pp. 158–75), and the Chemical Manufacturers Association (pp. 263–71).

[255]See the testimony in *Implementation* of Texas Railroad Commissioner James Nugent (pp. 53–69) and the Intrastate Gas Caucus (pp. 423–41).

[256]Ibid., p. 797.

[257]See *Natural Gas Policy*, pp. 605–31.

[258]Rush Moody and Allan Garten, "The Natural Gas Policy Act of 1978: Analysis and Overview," 25 *Rocky Mountain Institute* (New York: Matthew Bender, 1979), p. 2-1.

[259]*Implementation*, p. 552.

[260]Testimony of Texas Railroad Commissioner James Nugent. Ibid., pp. 53–54.

Table 8.6
OIL- VS. GAS-WELL ACTIVITY: 1979–82

Year	Oil Wells	Change	Gas Wells	Change
1979	20,689	+ 9%	15,166	+ 5%
1980	32,120	+55%	17,134	+13%
1981	42,510	+32%	19,742	+15%
1982	39,252	+ 8%	18,810	− 5%

SOURCE: American Petroleum Institute, *Basic Petroleum Data Book* (Washington, D.C.: API, 1992), sec. 3, table 2a.

stifled planning for many producers who collected revenues potentially subject to refund.[261] Stiff criminal penalties for "willful" violations of NGPA determinations made producers tread lightly.[262] One visible result of these problems was an unexpected dearth of incentive 102 gas applications relative to lower priced 103 gas, which involved less paperwork.[263]

A second major factor working against NGPA inducements was a severe underestimation of future oil prices upon which the act's price ceilings were set. A $15 per barrel price of oil was used to set NGPA prices, yet by January 1980, the market price for crude had doubled. Consequently, gas drilling, although increased, lagged noticeably behind the oil-drilling boom. As seen in table 8.6, between 1979 and 1982, the number of oil wells increased by 90 percent and the number of gas wells increased by 24 percent.

A third disincentive for gas producers was concern that, price incentives notwithstanding, discovered gas might be unmarketable. New supply was often not dedicated to a pipeline, and in the open market, fuel oil had an advantage over gas in industrial markets because of the incremental pricing provisions of the act. Commented

[261]"As a result . . . [of this] 'cloud' on producers' NGPA revenues . . . some producers, particularly small producers, have had to curtail precisely the type of exploration and development activities that the NGPA was intended to encourage." Testimony of the Domestic Petroleum Council. Ibid., p. 475.

[262]One producer suggested making a prison inmate a company officer to sign NGPA papers so that "the government won't have to spend money to put him in jail, and I can try to find oil and gas rather than marker wells." Quoted in Alexander Stuart, "A Bad Start on Gas Deregulation," *Fortune*, February 12, 1979, p. 89.

[263]Rush Moody and Allan Garten, "The Natural Gas Policy Act of 1978: Analysis and Overview," p. 2-35.

one executive on the artificial incentives of the NGPA, "The prices in the bill may be good enough to go look for gas, but what the hell good is it if you can't sell it?"[264]

Whatever boost the NGPA gave gas drilling compared to area and national rate incentives—which were still below market incentives—resources were unambiguously misdirected. Risky, high-cost gas was encouraged, which precluded the development of more logical prospects. Prominent in this regard was unregulated deep gas, which in 1982 fetched a price as much as three times the approximately $3 per Mcf price of gas from above 15,000 feet. Criticized Edward Erickson:

> It just defies economic and geologic common sense and ordinary logic that there are not vast quantities of gas that lie between 5,000 feet and 15,000 feet that would be cost effective at prices above the NGPA ceiling price, but well below the current prices that we are seeing for deep gas. In effect, we are embargoing our own access to an important segment of our own geology.[265]

Table 8.7 shows the relative surge of costly deep drilling, particularly at the expense of near-deep (10,000 to 15,000 feet) wells through 1982.

A vivid example of the malincentive of depth pricing concerned Amoco Production Company, which, after encountering gas, relocated a drilling rig to a nearby hill to break the 15,000-foot threshold and obtain unregulated prices.[266] Obviously, the expense of relocation and redrilling was pure waste from the viewpoint of an unregulated market.

Compared to the forgone alternative of full market incentives for low-cost prospects, a wasteful emphasis on high-cost gas was also encouraged by incentive prices given to tight-gas formations, stripper-well gas, geopressurized methane, coal-seam gas, and Devonian shale gas. All of these categories are low-yield, high-cost supply sources. As had occurred with stripper oil wells, incentive prices for stripper gas, as much as six times the price of certain regulated gas categories, created incentive to deplete gas fields and neglect

---

[264]Alexander Stuart, "A Bad Start on Gas Deregulation," p. 90.

[265]*Implementation*, p. 77.

[266]*Houston Post*, August 2, 1981, p. 18C. Another ploy used to qualify near misses was to trade out the measuring rod for an older, slightly bent rod to record several more necessary feet.

Table 8.7
NATURAL-GAS WELL COMPLETIONS

Year	Number	Change (%)	Average Cost ($)
		Below 5,000 Feet	
1979	7,899	3	98,174
1980	8,290	5	119,800
1981	9,606	16	143,818
1982	9,156	5	149,965
		5,000 to 10,000 Feet	
1979	4,306	9	457,194
1980	4,816	12	503,886
1981	5,425	13	619,097
1982	5,164	−5	650,097
		10,000 to 15,000 Feet	
1979	1,581	11	1,506,077
1980	1,750	11	1,732,918
1981	2,017	15	2,230,692
1982	3,098	4	2,537,375
		Over 15,000 Feet	
1979	293	5	3,799,627
1980	369	26	4,645,698
1981	485	31	6,199,374
1982	634	−30	7,388,126

SOURCE: American Petroleum Institute, *Joint Association Survey on Drilling Cost* (Washington, D.C.: API, 1979–82), table 2.

workovers to reduce output to qualifying levels.[267] The pricing advantage of new wells over older wells in the same field discouraged efficient development of proven reserves.[268] As a consequence, risky wildcat drilling was promoted, while existing supply was underutilized.

[267]Alexander Stuart, "The Blazing Battle to Free Natural Gas," *Fortune*, October 19, 1981, p. 158.

[268]*Natural Gas Policy*, p. 197.

Table 8.8
RESERVE ACTIVITY: 1978–82
(billion cubic feet)

Year	Beginning Reserves	Additions	Con- sumption	Net Revisions	Ending Reserves
1978	207,413	18,021	− 18,805	1,404	208,033
1979	208,033	14,704	− 19,257	− 2,483	200,997
1980	200,997	14,473	− 18,699	2,241	199,012
1981	199,012	17,220	− 18,737	4,235	201,730
1982	201,730	14,455	− 17,506	2,833	201,512

SOURCE: American Gas Association, *1991 Gas Facts* (Arlington, Va.: AGA, 1991), table 2.2.

Proponents of the NGPA emphasized the increase in gas drilling and production that took place after 1978 as evidence of the success of the act. This is a superficial assessment. The increase did not duplicate the market and in fact was obtained at unnecessarily high average and incremental cost.[269] Free-market conditions would have directed more effort toward lower cost prospects and encouraged greater production overall. Supply would have been less leveraged—and thus less susceptible to price volatility. Proven reserves, which declined by nearly 5 percent in the early NGPA period, cast doubt on the incentives of the act (table 8.8).

Price and Allocation Distortions. Opening price assignments under NGPA regulation ranged from $0.20 to over $2.00 per MMBtu, a disparity that widened further when deep gas was deregulated in November 1979. High prices were created in part by low prices. Because the good was the same, a regulated price that failed to clear the market sent excess demand to less regulated deep gas, high-cost gas, liquefied natural gas (LNG), and imports to raise their prices above the equilibrium levels of an unregulated market.

Pricing differentials had nonneutral effects depending on each pipeline's portfolio of categorized gas.[270] Certain pipelines with

[269]Independent Petroleum Asssociation of America head Kye Trout would testify that the NGPA "caused economic distortions that have raised everybody's costs and prices." *Natural Gas Regulation: 1,* p. 693.

[270]Unlike crude-oil refineries, natural-gas pipelines did not consider, much less implement, a scheme to equalize acquisition costs.

440

lower average acquisition costs had a cushion that pipelines with higher priced gas lacked. In addition to inequalities for end users,[271] two distortions were created that would strike at the heart of the NGPA. First, high-cushioned carriers could outbid low-cushioned carriers for new supply by rolling higher priced marginal purchases into relatively low average costs. Although this inequity was evident for a variety of interstate pipelines, a particular disparity was evident between interstate and intrastate carriers, with the former assigned cheaper 104 gas and the latter assigned higher priced 105 gas. A spot check of Texas intrastate carriers in 1979 showed average acquisition costs almost double those of major interstate carriers.[272]

The intrastate supply situation was further imperiled by regulations promulgated in response to the pre-1978 days of interstate curtailments and intrastate surpluses designed to divert gas from the former to the latter. The "permanent dedication rule" prevented expired interstate supply contracts from being renegotiated with an intrastate carrier. Intrastate pipelines were not allowed to contract for Outer Continental Shelf gas, imported gas, or gas available from an out-of-state intrastate carrier.

The interstate-intrastate distinction that was seemingly legislated away in 1978 reappeared with the tables turned—the intrastate market was now suffering from supply uncertainty, while the interstate market enjoyed surpluses ("gas bubbles") and lower prices.[273] Hence, gas-consuming businesses such as petrochemical plants that prior to the NGPA thrived in Texas and Louisiana were now threatened

---

[271]For disparate residential rates for eight cities as of May 1981, see *Implementation*, p. 196.

[272]Ibid., p. 74. By 1981, the cushion had narrowed to $1.53 per MMBtu for interstates and $1.72 per MMBtu for intrastates. With lower transmission costs for the latter, the disparity was effectively less. Robert Perdue, "FERC Natural Gas Regulation," Paper delivered at Executive Enterprise Conference, Houston, Texas, February 9, 1983, p. 26.

[273]The irony of the radically changed situation was not lost on at least one senator.

Texas Railroad Commissioner Jim Nugent: Interstate purchasers . . . will have an extreme advantage over intrastate purchasers. . . . We think it's time our consumers were given equal consideration with those of other states.

Senator Gordon Humphrey (R-N.H.): I have to say, Mr. Nugent, I think that is the first time I ever saw Texas come out on the short end of the stick anywhere.

Commissioner Nugent: I hope it's the last time, Senator!

Implementation, p. 55.

by regulatory-induced price and supply problems. The chickens came home to roost in the winter of 1980–81 when Texas and Louisiana experienced spot curtailments despite off-system sales from interstate carriers with excess deliverability under section 311 authority.[274]

Price inequalities under the NGPA also had an adverse effect on the interstate market. Many interstate pipelines with slack in their pass-through costs—defined as the difference between their average gas costs and a higher average cost at which fuel-oil substitution would occur—were able to purchase unregulated deep gas and imports at premium prices until average acquisition costs reached the competitive ceiling.[275]

In addition to providing needed supply, high-priced acquisitions meant lucrative contracts for pipeline production affiliates with deep gas or incentive-priced tight-sand gas. But the bonanza would not last long. Following sizable purchased-gas adjustment pass-throughs—with the incidence magnified for industrial users pursuant to Title II incremental pricing—the competitive price ceiling, the price of fuel oil, was soon reached.[276] (Once the switch price was reached, incremental pricing ceased to operate, but reaching this danger point was a problem created by Title II for an estimated 1,200 nonexempt gas users.) In mid-1982, one pipeline after another began to lower deep-gas prices and set price caps on tight-sand gas. That devastated many debt-financed deep-gas drillers, which had ramifications not only for the gas industry but for financial institutions as well.[277] Increased conservation, the recession, and declining

[274]Ibid., pp. 56, 333, 424, 892–93. Oklahoma and New Mexico also encountered tight supply. Ibid., p. 433. See the discussion in Catherine Abbott and Stephen Watson, "Pitfalls on the Road to Decontrol: Lessons from the Natural Gas Policy Act of 1978," in *The Deregulation of Natural Gas*, ed. Edward Mitchell (Washington, D.C.: American Enterprise Institute, 1983), pp. 58–62.

[275]Many deep-gas purchases were consummated at $9.00 per Mcf and more, which in Btu terms translated to $50 per barrel of oil. Such purchases balanced old gas that was regulated as low as $0.26 per Mcf, equivalent to $1.58 per barrel. *Implementation*, pp. 192–93.

[276]The FERC generally refused to block sizable purchased-gas adjustment filings pursuant to sec. 601(c) authority, finding that "fraud, abuse or similar grounds" did not apply.

[277]The deep-gas bust was a major factor, along with oil-rig and oil-service industry loans, in the Penn Square Bank and Continental Illinois failures and nationalization. Seafirst, Interfirst, Chase Manhattan, and other major banks were also hurt by a 50 percent decline in deep-gas prices in 1982–83.

fuel-oil prices made price reductions imperative if pipelines were to avoid devastating load losses occasioned by price-sensitive industrial customers and consequent price spirals with fixed costs allocated over fewer and fewer sales (the so-called death spiral). Higher prices under the NGPA also were fueled by "category creep," the legal (and sometimes illegal) transfer of gas from lower priced to higher priced categories and the replacement of depleting older, lower priced gas by newer, higher priced gas.[278]

Higher gas prices in the first years of the NGPA were encouraged by world events. The second round of OPEC price hikes in 1979 raised the price of fuel oil and other substitutes, which increased gas demand to increase its competitive price range. Higher world energy prices also meant higher import prices for gas received by U.S. firms that contributed to increased composite gas prices.

The result of the above forces was a price explosion for all gas consumers. Residents who paid on average $2.65 per Mcf in 1978 paid $4.29 per Mcf in 1981 and $6.08 per Mcf in October 1982. Industrial users and electric utilities paid similar increases.[279] By late 1982 and early 1983, composite gas prices approximated if not exceeded market-clearing levels, manifested by a total absence of shortages and the presence of excess deliverability. Not only exogenous events (depressed industrial conditions, declining substitute prices) but the rise of composite gas prices under the NGPA explains the unforeseen occurrence of usurped NGPA ceiling prices.[280] This suggests that not only did the act fail to properly encourage production, it failed to shield consumers from unregulated prices. Above-market unregulated prices "corrected," as it were, below-market prices to join price increases from other sources. The silver lining

---

[278]Between 1976 and 1982, interstate old gas (104 and 106 gas) declined by 10 percent per year. *Current Conditions in the Natural Gas Market,* Hearing before the Senate Committee on Energy and Natural Resources, 97th Cong., 2d sess. (Washington, D.C: Government Printing Office, 1982), p. 492.

[279]Michael Manning and Patrick Keeley, "Controversial Decontrol Legislation Proposed to Remedy Natural Gas Market Disorder," *Oil and Gas Analyst* (May 1983): 4.

[280]"We're telling clients to act as if the system were already deregulated. Market forces are becoming operative regardless of what the government does." John Sawhill of the consulting firm McKinsey and Co. Quoted in the *Wall Street Journal,* June 14, 1983, p. 56. In April 1982, Transco applied to FERC for a rate decrease, the first of its kind. See chapter 15, pp. 950–51.

was that disruptive shortages—industrial curtailments, closed businesses, and residential cut-offs—were avoided, unlike the situation in 1971–77. But this was a Pyrrhic victory. Inefficient production and a new variety of market disorder—excess deliverability and contract problems—were created.

When the problem of slack supply began to unfold in 1982, another NGPA-related distortion came to light: activated take-or-pay contracts that contributed to higher prices and oversupply. A paradigmatic case was Columbia Gas System, which in a highly publicized incident filed for a 20 percent Public Gas Association increase to pass along expensive gas purchases chosen over supply sources one-third the price.[281] What made this perverse behavior profit maximizing was a take-or-pay provision in the expensive gas contract that obligated Columbia to pay for 90 percent of deliverability even if less was actually taken. Rather than buy two batches of gas, only one of which was marketable, Columbia purchased the higher priced gas and applied for a pass-through adjustment.

While take-or-pay clauses were common in long-term gas sales contracts well before the 1970s—because producers desired a minimum cash flow and drainage protection from nonratable takes in a common reservoir—it was after this time that stringent provisions (80–90 percent of deliverability) became almost universal.[282] Although these provisions were voluntarily agreed to by buyer and seller, the role of government intervention in creating high-percentage take-or-pay situations initially and in skewing the terms in favor of the seller should not be overlooked. First, contract concessions by pipeline-purchasers substituted for *price competition*, which was prohibited by law.[283] Consequently, nonprice contractual provisions became very competitive; take-or-pay covenants (as well as escalator clauses upon decontrol) were often requisite for pipelines to secure long-term supplies desperately needed in the shortage days of the 1970s.

---

[281]*Washington Post*, September 2, 1982, p. A1.

[282]*Natural Gas Policy*, p. 673.

[283]Explained FERC chairman Mike Butler: "Because pipelines are limited in bidding for gas by offering a higher price, they can indirectly up their bids by making concessions on other contract terms. Generous price escalator clauses to become effective on deregulation are one example; high take-or-pay percentages are another." *Implementation*, p. 27.

Second, long-term contracts, the father of take-or-pay contracts, resulted in part from government intervention, namely the certification requirement that pipelines demonstrate a long-term supply base.[284] Without this certification requirement, less gas would have entered into long-run contracts, and contracts would not have been as long as twelve and twenty years. A third government-related reason for the take-or-pay problem was purchased-gas adjustment pass-throughs. The pipeline-to-distributor and distributor-to-consumers pass-throughs, which were routinely allowed, weakened incentives for pipelines to avoid risky contracts.[285] Fourth, stringent take-or-pay contracts for gas from the Outer Continental Shelf were directly related to Interior Department policy. Fifth, government pressure on pipelines during the 1976–77 supply crunch, including on Columbia Gas, which served the nation's capital, led to aggressive supply procurement with concern for risk secondary.[286] Sixth, gas fields that would have been unitized except for government intervention would have had lower take-or-pay provisions without drainage concerns.

Finally, the very existence of antagonistic relationships between gas buyers and gas sellers can be laid at the doorstep of government intervention. The advantages of integration in the oil industry were also present in the natural-gas industry. Yet while intervention discouraged integration in the oil industry, it had been wholly prevented in the natural-gas industry by legislative and administrative policy since the 1930s.[287] The result, as attorney Robert Perdue stressed, was the creation of a "3-headed monster"—consisting of gas producers, carriers, and distributors—that substituted adversarial uncertainty for cooperative relationships.[288] Resolution of this problem points to the wider question of gas *industry* deregulation rather than just gas *producer* deregulation, which is considered in the final chapter of the book.

---

[284]See chapter 15, pp. 937–38.

[285]Pipeline purchasers reasoned that, if activated take-or-pay clauses created consumer hardship (and hardship for pipelines from load loss), regulatory reform would alleviate the problem.

[286]Peter Holmes, "The Implosion at Columbia Gas," *Fortune*, May 2, 1983, p. 189.

[287]See chapter 29, p. 1797.

[288]Robert Perdue, Comments made at Executive Enterprise Conference, 1983.

Pipelines were put in a squeeze between honoring take-or-pay contracts and profitably marketing obligated supply. Some market-out clauses were activated by pipelines with excess deliverability problems, while others dubiously claimed force majeure.[289] Renegotiated contracts were also evidence of producers' and pipelines' common interest in marketable gas. Yet renegotiated contracts to ease the take-or-pay dilemma were hindered by two nonmarket elements. One, congressional bills affecting take-or-pay reduced purchaser incentive to renegotiate.[290] Second, antitrust questions about producers' sharing contract information created an informational vacuum around a common problem. If pipelines could have revealed contract specifics and worked toward nondiscriminatory, uniform proposals, settlements would have become more feasible.[291] Instead, unilateral action such as Tennessee Gas Transmission's emergency gas policy, announced April 29, 1983, provoked a flood of lawsuits against subcontract take levels.[292]

Whatever the final result of bargaining and lawsuits, a lesson was learned for future contracting between gas producers and pipelines. Transco chairman Jack Bowen spoke for the pipeline industry when he stated:

> Our future gas-buying contracts will have market-outs. We'll have a mechanism in them so that the gas contract will be flexible and sensitive to market signals—up or down. It will also have a more realistic take-or-pay procedure where the producer will get his rightful or pro rata share of our market.[293]

---

[289]Claims of force majeure are akin to breach of contract. Admitted one pipeline executive: "I think [force majeure] is a pretty thin reed. The recession and competition from other fuels may not apply as acts of God like the blowup of a compressor station might." *Houston Chronicle*, May 8, 1983, p. 4-10. Also see chapter 15, pp. 950–51.

[290]*Energy Daily*, September 7, 1984, p. 4.

[291]Antitrust made not only renegotiation but original contracting difficult. Remarked David Wilson, president of the Association for Equal Access to Natural Gas Markets and Supplies: "Producers have and are continuing to enter into contracts without a clear idea of the competitive market for their production. This occurs because of fear of antitrust implications of exchanging information.... Due to FERC protection, pipelines and their affiliates are able to have access to all contracts on their system, and then are able to use the most beneficial feature of each contract." *Natural Gas Legislation: 1*, pp. 856–57.

[292]See chapter 15, p. 951.

[293]*Energy Daily*, October 22, 1982, p. 3.

Without government influences creating necessary conditions for lopsided take-or-pay contracts—a seller's market with below-market gas prices and other supporting conditions—a recurrence of the take-or-pay problem cannot be expected.

Price misinformation, a problem of all price-control programs, was magnified under the NGPA. Prices for consumers were distorted in two major ways. Under Title I, myriad ceiling prices created wildly differing retail prices unexplainable by extraction cost or transportation expense. A second assault on scarcity prices was Title II's incremental-pricing provision, which required that household consumers be subsidized by industrial users of natural gas. Both regulations made informed decisions about the relative value of fuel-oil and coal burning versus natural-gas consumption impossible. Initial investment decisions about fuel-burning assets were hampered as were later retrofit decisions, and errors were made. Industrial boiler-fuel users were forced to overconserve and overconvert, while electric utilities and residential consumers behaved uneconomically.[294]

Producer decisions diverted private gain from efficient resource usage. Evaluating the myriad price tiers, one critic stated that

> gas producers are being told don't go out and look for gas where [you] have looked in the past. Don't go out and look in the same area at different depths. Don't go out and look in a close by area because . . . you won't be able to get as much money for it as if you look in more remote, less likely places, the places in the past where [you] didn't think it was worth looking. . . . [O]nly if you think the gas industry had a total misdirection of all their efforts for the last 50 years [does] that kind of policy make sense.[295]

Legislative Proposals

The election of President Reagan and the Republican gains in Congress in 1980 revived hopes for decontrol of natural gas—hopes that had been dormant since the 1954 election of Dwight Eisenhower. Deregulation of natural gas was one of Reagan's campaign promises

---

[294]Distortion also resulted from baseline or lifeline rate design on the state level that allocated costs disproportionately toward electric utilities and industrial users to subsidize residential users.

[295]Testimony of Charles Cicchetti, *Implementation*, p. 112.

along with decontrol of oil and the abolition of the Department of Energy. But like that of his Republican predecessor several decades before, Reagan's promise would fall victim to compromise.

During Reagan's first year in office, natural-gas reform was placed on the back burner. Deregulation of oil prices and allocation was the major energy initiative, and the intense lobbying effort that resulted in the Tax Reduction Act of 1980 occupied the day. The next year was an election year for Congress, and deregulation bills such as H.R. 5866 introduced by Phil Gramm (D-Tex.) and S. 2074 introduced by J. Bennett Johnston (D-La.) were not reported out of committee, in large part because the Reagan administration was reluctant to spend political capital on the area. Amendatory natural-gas legislation remained a volatile issue that required political care.

In 1983, a belated push for natural-gas reform was made. On February 28, President Reagan submitted a bill to Congress drafted by Department of Energy secretary Donald Hodel, entitled the Natural Gas Consumer Regulatory Reform Amendments of 1983.[296] The bill, as the title suggests, was not wholly deregulatory; it was a compromise of immediate deregulation, phased deregulation, reregulation, and new regulation involving the entire industry. The bill, noted Nolan Clark and Glenn Clark, was "a half-measure, a palliative written with political imperatives in mind."[297] The strategy, admitted Hodel, was to court consumer interests and "guarantee" price protection; first-year price declines of from $0.10 to $0.30 per Mcf were confidently predicted.[298]

Title I of the Reagan bill was not deregulatory but regulatory. As a compromise with deregulation elsewhere, it amended section 603 of the NGPA to expand FERC authority over interstate pipelines to rejecting gas cost pass-throughs if not "just, reasonable, and prudently incurred." More important, pass-throughs were limited to

[296]This bill was introduced in the Senate by James McClure (R-Idaho) as S. 615; the bill was introduced in the House with minor amendments by Tom Corcoran (R-Ill.) as H.R. 1760.

[297]Nolan Clark and Glenn Clark, "The Way to Deregulate Natural Gas," *Wall Street Journal*, May 4, 1983, p. 26.

[298]Said Hodel, "We concluded that no proposal we could present would have a real chance of passage or acceptance in Congress unless we could guarantee to provide protection for the consumer." U.S. Department of Energy, *Energy Insider*, March 1983, p. 1.

prior (NGPA) rates plus an inflation factor through 1985. After this date, FERC discretion came into play. New reporting requirements on volumes and prices of purchased gas were stipulated, and purchases of affiliate gas were constrained to ensure purchases of the least expensive gas.

Title II amended wellhead gas prices set by the NGPA. High-cost (107) gas was to be regulated at the higher of the current contract (NGPA) price or the "gas cap price" until deregulated on January 1, 1986. The cap was a composite national gas price averaged from the previous second, third, and fourth months. Prices for new (102) gas, new-onshore (103) gas, and rollover-contract (106) gas remained under NGPA ceilings until December 31, 1984, after which the gas cap price became the legal maximum. Beginning January 1, 1986, these categories were deregulated.

New contracts and 104 old gas, 105 dedicated-intrastate gas, 108 stripper-well gas, and 109 (other) gas were to be immediately deregulated. The NGPA provision to reregulate previously deregulated prices was repealed.

Title III amended existing take-or-pay contracts to set a maximum of 70 percent of available deliverability and provided for unilateral contract breaking ("market-out") by either the buyer or seller after January 1, 1985. Title IV introduced federal "just and reasonable" price review of all downstream parties involved with interstate gas—interstate pipelines, intrastate pipelines, and distribution companies. This was a consumerist provision to check unregulated wellhead prices. FERC authority to force carriage by interstate pipelines at a commission-determined price was authorized. Title V repealed sections of the Powerplant and Industrial Fuel Use Act of 1978 that forbade certain industrial customers to use natural gas and repealed incremental pricing of the NGPA to allow proportionate pass-through cost allocation among customer classes.

The most notable, and controversial, feature of the proposed amendments was the shift from wellhead regulation to pipeline and distribution regulation. If it was a phased deregulation bill for producers, it ensured effective regulation of the upstream industry because it had the potential to effectively reintroduce first-sale price control.

In congressional hearings, which produced 3,800 pages of testimony and supporting materials over an eight-day period, a wide split was evident in the gas industry depending on the particular situations of its members.[299] Favoring the Reagan bill were companies with large old-gas reserves, primarily the top twenty majors that controlled approximately 70 percent of old gas. Tenneco, whose gas portfolio contained primarily old gas, ardently lobbied for the bill through the American Petroleum Institute.[300] Also supporting the administration's bill were industrial end users who favored repeal of incremental pricing and the Fuel Use Act. Independent producers were cautiously supportive or cautiously opposed. Intrastate pipelines were generally supportive.[301]

Against the bill, or at least not favoring it, was everyone else—high-cost producers whose gas prices would be pulled down by unregulated competition, interstate pipelines with old-gas contracts (such as Northwest Energy) or carriers concerned about the automatic cost pass-through suspension, drilling contractors concerned about lower prices for deep-gas drilling, consumer groups complaining of price escalations, and gas distributors who were against old-gas deregulation and other features of the bill.[302] In addition to long-time opponents of gas deregulation, there were large banking and insurance companies fearful of the nullification of long-term contracts that supported their loans and investments.[303] For market-oriented critics, the concern was that an activist FERC could *increase*

---

[299]Senator Johnston commented: "This is, indeed, a great split within the gas industry. . . . Some in the industry oppose it, some are for it. There are some producers who are independent who strongly oppose the bill, some who are for it; some majors are undecided, some are for it, and I guess some are against it. Pipeline companies take every conceivable position." *Natural Gas Legislation: 1*, p. 68.

[300]Commented FERC chairman Mike Butler, "People are saying that the major oil companies are going to be substantially advantaged if we deregulate old gas and they are absolutely right." *Houston Post*, April 11, 1983, p. D-4.

[301]*Natural Gas Legislation: 1*, pp. 365, 424, 463–549, 693–707, 746–79, 791–802, 1182–88.

[302]Ibid., pp. 216–365, 746–79, 887–1001, 1358–65. A study for Northwest Energy by former deregulation advocate and FPC member Rush Moody is noteworthy for its anti-decontrol tone and "consumer protection" criteria. Ibid., pp. 824–44. Charles Butler, chairman of the FERC, commented, "Lawyers are paid to represent their clients, and Mr. Moody's analysis should be viewed in that light and not clothed with the trappings of the public interest." Ibid., p. 1064.

[303]*Wall Street Journal*, November 1, 1983, p. 25; and *OGJ*, April 25, 1983, p. 68.

price regulation over NGPA levels by stringent control of cost pass-throughs, which would reintroduce pre-*Phillips* uncertainty for producers and leave the gas industry as a whole more regulated. Alternative bills such as J. Bennett Johnston's S. 1715 to deregulate old gas, effective January 1, 1986, and Nancy Kassebaum's (R-Kans.) S. 60 to roll back prices and expand regulation became fringe proposals. All eyes were on Reagan's centralist bill.

Because the bill lacked a powerful enough constituency, the inertia of the status quo prevailed. The bill languished before being soundly rejected by the Senate in late 1983. The defeat proved, not so much that deregulation was politically unachievable, but that an intricate mix of regulation and deregulation to replace a different version of the same was politically unappealing. But the change in the parameters of the debate from the earlier "producer-vs.-consumer" configuration was noteworthy. Editorialized the *New York Times*:

> Decontrol of all gas would not further harm consumers [and] would add efficiencies. . . . It would provide a windfall for owners of old gas, but at the expense of the owners of now-decontrolled gas, not consumers. It sounds complicated, and it is, but consumer interests are not now at risk. Legislators choosing sides should know they are choosing only among producers.[304]

Election year 1984 would not threaten the durable NGPA. No bills were backed by Reagan, and none came to a vote. A Senate compromise bill, which would have scaled back take-or-pay obligations to between 50 and 60 percent, set escalator-clause ceilings, repealed incremental pricing, made gas pipelines common carriers, and subjected gas imports to scrutiny of the secretary of energy, got nowhere. "Consumer" bills that centered around price restrictions on escalator clauses covering deregulated gas and continued controls on old gas were not supported. Summarized Michael Manning:

> The divergent views among congressional leaders in the House and Senate, as well as industry groups, may have created an impasse. Many participants in the debate, especially in the Senate, appear to favor no action at all over a compromise. . . . No workable coalition has emerged.[305]

[304]*New York Times*, April 26, 1983, p. A22.

[305]Michael Manning, "Natural Gas Legislation before the Second Session of the 98th Congress," *Natural Gas* (August 1984): 28.

Regulation of Natural-Gas Prices in Retrospect

Comprehensive natural-gas price regulation at the wellhead has gone through four successive phases—individual ratemaking (1954–60), area ratemaking (1960–73), national ratemaking (1974–78), and formula ratemaking (1978).[306] The problems of each phase led to the next phase. Ex post, regulation of field prices cannot be considered satisfactory, but ex ante, was regulation necessary? Was there a case for regulation, with past failures attributable to *implementation* rather than *intent*? This important question will be considered below, followed by a review of the historical record during more than four decades of partial and comprehensive natural-gas regulation.

The Case for Regulation

Two leading proponents of field regulation of natural gas in the decisive 1950s were economist Alfred Kahn and Illinois Senator (and economist) Paul Douglas. In his testimony on behalf of utility interests in the 1958 *Champlin* case, Kahn used historical field data to demonstrate that concentration among producers was high and the responsiveness of supply to price was low. The gas market, consequently, was not "workably competitive," and gas contracting was spoiled by "significant monopoly exploitation."[307] "Thinned" competition among sellers due to long-term contracts and indefinite escalator clauses, apart from concentration, he stated elsewhere, "increase[d] the possibility, and accentuate[d] the possible influence, of monopoly power."[308] These conditions, he concluded, "may justify price regulation."[309]

The argument of Senator Douglas took the Kahnian view several steps further. Competitive problems existed not only in the field but at the burner tip. Residential consumers, not only pipelines, were

---

[306]If regulation of pipeline affiliates (1940–54) is included, five phases can be identified.

[307]Testimony before the FPC, *In the Matter of Champlin Oil Refining Co. et al.*, Docket G-9277, 1958, p. 4896.

[308]Alfred Kahn, "Economic Issues in Regulating the Field Price of Natural Gas," *American Economic Association Proceedings* (May 1960): 509.

[309]*In the Matter of Champlin*, p. 4896. Also see the succinct pro-regulation arguments of Randall Le Boeuf, "Chaos in the Natural-Gas Industry from the Distributor Viewpoint," *Georgetown Law Journal* (June 1956): 607–27.

"captive" to natural-gas producers once gas appliances were purchased.[310] Wellhead gas prices that doubled between 1946 and 1953, and more increases thereafter, were a consumer problem that regulation could and should address.[311] Douglas's analysis also emphasized how imperfect competition upstream—in the pipeline and distribution sectors—diminished rivalry at the wellhead. The "regulatory gap" at the field level allowed higher prices to enter the nexus to be fully passed through to the consumer. Price ceilings on gas production were needed to close the loophole.[312]

The senator made a final plea for price control on utilitarian grounds. "Pennies extracted from the many" by unregulated pricing, asserted Douglas, "mean millions for the few."[313]

In summary, interstate pipelines (and indirectly, gas utilities) in their comfortable public-utility position of passing through costs could not bargain, and were not bargaining, effectively with producers, which fueled an upward price spiral. New-gas supplies were not dependent on such higher prices. Consumers could not effectively substitute. With the intersection of inelastic demand and inelastic supply, price escalations benefited producers at the expense of consumers and had no redeeming social consequences. Regulation was consequently required to introduce price discipline in the field, while retaining the status quo of production.

The Case for Regulation Rebutted

Refutation of the case for regulation must tread a fine line between the historical performance of the gas industry and its hypothetical operation under purely market conditions. It is not enough, as several eminent economists have done, to draw upon the same pool of empirical data as Kahn did to reach the opposite conclusion—a

---

[310]Paul Douglas, "Federal Regulation of Independent Natural Gas Producers Is Essential," *Public Utilities Fortnightly* (October 13, 1955): 623.

[311]Ibid., p. 624.

[312]Ibid., p. 623; and idem, "The Case for the Consumer of Natural Gas," *Georgetown Law Journal* (June 1956): 587.

[313]Paul Douglas, "Federal Regulation of Independent Natural Gas Producers Is Essential," p. 633. Elsewhere, he added, "We submit that the 21 million families who use gas ... deserve more consideration than the oil-rich men, most of them northern absentees, who dominate the oil and gas producing states of the Southwest." Douglas, "The Case for the Consumer of Natural Gas," p. 576.

competitive and efficient industry and elastic supply and demand.[314] Attention must also be paid to existing government intervention that impinged on the effective operation of the field gas market.

Two prominent government interventions have distorted the gas market over the decades. Gas distributors have been protected by retail franchises, as noticed by Douglas, and potential gas carriers have had to satisfy the burden of proof to enter territories already served by interstate pipelines. With market competition restrained by law, cost-of-service pass-through at the carrier and retail level ensured that *internal* competition was minimized to leave only *external* competition, from coal and fuel oil, to carry the entire burden.[315] Unfettered upstream rivalry would have increased the need and desire of pipelines to drive harder bargains with producers and discover new cost-minimizing techniques.[316] Second, the interstate pipeline certification requirement that supply be dedicated for twenty years (later reduced to twelve years) "thinned" the market, as noticed by Kahn, in favor of large producers and large pipelines. To compensate sellers for such lengthy contracts, given inflationary trends and the historical growth of gas demand and prices, "one-way-street" escalator clauses became common.[317] Separately and together, mandated long-term agreements and cost-of-service pass-throughs in a public-utility environment imposed an anti-consumer element, which was legitimately criticized.[318] But to conclude that further government involvement is required to cure prior intervention is erroneous. Price intervention did not cure the "monopoly"

[314]See M. A. Adelman, in *In the Matter of Champlin*, p. 458; Leslie Cookenboo, *Competition in the Field Market for Natural Gas* (Houston: Rice Institute, 1958); and Paul MacAvoy, *Price Formation in Natural Gas Fields* (Westport, Conn.: Greenwood, 1962, 1976).

[315]The discipline of interfuel competition in major industrial and power-plant applications, however, would be severely weakened by 1970s gas regulation passed at the request on the coal lobby. But again, this is a regulatory, not a free-market, problem.

[316]The decline in pipeline-owned resources also tilted field bargaining toward producers and away from pipelines.

[317]Another reason for escalator clauses, although secondary to long-term price protection, was to reduce short-term costs for pipelines that had high front-end costs. Raymond Shibley and George Mickum, "The Impact of Phillips upon the Interstate Pipelines," p. 645.

[318]Other government interventions, of which Douglas was critical, are minimum wellhead gas prices imposed by several states and state prorationing. Paul Douglas, "The Case for the Consumer of Natural Gas," pp. 587–88.

problem; it added a new layer of government involvement and distortion while leaving the anti-competitive elements unaddressed. Other prominent arguments for regulation deserve rebuttal. Concentrated ownership of large gas reserves, if indeed it unambiguously exists, is not a priori anti-competitive. Competition is not the number of distinct competitors but the presence of unregulated entry and exit, which allows rivalry among entrepreneurial ideas.[319] Numbers aside, gas production was competitive because of unregulated entry. Price regulation, however, reduced economic incentives and thus entry to add to the "monopoly" situation price ceilings were intended to cure.

It is true that scale economies in exploration and production tend to encourage large size (although hardly a monopoly situation under any standard definition of the term). Chapter 4 explained why larger firms had certain advantages over smaller firms, other things the same. Reservoirs require singular or cooperative ownership to minimize drilling costs, and risk minimization requires that a firm be able to pool drilling prospects.[320]

The large rise in gas prices in the late 1940s and particularly in the early 1950s reflected not only the public-utility environment at the interstate transmission and distribution level but phenomenal growth of gas demand from new market connections. Rising prices were *competitively driven* to the extent that urban markets switched from coal, fuel oil, wood chips, and other sources of energy to gas because of the latter's competitive superiority. Early consumers did not benefit when later consumers bid up gas prices—necessitating higher priced contract renewals—but only if "consumers" is narrowly defined as preexisting users can exploitation be said to occur.

Inelastic supply and demand as a rationale for regulation is a fickle presumption and an irrelevant argument, broadly considered. Arguments based on the supposed insensitivity of supply and demand to price only assert that what happened in the past will continue to happen in the future. But not only does the future change, conclusions about the past are always tentative because surrounding causal factors assumed to be equal could have changed to falsify

---

[319]See chapter 1, pp. 32, 45.
[320]See chapter 4, p. 205.

the observed correlation.[321] For example, alleged price incentives in the post-1940 period and particularly after 1954 were dulled by regulatory-induced paperwork, delay, or uncertainty, which gave the appearance of price insensitivity not present in a true market situation. Second, technological and market considerations pointed to increasing price sensitivity of both supply and demand. Advances in exploration technology beginning in the 1960s made nonassociated gas drilling more precise. Originally a joint product found in the primary search for oil, gas supply has become more dependent on its own price rather than on oil prices. So *if* gas supply was once relatively inelastic to price, the future promised it would be less so. On the demand side, the 1950s and 1960s witnessed a competitive fray between fuel oil, a vested fuel, and natural gas, an attractive newcomer. Many consumers in urban areas were in the process of deciding whether to switch from the former to the latter—and make fixed asset commitments thereto—which was a price-driven decision. The number of conversions and "waiting-list " gas customers during this time speaks for itself—gas demand was sensitive to price. Third, to predict both supply and demand inelasticity for the present and foreseeable future is a very risky strategy for advancing consumerism. If *either* supply or demand is elastic or becomes sufficiently elastic to create an excess of demand over supply, disruptive shortages result, which turned out to be precisely the case. The market price, on the other hand, does not depend on empirical configurations under a central design to achieve coordination.

A major problem of the pro-regulation position is its lack of attention to its real-world problems vis-á-vis the "imperfect" market.[322]

---

[321]The FPC, while overlooking the methodological flaws of forecasting, pragmatically demoted the empirical approach after its poor performance: "While further quantitative studies of the elasticity of gas supply with respect to the wellhead price should be encouraged . . . the experience gained from previous considerations of this question demonstrates that reliable quantification is not possible with the present state of the art. . . . [T]o predict or quantify the precise level of new supplies . . . would be to 'demand the perfect at the expense of the achievable.' " Opinion 699, 51 FPC 2212 at 2233 (1974).

[322]What little Douglas said about the machinery of implementation proved dead wrong. He said in 1955: "Remarkable progress is being made in cleaning up the backlog [of certificate applications]. Thus there is no substance to the charge that regulation of producers is an impossible task which will bog down the commission." Paul Douglas, "Federal Regulation of Independent Gas Producers Is Essential," p. 630.

Substituting the "right" regulatory price for the "monopolistic" market price is a fallacy of constructivism. The goal of "set[ting] prices in all producing areas which will be adequate to maintain gas supplies needed by the consumers of the nation, but at prices that are no higher than are necessary to accomplish that purpose"[323] is a utopian mirage. It begs for perfect knowledge and exacting implementation, which are unrealizable. In the real world, the relevant questions of regulation are different: How can the "right" price be discovered and implemented, given ambiguous historical data and the absence of quantitative economic relationships?[324] What if the implemented price ceiling fails to clear the market? Are the pennies saved per Mcf a net gain if supply is curtailed or uncertain and businesses and even residential users can turn only to more expensive substitute fuels or have no substitutes at all? And even if discovering the "right" price were possible (which it is not), what assurance would there be that politically powerful lobbyists—coal and fuel-oil representatives, for example—would not selfishly tailor price regulation in nonsocial directions? Those intractable problems were conveniently left undiscussed by proponents of regulation in the 1950s to the detriment of gas producers *and* gas consumers in the 1960s and 1970s.

Results of Price Regulation

Economic Distortions. The landscape of NGA-NGPA producer regulation is littered with disincentives, malincentives, and distortion. More than a dozen major categories of unnecessary expenditure or inefficiency during the period from 1940 to 1984 can be identified.

1. Inflated administrative costs of firms' compliance with regulations and profit maximization under them. This also had an anti-competitive feature of threatening small producers less able to staff up or hire outside specialists.

---

[323]Testimony of the Federal Power Commission, *Phillips Petroleum Co.*, 24 FPC 547 (1960).

[324]The aforementioned difficulties of estimating subjective costs and separating joint costs are relevant here.

2. Taxpayer expense to create, administer, and adjudicate regulation. In 1978, state agencies assumed an active role under the NGPA to create a second layer of taxpayer involvement.[325]

3. Encouragement of high-cost production. From 1954 until 1977, cost-of-service regulation set prices from cost, which created incentive to pad expenses but still compete effectively with substitutes. Under the NGPA, incentive pricing and deregulated pricing for high-cost categories ensured that high-cost reserves would be located along with—if not before—low-cost reserves.

4. Discouragement of production by affiliates of regulated pipelines. From 1940 until 1954, price assignments for pipeline affiliates based on depreciated cost dried up a major source of exploration and production activity to increase independent bargaining power and field prices.[326]

5. Increased reservation demand to withhold natural gas from the market until better regulatory conditions emerged.[327] Numerous legislative drives to amend gas regulation and administrative leniency toward new discoveries encouraged wait-and-see strategies that distorted intertemporal production and consumption.

6. Reduced supply as a result of below-market pricing and high regulatory-related expenses. Marginal wells, in particular, were underdeveloped and prematurely retired until 1978 when incentive pricing began for them. At present, old-gas reserves remaining under price controls are threatened with inefficient extraction and premature retirement.

7. Discouragement of conservation. Federal regulations' artificially low prices and disincentives for interstate dedications clashed with state laws against flaring and other marginal and submarginal uses of gas.[328]

---

[325]For earlier estimates of regulatory costs for the regulators and regulated, see Paul MacAvoy, "The Effectiveness of the Federal Power Commission," *Bell Journal of Economics* (Autumn 1970): 282.

[326]See the discussion in J. J. Hedrick, "Regulation v. Pipe Line Production," *Gas Age*, April 21, 1955, p. 43.

[327]See Raymond Shibley and George Mickum, "The Impact of Phillips upon the Interstate Pipelines."

[328]Complained Texas Railroad Commissioner E. O. Thompson: "This situation [of federal price regulation] . . . will certainly ultimately destroy the great conservation

8. Delays between reserve discovery and dedication.[329] This exacerbated service to waiting markets seeking a lower cost alternative to fuel oil and coal.

9. The artificial advantage of major producing states in attracting gas-consuming industries away from northern importing states prior to the NGPA.[330] Interstate urban gas markets were hurt more by lower economic growth than were major gas-producing states.

10. Actual curtailments in the interstate markets in 1946–47 and 1970–77 when some residential communities experienced hardship, industry was shut down, and other activities were curtailed.

11. Higher energy prices as a result of reduced pipeline load, expensive gas imports, dependence on domestic high-cost gas, and substitution of higher cost fuels to bridge the supply gap in natural gas.[331]

12. Supply uncertainty and emergency preparation.

13. The preponderance of *political* over *economic* decisionmaking, resulting in inefficient public choices and regulatory inertia against reform.

14. The rise of the LNG industry, propane in particular, which escaped restrictive gas-price regulation by selling gas as a liquid to take advantage of high oil prices.[332] Stripping gas

---

work of the states. You cannot serve two masters." Quoted in Harry Fair, "The Natural Gas Dilemma—How, What, and Why?" p. 114.

[329]At one point in the natural-gas growth era, a two- to six-year wait was normal before gas discoveries could be marketed to an interstate pipeline. Lloyd Thanhouser, "Paradise Lost for Natural Gas," p. 638.

[330]"Ironically," noted Edmund Kitch, "the Natural Gas Act . . . achieved in part the objective of the producing states." Kitch, "Regulation of the Field Market for Natural Gas by the Federal Power Commission," p. 274.

[331]An overlooked fact is the importance of high pipeline utilization to spread fixed costs over more units of sales. Low gas prices by law, to the extent that pipeline supply is curtailed, can *increase* final prices despite lower gas-acquisition costs. See Tom Bethell, "The Gas Price Fixers," *Harper's*, June 1979, p. 104.

[332]Edward Mitchell identified the LNG industry as the major opponent of natural-gas decontrol during 1972 executive-branch discussions. Mitchell, *U.S. Energy Policy: A Primer* (Washington, D.C.: American Enterprise Institute, 1974), p. 4. A history of the early LNG industry and early regulation is contained in Henry Lippitt, "Regulatory Problems in the Development and Use of Liquid Methane," *Texas Law Review* (May 1969): 601–15.

into liquids was inefficient as demonstrated by the curtail-ment-period practice of transporting stripped gas interstate by truck to curtailed regions and regasifying it for consumption.

15. Price misinformation about relative scarcities of competing fuels complicated investment and consumption decisions. Not only below-market pricing in general but myriad different prices for an identical product made a mockery of the informa-tional aspects of scarcity pricing for producers and consumers.

16. Market disorder caused by excess deliverability, estimated at around 3 Bcf per day, that created financial problems and uncertainty in the production and transmission sectors.

Less supply and higher production costs caused interstate con-sumers to suffer despite the intention of regulation to lower their fuel bills. On the basis of the facts that interstate markets were cleared by regulated prices until the 1970s (although inventory, or proven reserves, was being invaded) and that unregulated intrastate prices were not noticeably above interstate prices until the late 1960s, it can be concluded that increased costs due to regulation resulted in prices not unlike those of the market. However, producer incen-tives to increase supply, and consequent lower prices, were reduced.

In the 1970s when supply became stagnant and prices failed to clear interstate markets, prices were driven *higher* than they would have gone if regulation had not been in place. Incremental supplies from nonregulated sources commanding premium prices were readily purchased, and as a result of a combination of increasing composite gas prices and declining demand, once again (by 1982), regulated pricing approached market pricing but at a regulatory premium.[333] If *some* consumers at *certain* times paid lower prices, it was at the expense of would-be consumers, consumers of reduced supply, and a gas market distorted by excess deliverability and take-or-pay liabilities.

Statistical Record. A much-cited effect of wellhead price regulation has been artificial encouragement of consumption and artificial dis-couragement of production. The statistical summary presented in

---

[333]Imported gas prices are discussed in chapter 15, pp. 963–70.

table 8.9 was the "proof of the pudding" that influenced the Federal Power Commission to liberalize prices.

Field price regulation has contributed to declining gas inventory since its beginning in 1940. In 1954, the causal relationship was made clear by the chilling effect of the *Phillips* decision and Order 174 on exploration activity and pipeline commitments. Shortages, the usual consequence of price ceilings, however, were postponed by large gas inventories that partly reflected the "mistakes" of drillers who in the search for oil found gas instead.[334]

The downward trend in inventory stabilized in the post-*Phillips* years but worsened in the late 1950s and early 1960s. The steady decline, measured by supply years, reached alarming levels by the late 1960s, which foreshadowed physical shortages that followed several years later. Although compilation of reserve data is necessarily imprecise, it *did* forewarn of the situation. The inventory deaccumulation that began in 1969 inspired legislative amendment, but deep-rooted distortions would not be "quick-fixed" away, absent fundamental reform. Indeed, deficit of consumption that exceeded new discoveries stubbornly continued edging downward until the early 1980s when market forces began to reassert themselves and gas reserves from the giant Prudhoe Bay field entered the picture. But as late as the spring of 1982, economist Edward Erickson commented that the natural gas market still was not clearing on a reserves-addition basis.[335]

Legacy of Regulation. Since 1982, gas markets have been in disarray. Unlike the shortage crises of the last decade, the new crisis has been oversupply. This anomaly resulted in part from increased gas deliverability under NGPA incentives but also from regulation-related demand distortions and price inflexibility. This inspired a variety of new approaches, described in appendix 15.1, to marketing spot gas in place of using jurisdictional supply to capture incremental markets.[336]

---

[334]An implication of the interrelationship between oil drilling and gas supply is that by keeping the price of oil artificially high by import restrictions, market-demand proration, and other intervention, the supply of gas was artificially encouraged to partially negate direct regulation.

[335]Edward Erickson, "Commentary," in *The Deregulation of Natural Gas*, p. 33.

[336]See chapter 15, pp. 949–59.

Table 8.9
Proven Reserves of Natural Gas: 1950–83 (Bcf)

Year	Beginning Reserves[a]	Reserve Additions[b]	Consumption[c]	Ending Reserves	Change	Supply Years[d]
1950	179,402	11,985	6,855	184,585	5,183	26.9
1951	184,585	15,966	7,924	192,786	8,201	24.3
1952	192,759	14,268	8,593	198,632	5,845	23.1
1953	198,632	20,341	9,188	210,299	11,667	22.9
1954	210,299	9,547	9,375	210,561	262	22.5
1955	210,561	21,898	10,063	222,483	11,922	22.1
1956	222,483	24,716	10,849	236,483	14,000	21.8
1957	236,483	20,008	11,440	245,230	8,747	21.4
1958	245,230	18,897	11,423	252,762	7,532	22.1
1959	252,762	20,621	12,373	261,170	8,409	21.1
1960	261,170	13,894	13,019	262,326	1,156	20.1
1961	262,326	17,166	13,379	266,274	3,947	19.9
1962	266,274	19,484	13,638	272,279	6,005	20.0
1963	272,279	18,165	14,546	276,151	3,872	19.0
1964	276,151	20,252	15,347	281,251	5,100	18.3
1965	281,251	21,319	16,252	286,469	5,217	17.6
1966	286,469	20,220	17,491	289,333	2,864	16.5
1967	289,333	21,804	18,381	292,908	3,575	15.9
1968	292,908	13,697	19,373	287,350	−5,557	14.8
1969	287,350	8,375	20,373	275,109	−12,241	13.3

Year					
1970	275,109	11,196	21,961	264,746	−10,362	12.1
1971[e]	264,746	9,825	22,077	252,806	−11,941	11.5
1972[e]	252,806	9,635	22,512	240,085	−12,721	10.7
1973[e]	240,085	6,825	22,605	223,950	−16,136	9.9
1974[e]	223,950	8,679	21,318	211,132	−12,818	9.9
1975[e]	211,132	10,484	19,719	202,200	−8,932	10.2
1976[e]	202,200	7,555	19,542	190,026	−12,174	9.7
1977[e]	190,026	11,852	19,447	182,878	−7,148	9.4
1978[e]	182,878	10,586	19,311	174,302	−8,577	9.0
1979[e]	174,302	14,286	19,910	168,917	−5,385	8.5
1980[f]	200,997	16,723	18,699	199,021	−1,976	10.6
1981[f]	199,021	21,446	18,737	201,730	2,709	10.8
1982[f]	201,730	17,288	17,506	201,512	−218	11.5
1983[f]	201,512	14,523	15,788	200,247	−1,265	12.7
1984[f]	200,247	13,521	17,193	196,575	−3,672	11.4

SOURCE: U.S. Department of Energy, Energy Information Administration, *Annual Energy Review, 1991* (Washington, D.C.: EIA, 1992), table 48; and American Gas Association, *1991 Gas Facts* (Arlington, Va.: AGA, 1991), table 2.2.

NOTE: Net storage injections or withdrawals will cause end reserves to deviate from arithmetic totals for each year.

[a]Reserve revisions, extensions, and discoveries.

[b]Equals production.

[c]Net of inventory adjustments.

[d]Also known as the reserve/production ratio.

[e]Figures exclude gas from Prudhoe Bay, Alaska (discovered in 1968), that is yet to be marketed. Associated reserves are estimated at 26 trillion cubic feet.

[f]Includes 26 trillion cubic feet from Prudhoe Bay, Alaska, that are yet to be marketed.

This most recent crisis of gas-market disequilibrium caps several decades of regulation-induced distortion of supply and demand. A more vivid case study of the errors of constructivism could not be cited. Neither the goal of protecting consumers or the goal of inciting producers has been achieved by price regulation and accompanying interventions. Only the spontaneous, ever-changing market price could have properly guided both producers and consumers. Morris Adelman's 1958 explanation of the necessity of spontaneous market order, one of the most classic statements of the entire gas-regulation debate, is equally relevant today.

> The competitive market price in itself is the price which is sufficient, but no more than sufficient, to encourage exploration for new supplies which will be needed by consumers. Unlike a human observer, who can only attempt to see and estimate *some* of the forces of supply and demand, a market mechanism registers all of them: that is its purpose. . . . In gas production, there is no question of the positive relation between price and supply. As with any commodity, it is most difficult, if not impossible, to measure that relationship precisely and more difficult to forecast. Like a giant calculating machine, competitive market price registers and weighs these variables of supply and demand, seeking to establish an equilibrium. Personally, I see no escape from the competitive market price for any regulatory body which seeks to establish just and reasonable prices for natural gas.[337]

As the fourth phase of natural-gas regulation continues to unfold—although market forces have become more dominant than ever before—the choice remains between the spontaneous order of the market and the predictable and unpredictable disorder of interventionism.

---

[337]Testimony given at the 1958 Champlin hearing. Quoted in Cecil Munn, "The Lesson of the Independent Gas Producer Regulatory Experiment," *Administrative Law Review* (Fall 1961): 57. The knowledge problem was recognized at the very beginning of comprehensive wellhead gas regulation. Argued Justice Douglas in his *Phillips* dissent, "Regulation of the business of producing and gathering natural gas involves considerations of which we know little and with which we are not competent to deal." 347 U.S. 672 at 960.

9. Regulation and Decontrol of Crude-Oil Prices: 1971–84

The decade-long experience with crude-oil price controls from 1971 to 1981 is a unique episode in American regulatory history. Not only were price controls initially imposed without industry support—a rarity in the annals of U.S. oil and gas policy—but the subsequent regulations represented one of the most ambitious peacetime attempts ever made to fine-tune a major industrial sector to satisfy simultaneously the needs of consumers and producers.

This chapter begins by reviewing the Nixon price-control program between 1971 and 1974. Particular distortions with petroleum, it is found, led to a continuation of controls after Phase IV with the Emergency Petroleum Allocation Act of 1973 (EPAA). The Arab embargo, associated by many with the EPAA, is determined to have been an extenuating circumstance that ensured quick passage of, instead of serving as the impetus for, the law itself. Amendments to the EPAA in major 1975 and 1976 legislation—and later administrative rulemakings that made price regulation progressively more complex—are then examined. Phased decontrol between 1979 and 1981 ends the historical review.

The next major section evaluates both the goals and the results of regulation. To this end, a statistical summary of quantity and price during and after regulation is presented. As was the case for wellhead natural-gas regulation, reviewed in the previous chapter, price controls on crude oil are determined to have been counterproductive. A major conclusion—that price controls predominantly redistributed wealth from producers and royalty owners to other parts of the industry rather than to consumers of petroleum products—will be further developed in later chapters on the crude-oil trading boom (chapter 12), the upsurge of small refiners (chapter 20), and retail regulation (chapter 27). Chapter 29, finally, brings together the major points of the three chapters to offer a concluding view of this bellwether regulatory episode.

Prelude to Price Control: The Economic Stabilization Act of 1970

Government "jawboning" to arrest rising prices has accompanied inflation and been second only to its root cause, expansionary monetary policy. Invariably, activist government military and social programs require expenditures in excess of tax receipts. Rather than borrow or raise taxes by the entire amount, part of the deficit traditionally has been monetized (i.e., financed by monetary creation by the Federal Reserve). Monetary creation, however, inflates general prices and causes economic dislocations therein. To quell public concern, government expediently substitutes effect for cause and publicly criticizes business firms for "causing" inflation by raising prices.

President Kennedy's verbal attack on U.S. Steel Corporation in 1962 was the beginning of the modern jawboning era.[1] The monetary creation, inflation, jawboning scenario continued in the Johnson administration with wage-price guidelines. In the early years of the Nixon administration, concern over rising prices led the Council of Economic Advisers to issue "inflation alerts" and the Federal Reserve Board to set wage guidelines on the assumption that inflation, running at 4 percent per annum, was of the "cost-push" variety.[2]

The oil industry became particularly sensitive to government persuasion. In late 1970, after a round of crude-oil and product price increases, Nixon announced an investigation by the Office of Emergency Preparedness, issued an inflation alert, and publicly denounced the increases in speeches and print. He also relaxed oil-quota regulations under the Mandatory Oil Import Program and liberalized federal regulation of offshore production to increase supply.[3]

Informal inflation fighting gave way to the Economic Stabilization Act on August 15, 1970, the result of election-year posturing by a Democratic Congress and Nixon. The act granted presidential

[1]For a history of similar earlier efforts beginning with the Truman presidency, see *Exhortation and Controls: The Search for a Wage Price Policy,* ed. Craufurd Goodwin (Washington, D.C.: Brookings Institute, 1975).

[2]The cost-push theory of inflation is criticized in this chapter, pp. 510–12.

[3]*Oil & Gas Journal,* December 1970, p. 20, and January 1971, pp. 31, 34. Cited hereafter as *OGJ.* See chapter 6, p. 284, and chapter 13, pp. 749–50.

authority to impose comprehensive wage, price, and rent controls.[4] Nixon pledged not to impose mandatory measures but signed the bill nonetheless.

General Wage and Price Controls: 1971–73

Phase I (Freeze 1)

Unexpectedly and against the better judgment of his economic advisers, President Nixon on August 15, 1971, imposed the first peacetime wage, price, and rent controls in U.S. history as part of a "New Economic Policy."[5] Previously, price controls had been implemented during the Revolutionary War by several states; during the Civil War by the South; and during World War I, World War II, and the Korean conflict by the federal government.[6] Nixon's surprise was by design. If businesses and labor were caught off guard, they could not raise prices and wages to weather the period of regulation.[7]

The ninety-day Phase I freeze lasted from August 6 until November 13, 1971. Headed by the newly established Cost of Living Council (CLC), administration of the program was delegated to the Office of Emergency Preparedness with local operations entrusted to the Treasury Department. Enforcement was assigned to the Internal Revenue Service. Prices, wages, and rents for petroleum firms, as for nonpetroleum firms excluding first sales of raw agricultural products and imports, were individually frozen at levels no greater than the price existing on May 25, 1970, or the price at which 10 percent or more of total transactions took place within a thirty-day period

[4]Public Law 91-379, 84 Stat. 796 (1970). The law stipulated that the base prices of any freeze not be less than those existing on May 25, 1970, and authorized price adjustments where needed to prevent "gross inequities."

[5]Executive Order 11588, 36 *Fed. Reg.* 15727 (August 17, 1971). The controls were upheld in *Amalgamated Meat Cutters* v. *Connally*, 337 F. Supp. 737 (D.D.C. 1971).

[6]For a brief review of these efforts, see Robert Schuettinger and Eamonn Butler, *Forty Centuries of Wage and Price Controls* (Washington, D.C.: Heritage Foundation, 1979). Wartime price controls on petroleum are examined in chapter 5 (exploration and production), chapter 12 (transportation), chapter 19 (refining), and chapters 23 and 24 (retailing).

[7]Authority to freeze dividends was not contained in the Economic Stabilization Act, but government jawboning achieved virtually total compliance during Phase I. Cost of Living Council, "Economic Stabilization Program Quarterly Report," August 15–December 31, 1971, p. 9.

ending August 14, 1971.[8] If no transactions were made on these dates, the nearest thirty-day period could be used. For new items, the base price was to be that of the nearest like product.

The effect of the freeze on crude-oil exploration and production was not pronounced; for most firms the current configuration of costs and revenues allowed near-normal activities to continue.[9] During the three-month freeze, market-demand factors in Texas, Louisiana, Oklahoma, and New Mexico remained at slack but rising levels.[10] Expectations undoubtedly were adversely altered from what they would have been in a regulation-free environment, but many if not most business people welcomed the "temporary" program for reasons popularized by the president.[11]

A few people eschewed the optimism of the day. In his weekly "Watching Washington" column, Gene Kinney of the *Oil & Gas Journal* prophetically stated, "If crude oil is kept under political price control, undesired foreign dependence will accelerate, and the result will be ... domestic shortages and outrageous prices for foreign supplies that are the only alternative."[12]

---

[8]Interstate natural-gas sales were unaffected because of prior price-control authority vested in the Federal Power Commission. Intrastate natural-gas transactions came under Phase I.

[9]Elsewhere in the petroleum industry, the effects of Phase I were more distortive. See chapter 20, pp. 1175–76, and chapter 27, pp. 1607–8.

[10]The market-demand factors during Phase I were as follows.

Date	Texas	Louisiana	Oklahoma	New Mexico[a]
1971				
August	66%	75%	75%	75%
September	65%	73%	75%	75%
October	63%	70%	75%	75%
November	63%	69%	75%	78%

[a]Average of Southeast and Southwest market-demand factors.

[11]An editorial in the *Oil & Gas Journal* typified general industry approval and support: "It goes without saying that oil companies and individuals will follow the letter of Nixon's new program. But more is required. Directors and administrators of company funds should ... fall in step with the spirit of the bold new plan." *OGJ*, August 23, 1971, p. 35. The freeze was also supported by broad-based business groups such as the U.S. Chamber of Commerce and the National Association of Manufacturers.

[12]*OGJ*, August 30, 1971, p. 43.

Phase II

Phase II commenced on November 14, 1971, and remained in force until January 10, 1973.[13] The Price Commission and the Pay Board were created to administer the regulations under the CLC.[14] Phase I ceiling prices remained as base prices for Phase II. Unlike before, cost increases, adjusted downward for productivity gains, could be passed through on a percentage basis to obtain higher selling prices if profit margins, defined as pretax profits divided by net sales, were not greater than they had been in two of the firm's last three fiscal years ending prior to August 15, 1971. For multiproduct firms, which included twenty-one large oil companies, term-limit pricing (TLP), under which a weighted average price increase of 2 percent was allowed, was introduced. Procedures to obtain higher prices depended on firm size. For companies with $100 million or more in yearly sales, thirty-day prenotification of the Price Commission was necessary. For firms with over $50 million but under $100 million in sales, quarterly reports detailing changes in prices, costs, or profits were stipulated. Firms with sales under $50 million were required only to obey the general rules; they were not subject to prenotification or reporting requirements.[15]

The change in regulatory emphasis from price to profit, signifying a liberalization of the price-control program, reflected a realization by authorities that some inflation, cited at 2 to 3 percent, was tolerable and indeed necessary to avoid major economic dislocation.[16] For crude-oil exploration and production, the modification was most

---

[13]Executive Order 11627, 36 *Fed. Reg.* 20139 (October 16, 1971). On December 22, 1971, the Economic Stabilization Act was extended until April 30, 1973, to continue the price-control program. Public Law 92-210, 85 Stat. 743 (1971).

[14]Other subagencies created for the effort were the Committee on Interest and Dividends and the Committee on State and Local Government Cooperation.

[15]"Heavy reliance was placed on self-administration of the standards for smaller units; these units were subject only to periodic review or a small probability of possible audit . . . in a way similar to the way the personal income tax is administered." Marvin Kosters, *Controls and Inflation: The Economic Stabilization Program in Retrospect* (Washington, D.C.: American Enterprise Institute, 1975), p. 19.

[16]Price Commission, Press release, November 11, 1971. Reprinted in C. Jackson Grayson and Louis Neeb, *Confessions of a Price Controller* (Homewood, Ill.: Dow-Jones-Irvin, 1974), p. 242.

pronounced for major companies that were required to prenotify authorities before effectuating a price change. In February 1972, Shell applied for a 2 percent price hike under the TLP system, the first major request under Phase II. Challenging the increase was the Independent Refiners Association of America, which lobbied for the weighted average increase to exclude crude oil. The Price Commission concurred with the refiners' association and allowed price increases for chemicals and minor petroleum products only. The prices of crude oil and major petroleum products such as gasoline and fuel oil, reasoned the commission, were "sensitive" to the economy and should not be changed.[17] This "limited TLP" set the tone for future oil-company requests.[18]

The emerging regulatory double standard for major companies and independents was enlarged on May 6, 1972, when the small business exemption became effective. Firms with less than $50 million in sales and fifty or fewer employees, excluding construction and health care companies, were exempted from price justification. This effectively deregulated independent producers at a time when a traditional buyer's market was turning into a seller's market. The *Oil & Gas Journal* reported in September 1972 that a "crude-supply squeeze" was emerging. Storage tanks and oil pipelines were at capacity, and market-demand proration states raised allowables to "capacity" as defined by maximum-efficient-rate (MER) and yardstick tables.[19] Independents began to increase posted prices and

[17] Robert Lanzillotti, Mary Hamilton, and Blaine Roberts, *Phase II in Review* (Washington, D.C.: Brookings Institution, 1975), p. 171; and *OGJ*, February 7, 1972, p. 32.

[18] Oil firms accounted for 22 of 187 TLP increases granted in the Phase II period. Increases of 2 percent, in addition to Shell Oil, were granted to Ashland Oil, Atlantic Richfield Co., Cities Service Company, Continental Oil Company, Diamond-Shamrock, Gulf Oil Company, Humble Oil Company, Kerr-McGee Corporation, Mobil Oil Corporation, Murphy Oil Company, Occidental Petroleum, and Pennzoil United. Increases of 1.8 percent were granted to Getty Oil Company, Phillips Petroleum, and Union Pacific/Champlin Petroleum. The overall average percentage increase was 2.6 percent, which made the petroleum industry average one of the lowest of all industrial sectors. In addition, low-profile products generally received the highest markup, while high-profile items, such as crude oil and gasoline, received the lowest. To an extent, consumers of lesser oil products subsidized purchasers of major products. Department of the Treasury, Office of Economic Stabilization, "Policy Planning," *Historical Working Papers on the Economic Stabilization Program: August 15, 1971 to April 30, 1974* (Washington, D.C.: Government Printing Office, 1974), part 1, pp. 3, 92. Cited hereafter as *Historical Working Papers*.

[19] *OGJ*, September 18, 1972, pp. 31–35. The escalation of state market-demand factors during Phase II was as follows.

receive "premiums" from refiners, while majors had to live with modest TLP adjustments. As of December 14, 1972, TLP increases averaged 2.1 percent for major companies compared to non-TLP company increases of 6.1 percent.[20]

Phase III

Phase III began on January 11, 1973, and continued until June 12, 1973.[21] The base price was each firm's price on the last day of Phase II, January 10. If cost-justified, a price could be increased by 1.5 percent or a greater amount if the firm's base-period (Phase II) profit level was not exceeded. The program, intended to begin a phaseout of controls, was described by officials as "voluntary and on a self-administered basis." To this end, the Price Commission and the Pay Board were abolished.[22] Phase II reporting requirements were revamped to apply only to firms with annual revenue over $250 million. Firms with revenue over $50 million were instructed to maintain records to submit if requested. The CLC, meanwhile, continued to monitor business and labor for standard violations.

Date	Texas	Louisiana	Oklahoma	Kansas	New Mexico[a]
1971					
November	63%	69%	75%	100%	80%
December	63%	69%	100%	100%	80%
1972					
January	68%	100%	100%	100%	100%
February	76%	100%	100%	100%	100%
March	86%	100%	100%	100%	100%
April–January					
1973	100%	100%	100%	100%	80–100%

[a]Northwest market-demand factor only.

[20]"Internal Data of the Economic Stabilization Program, *Historical Working Papers,* part 3, p. 9. Oil-field-machinery companies followed a similar pattern: TLP companies averaged a 2.75 percent increase, while non-TLP companies averaged 5.25 percent.

[21]Executive Order 11695, 38 *Fed. Reg.* 1473 (January 12, 1973).

[22]The "voluntary" description was not to be taken literally. The authority and machinery for price enforcement were in place and could—and would—be reactivated. In Charles Owens' estimation, "The Administration had the 'club in the closet.' " "History of Petroleum Price Controls," *Historical Working Papers,* part 2, p. 1239. The *Oil & Gas Journal* warned: "The CLC may step in to prevent violations [by] . . . issuing temporary orders, setting interim price and wage levels, holding hearings, and issuing special rules or orders. . . . Thus, for oilmen, whose crude and major product prices have been frozen, any significant increase might still face a federal rollback." *OGJ,* January 15, 1973, p. 43.

During the early days of Phase III, oil began to emerge as a trouble-some good for price controllers. Demand for petroleum products rose with industrial output, and prices edged upward. Hearings were held in February 1973 at which CLC deputy director James McLane characterized the oil price problem as

> a classic demand-pull situation . . . [t]he root causes [being] insuffi-cient domestic crude production, although we are pumping proven reserves out of the ground as fast as possible. . . . There currently is no way for a company to determine with any degree of certainty whether a proposed price increase is compatible with the goals of the program.

With the handwriting on the wall, McLane continued:

> The way to remove the uncertainty generated by Phase III and the controls program is to be specific about what pricing flexibility oil companies can exercise. . . . Therefore, administration of effective oil pricing policy by the Cost of Living Council during Phase III will require a coordinated and close-monitoring control system, not a piecemeal approach as is anticipated under self-administered and voluntary controls.[23]

On March 6, 1973, a semblance of strict price controls was reen-acted with Special Rule no. 1 (SR-1), which regulated prices of petro-leum firms with yearly sales of $250 million or more.[24] This included 25 petroleum firms that accounted for approximately 95 percent of industry sales.[25] SR-1, which was intended "to assure the American

[23]James McLane, quoted in *Historical Working Papers,* part 2, pp. 1240–41.

[24]CLC Release 219, 38 *Fed. Reg.* 6283 (March 8, 1973).

[25]Firms covered by the new rule and their 1972 gross operating revenue were:

1. Exxon ($20,310 million)	14. Cities Service ($1,862 million)
2. Mobil ($9,166 million)	15. Ashland ($1,780 million)
3. Texas ($8,693 million)	16. Ohio Standard ($1,447 million)
4. Gulf ($6,243 million)	17. Getty ($1,405 million)
5. Cal. Stand. ($5,829 million)	18. Amerada Hess ($1,334 million)
6. Ind. Stand. ($4,503 million)	19. Marathon ($1,278 million)
7. Shell ($4,076 million)	20. Pennzoil United ($810 million)
8. Continental ($3,415 million)	21. Kerr-McGee ($680 million)
9. ARCO ($3,321 million)	22. Skelly ($525 million)
10. Tenneco ($3,275 million)	23. Murphy ($378 million)
11. Phillips ($2,513 million)	24. Amer. Petrofina ($285 million)
12. Union ($2,098 million)	25. Clark ($279 million)
13. Sun ($1,918 million)	

consumer an adequate supply of oil at reasonable prices," allowed these firms a 1 percent increase without justification and a 1.5 percent increase in weighted average product prices if corroborated by post-March 6 cost escalations. Price increases above 1.5 percent required not only cost justification but CLC prenotification. The thirty-day notice requirement, as well as delays and other stalling tactics, made the process unattractive.[26] The result was a de facto freeze on crude prices because SR-1 companies refused to raise posted prices for purchased crude to avoid placing their refineries in a cost-price squeeze. Many independent producers with wells connected to distribution outlets of the major companies were adversely affected. Independents linked to non-SR-1 companies, on the other hand, were in a position to demand and receive higher prices since their crude was feedstock for products without price constraints. Almost immediately after SR-1 was passed, independents in Kansas and Oklahoma encountered firm posted prices of major companies and threatened drastic action unless there was "equitable pricing."[27] They also suffered from a cost-price squeeze between unchanged posted prices and rising prices of uncontrolled well service and supply companies. The Kansas Independent Oil and Gas Association floated a plan for state conservation agencies in Texas, Kansas, Louisiana, and Oklahoma to shut down wells in protest. Some Oklahoma independents tested the political waters to see if a $5.00 per barrel floor price could be established.[28] Although none of these actions took place, concessions were gained to lessen the price gap between independents that were locked into SR-1 companies and independents that were not.

The inexorable drift toward greater imports and less domestic output led President Nixon to abolish import quotas on April 18, 1973, and recommend extending the investment tax credit to crude exploration. The price-control program was hemorrhaging, and more fine-tuning was necessary. Noticed Charles Owens, "Inflation in the oil industry had completely outrun the controllers, and the

---

[26]The CLC was not above creating delays on purpose. One effective tactic was to hold public hearings where opponents could effectively delay or altogether kill a proposed price increase. Charles Owens "History of Petroleum Price Controls," p. 1248.

[27]*OGJ*, March 19, 1973, p. 32.

[28]Ibid.

distortions and dislocations caused by the Phase III rules were beginning to loom large in almost every sector of the industry."[29] The predicament led to an extension of the Economic Stabilization Program to April 30, 1974, and to an overhaul of Phase III.

Phase III (Freeze 2)

The failure of Phase III to constrain petroleum prices, more the result of allowed cost pass-throughs than of noncompliance, led President Nixon to reimpose formal price controls on June 13, 1973.[30] The sixty-day measure, which lasted through August 1, was intended to give regulators time to devise a more detailed program for petroleum. Individual prices were frozen at the highest level at which 10 percent or more of all transactions were priced between June 1 and 8, 1973. Price hikes made between June 9 and 13 had to be rolled back.[31] The ceilings applied to all petroleum companies, as they did to other industries. Exempted were first sales of agricultural products and wages, rents, dividends, and interest rates that remained under Phase III voluntary guidelines. Increases in import prices could be passed through dollar for dollar under certain conditions. Furthermore, companies with between $50 million and $250 million in annual revenues were instructed to submit quarterly reports of costs, profits, and prices for the first two quarters of 1973 to the CLC for audit purposes. Price ceilings, like the earlier Phase I version, froze dual prices for identical crude oil within and between fields. In West Texas, for example, similar crude was posted at $3.70 per barrel by Gulf and at $4.05 by Shell.[32] This and other distortions due to stopgap regulation led to a reformulation of controls designed as a first step toward decontrol.

Phase IV

Phase IV became effective August 12, 1973, for all industrial sectors except food and the primary petroleum phases—production, refining, and retailing.[33] Oil-drilling, service, and supply companies were covered. Base prices were either those at which 10 percent or more

---

[29]Charles Owens, "History of Petroleum Price Controls," p. 1250.

[30]Executive Order 11723, 38 *Fed. Reg.* 15765 (June 15, 1973).

[31]For some posted price rollbacks for crude oil, see *OGJ*, July 2, 1973, p. 30.

[32]Ibid.

[33]Executive Order 11723, 38 *Fed. Reg.* 15763 (August 12, 1973).

of all transactions took place during the second half of Phase III or the average price during the last fiscal quarter ending before January 11, 1973. Costs could be passed through dollar for dollar, subject to the profit-margin limitation used in Phase III. Small businesses with yearly sales under $50 million and with fewer than 60 employees were to file annual reports with the CLC, companies with over $50 million in sales were to submit quarterly reports, and companies with over $100 million in sales were to prenotify the CLC thirty days before scheduled price increases were to go into effect. Proposed petroleum regulations were announced August 19.[34]

The regulations were complex and comprehensive, covering each sector of the petroleum market transaction by transaction. Controllers knew from experience that partial regulation was ineffective. It was all or nothing, and the desire to phase out price controls to save face (outright termination would have entailed loss of face) led to the decision to begin the process from a full regulatory stance.[35]

Petroleum production was one of four industry sectors that came under tailor-made regulations in Phase IV.[36] The major regulation of exploration and production was a two-tiered ceiling price, effective September 1, 1973, corresponding to "old" and "new" oil.[37] New oil was the amount of crude produced monthly in excess of production on a particular property during the same month of 1972.[38] Old oil was the monthly 1972 amount, known as the Base Production Control Level (BPCL). Cumulative production for the year ending

---

[34]38 *Fed. Reg.* 22538 (August 22, 1973). The rules were first presented for comment July 19. Between this time and Phase IV's implementation, the CLC received 272 formal comments and met with an estimated 1,500 industry representatives. Charles Owens, "History of Petroleum Price Controls," p. 1264.

[35]"Controllers had learned the hard way that, even to have a chance to stem inflation in oil, the entire industry had to be controlled. They would not make the mistake they made in Phase III of creating two classes of sellers by controlling only part of the industry." Ibid., p. 1261.

[36]The other three were the reseller phase (see chapter 12), the refiner phase (see chapter 20), and the retailer phase (see chapter 27).

[37]Multiprice regulation, although new for crude oil, had a history in natural-gas price regulation beginning with area rate assignments in 1960. Statutory tier pricing for natural gas was implemented in 1978, very possibly influenced by crude-oil tiers established five years before. See chapter 8, pp. 426–29.

[38]If production did not occur in the corresponding month of 1972, a monthly average was to be used. If no production took place in the entire year, the oil was considered new oil.

with the 1973 month was to exceed the yearly amount at the end of the 1972 month by an amount equal to or greater than the added production of the current month. If not, new oil was limited to the cumulative difference.[39]

The importance of the two classifications of otherwise identical oil was that new oil was uncontrolled and free to fetch the market price, while old oil was pegged at its historic May 15, 1973, price plus $0.35 per barrel for each grade.[40] The May 15 base day, which controllers considered tranquil for the industry, was also the basis for price regulation in the other petroleum sectors.[41]

An additional incentive for new production under Phase IV regulation allowed old oil to become unregulated "released oil" by the amount new oil exceeded the BPCL amount. For example, if a property produced 100 barrels in October 1972 and 150 barrels in October 1973, then 50 barrels were old oil, 50 barrels were released oil, and 50 barrels were new oil. One hundred barrels would sell at the market price, and 50 barrels would be restricted to the May 15, 1973, price plus $0.35 per barrel.[42]

[39]Charles Owens, "History of Petroleum Price Controls," p. 1265.

[40]The $0.35 per barrel premium represented a hard-won victory for the independent-producer lobbying group, the Independent Petroleum Association of America. Defended on the grounds of increased production costs in the post–May 15 period, the premium prevented across-the-board rollbacks for producers.

[41]"On that day domestic crude oil postings reflected traditional domestic price parity. Historical differentials by field and by grade and gravity were operating with minor exceptions, and the . . . May 15 date preceded the initiation of the second round of crude price increases in 1973 that began on June 1." Charles Owens, "History of Petroleum Price Controls," p. 1266.

[42]Producers were initially concerned about purchaser discrimination, which was illegal under state common-purchaser statutes, caused by locked-in price differentials. To partially eliminate the problem, the CLC devised a weighted average price for old oil and released oil by the following formula.

$$P_{max} = P_c + \frac{(C_{pr} - 1)\,(P_m - P_c)}{(C_{bp})}$$

where

P_{max} = maximum price for nonnew oil ($/bl),
P_c = ceiling price of crude ($/bl),
C_{bp} = base period control level (bl),
C_{pr} = crude production for current month (bl), and
P_m = unregulated price ($/bl).

A major differential remained between the price of new oil and the weighted old oil–released oil average price that would lead to the refinery entitlements equalization program. See chapter 20, pp. 1205–8.

The first modification of Phase IV crude regulation came on November 16, 1973, when stripper oil was exempted from price regulation by section 406 of the Trans-Alaskan Pipeline Authorization Act.[43] The culmination of a long lobbying effort by independent producers, the exemption applied to all properties that produced less than 10 barrels per day of crude oil and condensate in the preceding calendar month.[44] The effect of the rule was dramatic: stripper output that previously sold at the controlled price of approximately $4.25 per barrel reached $10 per barrel by January 1974.[45] Not surprisingly, the number of wells producing under 10 barrels per day increased practically overnight. Simple economics told the producer to reduce production from wells in the 11 to 20 barrel per day range to achieve decontrolled status, a reclassification that was achievable with only a one-month dead period. This loophole, however, would soon be eliminated.[46]

Oil was now classified into four categories outside those of its innate gravity and sulfur content: old oil, priced at posted May 15, 1973, prices plus $0.35 per barrel; new oil and stripper oil, priced at market; and released oil, priced at a weighted average between old oil and new oil (but in fact commanding an uncontrolled price when not weighted).

By this time, the Arab embargo, announced October 7, was being felt, and on November 27, 1973, the EPAA, which gave the president additional authority to regulate crude oil prices, was passed.[47] For the time being, that act was moot; the Economic Stabilization Act was in effect with Phase IV specifications.

A second modification to Phase IV regulation of crude-oil prices occurred on December 21 when the May 15 price premium of $0.35 per barrel was raised to $1.35 to close the widening gap between controlled and uncontrolled crude.[48] CLC director John Dunlop

---

[43]Public Law 93-153, 88 Stat. 96 (1973).

[44]The "property" definition would be a source of much confusion and litigation from this point until the end of crude price controls in 1981. See this chapter, pp. 515–21.

[45]Charles Owens, "History of Petroleum Price Controls," p. 1308; and *OGJ*, January 14, 1974, p. 23.

[46]See this chapter, p. 488.

[47]Public Law 93-159, 87 Stat. 627 (1973).

[48]38 *Fed. Reg.* 34896 (1973).

called the existing $4.00 per barrel differential "potentially destabilizing," given the intention of Phase IV to phase out price controls by April 1974, not lock in restrictions that, once removed, would cause price explosions.[49]

The two Phase IV revisions were the only major ones affecting crude-oil pricing. It was expected that old oil would join the other three classifications, which would completely deregulate the crude market—as was envisioned for the rest of the economy (except for separately regulated natural-gas production and distribution). Speaking of sectoral decontrol in his Phase IV announcement, Nixon stated in a July 18, 1973, speech:

> There is no reason for me to reiterate my desire to end controls and return to the free market. . . . Our experience with the freeze has dramatized the essential difficulties of a controlled system—its interference with freedom, its inequities, its distortions, its evasions and the obstacles it places in the way of good international relations.[50]

Decontrol would not be petroleum's fate despite the industry-by-industry deregulation that began on October 25. On February 26, 1974, controls were dropped for manufacturers of oil-field machinery followed by the drilling service and supply industry on April 1.[51] Tubular goods (casing, tubing, and drill pipe) in short supply as a result of price controls—which stimulated demand and reduced supply—were decontrolled in early May.[52] Because regulatory-induced supply problems created industry demands for mandatory allocation, concentrated at the wholesale gasoline level, and because of import-price havoc caused by the Arab embargo, general price-control authority over crude-oil production did not terminate on April 30, 1974, as it did for other goods and services.

---

[49]*OGJ*, December 24, 1973, p. 18. Said Dunlop, "When we announced the final oil regulations in August, we stated that we would continually monitor the ceiling price toward achieving parity with world prices." Quoted in Charles Owens, "History of Petroleum Price Controls," p. 1309.

[50]Richard M. Nixon, quoted in Jonathan Brock and Roger Winsky, "Removing Controls: The Policy of Selective Decontrol," in *Historical Working Papers*, part 1, p. 869.

[51]39 *Fed. Reg.* 7796 (February 28, 1974); CLC Release 563, April 11, 1974; and *OGJ*, March 11, 1974, pp. 52–53, and April 8, 1974, p. 55.

[52]Executive Order 11781, 39 *Fed. Reg.* 15749 (May 6, 1974).

Phases I to IV in Retrospect

General Effects. The Nixon price-control program was a desperate supplement to Keynesian economic contracyclical policy that had become increasingly problematic since its formal implementation in the Full Employment Act of 1945.[53] Keynesian policy was as follows: By judiciously manipulating the economy's variables through fiscal and monetary policy, the government was to maintain a level of aggregate demand to steer the economy clear of inflation on the one hand and unemployment on the other. If prices were escalating, aggregate demand could be reduced by increasing taxes, decreasing government expenditure, and decreasing the money supply to achieve price stability. If unemployment was rising, aggregate demand could be increased by decreasing taxes, increasing government expenditure, and increasing the money supply to approach full employment. Aggregate demand was to be altered by government policy that went *against the economic cycle,* against the inflationary boom by reducing overheated demand and against depressionary unemployment by stimulating stagnant demand. But what if inflation and unemployment were simultaneously high, a real-world fact that uncovered a glaring anomaly in Keynesian theory?[54] How could economic planners concurrently increase and decrease aggregate demand to address both problems? This predicament plagued Keynesian policy practitioners—Truman, Eisenhower, Kennedy, Johnson, and particularly Nixon—and forced them into desperate postures of "exhortations and controls" to fight rising prices while stimulating the economy. The rationale was that "inflationary expectations" created the dilemma, and if moral suasion or formal controls could tame inflation by eliminating or reducing this psychological phenomenon, then unemployment could be reduced in a noninflationary way. This would not be the case, however, and thus was

---

[53]Public Law 79-304, 60 Stat. 23 (1946).

[54]For a theoretical explanation of simultaneous inflation and unemployment, called stagflation, see F. A. Hayek, *A Tiger by the Tail: The Keynesian Legacy of Inflation,* Cato Institute Paper no. 6 (Washington, D.C.: Cato Institute, 1979). Simplified, the explanation is that monetary creation spawns recession in addition to inflation because falsified interest rates and other errant prices misdirect resources into areas not consonant with true consumer preference. When monetary growth slows or fails to accelerate, malinvestments manifested by business failures and unemployment come to light.

signaled the decline—in theory if not practice—of the once sacrosanct Keynesian economics.[55]

Not unlike similar attempts over the centuries, the American price-control experience under Nixon failed to constrain prices and produced myriad undesirable side effects.[56] Inflationary psychology, the alleged culprit that the New Economic Policy was to tame, was never seriously threatened. It was business as usual at the Federal Reserve, and the control program was never intended for the long term. Indeed, if price controls were set for an extended time period, expectations of a worse kind would develop as government officials knew. Inflation, as can be seen in figure 9.1, continued a downward trend that began in 1970 during Phase I, the result of reduced monetary growth, and climbed during the remaining control period as a result of increased growth in the money stock. In fact, price controls *encouraged* inflation to the extent that pressure was reduced on the Federal Reserve to restrict monetary growth.[57]

Although there is not an exact quantitative relationship between money growth and prices—the subjective mind stands in between—

---

[55]Remarked renowned Keynesian J. R. Hicks: "There can yet be no doubt that the [postwar] boom was associated, in the minds of many, with the Keynesian policies, so when ... the boom itself began to falter, the authority of the policies that were supposed to have led to it inevitably began to be called in question. Instead of producing *real* economic progress (i.e., increasing employment) ... they were just producing inflation. Something, it seemed clear, had gone wrong.... So the issue which seemed closed is re-opened. We have to start, in a way, all over again." Hicks, *The Crisis in Keynesian Economics* (New York: Basic Books, 1974), pp. 3–4.

[56]The Phase I–Phase IV experience followed the typical path of other control programs in different countries and different eras. "Grandiose plans for regulating investment, wages, prices, and production are usually unveiled with great fanfare and high hopes. As reality forces its way in, however, the plans are modified a little more, then drastically altered, then finally allowed to vanish quietly and unmourned." Robert Schuettinger and Eamonn Butler, *Forty Centuries of Wage and Price Controls,* p. 9. For an inside view of the problematic task of controlling prices during Phase I–Phase IV, see C. Jackson Grayson and Louis Neeb, *Confessions of a Price Controller.*

[57]Observed Michael Darby: "The [Economic Stabilization Program] was supposed to reduce the expected rate of inflation and hence ease the adjustment to lower rates of money supply growth and inflation. Apparently the Fed did not get the message since it increased the money supply growth rate when it should have reduced it. So previous progress against inflation—achieved at a cost that included the 1969–1970 recession—was thrown away." Darby, "The U.S. Economic Stabilization Program of 1971–1974," in *The Illusion of Wage and Price Controls,* ed. Michael Walker (Vancouver: Fraser Institute, 1976), p. 153.

Figure 9.1
U.S. Inflation Rates: 1970–75

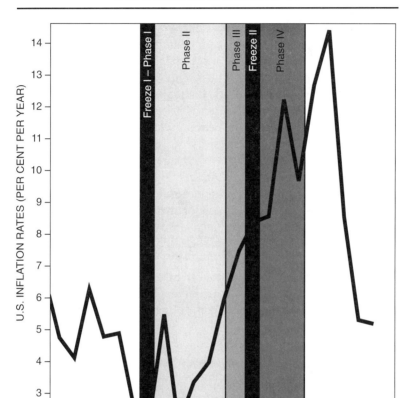

Source: U.S. Department of Commerce.

Source: Michael Darby, "The U.S. Economic Stabilization Program of 1971-1974," in *The Illusion of Wage and Price Control*, ed. Michael Walker (Vancouver: Fraser Institute, 1976), p. 146. Used by permission.

the correspondence between the two during Phases I–IV was only slightly dampened by the price-control experience, as shown in figure 9.2.

The gains against inflation made by regulation proved illusory. Not only did quality decline to maintain margins in the face of fixed selling prices, but government regulators purposely prevented increases for some of the 400 goods and services comprising the Consumer Price Index in return for granting liberal increases for "nonvisible" items not included in the price-index calculation.[58] Both effects *understated* inflation measured by the index.[59]

The particular methodology of the price-ceiling program, which constrained prices and profits to historical levels, created a number of distortions of normal profit-maximizing behavior. Price ceilings tied to previous sales locked in nonrepresentative (disequilibrium) prices and created multiple prices, not attributable to transportation differentials, for identical products. This created opportunities for middlemen to buy relatively underpriced items, including petroleum, and sell them at higher "market" prices.[60] The profit-margin limitation encouraged firms *not* to minimize costs by raising productivity and monitoring discretionary expenditure or to maximize revenue by altering new-product mixes or by integrating to stay within allowable profits.[61] As an alternative to the "inefficiency" route around regulation, firms employed "sham transactions" in which not-for-profit trades were made to lower the profit-to-sales margin to legal levels.[62] "Creative accounting"—whereby year-end inventory

---

[58]For examples within the petroleum sector, see chapter 27, pp. 1608–9.

[59]Michael Darby, focusing exclusively on quarterly adjusted real output, concludes that inflation was understated during Phases I and II and overstated during the second part of Phases III and Phase IV. Darby, "The U.S. Economic Stabilization Program, 1971–1974," pp. 147–52. This conclusion, however, crucially assumes a rigid relationship between output and employment (Okun's Law). The present analysis concludes that inflation was consistently understated because the Consumer Price Index calculators fell behind in their adjustments of quality changes, and the controllers purposely traded unrecorded inflation for reductions in Consumer Price Index inflation.

[60]See chapter 12, pp. 687–93.

[61]John Flory, "Price Control Mechanisms," in *Historical Working Papers*, part 1, pp. 293–96.

[62]For greater description of how firms "played the regulations" to minimize the effect of controls, see ibid., pp. 296–99.

Figure 9.2
U.S. MONEY AND PRICE GROWTH: 1964–77

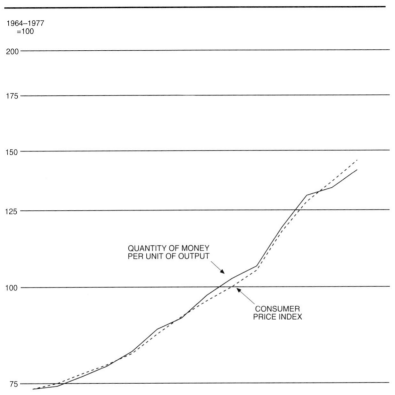

SOURCE: Milton Friedman and Rose Friedman, *Free to Choose: A Personal Statement* (New York: Harcourt Brace Jovanovich, 1979), p. 257. Used by permission.

483

was conservatively estimated to increase the cost of goods sold to reduce profit margins—was also employed.[63]

In a free market, prices and profits change with new circumstances to continually satisfy new consumer demands. Under regulation, locked-in prices and profit margins become obsolete with changed conditions of supply and demand and are unable to allocate supply to the most urgent uses, bring new opportunities to the attention of entrepreneurs, and reward efficiency. Resources, furthermore, are spent to formulate, administer, comply with, and circumvent controls. These costs, including that of production lost to disincentives and bottlenecks, had a price tag in the billions of dollars.[64] Because of these problems and the fact that the underlying cause of inflation—monetary growth—was never addressed, the wage- and price-control program could only be counterproductive.

Crude Oil Exploration and Production. The crude-oil price-control program could not have come at a more inopportune time for the wellhead industry or national welfare. The Organization of Petroleum Exporting Countries (OPEC), founded in 1960 in response to declining world oil prices and U.S. import restrictions, had long wanted to cartelize supply to control price.[65] This was not possible, however, unless the cartel could gain a large share of U.S. consumption and prevent the domestic industry from effectively responding to any cartel-type action OPEC might take. State proration regulation, by restricting output and increasing unit costs, gave OPEC a boost by increasing the competitive position of U.S. imports in the 1950s and 1960s, a situation that protectionist quotas were intended to negate. With price controls in the 1970s, which at once discouraged exploration and production and artificially stimulated demand (not unlike the situation in interstate natural-gas markets), OPEC received a godsend that would pave the way for later developments.[66]

---

[63]Michael Darby, "The U.S. Economic Stabilization Program of 1971–1974," p. 159.

[64]See Robert Bleiberg, "Wage and Price Controls," in *Champions of Freedom* (Hillsdale, Mich.: Hillsdale College Press, 1974), pp. 127–29.

[65]See chapter 13, pp. 758, 764.

[66]Statistics showing the gap between domestic production and consumption during Phases I–IV and the OPEC price explosion in late 1973 are presented in this chapter, pp. 522–23.

The general effect of Phase I through the first half of Phase III was to keep a depressed industry down. Prices remained artificially low, despite virtual deregulation of smaller firms, thanks to a direct link, in many cases, between independent producers and integrated companies. Phase IV, however, would create a series of distortions of its own.

The introduction of two-tiered pricing was accompanied by high hopes on the part of government officials. Here, they thought, was fine-tuning at its best: ceilings on old-oil prices for consumers and unregulated new-oil and released-oil prices to incite badly needed output. Assistant Secretary of the Interior Stephen Wakefield lauded the novel program as "a constructive balance . . . between the legitimate interests of both producers and consumers."[67] Indeed, the program provided comparatively greater incentive for producers, and the large supply of old oil was attractively priced for consumers. But this neglected the inherent distortions and perversities created by the "half slave, half free" pricing system. Seen in retrospect, the two-tiered pricing of Phase IV was the first stage of a regulatory nightmare that would last far beyond anyone's initial expectations.

The double pricing standard quickly led to opportunistic entrepreneurial behavior. Industry participants purchased controlled crude at regulated prices and processed the crude into uncontrolled product to sell at market prices. Arbitrage opportunities became so great that *crude-oil reselling* became an industry growth area.[68] At the wellhead, reports were heard of adjacent leaseholders' shutting down existing wells to redrill on new property to produce new oil exclusively.[69] Tremendous demand for price-controlled oil, substantially below market-clearing levels, sent excess demand toward new oil, released oil, and imports, which bid prices to levels *above* what an unregulated market would have allowed. Old-oil price ceilings, in

---

[67]*OGJ*, July 30, 1973, p. 90.

[68]See chapter 12, pp. 687–90.

[69]William Johnson, "The Impact of Energy Controls on the Oil Industry: How to Worsen an Energy Crisis," in *Energy: The Policy Issues,* ed. Gary Eppen (Chicago: University of Chicago Press, 1975), p. 111. Johnson also mentions the practice of "converting old oil to new oil merely by shuffling paper and redefining leaseholds" rather than by the more expensive practice of redrilling wells.

short, subsidized the other three.[70] Purchasers broke the distortion altogether—tie-in sales occurred in which new oil was bought at an inflated price to purchase old oil. A concerned CLC heard of one case in which a buyer paid a producer $50,000 for 1 barrel of new oil to obtain a batch of old oil.[71]

Economic inefficiency followed the distorted incentive to produce new oil at almost any cost. Artificially encouraged development wells were rapidly drilled and new pumping units were installed on existing wells to increase the amount of new oil. Old-oil wells were even shut down to increase neighboring new oil.[72] This spawned a mini-drilling boom held back only by material shortages, themselves a consequence of price controls.[73]

Another consequence of the once-heralded double-price program was the creation of political constituencies behind each oil tier. Behind uncontrolled oil were producers and royalty owners, who lobbied for price decontrol.[74] Lobbying for price controls were emerging consumer organizations and refineries that desired cheap feedstock.[75] The two-tiered crude-oil price scheme, the centerpiece of a "temporary" program, would resist decontrol for years to come.

Emergency Petroleum Allocation Act of 1973

On October 6, 1973, the Arab-Israeli War broke out over a long-standing dispute over territorial rights. A day later, the Arab countries, led by Saudi Arabia, unveiled the "oil weapon" by threatening

---

[70]For examples of new-oil price hikes, see *OGJ*, September 17, 1973, pp. 29–33, and January 14, 1974, p. 23. A similar thing occurred with natural gas when deep gas was deregulated in late 1978. See chapter 8, pp. 443–44.

[71]Charles Owens, "History of Petroleum Price Controls," p. 1307. Another "tie-in" example is given by William Johnson, "The Impact of Energy Controls on the Oil Industry," pp. 110–11. The National Petroleum Refiners Association lobbied for a single price ceiling because of the tie-in problem. *OGJ*, October 15, 1973, p. 63. In May 1974, a regulation against tie-in sales was issued. 39 *Fed. Reg.* 17766 (May 20, 1974).

[72]"Gerrymandering" is discussed in more detail in this chapter, p. 489.

[73]*OGJ*, October 22, 1973, pp. 11–14, and March 18, 1974, p. 39. Spot shortages of propane also idled drilling rigs. *OGJ*, May 21, 1973, p. 61.

[74]While the majors favored outright control, the Independent Petroleum Association of America pragmatically lobbied for higher prices for old oil.

[75]Charles Owens, "History of Petroleum Price Controls," p. 1306. Also see Milton Friedman, "Who Opposes Oil Decontrol?" *Newsweek*, September 15, 1975, p. 64.

to cut off oil exports to any country aiding Israel's war effort. Nonetheless, the United States continued to supply arms and spare parts to Israel, and on October 7, the Organization of Arab Petroleun Exporting Countries announced a general production cutback and an embargo on the export of oil to the United States and the Netherlands. Posted prices soared as a result of panic buying. A 2- to 3-million barrel per day shortfall, accounting for 10 to 17 percent of U.S. consumption, was predicted by U.S. officials.[76]

At the time of the embargo, a comprehensive oil-regulation bill, the EPAA, was well on its way to congressional approval. Shortages experienced prior to the cutoff by independent refiners, marketers, and farmer cooperatives as a result of price controls, and in particular as a result of SR-1, created political pressure for regulatory relief that the embargo only hastened.[77] On November 27, 1973, the EPAA was signed into law by Nixon.[78]

Although the EPAA was primarily concerned with government allocation of scarce oil supplies, it prominently regulated crude-oil prices.[79] Phase IV regulations remained in effect, but with the expiration of the Economic Stabilization Act on April 30, 1974, price controls under the EPAA began.[80]

Administered by the Federal Energy Office, which on December 26, 1973, took over petroleum matters from the CLC, the EPAA carried forward the Phase IV two-tiered program.[81] Old oil remained

[76]William Lane, *The Mandatory Petroleum Price and Allocation Regulations: A History and Analysis* (Washington, D.C.: American Petroleum Institute, 1981), p. 31. Imported crude prices rose by approximately 75 percent in October alone. *OGJ*, October 29, 1973, pp. 49–52.

[77]See John Kraft and Mark Rodekohr, "Crude Oil Price Controls: Their Purpose and Impact," *Denver Journal of International Law and Policy* (Winter 1979): 321. For greater discussion of passage of this act, see chapter 27, pp. 1624–26.

[78]Public Law 93-159, 87 Stat. 627 (1973).

[79]"The President shall promulgate a regulation providing for the mandatory allocation of crude oil ... at prices specified (or determined in a matter prescribed by) such regulation." Public Law 93-159, 87 Stat. 629 (1973).

[80]Executive Order 11748, 38 *Fed. Reg.* 33575 (December 6, 1973).

[81]The evolution of federal-level petroleum bureaucracy began in late 1972 when Nixon established a "super cabinet" position, the counselor to the president on natural resources. This was followed by the Oil Policy Committee (OPC) in early 1973 and the Energy Policy Office (EPO) soon thereafter to oversee the OPC. The EPO, in turn, was replaced by the Federal Energy Office (FEO) on December 6, 1973. See John Carver, "Government Regulation of Petroleum: 1973 Developments," *25 Oil and Gas Institute* (New York: Matthew Bender, 1974), pp. 2–8.

at its May 15, 1973, price plus $1.35 per barrel (approximately $5.25), and new oil, released oil, stripper oil, imported oil, and oil certified for export were allowed free determination.[82] Also contained in the act was a directive to establish "equitable pricing,"[83] first promulgated in the 1970 Economic Stabilization Act.

One change in the new law tightened the qualification for stripper oil. Previously, a property could qualify for stripper status if production from the previous month averaged less than 10 barrels per day; now production had to average less than 10 barrels per day for the preceding *calendar year* to qualify. This removed the exploited incentive to underproduce to qualify for uncontrolled prices three weeks after the original stripper exemption was passed.[84]

Strong sentiment to recontrol exempted crude surfaced soon after the EPAA became law. On February 21, 1974, an exemption given to state and local government sales of crude oil was rescinded.[85] A general rollback measure in early 1974 was soundly defeated in the Senate, but rising import and petroleum-product prices led to another bill a month later, the Energy Emergency Act, to roll back new oil, released oil, and stripper oil to the old-oil price of $5.25 per barrel.[86] President Nixon vetoed the bill, which was sustained in the Senate; this only postponed a rollback of more modest proportions that would occur later that year.

On May 27, 1974, petroleum regulation was transferred from the Federal Energy Office to the newly created Federal Energy Administration (FEA) with Simon in charge.[87] The FEA, while primarily concerned with mandatory allocation and the refinery-entitlements program, issued crude-oil price rulings in two troublesome areas: stripper-well qualification and "tie-in" sales of new oil and old oil.

---

[82]Public Law 93-159, 87 Stat. 630, sec. 4(b)(2)(B) (1973).

[83]Ibid., sec. 4(b)(1)(F).

[84]This would not discourage some firms from curtailing output to illegally classify production as stripper oil. See General Accounting Office, *Federal Energy Administration's Efforts to Audit Domestic Crude Oil Producers* (Washington, D.C.: Government Printing Office, 1975), pp. 6–7.

[85]39 *Fed. Reg.* 7176 (February 25, 1974).

[86]Energy czar William Simon, concerned about the high level of exempt prices, supported a rollback as long as it was not too low. To this end, he considered administratively ordering price reductions for exempt oil. *OGJ*, February 18, 1974, p. 46.

[87]Public Law 93-275, 88 Stat. 96 (1974).

Four rulings in late 1974 and early 1975, representing "the first real regulatory venture into the crude oil production segment of the oil industry since the original promulgation of the Phase IV pricing rules,"[88] clarified the qualifications for stripper-well exemptions:

1. Natural-gas liquids or condensate from gas wells did not qualify for stripper-well exemptions.[89]
2. Injection wells, shut-in wells, and disposal wells could not be added to producing wells to determine average well production for stripper classification.[90]
3. Casinghead gas, if treated and sold as crude oil at the lease, could qualify for the stripper-well exemption.[91]
4. Producing wells on a stripper property had to "operate at the maximum feasible rate of production and in accord with recognized conservation practices" to qualify for the exemption.[92]

The above clarifications were designed to tighten loopholes that allowed producers to maximize income by making perverse output decisions. But one loophole, "gerrymandering," remained: offset-well drilling to reduce average output per well from a particular property to reach stripper status.

"Tie-in" sales, in which new oil was purchased at inflated prices to secure underpriced old oil, had beset the crude-price program since the beginning of Phase IV. In response, the Federal Energy Office ruled that the "artificially high 'current free market price' for 'new' oil constitutes an attempt to evade the price limitations . . . applicable to crude oil."[93] Because it failed to set specific price standards, however, the ruling had little effect on the ongoing circumvention, which was fostered by growing discrepancies between controlled and uncontrolled oil throughout the EPAA period as shown in table 9.1.

Another ruling had particular importance for crude-oil production. On May 21, 1975, the FEA granted permanent stripper-well

---

[88]Jim Langdon, "Domestic Crude Oil Production—The New Regulatory Framework," *28 Oil and Gas Institute* (New York: Matthew Bender, 1977), p. 15.

[89]39 *Fed. Reg.* 44414 (December 24, 1974).

[90]Ibid.

[91]39 *Fed. Reg.* 44416 (December 24, 1974).

[92]40 *Fed. Reg.* 40828 (September 4, 1975).

[93]39 *Fed. Reg.* 17766 (May 20, 1974).

Table 9.1
TWO-TIERED WELLHEAD-PRICE REGULATION:
DECEMBER 1973–JANUARY 1976

Date	Controlled Oil Price ($/bl)[a]	Percent	Uncontrolled Oil Price ($/bl)[b]	Percent
1973				
December	5.25	–	6.70	–
1974				
January	5.25	60	9.82	40
February	5.25	62	9.87	38
March	5.25	60	9.88	40
April	5.25	60	9.88	40
May	5.25	62	9.88	38
June	5.25	63	9.95	37
July	5.25	64	9.95	36
August	5.25	66	9.98	34
September	5.25	67	10.10	33
October	5.25	66	10.74	34
November	5.25	67	10.90	33
December	5.25	66	11.08	34
1975				
January	5.25	58	11.28	42
February	5.25	61	11.39	39
March	5.25	60	11.47	40
April	5.25	61	11.64	39
May	5.25	62	11.69	38
June	5.25	63	11.73	37
July	5.25	62	12.30	38
August	5.25	63	12.38	37
September	5.25	63	12.46	37
October	5.25	63	12.73	37
November	5.25	64	12.89	36
December	5.25	63	12.95	37
1976				
January	5.02	54	12.99	46

SOURCE: Federal Energy Administration, *Monthly Energy Review,* various issues.
[a]Old oil.
[b]New, released, and stripper oil.

status to wells that qualified as stripper properties subsequent to December 31, 1972.[94] The stated rationale was to

> ensure that, as to properties that qualified for the stripper well lease exemption in 1973, but which exceeded the 10 barrel per well per day level in 1974 through workovers or other production stimulation techniques, the incentive to permit production again to decline naturally to stripper well levels will be removed, and further steps to maintain and increase production will be encouraged.[95]

The EPAA, due to expire on February 28, 1975, was extended six months to continue the existing network of price and allocation controls on crude oil and petroleum products.[96] Sentiment in Congress was strong that any rise in wellhead prices would translate into higher retail prices to worsen inflation and that a "windfall" from decontrol for producers was neither needed or deserved.[97]

Debate over a second EPAA extension revealed sharp political divisions. President Gerald Ford, who replaced Nixon on August 9, forwarded oil decontrol with a windfall profits tax as the centerpiece of his energy policy. Congress favored continued controls, mandatory allocation, and mandatory conservation. Ford's plan, it was charged, would result in increased inflation and more unemployment in a fragile economy.[98]

Throughout 1975, the White House and the FEA pushed phased decontrol at a skeptical Congress. After several delays, President Ford on April 30 instructed the FEA to prepare a bill to phase out price controls over a twenty-five-month period. On May 15, the House Commerce Committee killed the proposal. A second effort followed on July 14, this time extending the phaseout over thirty months, while setting a ceiling price of $13.50 per barrel on new oil

---

[94]40 *Fed. Reg.* 22123 (May 21, 1975).

[95]Ibid. Rep. Bob Eckhardt (D-Tex.) referred to the permanent status of stripper wells, even if output rose above 10 barrels per day, as the "Gypsy Rose Lee rule, that is once a stripper, always a stripper." *Stripper Oil Miscertification,* Hearing before the House Committee on Interstate and Foreign Commerce, 96th Cong., 2d sess. (Washington, D.C.: Government Printing Office, 1980), p. 1.

[96]Public Law 93-511, 88 Stat. 1608 (1975).

[97]Neil de Marchi, "The Ford Administration: Energy as a Political Good," in *Energy Policy in Perspective,* ed. Craufurd Goodwin (Washington, D. C.: Brookings Institution, 1981), p. 498.

[98]Ibid., pp. 482–93. This argument is critically examined in this chapter, pp. 510–12.

and released oil, which accounted for over one-fourth of domestic output.[99] When this met opposition, a third plan was quickly drafted that increased the phaseout to thirty-nine months with the lion's share of price increases scheduled after the 1976 elections. The controlled price of $11.50 applied to all domestically produced oil—old, new, released, and stripper.

Congress, particularly the House of Representatives laden with "Watergate freshmen," rejected the president's third and final compromise offer. President Ford retaliated on September 9 by vetoing an EPAA extension and was upheld by the Senate the next day. Technically, crude oil was decontrolled for all oil companies for the first time since August 1971.[100]

Concerned parties knew that oil was not decontrolled. Senators who made the margin of difference in sustaining Ford's veto voted on the understanding that they were supporting a thirty-nine-month phaseout, not immediate decontrol. The industry also knew that increasing prices to market levels would raise a furor and lead to retroactive rollbacks. Even before expiration, many oil companies embarked on a public-relations campaign to assure the public and lawmakers that price and allocation decisions would not noticeably change.[101]

On September 29, 1975, President Ford temporarily extended the EPAA to November 15.[102] As anticipated, the extension was retroactive to September 1, which forced some companies to refund money they had earned from price hikes in September.[103] The extension, followed by another for one month on November 14, was intended to give Congress time to devise a new bill palatable to the president.[104] Intense deliberations followed among the White House, the FEA,

[99]Ibid., p. 500.

[100]In Phase III prior to SR-1, however, from January 11 until March 6, 1973, unregulated pricing technically existed.

[101]OGJ, September 1, 1975, p. 54. Mobil Oil chairman Rawleigh Warner criticized total deregulation for its potential impact on "America's fragile economy recovery." Other major companies and independent producers favored immediate decontrol or a short phaseout.

[102]Public Law 94-99, 89 Stat. 481 (1975).

[103]OGJ, October 20, 1975, p. 29. Shell and Cities Service, for example, equalized their crude prices by increasing old-oil prices and reducing exempt-oil prices. OGJ, September 1, 1975, p. 54.

[104]Public Law 94-133, 89 Stat. 694 (1975).

and Congress to reach a compromise between phased decontrol and interim price ceilings. This was accomplished in late 1975 with the far-reaching, complicated legislation discussed next.

Energy Policy and Conservation Act of 1975

On December 22, 1975, the Energy Policy and Conservation Act (EPCA), signed after weeks of indecision by President Ford, became law.[105] The highly interventionist bill represented a victory for Congress and a painful compromise for a president whose original program of phased decontrol was scarcely recognizable.[106] With a stated purpose of increasing "the supply of fossil fuels in the United States through price incentives and production requirements," the act reestablished comprehensive price controls on the first sale of crude oil, broadly stipulated withdrawal rates from individual wells, and authorized imprisonment of persons who willfully violated the regulations. In addition, it closely regulated the other petroleum sectors, established a strategic petroleum reserve, and exhaustively detailed mandatory conservation measures for the general economy.[107] The act was the most interventionist piece of legislation in the peacetime history of the U.S. energy market, eclipsing the EPAA of 1973.

The act set "ceiling prices . . . applicable to any first sale of crude oil produced in the United States, such that the resulting actual weighted average first sale price for all such crude oil during such calendar month and each of the 39 months thereafter shall not exceed a maximum of $7.66 per barrel."[108] The president was given authority to adjust crude prices toward this limit and to increase the composite

---

[105]Public Law 94-163, 89 Stat. 871 (1975).

[106]Analysts interpreted Ford's decision to sign the bill after five weeks of indecision as a political maneuver to defeat upstart Ronald Reagan in the crucial New Hampshire Republican primary. See Neil de Marchi, "The Ford Administration: Energy as a Political Good," p. 507. Said William Simon, himself prone to compromise and regulatory advocacy in these years: "After long years of battling for a sensible energy policy, Ford caved in. Anxious for a quick political fix just before the New Hampshire and Florida primaries, he signed the bill. It may have got him a few votes in New Hampshire, but it lost him a great deal of moral support in his own party and was in part responsible for the conservative rebellion against him." Simon, *A Time for Truth* (New York: McGraw-Hill, 1978), p. 79.

[107]See chapter 17, pp. 1028–29, and chapter 27, pp. 1623–24, 1679, respectively.

[108]Public Law 94-163, 89 Stat. 945, sec. 401 (1975).

price ceiling to encourage production and account for inflation.[109] A special 3 percent "production incentive" could be awarded as long as it was within the 10 percent annual ceiling on discretionary increases. A higher cap required the approval of Congress. Increases were not allowed for old oil; they could apply only to newly established "upper-tier oil" (defined below), stripper oil (oil from wells historically producing 10 barrels or less per day excluding condensate), or crude produced in excess of a property's monthly average during 1972 or September through November 1975.[110]

Another provision of the 1975 law required government agencies to determine potentially enforceable production rates for individual oil and gas wells for standby implementation by the president.[111] For federal lands, the interior secretary was to calculate a MER, a temporary emergency production rate, and an above-MER rate capable of preserving total recoverability if maintained for less than ninety days. For nonfederal properties (i.e., state or private lands), the respective state conservation agencies were to calculate the MER and temporary emergency production rate. If provable reservoir damage occurred from such action, property owners were allowed to bring suit against the government to recover damages.[112]

Stage I

Pursuant to the EPCA, the FEA restructured the Phase IV EPAA two-tiered price, effective February 1, 1976, to meet the $7.66 per barrel weighted average statutory ceiling for crude oil. This was accomplished by reclassifying exempt-category crude (new, released, and stripper) as "upper-tier" oil subject to a ceiling price and redesignating controlled oil as "lower-tier" oil. The existing composite price of $8.19 per barrel was derived by estimating 60 percent of lower-tier oil at $5.25 per barrel and 40 percent of upper-tier oil at $12.60 per barrel. To achieve the legal limit of $7.66 per

---

[109]If the actual weighted average price exceeded the statutory limit, a price rollback was required.

[110]The addition of 1975 as a choice for base-period control level was designed to encourage output from declining properties. The 1975 option also had the advantage of eliminating any cumulative deficiency for producers attributable to the 1972 basis.

[111]Public Law 94-163, 89 Stat. 880, sec. 106 (1975).

[112]Ibid., pp. 880–81.

barrel, lower-tier oil remained at $5.25 per barrel (or more specifically, each property's May 15, 1973, price plus $1.35 per barrel as instructed by the EPAA), and upper-tier oil was rolled back to approximately $11.28 per barrel (the September 30, 1975, price minus $1.32 per barrel).[113] Additions to upper-tier oil were subject to the cumulative-deficiency proviso beginning February 1, 1976. Existing deficiencies were canceled.[114]

Stage II

The second implementation stage involved the first adjustment to the composite price. Effective March 1, 1976, the full 3 percent production incentive was granted along with a 6.8 percent inflation adjustment.[115] The 9.8 percent increase, equally applied to lower-tier and upper-tier oil, was within the 10 percent yearly maximum prescribed by law. The FEA also announced further six-month adjustments, subject to revision, for the remainder of the thirty-nine-month period.[116] Revisions would be necessary if errant predictions led to actual prices above or below the $7.66 composite. This was found to be the case when a June 1976 FEA study computed a $0.16 per barrel violation of the composite ceiling price during the first month of the program.[117] To correct the overage, Schedule 2 was

---

[113]The arithmetic formula was as follows.

Existing Price = Percent upper-tier (Price upper-tier) + Percent lower-tier (Price lower-tier)

$$= .4\ (\$12.60)\ +\ .6\ (\$5.25)$$
$$\$8.19 = \$5.04\ +\ \$3.15$$
Legal Price $= .4\ (x)\ +\ .6\ (\$5.25)$
$$\$7.66^a = .4x\ +\ \$3.15$$
$$.4x = \$4.51$$
$$x = \$11.275$$

aEPCA defined

[114]For greater detail on Stage I, see Jim Langdon, "Domestic Crude Oil Production—The FEA Regulatory Framework," pp. 19–24.

[115]41 *Fed. Reg.* 15566 (April 13, 1976).

[116]For a reprint of Schedule 1 adjustments through May 1979, see U.S. Senate Committee on Energy and Natural Resources, *Regulation of Domestic Crude Oil Prices*, 95th Cong., 1st sess. (Washington, D.C.: Government Printing Office, 1977), pp. 93–94.

[117]The computation was made by the FEA's new "Short Term Petroleum Forecasting Model," marking the entrance of direct econometric support in oil-price regulation. A decade before, econometrics was used by the FPC for natural-gas price regulation.

Table 9.2
PROJECTED VS. ACTUAL WELLHEAD-PRICE CHANGES:
JUNE–NOVEMBER 1976

| | Projected | | Actual | |
| | Lower Tier: | Upper Tier: | Lower Tier: | Upper Tier: |
Month	$3.90 plus	$12.60 minus	$3.90 plus	$12.60 minus
June	$1.48	$1.05	$1.48	$1.05
July	1.51	0.97	1.48	1.05
August	1.54	0.90	1.48	1.05
September	1.58	0.83	1.48	1.05
October	1.61	0.76	1.48	1.05
November	1.64	0.69	1.48	1.05

SOUCE: *Regulation of Domestic Crude Oil Prices,* pp. 93–96.

issued on June 30 to keep crude prices at current (June 1976) levels through July and August.[118] Schedule 3, issued on August 31, again held lower-tier and upper-tier prices at June 1976 levels through November.[119] Clearly, an output substitution of higher priced controlled oil for lower priced controlled oil was capturing the allowed 10 percent annual increase without any increase in the ceiling price per category. Part of this resulted from natural incentives; part resulted from a redefinition of the BPCL, effective July 1, 1976, to increase production incentive for lower-tier properties. This applied to properties that produced only lower-tier oil from February to July 1976 and properties that experienced declining production from 1972 to 1975. Operators could reduce their historic (1972 or 1975) BPCL by three-fourths of the decline. More lower-tier oil, consequently, would be reclassified as upper-tier; hence the rising composite price necessitated downward adjustments in price ceilings from projected levels published in Schedule 1, as shown in table 9.2.

The Schedule 1 price forecast was intended to reduce uncertainty for oil operators and investors and encourage greater production. Any credibility it had was squelched by revised schedules that disallowed projected price increases. The credibility of the crude-oil regulation program was not enhanced. Producer sentiment was expressed by A. V. Jones, president of the Independent Petroleum

[118]41 *Fed. Reg.* 27730 (July 6, 1976).
[119]41 *Fed. Reg.* 37311 (September 3, 1976).

Association of America: "This is a slam in the face to those who went out and searched for oil with what they thought were assurances of certainty as to crude-oil pricing."[120]

Energy Conservation and Production Act of 1976

On August 14, 1976, the Energy Conservation and Production Act (ECPA) was passed, which amended the Emergency Petroleum Allocation Act of 1973 as amended by the EPCA of 1975.[121] Intended to "provide an incentive for domestic production," the law represented a further effort to fine-tune improvement in a deteriorating domestic-production picture. Stripper oil, defined as oil from wells producing no more than 10 barrels daily at MER levels for a consecutive twelve-month period subsequent to December 31, 1972, was decontrolled effective September 1, 1976. Three tiers of domestic oil now existed: lower, upper, and uncontrolled (stripper). The stripper price was to be included in the composite price subject to the $7.66 per barrel limitation, which meant prices of upper-tier oil and particularly lower-tier oil would be penalized. Predictably, a vicious circle developed. Analogous to controlled oil's pushing up the price of uncontrolled (i.e., stripper and imported) oil, stripper price increases necessitated *lower* prices for lower-tier oil and upper-tier oil to maintain the legal composite price. These lower prices, in turn, sent more unfulfilled demand toward unregulated oil, which increased in price to begin the process anew. In any case, stripper oil once again was favored by government at the expense of lower cost oil.[122]

Another modification introduced by the ECPA removed the 3 percent production-incentive limitation, while retaining the 10 percent annual price ceiling. This allowed greater composite price increases than before if inflation was below 7 percent. This was intended to encourage production from high-cost recovery projects

---

[120]*OGJ*, March 7, 1977, p. 70.

[121]Public Law 94-385, 90 Stat. 1125 (1976).

[122]From 1930 until 1972, stripper oil benefited from state conservation law, which exempted such output from market-demand proration. With an exemption from price ceilings in the 1973 Trans-Alaskan Pipeline Authorization Act and reexemption in the 1976 ECPA, many high-cost stripper properties were saved from retirement. A study by Keplinger & Associates estimated that as of 1978, as many as 20 percent of the nation's 366,000 stripper wells were saved from retirement by post-1973 price-control exemptions. *OGJ*, May 29, 1978, p. 39.

and low-quality (high-sulfur "sour" or low-gravity "heavy") reservoirs. The former required special rule changes to "provide additional price incentives for bona fide tertiary enhanced recovery techniques."[123] Price imbalances between crude grades led the FEA to make adjustments, effective October 1, 1976, for heavy Alaskan and heavy Californian crude oil.[124]

The composite-price limitation continued to prove troublesome after the rule changes took effect. Schedule 4, effective November 30, 1976, extended the lower-tier and upper-tier price freeze begun by Schedule 2 another month through December.[125] Schedule 5, effective January 1, 1977, lowered the price of upper-tier oil by $0.20 per barrel and kept lower-tier prices the same.[126] Schedule 6, effective March 1, 1977, again reduced upper-tier prices by $0.45 per barrel and left lower-tier prices unchanged.[127] Controls were clearly tightening rather than loosening, contrary to the law's general intent to absorb inflation and provide production incentives. In February 1976, the first month of the EPCA, upper-tier prices were at $11.47 and lower-tier at $5.05 per barrel; in April 1977, upper-tier oil was below $11.00 and lower-tier was only $5.15 per barrel, a decrease when adjusted for inflation (table 9.3).

Crude-oil price controls, noticed Edward Erickson et al., had become "a political phenomenon with a life of their own."[128] No

---

[123]Section 122 of the EPCA defined such techniques as "extraordinary and high cost enhancement technologies of a type associated with tertiary applications including, to the extent that such techniques would be uneconomical without additional price incentives, miscible fluid or gas injection, chemical flooding, steam flooding, microemulsion flooding, in situ combustion, cyclic steam injection, polymer flooding, and caustic flooding and variations of the same."

[124]The existing discount for crude with a gravity differential above 34 degrees API was 6.2 percent per degree, the May 15, 1973, average. This was reduced to $0.02 per degree above 34 degrees (but below 40 degrees) and $0.03 per degree below 34 degrees. *Regulation of Domestic Crude Oil Prices*, pp. 10–11, 21–22. API gravity, expressed in degrees, is the standard industry measure of density of petroleum liquids. The higher the value of API gravity, the less dense, and more valuable, the petroleum liquid.

[125]41 *Fed. Reg.* 53333 (December 6, 1976).

[126]41 *Fed. Reg.* 1456 (January 7, 1977).

[127]42 *Fed. Reg.* 13013 (March 8, 1977).

[128]Edward Erickson, William Peters, Robert Spann, and Paul Tese, "The Political Economy of Crude Oil Price Controls," *Natural Resources Journal* (October 1978): 791.

Table 9.3
THREE-TIERED WELLHEAD-PRICE REGULATION:
FEBRUARY 1976–JUNE 1977

Date	Lower-Tier Oil Price ($/bl)	Percent	Upper-Tier Oil Price ($/bl)	Percent	Stripper Oil Price ($/bl)	Percent
1976						
February	5.05	56	11.47	44	—	—
March	5.07	57	11.39	44	—	—
April	5.07	57	11.52	43	—	—
May	5.13	57	11.55	43	—	—
June	5.15	56	11.60	44	—	—
July	5.19	56	11.59	44	—	—
August	5.18	56	11.62	44	—	—
September	5.17	53	11.65	34	13.21	13
October	5.15	52	11.62	35	13.35	13
November	5.17	50	11.62	37	13.31	13
December	5.17	50	11.64	36	13.30	14
1977						
January	5.17	51	11.44	37	13.27	13
February	5.18	50	11.39	37	13.32	13
March	5.15	49	11.03	37	13.31	14
April	5.15	49	10.97	37	13.28	14
May	5.18	48	10.98	37	13.26	14
June	5.16	49	10.92	37	13.28	14

SOURCE: U.S. Department of Energy, *Monthly Energy Review*, various issues.

fewer than fourteen price-schedule amendments would be forthcoming in the next twenty-six months, along with a variety of new tiers.[129] This was hardly the phaseout Ford originally desired.

A second era of ECPA multitiered pricing began when two new price-controlled categories of oil were established—Alaskan North Slope oil and naval petroleum reserve oil. The number of price-controlled categories now stood at five. Alaskan North Slope oil, considered low cost, was priced just above lower-tier oil, while naval petroleum reserve oil, considered high cost, was priced between upper-tier oil and exempt stripper oil. Since the percentage of naval reserve oil was small in comparison with North Slope oil, the composite price was not noticeably changed. Table 9.4 summarizes price changes under the five-tiered program.

During this period, the energy policies of President Carter were taking shape and being implemented. The Carter program was a further step toward national energy planning that continued the Energy Policy and Conservation Act, the Energy Conservation and Production Act, and the ill-fated $100 billion "Project Independence" proposal of the Ford administration. Carter, a constructivist through and through, brought the mentality of a trained engineer to bear on the problems of human action.[130] After assembling a team of like-minded energy planners led by James Schlesinger, a Harvard-trained economist enamored with centralized decisionmaking, Carter in 1977 presented lawmakers a national energy plan distinguished by quantitative forecasts of energy supply and energy demand according to regulatory constraints.[131] Politics—questionnaires were mailed to 450,000 citizens soliciting their ideas on solving the crisis—and

---

[129]William Lane, *The Mandatory Petroleum Price and Allocation Regulations: A History and Analysis*, p. 108.

[130]See James Cochran, "Carter Energy Policy and the Ninety–fifth Congress," in *Energy Policy in Perspective*, p. 547.

[131]When Schlesinger first presented the highly constructivist plan, even Carter stated concern about its complexity: "I am not satisfied with your approach. It is extremely complicated (I can't understand it). . . . A crucial element is simplicity. Even perfect equity can't be sold if Americans can't understand it. Their distrust is exacerbated by complexity." Jimmy Carter, *Keeping Faith* (New York: Bantam Books, 1982), pp. 96–97. The simplicity Americans were accustomed to, unrealized by Carter, was the spontaneous workings of free-market forces. In the end, Carter would accept complexity. He stated, "The total package [of energy bills] was extremely complicated, but far-reaching in its beneficial effect on our nation" (p. 107).

Table 9.4
FIVE-TIERED WELLHEAD-PRICE REGULATION: JULY 1977–MAY 1979

Date	Lower-Tier Oil Price ($/bl)	Percent	Upper-Tier Oil Price ($/bl)	Percent	Stripper Oil Price ($/bl)	Percent	North Slope Oil Price ($/bl)	Percent	Alaskan Reserve Oil Price ($/bl)	Percent
1977										
July	5.16	46.8	11.00	36.6	13.31	13.3	6.84	2.6	12.21	0.7
August	5.18	43.3	10.93	36.7	13.95	13.3	6.91	5.8	12.29	0.9
September	5.20	42.8	11.20	34.1	14.01	13.1	6.98	9.1	12.33	0.9
October	5.23	42.2	11.42	34.6	14.01	13.0	6.66	9.1	12.38	1.1
November	5.24	41.4	11.62	34.7	13.98	13.0	5.73	9.8	12.40	1.1
December	5.25	40.4	11.76	34.6	13.98	13.0	5.73	10.9	12.36	1.0
1978										
January	5.28	41.7	11.78	34.2	13.89	12.7	5.30	10.2	12.38	1.2
February	5.29	40.8	11.81	34.4	13.90	13.7	5.68	9.9	12.46	1.2
March	5.34	39.2	11.87	34.1	13.97	14.0	5.00	11.8	12.60	.9
April	5.35	38.0	11.94	34.0	13.95	13.7	5.15	13.3	12.67	1.0
May	5.38	38.2	11.98	34.0	13.93	13.8	4.87	13.0	12.70	1.0
June	5.46	36.8	12.08	35.0	13.95	13.9	5.63	13.5	13.08	0.8
July	5.46	37.6	12.16	34.4	13.95	13.9	5.26	13.5	13.07	1.0
August	5.50	36.5	12.22	34.4	13.93	14.4	5.09	13.7	13.04	1.0

(Continued on next page)

Table 9.4—Continued
FIVE-TIERED WELLHEAD-PRICE REGULATION: JULY 1977–MAY 1979

Date	Lower-Tier Oil Price ($/bl)	Percent	Upper-Tier Oil Price ($/bl)	Percent	Stripper Oil Price ($/bl)	Percent	North Slope Oil Price ($/bl)	Percent	Alaskan Reserve Oil Price ($/bl)	Percent
September	5.55	35.9	12.35	34.6	13.96	14.5	5.12	13.8	13.17	1.2
October	5.60	36.3	12.42	34.4	13.97	14.2	5.21	13.9	13.08	1.2
November	5.65	36.2	12.53	34.6	13.94	14.0	5.12	14.1	13.00	1.1
December	5.68	33.7	12.59	34.7	14.08	15.9	5.40	14.4	12.92	1.3
1979										
January	5.75	35.5	12.66	34.3	14.55	14.1	5.79	14.9	13.10	1.2
February	5.76	35.2	12.78	35.0	14.88	15.1	5.87	13.7	13.94	1.0
March	5.82	34.6	12.84	34.6	14.88	14.9	6.66	14.6	13.97	1.3
April	5.85	34.0	12.94	34.9	16.71	15.3	7.45	14.5	14.56	1.3
May	5.91	33.6	13.02	34.8	17.53	15.6	8.47	14.7	15.85	1.3

SOURCE: U.S. Department of Energy, Monthly Energy Review, various issues.

pseudoscientific model building and predictive econometrics were the order of the day.[132] Sober qualitative economic analysis, which invariably pointed to a market solution to energy problems initially created by nonmarket reliance, was no match for the constructivist impulse and political entrepreneurship of the president, Congress, and energy regulators.

Consonant with his centralist views on energy policy, President Carter created an executive-level Department of Energy (DOE), effective October 1, 1977.[133] The DOE replaced the Federal Energy Administration and assumed energy-related functions from other surviving agencies as well.[134] Crude-oil regulation was delegated to the newly formed Economic Regulatory Administration within the DOE.

On November 9, 1978, Carter's National Energy Act became law.[135] Its five component statutes—the Natural Gas Policy Act, the Energy Tax Act, the National Energy Conservation Policy Act, the Public Utilities Regulatory Policy Act, and the Powerplant and Industrial Fuel Use Act—bypassed reform of crude-oil price regulation. That would be the next order of business.

Phased Decontrol: 1979–81

On April 5, 1979, President Carter, under ECPA authority, announced his intent to deregulate crude-oil prices from June 1, 1979, to September 30, 1981.[136] The plan was to convert lower-tier oil to upper-tier oil in the twenty-seven-month period, while removing upper-tier controls over twenty-one months from January 1, 1980, until September 30, 1981.[137]

---

[132]Other grandstand plays were Carter's characterization of the energy crisis as "the moral equivalent of war"—first suggested by Schlesinger—and his "fireside chat" television broadcasts urging self-sacrifice and noneconomic behavior to endure and solve the crisis.

[133]Public Law 95-91, 91 Stat. 565 (1977). The DOE was officially formed by Executive Order 12009. 42 *Fed. Reg.* 46467 (September 15, 1977).

[134]For an examination of administrative changes under DOE regulation, see Donald Craven, "New Dimensions in Federal Regulation of Crude Oil and Petroleum Products under the Department of Energy," 29 *Oil and Gas Institute* (New York: Matthew Bender, 1978), pp. 1–37.

[135]Public Law 617, 92 Stat. 3117 (1978).

[136]Office of the White House Press Secretary, "Fact Sheet on the President's Program," April 15, 1979.

[137]44 *Fed. Reg.* 25168 (April 27, 1979); and 44 *Fed. Reg.* 66186 (November 19, 1979).

Table 9.5
CATEGORIES OF MARGINAL CRUDE OIL

Average Completion Depth (ft)	Barrels per day
2,000–3,999	20 or less
4,000–5,999	25 or less
6,000–7,999	30 or less
8,000–9,999	35 or less
Each additional 2,000 feet	5 additional barrels

SOURCE: 45 *Fed. Reg.* 47406 (July 14, 1980).

The decontrol plan was supported by virtually all independent producers and all majors but one. Mobil, relatively crude poor among majors, proposed the tradeoff of continued controls on existing oil for forgoing a windfall profits tax on undiscovered oil.[138] Relative competitive advantage continued to be a primary determinant of company policy.

On June 1, 1979, two new tiers of oil were established to join the existing five. Newly discovered oil, onshore oil produced from properties without output in 1978, and oil from Outer Continental Shelf properties leased after December 31, 1978, where no production previously existed, were exempt from price regulation.[139] Marginal crude oil was defined by output per well depth during calendar year 1978 (table 9.5).[140]

The BPCL for such properties was set at 20 percent of 1978 output to allow operators to receive prices corresponding to 20 percent lower-tier and 80 percent upper-tier oil. Total decontrol (zero BPCL) was reset for April 1, 1980, from the original January 1, 1980, date.[141]

[138]*Business Week*, May 21, 1979, pp. 32–33.

[139]44 *Fed. Reg.* 25828 (May 2, 1979). Discernible output from a property in 1978, even test-well production, precluded "newly discovered oil" certification. See David Tolin, "The Phased Deregulation of Crude Oil," in *Petroleum Regulation Handbook*, ed. Joseph Bell (New York: Executive Enterprises Publications, 1980), pp. 45–46.

[140]45 *Fed. Reg.* 47406 (July 14, 1980). The original definition of marginal crude was oil from properties producing 35 barrels per day or less at depths of 8,000 feet or more. This was revised and made retroactive to June 1, 1979, as a result of strong producer protest. The regulation was applicable to each property, with multiple wells averaged to determine the qualifying amount, if any.

[141]Executive Order 12209, 45 *Fed. Reg.* 26311 (April 16, 1980).

In addition to the creation of two new pricing tiers, several other steps were taken toward decontrol. Cumulative deficiencies were eliminated as of June 1, 1979. This allowed an estimated 9 percent of lower-tier oil to be reclassified as upper-tier oil for pricing purposes. Future deficiencies, restarted as of June 1, were relaxed to allow greater reclassifications of lower-tier oil as upper-tier oil.[142] New options for recalculating a property's BPCL were allowed, in keeping with the policy directive to replace lower-tier oil with upper-tier oil. A cumulative BPCL reduction of 1.5 percent per month from June to December 1979, followed by a 3 percent per month reduction in 1980, was granted.[143]

A third new tier classification, also effective June 1, involved perhaps the most straightforward regulatory blunder of the incentive-pricing phase of crude-oil price regulation. Pursuant to the ECPA, a notice of proposed rulemaking was issued by the ERA on January 12, 1977, to apply price incentives to crude oil produced as a direct result of enhanced-recovery projects.[144] Seven months later a "Notice of Decision" was issued that detailed the form the final regulations, to be issued in the "near future," would take.[145]

> Projects existing on the effective date of the final regulations will not generally be entitled to receive the incentive. . . . In general, only those projects commenced after the effective date of the regulations, and after receipt of the required certifications or expansions of preexisting projects after the effective date of the regulations and after the receipt of the required certifications, will be eligible for the incentive.[146]

While entrepreneurs delayed tertiary investments to ensure qualification for incentive pricing, the "near future" rule would not appear until almost a year later.[147] The new rule was immediately

---

[142]See James Carroll, "Department of Energy Crude Oil Producer Price Regulation: An Overview and an Update," *Natural Resources Lawyer* 12, no. 1 (1979): 333.

[143]For greater detail, see David Tolin, "The Phased Deregulation of Crude Oil," pp. 41–42.

[144]42 *Fed. Reg.* 2646 (January 12, 1977). This discussion is taken from William Lane, *The Mandatory Petroleum Price and Allocation Regulations*, pp. 111–13.

[145]42 *Fed. Reg.* 41572 (August 17, 1977).

[146]Ibid.

[147]43 *Fed. Reg.* 33679 (August 1, 1978). Bona fide oil-recovery techniques capable of certification were in situ combustion, unconventional steam drive injection, miscible fluid displacement, and microemulsion flooding.

lambasted by the *Oil & Gas Journal* for being "long on Utopian fine-tuning and short on basic economics."[148] Receiving a free-market price for *extra* production from tertiary methods instead of market prices for all production was scarcely adequate. Furthermore, the requirement to prove need, in terms of both time and expense for the applicants, made the incentive illusory. Not surprisingly, there were no takers when the program began on September 1, 1978.[149] The first project was not certified until April 1979, and in June of the same year, a new tier, incremental tertiary, was created. Thus two years of inactivity on tertiary recovery resulted from an amendment designed to promote such production. Despite the new categorization, certification was so complex that few applications were made, and not until late in the program.[150]

From June through August 1979, eight price tiers for crude oil were in place (table 9.6).

The next phase of oil decontrol established three more tiers of crude oil to bring the total to eleven. On August 17, 1979, price controls were removed from "heavy crude," oil with a weighted average gravity of not more than 16 degrees API gravity, calculated from the nearest month prior to July 1979.[151] This was changed to include all oil at or below 20 degrees API gravity effective December 21, 1979, to bring more high-cost crude under decontrol and incite greater output.[152] Based on this executive order, the DOE issued final rules to exempt heavy crude from price control on March 25, 1980.[153]

A second new pricing category, "tertiary incentive crude oil," allowed crude oil sold by an operator with an interest in tertiary-incentive property to be sold at market prices to generate "up-front" revenue to finance enhanced-recovery projects effective October 1, 1979.[154] Seventy-five percent of specified project costs could be

[148]*OGJ*, August 21, 1978, p. 15.

[149]*OGJ*, August 28, 1978, p. 42.

[150]Duke Ligon, "Crude Oil Pricing: Current Regulations and the Shift to Decontrol," 31 *Oil and Gas Institute* (New York: Matthew Bender, 1980), pp. 15, 19–20.

[151]Executive Order 12153, 44 *Fed. Reg.* 48949 (August 21, 1979).

[152]Executive Order 12186, 44 *Fed. Reg.* 76477 (December 27, 1979). This was clarified in an amendment issued January 16, 1980. 45 *Fed. Reg.* 3539 (January 18, 1980).

[153]45 *Fed. Reg.* 21206 (April 1, 1980).

[154]For ten "self-certifiable" enhanced oil recovery projects qualifying for cost-recoupment pricing, see David Tolin, "The Phased Deregulation of Crude Oil," p. 51.

Table 9.6
Eight-Tiered Wellhead-Price Regulation: June–August 1979

Month	Lower-Tier Oil		Upper-Tier Oil		Stripper Oil		Alaskan North Slope Oil		Alaskan Reserve Oil		Incremental Tertiary Oil		Newly Discovered Oil		Marginal Property Oil	
	Price ($/bl)	Percent	Price ($/bl)	Percent	Price ($/bl)	Percent	Price ($/bl)	Percent	Price ($/bl)	Percent	Price ($/bl)	Percent	Price ($/bl)	Percent	Price ($/bl)	Percent
June	5.95	29.3	13.14	38.2	20.24	16.0	8.97	13.6	16.02	1.3	11.98	0.1	22.97	0.6	13.61	0.8
July	5.98	27.0	13.25	16.0	24.76	16.0	13.35	15.9	20.13	1.4	15.09	0.02	26.69	1.1	13.18	1.1
August	6.09	26.0	13.33	36.7	25.71	16.9	14.14	15.8	20.77	1.3	16.14	0.2	26.63	1.7	13.37	1.3

Source: U.S. Department of Energy, *Monthly Energy Review*, various issues.

recouped up to a maximum of $20 million per project from market prices beginning January 1, 1980.[155] A third new tier was market-level new crude oil, called "other decontrolled oil." This category represented oil freed from price regulation under the phased-decontrol program, primarily upper-tier oil. The eleven tiers of price-controlled oil would continue for the rest of the regulated period (table 9.7).

In addition to converting lower-tier oil to upper-tier, upper-tier crude was incrementally deregulated beginning January 1, 1980. Market pricing was allowed each month for 4.6 percent of a property's previous month's upper-tier output.[156] This worked out to total decontrol in October 1981 when 100 percent of upper-tier oil, having consumed lower-tier oil, would become "market-level new crude oil" joining unregulated stripper oil, heavy crude oil, newly discovered oil, and tertiary-incentive crude. Another relaxation of regulation was exemption relief granted by the FEA's Office of Hearings and Appeals to firms judged to be suffering "serious hardship" or "gross inequity" from regulation.[157] Over a five- to six-year period, an estimated 300 to 400 producers received certification adjustments from a lower priced tier to a higher priced tier to reverse unprofitability.[158]

On January 28, 1981, eight months ahead of the schedule, President Reagan signed Executive Order 12287, which ended the decade-long experience with crude-oil price controls.[159] Intended to inaugurate a free-market approach to energy policy, the order would be a highlight of Reagan's first term.[160] After an initial increase in prices of

---

[155]44 *Fed. Reg.* 51148 (August 30, 1979). Windfall profit tax obligations effective March 1, 1980, were excluded to maintain incentive. 45 *Fed. Reg.* 40106 (June 13, 1980). After decontrol, officials were embarrassed when dozens of producers continued to qualify for reimbursements, many for forthcoming expenses, for tertiary projects that were uneconomical under price controls.

[156]For greater detail, see Michael Henke, "Enforcement, Exceptions, and FERC Review," in *Petroleum Regulation Handbook*, pp. 264–66.

[157]For greater detail, see ibid.

[158]U.S. Department of Energy, Memorandum to J. Erich Evered, August 3, 1981, p. 4. Copy in author's files.

[159]46 *Fed. Reg.* 9909 (January 30, 1981). The executive order was upheld in *Metzenbaum* v. *Edwards*, 510 F. Supp. 609 (D.D.C. 1981). Authority to reimpose price controls pursuant to the EPAA expired October 1, 1981.

[160]For a discussion of Reagan's first-term energy policies, see chapter 30, pp. 1861–64.

Table 9.7
ELEVEN-TIERED WELLHEAD-PRICE REGULATION: SEPTEMBER 1979–JANUARY 1981
(dollars per barrel)

Date	Incremental Tertiary Oil	Newly Discovered Oil	Marginal Property Oil	Heavy Crude Oil	Other Decontrolled Oil	Tertiary Incentive Oil	Lower-Tier Oil	Upper-Tier Oil	Actual Stripper Oil	Alaskan Reserve Oil	Naval Reserve Oil	Domestic Average
1979												
September	17.89	30.38	13.67	16.77	12.54	24.89	6.09	13.53	27.09	13.09	20.85	14.57
October	14.21	31.92	13.55	17.12	13.08	21.07	6.12	13.56	29.42	13.12	24.01	15.11
November	26.17	33.86	13.70	18.61	11.33	–	6.09	13.68	30.64	13.48	26.48	15.52
December	15.80	37.59	13.83	23.62	10.05	–	6.61	13.76	34.99	13.60	29.04	17.03
1980												
January	31.14	39.04	14.01	26.43	33.37	28.18	6.24	13.85	36.02	13.77	28.94	17.86
February	26.33	38.68	13.90	25.70	33.11	36.47	6.37	14.03	36.14	13.77	34.96	18.81
March	29.82	38.97	14.07	25.55	32.91	39.00	6.35	13.99	36.26	13.77	34.67	19.34
April	34.94	38.67	14.12	25.57	33.03	37.52	6.37	14.18	36.54	14.07	33.81	20.29
May	34.46	39.07	14.21	25.42	32.97	34.60	6.47	14.29	36.11	14.36	34.16	21.01
June	33.72	38.93	14.37	25.87	32.39	30.29	6.51	14.42	35.53	14.14	34.00	21.53
July	21.87	38.72	14.37	25.63	32.81	30.34	6.55	14.57	36.26	14.26	33.27	22.26
August	33.39	37.82	14.65	25.49	30.80	33.48	6.60	14.60	35.71	14.38	32.96	22.63
September	27.75	35.95	14.83	25.45	30.57	31.53	6.66	14.79	33.94	14.51	32.45	22.59
October	29.79	35.77	14.77	25.30	30.22	30.68	6.78	14.91	33.93	14.64	32.68	23.23
November	32.74	35.77	14.87	25.05	30.13	30.51	6.79	14.92	34.42	14.53	31.40	23.92
December	30.78	36.61	15.05	26.06	31.85	33.03	6.84	15.10	34.88	15.02	29.93	25.80
1981												
January	32.24	37.50	15.67	26.84	32.66	34.89	8.46	16.06	35.11	15.15	29.27	28.85

SOURCE: U.S. Department of Energy, *Monthly Energy Review*, June 1981, pp. 76–77.

petroleum products, part of which was attributable to an OPEC price hike, domestic prices from wellhead to retail began a downward trend that gave consumers long-awaited relief that price controls never did. By early 1982, prices had fallen below $30 per barrel from a decontrol high of around $34 per barrel, while import prices had fallen from as high as $39 per barrel to $35 per barrel. A year later, prices fell to 1979 levels. The price of domestic crude fell in 1983 and 1984 to around $26 per barrel. Ironically, by this time government concern had turned from rising prices to falling prices. On the federal level, falling windfall profit tax revenue lowered budget projections. Reduced severance taxes and royalty income hurt oil-producing states. The revenue outlook of oil-exporting Third World countries, many of which received major loans from U.S. banks, was devastated by the falling prices. Despite pronouncements to the contrary, many government entities were dependent on high oil prices and would feel the heat along with the upstream industry.

Wellhead Price Regulation in Retrospect

False Goals of Price Regulation

The mistaken purpose and distortive effects of price controls prior to the Arab embargo were unfortunate, but the continuation of controls through the crisis period proved disastrous. Ad hoc moralizing about "undeserved" producer profits and proven-reserve windfalls, buttressed with superficial, politically inspired rhetoric, replaced reasoned economic understanding and policy. Popular fallacies abounded. One was the belief that crude-oil price increases drove up the prices of petroleum-related goods and services—just about everything—by increasing costs (the "cost-push" theory), and consequently, immediate or phased decontrol would exacerbate an inflation already at high levels.[161] Politicians busily calculated new inflation estimates whenever new ceiling prices were proposed.

[161]The cost-push view was stated by economist Paul Samuelson: "Decontrolling oil and trying to promote U.S. independence from imports are bound to increase the rate of inflation. . . . Since wage rates tend to rise when consumer prices rise, it is to be feared that there will result a still further increase in costs and prices. And all this will be further aggravated by induced increases in airline costs and fares, and rises in prices of goods whose production depends on energy and which themselves set raw-material costs for production of other goods. Moreover, these days there is not only a pass-through of higher costs but also signs of a markup on such add-ons." Samuelson, "Oil Economics," *Newsweek*, September 29, 1975, p. 74.

510

The cost-push theory of inflation, and this particular application to oil prices, is an economic fallacy. Economic theory teaches that any increase in relative prices (e.g., those of crude oil) cannot cause all prices to rise; other things unchanged, the prices of complements (e.g., motorized vehicles) fall, while those of substitutes (e.g., unregulated gas, coal) rise.[162]

The general price explosion accompanying crude-oil price hikes, contrary to popular opinion, was primarily the result of monetary inflation by the Federal Reserve that prevented offset (oil-complement) prices from countering the rise of oil prices and oil-substitute prices. This explains why Japan and West Germany, totally dependent on OPEC imports and experiencing greater average increases in oil prices than the United States, had *lower* inflation rates in the 1979–80 period. Slower monetary growth in these countries explains the apparent anomaly.[163] Rising oil prices were "inflationary" only

[162]Seen another way, if the price of good A rises and the consumer continues to buy it as before, income and other things constant, then he has less money (less demand) for goods B through Z. Therefore, the prices of B through Z tend to fall. General prices can only rise if less production resulted from the relative price increase. But the gross national product did not fall by nearly the amount necessary to explain the large inflation in the 1973–81 period.

[163]High monetary growth in major industrial countries, lagged relationships between money growth and price increases, expectations, and methodological and data-collection errors prevent clear illustration of the theoretical point that inflation is always a monetary phenomenon, particularly with the 1974 oil-price experience. The following data for 1972 through 1980, particularly from 1979 to 1980, are nonetheless suggestive.

	Japan		West Germany		United States	
Year	Inflation Rate	Monetary Growth	Inflation Rate	Monetary Growth	Inflation Rate	Monetary Growth
1972	4.5	22.1	5.6	13.7	3.3	7.3
1973	11.7	26.1	6.9	5.0	6.3	6.8
1974	24.4	13.1	7.0	6.1	10.9	4.4
1975	11.8	10.3	6.0	14.1	9.2	4.5
1976	9.3	14.2	4.3	10.0	5.8	5.1
1977	8.0	7.0	3.7	8.1	6.5	7.2
1978	3.8	10.8	2.7	13.5	7.5	7.3
1979	3.6	9.9	4.1	7.2	11.3	7.6
1980	8.0	0.8	5.5	2.4	13.5	8.6
1981	4.9	3.7	5.9	0.9	10.4	5.2
1982	2.7	7.1	5.3	3.2	6.2	4.8

SOURCE: International Monetary Fund, *International Financial Statistics Yearbook, 1983* (Washington, D.C.: IMF, 1984) pp. 460–66.

to the extent the general output of the economy was directly reduced or inflationary expectations were increased.

Adherents to cost-push inflation assumed that price ceilings on domestic crude could lower refinery-input prices to restrain petroleum prices to end users. Lower oil-product prices, furthermore, would restrain energy prices in general. However, domestic controls pushed world crude prices to levels that were *higher* than they would have been if controls had not existed, and once domestic price exemptions were granted, these prices too were pushed artificially high. The refinery-entitlements program, discussed in chapter 20, was notorious for pushing prices of imported oil higher. All considered, weighted average crude prices were not significantly lower with controls than without controls (not to mention the high-price effect of reduced production caused by regulation). By the control advocates' own criteria, therefore, "restraining" inflation with domestic price restrictions increased inflation by reducing domestic supply and placing upward pressure on exempt and foreign crude.

Not only were prices of exempt crude higher than an unregulated market would have supported, refiner and retail petroleum prices were higher than advocates of price regulation believed. Because of price controls, a middleman explosion of *crude oil resellers* occurred that captured part of the economic rent denied by law to producers. After the crude was refined into products, more middlemen, *product resellers*, bid product prices toward market levels.[164] In fact, legislators would complain of "de facto decontrol" as a result of reseller activity.[165] When certain oil products became decontrolled, producers began to enter into agreements with refiners to distill price-controlled crude into uncontrolled product for the producer to sell at market prices.[166] So even if some domestic crude was attractively priced at the wellhead by law, this did not necessarily mean that refinery input or wholesale and retail product was similarly priced.

Another argument for wellhead controls was that an unadulterated wealth transfer to the petroleum sector from other economic

---

[164]See chapter 12, pp. 691–92.

[165]*The Case of the Billion Dollar Stripper,* Report of the House Committee on Interstate and Foreign Commerce, 96th Cong., 2d sess. (Washington, D.C.: Government Printing Office, 1980), p. 5.

[166]See *OGJ,* January 14, 1980, p. 50; and 45 *Fed. Reg.* 3060 (January 16, 1980).

sectors as a result of major increases in oil prices would cause economic dislocation and macroeconomic instability.[167] To alleviate destabilizing wealth effects, it was argued, prices should be restrained and other measures implemented, such as a neutralizing tax transfer.

This argument fails to distinguish between a market-adjustment situation, which it is, and an aggregate-demand problem, which it is not.[168] It is true that many oil-related firms benefit and expand, while petroleum-consuming firms must absorb higher costs or contract, or both. This is a microeconomic firm-by-firm phenomenon necessitated by relative price changes that can only be postponed or alleviated by falsifying economic reality. Such intervention does not correct the transition problem but misallocates resources and interferes with consumer service under changed conditions.

The misconception of the desirability (and ability) of price controls to restrain crude-oil and petroleum-product prices, salted with moralistic overtones, made the well-known case for a continuation of crude-price ceilings. As stated by President Carter in his 1977 National Energy Plan:

> The fourfold increase in world oil prices in 1973–74 and the policies of the oil exporting countries should not be permitted to create unjustified profits for domestic producers at consumer's expense. By raising the world price of oil, the oil-exporting countries have increased the value of American oil in existing wells. This increase in value has not resulted from free market forces or from any risk-taking by U.S. producers. *National energy policy should capture the increase in oil value for the American people.*[169]

These words clearly indicate a philosophical bent toward regulation. Increased profits and enhanced capital values of oil properties were "unjustified" because exogenous events were responsible. But

---

[167]For a 1980 restatement of this neo-Keynesian argument, see George Horwich, "Government Contingency Planning for Petroleum-Supply Interruptions: A Macroperspective," in *Policies for Coping with Oil-Supply Disruptions,* ed. George Horwich and Edward Mitchell (Washington, D.C.: American Enterprise Institute, 1982), pp. 33–65.

[168]See chapter 17, pp. 1043–47, for further analysis of this point.

[169]Executive Office of the President, Energy Policy and Planning, *National Energy Plan* (Washington, D.C.: Government Printing Office, 1977), p. xi. Emphasis in original. Although primarily an argument for the windfall profit tax, the quotation applies equally to price restraints to "capture" lower prices for consumers.

the same exogenous circumstances—the wealth of foreign oil deposits—had depressed the domestic-producer market for decades prior to 1973. Yet this is no better reason for government subsidization than it is an argument for penalization under opposite conditions. As a result of the nationalization of the Arabian-American Oil Company, the world oil situation radically changed. Carter's denial of this new reality and his anti-oil arguments were little more than political opportunism predicated on envy, a less than admirable trait under any circumstances but a destructive one upon which to predicate national energy policy. But with a scapegoat, constructivism could replace the spontaneous resolution of energy problems that oil as a free-market good, rather than a political good, could have achieved.

In his memoirs, Carter, while admitting that price controls had the threefold negative effect of inciting overconsumption, underproduction, and underdevelopment of alternative fuel sources, justified price regulation by saying that "there was no free market or effective competitive forces relating to world oil supplies and price."[170] While it is true that OPEC was a cartel of government monopolies, it still faced competition from the formidable U.S. petroleum industry. But because U.S. industry was *regulated*, which negated market processes, competition with OPEC was mitigated, and Carter's analysis was self-fulfilling, if incorrect. Carter's reason for regulation, in fact, was not an ex ante rationale but an ex poste explanation of how OPEC dictated events in the 1970s. The absence of a "free market or effective competition" called for repeal of existing domestic government intervention—from longstanding state wellhead regulation to federal-land policy—not a new layer of price and allocation controls and taxes to "fight" OPEC on economic grounds.

Waste and Prosecution from the "Property" Definition

Pervasive regulation in market situations is never a scientific endeavor above dispute. There are always a "gray" area and consequent self-interested interpretations. "Nonwillful" violations occur as do willful violations of relatively clear regulatory instruction. This was the case with regulated wellhead prices under the EPAA, EPCA, and ECPA.

---

[170]Jimmy Carter, *Keeping Faith*, pp. 94, 108.

Property Issues. The definition of property, around which crude-oil regulation revolved after Phase IV, was a crucial concept. Maximum crude prices depended not so much on purchaser valuation, as they would in a free market, as they did on when, where, how, and in what quantities oil was extracted from a particular *property*. The definition of property has been identified as "the cornerstone of the regulatory program controlling the first-sale price of crude oil and producer income."[171] Interpretation of the property definition by producers and regulators encouraged not only noneconomic output decisions but voluminous litigation involving legal prices and alleged overcharges.

Property was originally defined by regulators as "the right which arises from a lease or from a fee interest to produce domestic crude oil."[172] This created difficulty for an industry that had come to recognize the reservoir, not each separately owned lease interest, as the fundamental economic unit. As attorney David Beck explained, this definition entailed "the redetermination of nearly every oil property in the nation and . . . required oil producers to keep two sets of accounting on a property-by-property basis—one, the traditional property system for financial accounting, tax, and local regulatory purposes, and the other a new and different system for [federal regulatory purposes]."[173]

Regulators' concern with the lease definition of property arose from the incentive created to "gerrymander" leaseholds by shutting in certain wells to increase production of new oil and released oil from remaining wells.[174] FEA Ruling 1975–15, effective September 1975, clarified the original August 1973 ruling by requiring that the

[171]General Accounting Office, *Department of Energy Needs to Resolve Billions in Illegal Oil Pricing Violations* (Washington, D.C.: Government Printing Office, 1980), p. 29. Jim Langdon likened the computation of legal prices without a definition of property to a tax accountant's having all the relevant information for a group of taxpayers but not knowing how many separate tax cases exist and which return is which. Langdon, "Domestic Crude Oil Production—The New Regulatory Framework," p. 27.

[172]38 *Fed. Reg.* 2253 (August 22, 1973). For certain exceptions involving large or noncontiguous tracts, as well as partial unitization and separate tax or royalty accounting, see Randolph McManus, "Domestic Crude Oil Price Controls," in *Petroleum Regulation Handbook*, pp. 24–25.

[173]David Beck, "Department of Energy Audit Issues," *13 Oil and Gas Institute* (New York: Matthew Bender, 1979), p. 5.

[174]See *Pennzoil Co. v. DOE*, 680 F.2d 156 (1982).

BPCL for post-1972 unit agreements be calculated on a field-wide basis.[175] If unitization was artificially encouraged before, now it was artificially discouraged, reminiscent of earlier intervention of a different kind.[176] Owners of stripper wells, which enjoyed preferential prices, did not desire to enter a unit plan even if production rose because a redefinition to a lower priced tier meant less revenue in many cases. Similarly, the owner of a well with a high percentage of new oil would balk if unitization raised the BPCL to reclassify higher priced oil in a lower price category.[177] Amendments in February 1976 relaxed the ruling to allow the lease basis for post-January 1976 wells until enhanced recovery commenced or a significant change in production (generally, secondary unitization) resulted from unitization.[178] Another change allowed the BPCL to be calculated on a 1975 basis instead of a 1972 basis *or* on a twelve-month production average preceding a unit BPCL (i.e., when enhanced recovery or a major change in production occurred).[179] Unitization was now unambiguously encouraged.[180] Unit agreements made prior to February 1976, however, especially those made after 1972, were in a precarious position when it came to calculating BPCL on a lease basis, as discussed below.

The 1973–76 period was marked by regulatory confusion, hindering secondary unitization that was necessary to preserve or increase production from historic sources. Remarked William Lane, "Unitization projects were often delayed or postponed indefinitely because of the complexity and uncertainty regarding how much production from the unitized tract would qualify for treatment as upper-tier crude."[181] Regulators themselves were not sure of their own regulations. FEA deputy administrator John Hill testified before Congress,

[175]40 *Fed. Reg.* 40832 (September 4, 1975).

[176]See chapter 3, pp. 116–28, and chapter 4, pp. 205–11.

[177]41 *Fed. Reg.* 1570–71 (January 8, 1976). Exxon executive M. A. Wright recognized the problem in 1973 when he complained to Cost of Living Council director John Dunlop that unitization could "substantially extend the producing life of older fields without producing 'new' oil under the Phase IV rules." Quoted in *United States of America* v. *Exxon Corporation*, 561 F. Supp. (D.D.C. 1983).

[178]41 *Fed. Reg.* 4937 (February 3, 1976).

[179]Ibid., p. 4938.

[180]42 *Fed. Reg.* 4409 (January 25, 1977).

[181]William Lane, *The Mandatory Petroleum Price and Allocation Regulations*, pp. 110–11.

"It was not clear throughout that period [1973–76] exactly what the [property] regulation meant; it was not even clear to the agency itself."[182]

Not only unitization but production in general was hampered by the property-as-lease definition. If a lease property contained a shallow producing formation with declining output and a deeper untapped reservoir, the operator might not have been able to qualify for upper-tier prices because of a cumulative deficiency or a BPCL calculation on the property. The deeper formation in such cases would not be developed.[183] If the reservoir rather than the lease had been defined as property, deeper production would have qualified for upper-tier prices and become economical to deplete. But by stringently defining property without regard to the reservoir as the natural economic unit, price regulation had negative consequences that only oil-importing interests could applaud.

Effective September 1, 1976, producers were allowed to identify the reservoir, as long as "separate and distinct," as the property unit for determining crude tiers and legal prices.[184] This answered the question of whether vertical reservoirs, noncontiguous oil finds on the same lease, were one property or several. Producers favored separate treatment of vertical reservoirs, but the pre-September 1976 separation, similar to pre-February 1976 unitization using the lease-by-lease BPCL, was highly suspect under the law.[185]

Enforcement and Litigation. Enforcement of first-sale legal maximum pricing, essential to the government's policy of keeping prices below world levels for downstream cost-plus pricing, got off to a slow start. A General Accounting Office study in late 1974 revealed that little audit work had been performed to ensure compliance and recommended immediate action.[186]

---

[182]Quoted in Randolph McManus, "Domestic Crude Oil Controls," p. 22. Also see 41 *Fed. Reg.* 36174 (August 26, 1976).

[183]40 *Fed. Reg.* 40832. Also see William Lane, *The Petroleum Price and Allocation Regulations*, pp. 109–10.

[184]41 *Fed. Reg.* 36184 (August 26, 1976). Also see 42 *Fed. Reg.* 4409 (January 25, 1977).

[185]Ibid., p. 4411.

[186]General Accounting Office, *Problems in the Federal Energy Administration's Compliance and Enforcement Effort* (Washington, D.C.: Government Printing Office, December 6, 1974).

Belated enforcement coincided with the Project Manipulator (soon renamed Project Producer) report released by the FEA's Office of Compliance and Enforcement. Of an estimated 19,000 producers, 125 with the largest reported increases in new oil from September 1973 through October 1974 were targeted for audits. In early 1975, another 1,000 independent producers were added for review. By August 1975, approximately 200 investigations were completed, which resulted in 36 consent agreements with refunds of $3.2 million and penalties of $115,000. Fifty notices of probable violation were completed or being prepared, and over $11 million was at issue.[187] A typical violation was the improper computation of oil categories resulting in overestimated quantities of new oil or stripper oil.

A second General Accounting Office study released October 2, 1975, described these developments and made two major criticisms. One was inequitable procedures and penalties assessed by different regional enforcement offices. The other was exclusive focus on independents rather than major producers that accounted for 70 percent of U.S. output.[188]

Audits and prosecution of the majors would begin in earnest after 1975 and would culminate in over $3 billion in alleged overcharges in the 1978–81 period. The pendulum had swung the other way; independent producers became a low priority. In May 1984, ERA administrator Rayburn Hanzlik estimated restitution for alleged overcharges at between 10¢ and 15¢ on the dollar. A General Accounting Office report, prepared at the request of Rep. John Dingell (D-Mich.), a perennial critic of major oil companies, concluded in the same month that inadequate resources to expediently and fairly resolve litigation continued to be a problem.[189]

The two largest producer-overcharge disputes are paradigmatic of the many cases involving nonwillful "violations." The *Texaco* case involved separate treatment of vertical reservoirs to maximize higher priced oil categories between September 1973 and March 1979. Texaco interpreted property as the reservoir rather than the lease. This

[187]General Accounting Office, *Federal Energy Administration's Efforts to Audit Domestic Crude Oil Producers* (Washington, D.C.: Government Printing Office, October 2, 1975), p. 6.

[188]Ibid., pp. 1–2, 7–8.

[189]General Accounting Office, *Improvement Needed in the DOE Petroleum Pricing and Allocation Compliance Program* (Washington, D.C.: Government Printing Office, April 8, 1984).

decision was in accordance with Louisiana conservation regulations, which required unitization, under certain conditions, according to separate reservoirs. FEA first questioned Texaco's practice in late 1975, and on January 25, 1978, a notice of probable violation was issued followed by a proposed remedial order on May 1, 1979. In federal district court, Judge Walter Stapleton on May 6, 1980, decided against Texaco on grounds that the production in question predated a change in the law effective September 1, 1976, which made the reservoir rather than the lease area the property unit.[190]

The *Exxon* case concerned a secondary unitization plan for the Hawkins field, one of the largest in the United States, where lease-by-lease accounting was retained for crude-tier (maximum-price) determination.[191] As a result of not calculating the BPCL on a unit basis, 80 percent more new oil, released oil, and stripper oil was produced in place of old oil without a change in current output. This was possible through well consolidations whereby remaining wells produced more oil: stripper wells produced more stripper oil, and regular wells produced more new or upper-tier oil.

Secondary recovery through gas injection commenced on January 1, 1975. In the same year, the FEA defined a gray area by requiring unit operations to use a unit BPCL to avoid "gerrymandering." An amendment in February 1976 allowed the lease-by-lease property definition but only prospectively.[192] Prior units, including Hawkins, could not use that definition, and in early 1978, a notice of probable violation was issued, followed by a proposed remedial order six months later. In federal court, Judge Thomas Flannery sided with the government and approved payment of $1.636 billion in over-charges and interest to state treasuries for improperly certified oil between January 1, 1975, and the last day of controls, January 27, 1981.[193]

Of the various regulatory issues in *Exxon*, including ambiguous and retroactive government positions in the case, one stood out in the important verdict: that decreasing production by millions of

[190]*Texaco et al.* v. *DOE et al.*, 490 F. Supp. 874 (1980).

[191]*State of Louisiana* v. *Department of Energy*, 519 F.Supp. 351 (1981); 390 F.2d 180 (E.A. 1982); cert. den., 103 S. Ct. 1522 (1983).

[192]41 *Fed. Reg.* 4941 (February 3, 1976). The key phrase "significant alteration in producing patterns" was ambiguous and a source of much dispute.

[193]*United States of America* v. *Exxon Corporation*, 561 F. Supp. 816 (D.D.C. 1983).

Table 9.8
CRUDE-OIL OVERCHARGE LITIGATION
(thousands of dollars)

Firm	Date of Action	Alleged Overcharge	Firm	Date of Action	Alleged Overcharge
Texaco	05/01/79	888,329	Conoco	06/09/81	23,868
Exxon	06/08/78	685,152	Sohio	05/01/79	16,969
Gulf	05/01/79	577,959	Mobil	08/08/79	13,746
Shell	11/07/79	173,973	Exxon	11/07/79	12,424
Sun	11/07/79	104,526	Hess	11/07/79	12,264
Chevron	05/01/79	101,618	Cities		
Exxon	12/27/77	70,814	Service	06/14/78	7,860
Conoco	11/07/79	61,911	Exxon	07/02/81	5,691
Getty	06/27/78	46,958	Exxon	01/06/78	3,348
ARCO	05/01/79	42,024	Texaco	12/14/79	2,000
Murphy	01/28/81	39,300	Champlin	03/18/81	1,317
Marathon	05/01/79	29,064	Tesoro	03/19/81	964
Amoco	05/01/79	24,140	Fina	01/07/81	758

Total					$2,946,977

SOURCE: U.S. Department of Energy, Office of General Counsel, "Program Status Report," Internal report, 1981.

NOTE: Smaller settlements with independents totaling over $35 million as of mid-1982 are listed in the *Houston Chronicle,* September 5, 1982, p. 8-4.

barrels as a result of not unitizing (as would have been the case if lease-by-lease accounting had been prohibited) did not violate the EPAA goal of increased production because another goal—price restraint—was satisfied. Exxon's action, the court concluded, illegally "increased the average cost of crude oil of all refiners," which had to be rectified, albeit indirectly, by restitution.[194] The court, however, made a speculative assumption: that lower wellhead prices would have filtered through to final consumers instead of being largely dissipated within the industry nexus. As chapter 12 will substantiate, large quantities of old and lower-tier oil were miscertified as higher price categories or were price-inflated within the same category by middlemen's activity.

As of 1984, federal crude-oil overcharge suits against major companies totaled nearly $3 billion, as seen in table 9.8.

[194]Ibid., p. 852.

In 1980, an involved attorney remarked that the major cause of producer litigation was "the persistent failure of the government to interpret the petroleum regulations in a timely fashion."[195] In addition to creating much of the problem—indeed, *all* of the problem from the viewpoint of a deregulated market—the government itself was guilty of many of the alleged transgressions of private firms. Production from federal lands, supervised by the Department of the Interior, was linked to over $1 billion in overcharges attributable to illegitimate tier classification, illegal cost pass-throughs, and errant record keeping. Many refiners sued Interior for overcharging, and several dozen settlements were reached.[196] The DOE, however, declined to sue the Department of the Interior because of the embarrassing cast of characters involved, including Donald Hodel, who was second in charge at Interior during the violation heyday and was now the secretary of energy. Failure to prosecute guilty federal parties represents a double standard that is partial grounds for terminating litigation and settlements altogether.[197]

The Statistical Record: An Interpretation

Now that the mistaken purpose and questionable value judgments behind crude-price controls and the problematic nature of the regulatory effort from a legal-economic standpoint have been unmasked, a statistical examination of the 1970–84 era can be made to substantiate the failure of government intervention intended to restrain oil prices and imports of "artificially priced" oil. Three periods are identified in table 9.9: precontrol, control, and postcontrol.

The precontrol period was uneventful. The relatively high cost of U.S. extraction, partly the result of state conservation regulation and partly the result of inherent reservoir characteristics, made foreign production increasingly competitive with domestic output despite the locational advantages of the latter and federal protectionist legislation. Adjusted for inflation, crude prices were declining in the

---

[195]Paul Mode, "Judicial Review of Petroleum Regulations and Orders," in *Petroleum Regulation Handbook*, p. 286.

[196]*Wall Street Journal*, June 13, 1984 p. 27.

[197]Remaining to be resolved is who gets overcharge settlement money. The Office of Hearings and Appeals began evidentiary hearings in August 1984 to determine which first purchasers of crude were overcharged. Over $1 billion is in a stripper-well escrow fund, which has attracted many potential claimants armed with legal talent and economic consultants.

Table 9.9
SUMMARY OF DOMESTIC AND IMPORTED CRUDE OIL: 1970–84

| | U.S. Crude Output | | Crude Imports | |
	(000 bl/day)	Price ($/bl)	(000 bl/day)	Price ($/bl)
		I. Precontrol Era		
1970				
January	9,794	3.18	1,413	1.80
February	9,240	3.18	1,468	1.80
March	9,508	3.18	1,495	1.80
April	9,591	3.18	1,171	1.80
May	9,523	3.18	1,209	1.80
June	9,359	3.18	1,373	1.80
July	9,201	3.14	1,260	1.80
August	9,560	3.14	1,178	1.80
September	9,853	3.14	1,344	1.80
October	10,013	3.14	1,190	1.80
November	10,044	3.14	1,261	1.80
December	9,944	3.37	1,538	1.80
1971				
January	9,977	3.38	1,122	1.80
February	9,393	3.38	1,345	2.09
March	9,768	3.38	1,395	2.18
April	9,769	3.38	1,507	2.18
May	9,645	3.39	1,501	2.18
June	9,604	3.39	1,678	2.28
July	9,457	3.40	1,826	2.28
		II. Price-Control Era *Phase I*		
August	9,411	3.40	1,895	2.28
September	9,135	3.40	1,900	2.28
October	9,162	3.40	1,923	2.28
		Phase II		
November	9,139	3.40	1,985	2.28
December	9,100	3.40	2,128	2.28

	U.S. Crude Output		Crude Imports	
	(000 bl/day)	Price ($/bl)	(000 bl/day)	Price ($/bl)
1972				
January	9,418	3.36	2,046	2.35
February	9,336	3.36	2,081	2.48
March	9,462	3.37	2,067	2.48
April	9,513	3.37	2,004	2.48
May	9,614	3.38	2,160	2.48
June	9,522	3.39	2,085	2.48
July	9,496	3.39	2,182	2.48
August	9,483	3.40	2,112	2.48
September	9,508	3.40	2,364	2.48
October	9,482	3.40	2,516	2.48
November	9,426	3.40	2,299	2.48
December	9,335	3.40	2,667	2.48
		Phase III		
1973				
January	8,485	3.54	2,732	2.59
February	9,050	3.54	2,774	2.59
March	9,175	3.55	3,162	2.59
April	9,233	3.62	3,049	2.74
May	9,303	3.77	3,215	2.74
		Phase III.V		
June	9,209	3.87	3,220	2.90
July	9,195	3.88	3,501	2.96
		Phase IV		
August	9,161	3.88	3,593	3.07
September	9,077	4.11	3,471	3.07
October	9,172	4.11	3,740	3.06
November	9,144	4.30	3,452	5.18
		EPAA		
December	9,041	4.51	2,891	5.04
1974				
January	8,934	6.95	2,382	9.59
February	9,142	6.87	2,248	12.45

(Continued on next page)

Table 9.9—Continued
SUMMARY OF DOMESTIC AND IMPORTED CRUDE OIL: 1970–84

	U.S. Crude Output		Crude Imports	
	(000 bl/day)	Price ($/bl)	(000 bl/day)	Price ($/bl)
March	8,965	6.77	2,462	12.73
April	8,954	6.77	3,267	12.72
May	8,911	6.87	3,908	13.02
June	8,780	6.85	3,925	13.06
July	8,780	6.80	4,091	12.75
August	8,699	6.71	3,924	12.68
September	8,443	6.70	3,797	12.53
October	8,611	6.97	3,810	12.44
November	8,569	6.97	3,958	12.53
December	8,527	7.09	3,869	12.82
1975				
January	8,455	7.61	4,029	12.77
February	8,591	7.47	3,828	13.05
March	8,493	7.57	3,656	13.28
April	8,457	7.55	3,378	13.26
May	8,379	7.52	3,486	13.27
June	8,421	7.49	3,905	14.15
July	8,336	7.75	4,193	14.03
August	8,249	7.73	4,581	14.25
September	8,280	7.75	4,689	14.04
October	8,324	7.83	4,389	14.66
November	8,278	7.80	4,623	15.04
December	8,254	7.93	4,476	14.81
EPCA				
1976				
January	8,232	8.63	4,594	13.27
February	8,231	7.87	4,208	13.26
March	8,232	7.79	4,738	13.51
April	8,077	7.86	4,790	13.39
May	8,125	7.89	4,669	13.41
June	8,094	7.99	5,628	13.48
July	8,127	8.04	5,792	13.51
August	8,111	8.03	5,556	13.58

	U.S. Crude Output		Crude Imports	
	(000 bl/day)	Price ($/bl)	(000 bl/day)	Price ($/bl)
		ECPA		
September	8,150	8.39	5,875	13.47
October	8,063	8.46	5,689	12.38
November	8,080	8.62	5,946	12.38
December	8,061	8.62	5,925	12.38
1977				
January	7,854	8.50	6,281	13.00
February	8,139	8.57	6,659	13.00
March	8,090	8.45	6,699	13.00
April	8,145	8.40	6,821	13.00
May	8,075	8.49	6,818	13.00
June	8,102	8.44	7,065	13.00
July	8,105	8.48	7,068	13.66
August	8,307	8.62	6,395	13.66
September	8,480	8.63	6,429	13.66
October	8,573	8.72	6,409	13.66
November	8,579	8.72	6,248	13.66
December	8,487	8.77	6,248	13.66
1978				
January	8,360	8.68	6,126	13.66
February	8,377	8.84	5,655	13.66
March	8,720	8.80	6,031	13.66
April	8,818	8.82	5,519	13.66
May	8,825	8.81	5,594	13.66
June	8,832	9.05	6,322	13.66
July	8,756	8.96	6,175	13.66
August	8,758	9.05	6,251	13.66
September	8,800	9.12	6,829	13.66
October	8,820	9.17	6,400	13.66
November	8,741	9.20	6,643	13.66
December	8,662	9.47	6,751	13.66
1979				
January	8,457	9.46	6,656	14.34
February	8,498	9.69	6,344	14.34
March	8,585	9.83	6,240	14.34

(Continued on next page)

Table 9.9—Continued
SUMMARY OF DOMESTIC AND IMPORTED CRUDE OIL: 1970–84

	U.S. Crude Output		Crude Imports	
	(000 bl/day)	Price ($/bl)	(000 bl/day)	Price ($/bl)
April	8,533	10.33	6,145	15.64
May	8,585	10.71	6,163	15.64
		Phased Deregulation		
June	8,409	11.70	6,554	19.35
July	8,355	13.39	6,349	19.35
August	8,699	14.00	6,774	19.35
September	8,466	14.57	6,410	19.35
October	8,568	15.11	6,854	19.35
November	8,649	15.52	6,154	25.81
December	8,587	17.03	6,273	25.81
1980				
January	8,675	17.86	6,406	30.75
February	8,705	18.81	6,013	32.40
March	8,698	19.34	5,695	33.42
April	8,685	20.29	5,598	33.54
May	8,635	21.01	5,106	34.33
June	8,554	21.53	5,480	34.48
July	8,547	22.26	4,843	34.51
August	8,414	22.63	4,803	34.44
September	8,619	22.59	4,707	34.46
October	8,532	23.23	4,768	34.63
November	8,495	23.92	4,680	35.09
December	8,606	25.80	5,082	35.63
1981				
January	8,540	28.85	4,932	38.85
		III. Decontrol Era		
February	8,604	34.14	4,873	39.00
March	8,613	34.70	4,521	38.31
April	8,557	34.05	4,338	38.41
May	8,501	32.71	3,287	37.84
June	8,629	31.71	4,061	37.03
July	8,500	31.13	4,296	36.58
August	8,583	31.13	4,179	35.82

	U.S. Crude Output		Crude Imports	
	(000 bl/day)	Price ($/bl)	(000 bl/day)	Price ($/bl)
September	8,604	31.13	4,740	35.44
October	8,563	31.00	4,380	35.43
November	8,586	30.98	4,046	36.21
December	8,585	30.72	4,137	35.95
1982				
January	8,509	30.87	3,693	35.54
February	8,702	29.76	2,990	35.48
March	8,667	28.31	2,874	34.07
April	8,591	27.65	2,849	32.82
May	8,683	27.67	3,309	32.78
June	8,646	28.11	3,836	33.79
July	8,658	28.33	4,248	33.44
August	8,634	28.18	3,851	32.95
September	8,701	27.99	3,636	33.03
October	8,701	28.74	3,670	33.28
November	8,697	28.70	3,862	33.09
December	8,598	28.12	3,000	32.85
1983				
January	8,697	27.22	2,964	30.62
February	8,758	26.41	2,267	29.08
March	8,700	26.08	2,290	27.84
April	8,776	25.85	3,118	28.24
May	8,631	26.08	3,360	28.55
June	8,667	25.98	3,577	29.00
July	8,636	25.86	3,871	28.99
August	8,679	26.03	4,227	29.22
September	8,784	26.08	4,210	29.24
October	8,771	26.04	3,446	29.08
November	8,770	26.09	3,337	28.93
December	8,397	25.88	3,213	28.58
1984				
January	8,659	25.93	3,029	27.56
February	8,726	26.06	2,952	27.78
March	8,718	26.05	3,455	27.70
April	8,688	25.93	3,417	27.84

(Continued on next page)

Table 9.9—Continued
SUMMARY OF DOMESTIC AND IMPORTED CRUDE OIL: 1970–84

| | U.S. Crude Output | | Crude Imports | |
	(000 bl/day)	Price ($/bl)	(000 bl/day)	Price ($/bl)
May	8,752	26.00	3,927	27.87
June	8,743	26.09	3,410	27.78
July	8,769	26.11	3,646	27.19
August	8,781	26.02	3,244	27.29
September	8,759	25.97	3,294	27.14
October	8,847	25.92	3,751	27.15
November	8,846	25.44	3,552	26.91
December	8,797	25.03	3,126	26.76

SOURCES: Federal Energy Administration, *Monthly Energy Review*, various issues; U.S. Department of Energy, *Monthly Energy Review*, various issues; Bureau of Mines, *Petroleum Statistics Annual*, various issues; and Energy Economics Research Ltd. and Middle East Economic Survey, *International Crude Oil and Product Prices*, various issues.

NOTE: From January 1970 until December 1973, the posted price for Arabian 1 crude (34 degrees API) is used. From January 1973 until December 1981, the refiner acquisition cost of imported crude is used.

precontrol period as they had been in previous decades. Another reason for stagnant domestic oil production was price controls on interstate flows of natural gas that had existed since 1954 (and earlier with some interstate dedications). Because oil and gas frequently are produced together, disincentives for gas production also affected crude-oil production.[198]

The sudden implementation of price controls in 1971 did little more than preserve the precontrol stagnation. Domestic output began a slight downward trend, while petroleum demand rose as a result of a combination of economic growth, fuel-oil substitution during natural-gas shortages, and artificially low domestic crude prices as a result of controls. With domestic supply down and demand up, increased imports and inventory reductions made up the difference.

[198]Only below 15,000 feet can it be reasonably certain that crude oil will not be found with natural gas. Natural-gas price regulation that affected the petroleum situation is detailed in chapter 8.

As the Nixon price-control program wore on, the domestic producing industry began to weaken. Not only were many firms suffering from a cost-price squeeze, vital drilling equipment was in short supply because of price regulation.[199] Export-Import Bank subsidization of rig and drilling-material exports, even to Russia, left less for domestic use.[200] Relative price incentives under early controls encouraged the production of nonoil, energy-consuming goods rather than energy-producing goods such as tubular drilling goods.[201] Mandatory allocation of drilling supplies, last experienced during wartime, was avoided only by removing price regulation of this area during Phase IV. The majors, meanwhile, increasingly turned to nonoil ventures to maintain earnings, which gave rise to criticism both outside and inside the industry.[202]

Weakened by decades of state "conservation" regulation, which subsidized marginal wells by penalizing flush wells; long-standing price controls on natural gas and now crude oil, which discouraged exploration and production; and drilling-equipment shortfalls, which postponed some drilling projects and canceled others, the domestic industry was losing market share to foreign sources. It was also losing its ability to rebound in a timely manner should new incentives appear. This not only benefited OPEC in the short run, it would prove important in creating the conditions necessary for OPEC to engineer future conditions of world output and price.[203]

The Phase IV double-pricing standard, and the political reaction to foreign events embodied in the EPAA, set the tone for ensuing years of price and allocation control. Prices were to be fine-tuned to simultaneously satisfy consumer and producer needs. From a

[199]See, for example, *OGJ*, October 22, 1973, pp. 11–14.

[200]*OGJ*, May 6, 1974, p. 114.

[201]Complained an *Oil & Gas Journal* editorial: "While the administration talks about boosting domestic energy supply, its Cost of Living Council makes it more profitable for steel firms to sell abroad rather than at home. . . . To compound the problem, CLC has made it more profitable for U.S. steel producers to emphasize sheet and structural steel rather than tubular goods for drilling [and] production. Present price controls, thus, are channeling steel into energy-consuming uses—such as automobiles and air conditioners—rather than into energy-producing uses. This is misdirection at its worst." *OGJ*, October 22, 1973, p. 9.

[202]*OGJ*, October 15, 1973, p. 37.

[203]OPEC's new position was also the result of the Aramco nationalization, mentioned above, that put Saudi Arabia in control of its own prolific production.

529

two-tiered program beginning on September 1, 1973, price regulation
would expand to three tiers (September 1, 1976), five tiers (July 1,
1977), eight tiers (June 1, 1979), and eleven tiers (September 1, 1979)
before decontrol. Jim Langdon's early 1975 explanation of increasing
complexity was insightful and prophetic.

> The present program is a perfect example of the evolution toward
> complexity . . . [in the] attempt to bring equity into the program. . . .
> The motivation behind each regulatory modification is to remedy
> some unforeseen consequence which is creating inequitable results
> under the program. Ultimately, the increasing complexity aimed at
> increasing the equity reached a point of diminishing returns. The
> process of "successive approximations," as it has been called, never
> effectively hits the mark in terms of duplicating the market place.[204]

The complex schema was not increasing domestic output, reducing import dependence, or restraining composite prices. U.S. petroleum demand was not being mitigated to the extent necessary to
adjust to world conditions. The monthly statistics bear this out.
Imports steadily climbed throughout the period (except during the
embargo months in late 1973 and early 1974) despite higher prices.
Paradoxically, while 3.7 million barrels per day were demanded at
approximately $5.00 per barrel in November 1973, 3.9 million barrels
per day were purchased six months later at $13.00 per barrel. Acute
demand inelasticity would be evident again in late 1979 and early
1980 in the aftermath of the Iranian revolution. Normally, less supply
would be expected to be purchased at higher prices with conservation, interfuel substitution, and increased domestic production coming into prominent play, but therein lies the economic tragedy of
price controls. U.S. crude production was virtually paralyzed by
regulation and unable to anticipate and respond to changed world
conditions that provided undreamed-of incentives. As world prices
rose, domestic production responded as if $3.00 per barrel imports
were still the competition.[205] Even more telling, as domestic compos-

[204]Jim Langdon, "FEA Price Controls for Crude Oil and Refined Petroleum Products," 26 Oil and Gas Institute (New York: Matthew Bender, 1975), pp. 62–63.

[205]Joseph Kalt estimated that between 1975 and 1980 regulatory disincentives caused
U.S. producers to forgo between 300,000 and 1,500,000 barrels per day. Kalt, The
Economics and Politics of Oil Price Regulation (Cambridge, Mass.: MIT Press, 1981),
chap. 5. The discouraging effect of the windfall profit tax on existing production was
similar to that of price controls.

ite prices rose, domestic output remained unresponsive.[206] This resulted, in part, from the windfall profit tax, which after 1978 separated producers from first-sale revenues that would have encouraged new reserves and more extensive development of existing properties. This is also explained by the move toward "incentive pricing" of high-cost, low-yield production (of stripper, tertiary recovery, and "heavy" crude), which would remain relatively fixed in quantity under the best of conditions but which would disappear under unfavorable conditions. The rationale was that supply could be *maintained* by matching ceiling prices to different costs of oil to coax out supply with as little "producer surplus" as possible. Assuming the government could know this detailed information, which is highly questionable,[207] this is scarcely a recipe for *increasing* production—inciting exploration and creating new reserves to deplete—which was urgently needed. Only with establishment of "newly discovered oil" and phased decontrol in 1979 was the need for new discoveries seriously addressed by authorities, after which a drilling boom, which peaked in early 1981, began.[208] But this was at least six years too late. The damage of price controls had been done.

The opportunity cost of regulation was the free market. Although the effects of its operation will never be known, some of what would have occurred without government intervention in the crude-oil market can be surmised from economic theory. With the Aramco nationalization and warning signals of foreign unrest in critical oil regions, the prospect of higher future prices would have promoted inventory speculation and new drilling programs. Supply and service industries related to exploration and production would have

[206]Not even an exodus of rigs to the United States as a result of restrictive Canadian oil policy in late 1974 and again in late 1980 could counteract the malincentives of U.S. regulation. *OGJ*, October 14, 1974, p. 55, and December 15, 1980, p. 48.

[207]Explained Edward Erickson: "In a static sense the controllers must know the elasticities of supply of the various categories of domestic oil and the actual set of controlled prices must reflect these elasticities.... [Yet while] the knowledge requirements for the design and administration of even a statically efficient price control system are formidable ... the knowledge requirements for a dynamically efficient system are even more complexing." Erickson et al., "The Political Economy of Crude Oil Price Controls," pp. 793–94.

[208]U.S. oil exploration, development, and production expenditures increased from $9.4 billion in 1978 to $15.6 billion in 1979, $20.8 billion in 1980, and $30.7 billion in 1981. American Petroleum Institute, *Basic Petroleum Data Book* (Washington, D.C.: API, 1982), sec. 5, table 10.

followed in lockstep. With the actual cutoff and price hikes, inventories would have been drawn down and MER schedules would have been revised upward by entrepreneurs to counter the embargo and higher foreign prices. Consumers, on the other hand, would have adjusted to higher domestic and world prices by economizing on petroleum products. In the 1974–78 adjustment period, output from a drilling boom in the United States would have come on stream to partially replace imports, while implementation of new energy-efficient technologies as well as substitution of coal and natural gas would have reduced overall demand for crude oil. Demand for petroleum certainly would have been reduced before 1979–80 when the reduction finally occurred. These adjustments would have put pressure on OPEC to competitively price crude at lower levels or at least forgo price hikes. By no means could OPEC have doubled prices again in 1979, which dramatized the total helplessness of the domestic industry to take advantage of market incentives. "For six years," Richard Vietor concluded, "rent controls were allowed to stimulate demand, depress supply, and give OPEC the chance to do it again."[209] Given a petroleum market operating entirely upon market processes, domestic producers and consumers *could have* mitigated OPEC control of world output and prices years before mitigation finally occurred in 1981.[210] This was the error of crude-price constructivism, of the price *mis*information and *mal*incentives generated by regulation.

[209]Richard Vietor, *Energy Policy in America since 1945* (Cambridge, U.K.: Cambridge University Press, 1984), p. 349.

[210]Slight effects of the Iran-Iraq war "oil shock" in October 1980, accounting for a net reduction of over 2 million barrels per day, demonstrated growing strength of the U.S. oil industry under phased decontrol and expected deregulation.

10. Other Significant Intervention

In addition to the government intervention described in chapters 2 through 9, the exploration and production phase has been subject to other consequential government interventions, some unique to the industry and others experienced by the entire economy. This chapter attempts to chronicle and critically review these miscellaneous interventions.

Labor-market regulation and securities regulation are not unique to petroleum, but they have particular application to exploration and production. Accounting regulation, similarly, has particular application at the wellhead. Those regulations are examined. Loan subsidies to conventional fuels are surveyed, and a detailed examination of synthetic-fuel subsidization—which qualifies as oil and gas production—is provided. The chapter ends by describing a variety of local, state, and federal interventions to complete a comprehensive look at intervention in oil and gas exploration and production.

Labor-Market Intervention

Government intervention in the labor market has directly affected drilling operations and subsidiary industries. State and federal edicts, as well as court interpretations, have accorded unions special privileges—specified minimum wage rates, detailed working conditions, and set hours of employment. These regulations have helped some workers and employers, hurt others, and in all cases interfered with business costs and thus market prices for the affected goods and services.

Union Development and Early Regulation

The American labor union movement grew up alongside the petroleum industry. Early unions took shape after the Civil War, and there were 171 labor cooperatives by 1909. Particular gains were made between 1897 and 1904 when labor union membership quadrupled.[1]

In the first decades of exploration and production, local independent craft unions such as the Well Drillers' Union sprang up in the Pennsylvania-Ohio oil region. The first formal labor organization, the Federal Labor Union of Oil Field Workers (affiliated with the American Federation of Labor), was created in 1892. In 1899, the International Brotherhood of Oil and Gas Well Workers was chartered by the American Federation of Labor (AFL) to represent oil production workers of the Ohio Oil Company. This union called the first strike in the exploration and production sector in 1904.[2] The union claimed membership in fields in western Pennsylvania and California, but lack of worker interest led to its demise in 1906.[3] Only scattered oil-industry unions remained, such as the Guffey Oil and Gas Well Workers Local 11998, which was formed after a proposed 17 percent pay cut and waged a successful strike in several large Texas oil fields in 1905. Vestiges of unionism in Gulf Coast fields were removed by the 1907 depression.[4]

Formal collective bargaining by oil workers was limited by free-market conditions. The common law offered workers the right to unionize, but it also protected employers' right to set wages and other work conditions, criticize unions, prohibit union activity on company property, and hire and fire workers on nonunion conditions.[5] Modest capital investment per worker, compared with that of later decades, also limited the influence of labor and the "going wage." Except in certain highly skilled occupations, unions in search

---

[1]Allan Cartter and Ray Marshall, *Labor Economics: Wages, Employment and Trade Unionism* (Homewood, Ill.: Richard D. Irwin, 1972), p. 61.

[2]Herbert Werner, "Labor Organizations in the American Petroleum Industry," in Harold Williamson and Arnold Daum, *The Age of Illumination, 1859 to 1899,* vol. 1 of *The American Petroleum Industry* (Evanston, Ill.: Northwestern University Press, 1959), p. 830.

[3]Daniel Horowitz, *Labor Relations in the Petroleum Industry* (New York: U.S. Works Progress Administration, 1937), p. 58. A pro-union history blamed the failure of unionism in the oil industry on the "burning enmity of Standard Oil." Harvey O'Connor, *History of Oil Workers International Union* (Denver: Oil Workers International Union, 1950), p. 4.

[4]Ibid., pp. 4–5.

[5]Sylvester Petro, *The Labor Policy of the Free Society* (New York: Ronald Press Company, 1957), pp. 138–40.

of higher pay and better working conditions were artificial cartels that market forces discouraged and eliminated. The market discipline exerted against early unionization was what consumers were prepared to pay for final products rather than any inherent power or ruthlessness of management.

Until World War I, government intervention did not modify the common-law approach to labor-management questions. One common-law application, however, was not consonant with a free market. In a 1908 antitrust decision under the Sherman Act, the Supreme Court ruled against secondary boycotts by unions as a restraint of trade.[6] This was removed in 1914 by the Clayton Act,[7] which labor leaders considered the Magna Charta of the American labor movement." This amendment was joined in the same act by an intervention limiting an employer's right to use injunctions against undesired labor practices (such as picketing on management property). This modest beginning would be powerfully supplemented by other pro-labor laws in the 1930s.

On the state level, labor legislation also gained a foothold. Beginning with New Hampshire in 1847, several states passed maximum-hour legislation. Work-site safety law began in 1877 in Massachusetts, the state that also passed the first minimum wage law in 1912. Following Massachusetts with wage regulation, typically covering women and children, were Nebraska, Oregon, Utah, Washington, Wisconsin, California, Colorado, and Minnesota in 1913; Arkansas and Kansas in 1915; Arizona in 1917; the District of Columbia in 1918; and North Dakota and Texas in 1919.[8] More states followed during the New Deal.

War planning during World War I included unprecedented federal intervention in the labor market. Conscription began what workplace regulation and arbitration settlements by the National War Labor Board and the War Labor Policies Board continued. The government effort was clearly pro-union, and not surprisingly, unionism grew during the period. The Texas Federation of Labor and the Houston Trades Council visited oil fields in the state in the quest

---

[6]*Loewe* v. *Lawlor*, 208 U.S. 274 (1908). The so-called *Danbury Hatters'* decision was relatively unimportant because of the weak position of early unions.

[7]Public Law 212, 38 Stat. 730 (1914).

[8]Paul Douglas et al., *The Worker in Modern Economic Society* (Chicago: University of Chicago Press, 1925), p. 587.

for membership. The Goose Creek field, in particular, became heavily unionized with several thousand members. A strike idled fields in Texas and, to a lesser extent, Louisiana despite settlement efforts by the U.S. Conciliation Committee. Under the pretense of the war emergency, martial law was declared, and the National Guard policed the field, which helped replacement workers restore production.[9]

While Gulf Coast strikes failed to win concessions, California unions won their demands without striking for an eight-hour day (to replace the twelve-hour day) and a $4.00 per day minimum wage. With naval oil contracts at stake, these concessions were engineered by the president's Mediation Commission and enforced by a federal inspection board.[10] Several companies already had awarded similar concessions to preserve labor peace, which influenced other West coast firms to go along.

Wartime union growth led to the formation of the International Association of Oil Field, Gas Well and Refinery Workers of America in June 1918 to consolidate unions based in California, Texas, Oklahoma, Louisiana, and Kansas. Membership reached 24,800 in 1921 but declined precipitously the next year and remained low for the rest of the decade. Company-specific unions became more common. The introduction of company welfare plans that offered on-the-job disability insurance and retirement benefits, and incentive programs that increased productivity and reduced turnover, were important in the transformation. Stock subscription plans were introduced by Cities Service (1917) and Jersey Standard (1920); by 1928, sixteen large oil companies had employee stock ownership programs.[11] Pension plans were introduced in 1918 by California Standard, Jersey Standard, and Indiana Standard, and by 1929, over 200,000 workers in sixteen firms were participants. Jersey Standard inaugurated paid vacations in 1923. Dismissal compensation, health and accident insurance, and life insurance were other new policies of oil firms. These innovations came to a halt in 1929 with the crash of the stock

---

[9]Harvey O'Connor, *History of Oil Workers International Union*, pp. 5–7.

[10]Ibid., p. 11.

[11]These programs are described in Daniel Horowitz, *Labor Relations in the Petroleum Industry*, pp. 45–57.

market and ensuing Great Depression, a reversal that rekindled government pro-union policies.

Legislation in the 1930s

Pro-labor legislation passed during and immediately after the New Deal formed the basis of union privileges that have endured to this day. Falling wages and incomes were seen not as the effect but as the cause of the downturn, and higher labor incomes were promoted as a remedy. A second motivation was the strong perception that the worker was at an inherent bargaining disadvantage vis-á-vis the employer, an inequity that certain union rights could balance.

Within days of the October 24, 1929, crash, President Herbert Hoover called a series of White House conferences with leading businessmen to lobby for higher wage rates. Hoover desired to increase wage rates to precrash levels on the rationale that labor's ability to buy back the product would be increased (or in terms J. M. Keynes would soon popularize, aggregate demand would be increased).[12] On November 21, Jersey Standard's president Walter Teagle, with other leading businessmen, attended a White House session at which an informal agreement was made with Hoover that if the president would continue to coordinate policies with business input, they would resist pressures to reduce wages.[13] The tit for tat was observed. A second industrial policy was work sharing—hours per worker were shortened to hire more workers. In 1931, for example, Jersey Standard hired 3,000 workers under the banner of "job security by job sharing."[14]

The unintended result of high-wage policy was to *perpetuate* unemployment, which lowered labor's purchasing power and hindered

---

[12]This was not Hoover's first accommodation of labor. See Murray Rothbard, "Herbert Hoover and the Myth of Laissez-Faire," in *A New History of Leviathan*, ed. Ronald Radosh and Murray Rothbard (New York: E. P. Dutton, 1972), pp. 116–20.

[13]Murray Rothbard, *America's Great Depression* (Kansas City, Mo.: Sheed and Ward, 1963, 1972), pp. 187–88.

[14]Ibid., p. 294. Hoover later appointed Jersey Standard's Walter Teagle to head the National Employment Campaign, an organization dedicated to increasing employment by 1 to 2 million through work sharing, a plan endorsed by the AFL. *Oil & Gas Journal*, September 8, 1932, p. 10. Cited hereafter as *OGJ*.

economic recovery. Adjusted for deflation, wage rates were increasing, not decreasing as required to increase employment and hasten market readjustment.[15]

Hoover engineered several other labor-market interventions before his defeat by Franklin Roosevelt in 1932. Beginning in September 1930, immigration quotas were reduced by 90 percent and thousands of "undesirable" aliens were deported to reduce "excess" labor created in part by the industry-government above-market wage policy.[16] On March 23, 1932, Hoover signed the Norris-LaGuardia Act, which represented "the culmination of a fifty-year campaign by trade unionists and their allies in the academic community against 'government by injunction.' "[17] Stating that "the individual unorganized worker is commonly helpless to exercise actual liberty of contract and to protect his freedom of labor, and thereby to obtain acceptable terms and conditions of employment," the act made nonunion oaths as a condition of employment (yellow-dog contracts) unenforceable and weakened the right of employers to seek court injunctions against trespass, destruction of property, and intimidation.[18] With the rule of law suspended, union bullying could restrict the entry of new workers when union demands exceeded market levels to establish monopolistic cartels at the expense of displaced laborers, employers, and consumers.[19]

The National Industrial Recovery Act (NIRA), signed by Roosevelt on June 16, 1933, contained a labor section applicable to all industry codes.[20] Section 7 reaffirmed the Norris-LaGuardia Act and allowed the president to prescribe industry labor codes containing minimum wage rates and maximum hours with differentials according to "experience and skill of the employees affected and according to

[15]Murray Rothbard, *America's Great Depression*, pp. 290–94. For a refutation of the purchasing-power argument that higher wages increase demand to end resource idleness, see ibid., pp. 43–53. An exposition of the argument from a New Deal perspective is contained in Leverett Lyon et al., *The National Recovery Administration: An Analysis and Appraisal* (Washington, D.C.: Brookings Institution, 1935), pp. 756–75.

[16]Murray Rothbard, *America's Great Depression*, pp. 215–16.

[17]Morgan Reynolds, *Power and Privilege* (New York: Universe Books, 1984), p. 97.

[18]Public Law 65, 47 Stat. 70 (1932). A third purpose of the bill, which unlike the other provisions was consonant with the free market, was to exempt labor groups from antitrust law.

[19]See the discussion in Morgan Reynolds, *Power and Privilege*, pp. 101–4.

[20]Public Law 67, 48 Stat. 195 (1933).

the locality of employment.''[21] Article II of the Code of Fair Competition for the Oil Industry (Oil Code) was approved by Roosevelt on August 19 to formalize wage and hour regulation that Hoover previously approached by understanding and agreement.[22] For common labor, including drilling and drilling-related personnel, wage floors were tied to the location of work, ranging from $0.45 per hour in the South to $0.52 per hour in the West, North, and East. Clerical workers were not covered. Wages for skilled labor were set at the minimum wage plus "the differentia[l] between . . . the minimums established in this code [and the rates] existing in the industry in each geographical area on July 1, 1929.''[23] The Oil Code, as were other industry codes, was based on a belief that recovery could result from pricing labor as if boom conditions still existed. The New Deal, in this respect as in others, had Hooverian roots.

Maximum hours were set at 40 hours for oil and gas production personnel including clerical employees. Late in the program, on July 7, 1935, derrick- and rig-construction personnel were brought under hour law. The regulation had the effect of spreading the work around, particularly among common laborers, some of whom otherwise would have been priced out of the market by the minimum wage law.

On September 13, 1933, the Oil Code's labor provisions were revamped. At the request of owners complaining of sagging profits, stripper wells were exempted from hour ceilings, subject to approval from the Planning and Coordination Committee (PCC), the industry advisory group created to assist code administrator Harold Ickes. On July 1, 1929, the base-period differential for skilled labor was abolished in favor of wages determined on a discretionary basis by the PCC. This introduced flexibility not present with unskilled labor wage determination. The PCC then recommended on November 15 that established wages be retroactively applied to the day the code became effective—September 2, 1933.

---

[21]Ibid., p. 199.

[22]National Recovery Administration, *Code of Fair Competition for the Petroleum Industry* (Washington, D.C.: Government Printing Office, 1933), p. 6. Cited hereafter as *Oil Code*. Harvey O'Connor called the wage and hour regulations "the single greatest victory OWIU ever won for oil workers." O'Connor, *History of Oil Workers International Union*, p. 30.

[23]*Oil Code*, pp. 6–7.

The Petroleum Labor Policy Board was created on December 19, 1933, to replace the PCC labor subcommittees. Made up of three "impartial public representatives," the board had as its first order of business to devise minimum wage rates for skilled labor to recommend to the Petroleum Administration Board.[24] This resulted in a May 21, 1934, order that reverted to the 1929 standard for unskilled labor wage determination and set forth an extremely complicated set of adjustment factors based on hours of work, age, health, and work efficiency. The goal was equity, which, according to Myron Watkins, was "simply beyond the human powers of any administrative organization, however familiar with working conditions it might be."[25] The Petroleum Administration Board found this out firsthand and left wage determination to "mutual bargaining" beginning August 1. This was followed by a September 4, 1934, order exempting collective wage agreements from regulation.

In Texas, several measures were proposed to maximize oil employment. In mid-1933, the Independent Petroleum Association of Texas prepared a draft oil code that opposed unitization because rig-crew employment would be reduced.[26] An order from the Texas Railroad Commission, effective March 16, 1934, required operators of all wells in the state, estimated at nearly 18,000, to submit daily production reports attested to by employees on a twenty-four-hour watch. The "Watchman Order" was intended not only to detect hot oil but to create 40,000 jobs in the state.[27] The order was recognized as impractical and never became operative.

Federal wage and hour regulation ended with the *Schechter* decision in May 1935, which invalidated the NIRA and over 500 industry codes predicated on it.[28] Table 10.1 gives percentage changes from the 1929 base year to summarize the labor market under the two-year experiment.

The statistics indicate that employment and hourly wages significantly increased from May 1933 through the end of the code period.

---

[24]A summary of the activities of the Petroleum Labor Policy Board is contained in Daniel Horowitz, *Labor Relations in the Petroleum Industry*, pp. 68–70.

[25]Myron Watkins, *Oil: Stabilization or Conservation?* (New York: Harper & Brothers, 1937), p. 200.

[26]*Oil Weekly*, July 24, 1933, p. 7.

[27]*Oil Weekly*, March 19, 1934, pp. 9–10.

[28]*Schechter Poultry Corp.* v. *U.S.*, 295 U.S. 495 (1935).

Table 10.1

DRILLING AND PRODUCTION EMPLOYMENT STATISTICS PER CAPITA

Date	Employment		Payroll		Wage/Hour		Hours/Week		Earnings/Week	
	Majors	All	Majors	All	Majors	All	Majors	All	Majors	All
May 1929	100%	100%	100%	100%	100%	100%	100%	100%	100%	100%
May 1933	52	51	40	38	85	84	90	88	77	74
May 1934	76	80	58	60	128	116	61	65	78	75
July 1935	–	83	–	62	–	118	–	67	–	79

SOURCE: Myron Watkins, *Oil: Stabilization or Conservation?* p. 205.

This seems to contradict the theoretical position that statutory wage hikes *reduce* employment, but two circumstances intervened. The development of the huge East Texas field, with very low incremental development costs, contributed to increased employment. Second, government work-share policy increased employment by limiting weekly hours per worker. Relatively stagnant earnings reflected the tradeoff between higher wages and less work. Increased employment under the code, therefore, was an ambiguous gain compared with what might have occurred in a free market with unregulated wage scales and unregulated hours.

In an unregulated environment, a higher level of employment, longer weekly hours, and lower—but increasing—wages could have been expected. Weekly earnings could well have been lower after multiplying increased hours by lower wages. Total industry payroll, however, could have been higher without regulation because many more oil workers, especially the least skilled, would have been employed.

The experience of labor under New Deal regulation was unique. The primary purpose of New Deal labor legislation, not unlike that of subsequent labor legislation, was not improving the lot of the common worker. Explained Myron Watkins:

> The petroleum code, like most NRA codes, was not conceived fundamentally as an instrument for the alleviation of the conditions of labor. It was conceived as a means of fostering business recovery, and was so administered. Hence the wages and hours provisions of the code represented essentially concessions made by business interests in exchange for privileges accorded them.[29]

If New Deal labor legislation was a setback for nonunion workers without entry skills or seniority, it was a heyday for unions. The International Association of Oil Field, Gas Well and Refinery Workers of America's pre-NIRA membership of fewer than 300 workers climbed to 12,500 in 1934, 42,800 in 1935, and 75,000 in 1936.[30] Union demands were met by law; only minor strikes in Texas and the midcontinent fields were reported.

---

[29]Myron Watkins, *Oil: Stabilization or Conservation?* p. 200.

[30]Daniel Horowitz, *Labor Relations in the Petroleum Industry*, pp. 66–67. Also see Harvey O'Connor, *History of Oil Workers International Union*, pp. 30–35.

Unprecedented union power, both in numbers and political pull, ensured continued economic intervention on behalf of unions after the demise of the NIRA. For example, the National Labor Relations Act (Wagner Act) of July 5, 1935, reinstated and extended union guarantees previously contained in the NIRA.[31]

Premised on the "inequality of bargaining power" of workers, the law was replete with government intervention favoring labor at the expense of the property rights of employers. Management was forced to bargain with worker collectives (including locals of the newly renamed Oil Workers' International Union, representing the petroleum industry within the AFL) and were banned from taking actions on their property to prevent union organization. Discrimination against pro-union workers was illegal. Hiring new workers to break strikes was made difficult. The act also created a three-member National Labor Relations Board to investigate allegedly "unfair" labor practices by employers and assist in labor union matters. The oil industry, contrary to the initial interpretation by the industry, was covered by the federal law.[32]

The next major legislation to replace the NIRA was the 1938 Fair Labor Standards Act, administered by the Department of Labor (established 1913).[33] The law reinstituted the minimum wage, subject to certain criteria, set maximum hours, and delineated types of work permissible for persons from fourteen to eighteen years of age. These provisions applied to workers involved with interstate products, which covered over 50 percent of the nation's workforce.

Subsequent Developments

The Norris-LaGuardia and Wagner Acts, with minor amendments, continued to govern labor relations. The National Labor Relations Board, which began in 1936 with 140 employees, had almost

---

[31]Public Law 198, 49 Stat. 449 (1935). The Wagner Act was declared constitutional in *NLRB* v. *Jones and Laughlin Steel Corporation*, 301 U.S. 1 (1937).

[32]See Barbara Hinds, "Applicability of the Fair Labor Standards Act to the Oil Industry," *Texas Law Review* (December 1941): 204–12. Many states passed "little Labor Relations Acts" with similar union privileges.

[33]Public Law 718, 52 Stat. 1060 (1938). The law was upheld in *United States* v. *Darby*, 312 U.S. 100 (1941). Previously, federally financed projects set minimum wages, which corresponded to union rates pursuant to the Davis-Bacon Act of 1931 (Public Law 798, 46 Stat. 1494) and the Walsh-Healey Public Contracts Act of 1936 (Public Law 846, 50 Stat. 2036).

3,000 employees as of 1984. Administrative decisions, which in the beginning filled several volumes a year, now fill a weighty volume every few months.[34] Labor law is as rewarding for lawyers as it is complex for firms in the absence of a common-law, free-market resolution of labor questions.

The most amended area of labor regulation has been the Fair Labor Standards Act, which has periodically adjusted wage floors for inflation, growth, and political reasons. The major impact of this law in the oil and gas industry has been in gasoline retailing. Although the law is applicable to exploration and production, most pay scales for such work have been above minimum statutory levels, and work-site mobility has made noncompliance difficult to detect. Nonetheless, a bias was introduced that substituted capital for labor, increased costs, and reduced jobs for marginal (young, minority, unskilled) workers.

In addition to innumerable administrative interpretations and legislative amendments, several important new laws were enacted. The Labor Management Act of 1947 (Taft-Hartley Act), moderated the Wagner Act by specifying illegal union activity (including the closed shop) and reorganized the Federal Conciliation Commissioners as the Federal Mediation and Conciliation Service.[35] The 1940s were a decade of reaction against the virtual sweep of unions the decade before.

An important law for exploration and production was the Portal to Portal Act of 1947, which required employers to compensate workers for travel time to job sites.[36] If a worker took twenty hours to change drilling sites and spent fifteen minutes daily going to work thereafter, for example, the employer had to count the twenty hours plus each day's fifteen minutes as hours worked for compensation at the minimum wage or higher. This encouraged companies to hire nearby contract labor rather than company men to perform repair work and other unexpected chores at distant well sites.[37] Thus,

---

[34]Morgan Reynolds, *Power and Privilege*, pp. 110–11.

[35]Public Law 101, 61 Stat. 136 (1947). Another law moderating union power was the Landrum-Griffin Act of 1959 (Public Law 86-257, 73 Stat. 519).

[36]Public Law 49, 61 Stat. 84 (1947).

[37]Henrietta Larson and Kenneth Porter, *History of Humble Oil & Refining Company* (New York: Harper & Brothers, 1959), pp. 620–21.

a seemingly pro-employee law hurt some workers, particularly company men, while benefiting others, such as contract labor.

A new area of labor law began with the Occupational Safety and Health Administrative Act of 1970.[38] As originally promulgated, oil- and gas-well businesses were not classified under the General Industry Standards. In 1973, the Labor Department applied its Construction Safety Standards to oil-field supply companies on the rationale that hazards similar to the ones in the construction industry existed in the oil-field supply industry. This was disputed, and the Occupational Safety and Health Review Commission ruled that the assigned standards were inapplicable in a series of 1977–82 decisions.

Beginning in 1980, federal studies to measure and evaluate safety began at the wellhead. After a meeting with industry representatives, in particular the Association of Oil Well Servicing Contractors, a proposed ruling was released in late 1983 with 17 pages of regulations applicable to an estimated 47,000 drilling personnel and 48,000 servicing and special services employees.[39] Hearings were held at which industry opposition was voiced by the International Association of Drilling Contractors.

In March 1955, the Oil Workers International Union merged with the United Gas, Coke and Chemical Workers to form the Oil, Chemical and Atomic Workers' International Union. Representing 160,000 workers at its inception, the union as of 1984 claimed a membership of 130,000, which in the petroleum area is primarily oil field and refinery related.

Loan Subsidies

Reconstruction Finance Corporation

Another example of Hoover's activist policy to combat the Great Depression, the Reconstruction Finance Corporation Act was signed into law on January 22, 1932.[40] Based on the War Finance Corporation of World War I, the Reconstruction Finance Corporation (RFC), with

---

[38]Public Law 91-596, 84 Stat. 1590 (1970). Gasoline retail regulation under that act is described in chapter 28, pp. 1755–57.

[39]This history is taken from 48 *Fed. Reg.* 57202 (December 28, 1983). Also see *OGJ*, January 2, 1984, pp. 43–44.

[40]Public Law 2, 47 Stat. 5 (1932).

a $500-million budget, was instructed to lend public funds to failing banks—under Roosevelt the FRC was expanded to cover all business—to stop deflation and increase employment to foster recovery. From its beginning until 1945, when it joined the war effort as a subsidiary of the Defense Plant Corporation, the RFC was run by Texan Jesse Jones, who established a policy of not providing public funds to the oil and gas industry. He explained:

> Our policy of not lending to the oil industry was based on two considerations: first, the oil business was profitable; it was able to command money when other kinds of business could not; secondly, if we loaned a man money to drill an oil well and another man owning the adjoining property sought a loan for the same purpose, we would be honor-bound to accommodate him. So, as a policy, we simply decided against lending to the oil industry, although we had ample opportunity, from Texas and probably from another state or two.[41]

During World War II, the Defense Plant Corporation and the RFC actively financed pipelines and oil-carrying water vessels, as well as assisted refineries to convert from peacetime product slates to wartime production. In the postwar period, the RFC regained autonomy and continued to make loans to politically favored enterprises until it was replaced amid controversy by the Small Business Administration on July 30, 1953.[42] Small Business Administration loans to the petroleum industry were concentrated in gasoline marketing.[43]

Export-Import Bank

The Export-Import bank was created by Executive Order 6581 on February 2, 1934, to "facilitate exports and imports and the exchange of commodities between the United States and other nations or the agencies or nationals thereof." The bank could borrow, lend, guarantee debt, and "do a general banking business" with its $700-million budget.

The purpose of the Ex-Im Bank was to stimulate exports to create jobs and promote recovery. Imports, on the other hand, were discouraged by the Smoot-Hawley Tariff Act of 1930 and other protectionist

---

[41]Jesse Jones, *Fifty Billion Dollars* (New York: Macmillan, 1951), p. 234.

[42]Public Law 163, 67 Stat. 230 (1953).

[43]See chapter 25, pp. 1521–22.

legislation. The mercantilist notion of a favorable balance of trade—
dollar exports exceeding dollar imports—an inappropriate goal in
its own right, was contradicted by reduced export demand due to
import restrictions, which sent fewer dollars abroad for foreigners
to buy U.S. goods. Recovery, furthermore, was diminished by taxes,
intended to fund the Export-Import Bank, that reduced private-
sector demand.

After World War II, recovery was no longer deemed necessary
by the political establishment, and Ex-Im Bank lending became part
of the nation's foreign policy and foreign aid programs. In 1945, its
capital stock was increased to $1 billion, the first of many increases
associated with ever-expanding foreign commitments, both military
and economic, to counter perceived threats from Soviet communism.[44] As of 1983, Ex-Im Bank commitments are limited to $58.75
billion with a mix of $33.75 billion in direct loans and $25 billion in
guarantees and insurance. Commitments as of September 30, 1983,
totaled $23.7 billion in loans, $6.7 billion in guarantees, and $7.8
billion in insurance.[45]

A government-industry partnership of objectives has been behind
more than $100 billion in export support given in the history of Ex-
Im Bank.[46] The government's goal has been to help countries deemed
friendly to the United States; the exporters' goal has been to increase
demand for domestic products to make profits. Two private consortiums have been formed to act as a liaison between individual exporters and Ex-Im Bank. The Private Export Funding Corporation,
founded in 1970 and owned by fifty-four commercial banks and
several other groups, pays a fee to Ex-Im Bank for a $50-million
revolving line of credit and full loan guarantees for approved credits.
The Foreign Credit Insurance Association, founded in 1961 and
owned by fifty leading U.S. insurance companies, insures foreign
receivables against commercial risks. Ex-Im Bank, in turn, insures
political risks and reinsures part of the commercial risks. Much, if
not all, of this activity involves risks that are unacceptable to the
private sector.

[44]Public Law 173, 59 Stat. 526 (1945).
[45]Export-Import Bank of the United States, *Fiscal 1983 Annual Report* (Washington,
D.C.: Export-Import Bank, 1994), p. 27.
[46]*Exim News*, October 14, 1982, p. 4.

Major areas of Ex-Im Bank subsidization are electric power, aircraft, construction equipment, and communications. Beginning in the 1940s, loans were made to foreign countries to purchase U.S. equipment, including oil rigs, refinery parts, and pipeline equipment. Some of these loans were particularly controversial because of the expropriations of property of U.S. oil companies by beneficiary governments. Mexico's nationalization of U.S. oil properties in 1938 was followed by a loan of $30 million for roads in 1941, a $10-million refinery loan in 1943, and a $150-million loan for general development in 1950. A 1946 loan of $5.5 million to Bolivia for production, refining, and pipeline expenditure followed nationalization a decade before. A $125-million loan to Argentina in 1950 for general expenditure came just thirteen years after the oil industry had been taken over by authorities. A $300-million loan was made in 1950 to a thoroughly corrupt Brazilian government that would nationalize U.S. oil firms in 1964.[47]

More recent petroleum-related loans have gone to Mexico ($80 million in 1972), Burma ($2.8 million in 1971), Norway ($68 million in 1973), Taiwan ($11.3 million in 1973), Israel ($13.5 million in 1975), Britain ($71 million in 1975), Chile ($203 million in 1975), Norway ($44 million in 1975), Ivory Coast ($88 million in 1980), Brazil ($29 million in 1982), Indonesia ($333 million in 1982), New Zealand ($99 million in 1982), Cameroon ($54 million in 1982) and Angola ($45 million in 1983).[48] A $456-million loan and loan guarantee to New Zealand involved such well-known companies as Mobil and Phillips and sixteen major U.S. oil-field supply companies.[49] Many other industry leaders, such as Shell, Chevron, Getty, Occidental, and British Petroleum, have been beneficiaries of Ex-Im Bank largesse. Total oil and gas credits between 1975 and 1983 came to $3.5 billion. Other recipients of oil and gas loans were Algeria,[50] France, Hong Kong, Panama, Portugal, Yugoslavia, Belgium, Cayman Islands, Liberia, Japan, Spain, Peru, Romania, Singapore, Egypt, India, Sweden, and China.

---

[47]See Edward Chester, *United States Oil Policy and Diplomacy* (Westport, Conn.: Greenwood Press, 1983), pp. 131, 135, 137, 174, 189.

[48]Compiled from various Export-Import Bank annual reports from 1975 until 1983.

[49]*Exim News*, October 14, 1982, p. 1.

[50]Controversy surrounding Algerian liquefied natural gas imports made possible by Ex-Im Bank assistance is described in chapter 15, p. 930.

Securities Regulation

The lifeblood of the free market is savings and investment that underwrite the capital structure of the economy. Corporate finance with bonds and stocks is a major part of the system. Primary issues of stocks and bonds are handled by investment banking houses, while secondary trading is conducted on stock exchanges by means of buy-sell orders emanating from stock brokerage houses located across the country.

In the early nineteenth century, the New York Stock Exchange emerged as the major financial center in the United States. Many other regional exchanges also evolved to meet the financing and investment needs of clients. In the 1860s, oil stocks joined railroad securities and other securities on the local exchanges and in New York. For decades, little more than "let the buyer beware" governed investor decisions; in the next century, state regulation and then federal regulation would add "let the seller beware." This latter development is explored below with particular reference to oil and gas exploration and production.

Early Promotion and Regulation

Oil drilling, always a speculative business, was even more so in the years before scientific prospecting. Oil "smellers" and "divining rod" techniques made wildcatting a true gamble. If exploration was a gamble, investing in exploration companies was also. With every gusher, legions of oil companies were formed that descended upon the investing public with alluring promises of wealth. With little known about the location of undiscovered oil deposits, and with high costs for information about company track records and relevant factual data, a fine line existed between speculation and fraud in some cases.

"Speculation and fraudulent promotions," John Ise declared in 1926, "have been rampant in almost every oil field discovery since 1859."[51] There were a variety of "quick money" teasers in promotional literature, and sales pitches ranged from "Come with me to the golden lanes of wealth where the oil of old Mother Earth pours

---

[51]John Ise, *The United States Oil Policy* (New Haven, Conn.: Yale University Press, 1926), p. 187.

forth its riches" to "We can't miss the oil."[52] There was also unambiguous fraud—willful misinformation on acreage, past production, profits and dividends, and assets and liabilities—as well as false incorporations and violated written guarantees.[53] This was the province of common-law remedies, and some state agencies and federal agencies such as the Post Office, Justice Department, and Federal Trade Commission (FTC) became involved after the turn of the century.

Because of strong feelings about speculative losses and the magnitude of the problem in petroleum and other areas, states enacted blue-sky laws, which, in addition to prohibiting fraud, often required dealers to obtain licenses and register securities before their sale. Kansas passed the first law in 1911, and by 1933, all states except Nevada had followed suit.[54] Municipalities such as San Diego and Long Beach, California, passed stricter regulations.[55] On the private side, establishment of better business bureaus—one in Tulsa, Oklahoma, focused on oil securities—was one response; security standards pushed by the American Petroleum Institute and the National Vigilance Committee of the Associated Advertising Clubs were other responses.[56]

The public and private problem was summed up by Ise.

> The loss of hundreds of millions of dollars in unwise and fraudulent oil ventures has meant much more than the loss of this money. It has meant a great loss of confidence in all kinds of securities, not only legitimate oil stocks and bonds, but stocks and bonds of all kinds. Some of the large investment houses have often complained of the flow of money into worthless oil stock, not only because it meant so much of a subtraction from the funds available for productive uses, but because it made many people suspicious of all kinds of securities.[57]

[52]Ibid., pp. 200–201.

[53]Ibid., p. 196.

[54]Clair Wilcox, *Public Policies toward Business* (Homewood, Ill.: Richard D. Irwin, 1966), p. 616. The Kansas law in its first year was used to block 1,400 of 1,500 applications to sell the stock of "foreign" (i.e., out-of-state) firms. This left state investors primarily with in-state issues from which to choose. Gilbert Brach, "The Blue Sky Law," *Marquette Law Review*, 3 (1919): 143.

[55]John Ise, *The United States Oil Policy*, p. 200.

[56]Ibid., pp. 199–200. The National Vigilance Committee would become the National Better Business Bureau with offices in all major U.S. and Canadian cities.

[57]Ibid., p. 198.

While Ise's argument, thoroughly documented with examples, is intended to substantiate market failure and a need for regulation, the most obvious solution was a more efficient rendering of the common law's prohibitions and penalties against willful deceit. Beyond this, regulation entered the quagmire of trying to save investors from themselves. Investors make mistakes (sustained speculative losses), but investors as profit maximizers can be expected to learn from their mistakes.

In a business in which dry holes are far more numerous than oil strikes, many exploration investments can be expected to be barren. Today's development-well drilling programs improve the odds considerably, but yesterday's high percentage of wildcat wells made oil investments wildcats also. Imposing entry costs on security sales only narrowed investment options for consumers and raised expenses for security dealers to recover from their clients. Outside of fraud, separating "good" investments from "bad" investments by state commissions prior to maturity was itself speculative.

Early Federal Activity

During World War I and the postwar period, federal authorities intervened in the securities market, particularly that for oil and gas production. During the war, as mentioned in chapter 5, the Capital Issues Committee of the Treasury Department blocked new issues by prospective production firms because of alleged wartime scarcities.[58] After the war, the Capital Issues Committee continued its campaign against exploration and production securities because their popularity hurt the market for Liberty Bonds and war savings stamps. Explained Secretary of the Treasury Carter Glass:

> The offering of investments to the public competes with the offering of Government securities, and, as you are aware, the Treasury proposes to invite the public to subscribe to a very large issue of securities shortly. Stocks and securities of a legitimate investment character compete with the Government, but not nearly so much as highly speculative stocks. . . . The operations of the Government in the past, in endeavoring to induce persons of all classes to purchase Government bonds, have, to a large degree, brought into being a very large and new class of investors who are without experience or knowledge to guide them wisely. . . . But the very efforts of the Government

[58]See chapter 5, pp. 228–29.

agents, in persuading such persons to become investors, have prepared the way for promoters to place many worthless stocks. The result has been that those promoters have already displaced a very large amount of Government bonds by taking them in exchange for stock, and to such an extent as to undo the work which is so essential for the success of the Government's financial operations, because the Government cannot expect successful floatations of its own securities, or the preservation of a proper price therefore in the financial market, unless the great number of small buyers continue to hold their bonds.[59]

Pleas to the FTC by the Treasury Department to "protect" government bondholders by regulating securities as "articles of interstate commerce" did not succeed. This would wait until the New Deal.

New Deal Regulation

Federal security regulation, it is popularly explained, was a necessary outgrowth of ineffectual state regulation. Stated Clair Wilcox:

> [State] laws have afforded scant protection to investors. The funds provided for their enforcement have rarely been adequate to finance a real analysis of the statements that are filed. Little effort has been made to censor security prospectuses. . . . The laws do not prevent mismanagement of corporations. . . . Many transactions escape control, moreover, since the jurisdiction of state authorities does not extend to sales across state lines. It remained for Congress to make the first effective provision for the protection of investors when it enacted the securities laws in the early years of the New Deal.[60]

It took more than "failed" state regulation to pave the way for federal controls; it took an unprecedented securities crash in October 1929 and failed recovery to give government a rationale to intervene.[61] A lengthy investigation by the Senate Committee on Banking

---

[59]*OGJ*, March 14, 1919, p. 46. According to Gilbert Brach, "It has been estimated in responsible quarters that as much as $400,000,000 of Liberty Bonds placed with investors, have already fallen into the hands of dishonest brokers in the exchange for wildcat oil or mining issues." Brach, "The Blue Sky Law," p. 142.

[60]Clair Wilcox, *Public Policies toward Business*, p. 616.

[61]In the first years of the Great Crash, stocks and bonds listed on the New York Exchange fell from $138 billion to $45 billion. Ibid. Huge paper losses were also registered by investment trusts, public-utility holding companies, and nonlisted bonds.

and Currency and the FTC identified many 1920s bull-market practices as "abuses" and hinted that the security collapse could have
been avoided with proper regulation.[62] "In the opinion of many new
dealers," concluded Thomas McCraw, "unfettered trading on thin
margins represented a primary cause of the stock market crash and
the depression that followed."[63] Security practices, as it were, became
"whipping boys" of the Great Depression that was the necessary
aftermath of a speculative boom fueled by monetary expansion by
the Federal Reserve (founded 1913).[64]

The Federal Securities Act of 1933, similar to state blue-sky laws,
required full disclosure on security issues issued through the mails
or sold interstate to prevent fraud and misrepresentation.[65] However,
fraud was not the primary intent. House sponsor Sam Rayburn
(D-Tex.) admitted, "This bill is not so much a response to the frauds
of criminals as it is to the reticence of financiers."[66] Administration
was assigned to the FTC, which approved registrations conforming
to the act. Penalties accrued for "an untrue statement of a material
fact or [an] omitted . . . material fact required to be stated therein
or necessary to make the statements therein not misleading."[67] If a
stock price fell as the result of a misstatement or omission, the buyer
could sue for the difference upon sale. Although "of secondary
importance in a comprehensive program of social control over
finance," as noted by regulatory proponents William Douglas and

[62]See William Douglas and George Bates, "The Federal Securities Act of 1933," *Yale Law Journal* (December 1933): 171.

[63]Thomas McCraw, *Prophets of Regulation* (Cambridge, Mass.: Harvard University Press, 1984), p. 180.

[64]Monetary inflation and speculation were directly related. A vivid example was given by economist Percy Greaves. "In 1926, the banks could lend money on stock at 5 percent plus, and then discount loans at 4 percent at their Federal Reserve Banks. . . . [O]ne major New York bank was reported as borrowing $115 million from its Federal Reserve Bank on fifteen-day notes and lending it on stock exchange securities at from 6 percent to 7 percent. . . . As a result, stock market prices . . . moved up faster and faster as time passed." Greaves, *Understanding the Dollar Crisis* (Boston: Western Islands, 1973), p. 210. On monetary inflation during the 1920s and the artificial boom, see Murray Rothbard, *America's Great Depression*, Part II.

[65]Public Law 22, 48 Stat. 74 (1933). The act was also called the Truth in Securities Act.

[66]Quoted in Thomas McCraw, *Prophets of Regulation*, p. 173. The story of James Landis, who was the principal author of the 1933 law, is found in ibid., chap. 5, "Landis and the Statecraft of the SEC," pp. 153–209.

[67]Public Law 22, 48 Stat. 79–80 (1933).

George Bates, the act was an entering wedge that other New Deal legislation would buttress.[68] What the act did require was detailed, accurate reams of information that bared all financial secrets of a firm. But security floatations were not significantly restricted, and the investor was not saved from himself.

The Securities Exchange Act of 1934 was passed to "provide for the regulation of securities exchanges and of over the counter markets operating in interstate and foreign commerce . . . to prevent inequitable and unfair practices on such exchanges and markets."[69] The Securities and Exchange Commission (SEC) was established to assume authority from the FTC. "Any manipulative or deceptive device or contrivance" to inflate stock prices was prohibited.[70] Corporate officials were forbidden to trade stock on inside information. Brokers and dealers were required to register with the SEC and follow certain rules. Margin requirements, with the Federal Reserve Board in charge, were set at 55 percent of the stock's current price or its lowest price within thirty-six months to "preven[t] the excessive use of credit for the purchase or carrying of securities."[71] Authority to fix broker prices and set other rules was prescribed. Although the 1933 act was limited to new issues, the 1934 act governed securities in circulation.

The primary goal of the 1934 act, in the words of the first SEC chairman, Joseph Kennedy, was to "re-create, rebuild, and restore confidence" to end the depression.[72] Dedicated, talented young New Deal lawyers, who viewed economic problems as psychological rather than as crises of government intervention, produced pages of disclosure requirements and restrictions on stock transaction practices, which were futile. Economic recovery would not come, and the economy was saddled with another layer of regulation that impeded the flow of much-needed capital for business.

---

[68]William Douglas and George Bates, "The Federal Securities Act of 1933," p. 171.

[69]Public Law 291, 48 Stat. 881 (1934). Security was defined to include "any fractional undivided interest in oil, gas, or other mineral rights."

[70]Also forbidden was "false or misleading appearance of active trading." Ibid., p. 889.

[71]Ibid., p. 886. The Federal Reserve Board was given responsibility for rules governing purchase of stock on credit.

[72]Quoted in Thomas McCraw, *Prophets of Regulation*, p. 183.

A third New Deal act that contributed to "social control over finance" was the Public Utility Holding Company Act (Wheeler-Rayburn Act), which placed security sales of major electric and gas companies under SEC authority.[73] This is examined in chapter 15.[74]

Subsequent Amendments: An Overview

Subsequent statutes, such as the Maloney Act of 1938,[75] the Investment Company Act of 1940,[76] and the Security Acts Amendment of 1964,[77] extended control to the over-the-counter securities market and investment houses, strengthened the cartelization of the securities profession by limiting entry and preserving their rate-setting powers, and expanded SEC power over broker-dealer activities. Partial regulation, which began in 1933, was now comprehensive.

Far from its idealistic beginnings, securities regulation had created a cartel for private industry in the name of protecting the "public interest." The first crack in regulation came on December 5, 1968, when brokers were allowed to offer volume discounts from their regular per-share brokerage fee.[78] A more comprehensive move toward deregulation came with the Securities Acts Amendments of 1975.[79] The SEC was instructed to abrogate rules reducing competition, and it was stated that "no national securities exchange may impose any schedule or fix rates of commissions, allowances discounts or other fees to be charged by its members."[80] The New York Stock Exchange cartel was weakened, but licensing still restricted the

[73]Public Law 333, 49 Stat. 803 (1935). "Social control" could be politically wielded. For a sobering story of SEC prosecution of an independent oil man critical of Petroleum Administration Board head Harold Ickes, see J. Edward Jones, *And So—They Indicted Me* (New York: J. Edward Jones Publishing, 1938).

[74]See chapter 15, pp. 862–63.

[75]Public Law 719, 52 Stat. 1070 (1938).

[76]Public Law 768, 52 Stat. 789 (1940).

[77]Public Law 88-467, 78 Stat. 565 (1964).

[78]Hans Stoll, "Regulation of Securities Markets: An Examination of the Effects of Increased Competition," in U.S. Senate, Committee on Governmental Affairs, appendix to vol. 6 of *Study of Federal Regulation* (Washington, D.C.: Government Printing Office, 1978), p. 600.

[79]Public Law 94-29, 89 Stat. 97 (1975).

[80]Ibid., p. 107. For an initial examination of stock exchange broker commissions, see Alfred Kahn, *The Economics of Regulation*, 2 vols. (New York: John Wiley & Sons, 1971), vol. 2, pp. 193–209.

supply of security traders, and formal security registration ensured a fixed business. The rise of discount brokers in the 1980s was attributable to increased competition allowed by the 1975 amendments, but from the viewpoint of the free market, unnecessary cost, restricted entry, and overpricing of transactions remain. Fundamental reform would weaken or eliminate mandatory disclosure for public companies, requirements for security offerings, and restrictions on securities trading. Private standards with an eye toward investor goodwill and confidence would substitute.

Effects on the Oil and Gas Industry

After several years of observing the new federal regulation, the National Conference of Business Paper Editors concluded that "compliance with the provisions of the Securities Act has handicapped financing and increased the expense to the [oil] companies."[81] The problem inherent in state and federal securities regulation was stated by a former SEC attorney: "The hazardous and speculative nature of oil exploration, with the odds against any one venture, has made it especially difficult to design legislation adequate to protect the public from fraudulent promotions without unduly hindering bona fide efforts to finance exploratory operations.[82] By July 20, 1935, the deadline for security registration for the national security exchanges, over 100 oil and gas companies had registered.[83] Once-confidential information, such as stock holdings of principal officers, were now public information to the chagrin of many of those individuals.

In June 1936, pursuant to one of the SEC's first important administrative pronouncements, offering sheets had to be submitted and commission approval received for all gas and oil royalty sales prior to solicitation. Of the first batch, over 90 percent were amended or withdrawn after receiving initial disapproval.[84] The extensive questionnaire, which covered all aspects of the properties, was aimed at oil royalty "racketeers" who continued to be of great concern to regulators.

---

[81]*National Petroleum News*, May 29, 1935, p. 25. Cited hereafter as *NPN*.

[82]Julian Meer, "Oil Finance and the Securities Laws," *Texas Law Review* (June 1951): 885.

[83]*NPN*, July 24, 1935, p. 19.

[84]*Business Week*, August 15, 1936, p. 12.

Later administrative regulation continued to expand reporting requirements that rationed drilling programs in an attempt to save investors from themselves. After investor complaints in 1976–77, the SEC issued more disclosure requirements, which to independents were "more mire in the regulatory swamp."[85] This increased the long-standing practice of private placements to bypass the expense and delay of public offerings. Life insurance companies were one major source of private placements when direct negotiations sufficed in an unregulated environment.[86]

Distortions—in terms of increased expense, delay, and uncertainty—due to securities regulation in the oil- and gas-drilling industry were mitigated by greater-than-average reliance on internal financing. Such reinvestment resulted from favorable tax policies—intangible-drilling-cost expensing coupled with the depletion allowance, in particular—that lowered the industry's effective tax rate below that of other industries until the 1970s.[87]

Accounting Theory and Practice

"The fundamental purpose of accounting," stated Arthur Dewing, "is to determine whether or not the business is realizing a profit."[88] The practice of accountancy was not invented but evolved over centuries as certain bookkeeping methods were found to best provide a representative financial picture of business firms.[89]

In the United States, accounting emerged as a general practice in the 1870s, and in 1882, the first trade group was established in New York, the financial mecca of the country.[90] Although its original purpose was educational and scientific, its goals would shift to the political arena to achieve for its members the status and income

[85]*OGJ*, May 1, 1978, p. 36.

[86]Arthur Dewing, *The Financial Policy of Corporations*, 2 vols. (New York: Ronald Press, 1953), vol. 2, pp. 1112–14.

[87]See Harold Bloomenthal, "Securities Regulation of Oil and Gas and Mineral Transactions," 3 *Mineral Law Institute* (New York: Matthew Bender, 1957), p. 71.

[88]Arthur Dewing, *The Financial Policy of Corporations*, vol. 1, p. 509. This includes not only the income statement, which reveals profits during a period, but the balance sheet and subsidiary financial statements, which indicate the net worth of a company or the profit if sold.

[89]Ibid., p. 515.

[90]Wilmer Green, *History and Survey of Accountancy* (Brooklyn, N.Y.: Standard Text Press, 1930), p. 74.

that free-market conditions alone were slow to allow. From this beginning, regulation would extend into other areas of financial accounting and culminate, as far as the petroleum industry was concerned, debate in the 1970s over the estimation of hydrocarbon reserves.

State Licensing

In 1894, the American Association of Public Accountants, chartered in 1887 by New York State, approached the New York legislature about establishing educational requirements under the regents of New York University. Several tries later, the state passed An Act to Regulate the Profession of Public Accountants on April 17, 1896. Henceforth, only a certificated individual could be "styled and known as a Certified Public Accountant" (CPA).[91] A board of examiners was chosen, tests were given, and in 1898 the first prosecution of an noncertified individual advertising for-hire services as a CPA occurred.[92] Pennsylvania followed with certification in 1899 and was joined by Maryland in 1900, California in 1901, and Illinois and Washington in 1903. By 1913, over thirty states had passed CPA laws and established chapters in the American Association of Public Accountants. By 1921, all states had made accountancy a licensed profession.[93] Henceforth, the goal of state CPA organizations would be to keep entry-level standards high. The "public interest" in competent accountants fronted the effort; the more narrow motivation was the income and status to be gained from restricted membership.

Federal Influence

Federal licensing was never seriously considered because accounting was recognized as an intrastate matter. An important federal contribution, however, was to increase the demand for specialized bookkeeping through regulation and reporting requirements. Public-utility regulation created the Uniform System of Accounts that became a CPA-dominated matter. War contracts beginning during World War I were directed toward certified practitioners. Federal taxation of business income (1909), personal income (1913), excess

---

[91]The act is reprinted in James Edwards, *History of Public Accounting in the United States* (East Lansing: Michigan State University, 1960), p. 69.

[92]Ibid., pp. 72–73.

[93]Ibid., pp. 72, 109–10.

profit (1917), and well sales (1918) created lucrative areas of tax law that CPAs captured. In 1924, the U.S. Board of Tax Appeals ruled that along with certified lawyers, only certified accountants could come before the board.[94]

The capstone of regulatory-induced demand was the federal securities acts of the 1930s, which purported to better inform the investing public of the risks and prospects of stock offerings and the condition and prospects of publicly traded firms. This involved disclosure of financial information and mandatory audits for larger firms, which, in turn, required that, per SEC instruction, the public be properly informed of accounting alternatives. This gave the SEC a role in what hitherto had been predominately a professional, private concern—the formulation and implementation of accounting principles.

The role of the SEC would be important. In theory and practice, financially describing a business in a world of flux offers a range of accounting options that can be politically modified. This began in 1936 when the American Accounting Association, composed primarily of academic accountants, launched a march toward monolithic accounting by publishing *A Tentative Statement of Accounting Principles Underlying Corporate Financial Statements.*[95] Two years later, the American Institute of Certified Public Accountants (AICPA) was created to "narro[w] the areas of difference and inconsistencies" not only in accounting theory (like the American Accounting Association had begun to do) but in practice as well.[96] Sanctioned by the SEC and composed of government-licensed accountants, the AICPA through its subsidiary, the Committee on Accounting Procedures, renamed the Accounting Principles Board in 1959, had authority to issue "opinions" (formerly "bulletins") that had the status of *generally accepted accounting principles* (GAAP).[97]

The extent of SEC involvement with early efforts to impose uniform accounting is not altogether clear since market forces were also

[94]Ibid., p. 104.

[95]See Thomas Sanders, *A Statement of Accounting Principles* (New York: American Accounting Association, 1938), p. 45.

[96]Glenn Welsch, *Intermediate Accounting* (Homewood, Ill.: Richard D. Irwin, 1979), p. 6.

[97]From its inception until 1959, the Committee on Accounting Procedure issued bulletins; from 1959 until 1973, the Accounting Principles Board issued opinions. Both were considered GAAP.

working toward standardization. Before 1964, in any case, persuasion and scholarly debate were the main tools used to induce practitioners to conform with GAAP. But with Rule 203, issued in October 1964, the AICPA redefined the accountants' rule of ethics to require conformity with GAAP "unless the member can demonstrate that due to unusual circumstances the financial statements would otherwise have been misleading."[98] The force behind the ruling was that the "member" was a licensed practitioner who could be decertified if he did not follow professional ethics. Through the indirect use of government, monolithic accounting could be institutionalized.

The next government intrusion into accounting, leading to what Thomas Taylor called "the politicization of a profession," occurred when the SEC, along with some accountants, became dissatisfied with the quality and quantity of the opinions of the Accounting Principles Board.[99] At times, the SEC prevented opinions' becoming GAAP by refusing to back them. This led to the creation of the independent Financial Accounting Standards Board (FASB) in 1973, which received top sanction from the SEC to issue "statements" and "interpretations" for the profession to follow.

With the aid of an advisory council, the seven-member FASB, much like a formal regulatory body, issues final rulings. After a proposal of change is distributed, a public hearing is held after which an exposure draft is circulated. Then, after further comments, a final opinion, which automatically becomes GAAP, is reached. The SEC, on the other hand, directly influences accounting practices through reporting requirements. Regulation S-X, as amended and supplemented by the SEC's Accounting Series Releases, dictates how public firms report financial data and is augmented by special SEC "releases" and "staff accounting bulletins." Through these means and the quasi-governmental FASB, the government's voice in accounting theory and practice is heard.

Oil and Gas Accounting Controversies

The quest for monolithic accounting—along with new mandatory reporting requirements—reached a new pitch with federal oil and gas regulation in the energy-crisis decade of the 1970s. At issue were (1) a uniform method of disclosing on financial statements intended

[98]Glenn Welsch, *Intermediate Accounting*, p. 9.
[99]Thomas Taylor, "The Politicization of a Profession," *Policy Report* (June 1980): 4–7.

for investors the financial impact of drilling operations and (2) the compilation of broad financial and supply statistics to aid regulatory efforts.

Preceding the onslaught of federal petroleum regulation in the 1970s, a debate in the industry and accounting profession, not to mention the SEC, developed over the proper method of classifying costs associated with unsuccessful drilling. Traditionally, companies expensed dry-hole (noncommercial deposit) costs and capitalized costs associated with discoveries. This became known as the *successful efforts* method. In the 1960s, a second method came into use and received GAAP certification. Under the *full-cost* method, operators would capitalize all drilling expenses, generally on a companywide basis, on the reasoning that in the risky world of petroleum exploration, dry holes were the cost of discoveries. Dry-hole costs would then be amortized against revenue from extractions, subject to the limitation that costs not exceed revenues.

Use of full costing became popular with almost all of the smaller independent producing firms. The attraction was earnings and net worth stabilization. By postponing expenses until revenues were present, higher profits and net worth for the current period could be shown to better attract investor interest in upcoming drilling programs. Unless the sophisticated investor discounted full costing to equate it with successful efforts, capital costs appeared to be lower for these firms. The penalty, however, was higher taxes in a present-value sense. Major integrated companies, on the contrary, preferred successful efforts to full costing to minimize their tax obligations in a present-value sense. (Texaco, one of the few exceptions, switched to successful efforts in 1976.) Their capital requirements could be met by pledging fixed assets behind bank loans or issuing debentures and stock on the strength of historical earnings.

In 1964, the first sign of discontent over the dual option appeared when the AICPA commissioned a study on the alternative costs systems and recommended the better of the two.[100] Issued in 1969, the report recommended successful efforts. In a follow-up study, the AICPA's Committee on Extractive Industries reached a similar

---

[100]This discussion is taken from *Accounting: Professional Standards*, 3 vols. (Chicago: Commerce Clearing House, 1979), vol. 3, pp. 10, 477–88; and James Haverson, "An Analysis of the Oil and Natural Gas Reserve Reporting Problem," *27 Oil and Gas Institute* (New York: Matthew Bender, 1976), pp. 121–27.

verdict and recommended that the field, not the company, be recognized as the cost center.

Along with the accounting profession, the Federal Power Commission expressed its growing concern about the dual options. In late 1970, the commission, pursuant to its authority to regulate natural gas, issued a proposal to require full costing by natural-gas companies. After prolonged debate, with participation by the AICPA's Accounting Principles Board, the Federal Power Commission issued Order 440 on November 5, 1971, that required natural-gas producers to use full costing for leases acquired after October 6, 1969, with each county as the cost center.[101] This contradicted the profession's recommendation of successful efforts.

The debate resumed in 1973 when the Ad Hoc Committee on Full Cost Accounting was formed, primarily by integrated companies, to push for successful efforts. A technical study published a year later concluded that successful efforts more faithfully served investor needs than did full costing.

With the developing energy crisis and growing public suspicion about industry practices, a new era of federal regulation of accounting for exploration and production was set to begin. On December 22, 1975, President Gerald Ford signed the Energy Policy and Conservation Act, which empowered the SEC to

> prescribe rules applicable to persons engaged in the production of crude oil or natural gas, or make effective by recognition, or by other appropriate means indicating a determination to rely on accounting practices developed by the Financial Accounting Standards Board, if the Securities and Exchange Commission is assured that such practice will be observed by persons engaged in the production of crude oil or natural gas to the same extent as would result if the Securities and Exchange Commission had prescribed such practices by rule.[102]

The same section also required a compilation of various accounting information on exploration and production to create a national energy database. The act required each company to submit:

> (1) The separate calculation of capital, revenue, and operation cost information pertaining to—

[101]46 FPC 1148 (November 5, 1971).
[102]Public Law 94-163, 89 Stat. 871 (1975) at 958.

(A) prospecting,

(B) acquisition,

(C) exploration,

(D) development, and

(E) production,

including geological and geophysical costs, carrying costs, unsuccessful exploratory drilling costs, intangible drilling and development costs on productive wells, the cost of unsuccessful development wells, and the cost of acquiring oil and gas reserves by means other than development. Any such calculation shall take into account disposition of capitalized costs, contractual arrangements involving special conveyance of rights and joint operation, differences between book and tax income, and prices used in the transfer of products or other assets from one person controlled by controlling or under common control with such person.

(2) The full presentation of the financial information of persons engaged in the production of crude oil or natural gas, including—

(A) disclosure of reserves and operating activities, both domestic and foreign, to facilitate evaluation of financial information and result; and

(B) classification of financial information by function to facilitate correlation with reserve and operating statistics, both domestic and foreign.

(3) Such other information, projections, and relationships of collected data as shall be necessary to facilitate the compilation of such data base.[103]

Never before had government involvement in accounting practice been as meticulously prescribed by law. Before, the SEC role in accounting had been complementary and cooperative, although its ultimate authority was not in doubt. Now, the SEC—and all the special interests involved with government energy policy—became the driving force behind the FASB and the profession in general. The impetus for government intervention was less a concern for unscrupulous investors than it was to provide an informational foundation for the federal government's activist energy program.

Almost immediately, the FASB began deliberations over the changes mandated by the EPCA. The SEC, the Federal Power Commission, the Federal Energy Administration, the Oversight and Investigations Subcommittee of the House Committee on Interstate

[103]Ibid., p. 959.

and Foreign Commerce, the General Accounting Office, and the Cost Accounting Standards Board were involved. During the debate, several full-cost companies withdrew or canceled securities offerings.[104] The final report, issued December 22, 1977 (FASB 19), controversially mandated successful efforts instead of full-cost accounting for the fiscal years beginning after December 15, 1978. This was reversed nine months later by the SEC in Accounting Series Release (ASR) 253, which returned full costing to GAAP status. To the embarrassed FASB, this was a stark reminder that power over accounting rules lay not within the profession but within government. In February 1979, FASB 25 was issued to rescind FASB 19.

Controversy over whether to expense or capitalize dry-hole costs was joined by the question of whether a third alternative—to redefine income and subtract drilling costs as incurred—was better. On March 23, 1976, the SEC amended Regulation S-X with ASR 190 to require larger energy companies to disclose inventories and productive capacity and estimate oil and gas replacement cost in financial reports filed with the commission for fiscal years ending after December 24, 1976. Better accounting under inflationary conditions and better recognition of the financial worth of proven reserves, the chief asset of producing companies, were the reasons given for regulation. This began *reserve-recognition accounting* (RRA), also called discovery-value accounting and current-value accounting.

On May 12, 1976, the SEC, under the direction of Chairman Harold Williams and Chief Accountant A. Clarence Sampson, released Securities Act Release 5706 that required disclosure of information relating to exploration and production in reports filed with the commission.[105] ASR 253, released by the SEC on August 31, 1978, then suggested that historical cost be replaced with an accounting method based on proven-reserve valuation.

On September 24, 1979, RRA became mandatory as supplemental disclosure for all oil- and gas-production companies for the fiscal years ending after December 25, 1979. While the production industry flinched, petroleum-engineering companies, such as Keplinger and Associates, Ryder Scott, and DeGolyer and MacNaughton, geared

---

[104]*OGJ*, October 24, 1977, p. 71.

[105]For negative industry reaction, see *Forbes*, September 17, 1979, pp. 188, 192.

up for unprecedented business.[106] RRA entailed calculating a present value of proven hydrocarbon reserves for inclusion on the asset side of the balance sheet and changes in reserves and associated expenses recorded on the income statement. Under successful efforts and full costing, reserves were valued at cost pursuant to the lower of cost or market principal, only to be recognized as income when produced and sold, to adhere to the realization-of-revenue principle. To the SEC, however, traditional accounting principles were misleading to investors. This interpretation was controversial. Although RRA was not questioned as a theoretic ideal assuming perfect information, its use in practice was troublesome. Engineering estimates of reservoir quantities are imprecise, particularly when reservoirs are first located. It is not uncommon to have discovery-date estimates as much as 50 percent different from revised estimates five years later.[107] Dollar values assigned to reserves, moreover, are prone to obsolescence because future prices, interest rates (for discounting), technological changes, and withdrawal rates are variable. Wild swings in earnings without actual revenue was another distortion. For these reasons, a final computation could be as misleading as the conservative value derived from time-honored accounting principles. This was partially acknowledged by the SEC with ASR 289, released in February 1981, which abandoned the goal of incorporating RRA into primary financial statements. Stated the SEC:

> The Commission has determined that because of the inherent uncertainty of the recoverable quantities of proved oil and gas reserves, RRA does not presently possess the requisite degree of certainty to be accepted as a primary method of accounting. . . . [The SEC therefore] no longer considers Reserve Recognition Accounting to be a potential method of accounting in the primary financial statements.[108]

RRA remained mandatory for supplemental disclosures as stated in FASB 33. But the retreat would continue. In October 1981, the SEC again allowed firms to switch to dry-hole cost methods, "if the enterprise justifies the use of an accepted accounting principle on the basis that it is preferable." In late 1982, FASB 69 contained new disclosure rules that took RRA off the supplemental statements for

[106]*Forbes*, September 29, 1980, p. 109.
[107]*Business Week*, June 25, 1979, p. 102.
[108]46 *Fed. Reg.* 15496 (March 6, 1981).

fiscal years beginning after December 14, 1982.[109] A controversial episode of government-engineered accounting standards was over.

Evaluation

Government involvement in accounting theory and practice—from state licensing at the turn of the century to New Deal securities regulation in the 1930s to energy-crisis regulation in the 1970s—can be second-guessed. To the extent that government licensing proved more restrictive than professional licensing alone, the accounting profession achieved what could not be achieved in the market—cartelization. Nonmarket barriers may have achieved their purpose of increasing the economic rent accruing to CPAs, but it was done at the expense of consumers. To the extent fewer accountants and higher pricing reduced demand for accounting services, the "public-interest" end of licensing—better accounting services—was contradicted. In the absence of licensing, ratings by private institutions (such as the National Association of Security Dealers) and reputations would provide information for consumers to use in matching different tasks with different proficiencies. Increased competition in the absence of licensing would reduce accounting costs for all clients, particularly for approximately 7,500 firms with assets over $3 million and 5,000 or more owners; those firms must file audited annual reports.

Like other institutions of the social world, accountancy was "the result of human action but not of human design."[110] This body of knowledge was not invented by a genius or implemented by a series of government directives but was the result of contributions of countless individuals engaged in voluntary business pursuits over time.[111] From this perspective, government intervention in periodic

[109]Disclosure rules for publicly traded oil firms were strict for major companies and relaxed for smaller companies. See *OGJ*, December 20, 1982, pp. 24–25.

[110]See chapter 1, pp. 13–18.

[111]States Arthur Dewing: "Accounting has had a long and distinguished history. In its present form it was built up by a process of trial and error out of the data supplied by Italian and German merchants carrying on extended local and international trade during the fifteenth, sixteenth, and seventeenth centuries. There was no Newton or Mendel to lay a substantial theoretical basis on which the whole applied edifice could be erected; accountancy arose, slowly, as the formulation into commonly accepted usage of the practical expedients generally recognized by the merchants. Accountancy has remained set in this background ever since." Dewing, *The Financial Policy of Corporations*, vol. 1, p. 515.

moods of activism, interjecting "social" elements into time-honored accounting principles, seems petty and misplaced. Referring to cost-based regulation and the Uniform System of Accounts, one accountant in the 1940s complained of "a hopeless confusion between accounting principles and regulatory objectives."[112] The conflict expanded to other large publicly owned firms when section 13 of the 1934 Securities Exchange Act opened the door for the SEC to dictate private accounting standards and otherwise regulate security issues. Narrowing the choice of accounting standards to "improve" reporting and to "protect" investors was mistaken in purpose and costly.

The economy of analysis made possible by uniform accounting has value to the marketplace. Accounting standardization, indeed, was a major project of the American Petroleum Institute in the formative 1924–27 period. Greater confidence can be placed in a *private* decision reached through voluntary consensus than in *forced* uniformity, which bypasses the normal selection process and has proven superficial and distortive. With the past open to varying interpretation and the future marked by unexpected change, there cannot be a singular "scientific" representation of financial information. With different industries, companies within industries, management philosophies, and expectations, there is room for different accounting procedures to convey information. This is where financial and investment specialists perform their market function for the creditor and investor. By forcing monolithic accounting to combat "misrepresentation," the SEC itself misrepresented the heterogeneity of the business world. In Thomas Taylor's estimation:

> [The] bureaucratic approach fails to come to grips with the critical problem of the [dispersed] nature of knowledge in a highly complex society. . . . It is simplistic to think that accounting information can portray this reality through a single conceptual framework.[113]

The activist role of the SEC and other regulatory agencies in accounting theory and practice in the 1970s is open to further criticism. Forcing disclosure of sensitive information, such as oil and

---

[112]James Dohr, "Power Price Fixing," *Journal of Accountancy* (June 1945): 432. The tension between regulatory objectives and private accounting was verified by the Supreme Court's complaint of the "fetish of mere accounting." *FPC* v. *Hope Natural Gas Co.*, 320 U.S. 591 at 643 (1944).

[113]Thomas Taylor, "The Politicization of a Profession," p. 5.

gas reserves, causes rivalrous behavior to be replaced by nonmarket cooperation. Required presentation of reserves as supplemental information on financial statements at the highly inapproximate figure of market value (as opposed to cost) did not eliminate misrepresentation to the investor but added downside risk when estimates were overstated, as sometimes was the case.

Last, a national energy database is not preferable to nonregulation and inadequate (from the regulators' viewpoint) industry statistics. As detailed in other chapters, energy planning in the 1971–80 era not only failed but had no chance of succeeding. The accuracy and availability of data were not crucial to this failure.

With an end to the energy crisis, accounting controversies unique to oil and gas subsided. But as long as there is pervasive regulation of the economy and legislative blessing of "social accounting," controversial FASB pronouncements and SEC intervention remain an uncertainty that the energy industry and its investors cannot escape.

Subsidization of Synthetic Fuels

Pessimism about resources on the part of the federal government inspired subsidies to synthetically produced oil or gas, or both, from coal, shale, tar sands, agricultural and farming products, and waste materials. The original goal was to meet anticipated domestic oil and gas demand; later, the goal was expanded to ensuring national security by reducing dependence on imports. The history of this effort to date (1984) is summarized below.

Early Period

The production of synthetic fuels was a market phenomenon that predated oil-well drilling. Gas manufactured from coal, and to a lesser extent whale oil and rosin oil, was the "largest and fastest-growing branch of the illuminating industry in America" in the 1850s.[114] By 1860, an estimated 400 plants representing a $56-million investment had annual sales of $17 million.[115] Also in the 1850s, the coal-oil industry thrived. Shale oil, which reached peak production of 30,000 gallons a day in 1860, joined manufactured gas to replace candles for many Americans.[116]

---

[114]Harold Williamson and Arnold Daum, *The Age of Illumination*, p. 40.
[115]Ibid., p. 57.
[116]Ibid.

The fall of synthetic oil and gas was even more rapid than their rise. Oil from the Pennsylvania fields displaced coal oil in the early 1860s. When natural-gas wells were discovered near coal-gas markets, coal gasification was abandoned as uneconomical. Predictions of oil shortages by the Interior Department and the Department of the Navy, which led to the establishment of the naval petroleum reserves between 1912 and 1923, led the U.S. Geological Survey to conduct field studies on shale oil beginning in 1917. Shale-oil production in England served as a model. Another Interior agency, the Bureau of Mines, proposed to investigate the commercial feasibility of oil-shale plants. Federal authorities, the *Oil & Gas Journal* reported, considered the synfuels issue an "important question of conservation" and hoped to create "an oil supply more valuable even than the crude petroleum."[117]

A second brush with synfuels occurred in the 1925–29 period when the Bureau of Mines resumed research on shale-oil extraction. The commercial stage was reached, and 3,600 barrels of oil were extracted from 6,000 tons of Colorado oil shale. With the rise of the Texas and Oklahoma oil fields in the late 1920s, interest in synfuels waned; funding was halted until the mid-1930s when small quantities of gasoline were extracted from lignite and bituminous coal.[118]

Second Period: 1944–55

Oil-supply problems due to price controls and other anti-production policies during World War II renewed federal enthusiasm for the production of synthetic fuels. Congressional hearings began in the summer of 1942, and a year later a bill sponsored by coal-state congressmen to produce oil fuels and lubricants from coal, shale, and natural gas was debated.[119] Interior Secretary Harold Ickes pushed for similar legislation by arguing:

> The United States is losing ground as the outstanding producer of petroleum. Since 1938, the consumption of petroleum in the United States has exceeded the discovery of new reserves. I believe the time

[117]*OGJ*, February 22, 1917, p. 30.

[118]*NPN*, August 5, 1943, p. 19.

[119]Subcommittee on Mining and Natural Resources of the House Committee on Mines and Mining, *Production of Gasoline, Rubber, and Other Materials from Coal and Other Products*, 77th Cong., 2d sess., June 17–18, 25, July 15, 1942 (Washington, D.C.: Government Publishing Office, 1942).

is at hand for more intensive research in the production of synthetic fuels, especially with regard to larger-scale demonstration plants, both for possible war use and in the postwar era.[120]

Another argument within the Interior Department was that great advances in conversion were imminent, and if government, instead of a major company, uncovered the secrets, many small firms could carry on instead of one firm or several.[121]

Foremost in the minds of officials was Nazi Germany, which produced half of its gasoline synthetically.[122] Also encouraging was the domestic precedent of synthetic rubber production, which received a $750-million federal grant in 1941, administered by Jersey Standard. The prevailing opinion among officials was that the next war would find an even greater role for synfuels.[123]

Debate over the synfuel bill centered on the proposed $30-million allocation, which was well below amounts other countries were spending on similar commercialization. Secondary in the debate was the opportunity cost of federal-private development of synfuels, which was already under way. Stated A. W. Gauger, professor of mineral industry research at Pennsylvania State College:

> There has been a growing tendency to create new laboratories and agencies and to seek our men and men from other state or private organizations to man them. This process inhibits instead of accelerates progress and is at best a costly, wasteful procedure.[124]

On April 5, 1944, the Synthetic Liquid Fuels Act authorized $30 million for the Bureau of Mines for "construction and operation of demonstration plants to produce synthetic liquid fuels from coal, oil shales, agricultural and forestry products, and other substances, in order to aid the prosecution of the war, to conserve and increase

[120]*NPN,* August 5, 1973, p. 19.

[121]Craufurd Goodwin, "Truman Administration Policies toward Particular Energy Sources," in *Energy Policy in Perspective,* ed. Craufurd Goodwin (Washington, D.C.: Brookings Institution, 1981), p. 147.

[122]An overview of Germany's synfuel production is contained in J. Brian Eby, "Germany's Oil Fields and Synthetic Plants," *Oil Weekly,* February 4, 1946, pp. 12–18.

[123]Craufurd Goodwin, "Truman Administration Policies toward Particular Energy Sources," pp. 147–48.

[124]*NPN,* January 12, 1944, p. 5. University research, however, was primarily government financed.

the oil resources of the Nation, and for other purposes."[125] Within five years, one or more demonstration plants were to be built and maintained. Those plants were to be of a "minimum size which will allow the Government to furnish industry the necessary cost and engineering data," yet not be so large as to "constitute a commercially significant amount of the total national commercial sale and distribution of petroleum and petroleum products."[126] Any synfuels produced were to be sold at cost or below cost to the War Department or Navy Department on request. Remaining supply could fetch the going price on the private market.

The end of wartime did not diminish the zeal of the synthetic-fuels lobby. The coal industry faced unprecedented competition from natural gas, and problems with oil and gas supply during 1947 and 1948 reinforced the pessimistic view of government officials.[127] With expiration of the act set for mid-1949, Interior Secretary Julius Krug lobbied for a $9-billion commitment to synfuels with a five- to ten-year short-term production goal of 2 million barrels per day.[128] With current synfuel output at 50 barrels per day from a Rifle, Colorado, plant and 200 barrels per day from a Louisiana, Missouri, plant, and laboratories in Pennsylvania, West Virginia, and Wyoming without commercial capabilities, this goal was scarcely imaginable, even after surviving assets of and technical information from Germany's synthetic-fuels industry were secured.

Amid optimistic pronouncements from the Interior Department that "the unknowns are falling away one by one" and that the United States would realize "oil independence at any time that our dwindling . . . reserves make it necessary to turn to synthetic sources of gasoline,"[129] President Truman extended the program three years

---

[125]Public Law 290, 58 Stat. 190 (1944).

[126]Ibid.

[127]Postwar supply problems are described in chapter 24, pp. 1432–39.

[128]*NPN*, January 28, 1948, p. 19. Krug argued: "The country . . . is squeezed between increasing demand and decreasing productive capacity. The effect already is reflected in local shortages." For a pro-con debate on subsidized synfuel development, see James Boyd and A. L. Solliday, "Should the Government Build a Synthetic-Oil Industry?" *Modern Industry*, July 15, 1948, pp. 100–106.

[129]Quoted in Craufurd Goodwin, "Truman Administration Policies toward Particular Energy Sources," p. 149.

and doubled spending authority to $60 million.[130] Opposing the bill were the Independent Petroleum Association of America and individual producers who feared increased competition if demonstration production was significantly increased or a technological breakthrough occurred.[131]

On September 22, 1950, a second (and final) extension and expansion of the program became law.[132] Three more years made the total duration of the program eleven years, and $27.6 million was added to bring the cumulative authorization to $87.6 million. Although no breakthroughs had occurred to achieve cost parity and optimism was more guarded, the new emphasis was on *national security*. Secretary of Defense James Forrestal saw synfuels as a potential savior in "a major war effort" where demand "would exceed by at least 2 million [barrels per day] the now predictable production of the U.S."[133] The coal industry remained adamantly in favor of synthetic production to replace demand lost to fuel oil and particularly natural gas. Another constituency was the administering agency, the Bureau of Mines, and alliances favored one of the four particular synfuel processes: coal hydrogenation, shale-oil recovery, gas synthesis, and gas conversion to liquid fuel.[134]

The Korean conflict offered proponents of synfuels another chance to take the offensive. Bureau of Mines director James Boyd lobbied Interior Secretary Oscar Chapman for two 15,000 barrel per day coal-hydrogenation facilities at a cost of $326 million as a step toward "ultimate self-sufficiency in liquid fuels."[135]

Secretary Chapman lobbied the Defense Production Administration for $455 million, primarily for private-development incentives. In the commercialization debate, the oil industry more than ever before scrutinized the claims and results of the Bureau of Mines to find that, indeed, little progress toward competitive parity had been

---

[130]Public Law 443, 62 Stat. 79 (1948). One million dollars was appropriated to conduct research on secondary recovery from stripper wells and refining processes.

[131]*NPN*, May 5, 1948, p. 16.

[132]Public Law 812, 64 Stat. 905 (1950).

[133]*NPN*, March 2, 1949, p. 11.

[134]Craufurd Goodwin, "Truman Administration Policies toward Particular Energy Sources," p. 155.

[135]Ibid., p. 159. Boyd looked to the Defense Production Act of 1950 for funding authorization and predicted a profit within twelve years.

made. A National Petroleum Council study released in October 1951 estimated the cost of gasoline from coal hydrogenation at $0.414 per gallon compared to the government estimate of $0.11 per gallon.[136] Robert Wilson, chairman of Indiana Standard, complained that the Bureau of Mines understated cost, overstated revenue, and failed to account for risk in its capital-cost estimates.[137]

Retrospective study of the debate confirmed oil-industry concern. "What is most disillusioning about the debate over synthetic fuels that ranged within government during the Korean War," Craufurd Goodwin remarked, "is that more and more it was conducted by determined special interests making exaggerated claims on all sides."[138] Another factor that inhibited a major commitment to synfuels was scarce supplies of steel and other raw materials that would have to be withdrawn from other wartime uses on the gamble of a long-term payoff.

With the close of the Korean conflict, enlarged synfuel proposals were no longer seriously considered. In 1953, one of two major oil-shale demonstration plants was sold to private interests. In the same year, the head of the Bureau of Mines, W. C. Schroeder, resigned with the statement, "Now that the government is out of the synthetics development program, I am sure that private industry will go ahead with the Louisiana plant, and the information they gain will eventually be passed along to the public in the form of patents."[139] In April 1955, the Synthetic Liquid Fuels Act expired, although over $4 million earmarked for synthetic-fuel research was included in Interior's 1955 budget.[140] In eleven years, $82 million had been spent out of an $85.2-million allocation. Along with other Interior appropriations, synfuel subsidies totaled over $106 million as shown in table 10.2.

The eleven-year, $107-million allocation did not result in any major breakthroughs to make synfuels economical. This result was predictable, given the caution of private industry about major investments

[136]Ibid., p. 163. Other studies reduced the discrepancy but still found the government figures, which still were well below parity with conventional oil-lifting costs, understated.

[137]Ibid.

[138]Ibid., p. 158.

[139]*NPN*, September 9, 1953, p. 13.

[140]*NPN*, January 20, 1954, p. 19.

Table 10.2
ALLOCATIONS FOR SYNTHETIC FUELS
(thousands of dollars)

Date	Coal Research & Development	Coal Demonstration	Oil Shale Research & Development	Oil Shale Demonstration	Oil Shale Construction	Total
1945	2,750	340	585	915	2,403	6,993
1946	2,598	2,739	225	1,439	3,937	10,938
1947	1,371	2,120	429	1,330	2,124	7,374
1948	1,775	3,500	375	1,350	2,379	9,379
1949	2,771	8,379	500	2,100	7,680	21,430
1950	2,528	4,625	598	1,998	1,671	11,420
1951	2,335	3,754	510	1,800	718	9,117
1952	2,213	3,326	480	1,615	718	8,352
1953	4,886	3,193	482	1,475	2,850	12,886
1954	2,359	297	482	1,541	200	4,879
1955	2,305	—	477	1,257	—	4,039
Total	27,891	32,273	5,143	16,820	24,680	106,807

SOURCE: U.S. Department of the Interior, Bureau of Mines, *Synthetic Liquid Fuels Program, 1944–55* (Washington, D.C.: Government Printing Office, 1959), p. 4.

in the area. Cost parity between derived oil and gas and crude oil and natural gas remained elusive. As did other government energy programs before and after, the synfuels effort became more politicized and less focused over time. Pork-barrel influences transcended the scientific despite the limited scope of the effort.[141] If, indeed, a greater private role was economical, relaxation of antitrust law was called for to allow cooperative research and development through trade groups such as the American Petroleum Institute or a specially formed corporation. Instead, the majors were concentrating on developing foreign fields, which resulted in a level of imports in the 1950s that not only drowned the most optimistic hopes for synfuel commercialization but led to import quotas to protect domestic crude production.[142]

Third Period: 1971–84

The problems of the post-World War II synfuel effort were forgotten during the energy crises of the 1970s. New alarms were sounded, and "quick-fix" solutions were sought in research on and development and commercialization of synthetic fuels.

Research and Development. Newfound activism in energy policy began with a June 4, 1971, message to Congress by President Nixon, "A Program to Insure an Adequate Supply of Clean Energy in the Future." Nixon would later identify this as "the first message on energy policies ever submitted by an American President."[143] Oil supply was growing tighter, and natural gas was experiencing shortages in interstate markets. With abundant coal reserves and shale reserves, Nixon envisioned a greater future role for synfuels. He also announced that "in addition to its coal gasification work, the

---

[141]The debate over an expanded program during the Korean conflict led Craufurd Goodwin to state: "The prospect of substantial funds becoming available at last for synthetic fuel production drew the attention of those influential members of Congress who hoped for facilities to be constructed in their districts. It also brought one of the few direct interventions from [Truman] into the synthetics program in behalf of 'my good friend Harley O. Staggers' and the experimental station in Morgantown, West Virginia." Goodwin, "Truman Administration Policies toward Particular Energy Sources," p. 160.

[142]See chapter 13, pp. 726–35.

[143]Office of the President, *Executive Energy Documents* (Washington, D.C.: Government Printing Office, 1978), p. 14.

Department of the Interior has under way a major pilot plant program directed toward converting coal into cleaner liquid fuels," and proposed an "expanded program" to liquefy coal and "the orderly formulation" of shale-oil leasing on federal lands.[144]

Nixon's infatuation with new energy sources led to budget increases for synfuel-related Interior Department programs. The 1974 budget of $120 million for coal research and development was 300 percent above 1970 amounts. A roadblock to coal and shale conversion, however, was strip-mining reserves and coal emissions, which cooled Congress toward Nixon's request for a $10-billion, five-year crash program of energy research and development. Another unsuccessful Nixon initiative in troubled 1973 was a windfall profits tax to underwrite an energy development trust fund to undertake "a wide range of energy development and conservation projects which might not otherwise be feasible."[145]

President Ford continued Nixon's interest in alternative fuel development with a major emphasis on synthetic fossil fuels. On October 11, 1974, Ford signed the Energy Research and Development Administration Act into law, with a $2.2-billion budget and a 7,000-person staff taken largely from the abolished Atomic Energy Commission.[146] Synfuel programs within the Interior Department were transferred to the new agency, but the bulk of activity was in the nuclear and environmental areas. On January 19, 1975, the Energy Research and Development Administration (ERDA) was activated by executive order to "bear the responsibility for leading the National effort to develop the needed technology to assure that the United States will have ample and secure supplies of energy at reasonable prices."[147]

The Federal Non-Nuclear Energy Research and Development Act, passed several months later, declared that a $20-billion, ten-year research effort in nonnuclear areas was necessary and directed the ERDA administrator to present a comprehensive plan to Congress

[144]Ibid., pp. 1, 5, 7.

[145]Ibid., p. 114.

[146]Public Law 93-438, 88 Stat. 1233 (1974). Other alternative-fuel legislation in the solar and geothermal areas is surveyed in chapter 27, p. 1679. An overview of these research areas is contained in Richard Greeley, "Advanced Energy Technology," in *Free Market Energy*, ed. S. Fred Singer (New York: Universe Books, 1984), pp. 308–42.

[147]Office of the President, *Executive Energy Documents*, p. 249.

the next year.[148] Federal assistance to private-sector projects, such as price guarantees and loans, was authorized, although congressional approval was required for amounts over $50 million.

In his 1975 State of the Union address, President Ford set a goal of 1 million barrels per day of synfuels by 1985. After a request for $6 billion for loan guarantees and an oil-shale demonstration plant was rejected by the House after Senate approval, Ford unveiled a $100-billion plan, spearheaded by Vice President Nelson Rockefeller, to subsidize a variety of energy projects, prominently including synfuels, through the commercialization phase. Originally called the Energy Resources Finance Corporation and later changed to the Energy Independence Authority, the ten-year program with $25 billion in equity and $75 billion in Treasury credit was soundly rejected by fiscal conservatives and suspicious Democrats.[149]

President Carter shared the optimism of the previous two presidents about alternative energy sources and synthetic oil and gas production in particular. On November 17, 1979, Carter established the Energy Security Reserve within the Treasury Department with a $19-billion appropriation.[150] Of this amount, $1.5 billion was made available to the Department of Energy (DOE), formed on October 1, 1977, to consolidate the ERDA and many other energy-related agencies, "for purchases or production by way of purchase commitments or price guarantees of alternative fuels." Another $708 million was made available for immediate DOE use "to support preliminary alternative fuels commercialization activities": $100 million for project feasibility, $100 million for cooperative agreements, $8 million for administration, and $500 million to cover defaults of guaranteed indebtedness not to exceed $1.5 billion.

As of 1984, an estimated 2,000 contracts, amounting to over $2 billion, had been awarded by the DOE for research on and development of synthetic fuels. Grants ranged from underwriting laboratory chemists to funding major field projects. Twenty pilot plants in various synfuel areas were completed, and actual production came

---

[148]Public Law 93-577, 88 Stat. 1878 (1974).

[149]Neil de Marchi, "The Ford Administration: Energy as a Political Good," in *Energy Policy in Perspective*, p. 520.

[150]Public Law 96-126, 93 Stat. 970 (1979), pursuant to the Non-Nuclear Energy Research and Development Act, Public Law 93-575, 88 Stat. 1878 (1974).

on stream at sites in California, North Dakota, Tennessee, and Illinois.[151]

The Department of Energy Act authorized loan guarantees for alternative-fuel demonstration projects.[152] In July 1980, President Carter approved in principle a $1.5-billion loan guarantee to the Great Plains Coal Gasification Project, which had earlier failed to attract the interest of private investors. The tentative agreement expired, and in August 1981, Reagan approved a new proposal that was finalized on January 29, 1982.[153] The $2.02-billion nonrecourse loan, equivalent to 75 percent of the anticipated total cost of the project, was funded by the Treasury Department's Federal Financing Bank at 0.75 percent over that bank's variable rate. Repayment was to be within 20 years or within 90 percent of the expected useful life of the project assets. As a nonrecourse loan, default leaves the DOE with the assets of the project and no claim on project sponsors Tenneco (30 percent), American Natural Resources Company (25 percent), Transco (20 percent), MidCon Corporation (15 percent), and Pacific Lighting (10 percent). As of May 31, 1984, equity partners had contributed $463 million and federal borrowings were $1.17 billion.[154] In November 1984, production began at 50 percent of the plant's 137 million cubic feet per day capacity with the help of a guaranteed price contract.

Other major synfuel projects requested financial assistance under DOE authority but would wait until the synfuel program expanded in 1980.

Commercialization: The Synthetic Fuels Corporation. In April 1979, Carter proposed an energy security fund financed by a windfall profits tax, with 76 percent of its funding dedicated to alternative-fuel development. After five years of improved oil supplies, Congress was not motivated to underwrite a major program. It would take the summer gasoline lines in 1979 to set the sails of a new

---

[151]Conversation with Bob Porter, information officer, Fossil Energy Program, Department of Energy, November 6, 1984.

[152]Public Law 95-238, 92 Stat. 47 (1978).

[153]*OGJ*, August 10, 1981, p. 59, and February 8, 1982, p. 67.

[154]Government Accounting Office, "Status of the Great Plains Coal Gasification Project—May 31, 1984," September 18, 1984, p. 1.

synfuel commitment. During the second half of 1979, Congress rallied behind the White House for federally subsidized synfuel commercialization despite opposition from environmental and business groups. Opposition was also heard from quarters of the oil industry.

On June 30, 1980, the Energy Security Act became law.[155] To Carter, it was "the cornerstone of U.S. energy policy"; to critics, it was a "cookie-jar bill," prone to politics and misdirection of resources. With synfuel production targets of 500,000 barrels per day by 1987 and 2 million barrels per day by 1992, $88 billion was authorized for an Energy Security Reserve. Of this amount, $20 billion was available immediately to underwrite contracts, loan guarantees, and direct loans to private projects. Only as a last resort was public money to be used for federal projects. Net of previous funding by the DOE, $17.522 billion was earmarked for Title I with $12.212 billion for the corporation—$6 billion available on July 8, 1980, and $6.212 billion available on June 30, 1982.[156]

The commercialization program was to be administered by the United States Synthetic Fuels Corporation (SFC), which Congress modeled after a private corporate entity. The agency was to have a chairman, a board of directors, and regular financial audits. Strict congressional oversight was to prevent autonomous behavior and give Congress the high ground.

A companion bill to place up to seventy-five "critical" energy projects on a fast track by waiving environmental requirements failed. With coal and shale at the heart of the synfuel program, environmental exemptions by an energy mobilization board would have cut preparation cost and reduced delay to complement the Energy Security Act. Environmental interests were too strong for pro-Carter forces, and the House rejected the measure on June 27, 1980.

The unprecedented commitment to synfuels was a second chance for major projects that were stalled under the DOE's more limited authorization. It was also an invitation for new firms to enter the

---

[155]Public Law 96-294, 94 Stat. 611 (1980). Title I, Synthetic Fuels, was joined by other sections covering the alternative-fuel waterfront: Title II, Biomass Energy and Alcohol Fuels; Title V, Solar Energy and Energy Conservation; and Title VI, Geothermal Energy.

[156]Dana Contratto, "A Billion Here, a Billion There," *Energy Law Journal*, no. 2 (1980): 257–58. Further allocations required congressional approval.

area. The National Council on Synthetic Fuels Production, headed by a former draftsman of synfuel legislation, was opened in Washington, D.C., to represent businesses in pursuit of subsidies. The level of interest was indicated by 951 applications received in June 1980 by the DOE for $200 million for synfuel feasibility studies. With oil prices continuing to rise, a new industry seemed destined to develop.

Carter quickly staffed the SFC, and on November 21, 1980, the first solicitation for private-project aid was made. Despite the quick start, Carter's reelection defeat and a new budget-conscious administration raised uncertainty about the federal commitment. Despite advice from his transition team to abolish the program, Reagan filled open positions in the SFC and increased the sponsor-equity requirement of subsidized projects to 40 percent from 25 percent. As stated in the third *National Energy Policy Plan* released in July 1981:

> The Administration has restructured the National Synthetic Fuels Program to rely more heavily on private investment initiatives and less on the general taxpayer. Responsibility for commercializing the technologies of alternative fuels is shifting to the private sector, with potential support from the Synthetic Fuels Corporation.[157]

New life was pumped into synfuel subsidization in the summer of 1981 when Reagan broke a deadlock between White House aides and approved major DOE subsidies for three projects. On July 29, a $2-billion project of Union Oil to produce 50,000 barrels per day of crude oil from Colorado shale received $400 million in price guarantees and purchase commitments.[158] On August 5, a $2-billion loan guarantee was awarded to the Great Plains Coal Gasification Project, and a $1.1-billion loan guarantee was given to Tosco's portion of the Colony Oil Shale Project, jointly owned with Exxon. With these commitments, and previous subsidies to Ashland ($215 million for coal oil), Gulf ($90 million for coal oil), Northern Illinois ($50 million for coal gasification), Conoco ($38 million for coal gasification), and Memphis Light, Gas, and Water ($26 million for coal

---

[157]U.S. Department of Energy, *National Energy Policy Plan—III* (Washington, D.C.: Government Printing Office, 1981), p. 11.

[158]Union Oil of California was a veteran of synfuel proposals to government. In 1953, a 10,000 barrel per day shale-oil proposal for the same geographical area unsuccessfully sought federal assistance. *NPN*, October 28, 1953, p. 16.

gasification), the DOE synthetic-fuel program was terminated and transferred to the SFC, which was officially declared operational—ready to grant direct and indirect subsidies—on February 9, 1982.[159]

In the first solicitation period ending March 31, 1981, sixty-three proposals were submitted. Requests for supplemental information by January 4, 1982, narrowed the number to twenty-seven, which government screening reduced to eleven and then five. By mid-1982, only two coal projects remained under consideration, with many other proposals, some recycled, in the early stages of a second solicitation held from December 11, 1981, to May 31, 1982.[160]

Meanwhile, the bottom fell out of the synfuel market. With falling energy prices shattering optimistic projections of steadily rising prices to allow break-even points and profitability for synfuels in future decades, major projects were terminated. In March 1982, Panhandle Eastern suspended indefinitely a coal-gasification project in Wyoming. Two months later, Exxon abandoned the Colony Oil Shale Project and bought out Tosco pursuant to their agreement. Thanks to Exxon's prudence in not seeking guarantees—indeed, it was a critic of government largess in the area—no taxpayer loss resulted. Also in May, Ashland dropped plans for a $13-billion tar-sands project.[161] Other projects continued but only because of the lure of SFC bailouts. Union and Great Plains approached authorities for price supports to cut losses once production came on stream, sweetening earlier loan subsidies.

The new price reality, excess supply of conventional energy sources, and the slow pace of commitments brought heated criticism from Congress. Bills were introduced to abolish or scale down the program. Still, industry interest remained. As 1982 drew to a close, forty-six proposals were received in a third SFC solicitation.

In April 1983, the SFC made its first grant. The $820,750-subsidy, for design work on a project to convert carbonized vegetable tissue to methanol, was an ironic beginning to the Carter legacy. Not only was the project esoteric and puny, given several years of SFC solicitation and evaluation of over a hundred proposals, its financial

---

[159]*Forbes*, March 30, 1981, p. 36; and *Wall Street Journal*, July 30, 1981, p. 8, and August 6, 1981, p. 6.

[160]*OGJ*, January 11, 1982, p. 40, January 25, 1982, p. 94, and June 14, 1982, p. 40.

[161]*OGJ*, March 29, 1982, p. 53, and May 10, 1982, pp. 86, 94.

backers included many well-known Republican figures—former Federal Energy Administration head Frank Zarb, former ERDA head Robert Fri, Central Intelligence Agency director William Casey, and former deputy secretary of state Charles Robinson.[162] The same year, a $46.5-million loan guarantee was made to a California tar-sands project sponsored by Tenneco and four others, as was a $120-million price support award to the Cool Water Coal Gasification Project of Texaco and Southern California Edison. Another Tenneco project, co-owned with Occidental Petroleum, the Cathedral Bluffs Shale Oil Company, received a nonbinding commitment of $2.2 billion in loan guarantees and price guarantees equivalent to $60 per barrel.

SFC administration engendered controversy. In August 1983, President John Schroeder resigned after it was discovered that he had awarded consulting contracts to former business associates. His replacement, Victor Thompson, was forced to step down in May 1984 when it was revealed that, as a director of the SFC, he had attempted to sell stock in his ailing bank to sponsors of a pending synfuel request. With Thompson's resignation, the agency did not have a quorum, and the need for new appointments to reactivate the SFC put the ball in Reagan's court. Reagan used that leverage later in 1984 to cut $5.4 billion from its authorization in return for a promise to congressional synfuel proponents to fill the vacant posts and leave the remaining $8 billion authorization alone. Irregularities in the information in another project application added controversy to a troubled period.

Criticism also came from doctrinaire congressional synfuel advocates, not coincidentally representing coal and shale states, who faulted the SFC for not making commitments equal to budgeted authority, which left synfuel production far below targets set in the Energy Security Act of 1980. In an effort to achieve active status, commitments of $4.4 billion were granted to six projects in April 1984.[163] This increased opposition from the other side, the anti-synfuel legislators, who complained of corporate welfare and doubling a bad proposition. Union Oil received $2.7 billion in $60 per barrel price guarantees for a second-phase expansion, while its first phase

[162]*Houston Post*, April 14, 1983, p. A-24.

[163]*OGJ*, April 16, 1984, pp. 36–37. While new commitments were announced, a fourth solicitation was under way.

was behind schedule. Dow Chemical received price guarantees of $620 million for a coal-oil plant in Louisiana that equated to between $11.00 and $12.50 per million British thermal units. A Texas heavy-oil project received $60 million and a California heavy-oil project received $100 million in price and loan guarantees. A Kentucky tar-sands project received $543 million in price supports as high as $55 per barrel, and a Maine carbonization project received $365 million in price and loan guarantees. All of these projects had more in common than qualification as synfuels. They were uneconomic risks under market conditions made economic by potential calls on tax dollars.

In August 1984, the troubled Great Plains Coal Gasification Project received a letter of intent from the SFC for $709 million in price supports after threatening to walk away from the project leaving a $2-billion loan guarantee for authorities to retire. In October of the previous year, the price-support request had been denied, but upon reconsideration, 65 percent of the $2-billion request was tentatively awarded. Great Plains continued to face financial uncertainties, emblematic of the entire synfuel program in the face of continuing declines in energy prices through 1984.

Evaluation. A critical review of the history of synthetic-fuel development in the United States does not rest on crystal-ball assumptions of future supply and demand and thus the price of conventional oil and gas. While known reserves of synthetic-fuel feedstocks may outdistance proven and estimated reserves of crude oil and natural gas, and while synfuel commercialization is technologically feasible (and has been since at least World War II), forward-looking entrepreneurs dealing with relative prices (relative scarcities) have concluded again and again since the Pennsylvania oil strikes of the 1860s that oil and gas synthetics are uneconomic. While in the business world this means unprofitable, for society it means that resources capable of satisfying higher wants are expended on lesser wants.

Despite the market verdict, unfounded pessimism about future reserves of conventional fuels and unfounded optimism about imminent technological breakthroughs to achieve competitive parity have led to taxpayer subsidies and moral suasion by government to develop synthetic fuels. The experiences of 1944–55 and 1971–84 speak for themselves. Breakthroughs were not achieved, and in fact, conventional fuels increased their competitive advantage during both periods. In retrospect, shortcuts to energy prosperity were naive illusions.

The error of government synfuel subsidization can be fully appreciated in historical context. During World War II, wellhead regulation reduced incentives to produce and locate new reserves, which was worsened by downstream regulation to the point of physical shortages.[164] From this politically created predicament, the wrong conclusion was drawn, that supply was fixed and running out, and synthetic fuel research and development were necessary for a new energy era. In the 1970s, the same mistake was repeated in magnified form. Price and allocation controls dulled incentives for domestic exploration and production, drove up world energy prices, and created physical shortages.[165] To President Carter, the guilty regulations were necessary in their own right to prevent inflation and to equitably distribute supply. This left the problem of supply, which he attributed to the niggardliness of nature that synfuels in part could conquer. Without consequential government intervention in World War II and the 1970s, the supply problem would not have existed for a government "solution."

Much intellectual error in the synthetic-fuels debate could have been avoided if it had been realized that natural resources can— and have—become less scarce over time. Even so-called depletable resources are economically infinite because changing technology and prices change recoverable supply. In fact, improving technology or just plain luck can increase supply faster than it is consumed. Julian Simon has documented that a number of natural resources, including oil, have experienced flat or declining prices adjusted for inflation. While short-run dislocations such as "weather, war, politics, and population movements" may cause supply crises and higher prices, "human resourcefulness and enterprise . . . leave us better off than before the problem arose."[166] The behavior of oil and gas in the regulated 1970s—compared with the less regulated 1980s—is a case in point.

---

[164]See chapter 5, pp. 243–48, and chapter 24, pp. 1409–26.

[165]See chapter 9 and chapter 27 generally.

[166]Julian Simon, *The Ultimate Resource* (Princeton, N.J.: Princeton University Press, 1981), p. 345.

The more recent government-funded synfuel experience (still going on in 1984) is an example of inflexibility in the face of change. Despite every indication of failure, the program continued, albeit in reduced form, with new commitments and more solicitations. Past commitments had created demand for renegotiated commitments as falling energy prices caused project economics to deteriorate. In a game of taxpayer blackmail, firms have threatened to walk away from projects, leaving loan guarantees for the SFC to liquidate. (Faced with a $2-billion tab on one project, the government consented to new price supports.) With under $1 billion expended and nearly $7 billion on the line, the worst was yet to come for taxpayers. The same was true for shareholders of involved companies whose decision to take the government bait and take equity positions was increasingly being revealed as entrepreneurial error.

Miscellaneous

Oil-Well Torpedo Monopoly: 1866–79

In the first years of oil production, flowing wells were sometimes hindered by a waxy substance, paraffin, that crude oil left in the well tubing and well bottom.[167] Early efforts to remove residue involved injecting steam, boiling liquids, and air into a well's tubing. These mildly successful techniques were then replaced by a far superior alternative—oil-well torpedoing. Gun-powder explosions in water wells had been documented as early as 1808, and between 1860 and 1864, the technique was in use with oil wells as well. Despite its early use, Civil War Colonel E. A. L. Roberts claimed to have discovered the idea in 1862 at the Battle of Fredericksburg after witnessing the results of cannon fire into a water canal. On November 18, 1864, he applied to the U.S. Patent Office for "a process of increasing the productiveness of oil-wells by causing an explosion of gunpowder or its equivalent at or near the oil-bearing point, in connection with superincumbent fluid-pampering."[168] Despite similar patent applications from several well-shooting practitioners, two years later,

---

[167]This discussion comes from John McLaurin, *Sketches in Crude Oil* (Harrisburg, Pa.: John McLaurin, 1896), pp. 383–87; and Harold Williamson and Arnold Daum, *The Age of Illumination*, pp. 149–56.

[168]John McLaurin, *Sketches in Crude Oil*, p. 385.

Roberts received "the patent that was to become a grievous monopoly."[169]

In the same year his legal monopoly was issued, Roberts opened the Roberts Petroleum Torpedo Company in New York to manufacture bombs for use in the Pennsylvania oil region. He charged monopoly prices for his services. With production costs of between $15 and $20 per torpedo, he charged from $100 to $200 per torpedo and a one-fifteenth royalty on increased output after the explosion. Would-be competitors and disgruntled oil operators formed the Producers Union Association, raised $50,000 for legal expenses, and challenged the patent in U.S. district court. The challenge was denied in 1871. Nevertheless, competition arose as Roberts's exorbitant prices attracted a black market of moonlighters who risked their lives by strapping explosives to their backs to lower into wells for discharge under the cover of darkness. Not only was this done more cheaply, which forced Roberts to reduce his prices, new innovative techniques were introduced by the nocturnal monopoly breakers. In response, Roberts hired a network of informants, which resulted in nearly 2,000 arrests. Many were jailed, and settlements added to Roberts's company coffers. With his patent reissued in 1873 and again upheld in court despite a strong case documenting well shootings prior to 1864, the scope of the government grant was narrowed and legal competition began to emerge by 1880. A year later, E. A. L. Roberts—the man responsible for more litigation than any other person in U.S. history up until his time—died, leaving behind a great fortune memorialized by a torpedo-shaped tombstone above his grave.

The torpedo innovation represented a boon for oil production. Recognized in 1866 by the editor of *Scientific American* as the most beneficial technique known to enhance recovery, it not only rejuvenated pumping wells but turned near-miss dry holes into producing properties.[170] Nonetheless, the Roberts patent was a government intervention in the petroleum market. Going beyond the legitimate bounds of common-law copyright protection, it ignored independent discovery and prior use. Moreover, the patent was given for a general idea rather than a specific technological innovation. Thus,

[169]Ibid., p. 386.
[170]Harold Williamson and Arnold Daum, *The Age of Illumination*, p. 154.

when nitroglycerin replaced gun powder and new drop methods were adopted, some of which originated with the moonlighters, Roberts was protected by the original wording of his patent.

The consequences of the torpedo monopoly were both subtle and pronounced. By unnecessarily increasing costs of oil production, the monopoly meant lower supply and higher prices for consumers of petroleum products and lower economic rents for royalty owners and well operators. Those effects were subtle compared with the other consequence—clandestine operations leading to deaths and injuries. The precise number of fatalities among Roberts's daytime operators and the nighttime black marketeers is not well documented, but available evidence suggests a greater incidence of mishap for the latter group than for the former.[171] If that is so, this intervention ranks among the more consequential of the nineteenth century.

Government Drilling

State governments occasionally have authorized publicly financed petroleum exploration and production. In 1899, the Kansas legislature permitted the city of Paola to drill wells and produce natural gas for city residents and government buildings.[172] In 1984, the Texas land commissioner successfully drilled several wells on state land when attempts to lease the land to a private party to fulfill a lawsuit settlement failed.[173]

In its lone attempt, the federal government has had much less drilling success. From 1974 through 1980, twenty-two dry holes were drilled in the Alaskan Naval Reserve, the first seven by the Navy and the next fifteen by the Interior Department. The $700-million expenditure was 20 percent more expensive than normal because multiyear contracts with subcontractors were not allowed. Another problem was that the drilling locations were concentrated on one-eighth of the reserve for environmental reasons. If privately done, fewer wells would have been drilled at less cost on more dispersed sites to better evaluate the prospect. This failure was recognized

---

[171]See James McLaurin, *Sketches in Crude Oil*, pp. 390–98.

[172]Innis Harris, "Legal History of Conservation of Oil and Gas in Kansas," in American Bar Association, *Legal History of Conservation in Oil and Gas* (Baltimore: Lord Baltimore Press, 1939), p. 39.

[173]*Houston Chronicle*, May 21, 1984, pp. 1–7.

by Congress, and bills were introduced to lease acreage to private companies for future exploratory work.[174]

State and Local Discovery Rewards

State and local governments have offered rewards for oil and gas first discovered in their jurisdiction. In 1875, Nebraska offered a $15,000 reward for oil production above 50 barrels per day for sixty or more days and $15,000 for natural-gas production above 50 thousand cubic feet (Mcf) per day for thirty or more consecutive days. It was renewed in 1903 to give $15,000 to the first oil well to produce 50 barrels per day for sixty days or 58 Mcf per day of natural gas for thirty or more continuous days.[175]

In 1901, Nevada offered a $1,000 "bounty" to the first discoverer of 5 barrels of crude oil or 100 Mcf of natural gas.[176] Undoubtedly, these state legislatures reasoned that oil and gas were indiscriminately located and simply needed to be found in their areas as they had been elsewhere to provide local industry and tax revenue for the state.

In the 1950s, a second wave of discovery rewards began when Georgia offered $100,000 to the first oil well that produced 100 barrels per day. Several years later, the reward was increased to $250,000 with the amount divided among the royalty owner, the contractor, the operator, and the workers.[177] In 1953, Tennessee offered $50,000 for a well delivering 50 barrels per day of crude oil or 24 Mcf per day of natural gas for six straight months.[178] Oil and gas had been intermittently produced in small quantities in Tennessee since 1860, but large reservoirs had not been discovered. The offer expired without a claimant. The Oregon legislature considered a $150,000 reward for the state's first petroleum discovery in 1957 but did not act on the idea.

Statutory remuneration for oil and gas finds has not been confined to the state level. Soon after the discovery of the East Texas field in

[174]*Fortune*, November 3, 1980, p. 92.

[175]W. W. Thornton, *The Law Relating to Oil and Gas* (Cincinnati: W. H. Anderson, 1925), p. 2017.

[176]Ibid., p. 2029.

[177]Robert Sullivan, "Georgia," in *Conservation of Oil and Gas, a Legal History, 1958*, ed. Robert Sullivan (Chicago: American Bar Association, 1960), p. 66.

[178]Ibid., p. 217.

late 1930, Longview, Texas, proffered $10,000 for the first find within its trading district. Within a month, an extension of the East Texas field was struck, and the reward was dispensed.[179]

Discovery rewards, amounting to contingent government subsidies, have a wasteful side to their endearing character. In the event that the lure results in drilling activity and nondiscovery, resources literally have been gambled away as a consequence of government intervention. This occurred in Georgia where "a flurry of exploratory activity" followed the reward law with disappointing results.[180] With a qualifying discovery, a redistribution of wealth occurs from taxpayers to drilling interests. It is true that subsequent production-related taxation could reduce, nullify, or exceed the initial treasury payment, but this must be balanced with the risk that the reward will produce dry holes, as historically has been the case, and the probability that the uncovered reservoir eventually would have been found without taxpayer subsidy. Further, in the event of a discovery, an economic distortion could occur if operators adjusted flow rates away from normal present-versus-future profit calculations to meet the reward's conditions. Consumer preferences could be violated if production were reduced to a minimum to meet the longevity requirement or the reservoir were damaged by above-optimum withdrawal rates to meet the flow minimum. These potential problems have not occurred because discoveries of this kind have not been made under a reward situation.[181]

Affirmative Action

One intervention has concerned the offshore drilling industry exclusively. In 1978 amendments to the Outer Continental Shelf Lands Act, Congress directed the Interior Department to "take such affirmative action as deemed necessary to prohibit all unlawful employment practices and to assure that no person shall, on the grounds of race, creed, color, national origin, or sex be excluded from receiving or participating in any activity, sale, or employment

---

[179]Ruth Knowles, *The Greatest Gamblers* (New York: McGraw-Hill, 1959) p. 262.

[180]Robert Sullivan, "Georgia," p. 66.

[181]Other potential problems would be marginal finds produced only to receive the award, dishonesty, or legislative relief lowering qualification requirements.

conducted pursuant to the provisions of this act."[182] The rationale
and intent of Congress was echoed three years later by Interior
Secretary James Watt: "Since the oil and gas resources of the OCS
belong to all Americans . . . all Americans should have a fair shot
at contributing to the development of these resources."[183]

On December 3, 1980, the Interior Department under Secretary
Cecil Andrus issued a final rule setting forth a program designed
to force offshore companies to purchase equipment from women-
owned business enterprises and minority-owned firms.[184] By January
2, 1981, the effective date of the regulation, five women-owned businesses were positioned to benefit from the regulation. Tubular drill
pipe, however, the most salable piece of offshore equipment, was
in short supply as a legacy of price controls, and obtaining a distribu-
torship was next to impossible for these opportunistic firms.[185] This
problem, and general industry disfavor, led to repeal on January
16, 1981, on grounds that "the requirements of the regulations were
burdensome, unnecessary, and counterproductive."[186]

The free market penalizes true discrimination (i.e., the refusal to
buy a product of better quality or at a better price or to sell a product
at a higher price because of race, sex, or any other arbitrary criterion)
by penalizing profits. The discriminator must literally pay for his
choice because of the higher cost or lower revenue implications of
his actions.[187] George Smith, founder and president of Smith Pipe
and Supply, Inc., the nation's seventh largest black-owned company
in 1981, attested to this when he opined in response to the Interior
Department rule:

---

[182]Public Law 95-372, 92 Stat. 629 (1978). The law also stated, "Any rules promulgated under this section . . . shall be similar to those established and in effect under
Title VI and Title VII of the Civil Rights Act of 1964."

[183]U.S. Department of the Interior, News release, November 10, 1981.

[184]45 *Fed. Reg.* 80258 (December 3, 1980).

[185]*Houston Post*, January 11, 1981, p. C-22.

[186]46 *Fed. Reg.* 45951 (September 16, 1981).

[187]Adds Thomas Sowell, "Translating subjective preference into overt economic
discrimination is costly for profit-seeking firms, although less so for government,
public utilities, regulated industries like banking or non-profit organizations such as
universities or hospitals." Sowell, *Ethnic America* (New York: Basic Books, 1981),
p. 292. For a general critique of government intervention to prevent discrimination,
see Sowell, *Markets and Minorities* (New York: Basic Books, 1981).

I've tried not to build my business and hopes on laws that were passed. I've tried to build on the free enterprise system. . . . Most of my customers do business with me because I give good service. They will continue to do business with me as long as I give them service and a good product at a good price.[188]

Government-mandated business, on the other hand, penalizes the buying company, consumers of final products, and more competitive firms. Contrary to the law's intent, such edicts create ill will toward privileged firms and their principals.

Bankruptcy

Another intervention applies to business enterprise in general—bankruptcy law. The Bankruptcy Act of 1898, following three earlier short-lived federal bankruptcy statutes, first allowed extracontractual dissolution of obligations.[189] Amended by numerous laws, the most important of which were the Chandler Act of 1938 and the Bankruptcy Act of 1978, U.S. bankruptcy law has encouraged dishonesty and irresponsible financial behavior through legal forgiveness and penalized more worthy debtors by increasing the risk component of interest rates.[190]

Studies are unavailable on the degree to which production-related firms have benefited from or been hurt by bankruptcy law. Had the market run its course in the early 1930s in the Texas and Oklahoma oil fields, bankruptcy law might have hindered timely consolidation, but state conservation law intervened to protect marginal firms.

---

[188]*Houston Post*, January 11, 1981, p. C-22.

[189]Act of July 1, 1898, 30 Stat. 544.

[190]Public Law 696, 52 Stat. 840 (1938); and Public Law 95-598, 92 Stat. 2549 (1978). See Lawrence White, "Bankruptcy as an Economic Intervention," *Journal of Libertarian Studies* (Winter 1977): 281–88.

PART II

INTERVENTION IN TRANSPORTATION AND ALLOCATION

11. Early Intervention

This chapter describes the development of the transportation phase of the petroleum industry in the nineteenth century and the government intervention that affected it. The opening section describes transportation in the aftermath of the Pennsylvania oil strikes. The introduction of oil pipelines, in particular, rounded out what innovative waterway transport had begun. The next section describes pre-1860 government subsidies to roads, barges and waterways, and railroads that shaped the transportation nexus and, indirectly, the population centers that the oil industry inherited.

Regulation of oil pipelines, while not the first government intervention in the petroleum industry, represented the first systematic—and enduring—regulation of the industry. Pennsylvania, Ohio, New York, West Virginia, and Kansas, at the request of segments of the oil industry, passed laws mandating common carriage, eminent domain, common purchasing, and rate maximums for intrastate lines. Standard Oil was a target of such legislation beginning in the late 1870s. Discussion of federal regulation, which began in 1906 and was also inspired by Standard Oil, is postponed until chapter 14, which studies state and federal regulation in the twentieth century.

The next section focuses on regulation and subsidization of railroads from 1860 through 1900. The major development was entry and rate regulation placed on interstate lines in 1887. The Act to Regulate Interstate Commerce (Interstate Commerce Act) began as an anti-Standard bill to prohibit rebates but was expanded into a self-imposed antidote for "cutthroat" competition for many interstate lines.

The chapter concludes by critically evaluating the theory and practice of mode-specific regulation of intermodal transportation. The problems of specific intervention are found to be compounded by general transportation planning. On an empirical level, the intervention is found to have been counterproductive to a healthy transportation sector and efficient resource allocation in the economy as a whole.

Development of the Petroleum-Transportation Phase

The Titusville oil strike in 1859 immediately uncovered a problem of transportation.[1] The approximately 30,000 miles of railroad trackage existing in 1860 were not built with oil wells and refineries in mind. The closest railroad to Colonel Edward Drake's well was 25 miles away, and only ragged wagon trails, usable only under favorable weather conditions, existed. "Clearly," concluded Harold Williamson and Arnold Daum, "the mildest success in petroleum production would place a heavy burden on existing transport or handling facilities."[2]

The demand for transportation for crude oil literally had to create its supply. One recognized alternative to costly wagon transportation by teamster crews[3] was to move barreled oil by waterway. Early wells, drilled on the pregeological theory of "creekology," were near tributaries of the Allegheny River, which offered a direct route to the major Pittsburgh refining market. A problem existed, however, because low water levels on the Oil Creek tributary prevented passage during parts of the year. This obstacle invited ingenuity, and petroleum producers and shippers banded together to negotiate with nearby sawmill operators to open their dam floodgates to raise the water to navigable levels. *Pond fresheting*, as it was called, had been used on a smaller scale by lumbermen to float timber to market. A per barrel toll was arranged by shippers to purchase the dam owners' service, and a new transportation alternative was born.

With consistent navigability from Oil Creek to the Allegheny, a modest oil-shipping industry developed. Crude was transported by barrel or in bulk to Pittsburgh, the nation's leading petroleum refining, storage, and distribution center. By 1865, an estimated 2,000 oil transport vessels, mostly flatboats, populated the river. Twice weekly, fleets of flatboats carrying from 10,000 to 30,000 barrels

[1] This discussion is adopted from Harold Williamson and Arnold Daum, *The Age of Illumination, 1859 to 1899*, vol. 1 of *The American Petroleum Industry* (Evanston, Ill.: Northwestern University Press, 1959), chap. 5.

[2] Ibid., p. 86.

[3] An estimated 6,000 wagon crews worked in the teamster industry. An average trip moved around 5 or 6 barrels to railroad points twenty or thirty miles away at a charge of $2.50–$4.00 per barrel. The loss in oil and horses was high with this primitive mode of transport. See Paul Giddens, *The Early Petroleum Industry* (Philadelphia: Porcupine Press, 1974), pp. 101–3.

would ride the freshet to Oil City where the oil was reloaded for the 127-mile trip on the Allegheny River to Pittsburgh. Even river accidents brought forth profit-seeking activity as entrepreneurs salvaged spilt oil by strategically damming creek and river areas. Self-interest within a framework of quasi-private property rights was engendering a "spontaneous order" in the first years of crude oil distribution.[4]

Water transportation began to be replaced by rail transport in the middle 1860s. Venture capital financed local lines from the oil fields to existing trunk lines, which reduced crude loss, increased travel flexibility, and lessened cost.[5] The first operation was the locally financed Oil Creek Railroad, which brought in empty wooden barrels that were filled with crude for the return trip. Chartered in 1860, it commenced a 27-mile operation between Titusville and Corry, Pennsylvania, in the fall of 1862. Several other railroads, attracted by the handsome profits of the Oil Creek line, emerged in the middle 1860s to connect the Pennsylvania oil region with major trunk lines of the Atlantic and Great Western and Pennsylvania railroads for distribution to emerging refinery centers in Philadelphia, Cleveland, and the New York–New Jersey area.

Concurrent with the above was the birth of small "gathering" pipelines, modeled on existing water and manufactured-gas pipeline systems in urban areas, that connected oil wells and railroad pickup points.[6] Early proposals for such pipelines were aborted because of the Civil War–related capital and labor problems, political difficulties in obtaining charters, and deliberate destruction by oil-hauling teamsters. After five years of nonmarket setback, the first crude-oil pipeline, stretching 32,000 feet, was completed on October 10, 1865. Because of its success in undercutting alternative modes of transport and generating high profits, other lines soon followed, including

---

[4]Private ownership of the Allegheny and its tributaries did not exist, although oil entrepreneurs "rented" water levels through fresheting to make the river navigable.

[5]With waterway transportation, only one-third of the crude cargo reached its final Pittsburgh destination. An estimated one-third was lost through leakage prior to the trip, and another one-third was lost during transport. Paul Giddens, *Early Days of Oil* (Princeton, N.J.: Princeton University Press, 1948), p. 53.

[6]This summary is taken from Harold Williamson and Arnold Daum, *The Age of Illumination*, pp. 183–89.

"accommodation" lines, which connected oil-well storage tanks to gathering pipeline tanks.[7] These twin transport innovations connected oil wells to railroads, and a costly labor-intensive project was replaced by a far cheaper capital-intensive one, which freed wagon haulers for other employments, including construction and operation of oil pipelines.

Improvements in oil handling and storage were also the hallmark of the early years of crude-oil distribution. Improvements in railroad tank-car design reduced crude shrinkage and lessened explosion hazards. Small wooden storage vats were replaced by iron-reinforced cylindrical tanks to reduce leakage and increase storage capability. Storage capacity in the oil region increased from 300,000 barrels in early 1867 to 1.5 million barrels six years later.[8] This gave the titleholder of crude, whether producer, broker, or distributor, the flexibility to postpone sales until conditions were better, and thereby reduce price instability by taking inventory positions to counter the lows and highs of the market.

Setting the Stage: Pre-1860 Transportation Intervention

Prior to crude-oil distribution in the 1860s, the U.S. transportation system, consisting of roads and turnpikes, rivers and canals, and railroads, was subsidized by all levels of government—federal, state, county, and city (town). This had several important implications for the crude-oil market. The creation of transportation alternatives that private entrepreneurship alone would not have provided artificially dispersed the population. This complicated the problem of bringing petroleum to market despite the existence of an overbuilt, underpriced transportation network. Second, the most economical form of crude-oil distribution, oil pipelines, was placed at a competitive disadvantage by the subsidized competition. Because of that situation—and the direct use of these forms of transportation by the

---

[7]Alfred Smiley, builder of the first accommodation line, is also credited with devising the "run ticket" that remains an integral aspect of pipeline operations today. Other period innovations were "oil certificates" given by pipeline companies to titleholders of run oil and standard deductions of 2–3 percent of run oil to cover evaporation and leakage. Arthur Johnson, *The Development of American Petroleum Pipelines* (Ithaca, N.Y.: Cornell University Press, 1956), pp. 11–12.

[8]Harold Williamson and Arnold Daum, *The Age of Illumination*, p. 194.

crude-oil and product industry after 1860—a cursory examination of early government intervention in transport is warranted.

Subsidization of Roads

In the middle of the eighteenth century, travel over primitive trails and cleared areas brought forth several new forms of road transport. Between 1750 and 1790, a packhorse industry developed to carry goods in quantity to new markets. This was followed by wheeled vehicle transport—the stagecoach for passenger travel and the Conestoga wagon for goods transport. Dirt roads, however, remained largely unimproved.[9]

Beginning in the 1780s, improved roads or *turnpikes* began to emerge as entrepreneurs were granted permission by state authorities to charge users to cover construction outlays and provide a return. In 1794, the first privately financed turnpike was completed from Philadelphia to Lancaster, Pennsylvania.[10] With its stone foundation and gravel dressing, it set a new standard for workmanship. By 1800, 70 turnpike companies were chartered. That number swelled to 800 twelve years later.[11] By 1815, George Taylor stated, "Eastern Pennsylvania, New York, New Jersey, and southern New England were served by fairly good roads between the chief commercial centers."[12]

State and local governments expressed interest in promoting roads for reasons similar to those stated in the preamble to a 1788 Pennsylvania bill: "The opening of roads through the unsettled part of this State will greatly promote its settlement and population, and increase its domestic and foreign commerce, its manufacture and

---

[9]D. Philip Locklin, *Economics of Transportation* (Homewood, Ill.: R. D. Irwin, 1972), p. 102.

[10]Ibid., p. 103. Added Sidney Miller, "The old York road between New York City and Philadelphia, laid out in 1711, was the first important highway in the colonies, and it was not until 1792 that the first turnpike of broken stone was built." Miller, *Inland Transportation* (New York: McGraw-Hill, 1933), p. 573.

[11]Carter Goodrich, *Government Promotion of American Canals and Railroads* (New York: Columbia University Press, 1960), p. 21; and Frederick Cleveland and Fred Powell, *Railroad Promotion and Capitalization in the United States* (New York: Longmans, Green, and Co., 1909), p. 38.

[12]George Taylor, *The Transportation Revolution: 1815–1860* (New York: Rinehart, 1951), p. 18.

agriculture.''[13] Pennsylvania was the first state to subsidize road projects in the 1785–87 period, and in 1791, the unprecedented sum of $150,000 was appropriated for road and river projects.[14] Kentucky and Baltimore, Maryland, modestly subsidized road improvements prior to the turn of the century.[15]

In the first decades of the nineteenth century, Pennsylvania and Ohio provided several million dollars apiece for road projects.[16] New Jersey began aid in 1804. Maryland indirectly subsidized turnpike companies by requiring banks chartered in the state to subscribe to their stock. Between 1812 and 1831, $1.5 million, representing one-third of the capital requirements of the state's road companies, was raised in this manner.[17] In Virginia, an 1817 law allowed the state to provide up to 40 percent of a turnpike's capital, as did a South Carolina law in 1838. Indiana also became a partial owner of turnpikes.[18] Charters that would give advantages to existing firms were rarely denied. Said Taylor:

> With enthusiasm for turnpikes running high, state legislatures were generous in granting corporation charters. From 1815–1830 probably more charters were granted for this type of business than for any other, and by the twenties the common stocks issued by turnpike companies rivaled and possibly surpassed those which had been issued by state banks.[19]

The federal government confined its support to the interstate Cumberland Road, on which construction was begun in 1806. By 1818, it stretched from western Maryland to the eastern edge of Ohio, and in 1838, the road was completed to central Illinois at a taxpayer cost

---

[13]Quoted in Frederick Cleveland and Fred Powell, *Railroad Promotion and Capitalization in the United States,* p. 12. Other reasons, less consonant with the public weal, were also prominent as will be seen when waterway subsidization is examined below.

[14]Ibid., pp. 12–13.

[15]Ibid., p. 16.

[16]D. Philip Locklin, *Economics of Transportation,* p. 103.

[17]Frederick Cleveland and Fred Powell, *Railroad Promotion and Capitalization in the United States,* pp. 112–13.

[18]George Taylor, *The Transportation Revolution: 1815–1860,* pp. 23, 25.

[19]Ibid., p. 25.

of $6.8 million. Maintained by annual congressional appropriations, the nation's longest road was toll free for users.[20]

In the 1815–30 period, congressional support for federal roads rang loud from such stalwarts as John Calhoun of South Carolina and Henry Clay of Kentucky. Countering these statesmen were Presidents Monroe and Jackson, who vetoed road bills in states with above-average roads, particularly in the Northeast. For the time being, the states, not the federal government, would lead the way.[21]

Restrictive regulation sometimes accompanied government favor to turnpike companies. Several states incorporated maximum toll rates (directly with dollar amounts or indirectly with profit ceilings) and included minimum road standards in turnpike charters as a precondition for charging tolls.[22] This hindered expansion by successful road companies and made other roads unprofitable. Some fell into disrepair, and these and other roads abandoned because of unfavorable economics "reverted" to local governments for maintenance and commercial operation.[23] As a consequence, a tendency developed for government authorities to run lower quality, less commercial roads and private companies to operate higher quality, more commercial roads.[24]

As would be the case with canals and railroads, government support of improved roads went from public favor to disfavor. Overcapitalization—overbuilding—due in large part to generous state treasuries, hurt profitability for all. Ohio terminated stock subscriptions to road companies in 1842 and canceled all commitments to public-works projects, some in progress, in 1844.[25] Other states would

[20]D. Philip Locklin, *Economics of Transportation*, p. 104. For a history of earlier federal "post" roads, see *History of Transportation in the United States before 1860*, ed. B. H. Meyer (Washington, D.C.: Peter Smith, 1948), pp. 31–37.

[21]George Taylor, *The Transportation Revolution*, pp. 19–21.

[22]For some examples of rate regulation, see *History of Transportation in the United States before 1860*, pp. 70, 124–26, 303. For early turnpike laws in Maryland (1801), New York (1803), Massachusetts (1804), Connecticut (1806), New Hampshire (1807), and Vermont (1808), as well as specific charters, see M. H. Hunter, "The Early Regulation of Public Service Corporations," *American Economic Review*, no. 9 (1917): 569–81.

[23]Sidney Miller, *Inland Transportation*, p. 573.

[24]For the case of Ohio, see *History of Transportation in the United States before 1860*, p. 124.

[25]Ibid., p. 125. Ohio owned 50 percent of twenty-six companies, only nine of which returned dividends. George Taylor, *The Transportation Revolution*, pp. 26–27.

withdraw road aid along with canal and railroad support in the 1840s and 1850s.

Subsidization of Waterways

Government-aided canal building and river improvements, along with road support, were the forerunners to railroad subsidization. Although the first canals were privately built in 1800 and 1803, a combination of interests would impress upon lawmakers and the public the need for government sponsorship of waterway transport. Politicians were naturally attracted. Explained Harold Moulton, "The greater the work performed, the larger appears the statesmanship; and the more closely it appears the honor due the servant of the people."[26] Another reason was closely intertwined. Noticed Moulton:

> The expenditure of great sums of public money always carries with it a large amount of political patronage. . . . For the building of the public works contracts are given to private construction companies. These contracts may be let with the distinct understanding that there is to be given in return not only ordinary political support, but positive aid in elections, by cash contributions to campaign funds, and through direct influence upon the voting of laborers engaged upon the public works. Thus the party machine is strengthened.[27]

State by state, politicians extolled the benefits of the public waterways—lowered transportation costs to cheapen goods, increased commerce within the state, improved mobility for the citizenry, and a state revenue source from user charges for years to come.[28] Behind the scenes, special interests predominated—landowners near the waterways; businesses standing to gain construction contracts; companies poised to utilize the changed water flow for hydroelectric power; and "the representatives of lumber, coal, and other companies who hope[d] to be able to ship their goods at less cost to themselves, since on a public waterway part of the cost of transportation comes from the general public in the form of taxes to the Government, instead of entirely from shippers."[29] Only after negative experiences with waterway subsidization would the public recognize the

[26]Harold Moulton, *Waterways versus Railways* (New York: Houghton Mifflin, 1912), pp. 448–49.

[27]Ibid., p. 449.

[28]For examples of sensationalistic promises by state politicians, see ibid., pp. 440–45.

[29]Ibid., p. 450.

less-than-noble motivations behind the rhetoric and react with a vengeance.

In the early nineteenth century, Virginia and Maryland began a several-decade drive by state and local governments to improve waterway transportation by heavily subscribing to the stock of a Potomac River company. New York State also provided early assistance. Other states followed, including Pennsylvania, which by 1825 supplied $185,000 to water transportation companies and $180,000 to bridge businesses.[30] The pinnacle of state aid came in 1817 when construction began on the 364-mile Erie Canal, funded by New York State for $7 million.[31]

After its completion from Albany to Buffalo in 1825, the Erie generated much toll revenue, drastically reduced freight costs, and achieved a seven-year payout.[32] Its widely perceived success, coupled with the financing tool of state bonds, incited a burst of state and local aid to canal construction and river improvements in the 1825–40 era by authorities anxious to maintain or enhance their competitive position relative to other states.[33] Ohio in 1825, Illinois in 1835, and Michigan in 1837, in addition to Pennsylvania and New York State, began to assume heavy obligations in the high—if not outlandish—hope of a shortcut to progress via waterways. The propaganda ran particularly deep in Pennsylvania. As told in Avard Bishop's 1907 *State Works of Pennsylvania*:

> The advantages . . . were carefully documented: The farmer would find increased demand, brisker sales, and higher prices for his produce; the merchant, a wider field for his business; the manufacturer and mechanic, more certain employment and better pay for their

---

[30]Carter Goodrich, *Government Promotion of American Canals and Railroads*, pp. 62–63. For greater detail on early privately and publicly funded canal projects per state, see *History of Transportation in the United States*, chaps. 6–8.

[31]Philip Locklin, *Economics of Transportation*, p. 97.

[32]The success of the Erie was in part government created. For several years, New York State required railroads parallel to the Erie to charge an equal toll and forbade freight carriage except when the canal was closed. George Taylor, *The Transportation Revolution*, p. 75.

[33]Harold Moulton, *Waterways versus Railways*, p. 439. The Erie example inspired the Massachusetts State Commission to state in 1826, "To bring this theory [of canal feasibility] to the stern test of facts, it is only necessary to advert to the practical results, which the canals of New York abundantly furnish." Julius Rubin, *Canal or Railroad?* (Philadelphia: American Philosophical Society, 1961), p. 81.

industry; the capitalist, a better interest on his money; and the owner of lands and houses, a rise in rents of twenty-five or thirty percent. . . . It was predicted that the tolls would support the government and educate every child in the commonwealth.[34]

The canal-subsidy binge took the form not only of stock subscriptions but lottery privileges, exclusive franchises, banking charters, and guaranteed rates of return.[35]

Because of the unpopularity of higher taxes, the consequence of cash aid was state debt. With the panic of 1837, debt service for unproductive canals (as for other internal improvements) became strained, not to mention principal repayment, in major subsidy states. With $57.8 million in expenses and $40 million in debt incurred, Pennsylvania stopped interest payments in 1842 and considered default before raising taxes and stretching out payments beginning in 1845.[36] Ohio suspended canal assistance in 1842 due to an overburdened treasury.[37] In Ohio and other states, canals went unfinished and other canals were sold at a fraction of cost to private companies. Michigan took the unprecedented action of bond repudiation to rid the state of earlier waterway grants.[38] Illinois defaulted on interest payments before the debt balance was entirely repudiated.[39] Indiana stopped interest payments from 1847 to 1853 and assigned canal revenue to maturing principal.[40] New York State, proud builder of the Erie, suspended canal building.[41] Maryland, Virginia, South Carolina, and Massachusetts, among other states, had also unprofitably subsidized "internal improvements," which resulted in state finance problems and public disfavor.[42] New taxes and criticism from foreign bondholders were legacies of the previous excess.[43]

[34]Quoted in Harold Moulton, *Waterways versus Railways*, p. 440.

[35]George Taylor, *The Transportation Revolution*, pp. 50–52.

[36]Harold Moulton, *Waterways versus Railways*, p. 440; and Reginald McGrane, *Foreign Bondholders and American State Debts* (New York: Macmillan, 1935), chap. 4.

[37]*History of Transportation in the United States before 1860*, p. 292.

[38]Harold Moulton, *Waterways versus Railways*, p. 441.

[39]Ibid., p. 442.

[40]Reginald McGrane, *Foreign Bondholders and the American State Debts*, p. 139.

[41]George Taylor, *The Transportation Revolution*, p. 50.

[42]Carter Goodrich, *Government Promotion of American Canals and Railroads*, p. 273.

[43]See, generally, Reginald McGrane, *Foreign Bondholders and American State Debts*, chaps. 4–8.

It would be decades before talk of waterway subsidization again emerged, and even then, protagonists of government aid were plagued by memories of earlier experience.[44]

Subsidization of Railways

Government involvement with railroads has a unique place in U.S. regulatory history. Explains Clair Wilcox, "It is in the case of railroads that . . . government had its longest experience as a regulator and its greatest powers."[45] Government also had a long experience with railroad subsidization several decades before state and federal regulation reached full swing in the 1880s.

The first successful commercial railroad was the Baltimore and Ohio, which received a charter from the Ohio legislature in 1828 and began a 13-mile operation shortly thereafter. It was a totally private effort with capital raised from individuals confident of enduring returns.[46] But from this point until federal involvement began in the 1850s, state, city, and county governments aided railroads with property-tax exemptions, patriotic appeals for private investment, lottery sponsorships, bond guarantees, low-interest loans, donations of resources from state land (including timber and stone), exclusionary charters, the right of eminent domain, and bank charters.[47] Another subsidy came from the judiciary, which broke from common-law precedent to favor railroad activity in legal disputes. Nuisance and property-right violations were forgiven by the

---

[44]For a discussion of the "second waterways movement," which began in 1901, see Harold Moulton, *Waterways versus Railways*, pp. 1–17, 442–45.

[45]Clair Wilcox, *Public Policies toward Business* (Homewood, Ill.: Richard D. Irwin, 1966), p. 386.

[46]John Chamberlain, *The Enterprising Americans: A Business History of the United States* (New York: Harper and Row, 1961), p. 76. Earlier railroad charters in 1815 and 1822 failed to materialize into commercial operations because of lack of private funding.

[47]The "railroad bank" provided bank deposits as interest-free working capital for the railroad, which also could be used as a source of long-term debt (with interest charges) to facilitate capitalization. Frederick Cleveland and Fred Powell, *Railroad Promotion and Capitalization in the United States*, pp. 281–82. B. H. Meyer was to remark that "next to the grants of monopoly, perhaps the most frequent form of indirect aid was by means of banking privileges." *History of Transportation in the United States before 1860*, p. 559.

courts because transportation as a social good transcended the private good.[48] Several railroad companies, two in Pennsylvania and one in Georgia, were entirely state projects.

Statutes unfavorable to railroads were rare. Canal owners, which prominently included state governments, were the lone vested interest against railroads. Pennsylvania and Ohio taxed railroads into parity with nearby canals. New York kept railway tariffs high and restricted freight hauls. Massachusetts delayed its first railroad charter until 1830.[49]

Rate and dividend regulations existed but were rarely effective. Rate ceilings were generally set high, and dividend restrictions were circumvented by issuing stock bonuses.[50]

Of the above-mentioned legislative favors, the most basic was the special corporate charter, which gave franchise rights and eminent-domain privileges to the railroad firm.[51] With a franchise, pricing and service were not constrained by potential competition.[52] With condemnation, right-of-way costs could be reduced. Both facilitated stock subscriptions to capitalize operations. If this was inadequate, more direct favors such as cash subsidies and loan guarantees were often granted. Between 1840 and 1853, Pennsylvania gave an estimated $14 million to in-state railroads, including over two-thirds of the Pennsylvania Railroad's $9.9 million capitalization as of 1852.[53] Ohio passed a statute in 1837 to purchase one-third of all new stock issued by intrastate railroads. New York gave $4 million for early

[48]Canals also received preferential treatment on utilitarian grounds. See Morton Horwitz, *The Transformation of American Law* (Cambridge, Mass.: Harvard University Press, 1977), chap. 3.

[49]George Taylor, *The Transportation Revolution*, pp. 75–78.

[50]Ibid., pp. 88–89.

[51]"After determining the route and the territory to be served with transportation facilities, one of the most important financial considerations [was] the charter with provisions favorable to the enterprise." Frederick Cleveland and Fred Powell, *Railroad Promotion and Capitalization in the United States*, p. 155. B. H. Meyer noted that "the first railroad charters were patterned directly after turnpike charters." *History of Transportation in the United States before 1860*, p. 312.

[52]"A provision not infrequent in early American railroad charters is that by which the legislature renounces for a definite period of years the right to grant a charter over a competing route." Carter Goodrich, *Government Promotion of American Canals and Railroads*, p. 165.

[53]Clarence Carson, *Throttling the Railroads* (Indianapolis: Liberty Fund, 1971), p. 30.

projects, followed by another $36 million in ensuing decades. By 1857, Missouri counted $25 million in railroad loans. The southern states accounted for 55 percent of railroad capital in their area.[54] Maryland, Illinois, Minnesota, Iowa, Michigan, and other states also subsidized railroads extensively in the early period.[55]

Prior to 1850, federal aid to railroads consisted of route surveys, stock purchases, modest land grants, building materials found on public land, tariff exemptions on imported rail materials, inflated rates for mail delivery, and gratis right-of-way privileges through federal land. After this time, federal land grants reached new proportions.[56] Pursuant to the Act of September 30, 1850, 3.75 million acres were awarded to the Mobile and Ohio Railroad and the Illinois Central Railroad to build a line from Mobile, Alabama, to northern Illinois. The land was used as collateral for construction financing, and the 1,200-mile project was completed in 1857.[57] The act stipulated that federally owned land within six miles of each side of the tract was awardable, and over forty separate projects were attracted, many inefficiently built through sparsely populated areas to qualify for as much federal land as possible.[58]

Between 1830 and 1860, railroad trackage grew from 23 miles to 30,635 miles.[59] Implying that every mile less would have been a "market failure," George Taylor said:

> Had ample private capital been forthcoming, public grants might not have been thought advisable or necessary. But the capital needed to build 30,000 miles of railroad was simply not forthcoming. . . . The help of government agencies . . . was needed.[60]

But if market investment decisions are economically rational—profit-seeking entrepreneurs gauging the relative urgency of consumer demand—then a far different picture emerges. The portion

---

[54]George Taylor, *The Transportation Revolution*, pp. 93–94.

[55]Clarence Carson, *Throttling the Railroads*, pp. 30–31.

[56]For a list of government-funded railroad surveys beginning in 1824, see *History of Transportation in the United States before 1860*, pp. 598–600.

[57]Reduced iron tariffs between 1830 and 1843 saved an estimated $6 million in construction costs. George Taylor, *The Transportation Revolution*, p. 95.

[58]Carter Goodrich, *Government Promotion of American Canals and Railroads*, pp. 170–73.

[59]Emory Johnson, *American Railway Transportation* (New York: D. Appleton, 1903), p. 24.

[60]George Taylor, *The Transportation Revolution*, p. 88.

of 30,000 miles resulting from government favor, net of right-of-way land grants, taxes, and competition from government-sponsored transportation, represented *malinvestment*. It is erroneous to conclude that without government intervention a railroad industry would not have emerged.[61] The first railroads were private as were later ones. Technology, consumer demand, and domestic and foreign capital markets were present, and many beneficiaries—"merchants, small manufacturers, farmers, and professional men living along the proposed route of the new railroad"—were natural investors.[62] Patriotic investment by prominent town business leaders was also a source of capital. Businesses directly dependent on railroads such as cotton manufacturers, textile firms, iron foundries, and coal producers invested as a form of vertical integration.[63]

The legacies of railway subsidies were state budget crises in the 1840s and emergency tax legislation that followed. Another consequence was an overbuilt industry, which decades hence would engage in ruinous rate competition, unstable traffic alliances ("pools"), and, finally, the use of the political process to suppress rivalry.

Conclusion

Except for the Erie Canal project, the results of government intervention in canals, roads, and railroads were consistently disappointing. Aggregate state expenditures of $62.2 million for canals, $42.9 million for railroads, and $6.6 million for turnpikes prior to 1840[64] —and much more thereafter—did not create wealth but reduced private-sector consumption and investment and spawned malinvestments. Not only did government-aided projects encounter difficulty,[65] private projects suffered from the presence of advantaged

[61]Similarly, it is erroneous to conclude, as does Clarence Carson, that "virtually all the railroad trackage laid in the country was laid in consequence of some special privilege not granted to all enterprises." Carson, *Throttling the Railroads*, p. 32.

[62]George Taylor, *The Transportation Revolution*, p. 97. One example was the Auburn and Rochester Railroad, which was "financed almost exclusively by small investors living in the towns, villages, and farms along its route." Undoubtedly profit was their motive, but so were the general benefits of a line—higher land values, increased economic activity, and better mobility. Investment was a form of consumption for them.

[63]Ibid., pp. 98–99.

[64]Reginald McGrane, *Foreign Bondholders and American State Debts*, p. 6.

[65]The propensity of government-related projects to encounter unprofitability is explainable by the propensity of entrepreneurs to exploit the most profitable opportunities and leave less feasible projects for government consideration.

competition. Government-fostered overcapacity weakened the transportation industry as a whole and dislocated interregional trade. The irony was not only that states unnecessarily incurred expense to nullify the perceived advantages of rival-state aid, but that simultaneous subsidization of competing modes of transport worked at cross-purposes. Aiding canals disadvantaged roads and vice versa. Support for railroads disadvantaged canals and roads and vice versa. Subsidization and cross-subsidization were no substitute for impersonal market forces in answering the "when, where, and how much" questions about road, water, and rail transport. With a free market, less investment and much less malinvestment would have occurred. The result would have been a leaner, more stable industry serving fewer, stronger markets.

Intervention in Oil Pipelines: 1861–1905

The birth of intervention in petroleum transportation can be traced to the Pennsylvania legislature, which soon after the Titusville oil strike in 1859 became a battleground for competing transport interests seeking political favor. Oil pipelines were at the center of controversy. In late 186l, the first proposed pipeline was canceled when the legislature denied an incorporation charter to Heman James. Corporate charters, conferring special privileges, could be used to restrict entry altogether, and Pennsylvania lawmakers were under the influence of oil-hauling teamsters who recognized the competitive threat of pipe transport.[66] Three months later, the first pipeline charter was awarded to the Oil Creek Transportation Company on the political strength of oil producers distraught with horse-and-buggy transport and railroads interested in "feeder" pipelines to connect oil wells to tank-car terminals. The corporate charter awarded a monopoly grant to lay pipe or tubing from Oil Creek to either Oil City or connection points of the Philadelphia and Erie Railroad.[67]

While the Oil Creek's charter lay dormant, entrepreneur James Hutchings built in the oil region on a nonincorporated basis several

[66]No fewer than 4,000 teamsters descended upon the state capital of Harrisburg to lobby the lawmakers against the incorporation. John McLaurin, *Sketches in Crude Oil* (Westport, Conn.: Hyperion Press, 1902, 1976), pp. 265–66.

[67]Arthur Johnson, *The Development of American Petroleum Pipelines*, p. 5. Added Johnson, "Such legislative favors [monopoly grants] were not uncommon."

small lines that succumbed to mechanical failure and teamster sabotage. The first successful pipeline would wait until 1865 when Martin Van Sickle combined technical expertise and entrepreneurial innovation to minimize leakage and ward off teamsters from his two-inch-diameter line that stretched 32,000 feet from Pithole City, a production center, to the Oil Creek Railroad terminal at Miller's Farm, Pennsylvania. Behind his success was the importation of laborers with pugilistic talents in addition to regular work skills, which kept the teamsters at bay. After a full payout several months after operations began, a sister line was constructed by Van Sickle with significantly reduced rates.

Many competitors sprang up to profitably link new oil fields to railroad stations and river points for further transport. Teamster violence was ended once and for all when one victimized operator hired private detectives who made mass arrests and imprisoned the organizers.

With the teamsters silenced and corporate charters for local lines obtainable if the point of origin was not previously franchised, the next competitive challenge for oil pipelines was oil-carrying railroads (tank cars). The success of gathering and accommodation lines led to *trunk lines*, pipage of greater length, that connected oil wells directly to refineries and major distribution centers. With this development, the relationship of pipelines to railroads turned from complementary to rivalrous. This would have important implications not only in the economic realm but in the political realm as well.

In 1868, a consortium of producers and pipeline operators in Pennsylvania joined together to push for a statewide eminent-domain law for oil pipelines. Railroad charters, after all, commonly provided for condemnation rights as did the Oil Creek Transportation Company's amended pipeline charter of 1863.[68] Sentiment for the law reflected right-of-way difficulties that pipelines encountered from railroads that refused to allow pipage to cross their easements and landowners, some of whom were allied with railroads, wary of granting entrance to their property. The bill failed as did a second "free oil-carrying pipe line law" sponsored by the newly formed

[68]This company's right of eminent domain was revoked in early 1867 and restored later that year. Ibid., p. 13. The comprehensive charter prompted John McLaurin to recognize the Oil Creek line as "the only one empowered by the legislature to pipe oil to railway stations." McLaurin, *Sketches in Crude Oil*, pp. 267–68.

Petroleum Producers Association a year later. Railway interests, led by Tom Scott of the Pennsylvania Railroad, held sway over the legislature.

After a third denial in 1870, a new development shifted opinion against the railroads and toward their transportation rivals. In early 1872, a scheme came to light whereby the South Improvement Company, composed of the Pennsylvania, New York Central, and Erie railroads, planned to double rail rates for oil shipments. Traffic was to be split on a predetermined basis among the three lines. Rate discounts were assigned to refiners participating in the scheme as the buyers of the transported crude.[69] Indignation arose across the Pennsylvania oil region at what was to be the first of many railroad "pools," and new support was generated for a pipeline eminent-domain bill. With local oil interests united, outside support from New York refineries, and public opinion now on his side, the powerful Tom Scott was directly approached to write a free pipeline law for the Pennsylvania lawmakers to enact.

Scott's bill, passed on March 12, 1872, was a carefully crafted compromise. Eminent domain was allowed only in the eight counties that made up the oil region. Noticeably absent was Allegheny County where the major refinery center of Pittsburgh was located. Condemnation was not applicable within five miles of the state line if piped oil was destined for other states (i.e., the Ohio, New York, or New Jersey refining centers). The bill also contained a "railroad proviso" requiring oil destined for New York City, Baltimore, or Philadelphia to be piped at rates not less than those charged by the railroad "traveling the greatest distance in the state"—the Pennsylvania.[70] This blatant amendment caused a furor and was repealed a week later, leaving a restricted eminent-domain law as the only gain from the ill will created by the railroad cartelization scheme. The competitive position of the Pennsylvania line, which had a

---

[69]Making his first appearance in controversial matters as codeveloper of the plan was John D. Rockefeller, owner of a Cleveland refinery and part owner of the Allegheny Transportation Company. Also prominent in the scheme was Tom Scott, vice president of the Pennsylvania Railroad and notorious mover of the Pennsylvania legislature. See Austin Moore, *John D. Archbold and the Early Development of Standard Oil* (New York: Macmillan, 1930), pp. 67–91.

[70]Arthur Johnson, *The Development of American Petroleum Pipelines*, p. 22.

monopoly charter from the oil region to Pittsburgh, was little disturbed.

In Ohio, events leading to pipeline intervention were both similar to and different from those in Pennsylvania. With railroads enjoying eminent-domain privileges and wielding significant influence over the Ohio legislature, charters were denied would-be pipeline operators. This left Cleveland refineries at the mercy of the Baltimore and Ohio Railroad, which charged higher rates than the Pennsylvania Railroad charged Pittsburgh refineries, partly because of greater distance and partly because of foreclosed competition. The competitive solution was a trunk pipeline from the Pennsylvania oil region to Cleveland that, in the words of the *Cleveland Leader*, would "end . . . all monopolies, all warring with eastern corporations for just rates and all danger of defeat at the hands of our [refining] rivals."[71]

On April 15, 1872, an Ohio charter, the first of its kind, was awarded to lay pipe for the line. This was followed on April 29 by an eminent-domain law for all pipelines assuming common-carrier status. This stipulation, an apparent concession to Pennsylvania producers but in actuality a concession to Cleveland refiners, was intended to check the pipeline's privilege by forcing it to accept all tendered oil for shipment.[72] So, as was the case in the neighboring state to the east, in Ohio public opinion mobilized by the oil community overcame powerful railroad interests to turn the latter's monopoly position into a position shared with pipelines.

A second genre of pipeline legislation was passed in Pennsylvania on May 15, 1874, to require pipeline operators to present sworn monthly statements on the size and location of crude-oil inventory to the Pennsylvania Bureau of Statistics.[73] Oil producers, led by John Zane, convinced the legislature that oil pipelines, acting as speculators rather than common carriers, were "bearing" the market

---

[71]Quoted in Rolland Maybee, *Railroad Competition and the Oil Trade, 1855–1873* (Philadelphia: Porcupine Press, 1974), p. 375.

[72]Common-carrier statutes, adopted from the English common law for companies affected with a "public interest," were implicit in many charters of incorporation for transportation firms and later became explicit in conjunction with the right of eminent domain. See George Wolbert, *American Pipe Lines* (Norman: University of Oklahoma Press, 1951), pp. 114–15.

[73]Arthur Johnson, *The Development of American Petroleum Pipelines*, pp. 32–33.

by refusing to buy presented quantities.[74] Mandatory reporting could verify whether operators were refusing to buy because of "legitimate" storage limitations or "illegitimate" speculative activity. An amendment to require similar reporting by railroads, on the other hand, was quietly deleted before passage.

A year later, a bill was introduced in the Pennsylvania legislature to extend eminent domain to the entire state for crude-oil and petroleum-product pipelines, to declare such lines common carriers, to set maximum pipeline rates, and to prohibit pipelines from entering other phases of the petroleum industry.[75] Agitation for the law, sparked by the formation of a railroad-pipeline pool in 1874, came from two industry alliances. Producers, selected pipeline operators, and refiners were united in favor of eminent domain, which they believed would create new lines and lower transportation costs. In particular, the Columbia Conduit Company, chartered in 1872 to lay pipe from the oil region to Pittsburgh, was thwarted when the Pennsylvania Railroad, hitherto the monopolist of inland transportation to Pittsburgh, refused to allow pipe across its right-of-way. To proponents, eminent domain for pipelines would countervail the railroad's historic right of condemnation and prevent obstructionism. The second industry alliance was oil producers and refiners who not only desired lower pipeline rates to reduce transportation costs but sought to prevent new competition by outlawing integration should pipeline companies decide to enter a complementary phase. The intention of price regulation was to break the rate structure of the existing (and, in retrospect, short-lived) pipeline pool.

Opposition to the bill began with the railroads, particularly the Pennsylvania, and refiners, some of whom reversed earlier support. Pittsburgh refiners worried that a free pipeline law would encourage construction not only of projects to their gates, all well and good, but of trunk projects to refining centers elsewhere. Philadelphia and Baltimore refiners held comfortable positions in the newly established railroad-pipeline pool that could be disturbed by expansion under the bill. Another factor that would lead to the bill's defeat on

---

[74]Ibid. Part of the statute had common-law intent to protect contractual rights by detecting and prosecuting instances of oil-certificate fraud.

[75]Ibid., pp. 41, 46.

March 4, 1875, was the prospect of lower state revenue as a result of a shift from taxed rail transport to untaxed pipe transmission.[76]

The Columbia Conduit pipeline, shy of completion by the length of a railroad rail, resorted to wagon transport at a public crossing to break the Pennsylvania Railroad's obstruction. In mid-1875, after seven months, the railroad allowed the split line to be connected. The Pennsylvania now had inland competition year around to Pittsburgh, not just during the warm months when the waterways were usable.

The Standard Oil Company, rapidly expanding in the refining market, began to enlarge its pipeline holdings by purchasing the Empire Pipe Company from the Pennsylvania Railroad and the Columbia Conduit in 1877. With the consolidation came exclusive charter rights, and concerned producers took political and economic action to meet strength with strength. In January 1878, a sixth attempt at an unrestricted free pipeline law—and the second attempt since partial eminent-domain rights were granted in 1872—was initiated by the newly formed Petroleum Producers Union. That attempt, too, was blocked by the railroad lobby. A law passed on May 22, 1878, however, required pipelines to post the monthly amounts of crude and product received, sold, and held. This joined Pennsylvania's inventory record-keeping law of five years before.

Several months later, a plan was unveiled to build a trunk line toward the seaboard. The 115-mile project would go from Correyville to Williamsburg, Pennsylvania, from which the oil would be railed by tank car to the New York refining region. The Tide-Water Pipe Line was successfully completed without eminent-domain privileges on June 4, 1879, and effective competition was provided to traditional Pittsburgh and Cleveland routes. This trunk line ushered in a new era in crude-oil transport. Remarked oil pipeline historian Arthur Johnson:

> The successful completion and operation of the Tide-Water Pipe Line marked a turning point in the history of oil transportation. Just as pipelines had supplanted teams [of haulers] as a means of collecting oil in the fields, so now they were commencing to prove their potentialities as competitors of the railroads in long-distance crude oil transportation.[77]

[76]Ibid., p. 45.
[77]Ibid., p. 96.

The drive toward government involvement with crude-oil pipelines was not dampened by the defeat of the statewide free pipeline bill or the economic success of the Tide-Water line. New York State passed an eminent-domain law in 1878, the same year New Jersey defeated one. In 1879, West Virginia passed a common-carrier law for oil pipelines that outlawed rate discrimination between customers and set maximum rates.[78] In Pennsylvania, meanwhile, producers resorted to legal action against Standard Oil. It was charged that Standard's rebate program was inconsistent with its common-carrier status implicit in Pennsylvania law. Court action reached a stalemate, and an attempt to pass an explicit anti-discrimination bill with eminent-domain rights was defeated in 1879.

The preeminent position of Standard Oil in refining and pipeline transmission became the subject of journalistic fervor beginning in 1881 with an *Atlantic Monthly* article by Henry Demarest Lloyd, "Story of a Great Monopoly." "The forces of capital and industry," the article exclaimed, "have outgrown the forces of our government." If allowed to run its course, it was concluded, "the people will perish."[79] From this time until federal regulation began after the turn of the century, pipeline regulation would be inspired by hard-pressed Standard Oil competitors—small independents in all phases of the oil business—and sympathetic journalists, citizens, and lawmakers.

The real story of Standard's activities was different. As it had in the other petroleum sectors, Rockefeller's company pioneered big-business efficiencies in the storage and pipeline field.[80] Through the wholly owned affiliate National Transit Company (formed in 1881), "gargantuan" expansion resulted in 3,000 miles of gathering and trunk lines and 40 million barrels of storage capacity by the mid-1880s, and much more growth thereafter.[81] New wells were rapidly connected to give producers crucial outlets.[82] Right-of-way was

[78]Ibid., p. 93. The law also set evaporation and leakage allowances.
[79]Quoted in ibid., p. 112.
[80]See chapters 18 and 22 for Standard's contributions to refining and marketing.
[81]Ralph Hidy and Muriel Hidy, *Pioneering in Big Business, 1881–1911* (New York: Harper and Brothers, 1955), pp. 79, 83, 89. Standard's pipeline subsidiary was United Pipe Lines.
[82]Ibid., p. 78.

obtained by dollars, not legal force.[83] Pipe was laid deep for permanence, and only the best equipment was used to minimize leakage.[84] Storage records reflected "accuracy and integrity."[85] Innovative tank design reduced leakage and evaporation to benefit all parties.[86] Fire-prevention methods reduced ruinous tank-farm blazes.[87] All operations reflected "systematic administration."[88] The pricing strategy was to prevent entry by keeping rates low.[89] While these business successes may not have benefited certain competitors, they benefited customers and consumers of final products.

In 1883, Pennsylvania passed the long-sought unrestricted free pipeline law. The June 1 statute was followed four days later by a gauging law, similar to West Virginia's 1879 law, and twelve days later by an anti-consolidation law, which prohibited pipelines from entering the complementary phases of production and refining "under penalty of the loss of the entire property by escheat to the Commonwealth."[90] The spate of legislation was not the result of sudden zeal on the part of lawmakers for consumers and the common weal but of industry groups' seeking competitive advantage against Standard's formidable United Pipe Lines.[91] The degree of negative sentiment was evident in the 1887 Billingsly bill introduced in Pennsylvania, which was titled

> An act to punish corporations, companies, firms, associations and persons, and each of them engaged in the business of transporting by pipeline on lines or storing petroleum in tank or tanks, under certain restrictions and penalties from charging in excess of certain fixed rates for receiving, transporting, storing, and delivering petroleum, and to regulate deductions for losses caused to petroleum in pipelines and storage tanks by lightning, fire, storm, or other unavoidable causes.[92]

[83]Arthur Johnson, *The Development of American Petroleum Pipelines*, p. 114.
[84]Ibid., p. 102; and Ralph Hidy and Muriel Hidy, *Pioneering in Big Business*, p. 81.
[85]Ibid., p. 84.
[86]Ibid., p. 82.
[87]Ibid.
[88]Ibid., p. 83.
[89]Ibid., p. 84.
[90]Quoted in Arthur Johnson, *The Development of American Petroleum Pipelines*, p. 177. In 1895, the anti-consolidation bill was repealed.
[91]Ibid., p. 118.
[92]Quoted in ibid., p. 131.

Because of the stringent specifics of the bill—price ceilings for gathering and storage below cost and a reduction of customary shrinkage allowances—it was recognized that pipelines per se were put at risk. The bill was defeated as were similar bills in Maryland in 1882 and Ohio in 1887. Another regulatory attempt in Pennsylvania, the Burdick bill, failed in 1891.

Beginning in 1876, concern over Standard Oil was voiced on the federal level. Pennsylvania congressman James Hopkins introduced a bill to prohibit certain "monopolistic" railroad practices, which began the debate that several decades later would produce the Act to Regulate Interstate Commerce (Interstate Commerce Act of 1887).[93] No mention was made of pipelines in the bill. This was not only because lawmakers were not aware of Standard's vast pipeline holdings, which contributed significantly to its refining market share and leverage to dictate rate practices of rival railroads; it was because railroad interests that masterminded the bill believed their problems could be addressed by railroad regulation alone.[94] It would not be until 1906 that federal regulation of pipelines would supplement state statutes as occurred in 1887 for railroads.

Several other state pipeline laws were passed before 1906. In 1897, Texas prohibited integration of the production, transportation, and refining phases. This bill was directly aimed at Standard Oil and, along with the Texas Antitrust Law of 1889, discouraged competition to locally based, nonintegrated companies.[95] In 1905, Kansas specified "sound and wrought cast-iron or steel casings and pipes tested to at least four hundred pounds pressure per square inch" for oil pipelines in the state.[96] Kansas in the same year also passed an eminent-domain law for oil pipelines, designed to promote competition to Standard Oil by local firms, that also set maximum rates and made all lines common carriers. Overproduction of crude oil and consequent price declines were blamed on purchasers (Standard

---

[93]The implementation and effect of the Interstate Commerce Act are discussed in this chapter, pp. 622–23.

[94]Arthur Johnson, *The Development of American Petroleum Pipelines*, p. 201.

[95]Henrietta Larson and Kenneth Porter, *History of Humble Oil & Refining Company* (New York: Harper & Brothers, 1959), p. 700.

[96]W. W. Thornton, *The Law Relating to Oil and Gas* (Cincinnati: W. H. Anderson, 1904), p. 1322. Pennsylvania in 1885 passed the first safety-related law, which required pipe to be placed twenty-four inches below the surface.

being foremost), not producers operating under the rule of capture, which inspired the above legislation.

Subsidization and Regulation of Railroads: 1860–1900

Between 1860 and 1900, railroad trackage increased from under 31,000 miles to over 190,000 miles.[97] Part of this growth was attributable to the development of the oil industry: rail was laid between Pennsylvania oil regions and refining centers in Pennsylvania, Ohio, and seaboard states, as well as between refineries and retail markets. Before 1879, oil pipelines were subservient to oil-carrying railroads; after this time, long-distance "trunk" carriage began to displace oil-carrying railroads.[98] Nonetheless, tank-car transport would remain significant into the next century.

In the 1860–1900 period, four areas of government intervention in the railroad industry were in evidence: local aid for railroad construction, state regulation of railroad rates and practices, federal subsidization of railroad construction, and federal regulation of railroad activities. Each will be considered in turn.

Unsatisfactory experiences with transportation subsidies led to constitutional prohibitions on aid by Pennsylvania, New York, Maryland, Maine, Minnesota, Iowa, Kentucky, Kansas, Oregon, and California.[99] Local aid was not prohibited, and in the 1860–75 period, many municipalities subsidized railway construction with competitive fervor. Localities in Massachusetts, Ohio, New York, Illinois, Kansas, Texas, and Mississippi, in particular, subscribed heavily to railroad stock issues with generally disappointing results, which led to large reductions in—if not termination of—aid. A number of states amended their constitutions to prohibit local as well as state aid, including Michigan and Illinois (1870); California (1872); Missouri, Texas, Alabama, and Florida (1875); Colorado (1876); Georgia (1877); and Nevada and Massachusetts (1889).[100] Some states bucked the trend and pushed local subsidization in the post-1870 period,

---

[97]Emory Johnson, *American Railway Transportation*, p. 24.

[98]Arthur Johnson, *The Development of American Petroleum Pipelines*, p. 96.

[99]Carter Goodrich, *Government Promotion of American Canals and Railroads*, pp. 232–57.

[100]Ibid., pp. 214, 216–17, 245–53.

including New Mexico, Arizona, Virginia, North Carolina, South Carolina, and Maine.[101]

The era of state railroad subsidization was followed by an era of railroad *regulation*. Beginning in the 1840s and peaking in the 1870s and 1880s, as seen in table 11.1, over one-half of all states passed general regulatory statutes in contrast to specific charter provisions and established regulatory commissions to administer them. In the first decades, the commissions were mainly advisory; later, more detailed functions were assumed.

The inspiration and consequences of federal railroad regulation have been the subject of much scholarly debate. The common interpretation has been that while railroads sought and benefited from subsidization, they opposed and suffered from later regulation. In historian Sidney Miller's estimation, the railroads were forced to "bow to the public will."[102] This interpretation, however, has fallen into disrepute. Undoubtedly, some anti-railroad legislation stemmed from anti-railroad sentiment—to wit, long-standing charter provisions unfavorable to the railroads. But new regulation, such as maximum-rate legislation enacted in Illinois in 1871 and Wisconsin and Iowa in 1874, had roots outside the public-interest arena.[103] Prior to regulation, prices were falling from intense competition as a result of new entry, and the public was well served.[104] The source of complaint—and growing state regulation—was certain shippers (often farmers) who were in a disadvantageous bargaining position and complained about rebates received by their more adept competitors. Independent oil shippers, another major lobby, wanted to ban rebates to better compete against Standard Oil and spearheaded the first federal bill to do so—written by a lawyer of the Philadelphia and Reading Railroad.[105] Many railroads, which desired similar regulation to tame competition, joined the disgruntled shippers. Thus, "public-interest" regulation played into the hands of the regulated— as demonstrated by industry support of important provisions of

[101]Ibid., pp. 217–21, 253–55.

[102]Sidney Miller, *Railway Transportation* (New York: A. W. Shaw, 1924), p. 703.

[103]Ibid., p. 708. Administration problems and unsatisfactory results with maximum-rate regulation led to repeal or relaxation of the laws. Ibid., pp. 708, 722.

[104]Gabriel Kolko, *Railroads and Regulation* (New York: W. W. Norton, 1965), p. 7.

[105]Ibid., p. 21. Harold Williamson and Arnold Daum, *The Age of Illumination*, p. 431. Also see this chapter, pp. 622–23.

Table 11.1
ESTABLISHMENT OF STATE RAILROAD COMMISSIONS

State	Year	State	Year	State	Year
New Hampshire	1844	Minnesota	1874	Alabama	1881
Connecticut	1853	Wisconsin	1874	Kansas	1883
Vermont	1855	Missouri	1875	Mississippi	1884
Maine	1858	Virginia	1875	Nebraska	1885
Ohio	1867	California	1876	Colorado	1885
Massachusetts	1869	Iowa	1878	Texas	1891
Illinois	1871	South Carolina	1878	South Dakota	1897
Rhode Island	1872	Georgia	1879	Florida	1897
Michigan	1873	Kentucky	1880	Tennessee	1897

SOURCES: Albert Ellingwood and Whitney Coombs, *The Government and Railroad Transportation* (Boston: Ginn, 1930), p. 48; and Emory Johnson, *American Railway Transportation*, p. 362.

state regulation.[106] Price discrimination, which hindered efforts to pool traffic and standardize fares, was prohibited, as were formal attempts to pool. The ironic result was that while firms could not formally standardize rates under legal prohibitions against pooling, they could achieve a similar result at arm's length with individualized concessions and illegal secret discounts. Regulations setting maximum operating hours curtailed competition, reduced alternatives for shippers, and worked against fare reductions. Licensing, moreover, whereby each railroad had to continually meet minimum safety standards to be allowed to operate, reduced low-cost competition from potential and existing entrants. On balance, the so-called Granger laws favored the regulated as much as or more than they worked in favor of shippers and the public.

On the federal level, land grants of approximately 50 million acres were given to railroad companies between 1862 and 1864, primarily for Pacific Coast projects.[107] Counting earlier federal grants, a total of between one-fourth and one-ninth of ten different states were on the balance sheets of railway firms.[108] The Illinois Central Railroad, for one, was characterized by a financial analyst as "not a railway company" but "a land company."[109]

In addition to liberal land grants, $64.6 million in thirty-year government bonds was loaned to railways. With the U.S. Treasury taking second liens on railroad assets, repayment in the 1895–99 period would be over 95 percent.[110] This surprising result, considering the dismal record of earlier financial subsidization, mirrored the improved health of major railroad companies in the late nineteenth century, attributable in large part to federal regulation that reduced price competition and increased profitability, as explained below.

[106]For the favorable view of railroads toward state regulation, see William Shinn, "The Relations of Railways to the State," *Railway Review*, March 13, 1886, p. 122. Cited in Gabriel Kolko, *Railroads and Regulation*, p. 41.

[107]One motivation was to court California to neutralize the influence of the Confederate states.

[108]Frederick Cleveland and Fred Powell, *Railroad Promotion and Capitalization in the United States*, p. 251.

[109]Quoted in ibid., p. 225. Land tax problems that accompanied land grants are discussed in Leslie Decker, *Railroads, Lands, and Politics* (Providence, R.I.: Brown University Press, 1964).

[110]Frederick Cleveland and Fred Powell, *Railroad Promotion and Capitalization in the United States*, pp. 256–57.

Local, state, and federal assistance to railroads after 1830 had the general effect of creating artificially high capacity in the industry. Overcapacity, coupled with the cost economics of the business—high "sunk" fixed costs irrelevant to operating decisions and low variable costs that had to be covered by operations—bred fierce price wars between competitors on common routes. To deal with threatening rivalry, cooperative attempts to set traffic quotas and prices were made, which failed in the face of new entry and secret price concessions.[111] This would lead to a new chapter in railroad regulation.

The interstate railroad industry, tiring of unsuccessful attempts to tame rivalry by business arrangements, turned to political means to achieve stability. The result was An Act to Regulate Commerce, signed by President Grover Cleveland on February 4, 1887.[112] The law had distinct origins within the oil industry. The original 1878 proposal, introduced by Congressman Lewis Watson of Warren County, Pennsylvania, was conceived by Pennsylvania oilman E. J. Patterson and drafted by an attorney of the Petroleum Producers Union. It became the Reagan bill in committee, and with a pooling prohibition it became the Act to Regulate Commerce.[113]

Later renamed the Interstate Commerce Act, the law resembled earlier state attempts to regulate railroads that subtly favored the regulated.[114] While section 5 specifically banned formal pooling agreements, section 3 prohibited "any undue or unreasonable preference or advantage to any particular person, company, firm, corporation, or locality, or any particular description of traffic."[115] Rates were to be "published" and "just and reasonable."[116] While *formal*

---

[111]The difficulty of free-market cartelization is a major theme of the petroleum market. Also see chapter 3, pp. 88, 91; chapter 17, p. 1050; chapter 23, pp. 1330–44; and chapter 26, pp. 1542–44.

[112]24 Stat. 379 (1887).

[113]Gerald Nash, "Origins of the Interstate Commerce Act of 1887," *Pennsylvania History*, July 1957, p. 186; and George Wolbert, "The Recurring Spectre of Pipeline Divorcement," in *Oil's First Century*, ed. Ralph Hidy (Boston: Harvard Graduate School of Business Administration, 1959), p. 106.

[114]The law was also modeled after the British Railway and Canal Traffic Act of 1854. See Bruce Wyman, *Railroad Rate Regulation* (New York: Baker, Voorkis, 1915), pp. 43, 51.

[115]24 Stat. 380.

[116]Ibid., p. 381. Two years later, tariff amendments required a ten-day notice of fare increases and a three-day notice of fare decreases. 25 Stat. 855 at 856.

cartelization was outlawed to appease anti-railroad groups such as New York merchants and midwestern agriculturalists, backdoor standardization and cartelization were assured by the prohibitions on disparate business practices, the essence of competition. Indeed, major studies of ratemaking in the period have found that it was more concerted and monopolistic after 1887 than before.[117] This subtle but intended result was reinforced by section 4 of the act, the so-called Long-and-Short-Haul clause, which required pricing proportional to distance and prohibited higher charges for shorter distances than for longer distances on the same track.[118] However, the enforcing body, the Interstate Commerce Commission, founded on April 5, 1887, could grant exceptions upon request. This meant, as noticed by historian Gabriel Kolko, that "section 4 was theoretically capable of being applied whenever it aided a carrier, or being set aside if it damaged it."[119] This proved to be the case from the beginning with the Interstate Commerce Commission's *Louisville and Nashville Railroad* decision of June 15, 1887.[120] With this bent, and the virtual elimination of discounts and other special fare reductions as illegal discrimination, many railroads enjoyed a rate level hitherto unachievable.[121] This led a number of shipping interests, including the Producers Protective Association of the Pennsylvania oil region, to advocate repeal of the 1887 law.[122] Concluded Kolko, "The Interstate Commerce Act was a bitter harvest for the farmers and merchants."[123] The law was also a bitter harvest for oil producers, oil refiners, and consumers of petroleum products.

[117]See Paul MacAvoy, *The Economic Effects of Regulation* (Cambridge, Mass.: MIT Press, 1965); Robert Spann and Edward Erickson, "The Economics of Railroading: The Beginning of Cartellization and Regulation," *Bell Journal of Economics* (Autumn 1970): 227–44; and George Hilton, "The Consistency of the Interstate Commerce Act," *Journal of Law and Economics* (October 1966): 87–113.

[118]24 Stat. 380.

[119]Gabriel Kolko, *Railroads and Regulation*, p. 50.

[120]Ibid., p. 51. An 1897 Supreme Court decision made section 4 a dead letter. *ICC v. Alabama Midland Railway Co.*, 168 U.S. 144 (1897).

[121]"For about six months after the formation of the Commission, railroad income grew because of the termination of many rebates, elimination of passes, and general conformity to the Act." Gabriel Kolko, *Railroads and Regulation*, p. 57. This would continue into the next century. Ibid., pp. 232–33.

[122]Ibid., p. 53.

[123]Ibid. For greater detail concerning continued control of regulation by railroads and the benefits therein prior to 1916, including the central role played by industrialist J. P. Morgan, see ibid., chaps. 6–10.

Government Intervention and Early Oil Transport: An Analysis

The genesis of crude-oil transportation was earlier identified as an emerging spontaneous order: self-interested individuals pursuing their own monetary gain unintentionally promoting industry coordination and helping consumers. This laudatory assessment must be qualified to take into account government intervention that suppressed entry, spawned monopolistic behavior by privileged firms, and hampered the full development of an efficient crude-oil and oil-product distribution system. Property-right violations that the judiciary was slow to rectify were another retardant of the timely development of new industry institutions.

Three areas of government intervention during the 1830–1900 period were special charters, subsidies, and regulation. Charters restricted entry with franchise rights and capitalization minimums. Eminent domain subsidized right-of-way costs for the special few and then all entrants, creating competitive disparities along the way. Entrants were regulated by common-carrier provisions, rate maximums, and restrictions on stock ownership in other companies.[124] Integration of pipelines into production and refining was banned in several major oil states.

Railroad subsidies through loans, stock purchases, land donations, condemnation rights, and other means encouraged overentry on new routes and created artificial incentives for the geographical dispersement of population and industry. The general result in the case of railroads was to dampen rivalry where consumer demand was strong and to promote overextension into areas where demand was weak. Such perversity, the opposite of what free-market incentives would have achieved, resulted from a combination of local political favoritism toward influential railroad interests and governments' quest to extend populated areas.

A related distortion was the subsidization of competing modes of transport. Clearly, cross-subsidization worked against itself and had the net effect of overbuilding the transportation industry relative to other industrial sectors and consumer demand.

Another area of intervention unfavorably affected the supply of and demand for transportation-related investment. State and local

---

[124]Restrictive provisions, such as maximum-rate regulation, were often justified by the presence of favorable provisions, such as franchise rights and condemnation rights.

governments created a false euphoria about the financial prospects for new transportation ventures to gain taxpayer support for subsidization as well as to lure private investment. Acting on bad information, many individuals realized poor returns on their investments, which created ill will toward involved transportation companies and demand for "punitive" regulation.

A second major capital-market distortion was the federal government's propensity for expansionary monetary policy, which periodically created boom-and-bust cycles throughout the nineteenth century. General economic instability played havoc with an industry already prone to uneven growth.

Examination of the specific consequences borne by the petroleum industry reveals that the artificially secure position of subsidized railroads proved to be a barrier to crude-oil transportation in the 1860s. In particular, land grants well in excess of actually homesteaded areas not only induced overbuilding but gave railroads the means to obstruct pipeline projects. This stunted pipeline growth when pipelines' superiority to railcar transport was emerging, resulting in higher transportation costs that producers, refiners, and consumers had to bear.[125] Without government involvement, furthermore, the railroad industry would have been smaller and financially stronger to make capital markets more responsive to new transportation alternatives such as pipelines.

Joining intervention as a barrier to petroleum transportation was a property-rights problem. With a proper delineation of first title, pipeline obstructionism would not have been as prevalent. Under a homestead rule, unoccupied wilderness land would have been unowned until the railroad cleared the land for track construction. Land outside the cleared area would have remained unowned until further labor was performed on the land.[126] With less land, there would have been less obstruction. Under a thoroughgoing homestead theory, moreover, the pipeline seeking entry would have been able to cross below or above the homesteaded surface area if provable

[125]Railroads enjoyed condemnation rights much more frequently than did pipelines. The only advantage pipelines could claim over railroads was in the predominant oil state of Pennsylvania: the absence of a tonnage tax.

[126]Homesteading would have replaced land grants that extended as much as nine miles on each side of the track. This surplus land, in turn, was conveniently used to collateralize loans.

surface damage was not done.[127] Any need for direct entrance on the railroad's homesteaded surface property would have required negotiation to avoid trespass, but ingenuity in tunneling under or bridging the track without actual surface entry would have mitigated the powers of recalcitrant railroads to obstruct in "worst-case" situations.

Under that reformulation of property rights, the raison d'être of eminent-domain rights for pipelines (and other transportation modes) could have been challenged. Problems experienced by oil pipeline companies that "necessitated" condemnation rights were overwhelmingly connected with railroad obstructionism, not the absence of a right-of-way market. Examples exist of sizable projects completed without condemnation rights, such as the 115-mile Tide-Water pipeline completed in early 1878.[128] Standard Oil did not condemn land as company policy. It is true that at a certain price every project becomes unfeasible, and right-of-way costs can make the difference between project construction and project abandonment, but that is not a reason to prevent transactions at the market price, which must be defined as no more or less than the price mutually agreed upon by seller and buyer.[129] Advocates of condemnation rights are espousing forced transactions at below-market prices, which, as does any nonmarket price, conveys price misinformation and leads to inefficient entrepreneurial decisionmaking. Eminent-domain exponents contend that the "public interest" is served by taking the shortest, most economical route, and by making—by force if necessary—a market. Yet how do we measure and compare the benefits and costs of this policy? The potential losers include not only the coerced landowner or landowners but those exclusively involved with any alternate route (project) that might have been

[127]Damage bonds were customarily posted by the entering company to cover the event of damage to preexisting facilities. The same precaution could have been required by the surface owners under their homestead rights.

[128]Ingenuity on the part of Standard was required to escape recalcitrant landowners and obstruction, but Tide-Water prevailed. See Harold Williamson and Arnold Daum, *The Age of Illumination*, p. 441.

[129]It is fallacious to average the prices of past transactions deemed to be similar to determine a "fair" or "market" price as a basis for forced transactions. Historical transactions, particularly in the case of something as individualized as land rights-of-way, do not necessarily reflect the conditions surrounding present or future transactions.

used in the absence of condemnation law.[130] Only with ambiguity can their loss be said to be less than the gain to others, consumers included. An economic case cannot be made for such forced transactions, in short, without resorting to arbitrary judgments of interpersonal utility.

Hand in hand with eminent-domain privileges in corporate charters and state statutes came the obligation to serve as a common carrier, agreeing to transport all presented goods to capacity. Although the two may be statutorily related, the logic that supports one does not make a case for the other. Both are self-contained interventions that have separate beneficiaries and separate costs. Common-carrier regulation, ostensibly justified by the "public" nature of transportation, penalizes the regulated company in favor of marginal shippers—including crude-oil overproducers. As does condemnation, it denies the businessman the right to choose his clientele and terms of service. As argued in chapter 3, common-carrier regulations forced transactions between crude producers and transporters and discouraged wellhead consolidation and integration that were sorely needed to achieve unitized production during the troubled 1930s.[131]

As theory would predict, transportation interventionism in the nineteenth century turned out to be unsatisfactory. Subsidies, non-market charter provisions, and regulation proved to be a poor substitute for private entrepreneurship operating in a climate of government neutrality. Such intervention created a surmountable barrier that market forces eventually overcame. The result was generally efficient transportation services for crude oil and oil products, which contributed to the "spontaneous order" of the petroleum industry in its developmental stage.

---

[130]If right-of-way problems had killed the project in the absence of condemnation, the winners would have included other transportation modes that would have picked up the business and other industries that would have received freed capital resources.

[131]See chapter 3, pp. 118–19.

12. Regulation of Petroleum Allocation

Regulation of petroleum allocation has occurred in a variety of historical situations. Except for one instance, the common denominator has been effective maximum-price controls placed on crude oil and petroleum products. Price regulation during World War I, World War II, and the Korean conflict created imbalances between demand and supply that allocation and transportation directives attempted to address. Railroad tank cars and oil tankers were closely regulated during World War I, and during World War II, tank trucks were federally controlled as well. In the Korean conflict, precautionary regulation of tankers and rail cars was undertaken, although it was not as consequential as in the previous two wars.

Recent experience with oil price controls was accompanied by comprehensive allocation. Although the Emergency Petroleum Allocation Act of 1973 stopped short of setting preference hierarchies, the supplier-purchaser rule attempted to assign every barrel of domestic oil to the historic buyer. As important as direct allocation regulation in the 1970s was the emergence of a sizable oil-reselling industry that arose from regulatory opportunities. This saga of the unintended consequences of price and allocation controls is treated in depth in the final section of this chapter.

One major allocation episode did not concern price ceilings and inadequate supply. In the 1930s, record production and falling prices inspired regulation to limit crude output. Because the thousands of wells involved could not be adequately monitored, the strategy of state and federal authorities was to prevent the distribution of illegally produced oil and thus exert backpressure to stop wellhead overproduction. The saga of East Texas hot-oil regulation is examined in chronological sequence with the other allocation experiences.

The five regulatory episodes studied in this chapter do not entirely cover the allocation and transportation field. Transportation intervention that was not part of wartime planning is examined in chapters 11 and 16 for railroads, water vessels, and trucks. Intervention in oil pipelines, including wartime planning, is the subject of chapter 14. Natural-gas pipeline intervention and gas-curtailment priorities set during the 1971–72 and 1976–77 shortages are examined in chapter 15. Two major allocation programs under the Emergency Petroleum Allocation Act (EPAA), the buy-sell and entitlements programs, are described in chapter 20 on modern intervention in refining.

World War I Planning

Lever Act Authority

The Lever Act, signed August 10, 1917, authorized government intervention in the allocation of fuel oil as a wartime measure.[1] By executive order or proclamation, a licensing system could be activated for the "importation . . . storage . . . or distribution of such fuel."[2] It was declared illegal to waste, hoard, restrict, or monopolize "the supply of any necessaries."[3] Detailed record keeping for federal inspection could be ordered.[4] Governmental powers of requisition— the compulsory sale of assets deemed important to the war effort— were granted so long as "just compensation" was paid.[5] Price controls could be implemented only in the event of "unfair storage charge, commission, profit, or practice." In such cases, the president could substitute a "just, reasonable, nondiscriminatory, and fair" price.[6]

The Lever Act's limited authority placed a premium on industry cooperation with the U.S. Fuel Administration's Oil Division, headed by Mark Requa, that was formed in early 1918.[7] Authorities and the industry advisory group, the National Petroleum War Service Committee, had to rely on industry efforts. The Federal Trade Commission, established in 1914, however, was fit to wield antitrust

---

[1]Public Law 41, 40 Stat. 276 (1917). For greater detail on the evolution of World War I planning, see chapter 5, pp. 223–27.

[2]Public Law 41, 40 Stat. 276 (1917) at 277.

[3]Ibid.

[4]Ibid.

[5]Ibid., p. 279.

[6]Ibid., p. 278.

[7]For an organizational chart of the Oil Division, see appendix E, p. 1941.

law at interfirm pooling and other cooperative acts. Cooperative planning sanctioned by the Lever Act would win out.[8]

Transportation and Intervention

Federal transportation regulation, administered by the Interstate Commerce Commission (ICC) before the war, was not the product of cooperation but of confrontation. Rate-increase denials by the ICC beginning in 1910 weakened the financial health and the reinvestment capacity of railroads whose costs were rising as a result of inflation. This led to labor unrest and service breakdowns that culminated in the nationalization of major railroads in late 1917.[9] Not only was oil transportation disrupted; coal became unavailable as a result of transportation bottlenecks, and unprecedented pressure was placed on fuel oil to take up the slack.[10] Under government control, tank-car transportation continued to have problems between the field and refineries and between refineries and product bulk stations.[11]

International hostilities created a problem for waterway shipping. As early as 1914, a Jersey Standard tanker was detained by British authorities. When seizures ended two years later, German submarine attacks commenced. By the end of 1917, sinkings exceeded new construction by 2.5 million tons.[12]

The strain of meeting domestic and foreign fuel requirements inspired federal wartime intervention and invited more government involvement.[13] The U.S. Shipping Board and the Emergency Fleet Corporation increased their authority throughout 1917 and 1918. Beginning in April 1917, private chartering required shipping board approval, and outstanding contracts could be modified at will.[14]

---

[8]Gerald Nash, *United States Oil Policy* (Westport, Conn.: Greenwood Press, 1968, 1976), p. 36.

[9]See chapter 16, pp. 975–77.

[10]George Gibb and Evelyn Knowlton, *The Resurgent Years* (New York: Harper & Brothers, 1956), p. 229.

[11]*National Petroleum News,* June 12, 1918, pp. 9–10. Cited hereafter as *NPN.* Another problem cited by regulators was really a savior—tank-car diversions by product brokers. *Oil & Gas Journal,* May 30, 1918, p. 34. Cited hereafter as *OGJ.*

[12]George Gibb and Evelyn Knowlton, *The Resurgent Years,* p. 224.

[13]Ibid., p. 226.

[14]Gerald White called marine shipping "the most crucial of all shortages in World War I." White, *Formative Years in the Far West* (New York: Appleton-Century-Crofts, 1962), p. 544.

Requisitions were commonplace. In January 1918, a major requisition of oil vessels from the Pacific Coast to war duty on the Atlantic side abrogated contracts and forced consumers to turn to the higher priced spot market for fuel oil.[15]

Shipbuilding contracts were amended by the U.S. Shipping Board in favor of the builder, which resulted in significantly higher prices.[16] Insurance was subsidized by the U.S. Bureau of War Risk in cases in which private tanker protection was too expensive or too little.[17] On October 17, 1918, the U.S. Shipping Board requisitioned all cargo ships over 2,500 tons for reassignment.[18] Oil exchanges were ordered to reduce transportation distances.[19]

Transportation planning was rife with errors and inefficiency. One example was a shipping regulation that disrupted Mexican oil deliveries and idled border refineries.[20] The general problem was summarized George Gibb and Evelyn Knowlton:

> Federal policy fluctuated from week to week and the loose threads of federal administration were tangled. The good intentions of government agencies frequently were submerged in the ignorance, inexperience, and confusion of the times.[21]

Licensing and Allocation

On January 31, 1918, President Wilson invoked the Lever Act to license all fuel-oil refiners and distributors with yearly volumes of 100,000 barrels or more. This covered virtually the whole marketing sector.[22] Gasoline and kerosene were not affected. Fuel-transportation problems due to "traffic congestion on our railways" and lack

---

[15]*OGJ*, January 31, 1918, p. 36.

[16]George Gibb and Evelyn Knowlton, *The Resurgent Years*, p. 227. Sun Oil's shipbuilding subsidiary was one beneficiary of contract changes. See August Giebelhaus, *Business and Government in the Oil Industry* (Greenwich: Jai Press, 1980), p. 53.

[17]George Gibb and Evelyn Knowlton, *The Resurgent Years*, pp. 227–28.

[18]Gerald White, *Formative Years in the Far West*, p. 545.

[19]Ibid., p. 547.

[20]Simon Simon, *Economic Legislation of Taxation* (New York: Arno Press, 1979), p. 39.

[21]George Gibb and Evelyn Knowlton, *The Resurgent Years*, p. 227.

[22]Reprinted in *General Orders, Regulations and Rulings of the United States Fuel Administration* (Washington, D.C.: Government Printing Office, 1919), pp. 579–80. Cited hereafter as *General Orders*.

of available coastal steamships due to war-related transatlantic duty were cited as justifications for the licensing measure. Administered by the Oil Division, licensing was intended to ensure priority for "essential" industries or needs.[23] A preference hierarchy was established, and effective February 11, each licensed distributor east of the Rocky Mountains was instructed to satisfy demands of higher preference groups before meeting lower preference requests unless approved by the Fuel Administration. The classifications in order of preference were as follows.

1. Railroads and bunker fuel;
2. Export deliveries or shipments for the U.S. Army or Navy;
3. Export deliveries for the purposes of the Allies;
4. Hospitals that use fuel oil as fuel;
5. Public utilities and domestic consumers;
6. Shipyards under government contract;
7. Navy yards;
8. Arsenals;
9. Food-manufacturing plants;
10. Army and Navy cantonments where oil is in use;
11. Munitions manufacturers under government contract; and
12. All other classes.[24]

On March 19, an amendment was made to include oil refineries in the first category with railroads and bunker fuel.[25]

Oil Division administrator Mark Requa was not averse to regulation. In the spring of 1918 he stated:

> If zonal distribution of petroleum products is necessary to supply national needs, zonal distribution will be accomplished. If pooling of tank cars and ships will more efficiently meet national demands, those facilities will be pooled. . . . If licensing of jobbers and others is necessary, they will be licensed. . . . In short, whatever the national needs may be, everything that is necessary will be done to meet those requirements.[26]

---

[23]Ibid. Also see *OGJ*, February 7, 1918, p. 36.

[24]*General Orders*, p. 581.

[25]Ibid., pp. 581–82.

[26]*OGJ*, April 4, 1918, p. 49.

True to form, problems would be addressed by new regulation rather than by repudiating existing regulation.

Requa's first administrative action was taken on March 20, 1918. To supplement voluntary fuel-oil distribution, standby authority was given to pool fuel oil east of the Rockies. Private contracts were thus put on notice.[27] In June, Requa "suggested" a freeze in distribution channels to accompany "voluntary" maximum-price regulation that had been in effect since late May.[28] Following complaints that middlemen "profiteered" with crude oil and petroleum products, Requa hinted at more formal price regulation a month later.[29] Thomas O'Donnell of the Fuel Administration also jawboned the industry not to interrupt existing channels of distribution.[30]

Price and allocation controls were formalized under "the Plan." On August 9, 1918, ceiling prices were set, and crude distribution was frozen in May 17 channels unless approved by a local committee of the Petroleum War Service Committee, the Committee on Conciliation and Cooperation. This went beyond the bounds of the Lever Act, but the voluntary program, backed by veiled threats of enabling legislation, would suffice. The Petroleum War Service Committee and the Fuel Administration would review crude-allocation decisions throughout the planning period.[31]

With crude-oil allocation and fuel-oil distribution regulated for most companies, the next step was to bring remaining unregulated companies and fuels under planning. On September 23, 1918, President Wilson used emergency wartime powers to license virtually

---

[27]*OGJ*, March 21, 1918, p. 28. Requa's action was endorsed by an *OGJ* editorial, on March 28, 1918, "Fuel Oil Control Necessary," which said, "If sacrifices are required, they must be made" (p. 2).

[28]*OGJ*, June 28, 1918, p. 38. By this time, Requa had appointed the Advisory Committee on Distribution for the Atlantic Division, composed of representatives from fifteen leading oil companies, to voluntarily pool facilities and inventories to meet consumer requests.

[29]*OGJ*, May 30, 1918, p. 34.

[30]*OGJ*, July 5, 1918, p. 42.

[31]Northcutt Ely, "The Government in the Exercise of the War Power," in *Conservation of Oil and Gas: A Legal History, 1948*, ed. Blakely M. Murphy (Chicago: American Bar Association, 1949), p. 665; hereafter cited as *Legal History*, 1949; and William Kemnitzer, *Rebirth of Monopoly: A Critical Analysis of Economic Control in the Petroleum Industry of the United States* (New York: Harper & Brothers, 1938), p. 19.

the entire oil and gas industry.[32] Importers, refiners, distributors, and transporters of crude oil, gas oil, kerosene, and gasoline were affected. Distributors and transporters of natural gas, including integrated producers, were also included. Retailers of the above-mentioned products with annual sales below $100,000 were exempted. Producers were not licensed because of their sheer numbers. Authorities could now regulate the movement and price of all petroleum products to engineer a political solution to the "what, when, where, and how much" problem normally solved by spontaneous market forces.

Deregulation

Comprehensive regulation lived a short and uneventful life. The November 11, 1918, armistice was soon followed by deregulation. The license system was terminated December 7. Price and allocation controls under the Plan were lifted December 16. The U.S. Fuel Administration, reflecting the positive experience of the cooperative effort of the industry and regulators, survived until June 30, 1919.[33]

Evaluation

"The dire effects of tank-car and tank-steamer shortages," stated George Gibb and Evelyn Knowlton, "had been overcome by central planning and industry-wide cooperation."[34] This surprising assessment, given the authors' earlier characterization of transportation planning as "submerged in . . . ignorance, inexperience, and confusion," fails to correlate experienced problems with regulation and reflects an inability to perceive free-market solutions.[35] ICC regulation, not the free market, was responsible for railroad nationalization. Tanker deliveries, which were dependable before sinkings and requisitions became a way of life, were erratic under regulation. Tankers were always available at the right price to government as buyer or lessee, however, even if making them available required paying private parties to relax preexisting contracts.

---

[32]*General Orders*, pp. 582–88.

[33]The dissolution order of Fuel Administrator James Garfield is reprinted in *OGJ*, May 23, 1919, p. 2.

[34]George Gibb and Evelyn Knowlton, *The Resurgent Years*, pp. 242–43.

[35]Ibid., p. 227.

Planning banked on patriotism over self-interest. As Mark Requa told the industry:

> The war service of the petroleum industry is of the highest importance. It should be looked upon as a priceless privilege to assist in winning this war. The honor of patriotically, promptly, and efficiently performing that service should be guarded with the same jealous care with which you guard the welfare and sanctity of your homes.[36]

This world view had two fundamental shortcomings. One was the assumption that planning incentives could duplicate market incentives to elicit efficient outcomes. Second, even if incentives were present, the entrepreneurial discovery process could not be duplicated in the absence of market rivalry.[37]

Criticism of the novel government-industry petroleum alliance was discouraged as unpatriotic not only by authorities but within the industry. The *Oil & Gas Journal* lambasted a complaint about a permit denial by the Capital Issues Committee as "show[ing] an utter lack of fairness as well as . . . lack of knowledge."[38] Such journalistic patriotism prevented more planning errors from being exposed. But several things are known. Suspending competition, limiting firm entry, and pooling tasks on a cost-plus basis limited innovation through discovery.[39] No matter how great his patriotism, entrepreneurial contributions by the man on the spot were precluded by frozen chains of distribution and centralized decisions. Ostracism of low-cost firms for "profiteering" protected high-cost firms and allowed them to institutionalize inefficiency.[40]

[36]*OGJ*, April 4, 1918, p. 49.

[37]See chapter 1, pp. 32, 51.

[38]*OGJ*, October 25, 1918, p. 2.

[39]See this chapter, pp. 662–65, for further discussion on this point and a more detailed criticism of planning.

[40]A Federal Trade Commission study issued June 29, 1918, criticized "heavy profit made by the low-cost concern under a governmental fixed price for the whole country" as "inordinate greed and barefaced fraud." *OGJ*, July 5, 1918, p. 49. The *Texaco Star* took issue with the fallacious inference of the study: "It is the low-cost producer who's rendering the best service to the public. He is the leader, the explorer, the pathfinder in industry [who] . . . show[s] the way to the others." Furthermore, "by doing his work with a lower expenditure of labor, [the low-cost producer] releases labor for other work, a consideration quite as important as price." *Texaco Star*, September 1918, p. 8.

East Texas Hot-Oil Regulation: 1931–35

Along with alcohol prohibition (1920–33) and drug prohibition (1917–present), the legislative and administrative battle against hot-oil production in the 1931–35 period is one of the most illustrative cases of civil disobedience and lawbreaking ingenuity in U.S. history. Hot oil was defined as crude produced in excess of legal limits.[41] Unlike the situation with the other prohibited substances, detection and prevention of hot oil were eventually accomplished by a determined enforcement effort by federal and state authorities and supportive industry segments, and the task was made easier by the limited geographical area in which the contraband was to be found.[42]

The Battle over Production Limitation

The young Texas and Oklahoma proration efforts, limiting well output to a price-stabilizing "market demand," were severely tested in 1931 with the development of the East Texas field and, to a lesser extent, the Oklahoma City field. The mere threat of wide-open production led to declarations of martial law and shutdowns of the two great fields in August of that year.[43] When the fields were reopened with allowable assignments far below their per well potential, dissention among area producers, refiners, and shippers ran high, and hot oil began to be produced, transported, and refined along with allowable crude. Prices began to fall from wellhead to retail, and many established integrated companies began to experience losses despite high sales volume. Twenty-nine companies, which enjoyed cumulative profits of $497 million in 1929 and $271 million in 1930, suffered losses of $74 million in 1931.[44] This unfavorable development raised much concern and resolve within the industry to reduce price cutting and standardize retail practices via state-enforced wellhead proration and a marketing code of "fair competition."[45] Control of East Texas, however, would be no easy task; the

[41]The term hot oil was "borrowed from the argot of the peace officer, who for years had characterized stolen goods of any kind as 'hot.' " *NPN*, February 5, 1936, p. 430. Another source of the characterization was the high temperature that oil had from rapid withdrawal rates. *World Petroleum*, November 1937, p. 30.

[42]Allowable assignments by individual states such as Texas, California, and Kansas often exceeded federal recommendations, but this was not considered hot oil because the states had the sovereignty to set production quotas.

[43]See chapters 3, pp. 89–94, and chapter 4, pp. 138–41.

[44]*OGJ*, December 6, 1934, p. 12.

[45]On the drive for a marketing code, see chapter 23, pp. 1328–44.

effort to stabilize production and price would require four long years of struggle.

Rise of Hot Oil. The East Texas field was recognized as a destabilizing influence on the entire midcontinent region at the inaugural meeting of the Division of Production of the American Petroleum Institute in June 1931. Two months before, the first proration order for East Texas had been greeted by forty lawsuits that were "but the beginning of a ludicrous game of battledore and shuttlecock between the Commission and a minority element of East Texas."[46] Ten percent of the field's wells were suspected of violating state production rules, and the American Petroleum Institute sought unitization or a voluntary proration agreement to keep output below potentials.[47]

When the dust of martial law cleared a year later, evidence of overproduction and devious practices abounded. In response, an American Petroleum Institute committee audited the files of major pipeline companies in East Texas and compared the amount of shipped oil with the field's allowable to settle rumors of rampant supra-allowable production.[48] When suspicions of illegal production were confirmed, the Texas Railroad Commission (TRC) was pressured to hold hearings to field complaints and devise a plan of action. Numerous complaints about ineffective enforcement were aired in January 1933 hearings, and a striking example was showcased—the "Fortress of Gladewater," an oil well encased by a concrete blockhouse to thwart detection.[49] Another hundred proration violations were documented, whereupon a bellwether recommendation was made by Texas attorney general James Allred to concentrate enforcement on hot-oil transportation and leave the "little guys" (the independents) alone.[50] The TRC had jurisdiction over all forms of intrastate transportation (railroads, pipelines, and motor vehicles) in addition to oil production, and Commissioner E. O. Thompson

[46]Harry Harter, *East Texas Oil Parade* (San Antonio: Maylor, 1934), p. 102.
[47]*NPN*, June 3, 1931, p. 19.
[48]*Oil Weekly*, August 15, 1932, p. 8. Cited hereafter as *OW*.
[49]*OGJ*, January 19, 1933, p. 7.
[50]"If we are going to get at this thing, we need to check up on all pipelines. We want to know how the oil is getting out of the field, and how much." *OGJ*, January 19, 1933, p. 7.

announced his intent to expand mandatory reporting and require meters to be installed on pipelines.[51] Reform, however, would be slow. Hot-oil production would soon equal and then exceed the legal allowable of 400,000 daily barrels and prices would drop to under $0.25 per barrel.[52]

Enforcement of assigned allowables by the TRC was difficult and necessarily lax. A drilling spree, fostered in part by allowable assignments per well, spawned thousands of new wells, the policing of which was far beyond the limited staff and budget of the commission.[53] Wide use of injunctions by producers and refiners against the enforcement actions of the TRC allowed autonomous decisions that invariably favored supra-allowable output.[54] Even producers who supported proration overproduced in self-defense to maintain revenue at depressed prices. Other complicating factors were local independents' dislike of output quotas and the fact that locally elected policing authorities were sympathetic to local opinion. Bribes and financial support for elections in return for lax enforcement were common.[55] Not coincidentally, enforcement was relaxed before elections and strict after elections.[56]

The situation was not improved when new extensions of the East Texas field were discovered, and restless operators began to ignore their quotas. Asked an *Oil & Gas Journal* editorial in early 1933, "Is Proration Doomed?"[57]

[51]*OGJ*, January 5, 1933, p. 18.

[52]*OGJ*, January 19, 1933, p. 7; and *NPN*, February 1, 1933, p. 3.

[53]In 1932 alone, the number of wells increased from under 4,000 to over 9,000 in the several-hundred-square-mile field. See chapter 4, table 4.7, pp. 177–78. A similar problem existed in the eleven-square-mile Oklahoma City field, where approximately 500 wells were operating.

[54]See Robert Hardwicke, "Legal History of Conservation of Oil in Texas," in American Bar Association, *Legal History of Conservation of Oil and Gas* (Baltimore: Lord Baltimore Press, 1939), pp. 238–39.

[55]*OGJ*, August 25, 1932, p. 11. An editorial in the September 22, 1932, issue of the *OGJ* characterized the lawlessness between the regulators and the regulated as "a sad commentary on state enforcement and the mixing of politics with a vital business" (p. 7).

[56]*OW*, August 29, 1932, p. 9.

[57]*OGJ*, January 5, 1933, p. 18. A former member of the U.S. Department of Justice prohibition squad testified before the TRC that hot oil was more difficult to detect (and its producers more difficult to prosecute) than bootleg liquor. *NPN*, February 15, 1933, p. 25.

Federal Intervention and Control. With crisis at hand, major oil companies turned to their federal representatives and a sympathetic newly appointed secretary of the interior, Harold Ickes. It was resolved at a March 27, 1933, meeting between Ickes and the oil-state governors, the first meeting of its kind in peacetime, to ask President Roosevelt to temporarily shut in production and ban interstate hot-oil transportation as an emergency measure.[58] Although FDR did not act on the request, the meeting marked the beginning of attempts to supplement ineffective state efforts with federal regulation.

East Texas production would soon confirm the critics' worst fears. An open-flow test for maximum East Texas output with 401 of the field's 10,000 wells yielded a two-hour estimate of 2.7 million barrels, which was 700,000 barrels more than daily U.S. consumption.[59] By April 1, 1933, the field equaled its all-time production high of June 1931, and prices fell under $0.25 per barrel. An urgent message wired from the Longview Chamber of Commerce and fifty-two local oil producers to Secretary Ickes urged federal intervention.

> Conditions in largest oil field in the United States . . . rapidly approaching chaos. Injunctions and counter-injunctions of laws and rules, dissention in legislature, lack of respect of orders of state commission and widespread violations . . . are menacing our interests and whole industry and public good by dissipation of irreplaceable natural resources and threatened disorder. Armed men protecting leases and pipelines. Pipelines have been dynamited. The organization . . . believes that inability of state authorities to bring about effective control of production . . . justifies us in requesting immediate federal control of East Texas oil field.[60]

On April 6, the field was closed. It reopened on April 24 with a doubled allowable of 850,000 barrels per day, whereupon prices fell to $0.10 per barrel.[61] With hot-oil output rising, production approached 1 million barrels per day in May and June of 1933, which captured the national spotlight as single-handedly destabilizing the

---

[58]*OGJ*, March 30, 1933, pp. 7, 11.
[59]*NPN*, March 29, 1933, p. 8.
[60]Ibid.
[61]*NPN*, April 26, 1933, p. 11.

entire U.S. oil market. The 73rd Congress sympathetically entertained a host of bills that would eventually result in federal support for the fledgling TRC.[62]

In Oklahoma, a similar problem existed with the flush Oklahoma City field, although on a much smaller scale than in East Texas. Allowables enforcement was haphazard and legally hamstrung, and charges of racketeering among proration officials, including enforcement head Cicero Murray and other relatives of Governor Murray, made a mockery of the motives and sincerity of the state effort.[63] To save face, Governor Murray signed a new proration act on April 10, 1933, with stiff penalties for illegal production and the giving or taking of bribes.[64] Tenders and affidavits, consequently, surrounded oil production and transportation in the field. Although those measures were not entirely effective, the threat of destabilizing quantities of hot oil would not subsequently arise as it would in East Texas.[65]

On June 16, 1933, the eagerly sought interstate prohibition on transportation of hot oil became law in section 9(c) of the National Industrial Recovery Act.[66] The Connally amendment marked the entrance of federal intervention in state proration. Upon petition by

[62]Northcutt Ely, "The Use of Federal Powers to Supplement Those of the States," in *Legal History,* 1949, pp. 692–93.

[63]Court testimony alleged that bribes were taken not only to allow production of hot oil but to provide "protection" for shipments of the illegal oil. *OGJ,* February 9, 1933, p. 9; February 16, 1933, p. 11; February 23, 1933, p. 10; and March 2, 1933, p. 11. Also see *OW,* February 27, 1933, p. 8. The governor's cousin-in-law, Ray Walker, a hot-oil broker, was taperecorded saying: "They can't prove that I ever gave Cicero a nickel. The thing to do now is to protect Cicero. We've got to . . . help him. Cicero would do anything in the world for us." *NPN,* February 15, 1933, p. 22. Also see *NPN,* February 8, 1933, pp. 19–23. Governor Murray attempted to deport a witness against Walker. *NPN,* March 1, 1933 p. 21. The scandal ended short of a high-level prosecution when Cicero Murray refused to appear before the state senate investigative committee, citing an order from his brother that he was on duty to the governor and could not be arrested except for felony or treason. *NPN,* March 22, 1933, p. 14.

[64]*OGJ,* April 13, 1933, p. 24.

[65]*OGJ,* August 31, 1933, p. 14.

[66]"The President is authorized to prohibit the transportation in interstate and foreign commerce of petroleum and the products thereof produced or withdrawn from storage in excess of the amount permitted to be produced or withdrawn from storage by any State law or valid regulation or order prescribed thereunder. . . . Any violation of any order of the President issued under the provisions of this subsection shall be punishable by fine not to exceed $1,000, or imprisonment for not to exceed six months, or both." Public Law 67, 48 Stat. 200 (1933).

the Independent Petroleum Association of America, FDR by executive order invoked section 9(c) on July 11 and assigned federal agents to East Texas.[67] A week before, the Texas Petroleum Council had been formed to assist the floundering TRC by Texas oilmen who favored higher prices for controlled output. Together with federal officials, some of whom were situated in the field in anticipation of the order, they created a formidable alliance for the hot-oil industry to conquer. If hot-oil participants outfoxed the TRC in the first skirmish, they would have to beat organized federal and industry forces as well the second time around.

Less than a week after Interior's Oil Enforcement Unit settled in East Texas, rail shipments of contraband oil, the primary means of transport, virtually ceased.[68] Affidavits verifying oil as allowable were now required from all producers, refiners, and transporters. For the first time since the August 1931 shutdown, the great field was under control, although it would prove to be a lull, not dissolution and defeat, for the black marketeers.

On July 24, 1933, the federal clamp was extended to petroleum products manufactured by local refineries that routinely ran contraband oil.[69] On July 29, the TRC began supervising tenders' checks to clear up authorization disputes.[70] Flush with success, Ickes amended the hot-oil regulations on August 2 to apply only to the East Texas and Oklahoma City fields rather than to the country as a whole.[71]

Ickes's new concern was not destabilizing quantities of hot oil but state defiance of the Petroleum Administration Board's quota recommendations, which was a legal version of the same problem. States could eliminate hot oil by raising allowables, and in

---

[67]*OW*, July 17, 1933, p. 9. Three days later, Executive Order 6204 gave Interior Secretary Ickes full presidential powers under section 9(c).

[68]Prior to July 15, an average of 500 tank cars shipped crude each day from the East Texas field; on July 16, the number shrank to 33, and a day later to only 10 where it remained. *OW*, July 24, 1933, p. 11. Also see *NPN*, July 26, 1933, p. 31. Drafting the regulations for the field were Yale law professor and conservation-law expert J. Howard Marshall and conservation writer and former assistant solicitor of the Federal Power Commission Norman Myers.

[69]*OW*, July 31, 1933, p. 13. On September 7, refiners were required to submit daily reports of crude oil received and product movements. *NPN*, September 13, 1933, p. 16.

[70]*NPN*, August 2, 1933, p. 10.

[71]*OGJ*, August 10, 1933, p. 10.

October 1933, Ickes threatened Texas, Oklahoma, California, and Kansas with legal action if their liberal quotas, destabilizing to a fragile price structure, were not reduced. While Texas responded by lowering allowables below the federal board's recommendations, California did not and was brought to court by Ickes on December 14, 1933.[72]

Return of Hot Oil. The hot-oil industry would reappear in high form. This turn of events followed a ruling in the *Panama* case on February 21, 1934, that Interior Department activities in East Texas unconstitutionally interfered with a nonfederal matter.[73] The injunction again pitted the hot-oil industry against the TRC.

The advantage was not with the regulators for a number of reasons. The TRC had become financially overextended in the hot-oil effort and had to make severe personnel cutbacks.[74] Second, state penalties were modest fines—which to many were little more than a cost of doing business—rather than imprisonment.[75] Injunctions against TRC shutdown orders also kept the hot-oil business operating at a steady hum.[76]

Finally, ingenuity coupled with the sheer size of illegal activity was more than could be stopped under existing statutes by existing personnel. Night production under guard, bypass pipelines to run output undetected, and arrangements with nearby refineries to process crude into a variety of less detectable products were widely practiced.[77] The *Oil Weekly* summed up the problem for government regulators:

[72]*OW*, December 18, 1933, p. 9.

[73]*Panama Refining Co.* v. *Ryan*, 5 F. Supp. 639 (E.D. Tex. 1934). The decision was reversed by the Fifth Circuit Court of Appeals but was stayed pending Supreme Court review, which kept federal regulation at bay.

[74]*OW*, January 8, 1934, p. 7. Only seventy-two state employees remained to inspect over 14,000 wells. *OW*, September 24, 1934, p. 12. Budgetary problems were a sign that local sentiment favored—or at least was ambivalent toward—unrestricted production.

[75]*OGJ*, December 14, 1933, p. 10; and *OW*, January 8, 1934, p. 7.

[76]*OW*, March 5, 1934, p. 8.

[77]*OGJ*, December 14, 1933, p. R-10. Rivaling the "Fortress of Gladewater," one female well operator kept enforcement personnel at bay by conducting hot-oil operations from converted bathroom faucets. Summarized Ruth Knowles, "They devised more ingenious ways of running bootleg oil than the nation as a whole contrived to keep itself supplied with bootleg liquor." Knowles, *The Greatest Gamblers* (New York: McGraw-Hill, 1959), p. 265. For an inside look at some of the techniques used to secretly produce oil and the counterefforts of authorities to detect such production,

> It would require an army to watch all of the 12,500 wells in the field and another army to watch the watchers. . . . Ambitious agents find before them the glittering opportunity of quitting their jobs and "joining up" in the "hot" oil activities.[78]

By March 1934, hot-oil output in East Texas had reached 70,000 barrels per day. The flush Conroe field also attracted government attention as did reports of illegal output from California.[79] The situation led to a statewide meeting in April of Texas proration advocates to give Commissioner Thompson, an avid states-righter, an ultimatum: either plug the intrastate leak in the proration dike or prepare for expanded federal intervention. With the recent *Amazon* decision, the courts no longer stood in the way of state action.[80]

Attempts by state authorities to tighten regulation proved ineffective.[81] Hot-oil output soon reached 100,000 barrels per day, and talk of another East Texas shutdown arose. The hot-oil operators had overcome state authorities, and to save face the TRC fired its chief East Texas proration administrator.[82]

New Federal and Private Efforts. A renewed effort to tame hot oil by federal officials and private groups began in the spring of 1934. Federal interstate regulation was expanded on April 9 to require tender documents from oil-carrying water vessels that were transporting crude or crude products from Texas to the active California

---

see Elton Sterrett, "Checking Hot-Oil Flow in East Texas," *World Petroleum*, November 1937, pp. 28–35.

[78]*OW*, March 5, 1934, p. 8. Remarked Warren Platt, "The hot oilers' have contaminated, with something akin to money, a lot of the administration's special investigators sent to East Texas to get evidence on the crimes there." *NPN*, May 23, 1934, p. 9. Thirty-eight federal agents were discharged for irregularities.

[79]*OW*, March 5, 1934, p. 7, and April 2, 1934, p. 7.

[80]*Amazon Petroleum Corporation* v. *Railroad Commission*, 5 F. Supp. 633 (E.D. Tex. 1934); and *Panama Refining Co.* v. *Ryan*, 5 F. Supp. 639 (E.D. Tex. 1934).

[81]Remarked Andrew Rowley, "A majority of oil men have long ceased to look to the Texas Railroad Commission for . . . relief." *OGJ*, June 28, 1934, p. 11.

[82]The dismissed official, R. D. Parker, pinned blame on local court judges: "Indifference . . . constitutes a substantial obstacle in the prosecution of felony cases. The dockets in East Texas courts are terribly crowded on various and sundry other matters and quite naturally the officers in that territory are inclined to enforce those laws for which there is greatest popular demand." *OW*, June 25, 1934, p. 8. The *National Petroleum News* characterized the firing as politically motivated because Parker had dismissed political appointees in an effort to increase enforcement. *NPN*, June 27, 1934, pp. 7–10. Also see *Business Week*, July 14, 1934, p. 10.

market. The results were effective.[83] Effective June 10, 1934, a federal excise tax, to be applied to crude production from wells that had output of more than 5 barrels per day, was passed to give federal agents inspection authority to detect illegal oil. Agents from the Bureau of Internal Revenue would soon join their hamstrung brethren from the Interior Department in the field.[84] The small levy also proved effective in hampering hot-oil output.

On the private side, different actions were taken in the spring of 1934. Major companies in East Texas agreed to purchase gasoline from refineries promising not to process hot oil.[85] The Petroleum Committee of the Texas Bankers Association, interested in price stabilization to enhance the quality of their loan portfolios, was formed to assist the TRC. Promoted to the status of a public agency, the committee proposed to draft 100 experienced field men from the industry to detect the flow of bootleg oil.[86]

In conjunction with the federal excise tax, Ickes stiffened penalties and extended reporting requirements on July 20 to reclamation plants where illegally produced crude commonly found refuge.[87] A maximum penalty of $10,000 and ten years in jail was an unprecedented deterrent.[88] To strengthen detection, the TRC established the Oil Tender Committee for the East Texas Field (the "Little Commission") to certify oil for intrastate shipment and use. On August 4, a commission order required tenders for processed or "topped" crude to close the "hot-product" loophole. Such tenders had earlier proved successful until legal challenges nullified the decree.[89] Rule 11 was

---

[83]*OGJ*, April 16, 1934, p. 10, and April 23, 1934, p. 12.

[84]Public Law 216, 48 Stat. 680 (1934). See chapter 7, pp. 321–22.

[85]See chapter 19, pp. 1123–25.

[86]"[The bankers], in many cases, have large investments in the field and cannot afford to see their securities jeopardized because of illegal practices." *OW*, July 16, 1934, p. 7.

[87]The new regulations are reprinted in *NPN*, July 30, 1934, pp. 15, 44–45. Despite the *Panama* stay, the U.S. circuit court ruled that reporting requirements for producers, transporters, and refiners were legal. See *NPN*, June 6, 1934, p. 20-A.

[88]Political representatives of hot-oil interests defeated the Disney bill but failed to notice a change in the criminal code passed at the end of the session that promulgated heavy penalties for false statements in required reports. Public Law 394, 48 Stat. 996 (1934). Also see *NPN*, August 1, 1934, p. 3.

[89]*OGJ*, August 30, 1934, p. 9.

amended on August 16 to include gasoline and kerosene.[90] Refiners successfully moved to enjoin the order, which they described as the most far-reaching measure to limit East Texas production since the beginning of proration in 1931. This would be only a respite. Not only were the injunctions reversed, a strict federal affidavit became effective September 8, which required the shipper to give the transporter a signed statement that read:

> In tendering this shipment I certify that the products of crude petroleum so tendered were not manufactured from crude petroleum produced or withdrawn from storage in excess of the amount permitted to be produced or withdrawn from storage by any state law, provision, regulation or order prescribed thereunder by any board, commission officer or other duly authorized agency of a state.

While carriers were subject to a maximum $500 fine and six months in jail per offense, shippers came under the maximum $10,000 fine and ten years in jail.[91] Several problems existed, however, with the initiative. A number of producers and refiners who were enjoined under the pending *Panama* and *Amazon* cases did not have to make reports. The estimated 120,000 forms that were collected each month defied efforts at accurate identification, which was necessary for enforcement.[92] Almost 100,000 barrels per day of hot oil continued to leak.[93]

The next step was to pass a state law with similar provisions, and on September 28, Texas governor Mirian Ferguson signed Senate Bill no. 21 to this end.[94] But until December 25, the effective date of the statute, the hot-product loophole remained. Refineries, operating under enjoined shutdown orders, were not required to present tenders for intrastate shipments of product.

Government futility reached a new crescendo when Justice Department attorneys discovered that the amended hot-oil regulation signed by FDR on September 13, 1933, inadvertently, had no enforcement clause. That surprising omission meant that all federal prosecution and court action were without legal basis, and hot oil

[90]*NPN*, August 22, 1934, p. 7.
[91]*NPN*, September 12, 1934, p. 18.
[92]*NPN*, September 19, 1934, p. 11.
[93]*NPN*, September 26, 1934, p. 8.
[94]*OGJ*, October 4, 1934, p. 18.

in interstate commerce had been legal since the day FDR had signed his name. New regulations were then signed September 25, 1934, to make hot-oil production, transportation, and refining illegal.[95] For Warren Platt, whose *National Petroleum News* editorials regularly chastised state and federal officials for incompetent enforcement, this monumental error was the last straw. The typical government employee, he sniped, is "some hack who can't make a living elsewhere."[96]

Eager to take the offensive, and cognizant of the success of the Texas Tender Board, Ickes created the Federal Tender Board (FTB) on October 24, 1934, to issue "certificates of clearance" for interstate shipments of crude oil and petroleum products. Headquartered in the heart of the East Texas field and staffed by Department of Justice agents, the FTB survived injunction requests brought by hot-oil operators. Even *Panama* District Judge Randolph Bryant sided with the government. Consequently, railroads were forced to stop accepting untendered cargo. Whereas almost 15,000 tank cars left East Texas a month before the order, only 5,400 did so after federal certification was required.[97] Hot oil and hot product soon became bottlenecked in storage, and operators of illicit wellhead activities had little alternative but to cease. Fewer than thirty of the seventy-four refineries in the field were active. For the first time since the brief interlude following the implementation of section 9(c) of the oil code, East Texas output was near its legal bounds. Not only the field was affected. East Texas merchants complained that business was off by one-half.[98]

Hot Oil's Last Stand. In a game of cat and mouse under the double tender system, hot-oil merchants attempted to disguise oil trucks as moving vans to transport their clandestine cargos. This was an expensive and limited option, and the risk of detection by the Texas Highway Patrol was real.[99] By early 1935, hot-oil production was

[95]*NPN*, October 3, 1934, p. 13.

[96]Ibid., p. 12.

[97]*NPN*, December 12, 1934, p. 20-E.

[98]Ibid. Hot-oil production dropped from 130,000 barrels per day to 35,000 barrels per day within several weeks by some estimates. *OGJ*, November 15, 1934, p. 36. By the end of the year, hot oil was reported below 20,000 barrel per day. *NPN*, December 26, 1934, p. 3.

[99]*OGJ*, December 10, 1934, p. 15.

reportedly under 20,000 barrels per day.[100] The saga that seemed over would have one more episode when section 9(c) of the National Industrial Recovery Act was declared unconstitutional by the Supreme Court on January 7, 1935. Administrative authority to determine industry emergencies and to activate the interstate prohibition was now gone. Legislative instruction was necessary.[101]

For what would be the last time, the hot-oil industry swung into high gear with the FTB inactivated and interstate regulation removed. The Texas Tender Board, headed by a prominent East Texas banker, attempted to take up the slack by ordering thirty-four state railroads to require tenders, but motor vehicles and tank cars sped with impunity to interstate markets.[102] Noticed the *Oil & Gas Journal* in late January:

> The "hot oil artists" seem to be regaining their old-time nerve and fervor. . . . The field is of a "high temperature" if not "hot."[103]

Two circumventions came into wide use. A court ruling rendered pre–December 10, 1934, product inventory immune from state tender laws, and hot-oil producers subsequently filled storage to capacity—estimated between 1.5 million and 2.5 million barrels—and falsified documents declaring that oil unregulated.[104] Second, untendered gasoline was hauled to the Texas-Louisiana border where it was run from truck hoses through the proclaimed "shortest

[100]*NPN*, January 9, 1935, p. 7.

[101]*Panama Refining Company* v. *Ryan*, 293 U.S. 388 (1935).

[102]*NPN*, January 16, 1935, p. 20-A. The new chairman of the Texas Tender Board was Tucker Royall, chairman of the Royall National Bank of Palestine, the largest bank in East Texas whose portfolio was laden with area oil credits. Upon his appointment, an *Oil & Gas Journal* writer naively wrote of the "unusual man for the position: Mr. Royall . . . has no financial interest in the oil business and is not in politics. . . . He is intensely interested in the work, and although he had expected to be relieved on January 1 as they require so much of his time, he has decided now the work is so important he will continue . . . as long as his services are necessary." *OGJ*, January 17, 1935, p. 9.

[103]*OGJ*, January 31, 1935, p. 12.

[104]*OGJ*, January 17, 1935, p. 9; *NPN*, January 23, 1935, p. 20, and January 30, 1935, p. 24-A.

interstate pipeline in the world," measuring 32 feet, to escape Louisiana truck taxes and achieve interstate status for reloading and shipment to various destinations, including East Texas.[105] By mid-February, hot-oil output was over 50,000 barrels per day with untendered cargos numbering in the thousands.[106]

Regulators regained the high ground with the Interstate Transportation of Petroleum Products Act, signed February 22, 1935.[107] Known as the Connally Hot-Oil Act in recognition of sponsor Tom Connally (R-Tex.), it essentially was a remake of 9(c) without the latter's constitutional defects. With reinstalled authority, Ickes ordered the FTB, which had been only collecting field data since the Supreme Court decision, to resume tender activities on March 1. With interstate tenders again required, hot-oil output dropped from above 50,000 barrels per day to below 35,000 barrels per day.[108]

Despite the double tender system and new state legislation, the latter of which drastically increased penalties for intrastate hot-oil trucking and authorized state sales of confiscated oil, illegal production stubbornly remained for several reasons.[109] "New devices and tricks with which to hoodwink the authorities" allowed undetected hot-oil output.[110] Lakes of fuel oil, holding as much as 2.8 million barrels, were claimed as pre–December 10, 1934, inventory—legal and ready to be drawn down. Court orders to this effect served as tenders to transporters.[111] Because the 137 recorded oil pits were so difficult to measure, hot oil was put in as withdrawals were made. "It has been noted," the *National Petroleum News* stated, "that the level of some of these pits seems to remain about the same."[112] Much pit oil, it was discovered, was water covered with oil, which left red

---

[105]*NPN*, March 6, 1935, p. 13. After the TRC dismantled the line, the hot-oil truckers were manually handed pipe from the Louisiana side to perform the operation. *OGJ*, February 21, 1935, p. 15, and March 7, 1935, p. 18.

[106]*Business Week*, February 9, 1935, p. 9; and *NPN*, February 13, 1935, p. 24-F.

[107]Public Law 14, 49 Stat. 30 (1935).

[108]*NPN*, March 20, 1935, p. 20-A. Refiner lawsuits against federal tenders were unsuccessful.

[109]*NPN*, May 15, 1935, p. 19. The two new laws were the Truck Tender Shipping Bill, passed March 13, 1935, and the Texas Hot Oil Statute, passed May 11, 1935.

[110]*NPN*, July 17, 1935, p. 13.

[111]*NPN*, May 1, 1935, pp. 23-A, 24-A.

[112]Ibid., p. 24-A.

faces among regulators who blessed much more oil than was actually there. Tenders were used repeatedly to legalize shipments. Lax enforcement and dismissal of charges against guilty truckers by sympathetic justices of the peace encouraged illegal cargos.[113] Overstated refinery yields created "hot" product from "allowable" crude. Corruption and inefficiency multiplied illegal oil. Dozens of reclamation plants claimed "lost" oil found in creeks and ditches as allowable feedstock.[114] Millions of barrels of confiscated oil were resold—often to their original owners, who then had tendered oil instead of hot oil.[115]

In the spring and summer of 1935, hot-oil estimates ranged between 25,000 and 40,000 barrels per day.[116] One exception occurred during April when producers of hot oil agreed to produce at allowable levels so Commissioner Thompson could testify against federal oil legislation by saying that East Texas hot-oil output currently was at an "irreducible minimum."[117]

Near the close of 1935, overproduction was estimated at 15,000 barrels per day, low by historic field standards but evidence of continuing illegal activity.[118] In mid-1936, the figure was placed below 11,000 barrel per day, which prompted the *Oil & Gas Journal* to state, "With 21,013 well completions, hip-flasks can soon be used to transport the excess."[119] But not all wells were producing wells. A dry hole drilled in 1935 produced its allowable by taking oil from a nearby pipeline connection for five years.[120]

The FTB remained in East Texas until 1942 when Ickes replaced it with the Federal Petroleum Board. Federal tenders were no longer required, but the Interior Department's Petroleum Conservation

---

[113]*NPN*, July 17, 1935, p. 13.

[114]"Oil is being deliberately spilled or wasted, in some instances, so that [reclamation] plants may recover it and process it without . . . penalties." *NPN*, July 25, 1934, p. 20-B.

[115]*NPN*, August 28, 1935, p. 25.

[116]For example, see *NPN*, April 24, 1935, p. 24; June 19, 1935, p. 19; and July 17, 1935, p. 13.

[117]*NPN*, August 7, 1935, p. 26.

[118]*OGJ*, December 5, 1935, p. 17.

[119]*OGJ*, July 23, 1936, p. 20.

[120]East Texas Engineering Association, *East Texas Oil Field* (Kilgore, Tex.: East Texas Engineering Association, 1953), p. 168.

Division closely monitored interstate shipments.[121] After World War II, the TRC was assigned jurisdiction interstate as well as intrastate under authority of the Connally Hot-Oil Act, which was made permanent on June 22, 1942.[122]

Costs and Consequences

Natural economic incentives existed to produce oil in excess of allowables to supply ready markets west of the Rockies, along the Atlantic seaboard, in the midcontinent area, and along the Gulf Coast. In the unique case of the East Texas field, flush production was natural because of low lifting costs and the prevention of it unnatural, hence problematic. Focusing the effort on transportation, to strand illegal oil and product in inventory, discouraged hot-oil production. But it took four years of arduous effort, creating perverse consequences and significant cost.

The most obvious cost of the regulatory effort was the taxpayers' expenses for local, state, and federal enforcement and the heavy legal expenses of private companies resisting shutdowns and conservation orders. (Client fees made it possible for a number of attorneys to became East Texas operators.)[123] These "deadweight" costs also included the loaned employees and the legal war chests that proration advocates in the industry poured into the enforcement and lobbying effort.

Superfluous entrepreneurship also resulted from the existence of a market distorted by regulation. With official posted prices for allowable oil and myriad discount prices for hot oil, entrepreneurial resources were attracted to oil brokering (oil reselling) to exploit arbitrage opportunities as well as tender-falsification opportunities.[124] Another suboptimal dedication of resources (from the viewpoint of an unregulated market) was the subterfuges to circumvent the law: construction of secret well valves, bypass pipelines, dummy

[121]*OGJ*, November 5, 1942, p. 27. During the war effort, Ickes extended reporting requirements under the Hot-Oil Act to Louisiana, New Mexico, and other areas outside East Texas. *OGJ*, August 21, 1941, p. 29.

[122]Public Law 624, 56 Stat. 381 (1942).

[123]*OGJ*, January 17, 1935, p. 9.

[124]*OW*, July 24, 1933, p. 10; and *OGJ*, September 13, 1934, pp. 13, 44. The concept "superfluous entrepreneurship" and its applicability to regulatory-induced brokering opportunities for crude oil and petroleum product is further examined in this chapter, pp. 707–10.

derricks, and well pillboxes—all to qualify for greater allowables.[125] Inefficient transportation alternatives were used to legalize illegal cargos or ship undetected illegal crude and product. Those man-hours and capital goods would have been better used elsewhere in the absence of regulation. But given the regulations, resources employed in the hot-oil market were not misspent; in fact, they benefited consumers by increasing supply and lowering price.

Corruption and general disrespect for the law, characteristic of times when the law runs contrary to the self-interest of producers and consumers, were also present. Ickes's characterizations of hot-oil participants as hardened criminals never caught hold. The interior secretary unsuccessfully propagandized:

> You would not expect the American Bankers' Association to receive professional bank robbers as members in good standing. You would think that jewelers were a queer lot if they associated on friendly and intimate terms with men who make their living by smashing plateglass windows and grabbing handfuls of gems. . . . The same principles should control those in the oil industry. If you should refuse to associate with those who reek of "hot" oil, you would go far toward building up such a public opinion that these men could no longer withstand it.[126]

Ostracism did not occur to supplement industry efforts to stem illegal production. The fact was that the hot-oil business consisted of voluntary transactions, unlike the deeds of bank robbers and jewel thieves. Indeed, hot-oil as an offense could be eliminated instantaneously by deregulation. The illegal could have been legalized.

The haphazard method of regulation contributed to lawlessness. Widely varying East Texas allowables, set between 200,000 and 750,000 barrels per day, commented Erich Zimmermann, "virtually invited bootlegging"; what was illegal today, after all, might be legal tomorrow as a result of increased hot-oil production.[127] Perjury was

---

[125]Some "completed" wells in "shallow" sands were really only 100 feet deep and fed from a neighboring well or storage area. Harry Harter, *East Texas Oil Parade*, pp. 118–19, 122.

[126]Harold Ickes, "An Account of Stewardship," *15 Annual Proceedings* (New York: American Petroleum Institute, 1934), p. 30.

[127]Erich Zimmermann, *Conservation in the Production of Petroleum* (New Haven, Conn.: Yale University Press, 1957), p. 194.

committed without conscience to "legalize" illegal oil, and a black market for affidavits existed for the same purpose.[128] Government employees were prominent participants in the hot-oil racket. Evidence was presented in sensational court testimony in Oklahoma to show that the governor's nephew, Cicero Murray, and other proration umpires were bribed to ignore illegal practices and to give "protection" to hot-oil shipments.[129] An investigation for the Texas state legislature in 1935 reported that

> an almost vicious practice has been brought to light . . . the offering for sale by those claiming to have, and possibly having, an entree to official records, if not the keepers of such records, of increased potentials on wells together with the resultant increases in daily allowables. . . . The administration of this law has all but put the State in the "hot oil business" and has given rise to a form of legal racketeering.[130]

Conflicts of interest and outright illegalities were rife among the regulators. The son of a Texas Railroad Commissioner was charged with stealing oil from a pipeline. A TRC employee's relative was found with numerous signed tenders that were being dispensed across East Texas for a fee. The son of a major hot-oil refiner married the daughter of a proration official, a coincidence that was not lost on the oil community. A U.S senator's relative won a job with a notorious hot-oil company. A lawyer specializing in obtaining drilling exceptions in the East Texas field was the brother-in-law of a TRC official who granted drilling-exception permits. "Proration," complained Warren Platt in the exposé "His Sisters and His Cousins and His Aunts," "has too long been used by politicians as the vehicle through which relatives and friends are rewarded and maintained."[131]

Regulatory opportunism existed on the federal level as well. Congressional testimony was heard that the hot-oil crackdown was occurring only in East Texas where independents dominated the

---

[128]*OGJ*, January 17, 1935, p. 9

[129]See this chapter, p. 641.

[130]Committee of the Texas State Legislature, *Preliminary Report*, 1935. Quoted in William Kemnitzer, *Rebirth of Monopoly*, p. 120.

[131]*NPN*, July 11, 1934, p. 13.

field but not in other areas of the state and country where, allegedly, the majors ran hot oil with impunity.[132]

Lawlessness adversely affected related parties. Landowners were not paid royalties on supra-allowable oil because of its secret extraction. Thefts from storage tanks were passively resisted because lost allowables could be easily regained by increasing production.

Petroleum conservation was scarcely served by the proration effort. Oil haphazardly stored to escape detection was regulatory, not market, waste. When transportation bottlenecks were created by regulators, oil was left to evaporate or become contaminated in prolonged storage. Health hazards were also created. To escape detection, hot-oil operators avoided igniting (flaring) casinghead gas, which created a fire hazard in the vicinity of wells. At least three people burned to death by igniting free gas, one with automobile exhaust and two with a cooking fire.[133] It was illegal to let gas escape freely, but normal business practices were discouraged by conditions surrounding black-market operations.

World War II Planning

On the eve of wartime hostilities, tankers accounted for over 98 percent of all the petroleum delivered to major East Coast markets. The remainder was split between pipelines and, to a lesser extent, railroad tank cars and tank trucks.[134] This reflected the vastly superior cost economies of tanker transport and, in certain uses, pipeline transport, over railroad and truck transportation.

The European conflict first affected petroleum distribution in May 1941, when the U.S. Maritime Commission requisitioned twenty-five tankers to supply oil to Britain as part of the lend-lease program. Another twenty-five vessels were put on notice for similar duty.[135] This created logistic problems for the East Coast petroleum market where the tankers had been in service, and alternative forms

---

[132]*Petroleum Hearings before the Temporary National Economic Committee* (New York: American Petroleum Institute, 1942), p. 72.

[133]*OGJ*, January 1, 1934, p. 32. Unlike other well-known examples of racketeering, no deaths resulted from enforcement-related violence between operators and authorities.

[134]John Frey and H. Chandler Ide, *A History of the Petroleum Administration for War* (Washington, D.C.: Government Printing Office, 1946), p. 83.

[135]*OGJ*, May 8, 1941, p. 19.

of transportation were pressed into capacity use. Plans were pre-pared for the construction of major pipelines from Texas to the Northeast. Orders for new tankers and refurbishments of existing vessels were placed with shipyards.[136] Barge construction also rose substantially.[137] The market, in short, was responding to economic incentives to profitably meet consumer demands under altered con-ditions.[138] But the constructivist mentality was to prevail; planning and coordination of oil-carrying tankers, barges, railcars, trucks, and pipelines would soon replace market processes and rivalry.

On May 28, 1941, FDR created the Office of Petroleum Coordinator for National Defense and wrote Interior Secretary Ickes of the need for the "elimination or reduction of cross-hauling of petroleum and its products and the development of transportation facilities and of methods by which more efficient use can be made of existing transportation and storage facilities."[139] Inefficiency existed in the transportation system, but it was not due to entrepreneurial error. Long-standing intervention restricted entry and minimized rate competition by standardizing fares and prohibiting discrimination ("undue preference") among shippers. Such legislation had existed on the federal level for railroads since 1887, for pipelines since 1906, for ships since 1916 and 1940, and for motor trucks since 1935. Partially immune from competitive pressures under the regulatory umbrella of the ICC, inefficient practices such as cross-hauling (the simultaneous movement of like cargos from points A to B and B to A) and empty-load trips could be—and often were—profitable. President Roosevelt was aware that under wartime conditions reform was necessary, but instead of deregulating transportation, he opted for a government-industry partnership to increase utiliza-tion and efficiency by pooling transportational facilities.

Early planning was conducted by the Office of Defense Transpor-tation, formed on May 2, 1941, with a Division of Petroleum and Other Liquid Transport, and the Office of Petroleum Coordinator

---

[136]*OGJ*, May 29, 1941, pp. 10, 14.

[137]*OGJ*, June 5, 1941, p. 28.

[138]Some adjustment was prevented by the existing anti-cooperative philosophies of the Federal Trade Commission and the Justice Department, as well as state and Interstate Commerce Commission regulation.

[139]Quoted in John Frey and H. Chandler Ide, *A History of the Petroleum Administration for War*, pp. 374–75.

for National Defense (OPC). Ickes was appointed petroleum coordinator, and Ralph Davies, with equal authority, was appointed deputy coordinator of the OPC. The immediate problem was not oil supply per se but ample oil availability at points of consumption. Ickes publicly discussed rationing to encourage conservation in anticipation of transportation shortfalls.[140] "Voluntary" price ceilings that would create allocation problems for planning to "solve" began in June, the *National Petroleum News* noted the irony. "In trying to hold down, especially to unfairly low and even unprofitable levels, East Coast prices, is not the Administration at Washington contributing greatly to the shortage that it expects there?"[141]

After the size and capabilities of the petroleum-transport industry were surveyed, a series of OPC "recommendations" was issued for tanker, tank-truck, and tank-car transport. Tanker movements to Latin America and the Caribbean were curtailed or discontinued, and marine facilities in San Francisco were pooled to service the Pacific Coast.[142] Effective tanker capacity was increased beginning July 5 when a prewar regulation setting maximum capacity loads, intended to divide cargo over more vessels at a time when tankers were plentiful, was relaxed.[143] In conjunction with the government's increasingly active role in oil-tanker transportation, Ickes created the Tanker Control Board within the OPC on August 26 to coordinate tanker movements.[144] Implementation was delegated to the Maritime Commission, which set maximum tanker charter rates, effective September 1, for U.S. and foreign-flag vessels.[145] Another early action

[140]*OGJ*, June 12, 1941, p. 14.

[141]*NPN*, July 23, 1941, p. 18. The obvious free-market solution to growing scarcity was recommended: "Oil marketing companies on the East Coast right now should be permitted to raise their prices, even encouraged to raise them. The increase should ... make the East Coast a quite attractive market."

[142]Recommendation 2, part 1505 (July 24, 1941); recommendation 9, part 1505 (August 26, 1941); and recommendation 27, part 1505 (December 26, 1941). Recommendations and directives under wartime petroleum planning are reprinted in John Frey and H. Chandler Ide, *A History of the Petroleum Administration for War*, pp. 402–9. Early petroleum transport planning is described in S. F. Niness, "Wartime Regulations of Petroleum Carriers," in *Twenty-Third Annual Proceedings* (New York: American Petroleum Institute, 1942), pp. 69–71.

[143]*OGJ*, July 17, 1941, p. 17.

[144]John Frey and H. Chandler Ide, *A History of the Petroleum Administration for War*, p. 87.

[145]*OGJ*, August 28, 1941, p. 25.

was taken June 16 when Coordinator Ickes requested the Office of Export Control to prevent East Coast shipments of petroleum to Japan.[146]

Prewar government intervention with oil-carrying transportation inherited by the planning effort presented special problems. In particular, the increased role for railroads and trucks created by tanker diversions was complicated by protectionist legislation that hampered wartime adaptability. Thanks to federal regulation, truckers could not assume new interstate routes without obtaining "certificates of convenience and necessity" from the ICC, which was time consuming and otherwise difficult.[147] Railroads charged fixed fares, formulated by the Association of American Railroads and enforced by the ICC, which contributed to the fact that oil hauling was ten times more expensive by rail than by tanker.[148] Despite this differential, OPC Recommendation 5, issued August 18, ordered maximum use of railroad tank cars.[149] After predictable industry complaints, Ickes met with ICC chairman Joseph Eastman (soon to be director of the Office of Defense Transportation) to urge reductions in rail fares, whereupon the Association of American Railroads agreed to reduce freight fares across the board by 25 to 50 percent.[150]

The transformation to rail transport required constructing loading and unloading docks for railcars, and to handle related revenue deficits (petroleum-product prices had been "voluntarily" frozen since June and could not be raised to offset costs), Recommendation 12, issued September 30, allowed firms to prorate additional expenses incurred by using tank cars in the eastern states (District I) for possible government reimbursement.[151] Before the end of the

[146]*OGJ*, June 19, 1941, p. 23.

[147]Certificates were issued only after hearings at which it had to be shown that the general industry would benefit and the existing rate structure would not be disturbed. See chapter 16, pp. 991–92. Also see *OGJ*, September 4, 1941, p. 28.

[148]John Frey and H. Chandler Ide, *A History of the Petroleum Administration for War*, p. 86. See chapter 16, pp. 990–93, for a general discussion of ICC railroad regulation.

[149]John Frey and H. Chandler Ide, *A History of the Petroleum Administration for War*, p. 402.

[150]*OGJ*, September 11, 1941, p. 17.

[151]John Frey and H. Chandler Ide, *A History of the Petroleum Administration for War*, p. 403. The "Plan for Equitable Sharing of Revenues and Extra Transportation Expenses" created a "deficit pool," representing the extra cost of wartime overland transport over prewar tanker transport, that was to be offset by periodic relaxation of product-price controls. Price increases lagged behind the deficit pool, which reached $38 million by June 1942. This led to the "Petroleum Compensatory Adjustment

year, tank-car shipments increased from fewer than 5,000 to over 140,000 barrels per day.[152]

Another governmental impediment to transportation was strict state trucking regulations, which complicated interstate hauls because of varying requirements. This widely publicized inefficiency came under attack near the end of the neutral period, and in 1941, nineteen states amended their trucking laws to make them more uniform and lax. Texas, for example, increased its truck weight limit from 7,000 pounds to 38,000 pounds.[153] Problems remained with low limits, however, even on the municipal level, which raised industry protest.[154] State rate schedules for trucks and railroads were another issue that created conflicts over relative prices and relative market shares.

Several controversies surrounded federal transportation planning in late 1941. Tight East Coast conditions led to congressional hearings at which rumors of 20,000 idle tank cars were debated along with new transportation strategies to improve efficiency.[155] A second issue concerned a September 30 order by the Office of Production Management prohibiting gasoline shipments from Pennsylvania to Ohio to conserve gasoline for the East Coast. This was part of a wider regulation prohibiting gasoline exports from the defined shortage area— seventeen East Coast states and the District of Columbia—westward.[156] This threatened to create an "official and duly authorized 'shortage' for Ohio" and a gasoline surplus for Pennsylvania as a

---

Regulation no. 1," effective August 1, 1942, whereby expenses associated with "abnormal" transportation were directly absorbed by the government (see this chapter, pp. 660–61). Those government actions, coupled with the Marine War Risk Insurance Program, under which the government subsidized wartime insurance costs, lured private industry into providing what otherwise (given price controls) was an uneconomical service. The subsidies altogether approached $1 billion before the insurance program ended in April 1942. Recommendation 12 would not be terminated until August 25, 1945. Ibid., pp. 109, 362.

[152]Ibid., p. 86.

[153]Other changes are summarized in *OGJ*, August 27, 1941, p. 22. The Texas law, which previously limited trucks to only 1,000 gallons, now allowed loads of up to 4,500 gallons. The previous law not only subsidized railcars, it hurt the war effort by severely discouraging tank-truck construction. *NPN*, February 25, 1942, p. 19.

[154]*NPN*, November 19, 1941, p. 17.

[155]*OGJ*, September 11, 1941, p. 15; and *NPN*, September 10, 1941, pp. 7–8.

[156]*NPN*, October 8, 1941, p. 7.

result of large gasoline movements from the latter to the former.[157] Protests from affected refiners and jobbers postponed the order and exempted Appalachian refiners and then succeeded in canceling the entire order on October 27.[158] This setback for planners, however, did not deter authorities from seizing the offensive and increasing intervention after Pearl Harbor. On December 9, the OPC authorized pooling for aviation-fuel facilities and required all aviation-gasoline manufacture, storage, and distribution to receive prior approval.[159]

After the tanker situation improved in late 1941, the overall transportation situation quickly worsened when fifty American tankers were sunk by German submarines between February and May 1942.[160] On March 31, 1942, the OPC stepped up comprehensive planning by ordering a complicated rearrangement of transportation modes and schedules. The general thrust of the directives was to move crude oil and products eastward toward the Atlantic Coast where domestic consumption was concentrated and where petroleum could be dispensed for the European and African war theaters. Westward movements from the eastern states (District I) to the central states (District II), with minor exceptions, were to be terminated. Pipeline flows were to be reversed; new forms of transport were to be substituted; and exchanges, sales, and loans of supplies were ordered to implement what the *Oil & Gas Journal* described as "a revolutionary plan."[161] Government planning was increasingly replacing reliance on the price system and market entrepreneurship to direct petroleum supply to points of consumption.

Other directives were issued to complement the above regulations. Inventory was to be minimized to free oil for consumption.[162] Major tanker facilities on the Pacific Coast were coordinated into a single operating unit.[163] Scarce tanker space was to be allocated to firms that

---

[157]*NPN* October 15, 1941, p. 17.

[158]*NPN*, October 8, 1941, p. 13, October 22, 1941, p. 7, and October 29, 1941, p. 8.

[159]*OGJ* December 18, 1941, p. 22. Directive 77 on July 24, 1944, continued strict control over aviation gasoline until the end of the war. *NPN*, July 26, 1944, p. 27.

[160]John Frey and H. Chandler Ide, *A History of the Petroleum Administration for War*, p. 87. In the entire war, 140 tankers would be sunk or damaged by the enemy. See the listing in *NPN*, May 22, 1946, p. 32.

[161]*OGJ*, April 2, 1942, p. 26.

[162]Recommendation 33 (February 16, 1942).

[163]Recommendation 34 (February 9, 1942).

shipped oil to the Atlantic Coast between July 1939 and June 1941 according to actual usage.[164] War-risk cargo insurance was introduced March 1.[165] The War Production Board introduced a second gasoline-allocation plan, effective March 19, that set allocations at 80 percent of base-period supply for the East and Northwest.[166] District I importers and refiners were allowed to "bank" higher transportation costs, currently nonrecoverable, for later reimbursement out of future price increases.[167] A tank-car rationing plan, establishing a five-class hierarchy, was sent from the War Production Board to the Office of Defense Transportation in late March.[168] Plans for the federal Big Inch pipeline were finalized in May.[169] The Maritime Commission was authorized to construct tugs and barges for oil transport on the Mississippi River and intracoastal canals.[170] Empty tank cars at refineries were limited to a one-day supply.[171] A tank-car committee was formed to coordinate movements between the central, southwestern, and eastern sections of the United States.[172] A particularly important and confining regulation, issued by the Office of Defense Transportation, forbade the use of tank cars to move oil on routes shorter than 100 miles, effective June 1, 1942.[173] The aim was to use trucks for short hauls and leave railcars, which were already handling over 600,000 barrels per day, for longer East Coast trips.[174]

Although much of the petroleum-transportation sector was regimented by mid-1942, more regulation would follow to further centralize control. On August 19, 1942, tank-car shipments of gasoline

---

[164]Recommendation 36 (February 16, 1942). See *NPN*, February 25, 1942, p. 22, and March 11, 1942, p. 21.

[165]*NPN*, February 25, 1942, p. 22.

[166]*NPN*, March 18, 1942, p. 3.

[167]*NPN*, March 25, 1942, p. 4.

[168]*NPN*, April 30, 1942, p. 22.

[169]*OGJ*, June 4, 1942, p. 24. See chapter 14, pp. 801–2.

[170]*OGJ*, June 4, 1942, p. 24.

[171]Recommendation 44 (May 7, 1942).

[172]Directive 50 (May 7, 1942).

[173]ODT Order 7 (May 15, 1942).

[174]*OGJ*, May 14, 1942, p. 43, and May 21, 1942, p. 29.

were banned to twenty states—from Texas to Michigan to Tennessee—which forced substitution of pipelines, barges, and trucks.[175] Effective November 15, tank trucks were licensed by the Office of Defense Transportation with Certificates of War Necessity.[176] District I, District II, and District III were each ordered to pool transportation and storage equipment and maximize exchanges.[177] Effective October 10, 1942, the minimum haul for tank cars was increased by the Office of Defense Transportation from 100 miles to 200 miles, with certain exceptions, to redirect tank cars to longer hauls, with trucks filling the gap.[178]

Oil prices were controlled at the wellhead, and transporters at the refiner, wholesale, or retail levels could not pass on rising costs in their historic ceiling prices. District I importers were banking higher costs to be recouped in future increases in oil prices. This policy changed on July 25, 1942, when Jesse Jones of the Reconstruction Finance Corporation announced that the corporation would finance transportation deficits. In the first year alone, such payments totaled nearly $200 million.[179]

The first movement away from petroleum-transport planning came in October 1944, when the mileage division between tank cars and tank trucks was relaxed.[180] But it was not until several months after Germany surrendered on May 7 that several movements toward the free market were made. In mid-July, the Petroleum Administration for War and the War Production Board relaxed material rationing for transportation as well as for other sectors of the oil industry.[181] The Office of Defense Transportation removed the last of its transportation restrictions in mid-August, and on August 18, the Reconstruction Finance Corporation ended its subsidy plan for transportation. A major move toward decontrol came on August 25, just before Japan's surrender, when the Petroleum

---

[175]Directive 57 (August 19, 1942).

[176]General Order 21 (November 8, 1942).

[177]Directive 59 (September 25, 1942); Recommendation 65 (March 17, 1943); and Directive 67 (May 22, 1943).

[178]*NPN*, September 9, 1942, p. 21.

[179]*NPN*, July 29, 1942, p. 3, and September 29, 1943, p. 3.

[180]*NPN*, October 11, 1944, p. 42.

[181]*NPN*, July 18, 1945, p. 3.

Administration for War deregulated petroleum movements in Districts I–V.[182]

The Office of Price Administration belatedly removed tank-truck price ceilings in May 1946, which returned rate setting for interstate common carriers to the ICC.[183] The remaining order of business, disposal of government-constructed tankers, was delayed until after the 1947–48 oil-supply scare, a delay that created controversy in industry and government.[184]

Evaluation. The opportunity cost of pervasive government regimentation was decentralized decisionmaking, specifically the judgment of individual entrepreneurs and business units guided by profit making. After the sudden tanker requisition in May 1941, the industry responded with alternative transportation plans and new capital investments. Price controls and directives from the OPC intervened, however, which chilled incentives for a free-market solution. This fact was recognized by the *National Petroleum News*, which editorialized in August 1941:

> These . . . ideas of "reasonable" prices are still making it impossible for the ingenious minds of the oil industry to bring more river and lake barges of all sorts and descriptions, more tank cars and particularly more trunk transports and trucks into service to run petroleum products from mid-west marine and pipeline terminals and refineries to the East Coast.[185]

The wartime emergency could have been used to suspend special-interest regulation of transportation rather than to remove profit incentives and impose transportation directives. Restrictive load limits and vehicle-size maximums in the different states could have

---

[182]*NPN*, August 29, 1945, p. 8.

[183]*NPN*, May 22, 1946, p. 42.

[184]Henrietta Larson, Evelyn Knowlton, and Charles Popple, *New Horizons* (New York: Harper & Row, 1971), p. 670.

[185]*NPN*, August 20, 1941, p. 15. The same article noted that under Prohibition, which certainly presented trying circumstances, "untold millions of gallons of liquor were transported to every town in the country," suggesting that self-interested gain could solve any logistic problem with petroleum. Also see *NPN*, July 23, 1941, p. 18, and October 29, 1941, p. 11.

been eliminated.[186] Sundry laws, such as Texas's ban on Sunday oil hauls by truck, likewise could have been annulled either by patriotic action or by the state or federal wartime powers.[187] ICC certification and rate regulation could have been junked. Antitrust impediments to cooperative ventures also could have been eliminated in the neutral period to maximize opportunities for self-help.

An evaluation of oil-transportation planning does not have to be theoretical, hypothetically describing the forgone market alternative. Enough distortion was created to make it possible to clearly differentiate government planning from market order. Beginning in late 1941, the unsatisfactory East Coast supply situation led to congressional hearings to document rampant inefficiency. While the magnitude of the government's mistake—20,000 idle tank cars—was not sufficiently documented, the absence of market incentives unquestionably was responsible for unprecedented tight supply. The ill-fated order of September 30, 1941, which prohibited westward gasoline movements from "shortage" states, threatened to make established trade channels chaotic, particularly in Ohio and Pennsylvania, and was unceremoniously dropped. The arbitrary 100-mile division between trucks and railcars led to exceptions and amendments to stem the distortion.[188] Loss economics under price controls idled oil barges and tankers serving the Great Lakes and New York canal trade, thus hampering much-needed movements from District II to District I. A group of area mayors, led by New York's Fiorello La Guardia, complained to the Senate and the Office of Price Administration about the problem to little avail.[189] A major government plan to construct barges and tugboats for oil movement along the inland waterways became mired as a dozen government agencies with jurisdiction, including the army, navy, Office of Defense Transportation, Defense Plant Corporation, War Production

---

[186]While some states relaxed their laws in 1941, enough restrictive laws remained for Congress to consider a federal law setting uniform standards in 1942 and 1943. See *NPN*, January 27, 1943, p. 24. More states reformed their laws but only after the war. *NPN*, July 2, 1947, p. 43.

[187]*NPN*, February 25, 1942, p. 19.

[188]See, for example, *NPN*, July 15, 1942, p. 32. An unintended consequence of more truck usage was to increase demand for heavily rationed rubber.

[189]*NPN* June 17, 1942, p. 24, and July 1, 1942, p. 23.

Board, and Maritime Commission, debated various issues.[190] A Washington-Baltimore gasoline emergency was narrowly averted when ICC regulations were suspended to allow 100 trucks to rush gas to the area.[191] The incident, illustrative of how the market could provide timely corrective action, was in contrast to countless lesser emergencies that did not receive regulatory exceptions and were not avoided.

In 1944, Florida went from a summer gasoline surplus to a winter gasoline shortage, despite seasonal demand suggesting the opposite, because of transportation problems. This led the governor to ask for emergency powers to seize oil-transportation facilities.[192] Those powers were not granted. In the summer of 1944, to cite another example, hundreds of oil-carrying vehicles were idled because of a shortage of heavy-duty tires.[193]

For every major recognized distortion, there were countless other, smaller unreported ones. As an editorial in the *National Petroleum News* remarked:

> Government red tape and the regulatory agencies are blocking the oil industry's war effort. It is the story of a Wisconsin oil jobber who wants to use some of his idle truck time to haul for neighboring small jobbers; but he cannot, it seems, without . . . becoming a common carrier. . . . There must be thousands of such illustrations of red tape hampering full use of the oil industry's transportation facilities, as well as similar facilities of other industries. Government agencies cannot "plan" to discover all these little extra uses that ingenious businessmen can, and do, figure out. Yet, government agencies presume to do just that with the result that individual American ingenuity is not used or is not used to its full advantage in fighting this war.

The same article recommended a free-market solution.

> Since it is the maximum use of transportation facilities that this country is up against in order to win the war, why would it not be common sense to suspend all laws and regulations except those of safety, that in any way interfere with a truck owner's freedom of action with his own property? . . . Let the truck owner run his truck

[190]*NPN*, January 20, 1943, p. 30.

[191]*NPN*, June 16, 1943, p. 22.

[192]*NPN*, January 5, 1944, p. 4, and January 12, 1944, p. 6.

[193]*NPN*, July 26, 1944, p. 3; August 2, 1944, p. 3; August 23, 1944, p. 3; and September 6, 1944, p. 34.

anywhere ... and let him charge whatever he would ... without going to OPA for investigation, study and a probable "no."[194]

Planning during the Korean Conflict

Government planning lay in wait for another emergency. A four-year project by the National Security Resources Board completed in 1950 offered a twenty-section war-regulation bill in the event of wartime or a similar emergency.[195] In other sections of government, contingency planning was the order of the day in the post–Korean conflict period.[196]

North Korea's June 25, 1950, invasion of South Korea was followed on September 8 by the Defense Production Act, which gave the president discretionary power to impose price, allocation, and credit controls.[197] A month later, an emergency was declared by President Truman, and the Petroleum Administration for Defense (PAD), a remake of the Petroleum Administration for War, was created.[198]

Within the PAD, the Supply and Transportation Division evaluated transportation requirements and set administrative regulation. One early allocation issue was oil exports to China, which concerned two agencies, the Economic Cooperation Administration and the National Production Authority. Another important issue involved a "voluntary" tanker plan, which concerned the Supply and Transportation Division and the Military Sea Transportation Service.[199] The tanker plan was finalized in January, the same month the Maritime Administration licensed charters of U.S.-company foreign-flag vessels to foreigners.[200] A tanker emergency, however, would never develop. Tanker traffic was never at risk as in World War II, and

[194]*NPN*, September 16, 1942, p. 9.

[195]*NPN*, July 6, 1950, p. 28.

[196]The post–Korean conflict preoccupation with contingency planning is discussed in chapter 5, pp. 248–49.

[197]Public Law 774, 64 Stat. 798 (1950).

[198]For an organizational chart of the PAD, see appendix E, p. 1945.

[199]*NPN*, December 7, 1950, p. 53; and Bruce Brown, *Oil Men in Washington* (El Dorado, Ark.: Evanil Press, 1965), p. 36.

[200]*NPN*, January 31, 1951, p. 15.

the Korean "limited police action" hardly required the fuel the previous war had. By midyear, tankers were plentiful and rates were dropping.[201]

Tank-car supply became tight in early 1951, in part because of a railroad switchmen's strike.[202] As a precaution, the ICC assumed "emergency" control of tank cars for a six-month period ending July 31.[203] Both railroads and water vessels were subject to price controls, which limited prices to the highest price received between December 19 and 25, 1950.[204] Despite the intervention, the conflict did not become protracted enough to allow regulation to significantly distort these transport modes.

Specific oil-allocation regulations were not imposed. One general order, Regulation 1, allowed the PAD to "require adjustment in the distribution of petroleum products, gas and other material to promote the defense effort."[205] It was more a precautionary "standby" order than an operational directive; its use would be confined to requisitioning fuel oil for the navy.

The most used transportation-related regulation concerned material allocation to oil and gas pipelines.[206] New pipelines required PAD approval, and natural gas moved interstate required a certificate of public convenience and necessity from the Federal Power Commission.[207] Steel had been made scarce by war orders, and price controls precluded a natural ordering of demand and supply. Complicating the issue was that gas-transmission projects, which by custom preordered pipe, left little inventory for oil pipelines, which did not preorder. Without mandatory allocation to redirect available pipe to the oil side, few oil pipelines could be completed, much less begun.

---

[201]*NPN*, May 23, 1951, p. 39.

[202]*NPN*, January 10, 1951, p. 31; and Bruce Brown, *Oil Men in Washington*, p. 102.

[203]*OGJ*, February 15, 1951, p. 56.

[204]*OGJ*, February 1, 1951, p. 32; and *NPN*, February 7, 1951, p. 28. Earlier, the Economic Stabilization Agency froze prices, transportation tariffs included, at December 1, 1959, levels. *OGJ*, December 28, 1950, p. 31.

[205]Bruce Brown, *Oil Men in Washington*, p. 214; and *OGJ*, October 4, 1951, p. 156.

[206]Supply and Transportation director Richard Nelson stated, "One of PAD's principles has been to aid the oil and gas industries to obtain their fair share of those materials which were on hand." Nelson, "The Petroleum Administration and Pipe Lines," *33 Annual Proceedings* (New York: American Petroleum Institute, 1953), p. 64.

[207]Bruce Brown, *Oil Men in Washington*, pp. 124–25. Also see chapter 15, pp. 877–80.

To "allocate available materials fairly," PAD deputy administrator Bruce Brown reallocated pipe to oil projects from ongoing gas projects.[208] New oil and oil-product pipelines thus slowed down gas-line construction, which, combined with rate regulation by the Federal Power Commission, created spot natural-gas shortages in the winters of 1950–51 and 1951–52. This led to a PAD order that limited gas for "nonessential purposes" and permitted new pipe interconnects on June 25, 1951.[209]

Compared with the other two wartime planning experiences, transportation and allocation regulations during the Korea conflict were mild. Except for the initial demand for oil tankers, little pretense of emergency existed. The forgone alternative was simple reliance on the price system, with the government paying going rates for transportation instead of artificially cheapening its purchases with ceiling prices and requisitions. A second market strategy would have been to remove existing intervention, state truck regulation in particular.[210]

Modern Allocation Regulation: 1973–81

Except for hot-oil regulation, designed to detect and discourage illegal output, oil-allocation regulation concerned unusual supply uncertainty, whether perceived (Korean conflict) or real (World War I, World War II). Not coincidentally, these periods of abnormal scarcity—even shortage—accompanied price regulation that prevented a smooth incorporation of heightened demand or diminished supply, or both, into the terms of market exchange. In the absence of price controls, allocation regulation was never needed or implemented. A provision in the Oil Code of 1933 to "facilitate equitable access of refiners to the allowable supply of crude oil" was a dead letter.[211] The problem of the 1930s was quite different—*too much* supply and *falling* prices.

After a long absence, regulation of crude-oil and petroleum-product allocation reappeared in the 1970s. Allocation regulation was

[208]Bruce Brown, *Oil Men in Washington*, p. 122.

[209]Ibid., chap. 15. Oil and product pipelines completed during the war are listed in Richard Nelson, "The Petroleum Administration and Pipe Lines," p. 63.

[210]See *NPN*, November 14, 1951, pp. 65–67.

[211]National Recovery Administration, *Code of Fair Competition for the Petroleum Industry* (Washington, D.C.: Government Printing Office, 1933), art. 4.

preceded by price regulation, which began in August 1971 and continued for nearly a decade.

Because a variable price determination of who-gets-what was forsaken in favor of price ceilings set below market levels, shortages inevitably developed, which led to economic dislocation and industry hardship, sectoral pleas for "corrective" legislation, and allocation regulation to fine-tune an "equitable" and "efficient" solution to oil-supply problems. Six long years of allocation regulation would follow.

Developing Shortages and Policy Response

In late 1972 and early 1973, spot shortages of petroleum products first appeared.[212] The experience was new to most; not since World War II and briefly in the postwar period had the availability of petroleum been in question. Even with regulated imports, refiners or gatherers could always secure additional supply by increasing their nominations at proration hearings if prices were not destabilized; until the 1970s, there were always a few extra turns on the maximum efficient rate–yardstick allowable spigot. By early 1973, however, ominous trends materialized into stark reality. With market-demand factors in major producing states reaching 100 percent, the *Washington Post* reported that schools and factories were closed in eleven states because fuel was unavailable.[213] Also in January, shortages of diesel fuel curtailed or threatened to curtail trucking, railroad, bus, and airline operations.[214] Texaco, Shell, and Mobil announced wholesale rationing programs to limit heating fuel, diesel fuel, kerosene, and aviation fuel per customer.[215] Although the seasonally high demand of winter explained part of the increased scarcity, the causes of the shortfall were regulatory. High demand caused by economic growth and artificially low product prices could not be rationed by higher prices for available supply.[216] Without market pricing, more urgent uses could not be satisfied instead of less urgent uses.

[212]Early product shortages that first appeared in Phase II and grew in Phase III of President Nixon's price control program are described in chapter 27, pp. 1608–15.

[213]*Energy Crisis*, ed. Lester Sobel, 4 vols. (New York: Facts on File, 1974), vol. 1, p. 132.

[214]Ibid.; and *OGJ*, January 29, 1973, p. 67.

[215]*Energy Crisis*, vol. 1, p. 131.

[216]Regulation of the prices of products is discussed in chapter 27, pp. 1608–19.

Other policy-related distortions exacerbated the market-clearing price problem by either increasing petroleum demand or decreasing petroleum supply. The regulatory-induced shortage of natural gas increased the demand for fuel oil and especially scarce propane.[217] Domestic refining capacity was legislatively discouraged.[218] Imports of needed petroleum products were restricted by protectionist statutes left over from the oil-surplus days of the 1950s and 1960s[219] and by the "reseller rule" that prevented cost averaging of higher cost foreign supply.[220]

Early government measures to alleviate the developing crisis were to relax import restrictions on scarce petroleum products on January 17, 1973, and recommend conservation measures to 45,000 businesses in a letter from the Commerce Department dated February 16.[221] Under pressure from independent marketers and independent refiners concerned about competing for supply with their integrated rivals,[222] on April 30 Congress granted the president authority to allocate crude between refineries and product between marketers in the Economic Stabilization Act Amendments of 1973.[223] On May 10, a "voluntary" allocation program was announced by William Simon, chairman of the Oil Policy Committee and deputy secretary of the treasury, and William Johnson, energy advisor to the Treasury Department. With administration delegated to the Office of Oil and Gas (OOG) within the Interior Department, it was advised that

---

[217]Ibid., p. 1610.

[218]See chapter 20, pp. 1179–80.

[219]See chapter 13, pp. 748–50.

[220]See chapter 27, pp. 1613–14.

[221]*Energy Crisis*, vol. 1, pp. 132–33. If conservation measures could reduce demand, ceiling product prices could be brought closer to the market price to avert shortages in some cases.

[222]Lobby groups included the Independent Gasoline Marketers Council, the National Oil Jobbers Council, and the Independent Terminal Operators Association. *OGJ*, May 7, 1973, p. 32. Summarized Neil de Marchi: "The impetus behind allocation schemes was the complaints . . . of independent marketers and terminal operators. Protecting these independents (and the independent refiners) was *the* energy issue of 1973, not the Arab Embargo." De Marchi, "Energy Policy under Nixon: Mainly Putting Out Fires," in *Energy Policy in Perspective*, ed. Craufurd Goodwin (Washington, D.C.: Brookings Institution, 1981), p. 429. Also see chapter 27, p. 1620.

[223]Public Law 93-28, 87 Stat. 27 (1973).

> each producer, refiner, marketer, jobber and distributor . . . agree to make available in each state to each of its customers (including the spot market) the same percentage of its total supply of crude oil and products . . . provided during each quarter of a base period [the fourth quarter of 1971 and first three quarters of 1972].[224]

Priority allocations of oil products were established for food-producing industries, medical-service organizations, public transportation, long-distance private transportation, and state and local governments. Hearing procedures were established to handle complaints, and authority was vested with the OOG to impose mandatory measures on suppliers as a final resort. A letter from OOG director Duke Ligon to oil companies one day after Simon's announcement clearly exposed the club in the closet:

> We assume that you agree to participate fully in this program, unless you notify the Office of Oil and Gas to the contrary. The program, while voluntary, is backed up by the attached guidelines, a mechanism for providing continuing scrutiny of compliance with guidelines and the threat of imposition of a mandatory allocation program should this program fail.[225]

The march toward mandatory allocation had begun.

Within a month after the beginning of the program, it became obvious that the guidelines were being violated and that mandatory measures would be necessary to commandeer supply for threatened independents. The chief difficulty was hard-and-fast contracts that were incompatible with a return to historical relationships; the year that had elapsed since the base period had not been tranquil.[226] Uncertainty about antitrust violations under the guidelines, of particular concern to majors, also encouraged noncooperation with Simon's plan.[227] Meanwhile, the OOG exhorted companies to comply

---

[224]The program was first announced by Simon before a Senate committee on May 10, 1973. *OGJ*, May 21, 1973, p. 72; and *NPN*, June 1973, p. 9. A description of the program and slightly revised guidelines were published in 38 *Fed. Reg.* 13588 (May 23, 1973).

[225]Letter of May 11, 1973 (in author's files).

[226]See *NPN*, July 1973, p. 38. For evaluations of the voluntary program, see *NPN*, July 1973, p. 41, and August 1973, pp. 42–45. In congressional hearings, one company, Murphy Oil, announced outright that it was not complying with the voluntary program.

[227]*OGJ*, June 4, 1973, p. 35, and June 18, 1973, p. 47.

and worked feverishly to handle complaints, often expressed through members of Congress, by trying to locate available supplies, which was difficult at best.

On May 17, Senator Henry Jackson (D-Wash.) introduced the Emergency Fuels and Energy Allocation Act of 1973, to obligatorily allocate crude oil and products from wellhead to retail. As supply problems worsened, complaints grew, and the question of mandatory controls became not "if" but "when." The bill gained increasing support from both Congress and beleaguered industry segments.[228] The Nixon administration, particularly Nixon, Simon, and Charles DiBona and John Love of the newly formed White House Office of Energy Policy, weighed the political pros and cons of supporting the bill, usurping Congress with a bill of their own, or opposing mandatory controls altogether so as to be able to lay blame when the inevitable failures developed.[229] On August 9, Love unveiled a tentative mandatory allocation program, while reiterating that "we are not now planning to implement a mandatory program at any specific time in the foreseeable future."[230] As a further gesture of conciliation toward Congress, it was announced on August 31 and September 6 that mandatory-rationing plans were being readied for propane, heating oil, diesel fuel, and other distillates.[231] The administration was reluctant to act; it took a combination of anticipated winter shortages, growing recognition of the failure of voluntary allocation, and heavy congressional pressure to activate mandatory allocation authority under the Economic Stabilization Act.

[228]While independents heavily favored mandatory distribution, majors were split on the issue. See *OGJ*, June 18, 1973, p. 47.

[229]Neil de Marchi, "Energy Policy under Nixon: Mainly Putting Out Fires," pp. 439–40.

[230]Office of the White House Press Secretary, Statement of August 9, 1973, p. 4. Love's continued insistence on the voluntary program reflected his distaste for mandatory allocation: "Allocation schemes do not dampen demand, they do not increase demand. . . . They simply shift any actual shortage from one user to another" (p. 2). The proposed regulations were published in 38 *Fed. Reg.* 21797 (August 13, 1973).

[231]Of all fuels, propane was in the shortest supply and the most troublesome to regulate. Not only did the natural-gas shortage trigger propane substitution, Special Rule no. 1 (covering the top twenty-five firms) made the production of propane uneconomical, and diffuse points and terms of sale made centralized regulation difficult. Neil de Marchi, "Energy Policy under Nixon: Mainly Putting Out Fires," p. 441.

In early October, mandatory allocation came to pass when Love, upon instruction from Nixon, ordered the distribution of propane, heating oil, diesel fuel, kerosene, and jet fuel to be regulated. Propane was to be allocated according to priority guidelines, and middle distillates were to be apportioned according to 1972 monthly amounts.[232] A 5 percent set-aside for state allocation was also prescribed. Under the direction of Vice Admiral Eli Reich, deputy assistant secretary of defense for installations and logistics, the OOG dispensed personnel to all state capitals in conjunction with the right of each state to commandeer 10 percent of each supplier's distillate for priority allocation.[233]

In early November, a critical supply situation was complicated and worsened by the Arab embargo.[234] On November 7 in a nationally televised "Address on the Energy Emergency," President Nixon set the tone for the constructivist energy policy to follow by substituting Malthusian "doomsday" logic for sober economic reasoning. "Our growing demands have bumped up against the limits of available supply," he proclaimed, "because our economy has grown enormously . . . and luxuries [automobiles, air conditioning] are now considered necessities."[235]

Nixon's superficial analysis, politically inspired given the taboo of price decontrol, could appeal to the many untrained in economic cause and effect, whose opinions were based on surface observations only; left unexplained was the direct link between price regulation and declining energy supply, increasing energy demand, and the imbalance between the two, and how a removal of intervention could spontaneously reintroduce coordination. Drawing upon the Apollo space effort and World War II patriotism, Nixon's portrayal

---

[232]38 *Fed. Reg.* 27397 (October 3, 1973); and 38 *Fed. Reg.* 28660 (October 16, 1973).

[233]*OGJ*, October 15, 1973, p. 53; and *NPN*, November 1973, p. 10.

[234]The first effects of the embargo, announced October 17, were felt a month later. This corresponded to tanker travel time between the Middle East and the United States. The reduction was most pronounced in November and December, after which import substitutions from Canada, Iran, Nigeria, and Indonesia effectively replaced Arabian oil (but at higher world prices). William Lane, *The Mandatory Petroleum Price and Allocation Regulations: A History and Analysis* (Washington, D.C.: American Petroleum Institute, 1981), pp. 30–31.

[235]Address of November 7, 1973, in Office of the President, *Executive Energy Documents* (Washington, D.C.: Government Printing Office, 1978), p. 84.

of the emergency was as a problem to be conquered by government-engineered supply enhancement—quick-fix development of alternative fuel and greater petroleum production on federal land—and demand reduction—fuel-saving temperatures, slower driving, and other curtailments of energy use. Nixon also announced his intent to sign Senator Jackson's mandatory allocation bill, from which, indeed, the president's speech borrowed heavily.[236] Whatever earlier dissent the administration had faced was squelched; public reaction to the embargo and the general energy crisis, coupled the unraveling details of Watergate, made Nixon favor a dramatic constructivist energy program to demonstrate his capabilities as an activist leader during troubled times.

Allocation Regulation

General Programs. The administration's allocation program, described as on a "wartime footing," with the Interior Department's Office of Petroleum Allocation (formed November 1, 1973) in charge, was becoming more and more impotent as thousands of requests for special allocations overwhelmed the office's limited staff and budget, not to mention involved more oil than was available for redistribution.[237] What was needed, according to political consensus, was a bigger bureaucracy with full allocative powers to introduce conformity—hence equity—into the program. This led to the Emergency Petroleum Allocation Act, which superseded discretionary allocation authority under the Economic Stabilization Act effective November 27, 1973.[238] The new law, which required pursuant regulations to be effective within thirty days, covered all allocative decisions about crude oil and refined products—gasoline, kerosene, diesel fuel, liquefied petroleum gas (propane and butane only), middle distillates, and refined lubricating oils. After broadly defining its goals and identifying priority uses (agriculture; public services;

[236]"I met with the leaders of the Congress this morning, and I asked that they act on this legislation on a priority urgent basis.... Because of the hard work ... by Senators Jackson and Fannin, and others, I am confident that ... I will have the bill ... and will be able to sign it." Ibid., p. 83.

[237]By September, 7,000 requests were pending. Several months later, another 1,000 requests per week joined the backlog. *NPN*, October 1973, p. 11; and *OGJ*, November 19, 1973, p. 59. Also see *OGJ*, December 10, 1973, p. 59.

[238]Public Law 93-159, 87 Stat 627 (1973). Allocation regulation under the EPAA is also discussed in chapter 27, pp. 1624–30.

national defense; and the "public health, safety and welfare"), the act instructed that independent refiners and independent (nonbranded) marketers receive crude and product in amounts "not less than the amount sold or otherwise supplied to such marketer or refiner during the corresponding month of 1972," unless national supply was less than in 1972, in which case a proportionate share ("allocation fraction") corresponding to the deficit would be assigned.[239] Clearly, the law's intent was to protect independents from abnormal scarcity and shortage, base year 1972 being a "normal" business period of active independent involvement. To this end, the president was instructed to make monthly reports to Congress on the market share of nonbranded versus branded marketers to monitor the act's success. If unfavorable changes occurred, the president was instructed to order allocation adjustments to favor independents—thus penalizing majors—to reestablish the 1972 balance. Finally, the regulations were to remain in effect until February 28, 1975, unless it was demonstrated that the conditions that had given rise to the law no longer existed.

On December 12, 1973, regulations pursuant to the EPAA were proposed. Stated the newly established Federal Energy Office:

> Shortages of crude oil, residual fuel oil, and refined petroleum products caused by inadequate domestic production, environmental constraints, and the unavailability of imports sufficient to satisfy domestic demand, now exist or are imminent. Such shortages have created or may create severe economic dislocations and hardships, including increased unemployment, reduction of crop plantings and harvesting, and curtailment of vital public services, including the transportation of food and other essential goods. Such hardships and dislocations jeopardize the normal flow of commerce and constitute a national energy shortage which could threaten the public health, safety, and welfare and therefore requires prompt remedial action by the Executive Branch of the Federal Government.[240]

Allocation goals were specified as a percentage of 1972 crude runs between the wellhead and refinery, and as a percentage of 1972

---

[239]*Nonbranded* applied to marketers unaffiliated with refineries outside of their supply contracts; *branded* marketers were owned by their supplying refiner. *Independent* refiners obtained 70 percent or more of their throughput from nonaffiliated producers; *integrated* refiners obtained less than 30 percent of their supply from affiliate production.

[240]38 *Fed. Reg.* 34414 (December 13, 1973).

product allocations between the refinery and marketer. Two regulatory allocation programs were introduced: the *buy-sell program* designed to "equitably" distribute crude among refineries and the *supplier-purchaser rule* that attempted to lock in historical transactions for crude oil between wellhead and refinery and product transactions between refiner and marketer.[241] Under this rule, crude suppliers could not terminate existing relationships without thirty days' notice, and product suppliers were to continue to serve customers supplied between September 1, 1972, and November 30, 1973.

Final regulations issued December 27, 1973, relaxed the conditions underlying the buy-sell program; on January 15, 1974, final rules for the supplier-purchaser rule were released to specify new product allocation percentages with base-year 1972 and to freeze crude-oil relationships as of December 1, 1973.[242] This applied to all crude sales except exempt oil and could be terminated only by the mutual consent of the two parties or if the buyer declined to match a bona fide legal offer from another buyer. Several weeks later, it was added that new production could be sold to any person in a first sale, but once the sale was consummated, a frozen chain was established.[243]

The supplier-purchaser rule was designed to protect independent refineries from crude cutoffs by integrated companies to (1) maintain independent access to price-controlled crude and (2) establish base supply levels for the buy-sell program.[244] Many contracts, not coincidentally, were up for renewal in early 1974. In addition, reinforcement was given to the "normal business practice rule" to prevent circumvention of wellhead price maximums.[245] Specifically, tie-in sales were now verboten because the producer could no longer sell the uncontrolled portion of his output to the highest bidder whose quote was intended to cover the regulated portion also. Although

[241]While the supplier-purchaser rule is examined in detail in the next section, discussion of the buy-sell program is postponed until chapter 20, pp. 1195–1205.

[242]39 *Fed. Reg.* 744 (January 2, 1974); and 39 *Fed. Reg.* 1924 (January 15, 1974). The supplier-purchaser rule was upheld as constitutional in *Condor Operating Company* v. *Sawhill*, 514 F.2d 351 (1975).

[243]39 *Fed. Reg.* 3908 (January 30, 1974).

[244]Paul MacAvoy, *Federal Energy Administration Regulation* (Washington, D.C.: American Enterprise Institute, 1977), p. 26.

[245]39 *Fed. Reg.* 1936 (January 15, 1974). The rule states, "Nothing in this part is intended to exclude or supersede . . . operations which are normal . . . provided these procedures are not used to circumvent the intent of this part."

exempt oil could fetch its highest price, historic purchasers had the right of first refusal to all price-controlled supply.[246] The rule also removed opportunistic purchases of producing properties by refiners to "outbid" other refiners for price-controlled feedstock. Historic customers continued to have first refusal on production from sold properties. With these two circumventions removed, or at least made illegal, federal energy regulation became more binding.

In early 1974, the Federal Energy Office was busy on other allocation matters in addition to the above-mentioned two regulatory programs. Rumors of hoarding led Simon to threaten to investigate inventory levels and order stock reductions.[247] This was beyond the Federal Energy Office's reach, however, since firm-by-firm inventory levels were casually submitted for reports of the American Petroleum Institute, if at all. Simon thus continued down the interventionist path by advocating mandatory reporting by each firm on existing and anticipated inventory per location.[248] Effective February 22, weekly reports were required from refineries, bulk terminals, oil pipelines, and product pipelines; reports on product inventory, amounts, location, and any expected changes were also required.[249]

In the first month of the refiner buy-sell program, as discussed in more detail in chapter 20, a number of problems came to light. Industry pressure, including a lawsuit aimed at the heart of the program, prompted Simon to ask Congress for a revised allocation plan.[250] This led to a second version of the buy-sell program on June 1, 1974, but by this time the embargo had ceased. The new problem was the burgeoning price discrepancy between price-controlled oil and uncontrolled oil (including imports). This led to a refiner-acquisition-cost-equalization program on December 12, 1974, under which refiners operated until price decontrol in early 1981.[251]

[246]39 *Fed. Reg.* 31622 (August 30, 1974).

[247]Warned Simon: "Where we find people who have a 90-day supply or a 120-day supply and we deem 30 days reasonable we're going to roll them back. We're either going to reallocate their product . . . or not give them any additional supplies until they're back to a reasonable level." *OGJ*, January 14, 1974, p. 25.

[248]Despite existing authority to implement mandatory reporting, Simon urged specific legislation to "tail[or] sanctions and enforcement provisions" and to "expan[d] . . . mandatory reporting to other energy sources, such as coal and uranium." *OGJ*, January 21, 1974, p. 44.

[249]39 *Fed. Reg.* 5272 (February 11, 1974).

[250]See chapter 20, pp. 1196–98.

[251]See chapter 20, pp. 1205–37.

Crude Oil Supplier-Purchaser Rule. Early experience with the supplier-purchaser rule (freeze rule) brought publicized distortions.[252] On March 5, when changes were first sought to the original January 15 buy-sell rules, independent producers lobbied to revise the freeze rule as well because it "insure[d] the dominance of th[e] industry by its major purchasing segment" and discouraged sales to the highest bidder.[253] When the freeze rule was left unchanged,[254] Exxon filed suit to enjoin enforcement. Exxon had voluntarily supplied crude to independents in December 1973, during a period of tight supply, and was indefinitely frozen into sales of 130,000 barrels per day for its antiquated goodwill gesture. A preliminary injunction was denied in favor of defendants Ashland Oil and the Independent Refiners Association of America on grounds that Exxon's loss was the gain of others.[255]

Early operation of the supplier-purchaser rule also created detractors within government. John Weber, assistant administrator in charge of allocation for the Federal Energy Administration, criticized the rule for "eliminat[ing] competition . . . and preventing sales to be shifted from areas of decreased demand to areas of expanded demand."[256] He recommended relaxing the rule and substituting an arbitration process to handle disputes between sellers and buyers.

The supplier-purchaser rule continued in force with extensions of the EPAA. The Energy Policy and Conservation Act, signed December 22, 1975, in addition to extending the EPAA price and allocation rules, limited oil and product stocks to a ninety-day peak supply and prohibited "willfully accumulating crude oil [or products] . . . in excess of such person's reasonable needs."[257]

In 1975, two revisions to the freeze rule were made to exempt federal royalty oil and allow producers to change gatherers-resellers

---

[252]This discussion concerns crude-oil regulation only. Product regulation under the supplier-purchaser rule is discussed in chapter 27, pp. 1626–30.

[253]*OGJ*, April 1, 1974, p. 40.

[254]See 39 *Fed. Reg.* 15960 (June 1, 1974).

[255]*Exxon Corp.* v. *FEO*, 394 F. Supp 662 (D.D.C. 1974). Exxon also complained that 1,000 employees were involved with EPAA regulations. *OGJ*, June 24, 1974, p. 90.

[256]*OGJ*, September 9, 1974, p. 56.

[257]Sec. 458, sec. 459, and sec. 525 also significantly increased penalties for allocation (and price) violations.

with requisite notice.[258] The latter amendment was in response to producers' complaints that the rule "lessened . . . competition in the marketing of crude oil and has effectively prevented new entrants from having significant access to crude oil."[259]

The first major change to the freeze rule since its promulgation in early 1974 occurred when a new lock-in date of February 1, 1976, was established. Termination, as before, required mutual consent or the failure of the purchaser to match another bona fide price for stripper oil or new oil.[260] If production from a particular property rose or fell from December 1975 levels, historic purchasers had first-refusal rights to the reduction or excess in pro rata amounts. These changes continued the rule's favoritism toward purchasers, particularly independent refiners advantageously locked in to high-quality, lower tier crude. Proponents of the amended rule were independent refiners led by the Independent Refiners Association of America; opponents were independent producers and their lobbying arm, the Independent Petroleum Association of America.[261] Future amendments would also demonstrate the strength of the refining lobby. Producers were less influential, and resellers quietly squeezed their way into historical relationships on the coattails of independent refiners, despite legislative discouragement.

Several other changes were made before it was announced on August 18, 1980, that the supplier-purchaser rule would incrementally self-destruct with price decontrol.[262] Effective June 11, 1976, the mutual-consent proviso was replaced by the unilateral ability of a purchaser to terminate a relationship if all subsequent purchasers, including the refiner, agreed.[263] The intent of the change was to reduce transactions by middlemen, specifically opportunistic oil resellers. The producer was allowed to unilaterally terminate stripper-oil relationships if the replacement transaction was with a small

---

[258]40 Fed. Reg. 49297 (October 22, 1975); and 40 Fed. Reg. 54422 (November 24, 1975). Differentiation of reselling from gathering, first made in 40 Fed. Reg. 18182 (April 25, 1975), was significant given the importance of the regulation-spawned crude-reselling industry.

[259]40 Fed. Reg. 54422 (November 24, 1975).

[260]41 Fed. Reg. 7386 (February 18, 1976).

[261]OGJ, February 9, 1976, p. 50.

[262]45 Fed. Reg. 56732 (August 25, 1980).

[263]41 Fed. Reg. 24338 (June 16, 1976).

refiner (175,000 barrels per day or less) who processed the purchase. These complicating amendments increased flexibility for the regulated, but what began as a several-hundred-word regulation was now over five times that long.[264]

The phaseout announcement of August 18, 1980, effective October 1, terminated the rule for price-controlled crude sold directly by producers to large refiners (175,000 barrels per day or more) to free lower priced oil for small (mostly independent) refiners. Also included in what would be the final revisions to the rule was the "reseller substitution rule," which allowed either the producer or the refiner to alter a chain of distribution by eliminating a directly connected oil reseller as long as the ultimate beneficiary, the processing refiner, was not impaired. Like the previous rule, it was intended to discourage participation of middlemen. "The greatest economic efficiency and benefit to refiners" it was stated, "occurs in those instances where the distribution chain includes only those transactions necessary to ensure delivery of crude oil to the refiner."[265] This revision, however, was too late; the supplier-purchaser rule was so infested with the special-interest intent of protecting small refiners that it could never be used to derail activities that the U.S. Department of Energy (DOE) recognized as unnecessary and anti-consumer. Encouraging and protecting small refiners, as will be seen, was inherently pro-reseller.[266]

The supplier-purchaser rule was terminated on January 28, 1981, by Executive Order 12287, which ended the entire allocation program with minor exceptions.[267] Authority to allocate crude and oil products remained only during wartime emergencies pursuant to the Defense Production Act of 1950, as amended.[268] A determined attempt to pass a standby oil-allocation bill, sponsored by Senator James McClure (R-Ind.) with the support of major segments of the industry and various

---

[264]Remarked attorney Jay Elston, "The fact that this rule has been amended so many times is itself a commentary on its effectiveness, particularly the provisions designed to maintain competition." Elston, "The Crude Oil Supplier/Purchaser Regulations," Paper presented at Executive Enterprises Conference, Houston, Texas, September 4, 1980, p. 4.

[265]45 *Fed. Reg.* 56735 (August 25, 1980).

[266]See this chapter, pp. 687–88, 692–93.

[267]46 *Fed. Reg.* 9909 (January 30, 1981).

[268]The Defense Production Act was renewed seventeen times.

outside groups, failed on March 24, 1982, when the Senate narrowly upheld Reagan's veto.[269]

Allocation Regulation in Retrospect

Mandatory allocation regulation was a predictable failure. It never had the pretense of ending the crisis; it only meant to deal with it.[270] On the eve of mandatory regulation when "voluntary" allocation was on its last legs, William Simon acknowledged the futility of the situation:

> In allocating crude oil and product we have a situation not unlike the passengers on a sinking ship fighting for top position at the mast head. Unless we increase production we shall all sink sooner or later.[271]

The way to increase output and ration demand to bring the two into balance was to *deregulate prices,* which government officials were loathe to accept. Instead, stopgap measures such as the supplier-purchaser rule, the buy-sell program, and the entitlements program were implemented to appease politically powerful independent marketers and refiners. Arguments for "preserving competition" by protecting numerous small firms created under plentiful supply conditions of the 1960s were trotted out when, in fact, changed industry conditions necessitated consolidation to achieve scale economies and endure supply disruptions and lower sales. The supplier-purchaser rule substituted historical bygones for changing consumer preferences and supply conditions. The national distribution system,

---

[269]Supporting the Standby Petroleum Allocation Act of 1982 were eight major oil companies; petroleum marketing and refining organizations; and utility companies, as well as the National Governors' Association and labor, consumer, and agricultural groups. Against S. 1503 were smaller oil companies and various large product users such as Delta Air Lines, Eastern Airlines, Holiday Inns, General Motors, Goodyear, and Bethlehem Steel. *Congressional Quarterly,* March 27, 1982, p. 663.

[270]A House report stated that the EPAA was "not designed to increase supplies. . . . Instead this bill focuses on the short-term objectives of seeing to it that during times of shortage our priority needs are met and that whatever limited supplies we have are equitably distributed." *Small Business and the Energy Shortage,* Hearings before the Subcommittee on Special Small Business Problems of the House Committee on Small Businesses, 93rd Cong., 1st sess., House Report 721-8.1 (Washington, D.C.: Government Printing Office, 1973), p. 6.

[271]Quoted in Neil de Marchi, "Energy Policy under Nixon: Mainly Putting Out Fires," p. 433.

consequently, was out of date and backward looking rather than forward looking. Older firms "grandfathered" into distribution chains enjoyed monopoly privileges not enjoyed by outside, newer firms. The program was also patently biased toward crude buyers and against crude sellers; refiners routinely purchased oil not to refine but to resell at a profit.[272] Alert firms that increased inventory or entered into contracts after the base period were penalized, and less alert firms were rewarded. The winners were not consumers or properly scaled marketers and refiners. They were politically adept firms most vulnerable to highly competitive conditions, conditions created initially in part by government intervention. Allocation regulation was the proverbial "two wrongs don't make a right." A bad situation was made worse.

Regulatory Trading and the 1973–81 Oil-Trading Boom

The most important, yet least understood, consequence of oil-price and allocation regulation in the 1973–81 period was the dramatic growth of the crude-oil and oil-product reselling industry. The trading upsurge has been virtually overlooked by academicians purporting to identify the economic effects (inefficiencies, wealth redistribution) created by controls.[273] This is explained by the fact that most trading concerns sprang up overnight, were privately held, and kept a low profile.[274] Moreover, scholars did not

---

[272]Refiners refused to terminate seller ties even if the oil was needed for feedstock as a hedge against future supply problems, not to mention the profitability of resales. Paul MacAvoy, *Federal Energy Administration Regulation*, p. 101.

[273]For example, Joseph Kalt's *The Economics and Politics of Oil Price Regulation* (Cambridge, Mass.: MIT Press, 1981), described on the inside cover by Paul MacAvoy as "the definitive work to date" on the subject, neglects the trading industry and identifies only producers, refiners, and consumers as the important players in the regulatory saga. This omission is serious to a proper understanding of the "winners" and "losers" from price and allocation controls. Other works with a similar omission are Kenneth Arrow and Joseph Kalt, *Petroleum Price Regulation* (Washington, D.C.: American Enterprise Institute, 1979); Rodney Smith and Charles Phelps, *The Kaleidoscope of U.S. Price Regulation* (Santa Monica, Calif.: Rand Corporation, n.d.); and idem, *Petroleum Regulation: The False Dilemma of Decontrol* (Santa Monica, Calif.: Rand Corporation, 1977). Involved federal regulators, lawyers, and consultants, on the other hand, understood and emphasized the central role of regulatory reselling.

[274]Although trading firms numbered in the hundreds, the only lobby organization formed to represent them, the Petroleum Resellers Association of America, never claimed a wide membership and was not heard from after being founded in 1976. The unpublicized nature of trading is demonstrated by the fact that the *Oil Weekly* and the *Oil & Gas Journal*, two leading trade journals of the industry, not once reported on the spectacular growth of the industry and the reasons for it. The *Oil & Gas Journal*

681

know[275] what industry insiders did—the supplier-purchaser rule, which potentially forestalled the entry of opportunistic middlemen between producers and refiners and refiners and retailers, was not strictly enforced by regulators or observed by the industry; resellers could and did create new chains of "distribution" where profitable.

Only when widespread oil-tier miscertification came to light in 1980 did politicians and the press attempt to bring the intricate workings of crude-oil trading to the public. But much more than miscertification profiteering is of interest to scholars: large-scale opportunities to profit from properly certified crude and petroleum products, unintendedly created by price and allocation regulation, require explanation. To understand *regulatory trading*, the free-market, historical function of petroleum trading must first be explained.

Free-Market Trading

Imperfect knowledge and different geographical points of supply and demand create a market need for independent (or in-house) traders to coordinate refiner-purchasers with producer-suppliers on the one hand and wholesale purchasers and refiner-suppliers on the other.[276] Regarding imperfect knowledge, speculative sales and resales were made of physically undisturbed oil. Regarding geography, crude-oil suppliers from the beginning of the industry had

---

mentioned trading only in reporting on changes in reseller regulations, the position of producers and refiners toward reselling, and later, congressional investigation of miscertification. See *OGJ*, September 19, 1977, p. 99; September 26, 1977, p. 30; January 9, 1978, p. 26; October 27, 1980, p. 39; and November 10, 1980, p. 158. The *National Petroleum News*, very attuned to downstream petroleum activities, broke the silence of the trade press in mid-1979 with an in-depth story on regulatory trading, although exclusively concentrated on the oil-product side. See Marvin Reid, "Profiteering," *NPN*, August 1979, pp. 31–39.

[275]See, for example, Kenneth Arrow and Joseph Kalt, *Petroleum Price Regulation*, pp. 7, 10.

[276]For discussions of the historical (free-market) role of trading, see Ralph Cassady, *Price Making and Price Behavior in the Petroleum Industry* (New Haven, Conn.: Yale University Press, 1954), pp. 131–34, 166–74; Henry Ralph, "The Answer Is the Crude Oil Man," *OGJ*, November 14, 1955, pp. 180–96; Paul Davidson, "Public Policy Problems of the Domestic Crude Oil Industry," *American Economic Review* (March 1963): 100; Frank Bolton, "Problems Involved in the Sale and Transportation of Crude Oil," *25 Oil and Gas Institute* (New York: Matthew Bender, 1971), pp. 152–59; John Ryan, "The Domestic Crude Oil Market," Exxon Co., Houston, Tex., 1979, pp. 2–5, 22–26; and Robert Stobaugh, "Statement on Crude Oil Reseller Regulation before the U.S. Department of Energy," December 12, 1979 (copy in author's files). The Department of Energy summarized the gathering function in 42 *Fed. Reg.* 41257 (August 15, 1977).

performed the "location" function of aggregating and transporting oil from field stock tanks to refinery connection points.[277] When refineries became more sophisticated, the "quality-location" function emerged: suppliers were used to match crude types to refinery specifications. This not only meant locating the right crude at the lease to purchase, transport, and resell to the refiner, but it meant discovering opportunities to swap crude with other parties that had opposite needs.[278] Similarly, product traders could arrange for transportation between refineries and wholesale and retail points and arrange changes in product inventories so that consumers would have available the type and quantity of products desired at the desired time and place.

In the 1930s, field and transportation activities between the wellhead and the refinery gained autonomy as the *gathering* function. Before, gathering was predominantly an in-house activity of integrated companies; now, it was also a service offered by specialized independent companies. The subtle transformation resulted from the increased participation of independents in major new oil discoveries, the most prominent of which was East Texas. Proration and other state regulation that prevented major companies from assuming greater control in major fields were not inconsequential in this regard. Continued regulation and small-tract drilling by independents continued to propel demand for independent gathering services over the next decades.

Another service historically performed by traders in a free market is *time trading* or *exchanging* whereby crude or product is traded over time periods to synchronize inventory levels with throughput schedules for refineries and sales schedules for marketers.[279] Refiners

---

[277]*Oil & Gas Journal—Oil City Derrick*, August 27, 1934, p. 9; and Paul Giddens, *The Early Petroleum Industry*, (Philadelphia: Porcupine Press, 1974), p. 182. Related to time trading is futures trading, which is examined in chapter 17, pp. 1048–61.

[278]The economy of information provided by an independent trader can be appreciated from this example. Assuming that ten suppliers and ten buyers populate a market without any middlemen, one hundred informational links would need to be established; that is, each firm would have to connect with all the others to cover the market. With one trader between these firms, only twenty links, representing each firm's connection with the trader, would cover the market. See Robert Stobaugh, "Statement on Crude Oil Reseller Regulation before the U.S. Department of Energy," p. 6.

[279]Exchanges are often "even-Stephen" deals, adjusted for crude or product differentials, when performed by the principal parties.

(marketers) oversupplied with crude (product) reduce storage and carrying costs, while refiners (marketers) short of inventory can achieve proper levels of plant (outlet) utilization. Exchanging came of age in the early 1930s when depressed prices encouraged greater economy on the part of refiners to reduce freight costs.[280]

The quality-location-time service of trading reflects both an informational aspect—uncovering mutually beneficial trades—and in almost all cases a transportational aspect—overcoming locational differences to satisfy demand. The risks involved range from (1) the high risk of *position taking*, where a trader obtains inventory or "sells short" (promises to deliver what is not possessed) in the expectation that a price change will make it possible to profitably complete a trade; to (2) the normal risk of *possession* between the time the crude or product is bought and the time it is delivered;[281] to (3) the low risk of *arbitrage*, where a trader performs a simultaneous buy-sell trade without transportation or physical possession.[282] In this last category, informational errors have created underpriced crude that is profitably exploited by the trader. Although rare compared with transportation-related quality-time-location trading, arbitrage opportunities are available for alert resellers and will always exist, given imperfect knowledge.

It is important to note that the trading services of information and transportation can be inversely related. With supply and demand points distanced from one another, an important middleman service is to swap oil or product to reduce the travel between individual supply-demand points. This reduces cross-hauling (the simultaneous movement of oil from point A to B and from B to A), which lowers acquisition costs. Transportation assets, in addition, are freed

---

[280]*NPN*, May 6, 1942, p. 9. Later in the decade, growing brand identification and specialized refining techniques discouraged product swapping despite the locational advantages of doing so.

[281]Medium-risk trades can be reduced to low-risk ones by obtaining bank letters of credit to lock in payments and insurance to cover possession hazards.

[282]Crude and product brokers arbitrage from informational gaps by putting buyers and sellers together on a commission basis, whether it be producer to refiner, producer to trader, trader to refiner, refiner to wholesaler-retailer, trader to trader, refiner to refiner, or wholesaler-retailer to wholesaler-retailer. Brokers perform services without either taking title to or transporting oil, which reduces risk to a level comparable to that of arbitrage. In these low-risk situations, the financial risk of not covering costs remains, as it does in all financial enterprising.

to perform other duties as a result of ignorance discovered and removed.

Regulatory Trading before 1973

Regulatory trading refers to trading services offered in response to opportunities created by government intervention in the market. Before the 1970s, regulatory trading occurred during World War I, the hot-oil era of 1931–35, World War II, and the Korean conflict, primarily with crude oil but also product. In periods of price controls (World War I, World War II, and the Korean conflict), opportunities existed to "correct" artificially low prices between the producer and refiner.[283] Refiners (marketers) acquiesced to the resellers' "market-clearing" services and outbid competitors for desired supply as long as they could recoup middlemen's markups and retain their margins. The *Oil & Gas Journal* in 1918 pointed the finger at product brokers for wartime profiteering.

> The broker has been . . . playing both ends against the middle. . . . He has been buying fuel oil at $1.50 to $2.00 and reselling it as high as $3.50. The real offense lately has been . . . ordering carloads of products from refineries, with positive promises not to divert shipments, and later to divert several times. . . . It will not be surprising if the broker is limited [by regulation] to one diversion and prohibited from making more than one profit—that is to say there shall not be several commissions made.[284]

During the hot-oil days, resale opportunities were created by a dual-price market—posted prices for legal oil and discount prices for illegal oil.[285] Two-tiered pricing encouraged arbitrage trading to eliminate differentials (adjusted for risk) and encouraged tender

---

[283]Seen another way, middlemen (brokers and later independent gatherers) equilibrate the market in place of producers who by law cannot do so.

[284]*OGJ*, May 30, 1918, p. 34.

[285]Hot-oil discounts were estimated at between 10 and 80 percent below posted prices by *OW*, July 24, 1933, p. 11, and at between 25 and 60 percent below posted prices by John McLean and Robert Haigh, *The Growth of Integrated Oil Companies* (Boston: Harvard University Press, 1954), p. 593.

falsification to turn hot oil into "documented" allowable oil to fetch higher prices.[286]

On the product side, brokering became the scapegoat for price wars. The Oil Code of 1933 and industry suasion were geared toward keeping prices at profitable levels. Rather than precipitate price declines by selling surplus product through regular marketing channels, refiners quietly sold their surplus to brokers at a discount. The result was "a large number of desk-and-telephone brokers" each of whom

> buys where he can buy cheapest and sells at a higher price; that to keep his capital as low as possible, or even nil, he turns his purchases into sales as quickly as possible and at the least sign of a profit.[287]

In a series of editorials, *National Petroleum News* editor Warren Platt criticized brokers for demoralizing the market and recommended that majors not deal with them "in conformity to the conservation laws and the stabilization program."[288] Although part of the problem was that brokers were party to refined hot oil and tax-evaded product, the general circumstance was overproduction at the wellhead relative to the price levels the industry desired. As explained in chapter 24, consternation over wholesale and retail practices was occasioned by effects rather than causes.[289]

Between the Korean conflict and the 1970s, nonmarket trading occurred in one instance. Import rights given to inland refiners under the Mandatory Oil Import Program in the 1959–69 period were exchanged with majors for inland crude rights and a differential representing the value of lower priced imports.[290]

---

[286]Trade journal references suggest active crude brokering during the hot-oil boom. Idled refineries "function[ed] as crude brokers." *OW*, July 24, 1933, p. 10. "Brokers of crude in spot quantities . . . buy and sell oil considerably below the posted price." *OW*, August 29, 1932, p. 9. See also *OGJ*, April 26, 1934, p. 8., and September 13, 1934, pp. 13, 44.

[287]*NPN*, March 2, 1932, p. 13. Warren Platt remarked that no trade association had been formed for brokers as had been done for the other segments of the industry. Distress gasoline during the time of major company buying pools also attracted pure trading. See, for example, *NPN*, April 24, 1935, p. 41.

[288]*NPN*, March 9, 1932, p. 21.

[289]See chapter 23, pp. 1362–63.

[290]See chapter 13, pp. 738–39.

The Nixon price-control program, which began on August 28, 1971, set maximum prices for crude oil and petroleum products as well as for all other domestic goods and services. When price ceilings created abnormally tight supply, particularly of propane beginning in 1972, traders, as they had previously under price regulation, recognized market-clearing opportunities to purchase at regulated prices and profitably resell at prices approaching market levels. During Phase III, petroleum products were purchased from regulated firms for resale by unregulated companies. Stated Charles Owens, "The profit opportunities were obvious . . . and attracted a bevy of fly-by-night brokers and fast-buck seekers."[291]

The Petroleum Trading Boom: 1973–81

Price Regulation and "Daisy-Chain" Arbitrage. The trading boom in crude oil can be traced to September 1, 1973, the effective date of the two-tiered price program for crude oil.[292] The difference between the controlled price of old oil and the market price of new oil represented the economic rent, the *arbitrage differential*, which, by law, domestic producers and royalty owners could not receive but which was available for middlemen to capture. Two conditions existed that favored resellers' gaining the unclaimed economic rent. One, the supplier-purchaser rule was not effective until January 15, 1974, whereupon it was not strictly enforced and could be circumvented. Two, refiners who normally desired to minimize crude input costs were saddled with "cost-plus" margin restrictions capable of absorbing feedstock prices much higher than the wellhead regulated price—a price corresponding to the unregulated price.[293] Under the supplier-purchaser rule, traders could insert themselves into a chain by outbidding historical purchasers for a quantity of new oil to "tie

[291]Charles Owens, "History of Petroleum Price Controls," in *Historical Working Papers on the Energy Stabilization Program* (Washington, D.C.: Government Printing Office, 1974), p. 1244. Also see pp. 1296, 1298–99. The birth of regulatory reselling in the 1970s can be linked to price controls in general and particularly to Special Rule no. 1, effective March 6, 1973. See chapter 9, pp. 472–73.

[292]Testimony of the general counsel to the U.S. Department of Energy, Lynn Coleman, in *The Cost to the Consumer of Crude Oil Decontrol,* Hearing before the Subcommittee on Oversight and Investigation of the House Committee on Interstate and Foreign Commerce, 96th Cong., 2d sess. (Washington, D.C.: Government Printing Office, 1980), p. 48.

[293]Refinery price regulation is discussed in chapter 20, pp. 1181–89.

in" associated old oil (before amendments removed this practice) or become an extended part of the chain by purchasing oil from a refinery.[294] Alert resellers could become part of the first chain as new production and new refineries came on stream.[295]

Along with the above-mentioned legal entry, resellers "illegally" entered historical chains without complaint from traditional purchasers or prosecution by regulators. Therefore, if the rule was not circumvented, the previous chain was quasi-legally altered by the de facto consent of downstream members of the chain.[296]

Concurrent with multitiered pricing was the transformation of a long-standing buyer's market for crude oil to a seller's market. Proration was suspended, and increasing import prices and unfulfilled demand at regulated prices pushed prices of new oil further and further above those of old oil. This magnified arbitrage possibilities for traders who in 1974 were entering in great numbers, while the up market in general enhanced the profitability of position taking by traders.

[294]Incentive existed for refiners to postpone distillation and sell their crude to traders, extending the "frozen" distribution chain. The refiner could make a margin by the sale and later obtain the same oil (which all along remained in the refiner's inventory) at a higher price yet still make his maximum margin. Or the refiner could profitably exercise his resale rights with excess oil from the freeze rule.

[295]Said one small refiner: "A new refiner has no opportunity to buy crude at posted prices. Purchases are made primarily from resellers at markups well over posted prices." OGJ, March 20, 1978, p. 48. The small refiner boom is discussed in chapter 20, pp. 1209–19.

[296]In testimony, John Alan Zipp of the Department of Energy answered Rep. Alan Dingell's (D-Mich.) curiosity about how the resellers broke into chains given the supplier-purchaser rule:

Zipp: I asked [the Office of Special Investigation] why did you not enforce (the supplier-purchaser rule)? . . . And the response was, they cannot pursue a breach of the supplier-purchaser relationship unless there is a complaint by someone. . . . Their policy was that unless there was a complaint they would not try to enforce the regulation.

Dingell: Are you telling me that if the allocation regulations are enforced according to their terms . . . daisy chaining could have been prevented?

Zipp: In my judgement a substantial portion could have been prevented, yes, sir.

White Collar Crime in the Oil Industry, Hearings before the House Committee on Interstate and Foreign Commerce, 96th Cong., 1st sess. (Washington, D.C.: Government Printing Office, 1980), p. 122. Technically, new chain participants had to formally obtain the refiner's consent. The rule stated, "A new reseller may be substituted with the refiner's consent." 41 Fed. Reg. 24338 (June 16, 1976).

Another crucial element in the developing trading boom was the profit margins placed on each reseller. Because wellhead price controls on crude oil had to be complemented by downstream margin restrictions to prevent windfall gains (e.g., a firm's buying price-controlled oil to sell at unregulated prices), cost-plus margins were set for traders, refiners, and marketers alike. For traders, two sets of ceiling prices were prescribed. Historic gatherers (those in existence on or before May 15, 1973) were allowed cost plus their margin on or before May 15, 1973 (typically a $0.10 to $0.15 return on $3.00 per barrel oil); post–May 15 entrants were restrained to their first-sale margin plus cost.[297] For historic Class A resellers, approximately 39 firms closely identified with the traditional gathering function, the $0.10 to $0.15 margin became more restrictive as crude prices

[297]Margins for Class A resellers were first promulgated August 19, 1973, under the Phase IV regulations administered by the Cost of Living Council. 39 *Fed. Reg.* 22538 (August 22, 1973). From then until September 27 of the same year, margins were limited to average cost plus a margin equal to that of the last trade made on or before January 10, 1973. On September 28, the base day for margin computation was changed to May 15, 1973. For firms that entered after May 15 and before June 13, 1973, (later to be called Class B resellers along with firms entering until December 1, 1977), the first-sale price was the lawful maximum. Firms that began trading between June 13 and August 19, 1973, on the other hand, established a ceiling price by determining the "average price charged for the type of crude involved in a substantial number of current transactions in the applicable market by other persons selling comparable oil in the same marketing area." This price could only be increased to reflect dollar-for-dollar increases in crude-oil costs. The intent of the law was to determine a proxy May 15, 1973, price for new (Class B) firms comparable to that for existing (Class A) firms. The so-called new-item rule was extended to post–August 19 entrants to determine their legal price based on "transactions at the nearest comparable outlet on the day when the item is first offered for sale." 10 C.F.R. part 212, subpart F. The new-item rule created many problems for involved firms. An antitrust interpretation questioned the legality of basing prices on those of the nearest competitor (letter of December 28, 1979, from Department of Justice to William Scott, copy in author's personal files). Definitions of *transaction*, *nearest*, *comparable*, *item*, and *outlet* raised ambiguity. In late 1976, the Federal Energy Administration admitted that attempts to find a proxy price had "raised interpretative questions because of certain significant respects in which the historic methods of crude oil resellers differ from those generally employed by resellers of other covered products." Quoted in Thomas Houghton, "Application of 10 C.F.R. Part 212, Subpart F to Crude Oil Resellers," Paper presented at Executive Enterprises Conference, Houston, Texas, July 20, 1982, pp. 2–3. For a telling critique of subpart F's ambiguous method of determining lawful prices, see William DePaulo, "Bases for Resisting Applications of Subpart F to Crude Oil Resale Transactions Prior to January 1, 1978," Paper presented at Executive Enterprises Conference, Houston, Texas, September 4, 1980.

rose; for Class B resellers, a calculated first sale that locked in lucrative margins was possible and common. The general effect was to ensure that many trades would be made to arbitrage old oil to new-oil (market) levels; the specific effect was to place historic gatherers at a disadvantage compared with opportunistic entrants in exploiting pure profit opportunities created by statutorily underpriced crude. Over 100 new firms, the great majority of which did not have storage facilities or transportation equipment, would enter in the 1973–77 period, and many more would enter thereafter.

A hypothetical example of the trading activity created by the regulatory environment can be constructed. Assume that Class A gathering margins are $0.15 per barrel and Class B telephone-trading margins are $0.50 per barrel in August 1974, at which time old oil was at $5.25 per barrel and new oil was at a market price of $10.00 per barrel. The following scenario was typical.

- Step one: Gatherer A buys old oil at $5.25 per barrel at the lease and transports it to a pipeline connection point where it is sold to Reseller A for $5.40 per barrel.
- Step two: Reseller B sells to Reseller C for $5.90 per barrel.
- Step three: Reseller C sells to Reseller D for $6.40 per barrel.
- Step four: Reseller D sells to Reseller E for $6.90 per barrel.
- Step five: Reseller E sells to Reseller F for $7.40 per barrel.
- Step six: Reseller F sells to Reseller G for $7.90 per barrel.
- Step seven: Reseller G sells to Reseller H for $8.40 per barrel.
- Step eight: Reseller H sells to Reseller I for $8.90 per barrel.
- Step nine: Reseller I sells to Gatherer A for $9.40 per barrel.
- Step ten: Gatherer A ships the crude in his facilities to Refiner A who purchases it for refining at $9.55 per barrel.

Notice that historical services were performed only at steps one and ten; steps two through nine involved paperwork between reseller firms with the oil undisturbed. The seven "in-line" transfers, as it were, served the purpose of correcting the price of legally mispriced oil and little else. The refiner received "market-cleared" oil, which he refined and sold at a cost-plus price downstream to similarly restrained parties. Presumably, the $9.55 per barrel acquisition cost is able to absorb the forthcoming refiner, wholesaler, and retailer markups to be within the upper bound of trading-arbitrage possibilities.

There can be many variations on the foregoing example. Certain trading firms could participate in the chain more than once, which was not uncommon.[298] The eight $0.50 per barrel resales represent a minimum number of trades given full exploitation of the old-oil price; thirty-five trades averaging $0.10 per barrel could have taken place if resellers needed to average down profits from earlier trades made above legal levels.[299] Another possibility is that fewer traders could capture the unclaimed rent by violating their margin ceilings, or a single trader could claim the entire differential by recertifying old oil as new oil by adding a token markup to the falsified base price.[300] Finally, a refiner could have been involved in reseller trades for the aforementioned reasons instead of only passively receiving the daisy-chained oil.

In our example, of the $4.75 per barrel of the resource's market value denied to producers and royalty owners (the new-oil price minus the old-oil price), resellers captured $4.00 and the remaining $0.75 was received by a downstream party, possibly the consumer but more likely a product reseller. In other words, the crude-oil resellers had first opportunity to collect the floating economic rent, the product reseller the next opportunity, and the consumer the last opportunity.

The arbitrage example assumes sophisticated knowledge and the absence of legal or institutional barriers to prevent the movement of old-oil prices toward market levels. It is unlikely that, in the early days of the two-tiered program, resellers fully perceived their opportunities, and if they had done so, traditional buyer-seller relationships—whether established by regulation, contract, or custom— would have, at least to an extent, precluded daisy-chain activities.

---

[298]Stated the Economic Regulatory Administration, "Observations indicate that in many instances firms are not only purchasing and selling but often repurchasing and reselling identical volumes of crude oil." 45 *Fed. Reg.* 74438 (November 7, 1980).

[299]The maximum price a reseller could charge, the sum of the applicable cost and permissible margin, was not calculated on a transaction-by-transaction basis but on a monthly average. Therefore, high-margin trades would be made at the beginning of the month with later transactions made at small, zero, or even negative margins. This represented a subtle subsidization from skilled traders needing to average down to less skilled traders needing to average up.

[300]Such "miscertification" would be legal only if the trader regained balance at the end of the monthly trading period by an opposite tier switch. Tier switching is further examined in this chapter, pp. 696–99.

In such cases, the refinery would have refined underpriced oil and sold underpriced products, which would have presented opportunities for product resellers to trade to market-clearing levels. By most accounts, this is what occurred in the early years, particularly with fuel-oil sales to electric utilities.[301] This also occurred with motor gasoline, jet fuel, and other products, reflecting the traders' ability to penetrate traditional refiner-wholesaler-retailer relationships.

Energy officials worked to administratively choke off the oil-trading boom that was striking at the heart of the regulatory goal of keeping domestic oil prices below "artificial" world levels. The DOE identified regulatory trading as entirely superfluous.

> These firms do not own, operate or control the pipeline systems through which the crude oil is transported. Neither do they arrange or provide gathering services, accounting or reporting service for producers, or transportation, storage and handling services; nor do they find any new buyers to take crude oil off the pipelines or find any new end-users, i.e., refiners, for the crude oil. Furthermore, these firms do not at any time acquire, hold or exercise physical control, possession, or custody of the crude oil involved, but merely take title to the crude oil for brief periods and shortly pass that title to another firm at a higher selling price. In such in-line transfers, the firms involved do not serve as shippers of the crude oil in the pipeline involved. They do not pay transportation or other charges for shipment of the crude oil, deliver the crude oil to the pipeline for shipment, provide the necessary facilities for receiving the crude oil when it leaves the pipeline, or bear the risk of loss of the crude oil while it is in the pipeline. Neither do these firms serve as the final consignees of the crude oil or obtain title to the crude oil when it leaves the pipeline or assume the responsibility for removing it from the pipeline.[302]

The loophole in the grand "cost-plus" design that prevented a timely response to opportunistic reselling was the fact that oil and petroleum products can be traded infinitely, whereas crude oil is refined once and sold once to final consumers. With the supplier-purchaser rule, the government had a regulation that potentially could have locked out reseller arbitraging, but enforcement would

---

[301]See this chapter, pp. 699–701.
[302]45 *Fed. Reg.* 74438 (November 7, 1980).

have been a nightmare given the sheer size of the petroleum-distribution system and the pecuniary incentives to circumvent it. As it turned out, the rule scarcely hindered the middleman upsurge. With time, regulators and prosecutors got more serious and sophisticated about reselling. With new regulations and "harsh, retroactive interpretations," an attorney concluded, the "DOE's enforcement policy seems clearly designed to destroy the viability of most crude oil resellers."[303] Central to the government's effort was prohibition of profits where a reseller "performs no service or other function traditionally and historically associated with the resale of crude oil."[304] This struck at the heart of regulatory trading, which was almost entirely made up of paper transactions (or in DOE language, "sham transactions") in which markups were unaccompanied by storage or transportation services. But a problem existed with the DOE's justification of the "layering" rule. Trades without physical movement and without use of the purchaser's facilities *did* occur prior to 1973, a fact that DOE officials were inclined to admit after industry testimony on the point.[305] As one regulator remarked several years after the layering rule went into effect: "We do not have an adequate anti-layering rule. Trades [in-line transfers] are traditional and historical." How, then, could the DOE achieve its aim yet recognize this fact? Continued the official, "I think it is better to merely state that we *forbid layering which is a sequence of transactions designed to raise costs to consumers.*"[306] Regulators were between a rock and a hard place. They could do nothing and let the "racket" go on, or they could enforce a rule that, to quote its author, "threw the baby out with the bath water."[307]

---

[303]James Carroll, "Certification and Price Audit Issues," Paper presented at Executive Enterprises Conference, Houston, Texas, September 4, 1980, p. 1.

[304]42 *Fed. Reg.* 64863 (December 29, 1977).

[305]Testified W. S. Dumas before the DOE in late 1979: "While employed by a major oil company in 1970 and 1971, I was responsible for the crude oil trading activities amounting to several hundred thousand barrels per day. A substantial portion was done by in-line transfers in other companies' facilities [for] . . . *profit*, not simply for amusement." Copy of testimony in author's files.

[306]Letter from Daniel Thomas to Samuel Bradley, September 27, 1979. Copy in author's files. Emphasis added.

[307]Personal interview with F. Scott Bush, assistant administrator for regulations, Economic Regulatory Administration, July 23, 1981.

A second effort with similar intent and dilemmatic implications was the proposed margin limitation announced October 26, 1979. In response to complaints of "wide disparities in the average markups of apparently comparable resellers" and the fact that "in many instances the profit margins of [pure] traders . . . have exceeded [historic] resellers'," a transaction-by-transaction margin was proposed to limit traders to $0.25 per barrel for resold oil that was physically transported or stored and either $0.01 or nothing for traders not performing such services.[308] This sparked vigorous protest from both traditional and telephone traders who warned of bankrupting the industry in an attempt to control certain undesired practices. It was, again, a case of throwing the baby out with the bath water.[309] In the meantime, traders were allowed to continue to set margins on the new-item basis but were warned that a final margin rule would be retroactively enforced with refund liability.

On July 29, 1980, the DOE adopted the long-awaited margin liability rule to limit Class C resellers, firms making first sales after November 30, 1977, to $0.20 per barrel.[310] Firms that averaged over $0.20 per barrel in any month from the date of entry had to locate and identify a similar margin from a "nearest comparable seller" for justification. Given the antitrust implications of exchanging price information and the ambiguity of finding the "correct" nearest competitor, a group of Class C firms, through their attorneys, turned to a data-processing firm to gather nationwide reseller statistics on margin, crude type, location, and transaction date to create a master list of nearest comparable margins.

---

[308]44 *Fed. Reg.* 62848 (October 31, 1979). In the announcement, the DOE stated that the proposal was designed to "curb pricing abuses in the resale of crude oil"; specifically, "the accumulation of numerous, successive markups result[ing] in significantly higher prices for crude oil [which] . . . increases prices for consumers." *DOE News*, October 26, 1979, p. 1.

[309]An internal DOE memorandum expressed this point: the Economic Regulatory Administration "has reacted to what appears to be a substantial abuse of some resellers with a rule that would eliminate resellers all together. We originally questioned whether such a heavy handed approach did not risk throwing out the baby with the bath water. We are now convinced there is a baby. . . . A better course . . . would be to do nothing except to enforce the existing regulations concerning layering." T. Crawford Honeycutt to Dan Thomas, April 16, 1980. Letter in author's files.

[310]45 *Fed. Reg.* 52112 (August 5, 1980).

Effective December 1, 1980, the price regulations were revamped to set a uniform $0.20 per barrel margin for all traders, provided that historical services were performed.[311] For "in-line" specialists without gathering capabilities, *no margin was allowed*. The new rule was the regulators' revenge. But not only was it too late—decontrol was only two months away—ingenuity was exercised by traders who continued their opportunistic ways by moving traded oil short distances to qualify for a $0.20 per barrel margin.

Early resellers of oil products, like the crude reseller, refiner, jobber, and retailer, were limited to the May 15, 1973, margin in addition to cost.[312] Later entrants applied the "nearest comparable seller" or first-sale margin rule. As was the case with crude oil, early regulation did not differentiate between hardware jobbers and nouveau product traders with a telephone, telex, bank credit, and little more. The fuel-oil scandals in 1974 and 1975 brought attention to the difference, but it would not be until late 1979, two years after a crude-oil layering rule was enacted, that a layering rule was proposed to "prohibit unnecessary resales of gasoline for the purpose of artificially increasing retail selling prices."[313] The rule became effective May 1, 1980.[314]

Analogous to crude reselling (except for the absence of tier trading), product reselling exploited underpriced product; trades were made at the ceiling margin, which increased product prices toward market levels. This occurred for regulated products, not exempt products such as fuel oil and diesel (effective July 15, 1976), minor petroleum products (effective September 1, 1976), and jet fuel (effective October 1, 1976).[315] Covered products that would resist decontrol—gasoline, aviation fuel, butane, and propane—offered arbitrage opportunities. This was especially prominent with gasoline. With some products regulated and other products unregulated, bartered fuel trades (such as unregulated diesel for controlled gasoline) effectively circumvented the price ceilings.[316]

---

[311]45 *Fed. Reg.* 74432 (November 7, 1980).

[312]39 *Fed. Reg.* 1924 (January 15, 1974). In 1977, small resellers of propane, butane, and natural gasoline were deregulated. 42 *Fed. Reg.* 22131 (May 2, 1977).

[313]44 *Fed. Reg.* 69602 (December 3, 1979).

[314]45 *Fed. Reg.* 29546 (May 2, 1980).

[315]See chapter 27, pp. 1654–55.

[316]*NPN*, August 1979, pp. 37–38.

The motor-fuel shortages of 1974 revealed that the emerging prod-uct-reselling industry was underdeveloped, but in the 1975–78 period, resellers succeeded in capturing economic rent before it reached consumers. Shortages were prevented despite effective well-head ceilings, and refiner and retailer banks (unused allowable mar-gins) were growing.[317] The 1979 gasoline shortages again revealed inadequate market-clearing service by traders, attributable to sud-den supply problems resulting from the Iranian cutoff, but a bevy of new entries in late 1979 and 1980 would help reestablish market-clearing prices that continued until decontrol in early 1981.[318]

Certification Trading. In a free market, goods and services are sold on the basis of price, quality, and convenience. Under EPAA regula-tion, crude oil was also sold by its *tier certification*, determined by *when* the crude was discovered, *where* it was discovered, and *in what quantities* it was produced per well. These artificial determinants of value invited profitable correction by *tier trades* whereby certifica-tions were bought and sold with the physical oil undisturbed.

A *National Petroleum News* feature on product trading in mid-1979 gave the following example to illustrate the opportunities available with crude-oil paperwork.[319] A West Coast producer extracts low-grade stripper oil, which receives an unregulated $12.00 per barrel. An Oklahoma producer extracts high-quality ("Oklahoma sweet") crude that as old oil is limited to $5.00 per barrel. Recognizing that this batch of old oil is vastly underpriced, a trader swaps tiers. Although the California crude loses $7.00 per barrel and sells at $5.00 per barrel (plus a margin) in the transaction as old oil, the Oklahoma crude as stripper fetches a market price well above $12.00 per barrel to create a handsome profit for the trader. (Indeed, high-quality stripper crude could bring as much as $24.00 per barrel because of special refiner benefits discussed below.) Many more examples could be mentioned; suffice it to say that the quality-location trading function under the tier system created vast opportu-nities not present under free-market quality-location conditions.

Another prolific source of regulatory trading was servicing the refiners' demand for *entitlement-corrected cost minimization*. The

---

[317]See chapter 20, pp. 1188–90 and chapter 27, pp. 1649–62.
[318]See chapter 27, pp. 1683–84.
[319]*NPN*, August 1979, pp. 31–39.

crude-oil entitlements program, in operation from late 1974 until early 1981, was designed to equalize refinery acquisition costs, given the great disparity between the price of regulated crude and uncontrolled domestic and foreign oil. Refineries running more old oil than the national average had to purchase the right—the entitlement—to run relatively cheap crude from refineries running more expensive new oil or foreign oil. Cost of goods sold was to be made uniform by the former group of refineries' writing monthly checks to the latter that were on a list provided by the DOE.[320]

Smaller refineries received significant benefits under the entitlements program. These refiners running old oil were allowed to reduce or entirely forgo purchase obligations, as were firms obtaining special relief from the DOE. This not only encouraged new entry by small concerns, firms that coveted trader services to obtain feedstock given a tight market (created in part by the supplier-purchaser rule), it expanded opportunities for certification swapping.

The basic demand for trader services under the refinery-equalization program was to minimize cost on a postentitlements basis. Assume that for a particular month the national old-oil price averaged $8.00 per barrel, while that of new oil averaged $12.00 per barrel. The entitlement right is the difference, or $4.00 per barrel. Refineries, to the extent they needed to reduce cost to make their allowed margin or could draw down their banks, would be in the market to locate old oil under $8.00 and new oil under $12.00 to receive a net gain after the entitlements correction. Refiners not in a position to beat the entitlements spread, given their margin or bank situation, created a market for oil priced *above* the national average. These were mostly small refineries running old oil that were exempt from the program. They were not averse to purchasing old oil at prices above the national average as long as maximum profitability was observed and they could make a reseller margin by selling a certification.

A hypothetical example can be constructed. Assume an old-oil entitlements price of $8.00 per barrel, exempt Refiner A with $7.00 per barrel old oil, and nonexempt Refiner B with $9.00 per barrel old oil. Also assume Refiner A can maximize profit with feedstock

---

[320]See chapter 20, pp. 1205–34, for an analysis of the refinery entitlements program.

costs under $10.00 per barrel. Reseller X could perform a mutually profitable trade by buying oil from Refiner A for $7.25 to sell to Refiner B at $7.50, and replacing it with oil purchased from Refiner B at $9.00 per barrel to sell to Refiner A at $9.75 per barrel. The reseller makes $1.00 per barrel, Refiner A makes $0.25 per barrel, and Refiner B makes $0.50 per barrel instead of losing $1.00 per barrel on the entitlements spread.

At the new-oil bound of the entitlements calculation, *miscertification* created many profitable trading scenarios for reseller and refiner alike. Assume the national new-oil price is $12.00 per barrel with trader margins again at $0.50 per barrel.

- Step one: Reseller B sells old oil purchased for $7.50 from Reseller A to Reseller C for $8.00.
- Step two: Reseller C recertifies old oil as new oil and resells to Reseller D for $10.00.
- Step three: Reseller D sells new oil to Reseller E at $10.50.
- Step four: Reseller E sells new oil to Refiner A at $11.00.

While Refiner A achieves a net entitlement gain of $1.00 per barrel, all four traders make a profit, particularly Reseller C who makes an illegal gain of $1.50 per barrel, unless certification balance is achieved by recertifying a like quantity of new oil as old oil (a "wash transaction") within the legally prescribed monthly balancing period. As discussed below, this often was not done.

Many scenarios of varying degrees of legality could be constructed. Suffice it to say that the regulations—crude-price controls, tier assignments, margin restrictions, and the entitlements program—created opportunities for traders and refiners not inherent in free-market situations. The process involved certification swapping; physical crude generally stayed put, while its price and certification changed to profit-maximizing (cost-minimizing) positions.[321]

The DOE legally challenged certification swapping in its general effort to discourage middleman activity that did little more than raise prices toward market-clearing levels. At issue was the legality

---

[321]In the wake of an aborted takeover attempt, Gulf Oil accused Cities Service of employing trader services to minimize cost on a postentitlements basis, knowing that only by miscertification could expensive-tier oil be received at large discounts. *Wall Street Journal*, April 26, 1983, p. 33.

of *pooling*, in which oil is assumed to be homogeneous and certification papers are detached from the oil and used as the basis of exchange. The DOE favored *tracking*, in which the certification is affixed to the same oil (even abstractly in situations of commingling in storage).[322] The industry pragmatically practiced *balancing* (pooling), in which, at the end of each month, certifications bought and certifications acquired with beginning inventory equaled certifications sold and certifications held with ending inventory. Without this balance, a state of miscertification existed. Certificates thus were often sold "short" to exploit opportunities for profit with the expectation that a balancing purchase would be made in the same period (month). The question of legality was raised after the fact; traders routinely pooled oil and traded tiers throughout the regulated period, while the first legal challenge (notice of probable violation) was issued in early 1980. If the DOE had defined miscertification from the beginning as being out of balance *at any point in time*, trading flexibility to correct mispriced quality differentials and to help refineries achieve entitlement-corrected cost minimization would have been seriously impaired, and a major demand for trader services would not have existed. It was, from the regulatory viewpoint, another opportunity lost.

Prosecution. Regulation of trading activities was buttressed by prosecution of reselling firms and the principals involved. Enforcement would not begin in earnest until 1979, for reasons that included lack of manpower or expertise, or both; an anti-enforcement bias on the part of certain high-level energy regulators; and the ability of trading firms to creatively define, and inconspicuously perform within, legal bounds. The energy crisis of 1979, however, prompted regulators to make reseller firms "whipping boys" to divert blame from the inherent failings of national energy policy toward industry misbehavior.

In late 1974, press accounts of suspicious resales of fuel oil destined for utility consumption came to the attention of federal energy regulators. Testified DOE attorney Joseph McNeff:

> By the fall of 1974 FEA field personnel had become aware of these obvious and widespread schemes, particularly daisy chaining. . . .

[322]Elk Trading Company, Inc., U.S. Department of Energy, Office of Enforcement Case no. GAOXOO268 (January 10, 1980).

> The many field auditors and attorneys I have talked with that worked on the daisy chain investigations all agree that virtually every utility in the country paid widely inflated prices because of these chains.[323]

This early encounter with "daisy chaining" did not motivate the Federal Energy Administration and the Department of Justice to actively pursue inquiries or take legal action.[324] Project Escalator to investigate paper trading and other suspect industry activities, unveiled by FEA enforcement chief John Sawhill on December 17, 1974, was quietly shelved several weeks later when Sawhill resigned. One FEA enforcement official reported a "total refusal to look at criminal cases or to accept the fact that they were there" during the 1975–77 period.[325] Not until late 1977 would a daisy-chain case begin, based on charges of conspiracy and antitrust violations. It was followed by three more similar fuel-oil cases a year later.[326] Each case began at the local level with ambitious regional government attorneys pursuing leads and requesting support from Washington.

The preponderance of oil-product daisy chains over crude-oil daisy chains in the early years of regulation probably reflected the relatively effective operation of the supplier-purchaser rule between the producer and the refiner as opposed to between the refiner and the retailer. Crude reselling was also removed from the consumer and thus of less political interest. This allowed underpriced crude to turn into underpriced product for the product reseller to sell at market-clearing prices.[327] Utilities could pass through fuel-cost

[323] *White Collar Crime in the Oil Industry*, pp. 50–51.

[324] Ibid., pp. 50, 54, 133.

[325] Ibid., p. 62. For a sensationalistic but rare account of the investigative "cover-up," see Fred Cook, *The Great Energy Scam* (New York: Macmillan, 1982), chap. 5.

[326] The cases originated in Florida, Georgia, Illinois, and New York.

[327] Evidence exists that crude-oil daisy chains greatly accelerated in the 1978–79 period. DOE auditors examined two major crude pipelines, Shell's Rancho Pipeline and the Shipshoal Pipeline, to see how many times the oil was turned over by in-line transfers.

Date	Rancho Batches	Average Turnover	Shipshoal Batches	Average Turnover
May 1973	–	–	16	1.66
Nov. 1977	26	3.44	126	5.05
Sept. 1978	55	9.60	144	14.23
June 1979	86	20.45	149	15.30

SOURCE: *DOE Enforcement: RIF's and Budget Reductions I,* Hearings before the Subcommittee on Oversight and Investigations of the House Committee on Interstate and

increases to consumers in automatic rate hikes, so as crude resellers were selling to margin-regulated refineries, product resellers were advantageously situated to capture economic rent originally denied to producers and royalty owners. Even with regular jobber sales of petroleum products, successive markups were often within the final selling price of the fuel.

One product daisy chain received wide publicity in congressional hearings. A circulated letter from the LaGloria Oil and Gas Company dated November 7, 1974, read:

> Gentlemen:
>
> The following book transfer has been agreed to among all companies concerned and will be effective in October business.
>
> Product: No. 2 fuel oil
>
> Volume: 25,000 barrels
>
> Transfer sequence: LaGloria to Energy Marketing to Pedco to Gustafson to Conoco to LaGloria, Tyler, Tex.[328]

Five profitable trades were simultaneously made among companies with the oil's never leaving storage. Arbitrage paper transfers captured the economic rent denied by law to wellhead interests, with little social purpose as lawmakers noticed.

Prosecution of product resellers tapered off when prosecution of crude resellers became widespread in 1979. One reason was that audits of and court cases against the latter reduced the resources available to prosecute the former. A second was that the profitability of crude-oil trading reduced the economic rent available between the refining and retail stages.

Active prosecution of resellers of crude began in 1979. Legal action against product traders was all but a thing of the past compared with the over eighty notices of probable violation issued between this date and 1981 to crude-oil resellers.

The most active area of prosecution was instances in which firms reclassified crude from lower priced categories to higher priced categories and failed to get back in balance by a reverse certification

---

Foreign Commerce, 97th Cong., 1st sess. (Washington, D.C.: Government Printing Office, 1981).

[328]Reprinted in Fred Cook, *The Great Energy Scam*, p. 51.

Table 12.1
STRIPPER OIL: FIRST PURCHASES VS. REFINERY RECEIPTS
(barrels per day)

Date	Wellhead Stripper[a]	Refinery Stripper[b]	Stripper Increase
1979			
1st quarter	1,220,200	1,315,700	95,500
2nd quarter	1,306,900	1,473,400	166,500
3rd quarter	1,357,200	1,614,500	257,300
4th quarter	1,356,400	1,657,300	300,900
1980			
1st quarter	1,323,700	1,700,100	376,400
2nd quarter	1,322,300	1,783,700	416,400

SOURCE: *The Case of the Billion Dollar Stripper*, p. 21.
[a] Determined from First Purchase Reports (ERA-182), which began in February 1976.
[b] Determined from Entitlements Reports (ERA-49), which began in November 1974.

within the monthly designated period. In 1979, miscertification audits began, which led to indictments and fines of several firms.[329]

Miscertification reached new heights during 1979 and 1980, and congressional attention was directed to "the Case of the Billion Dollar Stripper" that allegedly cost consumers over $1 billion per year.[330] A tremendous temptation existed to take lower tier oil at approximately $6.00 per barrel and recertify it as stripper oil—which by June 1979 was $20.00 per barrel and by November 1979 reached $30.00 per barrel—without making a balance transaction. As table 12.1 indicates, for many, miscertification (the increase in stripper barrels between the wellhead and the refinery) was too lucrative to pass up.

[329]See the cases cited in *White Collar Crime in the Oil Industry*, pp. 144–46.

[330]*The Case of the Billion Dollar Stripper*, Hearings before the House Committee on Interstate and Foreign Commerce, 96th Cong., 2d sess. (Washington, D.C.: Government Printing Office, 1980). The first notice of miscertification—old oil becoming new oil or stripper oil between producer and refiner—was an April 15, 1977, letter from Mobil Oil to the Federal Energy Administration, which reported discrepancies between producer reports and refinery receipts. Reprinted in *White Collar Crime in the Oil Industry*, p. 130.

Not coincidentally, lower tier crude and upper tier crude were disappearing between the lease and the refinery gate in amounts similar to the increase in stripper oil.[331] At the heart of the problem were resellers, led by Robert Sutton, who, the DOE alleged, miscertified several hundred million barrels of lower priced oil as stripper oil in the 1976–80 period.[332] If true, this would make Sutton the first "regulatory billionaire" in U.S. history.

The second largest area of prosecution was *layering*, in which a markup is made on resold crude without providing traditional gathering and handling services. The DOE had ruled that profits could not be made under such circumstances. The largest case was against Langham Petroleum, with $107.9 million at stake.[333] Similar charges were brought against Carbonit Houston ($47.4 million) and FOSTI ($1.6 million), and the latter became one of the first cases to reach the proposed remedial order stage.[334] The FOSTI case concerned a company in bankruptcy proceedings and a deceased principal owner and thus an easy target for prosecutors. The Langham and Carbonit cases, as well as other smaller layering cases, were

---

[331]*The Case of the Billion Dollar Stripper*, p. 19. Miscertification by refiners trying to receive postentitlements windfall profits was far less frequent. See U.S. Department of Energy, "Validation of the Crude Oil Entitlements Information System," August 1981, p. 100.

[332]The Sutton story is a saga unequaled in the oil-trading patch. Beginning with a borrowed telephone in 1973 (he was delinquent on his phone bill, indicative of wider financial woes), the former postage-meter salesman began to broker oil. In 1976, he founded Bob's Petroleum Marketing (BPM, Ltd.). Conducting business on the principle, as recalled by a former employee, "we don't buy stripper—we sell stripper," he satisfied inquisitive employees that by use of a "trade secret" with the majors, certification balance was obtained. *Tulsa World*, May 5, 1982, p. 14-A. With his sizable proceeds, he built a lavish empire of over fifty companies. He was charged on October 29, 1981, with a fifteen-count indictment for illegally inflating the price of domestic crude oil and a two-count indictment for obstructing justice. All but the latter, which resulted in jail time, were dismissed on a technicality. On appeal, a federal judge found Sutton guilty of miscertifying 167 million barrels of crude and ordered refunds of $211 million. For an inside look at Sutton's activities and reselling in general, see the four-part series in the *Tulsa Tribune*, October 12–15, 1981; the *Wall Street Journal*, December 2, 1981 p. 27; and *Forbes*, August 1983, pp. 34–38.

[333]U.S. Department of Energy, Office of Enforcement Case no. 640X00433 (July 29, 1980).

[334]*Carbonit Houston*, U.S. Department of Energy, Office of Enforcement Case no. 650X00253 (July 18, 1980); and *Fuel Oil Supply and Terminaling, Inc.*, Case no. 650X00284 (March 17, 1982).

much more difficult to resolve, given the questionable government argument that "in-line" transfers did not exist prior to 1973, as well as procedural defects in the layering rule itself.[335]

Several notices of probable violation were issued against the margin determinations under the "new-item" rule. The DOE questioned the chosen "nearest comparable outlet," substituted a different firm, and recomputed the margin.[336] Several firms purchased uncertified crude (scrubber oil, tank-bottom oil, and "reconstituted crude" blended from residual fuel oil and naphtha) to sell as new oil or exempt oil. Notices of probable violation based on miscertification were issued against several firms.[337]

Major DOE suits against reselling firms are presented in table 12.2. Almost all cases are in the "notice of probable violation" stage, which follows the audit and begins the prosecution process. Several are in the remedial stage. The proposed remedial order, the second phase of the legal process, is followed by the final remedial order under which restitution is made by the firm and other penalties are assessed.[338] At the end of 1983, penalties of $4.2 million and refunds held in escrow of $120.2 million accounted for the government's effort.[339]

Market Readjustment. The trading boom wound down with phased decontrol and came to an end with total decontrol on January 28, 1981. With the end of price controls came the end of the arbitrage opportunities afforded by controlled prices. With the demise of tiers and refinery entitlements came the end of certification swapping. This forced telephone traders, to the extent they remained active,

---

[335]See James Carroll, "Certification and Price Audit Issues," pp. 16–18.

[336]*Southwestern States Marketing Corp.*, U.S. Department of Energy, Office of Enforcement Case no. GAOX00252 (July 19, 1979); and *Intercontinental Petroleum Corp.*, U.S. Department of Energy, Office of Enforcement Case no. C50X00282 (May 11, 1979).

[337]*Prime Resources Corp.*, U.S. Department of Energy, Office of Enforcement Case no. 6COX00234 (July 1, 1981); and *Doma Corp.*, U.S. Department of Energy, Office of Enforcement Case no. GAOX00111 (June 13, 1979).

[338]For a chart describing the DOE's case administration and appellate processes from the preliminary audit to the final remedial order, see Comptroller General of the United States, *Department of Energy Has Made Slow Progress Resolving Alleged Crude Oil Reseller Prices Violations* (Washington, D.C.: General Accounting Office, June 1, 1982), p. 16.

[339]U.S. Department of Energy, Office of Enforcement, Information Release, January 23, 1984.

Table 12.2
PETROLEUM-RESELLER LITIGATION AS OF 1981

Firm	Date of Action	Type of Action	Alleged Overcharge
Aweco	10-08-80	NOPV	$195,004,159
Langham Petroleum	07-29-80	NOPV	107,867,959
Aweco	07-20-79	NOPV	81,223,384
Carbonit	07-18-80	NOPV	47,445,880
Southwestern	07-19-79	NOPV	42,198,078
C. R. Rittenberry	11-07-79	NOPV	30,764,609
Permian	09-07-79	NOPV	25,434,839
Herndon	12-31-80	NOPV	22,763,539
Dalco Petroleum	05-25-79	NOPV	11,259,573
Hideca Petroleum	03-16-81	NOPV	7,847,940
Jack Holland	04-23-81	NOPV	7,109,043
Petrade	08-04-81	NOPV	7,092,277
Armour	12-31-80	NOPV	6,891,783
Intercontinental	05-11-79	NOPV	6,494,553
Prime Resources	12-24-80	NOPV	6,427,607
Thomas Petroleum	05-01-81	NOPV	6,239,562
Intercontinental	04-30-80	NOPV	5,318,898
Horizon Petroleum	04-16-80	NOPV	3,518,858
B & B Trading	03-06-80	NOPV	3,440,550
F.R.B. Petroleum	05-05-81	NOPV	3,383,487
Oil Tex. Petroleum	06-25-81	NOPV	3,152,825
Brazoria	10-23-79	NOPV	2,965,202
Merit Petroleum	01-29-81	NOPV	2,965,753
Crude Oil Pur.	06-02-80	NOPV	2,720,548
Merit Petroleum	04-03-80	NOPV	2,789,160
Northeast Petroleum	12-21-79	NOPV	2,274,625
Ryder Truck	09-26-80	NOPV	2,216,181
Concord Petroleum	08-25-80	NOPV	2,003,685
Doma Corp.	04-17-79	NOPV	1,965,149
Pel-Star Energy	12-20-79	NOPV	1,779,963
General Energy	04-12-79	NOPV	1,742,317
FOSTI	10-23-79	PRO	1,583,577
Ergon	07-17-81	NOPV	1,350,769
Total[a]			$657,236,332

SOURCE: U.S. Department of Energy, Office of Enforcement Information, *Program Status Report* (Washington, D.C.: DOE, 1981).
NOTE: PRO = proposed remedial order; NOPV = notice of probable violation.
[a] Approximately thirty-five more firms received NOPVs of under $1 million each.

to take inventory positions in anticipation of a favorable price change (purchasing inventory in the expectation of a price increase or selling short in the expectation of a price decline) or to search out market-error arbitrage opportunities. Not all firms were attracted to—or survived—the rigors of market trading. An estimated one-third of the approximately 400 trading firms that existed in 1980 were no longer operative a year after decontrol.[340] Firms such as FOSTI, Southwest Petroenergy, Minro Oil, and AWECO would declare bankruptcy soon after decontrol as a result of a down trading market and, in many cases, high debt service on fixed-asset acquisitions.[341] Langham Trading took advantage of a tax ruling and liquidated.[342] Hideca Petroleum "took its money and ran" by closing shop. But for other cash-rich, low-leveraged trading concerns, the market readjustment meant accepting lower returns—and accepting more risk to achieve returns—in order to be positioned for future trading opportunities, whether regulatory or market.[343] But not all would survive. Coral Petroleum, one of the largest nouveau reseller firms with a substantial net worth accumulated from trading between

[340]*Houston Chronicle*, March 21, 1982, p. 4–10.

[341]FOSTI and AWECO made millions trading directly with Sutton's BPM only to squander the money in the early decontrol period. After Sutton, FOSTI chairman Eddie Hadsell was the most notable of the rags-to-riches traders. Working out of a borrowed office after a severe business setback in 1975, Hadsell began to trade petroleum products. In 1978, he founded Fuel Oil Supply and Terminaling, Inc. (FOSTI) with a capitalization of $150,000. Over the next several years, approximately $10 million was earned on revenues of over $3.5 billion. The profit figure could have been much higher; millions were lavishly spent on employee perquisites, customer relations, charitable causes, and a national "accentuate the positive" advertising campaign. Unable to adjust expenses to decontrol, FOSTI filed for protection in October 1981, several months after which Hadsell died. Thus, FOSTI became an easy target for the DOE's first proposed remedial order concerning layering.

[342]Firms liquidating before December 31, 1981, were eligible for tax-reduced sales of last in, first out (LIFO) inventory. LIFO-basis inventory included controlled oil purchased during the control period, which had a low cost of goods sold to be subtracted from high postdecontrol prices to arrive at taxable net income. What in earlier years had been a postponement of taxable income by use of LIFO over first in, first out became a high-tax wash-sale cancellation.

[343]Daisy chains existed after decontrol, but unlike in the immediate past, in-line transfers represented risk taking more than arbitraging. See Ray Dafter, "On the Spot: Traders in Crude Find the Market More Speculative," *Houston Chronicle*, February 21, 1983, p. 2-2. Existence of postcontrol in-line trades once again refuted the government's rationale for the layering rule: that in-line trading did not exist prior to 1973.

1973 and 1980, entered bankruptcy proceedings in mid-1983 due to unsuccessful position taking on large cargos in addition to high debt service. Underscored by this development was that even the most successful at regulatory trading could be inadequate at market trading.

The Trading Boom in Retrospect. The seven-year trading boom represents a classic case of the unintended consequences of government intervention. The episode can even be identified as the most unusual in U.S. regulatory history. Never has regulation provided such large-scale opportunities for private gain. Hundreds of new trading companies possessing little more than telephonic equipment and bank letters of credit generated tens of billions of dollars in sales and several billion dollars in profits from back-to-back transactions.[344] Of equal importance to net profits was income after cost of goods sold and before general and administrative expenses. In light of the limited resources needed to trade profitably, most traders received huge salaries in the six to seven figure range[345] and entertained lavishly to ensure participation in chain trading to lower margins to allowable levels, avoid corporate income subject to double taxation, and limit retained earnings subject to refund liability in the event of prosecution. All told, a sizable amount of economic rent was captured by resellers in the price-control era that any economic analysis must take into account.

The trading boom has not only been misinterpreted by energy economists, it has been misinterpreted by politicians, federal regulators, and members of the press who have equated trading with miscertification. Consequently, trading represented, in the words of

---

[344]Aggregate sales and net income figures for the entire industry are unavailable. A very rough estimate of yearly activity in the 1979–81 period would be sales of $25 billion to $50 billion and profits of $2 billion to $5 billion. For example, three large trading companies in 1980 alone generated over $10 billion in sales. *Wall Street Journal,* September 28, 1981, p. 25, and April 19, 1982, p. 1; and *Tulsa Tribune,* October 13, 1981, p. 1. Profits calculated in 1979 and 1980 from stripper miscertification alone sum to a several-billion-dollar windfall for resellers. *The Case of the Billion Dollar Stripper,* p. 18.

[345]"There were 28-year-old traders, sometimes only three or four years out of college, making $1 million to $2 million a year." William Walker, *Houston Chronicle,* March 21, 1982, p. 4-10.

Representative Albert Gore (D-Tenn.), "the largest fraud, in monetary terms, that has ever been committed on the American public."[346] Unless one accepts a strict definition of the layering rule, reselling had a legal side whereby underpriced crude was incrementally traded to market-clearing levels. From 1973 to 1978, miscertification was not "in vogue" as it was later, and during 1979–80, judging from the absence of prosecution of a number of audited firms, many firms achieved certification balance.[347] If arbitrage and certification trading were done within legal limits to a greater extent than was purposeful miscertification, then fraud must have been secondary to opportunism as a characteristic of the trading boom.[348] Second and more important, the distortion and "crime" of the trading episode were not that consumers failed to gain the benefits from price regulation as intended by federal policy; they were that regulation prevented oil producers and royalty owners from receiving their full economic rent. The redistribution of wealth from producers to "superfluous entrepreneurs," those capitalizing on opportunities created not by the market but by government constraints on the market, represented a pernicious and grossly inefficient consequence from the viewpoint of the unhampered market. Politicians and lawmakers, not the industry, can be held accountable for those government constraints.[349]

From the market point of view, the trading boom represented superfluous entrepreneurship and the misdirection of resources. Resources that would have gone toward exploration and production

---

[346]"The Oil Game," *ABC News Close-Up*, June 20, 1982, p. 2. Federal Energy Administration administrator Hazel Rollins made essentially the same judgment when she testified: "We can call resellers rascals. We can call them violators of the law." *Stripper Oil Miscertification*, Hearing before the House Committee on Interstate and Foreign Commerce, 96th Cong., 2d sess. (Washington, D.C.: Government Printing Office, 1980), p. 6.

[347]*The Case of the Billion Dollar Stripper*, pp. 21, 24.

[348]Miscertification represented more of a circumvention of margin limitations than a separate act of "theft," since it reduced profit opportunities for downstream members of the trading chain.

[349]The term "superfluous entrepreneurship" is adopted from Israel Kirzner's "wholly superfluous discovery process" used to define pure profit opportunities created by government intervention. Kirzner, *Discovery and the Capitalistic Process*, (Chicago: University of Chicago Press, 1985), pp. 144–45. One broker commented, "As long as the government is telling you what you can and cannot do, you're going to maximize those few things that you can do." *NPN*, August 1979, p. 38.

instead went to a service industry known for its extravagant uses of money, if only to circumvent margin restrictions. Given the regulatory environment, however, *a case can be made that the reselling industry performed a positive "second-best" function by working to eliminate below-market price distortions.* Price rations low-priority users, and by substituting themselves in the oil nexus, traders served to equilibrate supply and demand at the refining and retail levels. For example, it was noticed that 1979 gas lines were worse in urban areas than rural areas because resellers generally supplied the latter while refiners directly supplied the former.[350] Jack Blum of the Independent Gas Marketers Council recognized that "the spot market and the traders who make it function was the only mechanism capable of easing the supply crisis and bringing supplies to the people that need them."[351] Without middlemen arbitrating, severe shortages of price-controlled domestic crude would have increased demand for exempt crude and foreign crude to fill the gap. This would have raised their prices and increased dependence on imports.[352]

Restated, price controls on crude oil caused two distortions, demanders overdemanding and suppliers undersupplying. Traders reduced the former distortion by their market-clearing activities, but the inability of producers to get higher prices to increase supply was left uncorrected. Costs of trader nonaction in the regulated market—increased imports and higher nonregulated prices—negated part of the costs associated with their activities. Except for "second-best" hypothesizing, it can be stated unequivocally that an absence of price and allocation regulation would have been a far better solution than the regulatory course chosen—and the unintended consequences created.

The oil-trading boom has come and gone. Two ex poste facto observations are enlightening. Commented the most notorious

---

[350]See the comments of Chevron marketing vice-president Donalt Mulit, *Federal Gasoline Allocation Process*, Hearings before the Subcommittee on Energy Regulation of the Senate Committee on Energy and Natural Resources, 96th Cong., 2d sess. (Washington, D.C.: Government Printing Office, 1980), p. 129.

[351]Ibid., pp. 153–54.

[352]Without the escape valve of exempt domestic oil and exempt crude imports, price-controlled oil not market cleared by middlemen would have led to product shortages, a situation more costly and wasteful (judging from the motor-fuel shortages in 1974 and 1979) than regulatory trading.

reseller, Robert Sutton: "They made it easy for us to make money—the rules did. If they are going to make it that easy—I had to take it."[353] Commented a Justice Department attorney: "There'll be no opportunity for regulatory millionaires again. This has just been a bizarre interlude in economic history."[354]

[353]*Tulsa World*, September 27, 1981, p. B-1.
[354]*Wall Street Journal*, December 2, 1981, p. 27.

13. History of Oil-Import Regulation

A long-standing government policy, most closely identified with seventeenth-century mercantilism, has been to regulate trade across sovereign boundaries. Primarily intended to raise revenue and protect domestic industry from entering merchandise, import taxes, or *tariffs*, and volume limitations, or *quotas*, have been imposed by government. Tariffs can be ad valorem, a percentage of estimated value, or specific, a fixed amount per item; quotas can be an absolute maximum or a trigger amount past which a tariff becomes effective ("tariff quota").

Export tariffs and quotas have been less common. Part of the protectionist doctrine is that, while imports are to be discouraged, exports are to be encouraged to achieve a favorable balance of trade.[1] Special-interest influences, however, have occasionally prevailed to limit exports. This has been the case in the U.S. petroleum market, as seen in the appendix to this chapter.

Protectionism has a long history in the United States. In 1789, a sizable tariff was placed on certain imported articles to raise revenue and protect "infant" industries. Two centuries later, tariffs and quotas covered a variety of goods. While less restrictive than other countries, the United States has not been a bastion of free trade.[2]

Foreign-trade restrictions were the exception rather than the rule in the first 125 years of the U.S. petroleum market. There have been decades of major tariff and quota regulation, but there has also been a century of predominantly free trade. Regarding natural gas, which much later crossed U.S. borders, "just and reasonable" price regulation under the Natural Gas Act of 1938 rather than protectionism has been the defining regulatory force.[3]

[1]The trade-balance fallacy is examined in chapter 17, p. 1044.

[2]A concise history of U.S. tariff policy is contained in J. J. Pincus, "Tariffs" in *Encyclopedia of American Economic History*, ed. Glen Porter, 3 vols. (New York: Charles Scribner's Sons, 1980), vol. 1, pp. 439–50.

[3]Import and export regulation of natural gas is discussed in appendix 15.2, pp. 961–70.

Petroleum tariffs emerged during the Civil War for revenue reasons and on the product side lingered past the turn of the century. From 1909 until the early 1930s, market incentives alone governed imports and exports. This would change when prolific domestic production created a strong independent-producer lobby that worked to reduce the market share of imports by legislation. The result was a comprehensive oil tariff, briefly joined by an oil quota, that would be reduced for Venezuela and Mexico. In 1947, oil tariffs were formalized as part of the General Agreement on Tariffs and Trade (GATT), which has been in effect ever since with one brief exception.

Protectionist sentiment came to the forefront after the petroleum-supply problems of World War II were overcome. The economic incentives to import oil overwhelmed existing tariffs, and market-demand factors were falling in Texas, Oklahoma, and other oil states. Voluntary import reductions were first tried, and in 1959, the Mandatory Oil Import Program (MOIP) began. It continued with many modifications until the early 1970s when market conditions dictated its demise. License fees were imposed in its place, and in 1979, the supplemental fees were abolished to leave long-standing tariffs, first set in 1932, between open and regulated trade. These duties, and selected export bans imposed by the United States against controversial foreign countries, are the extent of intervention in oil importing today.

The appendix to this chapter traces the rise of oil exports and the dominant role of Standard Oil therein. The relatively intermittent history of oil-export regulation is then examined.

Regulation and Free Trade, 1861–1930

Early Tariffs and Deregulation

Early imports of oil and derived products encountered government interference, although not sufficiently substantial to severely limit trade or misdirect investments. The Act of August 5, 1861, placed a $0.10 per gallon tariff on kerosene imports, which was increased to $0.30 for all oil products in 1864 and $0.40 in 1865. The Civil War revenue measure, equivalent to $16.80 per barrel, the highest tariff in industry history, would not be consequential until the 1880s because foreign competition was limited, reflecting the embryonic state of foreign refining.[4]

The Act of March 3, 1863, imposed a 20 percent ad valorem tax on crude imports, also as a war revenue measure, to completely regulate petroleum imports. It was repealed in May 1866, leaving only oil products taxed.[5] In 1868, congressional interest in a $0.25 per barrel tax on bonded oil (imported crude oil refined for export) was quelled by concern that domestic refinery capacity would be injured.

On July 24, 1897, petroleum-product tariffs were set at the foreign rate in an attempt to discourage foreign levies. This remained unchanged until countervailing duties were repealed in 1909, freeing the import market for the first time since 1861.[6] The effect of open trade on the dominant position of Standard Oil was more imports and new competitors. Stated Ralph and Muriel Hidy:

> Standard Oil marketers began also to feel more strongly the impact of foreign competition. The tariff act of 1909 left all petroleum products except residuum and tar totally unprotected for the first time in the history of the American industry.... The new tariff policy ... undoubtedly contributed to the decision of Royal Dutch-Shell to come into the American market in 1912.[7]

Free Trade from 1909 to 1930

Removal of countervailing tariffs, along with a maturing international oil industry, increased imports of kerosene fivefold by 1911. Lesser product imports such as paraffin wax rose from obscurity.[8] Another consequence, more subtle, was to improve the competitive position of U.S. oil in world markets. Standard Oil increased its kerosene shipments to Europe. Standard's strategy was to improve

---

[4]11 Stat. 292 (1861); 13 Stat. 491 (1865). Ralph Hidy and Muriel Hidy, *Pioneering in Big Business: 1882–1911* (New York: Harper & Brothers, 1955), p. 6.

[5]12 Stat. 742 (1863); and 14 Stat. 355 (1866).

[6]30 Stat. 151 (1897). W. W. Thornton, *The Law Relating to Oil and Gas*, 2 vols. (Cincinnati: W. H. Anderson, 1925), vol. 1, p. 121.

[7]Ralph Hidy and Muriel Hidy, *Pioneering in Big Business*, pp. 452–53.

[8]Ibid.

product quality—safety and reliability remained major problems—while pricing competitively, selling complementary items such as oil burners, and "getting nearer the market."[9]

With promising oil lands nearby in Mexico, U.S. oilmen began to export drilling capital and expertise along with oil. As exploration flowered into production, large shipments of Mexican oil began to arrive at Texas refineries, which precipitated the first show of protectionist sentiment in the twentieth century. On January 12, 1917, the Gulf Coast Oil Producers Association adopted a resolution asking Congress to tax Mexican crude in a tariff bill under consideration on equity grounds. The resolution read:

> Whereas, enormous amounts of crude oil are being shipped from Mexico into the United States free of duty, paying no tax whatever, bearing no share of the Government's expense, and
>
> Whereas, the oil producers and refiners of Texas especially, and all other parts of the United States, are paying their share of the Government's tax, as well as heavy State ad valorem and gross receipts taxes, be it
>
> Resolved . . . that you lay a portion of the burden of this taxation upon the oil imported into this country . . . in order that the burden of taxation may be more fairly distributed.[10]

Congress was not persuaded, however, and producing states were constitutionally powerless to restrict foreign trade.[11] The free-trade era continued.

World War I established the importance of petroleum as a military asset and inspired a postwar government policy of encouraging foreign-oil investments to augment U.S. supply. As of 1919, almost 40 percent of foreign production was by U.S. companies, representing an aggregate investment of $400 million; by 1929, with diplomatic aid from the State Department, an additional $1 billion was expended, doubling foreign output, although the world market

---

[9]Ibid., pp. 556–57. See the appendix to this chapter, pp. 766–69.

[10]Reprinted in *Oil & Gas Journal,* January 18, 1917, p. 36. Cited hereafter as *OGJ.*

[11]Protectionism by states was practiced in other ways such as employing state antitrust law against out-of-state corporations (see chapter 18, pp. 1074–81) and restricting natural-gas exports (see chapter 15, pp. 859–60).

share of U.S. firms would decrease to 30 percent.[12] With increased foreign output, a pattern developed to import cheap crude, primarily from Mexico and Venezuela, to refine into products for export.

A threefold increase in crude imports between 1918 and 1921 drove independent producers to seek a tariff on crude oil in 1921. The effort failed, as did a second attempt a year later. Strong opposition was registered by President Warren G. Harding, on national-security grounds; major companies that were active abroad; southwestern railroads and shipping interests that transported imported crude; and New England manufacturing interests that desired cheap fuel oil.[13] The official worry was that there was too little oil, not too much; government policy favored development of foreign reserves and, indirectly, greater importation.

The shift of the United States in 1923 from a net importing country to a net exporting country temporarily quieted independents' calls for petroleum tariffs. This would change with major Texas and Oklahoma oil discoveries beginning in 1926 and implementation of state-wide proration by the end of the decade. Mandatory proration was the majors' program, as discussed in chapter 4, and independents grew wary of enforced cutbacks in the face of unrestricted cheap imports. A 27 percent jump in imports in 1928 followed by a 19 percent increase the following year, coming at a time when domestic output was at its highest point in history despite proration, would awaken many independents into fervid action.

A summary of oil exports and imports between 1918 and 1929 is provided in table 13.1. That table shows a surge in crude imports in the early 1920s, which would subside for the rest of the decade. The threefold increase in crude imports between 1981 and 1921 drove independent producers to again seek a crude-oil tariff in 1921. It failed, as did a second attempt a year later.

Product imports increased steadily throughout the period, as did exports of both crude oil and refined products. In 1923, in fact, the

---

[12]Harold Williamson et al., *The Age of Energy, 1899 to 1959,* vol. 2 of *The American Petroleum Industry* (Evanston, Ill.: Northwestern University Press, 1959, 1963), p. 522. For accounts of foreign expansion by U.S. firms, particularly in the 1919–24 period, see ibid., pp. 506–32, and Gerald Nash, *United States Oil Policy* (Westport, Conn.: Greenwood Press, 1968, 1976), pp. 49–71.

[13]Ibid., pp. 53–55.

Table 13.1
OIL IMPORTS AND EXPORTS: 1918–29
(thousand barrels per day)

Year	Crude Oil		Refined Products		Total	
	Imports	Exports	Imports	Exports	Imports	Exports
1918	103	16	3	173	107	188
1919	145	17	4	158	148	175
1920	290	25	7	192	297	218
1921	343	26	9	171	353	197
1922	357	30	16	175	373	280
1923	225	48	48	232	273	204
1924	213	50	46	271	258	321
1925	169	37	45	276	214	312
1926	165	42	57	321	223	363
1927	160	43	37	346	197	390
1928	218	52	32	372	250	423
1929	216	72	82	375	298	447

SOURCE: American Petroleum Institute, *Basic Petroleum Data Book* (Washington, D.C.: API, 1973), sec. 9, table 11, and sec. 10, table 1.

United States became a net exporter, a position that would not change until after World War II.

Total United States participation in the world oil market, defined as the sum of total imports and exports, grew significantly in the twelve years under study. This reflected the major role of the United States in the world market and growing domestic and foreign demand for oil, not only for its traditional uses but as gasoline in the automobile age.

Toward Protectionism

Several months after an acrimonious meeting of the American Petroleum Institute in the summer of 1929, independent producers led by Wirt Franklin left this trade association to form the Independent Petroleum Association of America (IPAA). The independents now had a trade group to counter the major-dominated American Petroleum Institute, and the tariff-proration factions were clearly delineated. IPAA founder Wirt Franklin in an early speech voiced the independents' suspicion of their integrated, multinational brethren:

The true intent and purpose of those who had been fostering and promoting the so-called conservation program is to shut in domestic production and to turn the markets for petroleum in the United States over to a few large companies engaged in exploiting the petroleum reserves of South America and in importing the production thereof into the United States.[14]

As production mounted and prices continued to sag, the IPAA mobilized in early 1930. After a January cut in posted prices by Jersey Standard and New York Standard, a mass meeting was held in Tulsa, Oklahoma, and $50,000 was raised for a $100,000 war chest. The next week, 250 midcontinent producers boarded a train to Washington to personally voice their complaints.[15] Led by Franklin, the delegation sought an import tax of $1.00 per barrel on crude and an oil-product import tax of 50 percent of value. Congress, influenced by the administration and importing refiners, defeated the measure by a close vote in 1930.[16] But a conciliation would follow. Early the next year, Jersey Standard, Gulf, Indiana Standard, and Shell, accounting for 95 percent of U.S. imports, agreed to immediately cut imports by 25 percent and in the case of Shell, 50 percent. Coordinating the agreement was Secretary of Commerce Robert Lamont, who had been appointed by President Hoover in response to a Oil States Advisory Committee request in February 1931 to "negotiate" reductions. The involved majors closed ranks for one overriding reason: to buy independents' support of the fledgling proration program. Not only did imports drop noticeably in 1931— crude by 24 percent and products by 11 percent from 1930 levels— but the IPAA's debt of over $40,000 was quietly erased by several of the majors.[17] Another pragmatic consideration for the majors was the potential of a political setback; by adhering to voluntary limits,

---

[14]Norman Nordhauser, *The Quest for Stability* (New York: Garland, 1979), pp. 48–49.

[15]Ibid., p. 53. For a recollection of the independents' effort, see Warren Baker, "IPAA's First Trip to Capitol Hill," *Petroleum Independent,* February 1979, pp. 30–34. Also see *National Petroleum News,* February 5, 1930, p. 27. Cited hereafter as *NPN.*

[16]Behind the scenes in the tariff defeat were John Carroll, adroit lobbyist of Royal Dutch-Shell, and William Mellon, treasury secretary and major stockholder of Gulf Oil. *NPN,* March 26, 1930, pp. 30–31.

[17]William Kemnitzer, *Rebirth of Monopoly* (New York: Harper Brothers, 1938), p. 135. The import reduction brought crude imports down within the range of the 445,000 barrels per day advocated in a 1931 proposed import-quota bill, H.R. 16585.

they avoided a tariff and benefited from higher domestic prices. For its part, the IPAA would henceforth support proration and shape it its way, while the majors would acquiesce to import restrictions. But the politically maturing independents would want more: federal legislation to discourage imports and, if possible, import quotas as well.

First Protectionist Era: 1932–38

Internal Revenue Act of 1932

In early 1932, Wirt Franklin, complaining that "[t]here is hardly an independent oil company not now in the hands of its bankers," appeared before Congress to accuse majors of conspiring against independents. Franklin proposed "equalization" tariffs on foreign crude and product that he predicted would raise over $100 million annually. The proposal was unexpected—as was the attack on majors given the compromise of 1931—but it was most welcomed by legislators seeking revenue to narrow Hoover's record deficit.[18]

The improved chances of a tariff were reflected in higher tanker rates beginning in March as a result of a rush to ship South America oil to the United States.[19] Another reaction to the IPAA initiative was for importing majors to seek new foreign markets for their oil should it be displaced from domestic markets.[20]

On June 6, 1932, Hoover signed a comprehensive oil-tariff bill, which reflected the legislative aims of independents and, to a lesser extent, importing majors.[21] The tariff was applicable to domestically consumed imports; crude and heavy-crude products were taxed at $0.21 per barrel, gasoline and other motor fuels at $1.05 per barrel, lubricating oils at $1.68 per barrel, and wax products at $0.01 per pound.

---

[18]The *Oil Weekly* said of Franklin's pitch, "His song of predatory interests and rapacious oil trusts, accompanied by a melodious jingle of new taxes, is sung in a key to which the congressional ear is closely attuned." *Oil Weekly*, February 5, 1932, p. 12. Cited hereafter as *OW*. Although favoring a tariff, the same issue of the *Oil Weekly* denounced the conspiracy charge as baseless (p. 11).

[19]*OW*, March 11, 1932, p. 13. Venezuela, already hurt by the East Texas field, was very much against the tariff. *OW*, April 11, 1932, pp. 15–18.

[20]*OW*, April 18, 1932, p. 13.

[21]Public Law 154, 47 Stat. 169 at 259–60 (1932).

Three groups could claim victory. For independent producers, a tariff comprising 25 percent of the crude price strongly reinforced the voluntary quota. For independent refiners, relatively high product duties ensured that crude would be refined domestically. For government officials, the act was the "Bill-which-Balanced-the Budget."[22] For majors, not all was lost. Higher tariffs proposed by the IPAA were lowered by the House and Senate, low extraction costs of foreign fields allowed reduced imports to remain economical, and the prohibitive gasoline tax would protect domestic refinery investments. In this regard, domestic majors Jersey Standard and Gulf, relatively large crude importers, came out ahead of Shell, a large importer of inexpensive gasoline.[23] Broadly viewed, the bill was a victory for the domestic oil industry and Hoover's "New Deal" at the expense of U.S. consumers, foreign royalty interests, and foreign refineries. Domestic proration was now sealed from foreign competition, although industry troubles were not over— emblematic of, among other things, an unintended effect of import restriction.

The immediate effect of passage was to firm crude and product prices and increase imports before the effective date of June 21.[24] In fact, imports increased by 16 percent in the first half of 1932 to promote the very conditions that the tariff was intended to alleviate.[25] After the bill became effective, a dramatic drop in gasoline imports occurred—from 1.2 million barrels in June to under 100,000 barrels in July.[26] But some trouble spots remained for the protectionists. Cheap Romanian gasoline caused price wars in Detroit, which disturbed the IPAA.[27] Naphtha used as gasoline qualified for the lower

[22]George Stocking, "Stabilization of the Oil Industry: Its Economic and Legal Aspects," *American Economic Review* (March 1933): 62. The 1932 tax bill, "one of the greatest increases in taxation ever enacted in the United States in peacetime," contributed to a continuation of the Great Depression. Murray Rothbard, *America's Great Depression* (Los Angeles: Nash, 1963, 1972), p. 253.

[23]William Kemnitzer, *Rebirth of Monopoly*, p. 134.

[24]*OGJ*, June 9, 1932, p. 19, and June 23, 1932, p. 23.

[25]*OGJ*, July 28, 1932, pp. 13, 16.

[26]*OGJ*, November 3, 1932, p. 34. Higher domestic prices caused by fewer imports, according to supporters, contributed $500,000 to independents in the first year of the tariff. *The Conservationist*, February 4, 1933, p. 16.

[27]*NPN*, July 20, 1932, p. 17.

crude tax, which prompted an IPAA resolution calling for its reclassification as gasoline subject to a $0.025 per gallon duty. Customs
Commissioner F. X. A. Eble reclassified naphtha.[28] Gasoline kept
from the United States by the tariff went to world markets, displacing
gasoline exports of U.S. refineries.[29] Reconfirmed was the iron law
of international trade—import restrictions also restrict exports. Last
but not least, there was East Texas and the hot-oil war. Prolific
domestic production swamped import reductions and caused distress throughout the independent sector. One victim was Wirt Franklin, whose company went into receivership in mid-1933.[30]

The Oil-Code Quota of 1933

The Code of Fair Competition for the Production Industry,
approved August 19, 1933, by President Roosevelt as one of 500
industry codes under the National Industrial Recovery Act, contained a binding oil-import quota. Article IV stated:

> The importation of crude petroleum and the products thereof in large
> quantities is hereby declared to be unfair competition injuriously
> affecting interstate commerce. Therefore the President is requested
> to limit the daily imports of crude petroleum and the products
> thereof to an amount not exceeding the average imports into the
> United States during the last six months of 1932. Such imports [are]
> to be allocated to the various persons desiring to import such petro-
> leum and the products thereof in such equitable manners as the
> President may determine.[31]

Export regulation was also introduced in the code, lest a domestic
producer exceed his allowables and "dump" supply in foreign
commerce.

> It shall be deemed a waste of natural resources, unfair competition
> and a violation of this code if any person engaged in the petroleum

[28]*OGJ*, November 3, 1932, p. 30; and *NPN*, December 28, 1932, p. 16. The ruling
was effective January 21, 1933.

[29]*OGJ*, November 3, 1932, p. 13. Rerouted world trade also led to asset transfers
between firms, including the sale of a Venezuelan company by Indiana Standard to
Jersey Standard, the latter having foreign outlets for gasoline the former previously
sold domestically. *OW*, January 30, 1933, p. 14.

[30]*NPN*, June 7, 1933, p. 1.

[31]National Recovery Administration, *Code of Fair Competition for the Petroleum Industry* (Washington, D.C.: Government Printing Office, 1933), art. 4.

industry in any state shall produce crude petroleum or any product thereof in excess of [his] allotted share . . . and dump the same in interstate or foreign commerce.[32]

On September 2, 1933, Interior Secretary Ickes set an import quota of 98,000 barrels per day for crude and petroleum products for an indefinite period. This figure, representing less than 5 percent of domestic consumption, was calculated from a period of depressed imports—the second half of 1932—which were subject to tariffs, voluntary quotas, and an inventory buildup during the first half of the year in anticipation of the tax.

Federal officials reported compliance with the quota. The IPAA charged, however, that imports exceeded allowables by over 27,000 barrels per day for most of 1934.[33] Exports, too, were underreported by some accounts.[34]

On May 26, 1935, the Oil Code was annulled by the *Schechter* decision, which invalidated the National Industrial Recovery Act, and oil quota regulation was no more. But the 1932 tariffs remained, and voluntary oil quotas set in 1931 continued to be observed.

The protectionist era between 1931 and 1938, as seen in table 13.2, experienced a decline in crude-oil and product imports as a result of the voluntary quota, tariffs, and the formal quota. Crude-oil exports rose, serving as an escape valve for prolific domestic over-production. Product exports, on the other hand, declined markedly because of the tariff.

The net result of protectionism was a diminution of U.S. participation in the world oil market. In the five years after import restrictions (1931–35), total foreign oil trade involving the United States fell over 25 percent compared to the five-year average before the restrictions. This not only hurt consumers, it hurt the domestic industry. The "gain" of domestic producers from protectionism, ironically, was

---

[32]Ibid., art. 5.

[33]"[T]his quota was observed throughout the period of code enforcement [and] . . . did not necessitate specific allocations to individual members of the industry." Quoted in Northcutt Ely, "The Government in the Exercise of the Power over Foreign Commerce," in American Bar Association, *Conservation of Oil and Gas: A Legal History, 1948,* ed. Blakely M. Murphy (Chicago: American Bar Association, 1949), p. 657. Also see *NPN*, September 5, 1934, p. 16.

[34]Myron Watkins, *Oil: Stabilization or Conservation?* (New York: Harper and Brothers, 1937), pp. 104–5.

Table 13.2
OIL IMPORTS AND EXPORTS: 1930–38
(thousand barrels per day)

Year	Crude Oil		Refined Products		Total	
	Imports	Exports	Imports	Exports	Imports	Exports
1930	170	65	119	364	289	429
1931	129	70	106	271	236	341
1932	122	75	81	208	204	282
1933	87	100	37	192	124	292
1934	97	113	41	201	138	314
1935	88	141	56	212	144	353
1936	88	137	68	224	156	361
1937	75	184	81	289	157	474
1938	72	212	76	319	149	531

SOURCE: American Petroleum Institute, *Basic Petroleum Data Book*, 1973 ed., sec. 9, table 11, and sec. 10, table 1.

diluted by the loss of much-needed export markets, given the buyer's market at home.

Protectionist Vacillation: 1939–58

Regulatory Relaxation: 1939–49

In 1939, the first revision to the 1932 tariff act was enacted in a reciprocal trade agreement with Venezuela, the leading oil exporter to the United States.[35] Affected by the 1939 agreement were crude oil and certain heavy-crude products—topped crude, fuel oil, and gas oil. For quantities below 5 percent of domestically refined supply in the preceding year, a 50 percent tariff reduction (from $0.21 per barrel to $0.105 per barrel) was allowed; for imports above this amount, the full $0.21 per barrel remained. The 5 percent crude-import allowable was allocated to Venezuela (71 percent), the Netherlands and territories (20 percent), Colombia (4 percent), and other areas (5 percent).[36] Reflecting refiner sentiment, the gasoline tariff

[35]Presidential Proclamation, 54 Stat. 2375 (1939), signed November 6; the reduction was effective December 16, 1939.

[36]Northcutt Ely, "The Government in the Exercise of the Power over Foreign Commerce," p. 658.

of $1.05 per barrel and the lubricant tariff of $1.68 per barrel remained unchanged to severely discourage product imports.

A second tariff reduction was made in a trade agreement with Mexico in 1943.[37] The quota tariff of $0.105 per barrel above the 5 percent allowable was abolished, and duties on kerosene and liquid asphalt were reduced by half. Under a most-favored-nation clause, the reductions applied to all other countries including Venezuela. Stiff levies on gasoline and lubricants were left intact, continuing refinery protectionism.

With World War II petroleum planning in full swing, foreign-trade regulations became submerged into a wider supply-and-demand planning matrix for the Pacific and European war theaters as well as the United States. Domestic production was at full capacity, and efforts were made by the U.S. government to enhance output in Mexico and China and to gain favorable concessions for foreign production elsewhere.[38]

Despite conditions that were radically different from those of the decade before, the amended 1932 levies continued during the war years. The inertia of regulation and expectations of postwar normalization combined to preserve import restrictions. A February 28, 1944, preliminary report of the Petroleum Industry War Council's National Oil Policy Committee underscored the desire for policy "flexibility" to regulate imports as conditions required.

> (a) Our import policy, involving such questions as tariffs and quotas, should be kept flexible, so as to be readily adjusted from time to time to meet domestic need and general economic requirements.
>
> (b) The general principle of optimum-rate production for domestic oil fields will provide the basis for determining the economic need for imports, and to the extent that our requirements exceed such measure of domestic producibility, imports will be needed and will create economic balance.
>
> (c) Imports in excess of economic needs and not required in the national interest, will create conditions harmful to search for new

[37]E.A.S 311, 57 Stat. 833 (1942), signed December 23, 1942; it became effective January 30, 1943.

[38]John Frey and H. Chandler Ide, *A History of the Petroleum Administration for War* (Washington, D.C.: Government Printing Office, 1946), p. 25. For a summary of the Foreign Petroleum Supply Committee and foreign oil activities influenced by the U.S. government, see ibid., chaps. 15 and 16.

oil fields and the continuation of technologic progress in production and refining.[39]

Another sign of protectionist sentiment was the IPAA's adamant opposition to a 50 percent reduction in oil tariffs proposed in a 1945 trade bill.[40] Despite the problems of petroleum supply during the war, protectionist philosophy was alive and well in government and industry.

In the postwar period, a third relaxation of petroleum trade barriers was enacted. On October 30, 1947, the United States and twenty-two other nations signed the GATT to reduce import restrictions.[41] Long-standing gasoline and lubricant tariffs were cut in half to $0.525 per barrel for gasoline and $0.84 per barrel for lubricants, with a proviso that "in no event shall the rate of import tax . . . on topped crude petroleum, or fuel oil devised from petroleum be less than the rate of such tax applicable to crude petroleum."

This revision protected refiners and producers alike. But with reduced tariffs, protectionism was not the same. IPAA general counsel Russell Brown, referring to the period prior to 1947, remarked that "for thirteen years the tariff proved a great help."[42] The historical record of petroleum imports and exports in the 1939–49 period is shown in table 13.3.

Relaxed tariffs, abolished quotas, and higher prices, which reduced tariffs in real terms, led to new trade patterns in the period after 1930–38 protectionism.[43] Crude imports increased steadily to new records except during several war years when German submarine warfare was an effective deterrent. The threefold increase in crude imports between 1944 and 1949 set a new high of 421,000 barrels per day. Crude-oil exports were stagnant despite major postwar exports directed by the Office of International Trade under the Marshall Plan. Refined-oil exports shrank in the same six-year period, while product imports surged to virtually equal product

[39]Ibid., p. 396.

[40]*NPN*, May 16, 1945, p. 38.

[41]61 Stat. vol. 5, schedule XX (1947).

[42]Leonard Fanning, *The Story of the American Petroleum Institute* (New York: World Petroleum Policies, 1959), p. 136.

[43]For example, a 14.5-million-barrel allocation to over thirty countries was made in the first quarter of 1948. *NPN*, January 14, 1948, p. 18.

Table 13.3
OIL IMPORTS AND EXPORTS: 1939–49
(thousand barrels per day)

Year	Crude Oil		Refined Products		Total	
	Imports	Exports	Imports	Exports	Imports	Exports
1939	91	197	71	323	162	520
1940	117	141	112	216	229	356
1941	139	91	127	207	266	298
1942	34	93	65	228	99	320
1943	38	113	136	298	174	411
1944	122	94	130	474	252	567
1945	204	90	108	411	311	501
1946	236	116	141	303	377	420
1947	267	127	169	324	437	451
1948	353	109	161	259	514	367
1949	421	91	224	236	645	327

SOURCE: American Petroleum Institute, *Basic Petroleum Data Book*, 1973 ed., sec. 9, table 11, and sec. 10, table 1.

exports for the first time in U.S. history. Total petroleum imports steadily grew after the war to overtake declining exports and make the United States in 1948 a net importer for the first time since 1922. Contributing to this reversal were domestic supply problems brought on by lingering price regulation in the 1947–49 period.[44] The 1949 statistic of nearly 1 million barrels of oil per day in foreign trade involving the United States as buyer and seller, a record to date, reflected reduced trade barriers and growing demand for oil products.

By 1949, it was clear that conditions were ripe for protectionism. The Texas Railroad Commission and other state conservation agencies were prorating output in prewar fashion. Crude and product imports were setting new highs. The IPAA on May 3, 1949, raised anew a national-defense argument for import regulation before Congress.

> The nation's security and welfare of these many independent producers, their employees, and suppliers cannot be made subservient to the will of the ten principal importing companies. . . . Petroleum

[44]See chapter 24, pp. 1432–39, for a discussion of postwar supply problems.

reserves may be developed and refining facilities may be built in the theaters of future hostilities, but those will be a little value in time of war.[45]

Pleas by independent producers to "preserve the strength of the domestic industry" were unsuccessful, as was an attempt to persuade the U.S. Tariff Commission to activate an "escape clause" in the Venezuelan and Mexican agreements and return to full tariffs under the 1932 law. The Interstate Oil Compact Commission and oil-state congressmen joined the chorus. Political pressures would mount and lead to success in the next decade.

Back toward Protectionism: 1950–58

Winter of Discontent. The emergence of the United States as a net petroleum importer in 1948 was not wholly a natural phenomenon. After the war, proration resumed to prevent price declines, which made imports additionally competitive. Importing firms with domestic production were put in a peculiar position: the more they chose to import, the more state conservation commissions could shut in their wells. But the burden of proration fell relatively more on nonimporting independents, and clamor arose, as it had two decades before, for import restrictions to buoy domestic regulation.

In 1949 and early 1950, Congress heard many proposals—including a $1.00 per barrel tariff, a 5 percent quota, and an export-for-import certificate plan—for replacing the $0.105 per barrel crude import fee.[46] The 81st Congress held three investigations, and the Small Business Committee of the House of Representatives called for voluntary import curbs.

As the Texas Railroad Commission reduced allowables almost monthly, new pro-tariff allies joined the IPAA—the Railroad Brotherhoods and United Mine Workers, which both favored less oil for more coal, the CIO Oil Workers Union, and the (Texas) Statewide Citizens Economic Committee, which promoted Texas oil over foreign oil as vital to the state education and other public programs dependent on oil taxes.[47] In contrast, constituencies for free trade were relatively unorganized.

[45]Stuart Long, "The Oil Men's War," *Nation*, September 17, 1949, p. 272.

[46]*OGJ*, January 19, 1950, p. 29.

[47]*OGJ*, February 2, 1950, p. 25; and *Nation*, April 22, 1950, p. 358.

A tangible result of mounting protectionism was the decision of Texaco and Gulf to reduce imports to below 1949 levels. But before other companies had a chance to follow suit, combat broke out in Korea, and fears of a prolonged war against communism placed imports in a different light.

During the Korean conflict, several adjustments were made to tariff rates. With the termination of the Mexican trade agreement on December 31, 1950, the tariff structure reverted to that of the 1939 Venezuelan agreement: $0.105 per barrel below 5 percent and $0.21 per barrel above 5 percent for crude oil, fuel oil, and heavy products.[48] The quota level required allocation among countries exporting to the United States—Venezuela, Dutch West Indies, and others except Mexico, which had a one-tier tariff. On August 28, 1952, revisions were made to the 1939 Venezuelan agreement.[49] Effective October 11, crude oil and fuel oil of 25 degrees API or less were taxed at $0.525 per barrel with higher gravities taxed at $0.105 per barrel without reference to amounts.[50] Other product tariffs remained at the level set in 1947. This relaxation, coupled with proration, which protected the domestic price structure, encouraged importation.

Encountering little success at the federal level, independents persuaded the Texas Railroad Commission to require the majors, beginning in January 1953, to "nominate" anticipated imports for five upcoming months to compare to actual amounts. As M. A. Adelman noted, these reports "constituted an agreement between the commission and each importer to limit imports, which amounted also to an agreement among the importers themselves."[51] Mindful of industry relations and fearful of punitive legislation, majors restrained imports in 1953 and 1954 to amounts incrementally above 1952 levels. But even this level of importation crimped domestic output,

[48] Presidential Proclamation 2901, 15 *Fed. Reg.* 6063 (1950); and Presidential Proclamation 2916, 16 *Fed. Reg.* 109 (1951).

[49] Supplementary Trade Agreement with Venezuela, 3 U.S.T. 4195, T.I.A.S. 2565 (1952).

[50] API gravity, expressed in degrees, is the standard industry measure of density of petroleum liquids. The higher the value of API gravity, the less dense, and more valuable, the petroleum liquid.

[51] M. A. Adelman, *The World Petroleum Market* (Baltimore: Johns Hopkins University Press, 1972), p. 152.

as verified by falling market-demand factors in Texas, Oklahoma, Louisiana, and New Mexico.[52] Federal involvement would be needed to rescue the fragile domestic proration program and allow many independents to remain profitable.

"Voluntary" Import Controls. The influential IPAA, whose members accounted for 40 percent of U.S. production, went directly to the White House with a national-security argument for new protectionist legislation.[53] On July 30, 1954, President Eisenhower responded by appointing a Cabinet Committee on Energy Supplies and Resources Policy to study petroleum supply and demand conditions "with the aim of strengthening the national defense, providing orderly industrial growth, and assuring supplies for our expanding national economy and for any future emergency."[54] On February 26 of the following year, the committee recommended that crude imports and fuel-oil imports be kept at 1954 levels and hinted that mandatory means might be needed to replace voluntary means in the event of noncompliance.[55]

On May 25, 1955, Jersey Standard announced cooperation with the committee's findings. Several more firms followed suit.[56] But

---

[52]In the 1950s, market-demand factors fell from 76 to 33 percent in Texas, 30 to 23 percent in Oklahoma, 90 to 33 percent in Louisiana, and 74 to 49 percent in New Mexico. See table 13.5, p. 734.

[53]A 1954 ruling that domestic watchmakers merited protection from their Swiss counterparts in the interest of national security led IPAA general counsel Russell Brown, who was "quick to see the advantage," to "[hitch] the IPAA's star to 'national security.' Indeed lobbyists for coal and practically every other domestic industry rushed to Washington to get on the 'national security' bandwagon." Leonard Fanning, *The Story of the American Petroleum Institute,* p. 138.

[54]William Peterson, *The Question of Governmental Oil Import Restrictions* (Washington, D.C.: American Enterprise Association, 1959), p. 18.

[55]"The committee believes that if the imports of crude and residual oils should exceed significantly the respective proportions that these imports of oils bore to the production of domestic crude in 1954, the domestic fuels situation could be so impaired as to endanger the orderly industrial growth which assures the military and civilian supplies and reserves that are necessary to national defense. There would be an inadequate incentive for exploration and the discovery of new sources of supply." Report on Energy Supplies and Resources Policy, reprinted in Cabinet Task Force on Oil Import Control, *The Oil Import Question* (Washington, D.C.: Government Printing Office, 1970), pp. 163–68.

[56]William Peterson, *The Question of Governmental Oil Import Restrictions,* p. 19.

other firms remained ambivalent, which would inspire more voluntary—and finally mandatory—action.

On June 21, 1955, standby authority to curtail oil imports was enacted in the Reciprocal Trade Agreements Extension Act.[57] Section 7 read:

> Whenever the Director of the Office of Defense Mobilization has reason to believe that any article is being imported into the United States in such quantities as to threaten to impair the national security, he shall so advise the President, and if the President agrees that there is reason for such belief, the President shall cause an immediate investigation to be made to determine the facts. If, on the basis of such investigation, and the report to him of the findings and recommendations made in connection therewith, the President finds that the article is being imported into the United States in such quantities as to threaten to impair the national security, he shall take such action as he deems necessary to adjust the imports of such articles to a level that will not threaten to impair the national security.[58]

As a follow-up, Office of Defense Mobilization (ODM) director Arthur Fleming wrote the major importing companies on August 5 to request import data from 1954 and 1955 as well as projections for the first part of 1956.[59] With the club in the closet, "voluntary" import control was set to begin.

Phase I. Late in 1955, several months after importers were urged to reduce imports or face mandatory action, the ODM made public petroleum-import information received in response to its request of three months before. "Unless company policy changes were made,"

---

[57]Public Law 86, 69 Stat. 162 (1955). Section 2 of the Trade Agreements Act of 1954 (Public Law 464, 68 Stat. 360) prohibited tariff reductions if increased imports threatened national security.

[58]Public Law 86, 69 Stat. 166. Commented William Barber, "Though the language of this section was perfectly general, the legislative history of this provision leaves no doubt that it was drafted with the circumstances of the oil industry in mind." Barber, "The Eisenhower Energy Policy: Reluctant Intervention," in *Energy Policy in Perspective,* ed. Crauford Goodwin (Washington, D.C.: Brookings Institution, 1981), p. 230.

[59]"As a result," M. A. Adelman concluded, "the work of the Texas Railroad Commission was taken over by the Office of Defense Mobilization." Adelman, *The World Petroleum Market,* p. 153.

Table 13.4
CRUDE-OIL IMPORTS BY REGION: 1955–57
(thousand barrels)

Year	Venezuela	Canada	Other Western Hemisphere	Mideast & Other	Total
1955	148,829	16,395	9,590	113,197	294,170
1956	177,199	43,227	11,443	116,764	354,727
1957	209,049	53,804	10,619	109,550	386,209

SOURCE: Douglas Bohi and Milton Russell, Limiting Oil Imports (Baltimore: Johns Hopkins University Press, 1978), p. 28.

it was concluded, "imports would continue to be substantially above the standard recommendation (1954 levels) by the Advisory Committee."[60] Included was a more direct suggestion, marking the beginning of "voluntary" controls under ODM standby powers, to "reduce . . . planned imports of crude oil for the period April 1–December 31, 1955, by approximately 7 percent . . . with the exception of oil of Canadian and Venezuelan origin . . . if substantial conformity . . . is to be achieved.[61]

As could have been predicted, imports from Canada and Venezuela jumped considerably, while supplies from other sources fell slightly so as to not impair committed investments by domestic firms abroad. Total imports grew well beyond targeted levels despite repeated exhortations from the ODM (table 13.4).

On August 7, 1956, the IPAA and eighteen other domestic producer associations petitioned the ODM to activate section 7 of the Reciprocal Trade Act to grant compulsory powers to the president. After study, the ODM concluded that because the Suez crisis removed "surplus" oil, mandatory controls were not required. This veiled warning, said Douglas Bohi and Milton Russell, "signaled the end of the 'laissez-faire with bombast' policy and its replacement by administrative resolve not to let imports rise to their previously predicted levels."[62]

[60]William Barber, "The Eisenhower Energy Policy," p. 231.

[61]Ibid., p. 232. The exemptions reflected neighborly diplomacy and recognition that Western Hemisphere sources of supply were in the orbit of secure U.S. supply.

[62]Douglas Bohi and Milton Russell, Limiting Oil Imports, p. 40.

A second study by ODM released on April 23, 1957, surveyed imports under the voluntary program to conclude that imported crude was "in such quantities as to threaten to impair the national security."[63] This put the ball in the president's court, and Eisenhower demonstrated reluctance by forming a cabinet-level Special Committee to Investigate Crude Oil Imports to study the problem further and recommend solutions. Further "voluntary" action would be tried before a decision to formally inhibit trade would be made.

Phase II. On July 29, 1957, the special committee submitted its findings to President Eisenhower. The report, while admitting that "the low cost of imported oil is attractive," expressed concern that

> excessive reliance upon it in the short run may put the nation in a long-term vulnerable position. Imported supplies could be cut off in an emergency and might well be diminished by events beyond our control (leading to) a much higher cost, or even in the unavailability, of oil to consumers.[64]

With the best-of-all-worlds intent to permit "reasonable" imports and "stimulate a dynamic and vigorous exploratory and development effort in the country," a formal program for "voluntary" import controls was established for crude oil. Five planning districts formulated for World War II petroleum planning by the Petroleum Administration for War were dusted off with Districts I–IV, the area east of the Rockies, under import watch. District V, the West Coast area, was recognized as an oil-deficit area dependent upon imports to supplement local production. Imports were allowed to District V as long as they were "reasonably competitive" with domestic supply. Import assignments for Districts I–IV were allocated between "established importers," seven firms who were large-volume importers in 1954, and "new importers," fifteen firms who entered after 1954 or imported less than 20,000 barrels per day in 1954.[65] Quota assignments to "eliminate the threat of impairment to the

---

[63]Quoted in William Barber, "The Eisenhower Energy Policy," p. 236.

[64]Quoted in ibid., p. 239.

[65]In order of import amounts, the "established" firms were Gulf, Jersey Standard, Socony, California Standard, Sinclair, Atlantic, and Texaco; "new" firms were Sun, Cities Service, Tidewater, Great Northern, Eastern States, Indiana Standard, Phillips, International Refining, Northwestern, Gabriel, Lake Superior, Southwestern, Ohio Standard, Shell, and Lakehead.

national security" were set at 90 percent of 1954–56 imports for "established" firms and projected July 1957 amounts (if less than 1956 imports plus 12,000 barrels per day) for the other fifteen firms.[66] New entrants were to give the Oil Import Administration (OIA), a new agency established within the Interior Department to coordinate the program, six months' notice before commencing operation, and the OIA would assign new entrants quotas conforming to market conditions.

The program was voluntary to the extent that noncompliance was not subject to enforcement actions. But all knew that mandatory measures were possible and that the government was serious in its resolve to make the program work.

The program was not successful for a variety of reasons. First, petitions for increased quotas greeted the program—an obvious manifestation of the incentives created by the artificial situation. Second, increased importation through less scrutinized District V penalized importers elsewhere and weakened the effectiveness of quotas. Consequently, program director Matthew Carson brought District V into the program on December 12, 1957, with historical allocations per company.[67] Third, firms with investments committed to servicing imported crude petitioned for special relief in the form of increased quotas. Tidewater Oil had built a $200-million refinery and had related commitments, such as tanker charters, on the presumption that it would *become* a major importer; any quota based on historical purchases would endanger its investments.[68] These adjustments, and new entry, meant smaller shares for established importers. By September 1958, the number of nonestablished firms swelled from 15 to 55, and another 100 applications were pending.[69] Fourth, the loosely constructed cartel offered incentives for firms to import above their quotas, pay the nominal crude tariff, and undersell high-cost domestic supply.[70] One firm, Delta Refining, ignored

---

[66]William Barber, "The Eisenhower Energy Policy," p. 238.

[67]William Peterson, *The Question of Governmental Oil Import Restrictions*, pp. 23–24.

[68]Douglas Bohi and Milton Russell, *Limiting Oil Imports*, pp. 48–49.

[69]Torleif Meloe, *United States Control of Petroleum Imports* (New York: Arno Press, 1979), p. 68.

[70]Crude-acquisition-cost alternatives for an Indiana Standard refinery in September 1957 typified the natural incentives to import. The quality-adjusted delivered price for West Texas crude was $3.49 per barrel, while delivered Kuwaiti and Venezuelan crude sold for under $3.00 per barrel. Kenneth Dam, "Implementation of Import Quotas: The Case of Oil," *Journal of Law and Economics* (April 1971): 11.

the application process and began to import 20,000 barrels per day without any quota assignment.[71] Any program penalizing established firms while giving preferential treatment to newcomers and a "free ride" to noncompliers was not to survive long.

Another indication that the program was in trouble was the importation of slightly refined crude. It was ruled that "unfinished" oil and gasoline were not product for tariff purposes and not crude oil for quota purposes. This led to a flood of half-product imports. In 1957, approximately 73,000 barrels per day were imported; a year later, the figure had risen to 350,000 barrels per day.[72] To prevent further circumvention, unfinished gasoline and oil were brought into the program on June 4, 1958, by setting quotas at each firm's May–June 1958 average. But the damage had been done, and it was difficult to cajole firms into complying with even those high import levels.

Attempts were also made to put some bite behind the bark. The transition from voluntary to mandatory controls was made more probable by the Trade Agreements Extension Act of 1958, which required the president to ensure compliance—not just instigate further fact-finding—with an ODM national-security recommendation concerning import levels.[73] On March 27, 1958, the Buy American Act of 1933 was applied to oil imports to require all government purchases to be from firms holding a certificate of compliance from the OIA.[74]

By the end of 1958, the problems of the voluntary approach were obvious. Import restrictions had failed to hold the line against effective circumvention and scattered noncompliance. Noncompliance was spreading, and requests for increased quota assignments overwhelmed the OIA's ability to act rationally on them.[75] An attempt to

---

[71]Douglas Bohi and Milton Russell, *Limiting Oil Imports,* p. 53. OIA director Carson could only say, "In the event that Delta continues their pursuit, only the weight of public opinion could be brought to bear against them." *OGJ,* January 22, 1958, p. 124.

[72]William Peterson, *The Question of Governmental Oil Import Restrictions,* p. 25; and Torleif Meloe, *United States Control of Petroleum Imports,* p. 67.

[73]Public Law 85-686, 72 Stat. 673 (1958).

[74] Executive Order 10761, 23 *Fed. Reg.* 2067 (March 28, 1958).

[75]Publicly identified noncomplying firms were Sun Oil, Ohio Standard, Tidewater Oil (Getty Oil), and Eastern States Petroleum. Rene Manes, *The Effects of United States Oil Import Policy on the Petroleum Industry* (New York: Arno Press, 1961, 1979), p. 97.

Table 13.5
IMPORTS AND PRORATION: 1948–58
(thousand barrels)

Year	Crude Imports	Percent of U.S. Production	Allowables (%)			
			Tex.	N.Mex.	La.	Okla.
1948	129,093	6.4	100	63	–	–
1949	153,686	8.3	65	61	–	–
1950	177,714	9.6	63	69	–	–
1951	179,073	8.0	76	74	–	–
1952	209,591	9.2	71	68	–	–
1953	236,455	10.0	65	63	90	–
1954	239,479	10.3	53	57	61	–
1955	285,421	11.5	53	57	48	30
1956	341,833	13.1	52	56	42	27
1957	373,255	14.3	47	56	43	26
1958	348,007	14.2	33	49	33	23

SOURCE: American Petroleum Institute, *Basic Petroleum Data Book,* (Washington, D.C.: API, 1981), sec. 4, table 4, and sec. 9, table 2; and various state conservation agencies.

restructure the program on the basis of refinery capacity instead of import quotas ran aground for want of agreement. In December 1958, the program broke down. Previously, compliance had been identifiable; now noncompliance snowballed throughout the industry. In December, imports jumped 37 percent from 800,000 barrels per day to over 1 million barrels per day.[76] Protectionist interests petitioned for another national-security investigation, and on February 27, 1959, the ODM found that "crude oil and the principal crude oil derivatives and products are being imported in such quantities and under such circumstances as to threaten to impair the national security."[77] All signs pointed to mandatory controls.

The gravity of the situation on the eve of mandatory controls can be appreciated from table 13.5. Lower costs of extraction from

[76]Ibid.

[77]Reprinted in Cabinet Task Force on Oil Import Control, *The Oil Import Question,* pp. 207–10. In a March 4 supplement, it was emphasized that, while domestic demand increased by more than 15 percent between 1954 and 1958, domestic crude reserves increased by only 2.8 percent. Ibid., p. 211.

Table 13.6
OIL IMPORTS AND EXPORTS: 1950–58
(thousand barrels per day)

	Crude Oil		Refined Products		Total	
Year	Imports	Exports	Imports	Exports	Imports	Exports
1950	487	95	363	210	850	305
1951	491	78	354	344	844	422
1952	573	73	380	359	952	432
1953	648	55	386	347	1,034	402
1954	656	37	396	318	1,052	355
1955	782	32	466	336	1,248	368
1956	934	78	502	352	1,436	430
1957	1,023	138	552	430	1,574	568
1958	953	12	747	264	1,700	276

SOURCE: American Petroleum Institute, *Basic Petroleum Data Book*, 1973 ed., sec. 9, table 11, and sec. 10, table 1.

foreign fields, coupled with the high-cost implications of domestic proration, made the import "problem" feed on itself. Tariffs offered little protection. Inflation and rising crude prices made the $0.105 per barrel crude tariff fall in real terms. In 1952, the duty was 6.7 percent of the wellhead oil price; by 1958, it was less than 3 percent.[78] Throughout the voluntary-quota program, as in the postwar period, imports steadily increased their share of the U.S. market, while market-demand states lowered allowables to stabilize prices, which squeezed domestic producers with flush wells.[79] Table 13.5 compares growing crude imports with falling market-demand proration factors in four major oil states between 1948 and 1958. The record of crude and product imports and exports from 1950 through 1958 is given in table 13.6.

Mandatory Oil Import Program: 1959–73

Proclamation 3279

With the ODM finding of February 27, 1959, a similar recommendation with specific quota recommendations a week later by the

[78]Rene Manes, *The Effects of United States Oil Import Policy on the Petroleum Industry*, p. 62.

[79]Manes graphically presents the inverse relationship between imports and domestic allowables. Ibid., p. 52.

Special Committee to Investigate Crude Oil Imports, and political heat from independent producers and coal interests, President Eisenhower imposed mandatory import controls on March 10, 1959.[80] The proclamation ended five years of "hesitation, struggling, and indecisiveness" on the vexing oil-import question by a president concerned about higher oil prices and open international trade.[81]

After March 11, 1959, no crude or unfinished oil, and after April 1, 1959, no finished products, were to be imported ("entered for consumption or withdrawn . . . for consumption") without license from the secretary of the interior.[82] All fifty states and Puerto Rico were covered and divided for regulatory purposes into Petroleum Administration for Defense Districts I–IV, District V, and Puerto Rico.[83] District V, as had been the case under voluntary controls, received the most lenient treatment. Crude, unfinished oil, and finished oil could be imported into this district to satisfy demand not met by domestic supply if finished products did not exceed the 1957 import level and unfinished products did not exceed 10 percent of allowed crude and finished-oil imports. For each of the other districts, petroleum imports, except residual fuel oil, were to be no greater than 9 percent of total demand calculated by a Bureau of Mines forecast. A second ceiling was added that finished products (except fuel oil) could not be above their 1957 import level and unfinished oils could not exceed 10 percent of permitted crude and unfinished-oil imports. Residual fuel oil, on the other hand, was to be periodically reviewed by the interior secretary, and adjustments were to be made as needed. Puerto Rico, finally, was allowed an import quota for all petroleum equal to 1958 amounts, unless adjusted to meet changed demand.

[80]Presidential Proclamation 3279, "Adjusting Imports of Petroleum and Petroleum Products into the United States," 24 *Fed. Reg.* 1781 (March 12, 1959).

[81]Gerald Nash, *United States Oil Policy*, p. 206. For evidence of second thoughts by Eisenhower about his decision to regulate oil imports, see William Barber, "The Eisenhower Energy Policy," p. 251.

[82]Unfinished oil was defined as petroleum "to be further processed other than by blending by mechanical means." Finished oil was defined to include liquefied gases, gasoline, jet fuel, naphtha, fuel oil, lubricating oil, residual fuel oil, and asphalt.

[83]District V covered Alaska, Hawaii, California, Washington, Oregon, Nevada, and Arizona. In important respects, the West Coast was (and still is) a separate market from the oil market east of the Rockies. See the discussion in Torleif Meloe, *United States Control of Petroleum Imports*, pp. 82–85.

With aggregate import quotas defined, the next question was allocation. Quota assignments according to refinery capacity, first employed in September 1958 for the voluntary program, were resurrected in part for the mandatory program.[84] Although not entirely specific (detailed regulations were forthcoming), the guidelines were to allocate finished-product quotas to historic (1957) importers in relative amounts and to allocate crude and unfinished-product quotas according to refinery size and qualifying pipelines. This applied to Districts I–V. Puerto Rico's quota allocations for crude and unfinished products went to refiners according to 1958 amounts; finished oils went to importers in 1957 amounts. All allocations were to be "fair and equitable."

Failure to comply with assigned quotas or any regulation pursuant to Proclamation 3279 meant revocation or suspension of import licenses. An appeals board was established to hear complaints and make adjustments for "hardship, error, or other relevant special consideration" within the aggregate quota. One district's gain would necessitate another's loss.

The mandatory quota program, the first since the twenty-two-month import freeze in the 1930s, was a product of experience gained from the flaws of the voluntary program. *All* oil products and *all* areas were included. Complemented by modest crude and fuel-oil tariffs and higher gasoline and lubricant tariffs, effective protectionism was in place. However, strict regulation under a political program, which was contrary to the self-interest of importers and consumers, would be difficult.

Industry reaction to quota regulation was mixed. While domestic producers were pleased, importers and downstream parties were disappointed and concerned. The *National Petroleum News* editorialized that for downstream interests March 10 was "a day the oil industry will regret."[85] The regulatory program brought industry infighting (namely, a threat by the National Oil Jobbers Council to attack the depletion allowance in retaliation), international disfavor, and a margin squeeze for refiners caught between higher crude

---

[84]The throughput allocation plan is attributed to Under Secretary of Commerce Frederick Mueller and State Department consultant Herbert Hoover, Jr. William Barber, "The Eisenhower Energy Policy," p. 246.

[85]*NPN*, April 1959, p. 109.

costs and retail prices constrained by a government warning not to increase oil-product prices because of the quota.

Implementation

Several days after Eisenhower's proclamation, the machinery of protectionism was readied in the Department of the Interior. Licensing procedures were formulated, and an Oil Imports Appeals Board was established to join the OIA. On March 17, formal import regulations were released.[86] Quota ceilings of 738,570 barrels per day for all of Districts I–IV and 198,200 barrels per day for District V were set until June 30, 1959, whereafter six-month adjustments would be made. Individual import assignments were made to 136 firms, 76 more than had participated in the voluntary programs.[87] The high number of recipients came from the decision to grant quotas not only to historical importers but to all U.S. refineries. Historical firms received 80 percent of their previous (voluntary) quota to make room for the new recipients. Refinery allocations were scaled to daily throughput with a noticeable bias toward smaller firms.[88] Thus, the wealth redistribution from consumers to producers contained in oil-import restrictions now had a wealth effect on domestic refineries.

Strict rules governed oil exchanges and quota swaps. Because regulation in District V was less stringent than elsewhere, oil exchanges between District V and Districts I–IV were prohibited. Within the two areas, swaps could only be made to reduce cross-hauling or to time trade. Quota "tickets" could not be "sold, assigned, or otherwise transferred." This soon would be amended to mean that while a cash market in quotas was illegal, the exchange of imported crude for domestic crude was permissible if consummated within ninety days, reported to the OIA, and the oil was refined internally.[89] This revision was imperative for inland refiners

---

[86]24 *Fed. Reg.* 1907 (March 17, 1959).

[87]The firms and their quota assignments are listed in William Peterson, *The Question of Governmental Oil Import Restrictions*, pp. 31–34.

[88]The specific effects of the MOIP on domestic refineries, particularly smaller ones, are discussed in chapter 20, pp. 1160–75.

[89]Rene Manes, *The Effects of United States Oil Import Policy on the Petroleum Industry*, pp. 168–70.

who otherwise faced transportation expenses large enough to negate the value of their import tickets.

A natural trading pattern developed between coastal refineries near delivery points of foreign crude, the rights to which partly belonged to inland refineries, and inland refineries near domestic crude owned by coastal refineries. To minimize transportation costs, crude titles were exchanged to leave inland plants with inland crude and coastal plants with foreign crude.

Activity under the new program was described by the *Oil & Gas Journal* as "the biggest spate of horse trading in the history of the oil business."[90] Divergent terms came to be narrowed as the market discovered the relative values of the cost of foreign crude and the cost of domestic crude by location. Hundreds of exchanges took place, predicated on barrel differentials, to compensate quota holders for lower cost foreign crude. For example, if the landed cost of Kuwaiti crude was $2.80 per barrel and an exchange with a coastal refinery was made for West Texas crude priced at $3.20 per barrel, then the contract would stipulate an approximate ratio of 1.14 barrels of domestic crude per barrel of foreign crude, adjusted for transportation.[91] With cash consideration prohibited, the barrel ratio (and fringe benefits, if any) represented the value of an import "entitlement." This value was variously estimated at between $0.65 and $1.25 per barrel.[92]

Several aspects of the new program deserve mention. It was a mandatory rather than a voluntary program. Nonimporting refiners received a windfall from the premium exchange value of foreign crude quotas. A new dimension was given to the historical industry practice of exchanging, whereby firms employed new strategies to maximize relative positions. The results of the learning process, combined with external political considerations, would pressure MOIP into adjustment and revision.

Adjustment and Circumvention

An early complication of the program that required immediate correction was a threatened realignment of historic trading patterns

[90]*OGJ*, April 27, 1959, p. 83.

[91]In-depth discussions of exchange arrangements can be found in Rene Manes, *The Effect of United States Oil Import Policy on the Petroleum Industry*, pp. 172–209; and Torleif Meloe, *United States Control of Petroleum Imports*, pp. 229–87.

[92]Ibid., p. 245.

to the detriment of oil-export power and hemisphere ally Venezuela. Venezuela's problem was not direct but indirect, however. Canada, with its surplus oil blocked from export to the United States, was considering a pipeline from its western producing region to its eastern consuming region; oil carried by that pipeline would displace Venezuelan fuel oil. This tested already strained U.S.-Venezuelan relations, as the mandatory import program tested U.S. and Canadian ties.[93] Diplomatic pressure, coupled with an obvious lack of national-defense justification for the status quo, led to Presidential Proclamation 3290 on April 30 to exempt petroleum "entering the United States by pipeline, motor carriers or rail from the country of production."[94] This applied to Mexican and Canadian overland imports, but Venezuela was indirectly helped because it retained its eastern Canadian market.

The first years of the MOIP experienced imports in excess of targeted amounts set by authorities. One official reported to President Eisenhower that "experience under the mandatory oil import program indicates that the present formulae have resulted in a ratio of petroleum imports to domestic crude production above that contemplated when the program was initiated."[95] This had several causes, one of which was the overland exemption granted five weeks into the program. Nominally taxed Canadian crude (tariffs ranged from $0.525 per barrel to $0.105 per barrel) found a ready market at northern-tier refineries, while Venezuelan imports were increased to cover Canadian demand. Exempt Canadian oil in Districts I–IV increased from under 50,000 barrels per day on the eve of Proclamation 3290 to 70,000 barrels per day by year-end and more thereafter.[96] OIA administrator Matthew Carson jawboned Canadian producers

---

[93]While Venezuela sought to unite major oil-exporting nations to increase bargaining power over price, Canadian officials regularly complained to U.S. officials and hinted at trade reprisals.

[94]24 *Fed. Reg.* 3527 (May 2, 1959).

[95]Quoted in William Barber, "The Eisenhower Energy Policy," p. 258.

[96]Rene Manes, *The Effects of United States Oil Import Policy on the Petroleum Industry,* p. 136; and Douglas Bohi and Milton Russell, *Limiting Oil Imports,* p. 106. This particularly disadvantaged oil firms in the Far West, and Union Oil petitioned Interior Secretary Stewart Udall to place a quota on exempt overland imports. *NPN,* October 1962, p. 88.

to compete on a "fair basis," given the "super-abundance of domestic crude oil."[97] Mexico, on the other hand, increased imports from 7,000 barrels per day to over 40,000 barrels per day in a striking circumvention labeled the "Brownsville Shuffle" and "el loophole." With the apparent blessing of U.S. officials who feared that Petroleos Mexicanos oil would otherwise go to Cuban markets, a practice developed whereby Mexican cargos shipped by tankers to Brownsville, Texas, were unloaded in bond (thus free from tariff or quota restrictions) for export on tank trucks and motored across the Rio Grande into Mexico. The drivers then made U-turns to reenter the United States with overland exempt oil, which was reloaded on tankers for East Coast shipment and consumption.[98]

In addition to Canadian and Mexican imports that inflated actual imports above quota levels, a variety of other factors hurt the goals of the program. The Bureau of Mines' overestimate of petroleum demand led to overstated quotas for District V.[99] Relatively lenient regulation of residual fuel oil to appease Venezuelan suppliers and East Coast consumers, the objections of coal interests to the contrary notwithstanding, led to large residual import increases from pre-1959 levels.[100] Self-interested oilmen exploited another gap by increasing sales from District V to Districts I–IV to increase the former's supply deficit, which imports were allowed to cover. In the first year of the mandatory quota, sales between the two areas doubled. Increases in natural-gas liquid production swelled the ratio of imports to domestic production by increasing the denominator in the quota formula. Liquids were included in the definition of petroleum demand, while their use correspondingly reduced oil demand.[101] Puerto Rico as a mini free-trade zone encouraged refinery

[97]Rene Manes, *The Effects of United States Oil Import Policy on the Petroleum Industry,* p. 136.

[98]Douglas Bohi and Milton Russell, *Limiting Oil Imports,* pp. 132–33.

[99]The first six-month estimate was 3.5 percent overstated; the second six-month estimate was 2.5 percent high. Rene Manes, *The Effects of United States Oil Import Policy on the Petroleum Industry,* p. 111.

[100]Allocations rose from under 350,000 barrels per day at the beginning of the program to over 600,000 in early 1961. See the table in ibid., p. 283. From 1961 to 1965, imports of residual rose over 40 percent. See Torleif Meloe, *United States Control of Petroleum Imports,* p. 95.

[101]Edward Shaffer, *The Oil Import Program of the United States* (New York: Frederick Praeger, 1968), p. 49.

construction and increased crude imports for feedstock; refined products surplus to local demand went unrestricted to the contiguous United States for consumption.[102] The Oil Import Appeals Board, comprised representatives of the Departments of the Interior, Defense, and Commerce, finally allowed exemptions based on gross inequity or hardship.

Other factors that contributed to imports above anticipated levels were increased refinery yields, which made imported crude translate into more product, Defense Department oil purchases abroad, overestimates of refinery runs to qualify for more quota tickets, and inventory drawdowns from stocks built up during the voluntary period.[103] "The victory for the producing interests represented by the mandatory program," observed Douglas Bohi and Milton Russell, "was slipping away."[104] Between the program's beginning and 1961, exempt crude imports as a percentage of total crude imports had doubled, and it continued to increase thereafter.[105]

Program Revision

In the 1960–65 period, countermeasures were taken to shore up the program. In this period, exempt crude imports increased from 8 percent to almost 21 percent of total crude imports. Among the most important revisions was Proclamation 3509 on November 30, 1962, which replaced the leaky 9-percent-of-estimated-demand rule, established in late 1960 by Proclamation 3386, with a ceiling of 12.2 percent of prospective crude-oil and gas-liquid production in Districts I–IV.[106] While replacing one set of estimation problems with another, this served as a more effective ceiling. An overestimation in the first period under the new rule resulted in a quota reduction pursuant to an earlier rule change.[107] Effective action was also taken to stem eastward crude sales from District V. In 1960, sales above

[102]Ibid., p. 80; and Kenneth Dam, "Implementation of Import Quotas," pp. 44–45.

[103]See Rene Manes, *The Effect of United States Oil Import Policy on the Petroleum Industry*, pp. 120–23; Douglas Bohi and Milton Russell, *Limiting Oil Imports*, p. 109; and Yoram Barzel and Christopher Hall, *The Political Economy of the Oil Import Quota* (Stanford, Calif.: Hoover Institution, 1977), p. 36.

[104]Douglas Bohi and Milton Russell, *Limiting Oil Imports*, p. 107.

[105]Anthony Copp, *Regulating Competition in Oil* (College Station: Texas A&M University Press, 1976), p. 89.

[106]25 *Fed. Reg.* 13945 (December 30, 1960); and 27 *Fed. Reg.* 11985 (December 5, 1962).

[107]25 *Fed. Reg.* 13945 (December 30, 1960).

1958 levels were docked from the total demand figure used to calculate import allowables. This reduced District V's import quota by 11,500 barrels per day in the first half of 1961.[108] A second measure to discourage opportunistic District I–IV buying was implemented June 10, 1963. Proclamation 3541 reduced quotas by the anticipated amount of District V purchases.[109] Together, these changes dampened trading activity, although market reasons were also at work.[110]

The sharp rise of imports of residual fuel oil brought Interior Department action. In early 1961, Districts II–IV were granted flexible ceilings, but a fixed ceiling, based on Bureau of Mines' estimates, was left for District I.[111] Market and consumer pressure forced upward adjustments, however, and by 1966, residual imports were effectively decontrolled. Political pressure created import quotas; political pressure also restrained their effectiveness.

The growth of Puerto Rican crude imports and product exports led to Proclamation 3693 on December 10, 1965. Quota assignments were limited to 1964 levels, and product exports were capped at 1965 levels with greater amounts subtracted from the next period's ceiling.[112] This corrected the "transshipment problem" that Puerto Rico as a de facto free-trade zone created.

The largest problem area of the MOIP was the overland exemption, in particular, crude imports from western Canada to northern-tier refineries. Jawboning since 1960 had been ineffective; imports from Canada rose over 150 percent between 1959 and 1962.[113] Proclamation 3509 of November 30, 1962, attempted to affect the quota limit by subtracting exempt crude from the 12.2 percent ceiling.[114] If this did not stem the flow of Canadian oil (which it did not), it would (and did) crowd out Middle Eastern oil. Mexican overland imports began

[108]Rene Manes, *The Effects of United States Oil Import Policy on the Petroleum Industry*, p. 141.

[109]28 *Fed. Reg.* 5931 (June 13, 1963).

[110]Edward Shaffer, *The Oil Import Program of the United States*, p. 74.

[111]26 *Fed. Reg.* 507 (January 20, 1961). The complicated quota allocations with this highly prized commodity are described in Douglas Bohi and Milton Russell, *Limiting Oil Imports*, pp. 150–51.

[112]30 *Fed. Reg.* 15459 (December 16, 1965). In early 1968, a ceiling was reestablished for Puerto Rican exports to the United States. 33 *Fed. Reg.* 1171 (January 30, 1968).

[113]Torleif Meloe, *United States Control of Petroleum Imports*, p. 97.

[114]27 *Fed. Reg.* 11985 (December 5, 1962).

Table 13.7
IMPORTS AND DOMESTIC PRODUCTION: 1959–65
(thousand barrels per day)

Year	Crude Imports	Product Imports	Total Imports	Domestic Production	Crude Imports/ Domestic Production
1959	965	814	1,780	8,180	11.8%
1960	1,015	799	1,815	7,987	12.7
1961	1,045	872	1,917	8,174	12.8
1962	1,126	955	2,082	8,353	13.5
1963	1,131	1,000	2,130	8,641	13.1
1964	1,198	1,060	2,259	8,793	13.6
1965	1,238	1,229	2,468	9,014	13.7

SOURCE: American Petroleum Institute, *Basic Petroleum Data Book*, 1973 ed., sec. 9, table 11, and sec. 10, table 1.

to mushroom with the "Brownsville Loop," which led the OIA in May 1961 to reduce daily imports from a high of 50,000 barrels per day to 30,000 barrels per day. The country quota replaced the formality of truck hauls.[115]

Through formulation of strict import goals and program revisions to keep ceiling excesses under check, more effective regulation was achieved. A measure of the effective operation of the program was that quota tickets remained valuable in the period. As table 13.7 indicates, the growth of imports was partly counteracted by increasing domestic production and so remained between 12 and 14 percent.[116]

Complexity and Demise: 1966–73 The MOIP was not significantly modified by domestic political favor in the first half of its existence. Exploited loopholes were closed more than new loopholes were opened. This would change. Beginning in 1966, the protectionist pie would be sliced into more pieces to cover more constituencies, and apportionment would reflect concerns unrelated to national security.

[115]Douglas Bohi and Milton Russell, *Limiting Oil Imports*, p. 133.

[116]The 12.2 percent quota rule applied to District I–IV production and thus was not applicable to the percentages in table 13.7.

On May 25, 1966, petrochemical plants in addition to refineries began to receive import quotas.[117] Petrochemical plants were included on grounds of equity; import rights effectively lowered crude costs for inland refineries, which petrochemical plants could not match. Of sixty-five petrochemical facilities qualifying for quotas, twenty-five already had import entitlements under refinery status.[118] With allocation within the 12.2 percent maximum, apportioned on a straight sliding scale of input capacity to avoid subsidizing smaller facilities, yearly petrochemical allocations steadily increased as a result of lobbying pressure. Beginning at 30,000 barrels per day in 1966, the quota reached 90,000 barrels per day in the early 1970s.[119]

Before and after the petrochemical inclusion, several special deals were made under the MOIP that further evidenced the politicization of the program. Pursuant to Proclamation 3693, which allowed the interior secretary to make "allocations ... which ... will promote substantial expansion of employment in Puerto Rico through industrial development," arrangements that were far removed from the original goals of the quota program were made between companies and the Interior Department. In return for constructing a petrochemical plant in Puerto Rico, where unemployment was running at 11 percent, Phillips Petroleum was granted import rights to 50,000 barrels per day of Western Hemisphere crude (within the 12.2 percent quota) and the right to export 24,800 barrels per day to the continental United States. In 1968, another agreement was signed with Sun Oil whereby, in return for a $135-million Puerto Rican investment in refinery and support facilities and payments of $0.25 per barrel into a conservation fund, Sun would be allowed to import 66,000 barrels per day and export 29,500 barrel per day to the United

---

[117]Oil Import Regulation 1 (Revision 5), May 25, 1966. Authority to include petrochemicals in import allocations was granted by President Johnson on December 10, 1965. 30 *Fed. Reg.* 15459 (December 16, 1965). This created controversy because firms without existing or planned petrochemical plants were disadvantaged. *NPN,* March 1965, p. 53.

[118]Edward Shaffer, *The Oil Import Program of the United States,* p. 155. This overlap and the definitional problems therein led to charges of "double dipping" with quota assignments. See Douglas Bohi and Milton Russell, *Limiting Oil Imports,* pp. 163–64.

[119]See the table in ibid., p. 122. For special problems of defining petrochemical plants under the program, see Cabinet Task Force on Oil Import Control, *The Oil Import Question,* pp. 329–32.

States, gasoline excluded.[120] Other similar deals followed with Union Carbide and Commonwealth Oil Refining.

The Virgin Islands also received preferential treatment. Proclamation 3820 on November 9, 1967, sanctioned an arrangement between Hess Oil and Chemical and the Department of the Interior whereby Hess could export 15,000 barrels per day to the contiguous United States in return for investing $100 million in refinery and petrochemical facilities and payments of $7,500 per day to a Virgin Island conservation fund.[121] The ten-year agreement, made after similar requests from other firms were rejected by Interior Secretary Stewart Udall, became controversial when Hess failed to live up to it. The original construction deadline of December 1970 found Hess disputing the fine points of the agreement, which remained unresolved through the end of the quota program.[122]

In 1968, several proposals were considered for building refineries in Guam in return for product sales to the U.S. military (in lieu of importation rights to the U.S. mainland because of distance). One proposal accepted under this arrangement led to the establishment of Guam Oil and Refining.[123]

The original national-defense justification of the MOIP was joined by yet another consideration on July 16, 1967, when Proclamation 3994 authorized "bonus" quotas to refiners "who manufacture . . . residual fuel oil to be used as fuel, the maximum sulfur content of which is acceptable to [government officials]."[124] Air pollution in Los Angeles County was a pressing concern, and bonus allowables were given to District V refineries manufacturing low-sulfur fuel in compliance with federal pollution standards. Bonus quotas were awarded in Districts I–IV in December 1968 to three firms with desulfurization facilities capable of turning high-sulfur residual into low-polluting products. In 1970, the Oil Import Appeals Board made allocations to two utilities, Commonwealth Edison (Chicago) and Detroit Edison, to combat air pollution in both cities. The ad hoc

---

[120]As with Phillips, the 12.2 percent guideline applied, which meant other importers would be penalized.

[121]32 *Fed. Reg.* 15701 (November 15, 1967).

[122]See Douglas Bohi and Milton Russell, *Limiting Oil Imports*, pp. 176–77.

[123]Ibid., pp. 177–78.

[124]32 *Fed. Reg.* 10547 (July 19, 1967).

system of quota awards, remarked Kenneth Dam, had become "institutionalized."[125]

A noticeable difference from the first years of the program was the increased political presence of consumer interests and government awareness of their concerns. In 1966–67, the government repeatedly jawboned the industry to hold crude and product prices steady.[126] From this time forward, the "inflationary" effects of oil-price increases under the MOIP would inspire quota liberalization for major oil products.

In March 1966, Secretary Udall announced that the residual-fuel-oil quota in District I would be relaxed to "eliminate the premiums that have attached to import licenses and which have had the effect of forcing the smaller consumers to pay higher prices for residual fuel oil."[127] Eligibility for new licenses was broadened, while existing firms were to receive allocations adequate to meet "all existing contracts." The new policy represented a victory for the country's major consumer market, the East Coast, and "a decisive political defeat for the coal industry."[128]

From the beginning of the MOIP, sentiment existed to decontrol asphalt, a petroleum product that had a high profile because of its use on public roads. On April 10, 1967, Proclamation 3279 gave discretionary authority to the interior secretary to permit unregulated asphalt imports.[129] The appeals board also broke precedent to award a hardship allocation for asphalt. By 1970, quota assignments for this product doubled.

Home-heating (no. 2 fuel) oil was the third product in the late 1960s to receive a relaxed quota assignment. In late 1967 and early 1968, over a dozen hardship quotas were allotted by the appeals board to individual marketers. Several ticket awards went to shut-down refineries to pay debts and assist them in reopening.[130] In June 1970 and November 1971, no. 2 fuel oil quotas above the 12.2 percent figure and above the previous Western Hemisphere ceiling were

---

[125]Kenneth Dam, "Implementation of Import Quotas," p. 42.

[126]Douglas Bohi and Milton Russell, *Limiting Oil Imports,* p. 140.

[127]31 *Fed. Reg.* 5071 (March 29, 1966).

[128]Kenneth Dam, "Implementation of Import Quotas," p. 37.

[129]32 *Fed. Reg.* 5919 (April 13, 1967).

[130]Allan Demaree, "Our Crazy, Costly Life with Oil Quotas," *Fortune,* June 1969, p. 182.

reviewed.[131] These actions and other program liberalizations were necessitated by a changing domestic supply-demand picture that pointed to a greater role for product imports.

Along with regulatory changes, there was administrative change. Early in his first term, President Nixon transferred control of the oil-import program from the Interior Department to the White House where it was soon merged with the Office of Oil and Gas. Also in the spring of 1969, Nixon announced a thorough review of the import program, which resulted in the 393-page study, *The Oil Import Question,* released in early 1970. The study recommended replacing the quota system with tariffs. Despite growing momentum against the current program, Nixon's first response was to make it more binding by reducing crude-oil exemptions. On March 10, 1970, a quota was reimposed on overland Canadian shipments, which provoked protest from northern-state congressmen concerned about higher prices and possible shortages due to fewer imports to their areas.[132] In 1970, exempt crude imports fell to 116,000 barrels per day or 11 percent of total imports from 381,000 barrels per day or 35 percent of total imports a year before.[133] In 1971, exempt crude fell to only 29,000 barrels per day, but allowable crude imports increased 20 percent over 1968–70 levels.[134] This was indicative of changing domestic market conditions under price controls—namely, stagnant domestic production and rapidly growing demand.

Nineteen seventy-one and 1972 saw a major phasedown and the virtual elimination of the MOIP—which arguably started in 1966 with de facto decontrol of imports of residual fuel oil to the East Coast and continued with special program inclusions (petrochemicals), bonus quotas (West Coast refiners, utility companies), special allocations (Puerto Rico, Virgin Islands, Guam), and product-import relaxation (asphalt, no. 2 fuel oil, residual fuel oil). In 1970, the benchmark 12.2 percent standard was relaxed to allow more crude oil and product importation.[135] In early 1971, asphalt imports were

---

[131]35 *Fed. Reg.* 10091 (June 19, 1971); and 36 *Fed. Reg.* 21397 (November 9, 1971).

[132]See *Administration of the Oil Import Program,* Hearings before the Subcommittee on Administrative Practice and Procedure of the Senate Committee on the Judiciary, 92d Cong., 2d sess. (Washington, D.C.: Government Printing Office, 1971).

[133]Anthony Copp, *Regulating Competition in Oil,* p. 89.

[134]Ibid.

[135]35 *Fed. Reg.* 16357 (October 20, 1970); and 35 *Fed. Reg.* 19391 (December 23, 1970).

decontrolled despite opposition from Atlantic Richfield, Humble, and Mobil.[136] In the same period, the crude-oil quota for Districts I–IV was raised by 100,000 barrels per day.[137] In 1972, special quotas for gasoline were awarded by the appeals board, and by early 1973 such special allocations became frequent.[138] Several 1972 proclamations virtually ended quota ceilings if additional supply was required by increased demand.[139] In January 1973, with spot shortages in evidence, no. 2 fuel oil joined asphalt and natural-gas liquids from Canada as imports free of quota ceilings, and pragmatic adjustments were made to the overall product quota to legalize higher import volumes.[140] With all these liberalizations, one step remained— removal of all quotas. Already, the Consumers Union and a coalition of New England governors had filed suit against the program, and with domestic production reaching capacity, product shortages a distinct possibility, and a growing gap between domestic supply and demand that only imports could bridge, the political climate allowed—indeed encouraged—major program changes.[141]

On April 18, 1973, President Nixon announced,

> The current Mandatory Oil Import Program is of virtually no benefit any longer. Instead, it has the very real potential of aggravating our supply problems, and it denies us the flexibility we need to deal quickly and efficiently with our import requirements.[142]

[136]36 *Fed. Reg.* 775 (January 16, 1971); 36 *Fed. Reg.* 24115 (December 21, 1971); and *NPN*, February 1971, p. 17.

[137]36 *Fed. Reg.* 24203 (December 22, 1971).

[138]Yoram Barzel and Christopher Hall, *The Political Economy of the Oil Import Quota*, p. 43.

[139]37 *Fed. Reg.* 9543 (May 12, 1972); 37 *Fed. Reg.* 19115 (September 19, 1972); and 37 *Fed. Reg.* 28043 (December 20, 1972).

[140]38 *Fed. Reg.* 1719 (January 18, 1973).

[141]Despite growing obsolescence of import quotas, stubborn support remained in early 1973—such as independent producers organized as the Committee to Support the Mandatory Oil Import Program, privileged refiners, and top administration advisers, including John Ehrlichman and William Simon. *OGJ*, December 25, 1972, p. 45; February 5, 1973, p. 32; and February 26, 1973, p. 30. The *Oil & Gas Journal* editorialized against ending import regulation. *OGJ*, February 12, 1973, p. 27.

[142]Message from the President of the United States Concerning Energy Resources, April 18, 1973. Reprinted in *Energy Crisis*, ed. Lester Sobel, 4 vols. (New York: Facts on File, 1974), vol. 1, p. 148.

The same day, Proclamation 4210 replaced the MOIP with a tariff ("license") system to revert to pre-1959 protectionism.[143]

The demise of the MOIP was not due to convenience but necessity. Spurting domestic demand, coupled with stagnant domestic output, fostered in part by artificially low prices under Nixon's price-control program, made the choice relaxed importation or shortage.[144] Market-demand proration factors reached 100 percent in Kansas and Oklahoma (December 1971), Louisiana and New Mexico (January 1972), and Texas (April 1973). There was no more slack in the system. By late 1973, in fact, the landed cost of crude imports exceeded domestic crude prices for the first time in history.[145] Amid these developments, national-security considerations were a distant, secondary consideration. Table 13.8 shows the radically changed import situation in the early 1970s.

License-Fee Regulation: 1973–79

Proclamation 4210

Under authority of the Trade Expansion Act of 1962, Proclamation 4210 on April 18, 1973, ended fourteen years of quota regulation. The long-standing tariff structure, now part of GATT—$0.105 per barrel for most grades of crude oil, $0.525 per barrel for gasoline, and $0.84 per barrel for lubricating oil—was replaced with "license fees" similar in all but name.[146] Effective May 1, crude oil came under a $0.105 per barrel fee, residual fuel oil and middle distillates under a $0.15 per barrel fee, and gasoline and similar products under a $0.52 per barrel fee. These fees were to be increased in October 1973 to $0.13, $0.206, and $0.545 per barrel, respectively; in October 1974 to $0.18, $0.42, and $0.595 per barrel; in May 1975 to $0.21, $0.52,

---

[143]38 *Fed. Reg.* 9645 (April 19, 1973).

[144]An Interior Department memorandum dated December 8, 1972, stated, "The U.S. government will respond to every impending crude and product crisis by raising the import quotas." Quoted in Neil de Marchi, "Energy Policy under Nixon: Mainly Putting Out Fires," in *Energy Policy in Perspective*, p. 422.

[145]See table 9.9, pp. 522–28, for a comparison of average import and domestic crude prices.

[146]Charles Owens of the Cost of Living Council (established under Phase II of Nixon's price-control program) substituted the words "license fee" for "tariffs" in anticipation of a court challenge. Neil de Marchi, "Energy Policy under Nixon," p. 424. Behind tariff control were William Simon of the Oil Policy Committee, energy consultant Charles DiBona, and Treasury Secretary George Schultz. *OGJ*, March 26, 1973, p. 47.

Table 13.8
IMPORTS AND DOMESTIC PRODUCTION: 1966–72
(thousand barrels per day)

Year	Crude Imports	Product Imports	Total Imports	Domestic Production	Crude Imports/ Domestic Production
1966	1,225	1,348	2,573	9,579	12.8%
1967	1,128	1,409	2,537	10,220	11.0
1968	1,291	1,549	2,840	10,638	12.1
1969	1,409	1,757	3,166	10,839	13.0
1970	1,324	2,095	3,419	11,314	11.7
1971	1,681	2,245	3,926	11,172	15.4
1972	2,222	2,532	4,754	11,243	19.8

SOURCE: American Petroleum Institute, *Basic Petroleum Data Book*, 1973 ed., sec. 9, table 11, and sec. 10, table 1.

and $0.63 per barrel; and in October 1975 to $0.21, $0.63, and $0.63 per barrel. Import licenses were awarded by the Office of Oil and Gas upon payment of a fee. The fees did not apply to bonded imports or imports under January 1973 quota levels.

Quota levels for fee-free imports were 2,952,000 barrels per day in Districts I–IV, 950,000 barrels per day in District V, and 227,221 barrels per day in Puerto Rico. Canada was restricted to exporting 960,000 barrels per day to Districts I–IV and 280,000 barrels per day to District V. Mexico could export 32,500 barrels per day to the United States fee free. Residual oil was given special quotas apart from the rest of the program: 2.9 million barrels per day in District I, 42,000 barrels per day in Districts II–IV, and 75,600 barrels per day in District V. Imports above this level were taxable as were phased-in amounts below the quota. In seven years, all imports were scheduled to become taxable.[147] Historically protected refiners not only benefited from crude fees that were below product fees but from a license-fee exemption on 75 percent of throughput for five years. Moreover, refiners and marketers were eligible for the (Office

[147]The scale-down began on April 30, 1974, when 90 percent of January quotas were fee free and continued on April 30, 1975, at 80 percent; April 30, 1976, at 65 percent; April 30, 1977, at 50 percent; April 30, 1978, at 20 percent; and April 30, 1979, at 0 percent.

of Oil and Gas) appeals board's 50,000 barrels per day allocation of duty-free import quotas if hardship could be proven.

Political modification was a defining characteristic of the new program as the above differentials indicate. A number of other special provisions were made. Asphalt, butane, ethane, and propane were duty free. Canadian crude was tax free for one year (through May 1, 1974), after which a $0.57 per barrel fee for gasoline and a $0.03 per barrel fee for other products, with escalations toward parity with other product imports by May 1, 1980, applied. Puerto Rican imports were subject to regular fees, but exports to the U.S. mainland were not. The Virgin Islands imported duty free but exported to the United States under tariffs. Other exceptions for "small quantities" could be made by the interior secretary. These special-interest provisions led Thomas Preston to comment:

> By 1973, the Mandatory Program had become so complex and so torn by the pressures of diverse interests that no one could honestly maintain that it was a program with a distinct philosophy and direction. Yet incredibly, the license fee system was established with the same kind of crippling special interest provisions. Just as with price protection or the fee-free allocations, the accommodation of special interests reflects an effort to by-pass normal market forces.[148]

The new program, commented Oil Policy Committee chairman William Simon, was intended to "maintain import control and accountability without restricting the flow of essential oil into the United States."[149] Simon's message was that import quotas could reappear should idle domestic capacity and a buyer's market reappear. This would not occur. Instead, shortages would intensify and oil prices would quadruple between October 1973 and January 1974 to dilute tariffs to levels below regulatory intention. Revision would be necessary.

Revision and Termination

During the second half of 1973 and 1974, the new program went through a number of minor revisions that expanded fee exemptions for refiners and marketers as first purchasers of oil imports. In June

---

[148]Thomas Preston, "National Security and Oil Import Regulation: The License Fee Approach," *Virginia Journal of International Law* (Winter 1975): 417.

[149]*OGJ*, April 23, 1973, p. 20.

1973, import fees were relaxed for Canadian imports and imports of residual fuel oil above quota levels into District I. Fee prepayment was replaced by thirty-day payments, and new exemptions were awarded for American Samoa, Guam, the Virgin Islands, and foreign trade zones.[150] Imports from Canada, however, were temporarily halted by Canadian authorities who wished to redirect supply to home markets. Upon resumption of Canadian exports several months later, an export tax was applied, which began at $0.40 per barrel on October 1, 1973, and increased to $1.90 per barrel two months later.[151] Nationalism was joining the last remnants of protectionism as petroleum became more scarce.

On January 22, 1975, President Ford, under authority of the Trade Expansion Act of 1962, placed a supplemental license fee on petroleum imports and increased existing fees to promote domestic production and reduce dependence on imports.[152] The surcharge was $1.00 per barrel for imports of crude and all products except asphalt and natural-gas derivatives, effective February 1, 1975. Two similar increases, to $2.00 per barrel and $3.00 per barrel, respectively, were scheduled on the first day of the two following months. Product imports received rebates of $1.00 per barrel, $1.40 per barrel, and $1.80 per barrel to reduce the effective supplemental fee to zero in February, $0.60 per barrel in March, and $1.20 per barrel in April. Existing tariffs—$0.525 or $0.105 per barrel for crude imports, $0.105 per barrel for kerosene and naphtha, $0.525 per barrel for gasoline and fuel oil, and $0.84 per barrel for lubrication oil—continued to encourage domestic refining. These taxes were allowed as credit against other fees.[153] Another amendment allowed licenses to be sold if the sales were approved by the director of oil imports.[154] The new tariffs, coming on top of record import prices, were not intended as domestic incentives. (Judging from wellhead price controls, authorities were trying to rein in incentives.) The motivation was to force

[150]*OGJ*, June 25, 1973, p. 61.

[151]*OGJ*, September 24, 1973, p. 90; October 1, 1973, p. 33; October 22, 1973, p. 29; and November 12, 1973, p. 100.

[152]40 *Fed. Reg.* 3965 (January 23, 1975); and 40 *Fed. Reg.* 4771 (January 31, 1975). Ford's action was upheld in *FEA* v. *Algonquin SNG, Inc.,* 426 U.S. 548 (1976).

[153]40 *Fed. Reg.* 40143 (September 2, 1975).

[154]40 *Fed. Reg.* 59195 (December 22, 1975).

an antagonistic Congress to formulate acceptable alternative legislation.[155] After the first $1.00 per barrel installment was activated on February 1, the second installment was postponed several times before taking effect on June 1 at $2.00 per barrel for crude and $0.60 per barrel for products. The third and final increase never became effective.[156] Effective September 1, the $0.60 per barrel product fee was temporarily rescinded, and the $2.00 per barrel crude supplemental fee was revoked pursuant to the Energy Policy and Conservation Act of 1975.[157]

After the complicated license-fee fine-tuning in 1975, there remained the reestablished $0.63 per barrel fee on unfinished oil and products and the $0.21 per barrel levy on crude oil and natural-gas products. Over the next years, these amounts remained unchanged, but fee-free quota amounts, standing at 80 percent of 1973 import levels, were diminished. For 1976–77, the fee-free quota amount was reduced to 65 percent; for 1977–78 it fell to 50 percent; and in early 1979 it dropped to 20 percent except for imports of residual fuel oil into District I.[158] "Hardship" relief, in the form of fee-exempt licenses, was granted to importers of residual fuel oil on September 30, 1977.[159]

Growing supply problems and looming shortages led President Carter to abolish the fees effective April 1, 1979, and set import ceilings above which tariffs would be reactivated.[160] Set at 8.2 million barrels per day, the ceiling was so far above actual amounts as to make it superfluous. Only the formality of obtaining a license and incremental tariffs stood in the way of unregulated import trade, to the chagrin of refiners who benefited from license-fee differentials

[155]For discussion of the political seesaw between Ford, northern-state governors, and Congress, see *Energy Crisis*, vol. 2 pp. 114–15.

[156]40 *Fed. Reg.* 10437 (March 6, 1975); 40 *Fed. Reg.* 19421 (May 5, 1975); and 40 *Fed. Reg.* 23429 (May 30, 1975).

[157]Public Law 94-163, 89 Stat. 871 (1975). 41 *Fed. Reg.* 1037 (January 6, 1976).

[158]41 *Fed. Reg.* 17510 (April 26, 1976); 42 *Fed. Reg.* 20813 (April 22, 1976); 43 *Fed. Reg.* 59458 (December 20, 1978); and 44 *Fed. Reg.* 17960 (March 23, 1979).

[159]42 *Fed. Reg.* 54255 (October 5, 1977); and 43 *Fed. Reg.* 58077 (December 12, 1978).

[160]44 *Fed. Reg.* 21243 (April 10, 1979). The suspension was extended for additional six-month periods. 44 *Fed. Reg.* 39096 (June 20, 1979); 44 *Fed. Reg.* 72224 (December 13, 1979); and 45 *Fed. Reg.* 41899 (June 23, 1980).

and fee-free allocations, as they earlier had from import-quota assignments.[161]

Subsequent Developments

After the spring of 1979, all was not quiet on the import front. After the November 1979 seizure of the U.S. embassy in Iran, President Carter banned Iranian imports.[162] In March 1980, Carter briefly reimposed import fees on crude oil, and in June, licensing for crude oil and gasoline was extended.[163]

Allocation programs under the amended Emergency Petroleum Allocation Act influenced imports. The buy-sell program directly involved Canadian crude oil.[164] The entitlements program encouraged imports by lowering foreign-oil prices on a postentitlements basis—the opposite of what tariffs and quotas were designed to do. Regulation under the Emergency Petroleum Allocation Act also subjected entering imports to allocation regulation.[165]

In March 1982, President Reagan banned Libyan imports because of the alleged terrorist activities of Colonel Moammar Khadafy. However, crude exchanges in international markets and product imports refined in part from Libyan feedstock created leaks in the embargo.[166] The next intervention with imports was a tariff increase to discourage high levels of semirefined Chinese gasoline imports into the United States. Effective January 1, 1984, the U.S. Customs Service reclassified this product from motor gasoline to its chemical compounds, which increased the tax from $0.0125 to $0.088 per gallon. The announcement coincided with a visit to Peking by Reagan, who, ironically, was advocating greater trade between the two countries.[167]

---

[161]For the small refiners' displeasure over the suspension of tariff protectionism, see *OGJ*, May 28, 1979, p. 48.

[162]44 *Fed. Reg.* 65581 (November 12, 1979).

[163]Presidential Proclamation 4762, 94 Stat. 3760 (1980). 45 *Fed. Reg.* 39237 (June 10, 1980).

[164]See chapter 20, p. 1201.

[165]Issues concerning first sales in U.S. commerce are described in Robert Goodwin, "Regulation of Oil Imports and Exports," in *Petroleum Regulation Handbook*, ed. Joseph Bell (New York: Executive Enterprises, 1980), pp. 237–39.

[166]*OGJ*, March 8, 1982, p. 104, and March 15, 1982, p. 47.

[167]See *NPN*, September 1984, p. 28.

Table 13.9
OIL IMPORTS AND EXPORTS: 1973–84
(thousand barrels per day)

Year	Crude Oil Imports	Crude Oil Exports	Refined Products Imports	Refined Products Exports	Total Imports	Total Exports
1973	3,244	2	3,012	229	6,256	231
1974	3,477	3	2,635	218	6,112	221
1975	4,105	6	1,951	204	6,056	209
1976	5,287	8	2,026	215	7,313	223
1977	6,615	50	2,193	193	8,708	243
1978	6,356	158	2,008	204	8,364	362
1979	6,519	235	1,937	236	8,456	471
1980	5,263	287	1,646	258	6,909	545
1981	4,396	228	1,599	367	5,995	595
1982	3,488	236	1,625	579	5,113	815
1983	3,329	164	1,722	575	5,051	739
1984	3,426	181	2,011	541	5,437	722

SOURCE: American Petroleum Institute, *Basic Petroleum Data Book,* 1973 ed., sec. 9, table 11, and sec. 10, table 1.

Large import-fee increases to reduce reliance on foreign petroleum in the decontrol period were proposed without success. In 1980, Carter implemented a $4.62 per barrel tariff on gasoline as a "conservation fee," which brought court action and a congressional override.[168] In 1982, a proposal to tax imports at $5.00 per barrel to raise between $8 billion and $20 billion in revenue to reduce an anticipated fiscal year 1983 budget deficit of $150 billion, supported by members of the Reagan administration, was defeated by Congress.[169]

The post-1973 period was a radical break from the past. With domestic output stagnant, imports became the marginal supplier to meet record domestic consumption. Exports, on the other hand, virtually disappeared. Table 13.9 highlights U.S. import dependence that peaked in 1979 before declining thereafter.

Modest fees contained in the GATT remain through 1984: $0.105 per barrel for crude oil ($0.0525 per barrel under 25 degrees API gravity), $0.105 per barrel for kerosene and naphtha, $0.525 per

[168]45 *Fed. Reg.* 22864 (April 3, 1980); and Public Law 96-264, 94 Stat. 439 (1980).

[169]*OGJ,* April 19, 1982, p. 60, and April 26, 1982, p. 102.

barrel for gasoline and fuel oil, and $0.84 per barrel for lubricating oil. These most-favored-nation"rates were less than for certain communist nations such as the USSR that were subject to duties of $0.21 per barrel for crude oil, kerosene, and naphtha and $1.05 per barrel for gasoline. Imports of natural gas, asphalt, coke, and petroleum waxes were duty free for all nations.

With declining crude imports and growing diversification of foreign oil sources in the 1980s, national security as a rationale for protectionism faded, but weakening oil prices and poor refining margins renewed industry interest in higher import fees with appropriate differentials between crude and products. The formation in late 1984 of the Independent Refiners Coalition to lobby for higher gasoline tariffs is an example of a long domestic-industry tradition—competitive relief through government intervention at the international border.

Oil Protectionism Reconsidered

Oil Protectionism in Theory

In a market economy, production tends toward areas where relative production costs are lowest, net of transportation costs to market. For most of oil's first century, the United States was the world production leader as well as its consumption leader. As U.S. capital and expertise were exported to find oil abroad, first in South America and later in the Middle East, tension was created between low-cost foreign oil and higher cost oil from mature (and prorated) domestic deposits. This inspired protectionist sentiment among producers wed to marginal domestic oil deposits. To justify trade restrictions on foreign oil as more than self-serving, the best rationale was sought. The national-security argument was born.

As oilmen found a subterfuge for domestic proration in conservation, so they found "national security" a rationale for protectionism. The father of national-security oil protectionism was Wirt Franklin. Beginning in 1930, the founder of the Independent Petroleum Association of America argued before Congress that imports were closing thousands of stripper wells and thus impairing national defense. The argument emphasized that peacetime domestic output had to be maintained in case it was suddenly needed in a wartime or emergency situation in which the United States was isolated from foreign supply sources. Franklin's plea had two policy implications.

Marginal domestic wells, which would otherwise be retired by lower cost foreign fields, had to be protected to assure their maximum contribution. Second, incentives for exploration and additions to proven reserves had to be maintained. Both aspects required oil-import restrictions to create a domestic price structure high enough to make marginal domestic deposits and new discoveries the incremental domestic supplier.[170]

The national-security argument for petroleum protectionism invites rigorous censure. It was an open secret in the oil patch that national security was the public-relations side of government intervention desired and designed to protect investments dependent on the proration-maintained domestic price of oil.[171] Indeed, national-security considerations can be used equally well against trade barriers and for open trade. International tensions that create national-security uncertainty can be attributed initially to trade barriers in many cases. The oil-export ban against Japan in 1941 that precipitated the attack on Pearl Harbor and the 1959 quota regulation that led Venezuela to call the first meeting of oil-exporting countries are vivid examples. Free trade, in contrast, contributes to international goodwill, fosters interdependence of buyer and seller, and increases predictability of supply. A stated aim of U.S. trade policy has been ''to promote national security by expanding world trade'' for these reasons.[172]

Open access to major consuming markets, furthermore, encourages international petroleum development to diversify world production and increase the range of substitution when a region's supply is cut off. The United States has come to rely on foreign oil for foreign wars to minimize transportation cost and otherwise simplify

---

[170]A third national-security argument for maximum emergency production was the availability of excess (''surge'') capacity from restrictions on well output. For a critical look at this rationale for wellhead regulation, see chapter 4, pp. 190–91.

[171]A Nobel prize–winning economist described the national-security claim as ''a remark calculated to elicit uproarious laughter at the Petroleum Club.'' George Stigler, *The Citizen and the State* (Chicago: University of Chicago Press, 1975), p. 115.

[172]Cabinet Task Force on Oil Import Control, *The Oil Import Question*, p. 4. President Eisenhower himself said four years before he invoked the quota program, ''It is essential for the security of the United States and the rest of the free world that the United States take the leadership in promoting the achievement of those high levels of trade that will bring to all the economic strength upon which the freedom and security of all depend.'' Ibid., p. 4.

procurement. This was true during the Korea conflict and more true during the Vietnam War.

The "drain America first" consequence of oil protectionism lessens future self-sufficiency by exploiting domestic reserves before their economic time. Conservationist nonuse was once a public-interest argument, as was foreign oil development before abundant supply made regulatory price maintenance the top concern of domestic producers. Clarence Randall, chairman of the Council on Foreign Economic Policy, criticized the national-security argument during the Mandatory Oil Import Program years as follows:

> I think that the placing of any restrictions on oil imports is wrong. . . . Ostensibly, the program is based on national security, but if domestic petroleum reserves are required for our defense in war, or our recovery after war, I do not see how we advance toward that objective by using up our reserves. It seems to me that our policy should be to conserve that which we have, rather than to take measures which would cause our supplies to be exhausted more rapidly.[173]

The protectionist mentality underestimates the market-adjustment process that would cushion a sudden import cutoff.[174] When foreign supply is uncertain, incentives are created to enlarge inventory positions and enter into contingency agreements. A price premium also emerges to encourage conservation. New drilling programs, if only development wells from shallow prospects, become increasingly economical. All of these rational entrepreneurial responses protect consumers and the economy as a whole from the shock of a sudden import disruption.

Once a cutoff occurs, anticipatory entrepreneurship is joined by ameliorative entrepreneurship to "cushion the blow," so to speak. To the extent surge-production capacity is still available, it will be used to take advantage of high prices. Substitutions will be made to natural gas, coal, and purchased power in industrial and electric-generation markets to minimize the amount of oil burned. Marginal consumption by motorists and home owners will be eliminated by higher prices. These supply-demand adjustments bridge the gap

[173]Quoted in William Barber, "The Eisenhower Energy Policy," p. 247.

[174]This paragraph parallels some arguments made against crude-oil price regulation and the Strategic Petroleum Reserve. See chapter 9, pp. 528–32, and chapter 17, pp. 1041–47.

until longer run adjustments (new reserves, fuel-efficient technologies, new import supply networks) can be made. These long-run adjustments, to repeat an earlier point, would be facilitated by international goodwill, greater international supply-substitution capability, and more domestic drilling prospects in the historical absence of protectionism.

Finally, the protectionist argument entirely overlooks political modification of "national-security" regulation that is always likely and historically has occurred. The Cabinet Task Force on Oil Import Control found in its final report on the Mandatory Oil Import Program that

> the fixed quota limitations that have been in effect for the past ten years, and the system of implementation that has grown up around them, bear no reasonable relation to current requirements for protection either of the national economy or of essential oil consumption. The level of restriction is arbitrary and the treatment of secure foreign sources internally inconsistent. The present system has spawned a host of special arrangements and exceptions for purposes essentially unrelated to the national security.[175]

As is the case with every other nonmarket program, well-intentioned people who call for national-security protectionism must consider the risk of fatal political modification, other arguments notwithstanding.

On a different plane, there are the microeconomic and macroeconomic costs of tariff or quota protectionism that make it *unaffordable*. Although the precise extent of the rise in domestic oil prices caused by import regulation cannot be estimated, there is a significant pass-through to all energy users, particularly to energy-intensive consumers. A major tariff constitutes a multi-billion-dollar wealth transfer from oil consumers to oil producers and local, state, and federal governments (as tax collectors). While the microeconomic costs of such a policy can be gauged by identifying all the particular industries hard hit by higher energy bills (transportation, construction, road building, agriculture, chemical manufacturing, petroleum marketing), there are significant macroeconomic costs of forgone output and its interrelated negative effect on employment, prices, and economic growth. The Energy Information Administration, in a 1982

---

[175]Cabinet Task Force on Oil Import Control, *The Oil Import Question*, p. 128.

study of the effects of a $5.00 per barrel fee, concluded that federal collections would be diluted by a 1 percent rise in the Consumer Price Index and a 0.3 percent increase in unemployment. Regarding pass-through, a Congressional Budget Office study in the same year estimated that two-thirds of a tariff would be borne by domestic consumers and one-third by the exporting countries—$0.08 and $0.04 per gallon, respectively, for a $5 per barrel tariff.[176] Assuming this pass-through, domestic consumers (including the nation's largest consumer, the U.S. government) would incur approximately $18 billion a year in higher energy costs based on consumption of 15 million barrels per day.

The cost for domestic firms is magnified when competing internationally because world oil prices become depressed as imports kept from the United States flood the next-best markets. The domestic-foreign oil price differential created by oil tariffs and quotas thus represent a *tax* on exports and a *subsidy* for imports.

In addition to the above-discussed industry-oriented "national-security" argument, a decidedly academic argument has emerged in recent years to justify oil tariffs. Some economists have calculated that oil imports have a "social cost" greater than the price actually paid by importers. The *negative externality* of oil imports, measured by the divergence of private cost and social cost (called the "oil import premium"), is the result of the market's *underestimating*, or simply not being able to fully prepare for, import disruptions and consequent price "shocks" that impose such great costs on the economy.[177] To remove the externality, an "optimal" tariff is recommended to equate private with social costs. By imposing such a tariff, the United States "blunts" any disruption by having effective consumption and production habits in place.

Some of the arguments against the oil import premium rationale for tariffs overlap with the national-security argument. The market *can* be expected to alertly interpret foreign events affecting oil imports and anticipate worst-case events, given full profit incentives. Entrepreneurs in the 1970s, on the other hand, did *not* have adequate

[176]*OGJ*, April 19, 1982, p. 60.

[177]See Douglas Bohi and W. David Montgomery, *Oil Prices, Energy Security, and Import Policy* (Baltimore: Johns Hopkins University Press, 1982), chap. 5. Also see the variable import fee proposal in S. Fred Singer, "Restrictions on Oil Imports?" in *Free Market Energy*, ed. S. Fred Singer (New York: Universe Books, 1984), pp. 99–117.

profit incentives to anticipate and combat oil shocks because of pervasive price and allocation regulation. Economists who feel strongly that entrepreneurs cannot be trusted in this regard must explain why their knowledge is superior to the market, and indeed why "oil import premium" estimates have ranged all over the map.[178] The subjective calculation of the externality, assuming that qualitatively it exists (which is very much open to question), should make one cautious about policy recommendation. Moreover, as mentioned, there is the political problem that could turn an "accurate" estimate into "inaccurate" implementation.

Historical Record

The experienced consequences of oil protectionism reinforce the foregoing theoretical concerns. Each of the three experiences with oil tariffs and quotas has been counterproductive to the national interest.

Product protection for Standard Oil from inception until 1909 was a supreme irony for government policy that was otherwise dedicated to restraining trusts. In retrospect, the tariff was not crucial to Standard's success; the trust lost as an exporter much of what it gained from reduced competition from Russian refiners. Consumers, however, were unambiguously disadvantaged.

Protectionism in the 1930s was simply dollars and cents for domestic producers. Little pretense was made that tariffs had any major purpose other than to increase the landed cost of foreign oil to improve the competitive position of domestic prices. Foreign oil was no different from domestic hot oil; both were threats to the fragile domestic price structure.[179] The gain of domestic producers and government treasuries was the loss of consumers, importing majors, and foreign oil exporters. Ironically, only a decade before, the U.S. government had actively encouraged oil firms to establish foreign production to augment "dwindling" domestic supply. The policy reversal from State Department support for oil production in foreign lands to federal tariff barriers mocked industry entrepreneurship

---

[178]Douglas Bohi and W. David Montgomery, referring to the estimation problem as "more difficult than many expected," found sixteen estimates ranging from "zero to well over $100 per barrel, depending on assumptions and methodology." Bohi and Montgomery, *Oil Prices, Energy Security, and Import Policy*, p. 3.

[179]See *OW*, September 10, 1934, p. 10.

and reduced incentives to internationalize the petroleum industry to develop oil reserves in order of least cost.[180] Implementation of mandatory quotas in 1959 took protectionism a step beyond simple tariffs. The new program traded simplicity for complexity to mask the true effects of the program. A tariff or even cash payments for quota rights would have allowed quick calculation of the money transfers involved, which would have fomented controversy at a time when consumerism was maturing as a political force. Nonetheless, the redistribution of wealth under the fifteen-year program—in the tens of billions of dollars—was from domestic consumers, historic importers, foreign oil interests, and various transportation-related import interests (tankers, harbors, pipelines) to domestic producers, related service and supply industries, inland (nonhistoric) refiners, state and federal treasuries, and competing fuels (coal and natural gas).[181] Few sectors of the petroleum business were unaffected. Until 1973, the exploration and production phase was protected from imports that were around a dollar per barrel cheaper. Refineries, as detailed in chapter 20, received preferential treatment, especially small inland facilities.[182] Pipeline investments based on unregulated imports encountered profitability problems as new patterns of distribution developed under protectionism.[183] Marketers of gasoline and fuel oil found their relative competitive situations changed with the ebb and flow of program modifications and hardship rulings. In a publicized example of pure economic waste, importers of Mexican oil expended an estimated $15 million in transportation and handling expenses in Brownsville to qualify that oil for exempt status as an overland import.[184] For the industry as a whole, political uncertainty clouded major capital commitments,

---

[180]For an example of a major distress sale of foreign production properties as a result of the tariff, see Rene Manes, *The Effects of United States Oil Import Policy on the Petroleum Industry,* pp. 56–57.

[181]In 1962, the annual cost of oil quotas was estimated by M. A. Adelman at $4 billion. Adelman, "Efficiency of Resource Use in Crude Petroleum," *Southern Economic Journal* (October 1964): 105, 116, 122. The Cabinet Task Force on Oil Import Control estimated the cost at $5 billion for 1969 alone. *The Oil Import Question,* p. 22.

[182]See chapter 20, pp. 1160–75.

[183]George Wolbert, *U.S. Oil Pipe Lines* (Washington, D.C.: American Petroleum Institute, 1979), p. 153.

[184]Allan Demaree, "Our Crazy, Costly Life with Oil Quotas," p. 175.

and unnecessary costs were incurred to interpret and comply with the regulations and to maintain an active political presence.

Other regulatory costs and consequences of the Mandatory Oil Import Program are important. The program literally saved market-demand proration from extinction. On the eve of quota regulation, allowables in Texas, Oklahoma, Louisiana, and other oil states were at a low point and falling. Producers were becoming very restless. A continuation of import trends would have forced state commissions to either shut in domestic output more (a major political risk) or abandon proration altogether. The latter would have forced the belated retirement of many marginal wells and the consolidation of the independent sector. A mighty step toward free-market production and concentrated ownership to rationalize output under the rule of capture could have occurred. The fact that import regulation prevented these fundamental and necessary changes is a major cost of Eisenhower's fateful decree.

Another consequence of unprecedented peacetime federal intervention in the oil industry was a bonanza for "well-connected Washington lawyers and influential politicians."[185] The benefits for natural-gas lawyers from the Natural Gas Act were joined by benefits for oil lawyers from the Mandatory Oil Import Program.

A lingering negative consequence of U.S. petroleum protectionism was the awakening of oil-exporting giants by the 1959 quota, which locked out imports and depressed world prices. Diplomatic protests by Britain, the Netherlands, and Venezuela greeted MOIP; and Venezuela, as mentioned, organized the first meeting of what became the Organization of Petroleum Exporting Countries (OPEC) and provided crucial leadership in the early years of the organization.[186] As the MOIP developed, Middle Eastern countries found themselves more and more discriminated against by Western Hemisphere concessions that crowded out their allotment.

A second consequence of the mandatory quotas and license fees was a domestic price-world price differential that signaled foreign exporters that their oil was priced below what consumers in an open market were prepared to pay. This spurred the formation of OPEC

---

[185]Ibid., p. 180.

[186]See Douglas Bohi and Milton Russell, *Limiting Oil Imports*, pp. 134–35. Also see E. B. Brossard, *Petroleum: Politics and Power* (Tulsa: PennWell Books, 1983), pp. 63–64.

and invited renegotiation of concessions granted to U.S. companies, even unilateral contract breaking, to eliminate price discrimination. This led to price equalization in the early 1970s and much greater increases later; the oil-exporting community would do to U.S. consumers in the 1970s what U.S. regulation had done in the 1950s and 1960s.

Appendix to Chapter 13: Regulation of Oil Exports

As the long history of import regulation suggests, governmental concern over petroleum exports has been relatively infrequent. Exports, generally, have been welcomed to dispose of abundant domestic supply. There have been exceptions, however. In wartime, domestic supply has been licensed to guide its distribution in channels deemed proper by authorities; in peacetime, export control has been adjunct to a wider regulatory purpose.

Standard Oil and Early Oil Exporting

Two years after the Drake well in 1859, U.S. firms began to export oil across the Atlantic to Britain. In the next decades, the United States became the world's leading petroleum exporter with crude oil and refined products leaving the harbors of New York, Philadelphia, Baltimore, and Boston for Europe and other continents. Kerosene as an illuminating oil was the major product, along with lubricating oil and lesser specialty products. Crude oil was also a major export to foreign refineries. Petroleum imports, on the other hand, were displaced by growing volumes of domestic crude oil and refinery construction in the Pennsylvania oil region.

In contrast to government intervention, *self-regulation* of exports developed as a consequence of foreign-buyer pressure. The New York Produce Exchange established forty-four rules by 1874 to certify contract terms and monitor quality. Shipping had to be in barrels of specified quality, and illuminating oil, a safety hazard, had to be "standard white or better with a fire test of 110 degrees Fahrenheit or higher."[1]

---

[1]Harold Williamson and Arnold Daum, *The Age of Illumination, 1859 to 1899*, vol. 1 of *The American Petroleum Industry*, (Evanston, Ill.: Northwestern University Press, 1959), p. 503.

At landing points, U.S. oil faced a variety of import taxes and safety regulations.[2] Differential tariffs were also enacted by some countries to protect home refineries, which favored crude exports rather than product imports from the United States.

As was the case domestically, early export activity came to be dominated by Standard Oil investments. "It seemed absolutely necessary," stated John Rockefeller, "to extend the market for oil by exporting to foreign countries."[3] Overcoming "tariffs . . . local prejudice, and strange customs," Standard purchased oil-exporting firms and established new foreign marketing points to gain a secure foothold beginning in the 1870s.[4]

Standard's interest in a world market was strictly pecuniary— with highly social results. One company agent, attempting to secure export points in the Far East, wrote to the governor general of India:

> I may claim for petroleum that it is something of a civilizer, as promoting among the poorest classes of these countries a host of evening occupations, industrial, educational, and recreative, not feasible prior to its introduction; and if it has brought a fair reward to the capital ventured in its development, it has carried more cheap comfort into more poor homes than almost any discovery of modern times.[5]

Early Problems and Self-Regulation

Kerosene quality was a source of dispute between Standard and foreign buyers. A conference on the problem in Bremen, Germany, in early 1879 found Standard's insistence on improved lamps rather than improved refinery techniques unpopular. With 80 percent of its illuminant exports at stake, measures were taken by Standard to appease European buyers. New rules were adopted by the New

---

[2]"Practically every municipality, province, and national state in the world passed legislation and introduced regulations affecting the marketing of petroleum products [concerning] . . . color, specific gravity, fire, and flash test, and the like." Ralph Hidy and Muriel Hidy, *Pioneering in Big Business: 1882–1911* (New York: Harper & Brothers, 1955), p. 125.

[3]John Rockefeller, *Random Reminiscences of Men and Events* (New York: Doubleday, 1909), p. 82.

[4]Ibid., p. 63. Early Standard export activities are described in Harold Williamson and Arnold Daum, *The Age of Illumination*, pp. 498–99. Also see Ida Tarbell, *The History of Standard Oil Company*, 2 vols. (New York: Peter Smith, 1950), pp. 244–45.

[5]Quoted in Ralph Hidy and Muriel Hidy, *Pioneering in Big Business*, p. 137.

York Produce Exchange to improve the quality of barrels and illuminating oil, which influenced other shipping centers to follow suit. These improvements, according to Harold Williamson and Arnold Daum, represented

> a milestone in the handling of petroleum exports. By their actions on . . . the new rules, the Standard executives showed an awareness of how better regulations of this type might improve relations with foreign buyers.[6]

Improved product quality was not the result of abstract concern for foreign users. It was a competitive requirement. Standard Oil on the foreign side, as on the domestic side, was not a monopoly entrenched by government favor but a dominant firm seeking to outdistance the competition.[7] This became even more imperative with the rapid development of the Russian oil industry. In 1872, Russia imported over 80 percent of the kerosene it required from the United States; by 1880, imports from the United States were below 15 percent, and Russian kerosene and lubricating oil were ready to be exported from saturated home markets.[8]

In the 1880s, Standard sought new markets and innovated to keep existing ones from falling to the two leading Russian export groups, the Nobels and the Rothschilds.[9] The new challenge to Standard was not only price but quality of product, particularly of kerosene, which remained hazardous. Arrangements for foreign manufacture of lamp wicks better suited for Standard's kerosene was a major quality improvement; cheaper petroleum transport in steam tankers was another Standard innovation that favorably influenced price. The growth of exports to Canada, Latin America, and the Orient was yet another.[10]

---

[6]Harold Williamson and Arnold Daum, *The Age of Illumination,* p. 508. These regulations were not governmental but privately promulgated.

[7]Oil-product tariffs, previously described, were a hindrance to foreign competitors, however.

[8]Harold Williamson and Arnold Daum, *The Age of Illumination,* p. 512.

[9]Stated John Rockefeller, "The Standard is always fighting to the sell the American product against the oil produced from the great fields of Russia, which struggles for the trade of Europe, and the Burma oil, which largely affects the market in India." Rockefeller, *Random Reminiscences of Men and Events,* p. 63.

[10]Harold Williamson and Arnold Daum, *The Age of Illumination,* pp. 647, 657; and Ralph Hidy and Muriel Hidy, *Pioneering in Big Business,* pp. 254–68.

Export competition between U.S. firms joined export competition from other countries in the next decade. The Mellon interests integrated into foreign marketing in the early 1890s to complement their U.S. pipeline and refining investments before being acquired by Standard in 1895.[11] The Producers Oil Company, renamed Pure Oil in 1895, obtained the services of a leading European marketer and began shipping product to Germany. Other developments, such as the founding of Royal Dutch Shell in 1897, ensured continued international rivalry.

Export Regulation: 1917–53

During World War I, the Lever Act gave the president authority to license exports pursuant to broad wartime powers over petroleum distribution. License requirements followed as part of the U.S. Fuel Administration's inaugural planning effort with petroleum. With the armistice of November 1918, exports returned to their less scrutinized prewar state.

During World War II, export matters replaced prewar concerns about imports. The lend-lease program featured oil exports to the Allies at taxpayer-subsidized rates. On June 23, 1941, President Roosevelt placed all petroleum products under export control. Oil sales outside the Western Hemisphere, British Empire, and Egypt were banned to "meet a threatened shortage of petroleum products in the eastern United States." A second reason was to keep U.S. petroleum out of the hands of the enemy.[12] Licenses issued by the State Department covered only Atlantic Coast shipments because of tight transportation in District I.[13] A month later, an embargo of aviation fuel to Japan was announced, reflecting the U.S. government's support for China in its war with Japan. The embargo had a material effect on Japan's fuel supplies, and the strained relationship gave way to a surprise attack on Pearl Harbor and consequent U.S. entry into World War II.

With North Korea's invasion of U.S.-backed South Korea in 1950, petroleum exports to the enemy were banned. Export licenses, which had continued after World War II for shipments over $1,000, were

[11]Harold Williamson and Arnold Daum, *The Age of Illumination*, p. 651.

[12]*OGJ*, June 26, 1941, p. 36.

[13]Ibid., p. 25. Chiefly affected was lubricating oil shipped from North Atlantic Coast ports to the Far East. *OGJ*, June 26, 1941, p. 36.

required for cargos over $25.[14] Shipments to the Far East were halted to prevent oil from reaching North Korea's allies. Export control was administered by the Economic Cooperation Administration and the National Production Authority within the Petroleum Administration for Defense. After the July 1953 armistice, export-license requirements were relaxed to preconflict levels, which deregulated most industry shipments.[15]

Three peacetime regulatory episodes have also occurred with oil exports. The Oil Code of 1933, mentioned earlier with respect to imports, restricted exports as part of its domestic-production control program. Without this complementary intervention, hot oil could have escaped to foreign markets with destabilizing, albeit indirect, consequences for home markets.

Peacetime problems with oil supply in the winter of 1947–48 led to government regulation of exports to keep oil at home.[16] The winter scare was followed by a return to surplus conditions and with it, export decontrol.

Modern Export Regulation

With oil shortages in the 1970s, exports of domestic oil became of acute political interest. Regulation was accomplished under three laws: the Export Administration Act of 1973, the Trans-Alaskan Pipeline Authorization Act of 1973, and the Energy Policy and Conservation Act of 1975. The rise of Alaskan North Slope oil, in addition, inspired specific export regulation that reflected not only concerns about domestic supply but special privileges for U.S. shipping interests.

Export Administration Act

With first sales of crude oil and petroleum products in U.S. commerce subject to price regulation, a potential escape was to export petroleum to receive the unregulated world price. To seal this off, the Federal Energy Office in late 1973 placed crude, crude products, and natural-gas liquids on the Commodity Control List established by the Export Administration Act of 1969.[17] Administration was

---

[14]*OGJ*, July 13, 1950, p. 53, and August 31, 1950, p. 39.

[15]*NPN*, August 19, 1953, p. 32.

[16]Anthony Copp, *Regulating Competition in Oil*, p. 66.

[17]Public Law 91-184, 83 Stat. 841 (1969). 38 *Fed. Reg.* 34442 (December 13, 1973).

by the Office of Export Administration within the Department of Commerce. Beginning in 1974, quarterly quotas were set for each covered item, based on pre–Emergency Petroleum Allocation Act amounts, to prevent major export increases during the period of regulation.[18] Five percent of the quota was set aside for "hardship" distribution to exporters.

Amendments to the Export Administration Act in 1977, the year the Trans-Alaska Pipeline was completed, placed strict provisions on exports of Alaskan North Slope (ANS) oil. A presidential decision to relax restrictions was subject to veto by either house of Congress.[19] Further amendments two years later tightened the requirements. To permit exports, the president had to expressly find that such exports would not reduce the domestic supply of oil, would reduce refiner acquisition cost with 75 percent or more of the savings passed on at the marketing level, and would be in the national interest. Permitted exports had to be under interruptible contracts. Finally, both houses of Congress had to affirm the president's finding.[20] The reasons for this stringency, and the economic consequences of the ban, are discussed in the next section.

Trans-Alaska Pipeline Authorization Act

On November 16, 1973, this act amended the Mineral Leasing Act of 1920 by incorporating a new section to limit exports of domestic crude oil transported over federal domain.[21] Oil exchanges made "for convenience or increased efficiency" with a nearby country were not covered. Exports could be considered only if domestic supply was not diminished, the national interest was served, and the requirements of the Export Administration Act were satisfied. This law, although overshadowed by the Emergency Petroleum Allocation Act and the Export Administration Act, was a potential weapon against exports in other areas of the country.

---

[18]See, for example, the first-quarter allocation in 39 *Fed. Reg.* 3661 (January 29, 1974); and 39 *Fed. Reg.* 5311 (February 12, 1974).

[19]Public Law 95-52, 91 Stat. 235 (1977).

[20]Public Law 96-72, 93 Stat. 503 (1979).

[21]Public Law 93-153, 97 Stat. 584 (1973). Another similar law was the Naval Petroleum Reserves Production Act, Public Law 94-258, 90 Stat. 303 (1976).

Energy Policy and Conservation Act

Passed on December 22, 1975, this act gave the president authority to "restrict exports of . . . petroleum products, natural gas, or petrochemical feedstocks" when in the national interest.[22] On the other hand, a person engaged in petroleum activity could be required to allocate supply in international markets pursuant to an agreement by the United States with another country. The United States would subsequently enter into the International Energy Program Agreement to share oil with twenty-one other nations during an emergency.

Alaskan Oil Controversy

The prohibition on exporting ANS supply, which began before oil first reached the port of Valdez in 1977, was as much an economic perversity as a special-interest coup. Transportation economics dictate that the most logical market for ANS oil is the Pacific Rim countries such as Japan, with the West Coast serving as a residual market. With the export ban, however, surplus oil must either go to California or travel through the Panama Canal to the Gulf Coast or around Cape Horn to Caribbean refineries.

Because of greater distance and more competitive foreign shipping rates, a substantial transportation cost differential has been incurred. With 1982 transportation costs from Valdez to Japan estimated at $0.50 per barrel, from Valdez to the Gulf Coast at around $5.00 per barrel, and from the Persian Gulf to Japan and the Gulf Coast at $0.75 and $1.60 per barrel, respectively, the free-market scenario (ANS oil to Japan, Persian Gulf oil to the Gulf Coast) totals $2.10 per barrel compared to export-ban transportation of $6.00 per barrel (ANS oil to the Gulf Coast and Persian Gulf oil to Japan).[23] With over 500,000 barrels per day shipped to the Gulf of Mexico and other distant locales instead of to Japan, the estimated yearly cost of the export ban exceeded $600 million.

The infamous export ban resulted from two major sources of political pressure. Several weeks after the Arab embargo was

[22]Public Law 94-163, 89 Stat. 871 (1975).

[23]Estimates taken from the California Energy Commission, "Export Restrictions on Domestic Oil," November 1982, p. 3. Similar estimates can be found in Putnam, Hayes, and Bartlett, Inc., "The Export of Alaskan Oil," Cambridge, Mass., May 1983.

announced, the original 1973 prohibition was passed by congressmen concerned that ANS supply would bypass supply-short domestic markets. A second political force was U.S. shipping interests,
which under the Jones Act (section 27 of the Merchant Marine Act
of 1920) enjoyed a monopoly on cargos shipped between U.S. ports.[24]
Labor-union construction and operation made the domestic fleet
uncompetitive with foreign-flag vessels. The export ban, by bringing
the Jones Act into play, guaranteed the lucrative tanker business to
the high-cost home fleet.

Amendments in 1979, which strengthened the ban, were inspired
by the Iran cutoff and a desire to maximize U.S. supply. Heavy
lobbying by Jones Act interests, represented by such trade groups
as the American Maritime Association, the National Maritime Union,
the Maritime Trades Council, and the American Bulk Ship Owners
Committee, also was instrumental in preserving and tightening the
ban. Their interest reflects the fact that over 90 percent of U.S.-flag
shipping capacity—10 million deadweight tons—is dedicated to the
Alaskan oil trade.[25]

With changed supply conditions in the 1980s, critics targeted the
export prohibition for reform. With increased California production,
reduced product demand as a result of conservation, and a preference of area refineries for lighter crude, ANS oil dumped in California could only depress oil prices in Petroleum Administration for
Defense District V. Depressed prices also adversely affected ANS
owners Sohio, ARCO, and Exxon. With wellhead prices artificially
depressed by over $2.00 per barrel by artificially high transport costs,
production was depressed.[26] Lower prices and lower production
also meant less severance-tax revenue for Alaska and less windfall
profits tax for the federal treasury. Resource misallocations as a
result of the ban included the construction of the Northville Pipeline
across Panama, built to eliminate oil transfers from tankers to canal
boats. Another publicized problem, although more imagined than
real, was the negative trade balance with Japan, which could have

---

[24]Public Law 261, 41 Stat. 988 (1920). For discussion of the Jones Act, see chapter
16, pp. 1000–1001.

[25]Stephen Eule and S. Fred Singer, "Export of Alaskan Oil and Gas," in *Free Market
Energy,* p. 123.

[26]Milton Copulos, S. Fred Singer, and David J. Watkins, "Exporting Alaska's Oil
and Gas," Heritage Foundation Backgrounder no. 248, February 22, 1983, p. 9.

been eliminated almost overnight if the Alaskan oil-export market had been deregulated.

An attempt in 1981 to lift the export ban (H.R. 4346) was defeated, as was a more determined challenge in 1984 (S. 979) introduced by Senator Frank Murkowski (R-Alaska). Without active support from the Reagan administration, which was lacking because of opposition from the 15-million-member AFL-CIO in an election year, the amendment to lift the ban was defeated. Indeed, Reagan extended the prohibition by executive order until House and Senate conferences could complete amendments to the Export Administration Act.[27] In this as in other areas, energy policy during the "Reagan Revolution" fell short of its free-market beginnings.[28]

[27]48 *Fed. Reg.* 48215 (October 18, 1983); and 49 *Fed. Reg.* 13099 (April 3, 1984).
[28]See chapter 30, pp. 1861–64.

14. Regulation of Petroleum Pipelines

This chapter describes federal and state regulation of oil pipelines from the turn of the century to 1984.[1] Federal regulation enacted in 1906, like preceding state regulation, was designed to check the "monopolistic" practices of the Standard Oil Trust to benefit competitors. Standard, as other interstate oil pipelines, succeeded in avoiding Interstate Commerce Commission (ICC) jurisdiction, but the damage was done in 1911 when the trust's pipeline holdings were dismembered into almost a dozen companies.

In 1914, a major Supreme Court decision brought virtually the entire interstate oil pipeline industry under ICC authority. Rates were filed with the commission, but specific regulation was absent. This changed several decades later after shippers complained to the ICC. In 1940, an 8 percent profit ceiling on valued capital and a tender requirement to accept all batches up to 10,000 barrels were imposed on crude pipelines; a year later, a maximum 10 percent profit and a maximum 5,000-barrel tender requirement were implemented on oil product pipelines. An antitrust suit settlement in 1940 added an additional rate restriction for all seventy-nine interstate carriers—a 7 percent dividend ceiling payable to the parent. These regulations were overshadowed by federal pipeline projects in World War II and their postwar privatization.

ICC regulation of oil pipelines, unlike Federal Power Commission regulation of interstate natural-gas pipelines discussed in chapter 15, was light-handed and largely free of conflict from the 1940s through the 1960s. This changed in the 1970s with the *Williams I* and *Trans-Alaska Pipeline System* (*TAPS*) cases, which began as rate challenges but soon focused on the valuation methodology of the "Oak formula," which weighted replacement cost with original cost. These cases remained unsettled through 1984, but judicial instruction

---

[1] Pipeline regulation prior to 1900, entirely on the state level, is examined in chapter 11, pp. 609–18.

leaned toward traditional public-utility regulation based on depreciated original cost. Administration of the Hepburn Act fell to the Federal Energy Regulatory Commission (FERC), which assumed oil-pipeline regulatory matters from the ICC in 1977.

State pipeline regulation this century has followed lines similar to the ones it followed in the nineteenth century. The states were different, but events were familiar. Wellhead overproduction, precipitating pipeline refusals to buy or ship, led to producer-sponsored pipeline regulation in Texas, Oklahoma, Louisiana, New Mexico, Kansas, California, and other states. In addition to common-purchaser and common-carrier laws, rights of eminent domain were common. Rate regulation was less common.

This chapter concludes by evaluating traditional arguments for oil-pipeline regulation: excess profits and natural monopoly, market-share concentration, and capacity undersizing. The rationale for common-carrier law and rate regulation is also scrutinized to present a case for deregulating oil pipelines at the state as well as the federal level.

Oil Pipelines

The Pipeline Amendment of 1906

The misconception of common-carrier legislation as public-interest law has led to the puzzlement of why pipelines "escaped" federal regulation while railroads did not prior to 1906.[2] The mystery evaporates when it is recognized that statutory common-carriage and rate regulation did not have utilitarian roots; the Interstate Commerce Act of 1887 and its revisions in 1903 (Elkins Act) and in 1906 (Hepburn Act) became law on the strength of special-interest activism, which tailored social legislation toward short-term business needs. Railroads, as discussed in chapter 11, supported regulation as an alternative to competition.[3] Pipelines, on the contrary, *opposed* federal regulation but were no political match for other industry groups desiring intervention to achieve competitive advantage.

---

[2] Forrest Black, "Oil Pipe Line Divorcement by Litigation and Legislation," *Cornell Law Quarterly* (June 1940): 510.

[3] See chapter 11, pp. 619–23.

Federal regulation of oil pipelines was an outgrowth of state regulation, such as that of Texas (1899) and Kansas (1905).[4] The center of attention was Standard's "monopolistic" pipeline practices, which were criticized by independent producers, independent refiners, and their respective legislators. Independent producers blamed low prices on the purchasing leverage of Standard pipelines, which predominated over the Appalachian, Lima-Indiana, and Mid-continent fields, not competitive drilling and flush production. Independent refineries were discontent with low-cost competition from Standard refineries that benefited from integration and scale economies. Together, these groups used state law to legislate Standard into disadvantage,[5] and through sympathetic members of Congress, they interested the Bureau of Corporations, established in 1903 over the objection of Standard Oil, in investigating the nation's largest company in early 1905.[6] Under the direction of the commissioner of corporations, James Garfield, the final report in May 1906 concluded that Standard's pipeline rates and rebate alliances with railroads inflicted competitive damage on independents. It stated:

> The Standard Oil Company has all but a monopoly of the pipelines in the Unites States. Its control of them is one of the chief sources of its power. . . . The Federal Government has not as yet exercised any control over pipelines engaged in interstate commerce. The results that the charges made by the Standard for transporting oil through its pipelines for outside concerns are altogether excessive and in practice largely prohibitive. Since the changes far exceed the cost of service, the Standard has a great advantage over such of its competitors as are forced to use its pipelines to secure their crude oil.[7]

---

[4]See chapter 11, pp. 609–18.

[5]State antitrust action against Standard is discussed in chapter 18, pp. 1074–81, and chapter 22, pp. 1297–1305.

[6]The investigation, suggested to the bureau by Kansas Congressman Philip Campbell, reflected the views of Kansas producers who would complain to the agency: "We are hemmed in on all sides. Like prison guards, the railroads and the Standard Oil Company [pipelines] lurk on the borders of the State, gun in hand, ready to call a halt on any man . . . try[ing] to ship his oil . . . outside the borders of the State." Arthur Johnson, *Petroleum Pipelines and Public Policy* (Cambridge, Mass.: Harvard University Press, 1967), p. 23.

[7]U.S. Department of Commerce and Labor, Bureau of Corporations, *Report of the Commissioner of Corporations on the Transportation of Petroleum* (Washington, D.C.: Government Printing Office 1906), p. 37.

President Theodore Roosevelt, no friend of Rockefeller or Standard Oil, seized the findings to advocate passage of William Hepburn's (D-Ill.) anti-rebate bill, which included regulation of interstate oil pipelines.

The Hepburn bill was introduced in Congress on January 4, 1906. On April 16, the same day the Garfield report was released, Massachusetts Senator Henry Cabot Lodge proposed an amendment to the bill to extend common-carrier regulation to oil pipelines.[8] His motivation was not masked.

> Small well owners are absolutely at the mercy of pipelines. My object, I state frankly . . . is to bring the pipelines of the Standard Oil Company within the jurisdiction of the Interstate Commerce Commission.[9]

Lodge's amendment took on added significance on May 7 when Senator Stephen Elkins of West Virginia incorporated the so-called commodities clause in the Hepburn bill to prohibit common carriers from transporting produced or purchased goods. Intended to force divestiture of coal properties owned by coal-carrying railroads in West Virginia and other coal states, the amendment would be fatal to Standard's integrated structure. The same was true for other integrated oil companies, and united industry disfavor, including producer concern about stunting the growth of pipelines, led to the substitution of the words "railroad company" for "common carrier."[10] The first divestiture challenge to integrated oil pipelines was repelled.

[8]Earlier bills to regulate oil pipelines as common carriers had been introduced in the House by William Hearst of New York and in the Senate by Joseph Rhinock of Kentucky. Their versions were overshadowed by Lodge's amendment and dropped.

[9]40 *Congressional Record* 7000 (May 17, 1906). Considering the heavy railroad support for the Hepburn bill, it can be surmised that the railroad lobby favored the amendment to discourage Standard Oil's widespread rebate arrangements with oil-carrying railroads. On the railroad lobby, see Gabriel Kolko, *Railroads and Regulation* (New York: W. W. Norton & Company, 1965), chap. 7. In addition, Roosevelt's strong support of the pipeline amendment (and the bill in general) was likely influenced by his close relationship with railroad magnate J. P. Morgan, a personal and business rival of Rockefeller.

[10]Forrest Black, "Oil Pipe Line Divorcement by Litigation and Legislation," p. 511; and Arthur Johnson, *The Development of American Petroleum Pipelines* (Ithaca, N.Y.: Cornell University Press, 1956), pp. 227–28. Producers would continue to oppose later divestiture proposals for similar reasons. See George Wolbert, *U.S. Oil Pipe Lines* (Washington, D.C.: American Petroleum Institute, 1979), pp. 264–65.

With "the oil industry itself determin[ing] the outcome,"[11] the Hepburn bill easily passed both houses and was signed into law by Roosevelt on June 29, 1906, over the muted protest of Standard Oil.[12] Justification for the law was scant. Economic analysis had not been performed to survey past results in the free-market environment. Industry performance under the new law was not predicted. No pretense of consumerism was made in the debate or the language of the law. It was "producerist" regulation

> whose primary concern was higher prices and an easier life for the small businessman. . . . The people in the oil business who supplied the real impetus for the anti-Standard agitation were not bemused by vague abstractions about the beauties of perfect competition over the long run. Like businessmen since time immemorial, they were interested in money here and now. So the measures that they pushed were designed to cut down on Standard's take and to enhance theirs.[13]

The pipeline amendment read as follows:

> The provisions of this Act shall apply to any corporation or any person or persons engaged in the transportation of oil or other commodity, except water and except natural or artificial gas, by means of pipelines, or partly by pipelines and partly by railroad, or partly by pipelines and partly by water, who shall be considered and held to be common carriers within the meaning of this Act.[14]

Interstate oil pipelines with outside business were now legally obligated to charge "reasonable" (nondiscriminatory) rates to all parties desiring shipment and to file tariffs with the ICC. Rebates were prohibited and carried a triple-the-amount penalty pursuant to a 1903 amendment to the Interstate Commerce Act (Elkins Act). Although rate maximums could be prescribed under the law, they

---

[11]Arthur Johnson, *Petroleum Pipelines and Public Policy*, p. 31.

[12]Standard protested when the bill was first introduced but did not continue to lobby against it. See *The Economic Regulation of Business and Industry: A Legislative History of U.S. Regulatory Agencies*, ed. B. Schwartz, 5 vols. (New York: Chelsea House, 1973), vol. 2, pp. 915, 985.

[13]Opinion 154, Williams Pipe Line Company, 21 FERC 61670–71.

[14]Public Law 337, 34 Stat. 584 (1906). The law applied to oil pipelines located interstate, within the District of Columbia, or within territories of the United States.

were not. "Light-handed" regulation for the time being only mitigated the rate *differentials* about which producers were particularly concerned.

Regulation under the Hepburn Act: 1906–14

The practical effect of the law was not as great as intended. During debate over the pipeline amendment, the interstate pipelines began to devise ways to avoid common-carrier rank. On November 1, 1905, Standard Oil purchased several common-carrier lines (under state law) and reorganized them as private carriers by transporting only purchased crude. Also before the law's effective date, the Tide Water Pipe Line Company, Standard's foremost rival, ceased outside shipments in favor of purchased oil exclusively.[15] A more blatant circumvention took place when interstate lines separately incorporated state by state with pumping stations located at each border and tariffs calculated intrastate.[16] Finally, as was done on the state level, eminent-domain rights went unclaimed to avoid the obligation of common carriage.[17] As a result of these measures, a number of interstate oil pipelines did not file rate schedules with the ICC upon passage of the Hepburn Act.

For pipelines filing tariffs in open admission of common carriage, opportunities for use by outside shippers were limited by high tender minimums, specialized destination points, and high fares. In other words, while interstate pipelines were common carriers de jure, they remained private carriers de facto. Shipment terms were tailored to the specifications of the pipeline's refinery, and published rates were set high to discourage outside demand, which might crowd out internal throughput and lead to refinery underutilization.[18] Indeed, almost all trunk pipelines were integral parts of their respective refineries and were not built with outside use in mind. Minimum tender requirements, on the other hand, reflected not only the needs of the pipeline's refinery but the fact that running small

[15]Tide Water went private just six days before the Hepburn Act became effective, an action that the Bureau of Corporations interpreted as "an open defiance of the new act." Arthur Johnson, *Petroleum Pipelines and Public Policy*, p. 71.

[16]William Beard, *Regulation of Pipe Lines as Common Carriers* (New York: Columbia University Press, 1941), pp. 50–53.

[17]Of these companies, Standard Oil's Prairie Oil and Gas Company was the largest.

[18]The high rate for the integrated firm was only a transfer price—a bookkeeping item—without pecuniary consequence.

batches of oil of different grades resulted in mixing, which by industry custom reverted oil to the lowest grade with a corresponding price penalty.

With the June 18, 1910, passage of the Mann-Elkins Act, the ICC was empowered to investigate rates, veto proposed tariffs, and substitute rates.[19] Pursuant to this authority, investigation commenced to see if the aforementioned common-carriage barriers had monopolistic intent. Hearings in late 1911 and early 1912 failed to substantiate willful wrongdoing.[20] Pipeline practices were at once profit maximizing and commonsensical, a conclusion that rival producers could do little to dispel in congressional hearings. Arthur Johnson summarized the testimony as follows:

> Transportation for others and the revenue derived from such service was an incidental concern if it was a concern of pipeline managers at all. Pipelines were the refiner's life line to shifting centers of crude oil production, and a pipeline's cost had to be recovered as quickly as possible. Rates quoted to outside shippers reflected this fact. Minimum tender requirements were presented as necessary to insure efficient and economical pipeline operation.[21]

At the conclusion of the investigation, the ICC ordered sixty interstate pipeline firms to file tariffs. Thirteen, citing immunity from common carriage because of the aforementioned practices, did not.[22] A hearing was held on May 10, 1912, at which four defenses, one general (1) and three specific (2–4), were aired:

1. Interstate pipelines were private property; mandatory use by outsiders constituted "taking" of property in violation of the Fourteenth Amendment;

---

[19]Public Law 218, 36 Stat. 539 (1910).

[20]*In the Matter of Pipe Lines*, ICC Report 24, (June 1912–October 1912).

[21]Arthur Johnson, *Petroleum Pipelines and Public Policy*, p. 51. A detailed summary of the hearings can be found in the *Oil & Gas Journal*, September 28, 1911, pp. 8–16; October 5, 1911, pp. 6–22; and October 12, 1911, pp. 10–16. Cited hereafter as *OGJ*.

[22]The companies, five of which were affiliated with Standard Oil, are listed in Arthur Johnson, *Petroleum Pipelines and Public Policy*, p. 74. In addition to rates, standard ICC reporting requirements for firms included operating revenue and operating expense data effective January 1, 1911. William Beard, *Regulation of Pipelines as Common Carriers*, p. 58.

2. Common carriage did not apply to companies that historically did not act as common carriers, viz., did not transport outside oil or invoke eminent domain;

3. Common carriage did not apply to pipelines that, although interstate in a physical sense, were separately incorporated state by state; and

4. Common carriage did not apply to reincorporated (reorganized) private lines that previously had been interstate common carriers.[23]

The ICC rejected the constitutionality argument, the private-practice argument, and the circumvention practices. "Congress," the commission concluded, "intended to convert the interstate oil pipe lines of the country into common carriers."[24]

The thirteen firms were ordered to file tariffs by September 1, 1906. Six of the firms—four Standard affiliates, the Tide Water Pipe Line Company, and the Uncle Sam Oil Company—brought suit in U.S. Commerce Court (which existed from 1910 to 1913), where the order was enjoined.[25] The ICC immediately appealed to the U.S. Supreme Court.

Before the Supreme Court in the landmark *Pipe Line Cases of 1914,* the government stressed the utilitarian basis for regulation "in order to give the public adequate protection."[26] Pipeline attorneys rehashed their case that private businesses—companies not organized under state common-carrier law, not transporting oil for hire, and not embodied with rights of eminent domain—could not be forcibly transformed into common carriers without deprivation of property. In the majority opinion issued June 22, 1914, Justice Holmes sided with the government, speaking of Standard Oil as the "master of the fields without the necessity of owning them."[27] An

---

[23]This summary is adopted from discussions in Arthur Johnson, *Petroleum Pipelines and Public Policy,* pp. 74–76; and *OGJ,* May 16, 1912, pp. 10, 12.

[24]24 ICC 3 (1913). Another argument made by the companies was accepted by the commission: right-of way use with a public road or common-carrier railroad did not automatically convey common carriage on the pipeline. This, however, was secondary to the other three specific defenses and was not crucial to the issue.

[25]*Prairie Oil and Gas Company* v. *United States,* 204 F.2d 798 (1913).

[26]*The Pipe Line Cases,* 234 U.S. 548 (1914).

[27]Ibid., p. 559.

exception was made for Uncle Sam, which owned producing properties in Oklahoma linked by pipeline to its Kansas refinery. Such
interstate transportation, the court concluded, was "private" and
no more constituted "transportation" under the act than carrying
drawn water from a well to one's own house, "transportation being
merely an incident to use at the end."[28] This established a basis for
private carriage for interstate lines that would be further delineated
in future decisions. But outside of this narrow exemption, authority
of the ICC to regulate interstate oil pipelines was firmly established
after eight years of industry circumvention and legal challenges.

Along with the establishment of correlative rights in oil production, the regulation of interstate oil pipelines marked the beginning
of the Age of Interventionism in the petroleum industry. What began
as an "intraindustry conflict"—producers against pipelines or, more
precisely, producers against Standard Oil—had been elevated to a
"public calling" by the Supreme Court in its 1914 decision.[29] Law
journals hailed the verdict. The *Harvard Law Review*, for example,
trumpeted that "abstract principles of liberty and antiquated
economic theories can no longer be invoked to justify the abuse of
economic advantage, however honestly it may have been
acquired."[30]

Questions of the efficacy of regulation of interstate oil pipelines
can be recast as questions about whether consumers coincidentally
benefited from the political fray. The actual benefit of pipeline intervention to oil producers, the raison d'être of common-carrier law,
is a second question that is open to review.

Assuming the common case of Standard Oil as the only buyer
(monopsonist) in a field with numerous producer-sellers, the presumption has been that Standard exerted "economic advantage"
and possessed a "master relationship" in the field. This conclusion
is superficial. Producers could have banded together to counter seller

---

[28]Ibid., pp. 562–63.

[29]Arthur Johnson, *Petroleum Pipelines and Public Policy*, pp. 32, 80.

[30]"Application of the Police Power in the Insurance Rate and Pipe Line Cases,"
Harvard Law Review (November 1914): 86–87. Also see the similar reactions in A. P.
Matthew, "Validity of Act of Congress Declaring Pipe Lines Common Carriers,"
California Law Review (September 1914): 494–96; "Carriers of One's Own Property
across State Lines in Interstate Commerce," *Central Law Journal* (July 10, 1914): 20;
and "Pipe Lines as Common Carriers," *Columbia Law Review* (December 1914): 664–65.

advantage; indeed, this possibility encouraged vertical integration by pipeline firms in the first place.[31] If Standard was paying below-market prices at the wellhead and reaping abnormal profits, producers (or outsiders) could enter the pipeline field with the goodwill of the market—even with impenetrable long-term contracts—and leave the former monopsonist with a nonperforming or underutilized asset. The mere possibility of such action would give leverage to producers to obtain competitive prices for their oil. Moreover, with low variable costs, high utilization is needed by pipelines to achieve payout, which encourages the pipeline operator to price his services to attract volume.[32] The fact that producers did not choose the economic means—informal cooperation, formal consolidation, self-integration, or pipeline construction—to realign wellhead prices and pool throughput to meet tender requirements, but turned to the political means instead, suggests that Standard and other pipelines were scapegoats for producer problems created by unrestrained drilling and production.[33] Given unrestricted entry, free association, and entrepreneurial alertness to profitable opportunities, wellhead prices were not below market to make a case for pipeline regulation.[34]

Neither consumers nor oil producers benefited from common-carrier legislation. Producer welfare is directly dependent on the health and growth of pipeline transportation in place of more expensive transportation alternatives. Yet regulation that advantages producers at the expense of pipelines discourages incremental pipeline investments. Existing "sunk" pipeline investments may be hostage to political interference, but new lines and expansion of existing lines are not.

With the law forcing private carriers into public use, displacement of refinery feedstock would lead to imbalances for the integrated firm. This prospect would discourage construction of trunk lines

---

[31]See Benjamin Klein, Robert Crawford, and Armen Alchian, "Vertical Integration, Appropriable Rents, and the Competitive Contracting Process," *Journal of Law and Economics* (October 1978): 297–326.

[32]John McLean and Robert Haigh, *The Growth of Integrated Oil Companies* (Boston: Harvard Graduate School of Business Administration, 1954), p. 188.

[33]Criticism of Standard Oil by producers, not coincidentally, peaked during periods of unrestrained output.

[34]See Arthur Johnson, *Petroleum Pipelines and Public Policy*, p. 101.

(and gathering lines), not to mention refinery outlays, to the detriment of upstream producers and downstream consumers. Restated, investment risks will be avoided if the shipper can "free ride" on the other person's investment.

It is documented that for-hire firms suspended outside service to avoid common-carrier regulation, which forced involved producers to locate higher cost alternative transportation. What is not known is how many new pipelines and improvements in existing lines were delayed or altogether forgone because of the dark cloud of federal regulation of rates and other terms of service.

Critical mention of early intervention should include the direct costs of pipeline regulation—taxation to fund ICC activities and increased firm costs to comply with statutory requirements and cover court costs. Investments made only to circumvent regulation are another uniquely regulatory cost. These costs are borne either by pipelines as reduced earnings, producers in a reduced wellhead price, or consumers in an increased price paid for petroleum products.

Standard Oil Pipelines and the 1911 Dissolution Decree

Early government investigation of the oil industry focused on Standard Oil. Along with its refining and marketing practices, Congress recognized Standard's competitive advantage due to its pipeline network that stretched from the oil fields to refining affiliates. Efficiency from integration and scale economies, admitted a 1907 government study, was "more . . . than could possibly be secured under competition, even if the competing concerns were large," yet the report concluded that Standard "neither [had] legal nor moral claim to pocket all or the preponderant part of the gains due to its superior efficiency in the pipeline business."[35] The emotionalism of the day was poisoned against economic performance per se; big was bad, and that was that.

On November 15, 1906, the federal government began court action to dissolve the Standard Oil Trust on grounds of conspiring to

---

[35]U.S. Department of Commerce and Labor, Bureau of Corporations, *Report of the Commissioner of Corporations on the Petroleum Industry*, Part II: "Prices and Profits" (Washington D.C.: Government Printing Office, 1907), pp. 643, 649. This conclusion was similar to the emotional reasoning used to justify crude-oil price regulation in the 1970s. See chapter 9, pp. 513–14.

restrain trade in violation of the Sherman Antitrust Act of 1890. At stake was Standard's common ownership of interstate pipelines held in ten pipeline affiliates and two integrated firms. Over a fifteen-month period, government witnesses testified in U.S. district court that the company was not performing as a common carrier pursuant to the Hepburn Act. It was complained, as it would be again in 1911–12 hearings, that high rates, high tender requirements (a 300,000-barrel minimum), and inconvenient destinations effectively precluded outside use of Standard's pipelines. Standard argued that these service terms were tailored to internal refinery needs as were virtually all of the industry's trunk lines. State and federal common-carrier law, hence, was an artificiality that contradicted entrepreneurial decisionmaking. Specifically refuting the government charge that Standard "controlled" pipelines, company lawyers differentiated Standard's property from navigable rivers or public highways. "They argued that Standard Oil 'controlled' its common-carrier pipelines because it had paid for the rights-of-way, built the lines with its own money, and had owned them ever since."[36] The defense, noticed Arthur Johnson, "had reasonable explanations based in economics and not in predatory competitive practices,"[37] yet the crusade against monopoly was not to be sidetracked by economic considerations.

On November 20, 1909, the court unanimously reached a guilty verdict, which was upheld by the U.S. Supreme Court, after hearing similar arguments, on May 15, 1911.[38] Ten pipeline subsidiaries were severed from the trust: Buckeye Pipe Line Company, Crescent Pipe Line Company, Cumberland Pipe Line Company, Eureka Pipe Line Company, Indiana Pipe Line Company, National Transit Company, New York Transit Company, Northern Pipe Line Company, Southern Pipe Line Company, and South-West Pennsylvania Pipe Lines. Ohio Oil Company and Prairie Oil and Gas Company, both integrated Standard companies with sizable pipeline holdings, were also dissolved from trust ownership.

The effect of the dissolution, carried out over the next six months by prorating stock ownership from the trust to the shareholders of

---

[36]Arthur Johnson, *Petroleum Pipelines and Public Policy*, p. 63.
[37]Ibid., p. 64.
[38]*United States* v. *Standard Oil Co.*, 221 U.S. 1 (1911).

each individual company, was to undo an integration built up over three decades and fostered by the competitive requirements (natural incentives) of the petroleum business. But the government's competitive "correction" was window dressing; strong common bonds kept the companies close together. Even more important, Standard's market share since 1901 was being eroded by the rise of integrated rivals from the Southwest. They seized upon opportunities that Standard was slow to recognize—or unable to recognize given legislation in Kansas, Oklahoma, and Texas designed to discourage Standard's presence.[39]

In the older oil regions that Standard dominated, dissolution ended formal relationships that had created company self-sufficiency in transportation, refining, and marketing. This created imbalances and a loss of economies, which led to decisions to integrate—reintegrate—with particular emphasis on building or purchasing pipeline facilities to complement downstream operations. Dissolution, in other words, did not annul economic calculation but disrupted its prior result; integration and sizable scale economies would remain the order of the day.

Expansion of State Regulation: 1906–29

State regulation of oil pipelines prior to 1906 reflected producers' desire to counter purchaser (pipeline) power and thereby, in theory at least, receive higher prices at the wellhead. Outstanding examples were intrastate pipeline laws in Pennsylvania (1883) and Kansas (1905). Subsequent state intervention, as did federal intervention, followed the same theme—producers' turning to their state legislatures to achieve what they could not achieve in the marketplace.

Oklahoma. Federal pipeline regulation began just before Oklahoma became a state. In December 1906, Interior Secretary E. A. Hitchcock ordered that only common-carrier pipelines could cross Indian land in the Oklahoma Territory, and once a pipeline was constructed, its right-of-way could be revoked if Interior's rules were violated. This discouraged pipeline outlets for the Glenn Pool and other developing fields and contributed to storage waste until the order was rescinded in March 1909.[40]

---

[39]See chapter 18, pp. 1074–81.
[40]Arthur Johnson, *Petroleum Pipelines and Public Policy*, p. 40.

"Reasonable control and regulation" of intrastate pipelines were authorized upon statehood with article 9 of the Oklahoma Constitution of 1907. Producer discontent with purchasing practices in the Glenn Pool led the state legislature to pass a common-carrier law with rights of eminent domain two years later.[41] Also in 1909, a common-purchaser law was passed, the first of its kind, that instructed oil pipelines to "purchase all of the petroleum in the vicinity . . . reasonably reached . . . without discrimination in favor of one producer or one person against another."[42]

The new law was put to test in early 1914 in the low-cost, high-output Healdton field in southern Oklahoma. A problem arose when increasing supply and overestimated crude quality prompted the field's buyer, Magnolia Petroleum, to drop posted prices by one-third. This sent producers, many of whom based their business decisions on the prior posted price, to the Oklahoma Corporate Commission for relief. Similar developments in the prolific Cushing field intensified pressure for political action. On May 7, 1914, commission officials issued two orders for the respective fields. Order 813 designated a field umpire, with his salary paid by area pipeline companies, to handle ratable purchases for the Cushing field; Order 814, far more stringent, required Magnolia to buy daily minimums as well as buy storage facilities from producers and the oil therein at $0.50 per barrel.[43] "For the first time in the history of pipelining," noted Johnson, "government authority sought to regulate directly the conditions of doing business on a day-to-day basis."[44]

Oklahoma congressmen, meanwhile, began agitating for increased regulation if not more drastic remedies on the federal level. Talk was heard of building a government pipeline from the major Oklahoma fields to the Gulf of Mexico and having the War Department construct a 10,000-barrel storage facility for both the Cushing and Healdton fields.[45]

Federal inaction coupled with unsatisfactory results of Oklahoma pipeline regulation—common carriage (1909), common purchaser

[41]Ibid., pp. 101–2.
[42]*Revised Laws of Oklahoma*, section 4307 (1910). The law also required ratable purchases if the amount of oil tendered was greater than pipeline capacity.
[43]*OGJ*, May 14, 1914, pp. 28–29.
[44]Arthur Johnson, *Petroleum Pipelines and Public Policy*, p. 107.
[45]Ibid., pp. 107–8.

(1909), and Orders 813 and 814 (1914)—led to more government involvement, not less. Wellhead measures were undertaken to force producers, indirectly and later directly, to curtail output. Voluntary pipeline proration, under which purchasers bought predetermined maximum tenders equitably from each producer, was voluntarily implemented in May 1914 with little effect. An Oklahoma Corporation Commission order followed on July 1 to prohibit gathering lines from hooking up new wells in existing fields. This intervention pitted producer against producer, the historic producer versus the would-be (or expanding) producer. Price floors were resorted to in late 1914 with little success; pipeline companies either ignored the price orders or curtailed purchases. With the failure of these measures—confirming the erroneous belief of conspiratorial, monopolistic pipeline practices—the "solution" was found in direct producer regulation. Wellhead proration became Oklahoma law on February 11, 1915, to limit production to "market demand," defined as the capacity of transportation and marketing facilities.[46]

Texas. Oil-pipeline regulation in Texas originated from a political swap between producers and two local integrated companies, Texaco and Gulf. The "Texas Company Bill" sought to amend the state incorporation law to allow charters for fully integrated oil companies. Nonintegrated producers, in response, lobbied for common carriage and rate regulation for all intrastate oil pipelines as a condition to the new incorporation. After defeat of integrated incorporation in 1905 and a partial relaxation in 1915 to allow pipeline-refinery charters, full integration was enacted on February 20, 1917, but not without common-carrier rank and rate regulation for pipelines.[47] Specific regulations under the 1917 law became effective on July 26, 1919. Pipelines were to accept all tenders over 500 barrels and provide shippers with five days' free storage—specifications to which Texas's two largest producer trade groups were amenable. Pipelines, in return, were allowed liberal deductions from run quantities to account for evaporation, contamination, and impurities.[48] Common-purchaser regulation, sponsored by the Independent Petroleum Association of Texas with Humble Oil pipelines in mind, would

---

[46]See chapter 3, pp. 84–86.

[47]Arthur Johnson, *Petroleum Pipelines and Public Policy*, p. 115.

[48]Ibid., p. 194.

wait until early 1930 when "overproduction" became acute, but because of problems of enforcement and legal validity, the act would not be consequential.[49] Instead, as in Oklahoma, the quest for price stability would turn from purchaser (pipeline) regulation to producer regulation with eventual success.

Louisiana. Act 36 of 1906 designated all intrastate oil pipelines common carriers. In the same year, Act 39 granted powers of eminent domain to oil firms subject to a common-carrier obligation. Implementation of Act 36 was not of practical concern until over a decade later when large output and price deterioration led producers to press for legislative action. In early 1920, a common-carrier law was reenacted with common-purchaser provisions and a requirement that oil (warehouse) receipts be treated as negotiable financial instruments.[50]

Authority of the Louisiana Public Service Commission to regulate intrastate oil pipelines was exercised in regard to the common-carrier status of Louisiana Standard, the state's dominant pipeline company. At issue was Standard's posted price in the De Sota field. The matter was settled in late 1926 by a tariff rollback by Standard, which increased wellhead netbacks.[51] Behind the scenes was Huey Long, a Louisiana public service commissioner (and later governor and U.S. senator), who had a personal score to settle with Louisiana Standard as a result of a soured oil investment.[52]

Other. In 1905, Kansas declared all crude pipelines common carriers and set maximum rates. In 1909, Utah granted the right of eminent domain to intrastate pipelines as did Nevada in 1912 and New Jersey in 1918. In 1913, California passed a common-carrier law for

---

[49]Robert E. Hardwicke, "Legal History of Conservation of Oil in Texas," in American Bar Association, *Legal History of Conservation of Oil and Gas, 1938* (Baltimore: Lord Baltimore Press, 1939), p. 221; *National Petroleum News,* March 19, 1930, pp. 67, 69; cited hereafter as *NPN;* and Henrietta Larson and Kenneth Porter, *History of Humble Oil & Refining Company* (New York: Harper & Brothers, 1959), p. 323.

[50]Arthur Johnson, *Petroleum Pipelines and Public Policy,* p. 192.

[51]Ibid., p. 194.

[52]See T. Harry Williams, *Huey Long* (New York: Alfred A. Knopf, 1970), pp. 126–27, 138–40, 174–80.

all pipelines historically providing "for-hire services."[53] The Hepburn Act did not apply to intrastate pipelines, but California's Railroad Commission could now do what federal law could not.[54] In 1921, Montana passed a common-carrier statute to satisfy producers who claimed to be at the mercy of the state's two pipeline companies. In the same year, Nevada passed a similar law in anticipation of oil production (which would not occur until 1954) based on the reasoning and experience of other state common-carrier laws.[55] Other common-carrier laws were passed by Arizona and Idaho in 1913, Arkansas and South Dakota in 1921, New Mexico in 1927, and Michigan in 1929. Common-purchaser laws were enacted by Arizona and Idaho in 1913, Kentucky in 1920, Montana and Nevada in 1921, and Michigan in 1929.

Regulation of oil pipelines had less practical effect than legal significance after 1915. In Johnson's estimation, state regulation in the 1915–31 period was "largely *pro forma* . . . a fact largely attributable to the absence of shipper or producer complaints."[56] This did not result from a behavioral change by pipelines but from a new emphasis of wellhead interests on production regulation instead of pipeline regulation. The success of market-demand proration and related regulation raised price sufficiently so that pipeline rate reductions and other legislative favors beyond common-carriage and common-purchaser requirements were not required.

Federal Activity: 1915–40

To undo the damage of dissolution and respond to market incentives, many firms moved to integrate—and in many cases reintegrate—production and refining with pipeline facilities. It was, for many, "integrate or perish."[57] On the nonmarket side, the arena of

---

[53]*1913 California Statutes,* chap. 327.

[54]Companies desiring to remain private carriers had to pay $0.50 per barrel to cross public highways, and California Standard capitulated to common carriage to avoid the prohibitive fee. Other firms such as Associated Oil and Union Oil unsuccessfully brought suit to remain private carriers. Federal Trade Commission, *Report on the Pacific Coast Petroleum Industry* (Washington, D.C.: Government Printing Office, 1921) pp. 159–61.

[55]William Beard, *Regulation of Pipe Lines as Common Carriers,* pp. 18–19.

[56]Arthur Johnson, *Petroleum Pipelines and Public Policy,* pp. 194–95.

[57]Ibid., p. 168. The reintegration of three former Standard Trust companies, Prairie Pipe Line, National Transit, and Buckeye Pipe Line, is discussed in ibid., chap. 9.

politics and judicial decrees, investigation was commonplace but with little resulting administrative or judicial regulation.

Investigation and Legislative Proposals. A ready forum existed for complaints against oil pipelines on the federal level. If the complaint did not go directly to the ICC, the malcontent could ask his elected Washington representative to request an investigation either by Congress, the ICC, or the Federal Trade Commission (FTC), established in 1914 to replace the Bureau of Corporations. These requests were often granted.[58] State pipeline regulation was already in high gear, and in 1914, four bills were introduced in Congress by Oklahoma sponsors to have the federal government own and operate interstate crude pipelines.[59] The precedent of intervention was well established.

The first inquiry in the 1915–40 period was by the FTC in early 1916, in response to producer unrest in the Mid-Continent field. The *Report on Pipe-Line Transportation of Petroleum* reached familiar government conclusions—large tender requirements and high margins represented imperfect competition. The ICC entertained producer complaints during the 1915–19 period under Docket 4199, which was kept open from the *Pipeline* cases of 1914. No punitive action was taken, and the docket was closed on March 21, 1919.[60]

The next pipeline inquiry began in June 1922 as part of a general investigation of the price of gasoline, which by this time had become a major consumer product. Named for Wisconsin Senator Robert La Follette, the congressional inquiry served as an industrywide forum for malcontents and inevitably produced pipeline muckraking. Complaints were many—tenders were too high, connections too few, posted prices too low, and tariffs too high. The intraindustry feud had little consequence other than producing bad press for integrated companies for an unmoved public.[61]

The next investigative period was during the Great Depression, a time of destabilizing production for the industry.[62] On January 29,

[58]Ibid., p. 173.

[59]George Wolbert, "The Recurring Spectre of Pipeline Divorcement," in *Oil's First Century,* ed. Ralph Hidy (Cambridge, Mass.: Harvard Graduate School, 1960), pp. 107, 126.

[60]Arthur Johnson, *Petroleum Pipelines and Public Policy,* pp. 174, 195–96.

[61]Ibid., pp. 177–87.

[62]As Arthur Johnson noted, "Distress in the oil industry . . . and federal investigations of pipelines . . . bore a high correlation to one another." Ibid., p. 217.

1931, the first proposal for pipeline divorcement from integrated operations was introduced by Kansas Congressman Homer Hock. A year later, a resolution was passed by the House of Representatives to investigate oil and gas pipelines. Chaired by Texas Congressman Sam Rayburn, the House Committee on Interstate and Foreign Commerce assigned former University of Texas economist Walter Splawn to the investigation. The committee obtained detailed information from an estimated 95 percent of the country's pipelines, and its major finding was a free-market conclusion. "Oil pipe lines," the Splawn report concluded, "are found as a result of this investigation to be plant facilities in an integrated industry."[63] Mandatory carriage was thus a misuse of internal assets.

The *plant facilities* description of the report crystallized the argument of companies resisting common-carrier regulation. Yet it did not cause existing regulation to be reconsidered. Regulators were on the offensive, and interstate oil pipelines were on the defensive.

The 1933–35 New Deal period gave new life to special-interest agitation for pipeline investigation, regulation, and divorcement. On April 3, 1933, President Franklin D. Roosevelt recommended pipeline divorcement to Congress. In mid-1934, the Transportation Subcommittee of the Oil Code's Planning and Coordination Committee, upon request of Petroleum Administrator Harold Ickes, published the *Report upon Pipe Line Practices, Rates and Related Subjects,* which reaffirmed the conclusion of the Splawn report. In the same year, Congress held hearings to investigate the entire petroleum industry, and pipeline practices became a focus of interest. In addition to familiar arguments, several critics presented a new theory to justify divorcement. The argument was that "excessive" pipeline profits allowed integrated firms to take losses in their refining and marketing sectors to undercut the prices of downstream independent rivals. The testimony, however, was short on documentation and had a confusing logic. Legislators were not moved to action.

The "subsidy theory" deserves critical comment. The argument is little more than a backdoor admission of the advantages of integration wherein the loss of underscaled independents is the consumers' gain. Consumer interest, therefore, would dictate that the rigors of

---

[63]Ibid., p. 219.

the market not be weakened by regulation or annulled by divorcement. Second, the presence of subsidization between the stages of an integrated business is indeterminable given the problem of determining interdepartmental boundaries. Third, from the viewpoint of the company as a whole, subsidization is an empty concept. Standard Oil of New Jersey president Will Farish made this point in testimony: "How you could subsidize yourself by moving money from one pocket to another is a little disturbing to my way of thinking."[64]

Besides divorcement proposals, fifteen of which were introduced in Congress in the 1930s,[65] bills were introduced in the depression decade to prohibit stock ownership by integrated oil companies in oil pipelines and prohibit interstate pipelines from shipping oil that they directly or indirectly owned or controlled.[66] The bills were sponsored by independent producers and had a common goal—transferring economic rent from pipelines to producers.

The final major investigation of the U.S. petroleum industry prior to World War II was conducted by the Congressional Temporary National Economic Committee in September and October of 1939. The inquiry followed FDR's request for studies of all major industrial sectors for evidence of "monopoly" power in the wake of the 1937 downturn, a setback that cast doubt on the efficacy of New Deal policies in ending the depression. As had been the case in earlier investigations, integration rather than the pipeline business per se was on trial.[67] The buck stopped at pipelines nonetheless, and the subsidy theory was raised anew, primarily by independent marketers who advocated pipeline divorcement. The industry stocktaking produced more opinion than statutory reform but had one interesting development—the introduction of oil-product pipelines into political debate.[68]

---

[64]Quoted in Arthur Johnson, *Petroleum Pipelines and Public Policy*, p. 277.

[65]For a list of proposals and oil-state sponsors, see George Wolbert, "The Recurring Spectre of Pipeline Divorcement," p. 127. Contingent divorcement was also proposed in another bill.

[66]Ibid., p. 107.

[67]Arthur Johnson, *Petroleum Pipelines and Public Policy*, p. 278. A list of other pipeline hearings before Congress is contained in George Wolbert, "The Recurring Spectre of Pipeline Divorcement," pp. 127–28.

[68]Arthur Johnson, *Petroleum Pipelines and Public Policy*, p. 283.

Regulation. Mandatory reporting was a forerunner of active regulation of oil pipelines by the ICC. Interstate firms were ordered to file tariff schedules following the passage of the Hepburn Act in June 1906 and by letter were asked for information to be used to create a common oil-pipeline accounting system.[69] With the controversy over which pipelines were common carriers settled in June 1914, interstate pipelines almost universally filed their schedules.

With jurisdiction established, reporting requirements were expanded on January 1, 1915, to include statements of operating revenues and expenses as well as investments pursuant to the Valuation Act of 1913.[70] In mid-1919, "Form P" reports, annual reports for pipeline companies, became a yearly requirement for common carriers. In addition to financial data, the form required information on management, ownership, and operations.[71] Although this information would not be used to directly influence terms of service until several decades later, accountability was achieved should complaints be filed against a reporting company. Otherwise, ICC regulation was passive toward pipelines in the post-1915 period; the agency's efforts were concentrated on railroads.[72]

The first challenge to interstate crude-oil pipeline practices occurred on June 2, 1920, when two brothers in the oil-brokerage business filed a formal complaint with the ICC against the 100,000-barrel minimum tender requirement of the Prairie Pipe Line Company.[73] As an aside, the complaint included Prairie's general pipeline fares. After hearings, the ICC ordered a tender reduction to 10,000 barrels for several routes effective by July 16, 1922. The rate protest was

[69]20 ICC 62 (1906). This led to a rudimentary attempt to prescribe income and balance-sheet reporting (23 ICC 57 [1909]) and a standardized reporting form (24 ICC 31 [1910]). George Wolbert, *U.S. Oil Pipe Lines,* p. 309.

[70]Interstate Commerce Commission, *Classification of Investment in Pipe Lines, Pipe Line Operating Revenues and Pipe Line Operating Expenses of Carriers by Pipe Line, Effective on January 1, 1915* (1914). The Valuation Act was published in 37 Stat. 701 (1913).

[71]33 ICC 37 (1919).

[72]See chapter 16, pp. 974–78, for discussion of federal railroad activity. The ICC's preoccupation with railroads, along with a lack of complaint from shippers, was largely responsible for inactive pipeline regulation.

[73]*Brundred Brothers* v. *Prairie Pipe Line Co. et al.,* 68 ICC 458. In the same year as the Brundred complaint, a relatively minor protest concerning a proposed rate change was heard and settled by the ICC in *Crude Petroleum Oil from Kansas to Lacy Station, Pa.*

dismissed because of its generality and because the agency did not have a criterion for establishing yardstick fares.

The effect of the decision was academic in the practical sense but instructive in the legal sense. The reduced tender was still formidable to most shippers—only twenty tenders under 100,000 barrels (six of those tenders were at the 10,000 minimum) would be handled by Prairie between 1922 and 1931.[74] The decision demonstrated the leverage the ICC possessed over day-to-day operations of interstate pipelines.

The tranquil nature of oil-pipeline regulation in the 1906–30 period would drastically change in the next decade. A combination of general economic duress and industry price demoralization, specifically East Texas production, increased the political stock of pipeline interventionists.

The June 16, 1933, enactment of the National Industrial Recovery Act gave the president authority to initiate oil-pipeline proceedings before the ICC to ensure reasonable rates and other desired practices and to divorce pipelines from integrated operations as a last resort.[75] Although inclined toward divorcement, FDR would leave this authority unused. Pipeline intervention focused instead on section 9(c) of the same act that prohibited interstate shipments of illegally produced oil. Pursuant to this authority, the Federal Tender Board coordinated a program whereby all piped oil had to have tender documents verifying its legal status.

Of greater importance than New Deal regulation was a June 1934 complaint to the ICC that, according to one informed observer, "mark[ed] the beginning of a program of positive regulation of pipelines by the Interstate Commerce Commission."[76] Interestingly, *the complaint was not that pipelines rates were too high but that they were too low.* The protest was filed on behalf of the Louisiana-Arkansas Refiners' Association, representing eighteen independents who feared that reduced transportation costs for other refineries enjoying

---

[74]Arthur Johnson, *Petroleum Pipelines and Public Policy*, p. 206.

[75]National Industrial Recovery Act, title 1, secs. 9(a) and 9(b). 48 Stat. 200 (June 16, 1933).

[76]Roy Prewitt, "The Operation and Regulation of Crude Oil and Gasoline Pipe Lines," *Quarterly Journal of Economics* (February 1942): 206.

pipeline connections would endanger their ability to compete.[77] Whereas Petroleum Administration Board administrator Ickes had recently complained that tariffs were too high, he requested that the reductions be rescinded for the defendant pipelines Shell, Texas, Stanolind, and Texas-Empire, and asked for an investigation.[78] Noted Johnson, oil pipelines now "had to tread the difficult line between justifying rate reductions without at the same time admitting that prior rate levels had been unjustifiably high."[79]

Politics, not economics, continued to hallmark regulatory interest in pipelines, but higher prices were no political match for lower prices. On June 20, 1934, the ICC denied suspension of the proposed rate reductions and announced an investigation of other rates to see if they had been similarly lowered and if not, why not. The inquiry was broadened to include thirty-seven companies representing the majority of interstate trunk lines and gathering lines in the country. The information was assembled by the ICC's Bureau of Valuation, which had previously in the 1914–20 period appraised railroad properties for public-utility regulation. With industry cooperation, including assistance from the American Petroleum Institute, hearings were held in July 1936 and November 1938 and reports were received from ICC examiner J. Paul Kelley. Maximum rates (expressed as a percentage of historic rates) and tender minimums were at issue, and two integrated companies, Ohio Standard and the National Refining Company, broke ranks to take the government's side. With the majority of valuation work tentatively completed in 1939, a preliminary order was issued on December 23, 1940, by the ICC to universalize the 10,000-barrel tender minimum and *adopt an 8 percent annual return-on-capital ceiling.*[80] The return figure, acknowledged the ICC, was high relative to other industries to reflect the uncertainty of the commercial life of oil wells to which pipelines were wed. Twenty-one of the twenty-nine firms involved

---

[77]"Allowing the reductions to become effective will cause severe injury to protestant and the members of its association." *Reduced Pipe Line Rates and Gathering Charges,* ICC Docket no. 26570 (June 11, 1934).

[78]Ickes's about-face was influenced by the president of the refinery group, John Shatford, who was also a member of the Petroleum Administration Board's industry counterpart, the Planning and Coordination Committee.

[79]Arthur Johnson, *Petroleum Pipelines and Public Policy,* p. 242.

[80]*Reduced Pipe Line Rates and Gathering Charges,* 243 ICC 115 (1940).

were above the 8 percent ceiling in 1933 and were instructed to show just cause. Individual rates, however, were not challenged. Further action would be postponed—a December 18, 1941, hearing would be the last, because of the advent of World War II.

A final regulatory episode in the pre–World War II era was a case brought by the Valvoline Oil Company against the ICC, decided July 6, 1938.[81] Valvoline sought to avoid common carriage and valuation reporting on grounds analogous to those of the Uncle Sam Company exemption in 1914. The ICC ruled against Valvoline because the company purchased oil from numerous independents for interstate transport whereas Uncle Sam moved its own production—despite consideration that Valvoline's purchases were made in a competitive market unlike situations the Hepburn amendment was designed to countervail. On appeal, the Supreme Court upheld the ICC order, which further delineated the broad scope of federal oil-pipeline regulation. Noting that Valvoline was the sole purchaser and transporter for over 9,000 wells in Pennsylvania, West Virginia, and Ohio, the Supreme Court upheld regulation on anti-monopoly grounds.

> The practice of compelling producers to sell at the well before admitting their oil to the lines was widely used as a means of monopolizing the product before the Hepburn Amendment in 1906. . . . Certainly one would find a public interest in the sole means of transporting the commodity from thousands of wells for thousands of producers. This was covered by the *Pipe Line* decision.[82]

Taxation. Federal taxation of oil pipelines began in World War I when a 5 percent levy was placed on all interstate common-carrier transportation.[83] In 1918, the tax was raised to 8 percent and was extended to all oil piped by private as well as common carriers before its repeal in 1921.[84] Government attention to relatively high pipeline profits during the Great Depression led to reimposition of the tax in the Federal Revenue Act of 1932.[85] The 4 percent levy was applicable to oil and product lines. In 1940, as a wartime revenue

---

[81]*Petition of the Valvoline Oil Company in the Matter of the Valuation of Its Pipe Lines,* 48 ICC Valuation Reports 10 (1938).

[82]*Valvoline Oil Company* v. *United States,* 308 U.S. 141 at 144–45 (1939).

[83]Public Law 50, 40 Stat. 300 at 315 (1917).

[84]Public Law 254, 40 Stat. 1057 at 1102 (1919).

[85]Public Law 154, 47 Stat. 169 (1932). See *OGJ,* June 23, 1932, pp. 8–9.

measure, the rate was increased to 4.5 percent, where it would remain until after the war.[86]

World War II Policy

Regulatory Activity. The early response of interstate oil pipelines to expanded opportunities created by the widening European conflict occurred amid legal uncertainty. On September 30, 1940, the Antitrust Division of the Justice Department, under Thurman Arnold, filed a sweeping antitrust suit, consisting of sixty-nine charges against twenty-two major oil companies, their affiliates, and the American Petroleum Institute. Suits were simultaneously filed against three major pipeline firms, Phillips, Indiana Standard, and Great Lakes, alleging rebates in violations of the Elkins Act. Dividends from the pipeline companies to the parent equated to rebating and constituted discrimination against external shippers, it was held, although access and rates were the same for outside firms as for the integrated company. With firms liable for triple damages on their rebates made since January 1, 1939, a liability estimated at between $1.6 billion and $2.5 billion, and the government amenable to cooperation, given the looming war situation; a consent settlement was desired to settle the pipeline and antitrust suits. This gave prosecutors a welcomed chance at regulatory reform, normally the province of the ICC, and Arnold adamantly pressed for a new "reasonable" return standard despite the existing 8 percent return limitation.[87]

The settlement prescribed a maximum dividend of 7 percent on ICC valuation for crude and product lines, which was signed by twenty major oil firms and fifty-two pipeline companies on September 16, 1941, and made final on December 23.[88] The three pipeline suits were dismissed, while the so-called Mother Hubbard antitrust suit was postponed before finally being dropped in 1951.

Effective January 1, 1942, petroleum pipelines could not "credit, give, grant, or pay, directly or indirectly any earnings, dividends, sums of money or other valuable considerations . . . in excess . . . of seven percent (7%) of the valuation of such common carrier's property."[89] The dividend ceiling, however, did not automatically

[86]Public Law 656, 54 Stat. 516 at 523 (1940).
[87]Arthur Johnson, *Petroleum Pipelines and Public Policy*, pp. 288–89.
[88]*U.S. v. Atlantic Refining Company et al.*, Civil Action no. 14060 (D.C. District 1941).
[89]Quoted in Arthur Johnson, *Petroleum Pipelines and Public Policy*, p. 300.

translate into rate regulation or profit regulation. Profits in excess of 7 percent could be kept in a surplus account by the pipeline affiliate for either fixed asset reinvestment, retirement of existing debt, working capital, or future dividend payments to reach the maximum allowed. The dividend limit was for a firm's pipeline properties in total; unprofitable and marginally profitable lines could average down highly profitable lines to permissible dividend levels. This had uneconomic implications. Although the need to average up lessened the impact of regulation, the need to average down encouraged marginal investments that without regulation would not have been undertaken. "Padding the rate base," a perennial problem of public-utility regulation, made its entrance with interstate crude trunk lines.

Wartime operations under the consent decree required quick strategies by integrated companies to maximize profits under decree constraints. This, observed Johnson, would be difficult because "the possible variations . . . [were] virtually limitless."[90] One early move by the Great Lakes Pipe Line Company was to replace owners' equity with debt capital (bank loans or debentures), which had the advantages of providing interest expense to reduce earnings to the maximum dividend amount, freeing owner capital for other uses, and preserving firm valuation. The Justice Department partly removed the incentive by requiring the 7 percent maximum to include interest expense.[91]

Integrated companies with common-carrier pipelines had the following choices and combinations thereof:

1. Reinvest the 7 percent maximum on the strategy of maximizing long-run profits by increasing the firm's valuation base;
2. Pay the 7 percent maximum dividend and borrow funds, to be repaid from the cash flow provided by depreciation, to increase the firm's valuation base; and
3. Pay the 7 percent maximum dividend and reinvest any surplus although it would not increase the firm's valuation base.[92]

With the first option being too farsighted and the third alternative being too nearsighted, the middle choice became the most widely

[90]Ibid., p. 333.
[91]Ibid., p. 334.
[92]Ibid., p. 338.

used. The entire decisionmaking process, however, became tentative by 1943 when the ICC fell behind in accounting for valuation improvements made from a dividend fund or borrowings. Valuation work ceased entirely July 1, 1944.[93] Companies were left to their discretion to estimate valuation, which had to be tentative because ICC valuation methods were not public information. Integrated pipeline firms operated under this uncertainty throughout the war.

The tentative order of the ICC, limiting profits to an 8 percent return on a pipeline's property, came before the commission in a wartime case. In February 1942, the Minnelusa Oil Corporation and the Wasatch Oil Refining Company complained that tariffs charged by five pipeline companies for gathering-line and trunk-line services were unreasonable and discriminatory.[94]

In the first rate case in the thirty-six-year history of ICC jurisdiction, the commission sided with the plaintiffs and ordered rate reductions based on the 8 percent order. The reduction, ordered over the objection of competing railroads, was for trunk lines only; connected gathering-line charges were found reasonable and were left unchanged.[95]

Federal Pipelines. Growing incentives prior to the war and war-related tanker diversions beginning in mid-1941 encouraged firms to construct oil and oil-product pipelines to serve the major East Coast markets. In 1939, Jersey Standard began constructing the 812-mile Plantation Pipeline to carry gasoline from Louisiana to North Carolina. Soon after, Gulf Oil and Pure Oil began the 462-mile Southeastern Pipeline from Florida to Tennessee and Georgia. Both lines, however, encountered an age-old difficulty—obstruction by petroleum-carrying railroads. Seven Georgian railroads denied cross-rights to the pipelines, and the pipeline firms, unable to legally "homestead" their way over or below the surface property of the railroads, sought a political solution. A pipeline-sponsored eminent-domain bill was defeated by the Georgia legislature in March 1941, after which federal assistance was received. On the strength of the

---

[93]Ibid., p. 336.

[94]*Minnelusa Oil Corp. et al.* v. *Continental Pipe Line Co. et al.,* 258 ICC 41 (1944). This case also established ICC rate jurisdiction over interstate lines that carried oil intrastate if a contiguous stream went into interstate commerce.

[95]Arthur Johnson, *Petroleum Pipelines and Public Policy,* p. 397.

worsening European conflict, the Cole Act was passed on July 1 to give interstate pipelines deemed vital to national defense condemnation rights.[96] The Southeastern and Plantation lines were completed, respectively, in late 1941 and early 1942.

The Cole Act also authorized direct federal subsidization of pipelines built for the war effort. This federal effort was launched in early 1942 with a Tulsa, Oklahoma, meeting of industry experts who were to study supply-and-demand conditions and recommend new pipeline projects. Foremost in the resulting ten-point proposal was to "build *two big pipe lines* from the Texas area thru to the Atlantic Coast if tankers are not going to be available."[97] Not only did this recommendation materialize, its implementation would later prove to "revolutionize postwar American pipelining."[98]

Petroleum Administration for War Recommendation 49, issued May 11, 1942, gave general approval to implement the Tulsa plan. The centerpiece of the program, a 24-inch crude-oil trunk line from the Southwest to the eastern seaboard, was twice denied steel allocations by the War Production Board before approval was given on June 10, 1942. On June 26, formal plans were made final by the Defense Plant Corporation, a government agency that owned and operated physical assets associated with the war effort, and the War Emergency Pipelines, Inc., a consortium of eleven eastern oil companies working on government contracts. At a taxpayer cost of $79 million, the "Big Inch" crude pipeline was laid during the second half of 1942 from Longview, Texas, to Norris City, Illinois, and through to Linden, New Jersey. The 1,400-mile line, completed ahead of schedule and below budget, represented an engineering triumph that connected oil-rich East Texas to refinery centers in the Midwest and Northeast.[99]

A second major government pipeline, the "Little Big Inch" products line, stretched 1,700 miles from Beaumont, Texas, to Seymour, Indiana, and also through to Linden, New Jersey. Approved on

[96]Public Law 197, 55 Stat. 610 (1941). This law would be extended through June 30, 1946. Public Law 78, 59 Stat. 233 (1945).

[97]Arthur Johnson, *Petroleum Pipelines and Public Policy*, p. 316.

[98]Ibid., p. 317.

[99]For greater detail on the construction and operation of the Big Inch line, see John Frey and H. Chandler Ide, *A History of the Petroleum Administration for War* (Washington, D.C.: Government Printing Office, 1946), pp. 428–34.

January 26, 1943, the 20-inch line was placed in much-needed service a year later to the day. Built at a public expense of $68.6 million, the line linked the Beaumont-Port Arthur-Houston refining mecca with major consumer markets on the East Coast from which over two-thirds of the product was shipped to theaters of war.[100]

In addition to the Big Inch and Little Inch projects, four other pipelines were financed by the Reconstruction Finance Corporation, headed by New Dealer Jesse Jones. The overriding aim of the government pipeline program was to move oil east and north toward major consumption and shipping points. Pipelines were to replace tankers, which had previously moved crude and product from California and the Gulf Coast to the Atlantic seaboard. The projects were:

1. Southwest Emergency Pipe Line, which was built from Refugia to Pierce Junction, Texas, in October 1943 at a cost of $6.1 million. The 154-mile line would run over 52 million barrels of crude oil during wartime to feed the Big Inch line.
2. Florida Emergency Pipe Line, which was built in June 1943 from Carrabelle eastward to Jacksonville, Florida, for $4.2 million. The 200-mile line would carry over 19 million barrels of petroleum products during the war to link inland barge movements to the Atlantic Coast market.
3. Plantation Extension Pipe Line, which in February 1943 connected Greensboro, North Carolina, to Richmond, Virginia, at an expense of $3.4 million. The 175-mile project would carry 22 million barrels of crude oil during wartime to refineries in the central Atlantic states.
4. Ohio Emergency Pipe Line, which in 1943 was laid between Tiffin and Doylestown, Ohio, at a cost of $1.5 million. The 80-mile line would carry 17.7 million barrels of crude oil during the war to link two existing pipeline networks.[101]

The six government lines cost $163 million, ran just below 500 million barrels of crude and product in the 1942–45 period, and provided

---

[100]Ibid., pp. 434–37.

[101]Ibid., p. 370; and Arthur Johnson, *Petroleum Pipelines and Public Policy*, pp. 320–21. Also see Kendall Beaton, *Enterprise in Oil* (New York: Appleton-Century-Crofts, 1957), pp. 602–10.

tariff income of $193 million to show a $30-million surplus before general and administrative costs.[102]

Although in part usurped by the above-mentioned projects, burdened by wartime tax obligations, and restrained by strict material acquisitions from the War Production Board,[103] private projects in the war period exceeded government projects in pipe mileage and financial expenditure. In addition to converting existing pipage to new lines, expanding pump facilities to increase runs, and reversing flows, an estimated 2,200 miles of gathering lines and 9,850 miles of trunk lines were laid by the private sector at a cost of $179 million.[104] The extent of private initiative is all the more noteworthy given ICC rate regulation and dividend ceilings on integrated pipeline companies, which interfered with quick payouts needed to undertake war-demand projects whose peacetime profitability was less certain. Some disincentive was removed by the Accelerated Amortization Program, which allowed five-year writeoffs of fixed assets,[105] but overall, the regulatory environment encouraged federal substitution for private projects—as decided in part by pipeline executives in their advisory role to the Petroleum Administration for War, the Reconstruction Finance Corporation, and other federal agencies.

Postwar Readjustment

Privatization of Federal Pipelines. With the tide of war turned and peacetime envisioned, industry executives became concerned about federal ownership and operation of the Big Inch and Little Inch lines in the postwar era. The two pipelines were without equal and could dominate competitors. Once it became clear that federal operation

---

[102]John Frey and H. Chandler Ide, *A History of the Petroleum Administration for War,* p. 370.

[103]The most notable private project canceled because of lack of Petroleum Administration for War approval was the Pacific War Emergency Pipe Line, a proposed 20-inch-diameter line from Texas to California.

[104]A summary of the thirty-nine projects, twenty-seven of which came on stream during the war, is presented in John Frey and H. Chandler Ide, *A History of the Petroleum Administration for War,* pp. 418–25.

[105]To receive the tax break, a "certificate of necessity" was required from the War Production Board. Later, "nonnecessity certificates" were issued to shorter term projects, which allowed a writeoff for the duration of the war effort. Arthur Johnson, *Petroleum Pipelines and Public Policy,* p. 332.

would not be the case, the major issue became whether the two lines would continue to be used, and if so, for what purpose—oil, product, or natural-gas transport? Various opinions, reflecting the self-interest of various groups, were advanced. Taking the polar position of nonuse were coal interests represented by the National Coal Association, the Eastern States Retail Solid Fuel Conference, and the United Mine Workers and railroads represented by the Association of American Railroads. Their opinion was that the Big Inch and Little Inch should be mothballed as a "military asset" for use in a future emergency.[106] Taking a middle-ground position were motor-truck and tanker firms, oil pipelines, and Midwestern refineries that favored natural-gas transmission if the lines were to be operational at all. A free-market view, finally, was taken by the Independent Natural Gas Association, which favored sale of the lines to the highest bidder without use restrictions. Natural economics, it was believed, would dictate a match between the gas-rich Southwest and burgeoning Northeast markets.[107]

Immediate use of the two large-diameter lines was given to Tennessee Gas Transmission Company on December 2, 1946, in the wake of a major coal strike that natural-gas transmission could ease. Tennessee's use was limited to 120 days with deliveries capped at 150 million cubic feet per day under the watchful eye of the Interior Department. After disposal was decided upon by the government, bidding unsuccessfully took place in mid-1946 followed by a successful sale in early 1947. (The high bid of $66 million in 1946 was deemed too low.) The high bid of $143,127,000, announced February 14, 1947, was by the Texas Eastern Transmission Company, a paper corporation established for the bid by five investors including George and Herman Brown of the Brown and Root Company, a major defense contractor, and Everette DeGolyer, a former Petroleum Administration for War geologist who played a major role with the Big Inch.[108] The two lines were converted to natural-gas carriage, and high profits were immediately realized.

[106]Ibid., p. 345; and *NPN*, October 17, 1945, p. 44.

[107]For this reason, the Texas-based Commission for Conservation of Oil and Natural Gas supported natural-gas usage. Arthur Johnson, *Petroleum Pipelines and Public Policy*, p. 332.

[108]Raymond Klempin, "The Odyssey of Brown & Root: War Efforts," *Houston Business Journal*, September 6, 1982, p. 18; and *OGJ*, February 22, 1947, p. 101. Financing was obtained from $120 million in first-mortgage bonds purchased by twelve life insurance companies and $34 million raised from a stock issue. A footnote to this

The other four federal pipelines were disposed of with less fanfare: the Florida Emergency Pipeline was sold for scrap (metal) value; the Plantation Extension was sold for pipe value (removal to be relaid); the Southwest Emergency Pipe Line was sold for conversion to gas transmission; and the Ohio Emergency Pipe Line was sold for crude transport.[109]

Regulation. For oil pipelines, the postwar period was marked by technological advances and rapid expansion.[110] With crude producers and product consumers benefiting from these developments, pipeline criticism was at an all-time low. Federal regulation, consequently, was minimal. Except for tax incentives, oil pipelines received no preferential treatment during the Korean conflict of the early 1950s. Loan guarantees, requested by Texas Eastern to reconvert the Big Inch to crude carriage in 1955, by the American Pipe Line Company to build a Texas–East Coast crude line in 1955, and by Texas Eastern again to construct a Texas–New Jersey product line in 1958, were rejected by federal officials.[111] The extent of federal activity was to complete two pieces of unfinished regulatory business begun before the war. In 1948 and 1949, valuations were brought up to date for all fifty-five covered interstate oil pipelines. The second area of unfinished business concerned the ICC's tentative order, which set an 8 percent maximum return on valuation and a 10,000-barrel minimum tender in 1940. Firms violating the standards had been allowed to show just cause, but hearings were adjourned in late 1941 because of war conditions.

In 1948, the hearing on reduced pipeline rates and gathering charges was reopened. Drastic changes in the industry—increased trunk-line mileage, reduced fares, and lowered tender minimums— led ICC commissioner Clyde Aitchison to close the investigation. The 8 percent and 10,000-barrel parameters were not questioned as regulatory norms, but a rate decline averaging 40 percent and common use of 10,000-barrel tenders made further action superfluous.

---

sale is that Tennessee Gas, narrowly defeated by Texas Eastern's bid, would never do business with Brown and Root again during the tenure of Tenneco chairman Gardner Symonds.

[109] Arthur Johnson, *Petroleum Pipelines and Public Policy*, p. 347.

[110] For a list of fifteen major technological innovations in the pipeline industry in this period, see ibid., p. 354.

[111] Ibid., pp. 375, 377.

Oil pipelines, in short, had changed from plant facilities in the prewar era to carriers for hire, and given liberal computation of firm valuation—use of reproduction cost in addition to historical cost, a liberal interest return, and inclusion of debt capital in addition to owners' equity—the 8 percent ceiling represented a full market return for most. So what began as a complaint against a tariff reduction but turned into a high-rate and high-tender investigation became moot because of competitive conditions. Nonetheless, the consent decree was joined by a second layer of regulation.

The Korean Conflict

With hostilities in full swing in late 1950, the Petroleum Administration for Defense (PAD) pondered whether to allow accelerated tax amortization for new oil pipelines. The question was whether projects conceived prior to the war should receive benefits as new defense-designated projects did. Because other oil carriers (railroads, tankers, and barges) were receiving benefits, pipelines under construction were allowed to accelerate 40 percent of their investment (later 30 percent) with the balance depreciable at peacetime rates.[112]

Oil pipelines, already under either state or federal price and tender regulation, were not subject to PAD controls. The major area of pipeline regulation was materials acquisition. Deputy Administrator Bruce Brown described his agency's role:

> It has been, and continues to be, PAD's philosophy that the oil business is a private enterprise engaged in by very numerous groups of people and that PAD should not attempt to dictate what private enterprise groups do with their money. PAD has felt that its responsibility with respect to the allocation of controlled materials was merely that of a group of umpires making fair decisions as to which projects were likely to contribute to national security and hence should receive first priority attention. The whole priority system is merely a temporary regulation over the normal purchase and sale channels through which pipe and other equipment are acquired.[113]

The Controlled Materials Plan was controversial. Without free-market bidding to ration supply to demand, crucial decisions were

---

[112]Bruce Brown, *Oil Men in Washington* (El Dorado, Ark.: Evanil Press, 1965), pp. 171–72.

[113]Ibid., p. 278.

made on the basis of political value judgments and planners' forecasts. Oil pipelines competed directly with gas pipelines for pipage, and "the tension was terrific."[114] Whatever misallocation there was between pipeline types (not only crude oil and natural gas but oil product, too), there was reasoned speculation that steel and other materials were misallocated among industries. Bruce Brown complained:

> Steel has been diverted from line pipe manufacturers to "approved programs." So, while Detroit had its biggest week in automobile manufacturing, households will be cold next winter.[115]

Evidence of materials regulation was most obvious with the Platte oil pipeline, on which construction was begun prior to the conflict and which was left with a 591-mile gap in early 1951 because of an unapproved materials application.[116] After belated completion, it brought oil from the Rocky Mountains to midcontinent refineries. Unbuilt lines were a less obvious planning error. These problems would fade with the revocation of materials regulation in early 1953.

Federal Activity: 1956–84

Challenge to Consent-Decree Practices. In the mid-1950s, attention once again turned toward oil pipelines with the direct involvement of U.S. integrated companies in a foreign crisis.[117] Major integrated companies were multinationals as well, and an "oil lift" was performed in 1956 to supply Europe with petroleum that had been cut off by the closing of the Suez Canal. This accompanied a slight price rise at home, which, coupled with general suspicion about the majors' domestic and international practices, gave rise to hearings in early 1957 by the Subcommittee on Antitrust and Monopoly of the Senate Judiciary Committee. Coming on the heels of well-publicized hearings before the Texas Railroad Commission on well-connection

---

[114]Ibid., p. 200. Because construction of gas lines was generally further along than that of oil lines at the beginning of the materials rationing program, higher allocations went to the latter. In one quarter, 57 percent went to oil pipelines and 43 percent went to gas lines.

[115]Ibid., p. 175.

[116]Ibid., pp. 173–74.

[117]Not since the 1949 "Wherry Committee" hearings had oil pipelines come under criticism on the federal level.

decisions involving many of the same companies, discussed below, major companys' pipeline practices were once again in the spotlight. Effective counterarguments by the industry trade group, Committee for Oil Pipe Lines, explained the economics behind pipeline decisions to defuse the controversy. No legislative proposals followed the hearings.

In October of the same year, a more serious challenge to interstate oil pipelines developed when the chairman of the House Antitrust Subcommittee, Emanuel Celler, began an investigation to "ascertain how effective consent decrees have been to . . . restore a competitive climate in the industries concerned."[118] Immediately preceding the investigation—and probably prompted by its announcement in April—four court proceedings were initiated by the Justice Department against oil pipelines that questioned long-standing practices under the decree that, in retrospect, represented an attempt to increase regulation. Two motions against Tidal Pipe Line Company and Texas Pipe Line Company concerned the inclusion of leased (nonowned) property in the valuation base. A third motion against Service Pipe Line Company, a subsidiary of Indiana Standard, questioned adding firm betterments to the valuation base on a current, pro rata basis. The government contended that improvements and depreciation should be added the year after completion. The fourth motion was the most important, a challenge to debt-capital inclusion in the valuation base by Pure Oil's Arapahoe Pipe Line Company. The 7 percent dividend, Justice argued, could be based only on paid-in capital. The Texas Pipe Line motion was dropped in return for a $100,000 transfer into Texas's surplus account, and the remaining three cases were argued in federal district court.[119]

Judge Richmond Keech ruled against the three motions in March 1958 on grounds that the controverted actions, which had been going on for sixteen years without the ICC or the Justice Department's questioning them, did not result from malintent. On appeal, the U.S. Supreme Court upheld the lower court on June 8, 1959, with similar reasoning:

---

[118]Quoted in Arthur Johnson, *Petroleum Pipelines and Public Policy*, p. 440.

[119]*United States* v. *The Atlantic Refining Co. et al.*, Civil Action no. 14060 (D.C. District, March 25, 1958).

> Where the language of a consent decree in its normal meaning supports an interpretation; where that interpretation has been adhered to over may years by all the parties, including those government officials who drew up and administered the decree from the start; and where the trial court concludes that this interpretation is in fact the one the parties intended, we will not reject it simply because another reading might seem more consistent with the Government's reasons for entering into the agreement in the first place.[120]

The Justice Department's initiative to reregulate firms operating under the consent decree had been repelled.

The Celler investigation constituted a critical review of the commission's "Hear-No-Evil, See-No-Evil" approach.[121] In the 1941–55 period, thirty-one specialized interpretations of minor importance were made, and not until 1957 was there a major challenge to the industry's interpretation of the consent decree, viz., use of reproduction cost in addition to historical cost to determine valuation (unlike railroads), wholesale substitutions of debt for equity to maximize valuation, and liberal depreciation methods. Celler also censured congressional underfunding of ICC pipeline work, dependence on industry personnel for regulatory-related information, departmental turnover, an absence of prosecution of alleged decree violations, and poor liaison between the ICC and Justice Department.[122] Yet a reason for reregulation was not found; producers' complaints against pipeline practices had been virtually nonexistent, and no credible theory of inefficient performance existed. Whatever the intention of critics, the fact that pipeline regulation was lenient created industry growth that benefited producers, refiners, marketers, and ultimately consumers. Political opportunism, not economics, remained the foe of oil pipelines.[123]

---

[120]*United States* v. *Atlantic Refining Co. et al.*, 360 U.S. 19 at 23–24 (1959).

[121]This description of ICC inactivity was used by John Shenefield in testimony before the Senate Subcommittee on Antitrust and Monopoly on June 28, 1978. Reprinted in *Oil Pipelines and Public Policy*, ed. Edward Mitchell (Washington, D.C.: American Enterprise Institute, 1979), p. 198.

[122]*Report of the Antitrust Subcommittee on the Consent Decree Program of the Department of Justice*, House Committee on the Judiciary, 86th Cong., 1st sess. (Washington, D.C.: Government Printing Office, 1959).

[123]The minority report, written by three committee members, characterized the majority report as a political document by Democrat Celler against a Republican administration. Arthur Johnson, *Petroleum Pipelines and Public Policy*, pp. 450–51.

Controversies over Regulation of Public Utilities. From the 1940s through the 1960s, tranquility prevailed with interstate petroleum pipeline valuation and resulting rates. Rate regulation anchored on fair value "worked," judging from shipper acceptance and industry growth and performance.

In these years, the ICC formula was not publicly revealed, although the industry closely approximated its computation by comparing reported data and final valuations. The reason it was not formalized was because staff valuation work was subject to change by the commissioners.[124] The formula closely adhered to the final determination, however, and in 1977, veteran ICC valuation engineer Jesse Oak went public.[125] The basis of rate regulation, the "Oak Formula," was

$$V = 1.06 \, [O(O/O + R) + R(R/O + R)] \, R\text{-}D/R + (L_1 + L_2 + W)$$

where

V = valuation;
O = original cost;
R = cost of reproduction, new (replacement cost);
D = depreciation;
L_1 = land;
L_2 = right-of-way; and
W = working capital.

Described as "unique in the annals of rate regulation,"[126] the formula valued pipeline properties between original investment cost and current replacement cost of a similar facility. The cost mixing was called "fair value."[127] The particular weighting, devoid of rigorous explanation, had been controversial among traditional public-utility regulators and economists. The 1.06 multiplicand was

[124]Conversation between author and Jesse Oak, June 25, 1984.

[125]Testimony of Jesse Oak before the Federal Energy Regulatory Commission, FERC Docket no. OR 78-2 (March 25, 1977). Several months later, oil-pipeline regulation was transferred from the ICC to the Federal Energy Regulatory Commission by the Energy Reorganization Act, Public Law 95-91, 91 Stat. 584 (1977).

[126]Peter Navarro and Thomas Stauffer, "The Legal History and Economic Implications of Oil Pipeline Regulation," *Energy Law Journal* 2, no. 2 (1981): 296.

[127]"The basis of all calculations as to the reasonableness of rates . . . must be the fair value of the property being used. . . . The present as compared with the original cost of construction . . . are all matters for consideration, and are to be given such weight as may be just and right in each case." *Smyth* v. *Ames*, 169 U.S. 466 (1898). The fair-value doctrine was widely used for railroad valuation by the ICC and was reaffirmed by the Supreme Court in *Bluefield Company* v. *Public Service Commission,*

intended to represent the going interest rate (6 percent) to approximate the opportunity cost of capital, the "going-concern value," of the firm.[128] Depreciation was based on straight-line write-downs based on estimates of physical life that were revised upward with asset improvements. The addition of working capital, land valued at the higher of the appraisal price or one-half the purchase price, and right-of-way valued at depreciated cost based on estimated pipeline life resulted in a valuation that was distinctly higher than original cost, on which to base the allowed margin.

Given industry performance and the paucity of rate challenges, critics of the valuation formula have had to admit that "while its genesis [was] suspect . . . it functioned unexpectedly well."[129] Its success was not due to the equation itself but to the lack of constraint it placed on entrepreneurs and investors. Industry growth during four decades of Oak-formula regulation can be gleaned from table 14.1.

The plethora of rate cases that swelled the ICC-FERC dockets in the 1970s and early 1980s concerned the method of valuation for setting oil-pipeline rates. If a more stringent formula could be substituted for fair value—namely, standard public-utility original-cost valuation—shipping costs could be lowered and wellhead prices could be correspondingly increased.[130] With economic rent politically attainable, decades of peaceful coexistence between wellhead interests and pipeline interests were shattered; between 1969 and 1982, over 140 rate cases would be filed.

The *Trans-Alaska Pipeline System* case concerned crude-oil pipelines, although the *Williams I* case, involving a product line, set the

---

262 U.S. 679 (1923) and in *St. Louis O'Fallon Railway Company* v. *United States*, 279 U.S. 461 (1929). Fair-value ratemaking and alternative rate-base methodologies are examined in greater detail in chapter 15, pp. 929–33.

[128]See ICC testimony in Atlantic Pipe Line Co., Valuation Docket no. 1203, 47 ICC Val. Rep. 585 (1937).

[129]Peter Navarro and Thomas Stauffer, "The Legal History and Economic Implications of Oil Pipeline Regulation," p. 303. The formula is described by these economists as "bizarre . . . a mysterious collection of seemingly unrelated components that, through the wonders of jurists algebra, miraculously distill into a single simple sum" (p. 297).

[130]Rate reductions would not disrupt service as long as a pipeline's variable costs were covered. With pipelines built according to "fair-value" profitability, fixed-asset payouts could be jeopardized by regulatory changes in favor of wellhead or downstream interests.

Table 14.1
INTERSTATE OIL PIPELINE GROWTH: 1940–80

Year	Mileage	Employment	Average Haul (miles)	Revenue ($ millions)
1940	124,255	–	–	–
1945	137,545	–	–	–
1950	158,472	29,000	441	442
1955	188,540	27,000	454	678
1960	190,944	23,000	492	770
1965	268,275	20,000	489	904
1970	291,122	18,000	520	1,188
1975	313,178	17,000	546	1,184
1980	341,283	21,000	577	6,340

SOURCE: *Transportation in America,* ed. Frank Smith (Washington, D.C.: Transportation Policy Associates, various years).
NOTE: Mileage and employment are for intrastate and interstate pipelines; average haul and revenue are for interstate pipelines only. All figures refer to crude oil and product lines.

stage by bringing the entire ratemaking methodology under review in 1971.[131] The *TAPS* case grew out of the prolific Prudhoe Bay discovery in Alaska in 1968. In 1969, a consortium of eight companies began construction of an 800-mile crude line from the North Slope to the all-season shipping port of Valdez, Alaska. Ownership interests were held by Sohio (33.34 percent), ARCO (21 percent), Exxon (20 percent), British-Petroleum (15.84 percent), Mobil (5 percent), Phillips (1.66 percent), Union (1.66 percent), and Amerada Hess (1.5 percent). Construction was soon stopped by legal challenges filed by environmental groups pursuant to the National Environmental Policy Act of 1970. Years of delay and redesign followed, and with the help of the Trans-Alaska Pipeline Act of 1973, what had begun as a $900-million, three-year project was finally completed in eight years at a cost of over $9 billion.[132]

---

[131]*Williams I* is discussed in this chapter, pp. 827–32. According to John Cleary, who brought the original complaints in both cases, without the *Williams I* precedent, the *TAPS* challenge probably would not have occurred. Conversation with author, June 20, 1984.

[132]For some of the environment-related burdens placed on the project, which aggregated 1,500 man-years of environmental impact studies at a cost of $400 million, see Ruth Knowles, *America's Energy Famine* (Norman: University of Oklahoma Press, 1980), pp. 274–79.

In mid-1977, tariffs were first filed with the ICC based on a 7 percent return on valuation (per the consent decree), as was common industry practice. The alternative 8 percent return was not chosen so interest costs of the highly leveraged project could be expensed. Based on a huge pipeline investment, tariffs were calculated at over $6.00 per barrel, an astronomical figure, relatively speaking, which necessitated lower wellhead prices to be competitive. Formal protests were immediately filed by nonconsortium beneficiaries of maximum wellhead prices—the state of Alaska and the Arctic Slope Regional Corporation—as well as the ICC and Department of Justice, which recognized an opportunity to apply, and potentially expand, regulatory powers to oil pipelines as had been done during the 1970s "energy crisis" by regulators in other energy sectors. On grounds of "probable unlawfulness," the ICC denied the proposed tariffs on June 28, 1977, and substituted a substantially lower interim rate, recalculated at a 10 percent return (increased from 7 percent to allegedly compensate for increased risk) on a substantially reduced valuation.[133] A petition was filed by four of the owners in federal court to invalidate the order. They argued that it was illegal for the ICC to suspend the initial rates, traditionally calculated per the Oak formula, and to substitute interim rates. The court ruled against the owners to uphold the ICC action.[134] What began as a rate case became a dispute over valuation.

The Supreme Court upheld the authority and reasonableness of the commission's suspension in glowing language in a mid-1978 decision.[135] "What the Commission did," said the Court, "is an intelligent and practical exercise of its suspension power which is thoroughly in accord with Congress' goal . . . to strike a fair balance between the needs of the public and the needs of regulated carriers."[136] Upheld was the government's argument that a portion of

---

[133]Trans-Alaska Pipe Line System, 355 ICC 80 at 81 (1977). The commission opined: "Maintenance of excessively high rates could act as a deterrent to the use of the line by nonaffiliated oil producers and would also delay the Alaskan interests in obtaining revenue that depend on the well-head price of the oil." Interim rates were set between $4.68 and $5.10 per barrel, a reduction of between $1.13 and $1.67 per barrel for the eight carrier-owners.

[134]*Mobil Alaska Pipeline Co. v. United States,* 557 F.2d 775 (1977).

[135]Trans-Alaska Pipeline Rate Cases, 436 U.S. 631 (1978).

[136]Ibid., p. 653.

the $9-billion valuation represented project mismanagement and could not be included in the rate base.

By order of July 7, 1977, the commission referred the case to an administrative law judge to gather evidence and make a preliminary finding. Following *Williams I, TAPS* was divided into a generic inquiry into ratemaking methodology (Phase I) and a case-specific inquiry into operating and construction costs to determine "just and reasonable" rates (Phase II). On February 1, 1980, an initial decision of Phase I was made.[137] Administrative Judge Max Kane, with 131 volumes of testimony by his side, sided with the government that the traditional ICC methodology was improper, and thus the original tariff filings were not just and reasonable, while interim rates were. A federal court ruling in the parallel *Williams I* case was cited in support:

> It is for us "to build a viable modern precedent for use in future cases that not only renders the right result, but does so by way of ratemaking criteria free of the problems that appear to exist in the ICC's approach."[138]

Tiring of the prolonged proceedings, Alaska formally requested an expedited decision by the full ICC by September 1, 1982. Citing the "record's massive dimensions," the FERC with "genuine regret" denied the motion.[139] Attention was drawn to *Williams I*, which was to be the starting point for a tailored decision in *TAPS*. On November 30, 1982, the day of Opinion 154 in *Williams I*, a remand order allowed the *TAPS* litigants to submit new evidence in light of the decision.[140] The uniqueness of the case was reconfirmed; TAPS tariffs ten times the amount of other pipelines "may be of real moment to ultimate consumers."[141]

Pretrial evidence was presented before Administrative Judge Isaac Benkin in the second half of 1983. (Benkin served in the same capacity in *Williams I*.) In what he called "the largest case in America today," 60 thousand pages of manuscript were produced over several

[137]10 FERC 65174 (1980).

[138]10 FERC 65180.

[139]20 FERC 61095 (July 12, 1982).

[140]"This remand is limited and narrow. Its sole purpose is to obtain material that will enlighten us on the basic methodological issues." 21 FERC 61285 (1982). In *Williams I*, the FERC tipped its hand on *TAPS*. Noting that carriers and shippers were one and the same, the commission stated that "controls as stringent as those that the governing statute permits us to impose" might be necessary. 21 FERC 61600.

[141]Ibid.

hundred hearing days. The case was split into two phases. Phase I examined rate-base issues; Phase II was separated into cost of construction and non-cost of construction. Alaska held separate rate hearings. The first hint of a resolution was a proposed settlement submitted by ARCO in late 1984 that offered to reduce rates by 15 percent to $6.15 per barrel, equating to a 6.4 percent rate of return, roughly half of what was originally sought.

Vacation of the Consent Decree. On December 13, 1982, the Justice Department entered into an agreement with plaintiff oil companies to vacate the consent decree.[142] Party to the agreement were twenty oil companies, fifty-two pipeline companies, and seven affiliates or subsidiaries of major oil companies.[143] Throughout its forty-one-year

[142]*United States of America v. The Atlantic Refining Company et al.,* Civil Action no. 14060 (D.D.C. 1982).

[143]The defendants were the Atlantic Refining Company; Cities Service Company; Consolidated Oil Corporation; Continental Oil Company; Gulf Oil Corporation; Humble Oil & Refining Company; Mid-Continent Petroleum Corporation; Phillips Petroleum Company; Pure Oil Company; Shell Union Oil Corporation; Skelly Oil Company; Socony-Vacuum Oil Company, Incorporated; Standard Oil Company (Indiana); Standard Oil Company (Kentucky); Standard Oil Company (New Jersey); the Standard Oil Company (Ohio); Sun Oil Company; the Texas Company; the Texas Corporation; Tide Water Associated Oil Company; Ajax Pipe Line Corporation; Arkansas Fuel Oil Company; Arkansas Natural Gas Corporation; Arkansas Pipeline Corporation; Atlantic Pipe Line Company; Buffalo Pipe Line Corporation; Carter Oil Company; Cities Service Oil Company (Delaware); Continental Pipe Line Company; Detroit Southern Pipe Line Company; Empire Gas & Fuel Company; Empire Pipeline Company; Great Lakes Pipe Line Company; Gulf Refining Company; Humble Pipe Line Company; International Pipe Line Company; Kaw Pipe Line Company; Keystone Pipe Line Company; Lawrence Pipe Line Company; Magnolia Petroleum Company; Magnolia Pipe Line Company; Magnolia Pipe Line Company of Illinois; Middlesex Pipe Line Company; Oklahoma Pipe Line Company; Pan American Petroleum & Transport Company; Pan American Pipe Line Company; Phillips Pipe Line Company; Plantation Pipe Line Company; Portland Pipe Line Company; Pure Oil Pipe Line Company (Pennsylvania); Pure Transportation Company; Shell Pipe Line Corporation; Sinclair Refining Company; Sohio Pipe Line Company; Southeastern Pipe Line Company; Standard Oil Company of Louisiana; Standard Oil Company of New Jersey; Standish Pipe Line Company; Stanolind Pipe Line Company; The Sun Oil Line Company; Sun Oil Company of Michigan; Sun Pipe Line Company; Sun Pipe Line Company of Illinois; Sun Pipe Line, Inc.; Sun Transportation Company; Susquehanna Pipe Line Company; the Texas-Empire Pipe Line Company; the Texas-Empire Pipe Line Company of Texas; Texas-New Mexico Pipe Line Company; the Texas Pipe Line Company; the Tide Water Pipe Company, Limited; Tidal Pipe Line Company; Toledo Northern Pipe Line Company; Transit and Storage Company; Tuscarora Oil Company, Limited; United States Pipe Line Company; Utah Oil Refining Company; Wabash Pipe Line Company; and White Eagle Pipe Line Company, Inc.

history, the decree complicated existing regulation and incited abnormal business practices to modify its effects. Firms with frozen funds were instructed to establish a capital account to deplete within five years by enlarging working capital, retiring debt, or constructing or purchasing common-carrier facilities. Upon completion, signatory companies were "released from other obligations."[144] Authorities were allowed to file objections against disbursement plans, but this did not occur.

Investigation. A new area of federal oil-pipeline inquiry began in the early 1960s when jointly owned and operated lines, a common feature of the modern era of large-diameter pipelines, began to be investigated. In 1962, the FTC began to investigate the Colonial Pipeline; a year later that investigation was transferred to the Antitrust Division of the Department of Justice. The investigation revolved around the traditional regulatory question of shipper access in light of common-carrier obligations; little wrongdoing was substantiated, and the inquiry was closed in 1976. However, two proposed consortium purchases of the Gateway-Match and Glacier pipelines were blocked by the Justice Department on antitrust grounds and abandoned.[145]

Two actions involving pipelines occurred in the turbulent 1970s. In the wake of the Arab embargo, a 1971 investigation developed into a major antitrust suit filed on July 17, 1973, against the top eight majors.[146] Although bans on joint ventures and outright divorcement were suggested for oil pipelines, refinery operations within integrated operations were on the hot seat for the first time since the Rockefeller era. At issue was the competitive viability of independents in light of the practices of major companies.[147]

[144]*United States of America* v. *The Atlantic Refining Company et al.,* Civil Action no. 14060 (D.D.C. 1982), p. 6.

[145]Similar investigations were made of the TAPS, Explorer, and Olympic lines without action. George Wolbert, *U.S. Oil Pipe Lines,* p. 285.

[146]*In the matter of Exxon Corporation, et al.,* FTC Docket no. 8934 (1973). The suit alleged violation of section 5 of the Federal Trade Commission Act which read: "Unfair methods of competition in commerce and unfair or deceptive acts or practices in commerce, are declared unlawful." Joining the suit were the states of Arizona, California, Connecticut, Florida, Oregon, and Washington, each of which questioned Exxon's "monopoly" practices in their state. The case, combined with the *City of Long Beach* action, were consolidated as Multi-District Litigation, Docket no. 150 (MDL-150).

[147]The suit was dropped in 1981. See chapter 26, pp. 1561–62.

In June 1978, a staff report of the Subcommittee on Antitrust and Monopoly of the Senate Judiciary Committee, titled *Report on Oil Company Ownership of Pipelines* (Kennedy staff report), was released, which reinterpreted the history and purpose of oil-pipeline regulation with normative overtones of increased regulation.[148] On the basis of "overwhelmingly pervasive analysis," Senator Edward Kennedy (D-Mass.) petitioned the FTC on January 4, 1979, to begin groundwork on "a trade regulation rule declaring it to be an unfair trade practice for an oil company to have any ownership interest in petroleum pipelines of certain classes."[149] The renewed call for divestiture again reflected political opportunism.[150]

Safety Legislation. Federal safety regulation for oil pipelines began in 1921 when the Explosives Act of 1909 was amended to cover flammable liquids, including oil, natural gas, and petroleum products.[151] Pursuant to the act, the ICC conducted surveys of industry standards in 1930, 1935, and 1940 that led to a 1942 report recommending against setting federal safety standards to supplement industry norms. Federal safety authority for oil pipelines was eliminated in 1960 after decades of inactivity.[152] Indeed, public fatalities and injuries from pipeline leakage were both minimal and decreasing.[153] States, however, began to enact their own laws, and burdensome heterogeneous standards led the oil industry to ask for federal safety standards, which became law on July 27 in amendments to the Transportation of Explosives Act of 1965.[154]

---

[148]Staff of Subcommittee on Antitrust and Monopoly, Senate Committee on the Judiciary, 95th Cong., 2d sess., *Report on Oil Company Ownership of Pipelines* (Washington, D.C.: Government Printing Office, 1978). For a critical review of the report on factual and interpretive grounds, see George Wolbert, *U.S. Oil Pipe Lines*, pp. 293–99.

[149]"Petition for the Initiation of a Rulemaking Proceeding Prohibiting Ownership of Petroleum Pipelines by Petroleum Companies," Federal Trade Commission (1979).

[150]Senator Kennedy's action followed the second round of OPEC price hikes and the second prolonged occurrence of lines at the pump. Public distrust was at a high, and probably nowhere more than in his home state of Massachusetts.

[151]Public Law 400, 41 Stat. 1444 (1921). This discussion is taken from George Wolbert, *U.S. Oil Pipe Lines*, pp. 43–44.

[152]Transportation of Explosives and Other Dangerous Articles Act, Public Law 86-710, 74 Stat. 808 (1960).

[153]George Wolbert, *U.S. Oil Pipe Lines*, p. 43.

[154]Public Law 89-95, 79 Stat. 285 (1965).

ICC authority in this area was transferred on April 1, 1967, to the Department of Transportation, which by December of that year required accident reports. On April 1, 1970, that department promulgated the first federal safety code imposed on the oil-pipeline sector.[155]

The practical effect of federal safety intervention has been limited. Federal rules were predicated upon long-established industry standards formulated by the American Society of Mechanical Engineers with support from the American Petroleum Institute. Intervention aside, the safety record of oil-pipeline operations speaks for itself; good safety is good business given a free-market environment of insurance costs, accident liability, and company goodwill.

Environmental Regulation. Federal environmental regulation of onshore oil pipelines began with the National Environmental Policy Act of 1969, passed in the aftermath of the highly publicized Santa Barbara oil spill.[156] The "first shot" under that act was against the Trans-Alaska Pipeline System project, which had the misfortune of being built not only in treacherous wilderness area but on public land where politics rather than contractual arrangements would control the issue.[157] Occurring at a time when abundant, affordable oil was needed more than ever before (except during World War II), unanticipated costs and work stopages related to the act caused a five-year delay and inflated project costs that were easily passed through to consumers during the height of OPEC activism.

Other post-1970 pipeline projects experienced delay and expense—even cancellation—because of state and federal license requirements. In 1979, Sohio ended a quest to open a 1,000-mile pipeline between Long Beach, California, and Midland, Texas, to deliver 500,000 barrels per day of Alaskan crude. Seven hundred permits were obtained over a five-year period at an expense of $50 million, but enough required permits remained to make the project uncertain. Without the line, costly tanker transport through the Panama Canal, necessitated by the crude-oil export ban (examined in

---

[155]*Business Week,* January 31, 1970, pp. 68–69.

[156]Offshore pipeline construction is regulated under four acts: the Outer Continental Shelf Act of 1953, the Deepwater Port Act of 1974, the Water Pollution Control Act of 1972, and the Coastal Zone Management Act of 1972. See Frank Heard, "Energy Facility Siting—Pipelines," *Natural Resources Lawyer* 9 (1976): 517–25.

[157]Ruth Knowles, *America's Energy Famine,* p. 39.

chapters 13 and 16), continued.[158] A second proposed pipeline to carry North Slope oil, the Northern Tier Pipeline from Washington State to the Midwest, was abandoned in 1983 after 1,400 permits, eight years, and $50 million in expenses. Environmentalists in Washington State successfully argued that the benefits of the pipeline were outweighed by the hazards (spillage, fire, explosion) posed by a supertanker port at Puget Sound where the project began.[159] A third major pipeline, a proposed 1,200-mile line from California to Texas, the All-American Pipeline, was in the process of obtaining permits from fifty government agencies.

Accidents are destructive not only to the environment but to companies. Lost product, cleanup costs, downtime, tort liability, and loss of goodwill can threaten not only profitability but future operations. "Good ecology," in short, "is good business."[160] Internal determination of hazards, objectified by insurability and insurance costs, solves the environmental problem in a market setting where potentially damageable resources are privately owned, statutory liability maximums are not present, and condemnation does not falsify cost. Environmental overkill, on the other hand, hampers the entrepreneurial function of providing goods and services to consumers at least cost. Chapter 21 will explore a market balance between environmentalism and energy production.

Pipelines are noiseless, invisible to the eye at the earth's surface, and built to avoid leakage.[161] Also important, carriage by pipeline displaces other, more hazardous modes of transport—rail and truck. Environmental challenges constitute an anti-competitive restriction on entry, not unlike a certificate of public convenience and necessity in some cases, that cannot be described as pro-consumer.

State Regulation: 1930–84

State regulation of crude-oil and product pipelines has many facets. Before some of the more important laws are examined in historical context, currently applicable laws are reviewed.[162]

---

[158]H. A. Merklein and William Murchison, *Those Gasoline Lines and How They Got There* (Dallas, Tex.: Fisher Institute, 1980), pp. 121–26; and *Time*, March 26, 1979, p. 57.

[159]*Wall Street Journal*, April 21, 1983, p. 18; and *NPN*, June 1983, p. 31.

[160]George Wolbert, *U.S. Oil Pipe Lines*, p. 39.

[161]Ibid.

[162]This summary was compiled by the Office of Competition, U.S. Department of Energy. The author wishes to thank Director Leonard Coburn for summary sheets and explanations.

Current Laws. The most pervasive government involvement with oil pipelines, reflecting the industry's desire for inexpensive right-of-way, is eminent domain. Forty-two states allow condemnation, seventeen states in conjunction with common-carrier requirements.[163] Oregon alone requires intrastate lines to submit to federal regulation in return for eminent-domain rights. Nevada and Pennsylvania require a certificate of public convenience and necessity for condemnation. Instead of common carriage, Iowa requires a permit for the same. On the other hand, eight states practice right-of-way volunteerism—Connecticut, Hawaii, Illinois, Maine, Maryland, Massachusetts, Rhode Island, and Vermont. Illinois, in particular, boasts major pipeline networks built upon market procurement of right-of-way.

Certificates of public convenience and necessity, commonly associated with interstate natural-gas pipelines, are required by seven states. Tantamount to entry restrictions, certificates are in force in Alaska, Kentucky, Minnesota (crude pipelines only), Nevada, North Dakota, Pennsylvania, and Wyoming. The formality of permits, akin to a license for which an application fee is paid after satisfying a minimum-standards test, is required in Iowa, New Hampshire, New Mexico, Oklahoma, South Dakota, and Wyoming.

Rate regulation exists in thirteen states. "Reasonable" rates are required in Alaska, California, Kansas, Kentucky, Louisiana, Montana, Nevada, New Mexico, New York, North Dakota, Texas, West Virginia, and Wyoming. In all but three states—Kansas, Kentucky, and New Mexico—tariffs are required to be filed. Explicit power to suspend rates exists in Alaska, California, Texas, West Virginia, and Wyoming; other states can judge rates to be unreasonable and then suspend or change them.

Investigatory powers exist in Alaska, California, Kentucky, Louisiana, Michigan, Montana, Nevada, New Mexico (safety), New York (safety), Texas, and West Virginia. Service requirements, often to

[163]Common-carrier requirements exist in Florida, Georgia, Louisiana, Michigan, Minnesota, Mississippi, Montana, Nevada, New York, North Carolina, North Dakota, Ohio, Oregon, Pennsylvania, South Dakota, Texas, and Washington. States without requirements for condemnation are Alabama, Alaska, Arizona, Arkansas, California, Colorado, Delaware, Idaho, Indiana, Iowa, Kansas, Kentucky, Missouri, Nebraska, New Hampshire, New Jersey, New Mexico, Oklahoma, South Carolina, Tennessee, Vermont, Virginia, West Virginia, Wisconsin, and Wyoming.

order interconnections, are in force in Alaska, California, Kentucky, Montana, Nevada, North Dakota, Texas, and West Virginia. Reporting requirements are present in Alaska, Louisiana, Montana, Nevada, New York, North Dakota, South Dakota, Texas, West Virginia, and Wyoming.

Several types of pipeline regulation that began in the 1927–35 "overproduction" era remain. Seventeen states have common-carrier laws: Kansas (crude only), Kentucky, Louisiana, Michigan, Montana, Nebraska, Nevada, New Hampshire, New Mexico, New York, North Dakota, Ohio, Oklahoma, South Dakota, Texas, Washington, and Wyoming. Common-purchaser laws exist in Michigan, Nevada, Oklahoma (as an alternative to divestiture), and Texas. Anti-discrimination law, related to common-carrier and common-purchaser statutes but also covering rebates in most states, is in force in California, Louisiana, Michigan, Montana, Nevada, New York, North Dakota, Oklahoma, Tennessee, Texas, and Washington. Storage requirements for pipelines exist in Kansas and Louisiana. Texas, finally, has several unique interventions in force. Permits are required to abandon lines. And left over from the Standard Oil days, separate incorporation is required for petroleum pipelines owned by producers.

Eight states that do not have eminent-domain laws leave pipelines unregulated—Connecticut, Hawaii, Illinois, Maine, Maryland, Massachusetts, Rhode Island, and Vermont. They offer a case study of a free-market approach to the construction and operation of petroleum pipelines.

Selected Controversies. Several controversies that resulted in regulation beginning in 1930 deserve mention. As occurred in Oklahoma in 1909, overproduction and purchase reductions by pipeline companies led to a common-purchaser law in Texas in 1930.[164] In the same year, a statute was enacted that gave the Texas Railroad Commission (TRC) authority to order storage expansion and pipeline extensions. Pro-shipper and anti-carrier legislation, however, was no cure for overproduction; wellhead proration would soon take center stage over ineffectual pipeline proration.

---

[164]This discussion is adopted from Arthur Johnson, *Petroleum Pipelines and Public Policy*, pp. 215–16.

On August 14, 1931, a sweeping pipeline law was enacted by the TRC, again on the political strength of independent producers, that placed public-utility rate regulation on oil pipelines as was previously done in the state for natural-gas, electric, and water retailers.[165] Publicized statistics on the relatively high profitability of oil pipelines during the depression provided the support needed to gain passage on the state level as on the federal level. The same bill ordered pipelines not to disconnect a well without permission from either the lease owner or the TRC. Rate control would not be exercised until February 1933, when selected reductions were ordered, and on December 1, 1933, a schedule of intrastate oil-pipeline rates was first set by the TRC on the basis of fair value, similar to the federal methodology.[166]

In Kansas, production in excess of pipeline facilities led to the passage of a common-purchaser law for oil pipelines in 1939.[167] The law was inspired by distortions created by market-demand proration, which favored established producing areas in Oklahoma by precluding price competition by new fields in Kansas. Integrated companies had little incentive to build lines to new Kansas production when their nominations were fulfilled elsewhere. The result was that older Oklahoma wells had a market-demand factor much closer to their maximum efficient rate of production than did Kansas wells, and "overproduction" relative to nominations in Kansas led to demands for mandatory ratable purchases by pipelines.

A second pipeline controversy in Kansas concerned firms leaving areas of settled production for higher output fields. With stripper-well owners exerting political pressure, authorities in February 1939 ordered pipelines entering flush fields not to leave once production declined.[168] This had the undesired consequence of discouraging demand for replenishing supply within the state.

Another major producing state, New Mexico, joined Texas, Oklahoma, Louisiana, and Kansas with a common-purchaser law. As in other states, the law resulted from producer unrest when production outstripped the capacity of pipelines and other marketing facilities.

[165]Ibid., p. 215.
[166]Texas Railroad Commission, Oil and Gas Docket no. 139 (August 31, 1933).
[167]Jay Kyle, "Kansas, 1937–1948," in *Conservation of Oil & Gas: A Legal History, 1948,* ed. Blakely M. Murphy (Chicago: American Bar Association, 1949), p. 157.
[168]Ibid., p. 164.

The Ratable Purchase of Oil Act of 1941 was enacted to supplement New Mexico's 1935 market-demand law, without opposition from regulated companies.[169]

An important oil-pipeline controversy broke out in Texas in December 1956 when a group of independent producers, represented by the West Central Texas Oil and Gas Association, petitioned the TRC to investigate major company decisions to not connect wells in light of their legal obligations as common carriers. The complaint was that majors were importing foreign oil in lieu of connecting domestic wells, which left expensive truck transportation for some. Hearings were held the following year, and on June 4, 1958, the commission reaffirmed existing statutes concerning pipeline obligations but declined to order specific connections or place the burden of proof on pipelines to justify prospective well-connection decisions.[170] Legislative attempts by Texas producers to require connections as part of common carriage failed in the late 1950s, and the issue would not reappear thereafter.

The unconnected-well problem involved less than 5 percent of an estimated 168,930 wells in the state.[171] While import restrictions kept the number from being lower, regulatory obligations kept the number from being higher. Regulatory distortion notwithstanding, the choice for pipelines was basic economics—whether or not anticipated production from the well could make the connection profitable. To force uneconomic connections—hence encourage drilling and maintenance of uneconomic wells—would have been a wasteful dedication of resources and promised administrative difficulties, protracted court battles, and circumvention. Pipeline profitability, after all, would have been at stake. If connections were truly profitable and needed, producers themselves could build gathering lines (or offer the concessions necessary to have others do the same) to replace truck hauls to refineries or major pipeline connection points. That producers resorted to political favor instead underscored the superficiality of their case.

Petroleum-Product Pipelines

Petroleum-product pipelines came of age in the early 1930s, although as far back as the 1880s a kerosene line was in use between

[169]Ibid., pp. 312–14.
[170]Arthur Johnson, *Petroleum Pipelines and Public Policy*, p. 432.
[171]Ibid., p. 430.

the Pennsylvania oil region and the Atlantic seaboard. The sudden burst of gasoline-pipeline construction and conversions from crude pipelines to product carriers in 1930 and 1931, amounting to several thousand miles of pipage, was attributable to recent advances in pipeline technology that minimized leakage of the volatile fuel, expanded demand for motor gasoline, increased yields of gasoline from refined crude, and standardized gasoline specifications to facilitate pooled runs.[172] An additional factor was the high fare structure for product-hauling railroads, pursuant to the Transportation Act of 1920, which accelerated substitution of pipeline for tank-car transport.[173] John Shatford, president of the Louisiana-Arkansas Refiners' Association, labeled the ICC's railroad-rate policy "the mistake which created the gasoline pipelines."[174]

Product pipelines grew from 1,289 miles in 1930 to 4,471 miles in 1935 to over 8,000 miles by the end of the decade. Two of the largest lines were the earliest, the 1,240-mile Great Lakes line built in 1931 by a six-firm consortium from Oklahoma-Kansas refinery centers to major Midwest retail markets (renamed Williams in 1967), and the 735-mile Phillips line constructed in 1930 from the Texas Panhandle to Kansas City and St. Louis, Missouri. Both interstates, serving as plant facilities for their owners, with rates set at rail rates for similar distances to discourage external use, filed tariffs with the ICC despite the absence of rate or tender regulation.[175]

Rise of Regulation

As with crude-oil pipelines, product-pipeline regulation originated from sentiment within the petroleum industry. In 1938, a group of railroad-dependent independent refiners, jobbers, and retailers formed the Petroleum Rail Shippers Association to protest their deteriorating competitive position against major-company

---

[172]Ibid., pp. 252, 254–55.

[173]Section 15a of the 1920 act instructed the Interstate Commerce Commission to "initiate, modify, establish, or adjust such rates so that carriers as a whole will earn an aggregate annual net railway operating income equal, as nearly as may be, to a fair return upon the aggregate value of the railway property." Public Law 152, 41 Stat 456 (1920). See chapter 16, pp. 977–79, for railroad rate regulation.

[174]Quoted in Arthur Johnson, *Petroleum Pipelines and Public Policy*, p. 272.

[175]John DeGroot, "History and Development of Products Pipe Lines," *27 API Proceedings* (Washington, D.C.: American Petroleum Institute, 1949), p. 13.

rivals advantaged by lower cost transportation.[176] The primary complaint of the association was against railroad tariffs, but pipeline firms associated with the association's midwestern and north central gasoline markets were made parties to the complaint. It was charged that although rates were the same, the shipper-owners paid a lower effective rate because pipeline profits were dividends that allowed lower product prices to be set in downstream markets.

Detailed pipeline financial data were presented in hearings, and in March 1941, a decision was reached. Not only did the ICC order reduce fares for the Great Lakes and Phillips pipelines, rail fares were docked to reflect a "change in condition," namely the recent emergence of product-pipeline competition. The opportunity was also seized to prescribe rate and tender regulation for all interstate product pipelines.[177] Effective June 11, 1941, these firms were limited to a 10 percent return on ICC valuation with a minimum tender requirement of 5,000 barrels subject to shipment delay until 25,000 barrels could be pooled.

With ICC regulation for oil product pipelines, *all* interstate petroleum pipelines were now under federal tariff and tender regulation. But unlike crude pipelines, product lines of integrated companies were free of dividend constraints. And unlike their natural-gas counterparts, interstate oil lines were not tied to original-cost valuation exclusively, which made this application of public-utility regulation more "light handed" than "heavy handed."

Parameters of Regulation

Champlin I and II. With product-pipeline regulation in place, the next action by the ICC was to determine which common carriers were subject to federal authority as had been done with oil pipelines in 1914. In May 1941, the commission tested the waters by ordering

---

[176]*Petroleum Rail Shippers' Association* v. *Alton & Southern Railroad et al.*, 243 ICC 589 (1941).

[177]The product marketer-product pipeline riff also surfaced in the Temporary Economic National Committee hearings of late 1938, where the National Oil Marketers Association recommended divorcement because integrated company product lines "unfairly" subsidized their marketing arms. Arthur Johnson, *Petroleum Pipelines and Public Policy*, pp. 278–79. Crude-oil pipelines, long the butt of industry problems, were less criticized, given the success of proration law in curbing output and stabilizing prices by the late 1930s.

valuation data from Champlin Refinery Company, which had a 516-mile products pipeline from its Oklahoma refinery to wholesale marketing points in Oklahoma, Kansas, and Iowa. Champlin's line had been constructed without eminent domain and was always considered and used as a plant facility, and the company attempted to enjoin the order in federal district court. Failing there, Champlin appealed to the U.S. Supreme Court, which ruled five to four on November 18, 1946, that the interstate line was a common carrier to the extent of submitting valuation data to the ICC.[178] With that victory, the commission in early 1948 ordered Champlin to supplement its system of uniform accounts information with a tariff schedule to acknowledge for-hire status. This raised anew the common-carriage question despite the Supreme Court's language in *Champlin I*, where the firm was "not a common carrier in the sense of the common law carrier for hire."[179] Again taking the Uncle Sam defense—that "transportation" as defined by the 1906 act was inapplicable to internally used pipelines and compliance with the order would constitute taking of property in violation of the Fourteenth Amendment—Champlin filed suit in U.S. district court where the order was enjoined. The ICC then appealed to the Supreme Court, and on May 7, 1951, the Court ruled in favor of Champlin's private status, noting the absence of outside demand for Champlin's services and the diminutive size of Champlin's market share (*Champlin II*).[180] A line was drawn, however tenuous, between common carriage for filing financial information with the ICC and common carriage to file tariffs to become obligated as a common carrier. The Uncle Sam exemption for interstate oil pipelines now had a counterpart with product lines, albeit with slightly different reasoning.

Williams I. Until the 1970s, only one product-line rate case of significance arose. In 1962, several railroads protested to the ICC

---

[178]*Champlin Refining Company* v. *United States*, 329 U.S. 29 (1946). The court differentiated Champlin from the Uncle Sam Oil Company exemption by the former's pricing policy, which was couched in for-hire language, and the sale of transported product to outside parties.

[179]Ibid., p. 33.

[180]*United States et al.* v. *Champlin Refining Co.*, 341 U.S. 290 (1951).

when a competing propane pipeline reduced its rates. The commission rejected the contention that the reduction constituted "destructive competition," and the rate was left unchanged.[181]

In the 1970s, a controversy arose over interstate product-pipeline rates that became the most significant development since the beginning of federal rate regulation in 1941. At stake were both the method of valuation and the return allowed upon it. In 1971, a rate filing by the Williams Brothers Pipe Line Company, which in 1966 had purchased the Great Lakes pipeline, was challenged by Kerr-McGee, American Petrofina, Bell Oil, and several farmer cooperatives who shipped product on Williams.[182] New tariffs filed by Williams a year later inspired a second challenge by Petrofina et al., again on the method of valuation. Protestants challenged the fair-value inclusion of cost of reproduction, new, in the Oak formula, favoring instead exclusive use of original cost net of depreciation. Recognizing the importance of the first major rate challenge in decades, the ICC released a notice of proposed rulemaking and order (Ex Parte no. 308) on August 18, 1974, inviting all interested parties to testify on the valuation issue. An initial ruling June 6, 1974, by an ICC administrative law judge concluded that the rates were just and reasonable. After exceptions were filed by Petrofina, the case was heard by Division 2 of the ICC, which upheld the original verdict. Specific mention was made of the benefits of fair value in inflationary times to prevent capital erosion and earnings dissipation.[183] A recommendation, however, was made to the full commission that Ex Parte no. 308 be expanded to evaluate the appropriateness of the 10 percent return for product lines and the 8 percent return for crude lines. Division 2's affirmation and recommendation were upheld by the full commission on December 3, 1976, "because of the relative dearth of precedent concerning petroleum pipeline rates, and in view of the substantial sums of money at issue."[184] Upon reconsideration, the court affirmed continued adherence to ICC valuation. Petrofina,

---

[181]Pipeline Rates on Propane from Southwest to Midwest, 318 ICC 615 (1962).

[182]Williams Brothers Pipe Line Company, ICC Docket no. 1423 (1971).

[183]"Since a valuation base reflects to some degree the inflated cost of plant through the reproduction new value, it consequently helps to prevent capital exhaustion and attrition of earnings." Petroleum Products, Williams Bros. Pipe Line Company, 355 ICC 102 at 114 (1975).

[184]Petroleum Products, Williams Brothers Pipe Line Co., 355 ICC 479 at 481 (1976).

pressing the issue further, appealed to the D.C. Court of Appeals to continue the case into its sixth year.

While the case was pending, regulatory authority over oil and product pipelines was transferred from the ICC to the FERC, formerly the Federal Power Commission, which since the 1930s had regulated natural-gas pipelines and electric utilities on a strict public-utility basis. This changed the prospects of the case considerably. Whereas the ICC was allied with reproduction-cost valuation, the FERC was familiar with and inclined toward historical-cost valuation. Under these circumstances, the FERC asked the court to remand the case to the ICC for a "fresh look" at regulatory method. The court agreed but also opined on what the new formula should be. The Oak formula was described as "weak and outmoded," and several criticisms of fair value were made. The court in the *Farmers Union Central Exchange* decision, however, stopped short of recommending original cost.

> We may infer a congressional intent to allow freer play of competitive forces among oil pipeline companies. . . . We should be loath uncritically to import public utilities notions into this area without taking note of the degree of regulation and the nature of the regulated business.[185]

The general instruction in *Farmers I* was to develop a rate methodology to improve upon the ICC's long-standing Oak formula approach.

The issue had grown from the legality of the rates charged by a particular pipeline company to a generic case concerning rate-base valuation of all oil and product pipelines. With the consent decree vacated in December 1982, the balance of regulation hung on *Williams I*. The commission consolidated all rate cases into *Williams I* and began an evidentiary hearing in February 1979. (*Williams II*, concerning specific rates that Williams and the other plaintiffs were protesting, would be separately litigated.) Presiding Judge Isaac Benkin six weeks later issued an "Invitation to Submit Comments on Ratemaking Principles for Oil Pipeline Rate Cases." Seventy-six hearing days later, the FERC issued an order to transfer the case to

---

[185]*Farmers Union Central Exchange* v. *FERC*, 584 F.2d 408 at 413 (D.C. Cir. 1978), cert. den; *Williams Pipe Line Company* v. *FERC*, 439 U.S. 995 (1979). See the discussion in Brian O'Neill and George Knapp, "Oil Pipeline Regulation after *Williams*: Does the End Justify the Means?" *Energy Law Journal* 1 (1983): 63.

them. Arguments were heard on ratemaking methodology on June 30, 1980, and again on November 19, 1981, before a new set of commissioners. The case was now a decade old, and the plaintiffs— Kerr-McGee and the farmer co-ops, collectively called the Mid-Continent Petroleum Shippers—asked a federal court to set a deadline for a FERC opinion, which was granted.

On November 30, 1984, "the longest and most elaborate" decision in FERC history was released.[186] The 391-page opinion, complete with a panoramic overview of the history of oil-pipeline regulation that ranged from flippant to provocative, challenged the "just and reasonable" standard. Its original intent, the opinion argued, "was not 'public utility reasonableness,' but ordinary commercial 'reasonableness.'"[187] The 1906 Hepburn Act was not enacted for the public good but for the private good—for wellhead interests to increase their take at the expense of Standard Oil. Oil-pipeline rate regulation is not a consumer-protection measure. It probably was never intended to be. It is and was a producer-protection measure.[188]

Upon this revisionist foundation, conventional public-utility regulation was rejected because it "would not yield social benefit either to consumers or shippers sufficient to warrant the regulatory costs or the potential disruption of the industry."[189] This left the "light-handed method." The opinion concluded, "We see no cogent reason to depart from the rate base status quo."[190] Modifications of the Oak formula for ratemaking were prescribed, the most prominent being eight rate-of-return choices in place of the 8 percent/10 percent standard. While regulation was tightened, a pronounced break from light-handed regulation was not in evidence.[191]

The decision was immediately appealed to federal court by industry proponents of stricter regulation, and on March 9, 1984, the D.C.

[186]Press release, Opinion 154, 21 FERC 61568 (1982).

[187]Ibid., p. 61597.

[188]Ibid., p. 61584. In contrast, the Natural Gas Act of 1938, introducing public-utility regulation to interstate natural-gas pipelines, was identified as a consumer-protection law.

[189]Ibid., p. 61616.

[190]Ibid., p. 61631.

[191]Other changes—all tightening regulation—were to exclude leased property from the rate base, reduce working capital flexibility, and disallow a recomputation of original cost when a pipeline is sold.

Circuit Court unanimously reversed and remanded Opinion 154.[192] *Williams I* was characterized as an "apologia for virtual deregulation." The court substituted congressional intent for the law's motives to elevate "just and reasonable" to well-purposed and necessary regulation.[193] Implicit in *Farmers II* was that the free market was not sufficiently competitive to approximate the "just and reasonable" standard. There had to be, as Judge Patricia Wald paraphrased *Farmer II*, "an anchor to 'hold the terms just and reasonable to some recognizable meaning.' "[194] The anchor was cost, and the decision all but told the FERC that original cost was the proper ratemaking methodology.[195] Concluded attorney John Cleary, who had brought the original complaint against Williams thirteen years before:

> While not eliminating the discretion of the FERC to choose a nontraditional ratemaking method, the Farmers Union II Court drew fairly narrow bounds. . . . By eschewing the FERC's motive-oriented view of statutory construction and reestablishing actual costs as a yardstick for reasonableness, the *Farmers Union II* brought objectivity, and thus accountability, back to pipeline regulation.[196]

The FERC in *Williams I* would seriously consider a conventional public-utility standard or devise a new methodology and rationale for less stringent regulation free and clear of Opinion 154. In the absence of legislation, which failed in 1982 and 1983, more appeals were virtually certain; carriers were adamantly opposed to original-cost ratemaking, and a determined band of shippers was against Oak formula valuation.[197] In the meantime, a "regulatory chill" would

[192]*Farmers Union Central Exchange* v. *FERC, et al.,* Docket 82-2412, (D.D. Cir. 1984).

[193]Ibid., pp. 42–43.

[194]Ibid., p. 31.

[195]"The most useful and reliable starting point for rate regulation is an inquiry into costs." Ibid., p. 32. It was elaborated that "departures from cost based rates must be made, if at all, only when the non-cost factors are clearly identified and the substitute of supplemental ratemaking methods insure the resulting rate levels are justified by those factors" (p. 92).

[196]John Cleary, "*Farmers Union* v. *FERC:* Back to Ratemaking Basics," Paper presented at Executive Enterprises conference, Oil Pipeline Ratemaking, Houston, Tex., June 19, 1984, p. 22.

[197]The Oil Pipeline Regulatory Reform Act of 1983 (H.R. 2677), following two unsuccessful partial deregulation bills in 1982, retained common-carrier requirements but removed rate regulation. It was not reported out of committee. Favoring the bill was the Association of Oil Pipe Lines, representing ninety common-carrier pipelines comprising 95 percent of the interstate market. Expressing reservations about the bill, although in general agreement, were the Energy Department, Justice Department,

continue to envelope project planning in interstate petroleum-pipeline markets.[198]

Regulation of Oil Pipelines Reconsidered

The intellectual case for state and federal regulation is open to critical review. In addition, the practical effects of long-standing state and federal regulation can be shown to be inefficient. Together, the academic and practical combine to make a case against government intervention with oil pipelines.

Arguments for Regulation

In recent decades, theoretical arguments against unfettered oil-pipeline competition have been developed to supplement what hitherto has been industry infighting—transportation rivals complaining about displacement by oil pipelines, producers distraught over low posted prices paid by pipeline purchasers, producers complaining of access denial, and nonintegrated firms contending that integrated pipelines were subsidizing downstream affiliates. Two prominent theories alleging resource misallocation from industry incentives in a free market deserve analysis—the excess-profit, natural-monopoly argument and the undersizing argument. Both suggest the market failure of less supply at higher prices and resource misallocation.

Special-Interest Complaints. Special-interest arguments for oil-pipeline regulation were based on self-interest and were not part of a general argument for improved resource allocation in the economy as a whole. Displacement of less efficient transportation alternatives by pipelines lowered industry costs and final product prices, while releasing resources for urgent employments elsewhere. It was good

---

and the Office of Management and Budget. These parties desired continued regulation for certain monopolistic lines such as TAPS. The National Council of Farmer Cooperatives, the Independent Gasoline Marketers Council, and Crown Central Petroleum Corporation testified against the bill. They favored lower regulated rates over higher unregulated rates. See *Regulatory Reform of the Oil Pipeline Industry,* Hearings before the Subcommittee on Surface Transportation of the House Committee on Public Works and Transportation, 98th Cong., 1st sess. (Washington, D.C.: Government Printing Office, 1983).

[198]Stated Sun Pipeline president John DesBarres, "How do you explain to shareholders an investment decision when the reward side is uncertain?" Comments made at Executive Enterprises conference, Oil Pipeline Ratemaking, Houston, Tex., June 19, 1984. Commented the *OGJ* of May 31, 1982, "Managers cannot project future earnings in order to determine the economic feasibility of new projects" (p. 180).

for the industry and for the economy—not unlike other everyday occurrences of more efficient alternatives replacing (or "displacing") less efficient alternatives.

Low posted prices were a fact of flush production that producers wished to curb but could not, short of state prorationing beginning in the late 1920s and early 1930s. Pipelines may have *posted* lower prices, but they did not *create* lower prices. Overall conditions of supply (wellhead output) and demand (final product sales) established intermediary prices. Pipelines were in the middle, trying to attract supply to transport and sell to refineries or internally refine. If producers had felt that prices were artificially low, they could have withheld supply to force the pipeline's hand or turned to self-help alternatives such as arranging or building other carriage to market. They could even have collectively "blackmailed" the pipeline into selling out to them. Common-carrier regulation, however, precluded long-term sales agreements that were an important balancing mechanism between wellhead interests and pipelines. This is a regulatory problem rather than a market problem.

Denial of access, whether accidental or intended, was a profit-maximizing strategy crucial to pipeline investments in the first place. The record showed that outside use was not intended in almost all cases prior to World War II, and forced carriage disrupted asset complementarity between pipelines and refineries. Forced conversion of plant facilities to for-hire carriers was thus an attack on the pipeline investment itself, disrupting entrepreneurial plans and discouraging similar decisions to integrate. A later section will extend this argument to mandatory common carriage and fault producers for the predicament that regulation was intended to alleviate.[199]

A fourth area of shipper complaint concerned the alleged subsidization of downstream operations by the integrated pipeline. This argument was previously censured as an attack on integration per se and difficult to substantiate given the boundary problem.[200] The complaining party, in any case, could neutralize the "problem" by *self-integration*, whether by selling out to another firm, buying a

---

[199]See this chapter, pp. 843–44.
[200]See this chapter, pp. 793–94.

complementary firm, or expanding into a new phase. That the "self-help" route was eschewed in favor of political agitation is reason enough to depreciate the entire argument.

Excess Profits and Natural Monopoly. The technological fact of declining unit cost over a range of pipe sizes of increasing diameter, coupled with the high historic profitability of oil pipelines, has led some scholars to espouse public-utility regulation of such firms (if not the more drastic measure of divorcement) since natural monopoly characteristics are present.[201] Economies of scale and general profitability, however, do not necessarily imply improper industry incentives and practices or a need for regulation. As noted by attorney and oil-pipeline historian George Wolbert, the scale economies characteristic of oil pipelines have been illegitimately transformed into a natural-monopoly characteristic, classically defined as decreasing unit costs over the *demand* range rather than the *production* range, by tacitly assuming perfect foresight and static demand, whereby each pipeline is sized to capture the entire market to preclude eternal competition.[202] These assumptions are contradicted by the real world. Pipelines are rarely built to cover an entire market, and market growth over time leaves original capacity further and further behind. Moreover, scale economies with oil pipelines are not infinite but end in the 36-inch-diameter range, which necessitates multiple lines to major markets. Wolbert has argued that single lines serving major market areas would make the 48-inch-diameter TAPS line "look like a garden hose."[203] Multiple trunk lines are the rule rather than the exception between major producing and refining areas (and between major refining and wholesale centers with product pipelines), reflecting limited scale economies, imperfect knowledge, and changing (historically increasing) demand.[204]

---

[201]For example, see Donald Flexner, "Oil Pipelines: The Case for Divestiture," in *Oil Pipelines and Public Policy,* p. 4; and Thomas Spavins, "The Regulation of Oil Pipelines," in *Oil Pipelines and Public Policy,* p. 80. For a technological-economic explanation of cost-decreasing, large-diameter pipelines, see Leslie Cookenboo, *Crude Oil Pipelines and Competition in the Oil Industry* (Cambridge, Mass.: Harvard University Press, 1955), pp. 81–83; and George Wolbert, *U.S. Oil Pipe Lines,* pp. 98–100.

[202]George Wolbert, "Commentary," in *Oil Pipelines and Public Policy,* p. 57.

[203]Ibid., p. 106.

[204]In 1959, George Wolbert commented that "every refinery, not located specifically to receive crude by water or from an adjacent field, is served by one or more pipelines."

834

By theory and practice, the great majority of oil pipelines do not fall into the natural-monopoly mold. In those instances where one line envelops a market, however, regulation is not called for and, in fact, is counterproductive. As argued in chapter 1, competitive bidding before the fact and potential entry after the fact compel the "monopolist" to act similarly to head-to-head entrants.[205] The market is after the best deal, and competing proposals to build a line will bid down economic rents that a franchised monopolist would otherwise enjoy. The market can also act concertedly (a "monopsonist") to counter a single seller (a "monopolist"). Once the line is constructed, contracts will restrain the single provider from arbitrary behavior, but if such discipline is somehow absent, the goodwill of the market could go to a paper company that, with contracts in hand, could construct a wholly new line to leave the existing monopolist ruined. The existing line might not have any alternative but to sell out to the new company to avoid a total loss of value.

Related to the monopoly charge is the purported existence of above-average profits in the oil-pipeline sector, particularly in the pre-1940 era of nonregulated rates and most noticeably during the depression years.[206] Such profits, it is contended, if not prima facie evidence of natural monopoly, call for rate regulation to protect and benefit upstream and downstream parties.[207]

The above judgment is questionable on a number of interpretative grounds. Given the statistics, can profits be called unambiguously high? Profitability on borrowed and invested capital is lower than

---

"The Recurring Spectre of Pipeline Divorcement," p. 105. Specific examples of multi-line competition include the Gulf Coast–West Texas area, which is linked by thirteen lines and the Gulf Coast–East Texas area, which is served by nine lines. For these and other examples, see Wolbert, "Commentary," pp. 59, 148; and Michael Canes, "Commentary," in *Oil Pipeline Symposium* (Washington, D.C.: Department of Energy, 1980), p. 64.

[205]See chapter 1, p. 50.

[206]Between 1922 and 1940, the average before-tax return on depreciated investment for oil-pipeline firms reporting to the ICC ranged from 24 to 34 percent. In the 1940–53 period, the growth of competing pipelines and consent-decree regulation combined to drop returns to 12–19 percent of depreciated cost. Leslie Cookenboo, *Crude Oil Pipe Lines and Competition in the Oil Industry*, p. 98. Also see the somewhat lower profit percentages for borrowed and invested capital in John McLean and Robert Haigh, *The Growth of Integrated Oil Companies*, p. 193.

[207]See, for example, Thomas Spavins, "The Regulation of Oil Pipelines," p. 80.

profitability on depreciated cost, and profitability on reproduction cost would be lower still. Furthermore, when pipelines were predominantly plant facilities of integrated operations before World War II, rates were purposefully high to discourage outside demand that might disrupt internal needs. The resulting profits were "high" in the bookkeeping sense only. Any attempt to separate "true" pipeline profit was impossible for the integrated firm given the impossibility of defining relevant boundaries between phases for cost-revenue allocation.[208]

Third, to compare profits without differentiating risk is to mix apples and oranges. Pipelines can claim relatively high profitability, compared with other industries, from two sources of unique risk—one market and one regulatory. Once constructed, crude or product pipelines are hostage to the physical production of nearby reservoirs (refineries) and the willingness of producers (refiners) to continue to make short-term sales (purchases) to (from) them.[209] (Long-term contracts were discouraged by regulation.) If one of the two conditions does not hold, the pipelines' value plummets to scrap value. The anticipated return, therefore, has had to cover this risk, particularly prior to scientific reserve estimation and during periods of unrestrained production when well output could suddenly play out.

Regulatory risk has existed since 1906 when authority was granted to the ICC to regulate rates and other interstate trunk-line practices. Although strict rate regulation would not occur until 1940, the mere possibility of "changing the rules of the game"—which occurred with *TAPS* and was at stake in *Williams I*—was an uncertainty for which investors have had to be compensated. Given the conditions under which the profit figures were derived, judgments of profit "abnormality" must be qualified.

Derivation and risk aside, a methodological criticism of profit interpretation is in order. As argued previously, the chimera of a "just and reasonable" price and a "normal" return in market exchanges prevents differentiating a "monopolistic" price from a

---

[208]J. Howard Pew of Sun Oil testified in 1942 that one-third of his company's investment was not readily identifiable with any particular phase of Sun's business. Arthur Johnson, *Petroleum Pipelines and Public Policy*, p. 276.

[209]Remarked Thomas Spavins, "The system of regulation . . . has included a historic ICC hostility to long-term contracts for transportation services by ICC-regulated common carriers." "The Regulation of Oil Pipelines," p. 100.

normal price or an "excess" return from a normal return.[210] These terms are ethical judgments, not unlike the pronouncement that prices and profits be "good, true, and beautiful."[211] There are only the market price and profit, which result from the voluntary interaction of seller and buyer—a much more concrete event than the idle desires of critics that prices or profits be higher or lower.

Prices and profits are not "high" or "low" in an absolute sense. They reflect unique circumstances, which in oil-pipeline history have been the constant application of new entrepreneurial ideas and new technology to lower the cost of petroleum transport.[212] Profits have come from reduced costs; they constitute a return to entrepreneurial alertness and innovation with positive social implications, not a

---

[210]The difficulty of interpreting pipeline profits, either in the aggregate or individually, is discussed in Michael Piette, "Crude Oil and Refined Product Pipelines in the United States: An Examination of the Major Issues of Public Policy," in *Oil Pipeline Symposium*, pp. 26–28.

[211]Opinion 154, 21 FERC, para. 61260 (1982).

[212]The post–World War II period shows a remarkably steady level of oil-pipeline tariffs, in real terms, until the late 1970s (in dollars per barrel).

Year	Pipeline Rate[a]	CPI Prices[b]	Adjusted Rate[c]
1950	0.315	24	1.31
1955	0.322	24	1.34
1960	0.315	24	1.31
1965	0.279	21	1.33
1970	0.271	20	1.36
1975	0.368	28	1.31
1976	0.409	31	1.32
1977	0.617	47	1.31
1978	1.010	76	1.33
1979	1.115	84	1.33
1980	1.325	100	1.33
1981	1.452	110	1.32
1982	1.448	109	1.33
1983	1.616	122	1.32
1984	1.619	122	1.33

SOURCE: Transportation Policy Associates, Transportation in America, ed. Frank Smith (Washington, D.C.: TPA, 1992), p. 49.
[a]Average revenue per ton-mile.
[b]Wholesale price increases (1980 = 100), it should be noted, were less than consumer price increases.
[c]The adjusted (real) rate is calculated by dividing the nominal tariff by the price index.

return to "monopolistic power," which chapter 1 confined to a grant of special privilege from government.[213]

Critics of pipeline profits have failed to recognize several regulatory reasons why returns might have been above "competitive" levels. To the extent that regulation of oil-carrying railroads, tank trucks, barges, and tankers resulted in transportation charges over unregulated levels—which can be concluded given entry restriction, load maximums, and other restrictions[214]—oil pipelines have been able to enjoy less price-sensitive demand that has allowed higher tariffs. Second, to the extent that wellhead proration increased pipeline revenue over unregulated supply and price levels, profits have been greater than true market levels. Pro-consumer regulatory reform has been and is possible, but not in the direction many pipeline critics have been inclined to recommend.

Assuming that monopoly prices and monopoly profits exist in an unregulated pipeline market—which is highly debatable—the solution of rate-base regulation is a mirage. Cost-plus pricing does not automatically create "just and reasonable" pricing. Costs are increased above unregulated levels without the incentive to pare expenses and, more important, with the incentive to maintain and expand the rate base even when suboptimal from an unregulated market viewpoint.

Second, economic rent denied to pipelines does not automatically flow to consumers but lines the pockets of upstream and downstream parties. Shippers (including carrier-shippers) are the first in line to capture the floating economic rent, and not surprisingly, independent shippers (primarily producers) have been at the forefront of regulation, past and present, to this end.

Market Concentration. A formalization of a classic argument for government intervention was applied to interstate petroleum pipelines. Pursuant to congressional debate on whether to reform oil-pipeline regulation, the Department of Justice in May 1984 released

---

[213]The aggregate statistic of "average profit" also masks individual returns, which reveal instances of very high profit, which reflect particularly successful entrepreneurship, and instances of loss, which reflect inept entrepreneurship. For individual profits of interstate pipelines in 1920, 1925, and 1930, that ranged from 50 percent profit to 50 percent loss, see Harold Williamson et al., *The Age of Energy, 1899 to 1959*, vol. 2 of *The American Petroleum Industry* (Evanston, Ill.: Northwestern University Press, 1963), p. 359.

[214]See chapter 16 generally.

a preliminary report measuring competition for 150 interstate lines in the lower forty-eight states.[215] The study was intended to separate competitive firms from monopolistic ones, the latter possessing "economic power" to restrict throughout and "reduce economic welfare below the current level." With noncompetitive situations identified, selective deregulation was possible.[216]

The measure of competition is *market share,* calculated by the Herfindahl-Hirschman index (HHI), which squares each firm's percentage of the market to measure concentration levels between 0 (perfect competition) and 10,000 (pure monopoly).[217]

Individual market shares were assigned to pipelines, waterway carriers, and refineries. For pipelines, throughput capacity for June 1979 was used. Waterborne transportation was measured by 1980 deliveries between defined market areas. The refinery market percentage came from distillation capacity. While pipeline and waterway competition is direct, refineries were included because they compete for crude with crude lines, and refineries at the terminuses of product lines compete with product that is refined upstream and shipped.

From each of the three market-share areas, a percentage is derived per company. The "high-risk" threshold is an HHI of 2,500 or above (four firms with 20 percent shares or other combinations reaching a like result), which Justice defines as the "beginning point of concern."[218] This figure is above Justice's merger guideline figure of

---

[215]U.S. Department of Justice, Antitrust Division, *Competition in the Pipeline Industry: A Preliminary Report* (Washington, D.C.: Government Printing Office, 1984).

[216]Ibid., p. 9.

[217]Sample calculations are

1	firm with 100 percent market share	= 10,000 HHI (pure monopoly)
2	firms with 50 percent market share	= 5,000 HHI
3	firms with 33.3 percent market share	= 3,330 HHI
4	firms with 25 percent market share	= 2,500 HHI
5	firms with 20 percent market share	= 2,000 HHI
10	firms with 10 percent market share	= 1,000 HHI
100	firms with 1 percent market share	= 100 HHI
1,000	firms with 0.1 percent market share	= 10 HHI
Infinite firms		= 0 HHI (perfect competition)

[218]Firms in markets below a 2,500 HHI could be regulated as firms above 2,500 could be deregulated, depending on other evidence. Conversation with David Brown,

1,800 to account for the "social costs of pipeline regulation."[219] Amounts below 2,500, on the other hand, are judged either competitive or sufficiently competitive to not require regulation.

Calculations revealed that approximately one-third or 260 markets with HHI values between 2,500 and 10,000 were candidates for regulation. Product-origin markets were the least "monopolistic." Crude-origin markets were more "monopolistic" than crude-destination markets but were well below product-destination market concentration.

The HHI, like any concentration measure, embodies the tenet of neoclassical economic theory that more firms increase competition, thus lower prices and increase output (throughput), and fewer firms increase monopoly power, increasing price and reducing output. Competition in this view is a *state* that can be *measured* and even *modified* to achieve social ends. Another view of competition has been espoused throughout this book. It identifies competition as a *process* (not an outcome) that unfolds through entrepreneurial adjustments in response to incentives and information provided by the unregulated market. That process is inherently competitive because entrepreneurial *ideas* about entering, exiting, or modifying a product cannot be monopolized.[220] It is recognized that at any particular time inefficiency and error exist, even "monopolistic" behavior of overpricing and underproducing, but because processes are at work to exploit profitable opportunities and avoid loss situations that such "monopolistic" situations involve, resources are continually redeployed in better ways.

The institutional setting for this correctional process, the free market, is crucial. Market-share configurations, on the other hand, are not crucial to judgments of competition; they represent the economic history of a particular entrepreneurial process (modified or not by government intervention) at a certain place and time. For example, although Standard Oil in the 1890s had a very high HHI, a multiple of the "high-risk" Justice Department figure, the petroleum market

---

assistant chief, Energy Section, Antitrust Division of the Justice Department, June 27, 1984.

[219]See U.S. Department of Justice, Antitrust Division, *Competition in the Pipeline Industry*, p. 29.

[220]See chapter 1, pp. 16, 45.

was very competitive because free-market conditions were generally present.[221] Petroleum prices were falling, quantities sold were increasing, and industry investment was multiplying—all contradicting what neoclassical economics would suggest. What was true in the 1890s was true in the 1980s. Executives of "monopolistic" pipeline firms heard the Department of Justice and anointed economists speak of throughput cutbacks to raise tariffs and a lack of competition, yet they knew that competition was rigorous and unrelenting. They concluded that the economists' competitive model was an abstraction and that economic theory did not represent the "real world." In fact, they were right.

Many questionable empirical assumptions of the Department of Justice study should be mentioned, although such criticism is secondary to the methodological-theoretical problem of what is competitive and socially optimal. The 183 defined market areas delineated by the Commerce Department's Bureau of Economic Analysis are inherently arbitrary.[222] It can be complained that the divisions were not made with the oil industry in mind, and that redefined areas should be smaller or larger. A bottomless pit of analysis of the "relevant" geographics for pipeline competition could open, and even then interarea competition would need to be accounted for.

The 2,500-HHI threshold invites the question of why it is not a bit higher or lower. Having a round number for convenience does not make the delineation correct. Is the "social cost" of regulation really equivalent to 700 HHI? Regarding market share, the accuracy of June 1979 pipeline data can be questioned given the boom and bust of the industry over the 1979–84 period. Sole reliance on pipeline *capacity* neglects the more important indication of *utilization*. The exclusion of intrastate pipelines understates competition as defined in the study. Waterway *capacity* would be more relevant than actual usage to gauge substitutability, not to mention the use of data more current than 1980. Finally, the competitive role of crude and product imports—not to mention end-use conservation—is underemphasized, and much less quantifiable, in the study.

---

[221]One major blemish on the competitive operation of the early oil industry was oil-product tariffs between 1861 and 1909. See chapter 13, pp. 712–13.

[222]These areas are presented in U.S. Department of Justice, Antitrust Division, *Competition in the Pipeline Industry*, pp. 20–21.

Better data, better assumptions, and deeper research, however, are not the answer. The exercise is inherently biased by subjective approximations and must grow more suspect with time. By the time the data are compiled and a study is completed, it is time to begin again. Yet the study forthrightly claims to be the grist from which policy should be derived.

In summary, there are three fallacious assumptions behind the market-share exercise: (1) market concentration and other empirical factors can theoretically identify monopolistic market situations of less supply and higher price, (2) these situations can be uncovered by empirical investigation, and (3) government regulation can define competitive conditions to replace monopolistic outcomes with competitive prices and output.

Undersizing. Neoclassical monopoly theory portrays situations where a firm maximizes profit by reducing output to receive higher prices. An amount of profit, a *monopoly gain,* is made over the competitive situation of full supply sold at lower prices. As if to renounce the natural-monopoly argument where a single high-capacity firm dominates the market, a new argument is that oil pipelines are deliberately built at a low capacity to achieve monopoly power. With common-carrier obligations ruling out the excess-capacity route to monopoly gains, deliberate *undersizing* reaches a like end, the theory asserts, through interdepartmental profit transfers by integrated firms able to escape rate regulation.[223] The logic is that displaced oil shipped by higher cost modes sets the marginal transportation cost from which an average profit level settles upstream. The difference between the (higher) marginal transportation cost and the (lower) pipeline cost is the monopoly profit that the integrated pipeline company can retain in its unregulated production or marketing department. Because common-carrier law and rate regulation are circumvented, undersizing adherents have advocated further legislation, namely divestiture, to establish competitive conditions.

The undersizing argument, while a novel variant of "market failure," is fallacious. The existence of common-carrier law refutes the

---

[223]The undersizing theory originated within the Antitrust Division of the Department of Justice in 1976. Testimony of Assistant Attorney General John Shenfield before the Subcommittee on Antitrust and Monopoly, United States Senate, reprinted in *Oil Pipelines and Public Policy,* pp. 202–3.

argument because all shippers, the shipper-owner included, would share the pipeline and other transportation modes on a pro rata basis. The marginal transportation cost would be approximately equal for everyone and remove the incentive for the shipper-owner to undersize his line.[224] Economies of scale also suggest a lack of incentive to deliberately undersize a pipeline because it would be inefficient and invite entry by a lower cost, fully sized line that could potentially capture the existing market as well.[225]

The undersizing theory would suggest denial of access and continuous proration by undersized lines. Although scanty evidence was presented by the Justice Department, more rigorous examination suggests that restrictions on access and pipeline proration were not in evidence from entry until 1977 for five major pipeline systems under suspicion—the Buckeye, Colonial, Explorer, Plantation, and Williams lines.[226] This evidence has not been rebutted, and no recent evidence of undersizing has been presented. By theory and fact, the undersizing argument is without substance.

Weaknesses of Regulation

Common-Carrier Law. Common-carrier law, the obligation of a pipeline to accept all tendered oil at nondiscriminatory rates, was a product of producer distress. The law, however, fought the effects of the problem rather than its root cause, overproduction. Oil pipelines were the scapegoats of their upstream brethren; pipeline regulation was a poor substitute for more disciplined production.[227]

---

[224]George Wolbert, *U.S. Oil Pipe Lines,* pp. 388–89.

[225]See Michael Canes and Donald Norman, "Pipelines and Public Policy," in *Oil Pipelines and Public Policy,* p. 148.

[226]Edward Erickson, Gayle Linder, and William Peters, "The Pipeline Undersizing Argument and the Record of Access and Expansion in the Oil Pipeline Industry," in *Oil Pipelines and Public Policy,* pp. 15–55.

[227]The argument that pipelines circumventing common-carrier law were "a barrier to the free efforts of thousands of independent operators" (William Kemnitzer, *Rebirth of Monopoly* [New York: Harper & Brothers, 1938], p. 92) is not an argument against pipelines but an argument for their unfettered operation. Such "free efforts" constituted the problem of petroleum conservation; its discouragement by pipeline discipline represented a partial solution. Without common carriage, and with long-term contracts between producers and pipelines, less "spec" capacity would have come on the market.

In the pre-1940 era when pipelines were predominantly plant facilities adjacent to refinery operations, the negative potential of the law was at its greatest. The risk that internal throughput could be disrupted by outside shippers discouraged pipeline construction and investment in integrated refineries. Why should a refining entrepreneur bear the risk of building a line if once it is built, access is assured; why not let an independent build the line and take a "free ride" on a nonexclusive resource? Fortunately for independent producers (despite their short-run support of the law), circumvention of the law was possible and practiced. Through a costless bookkeeping charge, integrated firms could raise pipeline tariffs to limit external demand.[228]

A second deterrent to the practical operation of statutory common carriage was more natural than designed. Contamination between batches required tender minimums, which were often above the outside shipper's quantity without pooling arrangements. Nonetheless, with latitude over tariffs, integrated companies could minimize the inroads made by independents.

When rate and tender regulation emerged in the 1940s to achieve common carriage in practice as well as in law, technological changes were under way that minimized disruption to and disincentives for petroleum pipelines. Capacity expansion created a shift from plant-facility lines to for-hire lines. Improvements also allowed smaller runs without contamination. Consequently, common-carrier interventionism came of age with two major distortive consequences: the previously discussed free-rider problem and an inability of shipper-owners to transfer project risk to external shippers via long-term throughput contracts. Common carriage requires short-notice service, and preventing long-term shipping commitments by producers unnecessarily magnified project risk for for-hire pipeline projects.

Rate Regulation. Petroleum-pipeline tariffs have been indirectly set by ceilings on profits and dividends. For signers of the consent decree, a maximum 7 percent dividend could be paid by the pipeline

---

[228]The firm would merely show increased profits in the pipeline sector and reduced profits in the production sector (lower wellhead prices) or the refining sector (higher cost of goods sold). The only possible cost of this strategy would be if the rearrangement falsified internal accounting by preventing accurate cost-revenue matchups, but keeping two sets of books could prevent this.

subsidiary to the parent company from 1941 until 1982. For all pipe-lines, a maximum rate of return has been in force since the early 1940s: 8 percent for oil pipelines and 10 percent for product pipelines. For the seventy-nine consent-decree firms, the lower of the two was used; for independents, the 8 percent or 10 percent return was applicable.

Criticism of oil-pipeline profit and dividend regulation is aimed as much at what it could have done as at what it did do. Through a combination of "fair value," a 6 percent interest return (consent decree only), a 7 percent (or 8 percent to 10 percent) pure profit allowance, and the ability to average intrafirm pipeline projects, a quasi-market return was possible. Another factor that eased regulatory constraints for signers of the consent decree was substituting debt finance for equity finance to expense interest and applying the 7 percent allowable to remaining equity.[229] Nonetheless, "light-handed" public-utility regulation produced results that were inferior to those of the unregulated market.

As explained more fully in the next chapter, the pretense of public-utility regulation is that the unregulated price is "wrong" and that the "right" price can be derived from a "fair" valuation multiplied by a "normal" return.[230] But returns, either negative or positive, are never "normal." Cost-based valuation, either original or reproduction, is a throwback to the fallacious labor theory of value that equated expended effort with consumer want. Value is not cost but the subjective estimations of consumers manifested by the price paid for particular goods or services at a given point in time, something beyond the reach of public-utility valuation.

Cost-based valuation, as mentioned, disinclines the firm to minimize cost. If the firm perceives the allowed return to be restrictive, it becomes profit maximizing to bloat its cost of service and pad the rate base. This is waste from the viewpoint of the market where the firm would have maximized profit and left resources for use elsewhere in the economy.

A second prominent shortcoming of public-utility regulation is the uniform ceiling placed on profit (and in the case of integrated

---

[229]See George Wolbert, *U.S. Oil Pipe Lines*, pp. 314–29.
[230]See chapter 15 , pp. 928–33.

interstate crude pipelines, dividends), which overstimulates low-risk projects while discouraging high-risk ventures. Combined with common-carrier law, which prevents risk transfers from carriers to shippers via long-term throughput agreements, high-risk fields (reservoirs with uncertain production) are made less economical to connect, which leaves higher cost transport, generally by truck, as the next best alternative.

Rate averaging to meet the overall firm profit (dividend) maximum breeds inefficiency and creates an anti-competitive element. Instead of judging each project on a stand-alone basis, firms have undertaken marginal projects (submarginal without regulatory-induced incentives) to average down high-profit pipelines. This misdirects resources. Averaging also gives larger firms with multiple lines pricing flexibility over firms with fewer lines. This interferes with the latter's ability to compete profitably, particularly in average-down cases where a major pipeline competes directly with an independent line.

Rate-base price regulation creates nonmarket prices that deviate from scarcity values. A price too low creates overuse and artificially disadvantages competing pipelines and substitute transportation modes (in addition to the pipeline in question). A price too high penalizes shippers and artificially promotes alternative transport.

The consent-decree differential, 1 percent for oil lines and 3 percent for product lines, adds to tariff mispricing and competitive imbalances for users and transport substitutes. Moreover, *inherent* in Oak-formula and consent-decree ratemaking, and more so in original-cost public-utility ratemaking, is an intertemporal bias creating high present prices and low future prices from rate-base depreciation. "Front-end loading," and later the "vanishing rate base," misprices pipeline services throughout the life of the asset with concurrent resource misallocation.[231]

Recent judicial instruction to modify the valuation formula from fair value toward original cost represents a direct invitation to realize the potential distortions of conventional public-utility regulation. The most positive aspect of regulation, its relative leniency, would

---

[231]Peter Navarro, Bruce Petersen, and Thomas Stauffer, "A Critical Comparison of Utility-Type Ratemaking Methodologies in Oil Pipeline Regulation," *Bell Journal of Economics* (August 1981): 393–412.

be removed, and the aforementioned distortions and disincentives would become magnified to challenge the hitherto successful record of interstate crude-oil and oil-product pipelines.

15. Regulation of Natural-Gas Pipelines

For over 150 years, downstream manufactured- and natural-gas operations have been the most regulated sector of the U.S. oil and gas industry. The first gas distribution company was regulated in 1817, and by the early twentieth century, every state regulated investor-owned distribution companies as public utilities. Other distribution companies were municipally owned and operated.

In response to problems with local and state regulation, federal regulation of interstate pipelines began in 1938 with the Natural Gas Act (NGA). After describing the rise and "fall" of state public-utility regulation of the gas industry, the chapter focuses on the nearly fifty-year experience with the NGA. Price regulation is examined through the study of firm valuation and allowed rates of return. Certification regulation is described by examining Federal Power Commission (FPC), and later Federal Energy Regulatory Commission (FERC), policies on entry, exit, and service alterations. The record of regulation under the NGA is reviewed, and the case for public-utility regulation of interstate gas pipelines is reconsidered. The chapter ends with a cursory look at nonfederal intervention—regulation and taxation on state and Indian land.

Industry problems and innovative responses that have changed not only the structure of the industry but regulation itself are examined in appendix 15.1. Although much of the story would unfold after 1984, a clear trend toward spot-market gas purchases by end-users and transportation in place of traditional "bundled" utility service was evident. Appendix 15.2 studies gas import and export regulation, complementing the analysis of chapter 13 on petroleum import and export regulation.

Origins of Gas Usage and Regulation

Although instances of discovery, transmission, and use of natural gas are documented as far back as biblical times, commercial use of the vapor illuminant did not begin until the early nineteenth century.[1] In the United States, gas manufactured from soft (bituminous) coal was introduced for street lighting in 1917 by the Gas Light Company of Baltimore, four years after such lighting was inaugurated in England. Baltimore's example was followed by many U.S. cities in the East and then the Midwest and Pacific Coast. By 1870, manufactured gas provided lighting to forty-six cities.[2]

Natural gas from shallow reservoirs was also utilized by nearby light companies as a cheaper substitute for artificial gas. This added risk to an already untested industry, however; as the reservoir became depleted, curtailment of service if not outright termination occurred.

Pipelines to transport natural gas first operated in the 1860s and 1870s in Pennsylvania and New York. The longest line was twenty-five miles; long-distance pipelines would wait until the next century when large-scale markets, long-life fields, and advanced pipe technology came of age.

The introduction of gas lighting in major U.S. cities had some critics. Moralistic concerns were raised about violating the divine nature of darkened nights and encouraging drunkenness, and some medical professionals warned of physical harm from artificial light.[3] A more important hurdle was investor and consumer confidence. Explained Martin Glaeser:

> At first gas lighting was hardly more than a luxury or at most an expensive convenience. The industry had to sell its services to the consuming public and to establish its reputation for profitableness with investors. It had to experiment with production, transmission, and utilization problems in order to make service adequate, safe and continuous.[4]

---

[1]Malcolm Peebles, *Evolution of the Gas Industry* (New York: New York University Press, 1980), pp. 5–6, 21, 53.

[2]Ibid., pp. 53–54. Those cities included New York (1823), Brooklyn (1825), Boston (1829), Louisville and New Orleans (1832), Philadelphia (1834), Pittsburgh (1836), Cincinnati (1841), Albany (1845), Washington (1848), and Chicago (1850). Martin Glaeser, *Outlines of Public Utility Economics* (New York: Macmillan, 1927), p. 52. The beginning dates in thirty-six major U.S. cities are provided in Arlon Tussing and Connie Barlow, *The Natural Gas Industry: Evolution, Structure, and Economics* (Cambridge, Mass.: Ballinger, 1984), p. 13.

[3]Martin Glaeser, *Outlines of Public Utility Economics*, p. 53.

[4]Ibid.

Industry and Regulation

Before the 1880s, gas companies were for the most part unregulated, although government involvement existed in various degrees. Some companies were municipally owned.[5] In some jurisdictions, limited-duration franchises were awarded to promote entry. Liberal privileges on public property and eminent-domain rights on private property reduced the cost of laying pipe for gas companies. Multiyear lighting contract with municipalities closed the door to new entrants.

Punitive control of rates and service, and uniform accounting standards and reporting requirements, were infrequently prescribed or moderate in effect. In 1817, a Baltimore ordinance required the Gas Light Company to charge a price not greater than rates in effect for other forms of illumination.[6] From 1855 to 1870, gas companies in Massachusetts could not declare dividends in excess of 7 percent over any five-year period in return for their limited-duration franchises.[7] All considered, subsidization more than penalization hallmarked early relations between government and gas. "There was no public demand for regulation," John Gray stated, and "companies were inclined to let well enough alone, and to jog along as they have been doing for so long a time."[8]

The early era was highly profitable for gas companies, "even after carrying the heavy expenses of buying up competitors."[9] This dramatically changed in the 1880s when electric companies entered the scene and new gas firms attracted by high profits, some using

[5]Philadelphia in 1841 built and operated a gas manufacturing and distribution company. Other early municipal light companies were built in Hamilton, Ohio; Wheeling, West Virginia; and Charlottesville, Danville, and Richmond, Virginia. By the turn of the century, fifteen government gas companies were in operation, which by 1910 would balloon to over 100 before falling thereafter. Eliot Jones and Truman Bigham, *Principles of Public Utilities* (New York: Macmillan, 1931), p. 733.

[6]George Brown, *The Gas Light Company of Baltimore* (Baltimore: Johns Hopkins University Press, 1936), p. 18.

[7]Leonard White, "The Origin of Utility Commissions in Massachusetts," *Journal of Political Economy* (March 1921): 189.

[8]John Gray, "The Gas Commission of Massachusetts," *Quarterly Journal of Economics* (August 1900): 514–15. The courts supported the concept of free pricing and free choice of clientele for gas firms. See C. O. Ruggles, "Government Control of Business," *Harvard Business Review* (Autumn 1945): 40.

[9]John Gray, "The Gas Commission of Massachusetts," p. 514.

a more efficient water-gas process, entered in unprecedented numbers.[10] (Such new entry required overcoming legislatures "purchased" by the existing gas company in some cases.)[11] In 1887, for example, six gas companies were chartered to serve New York City.[12] Under the new competition, the "advance-guards of industrial progress," as Gray described them, "made the air heavy with complaints about monopolies, extortionate prices, inadequate service, fabulous profits, and antiquated management."[13] For trade groups, such as the Gas Light Association of America (founded 1872),

> the question before [had been] how to prevent state interference. It now became how to stimulate, direct, and control state interference so as to protect investments. . . . [They] recognized that the days of high charges and high profits . . . were gone forever, and that . . . they must . . . claim protection for "honest investments." They realized, also, that a request for protection would raise the cry of monopoly, which could be safely met only by an acknowledgment of the state's right to regulate the monopoly in the public interest. . . . The question now became simply how much of their previous claims the companies could afford to give up for the sake of state protection against rivals.[14]

[10]In 1880, coal-gas companies secured a Massachusetts law forbidding the sale of gas with 10 percent or more carbonic oxide, which precluded water-gas competition in the state. It was narrowly upheld in 1884 after a major legislative fight, which persuaded coal-gas firms to try another route for protection. Leonard White, "The Origin of Utility Commissions in Massachusetts," pp. 189–90.

[11]"If there was a gas company, the [city] council had usually been bought beforehand, and promoting an electric company involved outwitting both politicians and competitors." Forrest McDonald, *Insull* (Chicago: University of Chicago Press, 1962), p. 30.

[12]Ibid., p. 68. Other cities with multifirm gas service in the late nineteenth century included Chicago, Detroit, Brooklyn, San Francisco, New Orleans, Charleston, Indianapolis, Baltimore, Rochester, Memphis, St. Louis, Buffalo, Albany, Jersey City, Providence, Savannah, and Harrisburg. Burton Behling, *Competition and Monopoly in Public Utility Industries* (Urbana: University of Illinois Press, 1938), p. 20.

[13]John Gray, "The Gas Commission of Massachusetts," p. 515. Also see C. O. Ruggles, *Aspects of the Organization, Functions, and Financing of State Public Utility Companies* (Boston: Harvard Business School, 1937), p. 6.

[14]John Gray, "The Gas Commission of Massachusetts," pp. 515–16. He continued, "The remarkable thing was the suddenness and thoroughness with which the gas interests embraced the suggestion after so completely rejecting it for so many years" (p. 516).

Massachusetts was the opening shot in the gas manufacturers' and distributors' campaign to foreclose competition. With the help of all major state newspapers except one, public opinion was swayed toward regulation by the lure of improved service and lower prices. A bill was drafted by the Boston Gas Company, and after debate and revision "confined almost exclusively to the companies," An Act to Create a Board of Gas Commissioners became law on June 11, 1885.[15] The franchise clause read:

> In any city or town in which a gas company exists in active operation, no other gas company or any other person shall dig up and open the streets, lanes, and highways of such city or town, for the purpose of laying gas pipes therein, without . . . consent of the mayor and aldermen . . . after a public hearing . . . and notice to all parties interested.[16]

Despite the board's "summary powers as to rates and service" and the risk that restrictive provisions would be imposed, the trade-off proved beneficial for established firms.[17] Entry was frozen, even when contracts were signed with customers at considerably cheaper prices by the would-be company. In the first fifteen years of the law, all eighteen proposals for new entry were denied.[18] Rate and dividend regulation, to the extent it was effective, could be circumvented by overcapitalizing the firm to "lower" profits and dividends to permitted levels. High costs, including handsome salaries, could also benefit company interests yet satisfy regulatory confines intended to hold down consumer prices on a cost-plus basis. Dozens of new laws would be passed in Massachusetts to attempt to plug the regulatory gaps, but the law remained special-interest regulation

---

[15]Ibid., p. 518.

[16]John Gray, "Competition and Capitalization, as Controlled by the Massachusetts Gas Commission," *Quarterly Journal of Economics* (February 1901): 254.

[17]"To protect themselves . . . manufactures of coal gas secured the . . . act . . . with a veto power over competitive projects and as a consideration therefor submitted to regulation of the price and quality of gas and to publicity of their corporate affairs." Eliot Jones and Truman Bigham, *Principles of Public Utilities*, p. 164. Financial publicity, however, worked both ways. It could reveal a firm's high profits to its detriment, or it could reveal a competitor's strategies to discourage secretive price cutting and promote arm's-length cooperation.

[18]John Gray, "Competition and Capitalization, as Controlled by the Massachusetts Gas Commission," pp. 257–58.

by and for established coal-gas companies against upstart coal-gas and water-gas manufacturing companies.[19]

The creation of the Board of Gas Commissioners in Massachusetts was followed by similar regulation in other states—by industry demand. "Nearly all the gas associations of the United States for years recommended state commissions for all the states."[20] State authorities, in turn, welcomed a new sphere of influence and happily traded protection for restriction. Standby price regulation was authorized in South Carolina (1895), Tennessee (1896), Washington and Iowa (1897), Wisconsin (1898), and Mississippi (1899). Arkansas, California, Nebraska, Ohio, and the city of Chicago would soon follow. Regulation grew more prominent at the same time. Prices were fixed for a minimum period in Rhode Island (1891), Connecticut (1893), Florida (1897), and Illinois (1903).[21]

By this time, a powerful ally had come aboard. Beginning with an 1898 speech by electric-utility magnate Samuel Insull before the National Electric Light Association, a movement began to put the electric industry under state regulation. Competitive protection would be granted in return for regulation, a tradeoff similar to the one accepted earlier by gas companies (and railroads with the Interstate Commerce Act, as seen in chapter 11). Industry support was initially lacking, but within a decade, both the National Electric Light Association and the National Civic Federation endorsed Insull's plan. Allied with the gas industry and supportive state officials—and by documenting the history of franchises unaccompanied by regulation that left a trail of corruption and dissent—Insull prevailed.[22] Formal commissions and systematic regulation of rates and service would follow.

In 1905, New York State established the Commission of Gas and Electricity. In 1907, state and local regulation of public utilities

---

[19]Approximately ninety new laws and amendments were passed in Massachusetts between 1885 and 1900 to make the original law more effective. They included "wide-reaching inquisitorial powers" to investigate firms' finances and practices. Ibid., p. 271.

[20]John Gray, "The Gas Commission of Massachusetts," p. 516.

[21]Van Lindsley, *Rate Regulation* (New York: Banks Law Publishing, 1906), pp. 58–150.

[22]Forrest McDonald, *Insull*, pp. 84–88, 113–21; James Weinstein, *The Corporate Ideal in the Liberal State: 1900–1918* (Boston: Beacon Press, 1968), pp. 24–26, 34–35. The threat of municipal control also turned the electric and gas industries toward regulation.

reached a new plateau when New York expanded regulation with a new public service commission law, and Wisconsin and Georgia established formal utility commissions. States that subsequently created similar commissions were Vermont (1909); Maryland and New Jersey (1910); California, Connecticut, Kansas, Nevada, New Hampshire, Ohio, Oregon, and Washington (1911); Arizona and Rhode Island (1912); Colorado, Idaho, Illinois, Indiana, Maine, Missouri, Montana, North Carolina, Oklahoma, Pennsylvania, and West Virginia (1913); Virginia (1914); Alabama, North Dakota, and Wyoming (1915); Utah (1917); Michigan and Tennessee (1919); Louisiana (1921); and South Carolina (1922). By 1927, forty-eight states—railroad commissions had regulatory authority in the remainder—had jurisdiction over the distribution of natural gas along with electricity and other "public utilities."[23] So along with telephone, telegraph, water, and electric companies, manufactured- and natural-gas distributors came under public-utility regulation to become the first comprehensively regulated sector of the U.S. energy market. This would have important implications when a problem of regulatory boundaries created political pressures to extend regulation to interstate gas-transmission firms in the 1930s, and ultimately to natural-gas production in the 1940s and 1950s.

Some Misinterpretations

While the record is clear that gas companies spearheaded the movement to become regulated as public utilities, a misleading "textbook" view emerged that it was the public that had demanded regulation, and rightly so, because of the wastes of unregulated enterprise. Francis Welch expressed the traditional view:

> The public grew weary of the interminable rate wars which were invariably followed by a period of recoupment during which the victorious would attempt to take the price of the battle out of the consumers by way of increased rates. Investors suffered heavy losses through the manipulation of fly-by-night paper concerns operating with "nuisance" franchises. The industry suffered because such an erratic, unstable condition interfered with the necessary growth and improvement of service. Everybody suffered the inconvenience of

[23]Van Lindsley, *Rate Regulation*, pp. 170–72. For a list of state commissions and operating dates through 1936, see C. O. Ruggles, *Aspects of the Organization, Functions, and Financing of State Public Utility Companies*, pp. 4–5. Later commissions were established in Delaware and Alaska (1960).

855

city streets being constantly torn up and replaced by installation and location of duplicate facilities. The situation in New York City alone, prior to the major gas company consolidations, threatened municipal chaos.[24]

The preceding sketch of the historic wastes of utility competition, implying a need for government to foreclose competition and regulate a firm's operation at "competitive" levels, is open to historical revision and theoretical refutation. First, Welch reverses the historical sequence. It was primarily the industry, not the public, that "grew weary." The industry led the way to regulation and convinced the public while so doing. Second, many underhanded accounting practices that misled investors in the public-utility field occurred *after* regulation and not *before* regulation; regulation itself created perverse incentives to doctor financial reporting and engage in peculiar business practices. Observed George May:

> The [accounting] practices which had become discredited were more general in the regulated industries (and among the utility holding companies) and had spread from those fields to unregulated industry to only a minor extent where they had spread at all. This is true of the non-acceptance of the cost amortization concept of depreciation; of reappraisal and improper charges against capital surpluses resulting therefrom; of pyramiding of holding companies; of periodical stock dividends improperly accounted for; and of the practice of charging the surplus items which more properly belong in the income account.[25]

Restated, the book value of regulated companies was inflated and profits were understated to enable firms to charge higher rates,

[24]Francis Welch, "The Odyssey of Gas—A Record of Industrial Courage," *Public Utility Fortnightly*, October 12, 1939, p. 501. Referring to the Maryland experience, George Brown states, "The evils of the competitive era of gas companies—the trafficking in gas company charters, the failure of 'competing' companies to compete and the wanton tearing up of the streets—caused a decided change in public opinion and the actions of the legislature." Brown, *The Gas Light Company of Baltimore*, p. 74. A recent restatement of unregulated entry as a "wasteful duplication of facilities and services" is found in Richard Pierce, Gary Allison, and Patrick Martin, *Economic Regulation: Energy Transportation and Utilities* (New York: Bobbs Merrill, 1980), p. 87.

[25]George May, "Accounting and Regulation," *Journal of Accountancy*, October 1943, pp. 296–97. For greater detail, see May, *Financial Accounting: A Distillation of Experience* (New York: Macmillan, 1943), chaps. 7–9.

increase profits, and increase dividends within their cost-plus, franchised sphere.

Third, rate wars are erroneously assumed to be both wasteful and perpetual instead of a *process of discovery* whereby the most efficient firms emerge and a definite market structure is created. Without competition, it could not be known which firms are the most competent to assume a greater market share nor the optimum size of those firms. It is true that the discovery process might begin anew as a result of a new entry, but this ensures lowest cost provision of gas service. Potential competition is the omnipresent *check* on existing firms (including a "natural monopolist") and the correction for perceived existing inefficiency should actual entry take place. Capital is scarce, and calculating investors learn from experience. Entrance is not undertaken on a lark or for disruption's sake but to outdistance the competition and win profits. To the extent this is accomplished, consumers are better served than they would be had "destructive" competition not been allowed. New entry and "duplication," in fact, often represented new applications of technology, broadened markets, and cheapened service. These advantages remained with later consolidation.

Price is also of concern to Welch and other critics; it is too low during rate wars and too high after. Undeniably, price wars benefit consumers by lowering prices.[26] When price cutting has run its course and prices return to levels at or above fixed costs, in addition to variable costs, this must be considered the "right" price because it resulted from a market discovery process and is the payback to investors upon whom the service depends. A price that is perceived by the market as not "right" (e.g., a price reflecting too much cost or profit, or both) invites entry and a new round of discovery to once again reveal competitive conditions.

Criticism of the mainstream view does not imply that all was well in the early gas industry. Indeed, a careful reading of the complaints

---

[26]Burton Behling argues that "cut-throat competition favored the public for a time with low rates, but invariably at the expense of a deteriorated service." Behling, *Competition and Monopoly in the Public Utility Industries*, p. 20. That argument smuggles in the value judgment that higher cost, higher quality service is preferred to lower cost, lower quality service. This is particularly elitist when it is realized that home heating and lighting were in the process of changing from luxury goods for the few to conveniences for the many. It also neglects the consumer preference for lower prices in the short run, other things the same.

reveals that government intervention, as much as or more than the free market, was a source of industry problems. Government ownership of streets and their nonpriced use, as well as condemnation rights on private land, overencouraged subsurface construction.[27] Under private ownership and voluntary exchange, pipeline right-of-way costs would have reflected the financial costs of street downtime and paving repair to ration marginal projects. Duplication of facilities would have been discouraged, and the inconvenience of construction would have been reduced to "market" levels.

Government franchise rights gave politically adept firms paper assets for "nuisance" use by "fly-by-night" entrepreneurs. Franchising and exclusive municipal-lighting contracts also weakened the discovery process by fostering collusion and territorial agreements that could not be threatened by new entry. And, as was widely recognized, the power to issue monopolistic grants corrupted authorities, which ironically contributed to sentiment for further regulation to "cure" the effects of prior regulation.[28]

The case for replacing "market failure" with regulatory surrogate "competition" fails to forthrightly consider the drawbacks of the "correction." Public-utility textbooks drawing upon the nineteenth-century experience condemn market practices to espouse intervention. Then, in a different context, it is admitted that the corrective regulation was experimental, imperfect, and "evolving." This skirts a crucial point. It is not enough to lambast the market; the critic must also assess the political alternative to see if the correction is worse than the problem. The rationale and practice of public-utility regulation have pronounced shortcomings, as seen later in this chapter, that make a revaluation of the market alternative imperative.

Early State Regulation

Controversies surrounding oil pipelines since their introduction in the 1860s did not extend to manufactured- and natural-gas transmission until many decades later. This was primarily because (1) industry integration lessened the conflict between gas producers

---

[27]"The problem of excessive duplication of distribution systems is attributable to the failure of the community to set a proper price on the use of these scarce resources." Harold Demsetz, "Why Regulate Utilities?" *Journal of Law and Economics* (April 1968): 62.

[28]This major theme of regulation is explored in depth in chapter 29.

and gas pipelines and (2) gas pipelines did not displace other modes of transportation. State common-carrier laws excluded gas pipelines as did the Hepburn Act in 1906. This would change after the turn of the century as gas markets began to grow and wellhead interests emerged. But as discussed in chapter 4, natural gas was often unmarketable because of limited storage and transport, and even when it was connected by pipeline, gas did not command a high market price. This led discouraged producers to seek pipeline legislation to increase the marketability, if not the price, of natural gas. Common-carrier statutes for intrastate gas lines were passed by California (1913), Oklahoma (1915), Louisiana (1920), New Mexico (1927), Michigan (1929), and North Dakota (1933) among others; common-purchaser laws were enacted in Oklahoma (1913), Louisiana (1918), Kentucky (1920), Michigan (1929), Texas (1931), Mississippi (1932) and Kansas (1935). To the extent that the requirement to transport or purchase all tendered gas ratably discouraged pipeline investment, producers damaged their own interests by worsening the marketability (conservation) problem of natural gas.

State regulation of gas transmission attempted to restrict interstate commerce. In 1907, Oklahoma banned natural-gas exports to boost local industry at the expense of neighboring states. Challenged by a firm transporting gas from Oklahoma to Kansas, the statute was declared unconstitutional by the Supreme Court in 1911.[29] Undeterred, in early 1919 West Virginia passed the Steptoe bill that prohibited interstate gas sales unless the gas was unmarketable intrastate.[30] The intention was to avert a third straight winter of shortages that closed factories and schools and stop an exodus of firms to Ohio. West Virginia had a strict price-control law, and state production was increasingly being diverted where "competition and public regulation are the least, and the willingness of the public to pay for gas is the greatest."[31] This law was also declared in violation of the commerce clause of the Constitution by the nation's highest tribunal in 1923.[32] A final challenge to interstate gas transmission on the state level was made by Louisiana, which in 1924 forbade gas to be

---

[29]*Oklahoma* v. *Kansas Natural Gas Company*, 221 U.S. 229 (1911).

[30]*Oil & Gas Journal*, February 21, 1919, p. 48. Cited hereafter as *OGJ*.

[31]Philip Steptoe and George Hoffheimer, "Legislative Regulation of Natural Gas Supply in West Virginia," *West Virginia Law Quarterly* (June 1918): 262.

[32]*Pennsylvania* v. *West Virginia*, 262 U.S. 544 (1923).

exported for the manufacture of carbon black. Cloaked in conservation garb, the law was not legally challenged and enjoyed longevity.[33]

Rates were another area of state jurisdiction over gas pipelines. Since 1889, states had regulated intrastate pipelines' sales to gas distributors in conjunction with their authority to regulate the latter.[34] Along with limiting gas utilities to cost-plus rates to limit the rate of returns to 7 to 9 percent, state authorities could prohibit costs from being passed through if a cost study of the wholesaler revealed "unjustified" profits.[35] Indeed, without retail competition, wholesale demand was more price inelastic to the advantage of gas pipelines (and producers) and to the disadvantage of gas consumers. Moreover, firms integrated over the wholesale and retail sectors could escape regulation by receiving at wholesale the profit not allowed at retail. To close the loophole, authorities focused on the utilities' cost of goods sold and used their authority to regulate at retail to force pipeline firms to lower their city-gate prices to permitted passthrough levels.

The question remained whether *interstate* sales by gas-pipeline companies could be regulated as intrastate sales could be. This was no longer an academic question when long-distance gas transmission began to emerge in the 1920s. The first major case concerned a direct interstate sale to consumers, and the Supreme Court upheld a contention by New York State in 1920 that such transactions were local in nature, affected with a public interest, and subject to state regulation.[36] This left the area of wholesale interstate transactions unresolved, and in 1924, the Supreme Court drew the line on state authority by ruling that interstate pipeline firms were protected from price interference by the commerce clause.[37] This decision was joined two years later by a high-court decision that states could not regulate

---

[33]Yandell Boatner, "Legal History of Conservation of Oil and Gas in Louisiana," in American Bar Association, *Legal History of Conservation of Oil and Gas* (Baltimore: Lord Baltimore Press, 1939), p. 65.

[34]*OGJ*, June 30, 1938, p. 33.

[35]See the rate-of-return tables for gas utilities in Nelson Smith, *The Fair Rate of Return in Public Utility Regulation* (New York: Houghton Mifflin, 1932), pp. 131, 146–49.

[36]*Pennsylvania Gas Company* v. *Public Service Commission,* 252 U.S. 23 (1920).

[37]*Missouri* v. *Kansas Natural Gas Co.,* 265 U.S. 298 (1924). The same verdict was rendered for interstate electricity sales. *P.U.C. of Rhode Island* v. *Attleboro Steam and Electric Co.,* 273 U.S. 83 (1927).

interstate gas sold to gas distributors.[38] States could only regulate the production and intrastate consumption of natural gas.[39] These two rulings created a *regulatory gap* that encouraged pipeline investment in the interstate market, which became viable with the introduction of seamless pipe and the discovery of the prolific Amarillo (Texas) and Monroe (Louisiana) fields, and to sell at wholesale rather than directly to homes and businesses.[40] This free-market oasis was recognized by critics, but rather than promote intrastate deregulation to end regulatory problems, they began to press for federal authority to regulate interstate as well.

The Move toward Federal Regulation

Federal intervention with natural-gas pipelines began modestly in 1920 when the interior secretary was empowered to impose the "express condition" of common carriage on pipelines that received right-of-way on federal land.[41] In 1935, common-purchaser obligations were added to this requirement.[42] Whether Interior's authority extended to rate regulation would be the subject of later debate.[43]

Federal interest in interstate gas transmission began on February 15, 1928, when Senator Thomas Walsh (D-Mont.) introduced Senate Resolution 83 to investigate the market structure and economic performance of the electric and natural-gas industries and recommend policy. Congress approved a multiyear study by the Federal Power Commission, created in 1920 to regulate hydroelectric power, to investigate the need for regulation. Released in 1935, the findings strongly advocated a federal role with electricity and gas.

In 1934, President Franklin D. Roosevelt created by executive order the National Power Policies Commission to recommend legislation.

---

[38]*Peoples Natural Gas Co.* v. *Public Service Commission*, 270 U.S. 550 (1926).

[39]*Henderson Co.* v. *Thompson*, 300 U.S. 258 (1937).

[40]See Donald Libert, "Legislative History of the Natural Gas Act," *Georgetown Law Journal* (June 1956): 695–723. For a list of eighteen major new pipeline projects in the 1925–31 period, mostly interstate, see Arlon Tussing and Connie Barlow, *The Natural Gas Industry*, pp. 34–35. Before this time, only five short interstate lines had been built.

[41]Mineral Leasing Act, Public Law 146, 41 Stat. 437 at 449 (1920).

[42]Act of August 21, 1935, Public Law 297 1/2, 49 Stat. 674 at 678–79.

[43]See *Montana-Dakota Utilities Co.* v. *FPC*, 169 F.2d 392 (8th Cir.) cert. den. 315 U.S. 95 (1948); and *Chapman* v. *El Paso Natural Gas*, 204 F.2d 46 (D.C. Cir. 1953).

With the support of the FPC and draft input by the National Association of Railroad and Utilities Commissioners, H.R. 5423 was introduced on February 6, 1935, by Texas Representative Sam Rayburn to regulate interstate sales of electricity and natural gas. The bill had three parts: Title I regulating interstate public-utility holding companies, Title II regulating interstate electricity rates and entry, and Title III regulating rates and entry of interstate natural-gas pipelines. On August 26, 1935, Title I became law as the Public Utility Holding Company Act (Wheeler-Rayburn Act),[44] and Title II became the Federal Power Act.[45] Title III was deleted because pipeline firms were against common carriage, a certification provision favoring intrastate lines, strict determination of allowable costs, and the regulation of sales for resale to industrial users.[46]

The Public Utility Holding Company Act directly affected integrated gas operations that were 10 percent or more owned by a holding company. The Securities and Exchange Commission was empowered to scrutinize and disaggregate holding companies to address three alleged problems: investor misinformation due to an "absence of uniform standard accounts," inflated charges by nonregulated to regulated affiliates that were eligible for passthrough, and obstruction of state regulation.[47] Effective January 2, 1938, the commission after notice and hearing was to "limit the operations of the holding-company system of which such company is a part to a single integrated public-utility system, and to such other businesses as are reasonably incidental, or economically necessary or appropriate to the operations of such integrated public-utility system."[48] Exemptions were permitted if economies of scale were disrupted or the affiliates were located in one state.

Divestitures followed. Columbia Gas and Electric was split into an electric company and a gas company, with the latter spinning off Panhandle Eastern, an interstate gas-pipeline company. Jersey

[44]Title I, Public Law 333, 49 Stat. 803 (1935).

[45]Title II, Public Law 333, 49 Stat. 838 (1935).

[46]M. Elizabeth Sanders, *The Regulation of Natural Gas: Policy and Politics, 1938–1978* (Philadelphia: Temple University Press, 1981), p. 37. Objections to the gas bill were also raised by the coal industry, which feared that the common-carrier provision would increase the marketability of gas.

[47]Title I, sec. 1(b), Public Law 333, 49 Stat. 803-4 (1935).

[48]Ibid., p. 820.

Standard divested Consolidated Natural Gas Company. Cities Service Gas Company split along geographic lines into three companies. The prospective effect was also significant. Summarized Arlon Tussing and Connie Barlow:

> Fifteen years after the passage of the [Public Utilities Holding Company Act], holding company control of interstate gas pipeline mileage had shrunk from 80 to 18 percent. New interstate pipelines, organized and built after 1935, almost always chose to avoid the act's jurisdiction by remaining completely free of distributor entanglements.[49]

By 1950, the requirement of the Public Utilities Holding Company Act had been responsible for divestitures totaling $16 billion.[50]

Title III would be resurrected. The impetus for gas-pipeline regulation was a ninety-six-volume Federal Trade Commission report released during 1934 and 1935 that revealed a concentration of ownership among four interstate gas pipelines, which raised congressional fears of "holding-company control."[51] The study also cited a number of questionable practices suggesting a need for federal interstate regulation. These scrutinized practices included territorial divisions, abnormal profits between (unregulated) pipelines and (regulated) distributors that were affiliated, and artificial asset write-ups. Another concern was "discrimination" between wellhead purchases on the one hand and the rates charged commercial and industrial users on the other.[52] The widely recognized "breakdown of

---

[49]Arlon Tussing and Connie Barlow, *The Natural Gas Industry*, p. 208.

[50]Securities and Exchange Commission, *Fifteenth Annual Report* (Washington, D.C.: Government Printing Office, 1950), pp. 62–63.

[51]Senate Document no. 92 (1936). The four largest carriers—Columbia Gas and Electric, Cities Service, Electric Bond and Share Company, and Standard Oil of New Jersey—controlled 59 percent of the interstate gas-pipeline market in 1934. M. Elizabeth Sanders, *The Regulation of Natural Gas*, p. 28.

[52]The wellhead discrimination charge has been rebutted in regard to oil pipelines in chapter 14, pp. 783–85, 843–44. Producers could have formally consolidated to seek better terms from pipeline purchasers or built joint-venture pipelines to achieve competitive parity. M. Elizabeth Sanders argued that established pipelines could block new entry by their influence with the financial community and gas distributors. Ibid., p. 33. It is difficult, however, to see how any particular firm could persuade capital markets to forgo profitable opportunities. Regarding distributors, the absence of competition by law (franchise grants), not the free market, was primary.

regulation," it is important to note, was not linked to *existing regulation*—specifically franchise and rate-of-return regulation—but to the *absence of comprehensive regulation.*[53] The "regulatory gap" had to be closed by further intervention, not removed by deregulation. Favored firms dared not renounce public-utility regulation that was more protectionist than restrictive. While franchise rights offered territorial monopolies, cost-plus ratemaking in an environment of large rate bases and good relations with the public-utility commissions minimized regulatory risk. This backdoor result of "monopoly pricing" could easily be laid on the doorstep of the interstate pipelines' wholesale price of natural gas. "Public-utility status," after all, was

> the haven of refuge for all aspiring monopolists who found it too
> difficult, too costly, or too precarious to secure and maintain monopoly by private action alone. Their future would be assured if only
> they could induce government to grant them monopoly power and
> to protect them against interlopers, provided always, of course, that
> government did not exact too high a price for its favors in the form
> of restrictive regulation.[54]

The gas bill needed to be reworked before major interstate firms would support it as the electric utility industry had supported the Federal Power Act in 1935. By no means was regulation unwanted. Observed Gerald Nash:

> Representatives of gas companies were not at all unfriendly to the
> idea of federal regulation. For them, it promised uniformity and
> standardization in the interstate transmission of gas; this would
> reduce cutthroat competition and promote stabilization of the industry. At the same time, national regulation promised an escape from
> what they often considered onerous stipulations of state agencies.[55]

---

[53]A sampling of opinion on the anti-consumer nature of public-utility regulation through the early 1930s can be found in William Pendergast, *Public Utilities and the People* (New York: D. Appleton-Century, 1933), pp. 266–77.

[54]Horace Gray, quoted in Walter Adams, "The Role of Competition in the Regulated Industries," *American Economic Review*, May 1958, p. 528.

[55]Gerald Nash, *United States Oil Policy* (Westport, Conn.: Greenwood Press, 1968), pp. 212–13. Also see M. Elizabeth Sanders, *The Regulation of Natural Gas*, p. 195. The 1935 gas bill also included mandatory conservation by gas producers to "protect the investment" of pipelines.

While state control was not unwelcomed, federal regulation was seen as correcting its shortcomings and potentially offering more— the opportunity to tame rivalry and stabilize the industry with cost-plus rates and thus facilitate profitability and financing in the post-holding-company era.

In March 1936, a gas bill was reintroduced by Representative Clarence Lea (D-Calif.), a former state public-utility commissioner, that removed most of the pipeline industry's objections. Industry support was tentative rather than enthusiastic, however. In testimony before a House subcommittee the next month, Floyd Brown of Natural Gas Pipeline of America, who was a bit defensive because of his company's valuation tiffs with the Illinois Commerce Commission, stated:

> Possibly State regulation should be supplemented by Federal control of interstate activities. In some instances it might prove beneficial to the public as well as to the transmission company, and in others it would undoubtedly be detrimental to one or both. No gas company should fear or oppose Federal regulation and control if the authority so granted is administered fairly by the commission to whom these broad powers are entrusted. However, before creating a new bureau or a department under existing commissions, with the added expense for valuations, hearings, fields, and office administration and attendant delays under even the most harmonious proceedings, we should be fully convinced that there is need for this type of legislation and control.[56]

Brown, the only interstate-pipeline witness, also drew attention to the fact that natural gas under regulation would be less flexible to compete with coal and fuel oil, which were not subject to public-utility control.[57]

---

[56]*Natural Gas,* Hearing before a Subcommittee of the House Committee on Interstate and Foreign Commerce, 74th Cong., 2d sess. (Washington, D.C.: Government Printing Office, 1936), p. 102. Cited hereafter as *Natural Gas I.* Also see Kenneth Marcus, *The National Government and the Natural Gas Industry, 1946–1956* (New York: Arno Press, 1979), pp. 114–15. Representative Rayburn's interest in the bill waned (although he continued to favor it), presumably because of the exclusion of common carriage desired by Texas gas producers.

[57]"Prompt decision by management, without the delay of preparing valuations and holding rate hearings to meet the competition of any unregulated competitive fuels, is essential." *Natural Gas I,* p. 103.

John Battle of the National Association of Bituminous Coal Organization was also undecided about regulation that had the potential to either lower or raise gas prices. Although he complained of "unfair competition" from "unreasonably low" industrial gas prices, his position was that "if you are going to have the Federal Government going into that realm I think that it ought to make a good job of it."[58] The present bill was described as "practically nil insofar as benefiting anyone is concerned."[59]

In contrast, the government witnesses welcomed an expansion to interstate regulation with little reservation. Dozier DeVane of the FPC favorably compared the bill to the Federal Power Act to argue its constitutionality.[60] William Chantland of the Federal Trade Commission complained about "starvation . . . in the midst of plenty" with wellhead waste by producers on the one end and monopolistic pipelines restricting throughput to leave communities unserved on the other.[61] John Benton of the National Association of Railroad and Utilities Commissioners endorsed federal regulation to address the regulatory gap so long as existing state jurisdiction was not invaded.[62] Communications submitted to the subcommittee from the Missouri, Illinois, Kansas, and Alabama utility regulators also supported the bill. But while the House approved the bill, Senate confirmation was not forthcoming. Another try was necessary.

In early 1937, Lea again introduced a gas bill with an alteration that would prove to be the "winning formula"—restrictions on pipeline entry into occupied interstate markets.[63] Section 7(c) of the proposed bill required certificates from the FPC for new entrants, which put the burden of proof on would-be pipelines. This protective provision cajoled the pipeline industry into cautious support,

[58]Ibid., p. 79.
[59]Ibid., p. 71.
[60]Ibid., pp. 10–46.
[61]Ibid., pp. 55–56. Chantland did concede in questioning that excess capacity, even with storage capabilities, was attributable to the obligation to meet peak residential load during severe winter weather and to serve seasonal manufacturing industries (pp. 62–63).
[62]Ibid., pp. 84–98.
[63]M. Elizabeth Sanders, *The Regulation of Natural Gas,* p. 40; and Donald Libert, "Legislative History of the Natural Gas Act," p. 711.

enough when combined with outside support to ensure the bill's passage.

In House testimony in March 1937, the FPC, the Federal Trade Commission, and state regulatory bodies remained united behind interstate regulation. State utility regulators were frustrated by the regulatory gap, and federal officials recognized expanded career opportunities.[64] The National Coal Association (formerly the National Association of Bituminous Coal Organization), on the other hand, remained ambivalent. Even with section 7(c), they were not sure if natural-gas prices would be higher or lower. In testimony they reiterated their concern that the bill was ineffectual and not of benefit to anyone since their concern about industrial gas rates was not addressed.[65]

The interstate natural-gas industry again offered one witness. M. A. Dougherty, a New York lawyer, represented four interstates: Colorado Interstate Gas Co., Mississippi River Fuel Corporation, Interstate Natural Gas Co., and New York State Natural Gas Co. After suggesting a number of changes to the draft to reduce the expense and paperwork for the industry, Dougherty expressed his support for section 7(c) as a common covenant in interstate regulation and for promoting conservation. When asked about the industry's interest in the entire bill, Dougherty responded:

> We have no objection to the bill. We are not opposing it. . . . We think that generally it is sound regulation. It follows the lines of regulation in many of the states. Frankly, I think about the only result that will occur is increased cost both to the Federal Government . . . and to the companies. I do not believe that the expense that is going to be incurred by these companies, that ultimately must be paid by the rate payers and the consumer, is going to find its benefits in as greatly a reduced rate as some of these city officials feel that they will get; but we have no objection to the Federal Government stepping into this field of regulation.[66]

[64]M. Elizabeth Sanders, *The Regulation of Natural Gas*, pp. 46–53; and Kenneth Marcus, *The National Government and the Natural Gas Industry*, pp. 119–22.

[65]*Natural Gas*, Hearing before the House Committee on Interstate and Foreign Commerce, 75th Cong., 1st sess. (Washington, D.C.: Government Printing Office, 1937), pp. 120–23. Cited hereafter as *Natural Gas II.*

[66]Ibid., p. 135. When later asked by a congressman if the proposed legislation "contains any death sentence" for the industry, Dougherty replied: "No; I do not think so. We will keep on selling gas" (ibid.).

The sudden inclusion of section 7(c) after three years of legislative drafts and debate did not go unopposed in the committee hearings. Cities Alliance, an alliance of 100 midwestern cities dedicated to "securing natural gas at proper rates," stated,

> After 2 years of vigorous effort to free the natural-gas industry from unlawful monopolistic restraint, [we] are alarmed by any possibility that the Congress might, inadvertently, give its blessing to the practices and philosophy of monopolistic control now dominating the production, transportation, and distribution of natural gas throughput this nation.[67]

Ten reasons were given by Cities Alliance to delete the section:

1. It would "creat[e] a towering bureaucracy that feeds upon itself."[68]
2. It unnecessarily duplicates local and state authority already regulating gas service.
3. "It improperly assumes that a Federal bureau here at Washington has a better knowledge of just what constitutes 'public necessity and convenience' . . . than do the cities, counties, and States which are directly affected."[69]
4. It would discourage municipal ownership or service from a new distribution company.
5. It would indirectly promote waste by redirecting gas reserves toward inferior uses such as carbon-black manufacture and gas stripping.
6. "It would impose unfair and rigid requirements upon an industry which is still young and growing lustily."[70]
7. It discourages "legitimate freedom of opportunity."[71]
8. It gives the established pipeline the opportunity to simply expand its facilities to block an applicant.

---

[67]Ibid., p. 61.

[68]Ibid., p. 63.

[69]Ibid., p. 64.

[70]Ibid. Further, "Is it wise to clothe a toddling youngster in an old man's pantaloons and expect him to run a race against his older brothers—the oil, the coal, and the electric-power industries?" (p. 65).

[71]Ibid., p. 65.

9. New entry would be "subjected to unfair hazards incident to the delay in obtaining a Federal certificate."[72]

10. "It offers to powerful and wealthy pipe-line companies an endless opportunity to frustrate independent enterprise, frustrate the commission, and frustrate the public's own rate-reduction efforts by resorting to litigation . . . which is not available to them at this time."[73]

Permit hearings on the local and state levels, indeed, had witnessed coal and fuel-oil interests arguing to block entry of natural gas into their markets.[74]

Cities Alliance also rebutted the argument that section 7(c) was necessary to prevent a wasteful duplication of facilities. Cutthroat pricing, it was argued, would lower the rate of return to threaten the entrant's financing. If, on the other hand, lower prices could generate a bankable rate of return, consumers would benefit.[75]

Three congressmen defended section 7(c) in the face of Cities Alliance's challenge. Congressman Charles Halleck (R-Ind.) argued that "throughout the whole history of expanding government regulation and control of public utilities . . . a provision similar to . . . Section 7(c) has been applied."[76] He also asserted that competition had failed to bring gas prices down, a point that Cities Alliance vigorously denied.[77] Congressman Samuel Pettengill (D-Ind.) recognized a tradeoff between regulated rates and territorial protection. The first without the second, he opined, would hamper the incentive for natural-gas firms to expand to new markets.[78] Congressman Lea of California, who claimed authorship of the controversial section, stated that the certificate obligation was more necessary with gas than electricity because gas was a wasting asset in great need of conservation.[79] To him, fewer head-to-head confrontations assured more supply for consumers.

---

[72]Ibid.

[73]Ibid., pp. 65–66.

[74]See, for example, *Business Week*, November 11, 1933, p. 19.

[75]*Natural Gas II,* p. 62.

[76]Ibid., p. 76.

[77]Ibid., p. 82.

[78]Ibid., p. 77.

[79]Ibid., pp. 81, 83.

Although many of Cities Alliance's arguments could be used against interstate regulation (and intrastate regulation as well), the nation's first natural-gas consumer group decided to side with federal regulation. They had already used antitrust action to police the industry; they now proposed an amendment requiring compulsory pipeline extensions to nonserviced areas, although it would not be adopted.[80] This left the free-market alternative of removing state regulation to close the regulatory gap without a sponsor much less a champion. On June 14, the House approved H.R. 6586.

The Senate discussed natural-gas legislation but did not hold formal hearings. The Committee on Interstate Commerce recommended passage of the House version without amendment. This was due in large part to the popularity of the bill among state regulators and federal officials and an absence of reservation within the gas industry itself. It was noted again and again that there was no opposition from any quarter. Judging by Senate discussion, the gas industry had grown more comfortable with interstate regulation since the House hearings five months before. Senator Burton Wheeler (D-Mont.) attributed industry support to the fact that "they would rather have one body here in Washington regulate the interstate features of the matter than to have a lot of States try to regulate shipments."[81] He added:

> The authorities of cities like Columbus, Cleveland, Detroit, St. Louis, Chicago, Kansas City, and every single city in the United States that imports gas, have written me and begged me and pleaded with me to try to get this bill passed. Likewise . . . every State regulatory body has asked for it, and there has not been an objection that I know of coming from the transporters or producers of gas anywhere in the United States. In fact, one of them spoke to me abut the matter and said he hoped the bill would pass, because he felt that it would stabilize the industry, and stop the industry from being held up to ridicule.[82]

---

[80]Ibid., p. 66.

[81]*Congressional Record*, 75th Cong., 1st sess., 1937, p. 9312.

[82]Ibid., p. 9315. Added Texas Senator Tom Connally: "I have not had a letter for this bill, nor, so far as I recall, a letter against it. I have no particular interest in this matter, except that the bill does affect a large industry in my state. We want to sell our gas, of course, but we do not want to sell it at a price that is not just and fair" (ibid., p. 9316).

There was concern, as on the House side, about gas producers falling under regulation. Although the Senate was assured that state and not federal authority was controlling, its concern foreshadowed a difficult interpretive question under the just-and-reasonable standard that would surface in the 1940s and culminate with the 1954 *Phillips* decision.[83]

On June 7, 1938, the Senate passed H.R. 6586 with minor revisions. The House accepted all but one of the amendments on June 13, and the Senate concurred the next day. On June 21, President Roosevelt signed the NGA into law.[84] A \$2.5-billion industry serving 8 million customers in thirty-five states was now regulated. Major jurisdictional pipelines, which transported approximately one-fourth of all gas produced in the country, are listed in table 15.1.

The NGA of 1938

Effective six months after enactment, the NGA closely resembled the Federal Power Act of 1935 regulating electricity sales.[85] Prefaced on the "public interest" in interstate commerce, the act gave the FPC public-utility jurisdiction over rates, entry, and extension and abandonment of service. Rates were to be "just and reasonable," implying a market return on original cost, without "any undue preference or advantage" between city gates.[86] Tariffs were to be filed with the FPC and could not be changed for thirty days unless permitted by the commission. Filed tariffs could be challenged and brought to hearing by the FPC, but submitted rates, with a maximum five-month suspension period, could become effective if an escrow account was created to provide refunds should the approved rate fall below the interim rate. In no case could a hearing result in a rate determination above that filed; only reductions could be ordered.

Another major concern was entry, which was the most palatable aspect of the law to the interstate gas-pipeline industry. While an established firm could "enlarge or extend its facilities for the purpose of supplying increased market demands in the territory in which it

[83]See chapter 8, pp. 376–79.

[84]Public Law 688, 52 Stat. 821 (1938).

[85]Dozier DeVane, "Highlights of Legislative History of the Federal Power Act of 1935 and the Natural Gas Act of 1938," *George Washington Law Review* (December 1945): 38–39.

[86]Secs. 4(a) and 4(b), Public Law 688, 52 Stat. 821 at 822 (1935).

Table 15.1

JURISDICTIONAL PIPELINES UNDER THE NATURAL GAS ACT OF 1938

Year Completed	Company	From–To	Miles	Diameter (inches)
1925	Magnolia	Louisiana–Texas	214	14–18
1925	Dixie–Gulf	Louisiana–Texas	217	22
1926	Interstate	Louisiana–Texas	170	22
1927	Cities Service	Texas–Kansas	250	20
1928	Colorado Interstate	Texas–Colorado	350	20–22
1928	United	Texas–Mexico	141	18
1928	Mississippi Interstate	Texas–Missouri	350	20–22
1929	El Paso	New Mexico–Texas	218	16
1929	Southern Natural	Louisiana–Georgia	460	20–22
1929	Texas Gas Trans.	Louisiana–Tennessee	210	18
1929	Mountain Fuel	Wyoming–Utah	290	14–18
1930	Northern Natural	Texas–Minnesota	1,100	24–26
1931	Natural Gas America	Texas–Illinois	980	24
1931	Panhandle Eastern	Texas–Indiana	900	20–24
1931	Columbia	Kentucky–Wash., D.C.	467	20
1932	Western	Texas–Arizona	275	–
1936	Panhandle Eastern	Indiana–Michigan	300	–

SOURCE: Arlon Tussing and Connie Barlow, *The Natural Gas Industry*, pp. 34–35.

operates," new firms could not enter "a market in which natural gas is already being served by another natural-gas company" unless per hearing, a certificate of public convenience and necessity was obtained.[87] Service abandonments also required FPC approval.[88] On the other hand, a firm could be ordered to "extend or improve its transportation facilities" to supply gas distributors if existing service was not impaired.[89] Enlargement of mainline facilities could not be required.

Other sections of the NGA embellished the above-mentioned areas of jurisdiction. The commission could prescribe accounting methods, require records and reports, and undertake inspection and investigation. State conservation efforts were to be aided where informationally possible. Imports and exports of natural gas were to be regulated in the "public interest."[90] Executives of interstate pipeline firms were to forgo active trading of company securities. The remainder of the act prescribed the machinery of enforcement.

The parameters of the NGA can be better fathomed by noting what was not regulated. Security issues, consolidations, mergers, and gas-property sales were uncontrolled. Fixed-rate floors or ceilings were not prescribed. Conservation measures analogous to state natural-gas statutes were absent. So was the authority to regulate retail gas sales—state jurisdiction prevailed in both cases. It was specifically mentioned [section 1(b)] that the act "shall not apply . . . to the production or gathering of natural gas." Section 5(b), however, gave the FPC jurisdiction to "investigate and determine the cost of the production or transportation of natural gas." These two clauses would have important ramifications in the decades to follow.

The NGA has been described by Elizabeth Sanders as "cut from the same cloth as other New Deal economic regulatory statutes."[91] This is oversimplified. While industries wrote their own codes of fair competition under the National Industrial Recovery Act, the gas industry played a more reserved role with the NGA. Affected pipeline firms were moderately favorable if not apathetic toward

---

[87]Sec. 7(c), Public Law 688, 52 Stat. 825 (1935).
[88]Sec. 7(b), Public Law 688, 52 Stat. 824 (1935).
[89]Sec. 7(a), ibid.
[90]See appendix 15.2, pp. 961–70.
[91]M. Elizabeth Sanders, *The Regulation of Natural Gas*, p. 44.

federal regulation, whereas the National Industrial Recovery Act program was wholeheartedly endorsed by the involved industries. What the 1938 law represented was "but another example of the trend toward regulation of the interstate phases of industry by federal agencies."[92] The NGA was not born of FDR's "new" program of government intervention in the economy; it was a legacy of *Munn* v. *Illinois* (1877) and interstate regulation of transportation "affected with a public interest" that began with the Interstate Commerce Act of 1887. This point was made in a speech before the American Gas Association, shortly after the NGA was passed, by the president of the National Association of Railroad and Utilities Commissioners, an organization instrumental in passage of the NGA:

> I wish to dispel the thought that the regulations as we know it today is a child of the present decade, something novel or experimental. . . . With the background [of regulation] as it is, no one . . . can justly say that the enactment of . . . the federal natural gas act . . . unduly broadens the field of administrative control.[93]

Viewed from the gas-distribution angle, a vexing regulatory gap was closed; state authority over retail sales of interstate gas was now complemented by federal regulation of wholesale transactions of interstate gas. Nonetheless, while one gap may have been closed, another gap was opened. Although profits could be regulated to "normal" levels at the wholesale and retail levels, costs could not; indeed, as pipelines had previously, natural-gas producers occupied an advantageous position to receive premium prices as the unregulated link in a cost-plus industry that was franchised at the retail level. Restrictions on new entry in markets already served by gas pipelines reinforced this proclivity. While unrestricted entry could deter undisciplined practices by existing firms, protected markets all but assured the opposite. This was recognized by Cities Alliance (and coal interests favoring higher natural-gas prices), but it was

---

[92]*OGJ*, June 30, 1938, p. 105. FPC acting chairman Clyde Seavey similarly described the law as "a logical development . . . the next step in governmental regulation . . . merely extending to natural gas companies engaged in interstate commerce somewhat the same supervision that had been exercised over electric and transportation utilities." "Federal Regulation of Natural Gas," *Public Utilities Fortnightly,* October 13, 1938, p. 505.

[93]Alexander Mahood, "The Development of Regulatory Processes," *A.G.A. Proceedings—1938* (New York: American Gas Association, 1938), p. 43.

believed that cost-plus regulation, calculated on a specified return on investment, could neutralize section 7(c).[94]

Interstate gas-pipeline rates were made inflexible and susceptible to *political* rather than *economic* determination under the NGA. This complicated economic calculations by entrepreneurs and investors and spread misinformation throughout the economic system regarding the relative scarcities of competing fuels. Inflexibility was also imparted by limiting entry, requiring extensions, and blocking terminations. General and administrative expenses of firms were increased by reporting requirements and hearing defenses. Full public disclosure of business practices gave companies full knowledge of each other, which reduced the quest for competitive differentiation. The taxpayer, too, would share the burden; the FPC would be significantly enlarged to take on its new responsibilities.

Regulation under the NGA: 1938–84

For over four decades, interstate gas-transmission companies were regulated as public utilities with entry and exit, rates, and extension and abandonment of service controlled by the FPC (1938–77) and the Department of Energy's FERC (1977–84). With the NGA upheld as constitutional in 1942,[95] the FPC worked to define jurisdiction, implement an accounting framework to determine costs and revenue to determine cost of service, devise a valuation (rate-base) formula and a rate of return based on it, and settle various certification issues under the law. Although no legislative overhaul (or threat of the same) occurred with pipeline regulation as had happened with the field-price regulation of natural gas, several amendments were significant.

Jurisdictional Authority

The NGA encompassed interstate "sales for resale" of natural gas. This precluded regulation of gas-distribution companies and pipeline transactions with industrial users, which came under the

---

[94]The NGA addressed cost inflating in section 14(b), subjecting pipeline-company purchases of mineral acreage—that could be used to pad the rate base in the short run and yield large future production to sell at unregulated prices—to reasonableness reviews.

[95]*Federal Power Commission* v. *Natural Gas Pipeline Company of America*, 315 U.S. 575 (1942).

regulatory purview of state and local authorities.[96] Federal jurisdiction extended to interstate gas-transmission companies selling gas to distributors and, controversially, producers selling gas to interstate carriers.[97] The latter became the major area of jurisdictional dispute.

As discussed in chapter 8, the question arose of whether the FPC could regulate the gas-acquisition costs of interstate pipelines, which meant price control at the producer-gatherer-processor "field" level. Two commission decisions in 1940 set a precedent that arm's-length sales from producers to unaffiliated pipeline firms could be automatically passed through, while transactions between affiliated companies, creating situations where effective regulation could be circumvented, were subject to commission review and possible disqualification. This demarcation continued precariously over the next decade, although in several decisions the commission and courts employed language suggesting that the NGA extended to all producers by virtue of *sale* to interstate carriers *for resale*. This prompted legislative action by producers to amend the NGA to confine regulation to affiliated producers only, while exempting independents. A presidential veto in 1950 prevented this from taking place, and in 1954, long-foreshadowed comprehensive field regulation of natural gas came to pass in the Supreme Court's *Phillips* decision. This incited another legislative attempt in 1956 to exclude nonaffiliated producers from FPC regulation, which again met with a presidential veto.[98]

During the jurisdictional dispute, a related controversy was whether the FPC could regulate pipeline decisions intended to circumvent field regulation. It involved the commission's below-market valuation of reserves in the rate base, discussed in the next section, that penalized pipeline firms that internally supplied their gas needs rather than purchased gas from independents. In 1948, Panhandle Eastern Pipeline sold its producing properties to circumvent the discrimination. This was challenged by regulators who

---

[96]In 1947, states were granted authority to regulate sales from interstate pipelines to industrial customers, authority that Congress in 1942 refused to give to the FPC. See this chapter, pp. 883–84.

[97]A regulatory bias on the federal, state, and local levels has been to discourage gas-transmission companies from vertically integrating into residential and commercial retailing.

[98]See chapter 8, pp. 379–83.

feared higher gas-acquisition costs for distributors. Rejecting the agency's contention that it was its own jurisdictional judge, the Supreme Court in 1949 upheld Panhandle's reasoning that "ratemaking is not a precedent for regulation of any part of production and marketing," which was held to be local in nature.[99] If the long arm of the FPC reached the field price of natural gas under certain conditions, other field activities were left to the states to regulate or not.

A second jurisdictional question was whether an intrastate pipeline became subject to federal regulation if a sale or purchase was made with an interstate carrier. On February 14, 1949, the U.S. Court of Appeals ruled that the East Ohio Gas Company, a firm, wholly engaged in intrastate activities, that purchased gas from an interstate line for resale, was not covered by the NGA.[100] This was reversed by the Supreme Court, which held that "continuous flow of gas from other states through East Ohio's high-pressure lines constitutes interstate transportation."[101]

Amendments to the NGA

Section 7(a) of the original act empowered the FPC to compel a firm to "extend or improve its transportation facilities" and connect with distributors if "no undue burden will be placed upon such natural-gas company." Pipeline enlargement could not be required, and neither could forced connections "impair[ing] . . . [the firm's] ability to render adequate service to its customers." Section 7(b) prohibited a firm from abandoning all or part of its service without a "finding" by the FPC that "the present or future public convenience or necessity" would be maintained.

Section 7 Expansion: 1942. Next to the producer jurisdictional question, section 7(c) would prove to be the most crucial and problematical part of the act. Construction of a new line "to a market in which natural gas is already being served," or an ownership transfer of interstate gas-pipeline properties, required a certificate of public convenience and necessity. Activity in unserviced areas was free of federal permission but came under NGA regulation once service

---

[99]*Federal Power Commission* v. *Panhandle Eastern Pipe Line Company,* 337 U.S. 489 (1949).

[100]*East Ohio Gas Co.* v. *Federal Power Commission,* 173 F.2d 429 (1949).

[101]*Federal Power Commission* v. *East Ohio Gas Co. et al.,* 338 U.S. 464 (1949).

commenced. Reflecting the lobbying of Cities Alliance, who recognized the anti-competitive potential of certification, the concluding language of section 7(c) weakened the statute to limit protectionism for vested interstates and rival sources of energy (fuel oil and coal). The 1938 version read:

> In passing on applications for certificates of public convenience and necessity, the Commission shall give due consideration to the applicant's ability to render and maintain adequate service at rates lower than those prevailing in the territory to be served; it being the intention of Congress that natural gas shall be sold in interstate commerce for resale for ultimate public consumption for domestic, commercial, industrial, or any other use at the lowest possible reasonable rate consistent with the maintenance of adequate service in the public interest.[102]

After three years of operation, the gas industry, competing fuel interests, and state and federal regulators were ready to amend section 7(c) in anti-consumer directions. Cities Alliance was no longer a participant.

The gas industry and FPC both complained that tedious certification hearings were occurring for all new projects, not just those in areas that had existing service. This unintended result came from the ambiguity of the statute and the conservatism of creditors toward new projects. The phrase "market in which natural gas is already being served by another natural gas company" left the key terms "market" and "another natural gas company" undefined. Indeed, since the same companies were getting gas from the same general regions, and projects often criss-crossed on the way to markets, the companies sought a ruling from the commission.[103] A pipeline witness specifically mentioned his company's situation of trying to enter the Wisconsin market that two other firms proposed to enter.

---

[102]Public Law 688, 52 Stat. 825 (1938).

[103]William Dougherty, representing the same interstates as before, explained the industry's predicament: "Everyone who wants to build a line apparently feels that to be sure about these things they have either got to come into the Commission and either get a definition of jurisdiction or a certificate. . . . [Gas production] all originates either in Texas, Louisiana, or Oklahoma, and you radiate from that area, and every new pipe line is bound to cross the path of some existing pipe line." *Natural Gas Act Amendments,* Hearings before the House Committee on Interstate and Foreign Commerce, 77th Cong., 1st sess. (Washington, D.C.: Government Printing Office, 1941), p. 35.

Each of the three sought regulatory permission, so the Wisconsin Public Service Commission called a comparative hearing after the FPC declined.[104] State jurisdiction over interstate projects was not what the interstate pipeline industry desired. While the interstate industry pragmatically supported reform so long as several provisions were enacted (see below), the real winners from an expansion of certification regulation were the FPC and the alternate-fuel industries. The FPC welcomed an expansion of its charter to plug the regulatory gap by giving itself "an opportunity to scrutinize the financial set-up, the adequacy of the gas reserves, the feasibility of the proposed services, and the characteristics of the rate structure at a time when such vital matters can be revised and modified as the public interest demands."[105] Fuel-oil and coal interests, prominently including the railroad industry, sought expanded certification to achieve "the right to full participation" in commission hearings.[106] While the anti-gas lobby was already active before the FPC,[107] they now had full authority to intervene in hearings and block—or at least delay—gas-industry competition.

Effective February 7, 1942, section 7(c) certificates were required for all construction or extension of pipeline facilities in interstate commerce.[108] Two provisions were added at the request of the gas industry. The commission could authorize a temporary certificate "in cases of emergency, to assure maintenance of adequate service" without notice to intervening parties and a hearing. Second, existing lines built without a certificate were exempted from getting one. The authority for pipelines to use their original certificate to expand their facilities to meet increased demand in their service territories was retained and placed in section 7(f).

A new subsection, section 7(g), weakened the consumerist language of section 7(c) quoted above. It read,

> Nothing contained in this section shall be construed as a limitation upon the power of the Commission to grant certificates of public

---

[104]Ibid., p. 59.

[105]Ibid., p. 6.

[106]Ibid., p. 51.

[107]"[The commissioners] have been very patient with us and probably strained themselves a little bit to let us in." Testimony of John Battle, executive secretary of the National Coal Association. Ibid., p. 51.

[108]Public Law 444, 56 Stat. 83 at 84 (1942).

convenience and necessity for service of an area already being served by another natural-gas company.[109]

Section 7 was enlarged with two other subsections. Section 7(d) described the procedure for applying for certification, while section 7(e) gave the FPC authority to attach reasonable terms and conditions to the certificate as the "public convenience and necessity" may require.

The revised NGA was still "pluralist" to the extent that exclusive franchise rights were not given to the first entrant. But the competitive distortion of the original act was exacerbated by the extension of certification requirements. More red tape joined natural economic considerations between the entrepreneurial idea and reality of entry or expansion. Antagonistic parties—coal, fuel oil, and entrenched pipeline interests—were given a noneconomic means to forestall new gas service to industrial, commercial, and residential markets.

Rights of Eminent Domain: 1947. While rights of eminent domain were raised as an issue in the 1941 House hearings to amend the NGA,[110] they became a more urgent issue after the war. In House and Senate hearings in 1947, a variety of complaints and reasons for enacting a federal condemnation law for interstate lines was aired. Natural Gas Pipe Line was having trouble completing an FPC-authorized expansion to the growing Chicago market because of selected landowner holdouts.[111] Texas Eastern was seeking to assume the wartime condemnation rulings as part of its purchase of the Big Inch and Little Inch pipelines from the federal government. Texas Eastern also desired prospective eminent-domain rights to construct

---

[109]Ibid.

[110]See the testimony of J. J. Hedrick, representing Natural Gas Pipeline Company of America, who complained of railroad obstructionism against pipeline right-of-way "for the past 2 years." *Natural Gas Act Amendments*, p. 54.

[111]The reasons for landowner holdouts often were not petty. Stated one interstate representative: "The difficulties of this company are somewhat intensified by the fact that it is required to build its line through the relatively thickly settled and valuable Chicago suburban area, where every farmer envisions his tract as the site of a future subdivision and resents anything which will tend to minimize this possibility." *Amendments to the Natural Gas Act,* Hearings before the House Committee on Interstate and Foreign Commerce, 80th Cong., 1st sess. (Washington, D.C.: Government Printing Office, 1947), p. 557. For Senate testimony, see *Amendments to the Natural Gas Act,* Hearings before the Senate Committee on Interstate and Foreign Commerce, 80th Cong., 1st sess. (Washington, D.C.: Government Printing Office, 1947).

laterals to begin gas service off the former oil lines. Congress was sympathetic to the argument that higher right-of-way costs from holdout property owners were passed through to consumers. Interstate-pipeline interests complained that state condemnation rights often did not extend to interstate lines that went through the state but did not sell gas there. Other state eminent-domain laws did not apply to out-of-state corporations.

With the only opposition being from the alternate-fuel and manufactured-gas interests, section 7(h) was added to the NGA on July 25, 1947, to give federally certified pipelines eminent-domain rights for pipeline and adjacent-facility right-of-way.[112] While a victory for the interstate industry, especially prospective lines, condemnation would lower costs and thus reduce the rate base on which margins applied. Yet states such as Arkansas, Wisconsin, and Nebraska did not allow condemnation in their areas despite the rights conferred by federal certification.[113]

Not included with eminent domain was the obligation of common carriage, which potentially could have raised havoc for interstate pipelines externally financed on the strength of long-term contracts with producers and end-users. Section 28 of the Federal Lands Leasing Act of 1920, however, stated that right-of-way grants by the Department of the Interior had to be "under the express condition that such pipelines shall be constructed, operated and maintained as common carriers."[114] The U.S. Circuit Court of Appeals upheld this requirement for natural-gas pipelines in 1948.[115] In 1953, section 28 was amended to remove the common-carriage requirement where other municipal, state, or federal regulation was present.[116]

Legislative attempts in the 1950s to extend eminent domain to storage projects to join pipelines and compressor equipment failed.[117]

---

[112]Public Law 245, 61 Stat. 459 (1947).

[113]See William Mogel and John Gregg, "Appropriateness of Imposing Common Carrier Status on Interstate Natural Gas Pipelines," *Energy Law Journal*, no. 2 (1983): 172–73.

[114]Public Law 66-146, 41 Stat. 449 (1920).

[115]*Montana-Dakota Utilities Co.* v. *Federal Power Commission*, 169 F.2d 392 (8th Cir. 1948), cert. den. 315 U.S. 95 (1948).

[116]Public Law 83-253, 67 Stat. 557 (1953).

[117]Robert McGinnis, "Some Legal Problems in Underground Gas Storage," *17 Oil & Gas Institute* (New York: Matthew Bender, 1966), p. 70.

In 1974, however, it was ruled in federal district court that certificated firms could invoke eminent domain to acquire underground facilities to store natural gas as well.[118]

Hinshaw Exemption: 1954. The next major change to the NGA occurred when section 1(c) was added to exempt local distribution companies (LDCs) from federal regulation. The problem of "dual regulation" occurred when an LDC either built a "stub line" from the city gate to connect with an interstate or purchased gas for resale to another LDC or municipality. Both practices placed LDCs as natural-gas companies under the NGA, which resulted in costly federal filings in addition to state filings. Beginning in 1947, state public-utility commissions began lobbying Congress to exempt LDCs from federal oversight. When a 1950 Supreme Court decision[119] required federal jurisdiction over LDCs connected in interstate commerce or performing sales for resale, the FPC and National Association of Railroad and Utilities Commissioners went to work to amend section 1 of the Federal Power Act. In House hearings in 1953, various states documented the millions of dollars of costs, passed through to consumers, associated with federal filings.[120] "Of perhaps more importance," added one state commissioner, "are the delays incident to securing necessary approvals of the Federal Power Commission on matters such as extensions of gas facilities, changes or revisions in rates, in financing requirements of the utilities."[121]

The only opposition to the exemption came from some congressmen who felt that a move away from federal regulation was a bad precedent.[122] But with the cost and time advantages of removing dual regulation, H.R. 5976 was passed by Congress and signed into law by President Eisenhower on March 27, 1954.[123] Named after its

---

[118]*Natural Gas Pipeline Co. of America* v. *Iowa State Commerce Commission,* 369 F. Supp. 156 (D.C., S.D. Iowa, 1974).

[119]*Federal Power Commission* v. *East Ohio Gas Company,* 338 U.S. 464 (1950).

[120]*Natural Gas Act (Distribution),* Hearing before a Subcommittee of the House Committee on Interstate and Foreign Commerce, 83rd Cong., 1st sess. (Washington, D.C.: Government Printing Office, 1953), pp. 29, 34–35, 43, 47, 58.

[121]Ibid., p. 29.

[122]See, for example, *Congressional Record,* July 30, 1953, pp. 10563–65.

[123]Public Law 323, 69 Stat. 36 (1954). FPC Order 173, "Application for Exemptions from Provisions of the Natural Gas Act Pursuant to Section 1(c) Thereof," moderately reduced the backlog of cases that had worsened with the advent of producer price regulation.

House sponsor Carl Hinshaw (D-Calif.), the Hinshaw amendment was the bone given to gas producers in the wake of legislative and judicial setbacks to attempts to exempt field activities from federal regulation.

Industrial Sales-for-Resale Regulation: 1962. Since 1938, section 4 of the NGA had exempted sales for resale to industrial users from the Natural Gas Act. Only sales for resale in interstate commerce to residential and commercial users were subject to review, suspension, and refund by the commission. As industrial sales for resale became more important, sentiment surfaced to expand NGA regulation for the first time since 1942. The FPC began to lobby for comprehensive sale-for-resale regulation in 1951.[124] In congressional hearings in 1961 and 1962, the Midwest Industrial and Commercial Gas Users Association lobbied for its pro rata share of rate refunds from Cities Service Gas Company (estimated at $2 million between 1954 and 1961 alone).[125] The National Coal Association advocated closing "a serious gap" in regulation to make sure industrial rates represented a "fair share of the costs of pipeline operations" to "eliminate the incentive which now exists to divert gas to inferior uses."[126] In contrast, the American Gas Association opposed the amendment with the statement that "industrial rates are competitive."[127] Columbia Gas Systems found such industrial regulation "not objectionable" since it was a small part of their operations.[128] In fact, no interstate company, not even Cities Service with the most at stake, took a negative position.[129]

---

[124]Federal Power Commission, *Thirty-first Annual Report* (Washington, D.C.: Government Printing Office, 1951), p. 144.

[125]*Natural Gas for Resale for Industrial Use,* Hearing before a Subcommittee of the House Committee on Interstate and Foreign Commerce, 87th Cong., 2d sess. (Washington, D.C.: Government Printing Office, 1962), pp. 10–12.

[126]Ibid., p. 24.

[127]*Amendments to the Natural Gas Act,* Hearings before the Senate Committee on Commerce, 87th Cong., 1st sess. (Washington, D.C.: Government Printing Office, 1962), p. 171. The American Petroleum Institute and other oil interests took no position. Ibid., p. 135.

[128]Ibid., p. 186.

[129]Of the 100 interstate firms subject to NGA regulation, only 10 separated out their industrial sales to escape commission control. And of these ten, some firms voluntarily gave refunds to industrial customers along with residential and commercial users. Ibid., pp. 4–6, 9.

On May 21, 1962, the FPC received its desired authority to regulate interstate sales for resale to industrial users.[130] This increased the range of intervenors and stakes for all parties to discourage, delay, modify, or prevent a rate change. This left direct sales to industrial users as the only "gap" in interstate regulation. The FPC favored this expansion of authority, too, but the necessary constituency was not there to enact it.

Public-Utility Regulation

Revenue Pool. The pool of revenue a firm is allowed under public-utility regulation is the sum of its cost of service and capital return. Costs deemed by authorities to have been prudently incurred are passed through to consumers, and firms are allowed a rate of return on valued capital or the rate base. Within a broad legislative mandate for just, reasonable, and nonpreferential rates, the methodology of calculating the revenue pool has evolved from administrative practices and judicial instruction since the last century.

A fact of business life is that costs must be passed through (recovered) to have an ongoing concern. In public-utility regulation, costs deemed reasonable and necessary for the proper conduct of business are eligible for recoupment. "Unreasonable" outlays cannot be passed through in rates and instead represent a charge to utility investors.

Of the areas of allowable cost, tax expense is relatively straightforward—the sum of properly calculated local, state, and federal taxes. Common categories are income taxes, property taxes, gross receipt taxes, sales or use taxes, license or franchise taxes, public-utility taxes, and, where paid by the first purchaser, severance and production taxes. The dollar-for-dollar pass-through is interrupted only by rate change delays.[131] Depreciation, calculated pursuant to a standard formula in the Uniform System of Accounts, is also a standard pass-through.[132] Calling for greater judgment on the part of regulators

---

[130]Public Law 87-454, 76 Stat. 72 (1962).

[131]John Holtzinger and Helen Paeffgen, "Taxes Other Than Income Taxes," in American Gas Association, *Regulation of the Gas Industry*, 3 vols. (New York: Matthew Bender, 1981), vol. 2, chap. 27. The Louisiana First-Use Tax of $0.07 per thousand cubic feet, which was passed through by pipelines from 1978 to 1981, was declared unconstitutional and refunded to utility customers.

[132]For a discussion of allowed depreciation rates and historical controversies, see N. Knowles Davis, "Depreciation, Depletion, and Amortization," in American Gas Association, *Regulation of the Gas Industry*, vol. 2, p. 28.

are determinations of reasonable operating expenses.[133] The greatest expense for gas pipelines, gas-acquisition costs, must be the result of arm's-length transactions to be passed through as a cost of service. Under wellhead price controls, the regulated price would be the pass-through allowable.

When price escalations became routine in the 1970s, a purchased-gas adjustment provision was adopted to facilitate rate increases without laborious rate filings.[134] Later in the decade, purchased-gas-adjustment rate alternations were limited to two per year. In the early 1980s, with the take-or-pay predicament encouraging higher priced gas to be acquired instead of lower cost gas, the FERC introduced a "fraud and abuse" standard to discourage purchases at "excessive" prices.[135]

Other operating and maintenance expenses such as executive salaries, wages, pension contributions, rental expenses, transportation costs, and plant maintenance expenses are accepted at face value unless they are flagrantly high. Explained the Supreme Court,

> The Commission is not the financial manager of the corporation and it is not empowered to substitute its judgement for that of the directors of the corporation; nor can it ignore items charged by the utility as operating expenses [if] there is an abuse of discretion . . . by the corporate officers.[136]

Subject to scrutiny as potentially "unreasonable" are charitable donations, advertising expenses, and research, development, and demonstration costs.[137]

A firm's cost of service is taken for a test period, generally the most recent twelve months when the information is available, with

---

[133]This discussion is taken from John Stough and Helen Paeffgen, "Allowable Operating Expenses," in American Gas Association, *Regulation of the Gas Industry*, vol. 2, chap. 26.

[134]Order 452, 47 FPC 1049 (1972); Order 452-A, 47 FPC 1510 (1972); and Order 13, 43 *Fed. Reg.* 50167 (October 18, 1978).

[135]Sec. 601(c)(2), Public Law 92, Stat. 3; and 47 *Fed. Reg.* 6253 (February 11, 1982).

[136]*Southwestern Bell Telephone Co.* v. *PSC of Missouri*, 262 U.S. 276 at 289 (1923).

[137]While informational and conservation advertisements have continued to be allowed, promotional and goodwill messages became victims of the 1970s gas shortage. Research, development, and demonstration costs have included controversial "quick-fix" projects undertaken to increase gas supply. See this chapter, pp. 930–31, and chapter 10, pp. 580–83.

reasonably estimated changes when the final rate determination will apply. Cost regulation applies to jurisdictional costs only; revenues and expenses associated with nonregulated activities are separated before jurisdictional cost pass-throughs are calculated.

The company valuation or the *rate base* is an estimate of the company's worth to which a rate of return is applied to arrive at the total profit a firm is allowed over cost. Because economic value is subjective and not objective, this determination is not as simple as it might appear. As economist Alfred Kahn has noted, "Its determination has been by far the most hotly contested aspect of regulation, consuming by far the greatest amount of time of both commissions and courts."[138]

When federal regulation began in the 1930s, the FPC inherited the fair-value doctrine first established by the Supreme Court in 1898 for state regulatory commissions. In denying the exclusive use of original cost, desired by investors and regulated firms to increase valuation in a period of deflation, Justice John Harlan defined "fair value" as

> the original cost of construction, the amount expended in permanent improvements, the amount and market value of its bonds and stock, [and] the present as compared with the original cost of construction. . . . What the company is entitled to ask is a fair return upon the value of that which it employs for the public convenience.[139]

Thus, a middle figure between original cost and reproduction cost was made a constitutional requirement to avoid "the taking of private property for public use without just compensation or without due process of law."[140]

Unlike regulation of interstate oil pipelines, which from 1934 to the 1970s applied fair-value valuation under Interstate Commerce Commission regulation, FPC regulation of gas pipelines tended toward a more stringent valuation methodology. Under the NGA, the commission was given authority to "investigate and ascertain

---

[138]Alfred Kahn, *The Economics of Regulation: Principles and Institutions*, 2 vols. (New York: John Wiley & Sons, 1970), vol. 1, p. 36.

[139]*Smyth* v. *Ames*, 169 U.S. 466 at 547 (1898).

[140]Ibid., p. 523.

the actual legitimate cost of property of every natural-gas company."[141] The subjective word "legitimate" was interpreted by the
FPC to mean the *original cost* of gas reserves owned by interstate
transmission companies beginning in the early 1940s. This radically
understated the value of producing gas properties, and in 1942, the
Natural Gas Company of America brought suit against the FPC
to substitute fair value for original cost for determining just and
reasonable prices. Rejecting the challenge, Justice Stone opined for
the Supreme Court:

> The Constitution does not bind rate-making bodies to the service of
> any single formula or combination of formulas. Agencies to whom
> this legislative power has been delegated are free, within the ambit
> of their statutory authority, to make pragmatic adjustments which
> may be called for by particular circumstances. Once a fair hearing has
> been given, prior findings made and other statutory requirements
> satisfied, the courts cannot intervene in the absence of a clear show-
> ing that the limits of due process have been overstepped. If the
> Commission's order, as applied to the facts before it and viewed in
> its entirety, produces no arbitrary result, our inquiry is at an end.[142]

This decision opened the door for the "prudent investment" or
"actual legitimate cost" methodology, which valued the firm at
actual gross monetary outlays less depreciation (depletion) plus
working capital. A further burial of fair value was given two years
later in the *Hope* decision by Justice Douglas, who espoused an "end
result" or "capital attraction" criterion of just and reasonable rates
to balance consumer and investor needs.

> From the investor or company point of view it is important that
> there be enough revenue not only for operating expenses but also
> for the capital costs of the business. These include service on the
> debt and dividends of the stock. By that standard the return to the
> equity owner should be commensurate with returns on investments

---

[141]Public Law 52, Stat 824 (1938).

[142]315 U.S. 575. In a concurring opinion, Justices Black, Douglas, and Murphy plainly
recognized the importance of the majority decision: "While the opinion of the court
erases much which has been written in rate cases during the last half century, we
think it is an appropriate occasion to lay to rest the ghost of *Smyth* v. *Ames*, 169 U.S.
466, which has haunted utility regulation since 1898" (p. 602). The repudiation of
fair value was reaffirmed in the 1944 *Hope* case and by the FPC in the 1960 *Panhandle*
case (23 FPC 352).

in other enterprises having corresponding risks. That return, moreover, should be sufficient to assure confidence in the financial integrity of the enterprise, so as to maintain its credit and to attract capital.[143]

In two insightful dissents, Justices Frankfurter and Jackson decried the strict valuation of the Court. Frankfurter argued that the method of calculation should be open to judicial review case by case and that the "total public interest," embracing future consumers as well as current consumers, was not served by the majority's guidelines.[144] Justice Jackson took original cost to task by emphasizing how gas properties were different from a pipeline's physical facilities given that the high-risk characteristics of exploration made discovery cost well below market value.[145]

It would not be until the highly inflationary 1970s that depreciated original cost would come under judicial review. The interventionist bias of federal regulators and the courts, combined with industry growth that seemingly vindicated stringent valuation, explained the longevity and survival of the original-cost methodology. Another reason for its survival was the ability of firms to replenish the rate base with new investments as traditional investments "vanished" from depreciation. Many of these "replenishment" projects were not prudent on a stand-alone basis and, in retrospect, were fiscal blunders.[146] Inflation, in any case, would be accounted for in the rate of return.

The original-cost versus replacement-cost controversy was resurrected in the 1970s with oil pipelines. As seen in the last chapter, the FERC was instructed by the judiciary to value oil pipelines toward original cost instead of a combination of original and reproduction cost—another repudiation of "fair value."[147]

---

[143]*Federal Power Commission et al.* v. *Hope Natural Gas Co.*, 320 U.S. 591 at 603 (1944). Justice Douglas three decades later would similarly argue that just and reasonable rates required that "the financial health of the pipeline in our economic system remains strong." *Federal Power Commission* v. *Memphis Light, Gas, & Water Division*, 411 U.S. 458 at 474 (1973).

[144]320 U.S. 624–28.

[145]Ibid.

[146]See this chapter, pp. 929–31.

[147]See chapter 14, pp. 828–29.

Under either original cost or fair value, a "fair" rate of return is applied to derive profit. This return, summed with the firm's cost of service, is apportioned over the anticipated throughput of the pipeline to calculate individual pipeline tariffs. The rationale and guiding principle of determining the rate of return were stated by the Supreme Court in 1923.

> A public utility is entitled to such rates as will permit it to earn a return on the value of the property which it employs for the convenience of the public equal to that generally being made at the same time and in the same general part of the country on investments in other business undertakings which are attended by corresponding risks and uncertainties; but it has no constitutional right to profits such as are realized or anticipated in highly profitable enterprises or speculative ventures.[148]

Continuing in the language that Justice Douglas would rediscover two decades later in his "end result" doctrine.

> The return should be reasonably sufficient to assure confidence in the financial soundness of the utility and should be adequate, under efficient and economical management, to maintain and support its credit and enable it to raise the money necessary for the proper discharge of its public duties.[149]

In the first decade of federal regulation, allowed returns ranged from 6 to 6.5 percent.[150] Challenges to the yardstick seeking higher returns in 1944 (*Hope*) and 1945 (*Colorado Interstate*) were rebuffed by the Supreme Court.[151]

In 1952, a new methodology temporarily eclipsed the percentage-return approach. In the *Northern Natural Gas Company* case, the FPC unveiled the "cost-of-money" approach, which computed a 5.5 percent return. This was the first time under the NGA that a firm was allowed under 6 percent.[152] A manifestation of the end-result doctrine, the cost-of-money approach weighted the average of the

---

[148]*Bluefield Water Works and Improvement Co.* v. *Public Service Commission*, 262 U.S. 679 at 692–93 (1923).

[149]Ibid., p. 693.

[150]*Public Utilities Fortnightly*, November 20, 1952, p. 795.

[151]Kenneth Marcus, *The National Government and the Natural Gas Industry*, pp. 168, 173.

[152]Opinion 228, 11 FPC 123 (1952).

firm's contractual debt (bank loans and bonds) and equity.[153] A year later, a slightly liberalized cost-of-money formula resulted in a 6.25 percent return for the United Fuel Gas Company.[154] The new procedure tightened the regulatory clamp by lowering returns in some cases, increasing hearing costs for the firm, and prolonging the "locked-in" period for disputed rates. By January 1954, a backlog of forty-nine cases with $143 million in dispute resulted from the new return methodology.[155]

The cost-of-money approach became standard in the 1950s and provided a steady 6 percent return corresponding to steady borrowing costs and dividend rates.[156] The standard return, however, did not affect firms equally. Companies with high debt-to-equity capitalizations realized higher common-equity returns than low debt-to-equity companies because of favorable tax implications for the former.[157] This bias was exacerbated in the early 1960s when the FPC gave debt-intensive firms a return premium to compensate for the greater risk of having more fixed costs to cover.[158]

In the 1960s, despite escalating inflation, returns remained at 6 to 6.5 percent on net investment, a 10 to 12 percent equity return.[159] As late as 1968, the commission stubbornly refused to consider inflation

[153]A hypothetical example of computing a 5.6 percent cost-of-money allowance is

Type	Amount	% of Total	Rate	Weighted Cost
Bank debt	$1,000,000	0.20	8%	1.6%
Bond	2,000,000	0.40	6	2.4
Equity	2,000,000	0.40	4	1.6
		1.00%		5.6%

[154]In the Matter of the United Fuel Gas Company, FPC Docket G-1781 and G-2055, Opinion 258 (August 7, 1953); affirmed on rehearing, Opinion 258A (November 19, 1953).

[155]*Public Utilities Fortnightly,* January 21, 1954, p. 107. Field regulation of natural gas would add to the backlog problem.

[156]Walter Gallagher, "Rate of Return," in American Gas Association, *Regulation of the Gas Industry,* vol. 2, p. 30-55.

[157]Debt costs, unlike dividend payments, are expensed from gross income. By lowering taxable income, debt reduces the net cost of capital, which increases profit as a percentage of capital.

[158]In 1956, the FPC first tied the rate of return to a firm's capitalization. In 1962, a higher return was allowed for debt-intensive El Paso Natural Gas (Opinion 366) and in 1968 for similarly leveraged Panhandle Eastern (Opinion 543). Walter Gallagher, "Rate of Return," pp. 30-55 to 30-56.

[159]Ibid., p. 30-89.

in the return calculation. In one ruling, an inflation allowance was equated to fair-value ratemaking and rejected.[160] A second case the same year left the return calculations intact on grounds that "an assumption that an inflationary spiral will continue . . . would be pure speculation."[161] By the early 1970s, however, the FPC recognized inflation as a "present fact of life. . . . Its effects on cost must be acknowledged."[162] Similar judgments followed, and in a 1976 opinion, strong language was used to declare a break from the past to account for inflation: "The pendulum has definitely swung in a direction substantially contrary to the interests of the investor. A time of adjustment is clearly called for."[163] Higher rates of return, however, would not be automatic; the firm had to demonstrate why the adjustment was necessary for the public interest to be served.[164]

Record high rates of return were granted by the FERC in the inflationary 1975–80 years.[165] Future inflation allowances to prevent capital exhaustion seemed likely, but trends can change, not only politically (administratively) but with the inflation rate.

The allowed return is not a maximum rate or a guaranteed rate of profit. To some extent, profit is assured by entry restrictions (certification) and distribution franchises that make demand less sensitive to price. But actual returns can be below the maximum allowed. In such cases, unused returns cannot be carried forward to obtain a premium return in a future period; similarly, an above-maximum return from hidden rate-case opportunities cannot be balanced by a submaximum return in a future year.

Rate Structure. Prior to the Natural Gas Act, interstate pipeline firms entered into tailored agreements with local distributors and large industrial customers.[166] With an eye to overall profitability, pricing was determined according to demand sensitivity, with some customers valued for their contribution to fixed costs and other

---

[160]Opinion 543-A, 40 FPC 452 (1968).

[161]Opinion 543, 40 FPC 98 at 110 (1968).

[162]Opinion 659, 49 FPC 1154 at 1182 (1973).

[163]Opinion 769, 56 FPC 120 at 139 (1976).

[164]See, for example, 10 FERC 61041 (1980).

[165]See the return figures provided in Walter Gallagher, "Rate of Return," pp. 30-90 to 30-91.

[166]This discussion is taken in part from Paul Garfield and Wallace Lovejoy, *Public Utility Economics* (Englewood Cliffs, N.J.: Prentice-Hall, 1964), p. 178.

customers serving as profit makers because their rates covered fixed costs and more. (All purchasers paid rates above variable costs.) With the enactment of the NGA in 1938, rates were consolidated to conform to the just, reasonable, and nondiscriminatory provisions of the act. In 1940, the FPC released instructions to convert the myriad of contracts to systemwide tariffs. This was interrupted by wartime, and in 1948 the commission published a Tariff-and-Service Agreement form with which all firms were in compliance by 1950.[167] The agreements spelled out all service terms and conditions but left price as a variable. Without the flexibility to make long-term, fixed-price contracts, firms set short-term rates that could be changed with a new cost-of-service filing or commission decision.

Within the confines of nondiscriminatory pricing, assignment of variable cost was not difficult. Each customer would pay according to his physical consumption of gas. Fixed cost, however, which constituted between 80 and 90 percent of pipeline cost at the time, was judgmental. The choices were to assign fixed cost proportionally with variable cost or to skew fixed costs toward peak-demand users. The rationale of the latter approach was that idle capacity of natural-gas pipelines during off-peak periods (the summer in most markets) was the cost of providing peak, uninterrupted service to these customers, and they should pay for associated fixed costs. Prior to regulatory instruction, the practice developed of allocating fixed cost toward customers with the highest peak demand and charging proportionately less to customers whose demand alone would have required less pipeline capacity and less fixed cost.

In 1952, an FPC formula allocated 50 percent of the demand charge to the *demand* (firm service) component of sales and 50 percent to the *commodity* (volume) component of sales.[168] Compared to the prior approach, interruptible (nonpeak) customers paid more and noninterruptible (peak) customers paid less. The most detrimental consequence was to send nonpeak customers toward coal and fuel oil. This forced the commission to make pragmatic adjustments toward the pre-1952 formula to avoid load loss in some cases.[169] Thus, it

[167] Order 144, 13 *Fed. Reg.* 6371 (October 30, 1948).

[168] Atlantic Seaboard Corp., 11 FPC 43 (1952).

[169] Alfred Kahn, *The Economics of Regulation,* vol. 1, p. 99. For specific cases of demand component "tilting," see Francis Quinn and Cheryl Foley, "Pipeline Rates," in American Gas Association, *Regulation of the Gas Industry,* vol. 2, pp. 35-15 to 35-16.

was not surprising that "coal interests are the staunchest supporters of the *Atlantic Seaboard* formula."[170]

For over two decades the *Atlantic Seaboard* formula held sway, with certain exceptions. In 1973, a new formula received FPC sanction that tilted 75 percent of fixed cost to the commodity side.[171] The *United* formula was biased in favor of residential and commercial (peak) users at the expense of major industrial (nonpeak) users. The commission rationalized that average pipeline utilization would increase from this rate design.[172]

The political roots of the 75/25 percent apportionment were evident in Title II of the Natural Gas Policy Act of 1978, which instructed higher gas prices to be funneled toward industrial users to shield smaller users from higher fuel costs.[173] The unintended consequence, as before, was interfuel substitution away from gas, leaving captive customers with more fixed costs to shoulder. Exceptions to the *United* formula were made to place fixed cost on the demand component, such as the *Northern Border Pipeline* decision.[174]

With gas oversupply and load problems on interstate pipelines, flexible rate designs based on market-clearing considerations began to be introduced in 1983 and 1984.[175] In addition, Phase II of incremental pricing, intended to extend requirements from large industrial facilities to all industrial customers, was postponed and finally revoked by the FERC in March 1984.[176]

Geographical pricing relative to the pipeline supply source also came under FPC modification. An early commission dictum was, "In the absence of compelling reasons to the contrary, it is good and desirable practice to fix rates that are uniform."[177] The question arose

---

[170]Paul Garfield and Wallace Lovejoy, *Public Utility Economics*, p. 184.

[171]United Gas Pipe Line Co., Opinion 671, 50 FPC 1348 (1973), aff'd.; *Consolidated Gas Supply Corp.* v. *FPC*, 520 F.2d 1176 (D.C. Cir. 1975).

[172]Francis Quinn and Cheryl Foley, "Pipeline Rates," p. 35-10.

[173]Public Law 95-621, 92 Stat. 3371.

[174]11 FERC 61136 (1980).

[175]See J. Richard Tiano and Richard Bonnifield, "The Impact on Gas Distribution Companies of Federally Approved Special Marketing Programs," *Energy Law Journal*, no. 2 (1984): 293–95.

[176]49 *Fed. Reg.* 12207 (March 29, 1984).

[177]In the matter of *City of Cleveland* v. *Hope Natural Gas Co.*, 3 FPC 150 at 190 (1942).

whether equity implied uniform "postage-stamp" rates for customers or whether equality meant tiered prices progressively rising for distant customers. A 1955 decision by the FPC replaced uniform pricing with a three-zone system for the 600-mile Northern Natural pipeline.[178] Customers nearer the supply source argued that they subsidized distant customers; Northern argued that load requirements of distant markets subsidized nearer customers by permitting scale economies associated with a larger diameter pipeline. The zoning order also introduced thousand cubic feet-mile pricing into the *Atlantic Seaboard* formula. Other decisions went against zone pricing or mandated virtually identical prices geographically.[179]

Certification Issues. Upon the passage of the NGA, the FPC issued the Provisional Rules of Practice and Regulations under the Natural Gas Act, which became effective July 11, 1938. But it took a commission interpretation on October 24, 1939, in the *Kansas Pipeline* case, recognized by Carl Wheat as "a milestone in the development of Federal Power Commission administration under the statute," to delineate certification powers under section 7(c).[180] The FPC decided that its certification powers (1) could only be established on a factual case-by-case basis, (2) would cover "an area or territory of undefined extent bearing some reasonable relation to existing pipelines" (versus strips of land representing present occupation), and (3) did not encompass end-use considerations.[181]

The decision also provided guidelines specifying conditions for entry certification. The firm had to demonstrate

1. adequate financial resources to complete the project and become operational;
2. adequate demand for its service;
3. adequate supply to meet demand;
4. "full and complete" service; and

---

[178]Northern Natural Gas Co., 9 PUR 3d 8 (1955). See the discussion in Paul Garfield and Walter Lovejoy, *Public Utility Economics*, pp. 186–87.

[179]See, for example, Michigan Wisconsin Pipe Line Co., Opinion 471, 34 FPC 621 (1965).

[180]Carl Wheat, "Administration by the Federal Power Commission of the Certificate Provisions of the Natural Gas Act," *George Washington Law Review* (December 1945): 197.

[181]Kansas Pipe Line and Gas Co. et al., 2 FPC 29 (1939).

5. "adequate and reasonable" costs and rates.[182]

Reflecting the competitive language in the act, the commission concluded,

> Where there is not existing natural-gas service the convenience and necessity of the public . . . will be served by the introduction of that service provided that those who seek to render that service can meet certain minimum standards designed to secure such service on a continuous and adequate basis.[183]

These conditions applied to all firms entering the market, whether in occupied areas or not, which would bring complications. From 1940 to 1946, such matters were moot because of wartime steel shortages that postponed projects. With the resumption of entry in 1947 and universal certification, a trend began that has continued to this day—increasing complexity to satisfy entrance requirements. Noticed Cheatham:

> Since World War II numerous changes have been made to certification regulations . . . and generally these changes have required more data and details. As a result, a certificate application, with the necessary exhibits appended thereto, can now run into multiple volumes and thousands of pages.[184]

Interfirm competition was intended by the NGA despite the fact that proposals by interstates to enter occupied areas required hearings with the burden of proof on the potential entrant. In 1939, the FPC "began to give form to Congress' directive"[185] for nonexclusive territory by licensing the Louisiana-Nevada Transit Company to build a pipeline in the defined "market area" of the Arkansas-Louisiana Gas Company because of proposed lower rates.[186] A second

---

[182]See John Cheatham, "Regulation in the Post–World War II Period," in American Gas Association, *Regulation of the Gas Industry*, vol. 1, pp. 4-13 to 4-16.

[183]2 FPC 29 at 56 (1939).

[184]John Cheatham, "Regulation in the Post–World War II Period," p. 4-16. Regulations pertaining to section 7 of the NGA run over fifty pages, requiring (sec. 157.5) "all information necessary to advise the Commission fully concerning the operation, sales, service, construction, extension, or acquisition for which a certification is requested or the abandonment for which permission and approval is regulated." See American Gas Association, *Regulation of the Gas Industry*, vol. 4, p. 140-91.

[185]Walter Gallagher, "Rate of Return," p. 30-22.

[186]2 FPC 546 (1939).

decision two years later reaffirmed direct competition when Gas Transport, Incorporated, was certified to purchase and operate an unfinished gas-pipeline project in a market served by Hope Natural Gas for rate competition.[187] Amendments to the NGA in 1942 retained the commission's authority to deny exclusive territorial rights to a firm (which was soon exercised)[188] but extended the certification requirement to all entrants with a grandfather clause for established firms. The question of whether this clause would block entry in an occupied market was partly decided in March 1947 when the FPC awarded a certificate to the Michigan-Wisconsin Pipe Line Company to construct a line to Detroit, which hitherto had been exclusively served by Panhandle Eastern.[189] Detroit's demand for gas, however, did not present an "either-or" situation for the two firms; Michigan-Wisconsin was certified to serve the "growth load" above the capacity of Panhandle's line. Nonetheless, an important limitation was placed on grandfather rights. In the commission's words:

> It seems clear that any privileges conferred by a grandfather certificate issued under the Natural Gas Act should not, as a matter of law, be extended beyond "substantial parity" with the operation, service, transportation, or sale actually performed on February 7, 1942. It follows that any additional operation . . . not clearly covered by an existing grandfather certificate must be approved by a non-grandfather certificate.[190]

To the disappointment of established interstate pipelines, the protection envisioned from the 1942 amendments was confined to existing market share.

In the 1960s, entry applications for solely occupied areas significantly increased, which led to several opinions that better defined the FPC's view of head-to-head rivalry. Of $1.4 billion in proposals as of June 30, 1965, $1.1 billion was for occupied areas with the

---

[187]2 FPC 1079 (1941).

[188]Hope Natural Gas, 4 FPC 59 (1944). The argument of intervening coal and railroad interests—that a second pipeline represented an inferior use of gas—was rejected.

[189]Michigan-Wisconsin Pipeline Co., 6 FPC 1 (1947).

[190]Dissenting from this view in favor of quasi-franchise rights for established firms were the supposed consumer advocates, Commissioners Olds and Draper. *OGJ*, March 22, 1947, p. 132.

balance for virgin territory.[191] In keeping with its 1947 decision and the competitive language of the act, a series of FPC decisions in 1967 showed a clear preference for multifirm competition and low prices over certification protection. Stated the commission, "A monopoly . . . should not be automatically and consistently protected where it is demonstrated that competition would produce greater benefits to the public."[192] In 1967, the commission awarded a certificate to Texas Gas Transmission to pipe the supply previously moved by the Fuel Gas Company to Hamilton, Ohio, by virtue of better consumer service.[193] In the same year, Transcontinental Pipeline was awarded a certificate to sell gas to distributors in Washington, D.C., and northern Virginia despite a plea from the Atlantic Seaboard Corporation, sole supplier to the area, that Transco's entrance would destabilize its operation.[194] In another 1967 case, a distributor was allowed to switch pipeline suppliers to take advantage of cheaper rates.[195]

Thus, after twenty years area competition was confirmed with new entrants allowed to capture market growth. The FPC had let it be known that no existing market niche was immune from competition. But with the burden of proof on entrants and two decades of doubt, a strong anti-competitive legacy, which would continue, had been created.

Two other important FPC cases defined interfirm competition. Again in 1967, the commission initiated a section 7(a) proceeding to order Tennessee Gas to service Hartford, Connecticut, despite the fact that Algonquin Gas Transmission had applied for the extension.[196] While Tennessee's cost estimate for servicing Hartford was below Algonquin's, the unprecedented order was made to balance earlier decisions that leaned toward territorial rights on the rationale that two firms in a market were more competitive than one, even if created by edict.[197]

[191]John Cheatham, "Regulation in the Post–World War II Period," p. 4-20.

[192]Opinion 512, 37 FPC 130 (1967).

[193]Opinion 513, 37 FPC 209 (1967).

[194]Opinion 512, 37 FPC 118 (1967).

[195]Opinion 534, 38 FPC 1069 (1967). Aff'd *Alabama-Tennessee Natural Gas Co.* v. *FPC*, 417 F.2d 511 (5th Cir. 1969). Also see Alfred Kahn, *The Economics of Regulation*, vol. 2, pp. 166–67.

[196]Opinion 522, 37 FPC 1128 (1967).

[197]Carl Bagge, "The Federal Power Commission," *Boston College Industrial and Commercial Law Review* (May 1970): 702.

A second illustrative case occurred in the late 1960s when a comparative proceeding took place to decide which of three applicants, if not all, could meet the burgeoning demand of the southern California market. This market had been served by El Paso Natural Gas since 1946 and Transwestern since 1960, and both firms wished to expand service. A paper subsidiary of Tennessee Gas, Gulf Pacific Transmission Company, wanted to build an entirely new line. In 1958, the FPC denied an expansion by El Paso on grounds that gas demand was inadequate and the anticipated cost was too high. Use of fuel oil in place of natural gas had contributed to the area's worsening air-pollution problem, which gave new impetus for increased pipeline capacity to the state.

In 1968, the commission ruled against Gulf Pacific because "trends in nuclear energy, the development of remote coal-fired steam electric plants, and the build up in [extra-high-voltage] interregional interests will minimize the need for additional generation in Los Angeles county."[198] This decision would lead to second-guessing. With gas-supply curtailments in California in the mid-1970s, the ability of El Paso and Transwestern to satisfy demand was open to question; with dedicated reserves in tow, Gulf Pacific could have helped to bridge the gap, although partly at the expense of pipelines in other areas, given widespread shortages in interstate markets.

The prize of certification was also coveted by firms entering unserviced areas. In the late 1930s, Tennessee Gas and Transportation Company was organized to secure financing for a gas pipeline from southern Louisiana to the Tennessee Valley. A certification application was made to the FPC on November 25, 1942, and a year later the War Production Board, cognizant of looming gas shortages in the Appalachian region, granted a steel allocation subject to FPC approval.[199] With financing still a problem for Tennessee, Hope Natural Gas, a subsidiary of Jersey Standard, applied for a certificate to

[198]Opinion 500, 36 FPC 191 (1968). For Tennessee Gas this marked the end of an eight-year battle to enter the southern California market that had begun with a proposed pipeline through Mexico. Not only was it the most expensive certification lobbying effort by one company, it had the intrigue of a spy thriller. There were a bugging episode, sneak legislation, secret informants, alleged bribes, and secret evidence and obstructionism in hearings. For a story of certification at its worst, see Richard Smith, "They Play Rough in the Gas Business," *Fortune*, January 1966, pp. 132–35, 230–33.

[199]An earlier application in 1940 was dismissed for want of jurisdiction, which meant certification was not required in unserviced areas.

build a similar line commencing in the Hugoton field. Hope seemed the logical choice—financing was certain, it already had a line serving the targeted market, and its gas reserve base was strong. A day before hearings began on the Hope application, Tennessee's financing came through, and the commission orally awarded the exclusive franchise.[200] Tennessee's time-consuming completion of its certification requirements and secure steel rations figured prominently in the decision, but politics was also involved. "The company had more political than financial clout," stated Arlon Tussing and Connie Barlow. "It had not yet acquired any physical assets, but its presiding officer was the former son-in-law of President Roosevelt."[201] In 1944, the Tennessee Gas pipeline, enlarged to 1,265 miles to stretch from the Texas Gulf Coast to Cornwall, West Virginia, was completed at a cost of $4 million.

In 1950, competing applications to serve the New England market were made by Tennessee Gas Transmission and Texas Eastern Transmission.[202] The two companies were not cordial, and each relentlessly pursued an exclusive franchise to supply a major new market. Eastern states already receiving gas protested against both applications on the grounds that the FPC should not certify any new applications until their waiting-list customers were serviced. A compromise certification gave Texas Eastern (Algonquin) exclusive rights to Connecticut, Rhode Island, and eastern Massachusetts and gave Tennessee Gas a franchise to New York and remaining areas of Massachusetts.[203]

A mid-1970s certification tiff raised the level of complexity and delay to new heights. Three applications to transport natural gas from the Prudhoe Bay field in Alaska to the lower forty-eight states were submitted between March 1974 and July 1976—the Alcan Pipeline proposal to California, the Alaskan Arctic Gas Pipeline proposal to Illinois, and a tanker plan by El Paso to feed existing lines to California. The FPC used technical economic analysis to determine

---

[200]2 FPC 575 (1943). The certification was not only a setback for Hope but for coal intervenors who were against gas per se—the National Coal Association, United Mine Workers, Anthracite Institute, Southern Appalachian Coal Operators' Association, and Railway Labor Executives Association. Louisiana, which desired state gas to remain in home markets, was also against the certification.

[201]Arlon Tussing and Connie Barlow, *The Natural Gas Industry*, p. 42.

[202]This proceeding is also discussed in this chapter, pp. 936–37.

[203]Opinion 202, 9 FPC 271 (1950); and Opinion 206, 10 FPC 35 at 57 (1951).

the "Net National Economic Benefit" of each under a variety of assumptions. By the time the FERC inherited the stalemate in 1977, other branches of government had assumed jurisdiction over the decision. Finally, after U.S. officials narrowed the choice to two firms, the Canadian government chose the winner in mid-1977—Alcan.[204]

Another certification battle as of 1984 was between a $323-million Transcontinental Gas–Tennessee Gas–Texas Eastern proposal between Niagara Falls, New York, and Leidy, Pennsylvania, filed in January 1983, and an ANR Pipeline–Northern Natural 663-mile, $1-billion proposal between Ventura, Iowa, and Defiance, Ohio. Hearings on proposals to transport plentiful Canadian gas to the gas-poor Northeast began in 1985 with a resolution not expected for several years.

The foregoing decisions do not reveal any set procedure for awarding certification. Early applicants were rewarded (Tennessee, 1943) as were later applicants (Texas Eastern, 1952). Subjectively perceived "merits of the case," not excluding political factors, seem to have been a major factor in FPC decisions between competing interstate pipeline proposals.

Coal-related unions, railroads, producers, and distributors, led by the National Coal Association, participated directly in the debate over the Natural Gas Act in the 1935–38 period. The same parties were instrumental in expanding certification to all interstate activity in 1942. With their participation rights secure, alternate-fuel interests intervened regularly in FPC hearings in the 1940s, 1950s, and early 1960s, eager to forestall displacement of coal by cost-competitive, clean-burning gas.[205] Fuel-oil interests also actively opposed gas-pipeline licenses. As intervenors, they had to demonstrate that the public convenience and necessity were not served by displacement, which was argued first on *end-use* grounds—that gas as a premium fuel should not be used in "inferior" uses that relatively plentiful

---

[204]Further analysis of the regulatory issues surrounding Alaskan gas transportation is provided in this chapter, pp. 912–13.

[205]Testimony in the 1940s against a "free-trade" natural-gas policy was given by the National Coal Association, United Mine Workers of America, Railway Labor Executives Association, Brotherhood of Locomotive Engineers, American Retail Coal Association, Anthracite Institute, and Operators of Coal Docks on Lake Michigan and Lake Superior. See, for example, Ralph Huitt, "Federal Regulation of the Uses of Natural Gas," *American Political Science Review* 46 (1952): 455–69.

coal or fuel oil could meet—and second on grounds of employment and income loss from displacement. A third reason was championed by industry and utilities within gas-producing states who desired to retain gas in home markets to promote industrialization enjoyed by many gas-importing states.[206]

The original position of the FPC was that conservation and end-use considerations were outside of the certification process, which kept rival fuels at bay.[207] This September 1943 opinion was reversed less than a year later by the Supreme Court to give end-use material concern:

> When it comes to cases of abandonment or of extensions of service, we may assume that apart from the express exemptions contained in Section 7, considerations of conservation are material to the issuance of certificates of public convenience and necessity.[208]

Pursuant to this decision, the FPC released Docket G-508 calling for end-use evidence in future certification hearings. This opened the door for special interests threatened by natural-gas expansion. On June 10, 1944, the first end-use decision denied certification to Memphis Natural Gas because gas sold for boiler fuel was not a "superior" use of the fuel. Upon rehearing, certification was granted to Memphis, which led Louisiana, favoring intrastate use, to unsuccessfully seek reversal by the circuit court of appeals.[209]

With the issue opened, coal interests in 1943 and 1945 sought to amend the NGA to "give due consideration . . . to the conservation of natural gas resources, the adequacy of reserves and the social and economic effects of their depletion."[210] Although the majority of decisions would not go their way—indeed, a circuit court in 1951

---

[206]Ibid., pp. 460, 462–64.

[207]3 FPC 574 (1943). Also see "The First Five Years under the Natural Gas Act," *Federal Power Commission Report to the House Committee on Interstate and Foreign Commerce*, 78th Cong., 2d sess. (Washington, D.C.: Government Printing Office, 1944).

[208]*Federal Power Commission* v. *Hope Natural Gas Co.*, 320 U.S. 612 (1944).

[209]Also against certification were the National Coal Association, the United Mines Workers, and several railroad labor organizations; favoring certification were area gas distributors desiring lower prices, the Texas Railroad Commission, and the Independent Natural Gas Association of America. John Cheatham, "Regulation in the Post–World War II Period," p. 4-26.

[210]Carl Wheat, "Administration by the Federal Power Commission of the Certification Provisions of the Natural Gas Act," pp. 201–2.

ruled that while end use was an element to be considered in the complex of public convenience and necessity, it was not a determinative factor [211]—as late as 1959 the commission blocked an expansion of natural-gas service by New York's Consolidated Edison by ruling that gas use as a boiler fuel was "inferior."[212] In subsequent years, however, the ability of rivals to fend off natural gas diminished; gas was too cheap, plentiful, nonpolluting, and free of labor risks compared with coal. Natural-gas shortages and regulatory responses pushed coal back into the picture in the 1970s, but for the same reasons, active gas expansion into new markets was not present for coal interests to counter.

Section 7(a) of the NGA gave the FPC authority to order a firm to "extend or improve its transportation facilities or establish physical connection" to nearby distributors if "no undue burden" was placed on the firm's "ability to render adequate service to its customers."[213] This authority did not apply to enlargements constructed to handle load growth.

The first question under 7(a) was what constituted adequate service. Extensions to new areas could be stymied if the commission strictly interpreted the firm's obligation to its original clientele. In 1953, the court of appeals ruled that adequate service did not mean *full* service, defined as meeting demand in peak periods, and that extensions could be made short of this. Determination of "adequate service" was a factual matter to be decided case by case.[214]

A second case differentiated mandatory improvements from mandatory enlargements. In 1953, the FPC ordered Panhandle Eastern to eliminate customer discrimination by increasing the diameter of one of its pipelines. The order was reversed in circuit court; discrimination notwithstanding, it was ruled that forced expansion violated section 7(a) of the NGA.[215]

---

[211]*National Coal Association* v. *FPC*, 191 F.2d 462 at 467 (D.C. Cir. 1951).

[212]Opinion 315-A, 21 FPC 138 (1959). The constitutionality of end-use considerations was reconfirmed by the Supreme Court in *Federal Power Commission* v. *Transcontinental Pipe Line Corp.*, 365 U.S. 1 (1961).

[213]Public Law 688, 52 Stat. 824 (1938).

[214]*Manufacturers Light and Heat Co.* v. *FPC*, 206 F.2d 404 (3rd Cir. 1953).

[215]*Panhandle Eastern Pipe Line Co.* v. *FPC*, 204 F.2d 683 (3rd. Cir. 1953).

In 1962, the FPC ordered Mississippi River Fuel to reallocate pipeline volume away from direct industrial customers to increase deliveries to residential customers through their gas distributor.[216] The circuit court reversed on appeal because Mississippi was not unambiguously meeting the "present and reasonably foreseeable requirements [of] existing lawful customers."[217] Mandatory reallocation of supply between customers, the court ruled, was not permitted under 7(a).

Another important 7(a) decision occurred in 1964 when the FPC ordered Tennessee Gas to physically connect a gas-distribution company located near one of its pipelines. Commissioner Carl Bagge justified the "extraordinary action" as necessary to promote "vigorous pipeline competition in the Northwest."[218]

Issues concerning mandatory extensions and improvements of service became a thing of the past when the cumulative effects of field-price regulation of natural gas precipitated supply problems and even shortages in interstate markets in the late 1960s and 1970s. In sharp contrast to the previous era of rapid expansion, interpretations under the NGA took a complete turn from service extensions and improvements to abandonment and curtailment of service.

Offshore, the issue of forced service remained alive. Section 603 of the Outer Continental Shelf Land Act was designed to facilitate offshore pipeline connections, and the FERC followed with a statement of policy that Outer Continental Shelf hookups could be compelled.[219] Guidelines were not specified; presumably future opinions and court decisions would delineate them.[220]

Section 7(b) prohibited jurisdictional firms from abandoning service to any certificated customer without a commission "finding" that "the present or future public convenience or necessity permit such abandonment."[221] If any party was opposed to the proposed service termination, formal hearings were necessary.

[216]Opinion 355, 27 FPC 697 (1962).

[217]*Granite City Steel Co.* v. *FPC*, 320 F.2d 711 (D.C. Cir. 1963).

[218]37 FPC 1128 (1964). See John Cheatham, "Regulation in the Post–World War II Period," pp. 4-8 to 4-9.

[219]Order 92, 12 FERC 61069 (1980); and Order 92-A, 13 FERC 61215 (1980).

[220]Littman, Richter, Wright & Talisman, "Pipeline Service Obligations," in American Gas Association, *Regulation of the Natural Gas Industry*, vol. 1, p. 11-17.

[221]Public Law 688, 52 Stat. 824 (1938).

Termination clauses were not allowed in producer contracts. In the 1960 *Sunray* decision, a twenty-year certificate awarded by the FPC was found not to be a maximum period whereupon a producer could discontinue service but a certificate of unlimited duration.[222] The Fifth Circuit gave the following analogy.

> Like the ancient covenant running with the land, the duty to continue to deliver and sell flows with the gas from the moment of first delivery down to the exhaustion of the reserve, or until the commission, on appropriate terms, permits cessation of service under Section 7(b).[223]

The NGA gave the FPC wide discretion to tailor certifications "that the present and future public convenience and necessity require."[224] The commission's latent authority to make allocation decisions was first used between 1947 and 1951 when seven opinions were issued dealing with capacity problems of Panhandle Eastern in the Detroit area.[225] Other than this isolated instance, government allocation was confined to certification decisions about which waiting-list customers would be served. The issue was not moot. Between 1949 and 1952, Congress debated legislation that would deny service to new areas until existing areas were fully hooked up.[226]

In 1952, the FPC included service curtailment in the abandonment-of-service category.[227] In two later decisions, the Supreme Court upheld the interpretation.[228] Beginning in November 1970, section 7(b) would assume great importance when three major interstate

[222]*Sunray Mid-Continent Oil·Co.* v. *FPC,* 364 U.S. 137 (1960). In a 1978 decision, the "perpetual dedication rule" was extended to cover expired leases on gas properties. *California* v. *Southland Royalty Co.,* 436 U.S. 519 (1978).

[223]*Hunt* v. *FPC,* 306 F.2d 334 (5th Cir. 1962), rev'd on other grounds, 376 U.S. 515 (1964).

[224]Sec. 7(c), Public Law 688, 52 Stat. 825 (1938).

[225]See 6 FPC 196 (1947); 7 FPC 1 (1848); 7 FPC 48 (1948); 7 FPC 984 (1948); 8 FPC 1339 (1949); 9 FPC 1330 (1950); and 10 FPC 328 (1951). The earliest occurrence of mandatory natural-gas allocation was in 1918 when the U.S. Fuel Administration used its wartime powers to allocate gas according to a five-tiered priority schedule to relieve a gas shortage in New York State. *OGJ,* October 25, 1918, p. 2.

[226]See H. T. Koplin, "Conservation and Regulation: The Natural Gas Allocation Policy of the Federal Power Commission," *Yale Law Journal* (May 1955): 842–43.

[227]11 FPC 575 (1952).

[228]*Mid-Continent Oil Co.* v. *FPC,* 364 U.S. 137 (1960); and *United Gas Pipe Line Co.* v. *FPC* 395 U.S. 83 (1966).

pipelines, Arkansas-Louisiana, Transco, and United, announced pro rata curtailments in violation of contractual obligations.[229] With differences in customer need, volumetrically equal reductions were otherwise unequal, and hard choices had to be made about distributing the shortfall. "Human-need" customers such as the elderly, the young, and the sick, in particular, were less able to absorb a cutback than were commercial establishments or industrial users.

Instead of pipeline versus pipeline or fuel versus fuel, it was now customer versus customer with which the commission and courts had to contend. The stakes were high. For electric utilities that were curtailed, substitution to fuel oil could double customer bills. Curtailed industries turning to higher priced fuel oil could find their competitive positions threatened. In homes without adequate heat, illness or even tragedy could occur.

The first commission response was to have pipelines under curtailment develop and file tariff plans. Instructions for priority classes were also provided in the 1971 order.[230] In the same year, a curtailment plan was devised for United Gas.[231] The next action was a five-class priority curtailment plan for El Paso Natural Gas in 1972.[232] To formalize industry standards and replace voluntary arrangements, several commission orders were issued in early 1973 that set an eight-tiered hierarchical "end-use" plan, which was soon followed by a similar nine-tiered plan.[233]

[229]This section is adopted from Richard Merriman and Peyton Bowman, "The 1970s—A Period of Momentous Change," in American Gas Association, *Regulation of the Gas Industry*, vol. 1, chap. 5; and Jerome Muys, "Federal Power Commission Allocation of Natural Gas Supply Shortages: Prorationing, Priorities, and Perplexity," *20 Rocky Mountain Mineral Law Institute* (New York: Matthew Bender, 1975), pp. 301–58.

[230]Order 431, 45 FPC 570 (1971).

[231]Opinion 606, 46 FPC 786 (1971).

[232]Opinion 634, 48 FPC 931 (1972).

[233]Order 467, 49 FPC 85 (1973); Order 467-B, 49 FPC 583 (1973); and Order 467-C, 51 FPC 1199 (1974). Priority groups ranged from "high-priority" users captive to gas to "low-priority" industrial and electric power plants capable of substituting to oil to endure interrupted service. In order of priority, the hierarchy was (1) residential, small commercial users of under 50 Mcf per peak day; (2) large commercial users of over 50 Mcf per peak day, industrial firm requirements for plant protection, feedstock and process needs, and pipeline-customer storage-injection requirements; (3) all users not specified; (4) industrial boiler-fuel uses of 1.5 MMcf to 3 MMcf per day with alternate fuel capability; (5) industrial boiler uses of over 3 MMcf per day where substitution was available; (6) interruptible uses of between 0.3 MMcf and 1.5 MMcf per day where alternative fuels existed; (7) interruptible users of between 1.5 MMcf

Contract provisions for interruptible service and pro rata allocation were not allowed. Explained the commission:

> We are impelled to direct curtailment on the basis of end use rather
> than on the basis of contract simply because contracts do not neces-
> sarily serve the public interest requirement of efficient allocation. In
> times of shortage, performance of a firm contract to deliver gas for
> an inferior use, at the expense of reduced deliveries for priority uses,
> is not compatible with consumer protection.[234]

Strict implementation of the Order 467 series was overruled in
appeals court where it was opined that specific guidelines could only
be established per hearing.[235] Tailored curtailment plans followed
including those of Arkansas-Louisiana (eight tiers, 1973), United Gas
(five tiers, 1973), Southern Natural (seven tiers, 1975), and Transco
(nine tiers, 1976).[236]

FPC curtailment plans, as does any enforced rationing plan,
encountered difficulties. One early problem was the jurisdictional
status of direct industrial sales. If they were beyond commission
authority, only voluntary pro rata plans were possible, leaving local
distribution companies subject to FPC curtailment plans. The appeals
court agreed, but the Supreme Court came to the FPC's rescue with
an interpretative twist that the commission's authority over transportation, not rates, controlled the issue, hence curtailment orders
applied to direct sales as well as indirect sales.[237]

A second major issue involved compensation. Certain electric utilities dependent on natural gas as a boiler fuel, primarily in the South
and West, had to substitute fuel oil, which was over three times as

---

and 3 MMcf per day capable of substitution; (8) interruptible users of between 3
MMcf and 10 MMcf per day capable of substitution; and (9) interruptible users of
over 10 MMcf per day. In addition to human need, the bias toward domestic uses
over industrial uses was because of the hazards of restarting pilot lights in residences.

[234]Opinion 643, 49 FPC 53 at 66 (1973).

[235]*Pacific Gas & Electric Co.* v. *FPC*, 506 F.2d 33 (D.C. Cir. 1974).

[236]Opinion 643, 49 FPC 53 (1973); Opinion 647, 49 FPC 179 (1973); Opinion 747, 54
FPC 2298 (1975); and Opinion 778, 56 FPC 2134 (1976). Final plans became interim
plans, necessitating new hearings and opinions from court reversals. For example,
see *State of Louisiana* v. *FPC*, 503 F.2d 844 (5th Cir. 1974); and *State of North Carolina*
v. *FERC*, 584 F.2d 1003 (D.C.C., 1978).

[237]*Federal Power Commission* v. *Louisiana Power & Light Co.*, 406 U.S. 621 (1972).

expensive on a heating-value basis, while high-priority gas customers enjoyed relatively inexpensive gas. Noted Richard Merriman and Peyton Bowman, "A person with a gas stove and gas heat could escape practically unscathed from a gas shortage while the next-door neighbor with electric appliances encountered a doubling of utility bills."[238] Sentiment developed to have high-priority customers share the burden with other less fortunate customers, perhaps by a surcharge on the former. The commission refused jurisdiction in one such case but was reversed by the Fifth Circuit.[239] With jurisdiction, the commission refused to modify its end-use orders to apportion compensation.

Regional inequities were the most glaring problem of curtailment. Some pipelines, such as Transco and Texas Eastern, experienced severe supply problems in the pre-1978 period, while other inter-states such as Southern Natural and Pacific Gas Transmission met full demands. This meant that interruptible customers in states such as South Carolina and North Carolina were cut off, while the same customer class in Massachusetts and New Hampshire, served by lines with high reserves, were relatively unscathed.[240] Relative industrial development of states was directly affected; North Carolina, for example, was not considered for new plant location by thirty-four firms because of gas uncertainty.[241] "From the standpoint of economic efficiency," summarized Jeffrey Harrison and John Formby, "the administrative allocation of natural gas has been an unmitigated disaster."[242]

[238]Richard Merriman and Peyton Bowman, "The 1970s—A Period of Momentous Change," p. 5-20.

[239]*Mississippi Public Service Commission* v. *FPC*, 522 F.2d 1345 (5th Cir. 1975).

[240]Jeffrey Harrison and John Formby, "Regional Distortions in Natural Gas Allocations: A Legal and Economic Analysis," *North Carolina Law Review* (October 1978): 82–85. Severely curtailed states were North and South Carolina, Florida, Mississippi, Georgia, Alabama, Minnesota, Arizona, and Tennessee; above-average curtailed states were Arkansas, California, Nevada, Nebraska, Kansas, Louisiana, Iowa, Missouri, Virginia, Kentucky, Delaware, Ohio, and North Dakota; and moderately curtailed states were South Dakota, Maryland, West Virginia, Oregon, Wisconsin, New Mexico, Indiana, Utah, Pennsylvania, Washington, New York, and Connecticut. Little to no forced rationing was experienced in Illinois, Wyoming, Idaho, New Hampshire, Vermont, Colorado, Michigan, Texas, Oklahoma, Montana, Massachusetts, Rhode Island, and Maine.

[241]Ibid., p. 87.

[242]Ibid., p. 88.

Other mandatory-allocation problems were defining interruptible service, base-period levels, and alternate-fuel substitution. The unreliability of end-use data was the "Achilles heel of [the FPC] programs."[243] No customer class was satisfied unless it received priority. "In short," stated an FPC solicitor, "what we have is a group of petitioners none of which will concede that a program can ever be just and reasonable unless their individual gas supply is given highest priority and highest protection."[244] The customer clash was not only between direct (favored) and indirect (nonfavored) customers but between existing customers and new customers.

Not only did the FPC and the judiciary spring to action in the troubled 1970s. To supplement the NGA, the Emergency Natural Gas Act of 1977 was passed and immediately activated by President Carter.[245] FPC chairman Richard Dunham, appointed administrator of the act, promptly issued orders to reallocate gas between firms, establish emergency guidelines, and relax import and maritime regulations that hampered gas procurement.[246] With the end of the cold winter of 1976–77, curtailments eased, and the act was rescinded on April 1, 1977.

In 1946, the FPC ruled that interstate pipeline regulation extended to integral storage facilities.[247] As they did for pipeline projects, certification applications had to demonstrate funding, supply, demand, reasonable cost, and quality of service.[248] When requisite conditions were in doubt, temporary authorization was sometimes granted.[249]

A jurisdictional question concerning interstate pipeline storage facilities was whether an intrastate firm participating in a joint storage project with an interstate automatically became a "natural-gas company" under the NGA. A 1965 opinion found such a situation

[243]Jerome Muys, "Federal Power Commission Allocation of Natural Gas Supply Shortages," p. 327.

[244]Quoted in 503 F.2d 844 at 869.

[245]Public Law 95-20, 91 Stat. 1720 (1977). Proclamation 4485, 52 *Fed. Reg.* (February 2, 1977).

[246]See Richard Merriman and Payton Bowman, "The 1970s—A Period of Momentous Change," pp. 5-26 to 5-29.

[247]Opinion 620, 47 FPC 1527 (1972).

[248]Opinion 236, 11 FPC 366 (1952).

[249]John Cheatham, "Regulation in the Post–World War II Period," p. 4-32.

to be nonjurisdictional unless an inventory credit for compensation was granted to the interstate firm, which constituted a sale for resale by the intrastate firm.[250]

At the close of 1978, 216 underground gas-storage projects were operated by interstate carriers under FERC jurisdiction. Nine types of project facilities, all of which inject gas in "shoulder" periods to meet demand in "peak" periods, primarily residential demand in the winter, require separate certification.[251]

Antitrust and general monopolization issues have a long if infrequent history in the manufactured- and natural-gas industry. In 1889, an Illinois court ruled that the Chicago Gas Trust had to sell its stock interest in four other manufactured-gas companies because its monopoly position violated its corporate charter.[252] But a pure antitrust suit against a gas-transmission firm would come nearly seventy years later.

On December 23, 1957, a certificate of public convenience and necessity was awarded to El Paso Natural Gas, then the sole interstate supplier to the California market, to operate the recently acquired Pacific Northwest Pipeline Corporation, a 1,500-mile line from Seattle, Washington, to the San Juan Basin, despite an antitrust suit against the merger filed by the U.S. attorney general. This lawsuit represented the first major antitrust action against an interstate natural-gas line. The FPC had taken jurisdiction over the public-interest implications of the merger despite the pending suit and was upheld by the lower court. The Supreme Court reversed.[253] The suit was decided in 1964 by the Supreme Court, which ruled that an antitrust violation had taken place "unless Section 7 of the Clayton Act has no meaning in the natural gas field."[254] Divestiture of Pacific Northwest by El Paso was ordered, and after several divestiture plans were rejected by the courts, a separation agreement was approved

---

[250]Opinion 480, 34 FPC 1258 (1965). This qualification would be modified by the commission in a later decision.

[251]See S. K. Smith, Jr., "Pipeline Gas Supplies," in American Gas Association, *Regulation of the Gas Industry*, vol. 1, p. 12-48.

[252]*People* v. *Chicago Gas Trust Co.*, 130 Ill. 268 (1889). Cited in William Letwin, "Congress and the Sherman Antitrust Law: 1887–1890," *University of Chicago Law Review* (Winter 1956): 245.

[253]*California* v. *FPC*, 369 U.S. 482 (1962).

[254]*United States* v. *El Paso Natural Gas*, 376 U.S. 651 (1964).

on August 29, 1968. Court action continued until March 1973, and full separation was finally accomplished in 1979.[255]

The reduced bounds of its authority in light of the antitrust decision were recognized by the FPC in its 1966 annual report.

> The Commission's approval of an acquisition of assets does not exempt the transaction from subsequent prosecution under the antitrust laws. . . . The Commission cannot even make its statutory determination . . . as long as an antitrust action directed against the acquisition is pending in the courts.[256]

Subsequent rulings have been consistent with this pronouncement.[257] The Natural Gas Pipeline Safety Act, enacted on August 12, 1968, instructed the secretary of transportation to set minimum safety regulations for pipelines—intrastate gathering and trunk lines as well as interstate lines.[258] The industry had successfully followed a voluntary code, the American Standard Code for Pressure Piping, Gas Transmission, and Distribution Piping Systems, first established in 1942 by the American Society of Mechanical Engineers, yet many states chose to make the code mandatory. By 1968, all states except Nebraska and South Dakota had done so.[259] The FPC sought minimum federal safety standards beginning in 1950. In the next decade, the drive intensified to "sustai[n] and improv[e] . . . the voluntary code's present standards and mak[e] them mandatory in all States where pipelines operate."[260] The industry by this time was ready for a federal standard in place of forty-eight state standards, and this uniform standard was incorporated

---

[255]"In the past 16 years the case has come before the Supreme Court no fewer than eight times. Some 39 companies, Government agencies, and private citizens have joined the case over the years. At one point, a bill was introduced in Congress to exempt the . . . merger. . . . El Paso paid close to $16 million to lawyers and public relations men during its losing fight." *Time*, March 19, 1973, p. 73.

[256]Federal Power Commission, *1966 Annual Report* (Washington, D.C.: Government Printing Office, 1967), p. 10.

[257]See John Cheatham, "Regulation in the Post–World War II Period," pp. 4-29 to 4-30.

[258]Public Law 90-481, 82 Stat. 720 (1968).

[259]Martin Armstrong, "The Natural Gas Pipeline Safety Act of 1968," *Natural Resources Journal* (May 1969): 144.

[260]Federal Power Commission, *1966 Annual Report*, p. 136. Cited in John Cheatham, "Regulation in the Post–World War II Period," p. 4-40.

into certification requests. Prior to 1968, safety-related issues were discussed in commission hearings, and only accident reports were mandatory.

Despite constant amendments, numbering thirty-two in the federal law's first decade, prescribed "performance standards" were not a major impediment to pipeline construction and operation.[261] The law, in any case, was not born of necessity. It was testament to the urge to regulate, given the satisfactory safety record of the industry prior to the law.[262]

The National Environmental Policy Act of 1969 required environmental impact statements for all major federal actions directly affecting the environment.[263] The new requirements were incorporated into the certification process whenever a major environmental impact was judged present. This added to the heavy paperwork load of pipeline firms entering or exiting the market or expanding or curtailing service.

Pipeline right-of-way through public land and Indian land is closely supervised by federal authorities with environmental conditions in mind. Permits must be secured from the Interior Department with review and approval by different agencies and subagencies. Projects in national forests are reviewed by the Forest Service (U.S. Department of Agriculture); projects in Indian territory must be approved by the Bureau of Indian Affairs (Interior Department); projects in a wildlife refuge are evaluated by the Fish and Wildlife Service (Interior Department); projects in recreational or historic areas must secure approval from the Heritage Conservation and Recreation Service (Interior Department); and projects near or in water areas must be approved by the Army Corps of Engineers. In most cases, the Bureau of Land Management (Interior Department) has primary responsibility.

---

[261]Mel Martin, "Natural Gas Pipelines—Their Regulation and Their Current Problems," *30 Annual Institute on Oil and Gas* (New York: Matthew Bender, 1979), pp. 255–56.

[262]A study in 1966 revealed that only sixty-four fatalities occurred with some 800,000 miles of continuously run pipelines between 1950 and 1965. Federal Power Commission, *1966 Annual Report*, pp. 133–35. To Martin Armstrong, legislation in the face of the industry's safety record made pipelines "a scapegoat for the politically-motivated 'consumerism' which became a preoccupation of the [Johnson] administration." Armstrong, "The Natural Gas Pipeline Safety Act of 1968," p. 153.

[263]Public Law 91-190, 83 Stat. 853 (1970).

Unique in the annals of NGA regulation is the Alaska Natural Gas Transportation System, which was ten years in the making.[264] The 1968 discovery of the Prudhoe Bay field in northeastern Alaska was a major gas discovery in addition to the oil find, accounting for over 10 percent of U.S. proven gas reserves. The first proposal to pipe gas to the contiguous United States was presented to the FERC in March 1974 by a consortium of American and Canadian pipeline firms (Arctic Gas Proposal). Another proposal by the El Paso Alaska Company followed in September 1974. Slowing the certification process were both sponsors' requests for an "all events full cost of service tariff," which would have had consumers pay for all project costs regardless of gas delivery. Federal loan guarantees were also in the air.

A third proposal by the Alcan Pipeline Company in July 1976 did not formally propose an all-events tariff and government subsidies but offered little concrete evidence that investors would bear the risk instead of consumers and taxpayers. With the three mutually exclusive proposals, 250 days of hearings followed with over 250 volumes of testimony and exhibits. Other hearings were held before Congress and Canadian officials. Before the hearings ended on November 12, 1976, the Alaska Natural Gas Transportation Act was passed. In light of the severe gas shortage in the lower forty-eight states, the act imposed a May 1, 1977, deadline on the FERC to recommend one of the three proposed carrier systems to the president.[265] This gave Congress and the president jurisdiction to grant entry, prescribe regulations, and set tariffs. With the FERC deadlocked over the Arctic and Alcan proposals, the choice was given to Canadian authorities, who chose the Alcan plan on July 4, 1977. President Carter concurred, and in November 1977, Congress passed a joint resolution approving the choice.[266] Pursuant to the Natural Gas Policy Act, the field price was fixed at $1.45 per million British thermal units, adjusted for inflation from base-period April 1977, with no producer allowance for conditioning the gas, a matter that was disputed along with other financial issues.

---

[264]This discussion is taken K. S. Smith, Jr., "Pipeline Gas Supplies," pp. 12-74 to 12-83.

[265]Public Law 94-586, 90 Stat. 2903 (1976).

[266]Other joint resolutions in 1980 and 1981 encouraged the project. See Arlon Tussing and Connie Barlow, *The Natural Gas Industry*, p. 83.

Also in dispute was the ownership of the pipeline itself. In July 1977, the Department of Justice intervened to recommend that producers be banned from participating in the pipeline's financing because undersizing and nonaccess to outsiders would result. The position was accepted by the president and Congress; producers were banned from owning equity in the project, participating in management, or guaranteeing debt in the initial financing. But facing the fact that more delay was probable without the most logical financiers, the Department of Justice, under new leadership, consented to producer and pipeline sponsorship of the Alaska portion of the line in June 1980. Work began to join the Canadian and contiguous U.S. portions already under construction. But with the 4,800-mile project less than one-third complete, construction stalled amid financing woes. The new reality of falling gas prices made guaranteed cost recoupment in rates obsolete, and federal subsidy was out of the question. Regarding the former, natural-gas prices to industrial users were constrained by substitute-fuel prices, and any attempted cost pass-through would price the gas out of the market. The fate of the uncompleted portions of the pipeline and huge North Slope gas reserves was in question. Summarized Arlon Tussing in 1983:

> The upheaval that has occurred in natural-gas markets since 1980 means, effectively, that an Alaska gas-transportation project is either an idea whose time has yet to come or, more likely, one whose time has come and gone. . . . It is indeed conceivable that Prudhoe Bay gas will *never* be a marketable commodity. Before it can become such a commodity, the worldwide energy situation, the technological menu, or both, will have to change in ways that we cannot now foresee.[267]

NGA Regulation in Retrospect

For over four decades interstate gas pipelines have been subject to public-utility regulation, ostensibly to check natural-monopoly characteristics to keep prices and quantities competitive at the city gate. The theoretical calling and practical results of the regulatory effort, however, are open to complete review. Natural-gas pipelines

---

[267]Arlon Tussing and Connie Barlow, "An Epitaph for the Alaska Gas Pipeline?" *ARTA Energy Insights* (Summer 1983): 9, 20.

are not ipso facto natural monopolies, and even if they were, voluntary contracts and market processes can prevent "monopolistic" outcomes. Correcting a "lack" of competition with state franchises and the Natural Gas Act, moreover, is a "cure" far worse than the "disease." These government interventions are classically monopolistic, awarding government grants to exclusively or semiexclusively serve markets.

While restricting entry and rivalry, authorities have attempted to mimic the competitive environment by limiting rates to cost plus a prescribed rate of return on valued capital. The surrogate approach to market competition not only fails to recognize market decision-making as a *discovery process* and inherently competitive, it institutionalizes inefficient practices to maximize returns under regulatory constraints.

Although no empirical estimates will be made to arrive at a negative price savings for customer classes under the NGA, a review of the general record confirms the distortions and waste of public-utility regulation.[268] Unfortunately, what an unhampered market would have produced cannot be known—only surmised. What lines would have been built if customer contracts rather than certification had decided the issue? How much sooner would these lines have been built, and how many more "waiting-list" customers would have been served? What would the cost and rate structure have been for different markets? And finally, how much sooner would the revolutionary changes of the 1980s have been implemented without the public-utility status of the industry?

An interesting political fact should be emphasized at the outset to suggest that not all is well with the standard interpretation of the need for interstate natural-gas-pipeline regulation. The passage of the NGA and its subsequent operation have been generally supported by both consumer interests and the regulated pipeline industry. If it is assumed that consumers desire lower prices and pipelines desire higher prices and profits, then one group has misspecified its mean-ends framework by forsaking the free market for government

---

[268] An empirical study by Stephen Breyer and Paul MacAvoy on natural-gas-pipeline rate regulation in the early 1970s reached the "inescapable conclusion" that "the value of Federal Power Commission price-setting activities has been either very low or zero." Breyer and MacAvoy, *Energy Regulation by the Federal Power Commission* (Washington, D.C.: Brookings Institution, 1974), p. 54.

intervention. Given consumer unrest compared to that of the pipeline industry during the regulatory tenure, the political mistake seems to lie with the former.

Early Consequences

In congressional hearings in 1941, several Congressmen asked industry witnesses why interstate pipeline activity had slowed in the first three years of the Natural Gas Act. William Dougherty, representing four interstates, noted that a "lag in the construction of new facilities in the new areas" was because the FPC had not decided "the rate of return and other types of regulatory procedure." He added, "The first rate proceeding that was initiated was initiated in July 1938 and is not yet completed."[269]

The status of wellhead sales in interstate commerce was another major area of regulatory uncertainty. The first shot under the NGA concerned affiliate gas-acquisition costs between an interstate and its production subsidiary where interstate carriage was performed. Between 1940 and mid-1945, over $100 million in annual rate reductions was ordered.[270] Faced with calculating the allowable price on discovery cost instead of market value, many pipelines were forced to practically give their gas away.[271] The logical response was to not develop gas reserves and, where possible, to sell reserves to independents to receive full market value. In 1945, interstate carriers provided 35 percent of their own throughput; seven years later this dropped to 15 percent with the remainder purchased at arm's length.[272] This not only transferred market share to producers but discouraged a fertile source of reserve additions.

Later in the 1940s, a justifiable fear developed that FPC regulation would extend to independent producers by virtue of their sales contracts with interstate carriers. This encouraged intrastate sales in lieu of interstate agreements, withholding of supply from the market,

[269]*Natural Gas Act Amendments*, p. 34. Part of the slowdown was due to coal- or fuel-hauling railroads' refusing to grant right-of-way to pipelines entering new markets. See ibid., pp. 52–58.

[270]Marjorie Clark, "Protection of the Consumer under the Natural Gas Act—Refunds and Reparations," *George Washington Law Review* (December 1945): 271.

[271]See the concurring opinion of Justice Jackson, *Colorado Interstate Gas Co. et al. v. FPC*, 324 U.S. 610 at 611 (1945); and *Business Week*, September 6, 1952, p. 156.

[272]Robert Hardwicke, "Some Consequences of Fears by Independent Producers of Gas of Federal Regulation," *Law and Contemporary Problems* 19 (1954): 354–55.

and "escape-clause" contracts to void agreements should jurisdiction be claimed by the FPC.[273] Production incentive was dampened for independents as it already had been for pipeline affiliates. Flaring and other gas-conservation problems were encouraged. The regional advantage of gas-producing areas over gas-importing regions, now dependent on higher priced coal and fuel oil, was artificially enhanced.[274]

The low-price policies of the FPC, valuing reserves at depreciated cost, had adverse consequences for consumers and would-be consumers of gas. In the winter of 1946–47, a gas shortage occurred as demand outraced the capacity of Panhandle Eastern's pipeline to serve Detroit and other Michigan markets.[275] Although commonly interpreted as a war-related problem of rationed steel's preventing an expansion of the line, the problem was regulatory. Gas prices were prevented from rising to ration demand to available supply. In other words, depreciated-cost valuation failed to reproduce a market-clearing price that local distributors could pass along with their markup to consumers during peak demand periods. Material-acquisition problems may have limited pipeline capacity more than otherwise would have been the case, but price inflexibility made capacity short of demand.

The less obvious result of regulation in the 1940s and early 1950s was service delays to waiting-list areas. Although demand was present, long-term supply contracts, necessary to get pipelines from the drawing board to reality, discouraged by regulation or the threat thereof, were not. While serviced consumers gained by lower prices, would-be consumers were left with higher fuel-oil and coal bills— and when later connected, higher contract prices.[276] And to the extent

[273]Ibid., p. 355. See chapter 8, pp. 371, 385, 390–91.

[274]Robert Hardwicke, "Some Consequences of Fears by Independent Producers of Gas of Federal Regulation," pp. 356–59. The conservation distortion was a hotly debated point in Congress. See Kenneth Marcus, *The National Government and the Natural Gas Industry*, pp. 303, 305, 518.

[275]*OGJ*, December 21, 1946, p. 39; and Carl Wheat, "Administration by the Federal Power Commission of the Certificate Provisions of the Natural Gas Act." This was the third major instance of a natural gas shortage in the United States. In the winters of 1916–17 and 1917–18, West Virginia suffered industrial and civic shutdowns as a result of below-market pricing by the state's public-utility commission.

[276]Distributor regulation at the state level also played a major part in delaying expansion of gas service to eager markets. H. J. O'Leary cites one vivid example: "The introduction of natural gas in Wisconsin was delayed from 1941 to 1949. The Wisconsin legislature, which yielded to the opposition of coal, railroad and labor

that future supply was discouraged by artificially low interstate gas prices as a result of regulatory uncertainty, even short-run beneficiaries would pay for their bargain prices in higher renewal rates.

The growth of natural-gas pipelines in the late 1940s and early 1950s was both because of and in spite of regulation. A *Business Week* article in 1950 reported that between 1945 and 1950, ten major firms had raised $1.5 billion from "a relatively predictable future"— stable gas-acquisition costs, FPC-sanctioned 6 percent returns, certification barriers to new entrants, and strong demand.[277] Public-utility protection reinforced fundamental economics in this heyday. But less than two years later, the same magazine reported that the industry's phenomenal growth was threatened by regulation. Gas-acquisition prices had doubled as a result of declining affiliate production, reluctance of independents to sell new discoveries interstate, and FPC inaction on proposed rate hikes that tracked higher gas-acquisition costs.[278] The result was below-market pricing at the city gate, which led to the reappearance of spot shortages in the 1951–53 period. Although tremendous expansion was taking place, regulatory lag and other distortions from FPC intervention gathered strength as a counteracting force. Growth would continue but at a markedly slower rate than in the 1946–51 golden years when regulation helped more than hurt pipelines.[279]

In 1954, the discriminatory treatment of pipeline production was ended, and the independents' fear of contracting interstate was vindicated by comprehensive regulation of natural-gas field prices pursuant to the *Phillips* decision.[280] Numerous escape clauses were activated, and notices of withdrawn gas dedications were given by

---

interests, contributed to the delay by passing repressive legislation and excessive taxes applicable to natural gas service. . . . In the interval between 1941 and 1950 the buyer's market for natural gas was replaced by a seller's market. . . . The delay in securing gas cost Wisconsin distributors at least 30 to 50 percent more for gas at the city gate." O'Leary, "Distribution and Utilization of Natural Gas," *American Economic Review* (May 1953): 546.

[277]*Business Week,* November 25, 1950, pp. 96–98.

[278]*Business Week,* September 6, 1952, pp. 152–57.

[279]Between 1946 and 1950, $1.4 billion was raised for pipeline expansion. Despite inflation, only $2 billion in financing was raised between 1951 and 1961. Richard Rosan, "Post–World War II Growth of Gas Industry," in American Gas Association, *Regulation of the Gas Industry,* vol. 1, p. 3-14.

[280]See chapter 8, pp. 376–79.

interstate pipelines to their customers. Quick FPC action, however, later upheld by the courts, voided such clauses.[281]

Despite regulatory "certainty," problems had just begun. With interstate gas regulated and intrastate gas unregulated, interstate pipelines found twenty-year supply dedications scarce. It would be more than two years after *Phillips* before a major interstate project was announced, and the 574-mile pipeline from the Texas Gulf Coast to Miami, Florida, was finalized only because of nonregulated gas sales from producers to industrials. (This unregulated area became regulated in 1962.) The pipeline received a straight carriage fee for its services.[282] At about the same time, a second chilling blow to pipeline expansion occurred. In late 1957, a U.S. court of appeals ruled that cost pass-throughs by transmission companies did not have to be automatically allowed by the FPC, a ruling that shelved four major projects. The Supreme Court reversed in the *Memphis* decision, ending a one-year pipeline-construction moratorium.[283]

The record of major interstate-pipeline construction from the post-World War II boom until the slowdown in the late 1950s is shown in table 15.2.

Twilight and Crisis: 1960–80

The slowdown of the 1950s became a quagmire in the 1960s. The mature industry—consumers in all lower forty-eight states had gas service by 1966—was a major factor but not the only one.[284] Interstate price regulation began to transfer natural-gas growth to home-state markets to escape FPC jurisdiction. Interstate dedications became scarce as price controls became more stringent, beginning with President Kennedy's FPC appointments in the early 1960s. The 1960 *Sunray* decision, which perpetually dedicated gas reserves, was another reason for gas to stay in home states.

Certification denials joined wellhead policies to hinder the growth of interstate transmission. Attempts by pipelines to bypass regulation by entering into contracts to directly supply industrials and

---

[281]See this chapter, p. 885. Nonetheless, escape clauses were allowed where official certification had not been awarded, which doomed several planned projects.

[282]*Time*, January 14, 1957, p. 88.

[283]*Business Week*, December 13, 1958, p. 29.

[284]Arlon Tussing and Connie Barlow, *The Natural Gas Industry*, p. 55.

Table 15.2
INTERSTATE PIPELINE CONSTRUCTION: 1939–59

Date of Completion	Company	From–To	Miles	Diameter (inches)
1944	Tennessee	Tex. Gulf–Cornwall, W.Va.	1,265	24
1947	El Paso	West Tex.–So. Calif.	1,200	26–30
1949	Mich.-Wisc.	North Tex.–Detroit	1,609	24
1950	Transco	Tex. Gulf–NYC	1,840	26–30
1951	El Paso–Pacific	N.M.–San Fran.	–	24–34
1951	Tennessee	Penn.–Mass.	520	–
1951	Natural	Tex. Gulf–Chicago	1,300	26–30
1951	Trunkline	La. Gulf–Ill.	1,300	24–26
1953	Tex. Eastern	N.J.-Boston	–	–
1954	Gulf	La. Gulf–W.Va.	1,150	30
1956	Mich.-Wisc.	La.–Mich.	1,200	30
1956	Pacific-N.W.	Calif.–Wash.	1,487	22–26
1959[a]	Houston Corp.	Tex. Gulf–Florida	1,931	24
1959	Tennessee	Tenn.–Chicago	350	30

SOURCE: Arlon Tussing and Connie Barlow, *The Natural Gas Industry*, pp. 35–36.
NOTE: No pipelines were constructed between 1939 and 1944. In 1945, the "Big Inch" and "Little Inch" pipelines were converted from petroleum to natural gas.
[a] In 1957 and 1958, three foreign pipelines with U.S. destinations were built.

Table 15.3
INTERSTATE PIPELINE CONSTRUCTION: 1960–70

Year of Completion	Company	From–To	Miles	Diameter (inches)
1960	Tennessee	Minn.–Wisc.	504	24
1960	Transwestern	Tex.–Calif.	1,300	24–30
1961	Pacific Gas	Canada–Calif.	1,400	36
1967	Great Lakes	Minn.–Mich.	989	36

SOURCE: Arlon Tussing and Connie Barlow, *The Natural Gas Industry*, p. 37.
NOTE: No new pipelines were built in 1968–70.

electric-utility customers, including "most of the new interstate pipe-line proposals submitted in the early 1960s," were throttled.[285] Prominent casualties in the decade included projects to link Hugoton field gas to St. Louis industrials, Wyoming reserves to southern California, and a Tennessee Gas proposal to ship gas from Texas fields to Los Angeles utilities.

Activist regulation at the wellhead and transmission level resulted in only four major interstate projects in the 1960s compared to over a dozen the decade before. They are listed in table 15.3.

The 1970s would be an infamous decade for the natural-gas industry. In the 1970–71 winter season, curtailments by major pipelines began that continued the next year and returned in the 1974–75 and 1975–76 heating seasons. New pipeline construction was beyond contemplation; the question was, who would be curtailed and by how much. The scramble to find interstate dedications led to administrative actions to encourage producers and culminated in the Natural Gas Policy Act of 1978.[286] At the end of the decade, pipeline executives worked feverishly to contract for reserves to meet what seemed to be insatiable demand at any price. Supply proved adequate at the regulated price for the next several heating seasons, and by 1981, a new reality dawned—surplus or gas "bubble." The challenges to and responses of interstate pipelines—and the demoted role of regulation—are examined in appendix 15.1.

Public Utility Regulation Reconsidered

The Case for Regulation. Compared to interstate oil pipelines, which were subject to a weak form of public-utility regulation, interstate

[285]Ibid., p. 56. The Tennessee denial is discussed below.
[286]See chapter 8, pp. 423–30.

gas lines were under traditional public-utility control with original-cost ratemaking and entry and service subject to close administrative scrutiny. Such heavy-handed regulation was the result of a perception that pipelines are natural monopolies and create market failures. Economist James McKie made this argument:

> Competition will not work in the pipeline transmission of natural gas. The average throughput costs of pipelines tend to decrease with size to such an extent that there is seldom economic room for more than one pipeline to serve any point of consumption. Even the very largest consuming markets can be served by only two or three, and each of these two or three may pass through areas en route where it is the only supplier. . . . [Pipelines] cannot engage in price competition in the sale of gas. Direct costs are very low in relation to overhead costs. Price competition would amount to chronic price warfare. Furthermore, now that the pioneering stage of the industry is over, pipelines cannot determine that allocation of markets and routes among themselves by private decision and competitive bidding. Orderly development of the industry requires that the public authority do these things by franchise. In short, pipelines are public utilities.[287]

McKie's argument can be distilled into four components:

1. Gas pipelines are natural monopolies with a firm's range of decreasing cost covering the entire range of consumption;
2. Even where more than one firm serves a market, monopoly prevails from locational control (singular hookups);
3. High fixed costs and low variable costs make price wars—hence instability—"chronic"; and
4. Market-share decisions by pipeline firms cannot be rationally determined in the industry's mature stage.

Natural-gas users with alternate-fuel capability in a free market would face monopoly prices set at levels competitive with those of the inferior substitutes coal and fuel oil. Captive users would pay more—literally what the utility desired. Worse still, as occurred prior to regulation in the last century, gas users would be inconvenienced by inadequate service caused by disruptive rivalry. Enlightened regulation would correct these shortcomings. The competitive

---

[287]James McKie, *The Regulation of Natural Gas* (Washington, D.C.: American Enterprise Association, 1957), p. 15.

regulated price would replace the free-market monopolistic price by the rate-base method, and service regulation would ensure non-discriminatory service for the entire market and a minimum level of service from a strong, franchised industry.

The Case for Regulation Reconsidered. The case against regulation—which has scarcely attracted the same attention as the case for regulation—is developed at length in this section. The major arguments center on competition in the gas-pipeline industry, the protection of captive gas users at the distribution-company level, the problems of public-utility ratemaking, and the political problems of the regulatory solution.

A peculiarity of the public-utility argument is that free-market competition is criticized as too little (the "natural monopoly" argument) and too much (the "cutthroat competition" argument). A more balanced view is that free-market competition is neither insufficient nor overstimulated but continually *resource-adjusting* toward a consumer-dictated level of service. Competitive conditions are continually defined, which outside of this entrepreneurial discovery process cannot be known or implemented. When entry is needed (i.e., when profitable opportunities exist), entry takes place—despite the wishes of the entrenched supplier, which explains the origin of state franchise and federal certification law. When multiple entrants are suffering losses, consolidation efficiently redeploys resources. These are socially positive responses to unstable, unsustainable situations and are "equilibrating" toward efficient resource allocation.

The competitive process with high-fixed-cost assets such as gas pipelines is not perpetual chaos. Instability is not desired for its own sake. Potential competition "regulates" the existing firm or firms to discourage overpricing that leads to new entry. Long periods of stability as the result of competitive pricing can be imagined. Government intervention in the last century *prevented* the process from reaching this point—at the request of entrenched firms—but the free market cannot be blamed for leaving the job half done or undone.

Competition is omnipresent for interstate gas carriers in an unregulated market. There is potential competition, competition from substitutes, and, in many cases, pipeline-on-pipeline rivalry.

Potential competition is the possibility that a new pipeline will enter an occupied market to capture a growth load or attempt to replace the existing firm on the strength of executed contracts. The physical construction of a new pipeline or a purchase of existing facilities represents a new firm's displacing the traditional supplier or suppliers. It is to the consumers' advantage to allow timely entry and pipeline-on-pipeline competition that regulation can only discourage. Certification notwithstanding, the historical firm's market share is not set in concrete. Strong competitive pressure exists for firms in place to watch costs and profit so that the outside market does not view their pricing as uncompetitive and inviting of entry.[288] In short, potential entry makes firms compete as if a competitor already existed.

A traditional argument for price regulation is that a particular pipeline market is not "workably competitive." Thus, unregulated pricing would be above marginal cost and monopolistic. A major flaw of this argument is that the disincentive of regulated pricing will keep the market from being "workably competitive," whereas pure profits would incite new entry to make the market "workably competitive" or at least more so. Second, extraordinary profits are necessary for some markets to be served at all. It is much better that consumers—even captive users—have the choice of natural gas at unregulated prices than be left with phantom gas service at a "competitive" rate. One firm created by market conditions is wholly preferable to no firms created by regulatory conditions.

Substitute competition is a second competitive force bearing on interstate gas pipelines. Economist Charles Phillips noticed several decades ago that "the gas industry is subject to strong actual and potential competition from electricity, coal steam, and fuel oil."[289] This statement can be amended by adding nuclear power, hydroelectricity, and purchased power as rivals to gas in electric-power generation. In fact, natural gas has gone from a day-in, day-out *base-load* source in electric generation to a *swing* source in most markets, satisfying the last increment of demand.

[288]This is not to say that natural-gas pipeline markets are "perfectly contestable" where "entry is absolutely free and exit is absolutely costless." William Baumol, "Contestable Markets: An Uprising in the Theory of Industry Structure," *American Economic Review* (March 1982): 2. A useful criticism of this theory, centered on such unrealistic assumptions, is provided in William Shepherd, " 'Contestability' vs. Competition," *American Economic Review* (September 1984): 575–79.

[289]Charles Phillips, *The Economics of Regulation* (Homewood, Ill.: Richard Irwin, 1965), p. 362. Also see George Stigler and Claire Friedland, "What Can Regulators Regulate? The Case of Electricity," *Journal of Law and Economics* (October 1962): 11.

Since gas power plants and industrial boilers typically burn oil also, prices of residual fuel oil represent the upper boundary for gas prices, net of conversion costs. These alternatives, including conservation, make gas demand price sensitive. How much total revenue changes from price increases is an empirical question that varies from market to market and time to time, but recent experience indicates that gas prices are price-elastic as a result of strong interfuel competition and conservation.[290]

Pipeline-on-pipeline competition in major markets further questions the natural monopoly description of interstate pipelines. As with oil pipelines, scale economies do not necessarily imply natural monopoly. Entrepreneurial error, a finite range of scale economies, and demand growth often make one pipeline inadequate to serve a particular market.[291] It is naive to think of a pipeline as "one size fits all" to preclude the need for entry. McKie, writing in 1957, characterized interfirm rivalry as the exception rather than the rule. By the 1960s, one informed observer noticed "a marked increase in competition among pipelines," whereby "most major market areas today [1970] have two or even three sources of gas supply."[292] Examples include the New York-New Jersey area, which has been supplied by Texas Eastern (1945), Transco (1950), and Tennessee Gas (1955); Chicago, which is served by Peoples (1931) and Midwestern (1959); Detroit, which is served by Panhandle Eastern (1936), Michigan-Wisconsin (1949), and Great Lakes (1957); Washington, D.C., which is serviced by Atlantic Seaboard (1931) and Transco (1967); southern California, which is served by El Paso (1947) and Transwestern (1960); northern California, which is served by El Paso (1947) and Pacific Gas Transmission (1961); and Upper Michigan, which is served by Michigan Consolidated (1933) and Michigan-Wisconsin (1949). Numerous interstate pipelines offer strong potential entry by line "looping" should a neighboring market be inadequately served by its existing "monopolist."

States with multiple interstate pipelines are Texas (13), Louisiana (10), Oklahoma (8), Kansas (8), Illinois (8), Ohio (8), Arkansas (7),

[290]See appendix 15.1, pp. 949–57, on the increased competition in interstate gas markets.

[291]This point applies equally to any "undersizing" argument applied to gas pipelines. For a critique of the undersizing argument with oil pipelines, see chapter 14, pp. 842–43.

[292]Carl Bagge, "The Federal Power Commission," pp. 690, 701.

Kentucky (7), Mississippi (7), Missouri (7), New York (7), Colorado (6), Pennsylvania (6), Tennessee (5), New Jersey (5), Indiana (5), Alabama (5), New Mexico (4), Nebraska (4), Wyoming (4), Iowa (3), Maryland (3), Michigan (3), Virginia (3), West Virginia (3), Connecticut (2), Georgia (2), Massachusetts (2), Minnesota (2), Montana (2), South Carolina (2), Rhode Island (2), and Wisconsin (2).[293] Intrastate pipelines in gas-producing states offer more competition.

Multifirm competition aside, monopoly is claimed to be the rule rather than the exception because individual areas within broader markets have only one supplier. This is a tenuous theory of monopoly. All providers of goods and services have a geographical monopoly to one extent or another, which reduces to the truism, as noted by economist Murray Rothbard, that "only one thing can be in one place at one time."[294] Locational advantage, like price and service quality, is an integral aspect of real-world rivalry; only in the hypothetical world of perfect competition do consumers have infinite locational-nonspecific choices before them.

Defranchising gas distributors and decertifying pipelines would open the field to reveal true competitive conditions, but most certainly it would remain uneconomical for different suppliers to offer service to each consumer. As in many areas of the Midwest, one pipeline and one distributor may be the sole alternative to other fuels, but this "monopolistic" situation, unchecked by regulation, does not make consumers worse off because of the high-cost implications of the "competitive" solution. Dual pipelines in such situations would require prohibitive demand charges—certainly anti-consumer—and are noneconomic from the word go. Efficiency, in short, requires singular service. But far from justifying regulated pricing, such situations invite self-help solutions to integrate the consumers' bargain into the pricing equation as seen below.

---

[293]States with one interstate transmission company are California, Arizona, Idaho, Florida, New Hampshire, North Carolina, North Dakota, Oregon, South Dakota, and Washington; states without interstate natural-gas service are Alaska, Delaware, Hawaii, Maine, Nevada, and Vermont. *Implementation of Title I of The Natural Gas Policy Act of 1978,* Hearings before the Senate Committee on Energy and Natural Resources, 97th Cong., 1st sess. (Washington, D.C.: Government Printing Office, 1982), pp. 1107–11.

[294]Murray Rothbard, *Man, Economy, and State* (Los Angeles: Noah Publishing, 1970), p. 615. For a critique of locational monopoly price, see pp. 615–19.

While residential and commercial users of gas for space heating, water heating, cooking, and clothes drying do not have dual-fuel capability that sets an upper limit on price, this does not mean that they are at the whim of their local distribution company. Self-help and market processes can effectively substitute for public-utility ratemaking, not because the free-market alternative is perfect but because the regulatory solution, as argued later in this section, is relatively imperfect.

New residences and business establishments have energy alternates at the outset, although they become captive once the initial decision is made. New users choose between gas and electricity, and, in some cases, oil and coal. These choices in a nonregulatory environment invite long-term contracting to lock in acceptable rates and service terms. Failure to do so is not so much a market failure as buyer imprudence.

For existing captive users, contracting is also viable. Under regulation, the distributor has been able to offer its cost-plus rate as a "take it or leave it" proposition to customers in its franchise area. The only recourse for residential and other customer classes is political lobbying before state public-utility commissions. This would change in a free-market setting. On the one hand, the utility could offer an unregulated "take it or leave it" rate. If this default rate were unacceptable, an entrepreneurial opportunity would be created for consumers to organize to collectively bargain with the distribution company. In the jargon of economists, "monopoly" would be countervailed by "monopsony." An advantage of this approach for both parties is that regulatory costs are eliminated—leaving private contracting costs that presumably would be much less.

A contractual impasse could lead to new ownership of the gas firm or even customer ownership (the free-market equivalent of municipal ownership). Consumers could also fan public opinion to achieve a competitive solution. But there would be no public-utility commission or legislature to which to resort.

With newfound market discipline of gas distribution, hitherto absent, cost minimization would be exerted upstream to pipelines, intrastate and interstate, and producers.[295] The Natural Gas Act would no longer be needed, even from its proponents' perspective.

[295]Deregulation could lead to the integration—or reintegration—of the three industry phases for major companies, much as is the case in the oil industry.

Captive users have an *elasticity of demand* that sets an upper bound on prices. Budget-constrained consumers *conserve,* which is one way of saying that there is a tradeoff between price and quantity demanded. The profit-maximizing utility will rescind any price increase that reduces total revenue because of lost sales. Citing the nearly 20 percent drop in residential gas sales in the last decade as a result of increasing gas rates and other factors, Arlon Tussing and Connie Barlow concluded:

> The *price-elasticity of demand* is a far more formidable hazard because it begins to cut deeply into sales volume at gas prices well below those of competing fuels. . . . Residential customers turn down thermostats, stop heating unused rooms, and cover windows with plastic. And a gas-price rise which is expected to be permanent (even if gas prices are still well below those of alternative fuels), will prompt consumers to substitute capital for energy.[296]

"In a broad sense," Eli Clemens states, "the objective of public utility rate regulation is to achieve through regulation the same result that would be achieved through competition."[297] The "just and reasonable" price is derived by passing through prudent costs and limiting profit to depreciated cost multiplied by a "normal" return. The key is to limit profit; costs directly associated with providing the service are more or less given.

This seemingly straightforward methodology of rate determination proves problematic upon deeper reflection. First, there is no objective "just or reasonable" price or even a "zone of reasonableness." What is just and reasonable to one person or for one project may not be to another person or project. Consumers want low prices and suppliers desire high prices. Some consumers prefer higher prices and secure supply to lower prices and less certain supply. (Curtailments, even to high-priority users, made this choice very real in the 1970s.) High-risk projects require the potential for quick payouts, necessitating prices well above cost. A single "public-interest" price, even different prices tailored for each customer class, does not exist because preference and risk are heterogeneous.

---

[296] Arlon Tussing and Connie Barlow, "The Price Elasticity of Residential Gas Demand," *ARTA Energy Insights* (December 1983): 4–5.

[297] Eli Clemens, *Economics and Public Utilities* (New York: Appleton-Century-Crofts, 1950), p. 153.

The argument that "just and reasonable" is euphemistic for the "competitive" price is no escape. Competitive prices cannot be synthetically produced under regulated conditions as they can be in theory under simplifying assumptions (marginal-cost pricing). Only the market can reveal competitive conditions.[298]

A false presumption of public-utility regulation is that costs can be minimized, capital value can be measured, the right return can be calculated, and the "scientific findings" can be implemented in the political arena without suboptimal modification. These shortcomings are analyzed below.

Cost-of-Service Pass-Throughs. Profits are not added to a "given" cost in market situations but come out of cost as entrepreneurs succeed in reducing expense without impairing revenue. Under public-utility regulation, the situation is quite different. Costs are passed through, with minor exceptions, and a profit allowable is added. So long as a pipeline's rates can be increased without a loss of total revenue, a range of costs can be loosely managed without financial detriment to the firm. Wages, salaries, benefits, and rental and maintenance expenses are prime candidates; they are rarely scrutinized by authorities.[299] Other cost items must be arbitrarily dealt with by authorities who are placed in the position of substituting their judgment for the economic calculations of management—something the courts have limited the regulators' jurisdiction to do. What types of advertising, charity, and research expenses should be allowed, and how much? Particularly difficult is deciding what research and development expenses to allow—expenditures that may or may not benefit consumers in the future but must be paid by present ratepayers.

---

[298]Two major suggestions for regulatory pricing in place of "imperfect" market pricing, setting prices at marginal cost and according to the elasticity of demand, are defective substitutes. Marginal-cost pricing falsely assumes that cost is objective and discernable for implementation. It also begs the question of cost minimization. Marginal costs, not only average costs, can be artificially inflated without market incentives to maximize profits. Elasticity pricing (Ramsey pricing), on the other hand, assumes perfect knowledge for perfect market segmentation and lacks incentive for cost minimization. Only the lure of pure profit can ensure that a minimum amount of resources is expended to maximize production elsewhere.

[299]This is not to say that flagrant padding always occurs, but without full market discipline, there is less pressure to separate lean from fat where *known* or even to *recognize the difference* in many instances.

The regulatory alternative is not a free good. Taxpayers fund commission activities and ratepayers fund reporting, compliance, and legal expenses associated with regulation. Lawyers particularly benefit. The multitude of legal issues surrounding certification, rate-case, and other filings creates a voluminous demand for their services, the fees for which are passed through to consumers.

Problem of Regulatory Return Determination. Profit is derived from multiplying the depreciated cost of a firm's assets by a rate of return. The determination of the rate base, the maximum return rate, and the composite profit pool is arbitrary in method and distortive in practice.

Regarding the determination of the *rate base,* historical cost gives an imperfect estimate of the worth of a firm. Only in equilibrium are the two equal; outside of equilibrium, error and changed circumstances can make cost much lower or higher than value. Original cost is particularly prone to error during inflationary times when market value can race ahead of dollar cost. Value is not cost, historical or reproduction, but the subjective estimations of buyers and sellers as best reflected in the stock market.

In addition to incorrectly valuing the firm, the cost-plus ratemaking method does not incite cost minimization but the opposite. The incentive is to enlarge the rate base to increase the profit pool or at least counteract the "vanishing-rate-base" phenomenon created by depreciation.[300] There are many subtle ways a firm can do this—from buying an extra airplane to erecting a prestigious skyscraper for the home office. Whether or not such "discretionary" expenditures are needed cannot be proven or disproven a priori; it is something only economic calculation under free-market conditions can reveal.

Artificially maintaining and even "padding" the rate base are an institution in the interstate natural-gas industry (as elsewhere under public-utility regulation). Those practices are much less common for intrastate gas pipelines in such states as Texas where public-utility regulation has been light-handed or has not been applied. An example of artificially maintaining the rate base occurred in 1980 when Algeria ceased shipping liquefied natural gas (LNG) to a consortium

---

[300]This is particularly true when original-cost valuation during inflationary times shrinks the rate base to levels below the firm's achievable profit level.

of interstate purchasers. Rather than run the remaining LNG inventory through the regasification facility and close the plant after several days to minimize operating costs, El Paso, Columbia, and other partners ran LNG at minimum rates for eight months to maintain the projects' rate-base valuation.

The disastrous supplemental gas projects of the 1970s resulted not only from overly optimistic expectations during the energy boom but from *the fallback of rate-base treatment.* The rate base served as a safety net to allow marginal projects to contribute to a firm's income as much as stellar assets. LNG projects were at the forefront. A proposed LNG plant in California was shelved in 1982 with the majority of $400 million in preconstruction expenses put in the rate base for recovery (with a return) from utility customers.[301] This paled in comparison to an El Paso LNG project with Algeria's Sonatrach. With the help of a $400-million tanker loan guarantee under the Merchant Marine Act and a minimum bill tariff (minimum purchase requirement) to pass through costs, the regasification terminal began deliveries in 1978. With world prices escalating, the sovereign Sonatrach demanded and received a new contract in May 1978. A second renegotiation in December of the same year was nixed by the Department of Energy, and in April 1980, deliveries were terminated. The plant and tankers, lacking alternative uses, were almost complete losses, which forced El Paso to write off $365 million in associated investments. The federal government (taxpayers) had to retire its $400-million obligation. Private losses have gone into the rate bases for recovery, although court disputes, not to mention effective rate ceilings imposed by substitute-fuel competition, make full recovery in interstate gas rates unlikely.[302]

A third LNG venture of Panhandle Eastern, representing over $600 million in plant and tanker investments, weathered a renegotiation storm with Sonatrach, although the high price of liquefied gas boded ill for the project.[303]

A coal-to-gas project turned into an even bigger boondoggle than the aforementioned LNG projects. In the 1970s, many pipelines dedicated research and development funds to high-B thermal unit coal-gasification projects with rate-base pass-through. Several major projects were abandoned prior to construction—a $1.3-billion project

[301]Arlon Tussing and Connie Barlow, *The Natural Gas Industry*, p. 66.

[302]Ibid., pp. 65–69. Also see chapter 16 p. 1007.

[303]Arlon Tussing and Connie Barlow, *The Natural Gas Industry*, pp. 70–71.

of Texas Eastern and Pacific Lighting and a $3.5-billion project of Panhandle Eastern. But one $2-billion project, the Great Plains Coal Gasification Project, bullish on energy prices and flush with government subsidies, went ahead in 1981. The economics of the project fell apart with the reversal of natural-gas prices in 1982, and numerous subsidies and concessions were made by authorities.[304]

The lesson of supplemental gas failures is illustrative of the shortcomings of public-utility regulation, which discourages entrepreneurial innovation and cost minimization, while promoting risky capital projects that can be "bailed out" by rate-base treatment once certified. The bottom line is that a firm's cost is higher under public-utility regulation than under free-market conditions where the lower the cost, the higher the profit. In fact, the difference between regulated gas-acquisition costs and market-clearing gas prices has represented "a huge pork-barrel out of which the pipelines and distribution companies could finance steady expansion and upgrading of their regular facilities (even in the face of stagnant sales), as well as new investments in schemes to supply gas from unconventional sources (imported LNG, synthetic fuels, and gas from the Arctic) at costs many times the price of conventional suppliers."[305] These examples are consistent with the Averch-Johnson thesis: "If the rate of return allowed by the regulatory agency is greater than the cost of capital but is less than the rate of return that would be enjoyed by the firm were it free to maximize profit without regulatory constraint, then the firm will substitute capital for the other factors of production and operate at an output where cost is not minimized."[306]

---

[304]See chapter 10, pp. 580–83.

[305]Arlon Tussing, "Permanent Devolution: The Agonies of Half-Hearted Decontrol in the Natural-Gas Industry," American Enterprise Institute, Washington, D.C., 1984, p. 3.

[306]Harvey Averch and Leland Johnson, "Behavior of the Firm under Regulatory Constraint," *American Economic Review* (December 1962): 1053. Paul Joskow has questioned the Averch-Johnson thesis by claiming that to authorities, price changes are as important as, or more important than, rates of return. Consequently, firms will minimize costs to increase returns at a given price and will minimize costs to avoid a rate hearing to increase prices. Joskow, "Inflation and Environmental Concern: Structural Changes in the Process of Public Utility Price Regulation," *Journal of Law and Economics* (October 1974): 291–327. This point has some validity, but it is relatively minor compared to the virtually automatic rate increases approved by the FPC and FERC over nearly fifty years.

Original-cost valuation impedes asset transfers between pipeline firms because the assets remain at original cost in the rate base.[307] Prospective owners are limited to returns based on original depreciated cost and face the specter of the vanishing rate base. This discourages asset reallocations to entrepreneurs better able to employ them. Yardstick *rate-of-return* assignments treat entrepreneurship as a nonspecific talent. In the free market, entrepreneurs of varying ability perceive different opportunities and implement alternatives to perform regular tasks. Different profit-loss margins result and change with new developments. Public-utility standardization of profit treats every pipeline project as if it were equally desired by the market and equally managed by entrepreneurs. True profit-loss signals that alert the market that changes are needed are falsified. Many pipeline companies integrated into oil and gas production in the 1950s to receive unregulated returns.[308] In the next decades, these firms increasingly turned to nonenergy ventures with mixed results. In any case, public-utility regulation influenced firms to leave their primary areas and venture into fields in which their expertise was less.

A basic argument against standardized returns is the absence of an average or normal rate of return. Each project is unique. Profits from other industries or even fellow pipeline projects used to derive a common return reflect influences that are foreign to the project in question. Entrepreneurial talent and business situations are not accurately "priced" under public-utility regulation, which scrambles the signals that are used for economic calculation.[309]

Profit limitations on interstate gas carriers have a subtle consequence that dilutes the regulatory aim of limiting profit to limit price. Without large profits, and having a need to pay out a major portion of allowed margins as dividends to stockholders, pipelines have depended heavily on debt finance instead of retained earnings

---

[307]Walter Gallagher, "Rate of Return," pp. 30-92 to 30-94.

[308]*Business Week*, November 5, 1955, p. 120.

[309]One return methodology, the cost-of-money approach, has been blatantly criticized as "remov[ing] all incentive for obtaining cheap money and for efficient operation." Charles Francis, "Rate Regulation of Natural Gas Companies by the Federal Power Commission," *Law and Contemporary Problems* 19 (1954): 432. Also see Charles Francis, "Federal Regulation of Interstate Shipment and Sale of Gas," 4 *Institute of Oil and Gas Law* (New York: Matthew Bender. 1953), pp. 121–22.

to finance expansion. This has increased those firms' obligations, which have increased risk compared to less leveraged firms. This has forced the commission to allow higher profits—and higher rates for consumers—to compensate investors.[310]

Problems of Implementation: Bureaucratic Management, Politics, and Inefficiency. Pipeline regulation from beginning to end is political. It is born of a political mandate, is overseen by politically appointed commissioners of widely varying qualifications,[311] and is judicially reviewed by more political appointees. Politics, not the maximization conditions of neoclassical economics, controls the issue. This obvious fact would not need to be presented if many economists favoring regulation were not silent on the issue. Not only do they believe competitive conditions can be discovered by nonmarket means, an economic fallacy, it is assumed that they can be implemented without political modification. The experience with pipeline certification, as with other regulated goods and services, confirms this view as naive.

Inefficiency has hallmarked FPC activity with natural-gas pipelines. In the early 1950s, regulatory lag interfered with rate increases required to neutralize higher costs. This reduced profit margins and threatened continued expansion. The industry also complained about vague standards for rate determination and other important matters. Pleaded one lawyer in 1954:

> The least to which the natural gas industry is entitled after spending thousands of dollars, and days, weeks, and even months in the preparation of testimony . . . is that the Commission indicate where and to what extent it agrees or disagrees with that presentation. . . . The fact appears to be that the Commission either has been unwilling to clarify its position, or unable to do so because it has arrived at no final determination.[312]

The *Public Utilities Fortnightly* in the same year similarly observed:

> The [FPC] Staff also seems to have shown some propensity for "changing the rules" as each new case came up. . . . The Staff's

---

[310]Walter Gallagher, "Rate of Return," pp. 30-54 to 30-58.

[311]Monrad Wallgren, for example, a Truman crony, was a jeweler, optometrist, congressman, senator, and governor of Washington before becoming an FPC member from 1949 to 1951. *OGJ*, October 26, 1949, p. 23. A chart of commissioners and their previous occupations is contained in M. Elizabeth Sanders, *The Regulation of Natural Gas*, pp. 74–75.

[312]Charles Francis, "Rate Regulation of Natural Gas Companies by the Federal Power Commission," p. 431.

thinking . . . appears not to have "jelled" completely, with resulting variations which involve extra time and effort in the preparation of cases and considerable guesswork as to the final results of the orders.[313]

The situation worsened with wellhead regulation beginning in 1954 and has remained a problem to the present. Commenting on the 1950–69 period, one attorney remarked:

> The single most pervasive problem of FPC regulation since 1950 has been delay in the resolution of pending proceedings. . . . While the FPC has attempted from time to time to reform its procedures so as to expedite the regulatory process . . . delay and resulting uncertainty was characteristic.[314]

Not only the attorneys involved have noticed a lack of clarity about permitted industry practices and inconsistent reasoning in FPC decisions. In a spot check involving approximately 350 cases, totaling over a thousand pages, economist Paul MacAvoy complained that he was unable either to find substantive content or to decipher trends in the commission's 1969 caseload.[315]

Red tape has become a way of life for the regulated industry. Certification delays associated with the Alaska gas pipeline during the worst natural-gas shortage in history are eloquent testimony to the shortcomings of political decisionmaking. In an overview of pipeline ratemaking procedures, Francis Quinn and Cheryl Foley advised companies to expect as much as several years between the time a rate proposal is submitted to the FERC and the time it becomes effective. This period involves not only commission inactivity but court review as well.[316] The obvious consequence is the inability of

---

[313]*Public Utilities Fortnightly,* January 21, 1954, pp. 108–9.

[314]Richard Rosan, "Post–World War II Growth of Gas Industry," p. 3-38.

[315]"This review can only apply the burden of proof on the authors of the volume to show that there is some content in these cases—that a decision was made on an issue based on consistent reasoning, and that the decision had some economic effect on those involved or, later, on those carrying on the same activities." Paul MacAvoy, "The Formal Work-Product of the Federal Power Commissioners," *Bell Journal of Economics* (Spring 1971): 394.

[316]Francis Quinn and Cheryl Foley, "Procedures in Pipeline Ratemaking," in American Gas Association, *Regulation of the Gas Industry,* p. 36-6. Former FERC general counsel Charles Moore estimated that at any one time 16,000 or more dockets concerning production and transmission matters are before the FERC. *Houston Post,* September 14, 1983, p. 80.

firms and consumers to make informed decisions. Quick exploitation of recognized opportunities by entrepreneurs is prevented, while the hearings process bares all competitive secrets of a firm. Proposed rates can take effect after a suspension, but refunds can be ordered if a final decision does not allow any or all of the increase. In the meantime, economic calculation by the market participants borders on a sham. Do consumers conserve or substitute? Should the pipeline expand its facilities or earmark disputed revenue for other uses? The price system under the cloud of rate suspensions or refunds is not its reliable self.

Government certification of new projects and service modifications radically restricts the ability of entrepreneurs to effectively marshall resources in accordance with consumer preference. In its 1940 annual report, the FPC referred to the certification process as a "serious effort to control the unplanned construction of natural-gas pipelines with a view to conserving one of the country's valuable but exhaustible resources."[317] This view reflects the erroneous belief that bureaucrats in the political arena have better knowledge of the present and future state of consumer demand than do entrepreneurs working through capital markets. But whose money is on the line, and does not profit-loss reward business acumen and correct bad business judgment? That normally reliable entrepreneurs and investors, who supply thousands of goods and services in the economy, lose their bearings with pipe and vapor fuel is counterintuitive. The intrastate market, where pipelines have been much less regulated, can hardly be described as unplanned or chaotic. It has thrived and has avoided the rate-base boondoggles and shortages that have plagued the interstate market.

Insights about the efficiency of economic calculation in a free market apply to all economic objects, gas pipelines included. The hazards of government-as-entrepreneur, in contrast, are evident with pipelines as with other goods and services. The *Transwestern* case, in which a pipeline expansion was refused certification because forthcoming nuclear power was predicted to preempt its need, is a reminder of imperfect governmental decisionmaking.[318]

---

[317]Federal Power Commission, *Twentieth Annual Report* (Washington, D.C.: Government Printing Office, 1940), p. 78. Also see James McKie's argument in this chapter, pp. 921–92.

[318]See this chapter, p. 898.

Certification has meant many things to many people. To established interstate pipelines it was potentially a ticket to stability; to regulators it represented a significant expansion of authority; to rival fuels it was a new lease on life to avoid—or at least delay—displacement; and to consumer advocates it was the "price" of public-utility regulation that promised lower prices. The result of certification was to politicize entrepreneurial decisionmaking and slow the competitive process. As early as 1942, potential entrants in the interstate gas pipeline business were warned by attorney Carl Wheat:

> Careful preparation [of certification filings] seems . . . to be both desirable and essential, especially since objecting intervenors from the coal, railroad and labor interests have frequently appeared and participated in such proceedings. . . . Their presence and active participation in such proceedings have frequently served to prolong hearings to lengths unheard of in most certificate proceedings before other regulatory bodies.[319]

Coal-related and fuel-oil interests testified before the commission against certification applications until the 1960s when their influence waned. But "end-use" victories were won, and delays in many cases made the effort worthwhile. The entire "aggrieved-parties" effort was anti-consumer and a major cost of government regulation of entry.

Although regulation is potentially an instrument of monopoly—gas pipelines able to obtain certification to exclusively serve defined market areas—interfirm rivalry generally was allowed, reflecting the commission's preference for rivalry. But some applications were denied, and the burden of proof was always on the potential entrant, not on the historic firm. In all certification tussles, gas service to new consumers was delayed, which left them with more expensive energy substitutes. Two particular cases may be mentioned. Detroit, which regularly suffered winter gas shortages from an inability of Panhandle Eastern to handle peak demand, had to wait five years before the FPC (and the SEC regarding financing) awarded certification to the Michigan-Wisconsin Pipe Line Company.[320] In 1950, the "Battle of New England" between subsidiaries of Tennessee Gas

[319]Carl Wheat, "Administration of the Federal Power Commission of the Certificate Provisions of the Natural Gas Act," pp. 201–2.

[320]Newsweek, January 12, 1948, p. 63.

Transmission (TGT) and Texas Eastern Transmission (TET) and their respective chairmen, Gardiner Symonds and Reginald Hargrove, renewed a feud that had begun when TET narrowly outbid TGT for the lucrative Big Inch and Little Inch pipelines after World War II. TGT first applied to the FPC for certification to supply the entire New England market followed by TET. After several years of dispute, the FPC split the market between them. But the feud was not over. A vindictive Symonds obstructed completion of TET's line on legal technicalities to even the score.[321] A three-year delay caused by nonmarket elements was endured by consumers.

Other examples of the anti-consumer certification hearings could be chronicled. At one point the Justice Department entered the FPC's domain to file an antitrust suit against three companies who worked to keep a fourth company out of their territory through certification proceedings.[322] Although for naught, the action underscored the controversy involved in interstate-pipeline regulation designed to "protect" consumers.

Certification is a political contest between the "haves" and "have nots." Established fuel interests and established gas pipelines were given a forum in which to protect market share against new entrants. Consumers, especially those awaiting service, were victims of the "haves" along with potential entrants. In the free market, there has always been a role for new firms trying to compete their way into prominence. The certification process mitigated this process by substituting bureaucratic conservatism and politics for unfettered rivalry.

One noteworthy example of bureaucratic rigidity over competitive market flexibility may be mentioned. The FPC adopted a benchmark of twenty-year gas supply contracts to approve projects, while investors were inclined to finance projects with shorter throughput agreements.[323] To the detriment of waiting consumers, this precluded a number of pipeline projects that would have arisen on the free market. It is true that risk is higher with shorter supply contracts,

---

[321]Admitted Symonds: "They delayed us for two years . . . and made all the trouble they could. I'm just vindictive enough to want to do the same thing to them." *Time,* December 8, 1952, p. 96.

[322]*Business Week,* May 10, 1958, p. 29.

[323]Paul MacAvoy, "The Effectiveness of the Federal Power Commission," *Bell Journal of Economics* (Autumn 1970): 284.

but consumers could well prefer to save money in the interim and recontract for supply later. A new supply contract might be signed or another reserve-rich project might step into the breach if profitable. Long-term supply contracts with nonperformance penalties could easily cover the costs of reconversion in a worst-case situation. At least consumers could decide for themselves the merit of a pipeline, as did pipeline operators and investors; certification simply reduced the range of alternatives for all involved. Intrastate pipelines and their consumers have benefited without a supply-year minimum; only rarely has a carrier failed to honor supply commitments to distribution companies.[324]

Although clothed in public-interest garb, government regulation of entry, exit, and terms of service has been anti-competitive and anti-consumer. It has also been *anti-environmental*—natural-gas expansions have been delayed or blocked in favor of fuel oil and coal. These conclusions are not changed by the observation that certification has not been as restrictively employed as it could have been—and has been in other transportation fields under federal regulation, as seen in the next chapter.

Conclusion. Public-utility regulation constructs nonmarket retail and wholesale prices. If the resulting retail or wholesale prices are too low, the gas industry is weakened. Less pipeline expansion can be undertaken, exploration and production are discouraged, well abandonments increase, gas is wastefully used, and the specter of shortages is introduced.[325] If retail and wholesale rates are too high, consumer wealth is unnecessarily reduced and the industry is artificially stimulated. In both cases, price misinformation misaligns demand with the relative scarcity of gas versus alternative fuels.

---

[324]In Texas, for example, where reserve years are not a precondition for permits, only one pipeline in one period (Lo Vaca in 1973–75) encountered supply problems and broke contracts. Victimized customers successfully pursued legal remedies. Other prominent intrastates have delivered as agreed over many decades—Lone Star, Delhi, Enserch, El Paso, Tenneco, and Houston. It is self-interest that provides an adequate reserve base and a free-market environment that offers the reasonable opportunity to perform contractually.

[325]Natural gas shortages in the 1970s resulted not only from wellhead price controls but also from an inability of transmission companies to price incremental supplies at market-clearing rates at wholesale. For criticism of regulatory rate design at the pipeline and distributor level, see Richard Pierce, "Natural Gas Rate Design: A Neglected Issue," *Vanderbilt Law Review* (October 1978): 1089–1164.

What assurance is there that political processes can discover and implement the "right" price, and more fundamentally, how can "competitive conditions" be known outside of the rivalry of the market? Theory and experience suggest that under regulation, forces are at work to distort cost and price away from competitive levels. Political pressure exists to reduce prices as low as possible for residential users and other favored classes at the expense of suppliers and lower priority users, while barriers to competition and efficiency increase firm costs over unregulated levels. Public-utility regulation must be recognized not as the solution to a "defective" alternative but as a defective alternative in itself. The experience of interstate-gas-pipeline regulation in its four-decade history does not contradict this thesis.

Other Federal Regulation and Proposals

Other federal legislation in addition to the NGA has affected gas pipelines. Most of these laws, like the NGA itself, were born of crisis. In the 1930s, it was the breakdown of state regulation; in the 1970s, it was gas shortages and the general energy crisis.

In the late 1970s, new federal regulation joined the NGA. The Alaska Natural Gas Transportation Act of 1976 required owners and nonowners of this line to have equal access to transportation.[326] The nondiscrimination requirement for nonowners stopped short of common carriage.

The Emergency Natural Gas Act of 1977, as mentioned, gave emergency authority to the president to require transportation arrangements between interstate and intrastate carriers and construct required facilities.[327] These powers were readopted a year later in the Natural Gas Policy Act.[328] A second supplement to NGA regulation was the Outer Continental Shelf Lands Act Amendments of 1978 that made offshore gas pipelines common carriers.[329] Purchases and carriage were to be nondiscriminatory, even to the point of requiring expansion of throughput capacity. Commenting on the

---

[326]Public Law 94-586, 90 Stat. 2903 (1976).

[327]Public Law 95-2, 91 Stat. 4 (1977).

[328]Public Law 95-621, 92 Stat. 3350 (1978).

[329]Public Law 95-372, 92 Stat. 629 at 638–39 (1978). Previously, the Outer Continental Shelf Act of 1953 required purchase and transportation by pipelines without discrimination. Public Law 83-212, 67 Stat. 462 (1953).

pervasiveness of these laws in addition to the NGA, Mel Martin commented:

> Interstate natural gas pipeline companies can now be required, by federal regulation, to perform the functions of contract carriers, common carriers, and common purchasers. What else may be required?[330]

A companion bill to the NGPA was the Powerplant and Industrial Fuel Use Act, which sought to conserve natural gas and fuel oil, two highly regulated fuels experiencing supply problems, by limiting their use in existing and new power plants and major fuel-burning installations.[331] Existing plants were restricted to their current usage of natural gas until 1990 when an oil and gas ban was to take effect. New plants could not use oil or gas, which in effect restricted them to coal burning—despite cost and environmental considerations. With improving supply conditions, the Industrial Fuel Use Act was amended in 1981 to allow existing plants to increase natural-gas consumption. The 1990 ban was also removed.[332] The surviving prohibition on new plants' burning oil and gas gave an artificial advantage to existing plants and coal, but the surplus of the two restricted fuels promised further reform of the controversial 1978 law.

Pipeline safety was the focus of several laws beginning with the Hazardous Liquid Pipeline Safety Act of 1979.[333] The next year, the Comprehensive Environmental Response, Compensation, and Liability Act was passed to set a liability ceiling of $50 million "or such lessor amount as the President shall establish by regulation," but no less than $5 million.[334] Coupled with eminent-domain rights, two important costs for interstate transmission companies—right-of-way and insurance—were reduced by government favor.

Nonfederal Intervention through 1984

While their efforts have been overshadowed by the NGA, states have actively regulated and taxed intrastate gas lines. In addition,

---

[330]Mel Martin, "Natural Gas Pipelines—Their Regulation and Their Current Problems," *30 Annual Institute on Oil and Gas Law* (New York: Matthew Bender, 1979), p. 235.

[331]Public Law 95-620, 92 Stat. 3289 (1978).

[332]Omnibus Budget Reconciliation Act, Public Law 97-35, 95 Stat. 357 at 614 (1981).

[333]Public Law 96-129, 93 Stat. 989 (1979).

[334]Public Law 96-510, 94 Stat. 2767 at 2782 (1980).

a relatively new government entity, Indian tribal governments, have expanded their taxing powers to pipelines crossing their domain.

State Level

Regulation. All fifty states have public-utility commissions that have authority over domestic, commercial, and industrial sales of natural gas.[335] Since the beginning of the industry, residential and commercial sales have come under local and state regulation; in 1947, regulation of direct sales from interstate pipelines to industrial customers was also found by the Supreme Court to be a state and local function.[336] In addition, almost one-third of the 1,600 gas-distribution companies in the United States are government owned and operated.[337]

Intrastate gas pipelines, by virtue of their sales to franchised distributors, are under public-utility control in thirty-five states; entry, terms of service, and safety minimums are regulated.[338] All states but Nebraska indirectly regulate carriers by virtue of regulating rates of gas distributors. As did federal regulation, state commissions changed from fair-value to original-cost valuation in the 1940s for gas distributors and intrastate carriers.[339] The rate of return applied to the valuation figure approximated federal allowances—6 to 7 percent—until an inflation premium was added in the late 1970s.[340]

Cost-of-service determinations for pipelines have prominently included gas purchases. By 1975, forty-three states had automatic fuel adjustment charges to pass through to consumers price increases experienced by gas carriers.[341] Rate-increase requests on the state

---

[335]Only Nebraska does not regulate rates and service standards. American Gas Association, *Regulation of the Gas Industry*, vol. 3, Inf-10 to Inf-15.

[336]*Panhandle Eastern Pipe Line Co.* v. *Public Service Commission of Indiana et al.*, 332 U.S 507 (1947).

[337]Arlon Tussing and Connie Barlow, *The Natural Gas Industry*, p. 24.

[338]Ibid.

[339]N. Knowles Davis, "General Principles Applicable to Utility Rates," in *Regulation of the Gas Industry*, vol. 2, p. 25-6.

[340]William Diener, "State Regulation," in American Gas Association, *Regulation of the Gas Industry*, vol. 1, p. 4-68.

[341]*Public Utilities Fortnightly*, December 18, 1975, p. 6.

level have been generally automatic, as in Texas.[342] Michigan, on the other hand, eliminated purchased-gas adjustment clauses in 1982.[343] Land-use and zoning restrictions by state and local governments have shaped pipeline choices. Delay, restrictions, and paperwork costs, summarized Mel Martin, have made it difficult to "connect new wells [to pipelines] in a timely fashion."[344]

Surplus gas and rising burner-tip prices encouraged interest in *bypass* gas transactions, whereby end-users (primarily industrial customers) acquire their own gas and turn to their traditional supplier for transport services only.[345] Kentucky (1964, 1984), West Virginia (1983), New York (1984), and New Mexico (1984) required intrastate pipelines to accept tendered gas for shipment. Voluntary common carriage as a business strategy has been practiced in such states as Iowa, Indiana, Ohio, Illinois, and Maryland. Other states debating common-carrier requirements were California, Kentucky, and Kansas.[346] Further interest in natural-gas carriage on the part of both the private sector and regulators was encouraged by surplus gas.

Taxation. States have taxed intrastate natural-gas pipelines since the beginning of the century. Texas in 1905 and Oklahoma in 1907 enacted levies of 2 percent of gross revenue to underwrite their increasing oil and gas activities.[347] Today, most states tax gas pipelines within their boundaries. State taxation of interstate flows was ruled unconstitutional by the Supreme Court in two early cases and again in 1981.[348] Louisiana passed the First Use Tax Act of 1978 to tax all gas flows through the state that originated offshore or from

---

[342]Mel Martin, "Natural Gas Pipelines—Their Regulation and Their Current Problems," p. 247.

[343]*Houston Post,* May 2, 1983, p. 8A.

[344]Mel Martin, "Natural Gas Pipelines—Their Regulation and Their Current Problems," p. 246.

[345]Spot-gas transportation and bypass with interstate pipelines is the subject of appendix 15.1.

[346]See, generally, Connie Barlow, "Carriage of Customer-Owned Gas," *ARTA Energy Insights,* September 1984.

[347]Harold Williamson et al., *The Age of Energy, 1899 to 1959,* vol. 2 of *The American Petroleum Industry* (Evanston, Ill.: Northwestern University Press, 1963), pp. 50–51.

[348]*United Fuel Gas Co. v. Hallanan,* 257 U.S. 277 (1921); and *State Tax Commission v. Interstate Natural Gas Co.,* 284 U.S. 41 (1931).

another country. That act was challenged by eight eastern and mid-western states, and the Supreme Court on May 26, 1981, voided the $0.07 per thousand cubic feet (Mcf) levy as unconstitutionally burdening interstate commerce and conflicting with federal author-ity.[349] On June 15, the Court ordered a $600-million refund of col-lected taxes to rectify Louisiana's initiative at the expense of down-stream consumers.[350]

Indian Tribes

By their sovereignty and power to tax, Indian nations can be considered a branch of government along with federal, state, and local jurisdictions.[351] Their taxation power has been opportunistically used against pipeline firms. In one case, a twenty-year right-of-way renewal was unilaterally made subject to a "license and use agreement" by the involved tribe. Only when a $400,000 license was purchased could the twenty-year rental fee, negotiated at $6,000, be consummated with the Interior Department. In another case, as discussed in chapter 7, the Navajo Tribe enacted a 5 percent business activity tax on pipeline throughput across their reservation effective July 1, 1978.[352] Pipeline throughput qualified as a "Navajo service," subjecting both El Paso and Transwestern to millions of dollars in taxes and interest. Other instances exist in which "tribes have used their right of consent as a lever on industry."[353]

---

[349]*Maryland* v. *Louisiana*, 451 U.S. 725 (1981).

[350]40 U.S.L.W. 4709 (1981).

[351]See chapter 7, pp. 362–65.

[352]See chapter 7, pp. 363–64.

[353]Mel Martin, "Natural Gas Pipelines—Their Regulation and Their Current Prob-lems," p. 244.

Appendix 15.1: Market Ordering and Spot-Gas Transportation: 1975–84

This appendix examines the dawn of a new era in the natural-gas industry that is changing time-honored relationships and practices from the wellhead to the burner tip. Traditionally, pipelines have been *merchants,* buying gas at one point, selling it at another, and performing all the aggregating functions. Pipelines with storage capabilities also performed a load-balancing function between low- and high-sendout periods. Such services as transportation, gathering, and storage were "bundled" with sales rather than offered à la carte to parties who might have independently contracted for gas. Long-term contracts between producers and pipelines were the backbone of this industry structure, and rates were set at *cost of service* pursuant to regulatory instruction rather than *value of service* as in a free market.

The Natural Gas Act (NGA) and administrative regulation by the Federal Power Commission (FPC) both precluded spot-gas and contract-carriage transportation before the mid-1970s. The NGA precluded a spot market for gas by requiring long-term (ten- to twenty-year) producer contracts, perpetual dedication of supply, and formal certification hearings if a producer wished to change pipeline purchasers. The FPC explicitly blocked several attempts by the industry to substitute transportation for sales. Several industry initiatives designed to escape burdensome regulation were turned back by the FPC on narrow grounds, such as the gas was for an "inferior" end-use or the transaction price was above regulated levels.[1] On the other hand, several interstate pipeline projects were certified that escaped burdensome wellhead regulation by having end-users contract directly with producers and pay a straight transportation fee. A pipeline from Louisiana to West Virginia certified in 1954 by Gulf

---

[1] *Federal Power Commission* v. *Transcontinental Gas Pipe Line Corp.*, 365 U.S. 1 (1961); and *Arizona Public Service Co.* v. *FPC,* 483 F.2d 1275 (D.C. Cir. 1973).

Interstate and a line from Texas to Florida certified in 1959 by the Houston Corporation were the notable exceptions to commission policy.[2] But overall, the FPC was not ready to sanction "regulatory gaps" in its active agenda of economic control. Bundled sales were virtually instructed by law.

This regulatory and industry structure has changed. In recent years, many interstate pipelines have unbundled transportation from sales and moved spot gas sold by producers, brokers, and affiliates to industrial, commercial, and local distribution company (LDC) customers. Transportation rates have joined contract sales rates in pipeline tariff books, and many pipelines have transported growing volumes of nontraditional gas.

The natural-gas spot market did not begin with the natural-gas surplus of the 1980s. It began during curtailments when traditional certification was relaxed to facilitate the flow of gas from surplus areas to shortage areas. After the emergency transportation orders of the 1970s that created the opening that the surplus environment would exploit are identified, the market disorder of the new decade and the industry and regulatory responses to it are described.

Emergency Transportation: 1975–81

The forerunners to the spot-gas and carriage boom of the 1980s were the emergency transportation orders issued by the FPC (and after 1976 the Federal Energy Regulatory Commission, or FERC). The objective was to alleviate shortages by redirecting gas from amply supplied areas to threatened markets. As a result, a modest "spot" market for gas developed, although it was clearly tangential to pipeline sales from traditional system supply.

Special transportation began with Order 533 in August 1975, which allowed producers to sell gas directly from state waters to "high priority" industrial and commercial customers suffering from curtailment and arrange for pipeline carriage.[3] Process and feedstock gas, crucial to plant operations, was at the heart of the program. In the FPC's curtailment hierarchy, these gas uses were Priorities 2 and 3. Lower priority industrial and power-plant customers (Priorities

---

[2] See Connie Barlow, "Carriage of Customer-Owned Gas," *ARTA Energy Insights,* September 1984, pp. 2–3. Also see chapter 15, p. 918.

[3] Order 533, 54 FPC 821 (1975); and Order 533-A, 54 FPC 2058 (1975), affirmed, *American Public Gas Association* v. *FERC,* 587 F.2d 1089 (D.C. Cir. 1978).

4 and 5, respectively), as well as residential customers (Priority 1), were excluded from the self-help program.[4]

The "experimental" two-year program was intended to attract intrastate gas to interstate markets to keep plants open and workers from being laid off. The two incentives of the program were unregulated wellhead prices and legalized transportation. The commission recognized the half-regulated world that the order inaugurated.

> High priority customers might be able to buy gas directly from producers. Because such direct sales would not be subject to our rate jurisdiction, high priority customers could compete with the producer's intrastate customers for gas supplies not otherwise available to the interstate market. While the sale would be non-jurisdictional, the transportation of the gas from the producer to the buyer in interstate commerce would be subject to our jurisdiction. Such transportation would require a certificate of public convenience under Section 7(c) of the Act.[5]

By March 1977, nearly 8 billion cubic feet (Bcf) had been moved under the program, an amount that would have been greater except for the warm winter of 1975–76.[6] The FERC extended the program another two years, while warning that it would not "elevate an essentially stop-gap measure to the level of a permanent palliative to the natural gas shortage for the relatively small group of industrial concerns."[7]

While Order 533 opened the door for targeted transportation, section 311 of the Natural Gas Policy Act of 1978 (NGPA) provided a much more generic vehicle for spot-gas transportation. Like the

---

[4]For a discussion of gas shortages and consequent priority schedules, see chapter 15, pp. 904–8.

[5]54 FPC 823. Sales from producers to end-users were deemed nonjurisdictional (unregulated) because a *sale for resale* was not made pursuant to section 1(b) of the Natural Gas Act. But interstate *transportation* to effectuate the deal required certification—hence transportation orders finding that the public convenience and necessity were met.

[6]For discussion of the transportation program, see 43 *Fed. Reg.* 5362 (February 8, 1978). The FPC blessed the services of "intermediaries," or brokers, who "charge a fee for the various types of services performed, such as planning, purchasing, contracting for gathering systems, negotiating transportation agreements, and fulfilling administrative requirements" (p. 5368).

[7]Ibid., p. 5365. The commission decided not to extend the program to other existing customer classes or new customers.

wellhead provisions of the NGPA, the transportation section was intended to ease curtailments by facilitating interstate movements of gas. The pertinent section read:

> The Commission may, by rule or order, authorize any interstate pipeline to transport natural gas on behalf of i) any intrastate pipeline; and ii) any local distribution company [and] authorize any intrastate pipeline to transport natural gas on behalf of i) any interstate pipeline; and ii) any local distribution company served by any interstate pipeline.[8]

The "on behalf of" clause was very important. It had to be shown that the intrastate pipeline, interstate pipeline, or LDC received a clear economic benefit from the maximum five-year carriage contract.

Order 46, issued on August 30, 1979, implemented sections 311 and 312 of the NGPA.[9] Qualifying transportation contracts under two years in duration could be commenced without prior approval—only a filing within forty-eight hours of actual service was required. These "self-implementing" contracts could be extended at a later date. Contracts longer than two years had to receive a traditional section 7(c) certificate, which meant added expense and delay.

Order 63 the next year brought Hinshaw pipelines—intrastate pipelines exempt from federal regulation despite receiving gas from regulated interstate lines—within sections 311 and 312 of the NGPA.[10] Hinshaws now had the same rights as intrastate pipelines and local distribution companies (which with their pipeline facilities were already Hinshaws in most cases). This order had the same motivation as the previous ones. Stated the FERC: "The final rule is intended to further implement the Commission's policy of integrating the interstate and intrastate natural gas markets, removing administrative burdens from the sale of natural gas, and improving consumer access to natural gas."[11]

---

[8]Public Law 95-621, 92 Stat. 3351 at 3388–89 (1978). Section 312 gave the commission the power to "order" or "authorize" assignments of surplus gas from intrastate pipelines to interstates. 92 Stat. 3392.

[9]Order on rehearing of Order no. 46, 44 *Fed. Reg.* 66789 (November 21, 1979).

[10]45 *Fed. Reg.* 1872 (January 9, 1980).

[11]Ibid.

Section 608 of the Public Utility Regulatory Policies Act, along with section 311 of the NGPA, legalized transportation to alleviate natural-gas shortages. Section 7(c) of the NGA was amended by the 1978 law as follows.

> The Commission may issue a certificate of public convenience and necessity to a natural-gas company for the transportation in interstate commerce of natural gas used by any person for one or more high-priority uses . . . in the case of natural gas sold by the producer . . . and natural gas produced by such person.[12]

Pursuant to section 608, the FERC issued Order 27 to authorize interstate transportation of direct-sale gas for "essential agricultural users as certified by the Secretary of Agriculture, and all schools, hospitals, and similar institutions," effective April 23, 1979.[13] These recipients could be existing customers, curtailed or not, or entirely new customers within these groups. It was a general program bestowing privileges on certain politically endowed groups.

Order 27 marked the beginning of transportation for the benefit of the general market instead of as an expedient to alleviate curtailment. The market was turning from shortage to surplus, and the FERC recognized the advantage of improved pipeline utilization per se.[14]

Other expansions of direct-sale carriage were made in 1979. Order 30, issued on May 17, established procedures for transporting gas sold by intrastates and LDCs that would displace fuel oil.[15] Section 7(c) certification was required. The impetus of the order was the prospect of oil shortages that gas could help alleviate. Order 52, effective October 5, universalized Order 30 by pregranting certificates for direct sales and transportation that displaced fuel oil.[16] Transportation was now available for gas destined for "low-priority" boiler-fuel uses as well as "high-priority" industrial and commercial uses—all to alleviate different aspects of the energy crisis.

---

[12]Public Law 95-617, 92 Stat. 3117 at 3173 (1978).

[13]44 *Fed. Reg.* 24825 at 24827 (April 27, 1979). The maximum term was five years.

[14]See ibid., p. 24827.

[15]44 *Fed. Reg.* 30323 (May 25, 1979). This order was extended by 46 *Fed. Reg.* 30491 (June 9, 1981) and merged into Order 319; see chapter 15, pp. 954–55.

[16]44 *Fed. Reg.* 60080 (October 18, 1979). This order was extended past June 1, 1980, by Orders 30-B and 30-D, to May 31, 1981.

Another liberalization came with Order 60 of November 30, 1979, that gave blanket authorization for an interstate line to transport system supply for other interstate lines.[17] Contracts under this authority were limited to two years or less.

Section 603 of the Outer Continental Shelf Lands Act Amendments of 1978 instructed the FERC to facilitate interstate carriage of outer continental shelf (OCS) gas owned by an LDC to its service area.[18] Order 92, effective July 15, 1980, expanded expedited transportation for such gas under either section 7(c) or section 311 applications.[19]

The foregoing legislation and orders, along with a 1978 federal requirement that offshore pipelines offer nondiscriminatory transportation,[20] offered spot-gas carriage for "priority" industrial uses; "essential" agricultural uses; hospitals, schools, and "similar" institutions; and end-uses that could displace fuel oil. In many cases, transaction-by-transaction certification under section 7(c) of the NGA could be avoided by substituting expedited "blanket" approval.

A modest spot market was created by the aforementioned transportation orders. Regulation had precluded a spot-gas market in the decades before; regulation now encouraged a spot market to take shape. It was a "stopgap" market to equalize the disparities between the intrastate and interstate markets for short-run relief, however, not an institution that was expected to continue when gas markets got back into balance. Indeed, after approximately 8 Bcf were transported in the first two years of the program, volumes diminished as a result of the improved market balance caused by growing supply and declining demand. Section 311, however, was an open-ended, nonexperimental vehicle that awaited favorable conditions for regular use.

The Gas Surplus and Industry Responses: 1981–84

Pervasive natural-gas regulation created a legacy of industry disorder. A decade before, it was shortages and statutory allocation; beginning in 1981, the new problem was excess deliverability that

---

[17]Order 60, 44 *Fed. Reg.* 68819 (November 30, 1979).
[18]Public Law 95-372, 92 Stat. 629 at 694 (1978).
[19]45 *Fed. Reg.* 49247 (July 24, 1980).
[20]Public Law 95-372, 92 Stat. 629 at 638–39.

interstate pipelines could not market under the provisions of their contracts. A combination of rising gas prices, declining fuel-oil prices, new base-load coal and nuclear plants, the mild winters of 1981–82 and 1982–83, and an industrial recession significantly depressed demand for natural gas. Gas supply, meanwhile, was increasing because of incentive pricing under the NGPA and incentives under take-or-pay contracts to maximize deliverability from given reserves. For pipelines, lost load necessitated ever-increasing tariffs with fixed costs spread over fewer units, and alternate-fuel customers responded by switching to oil and coal. This also left pipelines with surplus supply, given their high take-or-pay obligations.[21]

Faced with a "death spiral" of increasing prices and decreasing demand, the industry needed a degree of market entrepreneurship foreign to its public-utility status.[22] The serenity of gas in, gas out and cost-plus billing would not suffice for pipelines that were caught between high-take purchase requirements (at high prices in many cases) and unmarketable supply. The job was to tiptoe out of a mine field between high prices on one side and minimum-take provisions on the other, with every self-help move requiring prenotification of and approval from the FERC.

Contract Remedies

Two early strategies were developed to arrest the related problems of high prices and excess deliverability. One was to enter into "dump-sale" contracts to dispose of excess supply at cost.[23] The second practice was to exercise "market-out" provisions in gas contracts to reduce purchase prices to market levels. This applied to unregulated "high-cost" gas, not regulated vintages for which NGPA ceiling prices also acted as price floors. In April 1982, Transco reduced the price for unregulated deep gas to $5.00 per Mcf, which was equitably done between affiliated and nonaffiliated production

---

[21]See chapter 8, pp. 442–44.

[22]Political entrepreneurship, on the other hand, was alive and well to get statutory or legislative relief from the "bad" contracts. President Reagan's unsuccessful Natural Gas Consumer Regulatory Reform Act of 1983, which would have annulled take-or-pay contracts above 50 percent of deliverability, was supported by Tenneco and other troubled interstate pipelines. A second nonmarket strategy was for pipeline companies to unilaterally break contracts and appeal to the FERC for support.

[23]*OGJ*, May 25, 1981, p. 46.

to avoid legal problems. Fifteen of the top twenty interstates followed within a year, and by the end of 1983, deep-gas prices averaged 50 percent below 1981 levels.[24] An estimated 3,100 market-out contract clauses were activated in this period.[25]

Other pipeline practices to mitigate take-or-pay claims were to reinterpret contracts on technicalities to force prices down and take refuge under state prorationing laws (particularly in Texas) that limited withdrawals to "market demand."[26]

Unfortunately for many interstate pipelines, the majority of their gas purchase contracts were not market sensitive even if new contracts were. This predicament led to unilateral take-reduction programs, based on force majeure, by Columbia (summer 1982), United (February 1983), Natural (April 1983), Consolidated (April 1983), and Tenneco (May 1983), which prompted a flood of lawsuits.[27] The "Act of God" contract-out traditionally meant a physical inability to perform because of unforeseen events (equipment failure or weather); it was now conveniently defined to mean an unforeseen change in the business climate (depressed demand and falling prices).

Many interstates began to file for rate decreases in April 1983 for the first time in decades, if not history. It had taken longer, but gas prices were now headed in the same direction as oil prices.

Early Spot-Market Activity: 1981–83

Contractual remedies were not nearly enough. Too many contracts, signed in an era of short supply and under malincentives

---

[24]Other firms were Michigan-Wisconsin (July 1982, $6.00 per Mcf); United (September 1982, $5.72 per Mcf); Tenneco (November 1982, $4.85 per Mcf); Natural (December 1982, $3.80 per Mcf); Florida (December 1982, $5.00 per Mcf); Northwest Central (January 1983, $3.30 per Mcf); Texas Eastern (January 1983, $5.00 per Mcf); Texas Gas (January 1983, $5.00 per Mcf); Transwestern (January 1983, $5.00 per Mcf); Panhandle (February 1983, $4.08 per Mcf); El Paso (March 1983, $5.00 per Mcf); and Colorado (April 1983, $5.00 per Mcf). El Paso, Natural, Northern, Tenneco, Texas Eastern, Transco, and United would drop deep-gas prices lower. U.S. Department of Energy, Energy Information Administration, "Recent Market Activities of Major Interstate Pipeline Companies," January 1984, p. 17.

[25]Jon Brunenkant, "State and Federal Take-or-Pay Issues," *Oil and Gas Analyst* (August 1983): 9.

[26]Connie Barlow, "Second- and Third-Tier Natural-Gas Markets," *ARTA Energy Insights* (October 1983): 3.

[27]See chapter 8, pp. 444–47, for further discussion of the take-or-pay problem.

from public-utility regulation, had inflexible price and take provisions.[28] New programs to turn jurisdictional gas into competitively priced spot gas were required. *Legalized* flexibility had worked against shortages; it now had to work against surpluses.

In late 1980, the FERC began granting case-by-case off-system sales certificates whereby interstate pipelines could take surplus system supply to other markets. The primary motivation for the commission and involved firms was take-or-pay relief. In the first two years of the ad hoc program, nearly 240 Bcf of an authorized 1 trillion cubic feet (Tcf) went to off-system markets.[29]

The worsening problems of surplus supply and take-or-pay liability led to a generic off-system sales program by the FERC in late 1981. Noticing that "now virtually all interstate pipelines have a supply surplus,"[30] the commission authorized interstates to sell excess gas in nontraditional markets if take-or-pay problems were being experienced, existing customers could be fully serviced, the transaction was priced at the higher of the pipeline's average section 102 wellhead price or the pipeline's average load factor rate, coal and other "plentiful" fuels were not displaced, and the incremental revenue benefited other pipeline customers. Off-system transactions also had to be interruptible, one year or less, and meet a demonstrable need of the buyer. Only new and high-cost gas was eligible for the program.

Firm customers, whether residential, commercial, or small industrial, could not participate in the program. These conditions reflected the concerns of intrastate pipelines about interstate spot-gas competition, interstate customers who did not want low-priced gas to go off system, and the interstates themselves who did not want spot gas to displace system supply in secure markets. Authority was limited to 954 Bcf and expired on June 30, 1982.

Although only 19 percent of the permitted volume was sold, a result attributable to strict regulatory stipulations, take-or-pay credit was achieved and the way was pointed toward a permanent spot market. The next step came on April 28, 1983, when Transco received

---

[28]See chapter 8, pp. 444–45, for the link between the contract problem and government intervention in natural-gas markets.

[29]The program is described in 23 FERC 61306 (1983).

[30]23 FERC 61305 at 61307. Surplus deliverability was estimated at between 2 and 3 Tcf annually.

952

permission in an uncontested rate settlement to reduce gas prices to compete with no. 6 fuel oil in threatened markets.[31] The Industrial Sales Program (ISP) hinged on blanket abandonment authority (in place of lengthy case-by-case review) for producers to withdraw dedicated reserves that Transco could reprice at competitive levels (determined by a net-back pricing formula based on monthly surveys of fuel-oil prices and substitution points) and sell to price-sensitive (fuel-switchable) customers. In return, Transco received a transportation fee in addition to take-or-pay relief. Several months later, the ISP was joined by the Common Carrier Program, under which outside parties matched supplier and buyer and hired Transco for transportation services.

From May to September 1983, Transco averaged 150 million cubic feet (MMcf) per day under its spot-market programs. This amount would have been greater if multiple prices had been allowed to meet the competition in distinct markets and the weighted-average-cost-of-gas price floor had been absent. As it was, there was much more supply than market. Nonetheless, the watershed programs benefited all parties, explaining why timely FERC approval was obtained initially. For Transco, take-or-pay credit and incremental transportation revenues were won. Higher pipeline utilization meant lower rates for all customers, residential and industrial. For producers, unmarketable gas was made marketable, and present money was received instead of uncertain revenue from take-or-pay litigation.[32] For targeted end-users, finally, the preferred boiler fuel of natural gas was made competitive with fuel oil.

[31]See Sheila Hollis, "Notable Recent Developments in Federal Natural Gas Regulation," *34 Oil and Gas Institute* (New York: Matthew Bender, 1973), pp. 40–41. Developments over the next several years, including a relaxation of pricing requirements to expand off-system sales, are described in J. Richard Tiano and Richard Bonnifield, "The Impact on Gas Distribution Companies of Federally Approved Special Marketing Programs," *Energy Law Journal* 5 (1984): 288–90.

[32]23 FERC, 61, 415 (1983). The proposal reflected not only the entrepreneurial alertness of such Transco executives as president Kenneth Lay but the fact that the company, in the words of chairman Jack Bowen, was "the first in the hospital." *Houston Chronicle,* January 1, 1985, p. 2-1. A decade earlier, Transco had experienced relatively severe curtailment problems, which not only incited many customers to install dual-fuel burners but led Transco into supply contracts with generous price terms and high take-or-pay levels.

Expedited Transportation

The spot market was given a solid transportational footing in the summer of 1983 when the FERC gave blanket certification to end-users to contract with producers, pipelines, and distributors to buy gas and hire an interstate for carriage. Order 234-B sanctified carriage for non-high-priority industrial and boiler-fuel customers (replacing Order 30) *and any end-user* so long as the gas was not dedicated interstate prior to November 8, 1978, and was purchased from an intrastate pipeline or was owned by either an LDC or the purchasing end-user.[33] The term was limited to 120 days. The two-year "experimental" program, which provided a special $0.05 per million Btu carriage fee for interstates, was intended to make gas competitive with fuel oil and thus increase pipeline throughput, benefit "high-priority" customers who otherwise would pay higher rates, and promote exploration and production. The commission recognized that traditional rolled-in (average-cost) pricing put these price-sensitive gas customers at risk and that only marginal-cost spot-market pricing could rectify the situation.

Order 319 awarded blanket transportation certification to Order 2 (high-priority) uses in place of transaction-by-transaction approval for contracts under five years in duration.[34] Eligible for expedited transportation were "high-priority" users; "essential" agricultural users; hospitals, schools, and "similar" institutions; commercial establishments using over 50 Mcf on a peak day; plants requiring gas for "protection"; and process and feedstock users. This included the system supply of another pipeline and all LDCs. Volumetric limitations established in earlier orders were dropped. The commission noted the difference between the old transportation orders and the new in Order 319.

---

[33]"Interstate Pipeline Blanket Certificates for Routine Transactions and Sales and Transportation by Interstate Pipelines and Distributors," Order 234-B, 48 *Fed. Reg.* 34872 (August 1, 1983). Order 319-A (48 *Fed. Reg.* 51436 [November 9, 1983]) clarified the requirement that eligible gas had to be internally developed by the end-user.

[34]"Sales and Transportation by Interstate Pipelines and Distributors; Expansion of Categories of Activities Authorized under Blanket Certificate," Order 319 (Phase II), 48 *Fed. Reg.* 34875 (August 1, 1983). Phase I of the commission's program (Order 234, 47 *Fed. Reg.* 24254 [June 4, 1982]) gave jurisdictional pipelines a blanket certificate for a variety of activities outside of transportation.

A direct sale program can serve a variety of policy objectives. Although these programs were originally designed to be a "stop-gap measure" rather than a permanent palliative to curtailment, the emphasis of the programs has shifted. . . . In the context of present natural gas markets, the primary objective of a direct sale program should be market ordering.[35]

The next commission transportation initiative to facilitate market ordering came with the Special Marketing Programs (SMPs), discussed below.

Spot-Market Expansion: 1983–84

In 1983, Connie Barlow observed, "The interstate pipeline business is fast becoming one of the most attractive management challenges for executives with entrepreneurial leanings—quite a contrast to its dreary utility image of the past."[36] Transco's special marketing program attracted imitators, but opposition slowed commission approval of the new programs. A Tenneco proposal was opposed by Texas intrastate pipelines such as Valero, Delhi, and Texas Oil that feared that freed spot gas would be used for "market-raiding transactions."[37] An application from Columbia Gas encountered stiff regulatory requirements because of industry dissent, which Columbia complained would "effectively preclude transportation of any significant volumes."[38]

Both applications were approved in November 1983 to give Transco competition outside the Blanket Certification Program. Tenneco's Tenneflex program was authorized to market surplus OCS gas if it was priced equal to or above the weighted average cost of pipeline gas.[39] Unlike Transco's ISP, Tenneco's program was a producer program that located buyers and made pipeline arrangements. Columbia's ISP was similar to Transco's with restrictions to limit the program to industrial customers only.[40]

[35]48 *Fed. Reg.* 34877 (August 1, 1983).

[36]Connie Barlow, "Second- and Third-Tier Natural-Gas Markets," p. 4.

[37]*Inside FERC*, December 5, 1983, p. 3. Other protestants were Mobil Oil and Texas Eastern.

[38]*Inside FERC*, December 12, 1983, p. 1.

[39]25 FERC 61601 (1983). Tenneflex would become a model for other gas-producer SMP applicants such as Cities Service Oil and Gas, Amoco, and TXP Operating Company (Transco).

[40]25 FERC 61561 (1983).

While other producer and pipeline special marketing programs were in the approval process, Transco's ISP ended in November 1983 because of firming oil prices that reduced pressure on gas. The Common Carrier Program continued until March 31, 1984, when both programs expired. Transco's decision not to renew was based on a January 16 FERC ruling that required 100 percent load factor rates as the pipeline carriage fee (the lower the throughput, the higher the rate) and required the gas to be priced no lower than contract gas.[41] Thereafter, "Common Carrier Program-type" transactions under the Blanket Certification Program, predominantly with off-system gas, kept Transco active in the spot market.[42]

The limiting provisions surrounding special marketing programs raised controversy in some gas-industry circles, although they appeased intrastate pipelines and other critics of unregulated spot-market activity. Worthwhile transactions were narrowed for Transco and the more recent ISPs of Columbia; Tenneco (Tempro, December 20, 1983); and Panhandle Eastern and Trunkline Gas (PanMark, March 19, 1984) and later Texas Eastern (TeenMark, June 29, 1984) and El Paso (STP, August 24, 1984). Only PanMark remained active in the third quarter of 1984. On the producer side, thirteen new programs were approved in 1984, and another six were pending, but only three, Transco's TransMart (July 24, 1984), Cities Service's cost of gas sold (June 29, 1984), and Amoco's SMP (August 20, 1984), registered volumes in the same period. Tenneflex led all pipeline and producer SMPs with nearly half of total period volume.[43] In all,

---

[41]26 FERC 61050 (1984).

[42]Transcontinental Gas Pipe Line Corp., "Overview of TGPL's Natural Gas Spot Market Programs: Mechanics and Experience to Date," Houston, Tex., December 31, 1984.

[43]Other approved producer SMPs were ARCO (August 23, 1984); Sun (October 9, 1984); Odeco (January 2, 1984); Champlin (December 17, 1984); ANR (December 17, 1984); and Cenergy (December 17, 1984). Pending producer SMP applications were from Texas Gas, Mesa Petroleum, Diamond Shamrock, American Petrofina, Union Texas, and Conoco. A natural-gas broker, Yankee Resources, also had an application pending. See Interstate Natural Gas Association of America, "Update on Special Marketing Programs," January 1985. These producer SMPs, in contrast to pipeline SMPs, were credited with more competitive pricing because of greater competition at the wellhead and less concern with customer targeting. See U.S. Department of Energy, *Increasing Competition in the Natural Gas Market*, the second report required by sec. 123 of the Natural Gas Policy Act of 1978 (Washington, D.C.: Government Printing Office, 1985), p. 83.

some 150 Bcf of spot gas were sold by SMPs between May 1983 and September 1984, an amount that would have been greater except for regulated producer contracts that could not be released into spot channels.[44]

Spot gas and transportation represented a partial but not total bypass of the LDCs. Once the focal point of gas transactions, the LDCs could now be third-party transporters for gas sales between producers (or marketers) and end-users. In addition to state and federal legalization of transportation, bypass was facilitated by the eradication of minimum bills between pipelines and LDCs in mid-1984 that previously locked out spot gas by locking in jurisdictional supply.[45] Total bypass of the LDCs, on the other hand, was achieved when interstates directly connected with end-users.[46]

Not only did onerous provisions reduce SMPs to a small part of the spot-market picture, complaints were heard that restricting the program to industrial customers and discouraging gas-on-gas competition with price floors represented "incremental pricing in reverse." While the NGPA directed higher gas prices toward industrial users, the FERC intended industrial customers to benefit from SMPs to leave residential customers and other captive users with "no alternative but to continue paying the pipeline's uncompetitive and often increasing regular rates, which caused the current load loss problems in the first place."[47]

The call for open competition impressed the FERC, and on September 26, 1984, new conditions were imposed on SMPs that replaced the pricing proviso with a requirement that up to 10 percent of a pipeline's firm-service demand could be raided by another firm's SMP.[48] The FERC's new agenda was to lower prices for *non-alternate-fuel* customers. This introduced gas-on-gas competition with a vengeance, and with most firms fearing deteriorations of take-or-pay

---

[44]Ibid., p. 72; and Connie Barlow, "Second- and Third-Tier Natural-Gas Markets," p. 12.

[45]Order 380, 49 *Fed. Reg.* 22778 (June 1, 1984).

[46]Connie Barlow, "Carriage of Customer-Owned Gas," pp. 11–12.

[47]Glen Howard, "Special Marketing Programs: Incremental Pricing in Reverse," *Natural Gas*, August 1984, p. 21.

[48]28 FERC 61684 (1984). Abolition of the fuel-switching eligibility rule, the commission noted, was partly to "avoid encouraging uneconomic investment in alternate fuel capability where the new investment is used not so much to utilize the alternate fuel as to qualify for cheaper natural gas." On rehearing, minor amendments were made to the 10 percent rule on December 21, 1984. 29 FERC 61697 (1984).

positions and lost throughput, only one firm, Texas Eastern, chose to renew its certificate. No volumes were carried.[49]

At the close of 1984, the spot market consisted of jurisdictional (regulated) areas such as gas sold under the Blanket Certification Program and nonjurisdictional (nonregulated) programs such as Transco's Market Retention Program (November 1984), which instructed producers on competitive pricing, and Tenneco's Tenngasco Exchange (October 1984), which set monthly spot-market prices for sellers and buyers. Deregulated gas was primarily involved. Another entrant into the spot market was the U.S. Natural Gas Clearinghouse, which offered brokerage services to the entire industry to reduce transaction costs. "As a neutrally positioned market maker," Transco's Bowen explained, "the clearinghouse will enable producers and users to satisfy their spot market gas requirements through a single national marketplace."[50] Equity partners were Transco, United Gas, Columbia, Colorado Interstate, Houston Natural Gas, the investment banking house Morgan Stanley, and the law firm of Akin, Gump. Other upstart brokers not affiliated with pipelines making markets in 1984 were Yankee Resources and Citizens Energy.

Another proliferation within the spot-gas market took the form of magazines, newsletters, consultants, and middlemen capitalizing on a market beginning to escape from a decades-old regulatory straightjacket. With multiple tiers of mispriced gas at the wellhead and similarly mispriced gas at the transmission and distribution levels, any relaxation of regulation offered bountiful opportunities. Arlon Tussing described the situation:

> The potential gains from arbitrage created by this mass of price and rate disparities measure in the tens of billions of dollars annually. They thus create an irrepressible provocation for thousands of entrepreneurially minded gas producers, pipeline and distribution company executives, industrial gas consumers, brokers, traders, and others to find holes in, and ways around, the regulatory and contractual obstacles to a continent-wide price equalization.[51]

---

[49]U.S. Department of Energy, *Increasing Competition in the Natural Gas Market*, p. 72.

[50]*OGJ*, June 25, 1984, p. 32.

[51]Arlon Tussing, "Permanent Devolution: The Agonies of Half-Hearted Decontrol in the Natural Gas Industry," unpublished manuscript, 1984, p. 9.

The spontaneous development of natural-gas spot markets to combat market disequilibrium changed the face of regulation as well. Tussing continues:

> It is the presence of these hustlers and deal makers that is the most drastic and irreversible change. . . . The infusion of entrepreneurship into a heretofore stodgy, legalistic, and unimaginative corporate leadership is a competitive genie that will refuse to return to its bottle, regardless of the wishes of state and federal utility commissioners or the members of Congress.[52]

Prior to natural-gas wellhead decontrol on January 1, 1985, the spot market had grown to a $6-billion-a-year industry, representing 15 percent of total U.S. gas consumption.[53] SMPs, because of FERC requirements, supplied no more than 10 percent of the total of nearly 1 trillion cubic feet, but benefits were reaped. In the first year of its SMP, Transco received $150 million in take-or-pay credit, and other firms accounted for several hundred million dollars more through 1984. With a continuing surplus, additional volumes of decontrolled gas under the NGPA, freed jurisdictional supply in the post-minimum-bill era, and new spot-market institutions, including a natural-gas futures market proposed by the New York Mercantile Exchange, continued growth was likely.[54]

The Perils of Regulation

As chapter 29 will substantiate, a recurring theme of this book is that government intervention creates distortions that necessitate relaxed regulation if market order is to reappear. Legalized transportation in the 1970s to arrest shortages and in the 1980s to ease surpluses is an outstanding example of this interventionist dynamic. But while expedited certification and the transportation orders are to be applauded, the market disorder they addressed was government created. Even relaxed regulation created problems compared with

---

[52]Ibid., p. 10.

[53]Benjamin Schlesinger & Associates, "Multi-Client Analysis of Natural Gas Spot Markets: Evolution and Consequences—1984 Update," Bethesda, Md., January 1985, p. I-2.

[54]Elting Treat, formerly the head of New York Mercantile Exchange, described the advantages of natural-gas futures as "an instantaneous price sampling device, a risk management forum for hedging future prices and supplies, and an arena for speculation." *Houston Chronicle,* May 8, 1983, p. 4-10.

less strict regulation and total administrative or legislative deregulation. Shortages in the early 1970s produced no market-oriented relief via direct contracting and transportation. When shortages again cursed interstate markets in the mid-1970s, relaxed regulation proved to be a mild palliative rather than a cure as the curtailments demonstrated. In the 1980s, the FERC's transportation orders were so encumbered with restrictions that, as during the shortages, a palliative replaced a cure. As Connie Barlow summarized:

> Events of the recent past and the present yield indisputable evidence of the limits—and dangers—of regulatory intervention. When the glut first became apparent, interstate pipelines attempted to execute off-system sales. Frustrated by FERC's resolve to impose the WACOG minimum-pricing standard (and worse yet, NGPA Section 102 price equivalency) for the sale of gas from one pipeline to another, companies invented industrial discount rates. Here again, FERC maintained a relatively strong commitment to fully allocated fixed costs and a WACOG price floor for the commodity charge. . . .
>
> More than anything else . . . regulators must come to realize that by trying to buck the inevitable, they may do more harm than good to their utility wards and the captive consumers of those utilities. . . . FERC and state PUC's may attempt to put the proverbial finger in the dike—but they have only so many fingers.[55]

Three major conclusions can be drawn from the early history of the natural-gas spot market: (1) scarcity short-term pricing of natural gas arrived to join long-term regulated contract prices; (2) the market drove pipeline regulation as much as or more than pipeline regulation drove the market after the passage of the Natural Gas Act; and (3) FERC attempts to monitor and shape the spot market were more impeding than encouraging within the framework of legalized transportation.

[55]Connie Barlow, "Second- and Third-Tier Natural-Gas Markets," pp. 19–20.

960

Appendix 15.2: Natural Gas Import-Export Regulation

In chapter 13, the long history of import and export regulation of petroleum was examined. This appendix turns to natural-gas import and export regulation, the history of which is relatively brief and noncontroversial. After a review of the statutory authority for international-trade regulation of natural gas, important certification issues are reviewed.

Statutory Authority

Statutory authority for natural-gas import and export regulation is found in section 3 of the Natural Gas Act of 1938:

> No person shall export . . . or import any natural gas . . . without first having secured an order of the Commission authorizing it to do so. The Commission may by its order grant such application . . . with such modification . . . and for good cause shown, make such supplemental order in the premises as it may find necessary or appropriate.[1]

A year after the NGA became law, an executive order instructed the FPC

> (1) to receive all applications for permits for the construction, operation, maintenance, or connection, at the borders of the United States, of facilities for the . . . importation of natural gas . . . for foreign countries, and (2) after obtaining the recommendations of the Secretary of State and the Secretary of War thereon, to submit each such application to the President with a recommendation as to whether the permit applied for should be granted, and if so, upon what terms and conditions.[2]

[1]Public Law 688, 52 Stat. 821 at 822 (1938).
[2]Executive Order 8202 (July 13, 1939). Quoted in 11 FPC 4 (1952).

An executive order in 1953 reiterated that licensing deliberations by the FPC for border facilities included a "favorable recommendation of the Secretary of State and the Secretary of Defense."[3] Cold-War politics, in addition to the first call of the domestic gas market, was a factor in this expansion of section 3 authority.

Natural-gas exports were specifically mentioned in the Alaskan Transportation Act of 1976.[4] Section 12 required the president to "make and publish an express finding that such exports will not diminish the total quantity or quality, nor increase the total price of energy available to the United States." This directive reflected gas shortages that plagued many consuming regions across the country.

In the Department of Energy Organization Act of 1977, natural-gas import-export regulation was transferred from the FPC to the newly created FERC within the U.S. Department of Energy.[5] The FERC inherited a vexing problem: whether to permit much-needed imports that were priced well above what the commission found to be "just and reasonable" for domestic gas.

Licensing Decisions

Federal regulation of natural-gas imports and exports affected imports from (and, to a lesser extent, exports to) Canada and Mexico and long-distance tanker shipments of liquefied natural gas (LNG). Most of this activity sprang up in the 1970s when domestic regulation of gas supplies created shortages that imports relieved.

Canada

The first section 3 ruling concerned Panhandle Eastern's 1951 request to export southwestern gas to Canada. The extension was denied because "in view of the demonstrated requirements of customers within the United States and the designed capacity of the Panhandle system (850 MMcf daily), no natural gas is available for exportation on a firm basis at this time."[6]

Two years later, the commission approved Tennessee Gas Transmission's application to export 62 MMcf per day of Gulf Coast gas

---

[3]18 *Fed. Reg.* 5397 (September 3, 1953).
[4]Public Law 94-586, 90 Stat. 2903 (1976).
[5]42 *Fed. Reg.* 46267 (September 15, 1977).
[6]10 FERC 329 at 339–40 (1951).

to Toronto and nearby markets.[7] The twenty-year contract was found to have "no material effect" on domestic reserves and, in fact, was well below volumes previously authorized for export to Mexico.[8] The first import application was approved in 1951 for Montana Power Company to deliver Canadian gas to the Anaconda Copper Mining Company, a war-related metals plant in Montana.[9] Another early application concerned a 400-mile pipeline carrying Canadian gas from Alberta to the Pacific Northwest. In a controversial 1954 ruling, the application was denied, which opened the door for a 1,400-mile extension of El Paso Pipe Line from the San Juan Basin in New Mexico and Colorado, connecting with Pacific Northwest Pipeline, to the same market.[10] The FPC based its denial on political uncertainties.

> The fullest possible . . . protection would not be afforded to any segment of the American people if its sole source of essential natural gas were through importation from a foreign country without some intergovernmental agreement assuring the continued adequacy of its supply. Otherwise, all control . . . would be in the hands of agencies of foreign governments whose primary interest would . . . always be . . . dependent upon public opinion within that country, rather than upon the interests of American consumers.[11]

The restrictive import policy of the FPC began to be reversed in the late 1950s, and by the late 1960s, the commission routinely approved applications to import Canadian gas to midwestern and northwestern markets. The growth of Canadian imports reflected this fact; by 1970, gas imports had grown from 104 Bcf a decade before to 768 Bcf.[12] With gas shortages over the next years, Canadian exports to the United States increased dramatically, and by 1974, 41 percent of Canada's gas went south.[13] Concern on the part of Canada's National Energy Board over excessive exports began in 1975,

[7]Opinion 261, 12 FPC 311 at 330 (1953).
[8]Ibid., p. 314.
[9]Opinion 223, 11 FPC 5 (1951).
[10]Opinion 223, 13 FPC at 235 (1954).
[11]Ibid.
[12]"Pipeline Gas Supplies," in American Gas Association, *Regulation of the Natural Gas Industry*, 4 vols. (New York: Matthew Bender, 1982), vol. 1, p. 12-67.
[13]Ibid.

but with only light-handed Canadian interference (unlike Canadian oil exports, which encountered heavy-handed intervention), volumes reached 1 Tcf in 1981.[14] U.S. regulators welcomed imports, but the high price of nearly $5.00 per Mcf was an unpleasant necessity given the alternative of inadequate supply. As of 1984, nineteen authorizations totaling 4.5 Bcf per day, a volume deemed surplus to home consumption, were in force at the (Canadian) regulated price at $4.94 per Mcf.[15] These allowables, significantly increased from the 1970s, were concentrated in California and the central United States.

Mexico

Mexico in the early 1960s began to export gas to the United States, and those exports averaged between 40 Bcf and 50 Bcf annually over the next decade.[16] A pricing dispute initiated by Mexico led to suspension of deliveries to the United States in 1975. Negotiations between Petroleos Mexicanos (PEMEX) and a consortium of U.S. gas suppliers, working through federal authorities, led to a resumption of imports in early 1980. Another pricing dispute initiated by Mexico resulted in a 23 percent price increase for Mexican gas to $4.32 per Mcf—at parity with Canadian gas—which was reluctantly granted by the Economic Regulatory Administration.[17] Although only a fraction of the amount of Canadian imports, high-priced Mexican gas served as a necessary supplement to domestic supply. As of 1983, only one authorization was in force: a 300 Mcf per day contract priced at $4.94 per Mcf.

The growth of gas imports in the 1960s and particularly in the troubled 1970s, and the increased prices that accompanied this growth, can be seen in table 15.A2-1.

Liquefied Natural Gas

High-priced imports, the wolf at the door of domestic natural gas regulation, were most clearly seen with LNG from Algeria (Sonatrach) and Indonesia (Pertamina). LNG reflects a capital-intensive

[14]David Muchow, "The Gas Industry: 1982–2000," in American Gas Association, *Regulation of the Gas Industry*, vol. 1, p. 6-18.

[15]Canadian export regulation is guided by two principles: (1) exports should not be priced below domestic sales, and (2) export quantities should be surplus to home consumption.

[16]"Pipeline Gas Supplies," p. 12-71.

[17]Ibid., p. 12-72.

Table 15.A2-1
NATURAL-GAS IMPORTS AND EXPORTS: 1960–84

	Imports		Exports		
Year	Total Imports (MMcf)	Avg. Price ($/Mcf)	Total Exports (MMcf)	Avg. Price ($/Mcf)	Net Imports (MMcf)
1960	155,646	–	11,332	–	144,314
1961	218,860	–	10,747	–	208,113
1962	401,534	–	15,814	–	385,720
1963	406,204	–	16,957	–	389,247
1964	443,326	–	19,603	–	423,723
1965	456,394	–	26,132	–	430,262
1966	479,780	–	24,639	–	455,141
1967	564,226	–	81,614	–	482,612
1968	651,885	–	93,745	–	558,140
1969	726,951	–	51,304	–	675,647
1970	820,780	–	69,831	–	750,949
1971	934,548	–	80,212	–	854,336
1972	1,019,496	0.31	78,014	0.31	941,482
1973	1,032,901	0.35	77,169	0.34	955,732
1974	959,284	0.55	76,789	0.55	882,495
1975	953,008	1.21	72,675	1.21	880,333
1976	963,768	1.72	64,710	1.72	899,058
1977	1,011,002	1.98	55,626	1.98	955,376
1978	965,545	2.13	52,533	2.13	913,012
1979	1,253,383	2.49	55,673	2.49	1,197,710
1980	984,767	4.28	48,731	4.28	936,036
1981	903,949	4.88	59,372	4.88	844,577
1982	933,336	5.03	51,728	5.03	881,608
1983	918,407	4.78	54,639	4.78	863,768
1984	843,060	4.08	54,753	4.08	788,307

SOURCE: U.S. Department of Energy, Energy Information Administration, *Natural Gas Monthly*, August 1992, p. 10; and American Gas Association, *1986 Gas Facts* (Arlington, Va.: 1987), p. 34; and American Gas Association, *1967 Gas Facts* (Arlington, Va.: 1968), p. 110.

process whereby natural gas is liquefied at extremely cold temperatures (−260°F) to condense the methane to 1/600 of its normal volume. It is then transferred from LNG terminals to special tankers for carriage to other LNG terminals where it is revaporized at pipe-line connection points.

LNG was first produced and commercially stored in the United States in 1939. Two decades later, transatlantic shipments commenced from the United States to Canvey Island, England. Small LNG imports began in 1968.

In March 1972, the FPC ruled that liquefied gas came within the meaning of the NGA and approved the first major LNG import project.[18] The commission also assumed jurisdiction over all LNG-related facilities—unloading terminals, storage areas, and regasification plants.[19]

Two major LNG cases in the 1970s attracted controversy because the FPC approved contract prices that were approximately double regulated domestic prices. One case concerned a 1970 application by Columbia LNG Corporation, Consolidated System LNG Company, and Southern Natural Gas Company for El Paso Natural Gas to purchase gas (liquefied in a $250-million plant owned by the Algerian government), ship it in special tankers to the United States, and regasify it for sale to Columbia, Southern, and Consolidated for interstate transportation and consumption.[20] FPC approval was given in June 1972 at $1.00 per Mcf, a rate two to three times the weighted average cost of gas of the three pipelines.[21] The irony of cost-based regulation, which created domestic-supply problems that created the demand for high-cost LNG, was explained by Commissioner Rush Moody.

> This inequity results from . . . cost-based pricing as the foundation for producer regulation. It is this system of regulation which produces discrimination against the lower cost energy source. . . . Cost-based regulation will encourage the capital intensive source, and will always favor that source which is most difficult to bring to the market; the more the importers spend on transport and processing facilities, the greater the dollar return.[22]

---

[18]Distrigas Corp., 47 FPC 752 (1972); and 47 FPC 1465 (1972).

[19]Distrigas Corp., 49 FPC 1145 (1973).

[20]The Algerian plant was 90 percent financed by the Export-Import Bank. Total U.S. Export-Import Bank involvement exceeded $400 million. *Energy Crisis*, ed. Lester Sobel, 4 vols. (New York: Facts on File, 1974), vol. 1, pp. 182–83.

[21]Opinion 622, 47 FPC 1624 (1972).

[22]Ibid., p. 1654.

The uncomfortable implications of the entire LNG project, despite his approval, led Moody to add:

> We place LNG customers, and the shareholders of three major pipe-lines, in dependence on a foreign power. Unilateral price escalation or interruption in service may be expected when foreign national interest so dictates. Only one force can effectively operate to hold down the costs of foreign supplies. We must have vigorous and effective competition from domestic producers.[23]

On rehearing, a new issue threatened the project—use of incremental over rolled-in pricing, which targeted the record high prices charged certain consumers.[24] This requirement threatened the project, and the sponsors filed suit and persuaded the court that the FPC went beyond their authority by requiring marginal-cost pricing.[25] The commission on remand approved rolled-in pricing in early 1977, and the project began after a six-year delay.[26]

A similar pricing dispute arose from a November 1973 request by Trunkline LNG Corporation to approve an import price that was double the price of domestic supply. The commission first required incremental pricing and suggested that the same rate design apply to all LNG projects.[27] After a storm of dissent—indeed, incremental pricing would either price LNG out of the market or seriously discriminate against certain users—an amendatory opinion was issued on June 30, 1977, to allow rolled-in pricing with regular curtailment contingencies.[28]

Licensing delays interfered with much-needed imports at the height of domestic-gas-supply emergencies.[29] Federal regulators were faced with a self-imposed regulatory dilemma—domestic shortage or program-defeating imports. The attorneys of one of the

---

[23]Ibid., p. 1653.

[24]Opinion 622-A, 48 FPC 723 (1972).

[25]*Columbia LNG Corporation* v. *FPC,* 491 F.2d 651 (5th Cir. 1974).

[26]Opinion 786, 57 FPC 354 (1977).

[27]Opinion 796, 58 FPC 726 (1977).

[28]Opinion 796-A, 58 FPC 2935 (1977).

[29]For regulatory delay problems of two California utilities desiring to purchase Indonesian LNG, see "A Funny Thing Happened on the Way to LNG," *Forbes,* September 18, 1981, pp. 52–56.

importers involved described the government's attitude as "'wavering,' 'uncertain' in many cases, and 'largely negative' toward LNG."[30] With an almost revengeful attitude, Department of Energy officials would turn against LNG imports when the gas emergency lightened.[31] In late 1978 and early 1979, energy czar James Schlesinger announced that LNG as a supply source was "at the end of the priority line," and two Algerian LNG applications were denied by officials because of an alleged lack of "overriding national or regional need for this gas."[32]

With increased volumes blocked by U.S. regulators, the Algerian government sought to increase revenue by again renegotiating higher prices with El Paso. A December 1979 renegotiation set the price at $1.95 per Mcf, with scheduled increases to $2.54 per Mcf in late 1980, but now the National Liberation Front government desired $6.11 per Mcf. El Paso brought in energy regulators to handle negotiations, and when they reached an impasse, shipments stopped on March 31, 1980. El Paso was losing $7 million a day, and after the seventh negotiating session failed, the company announced a $365.4-million writeoff covering seven LNG tankers and associated regasification facilities.[33] Commissioner Moody's 1972 warning about the perils of LNG imports came true with a vengeance.

Despite the El Paso debacle, LNG imports continued from Sonatrach to Everett, Massachusetts (Distrigas Corp.), and in September 1982, Panhandle Eastern began to receive LNG from Algeria, pursuant to a 1975 contract, priced at $3.92 per Mcf ($6.65 per Mcf landed). Given falling prices and surplus domestic gas, pressure from customers and legislators to amend the contract kept the pricing issue alive. Shipments continued at Panhandle's $580-million facility at Lake Charles, Louisiana.

With new gas-market conditions, pricing and other issues became vital to companies trying to remain competitive with substitute fuels

---

[30]"Pipeline Gas Supplies," p. 12-87.

[31]By analogy, LNG imports (and Canadian and Mexican gas imports) can be likened to the messenger with bad tidings who bears the brunt of the audience's (the regulators') anger.

[32]See David Muchow, "The Gas Industry—1982–2000," p. 6-25.

[33]"A Squeeze on LNG to Force up Prices," *Business Week*, July 7, 1980, p. 33; and Alexander Stuart, "El Paso Comes in from the Cold," *Fortune*, March 23, 1981, pp. 55–56.

in industrial markets. A policy announcement in early 1984 by the Department of Energy noted highly competitive gas markets and abolished federally set border prices to allow private contracting so long as "competitive" and in the "public interest."[34] The guidelines applied to new contracts, including fourteen pending applications for Canadian gas and two pending Algerian LNG applications. Import contracts remained regulated, but the burden of proof was shifted from applicants to intervenors. Combined with partial export deregulation on the Canadian side, growing gas imports into the United States from the north were evident as of 1984 with promise for greater volumes in the future.

Although less known, the United States was also an exporter of LNG. In 1967, Marathon Oil and Phillips Petroleum entered into a fifteen-year contract to supply several companies in Tokyo, Japan, with LNG from the North Cook Inlet and Kenai fields in Alaska. The first shipment arrived in Tokyo on November 4, 1969.[35] While Alaskan exports had remained steady since the early 1970s, energy analysts lamented the fact that North Slope gas, estimated at 10 percent of total reserves, had not been made available for export.[36] With restricted gas exports in the absence of a presidential finding, and the uneconomical prospects of the proposed Alaska Natural Gas Transportation System, recycling and flaring were the only alternatives. Without legislative impediment, a gas pipeline to Valdez (next to the Trans-Alaskan Pipeline System) or to the Kenai Peninsula (recommended by the Governor's Economic Committee on North Slope Natural Gas) was the most logical choice with Japan, which already has LNG facilities, and other Pacific Rim outlets as destinations.[37]

The rise and decline of LNG imports compared to LNG exports can be seen in table 15.A2-2.

[34]49 *Fed. Reg.* 6684 (February 22, 1984).

[35]Robert Hartig and John Norman, "Production, Conservation, and Utilization of Natural Gas in Alaska," *Natural Resources Lawyer* (November 1970): 699.

[36]A Heritage Foundation study identified a North Slope LNG industry as a potential "catalyst for establishing a stable industrial base in the 49th state." Milton Copulos, S. Fred Singer, and David Watkins, "Exporting Alaska's Oil and Gas," Heritage Foundation Backgrounder no. 248, February 22, 1983, p. 17.

[37]See the discussion in Stephen Eule and S. Fred Singer, "Export of Alaskan Oil and Gas," in *Free-Market Energy,* ed. S. Fred Singer (New York: Universe Books, 1984), pp. 118–43.

Table 15.A2-2
LNG FOREIGN TRADE 1969–84
(MMcf)

Year	Imports[a]	Exports[b]	Net Imports
1969	0	2,982	(2,982)
1970	757	44,257	(43,500)
1971	2,933	50,231	(47,298)
1972	2,262	47,882	(45,620)
1973	4,055	48,346	(44,291)
1974	0	50,258	(50,258)
1975	4,893	53,002	(48,109)
1976	10,155	49,779	(39,624)
1977	11,896	51,655	(39,759)
1978	84,422	48,434	35,988
1979	252,608	51,289	201,319
1980	85,850	44,732	41,118
1981	36,830	55,929	(19,099)
1982	55,136	49,861	5,275
1983	131,124	52,857	78,267
1984	36,191	52,840	(16,649)

SOURCE: U.S. Department of Energy, Energy Information Administration, *Natural Gas Monthly*, August 1992, pp. 10–11.
[a]From Algeria and, to a small extent, Canada.
[b]To Japan from Alaska.

16. Other Transportation Regulation

While oil and gas transportation is most closely identified with pipelines, crude oil, petroleum products, and natural-gas liquids can be moved by motor carriers, water carriers, and railroads. Table 16.1 shows the relative volumes of oil and derived products handled by each transportation mode from 1938 through 1980 in five-year increments. Oil pipelines have been the predominant mode of oil transportation for nearly one-half of the business. Water and motor carriers each have claimed around a quarter share of the market, with railcars carrying the shrinking residual.

In ton-miles, another measure of market share that was first tabulated in the early 1970s, the statistics are somewhat different, as seen in table 16.2. Oil pipelines held an even greater market share until the 1980s when their percentage fell to under 50 percent. Motor carriers, which held a quarter share of the market in raw tons, held only a 2 to 4 percent share in ton-miles; the big gainer was water carriers, which rival pipelines, with almost a 50 percent market share. As before, railroads held a small residual.

Those market-share statistics reflect fundamental market and regulatory forces. Continuing from chapter 11, the role of regulation in each of the four major modes will be examined along with the fundamental economics of each to assess the overall impact on oil transportation.

Railroad Regulation: 1900–84

The importance of railroad shipments of petroleum, as seen in table 16.1, has steadily declined since World War II. On short hauls, the flexibility provided by tank trucks has reduced the demand for tank cars; on long hauls, oil pipelines have proven more economical. Regulation, which stifled innovation and efficiency relative to less regulated transportation rivals, has also worked against railroads.[1]

---

[1] Relative regulation and subsidization of transportation modes are examined in this chapter, pp. 1016–19.

Table 16.1
INTERMODAL OIL TRANSPORTATION: 1938–80
(million tons)

Year	Total Volume	Pipelines Volume	Pipelines Share	Motor Carriers Volume	Motor Carriers Share	Water Carriers Volume	Water Carriers Share	Railroads Volume	Railroads Share
1938	354	139	39%	21	6%	138	29%	57	16%
1943	474	196	41	76	16	116	24	85	18
1948	686	262	38	121	18	238	35	65	10
1953	863	359	42	185	21	273	32	45	5
1958	1,017	433	43	252	25	299	29	33	3
1963	1,196	521	44	313	26	336	28	27	2
1968	1,563	726	46	450	29	361	23	26	2
1973	1,923	912	47	560	29	421	22	30	2
1978	2,124	982	46	613	29	503	24	26	1
1980	1,991	921	46	538	27	509	26	23	1

SOURCE: Association of Oil Pipelines, *Shifts in Petroleum Transportation* (Washington, D.C.: AOP, 1982), table 1.

Table 16.2
INTERMODAL OIL TRANSPORTATION: 1972–84
(billion ton-miles)

Year	Total Volume	Pipelines		Motor Carriers		Water Carriers		Railroads	
		Volume	Share	Volume	Share	Volume	Share	Volume	Share
1972	839	476	57%	23	3%	330	39%	10	1%
1976	868	515	59	33	4	307	35	13	2
1980	1,245	588	47	27	2	618	50	13	1
1984	1,180	568	48	29	2	571	48	12	1

SOURCE: Association of Oil Pipelines, *Shifts in Petroleum Transportation* (Washington, D.C.: AOP, 1986), table 1.

Only with deregulation beginning in 1976 did the railroad industry show signs of regaining its lost share of the petroleum market. Tank trains of twenty to eighty cars with quick petroleum loading and unloading capabilities were an innovation that promised to increase business for oil-carrying railroads in the future.[2]

Continuation of Protectionism: 1900–24

Chapter 11 described early government subsidization of railroads and later efforts of major railway firms to tame competition by federal regulation.[3] Near the turn of the century, the Supreme Court upheld state regulation of railroad rates as a public benefit.[4] Upon the foundation of *Smyth* v. *Ames*, railroad regulation, as regulation elsewhere in the economy, would expand.

The Elkins Anti-Rebating Act, a product of the Pennsylvania Railroad and its tireless president, Alexander Cassatt, became law on February 19, 1903.[5] This law reinforced section 5 of the 1887 Interstate Commerce Act to discourage individualized ratemaking (from rebates, concessions, underbilling, and the like) and encourage joint ratemaking. The open, published fare was the only legal fare; departures constituted a misdemeanor.[6] While pooling remained illegal under the original 1887 law, the 1903 amendment encouraged the same but in an indirect and *legal* manner. Private pooling had long

---

[2]George Wolbert, *U.S. Oil Pipe Lines* (Washington, D.C.: American Petroleum Institute, 1979), p. 135.

[3]See chapter 11, pp. 618–23.

[4]"A railroad is a public highway, and none the less so because constructed and maintained through the agency of a corporation deriving its existence and powers from the State. Such a corporation was created for public purposes. It performs a function of the State. Its authority to exercise the right of eminent domain and to charge tolls was given primarily for the benefit of the public." *Smyth* v. *Ames*, 169 U.S. 466 at 544 (1897).

[5]Public Law 103, 32 Stat. 847 (1903). "Most of the railroads were tired of rebating . . . and the Pennsylvania decided to resort to legislative means to end the costly institution." Gabriel Kolko, *Railroads and Regulation* (New York: W. W. Norton & Company, 1965), p. 95.

[6]In 1963, the Supreme Court identified the major purpose of the Elkins Act as to "prevent any kind of departure from published rates." *United States* v. *Braverman*, 373 U.S. 405 at 406. See David Boies, "Experiment in Mercantilism: Minimum Rate Regulation by the Interstate Commerce Commission," *Columbia Law Review* (April 1968): 607.

failed under market pressures. Statute-induced conformity—pooling in all but name—was far more promising.[7]

On June 29, 1906, a second major revision to the Interstate Commerce Act was enacted. The Hepburn Act, contrary to common interpretation, again advanced protectionism at the industry's request.[8] Published rates were frozen for thirty days instead of ten days, free travel was prohibited with certain exceptions, rebate fines were stiffened, prison sentences were introduced, and the Interstate Commerce Commission (ICC) was authorized (section 15) to "determine and prescribe . . . the just and reasonable rate . . . as the maximum to be charged" if a rate was challenged by a shipper.

Section 15, potentially limiting rates and profitability for the industry, was less of a threat to supportive firms than it seemed. Initial rate filings that had proven profitable remained unaffected, and formal complaints were prohibitively expensive for most shippers to file.[9] Section 20 standardized accounting for cost-of-service fare determination that shippers would have difficulty challenging. The 1906 amendments gave rebates a death blow, while steering clear of regulatory threats to profitable ratemaking.[10]

The Mann-Elkins Act of June 18, 1910, again advanced railroad protectionism to benefit the industry, but it also contained elements of pluralist legislation.[11] Public suspicion toward corporations, particularly railroads, made restrictive regulation politically opportune, and several shipper-oriented reforms to the Interstate Commerce Act were adopted. The long- and short-haul clause was resurrected after its de facto demise before the commission and courts several decades before.[12] Initial rates, whether for a new route or a rate

---

[7]In Gabriel Kolko's words, "Such a provision for maintaining rates accomplished the same end as pools and rate associations; this had been the goal of the railroads for three decades. The major railroads were delighted with the Elkins Act, for the legal machinery of the government was now to do what they had failed to accomplish themselves." Kolko, *Railroads and Regulation*, pp. 100–101.

[8]See the discussion in ibid., pp. 127–31.

[9]Ibid., p. 145. Informal complaints, on the other hand, were possible and would assume increasing importance. See Robert Harbeson, "Railroads and Regulation, 1877–1916: Conspiracy or Public Interest?" *Journal of Economic History* (June 1967): 236–37.

[10]Gabriel Kolko, *Railroads and Regulation*, p. 148.

[11]Public Law 218, 36 Stat. 539 (1910).

[12]See chapter 11, p. 623.

change on an existing route, could be suspended by the ICC for 120 days and then another six months, if necessary, if under review. Section 15 of the Interstate Commerce Act was now potentially anti-railroad if shippers could influence the commission, especially in times of inflation when unchanged rates meant declining rates. The railroads were not shut out, however. An amendment to section 4 weakened rate differentials based on unique routes, another blow to rate discounting.[13]

The 1910 amendments made regulation more risky than ever before for the regulated industry. Growing shipper influence had changed the law to allow administrative rate determination. The *Railway Age Gazette* still looked on the bright side.

> It does not necessarily follow that [Mann-Elkins] will either hurt or help anyone. Like the previous laws to regulate interstate commerce, its effects will depend on how it is administered and obeyed. . . . The present personnel and temper of the Interstate Commerce Commission encourage optimism.[14]

Administrative decisionmaking would exceed the railroads' worst expectations. Accelerated inflation was at the root of the problem. Prices had been stable or declining from the 1860s to the early 1900s; beginning in 1910 and particularly after 1915, they began to rise. Higher rates were required to stay even with higher costs, and in 1910, and again in 1915 and 1917, rate increases were denied in whole or in part by the commission. Increases were modest when granted.[15] Shippers had become more powerful and better organized, and the commissioners and President Taft himself made political hay by being "pro-consumer."

With rates falling below unregulated levels and earnings under siege, a vicious circle developed that would spell the end, at least temporarily, of private railroad ownership. With less profit and lower stock values, capital for expansion and modernization became scarce, and capacity to meet growing demand became more and more constrained. Inflation and labor unrest added fuel to the fire.

---

[13]David Boies, "Experiment in Mercantilism: Minimum Rate Regulation by the Interstate Commerce Commission," p. 608.

[14]Quoted in Gabriel Kolko, *Railroads and Regulation,* p. 195.

[15]Robert Harbeson, "Railroads and Regulation," p. 241.

It was a case, as documented by Albro Martin, of *enterprise denied*.[16] The irony of regulation's coming to haunt its original architects should not mask the fact that decades of gain had resulted from legislative protectionism. But now, regulation foreclosed entrepreneurial strategies to achieve profitability and growth.

With worsening problems and the unprecedented demands of World War I, the "breakdown" of railroad transportation was followed by a presidential order to nationalize the industry on December 28, 1917. Legislation to the same effect followed three months later.[17] In actuality, as the *New York Times* editorialized, it was regulation that had broken down, not the private railroad system.[18]

The newly formed United States Railroad Administration assumed control of the industry and instigated national pooling. Profits were guaranteed, and the bureaucratic chieftains were primarily railroad men wearing new hats.[19] The rationale for the unprecedented effort was wasteful duplication and general inefficiency under the "competitive" system; short shrift was given to how regulation stymied entrepreneurial efforts to restructure assets in a more efficient manner. After incurring over a billion dollars in deficits in twenty-six months of socialistic operation, the railroads were returned to private ownership and operation on February 29, 1920.[20]

The poor health of the privatized railroad industry, coupled with the close business-government relationship after the war, inspired the protectionist Transportation Act of 1920.[21] The act, noticed Gabriel Kolko, "was the logical culmination of more than forty years of agitation and education for comprehensive federal railroad regulation designed to provide rationalization and stability to the industry."[22] All pretense of being against railroad monopoly and noncompetitive practices was dropped. Pooling de jure was legalized to join pooling de facto. Minimum-rate authority was given to the commission. Mergers and consolidations were not only allowed but

---

[16] Albro Martin, *Enterprise Denied: Origins of the Decline of American Railroads, 1897–1917* (New York: Columbia University Press, 1971).

[17] Public Law 107, 40 Stat. 451 (1918).

[18] See Albro Martin, *Enterprise Denied*, p. 350.

[19] Gabriel Kolko, *Railroads and Regulation,* pp. 227–28.

[20] Clarence Carson, *Throttling the Railroads* (Indianapolis: Liberty Fund, 1971), p. 79.

[21] Public Law 152, 41 Stat. 456 (1920).

[22] Gabriel Kolko, *Railroads and Regulation,* p. 229.

invited by regulatory design. Intrastate tariffs set by state agencies could be changed—in the industry's eyes, raised—by the ICC. Public-utility ratemaking was adopted with "aggregate annual net railway operating income equal . . . to a fair rate return upon the aggregate value of the railway property."[23] Floor prices, in other words, would replace once-ruinous rate-increase denials. A recapture clause was added for firms with profits above the industry average for redistribution to firms below the aggregate average. Although profit was not guaranteed, the protected industry could relax cost discipline and still make the median profit.

Finally, the hitherto missing link in railroad cartelization prefaced on cost-plus ratemaking was added: *entry restriction.* New lines in occupied and unoccupied areas were required to obtain a certificate of public convenience and necessity with the burden of proof on new entrants.

Other regulation in the 1920 amendments, less favorable to the industry, came with the territory—abandonment preapproval, compulsory extension of facilities, and rate substitution by the ICC. Such detrimental actions would be rare. In the 1920s, the ICC would prove to be, in Kolko's words, "the shield of the railroads against the public."[24]

The Interstate Commerce Act, vintage 1920, embodied the legislative victory of the railroad industry's program over state regulation, which was less uniform, less predictable, and less favorable. The Supreme Court in 1924 recognized the "fostering guardianship and control" of the ICC "to promote [industry] growth and . . . safety."[25] A profitable financial future for the industry seemed assured. But if competition was legislatively restrained from within, it was not necessarily restrained from without. Intermodal competition would bring a new era to the railroad industry and require new legislative direction.

Intermodal Competition and Legislative Adjustment: 1925–84

If the railway industry had had a monopoly on freight transportation, existing legislation would have fostered financial stability for the industry despite internal inefficiencies. But freight in general,

---

[23]Public Law 152, 41 Stat. 488 (1920).

[24]Gabriel Kolko, *Railroads and Regulation,* p. 229.

[25]*Dayton-Goose Creek Railway* v. *United States,* 263 U.S. 456 at 478 (1924).

and oil in particular, increasingly had other transportation alternatives that thrived on artificially high rail rates. Pipelines and tank trucks would assume strong market positions at the expense of tank cars. Railroads, consequently, constrained by regulation to meet the challenge of intermodal competition, were driven to legislative reform, which marked a third era of federal railroad policy.[26]

In 1925, a congressional resolution was passed that signaled a major policy change for railroads. Freight rates, it was declared, should reflect "the conditions which at any given time prevail in our several industries."[27] Although largely symbolic, the message from Congress was that the ICC should allow rate reductions for agriculture (a politically favored industry) and generally promote rate flexibility to maintain traffic amid intermodal competition.

Legislative reform was more the idea of industry than the public. Continued growth of competition, particularly oil pipelines, led to a November 20, 1930, resolution to Congress by the Association of Railroad Executives

> to inquire whether, in the public interest, any [transportation companies] engaged in interstate commerce, should be regulated, or further regulated, whether existing governmental regulation of interstate commerce should be modified or amended, and to submit a report to the Congress . . . containing its recommendations thereon, together with a finding as to the effect of motor, water, air, and pipeline transportation on railroad revenues and with drafts of appropriate bills to carry into effect such recommendations as it may make.[28]

The Depression years witnessed several stopgap government actions to help railroads that were victimized not only by general economic conditions but by their own stagnate performance. Herbert Hoover's Reconstruction Finance Corporation and the Public Works Administration loaned $1.43 billion to railway firms beginning in

---

[26]The periods were the pre-1887 subsidization era, the 1887–1925 protectionist era, and the post-1925 regulatory adjustment era. The next era, examined below, would be the relaxed regulatory era dating from 1958.

[27]Resolution 17, 43 Stat. 801 (1925). See Harvey Mansfield, "The Hoch-Smith Resolution and the Considerations of Commercial Conditions in Rate-Fixing," *Cornell Law Quarterly* (April 1931): 339–58.

[28]*National Petroleum News*, February 18, 1931, p. 25. Cited hereafter as *NPN*.

1932.[29] A year later, the Bankruptcy Act of 1898 was amended to facilitate the financial reorganization of insolvent railroad companies.[30] Also in 1933, the Emergency Transportation Act established an office of Federal Coordinator of Transportation and provided several railroad-relief measures.[31] The recapture clause was abolished, and collected monies were returned to their respective firms. Fair-value ratemaking was liberalized to allow each firm to receive the profit required to operate "successfully." Other revisions brought rail firms face to face with the changing transportation scene. The ICC was instructed to consider "the effect of rates on the movement of traffic" to avoid pricing railroad services out of the market. Steps to lower railway operating costs were taken such as allowing greater pooling and consolidation to avoid the unnecessary duplication of facilities.

The Transportation Act of 1940 marked a complete shift of federal railway policy.[32] "The railroad problem," explained Clair Wilcox, "had now become a transport problem."[33] Cognizant of transportation as a whole, federal regulation called a truce between competing modes to preserve "the inherent advantages of each" against the "unfair or destructive competition" of the others.[34] When the ICC's jurisdiction was expanded to motor carriers in 1935 and water carriers in 1940, examined below, the agency would discourage price warring between jurisdictions or rate increases by one transportation mode to protect another mode. The burden of proof was now on the carrier that lowered its rates, while rate advances were not questioned with the welfare of competitors in mind. Pricing flexibility was replaced with rate "parity" to allow each carrier to have its "fair share" of traffic.[35]

---

[29]Frank Wilner, *Competitive Equity* (Washington, D.C.: Association of American Railroads, 1981), p. 40. Repayment of principal would exceed 99 percent.

[30]Public Law 420, 47 Stat. 1467 (1933).

[31]Public Law 68, 48 Stat. 211 (1933).

[32]Public Law 785, 54 Stat. 898 (1940).

[33]Clair Wilcox, *Public Policies toward Business* (Homewood, Ill.: R. D. Irwin, 1966), p. 401.

[34]Public Law 785, 54 Stat. 899 (1940).

[35]See Alfred Kahn, *The Economics of Regulation*, 2 vols. (New York: John Wiley and Sons, 1971), vol. 2, pp. 21–22.

The next accommodation to address the plight of the railroad industry was the Reed-Bulwinkle Act, enacted on July 6, 1948, over the veto of President Truman, that legalized concerted rate setting.[36] Subject to ICC approval, rates determined through industry trade associations ("rate bureaus") were immune from antitrust challenges. Several antitrust suits filed by the Department of Justice in 1944 were consequently put to rest.

By the 1950s, a multitude of deep-seated railway ills was obvious. Costs were inflated, and revenue could not be maximized because service was inflexible to consumer demand. Regulation was at fault. Whereas in earlier decades regulation had had a positive net effect on railroads except during the 1910–20 debacle, federal intervention now unintendedly acted as a straitjacket, preventing the reform necessary to create a lean, profitable industry. Regulatory problems were not only internal—labor-union featherbedding, restricted entry and exit, high state and federal taxation, inflexible routing and terms of service—but external. Federal policies subsidizing right-of-way costs advantaged competing modes of transportation at the expense of railroads.[37]

The industry recognized the new problem and sought relaxed regulation.[38] The railroads' new battle cry was the "freedom to compete on an equal basis."[39] The result of the new philosophy and lobbying initiative was the Transportation Act of 1958.[40] Federal railroad taxes were repealed. Union powers were curtailed. Abandonment proceedings were relaxed. Cost-saving routes could be more easily pursued. Section 15(a), importantly, was modified to allow pricing flexibility to meet a competitor's lower fares.[41] Relief from burdensome intrastate maximum-rate regulation was provided. These amendments represented a circuitous attempt at proactive deregulation—and tacit admission of the failure of regulation

[36]Public Law 622, 62 Stat. 472 (1948).

[37]Motor truck and waterway subsidies are examined in this chapter, pp. 984–1016.

[38]See the discussion in David Boies, "Experiment in Mercantilism: Minimum Rate Regulation by the Interstate Commerce Commission," pp. 624–25.

[39]Statement of the Association of American Railroads. Quoted in Carl Fulda, *Competition in the Regulated Industries: Transportation* (Boston: Little, Brown and Company, 1961), p. 27.

[40]Public Law 85-625, 72 Stat. 568 (1958).

[41]"Rates of a carrier shall not be held up to a particular level to protect the traffic of any other mode of transportation." Ibid., p. 572.

to achieve industry goals. More regulatory abatement was necessary, however, and would come.

The 1958 act—as was the legislation preceding it—was pragmatic and not the result of a consistent free-market philosophy. Evidence of this was a loan-guarantee program offering up to $5 million per line from a $500-million pool. Defaults of $107 million would result from this program.[42]

Frontal deregulation began with the Railroad Revitalization and Regulatory Reform Act of 1976.[43] In response to both deteriorating industry financial performance and malcontent shippers, the ICC was given the administrative discretion to deregulate commodities if competition was not impaired.[44] Abandonment of unprofitable low-density lines was permitted to redirect resources from low-demand areas to high-demand areas.[45] The burden of proof was placed on the complaining party to show that a price that made any contribution to fixed costs in addition to variable costs was unreasonable. Rates could also be changed by more than 7 percent in either direction without commission preapproval so long as "market dominance" was absent. The so-called 4-R Act was "a landmark—the first legislation to reduce regulation of any transportation sector in the history of the United States."[46]

The Staggers Rail Act, signed October 14, 1980, by President Jimmy Carter, advanced deregulation by increasing the latitude of decision-making by firms in major areas.[47] Continuing profitability problems convinced authorities and much of the industry that more legislative

[42]Frank Wilner, *Competitive Equity*, p. 51.

[43]Public Law 95-210, 90 Stat. 31 (1976).

[44]See, for example, 44 *Fed. Reg.* 18229 (March 27, 1979); and 45 *Fed. Reg.* 20484 (March 28, 1980).

[45]Excess capacity in branch lines alone was estimated to cost railroads $3 billion in unrecouped outlays in 1977 alone. Robert Harris, "Economic Analysis of Light Density Rail Lines," *Logistics and Transportation Review* (January 1980): 3–29. Other regulatory costs totaled in the billions of dollars. See Michael Babcock, "Efficiency and Adjustment: The Impact of Railroad Deregulation," Cato Institute Policy Analysis no. 33, January 31, 1984, p. 6.

[46]Thomas Moore, "Rail and Truck Reform—The Record So Far," *Regulation*, November–December 1983, p. 34.

[47]Public Law 96-448, 94 Stat. 1895 (1980). Carter's deregulatory position with railroads first crystallized with the appointment of free-market economists Darius Gaskins and Marcus Alexis to the commission.

reform than provided in 1976 was necessary. Requirements for extending or abandoning lines were eased. Merger applications were expedited. Rate maximums were eliminated for almost two-thirds of the industry, while rate minimums were relaxed to allow greater intermodal competition. For "market-dominant" firms, regulated rates were allowed to increase 6 percent above an industry inflation allowance (with an 18 percent overall ceiling), after which 4 percent annual escalations were allowed. Joint ratemaking, however, was prohibited as anti-competitive. The thirty-day rate-freeze requirement was reduced to ten days for rate decreases and twenty days for rate increases. Disputed rate proceedings were reduced from seven months to five months. The prohibition on discrimination between shippers, an original part of the Interstate Commerce Act in 1887, was relaxed. Discretionary authority for the ICC to deregulate railroads in competitive markets was given.

Another change would be particularly important—long-term shipping contracts in place of common-carrier offerings. By mid-1984, over 16,000 short-term and long-term contracts had been made. Agreements have ranged from several weeks to twenty years and had a variety of payment provisions, including front money for facility modernization.[48]

In late 1980, piggyback traffic (flatcar transport of trailer and container cars) was administratively deregulated.[49] Counting previous exemptions, nearly 80 percent of railway tonnage was deregulated after 1976.[50] The general consequence was lower costs and lower prices to revitalize the industry. Summarized Thomas Moore:

> The railroads have used their new freedom to cut rates when demand is low and equipment available, and raise them when demand is high and equipment in short supply. They have also offered low back-haul (return-trips) rates to fill containers and cars that previously had to return empty.[51]

[48]Comments of William Dempsey before the National Industrial Traffic League, November 18, 1982; comments of Richard Briggs before the Transportation Association of America, January 28, 1982, p. 11; and conversation with Thomas White, Association of American Railroads, August 20, 1984.

[49]45 *Fed. Reg.* 79123 (November 28, 1980).

[50]Frank Wilner, *Market Discipline and Modal Choice* (Washington, D.C.: Association of American Railroads, 1982), p. 30.

[51]Thomas Moore, "Rail and Truck Reform—The Record So Far," p. 35.

Many firms experienced a long-awaited return to profitability.[52] The main beneficiaries of deregulation were the food and coal industries, but petroleum participated as well. One example may be mentioned. In 1981, a ten-year contract to ship 3,600 tank cars of fuel oil annually was made by Conrail. Previously, with long-term contracts precluded by the common-carrier requirement, the oil had been barged across Lake Ontario at higher cost.[53] The flexibility provided by an innovative long-term contract closed the deal. For the first time since World War II, the declining market share of railroads was severely arrested if not reversed.

Motor Carrier Regulation: 1920–84

Although not competitively viable for long-distance petroleum transport, motor carriage is well suited to the flexibility requirements of low-volume, short-distance hauls. This is demonstrated by the fact that while trucking accounts for a large share of transported petroleum in raw tons, only a small percentage of ton-miles is carried, as was seen earlier.[54]

In the post–World War I period, for-hire trucking began to transform what hitherto had been a complementary relationship with railway carriage to a rivalrous relationship. Entry was easy, capitalization requirements were small, and the developing public road system opened new markets and reduced variable costs.[55] In 1924, the number of registered trucks had almost doubled from four years before.[56] A major reason for rapid industry growth, in addition to the public road subsidy, was the high fare structure of railroads, which was designed as if motor-carrier competition was nonexistent. Under the protective umbrella of the ICC, standardized rail fares

---

[52]See Michael Babcock, "Efficiency and Adjustment: The Impact of Railroad Deregulation," pp. 12–15; and Thomas Moore, "Rail and Truck Reform—The Record so Far," p. 36.

[53]Comments of Richard Briggs before the Pittsburgh Chapter, Delta Mu Alpha, April 14, 1982, p. 6 (copy in author's files).

[54]George Wolbert, *U.S. Oil Pipe Lines*, p. 347.

[55]"In the 1920s, you could get into the trucking business by having one truck, one driver, and one road connecting two points at which there were, respectively, a shipper and a receiver." John Spencer, "Trucking: A Retrospective," *Handling and Shipping Management*, October 1982, p. 3.

[56]Christopher Stone, "ICC: Some Reminiscences on the Future of American Transportation," *New Individualist Review* (Spring 1963): 9.

discriminated between high-volume agricultural goods and low-volume manufactured goods. High fares for the latter, where demand was assumed to be price-inelastic, played into the truckers' strength. Given their advantages of direct pickup and delivery, flexible hours, and rapid service, by merely matching rates motor carriers attracted merchandise that had previously gone by rail.[57] Rate regulation, in other words, boomeranged on the protected. Summarized Christopher Stone:

> The artificially high rate structure [of railroads] had a backlash to it, much as it had in the nineteenth century; but now, with the entry-stalling certificates of public convenience and necessity having closed the doors on rail expansion as an equalizer of investment possibilities, trucks were driving through the windows.[58]

State Regulation

The railroads, drawing upon a long history of government involvement, fought back against truckers in the legislative arena.[59] In 1923, a model statute was adopted by the National Association of Railroad and Utilities Commissioners to set rates and restrict entry for motor carriers. Already, Pennsylvania (1915), Utah (1917), Arizona and New Hampshire (1919), and Connecticut and Washington (1921) had motor-carrier laws, some with certification requirements. In the next four years, with railroad lobbying in full swing and established motor carriers, particularly bus companies, in general support, twenty-five states enacted regulation: California, Maine, Michigan, Montana, Ohio, Oklahoma, Rhode Island, and Virginia (1923); Indiana, Kansas, Wyoming, Iowa, Massachusetts, Minnesota, Nevada, North Carolina, North Dakota, Oregon, South Dakota, Vermont, and Wisconsin (1925); and Louisiana, Mississippi, Kentucky, and New Jersey (1926). By 1932, all states except Delaware had

---

[57] Alfred Kahn, *The Economics of Regulation,* vol. 2, pp. 14–15.

[58] Christopher Stone, "ICC: Some Reminiscences on the Future of American Transportation," p. 9.

[59] "The normal opposition in this country to extensions of public interference with business was, in this instance, kept from appearing by what may be called the momentum of two traditions: the tradition established in the case of railways of extensive regulation in the transportation field, and the far older tradition of looking upon the use of public highways as a place of business as a special privilege that may properly be denied or abridged in any way." G. Shorey Peterson, "Motor-Carrier Regulation and its Economic Basis," *Quarterly Journal of Economics* (May 1929): 607.

followed suit.[60] Also behind the surge were state public-utility commissions, which were easily persuaded to expand their authority. Typical of the language in the laws was a 1931 amendment to the Texas Truck Law of 1929 that limited supply to politically determined demand: "The rapid increase of motor traffic . . . [has] made it imperative . . . that the use of highways for the transport of property for hire may be restricted to the extent required by the necessity of the general public."[61]

Price regulation was the counterbalancing part of the regulatory covenant, along with certification requirements for common carriers. Cost-plus pricing was comfortable, although it was not a price or profit guarantee. Assigned rates could be stringent as well as lenient, depending on the relative political strength of constituencies influencing the commission. Thus, rate regulation was not relished as entry regulation was by railroads and motor carriers, although it was supported as an integral part of public-utility regulation.

Regulation of for-hire trucks had another dimension in addition to traditional rate and entry controls. Railroad interests were the primary architects, but unlike the case with other regulations, the regulated industry was disadvantaged and opposed to them. State laws that set weight and load maximums, length and width specifications, speed limits, equipment requirements, and travel areas blatantly discriminated against motor-vehicle transport and forced uneconomic substitutions of rail.

Not only railroads but big-city politics could hamper motor carriage. An outstanding example occurred in New York City. Until 1925, petroleum tank trucks were not allowed to directly service retail establishments in the city, ostensibly for safety reasons. This forced wooden barrels or steel drums to be distributed in the city. When tank trucks were legalized, the New York Hazardous Trades Board approved only one design, which was "virtually the specifications of one company." This company, not coincidentally, was

[60]D. Philip Locklin, *Economics of Transportation* (Homewood, Ill.: R. D. Irwin, 1972), pp. 673–74; and David Lilienthal and Irwin Rosenbaum, "Motor Carrier Regulation by Certificates of Necessity and Convenience," *Yale Law Journal* (December 1926): 164–66.

[61]Quoted in Edward Bailey, "Motor Truck Certificates and Permits in Texas," *Texas Law Review* (December 1941): 172. Said Bailey, "It is clear from the language of the new statute, as well as from the history of the period, that one of the predominant objectives of the new legislation was the protection of existing carriers, including the railroads, against unnecessary and harmful competition" (p. 171).

closely associated with the Tammany Hall interests that notoriously profited from graft and corruption.[62]

Over the next several years, several hundred heavily reinforced tank trucks ("Kenny tanks") were sold at over $3,000 per vehicle, compared to $1,500 for the regular make, while rival companies unsuccessfully tried to obtain certification. Competing designs fared well in rigorous testing, but authorities refused to budge. Even the American Petroleum Institute, headquartered in New York City, made an unprecedented appearance in local politics on behalf of would-be competitors, but to no avail.[63] A second design was finally approved in 1929 whereupon 75 new trucks entered a market capable of supporting 2,000 more, and Kenny tank prices dropped noticeably.[64] Other approvals would follow to dilute the tank-car monopoly, but burdensome design kept prices high to narrow the market and raise product prices for New York City consumers.

In 1932, Texas passed a law that limited trucks on state roads to 7,000 pounds. The special-interest railroad law had its intended effect—30,000 to 40,000 vehicles were forced from the road. Filling the void were not only railcars but light trucks, many coming out of retirement, which made state roads less safe, if less crowded.[65] In the same year, Kansas enacted a ton-mile tax that severely eroded motor-carrier profitability—again to benefit railroads. This led to a Supreme Court case in 1932 in which the right of states to regulate was unequivocally upheld despite the fact that railroads were patently advantaged at the expense of trucks.[66] This would encourage the railroad lobby to continue its legislative assault on truckers, whether by increasing labor costs and taxes, reducing speed limits, reducing tonnage ceilings, or requiring expensive safety features.

---

[62]*NPN*, July 4, 1928, p. 23. The company, Tank and Accessories Corporation, distributed tank cars in New York City through Interurban Delivery, Inc., a company managed by James Kenny, whose brother William was a major financial backer of New York governor Alfred Smith as well as co-owner of Interurban. The January 20, 1925, ordinance was written by J. J. Hoey, an insurance broker intimately associated with Tammany Hall, and revised on the advice of William Kenny.

[63]*NPN*, July 11, 1928, p. 23, and December 5, 1928, p. 23.

[64]*NPN*, June 19, 1929, p. 102.

[65]*NPN*, December 28, 1932, p. 25.

[66]"We need not consider whether the act in some other aspect would be good or bad. It is enough to support its validity that . . . one of its aims is to conserve the highways. "*Stephenson et al.* v. *Binford et al.*, 287 U.S. 251 at 276 (1932).

In 1933, Kentucky passed a truck law with onerous provisions, fathered by the legal division of the Louisville and Nashville Railroad, that led to forced truck sales, out-of-state transfers, diversions, closed shipper businesses, higher costs and final prices, and even retaliation by a neighboring state. Indiana trucks crossing the border could not meet Kentucky's strictly enforced requirements, so Indiana armed the border to harass Kentucky drivers that did not meet their legal technicalities. A similar clash over motor-carrier regulation occurred between Pennsylvania and New Jersey.[67]

Many irregular state regulations, reflecting the relative political strength of the railroad and motor-carrier lobbies in each jurisdiction, proved troublesome for petroleum planning during World War II. Federal jurisdiction prevailed, and inhibiting state rules were temporarily suspended under emergency wartime powers.[68] In peacetime, prior laws came back into effect; one 1946 study revealed that of 1,489 trade barriers between states, 301 concerned commercial-vehicle requirements.[69]

The influence of the railroad lobby waned in the next decade, and more states found it in their self-interest to adopt an "open-door policy," beginning with Kentucky in 1946.[70] A survey in 1956, however, showed noticeable differentials between states, although not as great as in the 1930s.[71] In fact, the nonuniformity problem continued. The truckers' strike in 1979, which negatively affected the entire U.S. economy, was partly intended to obtain uniform weight standards between states and remove other unpopular regulations.[72]

Another enduring issue in state motor-carrier regulation was relative rates of contract carriers and common carriers. With each faction trying to keep the other's rates high, fare reductions led to challenges before rate-setting boards. Oil jobbers were no exception. In 1963,

[67]*NPN*, January 4, 1933, pp. 15–17.

[68]See chapter 12, pp. 657–58.

[69]American Petroleum Institute, *Tax Economics Bulletin*, June 1946, p. 17. Also see *NPN*, June 7, 1944, pp. 31–36; August 2, 1944, p. 36; and January 23, 1946, p. 27.

[70]*NPN*, March 6, 1946, p. 48.

[71]See *1956 National Petroleum News Factbook* (Cleveland: NPN, 1957), p. 224.

[72]*Newsweek*, July 9, 1979, p. 26. Complained one trucker: "We have to live with innumerable rules and regulations that take up all of your time. You have to get 197 different permits if you drive in 48 states." *Time*, July 2, 1979, p. 22.

for example, the Colorado Petroleum Marketers' Association challenged a rate reduction application by contract truck jobbers before
the state public utilities commission because "heavy investments
. . . would become a loss."[73] The overall result of such infighting
was higher transportation costs and higher final petroleum prices,
which hurt consumers and encouraged oil refiners and retailers to
integrate to internalize the expense.

Federal Regulation

Congressional interest in federal trucking regulation began shortly
after the Supreme Court rebuffed state attempts to regulate interstate
trucking in 1925.[74] After collecting 5,000 pages of testimony from
hearings in sixteen cities, the ICC released a final report in 1928,
which advocated interstate regulation to close the "regulatory gap"
that the states encouraged.[75] This was also the position of railroads,
bus companies, and common-carrier trucking firms, which complained of "destructive" competition from "trucking gypsies" and
"wildcatters" who would freely enter and exit markets as profitable
opportunities dictated.

National Industrial Recovery Act Code. In the spring of 1933, two
interstate motor-carrier groups, the American Highway Freight
Association and the Federal Truck Association of America, began
to formulate an industry "Code of Fair Competition" pursuant to
the National Industrial Recovery Act.[76] From approximately ninety
submissions from various subgroups, a code was hammered out by
the newly formed American Trucking Associations. All for-hire firms
were required to sign the code by June 14, 1934, obligating themselves to maximum hours per worker, minimum wage levels, and,
most important, "minima for rates and tariff." Rebates or other
"discriminatory" actions were prohibited by the federally sanctioned code.[77]

---

[73]*NPN*, March 1963, p. 28.

[74]*Michigan Public Utilities Commission* v. *Duke*, 266 U.S. 570 (1925); *Buck* v. *Kuykendall*, 267 U.S. 307 (1925); and *Bush Co.* v. *Maloy*, 267 U.S. 317 (1925).

[75]This familiar theme of federal interstate regulation passed to complement intrastate regulation by the states is summarized in chapter 29, p. 1788.

[76]Public Law 67, 48 Stat. 195 (1933).

[77]Gary LaBella, *A Glance Back: A History of the American Trucking Industry* (Washington, D.C.: American Trucking Industry, 1977), pp. 18–20.

The maiden voyage of federal trucking regulation ran ashore when the National Industrial Recovery Act was declared unconstitutional in May 1935.[78] The short cooperative experience was not for naught— it "showed the truckers they could work together . . . and prepared the way for the rate bureaus."[79] Substitute regulation was the next order of business.

Motor Carrier Act of 1935. On August 9, 1935, the Motor Carrier Act, authored by the National Association of Railroad and Utility Commissioners from earlier drafts by the American Trucking Associations and the Association of Railroad Executives, became law.[80] Leading the effort to reinstall cartel-like regulation was the federal coordinator of transportation, Joseph Eastman, who argued that intermodal competition would be put "on a sounder and better plane." "Through routes and joint rates" were to replace "congestion and oversupply of transportation service."[81] Behind this banter was a well-recognized opportunity for railroads to recartelize inland transportation and for established truckers to forestall entry into a highly competitive business. Other trade groups supporting the Motor Carrier Act were the National Association of Motor Bus Operators, the Railroad Brotherhood Association, the American Railway Association, and, interestingly, the American Bar Association. Also seeking expanded ICC authority were Wall Street banking interests associated with major railway firms.[82] All told, a powerful alliance between railroad and trucking interests and federal transportation officials overwhelmed scattered opposition from farm interests, who received a special exemption in the law as appeasement, and smaller carriers.[83] Shippers, in contrast, were less organized.

The new law established the Bureau of Motor Carriers within the ICC, a condition necessary to ensure industry support, to regulate

[78]*Schechter Poultry Corp.* v. *United States,* 295 U.S. 495 (1935).

[79]John Spencer, "Trucking: A Retrospective," p. 4.

[80]Public Law 255, 49 Stat. 543 (1935). Carl Fulda, *Competition in the Regulated Industries: Transportation,* p. 12.

[81]Quoted in ibid. Eastman referred to himself as "the father of the Motor Carrier Act." Claude Fuess, *Joseph B. Eastman: Servant of the People* (New York: Columbia University Press, 1952), p. 249.

[82]Carl Fulda, *Competition in the Regulated Industries: Transportation,* pp. 11–12.

[83]David Boies, "Experiment in Mercantilism: Minimum Rate Regulation by the Interstate Commerce Commission," p. 658.

interstate trucking firms. Reporting requirements were issued, accounting standards were set, safety minimums were established, equipment standardization was prescribed, and maximum hours were fixed. The crux of the law concerned *entry* and *ratemaking,* examined below.[84]

Entry Regulation. Approximately 18,000 firms and their respective routes were "grandfathered" in by virtue of service on June 1, 1935.[85] Auxiliary rights did not come with certification. Firms on a particular route were not allowed to commence service to intermediate points if they did not do so on the required date. New commodities were not grandfathered for carriage. Return-trip hauls were restricted. Cost-minimization strategies were virtually outlawed; the flexibility to adapt service to unfolding opportunities was absent.[86] New routes for existing firms or entry by new firms required permits for contract carriers and certificates for common carriers. The burden of proof was on entrants who wished to break into grandfathered areas, and the ICC successfully protected established companies through strict licensing. Required notices in the *Federal Register* by firms seeking new authorizations gave established firms ample opportunity to challenge the applications. The mere fact of opposition was a key obstacle to approval. A typical ICC examiner recommendation,

---

[84]For a discussion of the Motor Carrier Act, see Edward Haid, "Regulation of Motor Carriers," *Washington University Law Quarterly* (December 1937): 1–46.

[85]These firms obtained approximately 27,000 certificates of public convenience and necessity. Sixty-two thousand certification applications were denied. Interstate Commerce Commission, *Annual Report, 1940* (Washington, D.C.: ICC, 1941). "These grants of authority," noticed John Snow in 1977, "still make up the vast majority of operating rights today." Snow, "The Problem of Motor Carrier Regulation and the Ford Administration's Proposal for Reform," in *Regulation of Entry and Pricing in Truck Transportation,* ed. Paul MacAvoy and John Snow (Washington, D.C.: American Enterprise Institute, 1977), p. 19.

[86]A stocktaking in 1941 revealed that 70 percent of the common carriers on regular routes were not allowed to fully serve intermediate points and 10 percent were not allowed any intermediate service. Sixty-two percent of motor carriers were restricted to special commodities and 40 percent to one commodity or commodity class. Thirty-three percent of intercity truckers were restricted on return-trip hauls and 10 percent were unable to do return business at all. Thomas Moore, "Deregulating Surface Freight Transportation," in *Promoting Competition in Regulated Markets,* ed. Almarin Phillips (Washington, D.C.: Brookings Institution, 1975), pp. 57–58. These figures did not substantially change in ensuing regulated decades.

which the full commission generally followed, illustrates the cavalier grounds of rejection.

> *Joseph E. Faltin, Manchester, N.H.*—Denial recommended for application to operate as common carrier of bulk petroleum products from Boston, Mass., and points and places within 20 miles of Boston, to points and places in Windsor and Windham Counties, Vt. . . . Rail carriers of New England opposed application, and joint board found public convenience and necessity does not require operation.[87]

Economist Alfred Kahn summarized several decades of ICC entry policy.

> The Commission has pursued an extremely restrictive policy with regard to the issuance of new licenses. The possibility that the applicants would take business away from existing carriers has been an important consideration in inducing it to refuse them. Time and again, it has turned down applications that enjoyed the support of shippers, on the ground that the service provided by existing carriers either was in its judgement sufficient *or could become so.* In short, even an admittedly poor performance by existing carriers [was] not necessarily a sufficient justification for permitting more competition.[88]

Rate Regulation. Rate regulation came of age with entry regulation. The 1935 act required all rates to be filed with the commission and to remain unchanged except with thirty-day notice and commission approval. Rates were to be standardized, at parity with railroad rates on similar routes, and above cost.

Following passage of the act, "rate conferences" were held between trucking firms and between the trucking and railroad industries with the full blessing of the ICC.[89] The result of concerted rate setting was predictable. "After 1935," John Spencer stated, "price competition was passé. The truckers had to win the traffic manager with service."[90] This bred overcapacity as documented by economic studies of the industry.[91]

[87]*NPN,* October 23, 1946, p. 44.

[88]Alfred Kahn, *The Economics of Regulation,* vol. 2, p. 15. In 1967, a district court labeled the ICC's protectionist entry philosophy the "invariable rule." Ibid., p. 16.

[89]Christopher Stone, "ICC: Some Reminiscences on the Future of American Transportation," p. 10.

[90]John Spencer, "Trucking: A Retrospective," p. 6.

[91]See Thomas Moore, "Deregulating Surface Freight Transportation," p. 58.

The commission's bias against fare reductions extended to petroleum shipments despite earlier opinions that the effect of railroad rate reductions on tank trucks was immaterial.[92] In 1951, competition between trucking and railroad firms for petroleum shipments forced the latter to reduce tariffs to regain lost business. Trucking firms complained to the Bureau of Motor Carriers that they could not meet the lower fares and remain in business, whereupon the commission suspended the reduced rate to "preserve" the "inherent advantages" of both rates.[93] The consequence of such decisions was preservation of the status quo of petroleum traffic, advantaging historic firms over more entrepreneurial ones. The commission's "fair-share" doctrine also meant higher transportation costs for the petroleum industry and its consumers.[94]

Industry Distortion and Policy Reform

The original 1935 act contained exemptions that created destabilizing "backdoor" competition for the protected industry. Agricultural carriers and private carriers (trucks operated by the shipper) were exempted, which created the incentive for farmer co-ops to carry nonfarm products and shippers to integrate into transportation. Petroleum was no exception. Other practices used to escape regulation were shippers' leasing trucks for private carriage and carriers' taking title to the shipped goods to resell after arrival.

The telltale consequence of federal regulation was the institutionalization of such inefficient practices as cross-hauling, circuitous routing, low-load backhauls, bloated labor costs, and inflexible service. Other signs of a distorted market were the high cash values

[92]See "Petroleum and Petroleum Products from California to Arizona," 241 ICC 21 (1940); and "Petroleum Products from Baltimore to Martinsburg, W. Va.," 246 ICC 496 (1941).

[93]Petroleum Products from Los Angeles to Arizona and New Mexico, 280 ICC 509 at 516 (1951). Similar verdicts were reached in Petroleum Products in Illinois Territory, 280 ICC 681 (1951); Petroleum Products in Southern Territory, 54 ICC 704 (1952); Southwestern Tank Truck Carriers Committee v. A & S Railway, 284 ICC 75 (1952); Petroleum Products in California and Oregon, 284 ICC 287 (1952); and Petroleum from Colorado and Wyoming to Western Trunkline Territory, 289 ICC 457 (1953). In a 1953 case (Petroleum from Los Angeles and El Paso to Arizona and New Mexico, 287 ICC 731), large fare reductions were granted to railroads to forestall construction of an oil pipeline.

[94]See the discussion in Jervis Langdon, "The Regulation of Competitive Business Fares: The Obstacle Race in Transportation," *Cornell Law Quarterly* (Fall 1955): 74–76.

of certificates,[95] overcapacity, erratic fare structures, and industry concentration unexplainable by scale economies. But so long as entry could be forestalled, industry profits could be maintained despite high-cost service.

With inflation taxing consumers and the energy crisis making fuel conservation imperative, trucking deregulation came of political age in the 1970s despite adamant industry opposition. Although failing to become law, President Ford's Motor Carrier Act of 1975, designed to "improve performance of our transportation industry by replacing Government regulation with competition," was seriously debated.[96] If legislative reform was slowed by vested interests, administrative reform did not have to be, and a pro-consumer ICC began to move toward administrative deregulation later in the decade. The time-honored policy of refusing new entry "endangering or impairing the operation of existing carriers,"[97] as the commission described it in a 1936 decision, was liberalized. The new emphasis was on *competition* over *protectionism*. The new blood at the commission proposed to grant certificates for general areas ("master certification") rather than by individual requests to facilitate and expedite entry.[98]

To prevent administrative deregulation, yet appease regulatory critics, the Motor Carrier Act of 1980 became law.[99] The protected industry, led by the American Trucking Associations, argued that historical regulation created stability out of chaos in the 1930s and was still needed. Joining the American Trucking Associations in favoring traditional regulation was the Teamsters Union, whose high wage structure captured much of the monopoly rent provided by protected markets.[100] A new group, Assure Competitive Transportation, Inc.," initiated a number of lawsuits that must be labeled 'ingenious,' if not downright bizarre . . . to fight deregulation."[101] Persuasively arguing against the status quo were academicians, large

---

[95]"Certificates are worth on the order of 15 to 20 percent of the annual sales of trucking firms." John Snow and Stephen Sabotka, "Certificate Values," in *Regulation of Entry and Pricing in Truck Transportation*, p. 153.

[96]Ibid., "Preface."

[97]Pan-American Bus Lines Operations, 1 ICC 190 at 203 (1936).

[98]Policy Statement on Motor Carrier Regulation, 44 *Fed. Reg.* 60296 (October 19, 1979).

[99]Public Law 96-296, 94 Stat. 793 (1980).

[100]James Annable, "The ICC, the IBT, and the Cartellization of the American Trucking Industry," *Quarterly Review of Economics and Business* (Summer 1973): 40.

[101]James Rakowski, "The Trucking Industry in the United States: A Study of Transportation Policy in Transition," *Transportation Quarterly* (October 1981): 625.

shippers, and pro-competition government bodies such as the Department of Transportation, the Department of Justice, and Congress. Protection created waste, they argued, and the trucking industry did not possess the characteristics of the classically regulated firm. All that was needed to go into the trucking business, reminded Thomas Moore, was "a used truck, a driver's license, and a rented terminal office."[102]

With the intent of reducing "unnecessary regulation by the Federal Government," the 1980 act eased entry certification and set a "zone of freedom" to allow prices to change 10 percent without government interference.[103] Previously, the entrant had to demonstrate "public convenience and necessity"; the requirement was now simplified to "fit, willing, and able." The burden of proof in application challenges was shifted from applicants to protestants. The commission was instructed to "not find diversion of revenue or traffic from an existing carrier to be in and of itself inconsistent with the public convenience and necessity."[104] To introduce consumer sovereignty and improve industry utilization, territorial and customer restrictions were set aside. Exemptions were expanded.

Although not wholly deregulatory, the new law sprang major leaks in the cartelist dike that sympathetic administrative interpretation could widen. This occurred. To the chagrin of long-established trucking interests, and the hurriedly formed Committee for Lawful Rates, "an unmistakable dismantling of . . . ratemaking" was administratively sanctioned.[105] Coupled with a "veritable blitz of new operating authorities," intense competition descended on the old order.[106]

---

[102]Thomas Moore, "Deregulating Surface Freight Transportation," p. 74.

[103]Public Law 96-296, 94 Stat. 793 (1980).

[104]Ibid., p. 794. One of the first orders of business after the law's effective date for established firms was to seek tax write-offs for once-valuable certificate values.

[105]Statement of Ross Gaussoin before the Surface Transportation Subcommittee of the House Committee on Public Works and Transportation, June 23, 1982 (copy in author's files).

[106]Statement of Bennett Whitlock before the Surface Transportation Subcommittee of the House Committee on Public Works and Transportation, June 23, 1982 (copy in author's files). Between 1978 and early 1982, Whitlock reported an unprecedented 35 percent increase in trucking firms.

By 1984, hundreds of firms, including some of the biggest names in the industry, entered bankruptcy proceedings. Meanwhile, over 10,000 new firms, many mom-and-pop operations operating well below union wage levels, entered and secured a market niche by discounting and offering specialized services. Not only deregulation but the recession and the higher taxes of the Surface Transportation Assistance Act of 1982 were responsible for the changed industry structure.[107] Minority-owned firms, no longer locked out by the vested interest of established firms, tripled. The value of trucking licenses plummeted from nearly $400,000 in 1975 to under $20,000 in the early 1980s.[108]

The pro-shipper gains on the federal level inspired Florida and Arizona to deregulate intrastate and led other states to debate the issue. Despite calls from the old order to "get rid of those 'free-market freaks' that remain at the ICC and get back to the responsible regulation," the forty-five-year gravy train seems to have ended for the formerly protected companies and the Teamsters.[109]

New business discipline and consumer gains were evident in the first years of partial deregulation. Thomas Moore calculated a 25 percent decline in rates between 1977 and 1982 despite significantly higher fuel costs.[110] Concluded a Federal Trade Commission staff report to the Motor Carrier Rate Making Study Commission:

> Competition among an increasing number of carriers has created downward pressure on rates and forced firms to increase productivity, e.g., by seeking removal of restrictions on operating certificates and by seeking concessions from labor. . . . Increased competition also means that the monopoly profits made possible by protective regulation are being squeezed out of the system.[111]

---

[107]This law increased gasoline taxes by $0.05 per gallon. See chapter 28, pp. 1742–43.

[108]Thomas Moore, "Rail and Truck Reform—The Record So Far," p. 37.

[109]*Wall Street Journal,* October 6, 1983, p. 31. Also see *Wall Street Journal,* October 20, 1983, p. 1; and *Reason,* August 1983, p. 14.

[110]Thomas Moore, "Rail and Truck Reform—The Record So Far," p. 39.

[111]Denis Breen, "Regulatory Reform and the Trucking Industry: An Evaluation of the Motor Carrier Act of 1980," Bureau of Economics, Federal Trade Commission, March 1982.

For the petroleum industry, relaxed trucking regulation reduced fares, enhanced service, and increased competition among oil pipe-lines, tank cars, and barges to improve overall oil transport performance. The longer run effects were to transfer market share from private motor carriage to the contract and common-carriage market and to make intermodal regulation more problematic and obsolete.

Waterway Regulation and Subsidization: 1887–1984

Federal involvement with waterway shipping has a history as old as the U.S. government itself. Free water right-of-way laws subsi-dized shipping from the beginning of the country. Federal acts, such as the Tariff Act of 1789 and the Cabotage Law of 1817, gave early preference to U.S. flag vessels.[112] State aid for canal construction, river improvements, and harbor building was common in the 1820–40 period.[113] This section focuses on four subsequent areas of federal involvement: rate and entry regulation, cargo-preference laws, direct subsidies, and water-port regulation.

Rate and Entry Regulation

Federal regulation of water carriers began in 1887. The Act to Regulate Commerce (Interstate Commerce Act) regulated shipments "partly by railroad and partly by water" if travel was continuous and under common arrangement. Port-to-port traffic was excluded.[114] Long-distance petroleum vessels, increasingly active in the burgeoning oil-export trade, were not regulated.[115]

In 1912, the Panama Canal Act forbade railroads to operate ship-ping facilities competing with the waterway. The first significant federal intervention was the Shipping Act of 1916, which created the U.S. Shipping Board within the ICC with jurisdiction over common

---

[112]1 Stat. 24 (1789); and 3 Stat. 351 (1817). See Irwin Heine, *The U.S. Maritime Industry* (Washington, D.C.: National Maritime Council, 1980), p. 4.

[113]See chapter 11, pp. 602–5.

[114]Act to Regulate Commerce, 24 Stat. 379 (1887).

[115]For an early history of oceangoing tank steamers, see Harold Williamson and Arnold Daum, *The Age of Illumination, 1859 to 1899*, vol. 1 of *The American Petroleum Industry* (Evanston, Ill: Northwestern University Press, 1959), pp. 637–43.

carriers in coastal or Great Lakes interstate trade.[116] Covered vessels were to file "just and reasonable" rates with the Shipping Board. Contract shippers, inland shippers, and carriers previously regulated by the ICC were exempt.

As was the rule rather than the exception, the 1916 law was supported by regulated parties who wanted to reduce price discounting and foster shipping conferences where rates and routes were jointly determined. Railroads also supported "rationalized" competition for water carriers. Competitive weapons that threatened to disrupt the cartel—deferred rebates, favorable insurance rates, and low-fare "fighting ships"—were prohibited. Section 19 banned rates "below a fair and remunerative basis with the intent of driving out or otherwise injuring a competitive carrier."[117] Section 15 required all agreements and understandings affecting price to be made public with the Shipping Board. Rate competition was restricted for part of the water-carrier industry to replace a problematic free-market cartel with a more effective government one.

The next major development extended federal authority to unregulated areas of the water shipping industry. On March 3, 1933, the Intercoastal Shipping Act required contract and common carriers traveling coast to coast through the Panama Canal to file rates and give at least thirty days' notice of changes.[118] Two years later, safety regulations were promulgated for "all vessels which shall have on board any inflammable explosives or like dangerous cargo."[119] In 1938, carriers previously regulated under the 1916 act were brought

---

[116]Public Law 260, 39 Stat. 728 (1916). The law also authorized $50 million to purchase or lease fifty vessels because of lost business from wartime conditions and high tariff policies. Expenditures astronomically exceeded this allocation, and the overbuilt industry collapsed in 1922. Ships that were purchased by the government at over $200 per ton were sold at less than 10 percent of cost in the fiscal disaster. Paul Zeis, *American Shipping Policy* (Princeton, N.J.: Princeton University Press, 1938), pp. 95–98, 125–41, 154–65.

[117]Public Law 260, 39 Stat. 735 (1916).

[118]Public Law 415, 47 Stat. 1425 (1933).

[119]Public Law 343, 49 Stat. 868 (1935). The regulations, which became law effective November 10, 1936, were formulated with the input of the American Petroleum Institute's Central Committee on Tanker and Barge Transportation, headed by J. Howard Pew. Enforcement was assigned to the Coast Guard. See Joseph Farley, "Regulation of the Movement of Oil by Water," *28 Annual Proceedings* (New York, American Petroleum Institute, 1948), pp. 63–66.

under the Intercoastal Shipping Act, and authority to impose minimum rates was established for all regulated ships except those in Great Lakes travel.[120] Administration was by the U.S. Maritime Commission, which replaced the Shipping Board in 1936 pursuant to the Merchant Marine Act.[121]

Comprehensive regulation of interstate water transportation, except for certain cargos, occurred in 1940 to join regulation of railroads (1887), oil pipelines (1906), and motor trucks (1935).[122] The ICC and railroads strongly supported the expansion of regulation; shippers and inland water carriers were opposed.[123]

The Water Carrier Act, part III of the Transportation Act of 1940, regulated entry and rates. Transoceanic ships were under the jurisdiction of the Maritime Commission, while inland coastwise ships reported to the ICC. Existing routes on January 1, 1940, were grandfathered; new routes required certification for common carriers and permits for contract carriers. For-hire firms were instructed to set "just and reasonable" rates with a thirty-day minimum, while contract vessels submitted minimum tariff schedules that also could not be changed for thirty days. The law also contained accounting and reporting requirements, a long- and short-haul clause, and a ban on shipper discounts and free passes.

Important exemptions made the law moot for most shipping runs. An important one was for bulk liquid cargos, including crude and petroleum products, which from the 1930s constituted the largest single shipped item. This meant that entry and rates of petroleum-carrying vessels were not regulated, although other consequential areas of federal involvement in water transport of petroleum would develop in the post-1940 period.

The Shipping Act of 1984 continued old themes with several revisions. While the act speaks of reduced regulation and efficient transportation, rate protectionism continues on the rationale of "encoura-g[ing] the development of [a] . . . United States liner fleet capable

[120]Public Law 704, 52 Stat. 953 (1938). In 1940, minimum rates were set by the ICC for common carriers in westbound intercoastal commerce to end a rate war.

[121]Public Law 835, 49 Stat. 1985 (1936). In the Reorganization Act of 1949 (63 Stat. 1069), the Maritime Commission would be renamed the Federal Maritime Board, which became the Federal Maritime Commission in 1961.

[122]Public Law 785, 54 Stat. 898 (1940).

[123]Samuel Huntington, "The Marasmus of the ICC: The Commission, the Railroads, and the Public Interest," *Yale Law Journal* (April 1952): 479.

of meeting national security needs."[124] Rates were to be made public, be fixed for thirty days or more, be nonpreferential, and be "just and reasonable." Discounting and price wars were verboten. The act broke from the past to exempt concerted agreements from anti-trust law and empower the ICC to impose protectionist measures on foreign vessels in retaliation for "unduly impaired access" of U.S. vessels to foreign ports.[125] Despite a policy declaration of "mini-mum . . . government intervention and regulatory costs," the 1984 law, quite unlike recent reform in the railroad and motor-carrier industries, preserved and extended monopoly privileges first given in 1916.

Cabotage and Cargo-Preference Regulation

In 1808 and 1817, the United States passed legislation reserving coastwise and intercoastal trade to U.S.-built and U.S.-registered vessels.[126] Section 27 of the Merchant Marine Act of 1920, commonly known as the Jones Act, reaffirmed this policy and extended it to the noncontiguous United States by declaring,

> No merchandise shall be transported by water . . . between points in the United States . . . in any other vessel than a vessel built in and documented under the laws of the United States and owned by persons who are citizens of the United States.[127]

Public Resolution 17 on March 26, 1934, expanded the U.S.-flag requirement to any shipper receiving a loan from the Reconstruction Finance Corporation or receiving any other government assistance.[128] On August 26, 1954, the Merchant Marine Act was amended pursu-ant to the resolution to require at least one-half of government cargos to be moved by private U.S.-flag ships.[129] This became particularly important with the Strategic Petroleum Reserve, which received imported oil by tanker. Although not adhered to early in the pro-gram, an agreement between the Department of Energy and the

[124]Public Law 98-237, 98 Stat. 67 (1984).

[125]Ibid., at 82.

[126]Wytze Gorter, *United States Shipping Policy* (New York: Harper and Brothers, 1956), p. 131.

[127]Public Law 261, 41 Stat. 988 (1920).

[128]Public Resolution 17, 48 Stat. 500 (1934). This would later apply to Export-Import Bank loans.

[129]Public Law 664, 68 Stat. 832 (1954).

Department of Transportation gave lucrative preference to American bottoms.[130]

Two other petroleum-related cabotage laws were passed in the 1970s. A provision in the Trans-Alaska Pipeline Authorization Act of 1973 banned exports of Alaskan oil unless strict conditions were met.[131] This special-interest coup single-handedly pushed water carriers past oil pipelines as the leading transportation source, measured in ton-miles, by 1980.[132] The logical scenario would have been to export oil by tanker to Japan and import more oil from traditional sources into the East Coast, but maritime interest groups pushed to "domesticate" Alaskan supply by requiring transport from Valdez in U.S.-flag vessels. The National Maritime Council reported that as of October 1, 1982, 75 U.S.-flag ships aggregating over 6.3 million deadweight tons were transporting crude through the Panama Canal to Gulf Coast and even East Coast refiners.[133] The export ban was still in effect as of 1984, although it was hotly debated by opponents who had documented the economic costs of violating least-cost import-export trade patterns.

A third protectionist element of petroleum transport by water came with an Interior Department appropriations bill in 1978 (Public Law 95-465) that gave a 50 percent entitlements benefit for oil shipped by U.S.-flag tankers to refineries located in the U.S. Virgin Islands. This political element raised acquisition costs and distorted the refinery equalization program, as is explained in chapter 27.[134]

Since the early 1970s, the maritime lobby had made a continuous effort to require a percentage of oil imports to be transported in American tankers. In 1972, a 50 percent cargo-preference proposal was defeated in the House; in 1974, President Ford vetoed a 20 percent proposal (with escalations to 30 percent by mid-1977); and in 1977, a 4.5 to 9.5 percent minimum requirement was again defeated in the House. Concern over the rising cost of oil imports prevented passage.

---

[130]See chapter 17, p. 1038.

[131]See the appendix to chapter 13, p. 771.

[132]See table 16.2, p. 973.

[133]National Maritime Council, Press release, December 21, 1982, p. 2.

[134]See chapter 27, p. 1678.

In 1983, a plan to require 5 percent of imports and exports to be carried by U.S.-built and U.S.-registered vessels, with the amount rising 1 percent a year until reaching 20 percent, titled the Competitive Shipping and Shipbuilding Act of 1983, was defeated. With under 5 percent of cargos currently on U.S. ships, the bill was estimated to cost consumers $10 billion per year and was opposed by the American Petroleum Institute.[135]

Forced use of higher cost U.S.-flag vessels benefited domestic water-carrier firms, shipbuilding companies, and associated labor. This advantage, however, was diluted because inflated shipping costs reduced the attractiveness of barge and tanker transport compared with other alternatives. Railroads and, to a lesser extent, trucking benefited.[136] With petroleum, trunk pipelines benefited on certain routes.[137] In fact, many have argued that protective maritime legislation weakened the industry on net and point to historic declines in the U.S.-flag fleet for substantiation.[138]

U.S. consumers were saddled with unnecessary oil-product costs. Economist Richard Mancke estimated that cabotage regulation of oil products shipped by tanker from Texas-Louisiana refining centers cost East Coast consumers over $100 million per year in the early 1970s.[139] The total differential between lower cost foreign-flag vessels and U.S.-flag vessels under the Jones Act, including the shipping of Alaskan oil and Strategic Petroleum Reserve oil in addition to coastwise transport, would bring Mancke's sum to much higher levels for subsequent years.

---

[135]*OGJ*, July 11, 1983, p. 43. The decline in U.S-flag ships' market share of oceanborne trade from 1940 to 1960 (in thousand long tons) is shown below.

Year	Cargo	Percent	Year	Cargo	Percent
1940	23,204	31	1965	27,361	8
1945	61,736	69	1970	26,527	6
1950	49,914	43	1975	31,347	5
1955	47,094	24	1980	28,199	4
1960	30,968	11	1983	36,711	6

SOURCE: Public Information Office, U.S. Maritime Administration.

[136]See the discussion in Wytze Gorter, *United States Shipping Policy*, pp. 133–34.

[137]George Wolbert, *U.S. Oil Pipelines*, p. 134.

[138]Richard Mancke, *The Failure of U.S. Energy Policy* (New York: Columbia University Press, 1974), p. 123.

[139]Ibid.

Construction and Operating Subsidies

Underpriced water right-of-way costs, cabotage and cargo-preference laws, and preferential rates for postal service cargos (pursuant to the Merchant Marine Act of 1928) were joined in 1936 by a law that "adopted a nationalistic and protectionist solution to the nation's shipping needs."[140] The Merchant Marine Act of 1936, the Magna Charta of the domestic maritime industry to its proponents, required U.S. ships to be built in domestic yards with U.S. labor and materials.[141] To defray higher associated costs, attributable to domestic wage rates several time higher than wage rates abroad, qualifying vessels received cash subsidies. The construction differential subsidy (CDS) compensated vessel owners for higher construction costs; the operating differential subsidy (ODS) covered higher subsequent operating costs. These subsidies, which between 1936 and 1970 provided cash payments of $4.3 billion, were not available for oil tankers as they were for other petroleum vessels.

Title XI of the 1936 act, providing loan guarantees for ship construction with the taxpayer liable for 87.5 percent of any principal in default, was available to oil-carrying vessels. It was not until the mid-1950s, however, that petroleum vessels participated. Under the "trade in and build" program in 1954 and the "trade out and build" program in 1956, oil tankers utilized Title XI.[142] During and after the 1956 Suez crisis, improved tanker markets offered oil companies opportunities for active dealing with the Maritime Administration.[143]

Up to 87.5 percent of total vessel cost was eligible for principal and interest guarantees. Firms receiving another subsidy were limited to 75 percent. New guidelines from the Office of Management and Budget beginning in 1982 set 75 percent as the limit for all vessels.

---

[140]Samuel Lawrence, *United States Merchant Shipping Policies and Politics* (Washington, D.C.: Brookings Institution, 1966), p. 49.

[141]Public Law 835, 49 Stat. 1985 (1936).

[142]Public Law 574, 68 Stat. 680 (1954). 21 *Fed. Reg.* 8588 (November 8, 1956). These respective programs allowed firms to sell aged tankers at a lucrative price to the government in return for building a new tanker in U.S. shipyards and allowed firms to sell older tankers abroad and receive subsidies for new tanker orders in U.S. shipyards.

[143]See Robert Engler, *The Politics of Oil* (Chicago: University of Chicago Press, 1961), pp. 176–77.

Table 16.3
TITLE XI SUBSIDIES TO OIL TANKERS: 1957–84
(thousands of dollars)

Year	No. of Tankers	Total Cost	Mortgage
1957	7	$ 66,645	$ 58,160
1958	11	127,473	110,668
1959	4	54,974	44,487
1960	8	88,836	76,802
1961	2	29,157	24,626
1962–66	0	–	–
1967	7	77,149	68,157
1968	5	54,279	47,623
1969	2	32,060	28,170
1970	2	36,472	28,270
1971	2	41,099	35,600
1972	14	344,079	261,995
1973	7	182,460	140,743
1974	22	713,681	557,940
1975	3	94,869	71,151
1976	1	6,483	5,400
1977	6	475,862	416,377
1978	1	56,471	42,850
1979	4	173,005	151,378
1980	13	662,121	579,347
1981	4	322,275	226,754
1982	4	95,130	71,585
1983	1	109,686	87,342
1984	–	–	4,148
Total	130	$3,844,266	$3,139,573

SOURCE: Public Information Office, U.S. Maritime Administration.

The stream of Title XI oil-tanker-construction subsidies is summarized in table 16.3. After the 1957–61 period, the subsidy program was dormant before picking up in 1967. In 1972, on the eve of the energy crisis when imports were escalating, a record $262 million in guaranteed mortgages was underwritten. A new record was set in 1980 when $579 million in mortgages was issued. In all, $3.1 billion in taxpayer-backed obligations was finalized between 1957 and 1984, 82 percent overall tanker expenditures of $3.84 billion.

A second era of active federal involvement with oil tankers began with the Merchant Marine Act of 1970, which amended the 1936 act to extend the CDS and ODS subsidy programs to tankers and oil barges.[144] The act, commented maritime historian Irwin Heine, "gave impetus to the largest peacetime building program of merchant ships."[145] CDS payments, now made directly to shipbuilders, were limited to 35 percent of total construction costs beginning July 1, 1975. When this proved inadequate to cover the differential, the subsidy was increased to 50 percent in the Negotiated Shipbuilding Act of 1976.[146]

Between 1981 and 1984, no new CDS grants were awarded as a result of Reagan administration cutbacks in the Maritime Administration budget. ODS contracts, covering fuel, wage, insurance, and noninsurance maintenance and repair expense differentials, also were not awarded after 1981. Contracts made prior to the cutoff continued to be honored. Oil-tanker subsidies prior to 1985 are totaled in table 16.4.

The oil-import boom of the 1970s, coupled with lower interest rates and less capital at risk as a result of Title XI guarantees and direct construction and operating cash grants, significantly expanded the U.S. oil-tanker fleet. In the 1960s, tanker growth was stagnant, thanks to the Mandatory Oil Import Program, which by discouraging oil imports discouraged additions to the tanker fleet. In the 1970s, with subsidies and regulation that encouraged oil imports, the U.S. fleet reached an all-time high. The swift decline in tanker demand in 1984 (table 16.5) revealed this buildup to have been artificial with government policy partly to blame. A painful retrenchment in the tanker fleet occurred thereafter.

The 1970s also witnessed an expansion of Title XI subsidies to new types of petroleum vessels. Increased offshore drilling led to new water-vehicle applications: moveable offshore drilling rigs, crew boats, and offshore-rig service ships. Tankers that carried liquefied natural gas also received subsidies. In a ten-year period ending in 1982, over $3 billion in construction costs was awarded these new vessel categories, according to the U.S. Maritime Administration.

---

[144]Public Law 91-469, 84 Stat. 1018 (1970).
[145]Irwin Heine, *The U.S. Maritime Industry*, p. 33.
[146]Public Law 94-372, 90 Stat. 1042 (1976).

Table 16.4
OIL-TANKER SUBSIDIES: 1972–84
(thousands of dollars)

Fiscal Year	CDS Paid Oil Tankers	CDS Paid LNG Tankers	ODS Paid Oil Tankers	ODS Paid Tugs & Barges
1972	533	–	–	–
1973	46,675	2,615	–	–
1974	70,803	11,705	962	–
1975	129,280	36,706	2,791	–
1976	124,816	49,589	6,815	–
1977	73,023	35,083	16,416	–
1978	30,109	23,570	17,917	–
1979	29,160	40,385	18,685	–
1980	2,128	32,092	26,589	–
1981	6,316	447	32,031	885
1982	23,914	509	38,793	3,285
1983	29,301	17	40,022	3,315
1984	8,561	1,372	58,800	–
Total	574,619	234,090	259,821	7,485

SOURCE: Public Information Office, U.S. Maritime Administration.

Table 16.5
U.S. OIL-TANKER FLEET: 1923–84

Year	Number	Gross Tons (000)	Year	Number	Gross Tons (000)
1923	380	2,314	1963	364	4,510
1928	360	2,295	1968	312	4,502
1933	365	2,449	1973	274	4,935
1938	373	2,631	1978	302	7,670
1946	894	7,894	1983	306	9,184
1952	458	4,237	1984	275	8,894
1957	232	3,509			

SOURCE: Public Information Office, U.S. Maritime Administration.

Barges owned by oil and gas companies also enjoyed Title XI loan guarantees. Recipients included East Texas Gas Transmission, Phillips Petroleum, Ashland Oil, Conoco, Exxon, Amoco, Mobil,

Shell, Kentucky Standard, Tenneco, Texaco, Union, Triangle Refineries, and Warren Petroleum. Outstanding loans to the inland barge industry as of mid-1980 totaled $456 million.[147] The decline in imports and offshore drilling as a result of falling oil prices in the 1980s brought to light a familiar consequence of government subsidization—overcapacity. The tanker market was in oversupply since imports had begun declining in early 1980, and many vessels were sold at scrap value. Offshore-rig vessels suffered through the worst slump in history in 1982 and 1983. Although the market could not have been expected to fully anticipate the extent of the decline in oil prices and imports, federal loan guarantees allowed a flood of speculative entry, which aggravated the miscalculation. A history of Title XI defaults through 1984 and terminations for oil-related vessels is presented in table 16.6.

As of March 31, 1984, outstanding mortgages totaled over $7.5 billion. Oil-related vessels constituted a large amount of taxpayer exposure; four liquefied-natural-gas tankers owned by El Paso Natural Gas led the list with Title XI mortgage guarantees of $475 million. A 1984 Freedom of Information Act request by the author for current exposure from oil- and liquefied-natural-gas-carrying vessels was denied with the explanation that "disclosure . . . could cause substantial competitive harm to companies with Title XI contracts."[148]

Government subsidies were not free for the subsidized. By virtue of acceptance, a number of restrictions in all areas of operation were assumed. Nonsubsidized carriers, in contrast, enjoyed a virtual free-market existence as seen in table 16.7.

The restriction that CDS tankers could not compete with nonsubsidized tankers would prove to be the former's undoing. Setting the stage was the fact that nonsubsidized tankers controlled domestic carriage, while ODS tankers were relegated to the import trade.

---

[147]Frank Wilner, *Competitive Equity,* pp. 56–57, 60–62. Barge subsidies have a long history. Summarizes Wilner: "Between 1879 and 1945, barge operators were the recipients of $4 billion in Federal aid, not including early land grants for canals and river improvements. From World War II to 1975, an additional $10.6 billion in Federal aid was bestowed upon barge operators. And, since 1975, the barge industry has been the recipient of around $800 million annually in outright subsidies for construction, operation, and maintenance of rights-of-way. This does not include additional subsidies for navigational aids and ice-breaking services, both provided by the Coast Guard" (p. 53).

[148]Letter from the U.S. maritime administration to author, September 11, 1984.

Table 16.6
TITLE XI DEFAULTS: OIL-INDUSTRY VESSELS
(thousands of dollars)

Year	Tankers		Drilling Vessels		Tugs & Supply Vessels	
	Number	Mortgage	Number	Mortgage	Number	Mortgage
1957	1	$ 7,000	–	–	–	–
1958–59	–	–	–	–	–	–
1960	1	5,635	–	–	–	–
1961–62	–	–	–	–	–	–
1963	3	31,300	–	–	–	–
1964	1	10,560	–	–	–	–
1965	–	–	–	–	–	–
1966	1	9,594	–	–	–	–
1967	1	9,487	–	–	–	–
1968	–	–	–	–	–	–
1969	2	4,500	–	–	–	–
1970	–	–	–	–	–	–
1971	1	21,856	–	–	–	–
1972–73	–	–	–	–	–	–
1974	2	12,533	3	$ 3,080	–	–
1975	6	172,073	1	7,200	–	–
1976	2	15,750	–	–	–	–
1977	13	477,647	–	–	–	–

Year						
1978	10	455,485	3	1,474	—	—
1979	—	—	5	12,922	—	—
1980	5	64,95	3	40,282	—	—
1981	1	11,859	—	—	1	$ 2,037
1982	2	15,792	—	—	—	—
1983	2	21,579	5	18,63	18	56,269
1984	—	—	1	21,987	4	9,084
Total	54	$1,347,604	21	$105,575	23	$67,390

SOURCE: Public Information Office, U.S. Maritime Administration.

Table 16.7
SUBSIDIZED VS. NONSUBSIDIZED REQUIREMENTS

Subsidized Requirements	Nonsubsidized Requirements
Must operate under long-term government-industry contracts	None
Must assume fixed ship-replacement obligations	None
Must operate normally under a twenty-five-year ship-life limitation	None
Must make predetermined mandatory deposits in capital-reserve funds for ship replacement	None
Operations are subject to rigid Maritime Administration surveillance	None
Must maintain extra administrative staffs for government accountability	None
Must meet required regular sailings; must sail even with vacant cargo space	None
Operations are limited to specific trade routes declared essential by U.S. government	None
May not normally vary from fixed and approved itineraries	None
Government approval generally required for modifying ports of call	None
May not unilaterally increase or diminish established ranges in yearly sailing schedules	None
Procurememt of ship supplies in United States is mandatory	None
Repair and maintenance of ships in United States is mandatory	None

1010

Subsidized Requirements	Nonsubsidized Requirements
Prohibited from owning, chartering, or operating ships in domestic commerce	None
Company wages and salaries paid under contract are limited	None
May not discriminate as to cargo but must operate unreservedly as a common carrier; may not choose customers	None (except for common carriers)
Must comply with "economical operations" provisions of 1936 Merchant Marine Act	None
Must comply with "prudent-business" provisions of the Merchant Marine Act	None
Ship construction in U.S. yards is mandatory	None
Must provide modern competitive ships on a rotating replacement basis	None (except for a three-year registration prior to transporting government-generated cargo in foreign-built ships)
Ship usage is limited by terms of government contract	None
May not own or operate foreign ships	None
Must successfully compete with all foreign competition in the trade	None
Must satisfy government that the objectives of the 1936 act are being met	None

SOURCE: Irwin Heine, *The U.S. Maritime Industry*, p. 54.

When import volumes began to fall, and with Alaskan oil leaving Valdez starting in 1977, fortunes became decidedly better on the domestic side. Owners of CDS tankers longed for a permanent reclassification in addition to six-month waiver stints, and in 1977, a newly completed CDS Seatrain tanker was allowed by the Maritime Administration to join the Alaskan trade in return for full repayment of its subsidy pursuant to section 506 of the Merchant Marine Act. This prompted a lawsuit by three firms active in Alaskan-crude shipping, including Shell Oil. The administrative action was upheld by the Supreme Court in 1980.[149]

To supplement the ad hoc waiver system, the Maritime Administration adopted an interim rule in October 1980, which restricted transfers to vessels over 100,000 deadweight tons, and then only in exceptional circumstances.[150] Another Seatrain tanker received a waiver the next month, which prompted a lawsuit from the U.S. Tanker Owners Committee, which favored the status quo for non-subsidized tankers. The rule was vacated on a technicality, but the particular waiver remained.[151] A proposed rule was released in early 1983 to allow CDS repayment and transfer, but legislative action prevented a final rule.[152] Through 1984, two tankers with permanent waivers and approximately forty CDS tankers with six-month waivers were the sole competition to traditional Jones Act carriers for Alaskan crude.

Water-Port Regulation

The Act of March 2, 1919, declared that "water terminals are essential to all cities and towns located upon harbors . . . and that at least one public terminal should exist . . . open to the use of all on public terms."[153] A year later, the Merchant Marine Act outlined siting, development, and operational rules for the U.S. Shipping Board to administer. This began the regulation of harbor development.[154] By the 1970s, over 50 federal agencies would be involved

[149]*Seatrain Shipbuilding Corp. et al. v. Shell Oil et al.*, 444 U.S. 571 (1980).

[150]45 *Fed. Reg.* 68393 (October 15, 1980).

[151]*Independent U.S. Tanker Owners Committee v. Lewis*, 690 F.2d 908 (D.D.C. 1982).

[152]48 *Fed. Reg.* 4408 (January 31, 1983); Public Law 98-78, 97 Stat. 453 (1983); Public Law 98-166, 97 Stat. 1071 (1983); and Public Law 98-411, 98 Stat. 1545 (1984).

[153]Public Law 323, 40 Stat. 1275 at 1286. See Henry Marcus et al., *Federal Port Policy in the United States* (Cambridge, Mass.: MIT Press, 1976), p. 25.

[154]Public Law 261, 41 Stat. 988 (1920).

in port activities and over 500 permit procedures would be required to satisfy environmental requirements.[155] The major law affecting shoreline ports has been the Coastal Zone Management Act of 1972, which supplemented earlier state efforts to balance economic and ecological priorities.[156]

With growing oil imports and the spectacular rise of supertankers in the 1965–70 period, demand accelerated for deep-water terminaling facilities.[157] Yet as of 1974, no such ports were located in the United States.[158] The reason was political, or, more precisely, environmental. As the executive director of the Texas Offshore Terminal Commission complained in 1973, federal agencies and citizens groups "could hold up development of a deep-water port facility indefinitely."[159]

To expedite certification, the Deep Water Port Act was signed into law by President Gerald Ford on January 4, 1975.[160] An eleven-month licensing procedure was formulated for port facilities beyond the three-mile U.S. territorial limit under the auspices of the Department of Transportation. Liability limits on damage—$50 million for the licensee and $20 million per vessel—were set, and individual states were given veto rights. One little-noticed provision would prove important. Section 7(b)(2) gave the U.S. attorney general the authority to challenge "any anticompetitive solution involved in the ownership, construction, or operation of a deep water port."

Proposed regulations were presented on May 7, 1975. After hearings and over one thousand suggestions, final rules were released on November 18, 1975. The first applications for a deep-water license were made concurrently in 1976 by the Louisiana Offshore Oil Port (LOOP) and Seadock, Inc., located off the Texas coast. The consortiums primarily involved major oil companies. Upon receipt of the

---

[155]National Research Council, *Public Involvement in Maritime Facility Development* (Washington, D.C.: National Academy of Sciences, 1979), p. 32. For a list of federal agencies and areas of involvement, see ibid., pp. 239–42.

[156]Public Law 92-583, 86 Stat. 1280 (1972). See Louis Brogaw et al., *The Challenge of Deepwater Terminals* (Lexington, Ky.: Lexington Books, 1975), pp. 76–77.

[157]Between 1965 and 1970, the number of supertankers above 100,000 deadweight tons grew from 19 to 319. Henry Marcus, "The U.S. Superport Controversy," *Technology Review* (March–April 1973): 49.

[158]Louis Brogaw et al., *The Challenge of Deepwater Terminals*, p. 29.

[159]Quoted in ibid., p. 101.

[160]Public Law 93-627, 88 Stat. 2126 (1975).

dual application, the Coast Guard contacted sixteen agencies and groups for LOOP and fifteen for Seadock for evaluation. Hearings were held locally and in Washington, D.C., followed by a conference on the competitive aspects of the proposed seaports held by the Department of Justice and the Federal Trade Commission. The major roadblock turned out to be antitrust law rather than environmentalism.[161]

Justice's antitrust challenge rested on a novel theory that both projects were intentionally *undersized* to exclude outside use and allow the owners to monopolize low-cost transport.[162] With outsiders resorting to higher cost alternatives, the argument went, downstream monopoly rents could be secured by deep-water port owners. This argument was analogous to the one used about owners of "undersized" oil pipelines examined in chapter 14.[163]

To rid the joint ventures of this alleged defect, "competitive rules" were established as a condition for certification. The rules were that ownership be open to all shippers, common-carrier service be available for all, ownership shares be continually revised to equate ownership to throughput percentages, and the port's pipeline facilities be enlarged at the request of any owner or shipper-guarantor.[164] For regulators, the rules ensured facilities large enough to provide low-cost service to all. For the owners, the conditions created unacceptable uncertainty, and the project was killed. Far from increasing competition, these rules ensured that there would be no alternative to "higher cost" transportation.[165]

[161]Safety and environmental considerations were embodied in the Ports and Waterways Safety Act of 1972 (Public Law 92-340, 86 Stat. 424) and the Port and Tanker Safety Act of 1978 (Public Law 95-474, 92 Stat. 1471), which closely regulated ship design, cargo, and operation to protect the marine environment and physical harbor structures from cargo leakage or explosion. Safety rules were also promulgated under the Outer Continental Shelf Amendments of 1978 (Public Law 95-372, 92 Stat. 628).

[162]Testified Assistant Attorney General John Shenefield of the Department of Justice's Antitrust Division on June 28, 1976, before the Senate Subcommittee on Antitrust and Monopoly, "[LOOP and Seadock's] initial sizing decisions were originally based almost exclusively on the needs of the owners, conservatively stated, rather than the shipping public at large." Testimony reprinted in *Oil Pipelines and Public Policy*, ed. Edward Mitchell (Washington, D.C.: American Enterprise Institute, 1979), p. 205.

[163]See chapter 14, pp. 842–43.

[164]John Shenefield, *Oil Pipelines and Public Policy*, p. 208.

[165]Lamented James Shamas, director of transportation for Getty Oil Company, "All the things Seadock had to do to meet the regulations made it an economic investment that got to be larger than could be justified." Quoted in ibid., p. 183.

Subsequent efforts by the Texas Deep Water Port Authority to revive the project failed. LOOP, on the other hand, presented an amended and restated shareholders' agreement and in August 1977 received a federal license good for twenty years with ten-year renewals thereafter. Construction began the following October and was completed in the fall of 1981, just in time to greet unfavorable market conditions. Through 1984, $700 million invested in a deep-water platform in the Gulf of Mexico near New Orleans, pipelines to shore, and eight underground reservoirs—representing an unloading capacity of 1.4 million barrels per day—was not profitable.

Deep-water ports offer several environmental advantages: reduced port congestion, bypassed dredging of ecologically sensitive areas, and more easily contained spills that are further from the shoreline. By discouraging and delaying implementation of deep-water ports, federal policies unintendedly blocked these benefits. Part of the political impasse centered around the political problems inherent in a nonowned "public" resource. But the bigger problem in this case was the antitrust objection based on the homemade economics of the Department of Justice. The undersizing argument is as tenuous for port pipelines as it is for onshore pipelines; the same telling arguments apply to both.[166] The "competitive rules," which second-guessed the legitimacy of firms entering new areas to outdistance the status quo of "expensive" transportation, were another controversial area. The benefits of innovation, the rules implied, should be shared equally to prevent certain firms from capturing abnormal gains. But to socialize advantage is to destroy the incentive necessary for socially beneficial resource allocation. It is because some firms lead that improvements over traditional methods are discovered for the benefit of not only the path-breaking firms and their consumers but more conservative firms that gain better market information from the pioneers. Immediate profit taking, albeit "abnormal," is the incentive or reward that alert entrepreneurs win before market adjustments lower profits. Interference with this fundamental process killed Seadock—indeed a case of undersizing if there ever was one—and effectively delayed LOOP, thereby hampering the financial success of the project.

[166]See chapter 14, pp. 842–43.

Financial difficulties led LOOP to appeal for deregulation in 1983 to adjust rates as market conditions dictated, make the license period open-ended, service foreign vessels not under bilateral agreements with the United States, and relax a $0.02 per barrel oil-spill cleanup fee.[167] Through 1984 such relief had not been granted.

Conclusion

From protectionism to enforced use of high-cost vessels to multi-billion-dollar differential subsidies to liberal loan guarantees, the effort to preserve historic market share for the U.S. maritime industry was a sizable boondoggle for taxpayers and an economic burden for shippers and consumers. For all the trouble, the market share of foreign oceanborne trade in U.S.-flag vessels fell from over 20 percent in the 1960s to under 15 percent in 1984.

The rationale for taxpayer and consumer subsidies to domestic shipping interests was national defense and national security. The experiences of World War I, World War II, and the Korean conflict were used to rationalize an enlarged home fleet. The Falklands conflict in 1983, during which England chartered tankers and other oil carriers, was showcased to appeal for increased shipping subsidies. Yet, as the American Petroleum Institute testified before Congress, "A definition of our defense needs has never been undertaken" by the maritime lobby.[168] In fact, any tangible translation of national need is arbitrary, prone to contamination by ulterior motives, and subject to the forecasting errors long associated with nonmarket decisionmaking. Subsidization also presumed that foreign vessels, heavily subsidized by fifty other countries, would be unavailable for hire or purchase to the extent that the U.S. industry underestimated market demand.[169] Only in very extreme circumstances, with a number of questionable assumptions, including a breakdown of entrepreneurship to build or buy vessels in anticipation of increased future demand, can proponents of subsidies concoct a case.

The Mirage of Intermodal Planning

The presumptuous aim of regulation of intermodal transportation was expressed in the Transportation Act of 1940:

[167] *Oil & Gas Journal,* August 8, 1983, p. 66.

[168] *Oil & Gas Journal,* July 11, 1983, p. 43.

[169] A summary of preferential shipping laws abroad as of 1979 is contained in Irwin Heine, *The U.S. Maritime Industry,* pp. 211–47.

> It is hereby declared to be in the national transportation policy of the Congress to provide for fair and impartial regulation of all modes of transportation subject to the provisions of this Act, so administered as to recognize and preserve the inherent advantages of each; to promote safe, adequate, economical, and efficient service and foster sound economic conditions in transportation and among the several carriers; to encourage the establishment and maintenance of reasonable charges for transportation services, without unjust discriminations, undue preferences or advantages, or unfair or destructive competition practices . . . to the end of developing, coordinating, and preserving a national transportation system by water, highway, and rail, as well as other means, adequate to meet the needs of the commerce of the United States.[170]

The goal of economic efficiency reflects the cardinal error of government planning: that the knowledge of the decentralized market and open competition can be synthetically constructed and implemented by regulation. The "knowledge problem" is compounded when close substitutes are involved; the greater the complexity, the more impractical "enlightened regulation" becomes.

The unyielding vagueness of Eastman's declaration reflected a mission without a sound rationale. What constitutes "fair and impartial regulation," "efficient service," "sound economic conditions," and "reasonable charges"? How does one establish priority among them when they conflict? David Boies recognized these problems clearly.

> The overriding weakness of the declaration . . . is that it says either too little or too much; almost every conceivable objective of transportation regulation is included, but no priorities are established. Further, the declaration gives no clue as to the meaning of its most important phrases. . . . Ordinarily the goals of the declaration would be taken as tautological consequences of a competitive equilibrium. Since the very existence of . . . regulation suggests that something other than a competitive equilibrium solution is intended, the lack

[170]Public Law 785, 54 Stat. 899 (1940). The heady expectations of comprehensive regulation of intermodal transportation were stated by ICC Chairman Joseph Eastman: "The new activity on which we are embarking is more than a mere experiment. . . . It is an essential part of a plan to give our country a well-ordered and stable system of transportation which will use such means of carriage to the best advantage without all manner of duplication and waste and with a reasonable expectation of fair profit for all." Quoted in Claude Fuess, *Joseph B. Eastman: Servant of the People*, p. 232.

of new definitions makes the declaration's effectiveness as a guide to interpretation limited at best.[171]

In lieu of satisfactory answers, the famous declaration should be recognized as little more than an all-inclusive attempt to coat the bitter pill of special-interest politics with the sugar of the public good. In practice, ICC administrative regulation and related court decisions were inconsistent with the 1940 declaration. With petroleum (and other commodities),[172] regulation favored some transportation modes over others by restricting rate changes, particularly rate decreases. The service of railroads and motor carriers became so inefficient that pressure built for policy reform—railroads from within (from poor financial performance) and truckers from without (from blatant inefficiency that hurt shippers). In the 1980s, partial deregulation rather than regulation became national transportation policy out of necessity.

The economic consequences of intermodal intervention were *higher priced* and *less flexible* transportation for shippers. The public interest in all respects was lost. Walter Adams deduced a historical principle from ICC trucking policy that applied to the agency's other transportation regulation as well.

> Once a commission is given power to dispense private privilege, it is almost compelled to validate the financial values predicated on such privilege and does so by suppressing competition wherever possible.[173]

Higher priced service resulted from entry restriction and minimum rate setting. This was most clearly revealed in trucking where deregulation found large established firms unable to compete in many cases with small carriers, many of them new entrants. Flexibility problems—the divergence between transportation choices and consumer demand—also resulted from legislative protectionism. Transportation resources were misdirected by prices that were not indicative of relative scarcities and an inability of entrepreneurs

---

[171]David Boies, "Experiment in Mercantilism: Minimum Rate Regulation by the Interstate Commerce Commission," p. 617.

[172]See, generally, ibid., pp. 618–34.

[173]Walter Adams, "The Role of Competition in the Regulated Industries," *American Economic Review* (May 1958): 538–39.

to exploit profit opportunities. Overcapacity of regulated carriers suggests that resources were overspent in transportation compared to other industrial sectors.

Within the transportation sector, the railroad industry can claim to have been the most disadvantaged by government intervention since it had been the least subsidized and most restrictively regulated of the four modes since the 1940s. Prior to the mid-1970s, railroads were completely regulated, which gave the advantage to less regulated truck, oil pipelines, and water tonnage. The most advantaged mode, on the other hand, was water carriers, which benefited from Jones Act protectionism, construction and operating subsidies, loan guarantees, and free usage of the water lanes.[174] Trucks, too, enjoyed subsidized routes. A study by the Department of Transportation in 1977 computed that of over $93 billion in direct federal aid to transportation in the post-World War II era, less than 2 percent went to railroads, with the balance going to trucks (87 percent) and water carriers (11 percent).[175]

Oil pipelines were ambiguously affected by federal transportation intervention. On the one hand, the Jones Act boosted the construction of long-distance oil pipelines; on the other hand, subsidies to motor and water carriers artificially constrained pipeline construction.

With partial deregulation of motor trucks and railroads, rational economic intermodal decisionmaking was facilitated for shippers. "The new flexibility given to the transportation industry," summarized Thomas Moore, "has undoubtedly strengthened the economy as a whole, and so has benefited us all."[176] The efficiency of petroleum carriage, particularly by pipelines, was increased, although the transportation market was by no means deregulated as of 1984. The "American experiment with mercantilism," as David Boies has described it, continued, but without some of its more flagrant historic features.

---

[174]In a private-property setting, initial ownership of water lanes would have gone to the first user, with the owner obtaining the right to sell or trade lane rights to another party.

[175]See Frank Wilner, *Competitive Equity*, pp. 14–15. While highway subsidies have gone only in small proportion to petroleum trucking, water-carrier subsidies have in large part aided water transportation of petroleum.

[176]Thomas Moore, "Rail and Truck Reform—The Record So Far," p. 41.

17. Other Significant Intervention

This chapter concludes part II on government intervention in transportation and allocation intervention by describing and evaluating regulation of oil and gas storage, federal oil stockpiling, and regulation of the oil-futures market.

Storage regulation began with state-level safety statutes in the nineteenth century and was joined by federal regulation designed to stabilize prices in the 1930s. During the energy crisis of the 1970s, inventory again became regulated, and beginning in 1977, federal authorities purchased and stored hundreds of millions of barrels of crude oil in anticipation of another oil-import crisis. The history and rationale of the Strategic Petroleum Reserve (SPR) are particularly prone to market-oriented criticism.

Natural-gas storage has become an integral part of both the intrastate and the interstate markets in recent decades. On the state level, such facilities have been accorded eminent-domain privileges. Natural-gas inventory has also been subject to price regulation along with other supply destined for interstate commerce.

The final section of the chapter chronicles three periods of oil-futures trading, with particular emphasis on the period that began in 1978. The institution of oil futures was a major development that reduced the influence of the Organization of Petroleum Exporting Countries (OPEC) on oil prices. The success of oil futures had to overcome regulatory scrutiny that delayed introduction of new contracts and hurt the competitiveness of several new contract offerings.

Intervention in Storage

Regulation of Storage

Oil. Surface storage of crude oil in the early era of the petroleum industry has been criticized as wasteful. "Perhaps the most unfortunate feature of Pennsylvania oil history," remarked John Ise, "was the waste of oil . . . running on the ground for lack of storage facilities."[1] Anti-pollution statutes focused on well plugging and casing to keep the water table separate from the oil table as described in chapters 3 and 4; surface regulation to arrest inventory leakage and overflows that contaminated creeks, rivers, and vegetation came later.

In the 1870s and 1880s, municipalities and states set storage regulations for refined oils deemed hazardous. Licenses were often required for large holders of petroleum, with limits on the amount that could be stored in one place. Chicago, Illinois, restricted storage to 5 barrels, and Galveston, Texas, limited aboveground storage to 40 barrels, for example.[2] The same family of regulations set flashpoint standards and inspection procedures for illuminants, described in chapter 22.[3]

In the next century, regulation by major southwestern producing states discouraged surface inventory and encouraged retaining oil in the reservoir. Surface mishandling and waste prevention were in the language of many market-demand proration statutes, but the primary intent was to restrain output to stabilize crude-oil prices. Reducing surface inventory made less "distress" oil available to drive down prices. Wellhead proration was a form of enforced storage that transferred present consumption to future consumption.[4] In the same vein, withdrawals of public land from petroleum activity and the set-aside of prime oil lands as Naval Petroleum Reserves were forms of intervention in storage and inventory.

States also included storage requirements in oil-pipeline regulation. A 1905 common-carrier law in Kansas aimed at Standard Oil Trust required oil pipelines to provide storage at the receipt point until the oil was shipped.[5] Other common-carrier laws, for example, a Michigan statute of 1929 and an Oklahoma statute of 1931, typically

---

[1]John Ise, *The United States Oil Policy* (New Haven, Conn.: Yale University Press, 1926), p. 25.

[2]Boverton Redwood, *A Treatise on Petroleum* (London: Charles Griffin, 1926), pp. 1052, 1061.

[3]See chapter 22, pp. 1290–92.

[4]Market-demand proration laws are discussed in chapter 4, pp. 162–65.

[5]Kansas Laws of 1905, chap. 315, sec. 2.

prohibited storage discrimination.[6] A 1925 Texas law declared oil-storage facilities open to general business as public utilities and put the Texas Railroad Commission in charge of rates and "inspection, grading, measurement, deductions for waste or deterioration, [and] the delivery of such products."[7] Common-purchaser oil-pipeline statutes, such as Michigan's 1929 law, often included ratable storage along with ratable purchase.[8]

The federal government regulated oil storage directly for the first time in 1933. The Code of Fair Competition for the Oil Industry for the Production Division, established pursuant to the National Industrial Recovery Act, declared that excess oil was presently in storage and prohibited drawdowns of over 100,000 barrels per day for the entire industry. The president was also empowered to regulate storage withdrawals to prevent "injurious" effects on interstate or foreign commerce.[9]

Direct federal regulation of oil storage reappeared in the Environmental Policy and Conservation Act of 1975. In conjunction with other broad powers to deal with energy shortages, the president was given the authority to

> require adjustments in the amounts of crude oil, residual fuel oil or any refined petroleum product which are held in inventory by persons who are engaged in the business of importing, producing, refining, marketing, or distributing such oils or products.[10]

Inventory-accumulation rates could be set, and inventory withdrawals at specified rates could be required. Another section of the act banned "willfully accumulating" oil and products "in excess of . . . reasonable needs" during a supply disruption.[11]

In the 1970s, states and the federal government regulated storage in conjunction with pollution-control laws. As described later, underground gasoline-storage tanks were not allowed to leak and

[6]See Northcutt Ely, *The Oil and Gas Conservation Statutes* (Washington, D.C.: Government Printing Office, 1933), pp. 212, 286.

[7]Texas Revised Statutes, 1925, title 102, art. 6049a, sec. 1.

[8]Northcutt Ely, *The Oil and Gas Conservation Statutes*, p. 211.

[9]*The Code of Fair Competition for the Petroleum Industry* (Washington, D.C.: Government Printing Office, 1933), art. 3.

[10]Public Law 94-163, 89 Stat. 871 at 954 (1975).

[11]Ibid.

aboveground tanks were required to have special tops to prevent evaporation.[12]

Natural Gas. Regulation of storage of natural gas began in the 1950s with the rapid growth of the natural-gas transmission and distribution industry. Once gas service was in place, the challenge became how to satisfy peak demand short of expensive new pipeline capacity. The other side of the coin was excess capacity during times of slack demand. The solution was to establish storage facilities. In a 1975 proposed rulemaking, the Federal Power Commission summarized the advantages of storage for all segments of the industry.

> (1) Storage tends to assure to independent producers a year-round cash flow which makes funds available for further exploration and development; (2) storage reduces the need for more expensive pipeline capacity and makes possible more efficient utilization of existing pipeline facilities, (3) storage benefits the high priority customers through the availability of natural gas during peak demand periods at the lowest reasonable costs; and (4) storage reduces the requirement for higher priced peak shaving [synthetic natural gas, liquefied natural gas], and other substitutes.[13]

Gas cannot be economically stored aboveground. The most viable option has been to utilize depleted oil and gas reservoirs—often near major markets. Eligible reservoirs had to be sealed to avoid leakage, porous to hold large quantities, and permeable to allow expeditious extraction of the gas. Qualifying reservoirs, however, required unanimous consent from surface owners pursuant to the common-law doctrine of ownership to the center of the earth. This magnified the transaction-cost problem of capture-rule production: whereas extraction holdouts from a unitization agreement had to incur the expense of drilling a well or face drainage, any surface owner over the reservoir could veto an entire project. A Kentucky court decision affirmed the absolute right of even the smallest surface owner to veto a project when it was ruled that injected gas without

---

[12]See chapter 28, pp. 1752–56.

[13]Quoted in American Gas Association, *Regulation of the Gas Industry*, 4 vols. (New York: Matthew Bender, 1982), vol. 1, p. 12-39. Gas is typically injected during the April through October "shoulder" months and withdrawn from November through March, the "peak" months. Seasonal variations and market characteristics change this cycle.

total consent of the surface owners lost its property title and once again was subject to the rule of capture.[14]

The practical difficulty of unanimity led to attempts, primarily on the part of gas-pipeline and utility companies, to force holdouts into agreement. To this end, eminent-domain laws were passed in West Virginia (1949); Kansas, Oklahoma, and Illinois (1951); Ohio and Missouri (1953); Montana and Pennsylvania (1955); Arkansas (1957); Indiana (1959); Kentucky (1962); Iowa, Nebraska, Louisiana, Colorado, New Mexico, Michigan, and New York (1963); Washington (1964); Georgia (1965); and Texas (1977).[15]

Condemnation typically requires a high percentage of voluntary agreement and cannot involve active oil or gas fields. A showing of "public purpose" is required to condemn not only underground storage space but associated surface areas.[16]

A federal eminent-domain law for underground gas-storage reservoirs was not passed. The Natural Gas Act was amended in 1947 to allow condemnation of pipeline right-of-way and associated property, but attempts in 1951 and 1953 to include underground reservoirs failed. Coal companies led the opposition to legislative favor for gas.[17] Consequently, state laws, if any, had to be used by interstate pipelines where voluntary agreement with reservoir landowners fell short. This changed in 1974, when a federal district court included acquisition and construction of gas-storage facilities within condemnation rights under section 7(h) of the Natural Gas Act.[18] Condemnation aside, all storage projects associated with interstate gas transmission required certification along with the pipeline itself under section 7(c) of the Natural Gas Act.

---

[14]*Hammonds* v. *Central Kentucky Natural Gas Co.*, 255 Ky. 685, 75 S.W.2d 205 (1934).

[15]See Stephen McDonald, *Petroleum Conservation in the United States* (Baltimore: Johns Hopkins University Press, 1971), pp. 255–70; and Robert McGinnis, "Some Legal Problems in Underground Gas Storage," 17 *Oil and Gas Institute* (New York: Matthew Bender, 1966), p. 53.

[16]Ibid., pp. 53–62.

[17]Ibid., p. 70.

[18]*Natural Gas Pipeline Co. of America* v. *Iowa State Commerce Commission*, 369 F. Supp. 156 (D.C., S.D. Iowa 1974). Section 7(h) gave eminent-domain rights to pipelines and "the necessary land for . . . the location of compressor stations, pressure apparatus, or other stations or equipment necessary to the proper operation of such pipe line." Public Law 245, 61 Stat. 450 (1947).

The rationale for eminent domain cannot be claimed to be within the conservation-law ethic of waste prevention and correlative-rights protection. Condemnation statutes are a "second-best" solution to a property-rights problem that substitutes a "tyranny of the majority" for a "tyranny of the minority." Reliance is placed on arbitrary court determinations of "fair value" instead of on true value as revealed by voluntary transactions. In one eminent-domain proceeding, the owner of a condemned property was awarded nothing because the court ruled that the storage easement across his property was "valueless."[19] Confiscatory verdicts are always potentially present when coercion is used.

Given the separability of subsurface storage and surface activities, surface owners should have no more interest in the innocuous workings of a gas reservoir beneath them than the movement of a satellite above their land—*so long as no material influence, real or potential, is present.* If reservoir use requires surface use, arrangement must be made with the landowner to avoid trespass. If damage or irritation occurs to the surface area as a result of reservoir mismanagement, whether in the form of destroyed vegetation, noxious fumes, or hazards, tort liability and retribution should apply.

With the surface owner justly considered, a homestead theory of oil and gas property law can be applied to reservoir ownership and use. The first finder of the oil and gas reservoir would continue to own the depleted formation unless sold or bequeathed to another party. Any use of the storage facility would require a lease between the owner or owners and the parties seeking storage. In cases in which the depleted reservoir was abandoned—the owner failing to keep proper legal documentation and not demonstrating intent to use—the reservoir would revert to a "state of nature" for a new first claimant to possess. In such cases, only a surface lease to operate the underground facility would be required.

Short of a homestead resolution to the transaction-cost problem, the "solution" of condemnation instead of unanimous agreement can be questioned. In recent decades, lease agreements have included provisions for reservoir rentals upon depletion to avoid the holdout problem. The large number of storage agreements made without

---

[19]*Midwestern Gas Transmission Company* v. *Mason*, 31 Ill. 2d 340, 201 N.E.2d 379 (1964).

condemnation suggests that pecuniary motives have made the transaction-cost problem surmountable. In Texas, prior to the Underground Gas Storage Act of 1977, for example, over a dozen reservoirs storing more than 150 million cubic feet each were in operation.[20]

As of March 31, 1981, there were 390 gas-storage reservoirs in twenty-six states with seasonal gas storage of 5.2 trillion cubic feet (Tcf) and capacity for 7.6 Tcf. Of the stored volumes, nearly 70 percent was cushion gas and the remainder working gas subject to withdrawal. Consuming states with the most gas-storage reservoirs and inventory were Michigan (44 and 989 billion cubic feet [Bcf]), Illinois (35 and 963 Bcf), Pennsylvania (55 and 826 Bcf), and Ohio (24 and 620 Bcf). Important producing states with the most reservoirs and storage were Texas (24 and 480 Bcf), Louisiana (7 and 439 Bcf), and Oklahoma (13 and 366 Bcf). California, a major consuming state with associated gas production, had nine reservoirs with 448 Bcf stored.[21]

The Strategic Petroleum Reserve

In the first decades of the twentieth century, fears of an imminent exhaustion of oil led to petroleum-land withdrawals and the reservation of oil-rich acreage for future military use. Four Naval Petroleum Reserves were set aside between 1912 and 1923.[22] With the discovery of major new oil fields in Oklahoma, Texas, and California in the late 1920s, the new fear—at least for the vested parts of the oil industry— became oversupply. A political response again resulted. State and federal regulation accommodated the price-stabilization ideal in the name of arresting waste as earlier chapters have chronicled.

The anti-production policies of World War II swung the pendulum back toward supply uncertainty. With peace in sight, the Petroleum Administration for War leased 10 million barrels of tank storage to house aviation gasoline. The Strategic Storage Program, in preparation for an assault on Japan, allowed full production of aviation fuel to continue.[23] A crude-oil stockpile was rejected because of high

---

[20]Texas Railroad Commission, *Annual Reports* for 1977 and 1978.

[21]U.S. Department of Energy, Energy Information Administration, "Underground Natural Gas Storage in the United States," DOE/EIA-0239(80), August 1981.

[22]See chapter 6, pp. 278–81.

[23]John Frey and H. Chandler Ide, *A History of the Petroleum Administration for War* (Washington, D.C.: Government Printing Office, 1946), pp. 363–64.

costs and the unknowns of belowground storage.[24] Oil would be supplied from normal production and inventory or stay in the ground as proven reserves.

History. In the 1970s, the federal government's storage strategy would change as part of a broad-based activist program to address the energy crisis.[25] Even before the Arab embargo of late 1973, bills began to surface in Congress to create a federal oil reserve to provide quick drawdown in case of foreign supply cutoffs.[26] The Petroleum Reserves and Import Policy Act, introduced by Senator Henry Jackson (D-Wash.) in April 1973, called for a ninety-day strategic supply, much like programs already in effect in Japan, Germany, Italy, France, and Britain.[27] That act, which lacked White House support or a well-defined constituency, was not passed.

In response to the "energy crisis"—the petroleum-product shortages both before and after the Arab embargo—and with government activism holding sway over deregulation and market solutions, the Energy Policy and Conservation Act became law.[28] One provision of the far-reaching law earmarked $1.1 billion for a Strategic Petroleum Reserve Office (project office) within the Federal Energy Administration to implement an Early Storage Reserve program by April 22, 1976, and an SPR program by December 15, 1976. The final goal was

[24]Ibid., pp. 395–96.

[25]The practice of federal stockpiling of strategic industrial goods began in 1939, and by 1980, some ninety-three commodities valued at $13 billion were stored by the government for contingency use. See David Weimer, *The Strategic Petroleum Reserve* (Westport, Conn.: Greenwood Press, 1982), p. 6.

[26]*Strategic Petroleum Reserve Program*, Hearings before the Subcommittee on Energy and Mineral Resources of the Senate Committee on Energy and Natural Resources, 97th Cong., 1st sess. (Washington, D.C.: Government Printing Office, 1981), part 2, p. 395. Academic discussion of a federal reserve began with an appendix to a 1970 report by the Cabinet Task Force on Oil Import Control, *The Oil Import Question, A Report on the Relationship of Oil Imports to the National Security* (Washington, D.C.: Government Printing Office, 1970), pp. 299–303, and a 1971 article by Walter Mead and Phillip Sorenson, "A National Defense Petroleum Reserve Alternative to Oil Import Quotas," *Land Economics* (August 1971): 211–24.

[27]David Weimer, *The Strategic Petroleum Reserve*, p. 10; and *Oil & Gas Journal*, August 6, 1973, p. 25. Cited hereafter as *OGJ*.

[28]Public Law 94-163, 89 Stat. 871 (1975). Section 151(a) stated that the stockpile's twin aims were to "diminish the vulnerability of the United States to the effects of a severe energy supply interruption, and provide limited protection from the short-term consequences of interruptions in supplies of petroleum products."

to stockpile 1 billion barrels of crude oil with an interim target of 150 million barrels by December 1978. An Industrial Petroleum Reserve program was also authorized under which crude importers and refiners would set aside 3 percent of their respective volumes for holding. As with the SPR, storage was to be "readily accessible" to each Federal Energy Administration region, and drawdown schedules and distribution were to be formulated.

Sixty percent of the reserve was to be intermediate-gravity (between 32 and 36 degrees API gravity)[29] crude oil. The remainder was to be one or two grades of low-sulfur (under 0.5 percent) crude oil of light to intermediate gravity. The advantages of having two or three types of crude were fewer separate storage facilities and the ability to meet the requirements of different refineries.[30]

On April 18, 1977, the SPR plan went into effect upon congressional approval.[31] Storage goals were 150 million barrels by December 22, 1978, 325 million barrels by December 22, 1980, and 500 million barrels by December 22, 1982. Salt-dome caverns in Texas and Louisiana were to be leached by water injection to create storage space. Storage in man-made containers such as tankers and steel drums was rejected because of cost. Petroleum products were not to be stored—only crude oil was. Private-sector "turnkey" arrangements, under which private contractors would prepare the storage area, fill the caverns, and turn over the finished project to the government, were prohibited.

In the first week of the program, three sites in Louisiana were acquired by the Corps of Engineers by eminent domain. Pipeline right-of-way was similarly acquired; appraisals below industry standards made condemnation necessary. This, however, did not reduce costs or trim start-up time as intended. The associated legal proceedings increased costs and created delay, and condemnation set the stage for political trading between Louisiana and federal officials in Washington, D.C.[32]

---

[29]American Petroleum Institute (API) gravity, expressed in degrees, is the standard industry measure of density of petroleum liquids. The higher the value of API gravity, the less dense, and more valuable, the petroleum liquid.

[30]Federal Energy Administration, *Strategic Petroleum Reserve Plan* (Washington, D.C.: Strategic Petroleum Reserve Office, 1976), p. 6.

[31]Energy Action no. 10, submitted to Congress February 16, 1977.

[32]David Weimer, *The Strategic Petroleum Reserve*, pp. 50–51. Among the concessions gained by Louisiana governor Edwin Edwards was to locate the SPR Project Office

Attention turned next to crude-oil acquisition policy. Imported crude received entitlement benefits to lower its effective purchase cost.[33] Domestic crude subject to price ceilings could not be sold above the maximum allowed or be part of a "tie-in sale."[34] Responsibility for procurement was assigned to the Defense Fuels Supply Center within the Department of Defense.

Early problems plagued the storage program. The rush to fill leached salt domes led to design problems, cost overruns, and poor planning "worthy of a defense contractor."[35] Expensive ad hoc barge transportation was chosen over cheaper term pipeline transport.[36] Fixed-price oil contracts in a declining market left middlemen with handsome arbitrage profits at taxpayers' expense.[37] Misestimated schedules overcommitted oil to storage sites; by the end of 1978, demurrage costs had reached $7 million.[38] Quality control problems allowed as much as 9 million barrels of lower grade crude to be substituted for higher grade contracted crude.[39] Nonstandard equipment led to breakdowns and delays. Land-acquisition and leaching costs were underestimated by 50 percent.[40] The failure to install withdrawal equipment or even formulate a drawdown plan prompted one critic to label the program "a useless boondoggle."[41] Environmental disputes concerning saltwater-brine disposal led to delays that increased construction costs by as much as $28 million. Crude acquisition costs were $400 million higher because of rising crude prices during the delay.[42] At one site, a five-day fire—which

---

in the state. Said Edwards, "If the federal government is going to pour money down a rat hole, I would just as soon it be a rat hole in Louisiana" (p. 51).

[33]42 *Fed. Reg.* 21761 (April 29, 1977). See chapter 20, pp. 1205–34, on the refinery entitlements program.

[34]42 *Fed. Reg.* 27908 (June 1, 1977). In a tie-in sale, price-controlled oil was sold to a particular buyer in return for purchasing unregulated oil at a higher price.

[35]Peter Kovler, "The Strategic Petroleum Rathole," *Inquiry*, April 16, 1979, p. 10.

[36]David Weimer, *The Strategic Petroleum Reserve*, pp. 40–41.

[37]*Business Week*, December 5, 1977, p. 36.

[38]David Weimer, *The Strategic Petroleum Reserve*, p. 41.

[39]Ibid.

[40]Ibid., pp. 46–47.

[41]*OGJ*, August 6, 1979, p. 49.

[42]David Weimer, *The Strategic Petroleum Reserve*, pp. 52–53.

was caused by a low-pressure blowout in September 1978 and which claimed one life and caused a serious injury and $12 million in damages—resulted from "inadequate attention to critical safety problems, procedures, and emergency response capability," according to a Department of Energy study.[43] Overpayments to contractors and subcontractors resulted from poor auditing and other management procedures, according to Defense Department auditors and the General Accounting Office.[44] Thefts by employees, including one incident where the prime contractor stole $400,000 worth of equipment, added to problems.[45]

Disruptive reorganizations compounded the problems for the infant program. In late 1977, the Federal Energy Administration merged with several other agencies to form the Department of Energy. The realigned bureaucratic hierarchy slowed decisionmaking. The deputy director of the SPR program estimated that 25 percent of the program's key personnel were lost to Department of Energy appointments.[46] The relocation of the project office from Washington, D.C., to New Orleans in May 1979 created large turnover and a six-month work stoppage on new planning and design.[47] By the end of 1979, the program had gone through five managers, hardly encouraging to the rest of the workforce and a contributing factor to general instability and inefficiency.[48] The accumulation of such problems, manifested in cost overruns and a failure to meet fillage goals, led to congressional inquiries and formal hearings beginning in 1981. Compliance with congressional requests and audit requests further burdened the project office, which by this time was streamlining its operations to eliminate some of the blatant errors of the past.[49] Complained Program Deputy Director Carlyle Hystad, "We have more reviewers than we had people working on

---

[43]Quoted in ibid., pp. 61–62. See also *Business Week*, October 23, 1978, p. 51.

[44]*Wall Street Journal*, September 28, 1982, p. 35.

[45]*Newsweek*, July 2, 1979, p. 62.

[46]Carlyle Hystad, "Lessons of the Strategic Petroleum Reserve," in *California and World Oil: The Strategic Horizon* (Sacramento: California Energy Commission, 1981), p. 255.

[47]David Weimer, *The Strategic Petroleum Reserve*, p. 44.

[48]Congressional Quarterly, *Energy Policy*, 2d ed. (Washington, D.C.: Congressional Quarterly, Inc., March 1981), p. 100.

[49]David Weimer, *The Strategic Petroleum Reserve*, p. 55.

1031

the program."[50] Despite heavy oversight, new problems and new controversy continued to surface in 1983 and 1984.

The fill rate of the reserve was never far from controversy. The political desire to reach ambitious targets was tempered by storage capacity, cost, world events, and international relations. Oil injections began in July 1977, but the aforementioned problems soon put the program behind schedule. The plan of Carter and energy czar James Schlesinger to accelerate Ford's targets by two years to reach 500 million barrels by 1980 soon was out of reach.[51] On December 22, 1978, the deadline for 150 million barrels, less than 69 million barrels were in place.

In November 1979, Carter suspended purchases because of escalating crude prices in the wake of the Iran crisis. The stoppage continued with the summer shortages of 1979. Resumption of purchases in late 1979 was slowed by a threat that Saudi Arabia would retaliate by initiating a new round of OPEC price increases. A visit to Saudi Arabia by Department of Energy head Charles Duncan in March 1980 reconfirmed the possibility.[52] Congress, however, was less intimidated, and on June 30, the Energy Security Act was enacted to require minimum fill rates of 100,000 barrels per day or else production from the Naval Petroleum Reserves, averaging 160,000 barrels per day, would be put into the reserve or shut in.[53]

The restart, against the wishes of the Carter administration, was led by Senator Robert Dole (R-Kan.) and freshman colleague Bill Bradley (D-N.J.). Purchases resumed on September 23, 1980, at 100,000 barrels per day, which coincided with an embarrassment of oil riches elsewhere. Industry inventory of crude and products was 260 million barrels over Department of Energy-defined "prudent" levels, and the Army was holding 100 million barrels and end-users 200 million barrels more.[54] The market, not the reserve's eight-day

[50]Carlyle Hystad, "Lessons of the Strategic Petroleum Reserve," p. 256. Between February 1977 and October 1981, the General Accounting Office released twenty-two reports evaluating the program.

[51]Public Law 95-70, 91 Stat. 275 (1977).

[52]Congressional Quarterly, *Energy Policy*, p. 101.

[53]Public Law 96-294, 94 Stat. 611 (1980). The Naval Petroleum Reserves' output provided annual revenue of over $2 billion, which was reason enough to observe the minimum fill rate.

[54]Juan Cameron, "Washington's Ill-Starred Efforts to Stash Crude," *Fortune*, September 8, 1980, p. 66.

supply of imports, was prepared for a supply emergency five years into the program.

Despite the checkered performance of the reserve program, high fill rates were good politics. The 1980 Republican platform called for "rapid filling" to avoid being "made hostage to the whims of foreign governments."[55] Reagan endorsed this view, and in August 1981, he signed into law the Omnibus Budget Reconciliation Act, which included a target fill rate of 300,000 barrels per day.[56] The average fill rate for fiscal 1981 was 292,000 barrels per day, which dwarfed previous rates of 4,000 barrels per day in 1980, 88,000 in 1979, 131,000 in 1978, and 3,000 in 1977.[57]

The SPR experienced a "Reagan Revolution"—although hardly of the free-market variety. Two reasons explained Reagan's bullish SPR policy. First, the reserve was the centerpiece of his "free-market" energy policy, which precluded the need for standby price and allocation controls to deal with future emergencies. Second, the reserve was an instrument of foreign policy should U.S. intervention and confrontation lead to reprisals by oil-exporting countries as they had in 1973 and 1979.

On August 3, 1982, the Energy Emergency Preparedness Act was approved, which required fill rates of 300,000 barrels per day or more until 500 million barrels was reached. This ambitious goal was subject to funding and could be reduced by "a finding by the President in his discretion for good cause that compliance with such rate would not be in the national interest."[58] With declining oil prices and growing fiscal pressures, on December 1 of the same year, Reagan made such a finding and reduced the fill rate to 220,000 barrels per day, which was again reduced to 186,000 barrels on October 1, 1983. A fiscal year 1985 request by the president for 145,000 barrels per day was increased to 159,000 barrels by Congress.

---

[55]"1980 Republican National Convention Platform," *Congressional Record*, 96th Cong., 2d sess., July 31, 1980, pp. 24.

[56]Public Law 97-35, 95 Stat. 357 (1981). President Reagan would later state, "We continue a firm policy of filling the reserve as fast as permanent storage can be made available." *OGJ*, August 9, 1982, p. 72.

[57]U.S. Department of Energy, *Strategic Petroleum Reserve Annual Report* (Washington, D.C.: DOE, 1984), p. 4.

[58]Public Law 97-229, 96 Stat. 248 at 249 (1982).

Average fill rates turned out to be 179,000 barrels per day in fiscal 1982, 228,000 barrels in fiscal 1983, and 191,454 barrels in fiscal 1984. On April 5, 1982, Phase I's target of 250 million barrels was reached. The inventory was composed of Saudi, Mexican, Egyptian, Ammon, North Sea, Dubai, and U.S. oil at one site in Texas and four in Louisiana. In early 1983, the 300 million barrel plateau was reached, and in mid-1984, 400 million barrels were in place. The Phase II target of 500 million barrels was anticipated to be met by 1986, and the final phase of 750 million barrels, a six-month import supply, was scheduled for 1990, although growing uncertainty due to a changing world oil market and fiscal pressures was likely to modify these goals.

Relative to expenditure, SPR appropriations were liberal during the Ford and Carter regimes. Through 1979, over $2.2 billion went unspent.[59] With the Reagan acceleration at a time of record crude prices, the reserve program became a major cost item, and with budget deficit problems, a group of proposals came forth to reduce cost while maintaining fill rates. Global settlements with refiners accused of product-price overcharges were one source tapped. Settlements with Chevron, Conoco, and Champlin yielded over $50 million in in-kind crude payments to the SPR. A proposal to transfer funds from the dormant Synthetic Fuels Corporation was rejected. Another revenue proposal by Senator Nancy Kassebaum (R-Kans.) to force oil companies to set aside a percentage of imports for the reserve also was blocked. A different approach was suggested by Representative Phil Gramm (D-Tex.) to sell "oil bonds" to speculators that could be redeemed for oil in an emergency or after ten years.[60]

The chosen solution was to go off budget. In May 1981, the program was entirely refinanced through U.S. borrowing, which conveniently removed the $3.9-billion cost item from the fiscal 1982 budget to "reduce" the deficit. Freed from budget scrutiny and deficit ceilings, the SPR received a five-year borrowing authority of $21.9 billion. To Senate sponsor Bennett Johnston (D-La.), going off

---

[59]Congressional Quarterly, *Energy Policy*, p. 231.

[60]For a discussion of Kassebaum's Strategic Petroleum Reserve Amendments of 1981 (S. 707) and Gramm's Private Equity Petroleum Reserve Act (H.R. 2304), see David Weimer, *The Strategic Petroleum Reserve*, pp. 72–76.

budget was "the direct dishonest thing to do."[61] The SPR had gone underground.[62]

Drawdown Policy. The Energy Policy and Conservation Act, which originally authorized the reserve in 1975, sanctioned drawdowns only if "required by a severe energy supply interruption or by obligations of the United States under the international energy program."[63] But it would not be until November 15, 1979, over two years after injections began, that sales procedures were unveiled by the Department of Energy. After the president issued a notice of sale detailing drawdown specifics (date, location, quantity), the Department of Energy would evaluate and award offers at *set* prices based on nearby sales of similar crude. The secretary of the Department of Energy was granted authority to allocate 10 percent of total supply per month at his discretion. Distribution was biased toward small refiners and was subservient to existing price and allocation regulation.[64]

In early 1981, the SPR drawdown plan was amended to conform to the end of price and allocation controls.[65] Specifically, allocation pursuant to the buy-sell program was removed. Still, only refiners could purchase crude from the reserve, and the 10 percent discretionary allocation rule applied.

The Energy Emergency Preparedness Act of 1982 required the president to submit a new drawdown plan to Congress by December 1, 1982.[66] Amendment no. 4 on the same day announced a sales policy based on competitive pricing. Four months later, a proposed rule was issued announcing that the "principal method of distributing SPR oil will be price competitive sale."[67] Government contracting was to be "flexible and expeditious" to "facilitate" the drawdown process. Proposed standard sales provisions were issued

[61]*Houston Post*, May 13, 1981, p. 8B; and *Wall Street Journal*, May 11, 1981, p. 4.

[62]For an overview of off-budget government expenditures and commitments, see James Bennett and Thomas DiLorenzo, *Underground Government* (Washington, D.C.: Cato Institute, 1983).

[63]Public Law 94-163, 89 Stat. 871 at 888 (1975).

[64]Department of Energy, Energy Action no. 5, October 21, 1979; 45 *Fed. Reg.* 55379 (August 19, 1980).

[65]46 *Fed. Reg.* 20508 (April 13, 1981).

[66]Public Law 97-229, 96 Stat. 248 at 252 (1982).

[67]48 *Fed. Reg.* 11125 at 11127 (March 16, 1983).

on June 15.[68] In addition to providing detailed model terms and conditions, the thirty-page proposal spelled out purchaser performance, financial guarantees, and objective standards for the awarded contracts.

In December 1983, the Department of Energy issued a final rule.[69] Strict limitations on the export of purchased oil were emphasized. All exports, regulated by license, had to be pursuant to the International Energy Program, another executive order, or after a finding that the oil could not "reasonably" be refined domestically.[70] An interim appendix to the interim final rule was published on January 20, 1984, revising the terms and language of the June proposal for standard sales provisions.[71] In conjunction with a simulated physical withdrawal in August 1983, the Department of Energy decided to allow greater flexibility for the bidders regarding the quantity purchased, how it would be removed, and when it would be removed.

Federal Stockpiling Reconsidered. The SPR is a "sacred cow" of U.S. energy policy. The case for the reserve assumes that another energy crisis lies around the corner, the reserve will be efficiently managed during the crisis to alleviate the emergency, and private inventories and entrepreneurship alone would be inadequate. The reserve is seen by proponents as the nation's insurance policy against the inherent instability of the world oil market.

The previous section, tracing the history of the reserve's early years, offered many performance miscues. This is not surprising. The SPR is susceptible to inefficiency because it is a government program outside the competitive marketplace where entrepreneurial discovery continually reallocates resources toward consumer preferences. Private business decisions under the discipline of profit and loss tailor costs toward expected revenue. Poor budgeting and cost overruns would be fatal with unforgiving consumers. Government programs such as the SPR, on the other hand, are heavily end-specific; expenditure is of secondary importance. Political considerations also prevail over fiscal prudence. The fate of the project is immune from cost overruns and performance failures. The program

---

[68]48 *Fed. Reg.* 27482 (June 15, 1983).
[69]48 *Fed. Reg.* 56538 (December 21, 1983).
[70]Ibid., p. 56539.
[71]49 *Fed. Reg.* 2692 (January 20, 1984).

is simply amended and continues as a luxury of tax finance and borrowing on the "full faith and credit" of the U.S. government.

An inventory program predicated on buying in low-demand (surplus) periods to sell in high-demand (shortage) periods should be very sensitive to price. Yet as prices increased to higher and higher levels, peaking in the first half of 1981, the capacity goals of the SPR remained unchanged. A purchase slowdown by one administration because of rising prices was followed by a major buildup by the next administration despite record prices. The result was a program costing much more than planned. In the original Strategic Petroleum Reserve Plan of December 15, 1976, the total cost of a 500 million barrel reserve was estimated at between $7.5 billion and $8 billion— between $15 and $16 per barrel.[72] Over twice this amount was spent with the 500 million barrel goal not yet reached. A fiscal-year summary of the federal storage program from inception through 1984 is presented in table 17.1.

The "insurance policy" of public oil stockpiling, incurring a $15-billion "premium" through 1984 with another $10 billion projected, is a case study in nonmarket decisionmaking. A sacrosanct, illusory end—"security"—justified the means of high taxpayer expense and incrementally higher world oil prices. Start-up problems often were multi-million-dollar mistakes. There is evidence that experience reduced the scope and severity of earlier errors—that the 1981–84 performance was superior to the 1977–79 performance—but new facets of the program have brought new problems.[73] Early purchases at "low" prices (between $15 and $20 per barrel) were canceled out by later purchases at "high" prices (between $30 and $38 per barrel). Combined with the $5 per barrel handling and storing expense, the overall market value of SPR oil was billions of dollars less than its embedded average cost of over $35 per barrel.[74] By any profit-loss

---

[72]Federal Energy Administration, *Strategic Petroleum Reserve Plan*, pp. 3, 182.

[73]The exchange program that began late in 1980, whereby the Project Office traded Naval Petroleum Reserve oil for SPR crude, for example, has come under criticism for poor trading strategies that cost taxpayers millions of dollars. These cumbersome trades were made to stay out of the world market to appease Saudi Arabia. David Weimer, *The Strategic Petroleum Reserve*, p. 71.

[74]The average acquisition cost of crude oil alone had been over $27 per barrel. This price is the average delivered price including import fees, Superfund taxes, terminaling costs, and a premium paid for delivery in U.S tankers. The approximately $8 per barrel balance covers all other facility and overhead costs. It is also net of entitlements benefits. Conversation with Howard Borgstrom, director of strategic planning, Strategic Petroleum Reserve, January 24, 1985.

Table 17.1
Strategic Petroleum Reserve Expenditures: 1976–84
(thousands of dollars)

Fiscal Year	Oil Purchases & Transportation	Storage, Acquisition & Operation	Other Cost	Total Cost
1976	$ 300,000	$ –	$ 13,975	$ 313,975
1977	–	440,000	7,824	447,824
1978	463,933	2,703,469	14,704	3,182,106
1979	632,504	2,356,456	18,111	3,007,071
1980	–	(2,022,272)[a]	22,462[b]	(1,999,810)
1981	108,168	3,205,094[c]	19,391	3,332,653
1982[d]	175,656	3,679,700	20,076	3,875,432
1983	222,528	2,074,060	19,590	2,316,178
1984	142,357	650,000	16,413	808,770
Total	$2,045,146	$13,086,507	$152,546	$15,284,199

Source: U.S. Department of Energy, *Strategic Petroleum Reserve Annual Report* (Washington, D.C.: DOE, 1984), p. 6.
[a]Recission from suspension of crude purchases.
[b]Reprogrammed from previous year's allocation to petroleum acquisition and transportation.
[c]Includes a $1.3-billion supplemental allocation from the loss of entitlements income.
[d]Beginning of off-budget status.

calculation, the program was fiscally problematic, underscoring why it was not considered, much less undertaken, by the private sector.

A second cost of the SPR, in addition to direct taxpayer expense, was far less quantifiable but real. Oil purchases for the reserve, mainly imports, supported world oil prices at the expense of the domestic economy since the United States is a net oil consumer.

Political factors contributed to the costly and inefficient performance of the stockpile program. The Jones Act increased transportation costs by as much as $1 per barrel by requiring Alaskan oil and one-half of the imported oil purchased by the reserve to be shipped on U.S.-flag vessels.[75] In late 1982, a major contract was signed with beleaguered Mexico as part of a U.S. aid package. (A year before, a 50,000 barrel per day contract for 110 million barrels was signed

[75]*Forbes*, July 5, 1982, p. 44. The Jones Act is examined in chapter 16, pp. 1000–1002.

with Pemex at market rates.) Reflecting its political nature, the terms of the contract were classified, but one publicized fact was one billion dollars in front money for Mexico. The loan was intended to help Mexico repay its debt to major U.S. banks, which made the SPR contract a taxpayer subsidy to a corrupt, socialistic government and its creditors.

Aboveground storage interests pounded the pavement of Capitol Hill for greater participation in the reserve program. In response to the "unmistakable aroma of pork," the steel industry, tank fabricators, oil-tanker owners, and steel-tank owners lobbied in 1982 for permanent surface storage at dispersed sites.[76]

The exclusive location of the oil reserves near Gulf Coast refineries sparked criticism and calls for geographical diversification. John Lichtblau of the Petroleum Industry Research Foundation recommended a residual-oil reserve for the East Coast. Senator Spark Matsunaga of Hawaii, noting that the reserves were as far away from his state as New York is from Istanbul, urged crude storage in Hawaii. At the time, SPR oil had to travel through the Panama Canal to reach the Pacific basin.[77]

The biggest political element was yet to come—who gets what, how much, and where in the event of an "emergency" drawdown. The fact that the "emergency" was not objectively defined practically ensured that the reserve would not be deployed in a timely manner—as all the positive net social cost calculations assumed.[78] The painstaking rules of the Standard Sales Provisions were yet to be tested in real emergencies. Only a real-life drawdown would unveil opportunities to game the program. While the potential for error is not unique to public-sector economic decisions, timely amendment would be burdened by procedural requirements.

---

[76]*Forbes*, July 5, 1982, p. 44. See the testimony of the American Iron and Steel Institute, the Steel Plate Fabricators Association, and the Independent Fuel Terminal Operators Association in Senate Committee on Energy and Natural Resources, *Current Condition of the Strategic Petroleum Reserve* (Washington, D.C.: Government Printing Office, 1982), pp. 278–330.

[77]Ibid., pp. 27–28, 222.

[78]"Any reserve size is cost beneficial if it is assumed that a shortfall *will* occur that would require use of the bulk of the Reserve." Federal Energy Administration, *Strategic Petroleum Reserve Plan*, p. 34.

The stockpile is a public good directed by temporary political majorities. What constitutes an emergency to trigger an SPR allocation is a political unknown, but when "it" occurs, a dogfight can be expected among members of Congress, different federal agencies, segments of the oil industry, and consumer groups. What should the minimum bid be, and how will discretionary supply be allocated? Should the oil go to government use (such as the military) or to the private sector? How will western U.S. interests, which are geographically removed from the oil, participate? Domestic producers will want as little drawdown as possible and sales at high prices to avoid being crowded out. Consumers will want as much supply as possible at low prices, with region competing against region, with the Northeast at the forefront.

The 1979 oil crisis found no drawdown capability and not even an allocation plan for the reserve. Although drawdown capacity and a procedural blueprint were developed later, not all was well. Assuming another crisis, fundamental questions such as when the drawdown should begin and how much should be withdrawn will receive political-bureaucratic answers, not entrepreneurial ones as in a market.

Policy contradictions proved to be no obstacle to the reputation of the SPR within academia and the political arena. The Elk Hills Naval Petroleum Reserve, originally intended to be a warehouse of proven oil reserves for emergency military use, was producing around 140,000 daily barrels for government sale and use, while the SPR was storing oil in similar quantities in the name of security. While the Naval Petroleum Reserve raised revenue, the SPR was a major cost item; while the SPR "increased" security, the naval reserve "decreased" it. The "wash" rarely involved transporting naval-reserve oil several thousand miles from California to Texas-Louisiana caverns, but the irony of the two government programs' working at cross-purposes should be noted even with the greater drawdown capacity of the SPR.

Another contraction was between public and private oil inventory. The massive government stockpile discouraged precautionary oil inventory held by the private sector for unforeseen emergencies. But the majority of the stockpile would *not* have been assumed by the private sector, underscoring the fact that the federal government misdiagnosed and overreacted to the energy crises of the 1970s. On the other hand, to the extent that the private market believed that the SPR would not be effectively used and that the reserve itself lessened the chance of reimposed price and allocation regulation, private inventories would be maintained.

The emergency supply and price buffer of the SPR reduced the potential need of alternative-fuel technologies in a crisis, which not only discouraged private synthetic-fuel development (to the extent there was still interest) but increased the cost-ineffectiveness of government-subsidized synfuel projects as well.

A fourth policy tension was the promotion of oil imports. While official U.S. policy decried our dependence on oil imports, the SPR from the start was hooked on them. A policy of reducing oil imports could have begun with reduced fillage of the reserve.

Finally, the promise of the reserve's thwarting higher oil prices during an oil import interruption contradicted another sacred pillar of U.S. energy policy—conservation. Consumers presumably would be more conservative about energy usage if they understood that they were not "protected" from the risks of the world oil market. "Insurance" in this case sent a wrong signal to not only energy suppliers but energy demanders.

The SPR was at odds with the nation's true first line of defense in a true oil emergency—private entrepreneurship. The government's hand was also strengthened for counterproductive short-run policies in a real emergency. The much-touted "insurance" of the SPR could be to negate bad government policy elsewhere—say the reimposition of price and allocation regulation—rather than consumer protection against an adverse change in the world oil market.

A technical literature has developed to justify import regulation and public oil storage to blunt a future oil emergency.[79] Through economic modeling and empirical estimation, the marginal social cost of imports is found to exceed marginal private import costs because importers do not factor the negative externalities associated with a potential supply disruption into their decisions. The price difference between (lower) private costs and (higher) social costs has been labeled *the oil import premium*.

Douglas Bohi and David Montgomery have argued for a government oil stockpile to mitigate the "macroeconomic dislocations that

---

[79]Also see the discussion in chapter 13, pp. 761–62.

are produced by an oil price shock and the economic cost of wealth transferred abroad when the price of imports rises."[80] Michael Barron makes a similar point when he states that "private incentives are insufficient to induce an appropriate stockpile level," necessitating a public reserve to "stabilize the general economy by limiting the inflation and loss of aggregate output and income induced by oil shortfalls."[81] Estimates of the oil-import premium vary, but one influential calculation, by the Congressional Budget Office in 1980, of the reduction in gross national product from a year-long cutoff was $146 billion, which gave a hypothecated SPR stockpile of 730 million barrels a social value of $200 per barrel.[82]

Before considering the legitimacy of the oil-import premium, one positive contribution of this technical literature should be acknowledged. Most critics of oil imports have acknowledged that the potential problem of oil-import dependence is higher prices and not physical shortages. If markets are free to clear, supply and demand will equalize; the price at which this occurs is the primary concern. Proponents of the SPR see the major benefit as preventing a price spike more than as preventing shortages.

The proof of a negative externality with oil imports rests upon questionable methodology and faulty assumptions. The key concept of social cost is computed as if cost were objectively measurable. This is incorrect. Cost—which economists define as the most attractive opportunity forgone—is notoriously subjective and open to varying estimation. It cannot be quantitatively expressed in the aggregate with scientific precision—which invites prejudice and political manipulation.[83] It is not surprising that twenty government and private studies favoring a stockpile found the "optimal" reserve to

---

[80]Douglas Bohi and David Montgomery, *Oil Prices, Energy Security, and Import Policy* (Baltimore: Johns Hopkins University Press, 1982), p. 130.

[81]Michael Barron, "Private-Sector Financing of Oil-Stockpile Acquisition," in *Policies for Coping with Oil-Supply Disruptions*, ed. George Horwich and Edward Mitchell (Washington, D.C.: American Enterprise Institute, 1982), pp. 112–13.

[82]Cited in *Fortune*, September 8, 1980, p. 67.

[83]For an explanation of subjective cost theory, see James Buchanan, *Cost and Choice* (Chicago: University of Chicago Press, 1969). For estimation problems involved in policy-oriented research, see Steven Cheung, *The Myth of Social Cost* (San Francisco: Cato Institute, 1980).

contain from as little as 250 million barrels to over 1 billion barrels.[84] The "optimum" depends on the assumptions and the philosophical outlook of the modeler.

Model building and "crystal-ball" predictions in the energy field have proven notoriously unreliable.[85] The case for a strategic stockpile, created out of the same cloth, is no more sturdy.

The externality literature assigns a high probability to an oil-import disruption and assumes an almost omniscient drawdown response from the reserve. Both pivotal assumptions are incorrect. As argued later in this section, the energy crises of the 1970s were caused by government intervention and not the mere fact of import dependence. A long era of oil oversupply and a buyer's market can be expected to reign so long as the free market reigns. Interruptions and the higher prices therein should be seen as the flip side of OPEC price wars and a general buyer's market. As such, higher oil prices in certain periods are akin to the "bad luck" of a cold winter or hot summer for energy ratepayers. It can happen and sometimes does— but it is not debilitating and reason for expensive and uncertain "insurance."

The "macroeconomic dislocation" of oil-import disruptions is also exaggerated. The two major externalities of private import decisions—inflation and an unfavorable balance of trade—are questionable building blocks for determining an oil-import premium. First, increasing oil imports can lead prices down and not up, as experience has shown. Second, higher oil prices are not necessarily inflationary. A change in relative prices cannot cause a general price change (short of a simultaneous increase in the money stock) *unless* the output of the economy is reduced or inflationary expectations are increased. Oil-substitute prices will increase as a result of higher oil prices, but oil-complement prices will go in the opposite direction.

---

[84]National Petroleum Council, *Emergency Preparedness for Interruption of Petroleum Imports into the United States* (Washington, D.C.: NPC, April 1981).

[85]"By now [1979] it should be clear that the predictions derived from energy models are subject to a great deal of imprecision. The derivation of coefficients that are necessary to generate forecasts often requires the modeler to make assumptions that cannot be completely substantiated, or to make assumptions that may obscure the representation of the system being analyzed." Robert Stobaugh and Daniel Yergin, "Limits to Models," in *Energy Future*, ed. Robert Stobaugh and Daniel Yergin (New York: Random House, 1979), p. 262. This evaluation would be even more valid five years later.

Indeed, as more income is spent on energy, less income is left to spend elsewhere, decreasing demand and thus prices. The net effect is a similar price "level," with the above qualifications, although the relative prices comprising the aggregate will be quite different.

Changed relative prices as a result of increased oil scarcity are not a Keynesian aggregate demand problem but an adjustment process that free-market forces can be expected to anticipate and absorb without triggering an economywide business cycle. The oil traumas of 1973–74 and 1979 are case studies of how government intervention prevented market forces from operating. The difficulties experienced did not result from exogenous price shocks to the market alone.

An "unfavorable" balance of trade—money leaving the United States with increasing oil-import dependence—invents more of a problem than it verifies. Greater imports, as mentioned, can well be at *lower* prices to make the net effect on the trade balance ambiguous. (On the other hand, import interruptions will create a tradeoff between higher prices and less imports.) But the whole trade balance issue, more fundamentally, is a nonproblem since exported dollars are "recycled"; they are either used to buy U.S. goods or are reinvested in the United States. The overlooked recycling effect means that the "negative" externality is counterbalanced by a "positive" externality.

Once its scientific gloss is removed, the case for an "optimal" tariff, quota, or public stockpile is revealed to be a mirage. In place of ambiguous oil-import premium derivations, qualitative discussion of market processes complements a historical reinterpretation of past oil-import reductions. The size of the reserve becomes secondary to whether the reserve can be justified at all. A market-process perspective concludes that the SPR fails the cost-benefit test and is superfluous, given the vicissitudes of the world petroleum market.

Without the SPR, the United States would not be helpless against the whims of the world petroleum market. The market's "insurance" policy is forward-looking *entrepreneurship unencumbered by tax and regulatory disincentives.*

The energy crises of the 1970s cannot be properly interpreted without understanding the role of government intervention in precipitating and exacerbating the crises. The "oil weapon" used to punish the United States in 1973 was a reaction to U.S. aid to Israel and in 1979 to long-standing U.S. intervention in Iranian politics.

A less interventionist foreign policy, a handmaiden to free-market domestic policy, would be less likely to arouse nationalistic and xenophobic sentiment to trigger retaliatory disruptions of petroleum imports. Furthermore, the world petroleum market diversified its output in the 1980s to lessen the chances of an effective embargo or concerted production cut. In late 1982, Mexico surpassed Saudi Arabia as the leading exporter of crude oil to the United States, and two years later Venezuela, Canada, Britain, and Nigeria rose to the top of the list as well. An embargo by Saudi Arabia or another country would only give rise to a highly profitable substitution of oil from other producing countries. Exporting countries' slack capacity was a growing phenomenon that made the worst-case scenario of oil-import interruptions much less likely and less consequential than it had been in the 1970s.

Turning from international to domestic policy, U.S. energy policy in the 1970s made the country dependent on and vulnerable to imports by artificially encouraging consumption, subsidizing imports, and discouraging production and inventory speculation. Price and allocation controls set the stage for OPEC profit maximization through higher prices and lower output. Specifically, as seen in previous chapters, domestic price ceilings lowered U.S. output to below unregulated levels, the refinery entitlements program subsidized the quantity and price of imports, allocation programs erased the profit potential of increased oil storage, and price ceilings delayed conservation and the development and implementation of new energy-efficient technologies. Gas lines and other symptoms of petroleum-product shortages, which created vast microeconomic distortions that adversely affected the national economy, were created by price controls and worsened by allocation controls. With decontrol in early 1981, the artificial props to imports were taken away, and crude prices and imports subsequently declined. The rationale for and anticipated use of the SPR became more and more questionable in the free-market 1980s.

The likelihood of a crisis aside, the presence of market forces to counter disruptions constitutes a strong case against federal stockpiling. Free-market entrepreneurship is an anticipatory function. Profits are gained by correctly anticipating the future state of supply and demand. When future supply is uncertain, profit seekers increase inventory to profitably use or sell when market conditions change.

1045

Storing in relatively plentiful times and selling in tight situations mitigate price fluctuations to better stabilize the market. In the 1970s, regulatory programs such as buy-sell, entitlements, and price controls removed incentive for firms to increase inventory to internally draw down or externally sell. Quite the opposite, firms with less inventory were rewarded and firms with more inventory were penalized.[86]

While market actions are anticipatory, another important market process is the adjustment to less supply and higher prices. Consumers reduce use and turn to other fuels, such as coal and natural gas, where possible. *Conservation* and *substitution* are key consumer strategies for adapting to the new reality. Producers increase crude output over normal levels (surge production) and sink development wells in existing fields. Wildcat drilling also becomes more economical. These are responses that state and federal regulation, from state output restrictions to federal price controls, have historically discouraged. Thus, broad-based market-oriented energy policies should be considered in lieu of the SPR.

Another market process that ensures adequate supply over time was delayed by regulation in the 1970s but made a grand appearance in the 1980s—the crude-oil and petroleum-product futures market. This institution has internalized expectations of supply and demand to prepare for the future, as discussed in the next section of this chapter.

A common defense for a reserve is that the market could be taken by complete surprise and have inadequate inventory to cushion a sudden import cutoff. This view tenuously assumes that market entrepreneurs as forecasters are inferior to government officials. If this were true, broad empirical support could be found for state bureaucratic direction of economic activity. The government could win profits, become self-financing, and enrich the economy in the process. Theory and experience, however, suggest the opposite.

---

[86]For a vivid example, see chapter 20, p. 1204. Unlike the situation during the 1973 and 1979 disruptions, the disruptions caused by the Iran-Iraq war in 1980, which reduced imports by 3 million barrels per day, were effectively countered by private-sector inventory drawdowns. Less restrictive regulation was at the forefront. Oil price ceilings were being phased out, and product prices were either deregulated or superfluous. Allocation regulation did not restrict inventory buildups, and with price incentives, quasi-market preparation and response were possible. The SPR, meanwhile, lacking drawdown capacity, was superfluous.

1046

Bureaucracy has *not* been able to discover and exploit profit opportunities. The record of the SPR and the Synthetic Fuels Program, predicated on a pessimistic world view of energy resources, attests to this fact.

In conclusion, the SPR is conceptually and empirically open to complete review. As the first decade of the program drew to a close, it was apparent that the government had mismanaged a program that could not be cost justified in the first place. With an embedded cost of around $35 per barrel, a multi-billion-dollar paper loss was incurred.

Government oil insurance is more than prohibitively expensive; it is unneeded. The free-market era in petroleum in the 1980s gave no hint of a repeat of the regulated 1970s. There will be no crisis for the reserve to mitigate so long as such counterproductive policies as price and allocation controls are not resorted to. (And even if they were, the SPR still would not be the savior.) Even if there were a crisis lurking around the corner, free-market entrepreneurship, not the uncertain utilization of a political asset, should be the nation's first line of defense. Chapter 31 will consider a nonpolitical, entrepreneurial future for the SPR.

The International Energy Agency

One of the two drawdown triggers for the SPR, in addition to a "severe energy supply disruption," is the energy-sharing program of the International Energy Agency (IEA). The IEA was founded in 1974 as a consuming-nation counterweight to OPEC. The United States joined in 1976. If any of the twenty-one member countries loses 7 percent or more of its crude, better situated countries, in theory at least, are obligated to share their supply. The IEA's major goals are to gather energy statistics to improve market information, promote conservation and international cooperation, and formulate sharing plans in the event of an actual disruption to mitigate price spikes and supply dislocations. Whether intended or not, the U.S. SPR, greater than the other member nations' stockpiles combined, has become the linchpin of this contingency sharing plan.

The IEA offers much downside and virtually no upside for U.S. consumers and taxpayers in worst-case events. The raison d'être of the organization is for "surplus" member nations to share supply with "deficit" member nations. Given the size and capability of the

SPR compared to other national stockpiles (many countries have no strategic reserves), the chances are that the SPR will aid foreign markets instead of foreign oil stockpiles' benefiting the United States. Under IEA guidelines, not only is the United States obligated to distribute SPR oil to any member country that loses more than 7 percent of its supply, the IEA secretariat decides at what price the transactions will take place.

The prospect of multinational price and allocation planning by an international energy czar is discomfiting. Price and allocation planning in the United States was a failure; expanding regulation to the multination "consumer cartel" will only compound the knowledge problem that inheres in central planning. Regulators cannot duplicate the efficiency of entrepreneurship and the market process.

This egalitarian world energy plan has a number of other problems. It forgives shortsightedness and penalizes foresight. Like the SPR, it has the potential to crowd out private-sector entrepreneurship by releasing crude to drive down prices. Private precautionary stocks—which can swing by over 100 million barrels in anticipation of oil disruptions or higher prices—are discouraged. The policy implication, discussed in the final chapter, is for the United States to reconsider its membership in the IEA whether or not policy reform takes place with the SPR.

Forward Markets and Futures Trading

The distribution of petroleum has not only a geographical dimension of physically moved supply but a *time* dimension of satisfying demand in future periods. In addition to immediate *spot sales*, petroleum can be traded in *contract sales* or *forward sales*. Contract sales are supply commitments over a period of time at either fixed or posted (variable) prices; in forward sales a price is immediately finalized for a transaction at a specified future date. When forward sales are common enough to become impersonal and standardized, liquid contracts and cash settlement predominating over physical possession, a *futures market* comes into being.

There are three categories of forward-futures participants. *Speculators*—"long buyers" anticipating a price increase and "short sellers" anticipating a price decrease—gamble on a favorable price change. *Hedgers*, short sellers who lock in a profit for current supply or long buyers who lock in future supply costs, are the risk-averse segment of the market. Hedging has the following attractions: setting fixed-price forward commitments, optimizing production and sales decisions, increasing volume, facilitating bank financing, participating anonymously in market exchanges, increasing the planning horizon, and economizing inventory.[87] There are also *arbitrageurs* who alertly identify price discrepancies between physically identical oil in different markets and simultaneously sell higher priced supply short and buy lower priced supply long to capture the price differential.

The general effect of forward-futures trading is to meet consumer demand over time, while simultaneously transferring uncertainty from risk averters to risk seekers. It is a free-market phenomenon born of self-interest and nurtured in an environment free of price and allocation regulation.

Forward and Futures Trading: 1865–1909

Forward trading began in the early years of the oil industry. To facilitate buying and selling crude, "oil exchanges" were formed in the late 1860s where sellers and buyers would physically congregate to deal in immediate "spot" oil delivery, ten-day "regular" oil delivery, and later "future" oil delivery.[88]

Some early oil exchanges set up shop in railcars that traversed the oil region; others were located on hotel sidewalks, the most famous being the Curbstone Exchange. Formal exchanges with telegraphic equipment followed in the Pennsylvania oil towns of Titusville, Franklin, and Oil City in 1871 and Pittsburgh, Petrolia, Parker, and Bradford soon after.[89]

Interest in forward trading outside of the oil region led to similar offerings at the Consolidated Stock and Petroleum Exchange in New York City and on exchanges in Philadelphia and Cincinnati. The gambling instinct of wildcat oilmen was particularly suited to forward trading, and price volatility kept interest high. Explained a commemorative issue of the *Oil & Gas Journal*:

> The buying and selling of oil for future delivery became a vocation in which fortunes were won or lost with ease. A 30-day option could

[87]Chicago Mercantile Exchange, "A Guide to Hedging in Petroleum Product Markets," no date, p. 6.

[88]*Oil & Gas Journal—Oil City Derrick*, August 27, 1934, p. 9.

[89]Paul Giddens, *The Early Petroleum Industry* (Philadelphia: Porcupine Press, 1974), pp. 188–91.

witness a wide change in the price of oil, with the result that a trade involving a few thousand barrels might raise a man from want to luxury, or the reverse.[90]

With such high stakes, attempts were made to manipulate price swings. The market was entirely unregulated; verbal and written agreements and open competition were the only "regulators." The alluring scheme was to "corner the market": contracts to take future delivery were executed followed by attempts to lock up the physical supply needed to make delivery. To honor their contracts, short sellers would have to buy oil from the instigators at inflated prices. The most famous attempt to corner an oil market occurred in Pittsburgh in 1869. A consortium ("oil ring") quietly purchased a number of futures contracts, most set to mature on December 31, and began to buy crude oil that would be needed by outsiders to meet delivery obligations. In the first several months, the scheme worked as purchased oil was profitably sold to liquidate contracts. Aiding the cause as a participant was the Allegheny Railroad, which refused to ship oil to Pittsburgh. This was important because dry weather had lowered the water level of the Allegheny River, which made barging impossible. As the important day of December 31 approached, however, the river became navigable and the oil ring was forced to step up its purchases. By the time the contracts matured, enough oil was available to retire the contracts, and falling prices forced the oil ring to sell its 500,000-barrel hoard at a loss.

Other attempted corners suffered a similar fate under the weight of market incentives to break them. "Generally," summarized Paul Giddens, "some petroleum dealer opened his tanks, broke the corner, and helped out the cornered individuals by furnishing oil."[91]

Forward oil speculation peaked in the 1880s and matured into futures trading with "little actual oil changing hands."[92] A Pennsylvania law passed on June 20, 1883, designated as legal tender certificates for petroleum that were transferable by signature. Those taking

[90]*Oil and Gas Journal—Oil City Derrick*, p. 9. High and low oil prices per year are listed in U.S. Geological Survey, *Mineral Resources of the United States* (Washington, D.C.: Government Printing Office, 1912) p. 364.

[91]Paul Giddens, *The Early Petroleum Industry*, p. 187.

[92]Harold Williamson and Arnold Daum, *The Age of Illumination, 1859 to 1899*, vol. 1 of *The American Petroleum Industry* (Evanston, Ill.: Northwestern University Press, 1959), p. 620.

delivery worked less through the exchange and more through producers. By 1887, speculative volumes began to fall, and the once-thriving oil exchanges began to exit.[93]

On January 22, 1895, the death knell for forward-futures trading was sounded when Standard Oil's purchasing arm in Oil City announced that small trading volumes on the exchange made its price quotes unreliable and daily quotations would be derived elsewhere.[94] Integration was replacing two-party transactions, and oil-price variations diminished.[95] The oil exchanges ceased operation with the demise of the Oil City and Bradford exchanges in 1909.

Second Period of Futures Trading: 1935

Interest in a petroleum futures market resurfaced in 1934. Price volatility created by the off-and-on production from the great southwestern fields spawned this market need. On October 22, an announcement was made by the New York Commodity Exchange:

> For some time the exchange has been contemplating the establishment of an oil futures market. Impetus has recently been given to this movement by the price war which has broken out in the industry. Trade papers have mentioned favorably the desirability of an oil exchange.[96]

Only the oldest members of the industry could recall futures trading on the Consolidated Stock and Petroleum Exchange in the 1880s and forward trading and futures trading on the other exchanges. The changing tide of the hot-oil war kept prices in flux, and commodity-futures brokers active in metals, rubber, silk, cocoa, cotton, and other commodities envisioned making profits by matching oil hedgers and speculators.

The board of directors of the American Petroleum Institute, representing primarily integrated majors, unanimously adopted a resolution against futures trading in November 1934 as a "speculative enterprise" that would be "harmful" to the petroleum industry.[97]

---

[93]Ibid.

[94]*Oil & Gas Journal—Oil City Derrick*, p. 13.

[95]The price range in 1893 was between $0.78 and $0.80 per barrel; in 1894 the range was between $0.9525 and $0.9575 per barrel. U.S. Geological Survey, *Mineral Resources of the United States*, p. 364.

[96]*OGJ*, October 25, 1934, p. 14.

[97]American Petroleum Institute, *15 Annual Proceeding* (New York: API, 1934) p. 47.

Sentiment for futures trading remained strong in other quarters, however, and in late December, the New York Commodity Exchange announced a gasoline-futures market to commence in February 1935. Several gasoline grades were specified with Gulf Coast and New York Harbor delivery. Crude-oil futures were also planned. Contract specifications were outlined, including a 30 percent margin requirement and a flat $25 broker's fee.[98] The Chicago Board of Trade soon followed with a petroleum-futures proposal.[99]

The New York Commodities Exchange mailed their completed proposal to oil executives to educate them on the function and procedure of futures trading. For refiners, price fluctuations could be contracted away. Risk for producers also could be hedged away. For marketers, inventory could be more flexibly managed. Brokers reported more speculative interest in upcoming oil futures than in oil stocks and bonds.[100]

After a one-month postponement, the New York Commodities Exchange opened crude-oil and gasoline trading on March 5, 1935. Twenty-five gasoline contracts for 1,000 barrels each and four crude contracts for 2,000 barrels each, with delivery either in the Houston-Galveston area or the Cushing-Drumright area, were traded in the opening period.[101] In the same month, the California Commodity Exchange in San Francisco announced a matching futures program for the West Coast industry.[102]

The flurry of early activity would soon be quieted. With Texas and Oklahoma regulators gaining the upper hand in the wellhead proration war, "dollar oil" took hold. With increased stability, both hedgers and speculators had little reason to play the futures market. If production control was not bad enough, price controls during World War II were. Not only petroleum but other more established futures markets were put out of business between 1942 and 1945 by stable prices set by law.

Third Period of Futures Trading: 1978–84

The absence of futures trading from 1910 to 1977, with several brief exceptions, reflected regulatory factors. Price stability due to

[98]*National Petroleum News*, December 26, 1934, p. 14. Cited hereafter as *NPN*.

[99]*Business Week*, January 5, 1935, p. 20.

[100]*NPN*, January 30, 1935, p. 24C.

[101]*NPN*, March 6, 1935, p. 14.

[102]*NPN*, March 20, 1935, p. 15.

state proration law, wartime price controls, federal import controls, and federal price controls curtailed fluctuations that attract hedgers and speculators.

The first futures offering since 1935 was a propane contract introduced by the New York Commodity Exchange in September 1967. Delivery problems limited trading, and the offering was ended after a three-year life. In 1971, the Petroleum Associates of the New York Cotton Exchange offered propane futures, which were traded for five years before interest waned.[103]

Volatile prices in late 1973 and early 1974 renewed interest in petroleum futures. In 1974, the New York Cotton Exchange began trading crude-oil and propane futures, but the trading was short-lived in the face of continuing price and allocation controls. Because of contract specification problems, success was also evasive abroad where the New York Mercantile Exchange (NYMEX) began futures trading with no. 2 oil and no. 6 oil on October 23, 1974. Trades could be made eighteen months forward with Rotterdam as the delivery point—beyond the jurisdiction of U.S. price regulation.[104]

With the decontrol of certain oil products in 1976, the opportunity surfaced to begin petroleum-futures trading with delivery in the United States. On November 14, 1978, the NYMEX began a market in home heating oil (no. 2 oil) and residual fuel oil (no. 6 oil) with delivery at New York Harbor. The 1,000-barrel contracts were standardized and interchangeable, a prerequisite for institutionalized trading. While the no. 2 oil offerings were successful, no. 6 oil failed to attract trading interest because of contract-specification problems with New York State pollution law and the automatic pass-through of fuel adjustment clauses by utilities.

No. 2 oil enjoyed a favorable response and record trading in 1979. By the summer of 1980, heating oil was among the top fifteen traded futures commodities in the United States.[105] On August 17, 1981,

---

[103]See Stephen Dinehart, "The Energy Futures Market," *Education Quarterly* (November 1983): 5.

[104]On April 6, 1981, the NYMEX was joined by the International Petroleum Exchange, which began heating-oil-futures trading in London with delivery in Amsterdam, Rotterdam, and Antwerp.

[105]*NPN*, August 1979, p. 11; U.S. Department of Energy, *The Economics and Regulation of Petroleum Futures Markets* (Washington, D.C.: DOE, August 1980), pp. 1.15–1.37; and NYMEX, *NYMEX Energy Futures* (New York: NYMEX, 1982), p. 11.

trading of no. 2 oil futures was enlarged to allow Gulf Coast delivery. With fewer than 2,000 contracts traded, this delivery point was terminated in early 1982.

On October 5, 1981, leaded-gasoline futures began trading on the NYMEX with New York Harbor delivery, and on December 14, 1981, a Gulf Coast delivery point was added. As had been that of heating oil contracts, futures trading was terminated several months later with only seventy-nine contracts traded.

Amid high expectations, crude-oil futures trading was inaugurated by the NYMEX on March 30, 1983, with delivery in the crude-oil mecca of Cushing, Oklahoma. By year end, 323,153 contracts were traded to make it easily the most successful petroleum offering in history and one of the most successful futures issues ever introduced. The next year, a phenomenal 1.8 million contracts were sold. All petroleum futures covered eighteen forward months and followed generally uniform rules and specifications.

In March 1984, with a growing spot market and price volatility, the NYMEX applied to the Commodity Futures Trading Commission (CFTC) for futures trading in natural gas. In July 1984, heating oil and crude options were also applied for. Commission approval would leave kerosene and residual fuel oil as two major products absent from the trading board.

The success of the NYMEX in gaining regulatory approval, structuring contracts, and attracting high industry interest led to imitations and variations by competitors. The Chicago Board of Trade (CBT) introduced unleaded futures in December 1982 and heating oil futures in April 1983 with delivery in the Texas Gulf Coast counties of Harris, Galveston, and Jefferson. Because of unpopular delivery procedures—paper certificates rather than physical "wet" barrels—trading became dormant. In March 1983, the CBT began crude futures with delivery in southern Louisiana. After an active opening, activity diminished due to contract requirements imposed by regulations. In April 1984, all three petroleum offerings ended, and an application for natural-gas futures trading was withdrawn.

As a result of the NYMEX's success and the CBT's failure, the Chicago Mercantile Exchange began trading heating-oil and leaded-gasoline futures on March 26, 1984, with Texas Gulf Coast delivery. Early trading averaged only 100 contracts per day for the four-month futures offerings, and in June, final trades were made. Pending

Table 17.2
ENERGY FUTURES TRADING: 1979–84
(thousands of contracts)

Exchange & Contract	1979	1980	1981	1982	1983	1984
NYMEX						
Heating oil	34	238	996	1,746	1,868	2,092
Leaded gasoline	–	–	7	104	407	654
Crude oil	–	–	–	–	323	1,840
CBT						
Heating oil	–	–	–	–	3	–
Unleaded gasoline	–	–	–	9	52	–
Crude oil	–	–	–	–	95	1
Chicago Mercantile Exchange						
Heating oil	–	–	–	–	–	5
Leaded gasoline	–	–	–	–	–	5

SOURCE: Stephen Dinehart, "The Energy Futures Market," *Education Quarterly* (November 1983): 6; New York Mercantile Exchange; Chicago Board of Trade; and Chicago Mercantile Exchange.

crude-futures contracts with delivery in Cushing, Oklahoma, were terminated along with leaded-gasoline and heating-oil contracts in mid-1984. This left only the NYMEX active in petroleum futures.[106] Aggregate trading of petroleum futures is shown in table 17.2.

Regulatory Influences and Consequences

The development of petroleum-futures trading in the 1860s and 1870s is a case study of the spontaneous orderly development of a market.[107] Self-regulation developed from business incentives, and schemes to monopolize trading were repelled by competitive market forces. A rare example of early regulation was an 1887 Illinois law that forbade "gambling" in petroleum where physical possession was not taken.

[106]For a brief history of modern petroleum-futures trading, see Steven Errera, "Exchanges and Their Contracts," in *Energy Futures,* ed. John Treat (Tulsa: PennWell Books, 1984), pp. 6–11.

[107]The origins of futures trading are discussed in Julius Baer and George Woodruff, *Commodity Exchanges* (New York: Harper and Brothers, 1929), chaps. 1 and 2.

Federal regulation would come decades later as, coincidentally, a second period of petroleum-futures trading was at an end. In 1936, the Commodity Exchange Act and the Grain Futures Act were passed to discourage speculative participation in the agricultural-futures market.[108] The rationale was that speculation destabilized markets and contributed to the lingering depression. It was not recognized that profitable speculation stabilizes prices while discovering true scarcity prices, and that restricting speculation would also curtail hedging. Through the Commodity Exchange Authority, regulation continued unabated until it was enlarged by the Exchange Act of 1968 to cover new futures products.[109]

In 1974, the Commodity Futures Trading Commission (CFTC) was established to replace the Commodity Exchange Authority.[110] A new criterion was promulgated by the CFTC in response to growing interest and applications for futures. Potential licensees had to meet an "economic-purpose" requirement by showing that the public interest would be served by the new offering. The Futures Trading Act of 1982 reauthorized the CFTC, distinguished its functions from those of the Securities and Exchange Commission, and established user fees on trading activity to partly finance its operation.[111]

Current (as of 1984) CFTC rules regulate petroleum futures in several ways. Proposed futures must pass a public-interest test by showing that a market need exists for the service and that contract terms and conditions will merit such demand.[112] Contract terms must "result in a deliverable supply which will not be conducive to price manipulation or distortion."[113] A CFTC official identified illegal activities as "corners, squeezes, futures manipulation, fraud and other noncompetitive trading practices."[114] Accordingly, daily price limits for petroleum were established—$0.03 per day with expanded

---

[108]Public Law 674, 49 Stat. 1491 (1936).

[109]Public Law 90-258, 82 Stat. 26 (1968).

[110]Public Law 93-463, 88 Stat. 1389 (1974).

[111]Public Law 97-444, 96 Stat. 2294 (1989).

[112]"Guidelines on Economic and Public Interest Requirements for Contract Market Designation," Commodity Futures Trading Commission (no date but current as of 1984).

[113]Ibid., p. 7.

[114]Remarks by James Culver, Commodity Futures Trading Commission, to Platt's Energy Futures Conference, New York, January 25, 1983, p. 3.

limits on the third consecutive limit day (150 percent), fourth day (200 percent), and fifth day (unlimited). Position limits were also set—a maximum of 5,000 contracts overall and a maximum of 1,000 contracts purchased within ten days of the lead month. Two fundamental CFTC functions, market surveillance and consumer protection and enforcement, revolve around this definition.

Futures regulation had three negative consequences: new offerings were delayed, price and quantity conditions narrowed profitable trading opportunities, and costs were increased.

Delays resulted from the cumbersome proof of market demand. In a free market, entrepreneurial commitments constitute prima facie proof of market need; further requirements are superfluous and reduce competition to established firms. An example is crude-oil futures trading on the NYMEX, which was delayed by the CFTC from March 1982 until March 1983 despite high market interest. Thousands of would-be speculators and hedgers were unable to actualize their preferences, and a much-needed crude index price was unavailable to increase market information. A second prominent example was natural-gas futures trading, which had been delayed since application was filed in March 1984. With a growing natural-gas spot market and seasonal volatility, a companion futures market was missed. On the other hand, futures offerings not conducive to market demand were quickly revealed, although regulatory delay prevented timely contract modification as an alternative to termination.

Of all the contract requirements imposed by the CFTC, the case of the CBT crude-futures contract stands out as a case study of the perils of regulation. With delivery in southern Louisiana, foreign crudes trading at a slight premium were a major factor in the CBT contract compared to the NYMEX's inland delivery of West Texas intermediate crude. The CBT requested to trade at par based on domestic-crude prices, but authorities required a fixed differential of $0.25 per barrel and unorthodox trading terms. After active opening interest, the market recognized the price-fixing distortion and interest waned. The CBT argued for relaxed requirements for one year, but the changes came too late to effectively compete with NYMEX. The CBT's crude and product futures were delisted.[115]

[115]Conversation with Peter Donnelly, manager, new products, Chicago Board of Trade, January 28, 1985.

Operating costs, which must be covered from commission fees paid to futures brokers, have been unnecessarily increased by license applications, mandatory reporting, and other regulatory paperwork. The bogey of speculation and the fear of free-market "monopoly" have introduced another distortion by setting daily price ranges that shut down trading when the limits are reached. This subtle form of price control disequilibrates supply and demand and misdirects resources as a result of false pricing. All the beneficial economic effects of the futures market, in short, are nullified when the limits are reached.

In addition to direct regulation of futures exchanges, government intervention has been felt in subtle ways. Artificial price stability as a result of regulation in the 1928–70 period usurped the need for futures trading, while in the 1970s, price and allocation controls rendered such activity impractical until late in the decade. Natural-gas futures have been legislatively discouraged for decades by the long-term contract requirement of federal certification and price controls.

Regulation continues to dampen trading in one petroleum futures market. Residual (no. 6) fuel oil has not been a major hedging prospect for electric distribution companies because risky cost-minimization techniques are discouraged by public-utility regulation, which allows such costs to be automatically passed through to ratepayers if prudently incurred.

As are other market institutions, the futures market is self-regulated by consumer demand, common-law protection against fraud and theft, and industry standards. The National Futures Association, formed in 1982 to audit records of member and nonmember companies and impose sanctions on violators of industry standards, has been successful—more successful than the CFTC.[116] The product of an unregulated market, futures exchanging not only promotes spontaneous order but signifies the existence of a free market itself.

Futures Trading and Efficiency

The development of oil-product trading has been widely hailed as a positive development. The congealing of innumerable bits of

---

[116]The National Futures Association's staff of 209 auditors, twice the size of the CFTC, had its $16.5-million 1984 budget funded by the industry. *Wall Street Journal*, October 3, 1984, p. 31.

dispersed knowledge into composite figures available across the country has replaced less comprehensive information via telephone calls, newsletters, and pricing services. "For the first time," reported one financial writer, "there will be clear and public pricing signals which those setting contract rates—OPEC, BNOC [British National Oil Corporation], and Mexico's Pemex oil company, for example—will ignore at their peril."[117] Futures pricing encourages better consumer and producer decisionmaking and provides a bridge between the spot market and the contract market. World pricing, once lead by OPEC, is now determined by the buy-sell orders of thousands of market participants. Forward planning by firms has been facilitated, profits have been locked in, and inventories have been minimized.[118] Risk has been reallocated among market participants more optimally than before. Speculators have found an attractive vehicle for risk taking. Active competition between futures exchanges has kept the market efficient, although certification by regulatory authorities of new contracts and delayed approval of contract changes have hindered rapid adjustment to consumer demand.

Another positive development in petroleum futures is the institutionalization of market exchanges eighteen months ahead. Government price and allocation regulation, although always possible, has an additional obstacle to implementation. Only with widespread abrogation of futures contracts could statutory pricing and allocation be introduced.

A far different view of the efficacy of oil futures has been advanced by petroleum consultant William Edwards, who has argued that such trading "is as socially redeeming as the Las Vegas roulette table."[119] Because speculators dominate the market over hedgers, he notes, prices vary more than if major refiners determined prices based on cost. The absence of cost-derived stability, in his view, has complicated industry conditions and led to malinvestments, particularly in the refining industry. Empirical support is derived

---

[117]Ray Dafter, "On the Spot: Traders in Crude Find the Market More Speculative," *Houston Chronicle*, February 21, 1983, p. 2-2.

[118]For hedging and inventory management benefits, see *NPN*, April 1982, pp. 47–50.

[119]Conversation with William Edwards, May 24, 1984. For brief presentations of his views, see *Houston Post*, July 26, 1983, pp. C-1, 4; and *Houston Post*, December 20, 1983, p. E-1.

from price fluctuations that are greater than before when speculation did not dominate futures trading.

Edwards also believes the futures market does not accurately or properly forecast. The forecasting errors of the winter of 1983–84 are cited. In December 1983, the market quoted prices below production cost and a month later quoted prices well above cost. The 40 percent gyration could have been avoided if cost-based prices had predominated over speculative prices, Edwards contends.

In addition to false prices, a second major concern of Edwards is the potential that major refiners could substitute futures deliveries for wet-barrel inventory or production. Paper barrels do not run cars or heat homes, he states, insinuating that inventories could become understocked and shortages could occur.

These criticisms follow from three misconceptions: stable prices per se are preferable, cost-based prices are correct, and errant predictions have a tendency to prevail and be perpetuated instead of being avoided and self-correcting.

The defining characteristic of the market is change. Consumers adjust their preferences and employ new ways to satisfy unchanged desires. Entrepreneurs change their menus and discover new methods to improve existing offerings. The flux of knowledge makes production cost a bygone, which can upset the status quo. But such instability is *creative* despite the fact that some entrepreneurs are penalized and new market conditions are created that force firms to lower costs or exit. The whole notion of profit and loss rests on the fact that value does not equal cost in a world of change and imperfect knowledge.

The futures market can—and has—incorrectly estimated the state of the market. But incorrect knowledge is no more a reason to close futures trading than entrepreneurial error is reason for ending other institutions. Moreover, the same misestimations and resource malinvestments might have prevailed without futures trading. Futures trading integrates correct knowledge into the market in a timely manner. Because error results in financial losses and correct forecasts win profits, good knowledge tends to drive out bad. Correct knowledge "wins out." This market process leads to a positive view of the futures market and, indeed, the entire market economy.

Futures trading allows cost minimization with inventory, which is positive from an individual and general perspective. Fears of inadequate inventory as a result of futures trading are pure assertion, and fears of shortages are unfounded, given the flexibility of price to equate supply and demand. An unpredicted cold snap in early 1984, following a mild early winter, found inventory lower than if the weather had been correctly forecast, but prices quickly increased to eliminate supply hardships and preserve market order. Even at its worst—even when the unanticipated occurs—the market learns and adjusts. As the petroleum-futures market continues to mature, greater sophistication of knowledge and greater benefits can be anticipated.

Part III

Intervention in Refining

Refining has been called "the keystone in the structure of the petroleum industry."[1] In this phase the raw material of crude oil is transformed by technological processes into a variety of consumer products essential to industrial, commercial, and residential activity.

The economic history of petroleum refining has largely been the story of growth and coordination provided by market forces. From simple distillation in "cheesebox stills" to catalytic cracking in fractionation towers, increased yields, improved quality, and reduced cost have resulted from the progressive march of applied science in an environment of economic calculation and free-market incentives.[2]

Until the 1960s and 1970s, government intervention was the exception rather than the rule in petroleum refining. Before World War I, state and federal antitrust action against Standard Oil was the only major refinery intervention. Prices were not regulated, and crude purchases and product sales by refiners were by voluntary contracts. Chapter 18 describes these early years and the Standard Oil controversy. The middle period in refining, from World War I until the Korean conflict, was one of intermittent regulation. Wartime planning during 1917–18, 1941–45, and 1951–53; East Texas hot-oil regulation between 1931 and 1935; and the National Industrial Recovery Act refinery program from 1933 to 1935, along with the subtle interaction between patents and proration, are studied in chapter 19. Chapter 20 describes the most interventionist period in the history of oil refining, which began with import regulation in 1959 and continued with price and allocation controls in the 1970s. Through three different programs—the Mandatory Oil Import Program (1959–73), the Buy/Sell Program (1973–74), and the Entitlements Program (1974–81)—small refiners were favored by government policy at the expense of their larger counterparts.

Chapter 21 chronicles environmental regulation, which came of age in the 1970s with implications for refinery siting, product quality, and emission control. With the demise of price and allocation regulation in 1981, environmental regulation began to define government intervention in the fourth, free-market phase in oil refining.

---

[1] Statement of Robert Wilson in *Petroleum Hearings before the Temporary National Economic Committee* (New York: American Petroleum Institute, 1942), p. 343.

[2] For an overview of refining technology from simple distillation to advanced cracking methods, see William Leffler, *Petroleum Refining* (Tulsa: PennWell Publishing, 1979).

18. Early Development and Intervention: 1861–1916

The early crude-oil-refining industry is primarily the story of John D. Rockefeller and the Standard Oil Company. Refineries in the Pennsylvania oil region had sprung up before Rockefeller's time, but beginning in the 1870s, Standard Oil secured a dominant position in oil distillation that continued until the Supreme Court dissolved the trust in 1911.

The evolution of Standard's growth is described in this chapter along with state and federal antitrust challenges against the trust. While industry critics have long employed the persona of Rockefeller and the Standard Oil Trust as an example of the dangers of unfettered enterprise and unchecked market power, the opposite conclusion is supported here. It is found that on economic grounds, Standard advanced consumer welfare by continually improving the quality and affordability of its products, primarily the illuminant kerosene. In contrast to a textbook monopolist, Standard *expanded* output and *decreased* prices during its four-decade tenure. The trust also promoted industry growth and coordination by concentrating on transportation, storage, refining, and marketing and by its decision in the late 1880s to actively explore for and produce crude thereafter.[1]

Standard was never "above" the marketplace. It was attuned to consumer demand both at home and abroad and was always influenced by potential and existing competition. Ironically, while the obligatory breakup officially closed the Standard Trust era, the relocation of the petroleum industry to the Southwest was in the process of doing the same.

---

[1]While this chapter concentrates on Standard's refining activities, Standard's equally dominant transportation network is studied in chapter 11, pp. 614–18. The trust's oil-marketing activities and antitrust challenges thereto are examined in chapter 22, pp. 1293–97. A major oil-product tariff that reduced foreign competition to Standard, while hurting the trust's export trade, is described in chapter 13, p. 713.

The oil trust was not without imperfections, both political and entrepreneurial. A sizable oil-product tariff, enacted in 1861 by a revenue-hungry Congress, prevented American consumers from fully benefiting from international competition.[2] This barrier helped Standard retain domestic markets yet hurt the trust's vibrant oil-export trade. It was not a protectionist or "pro-Standard" law. On the entrepreneurial side, there were regretted decisions (such as participation in the South Improvement Company in 1872), which hurt the trust's position, and instances of "chicanery and obstructionism." Predatory pricing, however, the most infamous alleged practice, was not among them. But such failings were scarcely significant compared with the triumphs of the trust and certainly not grounds for the Supreme Court verdict in 1911 that sought to use a pragmatic "rule of reason" with alleged monopoly.

Early Years

The refining industry was waiting for Drake's well and the subsequent Pennsylvania discoveries that inaugurated the U.S. petroleum industry. In the 1850s, coal-oil refineries were built in New York, Cincinnati, Boston, St.Louis, and Pittsburgh to distill oil from coal and then refine it into petroleum products, chiefly kerosene.[3] The basic process of underfiring an enclosed kettle to vaporize petroleum for condensation into products ("fractions") was in use, including *cracking* in which high temperatures would break hydrocarbon molecules into lighter components to increase product yields. Chemical treating was also employed to deodorize products and improve their appearance and burning qualities. These processes would find ready application in the next decade.

The development of the Pennsylvania oil region marked the decline of coal-oil refining and the ascent of crude-oil refining. One step in the distillation process was eliminated by substituting oil

[2]See chapter 13, pp. 712–13.

[3]To a lesser extent, shale oil, whale oil, and crude (seepage and salt-well) oil were used as feedstock in pre-1859 refineries. Coal-oil refining began with a 1850 patent by James Young in Glasgow, Scotland, to extract liquid hydrocarbons from shale and coal. Young's beginning was advanced in the 1850s by Abraham Gesner, Joshua Merrill, and Luther and William Atwood. Ralph Hidy and Muriel Hidy, *Pioneering in Big Business: 1882–1911* (New York: Harper and Bros., 1955), p. 5. Also see Kendall Beaton, "Founders' Incentives: The Pre-Drake Refining Industry," in *Oil's First Century,* ed. Ralph Hidy (Boston: Harvard Graduate Business School, 1959), pp. 7–19.

for coal. The first crude purchasers were coal-oil refineries, which numbered approximately eighty at their height, but soon "field refineries," many semiportable, would spring up in the oil region.[4] The first facility was completed in early 1861, and by 1867, over eighty refineries populated middle Pennsylvania.[5] In nearby cities, coal-oil plants switched to crude oil, while new refineries entered to service growing volumes of crude oil that lower prices allowed them to buy. By middecade, several hundred refineries were operating in Erie, Pittsburgh, Philadelphia, and Cleveland, as well as in the New York–New Jersey area.[6] Despite the large number of firms, output aggregated only 12,000 barrels per day by middecade, with field refineries averaging the least.[7] Tedious preparation between runs, unsophisticated firing and condensing methods, and rudimentary equipment were barriers to scale economies.

In the 1870s, refining grew alongside crude-oil output. Between 1866 and 1873, annual crude production grew from 3 million to 10 million barrels, and refining capacity swelled from 4.4 million to 17.5 million barrels annually. Product yields per crude barrel grew over 15 percent in the same period as a result of technological advances.[8] The number of refineries shrank by two-thirds as scale economies increasingly came into play.[9] "By the 1870s," observed Harold Williamson and Arnold Daum, "refining had attained an entirely new scale in plant and still sizes."[10] Most of these facilities concentrated on kerosene production and left higher and lower range products to smaller, specialized plants.

The early years of crude-oil distillation, while supportive of the spontaneous market order hypothesis, were not problem free. Much was yet to be learned to improve the quality and quantity of yields.

---

[4]Bill Berger and Kenneth Anderson, *Modern Petroleum: A Basic Primer* (Tulsa: Penn-Well Books, 1981), p. 208.

[5]*Oil & Gas Journal—Oil City Derrick*, August 27, 1934, p. 31.

[6]Harold Williamson and Arnold Daum, *The Age of Illumination, 1859–1899*, vol. 1 of *The American Petroleum Industry* (Evanston, Ill.: Northwestern University Press, 1959), p. 288.

[7]Ibid., p. 289. Crude throughput was roughly double product output.

[8]Ibid., p. 293.

[9]Ibid. See ibid., chap. 11, for a discussion of the major advances in refinery technology in the 1860s.

[10]Ibid., p. 273. Large refineries produced up to 3,500 barrels per day.

Fires and explosions were a constant worry. The "feast or famine" of production destabilized the refining industry as well. Outside of a $0.10 per barrel Civil War tax on refined oil that exacerbated industry profitability problems,[11] the market was at fault. But by the same token, opportunities existed to harness the potential of the refining business by technological improvement and managerial efficiency. Remarked Williamson and Daum, "No subsequent period was faced with as large a gap between the demands for throughput and the inadequacies of existing batch capacity."[12] This set the stage for the most innovative entrepreneur and the most dominant firm in the history of the oil business—John D. Rockefeller and the Standard Oil Company.

The Standard Oil Company and Antitrust Law

Rise of Standard Oil

In 1863, twenty-three-year-old Rockefeller invested $4,000 in a hometown Cleveland refinery. The 505 barrel per day facility, the largest in the city, prospered under Rockefeller and the able technical supervision of his partner, Samuel Andrews. For Rockefeller, it was a matter of being in the right place at the right time; refining was emerging as a growth industry along with crude-oil production and marketing, and Cleveland was well served by transportation on the crude side and was a major market on the product side. In 1886, a second Cleveland refinery was purchased, and with brother William, himself a budding entrepreneur, joining in, Rockefeller & Company was founded.

More expansion was called for, and the following year capital was attracted from Henry Flagler, who became managing partner, and Stephen Harkness. Business was good, and several integrations were made into manufacturing to lower product costs. In those early years, Rockefeller demonstrated the multifaceted entrepreneurial talents that would characterize his career—alertness to opportunity, cost minimization through cost internalization, "penny pinching," and sound judgment of executive talent.

---

[11]Revenue Act of July 1, 1862, 12 Stat. 432. Also see John Ise, *The United States Refining Policy* (New Haven, Conn.: Yale University Press, 1926), p. 24.

[12]Harold Williamson and Arnold Daum, *The Age of Illumination*, p. 266.

On January 10, 1870, Rockefeller and partners became incorporated as the Standard Oil Company of Ohio with a capitalization of $1 million and Rockefeller as president, William Rockefeller as vice-president, and Flagler as secretary.[13] The corporate assets were two refineries, which produced 1,500 barrels per day (one-fifth of Cleveland's capacity; one-twenty-fifth of U.S.capacity), a barrel-making operation and several manufacturing subsidiaries, a tank-car fleet, and storage facilities. Both horizontal and vertical integration were in evidence.

An integral part of Rockefeller's early strategy was to lower transportation cost, which represented as much as 20 percent of the selling price of refined products. This meant negotiating fare discounts with railroads in return for guaranteed shipment volumes, which, in turn, required large-scale refining. The discounts were taken in the form of rebates ("drawbacks") from regular railroad rates; published full fares were for less preferred customers to pay.

A well-positioned Standard Oil would immediately benefit from unstable conditions surrounding the refining industry. Rapid industry expansion during 1867–69 and again in 1870–71 became excess capacity when a business depression, precipitated by the U.S.Treasury's deflation of the money supply, reduced product prices to lower the spread between input and output prices.[14] During the first major consolidation in the history of oil refining, in 1872 Standard purchased twenty Cleveland refineries and bought several others in New York City to own a quarter of the city's capacity of 46,000 barrel per day. Rockefeller's plan was to merge "all oil refining firms and corporations into one great organization" to achieve internal and external economies of scale.[15]

The year 1872 was significant in another respect. Rockefeller and his partners joined a plan authored by Tom Scott of the Pennsylvania

---

[13]The following paragraphs are adopted from discussions in Harold Williamson and Arnold Daum, *The Age of Illumination;* Ralph Hidy and Muriel Hidy, *Pioneering in Big Business;* Allen Nevins, *Study in Power: John D. Rockefeller* (New York: Charles Scribner's Sons, 1953); Gilbert Montague, *The Rise and Progress of the Standard Oil Company* (New York: Harper & Bros., 1903); and Dominick Armentano, *Antitrust and Monopoly* (New York: John Wiley & Sons, 1982).

[14]See the discussion in Dominick Armentano, "The Petroleum Industry: A Historical Study in Power," *Cato Journal* 1, no. 1 (Spring 1981): 59–60.

[15]Quoted in Harold Williamson and Arnold Daum, *The Age of Illumination,* p. 354.

Railroad to form a railroad pool to profitably divide the oil-carrying business and assign rebates to participating refiners. Producer-shippers were on the short end of the proposed action that was intended to benefit participant railroads and refiners.

When the scheme became public, the Pennsylvania oil community became indignant, and an "oil war" ensued between regional producers and urban refiners. The consequences would prove the South Improvement Company Association to be among Rockefeller's greatest blunders, although Standard's role in the scheme was much smaller than commonly believed.[16] Retaliation by producers left Standard's refineries short of feedstock, while independent refineries in the oil region operated at capacity. In the longer run, a legacy of ill will, which would follow Standard for decades, was created with producers and the public.[17] It was, however, a lesson well learned. United producers were a powerful force; unified refiners could be too. Rockefeller would spend subsequent months organizing refiners into a cohesive front and appeasing producers by contracting for large quantities of crude at fixed and contingently escalating prices. The "Treaty of Titusville" brought peace to the oil region.[18]

In 1873, more Cleveland refineries were purchased, including several plants specializing in petroleum by-products. A major New York refinery was also absorbed, and by the end of the year Standard could claim a 30 to 40 percent national share of refining capacity, up from 10 percent two years before.[19] In the same year, aggressive purchases of gathering pipelines and marketing networks took place. Vertical integration to complement horizontal refinery integration was a less publicized part of Rockefeller's plan.

The years 1874 to 1876 brought Standard closer to Rockefeller's grand design. Philadelphia and Pittsburgh facilities were purchased with management intact followed by secretive penetration into the

---

[16]"Among subscribers for South-Improvement stock were certain holders of Standard stock and also their bitterest opponents; among those most active in giving the job its death-blow were prominent members of the Standard Oil Company. . . . [It] was not a Standard scheme. . . . Standard was made the scape-goat." John McLaurin, *Sketches in Crude Oil* (Westport, Conn.: Hyperion Press, 1902, 1976), p. 410.

[17]The value of goodwill would not again be underestimated by Rockefeller as shown by his later refinery purchases and other company practices.

[18]Harold Williamson and Arnold Daum, *The Age of Illumination*, p. 358.

[19]Ibid., p. 367.

West Virginia-Ohio refining market. The biggest coup was the patient courting of rival John Archbold, who merged his Pennsylvania oil region refinery with Standard in 1875 and became an important executive in Rockefeller's organization. (Archbold would eventually succeed Rockefeller as Standard's president.) This victory led to many other refinery mergers in the oil region to give Standard a stronghold in a traditionally independent area.

Further market penetration and profitable operation in the decade gave Standard a major share of the national refining market. In 1877, a head-to-head confrontation with a major Philadelphia refinery owned by the Empire Transportation Company resulted in a distress merger with Standard. The price war demonstrated Standard's longer staying power, which was due to more efficient operations and better capitalization. An important factor was Rockefeller's gathering-pipeline network, which by 1879 covered 80 percent of the market.[20] With more refineries in New York, Baltimore, Pittsburgh, and the oil region joining the fold in 1877 and 1878, Standard claimed a 90 percent market share—88,745 barrels per day of national capacity of 97,760 barrels per day.[21]

One of Standard's finest moments occurred in the next decade. New entry and increased competition pressured Standard into a major strategy change to integrate backward into production. Since 1878, Standard's involvement with production had been limited by company policy, but in late 1888, a decision was made to purchase a major interest in the Ohio-Indiana Lima fields. The multi-million-dollar investment gambled that a refining technique could be developed to remove sulfur from Lima crude to reduce its offensive odor and poor burning characteristics that hitherto had made it an undesired alternative to Pennsylvania crude. A crash program, led by company chemist Herman Frasch, yielded a solution, and large-scale refining began in 1889.[22] By 1890, over three-fourths of the area's production was sold to Standard refineries, a dedication that would surpass 90 percent several years later. Whereas in 1888 Standard accounted for less than 1 percent of national crude production,

---

[20]George Stocking, *The Oil Industry and the Competitive System* (Westport, Conn.: Hyperion Press, 1925, 1976), p. 17.

[21]Harold Williamson and Arnold Daum, *The Age of Illumination*, p. 466.

[22]Other refining methods for desulfurizing crude in this period were developed by independents. Ibid., pp. 617–18.

over 25 percent of U.S.output was produced by the company three years later.[23]

Standard's decision to concentrate downstream of the wellhead, and later to integrate into production, benefited all levels of the industry.

> By providing badly needed gathering lines and storage facilities the Trust undoubtedly prevented a wastage of crude such as had characterized earlier discoveries of flush fields. . . . Standard's more lasting contributions [were] . . . the intensive development of the fuel oil market which made it a permanent and major outlet for petroleum [and] . . . the perfection of a method of refining sulphur crude which could readily be applied to new discoveries of this type oil elsewhere in the United States.[24]

The 1890s witnessed the rapid expansion of national refining capacity with Standard at the forefront. Between 1884 and 1899, capacity tripled with Standard's market share increasing slightly to above 90 percent.[25] Interfirm competition was increasing. Many well-capitalized independents were entering the market, and Standard's export markets were under heavy pressure from Russian kerosene.[26] Another challenge to Standard, the least predictable and potentially most powerful of the three, came from a nonmarket source. Beginning in the 1890s, state and federal antitrust activity began its ascent. With the retirement of Rockefeller in 1895, this would be the problem of Standard's new leader, John Archbold.

Antitrust Challenges

State Level. Standard Oil's legal difficulties began in Ohio, although as far back as 1880 New York State investigated the company with sinister overtones. In February 1888, New York conducted a second investigation in which Rockefeller testified. In October 1889, Attorney General David Watson of Ohio serendipitously came upon Standard's trust agreement (dated 1882) and recognized that the charter given to Standard forbade monopolistic practices and

---

[23]Ibid., pp. 605, 607.

[24]Ibid., p. 613.

[25]Ibid., pp. 615, 627.

[26]Standard's export trade, discussed in the appendix to chapter 13 (pp. 766–69), was artificially diminished because of a heavy oil-product tariff that redirected foreign product from the United States to foreign markets.

foreign (out-of-state) control.[27] With control of the once Cleveland-based firm exercised from 26 Broadway in New York City, and under a broad definition of monopoly as a single seller, Standard was vulnerable. On May 8, 1890, Watson filed a quo warranto petition for Standard of Ohio to immediately cease illegal practices and dissolve the subsidiary.

On March 2, 1892, the Ohio Supreme Court unanimously sided with the state on both the foreign-control and monopoly issues. Justice Thaddeus Minshall's reasoning about the latter charge revealed the confused logic concerning the relationship between bigness and the public interest that would mark the Standard Oil controversy over the next decades.

> It may be true that [Standard] has improved the quality and cheapened the cost of petroleum and its products to the consumer. But such is not one of the usual or general results of a monopoly, and it is the policy of the law to regard not what may, but what usually happens. . . . [It] should be as much the policy of the laws to multiply the numbers engaged in independent pursuits . . . to cheapen the price to the consumer.[28]

Although punitive action was not taken, Standard quickly moved to reorganize. On April 1, 1892, the trust was dissolved into ninety-two geographical affiliates under twenty subsidiaries with its stock proportionally assigned to each holder of record. The complicated restructuring gave the appearance of eminent liquidation, but the close ownership left the ultimate control undisturbed without promise of further action.[29] This disturbed George Rice, an Ohio refiner whose personal activism against Standard was legendary. Rice persuaded the new Ohio attorney general, Frank Monnett, to reopen the case. Monnett, an opportunistic antitrust crusader with political ambitions, as well as the son of the president of Bucyrus Gas Company, a Standard competitor, filed suit against the trust in November 1897 on grounds similar to those alleged seven years before. Monnett

---

[27]This discussion of state antitrust activity against Standard borrows heavily from Bruce Bringhurst, *Antitrust and the Oil Monopoly* (Westport, Conn.: Greenwood Press, 1979), chaps. 1–4.

[28]Quoted in ibid., p. 16.

[29]In George Stocking's words, "Each hand received a new deal, but care was taken not to shuffle the cards." Stocking, *The Oil Industry and the Competitive System*, p. 43.

also secured a state antitrust law made to order against Standard that contained criminal penalties and charter revocation applicable to firms found guilty of willful violation. It became effective on July 1, 1898, and in November, antitrust suits were filed against each of the three Standard affiliates in Ohio. In January of the next year, another antitrust suit was filed against the parent, Standard of Ohio, which forced the company to belatedly turn to politics and public relations for relief.[30] Joseph Foraker, a U.S. senator from Ohio, was put on Standard's payroll to neutralize Monnett, and the Malcolm Jennings Advertising Agency was hired to prepare rebuttals that strategically found their way to the editorial pages of Ohio publications.[31] Although deceptive in the manner of presentation—the advertisements appeared as editorials—their content accurately and effectively portrayed the lawsuits as politically founded and economically unfounded. Stated one editorial:

> Whether the consumers of oil are getting a better quality at less cost and handling with greater safety than formerly is a question for the people to decide. In the commercial affairs of life it is things, not words, that count in making up the balance sheet of loss or gain, of benefit or injury. Monopoly and octopus, combines and trusts, are haughty words, but the best goods at lower prices are beneficial things. It is much easier to say harsh words than it is to make good things cheap.[32]

With the suits pending, sensationalistic events followed. Monnett charged that Standard offered bribes to influence the case and had destroyed evidence crucial to the government's case. Both revelations proved to be circumstantial at best, and Monnett's stock fell with the public. In 1899, he failed to win renomination, and his successor, John Sheets, discontinued the court fights, which led to their dismissal on December 11, 1900. The change of attorneys general was not coincidental; Standard's political presence helped to seal the fate of Monnett and paved the way for a candidate with different leanings.

[30]Standard first become politically active in the late 1880s and increased its activism with the Ohio antitrust actions in 1898. See Austin Moore, *John D. Archbold and the Early Development of Standard Oil* (New York: Macmillan, 1930), chap. 22.

[31]Standard also gave financial contributions to leading publications to generate goodwill. Ibid., p. 241.

[32]Quoted in Bruce Bringhurst, *Antitrust and the Oil Monopoly,* p. 28.

In 1899, Standard again reorganized as the Standard Oil Company (New Jersey). The choice of New Jersey reflected the leniency toward combinations of that state's incorporation laws, which in the absence of a federal incorporation law were controlling.

Ohio litigation was not at an end. In November 1906, Attorney General Wade Ellis filed three suits against Standard affiliates to "effectively separate the Ohio companies from the trust."[33] His term soon expired, and his successor, Ulysses Denman, played down the cases before dismissing them in 1911. The federal antitrust proceeding, he reasoned, was trial enough.

On January 10, 1901, an event occurred in Texas that marked the beginning of the relocation of the U.S. petroleum industry. On that day, a prolific gusher, Spindletop, was struck near Beaumont, and within a year hundreds of new companies were chartered in all phases of the oil business in the southern part of the state. Not since the Titusville strike forty-two years before had such a flurry hit the oil patch. But Standard was uncharacteristically slow to respond; upstarts such as Joseph Cullinan's Texas Company (Texaco) and William Mellon's Gulf Oil would gain prominence in Texas Gulf Coast production. Standard had changed its philosophy to become a major producer over a decade before, and indeed had backed Cullinan's Corsicana Petroleum Company in 1897, but the attitude of the New York headquarters toward Texas was one of wait and see. Although that attitude was attributed by some to a failing of entrepreneurial foresight, the hostile legal environment in Texas toward out-of-state companies and Standard in particular should not be overlooked. The Texas antitrust law, passed on March 30, 1889, was aimed at Standard and had Waters-Pierce, a petroleum-marketing company majority owned by Standard, on the brink of expulsion from the state. An educated guess was that a frontal attempt by Standard to enter the Gulf Coast market would invite further antitrust litigation.[34]

---

[33]Ibid., p. 37.

[34]An offer to Standard's Archbold by William Mellon to purchase Gulf and infuse the needed dose of capital was reputedly greeted with the words, "After the way Mr. Rockefeller has been treated by the state of Texas, he'll never put another dime in Texas." Quoted in Anthony Sampson, *The Seven Sisters* (New York: Viking Press, 1975), p. 47. Also see Harvey O'Connor, *The Empire of Oil* (New York: Monthly Review Press, 1955), pp. 13–14.

Future antitrust challenges would bear out this concern. Waters-Pierce walked the tightrope until it received a $1.6-million fine and "ouster" in 1909.[35] In 1907, Attorney General Robert Davidson moved against three Standard companies in Texas—two refineries and one tank-car concern—on prima facie evidence that they restrained competition.[36] In late 1909, an Austin judge revoked the two refinery charters (the third company had not been licensed and discontinued operations), placed three firms into receivership, and levied a $154,000 fine.[37] A judicial sale on the steps of an Austin hotel on December 7, 1909, was made to a partnership secretly dominated by Standard, and it was business as usual thereafter.

In 1923, an antitrust action against Humble Oil because of Jersey Standard's 60 percent interest was remindful of the inhospitable climate toward the Rockefeller legacy and the power of Texas antitrust law.[38]

Standard's newfound commitment to the exploration and production phase was manifested by the entrance of Forest Oil into undeveloped Kansas in 1895. In the first year alone, Standard drilled 129 wells and had 43 commercial finds.[39] Gathering facilities were built along with a refinery in 1897. These early years witnessed much excitement about and appreciation for the new industry on the part of state residents. Things, however, would sour in the next decade.

Yearly production in Kansas rose from under 200,000 barrels in 1901 to over 1 million barrels two years later and reached 5.6 million barrels in 1904 and 12 million barrels in 1905. High output was a positive development for Standard, whose production was receding

[35]See chapter 22, pp. 1298–1300.

[36]Standard's Security Oil (founded 1903) and Navarro Refining (founded in 1889 as Corsicana Refining), which refined 1.6 million and 1.1 million barrels of oil in 1906, respectively, provided competition to locally based Gulf Oil, a 3.9 million barrel refiner, and Texaco, a 0.9 million barrel refiner. Political pressure to favor locals over "monopolistic" Standard, along with a pecuniary incentive for the attorney general to successfully prosecute, more than an abstract concern about competition, inspired the antitrust suits.

[37]This fine, and particularly the more substantial fine levied against Waters-Pierce, was lucrative to Davidson, the prosecuting attorney, who by law received a 25 percent reward. Bruce Bringhurst, *Antitrust and the Oil Monopoly*, pp. 64–65.

[38]Henrietta Larson and Kenneth Porter, *History of Humble Oil & Refining Company* (New York: Harper & Brothers, 1959), pp. 81–82.

[39]Ralph Hidy and Muriel Hidy, *Pioneering in Big Business*, p. 275.

elsewhere, and major expansions into storage, pipelines, and refining were made. But for the multitude of new production firms and local investors that discovered oil only to see prices plummet—from $1.32 to $0.72 per barrel in 1904 alone—hopes were dashed.[40] Following industry precedent, blame was placed on the purchaser, Standard Oil, not the producer.

Politicians were quick to place blame and offer interventionist solutions. Leading the pack was Kansas governor Edward Hoch, himself the president of an embattled production firm. On January 9, 1905, the day after his inauguration, he made a dramatic proposal:

> Rather . . . than permit the great monopolies to rob us of the benefits of the vast reservoirs of oil which have been stored by the Creator beneath our soil, I am inclined to waive my objection to the socialistic phase of this subject and recommend the establishment of an oil refinery of our own in our own state for the preservation of our wealth and the protection of our people.[41]

A $410,000 appropriation request was made for a 1,000 barrel per day facility to be manned by convict labor.[42] "Prairie socialism" was endorsed by producers who turned against Standard, and lecturers of anti-Standard fame were imported to fan the flames. Ida Tarbell, whose 1904 work, *The History of the Standard Oil Company*, negatively portrayed the trust to a wide audience and who was rumored to be an "acting press agent" of Standard's purchasing rival, Shell Transport and Trading, spoke against the trust at producer meetings. Also active was Frank Monnett, who as Ohio's attorney general had been a thorn in Standard's side.[43]

[40]Bruce Bringhurst, *Antitrust and the Oil Monopoly*, p. 78.

[41]Quoted in ibid., p. 79. Governor Hoch later defended his state project by claiming: "The State refinery method of protecting State oil interests is not socialism. It is not the spirit of socialism, but the very reverse of it. It may have the semblance of socialism, but its soul is that of competition." Ibid., p. 84.

[42]A similar proposal in California several years later, again in response to the alleged dominance of Standard Oil, was rejected by the legislature.

[43]Ralph Hidy and Muriel Hidy, *Pioneering in Big Business*, p. 674. Tarbell's dislike for Standard was family based. Her father, Franklin Tarbell, was an independent producer in the Pennsylvania oil region who had boycotted Standard refineries and otherwise vigorously opposed the combination. Her brother William was a leading executive of Standard rival, Pure Oil Company. Ibid., p. 650; and Austin Moore, *John D. Archbold and the Early Development of Standard Oil*, p. 261.

While Tarbell's tome was exhaustive in scope, a bias toward independents per se and flawed interpretation of factual matters undermined its negative conclusions.

Tensions worsened when Standard announced it would cease purchasing heavy-grade oil and suspend work on a pipeline project. Plentiful high-grade Oklahoma crude was outcompeting Kansas output, and marketability problems for Standard forced the unpopular measures. These actions in early 1905 led to varied political responses. Along with the state refinery bill, the Kansas legislature passed pipeline regulations directed at Standard. Second, Attorney General C. C. Coleman filed an antitrust suit on March 2 against Prairie Oil and Gas, Standard's major Kansas arm, for restraint of trade. On the basis of a Bureau of Corporation investigation, the suit was extended to two other Kansas Standard affiliates in October 1906. The highly publicized antitrust suits were delayed until a state report was completed in 1911 that favorably commented on Standard's performance but acknowledged the firm's monopolistic position in the Kansas petroleum industry. A new attorney general sympathetic to Standard facilitated a negotiated settlement that was approved by the state judiciary on June 15, 1911. All three Standard affiliates, however, were restricted in what products they could sell, where they could be sold, and at what price. Production in Kansas by the trust was prohibited. Modest fines were also levied that went into the public-school fund.[44] The state refinery, meanwhile, failed a constitutional challenge and was never built.

The 1904–06 period was an active time for state antitrust activity against Standard affiliates. Tennessee (1904), Illinois (1904), Kentucky (1904–06), Missouri (1905), West Virginia (1905), Arkansas (1906), Oklahoma (1906), and Maryland (1906) joined Ohio, Texas, and Kansas in the legal attack.[45] These suits were not isolated. Observed Hidy and Hidy, "Prosecuting attorneys and attorney generals of the states flitted from state to state and to Washington, D.C.,

---

Henry Demarest Lloyd's earlier expose, *Wealth against Commonwealth* (New York: Harper & Brothers, 1894), was muckraking without foundation. Historical falsification and omission, incorrect theoretic understanding, and a negativist writing style marred the effort. See Allen Nevins, "Letter to the Editor," *American Historical Review* (April 1945): 676–89.

[44] Paul Giddens, *Standard Oil Company (Indiana)* (New York: Appleton-Century-Crofts, Inc., 1955), p. 129.

[45] See the chart in Ralph Hidy and Muriel Hidy, *Pioneering in Big Business*, p. 683. A Nebraska suit in 1899 was dropped two years later because of insufficient evidence. Later suits were filed in Mississippi (1909), Oklahoma (1910), Minnesota (1910), and Iowa (1911). The Oklahoma suit was settled with an agreement by Standard to construct a $150,000 refinery. Bruce Bringhurst, *Antitrust and the Oil Monopoly*, p. 102.

listening, conferring, and collecting data pertinent to their own local struggles with the embattled giant of the petroleum industry."[46] The cluster of suits reflected the same political currents that had earlier led to the passage of thirteen state antitrust laws in a seventeen-month period ending July 1890.[47] Bruce Bringhurst explained the attraction.

> There were potentially great political rewards for politicians who took on the oil monopoly. Furthermore the inevitable collapse of an antitrust suit was always far less visible than the well-publicized opening moves. Thus prosecutors had much to gain and very little to lose by taking the oil trust to court.[48]

All state actions would be subservient to the 1906–11 federal suit that proved to be Standard's undoing.

Federal Level. The Sherman Act of 1890, prohibiting business combinations in restraint of trade, was inherently dangerous to any major firm with unfavorable public and political relations.[49] "Restraint of trade" was a broad and nebulous term, hence potentially applicable to a wide spectrum of large-scale business activity. In 1900, the first of several major federal investigations into Standard Oil that reached negative conclusions was published.[50] Before 1906, however, there was little interest on the part of federal officials in legally challenging the trust despite numerous invitations to do so. George Rice wrote several dozen letters, some elaborate in factual and legal detail, to the Justice Department and President Theodore Roosevelt in the vain attempt to initiate a federal antitrust proceeding.[51] Rice claimed

[46] Ralph Hidy and Muriel Hidy, *Pioneering in Big Business*, p. 684.

[47] Bruce Bringhurst, *Antitrust and the Oil Monopoly*, p. 3.

[48] Ibid., p. 107. Marketing antitrust suits based on predatory pricing and other "unfair" practices are described in chapter 22, pp. 1297–1305.

[49] 26 Stat. 209 (1890). The July 2, 1890, law reflected, in part, strong political winds against bigness and monopoly. But behind the scenes were other reasons that were not public spirited but protectionist. See chapter 26, pp. 1526–31.

[50] U.S. Industrial Commission, *Report on Trusts and Industrial Combinations*, 13 vols. (Washington, D.C.: Government Printing Office, 1900).

[51] Approximately eighteen letters were sent to Attorney General John Griggs between November 5, 1898, and July 17, 1902. Roosevelt received nine letters between August 1, 1902, and the end of the year. The letter-writing campaign is discussed in Bruce Bringhurst, *Antitrust and the Oil Monopoly*, pp. 115–16, 124–27. An earlier attempt by refiner S. R. Kepler to interest U.S. Attorney General William Miller in a suit (letters of May 13, July 16, and August 17, 1892) led to a recommendation that a private suit be pursued, which Kepler did not do. Ibid., pp. 113–14.

that his refining business had been destroyed by the combination and called for "individual relief, but also in behalf of thousands of my conferees in the oil producing and refining business who are sorely oppressed."[52] Attempts by the Indiana Oil Men's League and individual oilmen from California, Minnesota, and West Virginia to aid an antitrust action were similarly unsuccessful.[53] In desperation, Rice filed a private antitrust suit on June 27, 1904, claiming the willful destruction of a $750,000 refinery investment as a result of concerted railroad discrimination and price undercutting by Standard. The case was dismissed for lack of evidence. What was needed was documentation that only the federal government had the resources and power to obtain.

Several changes at the Justice Department enhanced the plaintiff's ability to wage a successful suit. On February 14, 1903, the Bureau of Corporations was created within the new Department of Commerce and Labor. The bureau had the authority to investigate corporate practices and the power to secure internal business documents and compel testimony. In the same year, two acts were passed: the Expediting Act, which allowed the Justice Department to certify judges for antitrust suits of "general public importance," and the Deficiency Act, which earmarked manpower for antitrust cases and thus "marked the beginning of the Antitrust Division of the Justice Department."[54]

In 1906 and 1907, the Bureau of Corporations under James Garfield released two studies pertaining to the business practices of Standard Oil. The 1906 study, *Report on the Transportation of Petroleum*, was employed by Roosevelt to gain support for the Hepburn Act, which further outlawed railroad rebates and regulated interstate oil pipelines.[55] In the wake of the critical findings, Attorney General William Moody announced a preliminary antitrust investigation of Standard. On November 15, 1906, with the approval of Roosevelt, an antitrust suit alleging restraint of trade was filed against retired John Rockefeller, six fellow directors, and all Standard affiliates. During the suit, a second federal action against Standard developed over alleged

[52]Ibid., p. 115. It is worth noting that marketers were neglected in Rice's "class action" suit request for damage money.

[53]Ibid., pp. 126–27.

[54]Ibid., p. 123.

[55]See chapter 14, pp. 776–80, and chapter 16, pp. 974–75.

violations of the Elkins Act. It was charged that between September 1903 and March 1905, 1,462 carloads of oil were shipped at a price one-third the published rate in violation of the anti-rebate clause. Despite arguments that the discount was customary and similar to rates on a comparable route, Judge Kenesaw Landis, on August 3, 1907, ruled against Standard and assessed the maximum penalty of $20,000 per violation for a total of $29,240,000. The controversial decision led to a retrial where Judge Peter Grosscup, on July 22, 1908, overturned the record judgment.[56] Attention once again turned to the pending antitrust suit.

The presidential election of 1908 showed how much politics surrounded the Standard suit. Whereas prior to 1905 Roosevelt had disregarded the Standard question, it now became a theme of his party. The Republicans portrayed themselves as anti-Standard and the Democrats as pro-Standard. The plethora of state antitrust suits and their wide public support was not lost on Roosevelt or the Republican nominee William Taft. Political contributions from Standard were not accepted by Republicans, and Rockefeller's announced support of Taft was disowned. Roosevelt went so far as to blame the panic of 1907 on "the speculative folly and flagrant dishonesty of a few great men of wealth," Standard associates being foremost.[57] The election of Taft meant "continu[ing] the policy of exploiting public hostility toward Standard Oil."[58]

In February 1909, government lawyers completed their brief and began preparing a dissolution decree. Three years of preparatory work with testimony from hundreds of witnesses yielded twenty-three volumes totaling 12,000 pages. This and the two-volume *Report of the Commissioner of Corporations on the Petroleum Industry*, released in 1907, reached restraint-of-trade conclusions based on intent. After eight months of oral argument, a unanimous decision was reached on November 20, 1909, in federal district court in favor of the government, based on the prima facie evidence that the trust's thirty subsidiaries were a combination in restraint of trade. Judge William Hook's

---

[56]Discussions of the case can be found in Paul Giddens, *Standard Oil Company (Indiana)*, pp. 109–21; Austin Moore, *John D. Archbold and the Early Development of Standard Oil*, pp. 266–70; and Bruce Bringhurst, *Antitrust and the Oil Monopoly*, pp. 138–39.

[57]Ibid., p. 140.

[58]Ibid., p. 144.

opinion for the court was devoid of economic analysis or any standard of *reasonable* performance by a dominant firm, which had not yet become a criterion in antitrust law.

> A holding company, owning the stocks of other concerns whose commercial activities, if free and independent of common control, would naturally bring them into competition with each other, is a form of trust or combination prohibited by Section I of the Sherman Act. The Standard Oil Company of New Jersey is such a holding company.[59]

The lower court's decision was upheld by the Supreme Court on May 15, 1911.[60] Chief Justice Edward White's opinion for the Court, suspect in several important respects, was a fitting capstone to the legal challenges against Standard during the 1890–1911 period. The decision demonstrated the ambiguity of "restraint of trade" in general and White's "rule of reason" in particular. These points will be considered here; the Court's treatment of specific "unfair practices" by the trust will be considered in the next section.

Justice White defined illegal restraints of trade as "intent to do wrong to the general public and to limit the rights of individuals," manifested by lower output and higher prices.[61] *Reasonable* action, defined as the absence of intent to deprive or injure, was then differentiated to avoid blanket prosecution of large or dominant firms. This standard of economic performance was to be applied case by case. Applied to Standard, it was concluded that the firm *did* restrain commerce in contravention of the law. Practices such as rebating and predatory pricing demonstrated, in Justice White's words, "intent to drive others from the field and to exclude them from their right to trade."[62]

Before Standard is evaluated in terms of the rule of reason, a fundamental tension in the rule should be recognized. Restraints of individual trade in a free-market setting are not a "wrong to the general public." The voluntary purchases of consumers decide whose trade is restrained and whose trade is enlarged, the end

---

[59]*United States* v. *Standard Oil Company*, 173 F. 179 (1909). See the discussion in Dominick Armentano, *Antitrust and Monopoly*, pp. 68–69.

[60]*Standard Oil Company of New Jersey* v. *United States*, 221 U.S. 1 (1911).

[61]221 U.S. 58.

[62]Ibid.

process of which is the continual reallocation of resources to benefit the public at large. The "right of trade" of every market participant neglects unequal economic performance that requires some firms to contract and other firms to expand. Consolidation, integration, entry, and exit restrict the status quo, but such change is necessary for consumer preferences to be efficiently satisfied.[63] Consumer preference is not static but dynamic; resource allocation must be flexible, too.

The rule of reason applied to Standard Oil was a travesty of the standard. Justice White's 20,000-word opinion, devoid of facts and economic analysis, *asserted* misconduct on the prima facie evidence of intent to displace competition and "maintain . . . dominancy" from "aggregating so vast a capital."[64] Yet the rule purports to go beyond surface considerations to judge economic performance in addition to intent. Mergers frequently occurred that eliminated distinct competitors, and Rockefeller had a grand plan to make Standard the dominant firm in the industry. But more had to be proved—specifically, that the public was injured by the trust. The standard was introduced only to be half used.

A voluminous amount of government evidence was accumulated showing intent to increase market share at the expense of competitors, but Justice White's decision rested on theoretical presumptions against dominant firms, not on evidence of specific monopoly behavior—reduced output and higher prices. Company lawyers rebutted all major government charges on performance; in fact, *Standard presided over falling prices and expanding output*. Between 1874 and 1884, per capita consumption of kerosene rose from 1.5 gallons to 3.6 gallons a year; between 1880 and 1900, at the height of Standard's dominance, the output of petroleum products almost tripled.[65] Prices fell over the same period by approximately 50 percent.[66] As the nation's dominant refiner, Standard figured heavily in these output and pricing results. These decades of low-price, high-output practices were not undertaken to achieve long-run higher prices and

---

[63]"Efficiency is always exclusionary of less efficient competitors, but such exclusions are the very purpose of a competitive process." Dominick Armentano, *Antitrust and Monopoly*, p. 71.

[64]Quoted in ibid., p. 75.

[65]Harold Williamson and Arnold Daum, *The Age of Illumination*, p. 521.

[66]Ibid., pp. 524, 575.

curtailed production. Indeed, Standard's market share declined from a peak of 90 percent in the 1890s to 85 percent at the turn of the century and to 64 percent in the final years before dissolution.[67] Barring an entirely new set of facts and a new theory of why it is not self-interested to court consumers with lower prices, more supply, and better quality, only one conclusion can be reached—Standard passed the performance test of the rule of reason, which was neglected in favor of the intent-to-monopolize criterion. If performance had been a major consideration (as it should have been), the Supreme Court should have remanded the case to the trial court to decide the performance issue and then reevaluate intent versus performance on appeal.

The barren evidentiary case against the Standard Trust on the Supreme Court level was partly a legacy of the Sherman Act itself. Sponsor John Sherman (R-Ohio) spoke about limiting the ability of trusts to restrict output and "advance the cost to consumers."[68] But if the record of industrial output had been scrutinized, legislators would have discovered that it was increasing in virtually every "monopolized" sector.[69] Several members of Congress acknowledged that oil prices had fallen "immensely," but that the trust "destroyed" competitors and was "wrong" in principle.[70] This was "little-man" politics first and "common-good" economics last. Indeed, academic economists, some of whom specialized in antitrust, were never asked to testify on the Sherman bill, and if they had been asked, most would have defended trusts as natural, beneficial, and the wave of the future.[71] As discussed in chapter 26, the rationale of the Sherman Act was political, not economic.

[67]Bruce Bringhurst, *Antitrust and the Oil Monopoly*, p. 184.

[68]See Robert Bork, "Legislative Intent and the Policy of the Sherman Act," *Journal of Law and Economics* (October 1966): 15.

[69]Between 1880 and 1890 in twenty major industries, all but two products, castor oil and matches, increased in output, and production of many increased by 50 or 100 percent. The same expansion occurred in the next decade. See Thomas DiLorenzo, "The Origins of Antitrust: An Interest Group Perspective," Working paper, George Mason University, 1983, pp. 20–21.

[70]Sanford Gordon, "Attitudes towards Trusts prior to the Sherman Act," *Southern Economic Journal* (October 1963): 163.

[71]Thomas DiLorenzo, "The Origins of Antitrust," pp. 27–29; and Sanford Gordon, "Attitudes towards Trusts prior to the Sherman Act," pp. 161–67. Concluded George

Standard of New Jersey was instructed to dismember all thirty-seven subsidiaries within six months of June 21, 1911. This number was subsequently reduced to thirty-four, which with the parent Jersey Standard would create thirty-five distinct entities. On September 1, 1911, the separations took place, and stockholders received pro rata shares of each new company. Nineteen companies divided the refining empire, with Jersey Standard, Indiana Standard, California Standard, and Atlantic Refining parting with major facilities.

The irony of the antitrust "solution" was the modest effect of the dissolution on competition. Only the form of ownership and not the ownership itself was changed. Stockholders prior to September 1, primarily Rockefeller and his fellow company directors, owned the same amount of the Standard companies after that date. Consequently, management and the general interaction between former subsidiaries also could not be expected to be appreciably different. A stock-market analyst observed in late 1912 that

> the disintegration has not altered appreciably the natural commercial or trade relations between the various former subsidiaries. . . . Indeed they will continue to transact . . . as they did before the dissolution. Already it is obvious that each and every company is operated as efficiently and profitably today as before the disturbed intercorporate relations—through stock control.[72]

Stock ownership became more concentrated after the breakup to the chagrin of the dissolutionists. Many small stockholders sold "splinter" shares soon after dissolution only to see the stock values skyrocket when the true value of the historically undervalued firms came to light. Buying the stock were company insiders who acted quickly on a bargain.[73] Lamented President Roosevelt, "Not one particle of good resulted to anybody and a number of worthy citizens of small means were appreciably injured."[74]

Stigler, "One must regretfully record that in this period Ida Tarbell and Henry Demarest Lloyd did more than the American Economic Association to foster the policy of competition." Stigler, "Monopoly and Oligopoly by Merger," *American Economic Review* (May 1950): 30–31.

[72]Quoted in Bruce Bringhurst, *Antitrust and the Oil Monopoly*, p. 189.

[73]Paul Giddens, *Standard Oil Company (Indiana)*, p. 131.

[74]Quoted in ibid., p. 137.

Another irony of the decree was the declining market share of Standard and the rising star of new entrants such as Gulf, Texaco, and Sun. They, too, were integrated and well capitalized, and they quickly expanded into the prolific Gulf Coast and Mid-Continent producing regions. Other entrants that would grow into prosperous companies were Union Oil (California, 1890); Pure Oil (New Jersey, 1895); United Petroleum (California, 1899); Associated Oil (California, 1901); Indian Refining (Maine, 1904); National Refining (Ohio, 1906); American Petroleum (California, 1908); and American Oilfields (California, 1910).[75] Standard's share of national refining fell from a high of 90 percent or more to 65 percent in 1911, with independents accounting for 70 percent of fuel-oil output, 45 percent of lube-oil output, 30 percent of gasoline and wax production, and 25 percent of kerosene production.[76] "In a market characterized by a dwindling demand for kerosene and a rapidly expanding one for gasoline and industrial fuel oil," summarized Hidy and Hidy, "the changes were too quickly effected for the combination to keep pace with the growth of the industry."[77] From the point of view of Standard's critics, market forces were doing what dissolution did in a convoluted manner.

Internally, dissolution was also problematical. The trust's ongoing patent work was interrupted, and existing patent rights were fragmented. This slowed the adaptation of efficient new cracking methods of refining by several years and necessitated burdensome cross-licensing agreements between Standard companies in the 1920s and early 1930s.[78] Not only Standard but consumers lost in the process. Arbitrary geographical divisions and dismemberment of complementary phases led to companies strong in production and weak

[75]See John McLean and Robert Haigh, *The Growth of Integrated Oil Companies*, pp. 71–81, for discussion of the rise of integrated independents prior to 1911.

[76]Harold Williamson and Ralph Andreano, "Competitive Structure of the American Petroleum Industry, 1880–1911: A Reappraisal," in *Oil's First Century*, pp. 73–77.

[77]Ralph Hidy and Muriel Hidy, *Pioneering in Big Business*, p. 477.

[78]Melvin de Chazeau and Alfred Kahn, *Integration and Competition in the Petroleum Industry*, p. 295; and Harold Williamson et al., *The Age of Energy, 1899 to 1959*, vol. 2 of *The American Petroleum Industry* (Evanston, Ill.: Northwestern University Press, 1963), pp. 396–97. Patent controversies leading to the "Peace of 1931" are discussed in chapter 19, pp. 1114–16.

in marketing and vice versa.[79] A major beneficiary was British–Dutch Shell, whose worldwide presence was no longer rivaled by a unified Standard. Inevitably, pressures developed for reintegration through mergers, both between former Standard affiliates and with outside companies.[80] Active negotiations led only to several mergers; it was easier to mandatorily dismember in 1911 than it was to voluntarily reconsolidate in the 1920s and 1930s.

The unmistakable message of the historic breakup was that bigness and integration were to be discouraged by law to promote a competitive environment for smaller independents. One anti-competitive consequence was a reluctance by dismembered Standard affiliates to expand into a rival's market lest charges of monopolization be made.[81] This opened the door to independents, which added a final irony to the dissolution decree when competition in the late 1920s and 1930s was recognized as "excessive" with too much "independent capital" entering the market in the production and refining phases.[82]

Summary and Conclusions

Contributions of Standard Oil

Although focusing on government intervention, this book has highlighted the development of the U.S. oil and gas industry to illustrate the actual workings of market order. This is particularly relevant to Standard Oil. A résumé of the contributions of Standard Oil prior to dissolution offers an illuminating glimpse into entrepreneurship, the market process, and consumer service therein.

Rockefeller and the management team at Standard Oil can be credited with accelerating the maturation of the kerosene age in petroleum. Their entrance in the 1870s found an infant industry

---

[79]George Gibb and Evelyn Knowlton, *The Resurgent Years: 1911–1927* (New York: Harper & Brothers, 1956), pp. 111–13; and Henrietta Larson, Evelyn Knowlton, and Charles Popple, *New Horizons: 1927–1950* (New York: Harper & Row, 1971), p. 45.

[80]Ibid., pp. 46–47.

[81]Simon Whitney, *Antitrust Policies* (New York: Twentieth Century Fund, 1958), p. 105.

[82]For overproduction complaints on the refining front as early as 1918, see *Oil & Gas Journal*, July 5, 1918, p. 42, and September 13, 1918, p. 48. Production overinvestment is discussed in chapter 3 and chapter 4 generally.

prone to cyclical growth, undercapitalization, and coordination problems. Explained Williamson and Daum:

> Lack of balance between various segments of the industry appeared to be chronic; crude production, refinery capacity and throughput, and market demand were rarely in equilibrium. First, production would outrun throughput by refineries; the manufacturing capacity would exceed either current crude production or the rate at which refined products could be absorbed by the market. These more or less continuous maladjustments were reflected in wide fluctuations in prices of crude and refined products.[83]

Within the free-market environment, company and industry problems invited profitable solutions, and Rockefeller proved to be the right man at the right place and time. Standard strategically bypassed the unstable exploration and production phase, where drilling was risky and production often exceeded storage and demand capabilities, and concentrated instead on the manufacturing phase.[84] Demand for refined products was solid and growing, and the lure of a big strike would keep the drillers busy; Rockefeller's plan was to concentrate in the middle with storage, transportation, and refining to lower cost and add valve to the oil. The refining phase, in particular, was in need of great improvement. Summarized John McLaurin:

> The first refineries were exceedingly primitive and their processes simple. Much of the crude was wasted in refining, a business not financially successful as a rule until 1872, notwithstanding the high prices obtained. Methods of manufacture and transportation were expensive and inadequate. The product was of poor quality, emitting smoke and unpleasant odor and liable to explode on the slightest provocation. . . . Railroad-rates were excessive and irregular. . . . The cost of transportation and packages had been important factors in crippling the industry.[85]

[83]Harold Williamson and Arnold Daum, *The Age of Illumination,* p. 344.

[84]Company sentiment toward exploration and production was expressed by Charles Pratt: "Our business is that of manufacturers, and it is my judgement an unfortunate thing for any manufacturer or merchant to allow his mind to have the care and friction which attends speculative ventures." Ibid., p. 605.

[85]John McLaurin, *Sketches in Crude Oil,* p. 411.

Rockefeller clearly recognized the "manifold economies," to borrow biographer Allen Nevin's term, associated with large size.[86] Contracting in bulk lowered input prices and transportation rates. Diverse plant locations reduced the business risks of fire and explosion.[87] Improvements in distillation technology steadily lowered unit costs.[88] Integration into complementary phases (barrel making, pipelines, wagon production, storage, loading facilities, marketing) internalized profits and trimmed costs. By-products that other refiners treated as waste Rockefeller found uses for. Literally hundreds of by-products were distilled from each barrel of oil. Opportunities for efficient operation were discovered and implemented that set industry standards in favor of the consumer.

Internal efficiency was matched—and indeed fostered—by Standard's emphasis on cost accounting. Lewis Galantiere credits Standard with many advances in "that most baffling and fascinating department of business, corporate accounting."[89] Even the smallest of items, including the refinery bung (which had the value of a clothespin) did not escape attention on the financial ledgers.[90] Quarterly reports for internal planning and annual financial statements were pioneered.[91] With accurate and timely information, necessary adjustments could be made to changing market conditions.

As one of the first big businesses, Standard also pioneered major innovations in management organization. The trust arrangement

---

[86]Rockefeller reputedly stated, "I discovered something that made a new world, and I did not know it at the time." Matthew Josephson, *The Robber Barons* (New York: Harcourt, Brace, and Co., 1934), p. 116. While critics have used this phrase as evidence of a monopolization scheme, a fairer interpretation is Rockefeller's recognition of the cost and consumer advantages of integration and scale economies in the petroleum industry.

[87]John D. Rockefeller, *Random Reminiscences of Men and Events* (New York: Doubleday, Doran, 1937), p. 87. Standard kept a revenue fund to cover accidents. Because of improved safety, Standard's self-insurance became a profit center. Ibid., p. 88.

[88]Harold Williamson and Arnold Daum, *The Age of Illumination*, pp. 621–22.

[89]Lewis Galantiere, "John D.: An Academy Portrait," *New Republic*, December 9, 1940, p. 795.

[90]Ida Tarbell, *The History of the Standard Oil Company*, 2 vols. (New York: McClure, Phillips, and Company, 1904), vol. 2, p. 235. Also see Matthew Josephson, *The Robber Barons*, pp. 270–71. Said Rockefeller, "I learned to have great respect for figures and facts, no matter how small they were." *Random Reminiscences of Men and Events*, p. 21.

[91]Ralph Hidy and Muriel Hidy, *Pioneering in Big Business*, p. 36.

created by Standard became a model for other large businesses.[92] Middle management was inaugurated to provide the crucial link between field and plant activity and the New York office. Specialists were assigned to advisory committees to meet with senior management on important projects. A judicious mix of autonomy and coordination among managers attracted top talent and kept turnover low. Standard employees, as a whole, were a competent and content lot.[93] Company critic Ida Tarbell had only praise for Standard's work force.

> From Mr. Rockefeller himself . . . to the humblest clerk in the office of the remote marketing agency, everyone worked. There was not a lazy bone in the organization, not an incompetent hand, nor a stupid head. It was a machine where everybody was kept on his mettle by an extraordinary system of competition, where success met immediate recognition, where opportunity was wide as the world's craving for a good light to cheer its hours of darkness.[94]

The influence of Standard Oil on the oil industry in the 1870–1911 period can only be described as positive. Although not significantly involved in production until the late 1880s, Standard directly influenced wellhead activities. As the leading crude purchaser, Standard refused to buy excess crude created by production sprees. This discipline was manifested by voluntary proration in the Pennsylvania fields in the 1880s. Although not always dominant, a stabilizing influence was exerted on the upstream market by Standard. Noticed Ida Tarbell:

> The force of the combination has been greater because of the business habits of the independent body which has opposed it. To the Standard's caution the Oil Regions opposed recklessness; to its economy, extravagance; to its secretiveness, almost blatant frankness . . . far-sightedness . . . and . . . almost quixotic love of fair play. The Oil

---

[92] An economist at the time wrote: "The associated system of business is . . . recent. It took its life from the market and immediate success of the Standard Oil Trust, created in 1882. The career of this Titan agency has stimulated on all hands the most earnest efforts to imitate or rival it." E. B. Andrews, "Trusts According to Official Investigation," *Quarterly Journal of Economics* (January 1889): 121.

[93] Ralph Hidy and Muriel Hidy, *Pioneering in Big Business*, pp. 18–19, 580–87.

[94] Ida Tarbell, *The History of the Standard Oil Company*, vol. 2, p. 126.

> Regions had, besides, one fatal weakness—its passion for specula-
> tion. Now, Mr.Rockefeller never speculates. He deals only in those
> things which other people have proved sure.[95]

Once Standard was committed to exploration and production,
cost-saving techniques were implemented. Because Standard built
facilities for crude storage and pipelines, often on short notice, more
crude oil found a market. Reduced transportation costs allowed
refineries to be situated in consumer markets instead of the oil
regions.[96] For many refiners who wanted to sell out, Standard was a
ready buyer offering cash or stock. Rockefeller purchased inefficient
"teakettle" refineries if only to close them down to rid the market
of excess capacity.[97] As discussed in chapter 22, consumers benefited
from increasing volume, uniform quality (hence the company name),
and declining prices.[98] In virtually every petroleum sector, Standard
contributed technical, managerial, and entrepreneurial improvements.

The success of Standard resulted in sizable profits, which furthered
the company's winning ways. The absence of corporate taxation
allowed Standard an unmatched pool of retained earnings to use
for introducing the latest technology to existing operations, capitalizing on market opportunities by purchasing undervalued or under-
capitalized firms, and financing new projects. From the 1870s
through dissolution, Standard internally financed all projects and
was free of bankers and other financiers.[99] The entrance of Standard
into undeveloped Kansas in 1895 to drill wells, lay pipeline, construct
storage, and build refineries, for example, was as much a boon to
the state as it was profitable to Standard—all made possible by
yesterday's earnings.

---

[95]Ibid., vol. 2, pp. 253–54. This assessment can be qualified to acknowledge that
Rockefeller *did* speculate but in a reasoned manner. Examples would include the
desulfurization gamble that handsomely paid off for Standard upon its entrance into
exploration and production in the late 1880s.

[96]Austin Moore, *John D. Archbold and the Early Development of Standard Oil*, p. 219.

[97]Ralph Hidy and Muriel Hidy, *Pioneering in Big Business*, p. 107. Ida Tarbell recognized abandonments as prudent and not a means toward monopolization. *The History
of the Standard Oil Company*, vol. 2, p. 236.

[98]See chapter 22, pp. 1293–97.

[99]John Ise, *The United States Oil Policy* (New Haven, Conn.: Yale University Press,
1926), p. 49.

The contributions of Standard can be appreciated by imagining their absence. Greater industry instability, higher cost refining, less disciplined crude output, fewer crude outlets, and fewer consumer markets can be imagined in the absence of Rockefeller and the Standard plan. The advantages of large-scale integration surely would have been recognized; as McLean and Haigh state, "A failure to move in that direction might have represented a lack of business foresight," but the assumption that the thousands of opportunities would have been as fully and masterfully exploited without the entrepreneurial genius of Rockefeller or the scale economies of Standard is doubtful.

Unfair Practices Reconsidered

Critics of Standard Oil, while conceding many of the aforementioned points, might accuse the author of painting the picture with only bright colors. What about the other side of Standard's drive to power? Did the ends justify the means—preferential treatment from third parties over competitors, monopsony power to purchase crude at prices detrimental to producers, predatory pricing to eliminate rivals and raise prices, and excess profits gained at the expense of consumers? And what about land right-of-way obstructionism, buying into rivals to tame competition, establishing bogus companies, and spying on competitors? If these practices were legal, were they ethical? These points are considered below except for the monopsony argument, which was rebutted in chapter 14.[100]

It is worth noting at the outset that the complaints did not originate from consumers but from special interests within the industry. The critics were independent (non-Standard) producers, refiners, and marketers and sympathetic academicians and journalists who often had ulterior motives for their views.

Rebates. Price differentiation and individualized bargaining are essential aspects of competition. This is particularly true with railroads and other industries with relatively high fixed costs and low variable costs. Prices vary widely in such instances because incremental business covers at least variable costs.[101] The railway industry

---

[100]See chapter 14, pp. 783–84.

[101]This explains why rates were often nonproportional to distance. As Dominick Armentano states, "Distance, like technology, means little in economics; the value of services is determined by the relative strength of demand and supply at any given moment." Armentano, *Antitrust and Monopoly*, p. 61.

in Standard's day was very rivalrous, and railroads attempted to maximize revenue in each unique situation.

Before railroad interests passed protective legislation to discourage rebates, discussed in chapter 11, the industry custom was to set book rates that were discounted for special customers who provided steady, high-volume business. Standard was the prototype special customer.[102] Rebates off the book rate were, in Rockefeller's words, "the railroads' method of business."[103] As part of the competitive process, discounts were often kept secret and paid after the fact as rebates. Railroads did not desire to trigger open price wars, and customers preferred to keep their rivals guessing. Whether the rebate was money returned from a book price (rebates) or money received from competitors' shipments (drawbacks) was academic; preferred customers received lower rates than less preferred customers. Shippers with such scale economies were thus able to cheapen goods for consumers. If discounts could be prohibited by law, railroad interests would gain instead.

Critics of rebates have swallowed the railroad-industry line that rebates were "cutthroat" and bad, and therefore Standard was wrong for asking and receiving them. But rebates are price discounts that qualifying shippers and their consumers are entitled to negotiate in a free market. Moreover, as Standard stressed, rebating did not originate with them; was widely used by other shippers, competitors included; and was stopped once it became illegal in 1887.[104] Before rebates were replaced by regulatory-induced price cartelization, Standard's ability to negotiate them must be favorably viewed if consumer welfare and the interest of the recipient company are placed above the special interest of less able competitors and the railroad industry.

The last word on rebates was stated by Rockefeller in his memoirs when he recalled an oft-quoted statement: " 'I am opposed on principle to the whole system of rebates and drawbacks—unless I am in it.' "[105]

---

[102]Lower shipping rates given to Standard also resulted from the company's own insurance coverage and the use of its own loading and discharging facilities. John D. Rockefeller, *Random Reminiscences of Men and Events*, p. 109.

[103]Ibid., pp. 107–8.

[104]Ralph Hidy and Muriel Hidy, *Pioneering in Big Business*, pp. 680–81, 694.

[105]John D. Rockefeller, *Random Reminiscences of Men and Events*, p. 112.

Predatory Pricing. The most infamous practice associated with the Standard Trust, predatory pricing, was popularized by Lloyd, Tarbell, and other critics.[106] The charge was that in marketing and particularly in refining, Standard initiated price wars by selling at below cost to weaken competitors and buy them out at depressed prices. Then, with control of the market, prices could be raised to enjoy monopoly profits. This alleged practice attracted so much popular support and political attention that the Clayton Act extended antitrust law to ban "predatory" price discrimination in 1914.[107]

Economists have shown predatory pricing to be a highly risky and unprofitable strategy in theory, and evidence in the paradigmatic Standard case suggests it is historical myth as well.[108] Predatory intent—a conscious strategy to drive out competitors to restrict supply and raise price—was assumed but never tightly documented. The hard facts of increasing supply and falling prices in the period under review suggest that predation was not operative, whether intended or not. Indeed, many competitors that testified against the trust were profitable and expanding output in the heyday of Standard's expansion.[109]

More than seventy refineries were purchased and shut down by Standard to reduce overcapacity, but this signified obsolescence and asset replacement more than a strategy of permanently removing competition.[110] The industry by all accounts was overbuilt and inefficient, and Standard did the dirty work.[111] Standard actively

[106]In particular, see chapter 10 of Ida Tarbell's *The History of the Standard Oil Company*, entitled "Cutting to Kill."

[107]Public Law 212, 38 Stat. 730 (1914). The Clayton Act is discussed in chapter 26, pp. 1553–54.

[108]See Wayne Leeman, "The Limitations of Local Price-Cutting as a Barrier to Entry," *Journal of Political Economy* (August 1956): 329–34; and Murray Rothbard, *Man, Economy and State* (Los Angeles: Nash Publishing, 1970), pp. 602–4. On the Standard case, see John McGee, "Predatory Price-Cutting: The Standard Oil (New Jersey) Case," *Journal of Law and Economics* (October 1958): 137–69.

[109]Randall Mariger, "Predatory Price Cutting: The Standard Oil of New Jersey Case Revisited," *Explorations in Economic History* (October 1978): 347.

[110]John McGee, "Predatory Price-Cutting," p. 144.

[111]"Refineries were being built by the dozen, many of them by irresponsible men who had neither a knowledge of refining methods nor financial backing to insure success. The refineries were small, inefficient, wasteful, weak financially, and far too numerous. . . . Out of such chaotic conditions, monopoly developed easily." John Ise, *The United States Oil Policy*, p. 49.

consummated mergers during distress periods, particularly from 1872 to 1874, but not by predatory pricing.

"Standard Oil was not born with monopoly power," reminds John McGee.[112] Standard was able to weather the competitive storm because of lower costs. Natural incentives dictated that Standard buy and competitors sell. To competing firms, mergers often were a profitable way out of financial problems; for retained managements, they were a new lease on life with a promising company.[113] Certain examples of low purchase prices cited by critics were explainable by excess industry capacity and monetary deflation, which reduced market value below cost.[114] At least one plant was purchased substantially above book value to buy goodwill and management along with the tangible assets.[115] Rockefeller, the evidence suggests, purchased quite fairly; one publicized charge that Rockefeller vastly underpaid the widow and children for a deceased competitor's refinery has been exposed as fabrication.[116]

[112]John McGee, "Predatory Price-Cutting," p. 139.

[113]One example was given by Ralph Hidy and Muriel Hidy. "Harassed by depression, impressed by the accomplishments and integrity of Rockefeller and his associates, and assured equality of voice in management, the five [refiners] finally accepted the idea of joining the growing group of Standard Oil executives." *Pioneering in Big Business*, p. 18.

[114]Harold Williamson and Arnold Daum, *The Age of Illumination*, p. 355; and Dominick Armentano, *Antitrust and Monopoly*, p. 59. Owners of purchased refineries were offered cash or stock; many chose the former, which was often later regretted when the undervalued position of Standard's stock was revealed.

[115]Summarized John McGee after exhaustively researching the record, "Standard's purchase terms were generally good, and sometimes lavish." McGee, "Predatory Price-Cutting," p. 153. To John Bonham, a contemporary of Rockefeller, "nearly all" of Standard's purchases "were made at prices grossly in excess of the reasonable value of the material and business sold; the chief consideration being the absorption and accumulation of power which the monopoly was thereby acquiring." Quoted in Ralph Hidy and Muriel Hidy, *Pioneering in Big Business*, p. 202.

[116]Henry Demarest Lloyd charged that Standard, through cunning and trickery, bought a $400,000 refinery for $60,000 from Mrs. F. M. Backus and cheated her out of the payment. The source of the controversy was widow Backus, who complained bitterly about the sale until her death. But the facts were not sympathetic to her case. Not only did she approve the sale through her negotiator, Rockefeller, after learning of her displeasure, offered to sell it back to her or to trade cash for a stock interest that would let her participate in future earnings. This incident disturbed Rockefeller greatly despite a letter of apology from H. M. Backus, brother of the deceased refiner, for his sister-in-law's behavior and the full support of widow Backus's negotiator, who agreed that the purchase price was too high, if anything. Lloyd, *Wealth against Commonwealth*, pp. 73–83. See also John D. Rockefeller, *Reminiscences of Men and*

Standard avoided predatory tactics because of the business judgment of Rockefeller. He knew better than to engage in cutthroat pricing to subsidize consumers at the expense of company stockholders. As Leeman and McGee have explained, the decision to initiate a price war in hopes of a distress merger on very favorable terms—as opposed to making an immediate purchase at a price tending toward the firm's discounted profit stream—requires the dominant firm to forgo full margins for a period that can only be known afterward. The expense of a price war is great for the dominant firm since relatively more units are sold at depressed prices.[117] (In Standard's case, as much as 90 percent of the market would have to be price discounted.) The beleaguered refinery could hold on longer than expected thanks to investor interest or consumer goodwill or decide to temporarily shut down to reenter with new contracts when "monopoly" prices arose. In such cases, the predatory refinery could find itself mired with low prices. Standard, therefore, did not covet price wars with its high-volume business. Standard considered itself the "brand-name" supplier that received a premium for quality, compared to less established suppliers who discounted to attract consumer interest.[118]

As the dominant firm, Standard priced to discourage new entry. But this was not predatory pricing, and consumers were all the better off for this barrier to entry.[119]

Rockefeller's merger strategy, based on financial incentives rather than "fights to the finish," was not problem free. Sometimes Standard would buy a refinery only to have the displaced principals construct a new one.[120] Some rivals refused Standard's merger offers

---

Events, pp. 96–107; Allen Nevins, "Letter to the Editor," p. 677; and John McLaurin, Sketches in Crude Oil, p. 415.

[117]Wayne Leeman, "The Limitations of Local Price-Cutting as a Barrier to Entry," p. 331. John McGee's basic arguments against predatory pricing as a profit-maximizing strategy are rehashed and defended against critics in McGee, "Predatory Pricing Revisited," Journal of Law and Economics (October 1980): 289–330.

[118]See, for example, John McGee, "Predatory Price-Cutting," p. 154.

[119]For a "dominant-firm" interpretation of Standard's price and supply behavior, see Randall Mariger, "Predatory Price Cutting: The Standard Oil of New Jersey Case Revisited," pp. 341–67.

[120]Wayne Leeman, "The Limitations of Local Price-Cutting as a Barrier to Entry," p. 332.

and enjoyed long-lived profitability.[121] Standard gadfly George Rice would enter a Standard stronghold, cut prices, and "blackmail" Standard by raising his sellout price. While this worked in some cases, Rice tried it once too often when he tried to sell a $20,000 refinery plus subsequent improvements for $500,000. Standard's Archbold refused to pay.[122] Battered in competition by the trust, Rice spent his last years in court seeking to recover a sizable refinery investment lost as a result of "unfair" competition by Standard.[123]

The last word on Standard Oil and predatory pricing may be given to John McGee. After exhaustively studying Standard's pricing strategies, he concluded:

> Judging from the record, Standard Oil did not use predatory price discrimination to drive out competing refiners, nor did its pricing practice have that effect.... Standard Oil did not systematically, if ever, use local price cutting ... to reduce competition. To do so would have been foolish; and, whatever else has been said about it, the old Standard organization was seldom criticized for making less money when it could have made more.[124]

Monopoly and Monopoly Profits. If Standard is labeled a monopoly because of its large market share, a liberal application of the "single-seller" criterion, it should be recognized that outside of oil tariffs that Standard neither wanted nor needed, Standard was a free-market, not a governmental, monopoly. Standard had to continually offer quality products at competitive prices to gain and keep its dominant market share.[125] Lewis Galantiere observed with puzzlement that "this monopolist always produced as if he had competitors," incognizant of the fact that without domestic barriers to entry

[121]John McGee, "Predatory Price-Cutting," p. 154.

[122]Austin Moore, *John D. Archbold and the Early Development of Standard Oil,* pp. 159–60; and *Oil's First Century,* pp. 203–4.

[123]Holdouts such as Rice suffered the worst fate of all refinery sellers. Eyewitness John McLaurin explained, "Those who would neither improve, nor sell, nor combine sitting down placidly and believing they would be bought out later on their own terms, were soon left far behind, as they deserved to be." McLaurin, *Sketches in Crude Oil,* p. 412.

[124]John McGee, "Predatory Price-Cutting," p. 403.

[125]Analogies between the Standard Trust and OPEC's control and behavior in the 1973–81 period, consequently, are suspect and misleading.

(such as restrictive charters or siting permits), competition is omni-present whatever the number and size of individual firms.[126] This is because entrepreneurial ideas, awaiting fruition with the emer-gence of profit opportunities, can never be monopolized.[127]

Standard Oil had competitors throughout its history and increas-ingly so in the period of its antitrust troubles. In 1904, Standard's twenty-three refineries, although claiming over 80 percent of the market, competed against seventy-five independents.[128] By 1908, the number of independent refineries swelled to 125; three years later, the total was 147.[129] Potential entrants were virtually as important as actual entrants. In the 1880s and 1890s, Standard's efficient perfor-mance kept would-be competitors on the sidelines and encouraged consolidation. This resulted from a competitive process entirely con-sistent with the market virtue of lowest cost provision of goods and services.[130] There was also *substitute* competition; Standard's kerosene had to compete with coal gas and electricity in the all-important illuminant market. As John Chamberlain stated:

> Buyers always liked the company's product—they proved it by rushing to substitute petroleum kerosene for the old coal-oil and whale-oil illuminants. And buyers did not have any particular reason to complain of Standard's pricing policy: not only did kerosene cost less than older fluids, but it had to meet the competition of the Welsbach gas burner and Mr.Edison's carbon-filament electric light bulb. Standard could not have imposed a lighting monopoly even if it had tried.[131]

[126]Lewis Galantiere, "John D.: An Academy Portrait," p. 795.

[127]See chapter 1, pp. 16, 45.

[128]George Stocking, *The Oil Industry and the Competitive System*, p. 51.

[129]Ralph Hidy and Muriel Hidy, *Pioneering in Big Business*, p. 680; John McGee, "Predatory Price-Cutting," p. 156; and Dominick Armentano, "The Petroleum Indus-try," p. 69. In crude production, Standard peaked at one-third of national output in the late 1890s but fell to 11 percent by 1906 because of rising Southwest production. John McGee, "Predatory Price-Cutting," p. 142.

[130]As Wayne Leeman concludes: "*Potential* entry or expansion may be as effective as actual entry or expansion in insuring that a large and dominant firm behaves competitively.... For this reason one can never decide how competitive an industry is simply by counting the number of firms in the field or by looking at the proportion of the total business done by a given firm or group of firms." Leeman, "The Limitations of Local Price-Cutting as a Barrier to Entry," pp. 332–33.

[131]John Chamberlain, *The Enterprising Americans* (New York: Harper & Row, 1961), p. 147. For a defense of Standard on the product marketing side, see chapter 22, pp. 1302–5.

Critics seized upon Standard's dividend policies to assert that monopoly profits were made at the expense of consumers. Product margins increased over time, it was noted, and profits were unequaled as a percentage of capital.[132] Several observations can be made in regard to these facts. One, Standard's declared capital value was notoriously understated, as much as several hundred percent. Profits and dividends on the firm's *market* value were far more modest, estimated by Rockefeller himself at from 6 to 8 percent.[133] But more important, profits in a free market are a *positive* indication of economic performance. The higher the profits, other things being equal, the better the entrepreneurial correction between consumer demand and resource deployments. Profits won by Standard were available to other entrepreneurs, yet Standard prevailed and many independents did not. With anti-Standard sentiment spread by competitors and their political and academic allies, consumers had an extra reason to rethink product allegiance, but they remained with Standard. Higher profits from *artificially* high prices, on the other hand, would have opened the door to other firms.

Standard entered into agreements to "restrict" competition. For example, Standard initiated agreements with producers to reduce output to "marketable" quantities. Such agreements, however, far from fostering monopoly waste (less output at higher prices), promoted prudent resource management given the relative scarcity of refining capacity compared with crude production. On the refining side, Standard on different occasions tried to rationalize rivalry by entering into output and pricing agreements with fellow refiners. Some agreements proved their market mettle by lasting; many proved artificial and collapsed under the weight of self-interest.[134] The South Improvement Plan in 1872 was a bust as were the Petroleum Refiners Association and the Central Refiners Association cartels several years later.

Other. Gathering information on a competitor is part of the process of rivalry. According to Hidy and Hidy, "spying" had been a practice common in all phases of the oil business since the early days.[135]

---

[132]George Stocking, *The Oil Industry and the Competitive System*, pp. 29–33.

[133]John D. Rockefeller, *Random Reminiscences of Men and Events*, p. 90.

[134]John McGee, "Predatory Price-Cutting," pp. 150, 152, 155.

[135]Ralph Hidy and Muriel Hidy, *Pioneering in Big Business*, p. 8.

Whether or not such action turns from legal to illegal depends on the facts. Trespassing and contract breaking to gain information are clearly *invasion*; they are matters of tort law and may require restitution from the victimizer to the victim. Regulatory considerations have no role to play. Archbold answered a government accusation that Standard used such questionable competitive methods by declaring that it was not company policy, and "I would be only too thankful to have any such case brought to our attention."[136]

Use of hidden companies to give the impression of distinct competition, where, in fact, there was only one general firm in a geographical area, was a marketing practice used by Standard and other companies.[137] Bad public relations spawned by Standard's competitors and their allies, and prosecution by state governments in response to local opinion, encouraged hidden control by Standard. The practice, in other words, was more defensive than offensive. When this practice was found to be controversial, Standard discontinued its use in 1906.[138] Front companies still faced the same competitive pressures of the market that all other companies did—substitution and new entry.

Obstructionist practices, the most notorious being strategically purchased land rights-of-way to block construction of competing pipelines, are a flagrant example of unbridled rivalry within the competitive process. As with the other complaints, it was not a practice unique to Standard. But given the practice, it can be "competitively" overcome. "Self-help" alternatives are to beat the would-be obstructionist to the right-of-way or secure alternative routing. Another free-market solution is to sanction a homestead theory of property rights to weaken the ability to obstruct. Tunneling below or bridging above the impasse can be sanctioned under homestead law, whereas under prevailing law both actions are considered trespass.

Not all critics of Standard have decried the company's ethics. Many have praised them. John Ise commented that Standard established "standards of business practice which were in some ways

---

[136]Quoted in Austin Moore, *John D. Archbold and the Early Development of Standard Oil*, p. 164. Also see John D. Rockefeller, *Random Reminiscences of Men and Events*, p. 59. Several examples of over-zealous practices are described in Ida Tarbell, *The History of the Standard Oil Company*, vol. 2, pp. 38, 58.

[137]Ralph Hidy and Muriel Hidy, *Pioneering in Big Business*, p. 118.

[138]See chapter 22, p. 1303.

among the highest of the time."[139] Standard, in fact, was a rare example of an oil company that did not seek government favor but only grudgingly used the political process to repel threatening intervention designed by rivals. Unlike other trusts of the time, such as sugar and steel, Standard sought neither tariff protection nor subsidies, nor entry restrictions, price floors, nor public-land grants. On this score Standard towered not only above companies of its time but above the vast majority of future companies as well.

Ethical judgments of certain business practices employed by Standard are beyond the scope of economic evaluation, but one pertinent observation can be made. To the extent consumers and fellow firms resent particular business practices, a negative intangible is created that penalizes the guilty firm in subtle but real ways. As the nation's largest business entity and a pioneer in many areas, Standard undoubtedly entered the realm of the extralegal and controversial, which brought on problems. But this was part of entrepreneurial learning and the market's discovery process. It was not grounds for government intervention that would impede the competitive discovery process and create unforeseen problems.

Public Relations, Politics, and Prosecution

The major mistake of Standard Oil in its distinguished history was not a failing of economic performance. It was underestimating the need to present information to explain to the public and critics the virtues of integration and scale economies, particularly in petroleum. By following an explicit policy of secrecy until the late 1880s, Standard allowed opponents to get the upper hand in a public debate that for Standard would worsen at almost every turn, culminating in the 1911 decree.[140] Successful consumer service was considered by the company as its best strategy; it was not understood that competitors would be dissatisfied by the very fact that the public was so well served by Standard. Given the precedent of intervention

---

[139]John Ise, *The United States Oil Policy*, p. 48.

[140]As late as 1888, Standard executive Paul Babock wrote to Rockefeller, "I think this anti-trust fever is a craze which we should meet in a very dignified way and parry every question with answers which while perfectly truthful are evasive of bottom facts." Ralph Hidy and Muriel Hidy, *Pioneering in Big Business*, p. 214. Ida Tarbell credits Rockefeller with the statement, "We do not talk much—we saw wood." Tarbell, *The History of Standard Oil*, vol. 2, p. 127.

at all government levels, an offense would have been the best defense.

Prior to the onslaught of state antitrust activity, political action by Standard was occasional and defensive. Eminent-domain rights, tailored to the needs of Standard's pipeline competitors, and rate regulation of company pipeline and storage facilities, prompted Standard's entrance into state politics in the 1880s in Pennsylvania, Ohio, Maryland, and elsewhere to financially support friendly politicians.[141] In the late 1890s, federal politics became important to Standard, and Archbold made large contributions to favored candidates until a 1907 law prohibited corporate political contributions.[142] By this time, Standard regularly spoke for the public record, but it was too late. Numerically powerful producer interests, who blamed their cyclical difficulties on Standard, joined by hard-pressed independent refiners and marketers, inspired muckraking journalism that nudged the public to the "little man's" side. Tarbell's standard of goodness was not superior consumer service but "the right to do an independent business" and "free and equal transportation" for all.[143] The idea that consumers decide the structure and form of business and that in a free market less efficient firms—which she realized existed in the independent sector—must conform or perish had no part in her ethics, understanding, or sympathy.[144]

State and federal politicians, many with personal motives, readily capitalized on anti-Standard themes to seal the fate of the trust. Standard, meanwhile, had to wastefully redirect resources to the political fight when it found itself persecuted by regulation it neither sought nor benefited from. Standard's distaste of the political means to success, as opposed to the economic means of consumer service, was noticed and criticized by Ida Tarbell.

[141]Ralph Hidy and Muriel Hidy, *Pioneering in Big Business*, pp. 205, 213.

[142]Austin Moore, *John D. Archbold and the Early History of Standard Oil*, pp. 243–50.

[143]Ida Tarbell, *The History of Standard Oil*, vol. 2, pp. 255, 283.

[144]After describing the great lengths Standard went to for efficiency, Tarbell revealingly said: "The Oil Regions, which were notoriously extravagant in their business methods, resented this care and called it meanness, but the Oil Regions were wrong and Mr. Rockefeller was right. Take care of the bungs and the barrels will take care of themselves, is as good a policy in a refinery as the old saw it paraphrases is in financiering." Ibid., p. 235. The question that Tarbell must answer is, why should independents be guaranteed the right to compete when they are less efficient than dominant firms?

The notion that the business man must not appear in politics . . . save as a "stand-patter"—not even as a thinking, aggressive force— is demoralizing, intellectually and morally. Ever since 1872 the organization has appeared in politics only to oppose legislation obviously for the public good.[145]

But Tarbell was off the mark to idolize political activity. State and federal regulation of the day was the work product of special interests and unjustified from the consumers' point of view (although some consumers may have supported it). It is an enduring monument to Standard and Rockefeller that special privileges such as subsidies or tariffs were not sought. The company placed its fate in the hands of the consumer. It passed every test except the political one.

[145]Ibid., p. 290.